VOX

Compact

SPANISH

and

ENGLISH

Dictionary

English-Spanish / Spanish-English

Second Edition

Preface by
C. Edward Scebold
Executive Director, American Council on the
Teaching of Foreign Languages

Dictionary Compiled by
the Editors of Biblograf, S. A.

North American Edition Prepared by
the Editors of National Textbook Company

Printed on recyclable paper

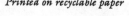

National Textbook Company
a division of *NTC Publishing Group* • Lincolnwood, Illinois USA

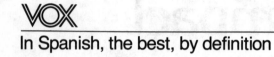

In Spanish, the best, by definition

1995 Printing

Published by National Textbook Company, a division of NTC Publishing Group.
© 1994, 1984 by NTC Publishing Group, 4255 West Touhy Avenue,
Lincolnwood (Chicago), Illinois 60646-1975 U.S.A.
Original copyright© Biblograf, S. A.
Manufactured in the United States of America.

Library of Congress Catalog Number: 84-61105

    6 7 8 9 0 AG 9 8 7 6 5 4

ISBN 0-8442-7985-4 (Hardcover Edition)
ISBN 0-8442-7986-2 (Softcover Edition)

CONTENTS

Maps/Mapas

PREFACE

The *Vox Compact Spanish and English Dictionary* contains all the elements for day-to-day reference. In a convenient size, with easily readable type, this dictionary is complete enough to answer the daily needs of a wide variety of students and general users—from those who are in their early stages of language learning to those who are fully proficient.

Although a concise reference, the *Vox Compact* has many features normally found only in larger, full-size dictionaries, such as grammar summaries in both English and Spanish; a separate listing of common English and Spanish suffixes; an easily accessible section of 3,500 Spanish and English idioms and expressions; a list of false cognates; tables of monetary units, weights and measures, numbers, and average temperatures; and six detailed maps. Best of all, the *Vox Compact* offers a lexicon that emphasizes contemporary, everyday language.

The many features that make the *Vox Compact* ideally suited to students also make this dictionary appealing to libraries, businesses, and the general user. To meet the needs of the widest possible audience, the *Vox Compact* has been specially edited to include only the most important words, with clear and accurate definitions and numerous examples. Students and occasional users alike will appreciate the easy-to-use pronunciation keys as well as the convenience of finding conjugations or models of irregular verbs under the verb entry instead of in an appendix, as is the case in many other dictionaries.

The *Vox Compact Spanish and English Dictionary* will satisfy anyone seeking a practical, yet comprehensive, Spanish and English dictionary of lasting value. Educators, in particular, can be assured of having a quality, all-purpose dictionary that they can confidently recommend to their students.

C. Edward Scebold
Executive Director, American Council on the
Teaching of Foreign Languages

PRÓLOGO

El *Vox Compact Spanish and English Dictionary* contiene todos los elementos necesarios para una buena obra de consulta de uso cotidiano. Presentado en un tamaño conveniente y con letra fácil de leer, este diccionario es una obra de consulta suficientemente completa para satisfacer las necesidades diarias de los estudiantes y del público en general—incluyendo las personas que hablan la lengua con fluidez.

Aunque es una obra de consulta concisa, el *Vox Compact* tiene muchas de las características que solamente se encuentran en diccionarios mayores, como: resúmenes de gramática en inglés y español; una lista separada de los sufijos más usados en inglés y español; una sección accesible de 3.500 expresiones idiomáticas; una lista de cognados falsos; tablas de unidades monetarias, pesas y medidas, números y temperaturas medias; y seis mapas detallados. Una de las principales características del *Vox Compact* es que ofrece un léxico que pone énfasis en el lenguaje contemporáneo.

Todas las características que hacen del *Vox Compact* el instrumento ideal para el uso de los estudiantes, también lo hacen muy atractivo para bibliotecas, negocios y el público en general. Para satisfacer las necesidades de un mayor número de lectores, el *Vox Compact* ha sido especialmente redactado para incluir solamente las palabras más importantes, con definiciones claras y precisas y con numerosos ejemplos. Los estudiantes y otras personas que usan el diccionario regularmente apreciarán lo fácil que es el uso de las guías de pronunciación como también la conveniencia de encontrar conjugaciones o modelos de verbos irregulares en la sección de verbos sin tener que referirse al apéndice, como es el caso en muchos otros diccionarios.

El *Vox Compact Spanish and English Dictionary* va a satisfacer a las personas que buscan un diccionario español e inglés que sea práctico, extensivo y a la vez duradero. Los educadores en particular pueden estar seguros de tener un diccionario de uso general, de calidad, que se podrá recomendar con toda confianza al estudiante.

C. Edward Scebold
Executive Director, American Council on the
Teaching of Foreign Languages

How to consult this dictionary

Gender of translation	**beast** [biːst] *n* bestia, animal *m*.	Género de traducción
	beastly [ˈbiːstlɪ] *adj* bestial.	
New grammatical category	**beat** [biːt] *n (of heart)* latido. **2** MUS ritmo. **3** *(of policeman)* ronda. — **4** *t (hit)* golpear; *(metals)* martillear; *(person)* azotar; *(drum)* tocar. **5** CULIN batir. **6** *(defeat)* vencer, derrotar. **7** *fam (puzzle)* extrañar. — **8** *i (heart)* latir. — **9** *adj fam* agotado,-a. ●*to ~ up t* dar una paliza a. ●*to ~ about the bush,* andarse por las ramas; MUS *to ~ time,* llevar el compás. ▲ *pt* **beat**; *pp* **beaten** [ˈbiːtən].	Cambio de categoría gramatical
Phrasal verb		Verbo preposicional
Phonetic transcription	**become** [bɪˈkʌm] *i (with noun)* convertirse en, hacerse; llegar a ser: *to ~ a doctor/teacher,* hacerse médico,-a/maestro,-a; *to ~ president,* llegar a la presidencia; *what has ~ of Peter?,* ¿qué ha sido de Peter? **2** *(with adj)* volverse, ponerse: *to ~ angry/sad,* enojarse/entristecerse. **3** *(suit)* favorecer. ▲ *pt* **became**; *pp* **become**.	Transcripción fonética
Interchangeable elements		Elementos intercambiables
Grammar note		Nota gramatical
Register label	**beef** [biːf] *n* carne *f* de vaca. — **2** *i fam* quejarse.	Etiqueta de registro lingüístico
Translation with explanation	**beefburger** [ˈbiːfbɜːgəʳ] *n* hamburguesa. **beefeater** [ˈbiːfiːtəʳ] *n* alabardero *de la Torre de Londres.* **beefsteak** [ˈbiːfsteɪk] *n* bistec *m*.	Traducción con explicación
Examples of use	**before** [bɪˈfɔːʳ] *prep (order, time)* antes de. **2** *(place)* delante de; *(in the presence of)* ante: *~ God,* ante Dios. — **3** *conj (earlier than)* antes de + *inf,* antes de que + *subj:* *~ you go,* antes de irte, antes de que te vayas. **4** *(rather than)* antes de (+ *inf).* — **5** *adv* antes. **6** *(place)* delante. ●*the day ~ yesterday,* antes de ayer.	Ejemplos de uso
Represents headword		Sustituye entrada
Cross-reference	**bled** [bled] *pt & pp →* **bleed**.	Envío
	blemish [ˈblemɪʃ] *n* imperfección. **2** *(on fruit)* maca. **3** *fig* mancha.	
Intransitive translated by reflexive	**blend** [blend] *n* mezcla, combinación. — **2** *t-i (mix)* mezclar(se), combinar(se). **3** *(match)* matizar, armonizar.	Intransitivo traducido por pronominal
Adverb of manner	**blind** [blaɪnd] *adj* ciego,-a. — **2** *n (on window)* persiana. — **3** *blindly adv* ciegamente, a ciegas. — **4** *t* cegar, dejar ciego,-a. **5** *(dazzle)* deslumbrar. ●*to be/go ~,* estar/quedarse ciego,-a.	Adverbio de manera
American English	**blinders** [ˈblaɪndəz] *npl* US anteojeras *fpl.*	Inglés americano
	blindfold [ˈblaɪndfəʊld] *n* venda. — **2** *t* vendar los ojos a. — **3** *adj-adv* con los ojos vendados.	

Guía para consultar este diccionario

Modelo de conjugación irregular	**disentir** [35] *i* to dissent, disagree. **diseñar** *t* to design. **diseño** *m* design. **disertación** *f* dissertation, discourse.	Irregular conjugation model
Preposiciones de régimen	**disertar** *t* to discourse (*sobre,* on/upon).	Prepositional complementation
Corresponde a la traducción del pronominal	**disfraz** *m* disguise. 2 *(vestido)* fancy dress. **disfrazar(se)** [4] *t-p* to disguise (o.s.).	Corresponds to translation of reflexive

Indicadores de contexto	**jubilación** *f (acción)* retirement. 2 *(dinero)* pension.	Indicators of context
Corresponde a la traducción del sustantivo	**jubilado,-a** *adj-m,f* retired (person). **jubilar(se)** *t-p (retirarse)* to retire. — 2 *t* to pension off; *fam fig* to get rid of, ditch. — 3 *i fml (alegrarse)* to rejoice.	Corresponds to translation of noun

Tecnicismo Fraseología	**margen** *m & f (extremidad)* border, edge. 2 *(de río)* bank. 3 *(papel)* margin. 4 COM margin. ●*dar ~ para,* to give scope for. **marginación** *f* exclusion. **marginado,-a** *adj* excluded. — 2 *m,f* drop-out. **marginar** *t* to leave out, exclude.	Field label Phraseology
Categoría gramatical de entrada	**maría** *f fam* EDUC easy subject. 2 *fam* housewife. 3 *arg (marihuana)* marijuana, pot.	Grammatical category of headword
Tabú	**marica***, **maricón*** *m* queer*.	Taboo

Español de Latinoamérica	**pena** *f (castigo)* penalty, punishment. 2 *(tristeza)* grief, sorrow. 3 *(lástima)* pity. 4 *(dificultad)* hardship, trouble. 5 AM *(vergüenza)* shame. ●*a duras penas,* with a great difficulty; *dar ~,* to arouse	Latin American Spanish
Nombres en construcciones fijas	pity; *valer la ~,* to be worth while. ■ *~ capital,* capital punishment. **penacho** *m* tuft (of feathers), crest.	Fixed noun combinations
Elemento opcional	**penal** *adj* penal. — 2 *m* penitentiary.	Optional element

Entrada doble	**resoplido, resoplo** *m* puff, pant.	Double headword
Verbo también pronominal	**resorte** *m* spring. 2 *fig* means. **respaldar(se)** *t* to support, back (up). — 2 *p* to lean back (*en,* on). **respaldo** *m* back. 2 *fig* support, backing. **respectar** *i* to concern. ●*por lo que a mí respecta,* as far as I'm concerned. ▲ *Used only in the 3rd pers. sing.*	Verb is also reflexive

INGLÉS-ESPAÑOL
ENGLISH-SPANISH

OBSERVACIONES

Al consultar este Diccionario, el lector ha de tener en cuenta que:

- Dentro de cada artículo, la palabra o el grupo de palabras correspondiente a cada una de las acepciones del vocablo inglés constituyen una entidad separada y numerada.

- Los ejemplos, frases y modos no se dan, como es corriente en esta clase de Diccionarios, al final del artículo, sino que van agregados a la acepción a que corresponden, con lo cual ilustran mejor el sentido de ésta.

- En general, los ejemplos, frases y modos, se dan, dentro de cada acepción, en el siguiente orden: grupos de nombre y adjetivo o compuestos formados por palabras separadas; oraciones con verbo expreso, y modos adverbiales, conjuntivos, etc.

- Las frases y modos no atribuibles a ninguna acepción determinada tienen lugar independiente y numerado dentro del artículo.

- Los compuestos formados por palabras separadas se encuentran en el artículo correspondiente a su primer elemento. Los compuestos cuyos elementos van unidos por un guión o formando una sola palabra se hallarán como artículos independientes.

- Los sinónimos y aclaraciones encerradas entre corchetes sirven para determinar el sentido en que han de tomarse las palabras que se dan como traducción.

- A este fin se usan también abreviaturas de materia, uso, etc., cuya interpretación se da en la lista correspondiente. (V. Abreviaturas usadas en este diccionario.)

- Inmediatamente después de cada entrada se da la transcripción fonética correspondiente.

Para completar las indicaciones de naturaleza gramatical que se dan en los artículos del Diccionario, se incluye una sección gramatical referente a temas concretos. No se trata de dar con ella, ni siquiera en resumen, toda la doctrina gramatical del inglés, sino de ofrecer al lector (especialmente de habla española) un medio rápido de consulta sobre los casos de dificultad más frecuentes.

- Un asterisco en el cuerpo de un artículo indica que la palabra española que precede sólo tiene uso en América.

El lector encontrará en este Diccionario secciones de referencia que facilitarán su aprendizaje y uso del idioma. Por ejemplo, en el centro del Diccionario se encuentra una lista de más de tres mil idiomas y expresiones: Español-Inglés e Inglés-Español.

Además se incluyen en los apéndices:

- False Cognates and "Part-Time" Cognates
- Monetary Units / Unidades monetarias
- Weights and Measures / Pesas y medidas
- Numbers / Numerales
- Temperature / La temperatura
- Maps/Mapas

ABREVIATURAS USADAS EN ESTE DICCIONARIO

abbr	*abbreviation* abreviatura	*irreg*	irregular
adj	adjetivo	JUR	jurisprudencia
adv	adverbio	LING	lingüística
AER	aeronáutico	*lit*	literario
AGR	agricultura	*m*	masculino
algn	alguien	*m & f*	género ambiguo
ANAT	anatomía	MAR	marítimo
ARCH	*architecture* arquitectura	MATH	matemáticas
art	artículo	MED	medicina
ART	arte	METEOR	meteorología
ASTROL	astrología	MIL	militar
ASTRON	astronomía	MUS	música
AUTO	automóvil	*n*	nombre
aux	verbo auxiliar	*neut*	neutro
AV	aviación	*o.s.*	*oneself*
BIOL	biología	*pej*	*pejorative* peyorativo
BOT	botánica	*pers*	personas; personal
CHEM	*chemistry* química	*phr*	*phrase* frase
CINEM	cinematografía	PHYS	*physics* física
COM	comercio	*pl*	plural
comp	comparativo	POL	política
COMPUT	*computers* informática	*poss*	*possessive* posesivo
conj	conjunción	*pp*	participio pasado
CULIN	culinario	*prep*	preposición
def	definido	*pres*	presente
ECON	economía	*prn*	nombre propio
EDUC	educación	*pron*	pronombre
ELEC	electricidad	*pt*	pretérito
esp	especialmente	®	marca registrada
etc	etcétera	RAD	radio
euph	*euphemism* eufemismo	*rel*	relativo
f	femenino	REL	religión
fam	familiar	sb.	*somebody*
fig	figurado	SEW	*sewing* costura
FIN	finanzas	*sing*	singular
fml	formal	*sl*	*slang* argot
gen	generalmente	SP	*sport* deporte
GEOG	geografía	sth.	*something*
GRAM	gramática	*subj*	subjuntivo
HIST	historia	*superl*	superlativo
i	verbo intransitivo	*t*	verbo transitivo
IND	industria	TECH	*technical* técnico
indef	indefinido	THEAT	*theater* teatro
indic	indicativo	TV	televisión
inf	infinitivo	ZOOL	zoología
interj	interjección	*	tabú
interrog	interrogativo	≈	aproximadamente equivalente a
inv	invariable	→	véase
iron	irónico		

SIGNOS DE LA A.F.I. EMPLEADOS EN LA TRANSCRIPCIÓN FONÉTICA DE LAS PALABRAS INGLESAS

Vocales

[iː]   como en español en *vida, tigre*.

[ɪ]   sin equivalencia en español. Parecida a [iː] pero aun más abierta.

[e]   como en español en *guerra, dejar*.

[æ]   sin equivalencia en español. Parecida a la [e] pero aun más abierta.

[ɑː]   como en español en *laurel, ahora*, pero enfatizada y alargada.

[ɔː]   como en español en *roca, manojo*, pero aun más abierta.

[ɒ]   sin equivalencia en español. Parecida a la [ɔː] pero aun más grave.

[uː]   como en español en *uno*, pero con el sonido más prolongado.

[ʊ]   sin equivalencia en español. Parecida a la [uː] pero aun más abierta.

[ʌ]   sin equivalencia en español. Sonido intermedio entre la *o* y la *e*.

[ɜː]   sin equivalencia en español. Sonido intermedio entre la *e* y la *r* inglesas.

[ə]   sin equivalencia en español. Parecida a la [ə] francesa en *venir, petit*.

[ə]   opcional. En algunos casos se pronuncia y en otros se omite.

Semiconsonantes

[j]   como en español en *labio, radio*.

[w]   como en español en *luego, huevo*.

Consonantes

[p]   como en español en *puerta, capa*, pero aspirada.

[t]   como en español en *todo, tienda*, pero aspirada.

[k]   como en español en *copa, queso*, pero aspirada.

[b]   como en español en *barco, vela*, pero aspirada.

[d]   como en español en *conde, candado*, pero aspirada.

[ð]   como en español en *adivinar, adorar*.

[g]   como en español en *guerra, gato*, pero aspirada.

[f]   como en español en *fuerza, fuego.*

[θ]   como en español en *hacer, ácido.*

[s]   como en español en *saber, silencio.*

[ʃ]   sin equivalencia en español. Fricativa palato-alveolar sorda. Parecida a la pronunciación de *chico*, si se alarga la consonante y se redondean los labios.

[v]   sin equivalencia en español. Fricativa labiodental. Al pronunciarla los incisivos superiores tocan el labio inferior y hay vibración de las cuerdas vocales. Es la pronunciación del francés en *avec.*

[z]   como en español en *mismo, asno.*

[ʒ]   sin equivalencia en español. Fricativa palato-alveolar sonora. Parecida a la pronunciación argentina de la *ll* pero con proyección de los labios.

[tʃ]   como en español en *chico, chocolate.*

[dʒ]   sin equivalencia exacta en español. Africada palato-alveolar sonora. Sonido semejante al de la *y* española en *cónyuge, yugo.*

[l]   como en español en *labio, cola.*

[m]   como en español en *madre, lima.*

[n]   como en español en *nota, notable.*

[ŋ]   como en español en *cuenca, ángulo.*

[r]   sonido fricativo parecido al de la *r* española en *pero.*

[h]   sonido parecido al de la *j* española en *jerga,* pero mucho más suave.

Otros signos

[']   indica el acento tónico primario.

[ˌ]   indica el acento tónico secundario.

[ː]   indica un alargamiento de la vocal.

[ʳ]   opcional. En algunos casos se pronuncia y en otros se omite.

Diptongos ingleses
(Sin equivalencia en español.)

[eɪ]   made [meɪd], way [weɪ], freight [freɪt].

[əʊ]   go [gəʊ], toe [təʊ], snow [snəʊ].

[aɪ]   lime [laɪm], thigh [θaɪ], try [traɪ].

[aʊ]   house [haʊs], cow [kaʊ].

[ɔɪ]   toy [tɔɪ], soil [sɔɪl].

RESUMEN DE LA GRAMÁTICA INGLESA

ARTÍCULO / ARTICLES

El inglés tiene dos clases de artículo: el definido y el indefinido.

- Artículo definido: **the**. Es invariable y corresponde a *el, la, los, las* y (en ciertos casos) *lo*.
- Artículo indefinido: **a** o **an**. Se usa para el singular en todos los géneros.
  —La forma **a** se usa: a) delante de consonantes (incluyendo entre ellas la **h** aspirada, la **w** y la **y**); b) delante de **u, eu** y **ew**, cuando suenan como en **use, European** y **ewe**, y delante de **o**, cuando suena como en **one**.
  —El plural español *unos* y *unas* se traduce al inglés por el adjetivo **some**: he had **some** papers in his hand, tenía unos papeles en la mano.

NOTA: El uso que hace el español del artículo determinado en expresiones como: me lavo *las* manos, ponte *el* sombrero, él se ha roto *el* brazo, no existe en inglés. Estas expresiones se traducen por: I wash **my** hands, put on **your** hat, he has broken **his** arm.

GÉNERO / GENDER

Por regla general, en inglés, son

- **Masculinos**. Los nombres que significan varón o animal macho: **man** (hombre); **knight** (caballero); **bull** (toro).
- **Femeninos**. Los que significan mujer o animal hembra: **woman** (mujer); **spinster** (solterona); **lady** (dama); **cow** (vaca).
- **Comunes**. Como en español, los de persona de una sola terminación para los dos géneros: **friend** (amigo, -ga); **neighbor** (vecino, -na); **companion** (compañero, -ra).
- **Neutros**. Los nombres de cosa concretos o abstractos; los de animales cuando no se especifica su sexo; los que significan niño [niño o niña indiferentemente] o niño de pecho como **child** o **baby**.

Excepciones:
- Los nombres de países, barcos y máquinas son generalmente del género femenino: **Poland** has lost **her** independence, Polonia ha perdido su independencia; **she** was a fine **ship**, era un hermoso barco.

Indicación del género

Hay cierto número de nombres que tienen palabras distintas para cada género: **man** (hombre); **woman** (mujer); **father** (padre); **mother** (madre); **widow** (viuda); **widower** (viudo); **bull** (toro); **cow** (vaca); **rooster** (gallo); **hen** (gallina), etc.

En los demás casos, el género se infiere del contexto (**she is an orphan**, ella es huérfana), o se distingue:

- Por medio de las terminaciones femeninas **-ess, -ix** o **-ine**: actor, **actress** (actor, actriz); duke, **duchess** (duque, duquesa); testator, **testatrix** (testador, testadora); hero, **heroine** (héroe, heroína).
- Por medio de **male, female, woman**, etc., en función de adjetivo o de los pronombres **he-, she-** como prefijos: **female fish** (pez hembra); **woman lawyer** (abogada, licenciada); **he-goat** (macho cabrío); **she-ass** (asna, jumenta).
- Por medio de palabras compuestas en que uno de los elementos expresa el género: **man-servant** (criado); **maidservant** (criada); **bull-elephant** (elefante), **doe-hare** (liebre hembra), **cock-sparrow** (gorrión).

PLURAL (Substantivos) / THE PLURAL OF NOUNS
Regla general

En inglés la desinencia del plural es una s que se añade a la forma propia del singular: bale, **bales**; chair, **chairs**.

Observ.: Los nombres terminados en se, ce, ge y ze ganan una sílaba en el plural al tomar la s, ya que la e muda se pronuncia como [i]: **fence** [fens], valla; pl. **fences** ['fensiz], vallas.

Excepciones y casos particulares
* Toman **es** en el plural:
  —Los nombres terminados en o precedida de consonante: virago, **viragoes**; potato, **potatoes**.

    Sin embargo, los nombres de formación moderna o de origen extranjero hacen el plural en s: auto, **autos**; contralto, **contraltos**; dynamo, **dynamos**; memento, **mementos**; piano, **pianos**.

  —Los nombres terminados en s, sh, ch (con sonido de *ch*), x y z: brass, **brasses**; bush, **bushes**; wrench, **wrenches**; box, **boxes**; chintz, **chintzes**.

  Observ.: Los terminados en ex hacen el plural en **exes** o **ices**; los terminados en ix lo hacen en **ixes** o **ices**: vortex, **vortexes** o **vortices**; appendix, **appendixes** o **appendices**.

* Los nombres terminados en f o fe hacen el plural en ves: half, **halves**; knife, **knives**; wolf, **wolves**.

  —Se exceptúan: **dwarf, gulf, safe, still-life, strife** y los terminados en **ff, ief** y **oof**, que hacen el plural en s: dwarf, **dwarfs**; cliff, **cliffs**; belief, **beliefs**; roof, **roofs**. Sin embargo, *thief* hace **thieves**.

  —Algunos tienen plural doble en fs y en ves, como: beef, **beefs** y **beeves**; hoof, **hoofs** y **hooves**; scarf, **scarfs** y **scarves**; wharf, **wharfs** y **wharves**.

* Los nombres terminados en **quy** o en y precedida de consonante hacen el plural cambiando la y en **ies**: colloquy, **colloquies**; cry, **cries**; oddity, **oddities**.

  —Sin embargo, los nombres propios terminados en y, con muy raras excepciones, hacen el plural en s: Henry, **Henrys**.

* Algunos nombres son invariables: **sheep** (carnero, carneros); **swine** (cerdo, cerdos). Otros tienen formas propias para el singular y para el plural: child, **children**; die, **dice**; foot, **feet**; man, **men**; mouse, **mice**; woman, **women**; tooth, **teeth**.

GENITIVO / THE GENITIVE CASE

En ciertos casos, el inglés expresa el genitivo añadiendo una s apostrofada (**'s**) al nombre del poseedor y poniendo sin artículo el nombre de lo poseído (**John's father**, el padre de Juan). Es lo que se llama *caso genitivo* o *genitivo sajón.*

Se omite la s (nunca el apóstrofe):
* Después de un nombre en plural terminado en s: the **birds'** nests, los nidos de los pájaros.

* Después de un nombre en singular cuya última sílaba empiece con s: **Moses'** law, la ley de Moisés.

* Después de un nombre propio latino, griego o extranjero terminado en s, es o x: **Cassius'** dagger, el puñal de Casio; **Achilles'** heel, el talón de Aquiles. Nótese, sin embargo: **Venus's** beauty, la hermosura de Venus.

* Después de un nombre terminado en s o **ce**, cuando va seguido de **sake**: for **goodness'** sake!, ¡por Dios!; for **conscience'** sake, por conciencia.

Casos especiales
* Puede usarse con elipsis del nombre de la cosa poseída cuando éste significa *iglesia, hospital, casa, tienda:* **St. Paul's**, la catedral de San Pablo; at my **aunt's**, en casa de mi tía; I am going to the **grocer's**, voy a la tienda de comestibles. También se usa con elipsis en casos como: this car is my **father's**, este coche es de mi padre; Is this your hat? No, it is **Mr. Brown's**; ¿Este sombrero es el suyo? No, es el del señor Brown.

* Si hay más de dos nombres propios de poseedor, el signo del genitivo se pone detrás del último: **Mary and Robert's** brother, el hermano de María y Roberto.

ADJETIVO / ADJECTIVES

El adjetivo inglés es invariable. Una misma forma sirve para todos los géneros en singular y en plural: an **old** man, un hombre viejo; an **old** house, una casa vieja; these trees are **old**, estos árboles son **viejos**.

Lugar del adjetivo

Por regla general, el adjetivo (cuando no tiene función de predicado) precede al substantivo que califica o determina: a **clever** man, un hombre inteligente; a **long** journey, un largo viaje.

El adjetivo va pospuesto:

- Cuando lleva un complemento: a man **worthy** of esteem, un hombre digno de aprecio.
- Cuando completa el sentido del verbo: he found the plot **absurd**, halló absurdo el argumento.
- Cuando equivale a una oración subordinada: the garden **proper** is not very large, el jardín propiamente dicho no es muy grande.
- Cuando significa de alto, de ancho, de edad, etc.: the tree is twenty feet **high**, el árbol tiene veinte pies de alto.
- Cuando califica un pronombre terminado en -thing o -body: there is nothing **strange** about that, eso no tiene nada de extraño.
- En algunas denominaciones de cargo, empleo, etc. y en ciertas expresiones procedentes del francés: accountant **general**, jefe de contabilidad; court **martial**, consejo de guerra.
- Los adjetivos **worth**, **ill**, **left** (que queda), **missing** y los compuestos con el prefijo a- suelen usarse sólo como predicados. Si alguno de ellos se aplica directamente al substantivo, debe ir detrás de éste: a life **worth** preserving, una vida que merece ser conservada; he has only three dollars **left**, sólo le quedan tres dólares.
- La palabra **alone** va siempre detrás del nombre o el pronombre: leave him **alone**, déjalo solo.

El substantivo usado como adjetivo

En inglés puede usarse un substantivo para calificar a otro substantivo. En este caso el primero va inmediatamente delante del segundo: **coal** ship, barco carbonero; **pocket** knife, navaja.

El comparativo y el superlativo

Al comparativo español *tan...como*, corresponde el inglés **as...as** para la afirmación, y **so...as** para la negación: my house is **as** beautiful **as** yours, mi casa es tan hermosa como la de usted; my house is not **so** beautiful **as** yours, mi casa no es tan hermosa como la de usted.

Al comparativo *más (o menos)...que*, corresponde el inglés **more (o less)...than**: my house is **more** (o **less**) beautiful **than** yours, mi casa es más (o menos) hermosa que la de usted.

El inglés no tiene desinencia propia para el superlativo absoluto. Este superlativo se forma anteponiendo al adjetivo los adverbios **very**, **most**, etc.: **very** high, altísimo; **most** excellent, excelentísimo.

Al superlativo relativo *el más* (o *el menos)... de*, corresponde el inglés **the most** (o **the least**)... **in** [delante de un nombre de lugar] u **of** [delante de los demás nombres]: **the most** populous quarter **in** town, el barrio más populoso de la ciudad; **the least** brave man **of** the regiment, el hombre menos valiente del regimiento.

Sin embargo, el comparativo correspondiente a *más...* y el superlativo correspondiente a *el más...* suelen formarse, cuando se trata de adjetivos monosílabos y de algunos bisílabos, añadiendo **-er** y **-est** a la forma del positivo. Así, de short (corto) se hace **shorter** (más corto) y **shortest** (el más corto).

Al agregar **-er** y **-est** a la forma del positivo, la terminación de éste queda modificada en los casos siguientes:

- Adjetivos terminados en **-e**. Pierden la **-e**: nice, **nicer**, **nicest**; large, **larger**, **largest**.
- Adjetivos terminados en **-y** precedida de consonante. Cambian la **-y** en **-i**: burly, **burlier**, **burliest**.
- Adjetivos monosílabos terminados en consonante precedida de vocal breve. Doblan la consonante: big, **bigger**, **biggest**; fat, **fatter**, **fattest**.

Observaciones:

No se pueden usar las formas en **-er** y **-est** con adjetivos compuestos con el prefijo a-, ni con los terminados en -al, -ed, -ful, -ic, -ile, -ive, -ose y -ous: alive, mortal, aged, rustic, fragile, massive, verbose, famous.

NUMERALES / NUMERALS

Algunas particularidades

Cardinales
- Los números compuestos de decenas y unidades (a partir de *veinte*) se expresan poniendo las unidades a continuación de las decenas, separadas por un guión: **twenty-one** (21); **forty-six** (46).

  También puede usarse la forma **one and twenty** o **one-and-twenty** (21), pero esto es menos corriente.

- Los números de cien, ciento, mil, un millón, etc., se expresan así: **a** o **one hundred; a** o **one thousand; a** o **one million**. Generalmente se usa **a** para los números redondos y **one** con los demás: **a hundred** men, cien hombres; **one hundred and sixty** dollars, ciento sesenta dólares.

  A doscientos, trescientos, dos mil, tres mil, etc., corresponden **two hundred, three hundred, two thousand, three thousand,** etc.

- En los números compuestos se pone **and** entre las centenas y las decenas o entre las centenas y las unidades, si no hay decenas: five hundred **and** thirty-six (536); five hundred **and** six (506).

  Después de **thousand** sólo se pone **and** cuando le sigue un número inferior a cien: three thousand **and** fifty-two (3.052).

Ordinales
- Los ordinales (excepto los tres primeros: **first, second, third**) se forman añadiendo **th** a la forma del cardinal: **four** (cuatro), **fourth** (cuarto); **seven** (siete), **seventh** (séptimo).

  Al recibir la desinencia del ordinal, el cardinal queda modificado en los casos siguientes:
  —**five** y **twelve** cambian la **v** en **f: fifth, twelfth**.
  —**eight** pierde la **t: eighth**.
  —**nine** pierde la **e: ninth**.
  —**twenty, thirty,** etc., cambian la **y** en **ie: twentieth, thirtieth,** etc.
  En los números compuestos, sólo toma la forma de ordinal el último elemento: **thirty-first, twenty-second, forty-third, fifty-eighth**.

- Cuando el ordinal se aplica al nombre de un soberano se escribe con mayúscula y se le antepone el artículo: Henry **the Fourth**, Enrique cuarto; Pius **the Twelfth**, Pío doce.

PRONOMBRE PERSONAL / PERSONAL PRONOUNS

Formas del pronombre personal

Personas	Oficio	Singular		Plural	
1.ª	sujeto complemento reflexivo	I me myself	masc. y fem.	we us ourselves	masc. y fem.
2.ª	sujeto complemento reflexivo	thou, you thee, you thyself, yourself	masc. y fem.	ye, you you yourselves	masc. y fem.
3.ª	sujeto complemento reflexivo	he (masc.) she (fem.) it (neut.) him (masc.) her (fem.) it (neut.) himself (masc.) herself (fem.) itself (neut.)		they them themselves	todos los géneros

Observaciones

- El pronombre complemento indirecto lleva la preposición to: she promised it **to me**, ella me la prometió.

  Sin embargo, con ciertos verbos, se puede omitir el to a condición de poner el complemento indirecto delante del directo: my father gave **me** this book, mi padre me dio este libro.

  Con **to tell** y **to answer**, se usa siempre esta última forma: he told **me** what had happened, me contó lo que había ocurrido.

- Después de los verbos seguidos de una partícula, el pronombre personal complemento directo se coloca entre el verbo y la partícula. Así a *he took off his coat* (se quitó el abrigo), corresponderá *he took it off*, se lo quitó.

- **All**, con un pronombre personal, se coloca después de éste; **all of**, delante: they **all**, **all of** them, todos, todos ellos o ellas.

- Después de las preposiciones **about, around, behind, with** y de las que indican movimiento, el inglés emplea el pronombre personal no reflexivo en vez del reflexivo: she brought her workbasket **with her**, ella trajo consigo su neceser de costura; he looked **behind him**, miró detrás de sí.

- El pronombre personal usado como antecedente de un relativo forma las expresiones **he who** o **that**, **she who** o **that**, etc., equivalentes a las españolas *el que, aquel que, la que*, etc.

  Sin embargo, en el lenguaje moderno no se dice **they who** o **that**, sino **those who** o **that**, los que, aquellos que.

- **They** puede ser sujeto de una oración impersonal, como: **they** say that, dicen que, se dice que.

- Las formas reflexivas del pronombre personal se usan también para reforzar el pronombre sujeto: I saw it **myself**, yo mismo lo vi.

POSESIVO (Adjetivo y pronombre) / POSSESSIVE ADJECTIVES AND PRONOUNS

Los adjetivos y pronombres posesivos ingleses son invariables por lo que se refiere a la cosa poseída. Sólo concuerdan con el nombre del posesor.

Adjetivos

Singular

1.ª persona:	**my**	mi, mis
2.ª persona:	**thy, your**	tu, tus*
3.ª persona:	**his**	su, sus [de él]
	her	su, sus [de ella]
	its	su, sus [de ello; de un animal o cosa en género neutro]

Plural

1.ª persona:	**our**	nuestro, nuestra, nuestros, nuestras
2.ª persona:	**your**	tu, tus; vuestro, vuestra; vuestros, vuestras; su, sus [de usted o ustedes]
3.ª persona:	**their**	su, sus [de ellos, ellas, tanto para el masc. y el fem. como para el neutro]

Observaciones:

- Cuando el adjetivo posesivo se refiere a dos o más nombres de género diferente se pone en masculino: all the pupils, **boys** and **girls**, were there, **each** carrying **his** little present, todos los alumnos, niños y niñas, estaban allí llevando cada uno su pequeño regalo.

- Cuando no hay idea de posesión, suele substituirse el adjetivo posesivo por el genitivo con **of**: the remembrance **of it**, su recuerdo; the directions for the use **of them**, las instrucciones para su uso.

Pronombres

Singular

1.ª persona:	**mine**	el mío, la mía, los míos, las mías
2.ª persona:	**thine, yours**	el tuyo, la tuya, los tuyos, las tuyas*
3.ª persona:	**his**	el suyo, la suya, los suyos, las suyas [de él]
	hers	el suyo, la suya, los suyos, las suyas [de ella]
	its own	el suyo, la suya, los suyos, las suyas [de un animal o cosa en género neutro]

Plural

1.ª persona:	**ours**	el nuestro, la nuestra, los nuestros, las nuestras
2.ª persona:	**yours**	el tuyo, la tuya, los tuyos, las tuyas; el vuestro, la vuestra, los vuestros, las vuestras; el suyo, la suya, los suyos, las suyas [de usted o de ustedes]
3.ª persona:	**theirs**	el suyo, la suya, los suyos, las suyas [de ellos, de ellas, tanto para el masc. y el fem. como para el neutro]

Observaciones:
- Cuando el pronombre posesivo va después del verbo **to be** puede traducirse también por el posesivo español sin artículo: this hat is **mine**, este sombrero es mío (o es el mío).
- El pronombre posesivo precedido de **of** equivale al adjetivo español *mío, tuyo,* etc., o *a uno de mis, de tus,* etc.: a friend **of mine**, un amigo mío, uno de mis amigos.

---

*El adjetivo posesivo **thy** y el pronombre **thine** sólo se usan en poesía, en la Biblia y en las oraciones. En el lenguaje corriente se usa **your** y **yours** para la segunda persona del singular, lo mismo que para la del plural.

CONJUGACIÓN DE VERBOS / CONJUGATION OF VERBS

La conjugación regular de un verbo inglés comprende un número de formas muy reducido. En todos los tiempos personales se usa la misma forma para todas las personas del singular y del plural, con excepción de la tercera persona del singular del presente de indicativo y de la segunda del singular del presente y el pretérito de indicativo.

Observación: La segunda persona del singular (que se forma añadiendo **st** a la forma propia del tiempo) sólo se emplea en poesía, en la oración y en la Biblia. En el lenguaje corriente se emplea la forma del plural, lo mismo para éste que para el singular. Así, **you dance** equivale, según los casos, a *tú bailas, usted baila, vosotros bailáis* o *ustedes bailan.*

Presente de indicativo

Tiene la forma del infinitivo sin **to** para la primera persona del singular y todas las del plural: I, we, you, they dance.

La tercera persona del singular

Se forma añadiendo **es** o **s** a la forma del infinitivo.

Toma **es:**
- En los verbos cuyo infinitivo termina en **ch, sh, ss, x** o **z**: reaches, brushes, passes, boxes, buzzes.
- En los verbos **to do** y **to go**: does, goes.

Toma **s:**
- En los verbos cuyo infinitivo termina en una **e** muda, una vocal o un diptongo: dances, lives, baas, sees, draws, knows.
- En aquellos cuyo infinitivo termina en una consonante que *no* es **ch, sh, ss, x** o **z**: sobs, packs, rings, kills, hears, bleats.

Observaciones:
- Los verbos terminados en y precedida de consonante cambian la y en ie: cry, cries; fly, flies. Los terminados en y precedida de vocal no cambian la y: buy buys; play, plays.

- Los verbos terminados en ce, se o ge y los terminados en ch, sh, ss, x o z, ganan fonéticamente una sílaba al tomar la desinencia de la tercera persona del singular: dance, danc·es; buzz, buzz·es; brush, brush·es.

Pretérito de indicativo

La forma del pretérito de indicativo distingue, una de otra, dos clases de verbos:

Verbos débiles
Forman el pretérito y el participio pasivo añadiendo ed, d o t a la forma del infinitivo: walk, walked; live, lived. Algunos acortan (no cambian) la vocal de la raíz y añaden t: keep, kept; sweep, swept.

Observaciones:
- Los verbos débiles terminados en y precedida de consonante cambian la y en ie al tomar la desinencia del pretérito y del participio pasivo: cry, cried; spy, spied. Los terminados en y precedida de vocal no cambian la y: cloy, cloyed; play, played. Por excepción, to lay y to pay hacen el pretérito y el participio pasivo en aid: laid y paid.

- Los verbos que terminan en una consonante dental ganan fonéticamente una sílaba al tomar la desinencia del pretérito y el participio pasivo: blind, blind·ed; wait, wait·ed.

- Los verbos monosílabos y los polisílabos acentuados en la última sílaba, cuando terminan en una vocal breve seguida de una sola consonante, doblan ésta en el pretérito, el participio pasivo y el gerundio: fit, fitted, fitting; bar, barred, barring; compel, compelled, compelling.
  Cuando la consonante final es l precedida de una sola vocal, pueden doblar la l aunque no estén acentuados en la última sílaba: travel, traveled o travelled.

Verbos fuertes
Forman el pretérito y el participio pasivo cambiando la vocal de la raíz y añadiendo o no e, en, n o ne. Generalmente tienen el pretérito diferente del participio pasivo: break, broke, broken; bear (llevar), born, borne.
Advertencia: Los pretéritos, participios pasivos y gerundios de los verbos fuertes, así como los de otros que ofrezcan particularidades de forma u ortografía, se encontrarán en el cuerpo de este Diccionario al final del artículo correspondiente a cada verbo.

Futuro de indicativo

Se forma anteponiendo shall o will al infinitivo sin to (véase lo referente al uso de shall y will en los respectivos artículos de este Diccionario): I shall come, yo vendré; we will come, nosotros vendremos; you will come, tú vendrás, usted vendrá, vosotros vendréis, ustedes vendrán; he will come, él vendrá; they will come, ellos vendrán.

Potencial

Se forma anteponiendo should y would al infinitivo sin to (véase lo referente al uso de should y would en los respectivos artículos de este Diccionario): I should come, yo vendría; we would come, nosotros vendríamos; you would come, tú vendrías, usted vendría, vosotros vendríais, ustedes vendrían; he would come, él vendría; they would come, ellos vendrían.

Imperativo

El imperativo inglés sólo tiene una forma propia que es la del infinitivo sin to y sólo se usa para las segundas personas: come, ven, venga usted, venid, vengan ustedes.
Para las personas 1.ª y 3.ª hay que recurrir a una oración formada con el verbo to let: let us see, veamos.

Tiempos compuestos

Se forman, como en español, con el verbo auxiliar **to have** (haber) y el participio pasivo.

Ejemplos:

I have played, yo he jugado; **he has played,** él ha jugado (pretérito perfecto).

I had played, yo había jugado o hube jugado (pretérito pluscuamperfecto o pretérito anterior).

I shall have played, yo habré jugado; **he will have played,** él habrá jugado (futuro perfecto).

I should have played, yo habría jugado; **he would have played,** él habría jugado (potencial compuesto o perfecto).

Conjugación continua

Además de esta forma de conjugación, el inglés tiene otra llamada *continua* que se forma con el auxiliar **to be** y el gerundio del verbo: **I am coming, I was coming.** Esta forma se usa para indicar una acción en curso de realización, o sea no terminada.

En el presente, corresponde a un presente español del verbo en cuestión o de una oración del verbo *estar:* **I am writing** a letter, escribo una carta o estoy escribiendo una carta.

En el pretérito simple corresponde a un imperfecto español: **he was writing** a letter, él escribía una carta o estaba escribiendo una carta.

Observación: La forma continua no puede usarse para expresar una acción instantánea o definitiva, como tampoco una acción habitual o permanente. Así no se dirá: **I am forgiving** him, **the sun is setting** every day, **he is being** her father, sino: **I forgive** him, **the sun sets** every day, **he is** her father.

INFINITIVO / THE INFINITIVE

Por regla general, el infinitivo va precedido de la partícula **to,** que en muchos casos equivale a las preposiciones *a* o *para.*

Infinitivo sin to

El infinitivo se usa sin **to:**

- Después de los auxiliares defectivos **shall, will, can, may** y **must: I shall write** to him, le escribiré; you **cannot speak** French, usted no sabe hablar francés; we **must be** quiet, hemos de callar.

  —Nótese que después de **ought** se usa el infinitivo con **to:** you **ought to know** it, usted debería saberlo.

- Después de **to dare** y **to need** usados como auxiliares: he **dared not speak** to him, él no se atrevió a hablarle; they **need not fear,** no tienen por qué temer.

- Después de los verbos que expresan sensación o percepción, como **to hear, to see, to feel, to behold, to observe, to watch,** etc.: **I hear** him **speak** in the hall, le oigo hablar en el vestíbulo; **I felt** the child **tremble** in my arms, sentí al niño temblar en mis brazos.

- Después de los verbos **to let** (dejar, permitir), **to bid** (ordenar, mandar) y **to make** (hacer que se ejecute una acción): **let me read** this letter, déjeme leer esta carta; he **bade** her **open** the door, le mandó abrir la puerta.

  —Sin embargo, en la voz pasiva, estos verbos van seguidos del infinitivo con **to: I was let to read** the letter, se me dejó leer la carta.

- Después de **and, or,** o **than** y **but** en oraciones como: they decided to stop there **and wait** for him, decidieron detenerse allí y esperarle; he was told to be quiet **or go,** se le dijo que se callara o que se fuera; she did nothing other **than laugh,** ella no hizo más que reír.

- En ciertas oraciones interrogativas o exclamatorias: a father not **love** his son!, ¡un padre no querer a su hijo!

- Después de las locuciones **had better, had rather, would rather,** etc.: you **had better wait,** vale más que espere.

Infinitivo traducido por el subjuntivo o el indicativo

El infinitivo inglés se traduce algunas veces por un subjuntivo y, aun, por un indicativo español.

Ejemplos: he asked me **to pay** the bill, me pidió que pagase la cuenta; the captain ordered the soldiers **to bring** the prisoner, el capitán ordenó a los soldados que trajesen el prisionero; I want him **to do** this, quiero que él haga esto; they expect him **to go** soon, esperan que se irá pronto.

GERUNDIO / THE GERUND

El gerundio inglés, o sea la forma verbal terminada en **-ing**, puede hacer varios oficios y generalmente se traduce, según los casos:

Como gerundio

Por el gerundio español: he was **waiting** for me, él me estaba esperando.

Como participio—adjetivo

- Por un participio activo: **cutting** tool, instrumento cortante; in a **surprising** manner, de un modo sorprendente.

- Por un participio pasivo: an **amusing** book, un libro entretenido; **lying** on a sofa, echado en un sofá.

- Por un adjetivo, o por una expresión equivalente a éste: a **calculating** person, una persona calculadora, interesada; **hunting** season, temporada de caza; **sewing** machine, máquina de coser.
  Observación: Por su naturaleza verbal puede tener un complemento directo. En este caso se traduce por *que* y un verbo en tiempo personal: a package **containing** six pairs of gloves, un paquete *que* contiene seis pares de guantes.

Como infinitivo o nombre verbal

- Por un infinitivo nominal: before **speaking**, antes de hablar; an organization for **helping** the poor, una organización para socorrer a los pobres.

- Por *que* y un verbo en tiempo personal (generalmente en subjuntivo): this door needs **painting**, esta puerta necesita que la pinten.

- Por un substantivo: he was engaged in the **reading** of that book, estaba ocupado en la lectura de aquel libro.

Observaciones:

—**On**, delante de la forma verbal en **-ing**, se traduce generalmente por *al* seguido de un infinitivo: on **arriving**, *al* llegar.

—Cuando un nombre va delante de la forma en **-ing**, debe ponerse en genitivo si es de los que lo admiten: my father was annoyed at Peter's **coming** so late, mi padre estaba enojado de que Pedro viniese tan tarde (o porque Pedro venía tan tarde).

—Si en lugar del nombre hay un pronombre, éste debe tomar la forma del posesivo: would you mind **my opening** the window?, ¿le molestaría que yo abriese la ventana?

NEGACIÓN / EXPRESSING NEGATION

Construcción de la oración negativa

- Cuando el verbo es **to be** o **to have**; **to dare** o **to need** (como auxiliares), o alguno de los defectivos **shall, will, can, may, must** o **ought**, la negación se expresa poniendo **not** inmediatamente después del verbo: they **are** not here, no están aquí; he **dared** not come, no se atrevía a venir; John **will** not win the prize, Juan no ganará el premio; if I **may** not go, si no puedo ir.
  Observ.: El presente **can** not se escribe en una sola palabra: **cannot**.

- Cuando el verbo es otro cualquiera en tiempo simple, la negación se expresa por medio del auxiliar **to do** seguido de **not**; el verbo toma la forma invariable del infinitivo sin **to**: I **do** not see it, no lo veo; he **does** not play, él no juega; her father **did** not come, su padre no vino.
  En los tiempos compuestos no se usa **do, does, did** y se pone **not** inmediatamente después del auxiliar: he **has** not seen it, él no lo ha visto.
  Observ.: Con **dare** la negación puede expresarse también así, pero el verbo regido lleva **to**: they **did** not dare **to** come, no se atrevieron a venir.

- En las oraciones interrogativas, **not** se pone después del sujeto si éste es un pronombre y antes de él si es un nombre: do you **not** see it?, ¿no lo ve usted?; **did** not (o **didn't**) your brother win the prize?, ¿no ganó el premio su hermano?

- En el infinitivo y en el gerundio se antepone **not** al verbo: **not** to understand, no entender; **not** understanding, no entendiendo.

- En el imperativo se antepone **do not** al verbo: **do not** (o **don't**) laugh, no rías (ría usted, rían ustedes, riáis); **do not** (o **don't**) let them come, que no vengan.

- En el lenguaje corriente **not** se contrae frecuentemente con **do** o con otros verbos: **don't** (do not); **didn't** (did not); **aren't** (are not); **can't** (cannot); **isn't** (is not); **won't** (will not); etc.

- Cuando el carácter negativo de la oración está determinado por palabras como **never**, **no**, **nobody**, **nothing**, **nowhere**, **by no means**, no se usa **not** ni el auxiliar **to do**: it is **never** too late, nunca es tarde; I have **no** time, no tengo tiempo.

INTERROGACIÓN / INTERROGATIVES

Construcción de la oración interrogativa

- Cuando el verbo es **to be** o **to have**; **to dare** o **to need** (como auxiliares) o algún defectivo como **shall**, **will**, **can**, **may**, **must** o **ought**, el sujeto va inmediatamente después del verbo: are they here?, ¿están aquí?; have you any money?, ¿tiene usted dinero?; dare you go there?, ¿se atreve usted a ir allí?; need he do it?, ¿necesita hacerlo?; can this boy write?, ¿sabe escribir este niño?

- Cuando el verbo es otro cualquiera en tiempo simple, la oración se construye con el auxiliar **to do**, que va delante del sujeto; el verbo toma la forma invariable del infinitivo sin **to**: do you see this tree?, ¿ve usted este árbol?; did your brother win the race?, ¿ganó la carrera su hermano?
  —En los tiempos compuestos no se usa **do**, **does**, **did** y el sujeto va inmediatamente después del auxiliar: have you seen the house?, ¿ha visto usted la casa?

- Cuando la oración empieza con un pronombre interrogativo sujeto del verbo o con un adjetivo interrogativo que acompaña al sujeto, no se usa **do**, **did** y no hay inversión del sujeto: **who** wins the prize?, ¿quién gana el premio?; **what** happened to him?, ¿qué le pasó?; **which** pillars support the arch?, ¿qué pilares sostienen el arco?

- Después de un adverbio interrogativo la oración se construye como se ha indicado: **how long** will they remain here?, ¿cuánto tiempo permanecerán aquí?

CONJUGACIÓN DE TO HAVE (TENER), HAD (TENÍA, TUVE), HAD (TENIDO)

INDICATIVO

	Afirmación	Negación	Interrogación (Negación)
Presente	*yo tengo* I have he, she, it has we, you, they have	*yo no tengo* I have not he, she, it has not we, you, they have not	*¿ (no) tengo yo?* have I (not)? has he, she, it (not)? have we, you, they (not)?
Pretérito (Past.)	*yo tenía, tuve* I had you had, etc.	*yo no tenía, tuve* I had not you had not, etc.	*¿ (no) tenía, tuve yo?* had I (not)? had you (not)?, etc.
Futuro simple	*yo tendré* I, we shall have you, he, they will have	*yo no tendré* I, we shall not have you, he, they will not have	*¿ (no) tendré yo?* shall I, we (not) have? will you, he, they (not) have?

	Afirmación	Negación	Interrogación (Negación)
Condicional simple	*yo tendría* I, we should have you, he, they would have	*yo no tendría* I, we should not have you, he, they would not have	*¿ (no) tendría yo?* should I, we (not) have? would you, he, they (not) have?
Pretérito perfecto	*yo he tenido* I, we, you, they have had he has had	*yo no he tenido* I, we, you, they have not had he has not had	*¿ (no) he tenido yo?* have I, we, you, they (not) had? has he (not) had?
Pretérito plusc.	*yo había tenido* I, you...had had	*yo no había tenido* I, you...had not had	*¿ (no) había tenido yo?* had I, you...(not) had?
Futuro perfecto	*yo habré tenido* I, we shall have had you, he, they will have had	*yo no habré tenido* I, we shall not have had you, he, they will not have had	*¿ (no) habré yo tenido?* shall I, we (not) have had? will he, you, they (not) have had?
Condicional compuesto	*yo habría tenido* I, we should have had you, he, they would have had	*yo no habría tenido* I, we should not have had you, he, they would not have had	*¿ (no) habría yo tenido?* should I, we (not) have had? would you, he, they (not) have had?

IMPERATIVO

Afirmación	Negación
tenga yo	*no tenga yo*
let me have have let him (her, it) have let us have have let them have	don't let me have don't have, etc.

PARTICIPIO PRES. GERUNDIO }	having *teniendo*
PARTICIPIO PAS.	had *tenido*
INFINITIVO SIMPLE	(not) to have *(no) tener*
INFINITIVO COMP.	to have had *haber tenido*

CONJUGACIÓN DE **TO BE** (SER, ESTAR), **WAS** (ERA, FUI), **BEEN** (SIDO)

INDICATIVO

	Afirmación	Negación	Interrogación (Negación)
Presente	*yo soy* I am he, she, it is we, you, they are	*yo no soy* I am not he, she, it is not we, you, they are not	*¿ (no) soy yo?* am I (not)? is he, she, it (not)? are we, you, they (not)?
Pretérito (Past.)	*yo era, fui* I, he was we, you, they were	*yo no era, fui* I, he was not we, you, they were not	*¿ (no) era, fui yo?* was I, he (not)? were we, you, they (not)?
Futuro simple	*yo seré* I, we shall be he, you, they will be	*yo no seré* I, we shall not be he, you, they will not be	*¿ (no) seré yo?* shall I, we (not) be? will you, he, they (not) be?
Condicional simple	*yo sería* I, we should be he, you, they would be	*yo no sería* I, we should not be he, you, they would not be	*¿ (no) sería yo?* should I, we (not) be? would you, he, they (not) be?
Pretérito perfecto	*yo he sido* I, we, you, they have been he has been	*yo no he sido* I, we, you, they have not been he has not been	*¿ (no) he sido yo?* have I, we, you, they (not) been? has he (not) been?
Pretérito plusc.	*yo había sido* I, you...had been	*yo no había sido* I, you...had not been	*¿ (no) había sido yo?* had I, you...(not) been?
Futuro perfecto	*yo habré sido* I, we shall have been you, he, they will have been	*yo no habré sido* I, we shall not have been you, he, they will not have been	*¿ (no) habré yo sido?* shall I, we (not) have been? will you, he, they (not) have been?
Condicional compuesto	*yo habría sido* I, we should have been you, he, they would have been	*yo no habría sido* I, we should not have been you, he, they would not have been	*¿ (no) habría yo sido?* should I, we (not) have been? would you, he, they (not) have been?

IMPERATIVO

Afirmación	Negación
sea yo let me be be let him (her, it) be let us be be let them be	*no sea yo* don't let me be don't be, etc.

PARTICIPIO PRES. GERUNDIO.	}	being *siendo*
PARTICIPIO PAS.		been *sido*
INFINITIVO SIMPLE		(not) to be *(no) ser*
INFINITIVO COMP.		to have been *haber sido*

CONJUGACIÓN DE UN VERBO REGULAR

to look (mirar), **looked** (miraba, miré), **looked** (mirado)

INDICATIVO

	Afirmación	Negación	Interrogación (Negación)
Presente	*yo miro* I look you look he, she, it looks we, you, they look	*yo no miro* I do not look you do not look he, she, it does not look we, you, they do not look	*¿ (no) miro yo?* do I (not) look? do you (not) look? does he, she, it (not) look? do we, you, they (not) look?
Pretérito (Past.)	*yo miré, miraba* I looked you looked he looked, etc.	*yo no miré, miraba* I did not look you did not look he did not look, etc.	*¿ (no) miré, miraba yo?* did I (not) look? did you (not) look? did he (not) look?, etc.
Futuro simple	*yo miraré* I, we shall look you, he, they will look	*yo no miraré* I, we shall not look you, he, they will not look	*¿ (no) miraré yo?* shall I, we (not) look? will you, he, they (not) look?
Condicional simple	*yo miraría* I, we should look you, he, they would look	*yo no miraría* I, we should not look you, he, they would not look	*¿ (no) miraría yo?* should I, we (not) look? would you, he, they (not) look?
Pretérito perfecto	*yo he mirado* I, we, you, they have looked he has looked	*yo no he mirado* I, we, you, they have not looked he has not looked	*¿ (no) he mirado yo?* have I, we, you, they (not) looked? has he (not) looked?
Pretérito plusc.	*yo había mirado* I, you...had looked	*yo no había mirado* I, you...had not looked	*¿ (no) había mirado yo?* had I, you...(not) looked?
Futuro perfecto	*yo habré mirado* I, we shall have looked you, he, they will have looked	*yo no habré mirado* I, we shall not have looked you, he, they will not have looked	*¿ (no) habré yo mirado?* shall I, we (not) have looked? will you, he, they (not) have looked?
Condicional compuesto	*yo habría mirado* I, we should have looked you, he, they would have looked	*yo no habría mirado* I, we should not have looked you, he, they would not have looked	*¿ (no) habría yo mirado?* should I, we (not) have looked? would you, he, they (not) have looked?

IMPERATIVO

Afirmación	Negación
mire yo	*no mire yo*
let me look	don't let me look
look	don't look, etc.
let him (her, it) look	
let us look	
look	
let them look	

PARTICIPIO PRES. ⎫ GERUNDIO ⎭	looking *mirando*
PARTICIPIO PAS.	looked *mirado*
INFINITIVO SIMPLE	(not) to look *(no) mirar*
INFINITIVO COMP.	to have looked *haber mirado*

CONJUGACIÓN DE UN VERBO IRREGULAR

to go (ir), **went** (iba, fui), **gone** (ido)

INDICATIVO

	Afirmación	Negación	Interrogación (Negación)
Presente	*yo voy* I go you go he, she, it goes we, you, they go	*yo no voy* I do not go you do not go he, she, it does not go we, you, they do not go	*¿ (no) voy yo?* do I (not) go? do you (not) go? does he, she, it (not) go? do we, you, they (not) go?
Pretérito (Past.)	*yo iba, fui* I went you went he went, etc.	*yo no iba, fui* I did not go you did not go he did not go, etc.	*¿ (no) fui, iba yo?* did I (not) go? did you (not) go? did he (not) go?, etc.
Futuro simple	*yo iré* I, we shall go you, he, they will go	*yo no iré* I, we shall not go you, he, they will not go	*¿ (no) iré yo?* shall I, we (not) go? will you, he, they (not) go?
Condicional simple	*yo iría* I, we should go you, he, they would go	*yo no iría* I, we should not go you, he, they would not go	*¿ (no) iría yo?* should I, we (not) go? would you, he, they (not) go?

	Afirmación	Negación	Interrogación (Negación)
Pretérito perfecto	*yo he ido* I, we, you, they have gone he has gone	*yo no he ido* I, we, you, they have not gone he has not gone	*¿ (no) he ido yo?* have I, we, you, they (not) gone? has he (not) gone?
Pretérito plusc.	*yo había ido* I, you...had gone	*yo no había ido* I, you...had not gone	*¿ (no) había ido yo?* had I, you...(not) gone?
Futuro perfecto	*yo habré ido* I, we shall have gone you, he, they will have gone	*yo no habré ido* I, we shall not have gone you, he, they will not have gone	*¿ (no) habré yo ido?* shall I, we (not) have gone? will you, he, they (not) have gone?
Condicional compuesto	*yo habría ido* I, we should have gone you, he, they would have gone	*yo no habría ido* I, we should not have gone you, he, they would not have gone	*¿ (no) habría yo ido?* should I, we (not) have gone? would you, he, they (not) have gone?

IMPERATIVO

Afirmación	Negación
vaya yo let me go go let him (her, it) go let us go go let them go	*no vaya yo* don't let me go don't go, etc.

PARTICIPIO PRES. GERUNDIO	} going *yendo*
PARTICIPIO PAS.	gone *ido*
INFINITIVO SIMPLE	(not) to go *(no) ir*
INFINITIVO COMP.	to have gone *haber ido*

SUBJUNTIVO / THE SUBJUNCTIVE MOOD

El inglés no tiene formas propias para el subjuntivo, excepto en el verbo **to be**, cuyo presente de subjuntivo es **be** y cuyo pretérito de subjuntivo es **were** para todas las personas del singular y del plural: whoever he **be**, quienquiera que sea; if I **were** in his place, si yo estuviese en su lugar.

En todo otro caso, el inglés expresa el subjuntivo mediante: a) el infinitivo; b) una forma de indicativo; c) una forma compuesta con los auxiliares **may** o **might** y **should**.

Por regla general:
- Cuando la acción expresada por el subjuntivo es pensada como cierta, se usa el infinitivo o el indicativo: tell him **to go away**, dígale que se vaya; as you **please**, como usted quiera o guste; wait till he **comes**, aguarde hasta que él venga.
- Cuando la acción es pensada como incierta, dudosa o simplemente deseada, se usa una forma compuesta con **may**, **might** o **should**.

  May, might se usan:
  —Para expresar la idea del verbo *poder*: however strong he **might be**, por fuerte que fuese.
  —Para expresar un deseo, una orden: **may** he live long, que viva muchos años.
  —En oraciones finales después de **that, in order that, so that** (para que, a fin de que): he went away **that** they **might** not **find** him in the house, se fue para que no le encontrasen en la casa.

  Se usa **should:**
  —Después de **that** (conjunción *que*): he seemed to expect **that** I **should** assent to this, parecía esperar que yo asintiese a esto; **that** I **should** be so unfortunate!, ¡que sea yo tan desgraciado!
  —Después de conjunciones condicionales o concesivas, como **if, though, even though,** etc.: if he **should** come, si él viniese; **though** he **should** come, aunque él viniese.
  —Después de **lest:** I shall keep your book **lest** you **should** lose it, guardaré tu libro para que no lo pierdas.

Observaciones:
- **If** puede omitirse en ciertos casos a condición de poner el sujeto detrás de **should, had** o **were:** should he know it, si él lo supiese; had I known it, si yo lo hubiese sabido; were I in his place, si yo estuviese en su lugar.
- Después de **for fear that** se usa **should** en el presente y **should** o **might** en el pretérito: he is running away **for fear that** his father **should** punish him, huye por miedo de que su padre le castigue; he ran away **for fear that** his father **should** (o **might**) punish him, huyó por miedo de que su padre lo castigase.

ADVERBIO / ADVERBS

El inglés tiene muchos adverbios derivados de adjetivo, análogos a los españoles terminados en *-mente*. Se forman añadiendo **-ly** al adjetivo. Así de **bad**, se forma **badly**; de **bright, brightly,** etc.

Esta forma de derivación tiene las siguientes alteraciones:
- Los adjetivos terminados en **-le** pierden esta terminación: possible, **possibly**; tolerable, **tolerably**.
- Los terminados en **-ue** pierden la e: due, **duly**; true, **truly**.
- Los terminados en **-ll** sólo añaden la y: dull, **dully**; full, **fully**.
- Los terminados en **-y** cambian esta letra en **i**: guilty, **guiltily**; showy, **showily**.

Lugar del adverbio

Cuando modifica una palabra que no es el verbo:
- Por regla general, va delante de la palabra que modifica: **seriously** ill, gravemente enfermo; **very** well, muy bien; **long** before, mucho antes.
  —Se exceptúan **enough**, que siempre va detrás de la palabra que modifica: good **enough** for me, suficientemente bueno para mí; y **ago**, que siempre va detrás de las palabras que expresan el período de tiempo: two years **ago**, hace dos años.

Cuando modifica al verbo:

- Si el verbo es transitivo, el adverbio no puede separar el verbo del complemento directo: va delante del verbo o después del complemento. En los tiempos compuestos, puede ir también después del verbo auxiliar: he **easily** defeated his opponent, he defeated his opponent **easily**, ha derrotado fácilmente a su adversario.

  —Sin embargo, cuando el complemento directo consta de muchas palabras o está complementado por una oración, el adverbio puede ir entre el verbo y el complemento directo: he rewarded **liberally** all those who had served his father, recompensó liberalmente a todos los que habían servido a su padre.

- Si el verbo es intransitivo, el adverbio va después del verbo, tanto en los tiempos simples como en los compuestos: she has sung **wonderfully**, ha cantado maravillosamente.

  —Sin embargo, algunos adverbios, como **suddenly, promptly**, etc., pueden ir después del auxiliar de los tiempos compuestos: the wind has **suddenly** risen, el viento ha soplado de pronto.

- Si el verbo es **to be**, el adverbio suele ir después del verbo o después del auxiliar de los tiempos compuestos: he is **always** silent, siempre está callado.

- Como en español, el adverbio va al principio de la oración cuando modifica la oración entera o cuando se quiere dar mayor fuerza a la expresión: **meanwhile**, I was writing the letter, entretanto yo escribía la carta.

Casos particulares

No yendo con el verbo **to be**, los adverbios **also, even, first, once** y **quite**, los de tiempo indefinido y los seminegativos como **almost, nearly, hardly, only** y **scarcely**, van siempre entre el sujeto y el verbo o después del auxiliar de los tiempos compuestos: he **never** spoke about it, él nunca ha hablado de ello.

En cambio, los adverbios de tiempo **early, late, today, tonight** y los polisílabos como **yesterday, presently**, etc.; los de lugar; los de cantidad, y los de modo **very well, badly** y **worse**, van al final de la oración: they arrived **late**, ellos llegaron tarde.

El comparativo y el superlativo

El comparativo y el superlativo de los adverbios se forman como los del adjetivo. Algunos tienen formas propias que se encontrarán en los artículos correspondientes de este Diccionario.

PREPOSICIÓN / PREPOSITIONS

Traslado de la preposición

La preposición mediante la cual el verbo rige a un complemento se puede trasladar al final de la oración:

- En las oraciones interrogativas: whom are you speaking **to**? (o sea: **to** whom are you speaking?), ¿a quién habla usted?

- En las subordinadas que empiezan por un pronombre relativo: I did not know the man whom I was speaking **with** (o the man **with** whom I was speaking), yo no conocía al hombre con quien estaba hablando.

Esta construcción es obligatoria cuando el pronombre relativo es **that**, ya sea expreso o elíptico: he has the book (**that**) you are looking **for**, él tiene el libro que usted busca.

Omisión de la preposición

En algunas frases adverbiales o prepositivas y en ciertas expresiones, se omiten las preposiciones:

at: (at) every moment, en todo momento; (at) full speed, a toda velocidad; (at) that hour, entonces; (at) the next moment, un momento después; he looked (at) me in the face, me miró a la cara.

of: on board (of) the ship, a bordo del buque; (of) what use is this to me?, ¿de qué me sirve esto?

with: (with) tooth and nail, con dientes y uñas, encarnizadamente, desesperadamente.

PRINCIPALES SUFIJOS
DE LA LENGUA INGLESA

-able, -ible   corresponden a los sufijos españoles **-able, -ible**.

-an, -ean, -ian   significa *de* o *originando de:* **American**, americano; **European**, europeo; **Californian**, californiano.

-dom   denota dignidad, cargo, dominio, jurisdicción, conjunto, condición, estado: **earldom**, condado; **kingdom**, reino; **Christendom**, cristiandad; **martyrdom**, martirio; **freedom**, libertad.

-ed, -d   es la terminación del pretérito y del participio pasivo de los verbos regulares.

-ed   significa también *que tiene, de:* **bearded**, barbado; **three-cornered**, de tres picos.

-ee   indica la persona que es objeto de la acción: **lessee**, arrendatario; **employee**, empleado.

-eer   indica ocupación u oficio: **mountaineer**, alpinista; **engineer**, ingeniero.

-er
- indica:
  —él o lo que hace, ejecuta, causa, etc., y suele corresponder a los españoles *-dor, -ra* (en sustantivos): **buyer**, comprador, -ra; **condenser**, condensador.
  —el residente o natural de: **New Yorker**, neoyorkino; **islander**, isleño.
  —ocupación u oficio: **baker**, panadero; **drummer**, tambor.
- es la terminación del comparativo de ciertos adjetivos o adverbios: **smaller**, más pequeño; **faster**, más de prisa.

-ese
- significa *de, perteneciente a, originando de:* **Japanese**, japonés.
- indica el residente o natural de: **Chinese**, chino.
- indica una lengua: **Siamese**, siamés.
- indica un estilo oratorio o literario (usualmente depreciativo): **journalese**, lenguaje periodístico.

-ess   forma el femenino de ciertos sustantivos: **hostess**, mesonera, anfitriona.

-est   es la terminación de ciertos superlativos: **shortest**, el más corto.

-fold   significa *veces:* **tenfold**, décuplo, diez veces.

-ful
- significa *lleno, que tiene* y a menudo corresponde a *-oso* y a *-ado, -ada:* **brimful**, lleno hasta el borde; **careful**, cuidadoso; **handful**, puñado; **spoonful**, cucharada.
- indica actitud, condición, estado, hábito: **heedful**, que hace caso; **needful**, necesitado, necesario; **forgetful**, olvidadizo.

-hood   indica condición, carácter, estado, grupo, y en muchos casos corresponde a *-dad, -ia, -ez:* **brotherhood**, hermandad, cofradía; **falsehood**, falsedad; **widowhood**, viudez.

-ie, -let   son terminaciones de diminutivo.

-ing   es la terminación del gerundio, del participio activo y del nombre verbal inglés. Corresponde a *-ando, -ante, -iente* y a *-dor, -ra* (en adjetivos) del español.

-ish
- forma adjetivos que indican nacionalidad: **Spanish**, español; **English**, inglés.
- forma adjetivos con el sentido de *de, que parece de, algo, que tira:* **brutish**, abrutado; **childish**, infantil, aniñado; **reddish**, rojizo.

-less   indica falta o ausencia de: **beardless**, sin barba; **endless**, sin fin.

-like   significa *de, propio de, que parece de, como, a manera de:* **deathlike**, mortal, cadavérico; **gentlemanlike**, de caballero o que lo parece; **catlike**, felino.

-ly
- es el sufijo adverbial que corresponde al español *-mente:* **divinely**, divinamente; **swiftly**, rápidamente.
- forma adjetivos como: **brotherly**, fraternal; **friendly**, amigable, amistoso; **daily**, diario; **yearly**, anual.

-ment, -tion   corresponden generalmente a los sufijos españoles *-miento* y *-ción.*

-ness   forma un número considerable de sustantivos abstractos derivados de adjetivos: **blackness**, negrura, oscuridad; **doggedness**, terquedad, obstinación. En algunos casos el adjetivo en **-ness** corresponde al artículo español *lo* seguido de un adjetivo: **the profoundness of her thought**, lo profundo de su pensamiento.

-ship
- forma sustantivos abstractos, a menudo con la equivalencia de *-dad, -tad, -ción, -esco,* etc.: **friendship**, amistad; **relationship**, relación, parentesco.
- indica:
  — arte, habilidad: **penmanship**, escritura, caligrafía.
  — título, cargo, oficio, ocupación, estado; su duración: **lordship**, señoría; **professorship**, profesorado; **apprenticeship**, aprendizaje.

-some   indica *que produce o causa, dado a:* **wearisome**, cansado, fatigoso, aburrido; **quarrelsome**, pendenciero.

-ty   forma sustantivos abstractos, a veces en correspondencia con el sufijo *-dad* español: **beauty**, belleza, beldad; **receptivity**, receptividad.

-ward, -wards   significa *hacia.*

-ways, -wise   significan manera, dirección, posición: **lengthways**, a lo largo, longitudinalmente; **clockwise**, como las agujas del reloj.

-y
- es un sufijo diminutivo.
- corresponde a las terminaciones españolas *-ia, -ía:* **memory**, memoria; **geology**, geología.
- significa *abundante en, lleno de, que tiene, que parece, que tira a,* etc., y a menudo corresponde a *-udo, -oso, -ado* del español: **hairy**, peludo, cabelludo; **mossy**, musgoso; **rosy**, rosado.

Tablas de verbos irregulares ingleses

Infinitivo	Pasado simple	Participio pasado
arise	arose	arisen
awake	awoke	awaked/awoken
bear	bore	borne/born
beat	beat	beaten
become	became	become
begin	began	begun
behold	beheld	beheld
bend	bent	bent
beseech	besought/beseeched	besought/beseeched
beset	beset	beset
bide	bode/bided	bided
bind	bound	bound
bite	bit	bitten
bleed	bled	bled
blow	blew	blown
break	broke	broken
breed	bred	bred
bring	brought	brought
broadcast	broadcast	broadcast
build	built	built
burn	burnt/burned	burnt/burned
burst	burst	burst
buy	bought	bought
cast	cast	cast
catch	caught	caught
choose	chose	chosen
cleave	cleft/cleaved/clove	cleft/cleaved/cloven
cling	clung	clung
clothe	clothed/clad	clothed/clad
come	came	come
cost	cost	cost
creep	crept	crept
crow	crowed/crew	crowed
cut	cut	cut
deal	dealt	dealt
dig	dug	dug
draw	drew	drawn
dream	dreamed/dreamt	dreamed/dreamt
drink	drank	drunk
drive	drove	driven
dwell	dwelt	dwelt
eat	ate	eaten
fall	fell	fallen
feed	fed	fed
feel	felt	felt
fight	fought	fought
find	found	found
flee	fled	fled
fling	flung	flung
fly	flew	flown
forbear	forbore	forborne
forbid	forbade	forbidden
forecast	forecast/forecasted	forecast/forecasted

for(e)go	for(e)went	for(e)gone
foresee	foresaw	foreseen
foretell	foretold	foretold
forget	forgot	forgotten
forgive	forgave	forgiven
forsake	forsook	forsaken
freeze	froze	frozen
get	got	got, US gotten
give	gave	given
grind	ground	ground
grow	grew	grown
hang	hung/hanged[1]	hung/hanged[1]
hear	heard	heard
hide	hid	hidden/hid
hit	hit	hit
hold	held	held
hurt	hurt	hurt
input	input	input
keep	kept	kept
kneel	knelt	knelt
knit	knit/knitted	knit/knitted
know	knew	known
lay	laid	laid
lean	leant/leaned	leant/leaned
leap	leapt/leaped	leapt/leaped
learn	learnt/learned	learnt/learned
leave	left	left
lend	lent	lent
let	let	let
light	lighted/lit	lighted/lit
lose	lost	lost
make	made	made
may	might	-
mean	meant	meant
meet	met	met
mislead	misled	misled
misread	misread	misread
misspell	misspelled/misspelt	misspelled/misspelt
mistake	mistook	mistaken
mow	mowed	mowed/mown
offset	offset	offset
outdo	outdid	outdone
outgrow	outgrew	outgrown
overcome	overcame	overcome
overdo	overdid	overdone
overhear	overheard	overheard
override	overrode	overridden
overrun	overran	overrun
oversee	oversaw	overseen
oversleep	overslept	overslept
overtake	overtook	overtaken
overthrow	overthrew	overthrown
pay	paid	paid
prove	proved	proved/proven
read	read	read
rebuild	rebuilt	rebuilt
rend	rent	rent

rid	rid/ridded	rid/ridded
ride	rode	ridden
ring	rang	rung
rise	rose	risen
run	ran	run
saw	sawed	sawed/sawn
say	said	said
see	saw	seen
seek	sought	sought
sell	sold	sold
send	sent	sent
set	set	set
sew	sewed	sewed/sewn
shake	shook	shaken
shear	sheared	sheared/shorn
shed	shed	shed
shine	shone	shone
shoe	shod	shod
shoot	shot	shot
show	showed	showed/shown
shrink	shrank	shrunk
shut	shut	shut
sing	sang	sung
sink	sank	sunk
sit	sat	sat
slay	slew	slain
sleep	slept	slept
slide	slid	slid
sling	slung	slung
slink	slunk	slunk
slit	slit	slit
smell	smelled/smelt	smelled/smelt
speak	spoke	spoken
speed	speeded/sped	speeded/sped
spell	spelled/spelt	spelled/spelt
spend	spent	spent
spill	spilled/spilt	spilled/spilt
spin	spun/span	spun
spit	spat	spat
split	split	split
spoil	spoiled/spoilt	spoiled/spoilt
spread	spread	spread
spring	sprang	sprung
stand	stood	stood
steal	stole	stolen
stick	stuck	stuck
sting	stung	stung
stink	stank/stunk	stunk
strew	strewed	strewed/strewn
stride	strode	stridden
strike	struck	struck
string	strung	strung
strive	strove	striven
sublet	sublet	sublet
swear	swore	sworn
sweep	swept	swept
swell	swelled	swollen

swim	swam	swum
swing	swung	swung
take	took	taken
teach	taught	taught
tear	tore	torn
think	thought	thought
thrive	throve/thrived	thrived/thriven
throw	threw	thrown
tread	trod	trodden/trod
undercut	undercut	undercut
undergo	underwent	undergone
understand	understood	understood
undertake	undertook	undertaken
underwrite	underwrote	underwritten
undo	undid	undo
unwind	unwound	unwound
wake	woke	woken
waylay	waylaid	waylaid
wear	wore	worn
wed	wedded/wed	wedded/wed
weep	wept	wept
win	won	won
withdraw	withdrew	withdrawn
withhold	withheld	withheld
withstand	withstood	withstood
wring	wrung	wrung
write	wrote	written

[1] Para la diferencia véase la entrada.

A

a [eɪ, ə] *indef art* un, una. **2** *(per)* por: *three times ~ week,* tres veces por semana; £2 ~ *kilo,* dos libras el kilo. ▲ *Se usa delante de las palabras que empiezan con sonido no vocálico.* → **an.**

aback [ə'bæk] *adv* hacia atrás. ●*to be taken ~,* asombrarse.

abacus ['æbəkəs] *n* ábaco. ▲ *pl* **abacuses.**

abandon [ə'bændən] *t* abandonar.

abashed [ə'bæʃ] *adj* confundido,-a.

abate [ə'beɪt] *i* menguar, amainar.

abatement [ə'beɪtmənt] *n* reducción.

abattoir ['æbətwɑːʳ] *n* matadero.

abbess ['æbes] *n* abadesa.

abbey ['æbɪ] *n* abadía.

abbot ['æbət] *n* abad *m.*

abbreviate [ə'briːvɪeɪt] *t* abreviar.

abbreviation [əbriːvɪ'eɪʃən] *n (shortening)* abreviación. **2** *(shortened form)* abreviatura.

abdicate ['æbdɪkeɪt] *t-i* abdicar.

abdication [æbdɪ'keɪʃən] *n* abdicación.

abdomen ['æbdəmən] *n* abdomen *m.*

abdominal [æb'dɒmɪnəl] *adj* abdominal.

abduct [æb'dʌkt] *t* raptar, secuestrar.

abduction [æb'dʌkʃən] *n* rapto, secuestro.

abductor [æb'dʌktəʳ] *n* secuestrador,-ra.

aberration [æbə'reɪʃən] *n* aberración.

abet [ə'bet] *t* incitar.

abeyance [ə'beɪəns] *in ~, adv* en desuso.

abhor [əb'hɔːʳ] *t* aborrecer, detestar.

abhorrence [əb'hɒrəns] *n* aborrecimiento, odio.

abhorrent [əb'hɒrənt] *adj* detestable, odioso,-a.

abide [ə'baɪd] *t (bear, stand)* soportar, tolerar. ◆*to ~ by t (promise)* cumplir con; *(rules, decision)* acatar.

ability [ə'bɪlɪtɪ] *n (capability)* capacidad, aptitud. **2** *(talent)* talento.

abject ['æbdʒekt] *adj* abyecto,-a.

ablaze [ə'bleɪz] *adj* ardiendo, en llamas. ●*fig ~ with light,* resplandeciente de luz.

able ['eɪbəl] *adj* que puede. **2** *(capable)* hábil, capaz. − **3** *ably adv* hábilmente. ●*to be ~ to,* poder.

abnormal [æb'nɔːməl] *adj (not normal)* anormal. **2** *(unusual)* inusual.

abnormality [æbnɔː'mælɪtɪ] *n* anomalía.

aboard [ə'bɔːd] *adv* a bordo.

abode [ə'bəʊd] *n fml* morada, domicilio.

abolish [ə'bɒlɪʃ] *t* abolir, suprimir.

abolition [æbə'lɪʃən] *n* abolición, supresión.

abominable [ə'bɒmɪnəbəl] *adj* abominable; *(terrible)* terrible, horrible.

abomination [əbɒmɪ'neɪʃən] *n* abominación.

aboriginal [æbə'rɪdʒɪnəl] *adj-n* aborigen *(mf).*

aborigine [æbə'rɪdʒɪnɪ] *n* aborigen *mf.*

abort [ə'bɔːt] *i* abortar.

abortion [ə'bɔːʃən] *n* aborto.

abound [ə'baʊnd] *i* abundar.

about [ə'baʊt] *prep (concerning)* sobre, acerca de: *to speak ~ ...,* hablar de ...; *what is the book ~?,* ¿de qué trata el libro?; *what did you do ~ ...?,* ¿qué hiciste con ...? **2** *(showing where)* por, en: *he's somewhere ~ the house,* está por algún rincón de la casa. − **3** *adv (approximately)* alrededor de: ~ £500, unas quinientas libras; *at ~ three o'clock,* a eso de las tres. **4** *(near)* por aquí/ahí: *there was nobody ~,* no había nadie. **5** *(available)* disponible. ●*to be ~ to ...,* estar a punto de ...; *how/what ~ a drink?,* ¿te apetece tomar algo?; *how/ what ~ going to Paris?,* ¿qué te parece ir a París?

above [ə'bʌv] *prep (higher than)* por encima de: ~ *our heads,* por encima de nuestras cabezas; *fig* ~ *suspicion,* por encima de toda sospecha; *fig only the manager is* ~ *him,* sólo el gerente está por encima de él. 2 *(more than)* más de/que: ~ *5,000 people,* más de 5.000 personas: *those* ~ *the age of 65,* los mayores de 65 años. − 3 *adv* arriba, en lo alto. 4 *(in writing)* arriba: *see* ~, véase arriba. ●~ *all,* sobre todo.

above-board [əbʌv'bɔːd] *adj* legítimo,-a, legal.

above-mentioned [əbʌv'menʃənd] *adj* arriba mencionado,-a.

abrasion [ə'breɪʒən] *n* abrasión.

abreast [ə'brest] *adv* de frente: *to walk four* ~, caminar cuatro de frente.

abridged [ə'brɪdʒd] *adj* abreviado,-a.

abroad [ə'brɔːd] *adv* en el extranjero: *to go* ~, ir al extranjero. 2 *fml (everywhere)* por todas partes.

abrupt [ə'brʌpt] *adj (sudden)* repentino,-a. 2 *(rude)* brusco,-a, arisco,-a.

abscess ['æbses] *n* absceso.

abscond [əb'skɒnd] *i* fugarse.

absence ['æbsəns] *n (of person)* ausencia. 2 *(of thing)* falta, carencia.

absent ['æbsənt] *adj* ausente. − 2 *t to* ~ *o.s.,* ausentarse. ▲ *En* 2 *(verbo)* [æb'sent].

absentee [æbsən'tiː] *n* ausente *mf.*

absent-minded [æbsənt'maɪndɪd] *adj* distraído,-a.

absinthe ['æbsɪnθ] *n* ajenjo.

absolute ['æbsəluːt] *n* absoluto,-a: *it's* ~ *rubbish,* es una perfecta tontería.

absolution [æbsə'luːʃən] *n* absolución.

absolutism ['æbsəluːtɪzəm] *n* absolutismo.

absolve [əb'zɒlv] *t* absolver.

absorb [əb'zɔːb] *t (soak up)* absorber; *fig (ideas etc.)* asimilar. ●*to be absorbed in sth.,* estar absorto,-a en algo.

absorbent [əb'zɔːbənt] *adj* absorbente.

absorbing [əb'zɔːbɪŋ] *adj* absorbente.

absorption [əb'zɔːpʃən] *n* absorción.

abstain [əb'steɪn] *i* abstenerse.

abstemious [æb'stiːmɪəs] *adj* abstemio,-a.

abstention [æb'stenʃən] *n* abstención.

abstinence ['æbstɪnəns] *n* abstinencia.

abstract ['æbstrækt] *adj (not concrete)* abstracto,-a. − 2 *n (summary)* resumen *m.* − 3 *t (summarize)* resumir. 4 *euph (steal)* sustraer. ▲ *En* 3 *y* 4 *(verbo)* [æb'strækt].

abstraction [æb'strækʃən] *n* abstracción. 2 *(absent-mindedness)* distracción, ensimismamiento.

abstruse [əb'struːs] *adj* abstruso,-a.

absurd [əb'sɜːd] *adj* absurdo,-a.

absurdity [əb'sɜːdɪtɪ] *n* disparate *m.*

abundance [ə'bʌndəns] *n* abundancia.

abundant [ə'bʌndənt] *adj* abundante.

abuse [ə'bjuːs] *n (verbal)* insultos *mpl;* *(physical)* malos tratos *mpl.* 2 *(misuse)* abuso. − 3 *t (verbally)* insultar; *(physically)* maltratar. 4 *(misuse)* abusar de. ▲ *En* 3 *y* 4 *(verbo)* [ə'bjuːz].

abusive [ə'bjuːsɪv] *adj (insulting)* injurioso,-a, insultante.

abysmal [ə'bɪzməl] *adj fam* malísimo,-a, fatal.

abyss [ə'bɪs] *n* abismo.

acacia [ə'keɪʃə] *n* acacia.

academic [ækə'demɪk] *adj-n* académico,-a.

academy [ə'kædəmɪ] *n* academia.

accede [æk'siːd] *i fml (agree)* acceder (*to,* a). 2 *(to throne)* ascender/subir (*to,* a).

accelerate [æk'seləreɪt] *t-i* acelerar(se).

acceleration [ækselə'reɪʃən] *n* aceleración.

accelerator [ək'seləreɪtəʳ] *n* acelerador *m.*

accent ['æksənt] *n* acento. − 2 *t* acentuar. ▲ *En* 2 *(verbo)* [æk'sent].

accentuate [æk'sentʃʊeɪt] *t* acentuar.

accentuation [æksentʃu'eɪʃən] *n* acentuación.

accept [ək'sept] *t (gift, offer, etc.)* aceptar. 2 *(admit to be true)* admitir, creer.

acceptable [ək'septəbəl] *adj (satisfactory)* aceptable. 2 *(welcome)* grato,-a, acepto,-a.

acceptance [ək'septəns] *n* aceptación, acogida.

access ['ækses] *n* acceso. ■ ~ *road,* carretera de acceso.

accessible [æk'sesɪbəl] *adj* accesible.

accession [æk'seʃən] *n (agreement)* asentimiento. 2 *(to throne)* advenimiento.

accessory [æk'sesərɪ] *n* accesorio. 2 *(accomplice)* cómplice *mf.*

accident ['æksɪdənt] *n* accidente *m: I'm sorry, it was an* ~, lo siento, lo hice sin querer. 2 *(coincidence)* casualidad. ●*by* ~, por casualidad.

accidental [æksɪ'dentəl] *adj* accidental, casual.

accident-prone ['æksɪdəntprəʊn] *adj* propenso,-a a los accidentes.

acclaim [ə'kleɪm] *n* aclamación. — **2** *t* aclamar.

acclamation [æklə'meɪʃən] *n* aclamación.

acclimatize [ə'klaɪmətaɪz] *t-i* aclimatar(se).

accolade ['ækəleɪd] *n* elogio.

accommodate [ə'kɒmədeɪt] *t (guests etc.)* alojar, hospedar. **2** *(satisfy)* complacer.

accommodating [ə'kɒmədeɪtɪŋ] *adj* servicial, complaciente.

accommodation [əkɒmə'deɪʃən] *n* alojamiento.

accompaniment [ə'kʌmpənɪmənt] *n* acompañamiento.

accompany [ə'kʌmpənɪ] *t* acompañar.

accomplice [ə'kɒmplɪs] *n* cómplice *mf.*

accomplish [ə'kɒmplɪʃ] *t* lograr.

accomplished [ə'kɒmplɪʃt] *adj* cumplido,-a, consumado,-a.

accomplishment [ə'kɒmplɪʃmənt] *n (act of achieving)* realización. **2** *(achievement)* logro. **3** *pl (skills)* aptitudes *fpl*, dotes *mpl*, habilidades *fpl*.

accord [ə'kɔːd] *n* acuerdo. — **2** *t (award)* conceder, otorgar. — **3** *i (agree)* concordar. •*of one's own ~,* espontáneamente, por propia voluntad; *with one ~,* unánimemente.

accordance [ə'kɔːdəns] *n in ~ with,* de acuerdo con.

according [ə'kɔːdɪŋ] *prep ~ to,* según: *~ to Philip/the paper/my watch,* según Philip/el periódico/mi reloj. **2** *(consistent with)* de acuerdo *(to,* con): *it went ~ to plan,* salió tal como se había previsto; *we were paid ~ to our experience,* se nos pagó de acuerdo con nuestra experiencia. — **3** *accordingly adv (appropriately)* de conformidad. **4** *(therefore)* por consiguiente.

accordion [ə'kɔːdɪən] *n* acordeón *m.*

accost [ə'kɒst] *t* abordar, dirigirse a.

account [ə'kaʊnt] *n* cuenta. **2** *(advantage)* provecho. **3** *(reason)* causa, motivo. **4** *(report)* relación, informe *m.* **5** *(importance)* importancia: *it is of no ~,* no tiene importancia. ◆*to ~ for i* explicar. •*on ~,* a cuenta; *on ~ of,* por, a causa de; *on no ~,* bajo ningún concepto; *there's no accounting for tastes,* sobre gustos no hay nada escrito; *to call sb. to ~,* pedir cuentas a algn; *to take into ~,* tener en cuenta; *to turn sth. to (good) ~,* sacar (buen) provecho de algo. ■ *current ~,* cuenta corriente; *deposit ~,* cuenta de ahorros.

accountable [ə'kaʊntəbəl] *adj* responsable *(to,* ante).

accountant [ə'kaʊntənt] *n* contable *mf.*

accounting [ə'kaʊntɪŋ] *n* contabilidad.

accredited [ə'kredɪtɪd] *adj* autorizado,-a, reconocido,-a.

accrue [ə'kruː] *i* FIN acumularse.

accumulate [ə'kjuːmjʊleɪt] *t-i* acumular(se).

accumulation [əkjuːmjʊ'leɪʃən] *n* acumulación.

accuracy ['ækjʊrəsɪ] *n (of numbers, instrument, information)* exactitud, precisión. **2** *(of shot)* certeza.

accurate ['ækjʊrət] *adj (numbers etc.)* exacto,-a, preciso,-a. **2** *(instrument)* de precisión. **3** *(shot)* certero,-a. **4** *(information etc.)* exacto,-a.

accusation [ækjuː'zeɪʃən] *n* acusación: *to bring an ~ against,* presentar una denuncia contra.

accusative [ə'kjuːzətɪv] *adj-n* acusativo,-a *(m).*

accuse [ə'kjuːz] *t* acusar *(of,* de).

accused [ə'kjuːzd] *n the ~,* el/la acusado,-a.

accuser [ə'kjuːzə] *n* acusador,-ra.

accustom [ə'kʌstəm] *t* acostumbrar *(to,* a).

accustomed [ə'kʌstəmd] *adj* acostumbrado,-a *(to,* a).

ace [eɪs] *n (cards)* as *m.* **2** *(tennis)* ace *m.* **3** *fam (expert)* as *m.* •*within an ~ of,* a dos dedos de.

ache [eɪk] *n* dolor *m.* — **2** *i* doler: *my head aches,* me duele la cabeza, tengo dolor de cabeza.

achieve [ə'tʃiːv] *t (finish)* realizar, llevar a cabo. **2** *(attain)* lograr, conseguir.

achievement [ə'tʃiːvmənt] *n (completion)* realización. **2** *(attainment)* logro. **3** *(feat)* hazaña, proeza.

aching ['eɪkɪŋ] *adj* dolorido,-a.

acid ['æsɪd] *adj-n* ácido,-a *(m).*

acidic [ə'sɪdɪk] *adj* ácido,-a.

acidity [ə'sɪdɪtɪ] *n* acidez *f.*

acknowledge [ək'nɒlɪdʒ] *t (admit)* reconocer, admitir: *to ~ defeat,* admitir la derrota. **2** *(an acquaintance)* saludar. **3** *(be thankful)* agradecer, expresar agradecimiento por. •*to ~ receipt of,* acusar recibo de.

acknowledgement [ək'nɒlɪdʒmənt] *n* reconocimiento. **2** *(thanks)* gratitud. **3** *(of letter etc.)* acuse de recibo.

acme ['ækmɪ] *n* apogeo, colmo.

acne ['æknɪ] *n* acné *f.*

acorn ['eɪkɔ:n] *n* bellota.

acoustic [ə'ku:stɪk] *adj* acústico,-a. − 2 *npl* acústica *f sing*.

acquaint [ə'kweɪnt] *t* informar (*with,* de): *to be acquainted with,* (*person*) conocer, tener trato con; (*subject*) conocer, tener conocimientos de.

acquaintance [ə'kweɪntəns] *n* (*knowledge*) conocimiento. 2 (*person*) conocido,-a.

acquiesce [ækwɪ'es] *i* consentir (*in,* en), conformarse (*in,* con).

acquiescence [ækwɪ'esəns] *n* aquiescencia, conformidad.

acquire [ə'kwaɪə^r] *t* adquirir. ●*to* ~ *a taste for sth.,* tomarle gusto a algo.

acquisition [ækwɪ'zɪʃən] *n* adquisición.

acquisitive [ə'kwɪzɪtɪv] *adj* codicioso,-a, acaparador,-ra.

acquit [ə'kwɪt] *t* absolver, declarar inocente.

acquittal [ə'kwɪtəl] *n* absolución.

acre ['eɪkə^r] *n* acre *m*.

acrid ['ækrɪd] *adj* acre. 2 *fig* (*remark*) cáustico,-a.

acridity [æ'krɪdɪtɪ] *n* acritud.

acrimonious [ækrɪ'məʊnɪəs] *adj* (*remark*) cáustico,-a; (*dispute*) enconado,-a, amargo,-a.

acrimony ['ækrɪmənɪ] *n* acritud, aspereza.

acrobat ['ækrəbæt] *n* acróbata *mf*.

acrobatics [ækrə'bætɪks] *npl* acrobacia *f sing*.

across [ə'krɒs] *prep* (*movement*) a través de: *to go* ~ *the road,* cruzar la carretera; *to swim* ~ *a river,* cruzar un río nadando/a nado; *to fly* ~ *the Atlantic,* sobrevolar el Atlántico. 2 (*position*) al otro lado de: *they live* ~ *the road,* viven enfrente. − 3 *adv* de un lado a otro: *it's 4 metres* ~, mide 4 metros de lado a lado; *he ran/swam* ~, cruzó corriendo/nadando.

acrostic [ə'krɒstɪk] *adj-n* acróstico,-a (*m*).

act [ækt] *n* acto, hecho, acción. 2 THEAT acto. 3 (*of parliament*) ley *f*. − 4 *i* obrar, actuar, conducirse. 5 THEAT actuar. ●*to catch sb. in the* ~, coger a algn. in fraganti. ■ ~ *of God,* fuerza mayor; *the Acts of the Apostles,* los Hechos de los Apóstoles.

acting ['æktɪŋ] *adj* interino,-a, en funciones. − 2 *n* THEAT (*profession*) teatro; (*performance*) representación.

action ['ækʃən] *n* acción. 2 MIL combate *m*, acción. 3 JUR demanda. ●*actions speak louder than words,* hechos son

amores y no buenas razones; *killed in* ~, muerto,-a en combate; *out of* ~, fuera de servicio; *to bring an* ~ *against sb.,* entablar una demanda contra algn.

activate ['æktɪveɪt] *t* activar.

active ['æktɪv] *adj* activo,-a. 2 (*volcano*) en actividad. 3 (*energetic*) vivo,-a, vigoroso,-a.

activity [æk'tɪvɪtɪ] *n* actividad.

actor ['æktə^r] *n* actor *m*.

actress ['æktrɪs] *n* actriz *f*.

actual ['æktʃuəl] *adj* real, verdadero,-a. − 2 *actually adv* en realidad, realmente, de hecho. ▲ 2 *nunca se traduce por "actualmente".*

actuary ['æktʃuərɪ] *n* actuario de seguros.

actuate ['æktʃueɪt] *t* (*make work*) accionar. 2 (*motivate*) mover, impulsar.

acuity [ə'kju:ɪtɪ] *n* agudeza.

acumen ['ækjumən] *n* perspicacia.

acute [ə'kju:t] *adj* (*keen*) agudo,-a; (*hearing etc.*) muy fino,-a; (*mind*) perspicaz. 2 (*severe*) agudo,-a, acusado,-a, grave.

ad [æd] *n fam* anuncio.

Adam ['ædəm] *n* Adán *m*. ■ *Adam's apple,* nuez *f* (de la garganta).

adamant ['ædəmənt] *adj* firme, inflexible.

adapt [ə'dæpt] *t-i* adaptar(se).

adaptable [ə'dæptəbəl] *adj to be* ~, saber adaptarse.

adaptation [ædəp'teɪʃən] *n* adaptación.

adaptor [ə'dæptə^r] *n* ELEC ladrón *m*.

add [æd] *t* añadir, agregar. − 2 *t-i* sumar. ◆*to* ~ *to* **t** aumentar. ◆*to* ~ *up* **t** sumar. − 2 *i fig* cuadrar.

adder ['ædə^r] *n* ZOOL víbora.

addict ['ædɪkt] *n* adicto,-a. 2 *fam* (*fanatic*) fanático,-a. ■ *drug* ~, drogadicto,-a; *heroin* ~, heroinómano,-a.

addicted [ə'dɪktɪd] *adj* adicto,-a.

addiction [ə'dɪkʃən] *n* adicción.

addictive [ə'dɪktɪv] *adj to be* ~, crear adicción.

addition [ə'dɪʃən] *n* adición, añadidura. 2 MATH adición, suma. ●*in* ~ *to,* además de.

additional [ə'dɪʃənəl] *adj* adicional.

address [ə'dres] *n* (*on letter*) dirección, señas *fpl*. 2 (*speech*) discurso, alocución. − 3 *t* (*speak to*) dirigirse a. 4 (*letter*) poner la dirección en. ■ *form of* ~, tratamiento.

addressee [ædre'si:] *n* destinatario,-a.

adduce [ə'dju:s] *t* aducir.

adenoids ['ædənɔɪdz] *npl* vegetaciones *fpl.*

adept ['ædept] *adj* experto,-a, perito,-a.

adequate ['ædɪkwɪt] *adj (enough)* suficiente. 2 *(satisfactory)* adecuado,-a.

adhere [əd'hɪəʳ] *i (stick)* adherirse, pegarse. ◆*to* ~ *to t (cause)* adherirse a. 2 *(rules)* observar.

adherence [æd'hɪərəns] *n (to cause)* adhesión. 2 *(to rules)* observación.

adherent [əd'hɪərənt] *adj* adherente. − 2 *n (supporter)* adherido,-a, partidario,-a.

adhesive [əd'hi:sɪv] *adj-n* adhesivo,-a *(m).*

adjacent [ə'dʒeɪsənt] *adj* adyacente.

adjective ['ædʒɪktɪv] *n* adjetivo.

adjoin [ə'dʒɔɪn] *t* lindar con. − 2 *i* colindar.

adjoining [ə'dʒɔɪnɪŋ] *adj (buliding)* contiguo,-a; *(land)* colindante.

adjourn [ə'dʒɜ:n] *t-i (postpone)* aplazar(se), suspender(se).

adjournment [ə'dʒɜ:nmənt] *n* aplazamiento, suspensión.

adjunct ['ædʒʌŋkt] *n* adjunto, accesorio.

adjust [ə'dʒʌst] *t* ajustar, arreglar. − 2 *i (person)* adaptarse.

adjustment [ə'dʒʌstmənt] *n* ajuste *m,* arreglo. 2 *(person)* adaptación.

administer [əd'mɪnɪstəʳ] *t (control)* administrar. 2 *(give)* administrar, dar.

administration [ədmɪnɪs'treɪʃən] *n* administración.

administrator [əd'mɪnɪstreɪtəʳ] *n* administrador,-ra.

admirable ['ædmɪrəbəl] *adj* admirable.

admiral ['ædmərəl] *n* almirante *m.*

admiration [ædmɪ'reɪʃən] *n* admiración.

admire [əd'maɪəʳ] *t* admirar.

admirer [əd'maɪərəʳ] *n* admirador,-ra.

admission [əd'mɪʃən] *n (to hospital)* ingreso. 2 *(price)* entrada. 3 *(acknowledgement)* reconocimiento.

admit [əd'mɪt] *t (allow in)* admitir; *(to hospital)* ingresar. 2 *(acknowledge)* reconocer.

admittance [əd'mɪtəns] *n* entrada. ●*no* ~, prohibida la entrada.

admittedly [əd'mɪtɪdlɪ] *adv* lo cierto es que.

admonish [əd'mɒnɪʃ] *t* amonestar.

admonition [ædmə'nɪʃən] *n* admonición.

ado [ə'du:] *n without further* ~, sin más (preámbulos); *much* ~ *about nothing,* mucho ruido y pocas nueces.

adolescence [ædə'lesəns] *n* adolescencia.

adolescent [ædə'lesənt] *adj-n* adolescente.

adopt [ə'dɒpt] *t* adoptar.

adoption [ə'dɒpʃən] *n* adopción.

adorable [ə'dɔ:rəbəl] *adj* adorable.

adoration [ædə'reɪʃən] *n* adoración.

adore [ə'dɔ:ʳ] *t* adorar.

adorn [ə'dɔ:n] *t* adornar.

adornment [ə'dɔ:nmənt] *n* adorno.

adrift [ə'drɪft] *adj* a la deriva.

adroit [ə'drɔɪt] *adj* diestro,-a, hábil.

adulation [ædju'leɪʃən] *n* adulación.

adult ['ædʌlt] *adj-n* adulto,-a *(m).*

adulterate [ə'dʌltəreɪt] *t* adulterar.

adulteration [ə'dʌltəreɪʃən] *n* adulteración.

adulterer [ə'dʌltərəʳ] *n* adúltero,-a.

adultery [ə'dʌltərɪ] *n* adulterio.

advance [əd'vɑ:ns] *n (movement)* avance *m.* 2 *(progress)* adelanto, progreso. 3 *(payment)* anticipo. − 4 *t (move forward)* adelantar, avanzar. 5 *(promote)* ascender. 6 *(encourage)* promover, fomentar. 7 *(pay)* adelantar, anticipar. − 8 *i (move forward)* adelantarse.

advanced [əd'vɑ:nst] *adj* avanzado,-a.

advancement [əd'vɑ:nsmənt] *n (promotion)* ascenso, promoción. 2 *(encouragement)* difusión, promoción.

advantage [əd'vɑ:ntɪdʒ] *n* ventaja. ●*to take* ~ *of, (thing)* aprovechar; *pej (person)* aprovecharse de.

advantageous [ædvən'teɪdʒəs] *adj* ventajoso,-a, provechoso,-a.

advent ['ædvənt] *n* advenimiento.

adventure [əd'ventʃəʳ] *n* aventura.

adventurer [əd'ventʃərəʳ] *n* aventurero.

adventuress [əd'ventʃərəs] *n* aventurera.

adventurous [əd'ventʃərəs] *adj* aventurero,-a. 2 *(risky)* arriesgado,-a.

adverb ['ædvɜ:b] *n* adverbio.

adversary ['ædvəsərɪ] *n* adversario,-a.

adverse ['ædvɜ:s] *adj* adverso,-a.

adversity [əd'vɜ:sɪtɪ] *n* adversidad.

advert ['ædvɜ:t] *n fam* anuncio.

advertise ['ædvətaɪz] *t* anunciar.

advertisement [əd'vɜ:tɪsmənt] *n* anuncio.

advertiser ['ædvətaɪzəʳ] *n* anunciante *mf.*

advertising ['ædvətaɪzɪŋ] *n* publicidad, propaganda.

advice [əd'vaɪs] *n* consejos *mpl.*

advisable [əd'vaɪzəbəl] *adj* aconsejable.

advise [əd'vaɪz] *t* aconsejar. **2** *(inform)* informar.

adviser [əd'vaɪzəʳ] *n* consejero,-a.

advocate ['ædvəkət] *n* abogado,-a. – **2** *t* abogar por, propugnar. ▲ *En 2 (verbo)* ['ædvəkeɪt].

aerial ['eərɪəl] *adj* aéreo,-a. – **2** *n* antena.

aerodrome ['eərədrəʊm] *n* aeródromo.

aerodynamics [eərəʊdaɪ'næmɪks] *n* aerodinámica.

aeronautics [eərə'nɔːtɪks] *n* aeronáutica.

aeroplane ['eərəpleɪn] *n* aeroplano, avión *m*.

aesthetic [iːs'θetɪk] *adj* estético,-a.

aesthetics [iːs'θetɪks] *n* estética.

affability [æfə'bɪlɪtɪ] *n* afabilidad.

affable ['æfəbəl] *adj* afable.

affair [ə'feəʳ] *n (matter)* asunto. **2** *(event)* acontecimiento. ▪ *foreign affairs,* asuntos exteriores; *love ~,* aventura amorosa.

affect [ə'fekt] *t* afectar. **2** *(move)* conmover, impresionar.

affectation [æfek'teɪʃən] *n* afectación.

affected [ə'fektɪd] *adj* afectado,-a, falso,-a.

affection [ə'fekʃən] *n* afecto, cariño.

affectionate [ə'fekʃənət] *adj* afectuoso,-a, cariñoso,-a.

affidavit [æfɪ'deɪvɪt] *n* declaración jurada, afidávit *m*.

affiliate [ə'fɪlɪət] *n* afiliado,-a.

affiliated [ə'fɪlɪeɪtɪd] *adj* afiliado,-a.

affiliation [əfɪlɪ'eɪʃən] *n* afiliación.

affinity [ə'fɪnɪtɪ] *n* afinidad.

affirm [ə'fɜːm] *t* afirmar.

affirmation [æfə'meɪʃən] *n* afirmación.

affix ['æfɪks] *n* afijo. – **2** *t* pegar, añadir. ▲ *En 2 (verbo)* [ə'fɪks].

afflict [ə'flɪkt] *t* afligir.

affliction [ə'flɪkʃən] *n* aflicción.

affluence ['æfluəns] *n* riqueza, prosperidad.

affluent ['æfluənt] *adj* rico,-a, próspero,-a.

afford [ə'fɔːd] *t* permitirse, costear: *I can't ~ to pay £750 for a coat,* no puedo (permitirme) pagar 750 libras por un abrigo; *how does she ~ it?,* ¿cómo se lo costea?; *can you ~ to reject his offer?,* ¿puedes permitirte el lujo de rechazar su oferta? **2** *fml* dar, proporcionar. ▲ *En 1 gen con* **can/be able***.*

affront [ə'frʌnt] *n* afrenta, insulto. – **2** *t* afrentar, insultar.

afield [ə'fiːld] *adv* far *~,* lejos.

afloat [ə'fləʊt] *adj* a flote.

afoot [ə'fʊt] *adv* something's *~,* se está tramando algo.

aforesaid [ə'fɔːsed] *adj* mencionado,-a, antedicho,-a.

afraid [ə'freɪd] *adj* temeroso,-a. ●*to be ~,* tener miedo.

afresh [ə'freʃ] *adv* de nuevo.

after ['ɑːftəʳ] *prep (time)* después de: *~ class,* después de la clase. **2** *(following)* detrás de: *we all went ~ the thief,* todos fuimos detrás del ladrón; *the police are ~ us,* la policía nos está persiguiendo. – **3** *adv* después: *the day ~,* el día después. – **4** *conj* después que; *~ he left, I went to bed,* después de que se marchara, me acosté.

after-effect ['ɑːftərɪfekt] *n* efecto secundario.

afterlife ['ɑːftəlaɪf] *n* vida después de la muerte.

aftermath ['ɑːftəmɑːθ] *n* secuelas *fpl*.

afternoon [ɑːftə'nuːn] *n* tarde *f*.

afters ['ɑːftəz] *npl fam* postre *m sing*.

aftershave ['ɑːftəʃeɪv] *n* loción para después del afeitado.

aftertaste ['ɑːftəteɪst] *n* regusto.

afterwards ['ɑːftəwədz] *adv* después, luego.

again [ə'gen, ə'geɪn] *prep* de nuevo, otra vez. ●*~ and ~,* repetidamente; *now and ~,* de vez en cuando.

against [ə'genst, ə'geɪnst] *prep* contra: *~ the wall,* contra la pared. **2** *(opposed to)* en contra de: *it's ~ the law,* va en contra de la ley; *I am ~ the plan,* me opongo al plan.

agate ['ægət] *n* ágata.

age [eɪdʒ] *n* edad. **2** *pl fam* años *mpl*: *it's ages since she left,* hace años que se marchó. – **3** *i-t* envejecer. ●*of ~,* mayor de edad; *under ~,* menor de edad. ▪ *old ~,* vejez *f,* senectud; *the Middle Ages,* la Edad Media.

aged ['eɪdʒɪd] *adj* viejo,-a, anciano,-a. **2** de (tantos años de) edad: *a boy ~ ten,* un muchacho de diez años. ▲ *En 2* [eɪdʒd].

agency ['eɪdʒənsɪ] *n* agencia.

agenda [ə'dʒendə] *n* orden *m* del día.

agent ['eɪdʒənt] *n* agente *mf*.

agglomeration [əglɒmə'reɪʃən] *n* aglomeración.

aggravate ['ægrəveɪt] *t (make worse)* agravar. **2** *fam (annoy)* irritar, molestar.

aggravation [ægrə'veɪʃən] *n (worsening)* agravamiento. **2** *(annoyance)* exasperación.

aggregate ['ægrɪgət] *n* agregado, totalidad.

aggression [ə'greʃən] *n* agresión.

aggressive [ə'gresɪv] *adj* agresivo,-a.

aggressor [ə'gresər] *n* agresor,-ra.

aggrieved [ə'gri:vd] *adj* afligido,-a, apenado,-a.

aghast [ə'gɑːst] *adj* horrorizado,-a.

agile ['ædʒaɪl] *adj* ágil.

agility [ə'dʒɪlɪtɪ] *n* agilidad.

agitate ['ædʒɪteɪt] *t (shake)* agitar. **2** *(worry)* inquietar, perturbar.

agitation ['ædʒɪ'teɪʃən] *n (shaking)* agitación. **2** *(worry)* inquietud, perturbación.

agitator ['ædʒɪteɪtər] *n* agitador,-ra.

aglow [ə'gləʊ] *adj* resplandeciente.

ago [ə'gəʊ] *adv* hace, atrás: *two years ~,* hace dos años.

agog [ə'gɒg] *adj* anhelante, deseoso,-a.

agonize ['ægənaɪz] *i* sufrir angustiosamente.

agony ['ægənɪ] *n (pain)* dolor muy agudo. **2** *(anguish)* angustia.

agrarian [ə'greərɪən] *adj* agrario,-a.

agree [ə'gri:] *i-t (be in agreement)* estar de acuerdo: *I ~ with you,* estoy de acuerdo contigo. **2** *(reach an agreement)* ponerse de acuerdo: *we agreed not to say anything,* nos pusimos de acuerdo en no decir nada. **3** *(say yes)* acceder, cosentir: *will he ~ to our request?,* ¿accederá a nuestra petición? **4** *(square)* concordar, encajar: *the two men's stories don't ~,* las historias de los dos hombres no encajan. **5** *(food)* sentar bien: *the prawns didn't ~ with me,* las gambas no me sentaron bien. **6** GRAM concordar.

agreeable [ə'gri:əbəl] *adj (pleasant)* agradable. **2** *(in agreement)* conforme.

agreement [ə'gri:mənt] *n* acuerdo. **2** GRAM concordancia. ●*in ~,* de acuerdo.

agricultural [ægrɪ'kʌltʃərəl] *adj* agrícola.

agriculture ['ægrɪkʌltʃər] *n* agricultura.

agriculturist [ægrɪ'kʌltʃərɪst] *n* ingeniero,-a agrónomo,-a.

aground [ə'graʊnd] *adv to run ~,* encallar, varar.

ahead [ə'hed] *adv (in front)* delante: *there's a police checkpoint ~,* hay un control de policía aquí delante; *Tom went on ~ to look for water,* Tom se adelantó a por agua; *we are ~ of the others,* llevamos ventaja sobre los otros. ●*go ~!,* ¡adelante!; *to plan ~,* planear para el futuro; *to think ~,* pensar en el futuro.

aid [eɪd] *n* ayuda, auxilio. – **2** *t* ayudar, auxiliar.

aids [eɪdz] *n* sida *m*.

ailing ['eɪlɪŋ] *adj* enfermo,-a.

ailment ['eɪlmənt] *n* dolencia, achaque *m*.

aim [eɪm] *n (marksmanship)* puntería. **2** *(objective)* meta, objetivo. ◆*to ~ at t* apuntar a. ◆*to ~ to t* tener la intención de. ●*to take ~,* apuntar; *to miss one's ~,* errar el tiro.

air [eər] *n* aire *m*. **2** *(feeling)* aire, aspecto. **3** *(affectation)* afectación, tono: *to put on airs,* darse tono. **4** MUS aire, tonada. – **5** *t (clothes)* airear, orear. **6** *(room)* ventilar. **7** *(opinions)* airear; *(knowledge)* hacer alarde de. ■ *~ conditioning,* aire acondicionado; *~ force,* fuerzas *fpl* aéreas; *~ gun,* pistola de aire comprimido; *~ hostess,* azafata; *~ mail,* correo aéreo; *~ raid,* ataque aéreo; *fresh ~,* aire fresco.

air-conditioned [eəkən'dɪʃənd] *adj* con aire acondicionado.

aircraft ['eəkrɑːft] *n* avión *m*. ■ *~ carrier,* portaaviones *m inv*.

airline ['eəlaɪn] *n* línea aérea.

airman ['eəmən] *n* aviador *m*.

airplane ['eəpleɪn] *n* aeroplano, avión *m*.

airport ['eəpɔːt] *n* aeropuerto.

airship ['eəʃɪp] *n* aeronave *f*.

airsick ['eəsɪk] *adj* mareado,-a (en el avión).

airspace ['eəspeɪs] *n* espacio aéreo.

airstrip ['eəstrɪp] *n* pista de aterrizaje.

airtight ['eətaɪt] *adj* hermético,-a.

airway ['eəweɪ] *n* línea/vía aérea.

airy ['eərɪ] *adj (ventilated)* bien ventilado,-a. **2** *(carefree)* despreocupado,-a.

aisle [aɪl] *n (in theatre)* pasillo. **2** *(in church)* nave *f* lateral.

ajar [ə'dʒɑːr] *adj* entreabierto,-a.

akimbo [ə'kɪmbəʊ] *adv* en jarras.

akin [ə'kɪn] *adj* parecido,-a.

alabaster ['æləbɑːstər] *n* alabastro.

alacrity [ə'lækrɪtɪ] *n* presteza.

alarm [ə'lɑːm] *n* alarma. **2** *(fear)* temor *m*, alarma. – **3** *t* alarmar, asustar. ■ *~ clock,* despertador *m*.

alarming [ə'lɑːmɪŋ] *adj* alarmante.

alas [ə'lɑːs] *interj* ¡ay!, ¡ay de mí!

albeit [ɔːl'biːɪt] *conj fml* aunque.

albino [æl'biːnəʊ] *adj-n* albino,-a.

album ['ælbəm] *n* álbum *m*.

albumen ['ælbjʊmɪn] *n* albúmina.

alchemy ['ælkɪmɪ] *n* alquimia.

alcohol ['ælkəhɒl] *n* alcohol *m*.

alcoholic [ælkə'hɒlɪk] *adj* alcohólico,-a.

alcove ['ælkəuv] *n* hueco, hornacina, cavidad.

ale [eɪl] *n* cerveza.

alert [ə'lɜ:t] *adj (quick to act)* alerta, vigilante. **2** *(lively)* vivo,-a. – **3** *n* alarma. – **4** *t* alertar, avisar. ●**on the** ~, alerta, sobre aviso.

algae ['ældʒi:] *npl* algas *fpl*.

algebra ['ældʒɪbrə] *n* álgebra.

algorithm ['ælgərɪðəm] *n* algoritmo.

alias ['eɪlɪəs] *adv-n* alias *(m)*.

alibi ['ælɪbaɪ] *n* coartada.

alien ['eɪlɪən] *adj-n (foreign)* extranjero,-a. **2** *(exterrestrial)* extraterrestre *(mf)*. **3** *(strange)* extraño,-a: *his ideas are* ~ *to me,* sus ideas me son ajenas.

alienate ['eɪlɪəneɪt] *t* alienar, enajenar.

alienation [eɪlɪə'neɪʃən] *n* alienación, enajenación.

alight [ə'laɪt] *adj* encendido,-a, ardiendo. – **2** *i fml* apearse. ◆**to** ~ **on** *t* posarse en.

align [ə'laɪn] *t-i* alinear(se).

alike [ə'laɪk] *adj* igual, semejante. – **2** *adv* igualmente: *dressed* ~, vestidos,-as iguales; *men and women* ~, tanto hombres como mujeres.

alimentary [ælɪ'mentərɪ] *adj* alimenticio,-a. ■ ~ *canal,* tubo digestivo.

alimony ['ælɪmənɪ] *n* pensión alimenticia.

alive [ə'laɪv] *adj (not dead)* vivo,-a, viviente. **2** *(lively)* vivo,-a, vivaz. ●~ *to,* consciente de; ~ *with,* lleno,-a de.

alkali ['ælkəlaɪ] *n* álcali *m*.

alkaline ['ælkəlaɪn] *adj* alcalino,-a.

all [ɔ:l] *adj* todo,-a; todos,-as: ~ *the money/ink,* todo el dinero/toda la tinta; ~ *the books/chairs,* todos los libros/todas las sillas; ~ *kinds of ...,* toda clase de ... . – **2** *pron (everything)* todo, la totalidad. **3** *(everybody)* todos *mpl,* todo el mundo. – **4** *adv* completamente, muy: *you're dirty!,* ¡estás todo sucio! ●*after* ~, después de todo; ~ *but,* casi; ~ *of a sudden,* de pronto, de repente; ~ *over,* en todas partes; ~ *right,* bueno,-a, competente, satisfactorio,-a: *are you* ~ *right?,* ¿estás bien?; ~ *the better,* tanto mejor; ~ *the same,* igualmente, a pesar de todo; *at* ~, *(emphatic negative)* en absoluto; *it's* ~ *the same to me,* me da lo mismo; *not at* ~, *(you're welcome)* no hay de qué.

allay [ə'leɪ] *t* calmar, apaciguar.

allegation [ælə'geɪʃən] *n* alegato.

allege [ə'ledʒ] *t* alegar.

allegiance [ə'li:dʒəns] *n* lealtad.

allegory ['ælɪgərɪ] *n* alegoría.

allergy ['ælədʒɪ] *n* alergia.

alleviate [ə'li:vɪeɪt] *t* aliviar, mitigar.

alley ['ælɪ] *n* callejuela, callejón *m*.

alliance [ə'laɪəns] *n* alianza.

allied ['ælaɪd] *adj* POL aliado,-a. **2** *(related)* relacionado,-a, afín.

alligator ['ælɪgeɪtə'] *n* caimán *m*.

allocate ['æləkeɪt] *t* asignar, destinar.

allocation [ælə'keɪʃən] *n (distribution)* asignación; *(of money)* distribución. **2** *(amount allocated)* cuota.

allot [ə'lɒt] *t* asignar, destinar.

allotment [ə'lɒtmənt] *n (of time etc.)* asignación; *(of money)* distribución. **2** *(land)* huerto.

allow [ə'lau] *t (permit)* permitir, dejar: *to* ~ *sb. to do sth.,* dejar que algn. haga algo; *dogs are not allowed in,* no se permite la entrada con perros. **2** *(set aside)* conceder, dar, asignar. ◆*to* ~ *for* *t* tener en cuenta.

allowance [ə'lauəns] *n (money)* pensión, subsidio. ●*to make allowances for,* tener en cuenta.

alloy ['ælɔɪ] *n* aleación.

allude [ə'lu:d] *i* aludir (*to,* a).

allure [ə'ljuə'] *n* atractivo, encanto. – **2** *t* atraer, seducir.

alluring [ə'ljuərɪŋ] *adj* seductor,-ra.

allusion [ə'lu:ʒən] *n* alusión.

alluvial [ə'lu:vɪəl] *adj* aluvial.

ally ['ælaɪ] *n* aliado,-a. – **2** *t-i* aliar(se).

almanac ['ɔ:lmənæk] *n* almanaque *m*.

almighty [ɔ:l'maɪtɪ] *adj* todopoderoso,-a.

almond ['ɑ:mənd] *n* almendra. ■ ~ *tree,* almendro.

almost ['ɔ:lməust] *adv* casi.

alms [ɑ:mz] *npl* limosna *f sing,* caridad *f sing.*

aloft [ə'lɒft] *adv* arriba, en lo alto.

alone [ə'ləun] *adj (unaccompanied)* solo,-a. – **2** *adv (only)* sólo, solamente.

along [ə'lɒŋ] *prep* a lo largo de. – **2** *adv* a lo largo. ●*all* ~, todo el tiempo; ~ *with,* junto con; *come* ~, *(sing)* ven; *(pl)* venid; *(including speaker)* vamos.

aloof [ə'lu:f] *adv* a distancia. – **2** *adj* distante.

aloud [ə'laud] *adv* en voz alta.

alphabet ['ælfəbet] *n* alfabeto.

alphabetical [ælfə'betɪkəl] *adj* alfabético,-a.

alpine [ɪ'ælpaɪn] *adj* alpino,-a.

already [ɔ:l'redɪ] *adv* ya.

also ['ɔ:lsəu] *adv* también.

altar ['ɔːltəʳ] *n* altar *m*.

altarpiece ['ɔːltəpiːs] retablo.

alter ['ɔːltəʳ] *t-i* cambiar(se), modificar(se).

alteration [ɔːltə'reɪʃən] *n* modificación.

altercation ['ɔːltɜː'keɪʃən] *n* altercado, disputa.

alternate [ɔːl'tɜːnət] *adj* alterno,-a. – 2 *t-i* alternar(se). ▲ *En* 2 *(verbo)* ['ɔːltɜːneɪt].

alternating ['ɔːltɜːneɪtɪŋ] *adj* ~ **current,** corriente alterna.

alternative [ɔːl'tɜːnətɪv] *adj* alternativo,-a. – 2 *n (option)* alternativa.

although [ɔːl'ðəʊ] *conj* aunque.

altitude ['æltɪtjuːd] *n* altitud, altura.

altogether [ɔːltə'geðəʳ] *adv (completely)* del todo. 2 *(on the whole)* en conjunto. ●*fam in the* ~*,* en cueros.

altruism ['æltrʊɪzəm] *n* altruismo.

altruist ['æltrʊɪst] *n* altruista *mf*.

aluminium [æljʊ'mɪnɪəm], us **aluminum** [ə'luːmɪnəm] *n* aluminio.

always ['ɔːlweɪz] *adv* siempre.

amalgam [ə'mælgəm] *n* amalgama.

amalgamate [ə'mælgəmeɪt] *t-i (metals)* amalgamar(se). 2 *(groups)* fusionar(se).

amass [ə'mæs] *t* acumular.

amateur ['æmətəʳ] *adj-n* aficionado,-a.

amaze [ə'meɪz] *t* asombrar, pasmar.

amazement [ə'meɪzmənt] *n* asombro, pasmo.

amazing [ə'meɪzɪŋ] *adj* asombroso,-a, pasmoso,-a.

Amazon ['æməzən] *n (river)* el Amazonas. 2 *(warrior)* amazona.

ambassador [æm'bæsədəʳ] *n* embajador,-a.

amber ['æmbəʳ] *n* ámbar *m*.

ambiguity [æmbɪ'gjuːɪtɪ] *n* ambigüedad.

ambiguous [æm'bɪgjʊəs] *adj* ambiguo,-a.

ambition [æm'bɪʃən] *n* ambición.

ambitious [æm'bɪʃəs] *adj* ambicioso,-a.

ambivalent [æm'bɪvələnt] *adj* ambivalente.

amble ['æmbəl] *i* deambular.

ambulance ['æmbjʊləns] *n* ambulancia.

ambush ['æmbʊʃ] *n* emboscada. – 2 *t* poner una emboscada a.

amen [ɑː'men] *interj* amén.

amenable [ə'miːnəbəl] *adj* susceptible: ~ *to reason,* razonable.

amend [ə'mend] *t-i (law)* enmendar(se). 2 *(error)* corregir(se).

amendment [ə'mendmənt] *n* enmienda.

amends [ə'mendz] *n* reparación, compensación: *to make* ~ *to sb. for sth.,* compensar a algn. por algo.

amenities [ə'miːnɪtɪz] *npl* servicios *mpl*, prestaciones *fpl*.

Americanism [ə'merɪkənɪzəm] *n* americanismo.

amiable ['eɪmɪəbəl] *adj* amable.

amicable ['æmɪkəbəl] *adj* amistoso,-a.

amid(st) [ə'mɪd(st)] *prep* en medio de, entre.

amiss [ə'mɪs] *adv-adj* mal. ●*to take* ~*,* tomar a mal.

ammonia [ə'məʊnɪ] *n* amoníaco.

ammunition [æmjʊ'nɪʃən] *n* municiones *fpl*.

amnesia [əm'niːzɪə] *n* amnesia.

amnesty ['æmnestɪ] *n* amnistía.

amoeba [æ'miːbə] *n* ameba.

amok [ə'mɒk] *adv to run* ~*,* volverse loco,-a.

among(st) [ə'mʌŋ(st)] *prep* entre.

amoral [æ'mɒrəl] *adj* amoral.

amorous ['æmərəs] *adj* amoroso,-a.

amorphous [ə'mɔːfəs] *adj* amorfo,-a.

amount [ə'maʊnt] *n* cantidad, suma. ◆*to* ~ *to t* ascender a; *fig* equivaler a.

amp(ere) ['æmp(eəʳ)] *n* amperio, ampere.

amphibian [æm'fɪbɪən] *n* anfibio.

amphibious [æm'fɪbɪəs] *adj* anfibio,-a.

amphitheatre ['æmfɪθɪətəʳ] *n* anfiteatro.

ample ['æmpəl] *adj (enough)* bastante. 2 *(plenty)* más que suficiente. 3 *(large)* amplio,-a.

amplifier ['æmplɪfaɪəʳ] *n* amplificador *m*.

amplify ['æmplɪfaɪ] *t (sound)* amplificar. 2 *(statement)* ampliar.

amplitude ['æmplɪtjuːd] *n* amplitud.

amputate ['æmpjʊteɪt] *t* amputar.

amputation [æmpjʊ'teɪʃən] *n* amputación.

amuck [ə'mʌk] *adv* → **amok**.

amuse [ə'mjuːz] *t* entretener, divertir.

amusement [ə'mjuːzmənt] *n (enjoyment)* diversión, entretenimiento. 2 *(pastime)* pasatiempo.

amusing [ə'mjuːzɪŋ] *adj (fun)* entretenido,-a, divertido,-a. 2 *(funny)* gracioso,-a.

an [ən, æn] *indef art* un,-a. 2 *(per)* por. ▲ *Se usa delante de las palabras que empiezan por un sonido vocálico;* ↔ **a**.

anachronism [ə'nækrənɪzəm] *n* anacronismo.

anaemia [ə'niːmɪə] *n* anemia.

anaemic [ə'niːmɪk] *adj* anémico,-a.

anaesthetic [ænəs'θetɪk] *n* anestético.

anaesthetist [ə'niːsθətɪst] *n* anestetista *mf.*

anaesthetize [ə'niːsθətaɪz] *t* anestetizar.

anagram ['ænəgræm] *n* anagrama *m.*

anal ['eɪnəl] *adj* anal.

analgesic [ænəl'dʒiːzɪk] *adj-n* analgésico,-a *(m).*

analogous [ə'næləgəs] *adj* análogo,-a *(to/with,* a).

analogy [ə'nælədʒɪ] *n* analogía, semejanza.

analyse ['ænəlaɪz] *t* analizar.

analysis [ə'nælɪsɪs] *n* análisis *m.* ▲ *pl analyses.*

analyst ['ænəlɪst] *n* analista *mf.*

anarchist ['ænəkɪst] *n* anarquista *mf.*

anarchy ['ænəkɪ] *n* anarquía.

anatomy [ə'nætəmɪ] *n* anatomía.

ancestor ['ænsəstər] *n* antepasado.

ancestral [æn'sestrəl] *adj* ancestral. ■ ~ *home,* casa solariega.

ancestry ['ænsəstrɪ] *n* linaje *m.*

anchor ['æŋkər] *n* ancla, áncora. – 2 *t-i* anclar.

anchovy ['æntʃəvɪ] *n (salted)* anchoa; *(fresh)* boquerón *m.*

ancient ['eɪnʃənt] *adj* antiguo,-a; *(monument)* histórico,-a. 2 *fam* viejísimo,-a.

ancillary [æn'sɪlərɪ] *adj* auxiliar.

and [ænd, ənd] *conj* y; *(before i- and hi-)* e.

anecdote ['ænɪkdəʊt] *n* anécdota.

anemone [ə'nemənɪ] *n* вот anémona.

anew [ə'njuː] *adv* nuevamente, de nuevo, otra vez.

angel ['eɪndʒəl] *n* ángel *m.*

angelic [æn'dʒelɪk] *adj* angélico,-a.

anger ['æŋgər] *n* cólera, ira. – 2 *t* encolerizar, enojar.

angle ['æŋgəl] *n* ángulo. – 2 *i* pescar (con caña).

angler ['æŋglər] *n* pescador,-ra (de caña). ■ ~ *fish,* rape *m.*

Anglican ['æŋglɪkən] *adj-n* anglicano,-a.

angling ['æŋglɪŋ] *n* pesca (con caña).

angry ['æŋgrɪ] *adj* colérico,-a, enojado,-a.

anguish ['æŋgwɪʃ] *n* angustia.

angular ['æŋgjʊlər] *adj* angular.

animal ['ænɪməl] *adj-n* animal *(m).*

animate ['ænɪmɪt] *adj* animado,-a, vivo,-a. – 2 *t* animar. 3 *fig* estimular. ▲ *En 2 (verbo)* ['ænɪmeɪt].

animated ['ænɪmeɪtɪd] *adj* animado,-a.

animation ['ænɪmeɪʃən] *n* animación. 2 *(life)* vida, marcha.

animosity [ænɪ'mɒsɪtɪ] *n* animosidad.

aniseed ['ænɪsiːd] *n* anís *m.*

ankle ['æŋkəl] *n* tobillo.

annals ['ænəlz] *npl* anales *mpl.*

annex [ə'neks] *t* anexar.

annexe ['ænəks] *n* anexo.

annihilate [ə'naɪəleɪt] *t* aniquilar.

annihilation [ənaɪə'leɪʃən] *n* aniquilación.

anniversary [ænɪ'vɜːsərɪ] *n* aniversario.

annotated ['ænəteɪtɪd] *adj (edition)* crítico,-a.

annotation [ænə'teɪʃən] *n* anotación.

announce [ə'naʊns] *t* anunciar, hacer saber.

announcement [ə'naʊnsmənt] *n* anuncio, declaración.

announcer [ə'naʊnsər] *n* TV RAD presentador,-ra, locutor,-ra.

annoy [ə'nɔɪ] *t* molestar.

annoyance [ə'nɔɪəns] *n* molestia.

annoying [ə'nɔɪɪŋ] *adj* molesto,-a, enojoso,-a.

annual ['ænjʊəl] *adj* anual.

annuity [ə'njuːɪtɪ] *n* renta vitalicia.

annul [ə'nʌl] *t* anular.

annulment [ə'nʌlmənt] *n* anulación.

anode ['ænəʊd] *n* ánodo.

anoint [ə'nɔɪnt] *t* untar, ungir.

anomalous [ə'nɒmələs] *adj* anómalo,-a.

anomaly [ə'nɒməlɪ] *n* anomalía.

anonymous [ə'nɒnɪməs] *adj* anónimo,-a.

another [ə'nʌðər] *adj-pron* otro,-a.

answer ['ɑːnsər] *n (reply)* respuesta, contestación. 2 *(solution)* solución. – 3 *t-i* responder, contestar. ◆*to* ~ *back t-i* replicar. ◆*to* ~ *for t* responder por/de.

answerable ['ɑːnsərəbəl] *adj* responsable *(to,* ante) *(for,* de).

ant [ænt] *n* hormiga. ■ ~ *hill,* hormiguero.

antagonism [æn'tægənɪzəm] *n* antagonismo.

antagonist [æn'tægənɪst] *n* antagonista *mf.*

antagonize [æn'təgənaɪz] *t* enemistarse con.

antecedent [æntɪ'siːdənt] *adj-n* antecedente *(m).*

antelope ['æntɪləʊp] *n* antílope *m.*

antenna [æn'tenə] *n* ZOOL antena. 2 TV RAD antena. ▲ *En 1 pl antennae* [æn'teniː]; *en 2 antennas.*

anthem ['ænθəm] *n* motete *m.* ■ *national* ~, himno nacional.

anthology [æn'θɒlədʒɪ] *n* antología.

anthracite ['ænθrəsaɪt] *n* antracita.

anthropologist [ænθrəˈpɒlədʒɪst] *n* antropólogo,-a.

anthropology [ˈænθrəˈpɒlədʒɪ] *n* antropología.

anti-aircraft [ˈæntɪˈeəkrɑːft] *adj* antiaéreo,-a.

antibiotic [ˈæntɪbaɪˈɒtɪk] *adj-n* antibiótico,-a *(m)*.

antibody [ˈæntɪbɒdɪ] *n* anticuerpo.

antics [ˈæntɪks] *npl* payasadas.

anticipate [ænˈtɪsɪpeɪt] *t (expect)* esperar. 2 *(get ahead of)* adelantarse a. 3 *(forsee)* prever.

anticipation [æntɪsɪˈpeɪʃən] *n (expectation)* expectación.

anticlockwise [æntɪˈklɒkwaɪz] *adj* en el sentido contrario al de las agujas del reloj.

anticyclone [ˈæntɪˈsaɪkləʊn] *n* anticiclón *m*.

antidote [ˈæntɪdəʊt] *n* antídoto.

antifreeze [ˈæntɪfriːz] *n* anticongelante *m*.

antipathy [ænˈtɪpəθɪ] *n* antipatía.

antiquated [ˈæntɪkweɪtɪd] *adj* anticuado,-a.

antique [ænˈtiːk] *adj* antiguo,-a. − 2 *n* antigüedad.

antiquity [ænˈtɪkwɪtɪ] *n* antigüedad.

antiseptic [æntɪˈseptɪk] *adj-n* antiséptico,-a *(m)*.

antithesis [ænˈtɪθəsɪs] *n* antítesis *f*.

antlers [ˈæntləʳ] *npl* cornamenta *f sing*.

antonym [ˈæntənɪm] *n* antónimo.

anus [ˈeɪnəs] *n* ano.

anvil [ˈænvɪl] *n* yunque *m*.

anxiety [æŋˈzaɪətɪ] *n (worry)* ansiedad, inquietud. 2 *(strong desire)* ansia, afán *m*.

anxious [ˈæŋkʃəs] *adj (worried)* ansioso,-a, inquieto,-a. 2 *(desirous)* ansioso,-a.

any [ˈenɪ] *adj (in questions)* algún,-una; *(negative)* ningún,-una; *(no matter which)* cualquier,-ra; *(every)* todo,-a: **have you got ~ money/gloves?**, ¿tienes dinero/guantes?; **he hasn't bought ~ milk/biscuits**, no ha comprado leche/galletas; **~ fool knows that**, cualquier tonto sabe eso; **without ~ difficulty**, sin ninguna dificultad; **~ old rag will do**, cualquier trapo sirve. − 2 *pron (in questions)* alguno,-a; *(negative)* ninguno,-a; *(no matter which)* cualquiera: **I asked for snails/caviar, but they hadn't got ~**, pedí caracoles/caviar pero no tenían. − 3 *adv I don't work there ~ more*, ya no trabajo allí; **do you want ~ more?**, ¿quieres más? ▲ *En preguntas y frases negativas no*

se usa **any** *sino* **a/an** *con substantivos contables en singular; en* 3 *(adverbio) generalmente no se traduce.*

anybody [ˈenɪbɒdɪ] *pron (in questions)* alguien, alguno,-a; *(negative)* nadie, ninguno,-a; *(no matter who)* cualquiera.

anyhow [ˈenɪhaʊ] *adv (despite that)* en todo caso. 2 *(changing the subject)* bueno, pues. 3 *(carelessly)* de cualquier forma.

anyone [ˈenɪwʌn] *pron* → **anybody**.

anything [ˈenɪθɪŋ] *pron. (in questions)* algo, alguna cosa; *(negative)* nada; *(no matter what)* cualquier cosa, todo cuanto.

anyway [ˈenɪweɪ] *adv* → **anyhow**.

anywhere [ˈenɪweəʳ] *adv (in questions) (situation)* en algún sitio; *(direction)* a algún sitio. 2 *(negative) (situation)* en ningún sitio; *(direction)* a ningún sitio. 3 *(no matter where) (situation)* donde sea, en cualquier sitio; *(direction)* a donde sea, a cualquier sitio.

aorta [eɪˈɔːtə] *n* aorta.

apart [əˈpɑːt] *adv* separado,-a: **these nails are too far ~**, estos clavos están demasiado separados. 2 *(in pieces)* en piezas. ●**~ from**, aparte de; **to take ~**, desarmar, desmontar; **to fall ~**, deshacerse.

apartment [əˈpɑːtmənt] *n* piso.

apathetic [æpəˈθetɪk] *adj* apático,-a.

apathy [ˈæpəθɪ] *n* apatía.

ape [eɪp] *n* simio. − 2 *t* imitar.

aperitif [əperɪˈtiːf] *n* aperitivo.

aperture [ˈæpətjəʳ] *n* abertura.

apex [ˈeɪpeks] *n* ápice *m*; *(of triangle)* vértice *m*.

aphorism [ˈæfərɪzəm] *n* aforismo.

aphrodisiac [æfrəˈdɪzɪæk] *adj-n* afrodisíaco,-a *(m)*.

apiece [əˈpiːs] *adv* cada uno,-a.

apologetic [əpɒləˈdʒetɪk] *adj* compungido,-a, arrepentido,-a. − 2 **apologetically** *adv* disculpándose.

apologize [əˈpɒlədʒaɪz] *i* disculparse, pedir perdón.

apology [əˈpɒlədʒɪ] *n* disculpa.

apoplexy [ˈæpəpleksɪ] *n* apoplejía.

apostle [əˈpɒsl] *n* apóstol *m*.

apostrophe [əˈpɒstrəfɪ] *n* apóstrofo.

appal [əˈpɔːl] *t* horrorizar.

appalling [əˈpɔːlɪŋ] *adj* horroroso,-a.

apparatus [æpəˈreɪtəs] *n (equipment)* aparatos *mpl*.

apparent [əˈpærənt] *adj (obvious)* evidente. 2 *(seeming)* aparente. − 3 **apparently**

adv (obviously) evidentemente; *(seemingly)* aparentemente.

apparition [æpə'rɪʃən] *n* aparición.

appeal [ə'pi:l] *n (request)* ruego, llamamiento; *(plea)* súplica. **2** *(attraction)* atractivo. **3** JUR apelación. — **4** *i (request)* pedir, solicitar; *(plead)* suplicar : *to ~ for help,* pedir ayuda. **5** *(attract)* atraer: *it doesn't ~ to me,* no me atrae. **6** JUR apelar.

appealing [ə'pi:lɪŋ] *adj (moving)* suplicante. **2** *(attractive)* atrayente.

appear [ə'pɪər] *i (become visible)* aparecer. **2** *(before a court etc.)* comparecer *(before,* ante). **3** *(on stage etc.)* actuar. **4** *(seem)* parecer. ●*to ~ on television,* salir en la televisión.

appearance [ə'pɪərəns] *n (becoming visible)* aparición. **2** *(before a court etc.)* comparecencia. **3** *(on stage)* actuación. **4** *(look)* apariencia, aspecto.

appease [ə'pi:ż] *t* aplacar, calmar.

append [ə'pend] *t* añadir.

appendage [ə'pendɪdʒ] *n* apéndice *m,* añadidura.

appendicitis [əpendɪ'saɪtɪs] *n* apendicitis *f inv.*

appendix [ə'pendɪks] *n* apéndice *m.*

appetite ['æpɪtaɪt] *n* apetito.

appetizer ['æpɪtaɪzər] *n* aperitivo.

appetizing ['æpɪtaɪzɪŋ] *adj* apetitoso,-a.

applaud [ə'plɔ:d] *t-i (clap)* aplaudir. — **2** *t (praise)* alabar.

applause [ə'plɔ:z] *n* aplausos *mpl.*

apple ['æpəl] *n* manzana. ■ *~ tree,* manzano.

appliance [ə'plaɪəns] *n* aparato. ■ *electrical ~,* electrodoméstico.

applicable ['æplɪkəbəl] *adj* aplicable.

applicant ['æplɪkənt] *n (for job)* candidato,-a.

application [æplɪ'keɪʃən] *n (for job)* solicitud. **2** *(of ointment, theory, etc.)* aplicación.

apply [ə'plaɪ] *t (ointment, theory, etc.)* aplicar. — **2** *i (be true)* aplicarse, ser aplicable. **3** *(for job)* solicitar: *to ~ for information,* pedir información.

appoint [ə'pɔɪnt] *t (person for job)* nombrar. **2** *(day, date, etc.)* fijar, señalar.

appointment [ə'pɔɪntmənt] *n (meeting)* cita: *to ask for an ~ (with the doctor),* pedir hora (con el médico). **2** *(person for job)* nombramiento.

apportion [ə'pɔ:ʃən] *t* repartir, distribuir. ●*to ~ blame to sb.,* echar la culpa a algn.

appraisal [ə'preɪzəl] *n* valoración, evaluación.

appraise [ə'preɪz] *t* valorar, evaluar.

appreciable [ə'pri:ʃəbəl] *adj* apreciable.

appreciate [ə'pri:ʃɪeɪt] *t (be thankful for)* agradecer. **2** *(understand)* entender. **3** *(value)* valorar, apreciar. — **4** *i* valorarse, valorizarse.

appreciation [əpri:ʃɪ'eɪʃən] *n (thanks)* agradecimiento, gratitud. **2** *(understanding)* comprensión. **3** *(appraisal)* evaluación. **4** *(increase in value)* apreciación, aumento en valor.

apprehend [æprɪ'hend] *t (arrest)* detener, capturar. **2** *(understand)* comprender.

apprehension [æprɪ'henʃən] *n (arrest)* detención, captura. **2** *(fear)* temor *m,* recelo.

apprehensive [æprɪ'hensɪv] *adj (fearful)* temeroso,-a, receloso,-a.

apprentice [ə'prentɪs] *n* aprendiz,-za.

apprenticeship [ə'prentɪsʃɪp] *n* aprendizaje *m.*

approach [ə'prəʊtʃ] *n (coming near)* aproximación, acercamiento. **2** *(way in)* entrada, acceso. **3** *(to problem)* enfoque *m.* — **4** *i (come near)* acercarse, aproximarse. — **5** *t (come near)* acercarse a, aproximarse a. **6** *(tackle) (problem)* enfocar, abordar; *(person)* dirigirse a. ■ *~ road,* vía de acceso.

approbation [æprə'beɪʃən] *n* aprobación.

appropriate [ə'prəʊprɪət] *adj* apropiado,-a, adecuado,-a. — **2** *t (allocate)* asignar, destinar. **3** *(steal)* apropiarse de. ●*at the ~ time,* en el momento oportuno. ▲ *En 2 y 3 (verbo)* [ə'prəʊprɪeɪt].

appropriation [əprəʊprɪ'eɪʃən] *n (allocation)* asignación. **2** *(seizure)* apropiación.

approval [ə'pru:vəl] *n* aprobación, visto bueno. **2** COM *on ~,* a prueba.

approve [ə'pru:v] *t* aprobar, dar el visto bueno a. ◆*to ~ of t* aprobar.

approximate [ə'prɒksɪmət] *adj* aproximado,-a. — **2** *i* aproximarse *(to,* a). — **3 approximately** *adv* aproximadamente. ▲ *En 2 (verbo)* [ə'prɒksɪmeɪt].

approximation [əprɒksɪ'meɪʃən] *n* aproximación.

apricot ['eɪprɪkɒt] *n* albaricoque *m.* ■ *~ tree,* albaricoquero.

April ['eɪprɪl] *n* abril *m.*

apron ['eɪprən] *n* delantal *m.*

apropos ['æprəpəʊ] *adj* oportuno,-a. — **2** *~ of adv* a propósito de.

apt [æpt] *adj (suitable)* apropiado,-a; *(remark)* acertado,-a. **2** *(liable to)* propenso,-a.
aptitude [ˈæptɪtjuːd] *n* aptitud.
aptness [ˈæptnəs] *n* lo acertado.
aquarium [əˈkweərɪəm] *n* acuario. ▲ *pl* **aquaria** o **aquariums**.
Aquarius [əˈkweərɪəs] *n* Acuario.
aquatic [əˈkwætɪk] *adj* acuático,-a.
aqueduct [ˈækwɪdʌkt] *n* acueducto.
aquiline [ˈækwɪlaɪn] *adj* aguileño,-a.
Arabic [ˈærəbɪk] *adj* arábigo,-a, árabe; ~ **numerals,** números arábigos. – **2** *n (language)* árabe *m.*
arable [ˈærəbəl] *adj* cultivable.
arbitrary [ˈɑːbɪtrərɪ] *adj* arbitrario,-a.
arbitrate [ˈɑːbɪtreɪt] *t-i* arbitrar.
arbitration [ɑːbɪˈtreɪʃən] *n* arbitraje *m.*
arc [ɑːk] *n* arco.
arcade [ɑːˈkeɪd] *n* pasaje *m.* ■ **shopping** ~, galerías *fpl* (comerciales).
arch [ɑːtʃ] *n* ARCH arco; *(vault)* bóveda. – **2** *t* arquear, enarcar. **3** *(vault)* abovedar. – **4** *i* arquearse. **5** *(vault)* formar bóveda.
archaeological [ɑːkɪəˈlɒdʒɪkəl] *adj* arqueológico,-a.
archaeologist [ɑːkɪˈɒlədʒɪst] *n* arqueólogo,-a.
archaeology [ɑːkɪˈɒlədʒɪ] *n* arqueología.
archaic [ɑːˈkeɪɪk] *adj* arcaico,-a.
archbishop [ˈɑːtʃˈbɪʃəp] *n* arzobispo.
archer [ˈɑːtʃər] *n* arquero.
archery [ˈɑːtʃərɪ] *n* tiro con arco.
archetypal [ˈɑːkɪtaɪp] *n* arquetípico,-a.
archipelago [ɑːkɪˈpelɪgəʊ] *n* archipiélago.
architect [ˈɑːkɪtekt] *n* arquitecto,-a.
architecture [ˈɑːkɪtektʃər] *n* arquitectura.
archives [ˈɑːkaɪvz] *npl* archivo *m* sing.
arctic [ˈɑːktɪk] *adj-n* ártico,-a *(m).*
ardent [ˈɑːdənt] *adj* apasionado,-a, fervoroso,-a.
ardour [ˈɑːdər] *n* ardor *m.*
arduous [ˈɑːdjuəs] *adj* arduo,-a.
are [ɑːr, ər] *2ª pers sing; 1ª, 2ª y 3ª pers pl del pres indic.* → **be.**
area [ˈeərɪə] *n (surface)* área, superficie *f.* **2** *(region)* región *f; (of town)* zona. **3** *(field)* campo. ■ SP **penalty** ~, área de castigo.
arena [əˈriːnə] *n (stadium)* estadio. **2** *(ring)* ruedo. **3** *fig* ámbito.
argue [ˈɑːgjuː] *i (quarrel)* discutir. **2** *(reason)* argüir, argumentar.

argument [ˈɑːgjumənt] *n (quarrel)* discusión, disputa. **2** *(reasoning)* argumento.
argumentative [ɑːgjʊˈmentətɪv] *adj* que discute/replica.
arid [ˈærɪd] *adj* árido,-a.
Aries [ˈeəriːz] *n* Aries *m.*
aridity [æˈrɪdɪtɪ] *n* aridez *f.*
arise [əˈraɪz] *i (crop up)* surgir. **2** *(old use)* levantarse. ▲ *pt* **arose**; *pp* **arisen** [əˈrɪzən].
aristocracy [ærɪsˈtɒkrəsɪ] *n* aristocracia.
aristocrat [ˈærɪstəkræt] *n* aristócrata *mf.*
aristocratic [ærɪstəˈkrætɪk] *adj* aristocrático,-a.
arithmetic [əˈrɪθmətɪk] *n* aritmética.
ark [ɑːk] *n* arca. ■ **Noah's** ~, el arca de Noé.
arm [ɑːm] *n* ANAT brazo. **2** *(of coat etc.)* manga; *(of chair)* brazo. **3** *pl (weapons)* armas *fpl.* – **4** *t-i* armar(se). ●~ *in* ~, cogidos,-as del brazo; *with open arms,* con los brazos abiertos; *to keep sb. at arm's length,* mantener a algn. a distancia. ■ **arms race,** carrera armamentística.
armaments [ˈɑːməmənt] *npl* armamentos *mpl.*
armchair [ˈɑːmˈtʃeər] *n* sillón *m.*
armful [ˈɑːmfʊl] *n* brazado.
armistice [ˈɑːmɪstɪs] *n* armisticio.
armour [ˈɑːmər] *n (suit of)* ~, armadura. **2** *(on vehicle)* blindaje *m.*
armoury [ˈɑːmərɪ] *n* armería.
armpit [ˈɑːmpɪt] *n* sobaco, axila.
army [ˈɑːmɪ] *n* ejército.
aroma [əˈrəʊmə] *n* aroma.
aromatic [ærəˈmætɪk] *adj* aromático,-a.
arose [əˈrəʊz] *pt* → **arise.**
around [əˈraʊnd] *adv (near, in the area)* alrededor: *is there anybody* ~?, ¿hay alguien (cerca)?; *don't leave your money* ~, *put it away,* no dejes tu dinero por ahí, guárdalo. **2** *(from place to place) they cycle* ~ *together,* van juntos en bicicleta. **3** *(available, in existence)* £1 *coins have been* ~ *for some time,* hace tiempo que circulan las monedas de una libra; *there isn't much fresh fruit* ~, hay poca fruta fresca. **4** *(to face the opposite way) turn* ~ *please,* dese la vuelta por favor. – **5** *prep (approximately)* alrededor de: *it costs* ~ £5,000, cuesta unas cinco mil libras. **6** *(near) there aren't many shops* ~ *here,* hay pocas tiendas por aquí. **7** *(all over) there were clothes* ~ *the room,* había ropa por toda la habitación. **8** *(in a circle or curve)* alrededor de: *he put his*

arms ~ *her,* la cogió en los brazos. ●~
the corner, a la vuelta de la esquina.
arouse [əˈraʊz] *t (awake)* despertar. **2**
(sexually) excitar.
arrange [əˈreɪndʒ] *t (hair, flowers)* arreglar; *(furniture etc.)* colocar, ordenar. **2**
(plan) planear, organizar. **3** *(agree on)*
acordar. ●*to* ~ *to do sth.,* quedar en hacer algo.
arrangement [əˈreɪndʒmənt] *n (of flowers)* arreglo (floral). **2** *(agreement)* acuerdo, arreglo. **3** MUS adaptación. **5** *pl
(plans)* planes *mpl; (preparations)* preparativos *mpl.*
arrears [əˈrɪəz] *npl* atrasos *mpl.*
arrest [əˈrest] *n* arresto, detención. − **2** *t*
arrestar, detener. **3** *fml (stop)* detener.
arrival [əˈraɪvəl] *n* llegada.
arrive [əˈraɪv] *i* llegar.
arrogance [ˈærəgəns] *n* arrogancia.
arrogant [ˈærəgənt] *adj* arrogante.
arrow [ˈærəʊ] *n* flecha.
arse* [ɑːs] *n* culo.
arsenal [ˈɑːsənəl] *n* arsenal *m.*
arsenic [ˈɑːsənɪk] *n* arsénico.
arson [ˈɑːsən] *n* incendio provocado.
art [ɑːt] *n (painting etc.)* arte *m.* **2** *(skill)*
arte, habilidad. **3** *pl (branch of know-
ledge)* letras *fpl.* ■ *arts and crafts,* artes
pl y oficios; *work of* ~, obra de arte.
artery [ˈɑːtərɪ] *n* ANAT arteria.
artful [ˈɑːtfʊl] *n* ladino,-a, astuto,-a.
arthritic [ɑːˈθrɪtɪk] *adj* artrítico,-a.
arthritis [ɑːˈθraɪtɪs] *n* artritis *f inv.*
artichoke [ˈɑːtɪtʃəʊk] *n* alcachofa.
article [ˈɑːtɪkəl] *n* artículo. ■ ~ *of clothing,* prenda de vestir; *leading* ~, editorial *m.*
articulate [ɑːˈtɪkjʊlət] *adj (person)* que se
expresa con facilidad; *(speech)* claro,-a.
− **2** *t* articular. **3** *(pronounce)* pronunciar.
▲ *En 2 y 3 (verbo)* [ɑːˈtɪkjʊleɪt].
artificial [ɑːtɪˈfɪʃəl] *adj (flowers, light, etc.)*
artificial. **2** *(limb, hair)* postizo,-a. **3**
(smile etc.) afectado,-a, fingido,-a.
artillery [ɑːˈtɪlərɪ] *n* artillería.
artisan [ɑːtɪˈzæn] *n* artesano,-a.
artist [ˈɑːtɪst] *n* artista *mf.* **2** *(painter)* pintor,-ra.
artistic [ɑːˈtɪstɪk] *adj* artístico,-a.
as [æz, əz] *adv* como: *he works* ~ *a clerk,*
trabaja de oficinista; *dressed* ~ *a monkey,* disfrazado,-a de mono. **2** *(in comparatives)* ~ *big* ~, tan grande como; ~
much ~, tanto,-a como. − **3** *conj (while)*
mientras; *(when)* cuando. **4** *(because)* ya
que. **5** *(although)* aunque. ●~ *a rule,*

como regla general; ~ *far* ~, hasta; ~
far ~ *I know,* que yo sepa; ~ *far* ~ *I'm*
concerned, por lo que a mí respecta; ~
for/regards, en cuanto a; ~ *if/though,*
como si; ~ *long* ~, mientras; ~ *of,* desde; ~ *soon* ~, tan pronto como; ~ *well*
~, además de; ~ *yet,* hasta ahora.
asbestos [æzˈbestəs] *n* amianto.
ascend [əˈsend] *t-i* ascender, subir.
ascendancy [əˈsendənsɪ] *n* ascendiente
m.
ascendant [əˈsendənt] *n* ascendiente *m.*
ascension [əˈsenʃən] *n* ascensión.
ascent [əˈsent] *n* subida.
ascertain [æsəˈteɪn] *t* averiguar.
ascetic [əˈsetɪk] *adj* ascético,-a. − **2** *n* asceta *mf.*
ascribe [əsˈkraɪb] *t* atribuir.
ash [æʃ] *n* ceniza. **2** *(tree)* fresno. ■ ~
tray, cenicero; *Ash Wednesday,* miércoles *m* de ceniza.
ashamed [əˈʃeɪmd] *adj* avergonzado,-a.
●*to be* ~ *of,* avergonzarse de, tener vergüenza de.
ashore [əˈʃɔːʳ] *adv (position)* en tierra;
(movement) a tierra. ●*to go* ~, desembarcar.
aside [əˈsaɪd] *adv* al lado, a un lado. − **2**
n THEAT aparte *m.* ●*to set* ~, apartar, reservar; *to step* ~, apartarse; *to take sb.*
~, separar a algn. (del grupo) para hablar aparte.
ask [ɑːsk] *t (inquire)* preguntar. **2** *(request)*
pedir. **3** *(invite)* invitar, convidar. ◆*to* ~
after/about t preguntar por. ◆*to* ~ *for*
t pedir. ◆*to* ~ *out t* invitar a salir.
askance [əsˈkæns] *adv to look* ~ *at,* mirar
con recelo.
askew [əsˈkjuː] *adv* de lado. − **2** *adj* ladeado,-a.
asleep [əˈsliːp] *adj-adv* dormido,-a: *to fall*
~, dormirse.
asp [æsp] *n* áspid *m.*
asparagus [æsˈpærəgəs] *n (plant)* espárrago; *(shoots)* espárragos *mpl.*
aspect [ˈæspekt] *n* aspecto. **2** *(of building)*
orientación.
asperity [æsˈperɪtɪ] *n* aspereza.
aspersions [əsˈpɜːʃənz] *npl to cast* ~ *on,*
difamar a.
asphalt [ˈæsfælt] *n* asfalto.
asphyxia [æsˈfɪksɪə] *n* asfixia.
asphyxiate [æsˈfɪksɪeɪt] *t* asfixiar.
aspic [ˈæspɪk] *n* CULIN gelatina.
aspirant [əsˈpaɪərənt] *n* aspirante *mf.*
aspirate [ˈæspəreɪt] *t* aspirar. − **2** *adj* as-
pirado,-a. ▲ *En 2 (adjetivo)* [ˈæspərət].

aspiration [æspə'reɪʃən] *n* LING aspiración. **2** *(ambition)* ambición.

aspire [əs'paɪəʳ] *i* aspirar *(to, a)*.

aspirin ® ['æspɪrɪn] *n* aspirina®.

ass [æs] *n* burro, asno. **2*** US culo.

assail [ə'seɪl] *t* asaltar.

assailant [ə'seɪlənt] *n* atacante *mf*, agresor,-ra.

assassin [ə'sæsɪn] *n* asesino,-a.

assassinate [ə'sæsɪneɪt] *t* asesinar.

assassination [əsæsɪ'neɪʃən] *n* asesinato.

assault [ə'sɔːlt] *n* MIL asalto. **2** JUR agresión. **– 3** *t* MIL asaltar. **4** JUR agredir.

assemble [ə'sembəl] *t* *(bring together)* reunir. **2** *(put together)* montar. **– 3** *i* reunirse.

assembly [ə'semblɪ] *n* *(meeting)* reunión. **2** TECH *(putting together)* montaje *m*.

assent [ə'sent] *n* asentimiento. **– 2** *i* asentir *(to, a)*.

assert [ə'sɜːt] *t* *(declare)* aseverar, afirmar. •*to ~ oneself,* imponerse.

assertion [ə'sɜːʃən] *n* aseveración.

assess [ə'ses] *t* *(value)* tasar, valorar. **2** *(calculate)* calcular. **3** *fig* evaluar.

assessment [ə'sesmənt] *n* *(valuation)* tasación, valoración. **2** *(calculation)* cálculo. **3** *fig* evaluación.

assessor [ə'sesəʳ] *n* asesor,-ra.

asset ['æset] *n* *(quality)* calidad positiva, ventaja. **2** *pl* COM bienes *mpl*.

assiduity [æsɪ'djuːɪtɪ] *n* asiduidad.

assiduous [ə'sɪdjʊəs] *adj* asiduo,-a.

assign [ə'saɪn] *t* *(allot)* asignar. **2** *(choose)* designar.

assignment [ə'saɪnmənt] *n* *(misión)* misión. **2** *(task)* tarea.

assimilate [ə'sɪmɪleɪt] *t-i* asimilar(se).

assimilation [əsɪmɪ'leɪʃən] *n* asimilación.

assist [ə'sɪst] *t* ayudar.

assistance [ə'sɪstəns] *n* ayuda.

assistant [ə'sɪstənt] *n* ayudante *mf*. ■ *~ manager,* subdirector,-ra; *shop ~,* dependiente *mf*.

associate [ə'səʊʃɪət] *adj* *(company)* asociado,-a. **2** *(member)* correspondiente. **– 3** *n* *(partner)* socio,-a. **– 4** *t-i* asociar(se). •*to ~ with sb.,* relacionarse con algn.

association [əsəʊsɪ'eɪʃən] *n* asociación.

assorted [ə'sɔːtɪd] *adj* surtido,-a, variado,-a.

assortment [ə'sɔːtmənt] *n* surtido, variedad.

assume [ə'sjuːm] *t* *(suppose)* suponer. **2** *(power, responsibility)* tomar, asumir. **3** *(attitude, expression)* adoptar.

assumption [ə'sʌmpʃən] *n* *(supposition)* suposición. **2** *(of power)* toma.

assurance [ə'ʃʊərəns] *n* *(guarantee)* garantía. **2** *(confidence)* confianza. **3** *(insurance)* seguro.

assure [ə'ʃʊəʳ] *t* asegurar.

assured [ə'ʃʊəd] *adj* seguro,-a.

asterisk ['æstərɪsk] *n* asterisco.

asthma ['æsmə] *n* asma.

asthmatic [æs'mætɪk] *adj-n* asmático,-a.

astonish [əs'tɒnɪʃ] *t* asombrar, sorprender.

astonishing [əs'tɒnɪʃɪŋ] *adj* asombroso,-a, sorprendente.

astonishment [əs'tɒnɪʃmənt] *n* asombro.

astound [əs'taʊnd] *t* pasmar, asombrar.

astray [ə'streɪ] *adv-adj* extraviado,-a. •*to go ~,* descarriarse.

astride [ə'straɪd] *prep* a horcajadas sobre.

astringent [əs'trɪndʒənt] *adj* astringente.

astrologer [əs'trɒlədʒəʳ] *n* astrólogo,-a.

astrology [əs'trɒlədʒɪ] *n* astrología.

astronaut ['æstrənɔːt] *n* astronauta *mf*.

astronomical [æstrə'nɒmɪkəl] *n* astronómico,-a.

astronomer [əs'trɒnəməʳ] *n* astrónomo,-a.

astronomy [əs'trɒnəmɪ] *n* astronomía.

astute [əs'tjuːt] *adj* astuto,-a, sagaz.

astuteness [əs'tjuːtnəs] *n* astucia.

asylum [ə'saɪləm] *n* asilo, refugio. ■ *mental ~,* manicomio; *political ~,* asilo político.

at [æt, ət] *prep* *(position)* en, a: *~ the door,* a la puerta; *~ home/school/work,* en casa/el colegio/el trabajo. **2** *(time)* a: *~ two o'clock,* a las dos; *~ night,* por la noche; *~ Christmas,* en Navidad; *~ the beginning/end,* al principio/final. **3** *(direction, violence)* *to shout ~ sb.,* gritarle a algn; *to shoot ~,* disparar contra; *to throw a stone ~ sb.,* lanzar una piedra contra algn. **4** *(rate)* a: *~ 50 miles an hour,* a 50 millas la hora; *~ £1000 a ton,* a mil libras la tonelada; *three ~ a time,* de tres en tres. **5** *(ability)* *he's good ~ French/painting/swimming,* va bien en francés/pinta bien/es buen nadador. •*~ first,* al principio; *~ last!,* ¡por fin!; *~ least,* por lo menos; *~ once,* en seguida.

ate [et] *pt* → **eat**.

atheism ['eɪθɪɪzəm] *n* ateísmo.

atheist ['eɪθɪɪst] *n* ateo,-a.
athlete ['æθli:t] *n* atleta *mf*.
athletic [æθ'letɪk] *adj* atlético,-a. **2** *(spor-ty)* deportista.
athletics [æθ'letɪks] *n* atletismo.
atlas ['ætləs] *n* atlas *m inv*.
atmosphere ['ætməsfɪəʳ] *n* atmósfera. **2** *(ambience)* ambiente *m*.
atoll ['ætɒl] *n* atolón *m*.
atom ['ætəm] *n* átomo. ■ ~ *bomb*, bomba atómica.
atomic [ə'tɒmɪk] *adj* atómico,-a.
atomizer ['ætəmaɪzəʳ] *n* atomizador *m*.
atone [ə'təʊn] *i to* ~ *for*, expiar.
atonement [ə'təʊnmənt] *n* expiación.
atrocious [ə'trəʊʃəs] *adj (cruel)* atroz. **2** *fam* fatal, malísimo,-a.
atrocity [ə'trɒsɪtɪ] *n* atrocidad.
attach [ə'tætʃ] *t (fasten)* sujetar. **2** *(tie)* atar. **3** *(stick)* pegar. **4** *(document)* adjuntar. ●*to* ~ *importance to,* considerar importante; *to be attached to,* tener cariño a.
attachment [ə'tætʃmənt] *n* TECH accesorio. **2** *(fondness)* cariño, apego.
attack [ə'tæk] *n* ataque. − **2** *t* atacar.
attain [ə'teɪn] *t (ambition)* lograr. **2** *(rank)* llegar a.
attainment [ə'teɪnmənt] *n (sth. achieved)* logro. **2** *(skill)* talento.
attempt [ə'tempt] *n (try)* intento, tentativa. − **2** *t* intentar. ●*to make an* ~ *on sb.'s life,* atentar contra la vida de algn.
attend [ə'tend] *t (be present at)* asistir a. **2** *(care for)* atender, cuidar. **3** *(accompany)* acompañar. − **4** *i (be present)* asistir. ◆*to* ~ *to t* ocuparse de. **2** *(in shop)* despachar.
attendance [ə'tendəns] *n (being present)* asistencia. **2** *(people present)* asistentes *mpl*.
attendant [ə'tendənt] *n (in car park, museum)* vigilante *mf*; *(in cinema)* acomodador,-ra.
attention [ə'tenʃən] *n* atención. **2** MIL ~*!,* ¡firmes! ●*to pay* ~*,* prestar atención; *to stand to* ~*,* cuadrarse.
attentive [ə'tentɪv] *adj* atento,-a. **2** *(helpful)* solícito,-a.
attic ['ætɪk] *n* desván *m*, buhardilla.
attire [ə'taɪəʳ] *n* traje *m*, vestido.
attitude ['ætɪtjuːd] *n* actitud.
attorney [ə'tɜːnɪ] *n* US abogado,-a. ■ GB *Attorney General,* Ministro,-a de Justicia.
attract [ə'trækt] *t* atraer. ●*to* ~ *attention,* llamar la atención.

attraction [ə'trækʃən] *n (power)* atracción. **2** *(thing)* atractivo. **3** *(incentive)* aliciente *m*.
attractive [ə'træktɪv] *adj (person)* atractivo,-a. **2** *(offer)* interesante.
attribute ['ætrɪbjuːt] *n* atributo. − **2** *t* atribuir. ▲ *En 2 (verbo)* [ə'trɪbjuːt].
attribution [ætrɪ'bjuːʃən] *n* atribución.
aubergine ['əʊbəʒiːn] *n* berenjena.
auburn ['ɔːbən] *adj* castaño,-a.
auction ['ɔːkʃən] *n* subasta. − **2** *t* subastar.
audacious [ɔː'deɪʃəs] *adj* audaz.
audacity [ɔː'dæsɪtɪ] *n* audacia.
audible ['ɔːdɪbəl] *adj* audible.
audience ['ɔːdɪəns] *n (spectators)* público. **2** *(interview)* audiencia.
audio-visual [ɔːdɪəʊ'vɪzjʊəl] *adj* audiovisual.
audit ['ɔːdɪt] *n* revisión de cuentas. − **2** *t* revisar.
audition [ɔː'dɪʃən] *n* prueba.
auditor ['ɔːdɪtəʳ] *n* revisor,-ra de cuentas.
auditorium [ɔːdɪ'tɔːrɪəm] *n* auditorio, sala.
augment [ɔːg'ment] *t-i fml* aumentar(se).
augur ['ɔːgəʳ] *t-i* presagiar. ●*to* ~ *well/ill,* ser de buen/mal agüero.
August ['ɔːgəst] *n* agosto.
august [ɔː'gʌst] *adj* augusto,-a.
aunt [ɑːnt] *n* tía.
auntie ['ɑːntɪ] *n fam* tía.
aura ['ɔːrə] *n (of person)* aura; *(of place)* sensación.
aural ['ɔːrəl] *adj* auditivo,-a.
auspices ['ɔːspɪsɪz] *npl* auspicios *mpl; under the* ~ *of,* bajo los auspicios de.
auspicious [ɔːs'pɪʃəs] *adj* propicio,-a, de buen augurio.
austere [ɒs'tɪəʳ] *adj* austero,-a.
austerity [ɒs'terɪtɪ] *n* austeridad.
authentic [ɔː'θentɪk] *adj* auténtico,-a.
authenticity [ɔːθen'tɪsɪtɪ] *n* autenticidad.
author ['ɔːθəʳ] *n* autor,-ra, escritor,-ra.
authoritative [ɔː'θɒrɪtətɪv] *adj (reliable)* autorizado,-a, fidedigno,-a. **2** *(authoritarian)* autoritario,-a.
authoritarian [ɔːθɒrɪ'teərɪən] *adj* autoritario,-a.
authority [ɔː'θɒrɪtɪ] *n* autoridad. ●*on good* ~*,* de buena tinta.
authorization [ɔːθəraɪ'zeɪʃən] *n* autorización.
authorize ['ɔːθəraɪz] *t* autorizar.
autobiographical [ɔːtəbaɪə'græfɪkəl] *adj* autobiográfico,-a.

autobiography [ɔ:təbaɪ'ɒgrəfɪ] *n* autobiografía.

autocracy [ɔ:'tɒkrəsɪ] *n* autocracia.

autocrat ['ɔ:təkræt] *n* autócrata *mf*.

autocratic [ɔ:tə'krætɪk] *adj* autocrático,-a.

autograph ['ɔ:təgrɑ:f] *n* autógrafo.

automatic [ɔ:tə'mætɪk] *adj* automático,-a.

automaton [ɔ:'tɒmətən] *n* autómata *m*.

automobile ['ɔ:təməbi:l] *n* automóvil *m*.

autonomous [ɔ:'tɒnəməs] *adj* autónomo,-a.

autonomy [ɔ:'tɒnəmɪ] *n* autonomía.

autopsy ['ɔ:təpsɪ] *n* autopsia.

autumn ['ɔ:təm] *n* otoño.

autumnal [ɔ:'tʌmnəl] *adj* otoñal.

auxiliary [ɔ:g'zɪljərɪ] *adj-n* auxiliar *(m)*.

avail [ə'veɪl] *n to no ~,* en vano. − **2** *t to ~ oneself of,* aprovecharse de.

available [ə'veɪləbəl] *adj (thing)* disponible: *it's ~ in four colours,* lo hay en cuatro colores. **2** *(person)* libre.

avalanche ['ævəlɑ:nʃ] *n* alud *m*; *fig* avalancha.

avarice ['ævərɪs] *n* avaricia.

avaricious [ævə'rɪʃəs] *adj* avaro,-a.

avenge [ə'vendʒ] *t* vengar.

avenger [ə'vendʒə'] *n* vengador,-ra.

avenue ['ævənju:] *n* avenida.

average ['ævərɪdʒ] *n* promedio, media. − **2** *adj* medio,-a. **3** *(not special)* corriente, regular. − **4** *t* hacer un promedio de: *I ~ 10 cigarettes a day,* fumo un promedio de 10 cigarrillos al día. **5** *(calculate)* determinar el promedio de. ●*above/below ~,* por encima/debajo de la media; *on ~,* por término medio.

averse [ə'vɜ:s] *adj* reacio,-a *(to,* a).

aversion [ə'vɜ:ʃən] *n* aversión.

avert [ə'vɜ:t] *t (avoid)* evitar. ●*to ~ one's eyes,* apartar la vista.

aviary ['eɪvjərɪ] *n* pajarera.

aviation [eɪvɪ'eɪʃən] *n* aviación.

aviator ['eɪvɪeɪtə'] *n* aviador,-ra.

avid ['ævɪd] *adj* ávido,-a.

avidity [ə'vɪdɪtɪ] *n* avidez *f*.

avocado [ævə'kɑ:dəʊ] *n ~ (pear),* aguacate *m*.

avoid [ə'vɔɪd] *t* evitar. **2** *(question)* eludir. **3** *(person)* esquivar.

avow [ə'vaʊ] *t* declarar.

await [ə'weɪt] *t fml* aguardar, esperar.

awake [ə'weɪk] *adj* despierto,-a. − **2** *t-i* despertar(se). ▲ *pt* **awoke**; *pp* **awaked** o **awoken**.

awaken [ə'weɪkən] *t-i* → **awake**.

award [ə'wɔ:d] *n (prize)* premio. **2** *(grant)* beca. **3** *(damages)* indemnización. − **4** *t (prize, grant)* otorgar, conceder. **5** *(damages)* adjudicar.

aware [ə'weə'] *adj* consciente. ●*to be ~ of,* ser consciente de; *to become ~ of,* darse cuenta de.

away [ə'weɪ] *adv* lejos, fuera, alejándose; *he lives 4 km ~,* vive a 4 km (de aquí); *the wedding is 6 weeks ~,* faltan 6 semanas para la boda. **2** *(indicating continuity)* *they worked ~ all day,* trabajaron todo el día. ●*to be ~,* estar fuera; *(from school)* estar ausente; *to go ~,* irse, marcharse; SP *to play ~,* jugar fuera; *to run ~,* irse corriendo.

awe [ɔ:] *n (fear)* temor *m*. **2** *(wonder)* asombro.

awful ['ɔ:fʊl] *adj (shocking)* atroz, horrible. **2** *fam (very bad)* fatal, horrible, espantoso,-a. − **3** *awfully adv fam* terriblemente.

awhile [ə'waɪl] *adv* un rato.

awkward ['ɔ:kwəd] *adj (clumsy)* torpe. **2** *(difficult)* difícil. **3** *(embarrassing)* embarazoso,-a, delicado,-a. **4** *(inconvenient)* inconveniente, oportuno,-a. **5** *(uncomfortable)* incómodo,-a.

awl [ɔ:l] *n* lezna.

awning ['ɔ:nɪŋ] *n* toldo.

awoke [ə'wəʊk] *pt* → **awake**.

awoken [ə'wəʊkən] *pp* → **awake**.

ax(e) [æks] *n* hacha.

axiom ['æksɪəm] *n* axioma *m*.

axiomatic [æksɪə'mætɪk] *adj* axiomático,-a.

axis ['æksɪs] *n* eje *m*.

axle ['æksəl] *n* eje *m*.

azure ['eɪʒə'] *adj-n* azul *(m)* celeste.

B

baa [bɑ:] *i* balar.

babble [ˈbæbəl] *t (excitedly)* barbullar. **2** *(meaninglessly)* balbucear. **3** *(water)* murmurar. – **4** *n (confused voices)* murmullo.

baboon [bəˈbu:n] *n* mandril *m*.

baby [ˈbeɪbɪ] *n* bebé *m*.

babyhood [ˈbeɪbɪhʊd] *n* infancia.

babyish [ˈbeɪbɪʃ] *adj* infantil.

baby-sit [ˈbeɪbɪsɪt] *i* hacer de canguro, cuidar niños.

baby-sitter [ˈbeɪbɪsɪtəʳ] *n* canguro *mf*.

bachelor [ˈbætʃələʳ] *n* soltero. ■ *Bachelor of Arts/Science,* Licenciado,-a en Filosofía y Letras/Ciencias.

back [bæk] *n* ANAT espalda. **2** *(of animal, book)* lomo. **3** *(of chair)* respaldo. **4** *(of cheque)* dorso. **5** *(of stage, room, cupboard)* fondo. **6** SP *(player)* defensa *mf*; *(position)* defensa *f*. – **7** *adj* trasero,-a, posterior. – **8** *adv (at the rear)* atrás; *(towards the rear)* hacia atrás; *(time)* hace: *several years* ~, hace varios años. – **9** *t (support)* apoyar, respaldar. **10** FIN financiar. **11** *(bet on)* apostar por. **12** *(vehicle)* dar march atrás a. – **13** *i* retroceder. **14** *(vehicle)* dar marcha atrás. ◆*to* ~ *away i* retirarse. ◆*to* ~ *down i* claudicar. ◆*to* ~ *out i* volverse atrás. ● ~ *to front,* al revés; *behind sb.'s* ~, a espaldas de algn.; *to answer* ~, replicar; *to be* ~, estar de vuelta; *to come/go* ~, volver; *to hit* ~, devolver el golpe; *fig* contestar a una acusación; *to have one's* ~ *to the wall,* estar entre la espada y la pared; *to put/give* ~, devolver; *to phone* ~, volver a llamar; *to turn one's* ~ *on,* volver la espalda a. ■ ~ *door,* puerta trasera; ~ *number,* número atrasado; ~ *pay,* atrasos *mpl*; ~ *seat,* asiento de atrás; ~ *street,* callejuela; ~ *wheel,* rueda trasera.

backbiting [ˈbækbaɪtɪŋ] *n* murmuración.

backbone [ˈbækbəʊn] *n* columna vertebral, espinazo. **2** *fig* carácter *m*.

backdated [bækˈdeɪtɪd] *adj* con efecto retroactivo.

backdrop [ˈbækdrɒp] *n* telón *m* de fondo.

backer [ˈbækəʳ] *n* FIN promotor,-ra. **2** *(supporter)* partidario,-a.

backfire [bækˈfaɪəʳ] *t* fallar: *our plan backfired,* nos salió el tiro por la culata.

background [ˈbækgraʊnd] *n* fondo. **2** *fig (origin)* origen *m*: *(education)* formación. ■ ~ *music,* música de fondo.

backhand [ˈbækhænd] *n* revés *m*.

backing [ˈbækɪŋ] *n (support)* apoyo, respaldo. **2** MUS acompañamiento.

backlash [ˈbæklæʃ] *n* reacción violenta y repentina.

backlog [ˈbæklɒg] *n* acumulación.

backside [bækˈsaɪd] *n fam* trasero.

backstroke [ˈbækstrəʊk] *n* espalda.

backward [ˈbækwəd] *adj* hacia atrás. **2** *(child)* atrasado,-a. **3** *(country)* subdesarrollado,-a. – **4** *adv esp* US → **backwards**.

backwards [ˈbækwədz] *adv* hacia atrás. **2** *(the wrong way)* al revés.

backwater [ˈbækwɔ:təʳ] *n* remanso.

bacon [ˈbeɪkən] *n* tocino, bacon *m*.

bacterium [bækˈtɪərɪəm] *n* bacteria. ▲ *pl bacteria* [bækˈtɪərɪə].

bad [bæd] *adj* malo,-a; *(before masc noun)* mal. **2** *(rotten)* podrido,-a. **3** *(serious)* grave. **4** *(harmful)* nocivo,-a, perjudicial. **5** *(naughty)* malo,-a, travieso,-a. **6** *(aches, illnesses)* fuerte. – **7** *n* lo malo. – **8** *badly adv* mal. **9** *(seriously)* gravemente. **10** *(very much)* muchísimo,-a. ◆*to come to a* ~ *end,* acabar mal; *to go* ~, pudrirse; *to go from* ~ *to worse,* ir de mal en peor. ▲ *comp worse; superl worst.*

baddie, baddy ['bædɪ] *n fam* malo,-a de la película.
bade [beɪd] *pt* → **bid**.
badge [bædʒ] *n* insignia, distintivo. 2 *(metallic)* chapa.
badger ['bædʒəʳ] *n* ZOOL tejón *m*. − 2 *t* acosar, importunar.
badminton ['bædmɪntən] *n* bádminton *m*.
badness ['bædnəs] *n* maldad.
baffle ['bæfəl] *t* confundir, desconcertar.
bag [bæg] *n (paper, plastic)* bolsa; *(large)* saco. 2 *(handbag)* bolso. 3 *fam (woman)* arpía. 4 *pl fam* pantalones *mpl*. − 5 *t* embolsar, ensacar. 6 *fam (catch)* cazar. ●*bags of,* montones de.
baggage ['bægɪdʒ] *n* equipaje *m*, bagaje *m*.
baggy ['bægɪ] *adj* holgado,-a, ancho,-a.
bagpipes ['bægpaɪps] *npl* gaita *f sing*.
bail [beɪl] *n* JUR fianza. ◆*to ~ out t* JUR conseguir la libertad de (algn.) bajo fianza. 2 *fig* sacar de un apuro. 3 MAR achicar.
bailiff ['beɪlɪf] *n* JUR alguacil *m*. 2 *(steward)* administrador,-ra.
bait [beɪt] *n* cebo. − 2 *t* cebar. 3 *(torment)* atosigar.
bake [beɪk] *t* cocer (al horno). − 2 *i* hacer mucho calor.
baker ['beɪkəʳ] *n* panadero,-a.
bakery ['beɪkərɪ] *n* panadería.
balance ['bæləns] *n* equilibrio. 2 *(scales)* balanza. 3 FIN saldo. 4 *(remainder)* resto. − 5 *t* poner en equilibrio. 6 FIN *(budget)* equilibrar; *(account)* saldar. − 7 *i* mantenerse en equilibrio. 8 FIN cuadrar. ●*to ~ the books,* hacer el balance.
balcony ['bælkənɪ] *n* balcón *m*. 2 US THEAT anfiteatro; *(gallery)* gallinero.
bald [bɔːld] *adj* calvo,-a. 2 *(tyre)* desgastado,-a. 3 *(style)* escueto,-a. − 4 *baldly adv* francamente.
baldness ['bɔːldnəs] *n* calvicie *f*, calvez *f*.
bale [beɪl] *n* bala. − 2 *t* embalar. ◆*to ~ out t* MAR achicar. − 2 *i* AER saltar (de un avión) en paracaídas.
balk [bɔːk] *t* poner obstáculos a, frustrar. − 2 *i* negarse.
ball [bɔːl] *n* pelota; *(football)* balón *m*; *(golf, billiards)* bola. 2 *(of paper)* bola; *(of wool)* ovillo. 3 *(dance)* baile *m*, fiesta. 4* *pl* cojones* *mpl*. ■ *~ bearing,* rodamiento de bolas.
ballad ['bæləd] *n* balada.
ballast ['bæləst] *n* lastre *m*.
ballerina [bælə'riːnə] *n* bailarina.

ballet ['bæleɪ] *n* ballet *m*.
ballistics [bə'lɪstɪks] *n* balística.
balloon [bə'luːn] *n* globo.
ballot ['bælət] *n (vote)* votación (secreta). 2 *(paper)* papeleta. − 3 *t* hacer votar. ■ *~ box,* urna.
ballpoint ['bɔːlpɔɪnt] *n ~ (pen),* bolígrafo.
ballroom ['bɔːlruːm] *n* sala de baile.
balm [bɑːm] *n* bálsamo.
balmy ['bɑːmɪ] *adj (weather)* suave.
balsam ['bɔːlsəm] *n* → **balm**.
balustrade [bælə'streɪd] *n* balaustrada.
bamboo [bæm'buː] *n* bambú *m*.
bamboozle [bæm'buːzəl] *t fam* engatusar.
ban [bæn] *n* prohibición. − 2 *t* prohibir.
banal [bə'nɑːl] *adj* banal.
banana [bə'nɑːnə] *n* plátano, banana.
band [bænd] *n* MUS banda; *(pop)* conjunto. 2 *(strip)* faja, tira. 3 *(youths)* pandilla; *(thieves)* banda. ◆*to ~ together,* acuadrillarse. ■ *elastic/rubber ~,* goma (elástica).
bandage ['bændɪdʒ] *n* venda, vendaje *m*. − 2 *t* vendar.
bandit ['bændɪt] *n* bandido,-a.
bandstand ['bændstænd] *n* quiosco de música.
bandwagon ['bændwægən] *n* ***to jump on the ~,*** subirse al tren.
bandy ['bændɪ] *adj* torcido,-a hacia fuera. ◆*to ~ about t* difundir. ●*to ~ words with,* discutir con.
bandy-legged ['bændɪleg(ɪ)d] *adj* estevado,-a.
bang [bæŋ] *n (blow)* golpe *m*. 2 *(noise)* ruido; *(of gun)* estampido; *(explosion)* estallido; *(of door)* portazo. − 3 *t-i* golpear. 4* *(have sex with)* follar*. − 5 *adv fam* justo: *~ in the middle,* justo en medio. ●*to ~ the door,* dar un portazo.
banger ['bæŋəʳ] *n (firework)* petardo. 2 *fam (sausage)* salchicha. 3 *fam (car)* tartana.
bangle ['bæŋgəl] *n* ajorca, brazalete *m*.
banish ['bænɪʃ] *t* desterrar.
banishment ['bænɪʃmənt] *n* destierro.
banister ['bænɪstəʳ] *n* barandilla.
banjo ['bændʒəʊ] *n* banjo.
bank [bæŋk] *n* FIN banco. 2 *(of river)* ribera; *(edge)* orilla. 3 *(mound)* loma; *(embankment)* terraplén *m*. 4 *(slope)* pendiente *f*. 5 *(sandbank)* banco. − 6 *t* ingresar, depositar. ◆*to ~ on t* contar con. ■ GB *~ holiday,* (día) festivo.
banker ['bæŋkəʳ] *n* banquero,-a.

banking ['bæŋkɪŋ] *n* banca.
bankrupt ['bæŋkrʌpt] *adj* quebrado,-a.
●*to go* ~, quebrar.
bankruptcy ['bæŋkrʌptsɪ] *n* bancarrota.
banner ['bænəʳ] *n* bandera. **2** *(placard)* pancarta.
banns [bænz] *npl* amonestaciones *fpl.*
banquet ['bæŋkwɪt] *n* banquete *m.*
banter ['bæntəʳ] *n* bromas *fpl*, chanzas *fpl.* – **2** *i* bromear.
baptism ['bæptɪzəm] *n* bautismo.
baptismal [bæp'tɪzməl] *adj* bautismal.
baptize [bæp'taɪz] *t* bautizar.
bar [bɑːʳ] *n (iron, gold)* barra. **2** *(prison)* barrote *m.* **3** *(soap)* pastilla. **4** *(chocolate)* tableta. **5** *(on door)* tranca. **6** *(gymnastics)* barra.‘**7** *(obstacle)* obstáculo. **8** *(counter)* barra, mostrador *m.* **9** *(room)* bar *m.* **10** JUR *the Bar,* el colegio de abogados. – **11** *t (door)* atrancar; *(road, access)* cortar. **12** *(ban)* prohibir, vedar. – **13** *prep* excepto.
barb [bɑːb] *n* púa, lengüeta.
barbarian [bɑː'beərɪən] *adj-n* bárbaro,-a.
barbaric [bɑː'bærɪk] *adj* bárbaro,-a.
barbarity [bɑː'bærɪtɪ] *n* barbaridad.
barbarous ['bɑːbərəs] *adj* bárbaro,-a.
barbecue ['bɑːbɪkjuː] *n* barbacoa.
barbed [bɑːbd] *adj* armado,-a con púas, punzante. ■ ~ *wire,* alambre *m* de púas.
barber ['bɑːbəʳ] *n* barbero. ■ *barber's shop,* barbería.
barbiturate [bɑː'bɪtʃurət] *n* barbitúrico.
bare [beəʳ] *adj (naked)* desnudo,-a; *(head)* descubierto,-a; *(feet)* descalzo,-a. **2** *(land)* raso,-a. **3** *(empty)* vacío,-a. **4** *(basic)* mero,-a. – **5** *t* desnudar; *(uncover)* descubrir.
barefaced ['beəfeɪst] *adj* descarado,-a.
barefoot ['beəfut] *adj* descalzo,-a.
bareheaded [beə'hedɪd] *adj* con la cabeza descubierta, sin sombrero.
barely ['beəlɪ] *adv* apenas.
bareness ['beənəs] *n* desnudez *f.*
bargain ['bɑːgən] *n (agreement)* trato. **2** *(good buy)* ganga. – **3** *i (negotiate)* negociar. **4** *(haggle)* regatear. ◆*to* ~ *for t* contar con.
barge [bɑːdʒ] *n* gabarra. – **2** *i* irrumpir *(through/into,* en).
baritone ['bærɪtəʊn] *n* barítono.
bark [bɑːk] *n (of tree)* corteza. **2** *(of dog)* ladrido. – **3** *i* ladrar. ●*to* ~ *up the wrong tree,* ir descaminado,-a.
barley ['bɑːlɪ] *n* cebada.
barmaid ['bɑːmeɪd] *n* camarera.

barman ['bɑːmən] *n* camarero, barman *m.*
barmy ['bɑːmɪ] *adj fam* chiflado,-a.
barn [bɑːn] *n* granero.
barnacle ['bɑːnəkəl] *n* percebe *m.*
barometer [bə'rɒmɪtəʳ] *n* barómetro.
baron ['bærən] *n* barón *m.*
baroness ['bærənəs] *n* baronesa.
baronet ['bærənət] *n* baronet *m.*
baroque [bə'rɒk] *adj* barroco,-a.
barrack ['bærək] *t* abuchear.
barracks ['bærəks] *n* cuartel *m.*
barrage ['bærɑːʒ] *n (dam)* presa. **2** MIL barrera de fuego. **3** *fig* bombardeo.
barrel ['bærəl] *n (of beer)* barril *m*; *(of wine)* tonel *m*, cuba. **2** *(of gun)* cañón *m.*
barren ['bærən] *adj* estéril.
barricade [bærɪ'keɪd] *n* barricada. – **2** *t* poner barricadas en.
barrier ['bærɪəʳ] *n* barrera.
barrister ['bærɪstəʳ] *n* abogado,-a *capacitado,-a para actuar en tribunales superiores.*
barrow ['bærəʊ] *n* carretilla.
barter ['bɑːtəʳ] *n* trueque *m.* – **2** *t* trocar.
basalt ['bæsɔːlt] *n* basalto.
base [beɪs] *n* base *f.* – **2** *t* basar. **3** MIL *(troops)* estacionar. – **4** *adj* bajo,-a, vil. **5** *(metal)* común.
baseball ['beɪsbɔːl] *n* béisbol *m.*
baseless ['beɪsləs] *adj* infundado,-a.
basement ['beɪsmənt] *n* sótano.
bash [bæʃ] *fam t* golpear. – **2** *n* golpe *m.* **3** *(try)* intento. ●*to have a* ~ *at sth.,* probar/intentar algo.
bashful ['bæʃful] *adj* vergonzoso,-a, tímido,-a, modesto,-a.
basic ['beɪsɪk] *adj* básico,-a. – **2** *npl the basics,* lo esencial.
basin ['beɪsən] *n (bowl)* cuenco. **2** *(wash-basin)* lavabo. **3** GEOG cuenca.
basis ['beɪsɪs] *n* base *f*, fundamento. ▲ *pl* **bases**.
bask [bɑːsk] *i* tumbarse al sol.
basket ['bɑːskɪt] *n* cesta, cesto.
basketball ['bɑːskɪtbɔːl] *n* baloncesto.
bass [bæs] *n (fish)* róbalo, lubina; *(fresh-water)* perca. **2** MUS *(singer)* bajo. **3** MUS *(notes)* graves *mpl.* – **4** *adj* MUS bajo,-a. ▲ *En 2, 3 y 4* [beɪs].
bassoon [bə'suːn] *n* fagot *m.*
bastard ['bæstəd] *adj-n* bastardo,-a.
baste [beɪst] *t* CULIN bañar. **2** SEW hilvanar.
bastion ['bæstɪən] *n* baluarte *m.*
bat [bæt] *n* ZOOL murciélago. **2** SP bate *m*; *(table tennis)* pala. – **3** *i* batear. – **4** *t* pes-

tañear. ●*without batting an eyelid,* sin inmutarse.

batch [bætʃ] *n* lote *m,* remesa; *(bread etc.)* hornada.

bated [ˈbeɪtɪd] *adj with* ~ *breath,* sin respirar.

bath [bɑ:θ] *n* baño. **2** *(tub)* bañera. **3** *pl* piscina *f sing* municipal. ‒ **4** *t-i* bañar(se). ●*to have a* ~, bañarse.

bathe [beɪð] *i* bañarse. ‒ **2** *t* MED lavar.

bather [ˈbeɪðəʳ] *n* bañista *mf.*

bathing [ˈbeɪðɪŋ] *n* baño. ■ ~ *costume/ suit,* traje *m* de baño.

bathrobe [ˈbɑ:θrəʊb] *n* albornoz *m.*

bathroom [ˈbɑ:θru:m] *n* cuarto de baño.

bathtub [ˈbɑ:θtʌb] *n* bañera.

baton [ˈbætən] *n (truncheon)* porra. **2** MUS batuta. **3** SP testigo.

batsman [ˈbætsmən] *n* bateador *m.*

battalion [bəˈtæljən] *n* batallón *m.*

batten [ˈbætən] *n* listón *m.* ◆*to* ~ *down t* sujetar con listones.

batter [ˈbætəʳ] *n* CULIN pasta para rebozar. **2** SP bateador,-ra. ‒ **3** *t* golpear, apalear. ●*in* ~, rebozado,-a.

battery [ˈbætəri] *n* ELEC *(wet)* batería; *(dry)* pila. **2** MIL batería.

battle [ˈbætəl] *n* batalla. ‒ **2** *i* luchar.

battlefield [ˈbætəlfi:ld] *n* campo de batalla.

battlements [ˈbætəlmənts] *npl* almenas *fpl.*

battleship [ˈbætəlʃɪp] *n* acorazado.

bauble [ˈbɔ:bəl] *n* baratija.

baulk [bɔ:k] *t* → **balk.**

bawdy [ˈbɔ:dɪ] *adj* grosero,-a.

bawl [bɔ:l] *i-t* chillar.

bay [beɪ] *n* GEOG bahía; *(large)* golfo. **2** *(tree)* laurel *m.* **3** ARCH hueco. **4** *(horse)* caballo bayo. ‒ **5** *i* ladrar. ●*at* ~, acorralado,-a. ■ ~ *leaf,* hoja de laurel; ~ *window,* ventana saliente; *loading* ~, cargadero.

bayonet [ˈbeɪənət] *n* bayoneta.

bazaar [bəˈzɑ:ʳ] *n (eastern)* bazar *m.* **2** *(at church etc.)* venta benéfica.

bazooka [bəˈzu:kə] *n* bazuca.

be [bi:] *i (permanent characteristic, essential quality, nationality, occupation, origin, ownership, authorship)* ser: *she's clever,* ella es inteligente; *diamonds are hard,* los diamantes son duros; *John's English,* John es inglés; *we are both teachers,* los dos somos profesores; *they are from York,* son de York; *this house is ours,* esta casa es nuestra; *this painting is by Fraser,* este cuadro es de Fraser. **2** *(lo-cation, temporary state)* estar: *Whitby is on the coast,* Whitby está en la costa; *how are you?,* ¿cómo estás?; *your supper is cold/in the oven,* tu cena está fría/ en el horno. **3** *(age)* tener: *Philip is 17,* Philip tiene 17 años. **4** *(price)* costar, valer: *a single ticket is £7.50,* un billete de ida sola cuesta £7.50; *prawns are cheap today,* las gambas están bien de precio hoy. ‒ **5** *aux (with pres p)* estar: *it is raining,* está lloviendo; *the train is coming,* viene el tren; *I am going to-morrow,* iré mañana. **6** *(passive)* ser: *it has been sold,* ha sido vendido,-a, se ha vendido. **7** *(obligation) you are not to come here again,* no debes volver aquí; *you are to do as I say,* tienes que hacer lo que yo te diga. **8** *(future) the King is to visit Egypt,* el Rey visitará Egipto. ●*there is/are,* hay; *there was/were,* había; *there will/would be,* habrá/habría. ▲ *pres 1st pers* **am;** *2nd pers sing & all persons pl* **are;** *3rd pers sing* **is;** *pt 1st & 3rd persons sing* **was;** *2nd pers sing & all persons pl* **were;** *pp* **been.**

beach [bi:tʃ] *n* playa. ‒ **2** *t* varar.

beacon [ˈbi:kən] *n (fire)* almenara. **2** AV MAR baliza.

bead [bi:d] *n (on necklace)* cuenta. **2** *(of liquid)* gota.

beak [bi:k] *n* pico.

beaker [ˈbi:kəʳ] *n* taza alta. **2** CHEM vaso de precipitación.

beam [bi:m] *n* ARCH viga. **2** *(of light)* rayo. **3** *(of ship)* manga. **4** *(smile)* sonrisa radiante. ‒ **5** *i (shine)* brillar. **6** *(smile)* sonreír. ‒ **7** *t* irradiar, emitir.

beaming [ˈbi:mɪŋ] *adj* radiante.

bean [bi:n] *n* alubia, judía, haba. **2** *(of coffee)* grano. ●*to be full of beans,* rebosar vitalidad; *to spill the beans,* descubrir el pastel. ■ *baked beans,* alubias *fpl* cocidas; *broad* ~, haba; *French/green/run-ner/string* ~, judía verde.

bear [beəʳ] *n* ZOOL oso. **2** FIN bajista *mf.* ‒ **3** *t (carry)* llevar. **4** *(weight)* soportar, aguantar. **5** *(tolerate)* soportar, aguantar. **6** *(fruit)* producir. **7** *(give birth)* dar a luz; *he was born in London,* nació en Londres. ◆*to* ~ *out t* confirmar. ◆*to* ~ *up i* mantenerse firme. ◆*to* ~ *with t* tener paciencia con. ●*to* ~ *in mind,* tener presente; *to* ~ *a grudge,* guardar rencor; *to* ~ *a resemblance to,* parecerse a. ▲ *pt* **bore;** *pp* **borne** *o* **born.**

bearable [ˈbeərəbəl] *adj* soportable.

beard [bɪəd] *n* barba.

bearded [ˈbɪədɪd] *adj* barbudo,-a.

bearer ['beərə'] *n (of news, cheque, etc.)* portador,-ra; *(of passport)* titular *mf.* 2 *(porter)* portador,-ra.

bearing ['beərɪŋ] *n (posture)* porte *m.* 2 *(relevance)* relación. 3 TECH cojinete *m.* 4 MAR orientación. ●*to lose one's bearings,* desorientarse; *fig* perder el norte.

beast [bi:st] *n* bestia, animal *m.*

beastly [bi:stlı] *adj* bestial.

beat [bi:t] *n (of heart)* latido. 2 MUS ritmo. 3 *(of policeman)* ronda. – 4 *t (hit)* golpear; *(metals)* martillear; *(person)* azotar; *(drum)* tocar. 5 CULIN batir. 6 *(defeat)* vencer, derrotar. 7 *fam (puzzle)* extrañar. – 8 *i (heart)* latir. – 9 *adj fam* agotado,-a. ●*to ~ up t* dar una paliza a. ●*to ~ about the bush,* andarse por las ramas; MUS *to ~ time,* llevar el compás. ▲ *pt* **beat**; *pp* **beaten** ['bi:tən].

beater ['bi:tə'] *n* CULIN batidora.

beatify [bɪ'ætɪfaɪ] *t* beatificar.

beating ['bi:tɪŋ] *n (thrashing)* paliza. 2 *(defeat)* derrota. 3 *(of heart)* latidos *mpl.*

beatitude [bɪ'ætɪtju:d] *n* beatitud. ■ *the Beatitudes,* las Bienaventuranzas.

beautician [bju:'tɪʃən] *n* esteticista *mf.*

beautiful ['bju:tɪfʊl] *adj* hermoso,-a, bonito,-a. 2 *(wonderful)* maravilloso,-a.

beautify ['bju:tɪfaɪ] *t* embellecer.

beauty ['bju:tɪ] *n* belleza, hermosura. ■ *~ spot, (on face)* lunar *m: (place)* lugar pintoresco.

beaver ['bi:və'] *n* castor *m.*

became [bɪ'keɪm] *pt* → **become**.

because [bɪ'kɒz] *conj* porque. – 2 *prep ~ of,* a causa de.

beckon ['bekən] *t* llamar por señas. – 2 *i* hacer señas.

become [bɪ'kʌm] *i (with noun)* convertirse en, hacerse; llegar a ser: *to ~ a doctor/teacher,* hacerse médico,-a/maestro,-a; *to ~ president,* llegar a la presidencia; *what has ~ of Peter?,* ¿qué ha sido de Peter? 2 *(with adj)* volverse, ponerse: *to ~ angry/sad,* enojarse/entristecerse. 3 *(suit)* favorecer. ▲ *pt* **became**; *pp* **become**.

becoming [bɪ'kʌmɪŋ] *adj (dress etc.)* que sienta bien. 2 *(behaviour)* apropiado,-a.

bed [bed] *n* cama. 2 *(of flowers)* macizo. 3 *(of river)* lecho, cauce *m; (of sea)* fondo. 4 GEOL capa, yacimiento. – 5 *t sl* acostarse con. ●*to go to ~,* acostarse; *fam* *to get out of ~ on the wrong side,* levantarse con el pie izquierdo.

bedbug ['bedbʌg] *n* chinche *m.*

bedclothes ['bedkləʊðz] *npl,* **bedding** ['bedɪŋ] *n* ropa de cama.

bedlam ['bedləm] *n* alboroto, jaleo.

bedpan ['bedpæn] *n* cuña.

bedraggled [bɪ'drægəld] *adj* desordenado,-a.

bedridden ['bedrɪdən] *adj* postrado,-a en cama.

bedroom ['bedru:m] *n* dormitorio.

bedside ['bedsaɪd] *n* cabecera. ■ *~ table,* mesita de noche.

bedsitter [bed'sɪtə'] *n* estudio.

bedspread ['bedspred] *n* cubrecama.

bedstead ['bedsted] *n* armazón *m* de la cama.

bedtime ['bedtaɪm] *n* la hora de acostarse.

bee [bi:] *n* abeja. ●*fam* *to have a ~ in one's bonnet,* tener una obsesión.

beech [bi:tʃ] *n* haya.

beef [bi:f] *n* carne *f* de vaca. – 2 *i fam* quejarse.

beefburger ['bi:fbɜ:gə'] *n* hamburguesa.

beefeater ['bi:fi:tə'] *n* alabardero *de la Torre de Londres.*

beefsteak ['bi:fsteɪk] *n* bistec *m.*

beefy ['bi:fɪ] *adj* robusto,-a.

beehive ['bi:haɪv] *n* colmena.

beeline ['bi:laɪn] *n* línea recta.

been [bi:n, bɪn] *pp* → **be**.

beer [bɪə'] *n* cerveza.

beetle ['bi:təl] *n* escarabajo.

beetroot ['bi:tru:t] *n* remolacha.

before [bɪ'fɔ:'] *prep (order, time)* antes de. 2 *(place)* delante de; *(in the presence of)* ante: *~ God,* ante Dios. – 3 *conj (earlier than)* antes de + *inf,* antes de que + *subj: ~ you go,* antes de irte, antes de que te vayas. 4 *(rather than)* antes de (+ *inf*). – 5 *adv* antes. 6 *(place)* delante. ●*the day ~ yesterday,* antes de ayer.

beforehand [bɪ'fɔ:hænd] *adv (earlier)* antes. 2 *(in advance)* de antemano, con antelación.

befriend [bɪ'frend] *t* ofrecer su amistad a.

beg [beg] *i* mendigar. – 2 *t (ask for)* pedir. 3 *(beseech)* suplicar, rogar. ●*I ~ your pardon?* ¿cómo ha dicho usted?

began [bɪ'gæn] *pt* → **begin**.

beggar ['begə'] *n* mendigo,-a. – 2 *t* empobrecer, arruinar; *fig* hacer imposible.

begin [bɪ'gɪn] *t-i* empezar, comenzar. ▲ *pt* **began**; *pp* **begun**.

beginner [bɪ'gɪnə'] *n* principiante *mf.*

beginning [bɪ'gɪnɪŋ] *n* principio.

beguile [bɪ'gaɪl] *t (cheat)* engañar. 2 *(seduce)* seducir, atraer.

begun [bɪ'gʌn] *pp* → **begin**.

behalf [bɪ'ha:f] *n on ~ of,* en nombre de, de parte de.

behave [bɪˈheɪv] *i* comportarse, portarse. ●*to* ~ *o.s.,* portarse bien.

behaviour [bɪˈheɪvjəʳ] *n* conducta, comportamiento.

behead [bɪˈhed] *t* decapitar.

beheld [bɪˈheld] *pt & pp* → **behold**.

behind [bɪˈhaɪnd] *prep (place)* detrás de. 2 *(in time)* después de. − 3 *adv* detrás. 4 *(late)* atrasado,-a. − 5 *n fam* trasero. ●~ *sb.'s back,* a espaldas de algn; ~ *schedule,* atrasado,-a; ~ *the scenes,* entre bastidores; *to leave sth.* ~, olvidar algo.

behindhand [bɪˈhaɪndhænd] *adv* en retraso. − 2 *adj* atrasado,-a, retrasado,-a.

behold [bɪˈhəʊld] *t* contemplar. ▲ *pt & pp* **beheld**.

beige [beɪʒ] *adj-n* beige *(m)*.

being [ˈbiːɪŋ] *n (living thing)* ser *m.* 2 *(existence)* existencia. ●*for the time* ~, por ahora.

belated [bɪˈleɪtɪd] *adj fam* tardío,-a.

belch [beltʃ] *n* eructo. − 2 *i* eructar. − 3 *t* vomitar.

belief [bɪˈliːf] *n* creencia. 2 *(opinion)* opinión. 3 *(faith)* fe *f.*

believe [bɪˈliːv] *t* creer: ~ *me,* créeme. 2 *(suppose)* creer, suponer: *he is believed to be dead,* se cree que está muerto. − 3 *i* creer (*in,* en): *we* ~ *in God,* creemos en Dios. 4 *(trust)* confiar (*in,* en). 5 *(support)* ser partidario,-a (*in,* de): *they* ~ *in free trade,* creen en el libre comercio.

believer [bɪˈliːvəʳ] *n* creyente *mf.*

belittle [bɪˈlɪtəl] *t* menospreciar.

bell [bel] *n (of church etc.)* campana. 2 *(handbell)* campanilla. 3 *(on bicycle, door, etc.)* timbre *m.* 4 *(cowbell)* cencerro. ●*that rings a* ~, esto me suena.

bellboy [ˈbelbɔɪ], US **bellhop** [ˈbelhɒp] *n* botones *m inv.*

belligerent [bɪˈlɪdʒərənt] *adj* beligerante.

bellow [ˈbeləʊ] *n* bramido. − 2 *i* bramar.

bellows [ˈbeləʊz] *npl* fuelle *m sing.*

belly [ˈbelɪ] *n (person)* vientre *m,* barriga. 2 *(animal)* panza. ■ *fam* ~ *button,* ombligo; ~ *laugh,* carcajada.

bellyache [ˈbelɪeɪk] *fam n* dolor *m* de barriga. − 2 *i* quejarse.

belong [bɪˈlɒŋ] *i* pertenecer (*to,* a), ser (*to,* de). 2 *(to a club)* ser socio,-a (*to,* de).

belongings [bɪˈlɒŋɪŋz] *npl* pertenencias *fpl.*

beloved [bɪˈlʌvd] *adj* querido,-a, amado,-a. − 2 *n* amado,-a. ▲ *En* 2 *(sustantivo)* [bɪˈlʌvɪd].

below [bɪˈləʊ] *prep* (por) debajo de. − 2 *adv* abajo. ●~ *zero,* bajo cero; *see* ~, véase abajo.

belt [belt] *n* cinturón *m.* 2 TECH correa. 3 *(area)* zona. − 4 *t fam* pegar. ●*to* ~ *along i* ir a todo gas. ●*to* ~ *up i fam* callarse. ●*a blow below the* ~, un golpe bajo. ■ *conveyor* ~, cinta transportadora; *safety/seat* ~, cinturón *m* de seguridad.

bemoan [bɪˈməʊn] *t* lamentar.

bemused [bɪˈmjuːzd] *adj* perplejo,-a.

bench [bentʃ] *n* banco. 2 JUR tribunal *m.*

bend [bend] *n (in road etc.)* curva. 2 *(in pipe)* ángulo. − 3 *t* doblar. 4 *(head)* inclinar. − 5 *i* doblarse. 6 *(road)* torcer. ●*to* ~ *down i* agacharse. ●*to* ~ *over i* inclinarse. ●*round the* ~, loco,-a perdido,-a. ▲ *pt & pp* **bent**.

beneath [bɪˈniːθ] *prep* bajo, debajo de. − 2 *adv* abajo, debajo.

benediction [benɪˈdɪkʃən] *n* bendición.

benefactor [ˈbenɪfæktəʳ] *n* benefactor.

benefactress [ˈbenɪfæktrəs] *n* benefactora.

beneficial [benɪˈfɪʃəl] *adj* beneficioso,-a, provechoso,-a.

beneficiary [benɪˈfɪʃərɪ] *n* beneficiario,-a.

benefit [ˈbenɪfɪt] *n (advantage)* beneficio, provecho. 2 *(good)* bien *m.* 3 *(allowance)* subsidio. − 4 *t-i* beneficiar(se). ■ *unemployment* ~, subsidio de desempleo.

benevolence [bɪˈnevələns] *n* benevolencia.

benevolent [bɪˈnevɒlənt] *adj* benévolo,-a.

benign [bɪˈnaɪn] *adj* benigno,-a.

bent [bent] *pt & pp* → **bend**. − 2 *adj* torcido,-a, doblado,-a. 3 *sl (corrupt)* corrupto,-a. 4 *sl (homosexual)* de la acera de enfrente. − 5 *n* inclinación. ●~ *on,* empeñado,-a en.

benzine [ˈbenziːn] *n* bencina.

bequeath [bɪˈkwiːð] *t* legar.

bequest [bɪˈkwest] *n* legado.

bereaved [bɪˈriːvd] *adj* desconsolado,-a.

bereavement [bɪˈriːvmənt] *n (loss)* pérdida. 2 *(mourning)* duelo.

bereft [bɪˈreft] *adj* privado,-a (*of,* de).

beret [ˈbereɪ] *n* boina.

berk [bɜːk] *n fam* capullo.

berry [ˈberɪ] *n* baya.

berserk [bəˈsɜːk] *adj* enloquecido,-a.

berth [bɜːθ] *n (in harbour)* amarradero. 2 *(on ship)* camarote *m,* litera. − 3 *t* poner en dique. − 4 *i* atracar.

beseech [bɪˈsiːtʃ] *t* implorar, suplicar. ▲ *pt & pp* **besought** *o* **beseeched**.

beset [bɪˈset] *t* acosar. ▲ *pt & pp* **beset**.

beside [bɪ'saɪd] *prep* al lado de. ●~ *o.s.,* fuera de sí; ~ *o.s. with joy,* loco,-a de alegría; ~ *the point,* que no viene al caso.

besides [bɪ'saɪdz] *prep (as well as)* además de. 2 *(except)* excepto. – 3 *adv* además.

besiege [bɪ'si:dʒ] *t* MIL sitiar. 2 *fig* asediar.

besought [bɪ'sɔ:t] *pt & pp* → **beseech.**

best [best] *adj (superl of good)* mejor. – 2 *adv (superl of well)* mejor. – 3 *n* lo mejor. ●*all the ~!,* ¡que te vaya bien!; *as ~ you can,* lo mejor que puedas; *at ~,* en el mejor de los casos; *the ~ part of,* la mayor parte de; *to do one's ~,* esmerarse; *to make the ~ of,* sacar el mejor partido de. ■ ~ *man,* padrino de boda.

bestial ['bestɪəl] *adj* bestial.

bestow [bɪ'stəʊ] *t (honour)* otorgar *(on,* a); *(favour)* conceder *(on,* a); *(title)* conferir *(on,* a).

best-seller [best'selə'] *n* best-seller *m,* superventas *m inv.*

bet [bet] *n* apuesta. – 2 *t-i* apostar.

betray [bɪ'treɪ] *t* traicionar. 2 *(secret)* revelar.

betrayal [bɪ'treɪəl] *n* traición.

betrothed [bɪ'trəʊðd] *adj-n* prometido,-a.

better ['betə'] *adj (comp of good)* mejor. – 2 *adv (comp of well)* mejor. – 3 *n* lo mejor. 4 *pl* superiores *mpl.* – 5 *t (improve)* mejorar. 6 *(surpass)* superar. ●~ *late than never,* más vale tarde que nunca; *had ~,* más vale que + *subj*: *we'd ~ be going,* más vale que nos vayamos; *so much the ~,* tanto mejor; *to get ~,* mejorar. ■ ~ *half,* media naranja.

betting ['betɪŋ] *n* apuestas *fpl.* ●*what's the ~ that ...,* ¿qué te apuestas a que ...?

bettor ['betə'] *n* apostante *mf.*

between [bɪ'twi:n] *prep* entre. – 2 *adv* en medio. ●~ *the lines,* entre líneas; ~ *you and me,* entre tú y yo, en confianza.

bevel ['bevəl] *n* bisel *m,* chaflán *m.* – 2 *t* biselar.

beverage ['bevərɪdʒ] *n* bebida.

bewail [bɪ'weɪl] *t fml* lamentar.

beware [bɪ'weə'] *i* tener cuidado *(of,* con).

bewilder [bɪ'wɪldə'] *t* desconcertar, confundir.

bewitch [bɪ'wɪtʃ] *t* hechizar; *fig* fascinar.

beyond [bɪ'jɒnd] *prep* más allá de. – 2 *adv* más allá. – 3 *n the ~,* el más allá.

●~ *belief,* increíble; ~ *doubt,* indudablemente; *it's ~ me,* no lo entiendo.

bias ['baɪəs] *n (prejudice)* parcialidad, prejuicio. 2 *(inclination)* tendencia. – 3 *t* predisponer.

bias(s)ed ['baɪəst] *adj* parcial.

bib [bɪb] *n* babero.

Bible ['baɪbəl] *n* Biblia.

biblical ['bɪblɪkəl] *adj* bíblico,-a.

bibliography [bɪblɪ'ɒgrəfɪ] *n* bibliografía.

biceps ['baɪseps] *n* bíceps *m inv.*

bicker ['bɪkə'] *i* discutir.

bicycle ['baɪsɪkəl] *n* bicicleta.

bid [bɪd] *n (at auction)* puja. 2 *(attempt)* intento. 3 *(offer)* oferta. – 4 *t (at auction)* pujar. 5 *(say)* decir. 6 *(order)* ordenar, mandar. 7 *(invite)* invitar. – 8 *i (at auction)* pujar. ▲ *En 4 y 8 pt & pp* bid; *en 5, 6 y 7 pt* bid/bade; *pp* bid/bidden.

bidder ['bɪdə'] *n* postor,-ra.

bidding ['bɪdɪŋ] *n (at auction)* puja. 2 *(order)* orden *f.*

bide [baɪd] *t-i to ~ one's time,* esperar el momento oportuno. ▲ *pt* bode *o* bided.

bidet ['bi:deɪ] *n* bidé *m.*

biennial [baɪ'enɪəl] *adj* bienal.

bifocal [baɪ'fəʊkəl] *adj* bifocal. – 2 *npl* lentes *fpl* bifocales.

big [bɪg] *adj* grande; *(before sing noun)* gran: *a ~ car,* un coche grande; *a ~ day,* un gran día. ●*too ~ for one's boots,* muy fanfarrón,-ona. ■ ~ *brother/sister,* hermano/hermana mayor; ~ *game,* caza mayor; ~ *noise/shot,* pez gordo.

bigamy ['bɪgəmɪ] *n* bigamia.

bighead ['bɪghed] *n* sabihondo,-a, creído,-a.

bigheaded [bɪg'hedɪd] *adj* sabihondo,-a, creído,-a.

big-hearted [bɪg'hɑ:tɪd] *adj* de buen corazón, generoso,-a.

bight [baɪt] *n* bahía.

bigmouth ['bɪgmaʊθ] *n* bocazas *mf inv.*

bigot ['bɪgət] *n* fanático,-a.

bigotry ['bɪgətrɪ] *n* fanatismo.

bigwig ['bɪgwɪg] *n fam* pez gordo.

bike [baɪk] *n fam (bicycle)* bici *f.* 2 *(motorcycle)* moto *f.*

bikini [bɪ'ki:nɪ] *n* biquini *m.*

bilateral [baɪ'lætərəl] *adj* bilateral.

bilberry ['bɪlbərɪ] *n* arándano.

bile [baɪl] *n* bilis *f,* hiel *f.*

bilge [bɪldʒ] *n* MAR agua de sentina. 2 *fig* tonterías *fpl.*

bilingual [baɪ'lɪŋgwəl] *adj* bilingüe.

bilious ['bɪlɪəs] *adj* bilioso,-a.

bill [bɪl] *n* factura; *(in restaurant)* cuenta. 2 *(law)* proyecto de ley. 3 US *(banknote)* billete *m*. 4 *(poster)* cartel *m*. — 5 *t* facturar. 6 THEAT programar. ●*to fit the ~,* cumplir los requisitos; THEAT *to top the ~,* encabezar el reparto. ■ *~ of exchange,* letra de cambio; *~ of lading,* conocimiento de embarque; *Bill of Rights,* declaración de derechos.

billboard ['bɪlbɔːd] *n* US valla publicitaria.

billiards ['bɪliədz] *n* billar *m*.

billion ['bɪliən] *n* GB billón *m*. 2 US mil millones *mpl*.

billow ['bɪləu] *n (of water)* ola. 2 *(of smoke)* nube *f*. — 3 *i (sea)* ondear. 4 *(sail)* hincharse.

billowy ['bɪləuɪ] *adj (sea)* ondoso,-a. 2 *(sail)* hinchado,-a.

billy-goat ['bɪlɪgəut] *n* macho cabrío.

bin [bɪn] *n* arca, cajón *m*. 2 *(for rubbish)* cubo de la basura; *(for paper)* papelera.

binary ['baɪnərɪ] *adj* binario,-a.

bind [baɪnd] *n fam* fastidio, molestia. — 2 *t (tie up)* atar. 3 CULIN ligar. 4 *(book)* encuadernar. 5 *(bandage)* vendar. 6 *(require)* obligar. ▲ *pt & pp* **bound**.

binder ['baɪndəˈ] *n* AGR agavilladora. 2 *(file)* carpeta. 3 *(of books)* encuadernador,-ra.

binding ['baɪndɪŋ] *n* SEW ribete *m*. 2 *(of skis)* fijación. 3 *(of book)* encuadernación. — 4 *adj* obligatorio,-a.

binge [bɪndʒ] *n* borrachera.

bingo ['bɪŋgəu] *n* bingo.

binocular [bɪ'nɒkjuləˈ] *adj* binocular. — 2 *npl* gemelos *mpl*.

biographer [baɪ'ɒgrəfəˈ] *n* biógrafo,-a.

biographical [baɪə'græfɪkəl] *adj* biográfico,-a.

biography [baɪ'ɒgrəfɪ] *n* biografía.

biological [baɪə'lɒdʒɪkəl] *adj* biológico,-a.

biologist [baɪ'ɒlədʒɪst] *n* biólogo,-a.

biology [baɪ'ɒlədʒɪ] *n* biología.

biopsy ['baɪɒpsɪ] *n* biopsia.

biorhythm ['baɪərɪðəm] *n* biorritmo.

biosphere ['baɪəsfɪəˈ] *n* biosfera.

bipartite [baɪ'pɑːtaɪt] *adj* bipartito,-a

biped ['baɪped] *adj-n* bípedo,-a *(m)*.

birch [bɜːtʃ] *n (tree)* abedul *m*. 2 *(rod)* vara (de abedul). — 3 *t* azotar.

bird [bɜːd] *n (large)* ave *f; (small)* pájaro. 2 GB *(girl)* chica. ●*a ~ in the hand is worth two in the bush,* más vale pájaro en mano que ciento volando; *to kill two birds with one stone,* matar dos pájaros de un tiro. ■ *~ of prey,* ave *f* de rapiña.

birdie ['bɜːdɪ] *n* pajarito. 2 *(golf)* birdie *m*.

birdseed ['bɜːdsiːd] *n* alpiste *m*.

bird's-eye view [bɜːdzaɪ'vjuː] *n* vista de pájaro.

bird-watcher ['bɜːdwɒtʃəˈ] *n* ornitólogo,-a.

Biro® ['baɪrəu] *n fam* boli *m*.

birth [bɜːθ] *n (of baby)* nacimiento. 2 MED parto. 3 *(descent)* linaje *m*. ●*to give ~ to,* dar a luz a. ■ *~ certificate,* partida de nacimiento; *~ control,* control *m* de (la) natalidad.

birthday ['bɜːθdeɪ] *n* cumpleaños *m inv*.

birthmark ['bɜːθmɑːk] *n* lunar *m*.

birthplace ['bɜːθpleɪs] *n* lugar *m* de nacimiento.

biscuit ['bɪskɪt] *n* galleta.

bisect [baɪ'sekt] *t* bisecar.

bisexual [baɪ'seksjuəl] *adj* bisexual.

bishop ['bɪʃəp] *n* obispo. 2 *(chess)* alfil *m*.

bishopric ['bɪʃəprɪk] *n* obispado.

bison ['baɪsən] *n* bisonte *m*.

bit [bɪt] *n (small piece)* trozo, pedacito. 2 *(small amount)* poco. 3 *(of bridle)* bocado. 4 *(of drill)* broca. 5 COMPUT bit *m*. 6 *(coin)* moneda. — 7 *pt →* **bite**. ●*~ by ~,* poco a poco; *bits and pieces,* trastos; *to come to bits,* romperse; *to take to bits,* desmontar; *fig to go to bits,* ponerse histérico,-a. ■ *a ~ of advice,* un consejo.

bitch [bɪtʃ] *n* hembra; *(of dog)* perra. 2 *pej (woman)* bruja. — 3 *i fam* quejarse.

bite [baɪt] *n (act)* mordisco. 2 *(of insect)* picadura. 3 *(of dog etc.)* mordedura. 4 *(of food)* bocado. — 5 *t-i* morder. 6 *(insect)* picar. 7 *(fish)* picar. ▲ *pt* **bit**; *pp* **bitten**.

biting ['baɪtɪŋ] *adj (wind)* cortante; *fig* mordaz.

bitten ['bɪtən] *pp →* **bite**.

bitter ['bɪtəˈ] *adj (gen)* amargo,-a. 2 *(weather)* glacial. 3 *(person)* amargado,-a. 4 *(fight)* enconado,-a. — 5 *n* cerveza amarga. 6 *pl* bíter *m sing*. — 7 *bitterly adv* con amargura: *~ disappointed,* terriblemente decepcionado,-a; *it's ~ cold,* hace un frío glacial.

bitterness ['bɪtənəs] *n (gen)* amargura. 2 *(of person)* amargura, rencor *m*.

bitty ['bɪtɪ] *adj* fragmentario,-a.

bitumen ['bɪtjumɪn] *n* betún *m*.

bivouac ['bɪvuæk] *n* vivaque *m*. — 2 *i* hacer vivaque. ▲ *pt & pp* **bivouacked**.

bizarre [bɪ'zɑːˈ] *adj* raro,-a, extraño,-a.

blab [blæb] *i fam* parlotear. 2 *(tell secret)* cantar, descubrir el pastel.

black [blæk] *adj* negro,-a. 2 *(gloomy)* aciago,-a, negro,-a. — 3 *n (colour)* negro. 4

(*person*) negro,-a. **5** (*mourning*) luto. **– 6** *t* (*make black*) ennegrecer. **7** (*boycott*) boicotear. ◆*to* ~ *out t* apagar las luces de. **– 2** *i* (*faint*) desmayarse. ●~ *and white*, blanco y negro; *fam* *to put down sth. in* ~ *and white*, poner algo por escrito. ■ ~ *coffee*, café solo; ~ *eye*, ojo morado/a la funerala; ~ *hole*, agujero negro; ~ *market*, mercado negro; ~ *marketeer*, estraperlista *mf*; *fig* ~ *sheep*, oveja negra.

black-and-blue [blækən'blu:] *adj* amoratado,-a.

blackberry ['blækbərɪ] *n* (zarza)mora.

blackbird ['blækbɜ:d] *n* mirlo.

blackboard ['blækbɔ:d] *n* pizarra.

blackcurrant [blæk'kʌrənt] *n* grosella negra.

blacken ['blækən] *t* ennegrecer. **2** *fig* (*defame*) manchar.

blackguard ['blægɑ:d] *n* pillo.

blackhead ['blækhed] *n* espinilla.

blackish ['blækɪʃ] *adj* negruzco,-a.

blackleg ['blækleg] *n* esquirol *m*.

blackmail ['blækmeɪl] *n* chantaje *m*. **– 2** *t* hacer un chantaje a.

blackmailer ['blækmeɪlər] *n* chantajista *mf*.

blackness ['blæknəs] *n* negrura, oscuridad.

blackout ['blækaʊt] *n* apagón *m*. **2** (*fainting*) pérdida de conocimiento.

blacksmith ['blæksmɪθ] *n* herrero.

bladder ['blædər] *n* vejiga.

blade [bleɪd] *n* (*of sword, knife, etc.*) hoja. **2** (*of iceskate*) cuchilla. **3** (*of propeller, oar*) pala. **4** (*of grass*) brizna.

blame [bleɪm] *n* culpa. **– 2** *t* culpar, echar la culpa a. ●*to be to* ~, tener la culpa; *to put the* ~ *on*, echar la culpa a.

blanch [blɑ:ntʃ] *t* CULIN escaldar. **– 2** *i* palidecer.

bland [blænd] *adj* soso,-a.

blank [blæŋk] *adj* (*page etc.*) en blanco. **2** (*look etc.*) vacío,-a. **– 3** *n* (espacio en) blanco. ●*my mind went* ~, me quedé en blanco; *fam* *to draw a* ~, no tener éxito. ■ ~ *cartridge*, cartucho de fogueo; ~ *cheque*, cheque *m* en blanco; ~ *verse*, verso blanco.

blanket ['blæŋkɪt] *n* manta. **– 2** *adj* general.

blare [bleər] *n* estruendo. ◆*to* ~ *out i* sonar muy fuerte.

blaspheme [blæs'fi:m] *t-i* blasfemar.

blasphemous ['blæsfɪməs] *adj* blasfemo,-a.

blasphemy ['blæsfɪmɪ] *n* blasfemia.

blast [blɑ:st] *n* (*of wind*) ráfaga. **2** (*of water, air, etc.*) chorro. **3** (*of horn etc.*) toque *m*. **4** (*explosion*) explosión, voladura. **5** (*shock wave*) onda expansiva. **– 6** *t* (*explode*) volar, hacer volar. **7** (*criticize*) criticar. **– 8** *interj* ¡maldito sea! ●*at full* ~, a todo volumen. ■ ~ *furnace*, alto horno.

blasted ['blɑ:stɪd] *adj* maldito,-a.

blast-off ['blɑ:stɒf] *n* despegue *m*.

blatant ['bleɪtənt] *adj* descarado,-a.

blaze [bleɪz] *n* (*fire*) incendio. **2** (*flame*) llamarada. **3** (*of light*) resplandor *m*. **– 5** *i* (*fire*) arder. **6** (*sun*) brillar con fuerza. ●*like blazes*, a toda pastilla, a todo gas; *to* ~ *a trail*, abrir un camino.

blazer ['bleɪzər] *n* chaqueta de deporte.

bleach [bli:tʃ] *n* lejía. **– 2** *t* blanquear.

bleak [bli:k] *adj* (*countryside*) desolado,-a. **2** (*weather*) desapacible. **3** (*future*) poco prometedor,-ra.

bleary ['blɪərɪ] *adj* (*from tears*) nubloso,-a. **2** (*from tiredness*) legañoso,-a.

bleat [bli:t] *n* balido. **– 2** *i* balar.

bleed [bli:d] *t-i* MED sangrar. ●*to* ~ *sb. dry*, sacarle a algn. hasta el último céntimo; *to* ~ *to death*, morir desangrado,-a. ▲ *pt & pp* **bled**.

bleeder ['bli:dər] *n sl* hijo,-a de tal.

bleeding ['bli:dɪŋ] *adj sl* puñetero,-a.

bleep [bli:p] *n* pitido. **– 2** *i* pitar. **– 3** *t* localizar con una busca.

bleeper ['bli:pər] *n* busca(personas) *m inv*.

bled [bled] *pt & pp* → **bleed**.

blemish ['blemɪʃ] *n* imperfección. **2** (*on fruit*) maca. **3** *fig* mancha.

blend [blend] *n* mezcla, combinación. **– 2** *t-i* (*mix*) mezclar(se), combinar(se). **3** (*match*) matizar, armonizar.

blender ['blendər] *n* CULIN batidora, minipímer® *m*.

bless [bles] *t* bendecir. ●~ *you!*, ¡Jesús!

blessed ['blesɪd] *adj* bendito,-a.

blessing ['blesɪŋ] *n* bendición. **2** (*advantage*) ventaja.

blew [blu:] *pt* → **blow**.

blight [blaɪt] *n fig* plaga.

blind [blaɪnd] *adj* ciego,-a. **– 2** *n* (*on window*) persiana. **– 3** *blindly adv* ciegamente, a ciegas. **– 4** *t* cegar, dejar ciego,-a. **5** (*dazzle*) deslumbrar. ●*to be/go* ~, estar/quedarse ciego,-a.

blinders ['blaɪndəz] *npl* US anteojeras *fpl*.

blindfold ['blaɪndfəʊld] *n* venda. **– 2** *t* vendar los ojos a. **– 3** *adj-adv* con los ojos vendados.

blindness ['blaɪndnəs] *n* ceguera.

blink [blɪŋk] *n* parpadeo. – **2** *i* parpadear.
● *fam on the* ~, averiado,-a.

blinkers ['blɪŋkəz] *npl* anteojeras *fpl*.

bliss [blɪs] *n* felicidad, dicha.

blister ['blɪstəʳ] *n* (*on skin*) ampolla. **2** (*on paint*) burbuja. – **3** *t-i* ampollar(se).

blithe [blaɪð] *adj* alegre.

blizzard ['blɪzəd] *n* tempestad de nieve.

bloated ['bləʊtɪd] *adj* hinchado,-a.

blob [blɒb] *n* gota. **2** (*of colour*) mancha.

bloc [blɒk] *n* POL bloque *m*.

block [blɒk] *n* bloque *m*. **2** (*of wood, stone*) taco. **3** (*building*) edificio, bloque *m*. **4** (*group of buildings*) manzana. **5** (*obstruction*) bloqueo. – **6** *t* (*pipe etc.*) obstruir, cegar, embozar. **7** (*streets etc.*) bloquear.
■ ~ *letters*, mayúsculas *fpl*.

blockade [blɒ'keɪd] *n* MIL bloqueo. – **2** *t* bloquear.

blockage ['blɒkɪdʒ] *n* obstrucción.

blockhead ['blɒkhed] *n* zoquete *mf*.

bloke [bləʊk] *n* GB *fam* tipo, tío.

blond [blɒnd] *adj-n* rubio,-a. ▲ *Suele escribirse* **blonde** *cuando se refiere a una mujer.*

blood [blʌd] *n* sangre *f*. **2** (*ancestry*) alcurnia. ■ ~ *group*, grupo sanguíneo; ~ *pressure*, tensión arterial; *high/low* ~ *pressure*, tensión alta/baja.

bloodcurdling ['blʌdkɜːdlɪŋ] *adj* horripilante.

bloodhound ['blʌdhaʊnd] *n* sabueso.

bloodless ['blʌdləs] *adj* (*pale*) pálido,-a. **2** (*revolution etc.*) incruento,-a, sin derramamiento de sangre.

bloodshed ['blʌdʃəd] *n* derramamiento de sangre.

bloodshot ['blʌdʃɒt] *adj* inyectado,-a de sangre.

bloodstream ['blʌdstriːm] *n* corriente sanguínea.

bloodthirsty ['blʌdθɜːstɪ] *adj* sanguinario,-a.

bloody ['blʌdɪ] *adj* (*battle*) sangriento,-a. **2** *sl* (*damned*) puñetero,-a, condenado,-a.

bloody-minded [blʌdɪ'maɪndɪd] *adj* tozudo,-a.

bloom [bluːm] *n* flor *f*. – **2** *i* florecer.

bloomer ['bluːməʳ] *n* GB *fam* metedura de pata.

bloomers ['bluːməz] *npl* pololos *mpl*.

blooper ['bluːpr] *n* US *fam* metedura de pata.

blossom ['blɒsəm] *n* flor. – **2** *i* florecer.

blot [blɒt] *n* (*of ink*) borrón *m*. – **2** *t* (*stain*) manchar. **3** (*dry*) secar. ◆*to* ~ *out* *t* (*hide*) ocultar. **2** (*memory*) borrar. ●*to* ~ *one's copybook*, manchar su reputación.

blotch [blɒtʃ] *n* mancha.

blotter ['blɒtəʳ] *n* papel *m* secante. **2** US registro.

blotting-paper ['blɒtɪŋpeɪpəʳ] *n* papel *m* secante.

blouse [blaʊz] *n* blusa.

blow [bləʊ] *n* golpe *m*. – **2** *i* (*wind*) soplar. **3** (*instrument*) tocar. **4** (*fuse*) fundirse. **5** (*tyre*) reventarse. – **6** *t* (*instrument*) tocar; (*whistle*) pitar; (*horn*) sonar. **7** *fam* (*money*) despilfarrar. ◆*to* ~ *out* *t-i* apagar(se). ◆*to* ~ *over* *i* (*storm*) amainar. **2** (*scandal*) olvidarse. ◆*to* ~ *up* *t* (*explode*) (hacer) volar. **2** (*inflate*) hinchar. **3** (*photograph*) ampliar. – **4** *i* (*explode*) explotar. **5** (*lose one's temper*) salirse de sus casillas. ●*fam euph* ~ *you!*, ¡vete a hacer puñetas!; *to* ~ *one's nose*, sonarse las narices; *to* ~ *one's top*, salirse de sus casillas. ▲ *pt* **blew**; *pp* **blown** [bləʊn].

blowlamp ['bləʊlæmp] *n* soplete *m*.

blowout ['bləʊaʊt] *n* AUTO reventón *m*. **2** *sl* comilona.

blowpipe ['bləʊpaɪp] *n* cerbatana.

blowtorch ['bləʊtɔːtʃ] *n* soplete *m*.

blubber ['blʌbəʳ] *n* grasa de ballena. – **2** *i* lloriquear.

blue [bluː] *adj* azul. **2** (*sad*) triste. **3** (*depressed*) deprimido,-a. **4** (*obscene*) verde. – **5** *n* azul *m*. ●*once in a* ~ *moon*, de Pascuas a Ramos; *out of the* ~, como llovido del cielo. ■ *the blues*, melancolía; MUS el blues.

blueberry ['bluːbərɪ] *n* arándano.

bluebottle ['bluːbɒtəl] *n* moscarda.

blue-eyed ['bluːaɪd] *adj* de ojos azules.
■ ~ *boy*, niño mimado.

blueprint ['bluːprɪnt] *n* cianotipo. **2** *fig* anteproyecto.

bluetit ['bluːtɪt] *n* herrerillo común.

bluff [blʌf] *n* farol *m*, fanfarronada. – **2** *i* tirarse un farol, fanfarronear. – **3** *adj* (*person*) francote, campechano,-a.

bluish ['bluːɪʃ] *adj* azulado,-a.

blunder ['blʌndəʳ] *n* plancha, metedura de pata. – **2** *i* meter la pata.

blunt [blʌnt] *adj* (*knife*) desafilado,-a; (*pencil*) despuntado,-a. **2** (*person*) franco,-a. – **3** *t* desafilar; (*pencil*) despuntar. – **4** **bluntly** *adv* sin rodeos.

blur [blɜːʳ] *n* borrón *m*.

blurred [blɜːd] *adj* borroso,-a.

blurt [blɜ:t] *t to* ~ *out,* soltar bruscamente.

blush [blʌʃ] *n* rubor *m,* sonrojo *m.* – 2 *i* ruborizarse, sonrojarse.

bluster ['blʌstəʳ] *n* fanfarronadas *fpl.* – 2 *t* fanfarronear.

blustery ['blʌstərɪ] *adj (windy)* ventoso,-a.

boa ['bəʊə] *n* boa.

boar [bɔ:ʳ] *n* verraco. ■ *wild* ~, jabalí *m.*

board [bɔ:d] *n (piece of wood)* tabla, tablero. 2 *(food)* comida, pensión. 3 *(committee)* junta, consejo. – 4 *t (ship etc.)* subirse a, embarcar en. – 5 *i (lodge)* alojarse. ●MAR *on* ~, a bordo; *fig above* ~, en regla, legal; *fig across the* ~, general.

boarder ['bɔ:dəʳ] *n* huésped,-da. 2 *(at school)* interno,-a.

boarding ['bɔ:dɪŋ] *n* embarque *m.* 2 *(lodging)* pensión, alojamiento. ■ ~ *card,* tarjeta de embarque; ~ *house,* casa de huéspedes; ~ *school,* internado.

boast [bəʊst] *n* jactancia. – 2 *i* jactarse. – 3 *t* ostentar, presumir de.

boastful ['bəʊstfʊl] *adj* jactancioso,-a.

boat [bəʊt] *n* barco; *(small)* barca; *(large)* buque *m; (launch)* lancha.

boating ['bəʊtɪŋ] *n to go* ~, dar un paseo en barca.

boatload ['bəʊtləʊd] *n fam* montón *m.*

boatswain ['bəʊsən] *n* contramaestre *m.*

bob [bɒb] *n (haircut)* pelo a lo chico. 2 *fam inv* chelín *m.* – 3 *t (hair)* cortar a lo chico. – 4 *i to* ~ *up/down,* subir/bajar.

bobbin ['bɒbɪn] *n* bobina.

bobby ['bɒbɪ] *n fam* poli *m.*

bode [bəʊd] *pt* → **bide.** – 2 *t-i* presagiar. ●*to* ~ *ill/well,* ser de buen/mal agüero.

bodice ['bɒdɪs] *n* corpiño.

bodily ['bɒdɪlɪ] *adj* físico,-a, corporal. – 2 *adv* físicamente. 3 *(en masse)* como un solo hombre.

body ['bɒdɪ] *n* cuerpo. 2 *(corpse)* cadáver *m.* 3 *(organization)* organismo, entidad. 4 *(of wine)* cuerpo. 5 *(main part)* parte *f* principal. ■ *heavenly* ~, cuerpo celeste.

body-building ['bɒdɪbɪldɪŋ] *n* culturismo.

bodyguard ['bɒdɪgɑ:d] *n* guardaespaldas *m inv.*

bodywork ['bɒdɪwɜ:k] *n* AUTO carrocería.

bog [bɒg] *n* pantano, cenagal *m.* 2 *sl (toilet)* meódromo. ◆*to* ~ *down t* atascar.

bogey ['bəʊgɪ] *n* fantasma *m.* 2 *(golf)* bogey *m.*

boggy ['bɒgɪ] *adj* pantanoso,-a.

bogus ['bəʊgəs] *adj* falso,-a.

bohemian [bəʊ'hi:mɪən] *adj-n* bohemio,-a.

boil [bɔɪl] *n* MED furúnculo. – 2 *t-i (water)* hervir; *(food)* hervir, cocer(se); *(egg)* cocer(se). ◆*to* ~ *down to t* reducirse a. ●*to come to the* ~, empezar a hervir.

boiler ['bɔɪləʳ] *n* caldera.

boiling ['bɔɪlɪŋ] *adj* hirviente. ■ ~ *point,* punto de ebullición.

boisterous ['bɔɪstərəs] *adj* bullicioso,-a.

bold [bəʊld] *adj (brave)* valiente. 2 *(daring)* audaz, atrevido,-a. 3 *(cheeky)* descarado,-a. ■ ~ *type,* negrita.

boldness ['bəʊldnəs] *n (courage)* valor *m.* 2 *(daring)* audacia. 3 *(cheek)* descaro.

bollard ['bɒlɑ:d] *n* MAR noray *m.* 2 AUTO baliza.

bolshie, bolshy ['bɒlʃɪ] *adj* GB *fam* rebelde.

bolster ['bəʊlstəʳ] *n* cabezal *m,* travesaño. – 2 *t* reforzar.

bolt [bəʊlt] *n (on door etc.)* cerrojo; *(small)* pestillo. 2 *(screw)* perno, tornillo. 3 *(lightning)* rayo. – 4 *t (lock)* cerrar con cerrojo/pestillo. 5 *(screw)* sujetar con pernos/tornillos. 6 *fam (food)* engullir. – 7 *i (person)* escaparse; *(horse)* desbocarse. ●~ *upright,* tieso,-a; *to make a* ~ *for it,* escaparse.

bomb [bɒm] *n* bomba. – 2 *t* MIL bombardear; *(terrorist)* colocar una bomba en. ■ *car* ~, coche-bomba *m.*

bombard [bɒm'bɑ:d] *t* bombardear.

bombastic [bɒm'bæstɪk] *adj* rimbombante, ampuloso,-a.

bomber ['bɒməʳ] *n* MIL bombardero. 2 *(terrorist)* terrorista *mf* que coloca bombas.

bombing ['bɒmɪŋ] *n* MIL bombardeo. 2 *(terrorist act)* atentado con bomba.

bomb-proof ['bɒmpru:f] *adj* a prueba de bombas.

bombshell ['bɒmʃel] *n* MIL obús *m.* 2 *fig* bomba. 3 *fam* mujer explosiva.

bona fide [bəʊnə'faɪdɪ] *adj* genuino,-a, auténtico,-a.

bond [bɒnd] *n (link)* lazo, vínculo. 2 FIN bono, obligación. 3 JUR fianza. 4 *(agreement)* pacto, compromiso. 5 *(adhesion)* unión. – 6 *t-i (stick)* pegar(se).

bondage ['bɒndɪdʒ] *n* esclavitud, servidumbre *f.*

bone [bəʊn] *n* hueso. 2 *(of fish)* espina. – 3 *t* deshuesar.

bone-idle [bəʊn'aɪdəl] *adj* holgazán,-ana.

bottom

bonfire [ˈbɒnfaɪəʳ] *n* hoguera. ▲ GB *Bonfire night* es la noche del cinco de noviembre; se celebra con hogueras y fuegos de artificio.

bonkers [ˈbɒŋkəz] *adj* GB *sl* chalado,-a.

bonnet [ˈbɒnɪt] *n (child's)* gorro, gorra. 2 AUTO capó *m*.

bonny [ˈbɒnɪ] *adj* hermoso,-a, lindo,-a.

bonus [ˈbəʊnəs] *n* prima.

bony [ˈbəʊnɪ] *adj* huesudo,-a.

boo [buː] *interj* ¡bu! – 2 *n* abucheo. – 3 *t-i* abuchear.

boob [buːb] *n fam* metedura de pata. 2 *pl* tetas *fpl*. – 3 *i* meter la pata.

booby trap [ˈbuːbɪtræp] *n* trampa explosiva. – 2 *booby-trap t* poner una bomba en.

booby prize [ˈbuːbɪpraɪz] *n* premio de consolación.

book [bʊk] *n* libro. 2 *(of tickets)* taco; *(of matches)* cajetilla. 3 *pl* COM libros *mpl*, cuentas *fpl*. – 4 *t (reserve)* reservar; *(contract)* contratar. 5 *(police)* multar; FTB amonestar. ■ *exercise* ~, cuaderno; *'phone* ~, listín *m*.

bookbinding [ˈbʊkbaɪndɪŋ] *n* encuadernación.

bookcase [ˈbʊkkeɪs] *n* librería, estantería.

booking [ˈbʊkɪŋ] *n* reservación. ■ ~ *office,* taquilla.

book-keeping [ˈbʊkkiːpɪŋ] *n* teneduría de libros.

booklet [ˈbʊklət] *n* folleto.

bookmaker [ˈbʊkmeɪkəʳ] *n* GB corredor,-ra de apuestas.

bookseller [ˈbʊkseləʳ] *n* librero,-a.

bookshop [ˈbʊkʃɒp], **bookstore** [ˈbʊkstɔːʳ] *n* librería.

bookworm [ˈbʊkwɜːm] *n fig* ratón *m* de biblioteca.

boom [buːm] *n (noise)* estampido, retumbo. 2 *fig (success)* boom *m*, auge *m*. 3 MAR botalón *m*. 4 *(of microphone)* jirafa. 5 *(barrier)* barrera. – 6 *i* tronar. 7 *(prosper)* estar en auge.

boomerang [ˈbuːməræŋ] *n* bumerang *m*.

boon [buːn] *n* bendición.

boor [bʊəʳ] *n* patán *m*.

boorish [ˈbʊərɪʃ] *adj* tosco,-a, zafio,-a.

boost [buːst] *n* empuje *m*. 2 *fig* estímulo. – 3 *t* aumentar. 4 *(morale)* levantar.

boot [buːt] *n* bota. 2 GB AUTO maletero. ◆*to* ~ *out t* echar (a patadas). ●*to* ~, además.

booth [buːð] *n* cabina. 2 *(at fair)* puesto.

bootlegger [ˈbuːtlegəʳ] *n* contrabandista *mf*.

booty [ˈbuːtɪ] *n* botín *m*.

booze [buːz] *fam n* bebida, alcohol *m*. – 2 *i* mamar.

boozer [ˈbuːzə] *n fam (person)* borracho,-a. 2 *(pub)* tasca.

bop [bɒp] *fam n* baile *m*. – 2 *i* bailar.

border [ˈbɔːdəʳ] *n (of country)* frontera. 2 *(edge)* borde *m*. 3 SEW ribete *m*. ◆*to* ~ *on t* lindar con; *fig* rayar en.

bore [bɔːʳ] *pt* → **bear**. – 2 *n (person)* pelmazo,-a, pesado,-a; *(thing)* lata, rollo. 3 *(of gun)* ánima, alma; *(calibre)* calibre *m*. – 4 *t* aburrir. 5 *(perforate)* horadar. ●*to* ~ *a hole in,* abrir un agujero en.

bored [bɔːd] *adj* aburrido,-a.

boredom [ˈbɔːdəm] *n* aburrimiento.

boring [ˈbɔːrɪŋ] *adj* aburrido,-a.

born [bɔːn] *pp* → **bear**. ●*to be* ~, nacer.

borne [bɔːn] *pp* → **bear**.

borough [ˈbʌrə] *n* ciudad. 2 *(district)* barrio.

borrow [ˈbɒrəʊ] *t* tomar/pedir prestado,-a.

borrower [ˈbɒrəʊəʳ] *n* prestatario,-a.

bosom [ˈbʊzəm] *n* pecho. 2 *(centre)* seno. ■ ~ *friend,* amigo,-a del alma.

boss [bɒs] *n fam* jefe,-a. ◆*to* ~ *around t* mangonear.

bossy [ˈbɒsɪ] *adj* mandón,-ona.

botanic(al) [bəˈtænɪk(əl)] *adj* botánico,-a.

botanist [ˈbɒtənɪst] *n* botánico,-a.

botany [ˈbɒtənɪ] *n* botánica.

botch [bɒtʃ] *n* chapuza. – 2 *t* remendar chapuceramente.

both [bəʊθ] *adj-pron* ambos,-as, los/las dos. – 2 *conj* a la vez: *it's* ~ *cheap and good,* es bueno y barato a la vez. ●~ *... and,* tanto ... como.

bother [ˈbɒðəʳ] *n (nuisance)* molestia. 2 *(problems)* problemas *mpl*. – 3 *t (be a nuisance)* molestar. 4 *(worry)* preocupar. – 5 *i (take trouble)* molestarse: *he didn't even* ~ *to ring,* ni se molestó en llamar. 6 *(worry)* preocuparse.

bothersome [ˈbɒðəsəm] *adj* fastidioso,-a.

bottle [ˈbɒtəl] *n* botella; *(small)* frasco. 2 *sl (nerve)* agallas *fpl*. – 3 *t (wine etc.)* embotellar; *(fruit)* envasar. ■ ~ *opener,* abrebotellas *m inv*.

bottleneck [ˈbɒtəlnek] *n fig* cuello de botella.

bottom [ˈbɒtəm] *n (of sea, box, garden, street, etc.)* fondo; *(of bottle)* culo; *(of hill,* *page)* pie *m; (of dress)* bajo; *(of trousers)* bajos *mpl.* 2 *(buttocks)* trasero, culo. – 3 *adj* de abajo. ●*to get to the ~ of sth.,* llegar al fondo de algo.

bottomless ['bɒtəmləs] *adj* sin fondo, insondable.

bough [baʊ] *n* rama.

bought [bɔːt] *pt & pp →* **buy**.

boulder ['bəʊldə^r] *n* canto rodado.

boulevard ['buːləvɑː] *n* bulevar *m.*

bounce [baʊns] *n (of ball)* bote *m.* 2 *fig (energy)* vitalidad. – 3 *i* (re)botar. 4 *(cheque)* ser rechazado,-a por el banco. – 5 *t* hacer botar.

bouncer ['baʊnsə^r] *n sl* gorila *m.*

bound [baʊnd] *pt & pp →* **bind**. – 2 *adj (tied)* atado,-a. 3 *(forced)* obligado,-a. 4 *(book)* encuadernado,-a. – 5 *n* salto, brinco. – 6 *i* saltar. ●*~ for,* con destino/ rumbo a; *to be ~ to,* ser seguro que: *Sue's ~ to win,* seguro que ganará Sue.

boundary ['baʊndəri] *n* límite *m,* frontera.

bounds [baʊndz] *npl* límites *mpl.*

bounteous ['baʊntɪəs], **bountiful** ['baʊntɪfʊl] *adj* generoso,-a. 2 *(abundant)* abundante.

bounty ['baʊntɪ] *n* generosidad. 2 *(reward)* prima.

bouquet [buː'keɪ] *n (flowers)* ramillete *m.* 2 *(wine)* aroma.

bourgeois ['bʊəʒwɑː] *adj-n* burgués,-esa.

bourgeoisie [bʊəʒwɑː'ziː] *n* burguesía.

bout [baʊt] *n (period)* rato. 2 *(of illness)* ataque *m.* 3 *(boxing)* encuentro.

boutique [buː'tiːk] *n* boutique *f,* tienda.

bow [baʊ] *n (with body)* reverencia. 2 MAR proa. 3 *(weapon)* arco. 4 *(of violin)* arco. 5 *(knot)* lazo. – 6 *i (in respect)* inclinarse, hacer una reverencia. 7 *(wall)* arquearse. ■ *~ tie,* pajarita. ▲ *En 3, 4, 5 y 7* [bəʊ].

bowel ['baʊəl] *n* intestino. 2 *pl* entrañas *fpl.*

bowl [bəʊl] *n (for soup)* escudilla. 2 *(for mixing)* cuenco. 3 *(for washing) (hands)* palangana; *(clothes)* barreño. 4 *(of toilet)* taza. 5 *pl (game)* bochas *fpl.* 6 *(ball)* bocha. – 7 *i (play bowls)* jugar a las bochas. 8 *(cricket)* lanzar la pelota.

bow-legged ['bəʊleg(ɪ)d] *adj* estevado,-a.

bowler ['bəʊlə^r] *n (hat)* bombín *m.* 2 *(cricket)* lanzador,-ra.

bowling ['bəʊlɪŋ] *n (game)* bolos *mpl.* ●*to go ~, (tenpin)* jugar a los bolos; *(bowls)* jugar a las bochas. ■ *~ alley,* bolera.

box [bɒks] *n* caja; *(large)* cajón *m.* 2 *(of matches)* cajetilla. 3 THEAT palco. 4 GB *fam (telly)* caja tonta. 5 BOT boj *m.* 6 *(blow)* cachete *m.* – 7 *t* poner en cajas, encajonar. – 8 *i* boxear. ■ *~ office,* taquilla.

boxer ['bɒksə^r] *n* boxeador,-ra. 2 *(dog)* bóxer *m.*

boxing ['bɒksɪŋ] *n* boxeo. ■ GB *Boxing Day,* día *m* de San Esteban.

boy [bɔɪ] *n (baby)* niño; *(child)* chico, muchacho; *(youth)* joven *m.* ■ *~ scout,* explorador *m.*

boycott ['bɔɪkɒt] *n* boicot *m.* – 2 *t* boicotear.

boyfriend ['bɔɪfrend] *n* novio.

boyhood ['bɔɪhʊd] *n* niñez *f.*

boyish ['bɔɪʃ] *adj* muchachil, juvenil.

bra [brɑː] *n →* **brassiere**.

brace [breɪs] *n (clamp)* abrazadera. 2 *(support)* riostra. 3 *(drill)* berbiquí *m.* 4 *(on teeth)* aparato. 5 *(two)* par *m.* 6 *pl* tirantes *mpl.* – 7 *t* reforzar. ●*to ~ o.s. for sth.,* prepararse para algo.

bracelet ['breɪslət] *n* brazalete *m.*

bracing ['breɪsɪŋ] *adj* tonificante.

bracket ['brækɪt] *n* paréntesis *m inv; (square)* corchete *m.* 2 *(for shelf)* soporte *m.* 3 *(group)* grupo, sector *m.*

brag [bræg] *n* jactancia. – 2 *i* jactarse *(about,* de).

braid [breɪd] *n* galón *m.* 2 US *(plait)* trenza.

Braille [breɪl] *n* braille *m.*

brain [breɪn] *n* cerebro. 2 *pl* inteligencia *f sing.* ■ *~ wave,* idea genial.

brainchild ['breɪntʃaɪld] *n* invento.

brainy ['breɪnɪ] *adj fam* inteligente.

brake [breɪk] *n* freno. – 2 *t* frenar.

bramble ['bræmbəl] *n* zarza.

bran [bræn] *n* salvado.

branch [brɑːntʃ] *n (tree)* rama. 2 *(road etc.)* ramal *m.* 3 COM sucursal *f.* – 4 *i* bifurcarse.

brand [brænd] *n* COM marca. 2 *(type)* clase *f.* 3 *(cattle)* hierro. – 4 *t* marcar.

brandish ['brændɪʃ] *t* blandir.

brand-new [bræn(d)'njuː] *adj* flamante.

brandy ['brændɪ] *n* brandy *m.*

brass [brɑːs] *n* latón *m.* 2 *sl (money)* pasta.

brassiere ['bræzɪə^r] *n* sujetador *m,* sostén *m.*

brat [bræt] *n fam* mocoso,-a.

brave [breɪv] *adj* valiente. – 2 *n* guerrero indio. – 3 *t* desafiar.

bravery ['breɪvərɪ] *n* valentía.

bravo! [brɑː'vəʊ] *interj* ¡bravo!

brawl [brɔːl] *n* reyerta, riña. − 2 *i* albo-rotar.

brazen ['breɪzən] *adj* desvergonzado,-a.

brazier ['breɪzjər] *n* brasero.

breach [briːtʃ] *n (opening)* brecha, aber-tura. 2 *(violation)* incumplimiento.

bread [bred] *n* pan. 2 *sl (money)* guita, pasta.

breadth [bredθ] *n* anchura.

break [breɪk] *n* rotura, ruptura. 2 *(pause)* interrupción, pausa. 3 *(chance)* oportu-nidad. − 4 *t* romper. 5 *(record)* batir. 6 *(promise)* faltar a. 7 *(news)* comunicar. 8 *(code)* descifrar. 9 *(fall)* amortiguar. 10 *(journey)* interrumpir. − 11 *i* romperse. 12 *(storm)* estallar. 13 *(voice)* cambiar. 14 *(health)* quebrantarse. ◆*to ~ down t* derribar. 2 *(analyse)* desglosar. − 3 *i (car)* averiarse; *(driver)* tener una avería. 4 *(appliance)* estropearse. ◆*to ~ in t* do-mar. ◆*to ~ into t (house)* entrar por la fuerza en; *(safe)* forzar. ◆*to ~ out i (pris-oners)* escaparse. 2 *(war etc.)* estallar. ◆*to ~ up t-i (crowd)* disolver(se). − 2 *i (marriage)* fracasar; *(couple)* separarse. 3 *(school)* empezar las vacaciones. ▲ *pt* **broke;** *pp* **broken.**

breakage ['breɪkɪdʒ] *n* rotura.

breakdown ['breɪkdaʊn] *n* avería. 2 MED crisis (nerviosa). 3 *(in negotiations)* rup-tura. 4 *(analysis)* análisis *m;* FIN desglose *m.*

breakfast ['brekfəst] *n* desayuno. − 2 *i* desayunar.

breakthrough ['breɪkθruː] *n* avance *m* importante.

breakwater ['breɪkwɔːtər] *n* rompeolas *m inv.*

breast [brest] *n* pecho. 2 *(of chicken etc.)* pechuga.

breaststroke ['breststrəʊk] *n* braza.

breath [breθ] *n* aliento. ●*out of ~,* sin aliento.

breathalyze ['breθəlaɪz] *t* hacer la prue-ba del alcohol a.

breathe [briːð] *t-i* respirar.

breathing ['briːðɪŋ] *n* respiración.

breathless ['breθləs] *adj* sin aliento, ja-deante.

bred [bred] *pt & pp* → **breed.**

breech [briːtʃ] *n (of gun)* recámara.

breeches ['brɪtʃɪz] *npl* pantalones *mpl.*

breed [briːd] *n* raza. − 2 *t* criar. − 3 *i* re-producirse. ▲ *pt & pp* **bred.**

breeding ['briːdɪŋ] *n* cría. 2 *(of person)* educación.

breeze [briːz] *n* brisa.

brethren ['breðrɪn] *npl* REL hermanos *mpl.*

brevity ['brevɪtɪ] *n fml* brevedad.

brew [bruː] *n (tea etc.)* infusión. 2 *(potion)* brebaje *m.* − 3 *t (beer)* elaborar. 4 *(tea etc.)* preperar. − 5 *i (tea etc.)* reposar.

brewery ['bruərɪ] *n* cervecería.

briar ['braɪər] *n* brezo.

bribe [braɪb] *n* soborno. − 2 *t* sobornar.

bribery ['braɪbərɪ] *n* soborno.

bric-a-brac ['brɪkəbræk] *n* baratijas *fpl.*

brick [brɪk] *n* ladrillo. 2 *(toy)* cubo (de ma-dera). ●GB *fam* **to drop a ~,** meter la pata.

bricklayer ['brɪkleɪər] *n* albañil *m.*

bridal ['braɪdəl] *adj* nupcial.

bride [braɪd] *n* novia, desposada.

bridegroom ['braɪdgruːm] *n* novio, des-posado.

bridesmaid ['braɪdzmeɪd] *n* dama de ho-nor.

bridge [brɪdʒ] *n* puente *m.* 2 *(of nose)* ca-ballete *m.* 3 *(on ship)* puente *m* de man-do. 4 *(game)* bridge *m.* − 5 *t (river)* tender un puente sobre.

bridle ['braɪdəl] *n* brida. 2 *t (horse)* em-bridar. − 3 *i* mostrar desagrado (at, por).

brief [briːf] *adj (short)* breve; *(concise)* con-ciso,-a. − 2 *n (report)* informe *m.* 3 JUR expediente *m.* 4 MIL instrucciones *fpl.* − 5 *t (inform)* informar. 6 *(instruct)* dar instrucciones a.

briefcase ['briːfkeɪs] *n* maletín *m,* carte-ra.

brigade [brɪ'geɪd] *n* brigada.

brigadier [brɪgə'dɪər] *n* brigadier *m.*

bright [braɪt] *adj (light, eyes, etc.)* brillan-te. 2 *(day)* despejado,-a. 3 *(colour)* vivo,-a. 4 *(future)* prometedor,-ra. 5 *(clever)* inteligente. 6 *(cheerful)* alegre, animado,-a.

brighten ['braɪtən] *i* animarse, avivarse. ◆*to ~ up i (weather)* despejarse. 2 *(per-son)* animarse. − 3 *t* animar, hacer más alegre.

brightness ['braɪtnəs] *n (light)* luminosi-dad. 2 *(of sun)* resplandor *m.* 3 *(of day)* claridad. 4 *(of colour)* viveza. 5 *(clever-ness)* inteligencia.

brilliance ['brɪljəns] *n (light)* brillo. 2 *(of person)* brillantez *f.*

brilliant ['brɪljənt] *adj* brillante, reluci-te. 2 *(person)* brillante, genial. 3 *fam* es-tupendo,-a, fantástico,-a.

brim [brɪm] *n (of glass)* borde *m.* 2 *(of hat)* ala. − 3 *i* rebosar (with, de).

brine [braɪn] *n* salmuera.

bring [brɪŋ] *t* traer: *he brought his sister to the party,* trajo a su hermana a la fiesta. **2** *(lead)* conducir: *he was brought before the court,* fue llevado ante el tribunal; *this path brings you to the church,* este camino te lleva a la iglesia. ◆*to ~ about t* provocar, causar. ◆*to ~ back t (return)* devolver. **2** *(reintroduce)* volver a introducir; *to ~ back memories of,* hacer recordar. ◆*to ~ down t (cause to fall)* derribar. **2** *(reduce)* rebajar. ◆*to ~ forward t* adelantar. ◆*to ~ in t (introduce)* introducir. **2** *(yield)* producir. **3** JUR *(verdict)* emitir. ◆*to ~ off t* conseguir, lograr. ◆*to ~ on t (illness)* provocar. ◆*to ~ out t* sacar (al mercado); *(book etc.)* publicar. ◆*to ~ round t (persuade)* persuadir, convencer. **2** *(revive)* hacer volver en sí. ◆*to ~ to t* hacer volver en sí. ◆*to ~ up t (educate)* criar, educar. **2** *(mention)* plantear. **3** *(vomit)* devolver. ●JUR *to ~ a charge against sb.,* acusar a algn. ▲ *pt & pp* **brought**.

brink [brɪŋk] *n* borde *m*. ●*on the ~ of,* a punto de.

brisk [brɪsk] *adj* enérgico,-a. ●*to go for a ~ walk,* caminar a paso ligero.

bristle ['brɪsəl] *n* cerda. – **2** *i* erizarse. ◆*to ~ with t fig* estar lleno,-a de.

brittle ['brɪtəl] *adj* quebradizo,-a, frágil.

broad [brɔːd] *adj (wide)* ancho,-a; *fig* amplio,-a, extenso,-a. **2** *(general)* general. **3** *(accent)* marcado,-a, cerrado,-a. – **4** *broadly adv* en términos generales. ●*in ~ daylight,* en pleno día.

broadcast ['brɔːdkɑːst] *n* RAD TV emisión. – **2** *t* RAD TV emitir, transmitir. **3** *(make known)* difundir. ▲ *pt & pp* **broadcast**.

broadcasting ['brɔːdkɑːstɪŋ] *n* RAD radiodifusión. **2** TV transmisión.

broaden ['brɔːdən] *t* ensanchar; *fig* ampliar.

broad-minded [brɔːd'maɪndɪd] *adj* liberal, tolerante.

broadside ['brɔːdsaɪd] *n* andanada.

brocade [brəʊ'keɪd] *n* brocado.

broccoli ['brɒkəlɪ] *n* brécol *m*, bróculi *m*.

brochure ['brəʊʃəʳ] *n* folleto.

broil [brɔɪl] *t* US asar a la parrilla.

broiler ['brɔɪləʳ] *n* CULIN pollo.

broke [brəʊk] *pt* → **break**. – **2** *adj fam* sin blanca.

broken ['brəʊkən] *pp* → **break**. – **2** *adj* roto,-a. **3** *(machine)* estropeado,-a. **4** *(bone)* fracturado,-a. **5** *(person)* destrozado,-a. **6** *(language)* chapurreado,-a.

broker ['brəʊkəʳ] *n* COM corredor *m*, agente *mf*.

brolly ['brɒlɪ] *n fam* paraguas *m inv*.

bromide ['brəʊmaɪd] *n* CHEM bromuro.

bromine ['brəʊmaɪn] *n* CHEM bromo.

bronchial ['brɒŋkɪəl] *adj* bronquial.

bronchitis [brɒŋ'kaɪtɪs] *n* bronquitis *f inv*.

bronze [brɒnz] *n* bronce *m*. – **2** *adj (colour)* bronceado,-a.

brooch [brəʊtʃ] *n* broche *m*.

brood [bruːd] *n (birds)* nidada. – **2** *i (hen)* empollar. **3** *fig* considerar, rumiar.

broody ['bruːdɪ] *adj (hen)* clueco,-a. **2** *(thoughtful)* pensativo,-a. **3** *(moody)* melancólico,-a.

brook [brʊk] *n* arroyo, riachuelo.

broom [bruːm] *n* escoba.

broomstick ['bruːmstɪk] *n* palo de escoba.

broth [brɒθ] *n* caldo.

brothel ['brɒθəl] *n* burdel *m*.

brother ['brʌðəʳ] *n* hermano.

brotherhood ['brʌðəhʊd] *n* hermandad.

brother-in-law ['brʌðərɪnlɔː] *n* cuñado.

brotherly ['brʌðəlɪ] *adj* fraternal.

brought [brɔːt] *pt & pp* → **bring**.

brow [braʊ] *n (eyebrow)* ceja. **2** *(forehead)* frente *f*. **3** *(of hill)* cresta.

browbeat ['braʊbiːt] *t* intimidar. ▲ *Se conjuga como* **beat**.

brown [braʊn] *adj* marrón. **2** *(hair etc.)* castaño,-a. **3** *(skin)* moreno,-a. – **4** *t* CULIN dorar. – **5** *t-i (tan)* broncear(se).

browse [braʊz] *i (animal) (grass)* pacer; *(leaves)* ramonear. **2** *(person in shop)* mirar: *to ~ through a book,* hojear un libro.

bruise [bruːz] *n* morado, magulladura, contusión. – **2** *t-i (body)* magullar(se), contusionar(se). **3** *(fruit)* machucar(se).

brunette [bruː'net] *adj-n* morena.

brunt [brʌnt] *n* *to bear the ~ of,* llevar el peso de.

brush [brʌʃ] *n (for teeth, clothes, etc.)* cepillo. **2** *(artist's)* pincel *m*. **3** *(house painter's)* brocha. **4** *(undergrowth)* maleza. – **5** *t* cepillar. **6** *(touch lightly)* rozar. ◆*to ~ up t* refrescar, repasar.

brush-off ['brʌʃɒf] *n* *to give sb. the ~,* no hacer ni el mínimo caso a algn.

brushwood ['brʌʃwʊd] *n (twigs)* broza. **2** *(undergrowth)* maleza.

brusque [bruːsk] *adj* brusco,-a, áspero,-a.

Brussels ['brʌsəlz] *prn* Bruselas. ■ *~ sprouts,* coles *fpl* de Bruselas.

bundle

brutal ['bruːtəl] *adj* brutal, cruel.
brutality [bruːˈtælɪtɪ] *n* brutalidad, cruel-dad.
brute [bruːt] *n* bruto,-a, bestia *mf.* − **2** *adj* brutal, bruto,-a.
brutish ['bruːtɪʃ] *adj* brutal, bestial.
bubble ['bʌbəl] *n* burbuja. − **2** *i* burbu-jear; CULIN borbotear.
bubbly ['bʌblɪ] *adj* burbujeante. **2** *(per-son)* vivaz.
buccaneer [bʌkəˈnɪər] *n* bucanero.
buck [bʌk] *n (gen)* macho; *(deer)* ciervo. **2** US *fam* dólar *m.* − **3** *i (horse)* corcovear. ◆**to ~ up** *t fam* ~ *your ideas up!,* ¡es-pabílate! − **2** *i* animarse. ●**to pass the ~ to sb.,** echar el muerto a algn.
bucket ['bʌkɪt] *n* cubo.
buckle ['bʌkəl] *n* hebilla. − **2** *t* abrochar. − **3** *i* torcerse. **4** *(knees)* doblarse.
bucolic [bjuːˈkɒlɪk] *adj* bucólico,-a.
bud [bʌd] *n (leaf)* yema; *(flower)* capullo. − **2** *i* brotar.
budding ['bʌdɪŋ] *adj* en ciernes.
buddy ['bʌdɪ] *n* US *fam* amigote *m.*
budge [bʌdʒ] *t-i* mover(se). **2** *(give way)* ceder.
budgerigar ['bʌdʒərɪgɑːr] *n* periquito.
budget ['bʌdʒɪt] *n* presupuesto. − **2** *t-i* presupuestar.
buff [bʌf] *n (colour)* color *m* del ante. **2** *(enthusiast)* aficionado,-a. − **3** *adj* de co-lor del ante. − **4** *t* dar brillo a.
buffalo ['bʌfələu] *n* búfalo.
buffer ['bʌfər] *n* tope *m.* **2** COMPUT me-moria intermedia.
buffet ['bʌfeɪ] *n (bar)* bar *m;* (*at station)* cantina. **2** *(meal)* bufet *m* libre. **3** *(slap)* bofetada. − **4** *t* abofetear. ▲ *En* **3** *y* **4** ['bʌfɪt].
buffoon [bʌˈfuːn] *n* bufón *m.*
bug [bʌg] *n* bicho. **2** *fam (microbe)* micro-bio. **3** *(microphone)* micrófono oculto. **4** *fam (interest)* afición. − **5** *t fam* ocultar micrófonos en. **6** *(annoy)* molestar.
bugbear ['bʌgbeər] *n* tormento.
bugger ['bʌgər] *n* sodomita *m.* **2*** *(person)* cabrón,-ona*. **3*** *(thing)* coñazo*. − **4*** *interj* ¡joder!* − **5** *t* sodomizar. ◆**to ~ about*** *i* hacer el gilipollas*. ◆**to ~ off*** *i* largarse. ◆**to ~ up*** *t* joder*.
bugle ['bjuːgəl] *n* corneta.
build [bɪld] *n (physique)* constitución. − **2** *t* construir. ◆**to ~ up** *t-i* acumular(se). ▲ *pt & pp* **built.**
builder ['bɪldər] *n* constructor,-ra.
building ['bɪldɪŋ] *n* edificio. **2** *(action)* construcción, edificación. ■ ~ **site,** obra; ~ **society,** sociedad hipotecaria.

build-up ['bɪldʌp] *n* aumento. **2** *(of gas)* acumulación. **3** *(of troops)* concentra-ción.
built [bɪlt] *pt & pp* → **build.**
built-in [bɪltˈɪn] *adj* incorporado,-a.
built-up [bɪltˈʌp] *adj* urbanizado,-a.
bulb [bʌlb] *n* BOT bulbo. **2** ELEC bombilla.
bulge [bʌldʒ] *i* bulto. − **2** *i* hincharse.
bulk [bʌlk] *n (mass)* volumen *m,* masa. **2** *(greater part)* mayor parte *f.* ●COM **in ~,** a granel.
bulky ['bʌlkɪ] *adj* voluminoso,-a.
bull [bʊl] *n* toro. **2** *(papal)* bula. **3** FIN al-cista *mf.*
bulldog ['bʊldɒg] *n* buldog *m.*
bulldozer ['bʊldəuzər] *n* bulldozer *m.*
bullet ['bʊlɪt] *n* bala.
bulletin ['bʊlɪtɪn] *n* boletín *m.* ■ **news ~,** boletín informativo/de noticias.
bullet-proof ['bʊlɪtpruːf] *adj* antibalas *inv.*
bullfight ['bʊlfaɪt] *n* corrida de toros.
bullfighter ['bʊlfaɪtər] *n* torero,-a.
bullfighting ['bʊlfaɪtɪŋ] *n* los toros; *(art)* tauromaquia.
bullion ['bʊljən] *n* oro/plata en barras.
bullock ['bʊlək] *n* buey *m.*
bullring ['bʊlrɪŋ] *n* plaza de toros.
bull's-eye ['bʊlzaɪ] *n (target)* diana. ●**to score a ~,** dar en el blanco.
bullshit* ['bʊlʃɪt] *n* mierda*.
bully ['bʊlɪ] *n* matón *m.* − **2** *t* intimidar, atemorizar.
bum [bʌm] *fam n* GB culo. **2** US *(tramp)* vagabundo,-a. **3** *(idler)* vago,-a. − **4** *t* go-rrear.
bumblebee ['bʌmbəlbiː] *n* abejorro.
bumbling ['bʌmblɪŋ] *adj* torpe.
bump [bʌmp] *n (swelling)* chichón *m.* **2** *(in road)* bache *m.* **3** *(blow)* choque *m,* ba-tacazo. − **4** *t-i* chocar *(into,* con), dar *(into,* contra). ◆**to ~ into** *t fam* encon-trar por casualidad, tropezar con. ◆**to ~ off** *t* matar.
bumper ['bʌmpər] *n* parachoques *m inv.* − **2** *adj* abundante.
bumpkin ['bʌmpkɪn] *n* paleto,-a.
bumpy ['bʌmpɪ] *adj (road)* lleno,-a de ba-ches.
bun [bʌn] *n (bread)* panecillo; *(sweet)* bo-llo. **2** *(cake)* ma(g)dalena. **3** *(hair)* moño.
bunch [bʌntʃ] *n* manojo. **2** *(flowers)* ramo. **3** *(grapes)* racimo. **4** *(people)* gru-po.
bundle ['bʌndəl] *n (clothes)* fardo. **2** *(wood)* haz *m.* **3** *(papers)* fajo.

bung [bʌŋ] *n* tapón *m*. − **2** *t fam (put)* poner. **3** *fam (throw)* lanzar.
bungalow ['bʌŋgələʊ] *n* bungalow *m*.
bungle ['bʌŋgəl] *t* chapucear.
bungler ['bʌŋglər] *n* chapucero,-a.
bunion ['bʌnjən] *n* juanete *m*.
bunker ['bʌŋkər] *n (for coal)* carbonera. **2** *(golf)* búnker *m*. **3** MIL búnker *m*.
bunny ['bʌnɪ] *n fam* conejito.
buoy [bɔɪ] *n* boya.
buoyant ['bɔɪənt] *adj* flotante. **2** FIN con tendencia alcista. **3** *(person)* animado,-a.
burden ['bɜːdən] *n* carga. − **2** *t* cargar.
bureau ['bjʊərəʊ] *n (desk)* escritorio. **2** *(office)* oficina. ▲ *pl* **bureaus** *o* **bureaux**.
bureaucracy [bjʊəˈrɒkrəsɪ] *n* burocracia.
bureaucrat ['bjʊərəkræt] *n* burócrata *mf*.
bureaucratic [bjʊərəˈkrætɪk] *adj* burocrático,-a.
burglar ['bɜːglər] *n* ladrón,-ona.
burglary ['bɜːglərɪ] *n* robo.
burgle ['bɜːgəl] *t* robar.
burial ['berɪəl] *n* entierro.
burly ['bɜːlɪ] *adj* corpulento,-a.
burn [bɜːn] *n* quemadura. − **2** *t* quemar. − **3** *i* arder, quemarse. ◆*to* ~ *down* t-i incendiar(se). ◆*to* ~ *out* i *(fire)* extinguirse. **2** *(person, machine)* gastarse. ▲ *pt & pp* **burnt**; **burnt** *o* **burned** *cuando es intransitivo*.
burner ['bɜːnər] *n* quemador *m*.
burning ['bɜːnɪŋ] *adj (on fire)* incendiado,-a, ardiendo. **2** *(passionate)* ardiente. ■ ~ *question,* cuestión candente.
burnt [bɜːnt] *pt & pp* → **burn**.
burp [bɜːp] *n fam* eructo. − **2** *i* eructar.
burrow ['bʌrəʊ] *n* madriguera. − **2** *i* excavar una madriguera.
burst [bɜːst] *n* explosión, estallido. **2** *(of tyre)* reventón *m*. **3** *(of activity)* arranque *m*. **4** *(of applause)* salva. **5** *(of gunfire)* ráfaga. − **6** *t (balloon)* reventar. − **8** *i (balloon, tyre, pipe, etc.)* reventarse. ◆*to* ~ *into tears,* echarse a llorar; *to* ~ *out crying/laughing,* echarse a llorar/reír; *(river) to* ~ *its banks,* salirse de madre. ▲ *pt & pp* **burst**.
bury ['berɪ] *t* enterrar.
bus [bʌs] *n* autobús *m*. ■ ~ *stop,* parada de autobús.
bush [bʊʃ] *n (plant)* arbusto. **2** *(land)* monte *m*.
bushy ['bʊʃɪ] *adj* espeso,-a, tupido,-a.
business ['bɪznəs] *n (commerce)* los negocios. **2** *(firm)* negocio, empresa. **3** *(duty)* deber *m*. **4** *(affair)* asunto.

businesslike ['bɪznəslaɪk] *adj* formal, serio,-a.
businessman ['bɪznəsmən] *n* hombre *m* de negocios, empresario.
busker ['bʌskər] *n* GB músico,-a callejero,-a.
bust [bʌst] *n* busto. − **2** *t fam* romper. − **3** *adj fam* roto,-a. ●*fam to go* ~, quebrar.
bustle ['bʌsəl] *n* bullicio. ◆*to* ~ *about i* ir y venir, no parar.
busy ['bɪzɪ] *adj (person)* ocupado,-a, atareado,-a. **2** *(street)* concurrido,-a. **3** *(day)* ajetreado,-a. **4** *(telephone)* ocupado,-a. ●*to* ~ *o.s. doing sth.,* ocuparse en hacer algo.
busybody ['bɪzɪbɒdɪ] *n* entremetido,-a.
but [bʌt] *conj* pero: *it's cold,* ~ *dry,* hace frío, pero no llueve; *I'd like to,* ~ *I can't,* me gustaría, pero no puedo. **2** *(after negative)* sino: *not two,* ~ *three,* no dos, sino tres. − **3** *adv* sólo: *had I* ~ *known ...,* si lo hubiese sabido ...; *she is* ~ *a child,* no es más que una niña. − **4** *prep* excepto, salvo, menos: *all* ~ *me,* todos menos yo. ●~ *for, (past)* si no hubiese sido por; *(present)* si no fuese por: ~ *for his help, we would have failed,* si no hubiese sido por su ayuda, habríamos fracasado.
butane ['bjuːteɪn] *n* butano.
butcher ['bʊtʃər] *n* carnicero,-a.
butler ['bʌtlə] *n* mayordomo.
butt [bʌt] *n (of cigarette)* colilla. **2** *(of rifle)* culata. **3** *(barrel)* tonel *m*. **4** *(target)* blanco. **5** US *fam* culo. **6** *(with head)* cabezazo. − **7** *t (with head)* topet(e)ar. ◆*to* ~ *in i* entrometerse.
butter ['bʌtər] *n* mantequilla. − **2** *t* untar con mantequilla. ◆*to* ~ *up t fam* dar coba a. ●*to look as if* ~ *wouldn't melt in one's mouth,* parecer una mosquita muerta.
butterfingers ['bʌtəfɪŋgəz] *n* manazas *mf inv*.
butterfly ['bʌtəflaɪ] *n* mariposa.
buttock ['bʌtək] *n* nalga.
button ['bʌtən] *n* botón *m*. − **2** *t-i* abrochar(se).
buttonhole ['bʌtənhəʊl] *n* ojal *m*.
buttress ['bʌtrɪs] *n* contrafuerte *m*.
butty ['bʌtɪ] *n fam* bocata *m*.
buxom ['bʌksəm] *adj* rollizo,-a.
buy [baɪ] *n* compra. − **2** *t* comprar. **3** *(bribe)* sobornar. **4** *fam (believe)* tragar. ▲ *pt & pp* **bought**.
buyer ['baɪər] *n* comprador,-ra.
buzz [bʌz] *n* zumbido. **2** *fam* telefonazo. − **3** *i* zumbar.

byte

buzzer [ˈbʌzəʳ] *n* zumbador *m*.

by [baɪ] *prep (showing agent)* por: *painted ~ Fraser,* pintado,-a por Fraser. **2** *(manner)* por: *~ air/road,* por avión/carretera; *~ car/train,* en coche/tren; *~ hand,* a mano; *~ heart,* de memoria. **3** *(showing difference)* por: *I won ~ 3 points,* gané por tres puntos; *better ~ far,* muchísimo mejor. **4** *(not later than)* para; *I need it ~ ten,* lo necesito para las diez. **5** *(during)* de: *~day/night,* de día/noche. **6** *(near)* junto a, al lado de: *sit ~ me,* siéntate a mi lado. **7** *(according to)* según: *~ the rules,* según las reglas. **8** *(measurements)* por: *6 metres ~ 4,* 6

metros por 4. **9** *(rate)* por: *paid ~ the hour,* pagado,-a por horas; *two ~ two,* de dos en dos. **— 10** *adv to go ~,* pasar (de largo). **12** *~ and ~,* con el tiempo. ●*~ o.s.,* solo,-a.

bye [baɪ] *interj fam* ¡adiós!, ¡hasta luego!

by-law [ˈbaɪlɔ:] *n* ley *f* municipal.

bypass [ˈbaɪpɑ:s] *n* AUTO variante *f*. **2** MED by-pass *m*.

by-product [ˈbaɪprɒdʌkt] *n* subproducto, derivado.

bystander [ˈbaɪstændəʳ] *n* espectador,-ra.

byte [baɪt] *n* COMPUT byte *m*.

C

cab [kæb] *n* taxi *m*. **2** HIST cabriolé *m*. **3** *(in lorry)* cabina de conductor; *(in train)* cabina de maquinista.

cabaret ['kæbəreɪ] *n* cabaret *m*.

cabbage ['kæbɪdʒ] *n* col *f*, berza, repollo.

cabin ['kæbɪn] *n (wooden)* cabaña. **2** MAR camarote *m*. **3** AER cabina.

cabinet ['kæbɪnət] *n (ministers)* gabinete *m*. **2** *(furniture)* armario; *(glass fronted)* vitrina.

cable ['keɪbəl] *n* cable *m*. — **2** *t* cablegrafiar.

cackle ['kækəl] *n* cacareo. **2** *(laugh)* risotada. — **3** *i* cacarear. **4** *(laugh)* reír.

cactus ['kæktəs] *n* cacto, cactus *m*.

cad [kæd] *n* GB *fam* canalla *m*.

caddie ['kædɪ] *n* cadi *m*.

caddy ['kædɪ] *n* cajita/lata para el té.

cadence ['keɪdəns] *n* cadencia.

cadet [kə'det] *n* cadete *m*.

cadge [kædʒ] *t-i fam* gorronear.

cadger ['kædʒər] *n fam* gorrón,-ona *m,f*.

café ['kæfeɪ] *n* cafetería.

cafeteria [kæfɪ'tɪərɪə] *n* cafetería, autoservicio.

caffeine ['kæfi:n] *n* cafeína.

cage [keɪdʒ] *n* jaula. — **2** *t* enjaular.

cagey ['keɪdʒɪ] *adj fam* cauteloso,-a.

cagoule [kə'gu:l] *n* canguro.

cajole [kə'dʒəʊl] *t* engatusar, camelar.

cake [keɪk] *n* pastel *m*, tarta. ●*to sell like hot cakes,* venderse como rosquillas; *fam it's a piece of* ~, está chupado,-a.

calamity [kə'læmɪtɪ] *n* calamidad.

calcium ['kælsɪəm] *n* calcio.

calculate ['kælkjʊleɪt] *t* calcular. — **2** *i* hacer cálculos.

calculating ['kælkjʊleɪtɪŋ] *adj* calculador,-ra.

calculation [kælkjʊ'leɪʃən] *n* cálculo.

calculator ['kælkjʊleɪtər] *n* calculador *m*, calculadora.

calculus ['kælkjʊləs] *n* cálculo.

caldron ['kɔːldrən] *n* → **cauldron**.

calendar ['kælɪndər] *n* calendario.

calf [kɑːf] *n* ZOOL ternero,-a, becerro,-a. **2** ANAT pantorrilla. ▲ *pl* **calves**.

calibrate ['kælɪbreɪt] *t* calibrar, graduar.

calibre ['kælɪbər] *n* calibre *m*.

calico ['kælɪkəʊ] *n* calicó *m*.

call [kɔːl] *n* grito, llamada. **2** *(telephone)* llamada. **3** *(of animal)* reclamo. **4** *(demand)* demanda. **5** *(summons)* llamada, llamamiento. **6** *(visit)* visita corta. **7** *(need)* necesidad. — **8** *t (gen)* llamar a, telefonear. **9** *(on telephone)* llamar. **10** *(meeting)* convocar. — **11** *i (gen)* llamar(se). **12** *(visit)* pasar. **13** *(train)* parar *(at,* en*)*. ◆*to* ~ *for t (pick up)* pasar a buscar. **2** *(demand)* exigir. **3** *(need)* necesitar: *this calls for a celebration,* esto hay que celebrarlo. ◆*to* ~ *off t (suspend)* suspender. ◆*to* ~ *on t (visit)* visitar. **2** *fml (urge)* instar: *he called on them to negotiate,* les instó a negociar. ◆*to* ~ *out t (troops)* sacar a la calle. **2** *(doctor)* hacer venir. **3** *(workers)* llamar a la huelga. — **4** *i* gritar. ◆*to* ~ *up t* MIL llamar a filas. **2** *(telephone)* llamar. ●*on* ~, de guardia; *to* ~ *into question,* poner en duda; *to* ~ *to mind,* traer a la memoria; *to pay/make a* ~ *on,* visitar; *fam let's* ~ *it a day,* dejémoslo estar/correr. ■ GB ~ *box,* cabina telefónica; ~ *girl,* prostituta.

caller ['kɔːlər] *n* visita *mf*, visitante *mf*. **2** *(telephone)* persona que llama.

calligraphy [kə'lɪgrəfɪ] *n* caligrafía.

calling ['kɔːlɪŋ] *n* vocación.

callipers ['kælɪpəz] *npl* TECH calibrador *m sing*. **2** MED aparato *m sing* ortopédico.

callous ['kæləs] *adj* duro,-a, insensible.

calm [kɑːm] *adj (sea)* en calma, sereno,-a. **2** *(person)* tranquilo,-a, sosegado,-a. – **3** *n (of sea)* calma. **4** *(of person)* tranquilidad, serenidad. – **5** *t-i to ~ (down),* calmar(se), sosegar(se).

calmness ['kɑːmnəs] *n* tranquilidad, calma.

calorie ['kælərɪ] *n* caloría.

calumny ['kæləmnɪ] *n* calumnia.

came [keɪm] *pt* → **come**.

camel ['kæməl] *n* camello.

camellia [kə'miːljə] *n* camelia.

cameo ['kæmɪəʊ] *n* camafeo.

camera ['kæmərə] *n* cámara/máquina fotográfica. ●*in ~,* a puerta cerrada.

cameraman ['kæmərəmən] *n* cámara *m*.

camomile ['kæməmaɪl] *n* BOT manzanilla, camomila.

camouflage ['kæməflɑːʒ] *n* camuflaje *m*. – **2** *t* camuflar.

camp [kæmp] *n* campamento. – **2** *i* acampar. ■ ~ *bed,* cama plegable; ~ *site,* camping *m*, campamento.

campaign [kæm'peɪn] *n* campaña. – **2** *i* hacer campaña *(for,* en favor de).

camper ['kæmpə^r] *n* campista *mf*. **2** US *(vehicle)* caravana.

camphor ['kæmfə^r] *n* alcanfor *m*.

camping ['kæmpɪŋ] *n to go ~,* ir de camping. ■ ~ *site,* camping *m*, campamento.

campus ['kæmpəs] *n* campus *m*.

can [kæn] *n (for food, drinks)* lata. **2** *(for oil etc.)* bidón *m*. – **3** *t (put in cans)* enlatar. – **4** *aux (be able to)* poder: *~ you come tomorrow?,* ¿puedes venir mañana? **5** *(know how to)* saber: *he ~ swim/speak Chinese,* sabe nadar/hablar chino. **6** *(be allowed to)* poder: *you can't smoke here,* no se puede fumar aquí. **7** *(be possible)* poder: *he can't be here already!,* ¡no puede ser que ya haya llegado!; *what ~ it mean?,* ¿qué querrá decir? ▲ *pt & cond* **could**.

canal [kə'næl] *n* canal *m*.

canary [kə'neərɪ] *n* canario.

cancel ['kænsəl] *t* cancelar. **2** COM anular. **3** *(cross out)* tachar.

cancellation [kænsə'leɪʃən] *n* cancelación. **2** COM anulación.

cancer ['kænsə^r] *n* MED cáncer *m*. **2** *Cancer,* ASTROL ASTRON Cáncer *m inv*.

candid ['kændɪd] *adj* franco,-a, sincero,-a.

candidate ['kændɪdɪt] *n* candidato,-a. **2** *(in exam)* opositor,-ra.

candied ['kændɪd] *adj* confitado,-a.

candle ['kændəl] *n* vela; *(in church)* cirio.

candlestick ['kændəlstɪk] *n* candelero, palmatoria.

candour ['kændə^r] *n* franqueza, sinceridad.

candy ['kændɪ] *n* US caramelo.

cane [keɪn] *n* BOT caña. **2** *(stick)* bastón *m*; *(for punishment)* palmeta. **3** *(furniture)* mimbre *m*. – **4** *t* castigar con la palmeta.

canine ['keɪnaɪn] *adj* canino,-a.

canister ['kænɪstə^r] *n* bote *m*, lata.

canned [kænd] *adj* enlatado,-a. **2** *sl (drunk)* mamado,-a.

cannery ['kænərɪ] *n* fábrica de conservas.

cannibal ['kænɪbəl] *adj-n* caníbal *(mf)*.

cannon ['kænən] *n* cañón *m*. **2** *(billiards)* carambola.

cannot ['kænɒt] *forma compuesta de* **can** + **not**.

canoe [kə'nuː] *n* canoa, piragua.

canon ['kænən] *n (rule)* canon *m*. **2** *(priest)* canónigo.

canonize ['kænənaɪz] *t* canonizar.

canopy ['kænəpɪ] *n* dosel *m*.

cant [kænt] *n* hipocresías *fpl*. **2** *(slang)* jerga.

can't [kɑːnt] *contracción de* **can** + **not**.

cantankerous [kən'tæŋkərəs] *adj* intratable.

canteen [kæn'tiːn] *n (restaurant)* cantina. **2** *(cutlery)* juego de cubiertos. **3** *(flask)* cantimplora.

canter ['kæntə^r] *n* medio galope. – **2** *i* ir a medio galope.

canvas ['kænvəs] *n* lona. **2** ART lienzo.

canvass ['kænvəs] *i* hacer propaganda política.

canyon ['kænjən] *n* cañón *m*.

cap [kæp] *n (man's)* gorro; *(soldier's)* gorra; *(nurse's)* cofia. **2** *(of pen)* capuchón *m*; *(of bottle)* chapa. **3** MED **(Dutch)** ~, diafragma *m*. – **4** *t (crown)* cubrir; *fig* coronar. ●*to ~ it all,* para colmo.

capability [keɪpə'bɪlɪtɪ] *n* capacidad, aptitud, habilidad.

capable ['keɪpəbəl] *adj* capaz.

capacity [kə'pæsɪtɪ] *n (of container)* capacidad, cabida. **2** *(of theatre)* capacidad, aforo. **3** *(ability)* capacidad. **4** *(position)* condición, calidad. ●*to be filled to ~,* estar al completo.

cape [keɪp] *n* GEOG cabo. **2** *(garment)* capa corta.

caper ['keɪpə^r] *n (jump)* brinco. **2** *(prank)* travesura. – **4** *i* brincar.

capital ['kæpɪtəl] *n* GEOG capital *f*. **2** FIN capital *m*. **3** *(letter)* mayúscula. – **4** *adj*

GEOG JUR capital. **5** *(letter)* mayúscula: ~. *A,* A mayúscula. ■ ~ *punishment,* la pena capital.

capitalism ['kæpɪtəlɪzəm] *n* capitalismo.

capitalist ['kæpɪtəlɪst] *adj-n* capitalista *(mf).*

capitulate [kə'pɪtjʊleɪt] *i* capitular.

capitulation [kəpɪtjʊ'leɪʃən] *n* capitulación.

caprice [kə'priːs] *n* capricho, antojo.

capricious [kə'prɪʃəs] *adj* caprichoso,-a, antojadizo,-a.

Capricorn ['kæprɪkɔːn] *n* Capricornio *m inv.*

capsize [kæp'saɪz] *i* zozobrar. – **2** *t* hacer zozobrar.

capstan ['kæpstən] *n* cabrestante *m.*

capsule ['kæpsjuːl] *n* cápsula.

captain ['kæptɪn] *n* capitán *m.*

caption ['kæpʃən] *n* leyenda, pie *m.*

captivate ['kæptɪveɪt] *t* cautivar, fascinar.

captive ['kæptɪv] *adj-n* cautivo,-a.

captivity [kæp'tɪvɪtɪ] *n* cautiverio.

capture ['kæptʃəʳ] *n (of person)* captura, apresamiento; *(of town)* toma. – **2** *t (person)* capturar, apresar; *(town)* tomar. **3** *fig (mood etc.)* captar.

car [kɑːʳ] *n* AUTO coche *m,* automóvil *m.* **2** *(railways)* vagón *m,* coche *m.* ■ ~ *wash,* túnel *m* de lavado; *dining/sleeping* ~, coche restaurante/cama.

caramel ['kærəmel] *n* CULIN azúcar quemado. **2** *(sweet)* caramelo.

carat ['kærət] *n* quilate *m.*

caravan [kærə'væn] *n* AUTO caravana. **2** *(gypsy)* carruaje *m* de gitanos.

caraway ['kærəweɪ] *n* alcaravea.

carbohydrate [kɑːbəʊ'haɪdreɪt] *n* hidrato de carbono.

carbon ['kɑːbən] *n* CHEM carbono. ■ ~ *dioxide/monoxide,* dióxido/monóxido de carbono; ~ *paper,* papel *m* carbón.

carbuncle ['kɑːbʌŋkəl] *n* MED carbunco.

carburettor ['kɑːbjʊrətəʳ] *n* carburador *m.*

carcass ['kɑːkəs] *n* res muerta. **2** *(at butcher's)* res abierta en canal.

carcinogenic [kɑːsɪnə'dʒenɪk] *adj* MED cancerígeno,-a, carcinógeno,-a.

card [kɑːd] *n (playing card)* carta, naipe *m.* **2** *(business, credit, etc.)* tarjeta. **3** *(in file)* ficha. **4** *(membership, identity)* carnet *m,* carné *m.* **5** *(Christmas, birthday)* felicitación. **6** *(stiff paper)* cartulina.

cardboard ['kɑːdbɔːd] *n* cartón *m.*

cardiac ['kɑːdɪæk] *adj* cardíaco,-a. ■ ~ *arrest,* paro cardíaco.

cardigan ['kɑːdɪgən] *n* rebeca, chaqueta de punto.

cardinal ['kɑːdɪnəl] *adj* cardinal. – **2** *n* REL cardenal *m.*

care [keəʳ] *n (attention, protection, carefulness)* cuidado. **2** *(worry)* preocupación, inquietud. **3** *(custody)* custodia. – **4** *i (be worried)* preocuparse: *he doesn't* ~ *about others,* no le importan los demás; *I don't* ~, me tiene sin cuidado. **5** *fml (like, want)* gustar: *would you* ~ *to dance?,* ¿te gustaría bailar? ◆*to* ~ *for t (look after)* cuidar. **2** *(like)* gustar, interesar. ●*to take* ~ *of, (child etc)* cuidar; *(business, matters)* ocuparse de, hacerse cargo de; *to take* ~ *not to do sth.,* tener cuidado de no hacer algo.

career [kə'rɪəʳ] *n (profession)* carrera. **2** *(working life)* vida profesional. – **3** *i* correr a toda velocidad.

careful ['keəfʊl] *adj* cuidadoso,-a. **2** *(cautious)* prudente: *a* ~ *driver,* un conductor prudente. – **3** *carefully adv* cuidadosamente; *(cautiously)* con cuidado: *drive carefully,* conduce con cuidado.

careless ['keələs] *adj* descuidado,-a; *(driving)* negligente; *(work)* dejado,-a.

carelessness ['keələsnəs] *n* despreocupación, negligencia.

caress [kə'res] *n* caricia. – **2** *t* acariciar.

caretaker ['keəteɪkəʳ] *n (in school etc.)* conserje *m;* *(in flats)* portero,-a.

cargo ['kɑːgəʊ] *n* carga, cargamento.

caricature ['kærɪkətjʊəʳ] *n* caricatura. – **2** *t* caricaturizar.

caries ['keərɪz] *n* caries *f inv.*

carnage ['kɑːnɪdʒ] *n* carnicería.

carnal ['kɑːnəl] *adj* carnal.

carnation [kɑː'neɪʃən] *n* clavel *m.*

carnival ['kɑːnɪvəl] *n* carnaval *m.*

carnivorous [kɑː'nɪvərəs] *adj* carnívoro,-a.

carol ['kærəl] *n* villancico.

carouse [kə'raʊz] *i* ir de juerga.

carp [kɑːp] *n (fish)* carpa. – **2** *i* refunfuñar.

carpenter ['kɑːpɪntəʳ] *n* carpintero.

carpentry ['kɑːpɪntrɪ] *n* carpintería.

carpet ['kɑːpɪt] *n* alfombra. – **2** *t* alfombrar.

carriage ['kærɪdʒ] *n* HIST carruaje *m.* **2** *(railway)* vagón *m,* coche *m.* **3** TECH carro. **4** *(transport)* transporte *m.* **5** *(bearing)* porte *m.*

carriageway ['kærɪdʒweɪ] *n* GB calzada.

carrier ['kærɪəʳ] *n (company, person)* transportista *mf.* **2** MED portador,-ra. ■ MAR

aircraft ~, portaaviones *m inv*; ~ *bag,* bolsa de papel/plástico.
carrion ['kærɪən] *n* carroña.
carrot ['kærət] *n* zanahoria.
carry ['kærɪ] *t (gen)* llevar; *(money etc.)* llevar (encima). **2** *(goods etc.)* transportar. **3** ARCH *(load)* sostener. **4** COM tener (en existencia). **5** *(responsibility, penalty)* conllevar. **6** *(news, story)* publicar. **7** *(vote etc.)* aprobar. **8** *(disease)* ser portador,-ra de. – **9** *i (sound)* oírse. ◆*to* ~ *forward t* llevar a la columna/página siguiente. ◆*to* ~ *off t* realizar con éxito. **2** *(prize)* llevarse. ◆*to* ~ *on t-i* continuar, seguir. – **2** *i fam* exaltarse. ◆*to* ~ *on with t* estar liado,-a con. ◆*to* ~ *out t* llevar a cabo, realizar; *(order)* cumplir. ●*to get carried away,* exaltarse.
cart [kɑːt] *n (horse-drawn)* carro. **2** *(handcart)* carretilla. – **3** *t* carretear.
cartel [kɑːˈtel] *n* cártel *m.*
cartilage ['kɑːtɪlɪdʒ] *n* cartílago.
cartography [kɑːˈtɒgrəfɪ] *n* cartografía.
carton ['kɑːtən] *n (of cream)* bote *m.* **2** *(of cigarettes)* cartón *m.*
cartoon [kɑːˈtuːn] *n* caricatura. **2** *(film)* (película de) dibujos *mpl* animados.
cartridge ['kɑːtrɪdʒ] *n* MIL cartucho. **2** *(for pen)* recambio.
cartwheel ['kɑːtwiːl] *n* voltereta.
carve [kɑːv] *t (wood)* tallar. **2** *(stone)* esculpir. **3** *(meat)* cortar, trinchar.
carver ['kɑːvəʳ] *n (of wood)* tallista *mf.* **2** *(of stone)* escultor,-ra. **3** *(knife)* trinchante *m.*
carving ['kɑːvɪŋ] *n (of wood)* talla. **2** *(of stone)* escultura. ■ ~ *knife,* trinchante *m.*
cascade [kæsˈkeɪd] *n* cascada.
case [keɪs] *n (gen)* caso. **2** JUR causa. **3** *(suitcase)* maleta. **4** *(box)* caja. **5** *(for glasses)* estuche *m,* funda. **6** *(type)* caja. ●*in any* ~, en todo/cualquier caso; *in* ~, por si; *in* ~ *of,* en caso de; *just in* ~, por si acaso. ■ *upper/lower* ~, caja alta/ baja.
casement ['keɪsmənt] *n* ventana de bisagras.
cash [kæʃ] *n* efectivo, metálico. – **2** *t (cheque)* cobrar. ●~ *down,* a toca teja; ~ *on delivery,* contra reembolso; *to pay* ~, pagar al contado/en efectivo. ■ ~ *desk,* caja; ~ *register,* caja registradora.
cash-and-carry [kæʃənˈkærɪ] *n* comercio al por mayor.
cashew [kəˈʃuː] *n* anacardo.
cashier [kæˈʃɪəʳ] *n* cajero,-a. – **2** *t* MIL separar del servicio.

cashmere [kæʃˈmɪəʳ] *n* cachemira.
casino [kəˈsiːnəʊ] *n* casino.
cask [kɑːsk] *n* tonel *m,* barril *m.*
casket ['kɑːskɪt] *n* cofre *m.*
casserole ['kæsərəʊl] *n (dish)* cazuela. **2** *(food)* guisado.
cassette [kəˈset] *n* casete *f.* ■ ~ *player/ recorder,* casete *m.*
cassock ['kæsək] *n* sotana.
cast [kɑːst] *n (throw)* lanzamiento. **2** THEAT reparto. **3** TECH molde *m.* – **4** *t (fishing)* lanzar. **5** *(shadow)* proyectar. **6** *(vote)* emitir. **7** THEAT *(play)* hacer el reparto de; *(part)* dar el papel de. **8** TECH moldear. ◆*to* ~ *off t* desechar. – **2** *i* cerrar los puntos. **3** MAR soltar amarras. ●*to be* ~ *away,* naufragar; *to* ~ *a spell on,* hechizar; *to* ~ *doubts on,* poner en duda; *to* ~ *suspicion on,* levantar sospechas sobre. ■ ~ *iron,* hierro colado; *plaster* ~, escayola. ▲ *pt & pp* cast.
castanets [kæstəˈnets] *npl* castañuelas *fpl.*
castaway ['kɑːstəweɪ] *n* náufrago,-a.
caste [kɑːst] *n* casta.
caster ['kɑːstəʳ] *n* ruedecilla. ■ ~ *sugar,* azúcar extrafino.
casting ['kɑːstɪŋ] *n* TECH (pieza de) fundición. **3** THEAT reparto de papeles. ■ ~ *vote,* voto de calidad.
castle ['kɑːsəl] *n* castillo. **2** *(chess)* torre *f.*
castor oil [kɑːstərˈɔɪl] *n* aceite *m* de ricino.
castrate [kæsˈtreɪt] *t* castrar, capar.
castration [kæsˈtreɪʃən] *n* castración.
casual ['kæʒjʊəl] *adj* fortuito,-a, casual. **2** *(clothes)* (de) sport. **3** *(not serious)* superficial. **4** *(worker)* ocasional. – **5** *casually adv* sin darle importancia.
casualty ['kæʒjʊəltɪ] *n* MIL baja. **2** *(of accident)* herido,-a. **3** *fig* víctima. ■ ~ *department,* departamento de traumatología.
cat [kæt] *n* gato,-a. ●*fam to let the* ~*out of the bag,* descubrir el pastel; *fam to put the* ~ *among the pigeons,* meter los perros en danza.
cataclysm ['kætəklɪzəm] *n* cataclismo.
catacomb ['kætəkuːm] *n* catacumba.
catalogue, US **catalog** ['kætəlɒg] *n* catálogo. – **2** *t* catalogar.
catalyst ['kætəlɪst] *n* catalizador *m.*
catapult ['kætəpʌlt] *n (weapon)* catapulta. **2** *(toy)* tirador *m.* – **3** *t* catapultar.
cataract ['kætərækt] *n (waterfall)* catarata, cascada. **2** MED catarata.
catarrh [kəˈtɑːʳ] *n* catarro.

catastrophe [kə'tæstrəfɪ] *n* catástrofe *f*.

catcall ['kætkɔ:l] *n* silbido.

catch [kætʃ] *n (of ball)* parada. **2** *(of fish)* captura. **3** *fam (trick)* pega. **4** *(fastener)* cierre *m*, pestillo. — **5** *t (gen)* coger; *(take, capture)* coger, atrapar. **6** *(fish)* pescar. **7** *(train etc.)* coger, tomar, AM agarrar. **8** *(surprise)* pillar, sorprender. **9** *(hear)* oír. — **10** *i (sleeve etc)* engancharse **(on,** en). ◆**to ~ on** *i* caer en la cuenta. **2** *(get the hang)* coger el truco. **3** *(become popular)* hacerse popular. ◆**to ~ out** *t* pillar, sorprender. ◆**to ~ up** *t* atrapar, alcanzar. **2** *(with news)* ponerse al día. ●**to ~ a cold,** coger un resfriado; **to ~ fire,** prender fuego, encenderse; **to ~ hold of,** agarrar, echar mano a; **to ~ sb.'s eye,** captar la atención de algn.; **to ~ sight of,** entrever. ▲ *pt & pp* **caught.**

catching ['kætʃɪŋ] *adj* contagioso,-a.

catchy ['kætʃɪ] *adj* pegadizo,-a.

catechism ['kætɪkɪzəm] *n* catecismo.

categoric(al) [kætɪ'gɒrɪk(əl)] *adj* categórico,-a.

category ['kætɪgərɪ] *n* categoría.

cater ['keɪtəʳ] *i (food)* proveer comida: **to ~ for sb.'s needs,** atender a las necesidades de algn.

caterer ['keɪtərəʳ] *n* proveedor,-ra.

caterpillar ['kætəpɪləʳ] *n* oruga.

cathedral [kə'θi:drəl] *n* catedral *f*.

Catholic ['kæθəlɪk] *adj-n* REL católico,-a.

Catholicism [kə'θɒlɪsɪzəm] *n* REL catolicismo.

catkin ['kætkɪn] *n* amento.

catnap ['kætnæp] *n* cabezadilla.

Catseye® ['kætsaɪ] *n* GB catafaro.

cattle ['kætəl] *n* ganado vacuno.

caught [kɔ:t] *pt & pp* → **catch.**

cauldron ['kɔ:ldrən] *n* caldero.

cauliflower ['kɒlɪflaʊəʳ] *n* coliflor *f*.

cause [kɔ:z] *n (gen)* causa. **2** *(reason)* razón *f*, motivo. — **3** *t* causar. ●**to ~ sb. to do sth.,** hacer que algn. haga algo.

caustic ['kɔ:stɪk] *adj* cáustico,-a.

cauterize ['kɔ:təraɪz] *t* cauterizar.

caution ['kɔ:ʃən] *n* cautela, precaución. **2** *(warning)* aviso, advertencia. — **3** *t* advertir, amonestar.

cautious ['kɔ:ʃəs] *adj* cauteloso,-a, prudente.

cautiousness ['kɔ:ʃəsnəs] *n* cautela, precaución, prudencia.

cavalier [kævə'lɪəʳ] *n* caballero. — **2** *adj* arrogante.

cavalry ['kævəlrɪ] *n* caballería.

cave [keɪv] *n* cueva. ◆**to ~ in** *i* hundirse, derrumbarse.

caveman ['keɪvmæn] *n* cavernícola *m*.

cavern ['kævən] *n* caverna.

caviar(e) ['kævɪɑ:ʳ] *n* caviar *m*.

cavity ['kævɪtɪ] *n* cavidad. **2** *(in tooth)* caries *f inv*.

caw [kɔ:] *n* graznido. — **2** *i* graznar.

cease [si:s] *i-t* cesar. ●MIL **to ~ fire,** cesar el fuego.

cease-fire [si:s'faɪəʳ] *n* alto el fuego.

ceaseless ['si:sləs] *adj* incesante.

cedar ['si:dəʳ] *n* cedro.

cede [si:d] *t* ceder.

ceiling ['si:lɪŋ] *n* techo. **2** *(limit)* tope *m*. ●*fam* **to hit the ~,** ponerse histérico,-a.

celebrate ['selɪbreɪt] *t-i* celebrar.

celebrated ['selɪbreɪtɪd] *adj* célebre.

celebration [selɪ'breɪʃən] *n* celebración. **2** *pl* festejos *mpl*.

celebrity [sɪ'lebrɪtɪ] *n* celebridad.

celery ['selərɪ] *n* apio.

celestial [sɪ'lestɪəl] *adj* celestial. **2** ASTRON celeste.

celibacy ['selɪbəsɪ] *n* celibato.

celibate ['selɪbət] *adj-n* célibe *(mf)*.

cell [sel] *n (prison etc.)* celda. **2** BIOL célula.

cellar ['seləʳ] *n* sótano. **2** *(for wine)* bodega.

cellist ['tʃelɪst] *n* violoncelista *mf*.

cello ['tʃeləʊ] *n* violoncelo.

cellophane® ['seləʊfeɪn] *n* celofán *m*.

celluloid ['seljʊlɔɪd] *n* celuloide *m*.

cellulose ['seljʊləʊs] *n* celulosa.

cement [sɪ'ment] *n* cemento. **2** *(concrete)* hormigón *m*. — **3** *t* unir con cemento. **4** *fig* cimentar. ■ **~ mixer,** hormigonera.

cemetery ['semɪtrɪ] *n* cementerio.

censor ['sensəʳ] *n* censor,-ra. — **2** *t* censurar.

censorship ['sensəʃɪp] *n* censura.

censure ['senʃəʳ] *n* censura. — **2** *t* censurar.

census ['sensəs] *n* censo, padrón *m*.

cent [sent] *n* centavo, céntimo. ●**per ~,** por ciento.

centenary [sen'ti:nərɪ], US **centennial** [sen'tenɪəl] *n* centenario.

centigrade ['sentɪgreɪd] *adj* centígrado,-a.

centimetre ['sentɪmi:təʳ] *n* centímetro.

centipede ['sentɪpi:d] *n* ciempiés *m inv*.

central ['sentrəl] *adj* central. ■ **~ heating,** calefacción central.

centralization [sentrəlaɪ'zeɪʃən] *n* centralización.

centralize ['sentrəlaız] *t* centralizar.
centre ['sentə'] *n* centro. − **2** *t* centrar.
■ SP ~ *forward*, delantero centro.
centrifugal [sentrı'fju:gəl] *adj* centrífugo,-a.
centurion [sen'tjuərıən] *n* centurión *m*.
century ['sentʃərı] *n* siglo.
ceramic [sı'ræmık] *adj* cerámico,-a. − **2** *npl* cerámica *f sing*.
cereal ['sıərıəl] *n* cereal *m*.
cerebral ['serıbrəl] *adj* cerebral.
ceremonial [serı'məunıəl] *adj* ceremonial.
ceremonious [serı'məunıəs] *adj* ceremonioso,-a, ceremoniero,-a.
ceremony ['serımənı] *n* ceremonia.
certain ['sɜ:tən] *adj (sure)* seguro,-a: *she's ~ to pass*, seguro que aprobará. **2** *(moderate)* cierto,-a. **3** *(unknown)* cierto,-a: *a ~ Mr Buck*, un tal Sr Buck. − **4** *certainly adv* desde luego, por supuesto; *certainly not*, por supuesto que no. ●*for ~*, con toda seguridad; *to a ~ extent*, hasta cierto punto; *to make ~ of*, asegurarse de.
certainty ['sɜ:təntı] *n* certeza. ●*it's a ~ that*, es seguro que.
certificate [sə'tıfıkət] *n gen* certificado. **2** EDUC diploma. ■ *birth ~*, partida de nacimiento; *death ~*, certificado de defunción.
certify ['sɜ:tıfaı] *t* certificar.
cervical ['sɜ:vıkəl] *adj (neck)* cervical. **2** *(uterus)* del útero.
cervix ['sɜ:vıks] *n (neck)* cerviz *f*, cuello. **2** *(uterus)* cuello del útero. ▲ *pl cervixes o cervices*.
cessation [se'seıʃən] *n* cese *m*.
cesspit ['sespıt] *n* pozo negro.
chafe [tʃeıf] *t* rozar, escoriar. − **2** *i* enfadarse *(at, por)*.
chaff [tʃæf] *n* barcia.
chaffinch ['tʃæfıntʃ] *n* pinzón *m*.
chain [tʃeın] *n* cadena. **2** *(mountains)* cordillera. **3** *fig* serie *f*. − **4** *t* encadenar.
chair [tʃeə'] *n* silla. **2** *(with arms)* sillón *m*. **3** *(position)* presidencia. **4** *(university)* cátedra. − **5** *t* presidir.
chairman ['tʃeəmən] *n* presidente *m*.
chairmanship ['tʃeəmənʃıp] *n* presidencia.
chairperson ['tʃeəpɜ:sən] *n* presidente,-a *m,f*.
chairwoman ['tʃeəwumən] *n* presidenta.
chalet ['ʃæleı] *n* chalet *m*, chalé *m*.
chalice ['tʃælıs] *n* cáliz *m*.

chalk [tʃɔ:k] *n* creta. **2** *(for writing)* tiza. ◆*to ~ up* *t fam* apuntarse.
challenge ['tʃælındʒ] *n* reto, desafío. − **2** *t* retar, desafiar. **3** MIL dar el alto a. **4** JUR recusar.
challenger ['tʃælındʒə'] *n* SP aspirante *mf* (a un título).
chamber ['tʃeımbə'] *n* cámara. **2** *(of gun)* recámara. ■ ~ *music*, música de cámara.
chambermaid ['tʃeımbəmeıd] *n* camarera.
chamberpot ['tʃeımbəpɒt] *n* orinal *m*.
chameleon [kə'mi:lıən] *n* camaleón *m*.
champagne [ʃæm'peın] *n* champán *m*; *(Catalan)* cava *m*.
champion ['tʃæmpıən] *n* campeón,-ona. **2** *fig (defender)* defensor,-ra. − **3** *t fig* defender.
championship ['tʃæmpıənʃıp] *n* campeonato.
chance [tʃɑ:ns] *n (fate)* azar *m*. **2** *(opportunity)* oportunidad. **3** *(possibility)* posibilidad. **4** *(risk)* riesgo. − **5** *adj* fortuito,-a. − **6** *t* arriesgar. ●*by ~*, por casualidad; *on the (off) ~*, por si acaso; *to ~ on sth.*, encontrar algo por casualidad; *to ~ to do sth.*, hacer algo por casualidad; *to have a good ~ of doing sth.*, tener buenas posibilidades de hacer algo.
chancellor ['tʃɑ:nsələ'] *n* canciller *m*. **2** GB *(of university)* rector,-ra. ■ GB *Chancellor of the Exchequer*, ministro,-a de Hacienda.
chancy ['tʃɑ:nsı] *adj fam* arriesgado,-a.
chandelier [ʃændı'lıə'] *n* araña (de luces).
change [tʃeındʒ] *n* cambio. **2** *(money)* cambio, vuelta. − **3** *t* cambiar (de). − **4** *i* cambiar(se). ●*for a ~*, para variar; *to ~ one's mind/the subject*, cambiar de opinión/de tema; *to ~ clothes, to get changed*, cambiarse (de ropa); *to ~ into*, convertirse/transformarse en; *fig to ~ hands*, cambiar de dueño. ■ ~ *of clothes*, muda de ropa; ~ *of heart*, cambio de parecer.
changeable ['tʃeındʒəbəl] *adj (weather)* variable. **2** *(person)* inconstante.
changing ['tʃeındʒıŋ] *adj* cambiante. ■ ~ *room*, vestuario.
channel ['tʃænəl] *n* GEOG canal *m*. **2** RAD TV canal, cadena. − **3** *t* canalizar, encauzar. ●*through the official channels*, por los conductos oficiales. ■ *English Channel*, Canal de la Mancha.

chant [tʃɑːnt] *n* REL canto litúrgico. 2 *(of crowd)* eslogan *m*. − 3 *t-i* REL cantar. 4 *(crowd)* corear.

chaos ['keɪɒs] *n* caos *m*.

chaotic [keɪ'ɒtɪk] *adj* caótico,-a.

chap [tʃæp] *n fam* tío.

chapel ['tʃæpəl] *n* capilla.

chaperon(e) ['ʃæpərəʊn] *n* carabina. − 2 *t* hacer de carabina a.

chaplain ['tʃæplɪn] *n* capellán *m*.

chapter ['tʃæptər] *n (in book)* capítulo. 2 REL cabildo.

char [tʃɑːr] *n* GB *fam* asistenta. − 2 *t (burn)* carbonizar.

character ['kærɪktər] *n* carácter *m*. 2 THEAT personaje *m*. 3 *fam* tipo. 4 *(letter)* carácter.

characteristic [kærɪktə'rɪstɪk] *adj-n* característico,-a *(f)*.

characterize ['kærɪktəraɪz] *t* caracterizar.

charade [ʃə'rɑːd] *n (farce)* farsa. 2 *pl (game)* charadas *fpl*.

charcoal ['tʃɑːkəʊl] *n* carbón *m* de leña. 2 ART carboncillo.

charge [tʃɑːdʒ] *n (price)* precio, coste *m*. 2 *(responsibility)* cargo. 3 JUR cargo. 4 MIL carga, ataque *m*. 5 *(explosive)* carga explosiva. 6 ELEC carga. − 7 *t* cobrar. 8 JUR acusar (**with**, de). 9 ELEC cargar. 10 MIL cargar contra, atacar. − 11 *i* ELEC cargar. 12 MIL cargar, atacar. ●*to be in ~ of,* estar a cargo de; *to bring a ~ against sb.,* formular una acusación contra algn.; *to ~ sb. with murder,* acusar a algn. de asesinato; *to take ~ of,* hacerse cargo de.

charger ['tʃɑːdʒər] *n* ELEC cargador *m*. 2 *(horse)* corcel *m*.

chariot ['tʃærɪət] *n* carro (de guerra).

charisma [kə'rɪzmə] *n* carisma *m*.

charismatic [kærɪz'mætɪk] *adj* carismático,-a.

charitable ['tʃærɪtəbəl] *adj (person)* caritativo,-a. 2 *(organization)* benéfico,-a.

charity ['tʃærɪtɪ] *n* caridad. 2 *(organization)* institución benéfica.

charlatan ['ʃɑːlətən] *n* charlatán,-ana.

charm [tʃɑːm] *n* encanto. 2 *(object)* amuleto. 3 *(spell)* hechizo. − 4 *t* encantar. ●*to work like a ~,* funcionar a las mil maravillas.

charming ['tʃɑːmɪŋ] *adj* encantador,-ra.

chart [tʃɑːt] *n* tabla; *(graph)* gráfico. 2 MAR carta de marear. 3 MUS *the charts,* la lista de éxitos. − 4 *t (make a map of)* hacer un mapa de; *fig this book charts*

her rise to fame, este libro describe su ascenso a la fama.

charter ['tʃɑːtər] *n* carta. − 2 *t (plane etc.)* fletar. ■ ~ *flight,* vuelo chárter.

charwoman ['tʃɑːwʊmən] *n* asistenta.

chary ['tʃeərɪ] *adj fam* cauteloso,-a, cauto,-a.

chase [tʃeɪs] *n* persecución. − 2 *t* perseguir.

chasm ['kæzəm] *n* GEOG sima. 2 *fig* abismo.

chassis ['ʃæsɪ] *n* chasis *m inv*.

chaste [tʃeɪst] *adj* casto,-a.

chasten ['tʃeɪsən], **chastise** [tʃæs'taɪz] *t* castigar.

chastisement ['tʃæstɪzmənt] *n* castigo, corrección.

chastity ['tʃæstɪtɪ] *n* castidad.

chat [tʃæt] *n* charla. − 2 *i* charlar. ◆*to ~ up t fam* (intentar) ligar con.

chatter ['tʃætər] *n* cháchara, parloteo. 2 *(of teeth)* castañeteo. − 3 *i* chacharear, parlotear. 4 *(teeth)* castañetear.

chatterbox ['tʃætəbɒks] *n* parlanchín,-ina.

chatty ['tʃætɪ] *adj* hablador,-ra, parlanchín,-ina.

chauffeur ['ʃəʊfər] *n* chófer *m*.

chauvinism ['ʃəʊvɪnɪzəm] *n* chovinismo. ■ *male ~,* machismo.

chauvinist ['ʃəʊvɪnɪst] *adj-n* chovinista *(mf)*. ■ *male ~,* machista *m*.

cheap [tʃiːp] *adj* barato,-a, económico,-a. 2 *(contemptible)* vil, bajo,-a. ●*fig to feel ~,* sentir vergüenza.

cheapen ['tʃiːpən] *t* abaratar. 2 *fig* degradar.

cheapness ['tʃiːpnəs] *n* baratura.

cheat [tʃiːt] *n* tramposo,-a. − 2 *t* engañar. − 3 *i* hacer trampa.

check [tʃek] *n* comprobación, verificación. 2 US → **cheque.** 3 US *(bill)* nota. 4 *(chess)* jaque *m*. 5 *(pattern)* cuadro: *a ~ shirt,* una camisa a cuadros. − 6 *t* comprobar, revisar, verificar. 7 *(stop)* detener. 8 *(hold back)* contener, refrenar. 9 *(chess)* dar jaque a. ●*to keep in ~,* contener.

checkbook ['tʃekbʊk] *n* talonario (de cheques).

checkers ['tʃekəz] *npl* damas *fpl*.

checkmate ['tʃek'meɪt] *n* mate *m*. − 2 *t* dar mate a.

checkup ['tʃekʌp] *n* chequeo, reconocimiento.

cheek [tʃiːk] *n* ANAT mejilla. 2 *fig* descaro.

cheekbone ['tʃiːkbəʊn] *n* pómulo.

cheeky ['tʃiːkɪ] *n* descarado,-a.
cheep ['tʃiːp] *n* pío. – **2** *i* piar.
cheer [tʃɪəʳ] *n* viva *m*, vítor *m*. – **2** *t-i* vitorear, aclamar. ◆*to* ～ *up* *t-i* animar(se), alegrar(se).
cheers [tʃɪəz] *interj* ¡salud! **2** *(thanks)* ¡gracias!
cheerful ['tʃɪəfʊl] *adj* alegre.
cheese [tʃiːz] *n* queso.
cheesecake ['tʃiːzkeɪk] *n* tarta de queso.
cheesecloth ['tʃiːzklɒθ] *n* estopilla.
cheesed off [tʃiːzd'ɒf] *adj* GB *fam* harto,-a.
cheetah ['tʃiːtə] *n* guepardo.
chef [ʃef] *n* chef *m*, cocinero.
chemical ['kemɪkəl] *adj* químico,-a. – **2** *n* producto químico.
chemist ['kemɪst] *n* químico,-a. **2** GB farmacéutico,-a. ■ *chemist's (shop),* farmacia.
chemistry ['kemɪstrɪ] *n* química.
cheque [tʃek] *n* cheque *m*, talón *m*. ■ ～ *book,* talonario (de cheques).
chequered ['tʃekəd] *adj (cloth)* a cuadros. **2** *fig* con altibajos.
cherish ['tʃerɪʃ] *t* apreciar, querer. **2** *(hope)* abrigar.
cherry ['tʃerɪ] *n* cereza. ■ ～ *tree,* cerezo.
cherub ['tʃerəb] *n* querubín *m*. ▲ *pl cherubs o cherubim.*
chess [tʃes] *n* ajedrez *m*.
chesspiece ['tʃespiːs] *n* pieza de ajedrez.
chessboard ['tʃesbɔːd] *n* tablero de ajedrez.
chessmen ['tʃesmən] *npl* piezas *fpl* de ajedrez.
chest [tʃest] *n* cofre *m*, arca. **2** ANAT pecho. ●*to get sth. off one's* ～, desahogarse. ■ ～ *of drawers* cómoda.
chestnut ['tʃesnʌt] *n* BOT *(nut)* castaña. – **2** *adj-n* castaño,-a *(m)*. **3** *(horse)* alazán,-ana. ■ ～ *tree,* castaño.
chew [tʃuː] *t* mascar, masticar. ●*to* ～ *sth. over,* darle vueltas a algo.
chewing gum ['tʃuːɪŋɡʌm] *n* goma de mascar.
chewy ['tʃuːɪ] *adj* correoso,-a.
chic [ʃiːk] *adj* elegante.
chick [tʃɪk] *n* polluelo.
chicken ['tʃɪkɪn] *n* pollo. **2** *fam (coward)* gallina *mf*. – **3** *adj fam* gallina. ◆*to* ～ *out i fam* rajarse.
chickenpox ['tʃɪkɪnpɒks] *n* varicela.
chickpea ['tʃɪkpiː] *n* garbanzo.
chicory ['tʃɪkərɪ] *n* achicoria.

chief [tʃiːf] *n* jefe *m*. – **2** *adj* principal. – **3** *chiefly adv* principalmente, mayormente. **4** *(especially)* sobre todo.
chieftain ['tʃiːftən] *n* cacique *m*.
chiffon ['ʃɪfɒn] *n* gasa.
chihuahua [tʃɪ'wɑːwə] *n* chihuahua *m*.
chilblain ['tʃɪlbleɪn] *n* sabañón *m*.
child [tʃaɪld] *n* niño,-a. **2** *(son)* hijo; *(daughter)* hija. ▲ *pl children.*
childbirth ['tʃaɪldbɜːθ] *n* parto.
childhood ['tʃaɪldhʊd] *n* infancia, niñez *f*.
childish ['tʃaɪldɪʃ] *adj* pueril, inmaduro,-a.
childlike ['tʃaɪldlaɪk] *adj* infantil, inocente.
children ['tʃɪldrən] *npl* → **child.**
chill [tʃɪl] *n* MED resfriado. **2** *(coldness)* frío. – **3** *adj* frío,-a. – **4** *t (wine)* enfriar.
chilly ['tʃɪlɪ] *adj* frío,-a. ●*to feel* ～, tener frío.
chime [tʃaɪm] *n* carillón *m*. – **2** *i (bells)* tocar. **3** *(clock)* dar.
chimney ['tʃɪmnɪ] *n* chimenea. ■ ～ *sweep,* deshollinador *m*.
chimpanzee [tʃɪmpæn'ziː] *n* chimpancé *m*.
chin [tʃɪn] *n* barbilla, mentón *m*.
china ['tʃaɪnə] *n* loza, porcelana.
chink [tʃɪŋk] *n (crack)* grieta. **2** *(noise)* tintineo. – **3** *t-i* tintinear.
chip [tʃɪp] *n* CULIN patata frita. **2** COMPUT chip *m*. **3** *(of wood)* astilla. **4** *(of stone)* lasca. **5** *(in plate, glass)* desportilladura. **6** *(in casino)* ficha. – **7** *t-i (wood)* astillar(se). **8** *(stone)* resquebrajar(se). **9** *(plate, glass)* desportillar(se). **10** *(paint)* descascarillar(se).
chiropodist [kɪ'rɒpədɪst] *n* podólogo,-a, pedicuro,-a.
chirp [tʃɜːp] *i (insect)* chirriar. **2** *(bird)* gorjear.
chisel ['tʃɪzəl] *n (for wood)* formón *m*, escoplo. **2** *(for stone etc)* cincel *m*. – **3** *t (wood)* escoplar. **4** *(stone)* cincelar.
chit [tʃɪt] *n* nota.
chitchat ['tʃɪttʃæt] *n fam* palique *m*.
chivalrous ['ʃɪvəlrəs] *adj* caballeroso,-a.
chivalry ['ʃɪvəlrɪ] *n* caballerosidad.
chloride ['klɔːraɪd] *n* cloruro.
chlorine ['klɔːriːn] *n* cloro.
chloroform ['klɒrəfɔːm] *n* cloroformo.
chock [tʃɒk] *n* calzo, cuña.
chock-a-block [tʃɒkə'blɒk], **chock-full** [tʃɒk'fʊl] *adj fam* hasta los topes.
chocolate ['tʃɒkələt] *n* chocolate *m*. **2** *pl* bombones *mpl*.

choice [tʃɔɪs] *n* selección. 2 *(option)* opción, alternativa. — 3 *adj* selecto,-a. ●*to make a ~,* escoger.

choir ['kwaɪəʳ] *n* coro.

choke [tʃəʊk] *t-i* ahogar(se), sofocar(se). — 2 *t (block)* atascar. — 3 *n* AUTO stárter *m.* ●*to ~ back t* contener.

cholera ['kɒlərə] *n* cólera *m.*

choose [tʃu:z] *t* escoger, elegir. 2 *(decide)* decidir. ●*there's not much to ~ between them,* son muy parecidos,-as. ▲ *pt chose; pp chosen.*

choos(e)y ['tʃu:zɪ] *adj fam* exigente.

chop [tʃɒp] *n* golpe *m.* 2 CULIN chuleta. — 3 *t* cortar. ●*to ~ down t* talar. ●*to ~ up t* cortar en trozos. 2 CULIN picar. ●*fam to get the ~,* ser despedido,-a (de un trabajo).

choppy ['tʃɒpɪ] *adj (sea)* picado,-a.

choral ['kɔ:rəl] *adj* coral.

chord [kɔ:d] *n* MATH cuerda. 2 MUS acorde *m.*

chore [tʃɔ:ʳ] *n* quehacer *m.*

chorus ['kɔ:rəs] *n* coro. 2 *(of song)* estribillo.

chose [tʃəʊz] *pt →* **choose.**

chosen ['tʃəʊzən] *pp →* **choose.**

Christ [kraɪst] *n* Cristo.

christen ['krɪsən] *t* bautizar.

christening ['krɪsənɪŋ] *n* bautizo.

Christian ['krɪstɪən] *adj-n* cristiano,-a. ■ *~ name,* nombre *m* de pila.

Christmas ['krɪsməs] *n* Navidad. ■ *~ card,* tarjeta de navidad, christmas *m; ~ carol,* villancico; *~ Eve,* Nochebuena.

chrome [krəʊm], **chromium** ['krəʊmɪəm] *n* cromo.

chronic ['krɒnɪk] *adj* crónico,-a.

chronicle ['krɒnɪkəl] *n* crónica. — 2 *t* narrar.

chronological [krɒnə'lɒdʒɪkəl] *adj* cronológico,-a.

chronology [krə'nɒlədʒɪ] *n* cronología.

chrysalis ['krɪsəlɪs] *n* crisálida.

chrysanthemum [krɪ'sænθəməm] *n* crisantemo.

chubby ['tʃʌbɪ] *adj* regordete.

chuck [tʃʌk] *n (of drill)* portabrocas *m inv.* — 2 *t (throw)* tirar. ●*to ~ out t (person)* echar. 2 *(thing)* tirar.

chuckle ['tʃʌkəl] *i* reír en silencio. — 2 *n* risita.

chum [tʃʌm] *n fam* compinche *mf.*

chunk [tʃʌŋk] *n fam* cacho, pedazo.

church [tʃ3:tʃ] *n* iglesia.

churchgoer ['tʃ3:tʃgəʊəʳ] *n* practicante *mf.*

churchyard ['tʃ3:tʃja:d] *n* cementerio.

churlish ['tʃ3:lɪʃ] *adj* rudo,-a.

churn [tʃ3:n] *n* GB *(for milk)* lechera. 2 *(for butter)* mantequera. — 3 *i (stomach)* revolverse. ●*to ~ out t* producir en serie.

chute [ʃu:t] *n* tobogán *m.*

cider ['saɪdəʳ] *n* sidra.

cig [sɪg] *n fam* pitillo.

cigar [sɪ'gɑ:ʳ] *n* (cigarro) puro.

cigarette [sɪgə'ret] *n* cigarrillo. ■ *~ case,* pitillera; *~ holder,* boquilla; *~ lighter,* encendedor *m.*

cinch [sɪntʃ] *n fam* it's *a ~,* está chupado.

cinder ['sɪndəʳ] *n* ceniza.

cinema ['sɪnɪmə] *n* cine *m.*

cinnamon ['sɪnəmən] *n* canela.

cipher ['saɪfəʳ] *n* código.

circle ['s3:kəl] *n* círculo. 2 THEAT piso. — 3 *t* rodear. — 4 *i* dar vueltas. ●*fig to come full ~,* completar un ciclo; *to go round in circles,* dar vueltas.

circuit ['s3:kɪt] *n* circuito. 2 *(of track)* vuelta.

circuitous [sə'kju:ɪtəs] *adj* tortuoso,-a, indirecto,-a.

circular ['s3:kjʊləʳ] *adj-n* circular *(f).*

circulate ['s3:kjʊleɪt] *i* circular. — 2 *t* hacer circular.

circulation [s3:kjʊ'leɪʃən] *n* circulación. 2 *(newspaper)* tirada.

circumcise ['s3:kəmsaɪz] *t* circuncidar.

circumcision [s3:kəm'sɪʒən] *n* circuncisión.

circumference [sə'kʌmfərəns] *n* circunferencia.

circumflex ['s3:kəmfleks] *adj* circunflejo,-a.

circumlocution [s3:kəmlə'kju:ʃən] *n* circunloquio.

circumscribe ['s3:kəmskraɪb] *t* circunscribir.

circumspect ['s3:kəmspekt] *adj* circunspecto,-a, prudente.

circumstance ['s3:kəmstəns] *n* circunstancia. ●*in/under no circumstances,* en ningún caso, bajo ningún concepto.

circumstantial [s3:kəm'stænʃəl] *adj* circunstancial.

circumvent [s3:kəm'vent] *t* burlar, evitar.

circus ['s3:kəs] *n* circo. 2 GB *(junction)* plaza redonda.

cirrhosis [sɪ'rəʊsɪs] *n* cirrosis *f inv.*

cistern ['sɪstən] *n* cisterna.

citadel ['sɪtədəl] *n* ciudadela.

cite [saɪt] *t* citar.

citizen ['sɪtɪzən] *n* ciudadano,-a.

citizenship ['sɪtɪzənʃɪp] *n* ciudadanía.
citric ['sɪtrɪk] *adj* cítrico,-a.
citrus fruits ['sɪtrəsfruːts] *npl* agrios *mpl*.
city ['sɪtɪ] *n* ciudad. ■ *the City*, el centro financiero de Londres.
civic ['sɪvɪk] *adj* cívico,-a.
civics ['sɪvɪks] *n* educación cívica.
civil ['sɪvəl] *adj* civil. 2 *(polite)* cortés. ■ ~. *law,* derecho civil; ~ *rights,* derechos *mpl* civiles; ~ *servant,* funcionario,-a; ~ *service,* administración pública; ~ *war,* guerra civil.
civilian [sɪ'vɪljən] *adj-n* civil *(mf)*.
civility [sɪ'vɪlɪtɪ] *n* cortesía.
civilization [sɪvɪlaɪ'zeɪʃən] *n* civilización.
civilize ['sɪvɪlaɪz] *t* civilizar.
clad [klæd] *pt & pp* → **clothe**. – 2 *adj* vestido,-a.
claim [kleɪm] *n (assertion)* afirmación. 2 *(demand)* reclamación. 3 *(right)* derecho. – 4 *t (assert)* afirmar, sostener. 5 *(property, right, etc.)* reclamar. ●*to lay* ~ *to,* reclamar el derecho a.
claimant ['kleɪmənt] *n* reclamante *mf*. 2 JUR demandante *mf*.
clairvoyance [kleə'vɔɪəns] *n* clarividencia.
clairvoyant [kleə'vɔɪənt] *adj-n* clarividente *(mf)*.
clam [klæm] *n* almeja. ◆*to* ~ *up* i *fam* callarse.
clamber ['klæmbəʳ] *i* trepar.
clammy ['klæmɪ] *adj (weather)* bochornoso,-a. 2 *(hand)* pegajoso,-a.
clamour ['klæməʳ] *n* clamor *m*, griterío. – 2 *i* clamar: *to* ~ *for sth.,* pedir algo a gritos.
clamp [klæmp] *n* abrazadera. – 2 *t* sujetar. ◆*to* ~ *down on* t dirigir una campaña contra. ■ *wheel* ~, cepo.
clampdown ['klæmpdaʊn] *n* campaña en contra.
clan [klæn] *n* clan *m*.
clandestine [klæn'destɪn] *adj* clandestino,-a.
clang [klæŋ] *n* sonido metálico fuerte. – 2 *i* sonar. – 3 *t* hacer sonar.
clanger ['klæŋəʳ] *n fam* metedura *f* de pata, plancha. ●*to drop a* ~, meter la pata, hacer una plancha.
clank [klæŋk] *n* sonido metálico seco. – 2 *i* sonar. – 3 *t* hacer sonar.
clap [klæp] *n (noise)* ruido seco: *a* ~ *of thunder,* un trueno. 2 *(applause)* aplauso. 3 *(tap)* palmada. – 4 *t-i (applaud)* aplaudir. ●*to* ~ *eyes on,* ver; *to* ~ *one's hands,* dar una palmada; *to* ~ *sb. on the*

back, dar una palmada en la espalda a algn.
clapper ['klæpəʳ] *n* badajo.
clapping ['klæpɪŋ] *n* aplausos *mpl*.
claptrap ['klæptræp] *n fam* disparates *mpl*.
clarification [klærɪfɪ'keɪʃən] *n* aclaración, clarificación.
clarify ['klærɪfaɪ] *t-i* aclarar(se), clarificar(se).
clarinet [klærɪ'net] *n* clarinete *m*.
clarity ['klærɪtɪ] *n* claridad.
clash [klæʃ] *n (fight)* choque *m*. 2 *(conflict)* conflicto. 3 *(noise)* estruendo. – 4 *i (opposing forces)* chocar. 5 *(dates)* coincidir. 6 *(colours)* desentonar. 7 *(cymbals)* sonar.
clasp [klɑːsp] *n (on jewellery)* broche *m* (de cierre). 2 *(on belt)* hebilla. 3 *(grasp)* apretón *m*. – 4 *t* asir, agarrar.
class [klɑːs] *n gen* clase *f*. – 2 *t* clasificar.
classic ['klæsɪk] *adj-n* clásico,-a *(m)*.
classical ['klæsɪkəl] *adj* clásico,-a.
classification [klæsɪfɪ'keɪʃən] *n* clasificación.
classified ['klæsɪfaɪd] *adj* clasificado,-a. 2 *(secret)* secreto,-a. ■ ~ *advertisements,* anuncios *mpl* por palabras.
classify ['klæsɪfaɪ] *t* clasificar.
classmate ['klɑːsmeɪt] *n* compañero,-a de clase.
classroom ['klɑːsrʊm] *n* aula, clase *f*.
classy ['klɑːsɪ] *adj sl* con clase.
clatter ['klætəʳ] *n* ruido, estrépito. – 2 *i* hacer ruido.
clause [klɔːz] *n* cláusula. 2 GRAM frase *f*.
claustrophobia [klɔːstrə'fəʊbɪə] *n* claustrofobia.
claustrophobic [klɔːstrə'fəʊbɪk] *adj (person)* que padece claustrofobia. 2 *(place)* claustrofóbico,-a, que produce claustrofobia.
clavicle ['klævɪkəl] *n* clavícula.
claw [klɔː] *n (of bird, large animal)* garra. 2 *(of cat)* uña. 3 *(of crab)* pinza. – 4 *t* arañar.
clay [kleɪ] *n* arcilla.
clean [kliːn] *adj* limpio,-a. – 2 *t* limpiar. ◆*to* ~ *out* t limpiar a fondo. 2 *fam* dejar sin blanca a. ◆*to* ~ *up* t limpiar.
clean-cut [kliːn'kʌt] *adj* definido,-a, nítido,-a.
cleaner ['kliːnəʳ] *n (person)* encargado,-a de la limpieza. 2 *(product)* limpiador *m*.
cleaner's ['kliːnəz] *n* tintorería. ●*to take sb. to the* ~, dejar a algn sin blanca.
cleanliness ['klenlɪnəs] *n* limpieza, aseo.

cleanly ['klenlɪ] *adj* limpio,-a, aseado,-a.
− 2 *adv* limpiamente. ▲ *En* 2 ['kli:nlɪ].

cleanse [klenz] *t* limpiar.

clear [klɪərʳ] *adj (glass etc.)* transparente. 2
(sky, road, view, etc.) despejado,-a. 3
(writing, voice) claro,-a. 4 *(television picture)* nítido,-a. 5 *(thinking, mind)* lúcido,-a. 6 *(obvious)* claro,-a, patente. − 7
t-i (room, desk, etc.) despejar(se), va-
ciar(se). 8 *(pipe)* desatascar(se). − 9 *t (table after a meal)* levantar. 10 *(accused
person)* absolver. 11 *(plans etc.)* aprobar.
12 *(debt)* liquidar. 13 *(obstacle)* salvar. −
14 *i (fog, clouds, smoke)* despejarse. 15
clearly adv claramente, con claridad. 16
(obviously) evidentemente, obviamente.
◆*to ~ away t* quitar. ◆*to ~ off i fam*
largarse. ◆*to ~ out i* largarse. − 2 *t
(room etc.)* vaciar. 3 *(old things)* tirar. ◆*to
~ up t (solve)* aclarar. 2 *(tidy)* ordenar. −
3 *i (weather)* mejorar. ●*to be ~ about
sth.,* tener algo claro; *to ~ one's throat,*
aclararse la garganta; *to have a ~ conscience,* tener la conciencia limpia; *to
make o.s. ~,* explicarse (con claridad);
fam in the ~, (danger) fuera de peligro;
(suspicion) fuera de toda sospecha.

clearance ['klɪərəns] *n (of area)* despejo
m. 2 *(space)* espacio libre. 3 *(permission)*
permiso, autorización. ■ COM *~ sale,* liquidación.

clear-cut [klɪə'kʌt] *adj* bien definido,-a.

clear-headed ['klɪə'hedɪd] *adj* lúcido,-a.

clearing ['klɪərɪŋ] *n (in wood)* claro.

clearness ['klɪənəs] *n* claridad.

clear-sighted [klɪə'saɪtɪd] *adj* clarividente, perspicaz.

cleavage ['kli:vɪdʒ] *n fam (in dress)* escote
m.

cleave [kli:v] *t* hender, partir. ▲ *pt cleft o
cleaved o clove; pp cleft o cleaved o cloven.*

clef [klef] *n* MUS clave *f.*

cleft [kleft] *pt & pp* → **cleave.** − 2 *adj*
hendido,-a. − 3 *n* hendidura.

clemency ['klemənsɪ] *n* clemencia.

clement ['klemənt] *adj (weather)* suave.

clench [klentʃ] *t* agarrar. 2 *(teeth, fist)*
apretar.

clergy ['kle:dʒɪ] *n* clero.

clergyman ['kle:dʒɪmən] *n* clérigo, eclesiástico.

clerical ['klerɪkəl] *adj* REL eclesiástico,-a.
2 *(to do with clerks)* de oficinista.

clerk [klɑ:k, US kle:rk] *n* oficinista *mf.* 2
US *(in shop)* dependiente *mf.* ■ *~ of the
court,* secretario,-a de juez; *town ~,* secretario,-a del ayuntamiento.

clever ['klevəʳ] *adj (person)* listo,-a, espabilado,-a. 2 *(idea)* ingenioso,-a. ■ ~
Dick, sabelotodo *mf.*

cleverness ['klevənəs] *n* inteligencia. 2
(skill) destreza, habilidad.

cliché ['kli:ʃeɪ] *n* cliché *m.*

click [klɪk] *n* clic *m.* 2 *(with tongue)* chasquido. − 3 *t (tongue)* chasquear. − 4 *i
(make noise)* hacer clic. 5 *(realize)* caer en
la cuenta. 6 *(be successful)* tener éxito.

client ['klaɪənt] *n* cliente *mf,* clienta.

cliff [klɪf] *n* acantilado.

cliffhanger ['klɪfhæŋəʳ] *n* película/histo-
ria etc. de suspense.

climactic [klaɪ'mæktɪk] *adj* culminante.

climate ['klaɪmət] *n* clima *m.*

climatic [klaɪ'mætɪk] *adj* climático,-a.

climax ['klaɪmæks] *n* clímax *m,* punto
culminante. 2 *(orgasm)* orgasmo. − 3 *i*
culminar.

climb [klaɪm] *n* subida, ascenso. − 2 *t* subir. 3 *(tree)* trepar a. 4 SP escalar. − 5 *i*
subirse. 6 *(plant)* trepar. ◆*to ~ down i*
bajarse. 2 *fig* volverse atrás.

climber ['klaɪməʳ] *n* SP alpinista *mf,* escalador,-ra. ■ *social ~,* arribista *mf.*

clinch [klɪntʃ] *fam n* abrazo. − 2 *t (deal)*
cerrar.

cling [klɪŋ] *i* asirse *(to,* a), aferrarse *(to,* a).
▲ *pt & pp clung.*

clinic ['klɪnɪk] *n* clínica. 2 *(part of hospital)*
ambulatorio.

clinical ['klɪnɪkəl] *adj* clínico,-a.

clink [klɪŋk] *n (noise)* tintineo. 2 *sl (prison)*
chirona. − 3 *i-t* (hacer) tintinear.

clip [klɪp] *n* clip *m.* 2 *(for hair)* pasador *m.*
3 *(of film)* clip. 4 *fam (blow)* cachete *m.*
− 5 *t (cut)* cortar. 6 *(sheep)* esquilar. 7
fam (hit) dar un cachete a.

clipper ['klɪpəʳ] *n* clíper *m.*

clippers ['klɪpəz] *npl (for nails)* cortauñas
m inv.

clipping ['klɪpɪŋ] *n* recorte *m* de periódico.

clique [kli:k] *n* camarilla, pandilla.

clitoris ['klɪtərɪs] *n* clítoris *m inv.*

cloak [kləʊk] *n* capa. − 2 *t* encubrir.

cloakroom ['kləʊkrʊm] *n* guardarropa. 2
GB *(toilet)* servicios *mpl.*

clock [klɒk] *n* reloj *m* (de pared). 2 AUTO
fam cuentakilómetros *m inv.* ◆*to ~ on
i* fichar (a la entrada). ◆*to ~ off i* fichar
(a la salida). ◆*to ~ up t (miles)* hacer.
●*against the ~,* contra reloj; *round the
~,* día y noche; *to put the ~ back/for-
ward,* atrasar/adelantar el reloj.

clockwise ['klɒkwaɪz] *adj-adv* en el sentido de las agujas del reloj.
clockwork ['klɒkwɜːk] *n* mecanismo de relojería. ●*like ~,* como una seda.
clod [klɒd] *n* terrón *m.*
clog [klɒg] *n* zueco. − 2 *t-i* obstruir(se).
cloister ['klɔɪstə*ʳ*] *n* claustro.
close [kləʊz] *n (end)* fin *m,* conclusión. − 2 *t-i* cerrar(se). − 3 *adj (near)* cercano,-a. 4 *(stuffy)* cargado,-a. 5 *(weather)* bochornoso,-a. 6 *(friend)* íntimo,-a. 7 *(relative)* cercano,-a. 8 *(detailed)* detallado,-a. 9 *(secretive)* reservado,-a. − 10 *adv* cerca. − 11 *closely adv* estrechamente. 12 *(attentively)* de cerca: *to follow sth. closely,* seguir algo de cerca. ◆*to ~ down t-i* cerrar(se) definitivamente. ◆*to ~ in i (days)* acortarse. 2 *(night)* caer. ◆*to bring to a ~,* concluir; *to ~ ranks,* cerrar filas; *to draw to a ~,* tocar a su fin; *to keep a ~ watch on,* vigilar estrechamente. ■ *~ season,* época de veda.
closed [kləʊzd] *adj* cerrado,-a. ■ *~ circuit television,* circuito cerrado de televisión.
close-fitting [kləʊs'fɪtɪŋ] *adj* ceñido,-a.
close-knit [kləʊs'nɪt] *adj* unido,-a.
closeness ['kləʊsnəs] *n (nearness)* proximidad.
closet ['klɒzɪt] *n* US armario.
close-up ['kləʊsʌp] *n* primer plano.
closing ['kləʊzɪŋ] *n* cierre *m.* ■ *~ ceremony,* acto de clausura; *~ time,* hora de cerrar.
closure ['kləʊʒə*ʳ*] *n* cierre *m.*
clot [klɒt] *n (of blood)* coágulo. 2 GB *fam* tonto,-a. − 3 *t-i* coagular(se).
cloth [klɒθ] *n (fabric)* tela. 2 *(rag)* trapo.
clothe [kləʊð] *t* vestir. ▲ *pt & pp clothed o clad.*
clothes [kləʊðz] *npl* ropa *f sing.* ●*in plain ~,* de paisano,-a. ■ *~ hanger,* percha; *~ line,* tendedero; *~ peg,* pinza.
clothing ['kləʊðɪŋ] *n* ropa.
cloud [klaʊd] *n* nube *f.* ◆*to ~ over i* nublarse. ●*every ~ has a silver lining,* no hay mal que por bien no venga; *under a ~,* bajo sospecha.
cloudburst ['klaʊdbɜːst] *n* aguacero.
cloudy ['klaʊdɪ] *adj (sky)* nublado,-a. 2 *(liquid)* turbio,-a.
clout [klaʊt] *fam n* tortazo. 2 *(influence)* influencia. − 3 *t* dar un tortazo a.
clove [kləʊv] *pt →* **cleave.** − 2 *n (spice)* clavo. 3 *(of garlic)* diente *m.*
cloven ['kləʊvən] *pp →* **cleave.** − 2 *adj* hendido,-a.
clover ['kləʊvə*ʳ*] *n* trébol *m.*

clown [klaʊn] *n* payaso. ◆*to ~ about/around t* hacer el payaso.
club [klʌb] *n* club *m,* sociedad. 2 *(stick)* porra, garrote *m.* 3 *(in golf)* palo. 4 *(cards)* trébol *m.* − 5 *t* aporrear. ◆*to ~ together i* pagar a escote.
cluck [klʌk] *n* cloqueo. − 2 *i* cloquear.
clue [kluː] *n* pista, indicio; *he hasn't got a ~,* no tiene (ni) idea.
clump [klʌmp] *n (of trees)* grupo. 2 *(of plants)* mata. 3 *(of earth)* terrón *m.* − 4 *i* andar pesada y ruidosamente.
clumsiness ['klʌmzɪnəs] *n* torpeza.
clumsy ['klʌmzɪ] *adj* torpe.
clung [klʌŋ] *pt & pp →* **cling.**
cluster ['klʌstə*ʳ*] *n* grupo. − 2 *i* agruparse, apiñarse.
clutch [klʌtʃ] *n* TECH embrague *m.* − 2 *t* estrechar. ◆*to ~ at t* intentar agarrar. ●*in sb.'s clutches,* en las garras de algn.
clutter ['klʌtə*ʳ*] *n* trastos *mpl.* − 2 *t* llenar, atestar: *cluttered (up) with toys,* atestado,-a de juguetes.
coach [kəʊtʃ] *n* AUTO autocar *m.* 2 *(carriage)* carruaje *m.* 3 *(on train)* coche *m.* 4 *(tutor)* profesor,-ra particular. 5 *(trainer)* entrenador,-ra. − 6 *t* preparar. ■ *~ station,* terminal *f* de autobuses.
coachman ['kəʊtʃmən] *n* cochero.
coachwork ['kəʊtʃwɜːk] *n* carrocería.
coagulate [kəʊ'ægjʊleɪt] *t-i* coagular(se).
coal [kəʊl] *n* carbón *m,* hulla. ●*to haul sb. over the coals,* echar un rapapolvo a algn. ■ *~ mine,* mina de carbón; *~ mining,* minería del carbón.
coalesce [kəʊə'les] *i* unirse, fundirse.
coalition [kəʊə'lɪʃən] *n* coalición.
coarse [kɔːs] *adj (material)* basto,-a. 2 *(person)* grosero,-a, vulgar.
coast [kəʊst] *n* costa, litoral *m.* − 2 *i (in car)* ir en punto muerto. 3 *(on bicycle)* ir sin pedalear. ●*fam the ~ is clear,* no hay moros en la costa.
coastal ['kəʊstəl] *adj* costero,-a.
coastguard ['kəʊstgɑːd] *n* guardacostas *m inv.*
coastline ['kəʊstlaɪn] *n* costa, litoral *m.*
coat [kəʊt] *n (garment)* abrigo. 2 *(of paint)* capa, mano *f.* 3 *(of animal)* pelaje *m.* − 4 *t* cubrir *(with,* de). ■ *~ of arms,* escudo de armas.
coating ['kəʊtɪŋ] *n* capa, baño.
coax [kəʊks] *t (person)* engatusar. ●*to ~ sth. out of sb.,* sonsacar algo a algn.
cob [kɒb] *n* mazorca.
cobalt ['kəʊbɔːlt] *n* cobalto.

cobble ['kɒbəl] *n* adoquín *m*. ◆*to* ~ *together t* amañar, apañar.

cobbled ['kɒbəld] *t* adoquinado,-a.

cobbler ['kɒblə^r] *n* zapatero (remendón). **2*** *pl* huevos* *mpl*. **3*** *pl (nonsense)* chorradas *fpl*.

cobra ['kəubrə] n cobra.

cobweb ['kɒbweb] *n* telaraña.

cocaine [kə'keɪn] *n* cocaína.

cock [kɒk] *n (male hen)* gallo. **2** *(any male bird)* macho. **3*** polla*. − **4** *t* alzar, levantar. ◆*to* ~ *up t* GB *sl* chapucear.

cockatoo [kɒkə'tu:] *n* cacatúa.

cockerel ['kɒkərəl] *n* gallito.

cockle ['kɒkəl] *n* berberecho.

cockney ['kɒknɪ] *adj-n* londinense *(mf)* del East End.

cockpit ['kɒkpɪt] *n (in plane)* cabina del piloto. **2** *(in car)* puesto de pilotaje.

cockroach ['kɒkrəutʃ] *n* cucaracha.

cocktail ['kɒkteɪl] *n* cóctel *m*.

cockup ['kɒkʌp] *n* GB *sl* chapuza.

cocky ['kɒkɪ] *adj fam* creído,-a.

cocoa ['kəukəu] *n* cacao.

coconut ['kəukənʌt] *n* coco.

cocoon [kə'ku:n] *n* capullo.

cod [kɒd] *n* bacalao.

code [kəud] *n* código. **2** *(secret)* clave *f*. − **3** *t* poner en clave, codificar.

codify ['kəudɪfaɪ] *t* codificar.

codswallop ['kɒdzwɒləp] *n sl* chorradas *fpl*.

coeducation [kəuedjʊ'keɪʃən] *n* enseñanza mixta.

coefficient [kəuɪ'fɪʃənt] *n* coeficiente *m*.

coerce [kəu'ɜ:s] *t* coaccionar.

coercion [kəu'ɜ:ʃən] *n* coacción.

coexist [kəuɪg'zɪst] *i* coexistir.

coexistence [kəuɪg'zɪstəns] *n* coexistencia.

coffee ['kɒfɪ] *n* café *m*. ■ ~ *cup*, taza para café; ~ *grinder*, molinillo de café; ~ *shop*, cafetería; ~ *table*, mesita de café; *black* ~, café solo; *white* ~, café con leche.

coffeepot ['kɒfɪpɒt] *n* cafetera.

coffer ['kɒfə^r] *n* arca.

coffin ['kɒfɪn] *n* ataúd *m*, féretro.

cog [kɒg] *n* diente *m* (de engranaje). **2** *fig* pieza.

cogent ['kəudʒənt] *adj* convincente.

cognac ['kɒnjæk] *n* coñac *m*.

cognate ['kɒgneɪt] *adj* afín. − **2** *n* palabra afín.

cogwheel ['kɒgwi:l] *n* rueda dentada.

cohabit [kəu'hæbɪt] *i* cohabitar.

coherence [kəu'hɪərəns] *n* coherencia.

coherent [kəu'hɪərənt] *adj* coherente.

cohesion [kəu'hi:ʒən] *n* cohesión.

cohesive [kəu'hi:sɪv] *adj* cohesivo,-a.

coil [kɔɪl] *n (of rope)* rollo. **2** *(of hair)* rizo. **3** TECH bobina. **4** MED *(IUD)* espiral *f*, DIU *m*. − **5** *t* enrollar. − **6** *i* enroscarse.

coin [kɔɪn] *n* moneda. − **2** *t* acuñar. **3** *fig* inventar.

coincide [kəuɪn'saɪd] *i* coincidir.

coincidence [kəu'ɪnsɪdəns] *n* coincidencia.

coitus ['kəuɪtəs] *n* coito.

coke [kəuk] *n* coque *m*. **2** *sl (drug)* coca.

colander ['kʌləndə^r] *n* colador *m*.

cold [kəuld] *adj* frío,-a. − **2** *n* frío. **3** MED resfriado, catarro. ●*to be* ~, *(person)* tener frío; *(thing)* estar frío,-a; *(weather)* hacer frío; *to catch* ~, resfriarse; *to feel the* ~, ser friolero,-a; *to give sb. the* ~ *shoulder*, tratar a algn. con frialdad; *to have a* ~, estar resfriado,-a; *to knock sb. out* ~, dejar a algn. inconsciente. ■ ~ *war*, guerra fría; ~ *sore*, herpe(s) *m*.

cold-blooded [kəuld'blʌdɪd] *adj* ZOOL de sangre fría. **2** *fig* cruel.

cold-hearted [kəuld'hɑ:tɪd] *adj* insensible.

coldness ['kəuldnəs] *n* frialdad.

coleslaw ['kəulslɔ:] *n* ensalada de col.

collaborate [kə'læbəreɪt] *i* colaborar.

collaboration [kəlæbə'reɪʃən] *n* colaboración.

collaborator [kə'læbəreɪtə^r] *n* colaborador,-a. **2** POL colaboracionista *mf*.

collapse [kə'læps] *n (falling down)* derrumbamiento. **2** *(falling in)* hundimiento. **3** MED colapso. − **4** *i (fall down)* derrumbarse. **5** *(fall in)* hundirse. **6** *(person)* desplomarse.

collapsible [kə'læpsɪbəl] *adj* plegable.

collar ['kɒlə^r] *n (of shirt etc.)* cuello. **2** *(for dog)* collar *m*. − **3** *t fam* pillar, pescar.

collarbone ['kɒləbəun] *n* clavícula.

collateral [kə'lætərəl] *n* FIN garantía subsidiaria. − **2** *adj* colateral.

colleague ['kɒli:g] *n* colega *mf*.

collect [kə'lekt] *t (gather)* recoger, juntar. **2** *(stamps etc.)* coleccionar. **3** *(taxes)* recaudar. **4** *(for charity)* hacer una colecta. **5** *(pick up, meet)* ir a buscar, recoger. − **6** *i (things)* acumularse. **7** *(people)* congregarse. ●us *to call* ~, llamar a cobro revertido; *to* ~ *o.s.*, serenarse.

collected [kə'lektɪd] *adj* dueño,-a de sí mismo,-a.

collection [kə'lekʃən] *n (of stamps etc.)* colección. **2** *(for charity)* colecta. **3** *(of mail)* recogida. **4** *(of taxes)* recaudación.
collective [kə'lektɪv] *adj* colectivo,-a. **– 2** *n* cooperativa.
collector [kə'lektər] *n (of stamps etc.)* coleccionista *mf*.
college ['kɒlɪdʒ] *n* colegio. **2** *(of university)* colegio mayor.
coilide [kə'laɪd] *i* colisionar, chocar.
collier ['kɒlɪər] *n* minero (de carbón).
colliery ['kɒljərɪ] *n* mina de carbón.
collision [kə'lɪʒən] *n* colisión, choque *m*.
colloquial [kə'ləʊkwɪəl] *adj* familiar, coloquial.
colloquialism [kə'ləʊkwɪəlɪzəm] *n* expresión coloquial.
collusion [kə'luːʒən] *n* confabulación; JUR colusión.
cologne [kə'ləʊn] *n* (agua de) colonia.
colonel ['kɜːnəl] *n* coronel *m*.
colonial [kə'ləʊnɪəl] *adj* colonial.
colonialism [kə'ləʊnɪəlɪzəm] *n* colonialismo.
colonist ['kɒlənɪst] *n (inhabitant)* colono. **2** *(colonizer)* colonizador,-ra.
colonize ['kɒlənaɪz] *t* colonizar.
colony ['kɒlənɪ] *n* colonia.
colossal [kə'lɒsəl] *adj* colosal.
colour ['kʌlər] *n* color *m*. **2** *pl* bandera *f sing*, enseña *f sing*. **– 3** *t* colorear. **4** *fig* influenciar. **– 5** *i* enrojecerse, ruborizarse. ● *in full* ~, a todo color; *to be off* ~, no encontrarse bien; *to lose* ~, palidecer. ■ ~ *bar*, discriminación racial; ~ *blindness*, daltonismo; ~ *film*, película en color; ~ *television*, televisión en color.
colour-blind ['kʌləblaɪnd] *adj* daltónico,-a.
coloured ['kʌləd] *adj (drawing etc.)* en color. **2** *euph (person)* de color. **– 3** *n euph* persona de color.
colourful ['kʌləfʊl] *adj (with colour)* lleno,-a de color. **2** *fig* vivo,-a, lleno,-a de colorido. **3** *(person)* pintoresco,-a.
colouring ['kʌlərɪŋ] *n (substance)* colorante *m*. **2** *(colour)* colorido.
colourless ['kʌlələs] *adj* incoloro,-a. **2** *fig* soso,-a.
colt [kəʊlt] *n* potro.
column ['kɒləm] *n* columna.
columnist ['kɒləmnɪst] *n* columnista *mf*.
coma ['kəʊmə] *n* MED coma *m*.
comatose ['kəʊmətəʊs] *adj* MED en estado comatoso.

comb [kəʊm] *n* peine *m*. **2** *(of bird)* cresta. **– 3** *t* peinar. **4** *(search)* rastrear, peinar.
combat ['kɒmbət] *n* combate *m*. **– 2** *t-i* combatir.
combatant ['kɒmbətənt] *n* combatiente *mf*.
combination [kɒmbɪ'neɪʃən] *n* combinación.
combine ['kɒmbaɪn] *n* grupo de compañías. **– 2** *t-i* combinar(se). **3** *(unite)* unir(se), fusionar(se). ▲ *En 2 y 3 (verbo)* [kəm'baɪn].
combustible [kəm'bʌstɪbəl] *adj* combustible.
combustion [kəm'bʌstʃən] *n* combustión. ■ ~ *engine*, motor *m* de combustión.
come [kʌm] *i* venir: *can I* ~ *with you?*, ¿puedo ir contigo?; *coming!*, ¡ya voy! **2** *(arrive)* llegar. **3** *sl* correrse. ◆*to* ~ *about i* ocurrir, suceder. **– 2** *i to* ~ *across t* encontrar por casualidad. **– 2** *i to* ~ *across well/badly*, causar buena/mala impresión. ◆*to* ~ *along i* progresar, avanzar. **2** *(arrive)* presentarse. ◆*to* ~ *apart i* romperse, partirse. ◆*to* ~ *at t* atacar. ◆*to* ~ *back i* volver, regresar. ◆*to* ~ *before t* preceder. **2** *fig* ser más importante que. ◆*to* ~ *by t* adquirir, obtener. ◆*to* ~ *down i* caer. **2** *(prices)* bajar. ◆*to* ~ *down with t fam (illness)* coger. ◆*to* ~ *forward i* avanzar. **2** *(volunteer)* ofrecerse. ◆*to* ~ *from t* ser de. ◆*to* ~ *in i* entrar. **2** *(train)* llegar. ◆*to* ~ *in for t* ser objeto de. ◆*to* ~ *into t (inherit)* heredar. ◆*to* ~ *off i (happen)* tener lugar. **2** *(be successful)* tener éxito. **3** *(break off)* desprenderse. ◆*to* ~ *on i* progresar, avanzar. **2** *fam (start)* empezar. ◆*to* ~ *out i* salir: *when the sun comes out*, cuando salga el sol. **2** *(stain)* quitarse. **3** GB *(on strike)* declararse en huelga. **4** *(in society)* ponerse de largo. ◆*to* ~ *out with t* soltar. ◆*to* ~ *round i (regain consciousness)* volver en sí. **2** *(be persuaded)* dejarse convencer, ceder. **3** *(visit)* visitar. ◆*to* ~ *through i (arrive)* llegar. **– 2** *t (survive)* sobrevivir. ◆*to* ~ *to i (regain consciousness)* volver en sí. **– 2** *t (total)* subir a, ascender a. ◆*to* ~ *up i (arise)* surgir. **2** *(approach)* acercarse. **3** *(sun)* salir. ◆*to* ~ *up against t* topar con. ◆*to* ~ *up to t* llegar a. ◆*to* ~ *up with t (idea)* tener; *(solution)* encontrar. ◆*to* ~ *upon t* encontrar. ● ~ *what may*, pase lo que pase; *to* ~ *down in the world*, venir a menos; *to* ~ *in handy*, ser útil; *to* ~ *into fashion*, ponerse de moda; *to* ~ *into force*, entrar en vigor; *to* ~ *of age*, llegar

a la mayoría de edad; **to ~ out in favour of/against,** declararse a favor de/en contra de; **to ~ to an end,** acabar, terminar; **to ~ together,** juntarse; **to ~ to one's senses,** volver en sí; *fig* recobrar la razón; **to ~ to pass,** acaecer; **to ~ true,** convertirse en realidad; **to ~ under attack,** ser atacado,-a; *fam ~ again?,* ¿cómo?; *fam* **to ~ out in spots,** salirle un sarpullido a uno. ▲ *pt* **came;** *pp* **come.**

comeback ['kʌmbæk] *n fam (of person)* reaparición. **2** *(reply)* réplica.

comedian [kə'mi:djən] *n* cómico.

comedienne [kəmi:dɪ'en] *n* cómica.

comedy ['kɒmɪdɪ] *n* comedia.

comet ['kɒmɪt] *n* cometa *m.*

comfort ['kʌmfət] *n (well-being)* comodidad. **2** *(consolation)* consuelo. **– 3** *t* consolar.

comfortable ['kʌmfətəbəl] *adj (chair etc.)* cómodo,-a. **2** *(patient)* tranquilo,-a. ●*to make o.s. ~,* ponerse cómodo,-a.

comforter ['kʌmfətəʳ] *n* consolador,-ra. **2** *(scarf)* bufanda. **3** *(dummy)* chupete *m.*

comforting ['kʌmfətɪŋ] *adj* reconfortante.

comfy ['kʌmfɪ] *adj fam* cómodo,-a.

comic ['kɒmɪk] *adj-n* cómico,-a. **– 2** *n (magazine)* tebeo.

comical ['kɒmɪkəl] *adj* cómico,-a.

coming ['kʌmɪŋ] *adj* próximo,-a. **2** *(generation)* venidero,-a. **– 3** *n* venida.

comma ['kɒmə] *n* coma. ■ *inverted ~,* comilla.

command [kə'mɑ:nd] *n (order)* orden *f.* **2** *(control)* mando: **under the ~ of the king,** bajo el mando del rey. **3** *(knowledge)* dominio: **he has a good ~ of Greek,** domina el griego. **– 4** *t-i (order)* mandar, ordenar. **5** MIL mandar. **– 6** *t (respect)* infundir.

commandant ['kɒməndænt] *n* comandante *m.*

commandeer [kɒmən'dɪəʳ] *t* requisar.

commander [kə'mɑ:ndəʳ] *n* comandante *m.*

commandment [kə'mɑ:ndmənt] *n* mandamiento.

commando [kə'mɑ:ndəʊ] *n* comando.

commemorate [kə'meməreɪt] *t* conmemorar.

commemoration [kəmemə'reɪʃən] *n* conmemoración.

commemorative [kə'memərətɪv] *adj* conmemorativo,-a.

commence [kə'mens] *t-i fml* comenzar, empezar.

commencement [kə'mensmənt] *n fml* comienzo.

commend [kə'mend] *t (praise)* elogiar. **2** *(entrust)* encomendar.

commendable [kə'mendəbəl] *adj* encomiable.

commensurate [kə'menʃərət] *adj* en consonancia (**with,** con).

comment ['kɒment] *n* comentario. **– 2** *i* comentar.

commentary ['kɒməntərɪ] *n* comentario.

commentate ['kɒmənteɪt] *i* comentar.

commentator ['kɒmənteɪtəʳ] *n* comentarista *mf.*

commerce ['kɒmɜ:s] *n* comercio.

commercial [kə'mɜ:ʃəl] *adj* comercial. **– 2** *n* TV anuncio. ■ *~ traveller,* viajante *mf.*

commercialize [kə'mɜ:ʃəlaɪz] *t* comercializar.

commiserate [kə'mɪzəreɪt] *i* compadecerse (**with,** de).

commiseration [kəmɪzə'reɪʃən] *n* conmiseración.

commission [kə'mɪʃən] *n* comisión. **2** MIL despacho (de oficial). **– 3** *t* MIL nombrar. **4** *(order)* encargar, comisionar.

commissionaire [kəmɪʃə'neəʳ] *n* portero, conserje *m.*

commissioner [kə'mɪʃənəʳ] *n* comisario.

commit [kə'mɪt] *t (crime)* cometer. ●*to ~ o.s. (to do sth.),* comprometerse (a hacer algo); **to ~ suicide,** suicidarse; **to ~ to memory,** memorizar; **to ~ to prison,** encarcelar.

commitment [kə'mɪtmənt] *n* compromiso.

committee [kə'mɪtɪ] *n* comité *m,* comisión.

commodity [kə'mɒdɪtɪ] *n* producto, artículo.

common ['kɒmən] *adj (not special)* corriente, usual, ordinario,-a. **2** *(shared)* común. **3** *(vulgar)* vulgar, bajo,-a, ordinario,-a. **– 4** *n* terreno común. ●*in ~,* en común; **to be ~ knowledge,** ser de dominio público. ■ *~ cold,* resfriado común; *~ denominator,* denominador *m* común; *~ factor,* factor *m* común; *Common Market,* Mercado Común; *~ sense,* sentido común; *House of Commons,* Cámara de los Comunes.

commoner ['kɒmənəʳ] *n* plebeyo.

commonplace ['kɒmənpleɪs] *adj* corriente.

commotion [kəˈməʊʃən] *n* alboroto, agitación.

communal [ˈkɒmjʊnəl] *adj* comunal, comunitario,-a.

commune [ˈkɒmjuːn] *n* comuna, comunidad. − **2** *i* comulgar, estar en comunión (**with**, con). ▲ *En* **2** *(verbo)* [kəˈmjuːn].

communicate [kəˈmjuːnɪkeɪt] *t-i* comunicar(se).

communication [kəmjuːnɪˈkeɪʃən] *n* comunicación. **2** *(message)* comunicado.

communicative [kəˈmjuːnɪkətɪv] *adj* comunicativo,-a.

communion [kəˈmjuːnjən] *n* comunión.

communiqué [kəˈmjuːnɪkeɪ] *n* comunicado.

communism [ˈkɒmjʊnɪzəm] *n* comunismo.

communist [ˈkɒmjʊnɪst] *adj-n* comunista *(mf)*.

community [kəˈmjuːnɪtɪ] *n* comunidad. ■ ~ *centre,* centro social; *local* ~, vecindario.

commute [kəˈmjuːt] *i* viajar diariamente de casa al lugar de trabajo. − **2** *t* conmutar.

commuter [kəˈmjuːtəʳ] *n* persona que diariamente viaja hasta su lugar de trabajo.

compact [kəmˈpækt] *adj* compacto,-a. − **2** *n* polvera de bolsillo. **3** *(pact)* pacto. ■ ~ *disc,* disco compacto. ▲ *En* **2** *y* **3** *(sustantivo)* [ˈkɒmpækt].

companion [kəmˈpænjən] *n* compañero,-a. **2** *(nurse)* acompañante *mf*.

companionable [kəmˈpænjənəbəl] *adj* sociable.

companionship [kəmˈpænjənʃɪp] *n* compañía.

company [ˈkʌmpənɪ] *n* compañía. **2** *fam (visitors)* visita. ●*to keep sb.* ~, hacer compañía a algn; *to part* ~, separarse (*with*, de).

comparable [ˈkɒmpərəbəl] *adj* comparable.

comparative [kəmˈpærətɪv] *adj* comparativo,-a. **2** *(relative)* relativo,-a. **3** *(subject)* comparado,-a. − **4** *n* comparativo. − **5** *comparatively adv* relativamente.

compare [kəmˈpeəʳ] *t-i* comparar(se). ●*beyond* ~, sin comparación.

comparison [kəmˈpærɪsən] *n* comparación. ●*there's no* ~, no hay punto de comparación.

compartment [kəmˈpɑːtmənt] *n* compartimiento.

compass [ˈkʌmpəs] *n (magnetic)* brújula. **2** *(for drawing)* compás *m*.

compassion [kəmˈpæʃən] *n* compasión.

compassionate [kəmˈpæʃənət] *adj* compasivo,-a.

compatibility [kəmpætəˈbɪlɪtɪ] *n* compatibilidad.

compatible [kəmˈpætɪbəl] *adj* compatible.

compatriot [kəmˈpætrɪət] *n* compatriota *mf*.

compel [kəmˈpel] *t* obligar, forzar, compeler.

compendium [kəmˈpendɪəm] *n* compendio.

compensate [ˈkɒmpənseɪt] *t* compensar. **2** *(money)* indemnizar.

compensation [kɒmpənˈseɪʃən] *n* compensación. **2** *(money)* indemnización.

compere [ˈkɒmpeəʳ] GB *n* presentador,-ra. − **2** *t* presentar.

compete [kəmˈpiːt] *i* competir.

competence [ˈkɒmpɪtəns] *n* competencia.

competent [ˈkɒmpɪtənt] *adj* competente.

competition [kɒmpɪˈtɪʃən] *n (contest)* concurso, competición. **2** *(rivalry)* competencia, rivalidad.

competitive [kəmˈpetɪtɪv] *adj (person)* de espíritu competitivo. **2** *(price etc.)* competitivo,-a.

competitor [kəmˈpetɪtəʳ] *n (rival)* competidor,-ra. **2** *(in race etc.)* participante *mf*. **3** *(in quiz etc.)* concursante *mf*.

compilation [kɒmpɪˈleɪʃən] *n* compilación, recopilación.

compile [kəmˈpaɪl] *t* compilar, recopilar.

complacency [kəmˈpleɪsənsɪ] *n* complacencia.

complacent [kəmˈpleɪsənt] *adj* satisfecho,-a de sí mismo,-a.

complain [kəmˈpleɪn] *t* quejarse.

complaint [kəmˈpleɪnt] *n* queja. **2** COM reclamación. **3** MED enfermedad. ●*to make a* ~, presentar una reclamación.

complement [ˈkɒmplɪmənt] *n* complemento.

complementary [kɒmplɪˈmentərɪ] *adj* complementario,-a.

complete [kəmˈpliːt] *adj* completo,-a. **2** *(finished)* acabado,-a, terminado,-a. **3** *(utter)* total. − **4** *t* completar. **5** *(finish)* acabar, terminar. − **6** *completely adv* por completo, completamente.

completion [kəmˈpliːʃən] *n* finalización, terminación.

complex ['kɒmpleks] *adj-n* complejo,-a *(m)*.

complexion [kəm'plekʃən] *n* cutis *m*, tez *f*. 2 *fig* aspecto.

complexity [kəm'pleksɪtɪ] *n* complejidad.

compliance [kəm'plaɪəns] *n* conformidad. •*in* ~ *with,* de acuerdo con.

compliant [kəm'plaɪənt] *adj* sumiso,-a.

complicate ['kɒmplɪkeɪt] *t* complicar.

complicated ['kɒmplɪkeɪtɪd] *adj* complicado,-a.

complication [kɒmplɪ'keɪʃən] *n* complicación.

complicity [kəm'plɪsɪtɪ] *n* complicidad.

compliment ['kɒmplɪmənt] *n* cumplido. 2 *pl* saludos *mpl*: *my compliments to the chef,* felicite al cocinero de mi parte. – 3 *t* felicitar (*on,* por). •*with the compliments of ...,* obsequio de .... ▲ *En 3 (verbo)* ['kɒmplɪment].

complimentary ['kɒmplɪ'mentərɪ] *adj* elogioso,-a, lisonjero,-a. 2 *(free)* gratuito,-a.

comply [kəm'plaɪ] *i (order)* obedecer (*with,* a): *it complies with European standards,* cumple con la normativa europea.

component [kəm'pəʊnənt] *adj-n* componente *(m)*.

compose [kəm'pəʊz] *t* componer. •*to be composed of,* componerse de; *to* ~ *o.s.,* calmarse, serenarse.

composed [kəm'pəʊzd] *adj* sereno,-a, sosegado,-a.

composer [kəm'pəʊzə^r] *n* compositor,-ra.

composite ['kɒmpəzɪt] *adj* compuesto,-a.

composition [kɒmpə'zɪʃən] *n* composición. 2 *(essay)* redacción.

compost ['kɒmpɒst] *n* abono.

composure [kəm'pəʊʒə^r] *n* calma, serenidad.

compound ['kɒmpaʊnd] *adj-n* compuesto,-a. – 2 *n* compuesto. 3 *(enclosure)* recinto. – 4 *t* componer. 5 *(worsen)* agravar. ▲ *En 4 y 5 (verbo)* [kəm'paʊnd].

comprehend [kɒmprɪ'hend] *t* comprender.

comprehensible [kɒmprɪ'hensəbəl] *adj* comprensible.

comprehension [kɒmprɪ'henʃən] *n* comprensión.

comprehensive [kɒmprɪ'hensɪv] *adj (thorough)* completo,-a. 2 *(broad)* amplio,-a, extenso,-a. ■ ~ *insurance,* se-

guro a todo riesgo; GB ~ *school,* instituto de segunda enseñanza.

compress ['kɒmpres] *n* compresa. – 2 *t* comprimir. 3 *fig* condensar. ▲ *En 2 y 3 (verbo)* [kəm'pres].

compression [kəm'preʃən] *n* compresión.

compressor [kəm'prəsə^r] *n* compresor *m*.

comprise [kəm'praɪz] *t (consist of)* constar de. 2 *(include)* incluir.

compromise ['kɒmprəmaɪz] *n* pacto, acuerdo. – 2 *i* pactar. – 3 *t* comprometer.

compromising ['kɒmprəmaɪzɪŋ] *adj* comprometido,-a.

compulsion [kəm'pʌlʃən] *n* obligación, coacción. 2 *(urge)* necesidad creada.

compulsive [kəm'pʌlsɪv] *adj (book etc.)* fascinante. 2 *(person)* empedernido,-a.

compulsory [kəm'pʌlsərɪ] *adj* obligatorio,-a.

compunction [kəm'pʌŋkʃən] *n* remordimiento.

compute [kəm'pjuːt] *t* computar, calcular.

computer [kəm'pjuːtə^r] *n* ordenador *m*, computadora. ■ ~ *programmer,* programador,-ra de ordenador; ~ *science,* informática.

computerize [kəm'pjuːtəraɪz] *t* informatizar.

computing [kəm'pjuːtɪŋ] *n* informática.

comrade ['kɒmreɪd] *n* compañero,-a; POL camarada *mf*.

comradeship ['kɒmreɪdʃɪp] *n* compañerismo, camaradería.

con [kɒn] *sl n* estafa, timo. – 2 *t* estafar, timar. ■ ~ *man,* estafador *m*; *pros and cons,* pros y contras.

concave ['kɒnkeɪv] *adj* cóncavo,-a.

conceal [kən'siːl] *t* ocultar.

concede [kən'siːd] *t* conceder. – 2 *i* admitir la derrota.

conceit [kən'siːt] *n* vanidad, presunción.

conceited [kən'siːtɪd] *adj* engreído,-a, presuntuoso,-a.

conceivable [kən'siːvəbəl] *adj* concebible. – 2 *conceivably adv* posiblemente.

conceive [kən'siːv] *t-i* concebir.

concentrate ['kɒnsəntreɪt] *n* concentrado. – 2 *t-i* concentrar(se).

concentrated ['kɒnsəntreɪtɪd] *adj* concentrado,-a.

concentration [kɒnsən'treɪʃən] *n* concentración. ■ ~ *camp,* campo de concentración.

concentric [kən'sentrɪk] *adj* concéntrico,-a.

concept ['kɒnsept] *n* concepto.

conception [kən'sepʃən] *n* 'MED concepción. **2** *(idea)* concepto, idea.

concern [kən'sɜːn] *n (matter)* asunto. **2** *(worry)* preocupación, inquietud. **3** COM negocio. − **4** *t (affect)* afectar, concernir, importar a. **5** *(worry)* preocupar. **6** *(have to do with)* tener que ver con. ●*as far as I'm concerned*, por lo que a mí se refiere; *it's no ~ of mine,* no es asunto mío; *there's no cause for ~,* no hay motivo de preocupación; *to whom it may ~,* a quien corresponda.

concerned [kən'sɜːnd] *adj (affected)* afectado,-a, involucrado,-a. **2** *(worried)* preocupado,-a.

concerning [kən'sɜːnɪŋ] *prep* referente a, en cuanto a.

concert ['kɒnsət] *n* concierto.

concerted [kən'sɜːtɪd] *adj* concertado,-a.

concerto [kən'tʃeətəʊ] *n* concierto.

concession [kən'seʃən] *n* concesión.

conciliate [kən'sɪlɪeɪt] *t* conciliar.

conciliation [kənsɪlɪ'eɪʃən] *n* conciliación.

conciliatory [kən'sɪlɪətərɪ] *adj* conciliatorio,-a.

concise [kən'saɪs] *adj* conciso,-a. − **2** *concisely adv* con concisión.

concision [kən'sɪʒən] *n* concisión.

conclude [kən'kluːd] *t-i* concluir.

conclusion [kən'kluːʒən] *n* conclusión. **2** *(end)* final *m.*

conclusive [kən'kluːsɪv] *adj* concluyente.

concoct [kən'kɒkt] *t* confeccionar. **2** *fig* inventar.

concoction [kən'kɒkʃən] *n* mezcla; *(drink)* brebaje *m.*

concord ['kɒŋkɔːd] *n* concordia.

concordance [kən'kɔːdəns] *n* concordancia.

concourse ['kɒŋkɔːs] *n (hall)* vestíbulo. **2** *(people)* concurrencia.

concrete ['kɒŋkriːt] *adj* concreto,-a, específico,-a. − **2** *n* hormigón *m.* − **3** *t* revestir de hormigón.

concur [kən'kɜː] *i* coincidir.

concurrent [kən'kʌrənt] *adj* simultáneo,-a, concurrente.

concussion [kən'kʌʃən] *n* conmoción cerebral.

condemn [kən'dem] *t* condenar. **2** *(building)* declarar inhabitable.

condemnation [kɒndem'neɪʃən] *n* condenación.

condensation [kɒnden'seɪʃən] *n* condensación. **2** *(on window)* vaho.

condense [kən'dens] *t-i* condensar(se). − **2** *t (shorten)* abreviar.

condescend [kɒndɪ'send] *i* dignarse.

condescending [kɒndɪ'sendɪŋ] *adj* condescendiente.

condescension [kɒndɪ'senʃən] *n* condescendencia.

condiment ['kɒndɪmənt] *n* condimento.

condition [kən'dɪʃən] *n* condición. − **2** *t* condicionar. **3** *(treat)* acondicionar. ●*in good/bad ~,* en buen/mal estado; *on ~ that,* a condición de que; *to be out of ~,* no estar en forma.

conditional [kən'dɪʃənəl] *adj-n* condicional *(m).*

conditioner [kən'dɪʃənəʳ] *n* acondicionador *m.*

condolences [kən'dəʊlənsɪz] *npl* pésame *m sing.* ●*please accept my ~,* le acompaño en el sentimiento; *to send one's ~,* dar el pésame.

condom ['kɒndəm] *n* condón *m,* preservativo.

condone [kən'dəʊn] *t* consentir.

condor ['kɒndɔːʳ] *n* cóndor *m.*

conducive [kən'djuːsɪv] *adj* propicio,-a *(to,* para).

conduct ['kɒndəkt] *n* conducta. − **2** *t* conducir. **3** *(heat etc.)* ser conductor,-ra de. − **4** *t-i* MUS dirigir. ▲ *En 2, 3 y 4 (verbo)* [kən'dʌkt].

conductor [kən'dʌktəʳ] *n (of heat etc.)* conductor *m.* **2** MUS director,-ra. **3** *(on bus)* cobrador *m.*

conductress [kən'dʌktrəs] *n (on bus)* cobradora.

cone [kəʊn] *n* cono. **2** *(ice cream)* cucurucho. **3** *(of pine etc.)* piña.

confectioner [kən'fekʃənəʳ] *n* confitero,-a.

confectionery [kən'fekʃənərɪ] *n* confitería.

confederacy [kən'fedərəsɪ] *n* confederación.

confederate [kən'fedərət] *adj* confederado,-a. − **2** *n* confederado,-a. **3** JUR cómplice *m.* − **4** *t-i* confederar(se). ▲ *En 4 (verbo)* [kən'fedəreɪt].

confederation [kənfedə'reɪʃən] *n* confederación.

confer [kən'fɜːʳ] *t (award)* conferir, conceder. − **2** *i (consult)* consultar (*with,* con).

conference ['kɒnfərəns] *n* congreso. **2** *(meeting)* reunión.

confess [kən'fes] *t-i* confesar(se).

confession [kən'feʃən] *n* confesión.

confessional [kən'feʃənəl] *n* confesionario.

confetti [kən'feti] *n* confeti *m*.

confidant ['kɒnfɪdænt] *n* confidente *m*.

confidante ['kɒnfɪdænt] *n* confidenta.

confide [kən'faɪd] *t-i* confiar.

confidence ['kɒnfɪdəns] *n* confianza, fe *f*. **2** *(secret)* confidencia.

confident ['kɒnfɪdənt] *adj* seguro,-a. – **2** *confidently adv* con seguridad.

confidential [kɒnfɪ'denʃəl] *adj* confidencial.

confine [kən'faɪn] *t* encerrar. **2** *fig* limitar.

confinement [kən'faɪnmənt] *n* reclusión. **2** MED alumbramiento.

confines ['kɒnfaɪnz] *npl* límites *mpl*.

confirm [kən'fɜːm] *t* confirmar.

confirmation [kɒnfə'meɪʃən] *n* confirmación.

confirmed [kən'fɜːmd] *adj* confirmado,-a. **2** *fig* empedernido,-a, inveterado,-a.

confiscate ['kɒnfɪskeɪt] *t* confiscar.

confiscation [kɒnfɪs'keɪʃən] *n* confiscación.

conflagration [kɒnflə'greɪʃən] *n* conflagración.

conflict ['kɒnflɪkt] *n* conflicto. – **2** *i* chocar, estar en conflicto. ▲ *En 2 (verbo)* [kən'flɪkt].

conflicting [kən'flɪktɪŋ] *adj (evidence)* contradictorio,-a. **2** *(opinions)* contrario,-a.

confluence ['kɒnfluəns] *n* confluencia.

conform [kən'fɔːm] *i* conformarse. **2** *(to rules etc.)* ajustarse *(to/with,* a).

conformist [kən'fɔːmɪst] *adj-n* conformista *(mf)*.

conformity [kən'fɔːmɪtɪ] *n* conformidad. ●*in* ~ *with,* conforme a.

confound [kən'faʊnd] *t* confundir. ●~ *it!,* ¡maldito sea!

confounded [kən'faʊndɪd] *adj fam* maldito,-a, condenado,-a.

confront [kən'frʌnt] *t* confrontar.

confuse [kən'fjuːz] *t (thing)* confundir. **2** *(person)* dejar confuso,-a a, desconcertar.

confused [kən'fjuːzd] *adj (person)* confundido,-a. **2** *(mind, ideas)* confuso,-a.

confusing [kən'fjuːzɪŋ] *adj* confuso,-a.

confusion [kən'fjuːʒən] *n* confusión.

congeal [kən'dʒiːl] *t-i* coagular(se).

congenial [kən'dʒiːnjəl] *adj* agradable.

congenital [kən'dʒenɪtəl] *adj* congénito,-a.

conger ['kɒŋɡəʳ] *n* ~ *(eel),* congrio.

congested [kən'dʒestɪd] *adj (roads etc.)* colapsado,-a, congestionado,-a. **2** MED congestionado,-a.

congestion [kən'dʒestʃən] *n* congestión.

conglomerate [kən'ɡlɒmərət] *n* conglomerado. – **2** *t-i* conglomerar(se). ▲ *En 2 (verbo)* [kən'ɡlɒməreɪt].

congratulate [kən'ɡrætjʊleɪt] *t* felicitar *(on,* por).

congratulation [kənɡrætjʊ'leɪʃən] *n* felicitación. **2** *pl* felicitaciones *fpl*, enhorabuena *f sing*.

congregate ['kɒŋɡrɪɡeɪt] *t-i* congregar(se).

congregation [kɒŋɡrɪ'ɡeɪʃən] *n* fieles *mpl*.

congress ['kɒŋɡres] *n* congreso.

congruent ['kɒŋɡruənt] *adj* congruente.

conical ['kɒnɪkəl] *adj* cónico,-a.

conifer ['kɒnɪfəʳ] *n* conífera.

coniferous [kə'nɪfərəs] *adj* conífero,-a.

conjecture [kən'dʒektʃəʳ] *n* conjetura. – **2** *t* conjeturar.

conjugal ['kɒndʒʊɡəl] *adj* conyugal.

conjugate ['kɒndʒʊɡeɪt] *t* conjugar.

conjugation [kɒndʒʊ'ɡeɪʃən] *n* conjugación.

conjunction [kən'dʒʌŋkʃən] *n* conjunción. ●*in* ~ *with,* conjuntamente con.

conjure ['kʌndʒəʳ] *i* hacer magia, hacer juegos de manos. – **2** *t* hacer aparecer. ◆*to* ~ *up t* imaginar. **2** *(memories)* evocar.

conjurer, conjuror ['kʌndʒərəʳ] *n* mago,-a, prestidigitador,-ra.

connect [kə'nekt] *t (link)* unir, enlazar, conectar. **2** *(join)* juntar. **3** *(associate)* relacionar, asociar. **4** *(on telephone)* poner (en comunicación). – **5** *i* unirse. **6** *(rooms)* comunicarse.

connection, connexion [kə'nekʃən] *n* unión, enlace *m*. **2** ELEC TECH conexión. **3** *fig* relación. **4** *(railways)* correspondencia, conexión.

connivance [kə'naɪvəns] *n* connivencia.

connive [kə'naɪv] *i* conspirar, confabularse. ●*to* ~ *at,* hacer la vista gorda a.

connoisseur [kɒnə'sɜːʳ] *n* conocedor,-ra.

connotation [kɒnə'teɪʃən] *n* connotación.

conquer ['kɒŋkəʳ] *t (lands)* conquistar. **2** *(enemy)* vencer a.

conqueror ['kɒŋkərəʳ] *n* conquistador,-ra, vencedor,-ra.

conquest ['kɒŋkwest] *n* conquista.

conscience ['kɒnʃəns] *n* conciencia.

conscientious [kɒnʃɪ'enʃəs] *adj* concienzudo,-a. ■ ~ *objector,* objetor,-ra de conciencia.

conscientiousness [kɒnʃɪ'enʃəsnəs] *n* escrupulosidad.

conscious ['kɒnʃəs] *adj* consciente.

consciousness ['kɒnʃəsnəs] *n* conciencia. 2 MED conocimiento.

conscript ['kɒnskrɪpt] *n* recluta. – 2 *t* reclutar. ▲ *En 2 (verbo)* [kən'skrɪpt].

conscription [kən'skrɪpʃən] *n* reclutamiento (forzoso), servicio militar obligatorio.

consecrate ['kɒnsɪkreɪt] *t* consagrar.

consecration [kɒnsɪ'kreɪʃən] *n* consagración.

consecutive [kən'sekjʊtɪv] *adj* consecutivo,-a.

consensus [kən'sensəs] *n* consenso.

consent [kən'sent] *n* consentimiento. – 2 *i* consentir (*to,* en). ■ *age of ~,* edad núbil.

consequence ['kɒnsɪkwəns] *n* consecuencia. ●*it is of no ~,* no tiene importancia.

consequent ['kɒnsɪkwənt] *n* consiguiente. – 2 *consequently adv* por consiguiente.

conservation [kɒnsə'veɪʃən] *n* conservación.

conservationist [kɒnsə'veɪʃənɪst] *n* ecologista *mf.*

conservatism [kən'sɜ:vətɪzəm] *n* POL conservadurismo.

conservative [kən'sɜ:vətɪv] *adj* cauteloso,-a. 2 POL conservador,-ra. – 3 *n* conservador,-ra.

conservatory [kən'sɜ:vətrɪ] *n* MUS conservatorio. 2 *(for plants)* invernadero.

conserve [kən'sɜ:v] *t* conservar. – 2 *n* conserva.

consider [kən'sɪdəʳ] *t* considerar.

considerable [kən'sɪdərəbəl] *adj* importante, considerable. – 2 *considerably adv* bastante.

considerate [kən'sɪdərət] *adj* considerado,-a.

consideration [kənsɪdə'reɪʃən] *n* consideración. ●*to take into ~,* tener en cuenta.

considering [kən'sɪdərɪŋ] *prep* considerando (que).

consign [kən'saɪn] *t* consignar. 2 *(entrust)* confiar.

consignment [kən'saɪnmənt] *n* remesa, envío.

consist [kən'sɪst] *i* consistir (*of,* en). 2 *(comprise)* constar (*of,* de).

consistency [kən'sɪstənsɪ] *n* consecuencia, coherencia. 2 *(firmness)* consistencia.

consistent [kən'sɪstənt] *adj* consecuente, coherente.

consolation [kɒnsə'leɪʃən] *n* consolación, consuelo.

console ['kɒnsəʊl] *n* consola. – 2 *t* consolar. ▲ *En 2 (verbo)* [kən'səʊl].

consolidate [kən'sɒlɪdeɪt] *t-i* consolidar(se).

consolidation [kənsɒlɪ'deɪʃən] *n* consolidación.

consommé ['kɒnsɒmeɪ] *n* consomé *m.*

consonant ['kɒnsənənt] *n* consonante *f.*

consort ['kɒnsɔ:t] *n* consorte *mf.* – 2 *i* asociarse (*with,* con). ▲ *En 2 (verbo)* [kən'sɔ:t].

conspicuous [kəns'pɪkjʊəs] *adj* llamativo,-a, visible. 2 *(obvious)* evidente, obvio,-a.

conspiracy [kən'spɪrəsɪ] *n* conspiración.

conspirator [kən'spɪrətəʳ] *n* conspirador,-ra.

conspire [kən'spaɪəʳ] *i* conspirar.

constable ['kʌnstəbəl] *n* policía *mf,* guardia *mf.*

constabulary [kən'stæbjʊlərɪ] *n* GB policía *f.*

constancy ['kɒnstənsɪ] *n* constancia.

constant ['kɒnstənt] *adj (unchanging)* constante. 2 *(continuous)* continuo,-a. 3 *(loyal)* leal. – 4 *n* constante *f.*

constellation [kɒnstə'leɪʃən] *n* constelación.

consternation [kɒnstə'neɪʃən] *n* consternación.

constipated ['kɒnstɪpeɪtɪd] *adj* estreñido,-a.

constipation [kɒnstɪ'peɪʃən] *n* estreñimiento.

constituency [kən'stɪtjʊənsɪ] *n* circunscripción/distrito electoral.

constituent [kəns'tɪtjʊənt] *adj* constitutivo,-a. 2 POL constituyente. – 3 *n* componente *m.* 4 POL elector,-ra.

constitute ['kɒnstɪtju:t] *t* constituir.

constitution [kɒnstɪ'tju:ʃən] *n* constitución.

constitutional [kɒnstɪ'tju:ʃənəl] *adj* constitucional.

constrain [kəns'treɪn] *t* constreñir, obligar.

constraint [kən'streɪnt] *n* constreñimiento, coacción.

constrict [kən'strɪkt] *t* apretar, constringir.

constriction [kən'strɪkʃən] *n* constricción.

construct [kəns'trʌkt] *t* construir.

construction [kən'strʌkʃən] *n* construcción.

constructive [kən'strʌktɪv] *adj* constructivo,-a.

construe [kən'stru:] *t* interpretar.

consul ['kɒnsəl] *n* cónsul *mf*.

consular ['kɒnsjʊləʳ] *adj* consular.

consulate ['kɒnsjʊlət] *n* consulado.

consult [kən'sʌlt] *t-i* consultar.

consultant [kən'sʌltənt] *n* asesor,-ra. 2 MED especialista *mf*.

consultation [kɒnsəl'teɪʃən] *n* consulta.

consume [kən'sju:m] *t-i* consumir.

consumer [kən'sju:məʳ] *n* consumidor,-ra.

consummate ['kɒnsəmət] *adj* consumado,-a. – 2 *t* consumar. ▲ *En 2 (verbo)* ['kɒnsəmeɪt].

consummation [kɒnsə'meɪʃən] *n* consumación.

consumption [kən'sʌmpʃən] *n* consumo. 2 MED tisis *f*.

contact ['kɒntækt] *n* contacto. – 2 *t* ponerse en contacto con, contactar con. ■ ~ *lenses*, lentillas *fpl*, lentes *fpl* de contacto.

contagious [kən'teɪdʒəs] *adj* contagioso,-a.

contain [kən'teɪn] *t* contener. 2 *(restrain)* contener, controlar.

container [kən'teɪnəʳ] *n* recipiente *m*, envase *m*. 2 COM container *m*.

contaminate [kən'tæmɪneɪt] *t* contaminar.

contamination [kəntæmɪ'neɪʃən] *n* contaminación, polución.

contemplate ['kɒntempleɪt] *t* contemplar. 2 *(consider)* considerar.

contemplation [kɒntem'pleɪʃən] *n* contemplación.

contemplative ['kɒntempleɪtɪv] *adj* contemplativo,-a.

contemporaneous [kəntempə'reɪnjəs] *adj* contemporáneo,-a.

contemporary [kən'tempərərɪ] *adj-n* contemporáneo,-a.

contempt [kən'tempt] *n* desprecio, menosprecio. 2 JUR desacato. ●*to hold in* ~, despreciar.

contemptible [kən'temptəbəl] *adj* despreciable.

contemptuous [kən'temptjʊəs] *adj (attitude)* despreciativo,-a, despectivo,-a. 2 *(person)* desdeñoso,-a.

contend [kən'tend] *i (compete)* contender, competir. – 2 *t (claim)* sostener.

content ['kɒntent] *n* contenido. 2 *pl* contenido *m sing*. 3 *pl (table)* índice *m sing* de materias. – 4 *adj* contento,-a. – 5 *t* contentar. ●*to* ~ *o.s. with*, contentarse con. ▲ *En 4 y 5 (adjetivo y verbo)* [kən'tent].

contented [kən'tentɪd] *adj* contento,-a, satisfecho,-a.

contention [kən'tenʃən] *n (opinion)* parecer *m*. 2 *(dispute)* controversia, contienda. ■ *bone of* ~, manzana de la discordia.

contentious [kən'tenʃəs] *adj* contencioso,-a.

contentment [kən'tentmənt] *n* contento, satisfacción.

contest ['kɒntest] *n (competition)* concurso. 2 *(struggle)* contienda, lucha. – 3 *t (fight for)* luchar/competir por. 4 *(appeal against)* impugnar. ▲ *En 3 y 4 (verbo)* [kən'test].

contestant [kən'testənt] *n* concursante *mf*.

context ['kɒntekst] *n* contexto.

continent ['kɒntɪnənt] *adj-n* continente *(m)*.

continental [kɒntɪ'nentəl] *adj* continental. 2 GB europeo,-a. ■ ~ *breakfast*, desayuno con tostadas, croissants *mpl* con café o té.

contingency [kən'tɪndʒənsɪ] *n* contingencia, eventualidad.

contingent [kən'tɪndʒent] *adj-n* contingente *(m)*.

continual [kən'tɪnjʊəl] *adj* continuo,-a, incesante.

continuation [kəntɪnjʊ'eɪʃən] *n* continuación.

continue [kən'tɪnju:] *t-i* continuar, seguir.

continuity [kɒntɪ'nju:ɪtɪ] *n* continuidad.

continuous [kən'tɪnjʊəs] *adj* continuo,-a.

contort [kən'tɔ:t] *t* retorcer. 2 *(face)* contraer.

contortion [kən'tɔ:ʃən] *n* contorsión.

contour ['kɒntʊəʳ] *n* contorno. ■ ~ *line*, línea de nivel.

contraband ['kɒntrəbænd] *n* contrabando.

contraception [kɒntrə'sepʃən] *n* anticoncepción.

contraceptive [kɒntrə'septɪv] *adj-n* anticonceptivo,-a *(m)*.

contract ['kɒntrækt] *n* contrato. — 2 *i (become smaller)* contraerse. 3 *(agree)* contractar, hacer un contrato. — 4 *t (illness, marriage)* contraer. ▲ *En 2, 3 y 4 (verbo)* [kən'trækt].

contraction [kən'trækʃən] *n* contracción.

contractor [kən'træktəʳ] *n* contratista *mf.*

contradict [kɒntrə'dɪkt] *t* contradecir.

contradiction [kɒntrə'dɪkʃən] *n* contradicción.

contradictory [kɒntrə'dɪktərɪ] *adj* contradictorio,-a.

contralto [kən'træltəʊ] *n (voice)* contralto *m.* 2 *(singer)* contralto *f.*

contraption [kən'træpʃən] *n* cacharro, artefacto.

contrariness [kɒn'treərɪnəs] *n* terquedad.

contrary ['kɒntrərɪ] *adj* contrario,-a. 2 *(stubborn)* terco,-a. — 3 *n* contrario. ●~ *to,* en contra de; *on the* ~, al contrario. ▲ *En 2* [kɒn'treərɪ].

contrast ['kɒntræst] *n* contraste *m.* — 2 *t-i* contrastar. ▲ *En 2 (verbo)* [kɒn'træst].

contravene [kɒntrə'viːn] *t* contravenir.

contravention [kɒntrə'venʃən] *n* contravención.

contribute [kən'trɪbjuːt] *t-i* contribuir. — 2 *i (to newspaper etc.)* colaborar *(to,* en).

contribution [kɒntrɪ'bjuːʃən] *n* contribución. 2 *(to newspaper)* colaboración.

contributor [kən'trɪbjʊtəʳ] *n* contribuyente *mf.* 2 *(to newspaper)* colaborador,-ra.

contributory [kən'trɪbjʊtərɪ] *adj (factor)* contribuyente. 2 *(pension etc.)* contributorio,-a.

contrivance [kən'traɪvəns] *n* artefacto, cacharro.

contrive [kən'traɪv] *t* idear, inventar. ●*to* ~ *to do sth.,* conseguir hacer algo.

contrived [kən'traɪvd] *adj* artificial, forzado,-a.

control [kən'trəʊl] *n* control *m.* 2 *(device)* mando, control. 3 *(restraint)* dominio. — 4 *t* controlar. ●*out of* ~, fuera de control; *to be in* ~, estar al mando; *to bring under* ~, conseguir controlar; *to go out of* ~, descontrolarse; *to lose* ~, perder

el control, *under* ~, bajo control. ■ ~ *tower,* torre *f* de control.

controller [kən'trəʊləʳ] *n* FIN interventor,-ra. 2 RAD TV director,-ra de programación. 3 AV controlador aéreo.

controversial [kɒntrə'vɜːʃəl] *adj* controvertido,-a, polémico,-a.

controversy [kən'trɒvəsɪ] *n* controversia, polémica.

contusion [kən'tjuːʒən] *n* contusión.

conurbation [kɒnɜː'beɪʃən] *n* conurbación.

convalesce [kɒnvə'les] *i* convalecer.

convalescence [kɒnvə'lesəns] *n* convalecencia.

convalescent [kɒnvə'lesənt] *adj* convaleciente.

convection [kən'vekʃən] *n* convección.

convene [kən'viːn] *t* convocar. — 2 *i* reunirse.

convenience [kən'viːnjəns] *n* conveniencia, comodidad. ■ GB *public* ~, servicios *mpl* públicos.

convenient [kən'viːnjənt] *adj* conveniente, oportuno,-a. 2 *(place)* bien situado,-a.

convent ['kɒnvənt] *n* convento.

convention [kən'venʃən] *n* convención.

conventional [kən'venʃənəl] *adj* convencional.

converge [kən'vɜːdʒ] *i* converger, convergir.

convergent [kən'vɜːdʒənt] *adj* convergente.

conversant [kən'vɜːsənt] *adj* versado,-a *(with,* en).

conversation [kɒnvə'seɪʃən] *n* conversación.

conversational [kɒnvə'seɪʃənəl] *adj* coloquial.

converse ['kɒnvɜːs] *adj* opuesto,-a. — 2 *n* lo opuesto. — 3 *i* conversar. ▲ *En 3 (verbo)* [kən'vɜːs].

conversion [kən'vɜːʃən] *n* conversión.

convert ['kɒnvɜːt] *n* converso,-a. — 2 *t-i* convertir(se). ▲ *En 2 (verbo)* [kən'vɜːt].

convertible [kən'vɜːtəbəl] *adj* convertible. 2 AUTO descapotable . — 3 *n* AUTO descapotable *m.*

convex ['kɒnveks] *adj* convexo,-a.

convey [kən'veɪ] *t* llevar, transportar. 2 *(ideas etc.)* comunicar. 3 JUR transferir.

conveyor belt [kən'veɪəbelt] *n* cinta transportadora.

convict ['kɒnvɪkt] *n* presidiario,-a. — 2 *t* JUR declarar culpable. ▲ *En 2 (verbo)* [kən'vɪkt].

conviction [kən'vɪkʃən] *n* convicción. **2** JUR condena.

convince [kən'vɪns] *t* convencer.

convincing [kən'vɪnsɪŋ] *adj* convincente.

convivial [kən'vɪvɪəl] *adj (party)* alegre. **2** *(person)* sociable.

convoke [kən'vəʊk] *t* convocar.

convoy ['kɒnvɔɪ] *n* convoy *m.*

convulse [kən'vʌls] *t* convulsionar. ●*to be convulsed with laughter,* troncharse de risa.

convulsion [kən'vʌlʃən] *n* convulsión.

coo [kuː] *i* arrullar.

cook [kʊk] *n* cocinero,-ra. − **2** *t* guisar, cocinar; *(meals)* preparar. − **3** *i* cocinar, cocer.

cooker ['kʊkə^r] *n* cocina.

cookery ['kʊkərɪ] *n* cocina. ■ ~ *book,* libro de cocina.

cookie ['kʊkɪ] *n* US galleta.

cooking ['kʊkɪŋ] *n* cocina. ●*to do the* ~, cocinar.

cool [kuːl] *adj* fresco,-a. **2** *(unfriendly)* frío,-a. **3** *(calm)* tranquilo,-a. − **4** *n* fresco, frescor *m.* **5** *sl* calma. − **6** *t-i* refrescar(se), enfriar(se). ◆*to* ~ *down t-i* enfriar(se); *(person)* calmar(se). ●*to lose one's* ~, perder la calma.

coolness ['kuːlnəs] *n* fresco, frescor *m.* **2** *(unfriendliness)* frialdad. **3** *(calm)* serenidad.

coop [kuːp] *n* gallinero. ◆*to* ~ *up t* encerrar.

cooperate [kəʊ'ɒpəreɪt] *i* cooperar.

cooperative [kəʊ'ɒpərətɪv] *adj* cooperativo,-a. **2** *(helpful)* cooperador,-ra. − **3** *n* cooperativa.

coordinate [kəʊ'ɔːdɪneɪt] *t* coordinar.

coordination [kəʊɔːdɪ'neɪʃən] *n* coordinación.

cop [kɒp] *sl n (policeman)* poli *mf.* − **2** *t* pillar, pescar. ◆*to* ~ *out i* rajarse. ●*it's not much* ~, no es nada del otro jueves.

cope [kəʊp] *i* arreglárselas: *I just can't* ~*!,* ¡es que no doy abasto! ◆*to* ~ *with t* poder con.

copious ['kəʊpjəs] *adj* copioso,-a.

copper ['kɒpə^r] *n (metal)* cobre *m.* **2** GB *fam (coin)* pela, perra. **3** *sl (policeman)* poli *mf.*

copulation [kɒpjʊ'leɪʃən] *n* copulación.

copy ['kɒpɪ] *n* copia. **2** *(of book etc.)* ejemplar *m.* − **3** *t-i* copiar.

copycat ['kɒpɪkæt] *n fam* copión,-ona.

copyright ['kɒpɪraɪt] *n* copyright *m.*

coral ['kɒrəl] *n* coral *m.*

cord [kɔːd] *n (string, rope)* cuerda. **2** ELEC cordón *m.* **3** *pl fam* pantalones *mpl* de pana.

cordial ['kɔːdjəl] *adj* cordial. − **2** *n (soft drink)* zumo de fruta. **3** *(liqueur)* licor *m.*

cordon ['kɔːdən] *n* cordón *m.* − **2** *t to* ~ *(off),* acordonar.

corduroy ['kɔːdərɔɪ] *n* pana.

core [kɔː^r] *n* núcleo, centro; *(of apple etc.)* corazón *m.* ●*fig to the* ~, hasta la médula.

cork [kɔːk] *n (material)* corcho. **2** *(stopper)* tapón *m,* corcho. − **3** *t* encorchar. ■ ~ *oak,* alcornoque.

corkscrew ['kɔːkskruː] *n* sacacorchos *m inv.*

cormorant ['kɔːmərənt] *n* cormorán *m* grande.

corn [kɔːn] *n* cereales *mpl.* **2** *(maize)* maíz *m.* **3** MED callo. ■ *sweet* ~, maíz.

cornea ['kɔːnɪə] *n* córnea.

corner ['kɔːnə^r] *n* ángulo. **2** *(exterior angle)* esquina. **3** *(interior angle)* rincón *m.* − **4** *t* arrinconar. **5** COM acaparar. ●*in a tight* ~, en un aprieto; *just round the* ~, a la vuelta de la esquina. ■ *(football)* ~ *kick,* córner *m.*

cornerstone ['kɔːnəstəʊn] *n* piedra angular.

cornet ['kɔːnɪt] *n* MUS corneta. **2** GB *(ice-cream)* cucurucho.

cornflakes ['kɔːnfleɪks] *npl* copos *mpl* de maíz.

cornflour ['kɔːnflaʊə^r], US **cornstarch** ['kɔːnstɑːtʃ] *n* harina de maíz, maizena®.

corny ['kɔːnɪ] *adj fam (joke)* gastado,-a, sobado,-a. **2** *(film)* sensiblero,-a.

corollary [kə'rɒlərɪ] *n* corolario.

coronary ['kɒrənərɪ] MED *adj* coronario,-a. − **2** *n* trombosis *f inv* coronaria.

coronation [kɒrə'neɪʃən] *n* coronación.

coroner ['kɒrənə^r] *n* juez *mf* de instrucción.

corporal ['kɔːpərəl] *adj* corporal. − **2** *n* MIL cabo. ■ ~ *punishment,* castigo corporal.

corporation [kɔːpə'reɪʃən] *n* COM corporación. **2** GB *(council)* ayuntamiento.

corps [kɔː^r] *n* cuerpo. ▲ *pl corps* [kɔːz].

corpse [kɔːps] *n* cadáver *m.*

corpulence ['kɔːpjʊləns] *n* corpulencia.

corpulent ['kɔːpjʊlənt] *adj* corpulento,-a.

corpuscle ['kɔːpʌsəl] *n* corpúsculo, glóbulo.

correct [kə'rekt] *adj gen* correcto,-a, exacto,-a. **2** *(behaviour)* formal. − **3** *t* corregir.

correction [kəˈrekʃən] *n* corrección.

corrective [kəˈrektɪv] *adj-n* correctivo,-a *(m)*.

correctness [kəˈrektnəs] *n* exactitud. **2** *(behaviour)* corrección.

correlate [ˈkɒrəleɪt] *t* correlacionar. **– 2** *i* tener correlación.

correlation [kɒrəˈleɪʃən] *n* correlación.

correspond [kɒrɪsˈpɒnd] *i* corresponder(se). **2** *(write)* escribirse.

correspondence [kɒrɪsˈpɒndəns] *n* correspondencia. **2** *(mail)* correo.

correspondent [kɒrɪsˈpɒndənt] *n* corresponsal *mf*.

corresponding [kɒrɪsˈpɒndɪŋ] *adj* correspondiente.

corridor [ˈkɒrɪdɔːʳ] *n* corredor *m*, pasillo.

corroborate [kəˈrɒbəreɪt] *t* corroborar.

corroboration [kərɒbəˈreɪʃən] *n* corroboración.

corrode [kəˈrəʊd] *t* corroer.

corrosion [kəˈrəʊʒən] *n* corrosión.

corrosive [kəˈrəʊsɪv] *adj* corrosivo,-a.

corrugated [ˈkɒrəgeɪtɪd] *t* ondulado,-a.

corrupt [kəˈrʌpt] *adj* corrompido,-a, corrupto,-a. **– 2** *t-i* corromper.

corruption [kəˈrʌpʃən] *n* corrupción.

corset [ˈkɔːsɪt] *n* corsé *m*.

cortège [kɔːˈteɪʒ] *n* cortejo.

cortisone [ˈkɔːtɪzəʊn] *n* cortisona.

cosh [kɒʃ] GB *n* porra. **– 2** *t* dar un porrazo a.

cosmetic [kɒzˈmetɪk] *adj-n* cosmético,-a *(m)*. ■ ~ *surgery,* cirugía estética.

cosmic [ˈkɒzmɪk] *adj* cósmico,-a.

cosmonaut [ˈkɒzmənɔːt] *n* cosmonauta *mf*.

cosmopolitan [kɒzməˈpɒlɪtən] *adj* cosmopolita.

cosmos [ˈkɒzmɒs] *n* cosmos *m inv*.

cost [kɒst] *n* coste *m*, costo, precio. **2** *pl* JUR costas *fpl*. **– 3** *i* costar, valer. ●*whatever the ~,* cueste lo que cueste. ■ ~ *of living,* coste de la vida. ▲ *pt & pp* **cost**.

co-star [ˈkəʊstɑːʳ] *n* coprotagonista *mf*.

costly [ˈkɒstlɪ] *adj* costoso,-a.

costume [ˈkɒstjuːm] *n* traje *m*, vestido. **2** *pl* THEAT vestuario *m sing*. ■ *bathing/ swimming ~,* bañador *m*, traje *m* de baño; ~ *jewellery,* bisutería.

cosy [ˈkəʊzɪ] *adj* acogedor,-ra.

cot [kɒt] *n* cuna.

cottage [ˈkɒtɪdʒ] *n* casa de campo. ■ ~ *cheese,* requesón *m*.

cotton [ˈkɒtən] *n* algodón *m*. **2** *(thread)* hilo. ●*to ~ on i* caer en la cuenta. ■ ~

wool, algodón hidrófilo; ~ *plant,* algodonero.

couch [kaʊtʃ] *n* canapé *m*, sofá *m*. **– 2** *t* expresar.

couchette [kuːˈʃet] *n* litera.

cough [kɒf] *n* tos *f*. **– 2** *i* toser. ●*to ~ up fam t* soltar. **– 2** *i* desembolsar, aflojar la pasta.

could [kʊd, kəd] *pt* → **can**.

council [ˈkaʊnsɪl] *n* consejo. **2** *(town, city)* ayuntamiento. **3** REL concilio.

councillor [ˈkaʊnsɪləʳ] *n* concejal *mf*.

counsel [ˈkaʊnsəl] *n* *(advice)* consejo. **2** JUR abogado,-a. **– 3** *t* aconsejar.

counsellor [ˈkaʊnsələʳ] *n* consejero,-a. **2** US abogado,-a.

count [kaʊnt] *n* cuenta. **2** *(noble)* conde *m*. **– 3** *t* contar. **4** *(consider)* considerar: ~ *yourself lucky you weren't fined,* suerte tienes que no te multaron. **– 5** *i* contar. ●*to ~ in t fam* incluir, contar con. ●*to ~ on t* contar con. ●*to ~ out t* ir contando. **2** *(boxer)* declarar fuera de combate. **3** *fam* no contar con.

countable [ˈkaʊntəbəl] *adj* contable.

countdown [ˈkaʊntdaʊn] *n* cuenta atrás.

countenance [ˈkaʊntɪnəns] *fml n* rostro, semblante *m*. **– 2** *t* aprobar.

counter [ˈkaʊntəʳ] *n* *(in shop)* mostrador *m*. **2** *(which counts)* contador *m*. **3** *(in game)* ficha. **– 4** *t* contrarrestar. **– 5** *adv* en contra *(to,* de).

counteract [kaʊntəˈrækt] *t* contrarrestar.

counterattack [ˈkaʊntərətæk] *n* contraataque *m*.

counterbalance [ˈkaʊntəbæləns] *n* contrapeso. **– 2** *t* contrapesar.

counterclockwise [kaʊntəˈklɒkwaɪz] *adj & adv* US en sentido contrario al de las agujas del reloj.

counterespionage [kaʊntərˈespɪənɑːʒ] *n* contraespionaje *m*.

counterfeit [ˈkaʊntəfɪt] *adj* falso,-a, falsificado,-a. **– 2** *n* falsificación. **– 3** *t* falsificar.

counterfoil [ˈkaʊntəfɔɪl] *n* matriz *f*.

countermeasure [ˈkaʊntəmeʒəʳ] *n* contramedida.

counterpane [ˈkaʊntəpeɪn] *n* colcha, cubrecama *m*.

counterpart [ˈkæʊntəpɑːt] *n* homólogo,-a.

counterpoint [ˈkaʊntəpɔɪnt] *n* contrapunto.

counterproductive [kaʊntəprəˈdʌktɪv] *adj* contraproducente.

countersign [ˈkaʊntəsaɪn] *t* refrendar.

countess ['kaʊntəs] *n* condesa.

countless ['kaʊntləs] *adj* incontable, innumerable.

country ['kʌntrɪ] *n (political)* país *m*. **2** *(homeland)* patria. **3** *(rural area)* campo. **4** *(region)* tierra, región.

countryman ['kʌntrɪmən] *n* campesino. **2** *(compatriot)* compatriota *m*.

countryside ['kʌntrɪsaɪd] *n* campo. **2** *(scenery)* paisaje *m*.

countrywoman ['kʌntrɪwʊmən] *n* campesina. **2** *(compatriot)* compatriota.

county ['kaʊntɪ] *n* condado.

coup [ku:] *n* golpe *m*. ■ ~ *d'état,* golpe de estado.

coupé ['ku:peɪ] *n* coupé *m*, cupé *m*.

couple ['kʌpəl] *n (things)* par *m*. **2** *(people)* pareja. – **3** *t (connect)* acoplar, conectar. – **4** *i (mate)* aparearse.

coupon ['ku:pɒn] *n* cupón *m*. **2** GB SP boleto.

courage ['kʌrɪdʒ] *n* valor *m*, valentía.

courageous [kə'reɪdʒəs] *adj* valeroso,-a, valiente.

courgette [kʊə'ʒet] *n* calabacín *m*.

courier ['kʊərɪəʳ] *n (messenger)* mensajero,-a. **2** *(guide)* guía *mf* turístico,-a.

course [kɔ:s] *n (of ship, plane)* rumbo; *(on chart)* derrotero. **2** *(of river)* curso. **2** *(series)* serie *f*, ciclo. **3** *(lessons)* curso; *(short)* cursillo. **4** *(university)* curso; *(subject)* asignatura. **5** *(of meal)* plato. **6** *(for golf)* campo. **7** *(of bricks)* hilada. ●*during the* ~ *of,* durante; *in due* ~, a su debido tiempo; *in the* ~ *of time,* en el transcurso del tiempo; *of* ~, desde luego, por supuesto.

court [kɔ:t] *n* JUR tribunal *m*. **2** *(royal)* corte *f*. **3** *(tennis etc.)* pista. **4** *(courtyard)* patio. – **5** *t* cortejar. ●*to take sb. to* ~, llevar a algn. a juicio. ■ *high* ~, tribunal supremo.

courteous ['kɜ:tɪəs] *adj* cortés.

courtesy ['kɜ:tɪsɪ] *n* cortesía.

courtier ['kɔ:tjəʳ] *n* cortesano.

court-martial [kɔ:t'mɑ:ʃəl] *n* consejo de guerra.

courtship ['kɔ:tʃɪp] *n* cortejo.

courtyard ['kɔ:tjɑ:d] *n* patio.

cousin ['kʌzən] *n* primo,-a.

cove [kəʊv] *n* cala, ensenada.

covenant ['kʌvənənt] *n* convenio, pacto.

cover ['kʌvəʳ] *n* cubierta; *(lid)* tapa. **2** *(of book)* cubierta; *(of magazine)* portada. **3** *(insurance)* cobertura. **4** *fig* abrigo, protección. – **5** *t* cubrir *(with,* de); *(floor etc.)* revestir *(with,* de). **6** *(with lid)* tapar. **7** *(book)* forrar. **8** *(hide)* encubrir. **9** *(pro-* *tect)* proteger, abrigar. **10** *(insurance)* asegurar. **11** *(deal with)* abarcar. **12** SP marcar. ●*to* ~ *up t* cubrir. **2** *(hide)* encubrir. – **3** *i* cubrirse, taparse. ●*to take* ~, abrigarse, refugiarse; *under* ~, *(in hiding)* clandestinamente; *under separate* ~, por separado. ■ ~ *charge,* precio del cubierto; GB ~ *note,* seguro provisional.

coverage ['kʌvərɪdʒ] *n* reportaje *m*. **2** *(insurance)* cobertura.

covering ['kʌvərɪŋ] *n* cubierta, envoltura.

covert ['kʌvət] *adj* secreto,-a, disimulado,-a.

cover-up ['kʌvərʌp] *n* encubrimiento.

covet ['kʌvɪt] *t* codiciar.

cow [kaʊ] *n* vaca.

coward ['kaʊəd] *n* cobarde *mf*.

cowardice ['kaʊədɪs] *n* cobardía.

cowardly ['kaʊədlɪ] *adj* cobarde.

cowboy ['kaʊbɔɪ] *n* vaquero.

cowl [kaʊl] *n* capucha. **2** *(of chimney)* sombrerete *m*.

coy [kɔɪ] *adj* tímido,-a.

crab [kræb] *n* cangrejo. **2** BOT ~ *apple,* manzana silvestre.

crack [kræk] *t (split)* rajar; *(bone)* fracturar. **2** *(safe)* forzar; *(egg, nut)* cascar. **3** *(whip)* hacer restallar. **4** *fig (problem)* solucionar; *(joke)* soltar. – **5** *i* rajarse, agrietarse. **6** *(voice)* cascarse. – **7** *n (in cup)* raja; *(in ice etc.)* grieta. **8** *(of whip)* restallido. **9** *fam (blow)* golpetazo. – **10** *adj* sl de primera. ●*fam to get cracking,* poner manos a la obra.

crackbrained ['krækbreɪnd] *adj fam* chalado,-a, chiflado,-a.

cracker ['krækəʳ] *n (biscuit)* galleta de hojaldre.

crackle ['krækəl] *n* chasquido. – **2** *i* chasquear.

cradle ['kreɪdəl] *n* cuna. **2** *(construction)* andamio volante. – **3** *t* acunar.

craft [krɑ:ft] *n (skill)* habilidad, destreza. **2** *(occupation)* oficio. **3** *(boat)* embarcación.

craftsman ['krɑ:ftsmən] *n* artesano.

craftsmanship ['krɑ:ftsmənʃɪp] *n* arte *m*, habilidad.

crafty ['krɑ:ftɪ] *adj* astuto,-a, taimado,-a.

crag [kræg] *n* risco, peñasco.

cram [kræm] *t* henchir, atestar *(with,* de). – **2** *i fam* empollar.

cramp [kræmp] *n* calambre *m*, rampa. – **2** *t* limitar, restringir. ●*fam to* ~ *sb.'s style,* cortar el vuelo a algn.

crane [kreɪn] *n* ZOOL grulla común. **2** *(device)* grúa. – **3** *t (neck)* estirar.

cranium ['kreɪnɪəm] *n* cráneo.
crank [kræŋk] *n* cigüeñal *m*. **2** *(starting handle)* manivela. **– 3** *t to* ~ *(up),* arrancar con manivela.
cranky ['kræŋkɪ] *adj fam* chiflado,-a, eccéntrico,-a.
crap [kræp] *n fam* mierda.
crash [kræʃ] *i* chocar *(into,* con); *(car, plane)* estrellarse *(into,* contra). **2** COM quebrar. **– 3** *n (noise)* estallido, estrépito. **4** *(collision)* choque *m*. **5** COM quiebra.
crass [kræs] *adj* grosero,-a.
crater ['kreɪtəʳ] *n* cráter *m*.
crave [kreɪv] *i* ansiar *(for,* -).
craving ['kreɪvɪŋ] *n* ansia; *(in pregnancy)* antojo.
crawfish ['krɔːfɪʃ] *n* langosta.
crawl [krɔːl] *i* arrastrarse; *(baby)* gatear; *(car)* avanzar lentamente. **– 2** *n* DEP crol *m*. ●*to* ~ *with,* estar apestado,-a de; *to make sb.'s flesh* ~, poner los pelos de punta a algn.
crayfish ['kreɪfɪʃ] *n* cangrejo de río.
crayon ['kreɪɒn] *n* lápiz *m* pastel.
craze [kreɪz] *n* manía, moda.
crazy ['kreɪzɪ] *adj fam* loco,-a, chiflado,-a. ●*to drive sb.* ~, volver loco,-a a algn.
creak [kriːk] *i* crujir; *(hinge)* chirriar. **– 2** *n* crujido; *(of hinge)* chirrido.
cream [kriːm] *n* crema; *(of milk)* nata. **2** *(cosmetic)* crema. **3** *fig the* ~, la flor y nata. **– 4** *t (milk)* desnatar. **5** *(mix)* batir. ■ ~ *cheese,* queso cremoso; *double* ~, nata para montar; *whipped* ~, nata montada.
crease [kriːs] *n (wrinkle)* arruga; *(ironed)* raya. **– 2** *t (wrinkle)* arrugar; *(with iron)* hacer la raya. **– 3** *i* arrugarse.
create [kriːˈeɪt] *t* crear. **2** *fig* producir, causar.
creation [kriːˈeɪʃən] *n* creación.
creative [kriːˈeɪtɪv] *adj* creativo,-a.
creature ['kriːtʃəʳ] *n (animal)* criatura. **2** *(human being)* ser *m*.
credentials [krɪˈdenʃəlz] *npl* credenciales *fpl*.
credibility [kredɪˈbɪlɪtɪ] *n* credibilidad.
credible ['kredɪbəl] *adj* creíble.
credit ['kredɪt] *n* mérito, reconocimiento. **2** *(benefit)* honor *m*. **3** COM crédito; *(in accountancy)* haber *m*: ~ *and debit,* debe y haber. **4** *pl* CIN TV ficha *f sing* técnica. **– 5** *t* creer, dar crédito a. **6** COM abonar, acreditar. ●*on* ~, a crédito; *to do sb.* ~, honrar a algn.; *to take* ~ *for sth.,* atribuirse el mérito de algo. ■ ~ *card,* tarjeta de crédito.

creditor ['kredɪtəʳ] *n* acreedor,-ra.
credulous ['kredjʊləs] *adj* crédulo,-a.
creed [kriːd] *n* credo.
creek [kriːk] *n* GB cala. **2** US riachuelo.
creep [kriːp] *i (insect)* arrastrarse; *(animal)* deslizarse; *(plant)* trepar. **– 2** *n fam (person)* pelota *mf*. ●*to* ~ *in/out,* entrar/salir sigilosamente. ▲ *pt & pp* **crept**.
creeper ['kriːpəʳ] *n* trepadora.
cremation [krɪˈmeɪʃən] *n* incineración.
crematorium [kreməˈtɔːrɪəm] *n* (horno) crematorio.
crept [krept] *pt & pp* → **creep**.
crescent ['kresənt] *n* medialuna.
crest [krest] *n (of cock, wave)* cresta. **2** *(of hill)* cima, cumbre *f*. **3** *(heraldry)* blasón *m*.
crestfallen ['krestfɔːlən] *adj* abatido,-a.
cretin ['kretɪn] *n* cretino,-a.
crevice ['krevɪs] *n* raja, hendedura.
crew [kruː] *n* AV MAR tripulación. **2** *(team)* equipo. **– 3** *pt* → **crow**.
crib [krɪb] *n (manger)* pesebre *m*. **2** *(baby's)* cuna. **– 3** *t fam* plagiar. ■ *fam* ~ *note,* chuleta.
crick [krɪk] *n* tortícolis *f inv*.
cricket ['krɪkɪt] *n (insect)* grillo. **2** SP cricquet *m*.
crime [kraɪm] *n* crimen *m*. **2** *(act)* delito.
criminal ['krɪmɪnəl] *adj-n* criminal *(mf)*.
crimson ['krɪmzən] *adj-n* carmesí *(m)*.
cringe [krɪndʒ] *i* abatirse, encogerse.
crinkle ['krɪŋkəl] *t-i* arrugar(se).
cripple ['krɪpəl] *n* lisiado,-a. **– 2** *t* dejar cojo,-a; *fig* paralizar.
crisis ['kraɪsɪs] *n* crisis *f inv*. ▲ *pl* **crises** ['kraɪsiːz].
crisp [krɪsp] *adj (toast etc.)* crujiente. **2** *(lettuce)* fresco,-a. **3** *(weather)* frío,-a y seco,-a. **4** *(style)* directo,-a. **– 5** *n* GB patata frita (de churrería).
crisscross ['krɪskrɒs] *t-i* entrecruzar(se).
criterion [kraɪˈtɪərɪən] *n* criterio.
critic ['krɪtɪk] *n* crítico,-a.
critical ['krɪtɪkəl] *adj* crítico,-a. ●*in* ~ *condition,* grave.
criticism ['krɪtɪsɪzəm] *n* crítica.
criticize ['krɪtɪsaɪz] *t-i* criticar.
croak [krəʊk] *n (of raven)* graznido; *(of frog)* canto. **2** *(of person)* voz *f* ronca. **– 3** *i (raven)* graznar; *(frog)* croar. **4** *(person)* hablar con voz ronca.
crochet ['krəʊʃeɪ] *n* ganchillo. **– 2** *i* hacer ganchillo.
crockery ['krɒkərɪ] *n* loza.
crocodile ['krɒkədaɪl] *n* cocodrilo.
crocus ['krəʊkəs] *n* azafrán *m*.

crony [ˈkrəʊnɪ] *n* compinche *mf*.

crook [krʊk] *n* gancho. **2** *(shepherd's)* cayado. **3** *fam* caco.

crooked [ˈkrʊkɪd] *adj* torcido,-a. **2** *fam* deshonesto,-a.

crop [krɒp] *n* cultivo; *(harvest)* cosecha. **2** *(hair)* pelado corto. **3** *(of bird)* buche *m*. — **4** *t* *(grass)* pacer. **5** *(hair)* cortar al rape. ◆*to* ~ *up fam* surgir.

croquet [ˈkrəʊkeɪ] *n* croquet *m*.

cross [krɒs] *n* cruz. **2** *(breeds etc.)* cruce *m*. **3** *(sewing)* sesgo *m*. — **4** *t* cruzar. **5** REL *to* ~ *oneself,* santiguarse. — **6** *i* cruzar(se). — **7** *adj* transversal. **8** *(angry)* enojado,-a. ◆*to* ~ *off/out* *t* borrar, tachar. ◆*to* ~ *over* *t* pasar, atravesar. ●*it crossed my mind that ...,* se me ocurrió que ... . ■ *Red Cross,* Cruz Roja.

crossbar [ˈkrɒsbɑː^r] *n* travesaño.

crossbow [ˈkrɒsbəʊ] *n* ballesta.

crossbred [ˈkrɒsbred] *adj-n* híbrido,-a.

cross-country [krɒsˈkʌntrɪ] *adj-adv* campo través. ■ DEP ~ *race,* cros *m*.

cross-examine [krɒsɪgˈzæmɪn] *t* interrogar.

cross-eyed [ˈkrɒsaɪd] *adj* bizco,-a.

crossing [ˈkrɒsɪŋ] *n* cruce *m*. **2** MAR travesía. ■ *pedestrian* ~, paso de peatones.

cross-reference [krɒsˈrefərəns] *n* remisión.

crossroads [ˈkrɒsrəʊdz] *n* encrucijada.

crosswise [ˈkrɒswaɪz] *adv* de través.

crossword [ˈkrɒswɜːd] *n* ~ *(puzzle),* crucigrama *m*.

crotch [krɒtʃ] *n* entrepierna.

crotchet [ˈkrɒtʃɪt] *n* negra.

crotchety [ˈkrɒtʃɪtɪ] *adj fam* cascarrabias *inv*.

crouch [kraʊtʃ] *i* agacharse, agazaparse.

crow [krəʊ] *n* cuervo. — **2** *i* *(cock)* cantar. ■ *crow's-feet,* patas *fpl* de gallo. ▲ *pt crowed o crew*.

crowbar [ˈkrəʊbɑː^r] *n* palanca.

crowd [kraʊd] *n* multitud, gentío. — **2** *t* llenar, atestar. — **3** *i* apiñarse.

crown [kraʊn] *n* corona. **2** ANAT coronilla. **3** *(of hat, tree)* copa. — **4** *t* coronar.

crucial [ˈkruːʃəl] *adj* crucial, decisivo,-a.

crucifix [ˈkruːsɪfɪks] *n* crucifijo.

crucify [ˈkruːsɪfaɪ] *t* crucificar.

crude [kruːd] *n* *(manner)* tosco,-a, grosero,-a. **2** *(oil)* crudo,-a.

crudeness [ˈkruːdnəs] *n* crudeza, tosquedad.

cruel [kruːəl] *adj* cruel.

cruelty [ˈkruːəltɪ] *n* crueldad.

cruet [ˈkruːɪt] *n* ~ *set,* vinagreras *fpl*.

cruise [kruːz] *i* hacer un crucero. — **2** *n* crucero.

cruiser [ˈkruːzə^r] *n* crucero.

crumb [krʌm] *n* miga, migaja.

crumble [ˈkrʌmbəl] *t* desmenuzar, desmigar. — **2** *i* desmoronarse.

crumple [ˈkrʌmpəl] *t-i* arrugar(se).

crunch [krʌntʃ] *t* *(food)* mascar. **2** *(with feet etc.)* hacer crujir. — **3** *i* crujir.

crusade [kruːˈseɪd] *n* cruzada.

crusader [kruːˈseɪdə^r] *n* cruzado.

crush [krʌʃ] *t* aplastar. — **2** *n* aplastamiento. **3** *fam* enamoramiento.

crust [krʌst] *n* *(of bread)* corteza. **2** *(pastry)* pasta. **3** *(of earth)* corteza.

crustacean [krʌˈsteɪʃən] *adj-n* crustáceo,-a (*m*).

crutch [krʌtʃ] *n* muleta.

crux [krʌks] *n* quid *m*, meollo.

cry [kraɪ] *t-i* *(shout)* gritar. — **2** *i* llorar, lamentarse. — **3** *n* grito. **4** *(weep)* llanto. ◆*to* ~ *out* *i* gritar; *fig to* ~ *out for sth.,* pedir algo a gritos.

crying [ˈkraɪɪŋ] *n* llanto. — **2** *adj fig* apremiante.

crypt [krɪpt] *n* cripta.

cryptic [ˈkrɪptɪk] *adj* enigmático,-a.

crystal [ˈkrɪstəl] *n* cristal *m*.

crystallize [ˈkrɪstəlaɪz] *t-i* cristalizar(se).

cub [kʌb] *n* cachorro,-a.

cube [kjuːb] *n* MAT cubo. **2** *(of sugar)* terrón *m*. — **3** *t* MAT elevar al cubo. ■ ~ *root,* raíz cúbica.

cubic [ˈkjuːbɪk] *adj* cúbico,-a.

cubicle [ˈkjuːbɪkəl] *n* cubículo.

cubism [ˈkjuːbɪzəm] *n* cubismo.

cuckoo [ˈkʊkuː] *n* cuco común. — **2** *adj fam* majareta, pirado,-a.

cucumber [ˈkjuːkʌmbə^r] *n* pepino.

cuddle [ˈkʌdəl] *t* abrazar, acariciar. — **2** *i* abrazarse. — **3** *n* abrazo.

cudgel [ˈkʌdʒəl] *n* porra. — **2** *t* aporrear. ●*to take up the cudgels for sb.,* salir en defensa de algn.

cue [kjuː] *n* señal *f*. **2** THEAT pie *m*. **3** *(billiards)* taco.

cuff [kʌf] *n* *(of sleeve)* puño. — **2** *t* abofetear. ■ ~ *links,* gemelos *mpl*.

cul-de-sac [ˈkʌldəsæk] *n* calle *f* sin salida.

culminate [ˈkʌlmɪneɪt] *t* culminar.

culmination [kʌlmɪˈneɪʃən] *n* culminación, apogeo.

culpable [ˈkʌlpəbəl] *adj* culpable.

culprit [ˈkʌlprɪt] *n* culpable *mf*.

cult [kʌlt] *n* culto.

cultivate [ˈkʌltɪveɪt] *t* cultivar.

cultivated [ˈkʌltɪveɪtɪd] *adj (person)* culto,-a. **2** *(land etc.)* cultivado,-a.
cultivation [kʌltɪˈveɪʃən] *n* cultivo.
culture [ˈkʌltʃəʳ] *n* cultura.
cultured [ˈkʌltʃəd] *adj (person)* culto,-a.
cumbersome [ˈkʌmbəsəm] *adj (awkward)* incómodo,-a.
cum(m)in [ˈkʌmɪn] *n* comino.
cunning [ˈkʌnɪŋ] *adj* astuto,-a. − **3** *n* astucia, maña.
cup [kʌp] *n* taza. **2** SP copa.
cupboard [ˈkʌbəd] *n (for clothes, books)* armario; *(on wall)* alacena.
cupola [ˈkjuːpələ] *n* cúpula.
cur [kɜːʳ] *n pey* chucho. **2** *(person)* canalla.
curable [ˈkjʊərəbəl] *adj* curable.
curate [ˈkjʊərət] *n* cura *m*, coadjutor *m*.
curator [ˈkjʊəreɪtəʳ] *n* conservador,-ra.
curb [kɜːb] *n (for horse)* barbada. **2** *fig* freno. − **3** *t (horse)* refrenar. **4** *fig* contener.
curd [kɜːd] *n* cuajada.
curdle [ˈkɜːdəl] *t-i (milk)* cuajar(se), cortar(se). **2** *fig* helar(se).
cure [kjʊəʳ] *t* curar. − **2** *n* cura.
curfew [ˈkɜːfjuː] *n* toque *m* de queda.
curiosity [kjʊərɪˈɒsɪtɪ] *n* curiosidad.
curious [ˈkjʊərɪəs] *adj* curioso,-a.
curl [kɜːl] *t-i* rizar(se). − **2** *n* rizo, bucle *m*; *(tight)* tirabuzón *m*. **3** *(of smoke)* espiral *f*.
curlew [ˈkɜːljuː] *n* zarapito real.
curling [ˈkɜːlɪŋ] *adj* ~ *tongs,* tenacillas *fpl* de rizar el pelo.
currant [ˈkʌrənt] *n* pasa (de Corinto). **2** *(fruit)* grosella.
currency [ˈkʌrənsɪ] *n* moneda. ■ *foreign* ~, divisa; *hard* ~, divisa fuerte.
current [ˈkʌrənt] *adj* general; *(phrase)* actual; *(month etc.)* en curso. **2** FIN corriente. − **3** *n* corriente *f*.
curry [ˈkʌrɪ] *n* curry *m*. − **2** *t fig to* ~ *favour (with sb.),* congraciarse (con algn.).
curse [kɜːs] *n* maldición. **2** *(oath)* palabrota. **3** *fig* azote *m*. − **4** *t-i* maldecir.
cursory [ˈkɜːsərɪ] *adj* rápido,-a, superficial.
curt [kɜːt] *adj* seco,-a, brusco,-a.
curtail [kɜːˈteɪl] *t* reducir.
curtain [ˈkɜːtən] *n* cortina; THEAT telón *m*. ●*to drop/raise the* ~, bajar/alzar el telón.

curts(e)y [ˈkɜːtsɪ] *n* reverencia.
curvature [ˈkɜːvətʃəʳ] *n* curvatura.
curve [kɜːv] *n* curva. − **2** *t* encorvar. − **3** *i* torcer.
cushion [ˈkʊʃən] *n* cojín *m*; *(large)* almohadón *m*. − **2** *t fig* suavizar.
custard [ˈkʌstəd] *n* natillas *fpl*.
custodian [kʌsˈtəʊdɪən] *n* conserje *mf*.
custody [ˈkʌstədɪ] *n* custodia. ●*to take into* ~, detener.
custom [ˈkʌstəm] *n* costumbre *f*.
customary [ˈkʌstəmərɪ] *adj* acostumbrado,-a, habitual.
customer [ˈkʌstəməʳ] *n* cliente *mf*.
customs [ˈkʌstʌmz] *n sing or pl* aduana.
cut [kʌt] *t* cortar. **2** *(stone, glass)* tallar; *(record)* grabar. **3** *(divide up)* dividir. **4** *(reduce)* recortar. − **5** *n* corte *m*. **6** *(of meat)* tajada. **7** *(share)* parte *f*. **8** *(reduction)* recorte *m*; *(discount)* descuento. **9** *(insult)* desaire *m*. − **10** *adj* cortado,-a; *(price)* reducido,-a. ◆*to* ~ *down t* talar, cortar. **2** *fig to* ~ *down (on),* reducir. ◆*to* ~ *in i* meter baza. ◆*to* ~ *off t* cortar; *fig* desheredar. ◆*to* ~ *out t* recortar; *(dress)* cortar. **2** *fig* suprimir. ●*to* ~ *one's hair,* cortarse el pelo; *fig to* ~ *corners,* recortar presupuestos. ■ *cold cuts,* fiambres *mpl*; *short* ~, atajo. ▲ *pt & pp* **cut**.
cute [kjuːt] *adj* mono,-a.
cuticle [ˈkjuːtɪkəl] *n* cutícula.
cutlery [ˈkʌtlərɪ] *n* cubiertos *mpl*, cubertería.
cutlet [ˈkʌtlət] *n* chuleta.
cutting [ˈkʌtɪŋ] *n* recorte *m*. **2** BOT esqueje *m*. − **3** *adj* cortante.
cuttlefish [ˈkʌtəlfɪʃ] *n* jibia, sepia.
cyanide [ˈsaɪənaɪd] *n* cianuro.
cycle [ˈsaɪkəl] *i* ir en bicicleta.
cycling [ˈsaɪklɪŋ] *n* ciclismo.
cyclist [ˈsaɪklɪst] *n* ciclista *mf*.
cyclone [ˈsaɪkləʊn] *n* ciclón *m*.
cylinder [ˈsɪlɪndəʳ] *n* cilindro. **2** *(gas)* bombona.
cymbal [ˈsɪmbəl] *n* címbalo.
cynic [ˈsɪnɪk] *n* cínico,-a.
cynical [ˈsɪnɪkəl] *adj* cínico,-a.
cynicism [ˈsɪnɪsɪzəm] *n* cinismo.
cypress [ˈsaɪprəs] *n* ciprés *m*.
cyst [sɪst] *n* quiste *m*.
czar [zɑːʳ] *n* zar *m*.

D

dab [dæb] *n* toque *m*. **2** *(fish)* acedía. **– 3** *t* tocar ligeramente. **4** *(with paint)* dar pinceladas a.

dabble ['dæbəl] *i* aficionarse *(in,* a).

dad [dæd], **daddy** ['dædɪ] *n fam* papá *m*.

daffodil ['dæfədɪl] *n* narciso.

daft [dɑːft] *adj fam (person)* chalado,-a; *(idea)* tonto,-a.

dagger ['dægəʳ] *n* daga, puñal *m*.

daily ['deɪlɪ] *adj* diario,-a, cotidiano,-a. **–** **2** *adv* diariamente. **– 3** *n* diario.

dainty ['deɪntɪ] *adj (delicate)* delicado,-a. **2** *(refined)* refinado,-a.

dairy ['deərɪ] *n (on farm)* vaquería. **2** *(shop)* lechería. ■ **~ farming,** industria lechera.

dais ['deɪɪs] *n* tarima, estrado.

daisy ['deɪzɪ] *n* margarita.

dam [dæm] *n (barrier)* dique *m*. **2** *(reservoir)* embalse *m*, presa. **– 3** *t* represar, embalsar. **4** *fig* **to ~ (up),** reprimir.

damage ['dæmɪdʒ] *n* daño. **2** *fig* perjuicio. **3** *pl* daños *mpl* y perjuicios. **– 4** *t* dañar. **5** *fig* perjudicar.

damaging ['dæmɪdʒɪŋ] *adj* perjudicial.

dame [deɪm] *n (title)* dama. **2** *US fam* mujer *f,* tía.

damn [dæm] *interj fam* **~ (it)!,** ¡maldito,-a sea! **– 2** *adj s|* maldito,-a. **– 3** *t* condenar. ●*I don't give a ~,* me importa un bledo.

damned [dæmd] *adj* maldito,-a.

damp [dæmp] *adj* húmedo,-a; *(wet)* mojado,-a. **– 2** *n* humedad.

dampen ['dæmpən] *t* humedecer. **2** *fig* desalentar.

dampness ['dæmpnəs] *n* humedad.

dance [dɑːns] *n* baile *m; (classical, tribal)* danza. **– 2** *i-t* bailar.

dancer ['dɑːnsəʳ] *n* bailador,-ra. **2** *(professional)* bailarín,-ina.

dandelion ['dændɪlaɪən] *n* diente *m* de león.

dandruff ['dændrəf] *n* caspa.

danger ['deɪndʒəʳ] *n* peligro. **2** *(risk)* riesgo.

dangerous ['deɪndʒərəs] *adj* peligroso,-a. **2** *(illness)* grave.

dangle ['dæŋgəl] *t-i* colgar, balancear(se) en el aire.

dank [dæŋk] *adj* húmedo,-a y malsano,-a.

dappled ['dæpəld] *adj* moteado,-a; *(horse)* rodado,-a.

dare [deəʳ] *i* atreverse *(to,* a), osar. **– 2** *t (challenge)* desafiar. **– 3** *n* reto, desafío. ●*I ~ say,* creo (que sí).

daredevil ['deədevəl] *adj-n* atrevido,-a.

daring ['deərɪŋ] *adj* audaz, osado,-a. **– 2** *n* osadía, atrevimiento.

dark [dɑːk] *adj* oscuro,-a. **2** *(hair, skin)* moreno,-a. **3** *fig (gloomy)* triste; *(future)* negro,-a. **4** *fig (secret)* misterioso,-a. **– 5** *n* oscuridad. **6** *(nightfall)* anochecer *m*. ●*fig* **to be in the ~,** estar a oscuras, no saber nada.

darken ['dɑːkən] *t-i* oscurecer(se). **2** *fig* entristecer(se).

darkness ['dɑːknəs] *n* oscuridad, tinieblas *fpl*. ●*in ~,* a oscuras.

darling ['dɑːlɪŋ] *n* querido,-a, amado,-a. **– 2** *adj* querido,-a. **3** *fam* precioso,-a.

darn [dɑːn] *n* zurcido. **– 2** *t* zurcir. **– 3** *interj fam euph* ¡mecachis!

dart [dɑːt] *n* dardo. **2** *(rush)* movimiento rápido. **3** SEW pinza. **– 4** *t* echar. **– 5** *i* lanzarse, precipitarse.

dartboard ['dɑːtbɔːd] *n* blanco de tiro.

dash [dæʃ] *n (rush)* carrera. **2** *(small amount)* poco; *(of salt etc.)* pizca; *(of liquid)* chorro. **3** *(mark)* raya. **4** *(style)* elegancia. **– 5** *t* lanzar, arrojar. **6** *(smash)* romper, estrellar; *fig* desvanecer. **– 7** *i*

(rush) correr. ◆*to ~ off t* escribir deprisa y corriendo. − **2** *i* salir corriendo.
dashboard [ˈdɑːʃbɔːd] *n* salpicadero.
data [ˈdeɪtə] *npl* datos *mpl*. ■ COMPUT ~ *base,* base *f* de datos; ~ *processing,* *(science)* informática.
date [deɪt] *n* fecha. **2** *(appointment)* cita, compromiso. **3** BOT dátil *m*. − **4** *t* fechar, datar. **5** US *fam (go out with)* salir con. ●*out of ~,* anticuado,-a; *up to ~,* actualizado,-a; *fig to be up to ~ (on sth.),* estar al corriente (de algo). ■ ~ *palm,* (palmera) datilera.
dated [ˈdeɪtɪd] *adj* anticuado,-a.
dative [ˈdeɪtɪv] *adj-n* dativo.
daub [dɔːb] *n* revestimiento, capa. − **2** *t* embadurnar; *(with oil)* untar. − **3** *i fam* pintarrajear.
daughter [ˈdɔːtəʳ] *n* hija.
daughter-in-law [ˈdɔːtərɪnlɔː] *n* nuera.
daunt [dɔːnt] *t* intimidar.
dawdle [ˈdɔːdəl] *i* ir despacio. **2** *(waste time)* perder el tiempo.
dawn [dɔːn] *n* alba, aurora, amanecer *m*. **2** *fig* albores *mpl*. − **3** *i* amanecer, alborear. ●*it dawned on me that ...,* caí en la cuenta de que ... .
day [deɪ] *n* día *m*. **2** *(period of work)* jornada. **3** *(era)* época, tiempo. ●*by ~,* de día; *the ~ after tomorrow,* pasado mañana; *the ~ before yesterday,* anteayer; *these days,* hoy en día. ■ ~ *off,* día libre.
daybreak [ˈdeɪbreɪk] *n* amanecer *m*, alba.
daydream [ˈdeɪdriːm] *n* ensueño. − **2** *i* soñar despierto,-a.
daze [deɪz] *n* aturdimiento. − **2** *t* aturdir.
dazzle [ˈdæzəl] *n* deslumbramiento. − **2** *t* deslumbrar.
deacon [ˈdiːkən] *n* diácono.
dead [ded] *adj* muerto,-a. **2** *(still)* estancado,-a. **3** *(numb)* entumecido,-a. **4** *(sound)* sordo,-a. **5** *(total)* total, absoluto,-a: ~ *silence,* silencio total. − **6** *n in the ~ of night/winter,* en plena noche/pleno invierno. − **7** *adv (totally)* totalmente. **8** *(exactly)* justo. ●*to stop ~,* pararse en seco. ■ ~ *calm,* calma chicha; ~ *end,* callejón *m* sin salida.
deadline [ˈdedlaɪn] *n* fecha/hora tope, plazo.
deadlock [ˈdedlɒk] *n* punto muerto.
deadly [ˈdedlɪ] *adj* mortal; *(weapon, gas)* mortífero,-a.
deaf [def] *adj* sordo,-a. ●*to turn a ~ ear,* hacerse el sordo/la sorda.
deaf-and-dumb [defənˈdʌm] *adj* sordomudo,-a.

deafen [ˈdefən] *t* ensordecer.
deafness [ˈdefnəs] *n* sordera.
deal [diːl] *n* trato, pacto. **2** *(amount)* cantidad: *a great ~ of noise,* mucho ruido. **3** *(cards)* reparto. − **4** *t (give)* dar; *(blow)* asestar. **5** *(cards)* repartir. − **6** *i* comerciar *(in,* en). ◆*to ~ with t* COM tratar con. **2** *(manage)* abordar, ocuparse de. **3** *(treat)* tratar de. ▲ *pt & pp* **dealt**.
dealer [ˈdiːləʳ] *n* comerciante *mf*. **2** *(cards)* repartidor,-ra.
dealings [ˈdiːlɪŋz] *npl* trato *m sing*. **2** COM negocios *mpl*.
dealt [delt] *pt & pp* → **deal**.
dean [diːn] *n* REL deán *m*. **2** EDUC decano,-a.
dear [dɪəʳ] *adj* querido,-a. **2** *(in letter)* querido,-a. *fml* apreciado,-a, estimado,-a. **3** *(expensive)* caro,-a. − **4** *n* querido,-a, cariño. − **5** *interj* oh ~!/~ *me!,* ¡caramba!, ¡vaya por Dios! − **6** *adv* caro. − **7** *dearly adv* mucho. ●*Dear Sir,* Muy señor mío.
death [deθ] *n* muerte *f*. ●*on pain of ~,* bajo pena de muerte. ■ ~ *certificate,* certificado de defunción; ~ *penalty/sentence,* pena de muerte.
deathly [ˈdeθlɪ] *adj* sepulcral.
deathtrap [ˈdeθtræp] *n fam* lugar peligroso.
debar [dɪˈbɑːʳ] *t* excluir *(from,* de).
debase [dɪˈbeɪs] *t (degrade)* desvalorizar. **2** *(humiliate)* degradar.
debatable [dɪˈbeɪtəbəl] *adj* discutible.
debate [dɪˈbeɪt] *n* debate *m*, discusión. − **2** *t-i* debatir, discutir.
debauchery [dɪˈbɔːtʃərɪ] *n* libertinaje *m*, corrupción.
debilitate [dɪˈbɪlɪteɪt] *t* debilitar.
debit [ˈdebɪt] *n* FIN débito. − **2** *t* cargar en cuenta. ■ ~ *balance,* saldo negativo.
debrief [diːˈbriːf] *t* interrogar, pedir un informe a.
debris [ˈdeɪbriː] *n* escombros *mpl*.
debt [det] *n* deuda. ●*to get into/run up debts,* contraer deudas.
debtor [ˈdetəʳ] *n* deudor,-ra.
debunk [diːˈbʌŋk] *t fam* desmitificar, desenmascarar; *(idea, belief)* desacreditar.
debut [ˈdeɪbjuː] *n (show)* estreno; *(person)* debut *m*.
decade [ˈdekeɪd] *n* década, decenio.
decadence [ˈdekədəns] *n* decadencia.
decadent [ˈdekədənt] *adj* decadente.
decaffeinated [dɪˈkæfɪneɪtɪd] *adj* descafeinado,-a.
decant [dɪˈkænt] *t* decantar.
decanter [dɪˈkæntəʳ] *n* jarra.

decapitate [dɪˈkæpɪteɪt] *t* decapitar.

decay [dɪˈkeɪ] *n* descomposición. **2** *(ruin)* deterioro. **3** *(of teeth)* caries *f inv.* **4** *fig* decadencia. **– 5** *i* descomponerse. **6** *(deteriorate)* desmoronarse. **7** *(teeth)* cariarse. **8** *fig* corromperse.

deceased [dɪˈsiːst] *adj-n* difunto,-a, fallecido,-a.

deceit [dɪˈsiːt] *n* engaño, falsedad.

deceitful [dɪˈsiːtfʊl] *adj* falso,-a, mentiroso,-a.

deceive [dɪˈsiːv] *t* engañar.

decelerate [diːˈseləreɪt] *i* reducir la velocidad.

December [dɪˈsembəʳ] *n* diciembre *m.*

decency [ˈdiːsənsɪ] *n* decencia.

decent [ˈdiːsənt] *adj* decente. **2** *(adequate)* adecuado,-a, razonable. **3** *fam (kind)* bueno,-a.

decentralize [diːˈsentrəlaɪz] *t* descentralizar.

deception [dɪˈsepʃən] *n* engaño, mentira, decepción.

deceptive [dɪˈseptɪv] *adj* engañoso,-a, falso,-a.

decibel [ˈdesɪbel] *n* decibelio.

decide [dɪˈsaɪd] *t-i* decidir(se). ●*to ~ on,* optar por.

decided [dɪˈsaɪdɪd] *adj (resolute)* decidido,-a. **2** *(clear)* marcado,-a. **– 3** *decidedly adv* decididamente; *(clearly)* sin duda.

deciding [dɪˈsaɪdɪŋ] *adj* decisivo,-a.

decimal [ˈdesɪməl] *adj-n* decimal *(m).*

decimate [ˈdesɪmeɪt] *t* diezmar.

decipher [dɪˈsaɪfəʳ] *t* descifrar.

decision [dɪˈsɪʒən] *n* decisión.

decisive [dɪˈsaɪsɪv] *adj* decisivo,-a. **2** *(firm)* decidido,-a.

deck [dek] *n* cubierta. **2** *(of bus, coach)* piso. **3** US *(of cards)* baraja. **– 4** *t* adornar.

declaration [dekləˈreɪʃən] *n* declaración.

declare [dɪˈkleəʳ] *t* declarar, manifestar. **– 2** *i to ~ for/against,* pronunciarse en contra/a favor de.

decline [dɪˈklaɪn] *n (decrease)* disminución. **2** *(decay)* deterioro; *(health)* empeoramiento. **– 3** *i* disminuir. **4** *(decay)* deteriorarse; *(health)* empeorarse. **– 5** *t (refuse)* rehusar, rechazar. **6** GRAM declinar.

decode [diːˈkəʊd] *t* descifrar.

decompose [diːkəmˈpəʊz] *t-i* descomponer(se).

decor, décor [ˈdeɪkɔːʳ] *n* decoración. **2** THEAT decorado.

decorate [ˈdekəreɪt] *t* decorar, adornar. **2** *(honour)* condecorar. **– 3** *t-i (paint)* pintar; *(wallpaper)* empapelar.

decoration [dekəˈreɪʃən] *n* decoración. **2** *(medal)* condecoración.

decorative [ˈdekərətɪv] *adj* decorativo,-a.

decorum [dɪˈkɔːrəm] *n fml* decoro.

decoy [ˈdiːkɔɪ] *n (bird)* cimbel *m;* *(artificial)* señuelo. **2** *fig* señuelo. **– 3** *t* atraer con señuelo.

decrease [dɪˈkriːs] *n* disminución. **– 2** *i* disminuir, reducir.

decree [dɪˈkriː] *n* decreto. **– 2** *t* decretar.

decrepit [dɪˈkrepɪt] *adj* decrépito,-a.

dedicate [ˈdedɪkeɪt] *t* dedicar, consagrar.

dedication [dedɪˈkeɪʃən] *n* dedicación, entrega. **2** *(in book etc.)* dedicatoria.

deduce [dɪˈdjuːs] *t* deducir, inferir.

deduct [dɪˈdʌkt] *t* restar, descontar.

deduction [dɪˈdʌkʃən] *n* deducción.

deed [diːd] *n (act)* acto. **2** *(feat)* hazaña. **3** JUR escritura.

deem [diːm] *t* juzgar, considerar.

deep [diːp] *adj* hondo,-a, profundo,-a. **2** *(sound, voice)* grave. **3** *(colour)* oscuro,-a. **4** *(serious)* grave. **– 5** *adv* profundamente. **– 6** *n* profundidad. **– 7** *deeply adv* profundamente. ●*it's ten metres ~,* tiene diez metros de profundidad; *fig to be ~ in thought,* estar absorto,-a.

deepen [ˈdiːpən] *t-i* ahondar(se). **2** *(colour, emotion)* intensificar(se). **3** *(sound, voice)* hacer(se) más grave.

deer [dɪəʳ] *n inv* ciervo.

deface [dɪˈfeɪs] *t* desfigurar.

defamation [defəˈmeɪʃən] *n* difamación.

defamatory [dɪˈfæmətərɪ] *adj* difamatorio,-a.

default [dɪˈfɔːlt] *n* negligencia. **2** *(failure to pay)* incumplimiento de pago. **3** JUR rebeldía. **4** SP incomparecencia. **– 5** *i* faltar a un compromiso, imcumplir. **6** JUR estar en rebeldía. **7** SP no comparecer.

defeat [dɪˈfiːt] *n* derrota. **2** *fig* fracaso. **– 3** *t* derrotar, vencer. **4** *fig* frustrar.

defecate [ˈdefəkeɪt] *i fml* defecar.

defect [ˈdiːfekt] *n* defecto; *(flaw)* desperfecto. **– 2** *i* desertar. ▲ *En 2 (verbo)* [dɪˈfekt].

defection [dɪˈfekʃən] *n* deserción, defección.

defective [dɪˈfektɪv] *adj* defectuoso,-a. **2** *(lacking)* deficiente. **3** GRAM defectivo,-a.

defector [dɪˈfektəʳ] *n* tránsfuga *mf.*

defence [dɪ'fens] *n* defensa.
defenceless [dɪ'fensləs] *adj* indefenso,-a.
defend [dɪ'fend] *t* defender.
defendant [dɪ'fendənt] *n* demandado,-a, acusado,-a.
defender [dɪ'fendə^r] *n* defensor,-ra.
defending [dɪ'fendɪŋ] *adj* SP ~ *champion,* campeón,-ona titular. **2** JUR ~ *counsel,* abogado,-a defensor.
defensive [dɪ'fensɪv] *adj* defensivo,-a. − **2** *n* defensiva.
defer [dɪ'fɜ:^r] *t* aplazar, retrasar. − **2** *i* deferir.
deference ['defərəns] *n* deferencia, consideración.
defiance [dɪ'faɪəns] *n* desafío. ●*in* ~ *of,* a despecho de.
defiant [dɪ'faɪənt] *adj* desafiante, provocativo,-a.
deficiency [dɪ'fɪʃənsɪ] *n* deficiencia.
deficient [dɪ'fɪʃənt] *adj* deficiente. ●*to be* ~ *in sth.,* estar falto,-a de algo.
deficit ['defɪsɪt] *n* déficit *m.*
defile [dɪ'faɪl] *n* desfiladero. − **2** *t* ensuciar, contaminar. **3** *(desecrate)* profanar.
define [dɪ'faɪn] *t* definir.
definite ['defɪnət] *adj* definido,-a. **2** *(clear)* claro,-a, preciso,-a. **3** *(fixed)* determinado,-a. − **4** *definitely adv* definitivamente. ■ GRAM ~ *article,* artículo determinado.
definition [defɪ'nɪʃən] *n* definición. **2** *(clarity)* nitidez *f.*
definitive [dɪ'fɪnɪtɪv] *adj* definitivo,-a.
deflate [dɪ'fleɪt] *t-i* desinflar(se), deshinchar(se).
deflation [dɪ'fleɪʃən] *n* desinflamiento. **2** ECON deflación.
deflect [dɪ'flekt] *t-i* desviar(se).
deform [dɪ'fɔ:m] *t* deformar, desfigurar.
deformed [dɪ'fɔ:md] *adj* deforme.
defrost [di:'frɒst] *t-i* descongelar(se).
deft [deft] *adj* diestro,-a, hábil.
defunct [dɪ'fʌŋkt] *adj* difunto,-a.
defy [dɪ'faɪ] *t* desafiar; *(law)* desobedecer. **2** *(challenge)* retar.
degenerate [dɪ'dʒenərət] *adj-n* degenerado,-a. − **2** *i* degenerar. ▲ *En 2 (verbo)* [dɪ'dʒenəreɪt].
degeneration [dɪdʒenə'reɪʃən] *n* degeneración.
degrade [dɪ'greɪd] *t* degradar, rebajar.
degrading [dɪ'greɪdɪŋ] *adj* degradante.
degree [dɪ'gri:] *n* grado. **2** *(stage)* punto, etapa. **3** EDUC título. ●*by degrees,* poco a poco; *to some* ~, hasta cierto punto;

to take a ~ *(in sth.),* licenciarse (en algo). ■ *first* ~, licenciatura; *honorary* ~, doctorado "honoris causa".
dehydrate [di:haɪ'dreɪt] *t* deshidratar.
de-ice [di:'aɪs] *t* quitar el hielo a, deshelar.
deign [deɪn] *i* dignarse *(to,* a).
deity ['deɪtɪ] *n* divinidad, deidad.
dejected [dɪ'dʒektɪd] *adj* abatido,-a, desanimado,-a.
delay [dɪ'leɪ] *n* retraso. − **2** *t* *(defer)* aplazar, diferir. − **3** *t-i* retrasar(se); *(person)* entretener(se).
delegate ['delɪgət] *adj-n* delegado,-a. − **2** *t* delegar. ▲ *En 2 (verbo)* ['delɪgeɪt].
delegation [delɪ'geɪʃən] *n* delegación.
delete [dɪ'li:t] *t* borrar, suprimir.
deliberate [dɪ'lɪbərət] *adj* deliberado,-a, premeditado,-a. **2** *(slow)* pausado,-a, lento,-a. − **3** *t-i* deliberar. ▲ *En 3 (verbo)* [dɪ'lɪbəreɪt].
deliberation [dɪlɪbə'reɪʃən] *n* deliberación.
delicacy ['delɪkəsɪ] *n* delicadeza. **2** *(fragility)* fragilidad. **3** *(food)* manjar (exquisito).
delicate ['delɪkət] *adj* delicado,-a; *(handiwork)* fino,-a. **2** *(fragile)* frágil. **3** *(subtle)* suave.
delicatessen [delɪkə'tesən] *n* charcutería selecta.
delicious [dɪ'lɪʃəs] *adj* delicioso,-a. *(taste, smell)* exquisito,-a.
delight [dɪ'laɪt] *n* placer *m,* gusto. **2** *(source of pleasure)* encanto, delicia. − **3** *t* deleitar, encantar, dar gusto. − **4** *i* deleitarse *(in,* en/con).
delighted [dɪ'laɪtɪd] *adj* encantado,-a.
delightful [dɪ'laɪtful] *adj* *(pleasant)* encantador,-ra, ameno,-a. **2** *(delicious)* delicioso,-a.
delinquency [dɪ'lɪŋkwənsɪ] *n* delincuencia.
delinquent [dɪ'lɪŋkwənt] *adj-n* delincuente *(mf).*
delirious [dɪ'lɪrɪəs] *adj* delirante.
deliver [dɪ'lɪvə^r] *t* *(goods etc.)* entregar, repartir. **2** *(hit, kick)* dar. **3** *(say)* pronunciar. **4** *(doctor)* asistir al parto de. **5** *fml (free)* liberar.
deliverance [dɪ'lɪvərəns] *n fml* liberación, rescate *m.*
delivery [dɪ'lɪvərɪ] *n* *(of goods etc.)* entrega, reparto; *(of mail)* reparto. **2** *(of speech etc.)* elocuencia, dicción. **3** *(of baby)* parto, alumbramiento. ●*cash on* ~, entrega contra reembolso. ■ ~ *man,* repartidor *m;* ~ *note,* albarán *m* de entrega;

~ *room,* sala de partos; GB ~ *van,* furgoneta de reparto.

delta ['deltǝ] *n* delta *m.*

delude [dɪ'luːd] *t* engañar.

deluge ['deljuːdʒ] *n* diluvio. 2 *(flood)* inundación. — 3 *t* inundar (*with,* de).

delusion [dɪ'luːʒǝn] *n* engaño. 2 *(false belief)* ilusión.

de luxe [dǝ'lʌks] *adj inv* de lujo.

delve [delv] *i* hurgar (*into,* en). 2 *fig (past)* escarbar (*into,* en).

demand [dɪ'mɑːnd] *n* solicitud; *(for pay rise etc.)* reclamación, petición. 2 *(claim)* exigencia. 3 ECON demanda: *there's a big ~ for computers,* hay una gran demanda de ordenadores. — 4 *t* exigir; *(rights etc.)* reclamar. ●*on ~,* a petición.

demanding [dɪ'mɑːndɪŋ] *adj* exigentte. 2 *(tiring)* agotador,-ra.

demean [dɪ'miːn] *i fml* rebajar.

demeanour [dɪ'miːnǝʳ] *n fml* comportamiento, conducta. 2 *(bearing)* porte *m.*

demented [dɪ'mentɪd] *adj* demente.

demise [dɪ'maɪz] *n* fallecimiento, defunción.

demist [diː'mɪst] *t* desempañar.

demobilize [diː'mǝʊbɪlaɪz] *t* desmovilizar.

democracy [dɪ'mɒkrǝsɪ] *n* democracia.

democrat ['demǝkræt] *n* demócrata *mf.*

democratic [demǝ'krætɪk] *adj* democrático,-a. ■ US *Democratic party,* partido demócrata.

demolish [dɪ'mɒlɪʃ] *t* derribar, demoler. 2 *fig* destruir.

demolition [demǝ'lɪʃǝn] *n* demolición, derribo.

demon ['diːmǝn] *n* demonio, diablo.

demonstrate ['demǝnstreɪt] *t* demostrar. 2 *(show)* mostrar. — 3 *i (protest)* manifestarse.

demonstration [demǝn'streɪʃǝn] *n* demostración. 2 *(march)* manifestación.

demonstrative [dɪ'mɒnstrǝtɪv] *adj (person)* abierto,-a, franco,-a. 2 GRAM demostrativo,-a.

demonstrator ['demǝnstreɪtǝʳ] *n* manifestante *mf.*

demoralize [dɪ'mɒrǝlaɪz] *t* desmoralizar.

demote [dɪ'mǝʊt] *t* degradar.

demur [dɪ'mɜːʳ] *i fml* oponerse.

demure [dɪ'mjʊǝʳ] *adj* recatado,-a, discreto,-a.

den [den] *n* guarida.

denial [dɪ'naɪǝl] *n* mentís *m inv.* 2 *(refusal)* denegación, negativa.

denomination [dɪnɒmɪ'neɪʃǝn] *n (belief)* confesión. 2 *(value)* valor *m.*

denominator [dɪ'nɒmɪneɪtǝʳ] *n* denominador *m.* ■ *common ~,* común denominador.

denote [dɪ'nǝʊt] *t* denotar, indicar. 2 *(position, weight)* marcar.

denounce [dɪ'naʊns] *t* denunciar, censurar.

dense [dens] *adj* denso,-a, espeso,-a. 2 *fam (person)* corto,-a.

density ['densɪtɪ] *n* densidad.

dent [dent] *n* abolladura. — 2 *t* abollar.

dental ['dentǝl] *adj* dental. ■ ~ *surgeon,* odontólogo,-a.

dentist ['dentɪst] *n* dentista *mf.*

dentistry ['dentɪstrɪ] *n* odontología.

dentures ['dentʃǝz] *npl* dentadura *f sing* postiza.

denude [dɪ'njuːd] *t* desnudar, despojar.

denunciation [dɪnʌnsɪ'eɪʃǝn] *n* denuncia, condena.

deny [dɪ'naɪ] *t* negar.

deodorant [diː'ǝʊdǝrǝnt] *n* desodorante *m.*

depart [dɪ'pɑːt] *i fml* partir, salir. 2 *fig* desviarse, apartarse (*from,* de).

departed [dɪ'pɑːtɪd] *adj euph* difunto,-á.

department [dɪ'pɑːtmǝnt] *n* departamento; *(in office, store)* sección. ■ ~ *store,* grandes almacenes *mpl.*

departure [dɪ'pɑːtʃǝʳ] *n* partida, marcha; *(of plane, train, etc.)* salida. 2 *fig* desviación.

depend [dɪ'pend] *i* depender (*on,* de). ◆*to ~ on/upon t (trust)* confiar en, fiarse de. 2 *(vary, be supported by)* depender de. ●*that/it (all) depends,* según, (todo) depende.

dependable [dɪ'pendǝbǝl] *adj* fiable.

dependence [dɪ'pɒndǝns] *n* dependencia (*on/upon,* de).

dependent [dɪ'pendǝnt] *adj* dependiente. ●*to be ~ on,* depender de.

depict [dɪ'pɪkt] *t* pintar, representar, retratar. 2 *fig* describir.

depilatory [dɪ'pɪlǝtǝrɪ] *n* depilatorio.

deplete [dɪ'pliːt] *t fml* reducir.

depletion [dɪ'pliːʃǝn] *n fml* reducción.

deplorable [dɪ'plɔːrǝbǝl] *adj* deplorable, lamentable.

deplore [dɪ'plɔːʳ] *t* deplorar, lamentar.

deploy [dɪ'plɔɪ] *t fig* desplegar.

deployment [dɪ'plɔɪmǝnt] *n* despliegue *m.*

deport [dɪ'pɔːt] *t* deportar.

deportation [dɪːpɔːˈteɪʃən] *n* deportación.

depose [dɪˈpəʊz] *t* deponer, destituir.

deposit [dɪˈpɒzɪt] *n* sedimento. **2** *(mining)* yacimiento. **3** *(wine)* poso. **4** *(bank)* depósito. **5** COM depósito; *(first payment)* entrada. − **6** *t* depositar. **7** *(into account)* ingresar. ■ ~ *account,* cuenta de ahorros/a plazo fijo.

depot [ˈdepəʊ] *n (storehouse)* almacén *m*; MIL depósito. **2** US *(railway)* estación de ferrocarriles.

deprave [dɪˈpreɪv] *t* depravar.

depravity [dɪˈprævɪtɪ] *n* depravación.

deprecate [ˈdeprɪkeɪt] *t fml* desaprobar, censurar.

depreciate [dɪˈpriːʃɪeɪt] *i* depreciarse.

depreciation [dɪpriːʃɪˈeɪʃən] *n* depreciación, desvalorización.

depress [dɪˈpres] *t* deprimir. **2** *(reduce)* reducir, disminuir.

depressing [dɪˈpresɪŋ] *adj* deprimente.

depression [dɪˈpreʃən] *n* depresión. **2** ECON crisis *f inv* (económica).

depressive [dɪˈpresɪv] *adj* depresivo,-a.

deprivation [deprɪˈveɪʃən] *n* privación.

deprive [dɪˈpraɪv] *t* privar/despojar *(of,* de).

depth [depθ] *n* profundidad; *(of cupboard etc.)* fondo. **2** *(of sound, voice)* gravedad. **3** *(of emotion, colour)* intensidad. ●*in* ~, a fondo; *in the depths of the forest,* en el corazón del bosque; *to be out of one's* ~, perder pie; *fig* meterse en camisa de once varas.

deputation [depjʊˈteɪʃən] *n* delegación.

deputy [ˈdepjʊtɪ] *n (substitute)* su(b)stituto,-a, suplente *mf.* **2** POL diputado,-a. ■ ~ *chairman,* vicepresidente,-a.

deranged [dɪˈreɪndʒd] *adj fml* trastornado,-a, loco,-a.

derelict [ˈderɪlɪkt] *adj* abandonado,-a.

deride [dɪˈraɪd] *t* burlarse de, ridiculizar.

derision [dɪˈrɪʒən] *n* mofa, irrisión.

derisive [dɪˈraɪsɪv] *adj* burlón,-ona, irónico,-a.

derisory [dɪˈraɪsərɪ] *adj* irrisorio,-a.

derivation [derɪˈveɪʃən] *n* derivación.

derivative [deˈrɪvətɪv] *adj pej* poco original. − **2** *n* derivado.

derive [dɪˈraɪv] *t* derivar, sacar *(from,* de). − **2** *i* GRAM derivar(se).

derogatory [dɪˈrɒgətərɪ] *adj* despectivo,-a, peyorativo,-a.

derrick [ˈderɪk] *n* grúa. **2** *(oil)* torre *f* de perforación.

descend [dɪˈsend] *t-i* descender, bajar. ◆*to* ~ *on/upon t* atacar. **2** *fig* visitar: *they descended on us at dinnertime,* se dejaron caer por casa a la hora de cenar. ◆*to* ~ *to t* rebajarse a.

descendant [dɪˈsendənt] *n* descendiente *mf.*

descent [dɪˈsent] *n* descenso, bajada. **2** *(slope)* pendiente *f.* **3** *(family origins)* ascendencia.

describe [dɪˈskraɪb] *t* describir. **2** *(arc etc.)* trazar.

description [dɪˈskrɪpʃən] *n* descripción. ●*of some* ~, de alguna clase.

descriptive [dɪˈskrɪptɪv] *adj* descriptivo,-a.

desecrate [ˈdesɪkreɪt] *t* profanar.

desert [ˈdezət] *n* desierto. − **2** *t* abandonar, dejar. − **3** *i* MIL desertar. ▲ *En 2 y 3 (verbo)* [dɪˈzɜːt].

deserter [dɪˈzɜːtər] *n* desertor,-ra.

desertion [dɪˈzɜːʃən] *n* abandono. **2** MIL deserción.

deserve [dɪˈzɜːv] *t* merecer(se): *you* ~ *a rest,* te mereces un descanso.

deservedly [dɪˈzɜːvədlɪ] *adv* merecidamente, con (toda) razón.

deserving [dɪˈzɜːvɪŋ] *adj (person)* que vale, digno,-a. **2** *(action, cause)* meritorio,-a.

design [dɪˈzaɪn] *n* dibujo; *(of fashion)* diseño, creación. **2** *(plan)* plano, proyecto. **3** *(sketch)* boceto. **4** *fig* plan *m*, intención. − **5** *t* diseñar; *(fashion)* crear. **6** *(develop)* concebir, idear. − **7** *i* diseñar.

designate [ˈdezɪgneɪt] *t fml (indicate)* indicar, señalar. **2** *(appoint)* designar. − **3** *adj* designado,-a. ▲ *En 3 (adj)* [ˈdezɪgnət].

designation [dezɪgˈneɪʃən] *n fml* designación.

designer [dɪˈzaɪnər] *n* diseñador,-ra.

desirable [dɪˈzaɪərəbəl] *adj* deseable, atractivo,-a. **2** *(residence)* de alto standing. **3** *(advisable)* conveniente.

desire [dɪˈzaɪər] *n* deseo. − **2** *t* desear.

desist [dɪˈzɪst] *i* desistir *(from,* de).

desk [desk] *n (in school)* pupitre *m*; *(in office)* escritorio. ■ ~ *work,* trabajo de oficina.

desolate [ˈdesələt] *adj (place)* desolado,-a, desierto,-a. **2** *(person) (sad)* triste, desconsolado,-a; *(lonely)* solitario,-a.

desolation [desəˈleɪʃən] *n (of place)* desolación. **2** *(of person)* desconsuelo, aflicción.

despair [dɪsˈpeəʳ] *n* desesperación. — **2** *i* desesperar(se), perder la esperanza (*of,* de).

despatch [dɪsˈpætʃ] *n-t* → **dispatch.**

desperate [ˈdespərət] *adj (wild)* desesperado,-a. **2** *(critical)* grave. **3** *(need)* apremiante, urgente. — **4** *desperately adv* desesperadamente.

desperation [despəˈreɪʃən] *n* desesperación.

despicable [dɪˈspɪkəbəl] *adj* despreciable, vil, bajo,-a.

despise [dɪˈspaɪz] *t* despreciar, menospreciar.

despite [dɪˈspaɪt] *prep* a pesar de.

despondent [dɪˈspɒndənt] *adj* desalentado,-a, desanimado,-a.

despot [ˈdespɒt] *n* déspota *mf.*

despotism [ˈdespətɪzəm] *n* despotismo.

dessert [dɪˈzɜːt] *n* postre *m.*

dessertspoon [dɪˈzɜːtspuːn] *n* cuchara de postre. **2** *(measure)* cucharadita (de postre).

destination [destɪˈneɪʃən] *n* destino.

destined [ˈdestɪnd] *adj* destinado,-a. **2** *fig* condenado,-a: ~ *to fail,* condenado,-a al fracaso. **3** *(bound)* con destino (*for,* a).

destiny [ˈdestɪnɪ] *n* destino.

destitute [ˈdestɪtjuːt] *adj* indigente, mísero,-a. ●~ *of,* desprovisto,-a de.

destitution [destɪˈtjuːʃən] *n* indigencia, miseria.

destroy [dɪˈstrɔɪ] *t* destruir. **2** *(animal)* matar.

destroyer [dɪˈstrɔɪəʳ] *n (warship)* destructor. **2** *(person, thing)* destructor,-ra.

destruction [dɪˈstrʌkʃən] *n* destrucción.

destructive [dɪˈstrʌktɪv] *adj* destructor,-ra; *(tendency, power)* destructivo,-a.

detach [dɪˈtætʃ] *t* separar.

detached [dɪˈtætʃt] *adj* separado,-a, suelto,-a. **2** *(impartial)* desinteresado,-a, imparcial. ■ ~ *house,* casa independiente; ~ *retina,* retina desprendida.

detachment [dɪˈtætʃmənt] *n* separación. **2** *(aloofness)* desapego, indiferencia. **3** MIL destacamento.

detail [ˈdiːteɪl] *n* detalle *m,* pormenor *m.* **2** *pl (information)* información *f sing.* **3** MIL destacamento. — **4** *t* detallar, enumerar. **5** MIL destacar. ●*to go into* ~, entrar en detalles.

detain [dɪˈteɪn] *t (hold)* detener. **2** *(delay)* retener, entretener.

detect [dɪˈtekt] *t* detectar, descubrir.

detection [dɪˈtekʃən] *n* descubrimiento.

detective [dɪˈtektɪv] *n* detective *mf.* ■ ~ *story,* novela policíaca.

detector [dɪˈtektəʳ] *n* detector *m.*

detention [dɪˈtenʃən] *n* detención, arresto. ●*to get* ~*rr, (in school)* quedar(se) castigado,-a.

deter [dɪˈtɜː] *t* disuadir (*from,* de).

detergent [dɪˈtɜːdʒənt] *n* detergente *m.*

deteriorate [dɪˈtɪərɪəreɪt] *i* deteriorar, empeorar.

deterioration [dɪtɪərɪəˈreɪʃən] *n* deterioro, empeoramiento.

determination [dɪtɜːmɪˈneɪʃən] *n* decisión.

determine [dɪˈtɜːmɪn] *t* determinar.

determined [dɪˈtɜːmɪnd] *adj* decidido,-a, resuelto,-a.

deterrent [dɪˈterənt] *adj* disuasivo,-a. — **2** *n* fuerza disuasoria.

detest [dɪˈtest] *t* detestar.

detestable [dɪˈtestəbəl] *adj* detestable.

detonate [ˈdetəneɪt] *i* estallar. — **2** *t* hacer estallar.

detonator [ˈdetəneɪtəʳ] *n* detonador *m.*

detour [ˈdiːtuəʳ] *n* desvío.

detract [dɪˈtrækt] *t* quitar mérito (*from,* a).

detractor [dɪˈtræktəʳ] *n* detractor,-ra.

detriment [ˈdetrɪmənt] *n fml* detrimento, perjuicio.

detrimental [detrɪˈmentəl] *adj fml* perjudicial (*to,* para).

devaluation [diːvæljuːˈeɪʃən] *n* devaluación.

devalue [diːˈvæljuː] *t* devaluar.

devastate [ˈdevəsteɪt] *t* devastar.

devastating [ˈdevəsteɪtɪŋ] *adj* devastador,-ra.

develop [dɪˈveləp] *t-i* desarrollar(se). — **2** *t (resources)* explotar; *(site etc.)* urbanizar. **3** *(film)* revelar.

development [dɪˈveləpmənt] *n* desarrollo. **2** *(advance)* avance *m.* **3** *(change)* cambio, novedad. **4** *(of resources)* explotación; *(of site etc.)* urbanización. **5** *(of film)* revelado. ■ *housing* ~, conjunto residencial.

deviate [ˈdiːvɪeɪt] *i* desviarse.

deviation [diːvɪˈeɪʃən] *n* desviación.

device [dɪˈvaɪs] *n* mecanismo, dispositivo. **2** *(plan)* ardid *m,* estratagema. ■ *explosive* ~, artefacto explosivo.

devil [ˈdevəl] *n* diablo.

devilish [ˈdevəlɪʃ] *adj* diabólico,-a.

devious [ˈdiːvɪəs] *adj* tortuoso,-a.

devise [dɪˈvaɪz] *t* idear, concebir.

devoid [dɪ'vɔɪd] *adj* falto,-a, desprovisto,-a.

devolution [di:və'lu:ʃən] *n* POL transmisión de poderes.

devolve [dɪ'vɒlv] *i* recaer (*on,* sobre).

devote [dɪ'vəʊt] *t* consagrar, dedicar.

devoted [dɪ'vəʊtɪd] *adj* fiel, leal (*to,* a).

devotion [dɪ'vəʊʃən] *n* consagración, dedicación. **2** *(fondness)* afecto, cariño. **3** REL devoción.

devour [dɪ'vaʊəʳ] *t* devorar.

devout [dɪ'vaʊt] *adj* devoto,-a, piadoso,-a. **2** *(sincere)* sincero,-a.

dew [dju:] *n* rocío.

dexterity [dek'sterɪtɪ] *n* destreza, habilidad.

dext(e)rous ['dekstrəs] *adj* diestro,-a, hábil.

diabetes [daɪə'bi:ti:z] *n inv* diabetes *f inv.*

diabetic [daɪə'betɪk] *adj-n* diabético,-a.

diabolical [daɪə'bɒlɪkəl] *adj* diabólico,-a.

diagnose ['daɪəgnəʊz] *t* diagnosticar.

diagnosis [daɪəg'nəʊsɪs] *n* diagnóstico. ▲ *pl* **diagnoses** [daɪəg'nəʊsi:z].

diagnostic [daɪəg'nɒstɪk] *adj* diagnóstico,-a.

diagonal [daɪ'ægənəl] *adj-n* diagonal (*f*). — **2 diagonally** *adv* en diagonal.

diagram ['daɪəgræm] *n* diagrama *m,* esquema *m*; *(graph)* gráfico.

dial ['daɪəl] *n* (*of clock, barometer*) esfera. **2** (*on radio*) dial *m*. **3** (*telephone*) disco. — **4** *t* marcar.

dialect ['daɪəlekt] *n* dialecto.

dialogue ['daɪəlɒg] *n* diálogo.

diameter [daɪ'æmɪtəʳ] *n* diámetro.

diamond ['daɪəmənd] *n* diamante *m*. **2** *(shape)* rombo.

diaper ['daɪəpəʳ] *n* US pañal *m*.

diaphragm ['daɪəfræm] *n* diafragma *m*.

diarrhoea [daɪə'rɪə] *n* diarrea.

diary ['daɪərɪ] *n* diario. **2** *(agenda)* agenda.

dice [daɪs] *n inv* dado. — **2** *t* cortar en dados.

dichotomy [daɪ'kɒtəmɪ] *n* dicotomía.

dictate ['dɪkteɪt] *n* mandato. — **2** *t* dictar; *(impose)* imponer. — **3** *i* mandar. ▲ *En 2 y 3 (verbo)* [dɪk'teɪt].

dictation [dɪk'teɪʃən] *n* dictado.

dictator [dɪk'teɪtəʳ] *n* dictador,-ra.

dictatorial [dɪktə'tɔ:rɪəl] *adj* dictatorial.

dictatorship [dɪk'teɪtəʃɪp] *n* dictadura.

diction ['dɪkʃən] *n* dicción.

dictionary ['dɪkʃənərɪ] *n* diccionario.

did [dɪd] *pt* → **do**.

didactic [dɪ'dæktɪk] *adj* didáctico,-a.

diddle ['dɪdəl] *t fam* estafar, timar.

didn't ['dɪdənt] *contracción de* **did** + **not**.

die [daɪ] *i* morir(se). — **2** *n* (*for coins*) cuño, troquel *m*. ◆*to* ~ *away i* desvanecerse. ◆*to* ~ *down i* extinguirse. **2** *fig* disminuir. ◆*to* ~ *off i* morir uno por uno. ◆*to* ~ *out i* perderse, desaparecer. ●*fam to be dying for/to,* morirse de ganas de.

diehard ['daɪhɑːd] *n* intransigente *mf.*

diesel ['di:zəl] *n* gasóleo. ■ ~ *engine,* motor *m* diesel.

diet ['daɪət] *n* dieta. **2** *(for slimming)* régimen *m*.

differ ['dɪfəʳ] *i* diferir/diferenciarse (*from,* de). **2** *(disagree)* discrepar.

difference ['dɪfərəns] *n* diferencia. **2** *(disagreement)* desacuerdo.

different ['dɪfərənt] *adj* diferente, distinto,-a. — **2 differently** *adv* de otra manera.

differential [dɪfə'renʃəl] *n* MATH diferencial *f*. **2** *(between rates etc.)* diferencia.

differentiate [dɪfə'renʃɪeɪt] *t-i* diferenciar, distinguir.

difficult ['dɪfɪkəlt] *adj* difícil.

difficulty ['dɪfɪkəltɪ] *n* dificultad. **2** *(problem)* apuro, aprieto.

diffident ['dɪfɪdənt] *adj* discreto,-a, reservado,-a.

diffuse [dɪ'fju:s] *adj* difuso,-a. **2** *pej* prolijo,-a. — **3** *t-i* difundir(se). ▲ *En 3 (verbo)* [dɪ'fju:z].

diffusion [dɪ'fju:ʒən] *n* difusión.

dig [dɪg] *n* codazo. **2** *fam (gibe)* pulla. **3** *pl* GB alojamiento *m sing*. — **4** *t* cavar; *(tunnel)* excavar. **5** *(thrust)* clavar, hincar. ◆*to* ~ *out/up t* desenterrar. ▲ *pt & pp* **dug**.

digest ['daɪdʒest] *n* resumen *m,* compendio. — **2** *t-i* digerir. ▲ *En 2 (verbo)* [dɪ'dʒest].

digestion [dɪ'dʒestʃən] *n* digestión.

digger ['dɪgəʳ] *n (machine)* excavadora. **2** *(person)* excavador,-ra.

digit ['dɪdʒɪt] *n* dígito.

dignified ['dɪgnɪfaɪd] *adj* solemne, serio,-a.

dignify ['dɪgnɪfaɪ] *t* dignificar, enaltecer.

dignitary ['dɪgnɪtərɪ] *n* dignatario.

dignity ['dɪgnɪtɪ] *n* dignidad.

digress [daɪ'gres] *i* hacer digresiones.

digression [daɪ'greʃən] *n* digresión.

dike [daɪk] *n* US → **dyke**.

dilapidated [dɪ'læpɪdeɪtɪd] *adj* estropeado,-a, en mal estado; *(falling apart)* desvencijado,-a.

dilate [daɪ'leɪt] *t-i* dilatar(se).

dilemma [dɪ'lemə] *n* dilema *m*.

diligence ['dɪlɪdʒəns] *n* diligencia.
diligent ['dɪlɪdʒənt] *adj* diligente.
dilute [daɪ'luːt] *t-i* diluir(se). – **2** *t* aguar. **3** *fig* atenuar, suavizar.
dim [dɪm] *adj (light)* débil, difuso,-a, tenue. **2** *(hazy)* oscuro,-a. **3** *(memory etc.)* borroso,-a. **4** *fam (person)* tonto,-a. – **5** *t (light)* bajar. **6** *(eyes)* empañar. **7** *fig (memory)* borrar, difuminar.
dime [daɪm] *n* US moneda de diez centavos.
dimension [dɪ'menʃən] *n* dimensión.
diminish [dɪ'mɪnɪʃ] *t-i* disminuir(se), reducir(se).
diminutive [dɪ'mɪnjʊtɪv] *adj* diminuto,-a. – **2** *n* diminutivo.
dimness ['dɪmnəs] *n (of light)* palidez *f*. **2** *(of area)* semioscuridad, penumbra. **3** *fam (of person)* torpeza.
dimple ['dɪmpəl] *n* hoyuelo.
din [dɪn] *n* alboroto, estrépito.
dine [daɪn] *i* cenar.
diner ['daɪnə^r] *n (person)* comensal *mf*. **2** US restaurante *m* barato.
dinghy ['dɪŋgɪ] *n* bote *m*.
dingy ['dɪndʒɪ] *adj (dirty)* sucio,-a, sórdido,-a. **2** *(faded)* desteñido,-a.
dining room ['daɪnɪŋrʊm] *n* comedor *m*.
dinner ['dɪnə^r] *n (midday)* comida; *(evening)* cena. ■ ~ *jacket,* esmoquin *m*; ~ *service,* vajilla; ~ *table,* mesa de comedor.
dinosaur ['daɪnəsɔː^r] *n* dinosaurio.
diocese ['daɪəsɪs] *n* diócesis *f inv*.
dioxide [daɪ'ɒksaɪd] *n* dióxido.
dip [dɪp] *n (drop)* declive *m*, pendiente *f*. **2** *fam (bathe)* chapuzón *m*. – **3** *t* sumergir, bañar, mojar. – **4** *i (drop)* bajar. ◆*to* ~ *into t (glance through)* hojear. **2** *(savings etc.)* echar mano de. ●AUTO *to* ~ *the lights,* poner las luces de cruce.
diphthong ['dɪfθɒŋ] *n* diptongo.
diploma [dɪ'pləʊmə] *n* diploma *m*.
diplomacy [dɪ'pləʊməsɪ] *n* diplomacia.
diplomat ['dɪpləmæt] *n* diplomático,-a.
diplomatic [dɪplə'mætɪk] *adj* diplomático,-a.
dire ['daɪə^r] *adj* extremo,-a. **2** *(terrible)* terrible.
direct [dɪ'rekt, 'daɪrekt] *adj* directo,-a. **2** *(person, manner)* franco,-a, sincero,-a. – **3** *adv* directamente; *(flight)* directo; *(broadcast)* en directo. – **4** *t (lead)* dirigir. **5** *fml (instruct)* mandar, ordenar. – **6** *directly adv* directamente. **7** *(speak)* francamente, claro. ■ ~ *object,* complemento directo.

direction [dɪ'rekʃən, daɪ'rekʃən] *n* dirección. **2** *pl (to place)* señas *fpl*; *(for use)* instrucciones *fpl*, modo *m sing* de empleo.
directness [dɪ'rektnəs, daɪ'rektnəs] *n* franqueza, sinceridad.
director [dɪ'rektə^r, daɪ'rektə^r] *n* director,-ra. ■ *board of directors,* consejo de administración, (junta) directiva; *managing* ~, director,-ra, gerente *mf*.
directory [dɪ'rektrɪ, daɪ'rektrɪ] *n (telephone)* guía telefónica. **2** *(street)* ~, callejero.
dirt [dɜːt] *n* suciedad. **2** *(earth)* tierra. ●*to treat sb. like* ~, tratar mal a algn.
dirty ['dɜːtɪ] *adj* sucio,-a. **2** *(indecent)* indecente; *(joke)* verde. **3** *fam (low)* bajo,-a, vil. – **4** *t-i* ensuciar(se). ●*to get* ~, ensuciarse; *to give sb. a* ~ *look,* fulminar a algn. con la mirada. ■ ~ *trick,* cochinada; ~ *word,* palabrota.
disability [dɪsə'bɪlɪtɪ] *n (condition)* invalidez *f*. **2** *(handicap)* impedimento, hándicap *m*.
disabled [dɪs'eɪbəld] *adj* minusválido,-a.
disadvantage [dɪsəd'vɑːntɪdʒ] *n* desventaja. **2** *(obstacle)* inconveniente *m*.
disadvantageous [dɪsædvɑːn'teɪdʒəs] *adj* desventajoso,-a, desfavorable.
disagree [dɪsə'griː] *i (differ)* discrepar *(with,* con). **2** *(food)* sentar mal *(with,* -).
disagreeable [dɪsə'grɪəbəl] *adj* desagradable.
disagreement [dɪsə'griːmənt] *n* desacuerdo.
disallow [dɪsə'laʊ] *t fml* denegar; *(goal)* anular.
disappear [dɪsə'pɪə^r] *i* desaparecer.
disappearance [dɪsə'pɪərəns] *n* desaparición.
disappoint [dɪsə'pɔɪnt] *t* decepcionar.
disappointment [dɪsə'pɔɪntmənt] *n* desilusión, decepción.
disapproval [dɪsə'pruːvəl] *n* desaprobación.
disapprove [dɪsə'pruːv] *t* desaprobar *(of,* -).
disarm [dɪs'ɑːm] *t-i* desarmar(se).
disarmament [dɪs'ɑːməmənt] *n* desarme *m*.
disarray [dɪsə'reɪ] *n* desorden *m*.
disaster [dɪ'zɑːstə^r] *n* desastre *m*.
disastrous [dɪ'zɑːstrəs] *adj* desastroso,-a.
disband [dɪs'bænd] *t-i* dispersar(se), desbandar(se).
disbelief [dɪsbɪ'liːf] *n* incredulidad.

disbelieve [dɪsbɪˈliːv] *t* no creer, dudar de.

disc [dɪsk] *n* disco. ■ ~ *jockey,* disc-jockey *m.*

discard [dɪsˈkɑːd] *t* desechar, deshacerse de. 2 *fig* descartar.

discern [dɪˈsɜːn] *t* percibir, discernir.

discerning [dɪˈsɜːnɪŋ] *adj* perspicaz, sagaz.

discharge [ˈdɪstʃɑːdʒ] *n* ELEC descarga. 2 *(of smoke)* emisión. 3 *(of gas)* escape *m.* 4 *(of prisoner)* liberación, puesta en libertad. 5 *(of patient)* alta. 6 MIL licencia. 7 *(of worker)* despido. − 8 *t-i (pour)* verter. 9 *(unload)* descargar. 10 *(let out)* emitir. − 11 *t (prisoner)* liberar, soltar. 12 *(patient)* dar de alta. 13 MIL licenciar. 14 *(dismiss)* despedir. 15 *(pay)* saldar. ▲ *De 8 a 15 (verbo)* [dɪsˈtʃɑːdʒ].

disciple [dɪˈsaɪpəl] *n* discípulo,-a.

discipline [ˈdɪsɪplɪn] *n* disciplina. 2 *(punishment)* castigo. − 3 *t* disciplinar. 4 *(punish)* castigar; *(official)* expedientar.

disclaim [dɪsˈkleɪm] *t* negar, rechazar.

disclose [dɪsˈkləʊz] *t* revelar.

disclosure [dɪsˈkləʊʒəʳ] *n* revelación.

discolour [dɪsˈkʌləʳ] *t-i* descolorar(se).

discomfort [dɪsˈkʌmfət] *n* incomodidad. 2 *(pain)* malestar *m,* molestia.

disconcert [dɪskənˈsɜːt] *t* desconcertar.

disconnect [dɪskəˈnekt] *t* desconectar; *(gas etc.)* cortar.

disconnected [dɪskəˈnektɪd] *adj* desconectado,-a. 2 *(gas etc.)* cortado,-a. 3 *fig* deshilvanado,-a.

discontent [dɪskənˈtent] *n* descontento.

discontinue [dɪskənˈtɪnjuː] *t* suspender.

discord [ˈdɪskɔːd] *n* discordia. 2 MUS disonancia.

discordant [dɪsˈkɔːdənt] *n* discordante.

discotheque [ˈdɪskətek] *n* discoteca.

discount [ˈdɪskaʊnt] *n* descuento. − 2 *t* descontar, rebajar. 3 *(disregard)* descartar. ▲ *En 2 y 3 (verbo)* [dɪsˈkaʊnt].

discourage [dɪsˈkʌrɪdʒ] *t* desanimar, desalentar. 2 *(deter)* disuadir *(from,* de).

discouragement [dɪsˈkʌrɪdʒmənt] *n* desaliento, desánimo. 2 *(dissuasion)* disuasión.

discouraging [dɪsˈkʌrɪdʒɪŋ] *adj* desalentador,-ra.

discourteous [dɪsˈkɜːtɪəs] *adj* descortés.

discover [dɪsˈkʌvəʳ] *t* descubrir.

discoverer [dɪsˈkʌvərəʳ] *n* descubridor,-ra.

discovery [dɪsˈkʌvərɪ] *n* descubrimiento.

discredit [dɪsˈkredɪt] *n* descrédito. − 2 *t* desacreditar, desprestigiar.

discreet [dɪˈskriːt] *adj* discreto,-a.

discrepancy [dɪˈskrepənsɪ] *n* discrepancia.

discretion [dɪˈskreʃən] *n* discreción. ●*at the* ~ *of,* a juicio de.

discriminate [dɪˈskrɪmɪneɪt] *i pej* discriminar *(against,* -).

discriminating [dɪˈskrɪmɪneɪtɪŋ] *adj* entendido,-a, selecto,-a. 2 *pej* parcial.

discrimination [dɪskrɪmɪˈneɪʃən] *n pej* discriminación. 2 *(taste)* buen gusto.

discus [ˈdɪskəs] *n* disco.

discuss [dɪˈskʌs] *t-i* discutir. − 2 *t (talk over)* hablar de.

discussion [dɪˈskʌʃən] *n* discusión, debate *m.*

disdain [dɪsˈdeɪn] *n* desdén *m,* menosprecio. − 2 *t* desdeñar, menospreciar.

disdainful [dɪsˈdeɪnfʊl] *adj* desdeñoso,-a.

disease [dɪˈziːz] *n* enfermedad.

disembark [dɪsɪmˈbɑːk] *t-i* desembarcar.

disembarkation [dɪsɪmbɑːˈkeɪʃən] *n (of people)* desembarco; *(of goods)* desembarque *m.*

disenchanted [dɪsɪnˈtʃɑːntɪd] *adj* desencantado,-a.

disengage [dɪsɪnˈgeɪdʒ] *t (free)* soltar, desprender. 2 *(clutch)* desembragar. − 3 *i* MIL retirarse.

disentangle [dɪsɪnˈtæŋgəl] *t* desenredar, desenmarañar.

disfigure [dɪsˈfɪgəʳ] *t* desfigurar.

disgrace [dɪsˈgreɪs] *n* desgracia. 2 *(shame)* escándalo, vergüenza. − 3 *t* deshonrar.

disgraceful [dɪsˈgreɪsfʊl] *adj* vergonzoso,-a.

disguise [dɪsˈgaɪz] *n* disfraz *m.* − 2 *t* disfrazar *(as,* de). 3 *fig* disimular. ●*in* ~, disfrazado,-a.

disgust [dɪsˈgʌst] *n* asco, repugnancia. − 2 *t* repugnar, dar asco.

disgusting [dɪsˈgʌstɪŋ] *adj* asqueroso,-a, repugnante. 2 *(intolerable)* intolerable.

dish [dɪʃ] *n* plato; *(for serving)* fuente *f.* ◆*to* ~ *out t fam* repartir. ◆*to* ~ *up t* servir.

dishcloth [ˈdɪʃklɒθ] *n* paño de cocina.

dishearten [dɪsˈhɑːtən] *t* descorazonar.

dishevelled [dɪˈʃevəld] *adj (hair)* despeinado,-a; *(appearance)* desaliñado,-a, desarreglado,-a.

dishonest [dɪsˈɒnɪst] *adj (person)* deshonesto,-a, poco honrado,-a. 2 *(means)* fraudulento,-a.

dishonesty [dɪs'ɒnɪstɪ] *n* deshonestidad, falta de honradez. **2** *(of means)* fraude *m*.

dishonour [dɪs'ɒnəʳ] *n* deshonra. − **2** *t* deshonrar. **3** *(cheque)* no pagar por falta de fondos.

dishonourable [dɪs'ɒnərəbəl] *adj* deshonroso,-a.

dishwasher ['dɪʃwɒʃəʳ] *n* lavavajillas *m inv.*

disillusion [dɪsɪ'luːʒən] *t* desilusionar.

disinfect [dɪsɪn'fekt] *t* desinfectar.

disinfectant [dɪsɪn'fektənt] *adj-n* desinfectante *(m)*.

disinherit [dɪsɪn'herɪt] *t* desheredar.

disintegrate [dɪs'ɪntɪgreɪt] *t-i* desintegrar(se), disgregar(se).

disintegration [dɪsɪntɪ'greɪʃən] *n* desintegración.

disinterested [dɪs'ɪntrəstɪd] *adj* desinteresado,-a, imparcial.

disjointed [dɪs'dʒɔɪntɪd] *adj fig* inconexo,-a.

disk [dɪsk] *n* disco. ■ COMPUT ~ *drive,* disquetera.

diskette [dɪs'ket] *n* disquete *m*.

dislike [dɪs'laɪk] *n* aversión, antipatía. − **2** *t (sth.)* no gustarle a uno; *(sb.)* tener antipatía a.

dislocate ['dɪsləkeɪt] *t* dislocar.

dislodge [dɪs'lɒdʒ] *t* desalojar, sacar.

disloyal [dɪs'lɔɪəl] *adj* desleal.

disloyalty [dɪs'lɔɪəltɪ] *n* deslealtad.

dismal ['dɪzməl] *adj* triste, sombrío,-a.

dismantle [dɪs'mæntəl] *t-i* desmontar(se).

dismay [dɪs'meɪ] *n* consternación. − **2** *t* consternar, acongojar.

dismiss [dɪs'mɪs] *t (employee)* despedir; *(official)* destituir. **2** *(send away)* dar permiso para retirarse. **3** *(put aside)* descartar. **4** JUR desestimar, denegar.

dismissal [dɪs'mɪsəl] *n (sacking)* despido; *(of official)* destitución. **2** *(rejection)* abandono. **3** JUR desestimación, denegación.

dismount [dɪs'maʊnt] *i* desmontar(se).

disobedience [dɪsə'biːdɪəns] *n* desobediencia.

disobedient [dɪsə'biːdɪənt] *adj* desobediente.

disobey [dɪsə'beɪ] *t-i* desobedecer. − **2** *t (law)* violar.

disorder [dɪs'ɔːdəʳ] *n* desorden *m*.

disorderly [dɪs'ɔːdəlɪ] *adj (untidy)* desordenado,-a. **2** *(unruly)* alborotado,-a, escandaloso,-a.

disorganization [dɪsɔːgənaɪ'zeɪʃən] *n* desorganización.

disorganized [dɪs'ɔːgənaɪzd] *t* desorganizado,-a.

disorient(ate) [dɪs'ɔːrɪənt(eɪt)] *t* desorientar.

disown [dɪs'əʊn] *t* no reconocer.

disparage [dɪ'spærɪdʒ] *t* menospreciar.

disparaging [dɪ'spærɪdʒɪŋ] *adj* despreciativo,-a. − **2** *disparagingly adv* con desprecio.

disparity [dɪ'spærɪtɪ] *n fml* disparidad.

dispassionate [dɪs'pæʃənət] *adj* desapasionado,-a.

dispatch [dɪ'spætʃ] *n (report)* despacho, parte *m*, comunicado. **2** *(press)* reportaje *m* (de corresponsalía). **3** *(sending)* despacho, envío. **4** *fml (haste)* prontitud. − **5** *t* enviar, expedir, despachar. ■ ~ *rider,* mensajero.

dispel [dɪ'spel] *t* disipar.

dispensary [dɪ'spensərɪ] *n* dispensario.

dispensation [dɪspen'seɪʃən] *n* dispensa.

dispense [dɪ'spens] *t* distribuir, repartir. **2** *(provide)* suministrar, administrar. **3** *(medicines)* preparar y despachar. ◆*to* ~ *with t* prescindir de, pasar sin.

dispenser [dɪ'spensəʳ] *n* máquina expendedora. ■ *cash* ~, cajero automático.

dispersal [dɪ'spɜːsəl] *n* dispersión.

disperse [dɪ'spɜːs] *t-i* dispersar(se).

dispirited [dɪ'spɪrɪtɪd] *t* desanimado,-a.

displace [dɪs'pleɪs] *t* desplazar; *(bone)* dislocar. **2** *(replace)* sustituir, reemplazar. ■ *displaced person,* expatriado,-a.

displacement [dɪs'pleɪsmənt] *n* desplazamiento. **2** *(replacement)* reemplazo.

display [dɪ'spleɪ] *n (of goods)* exposición. **2** *(of force, military)* exhibición, despliegue *m*. **3** COMPUT visualización. − **4** *t* exhibir, mostrar; *(goods)* exponer. **5** COMPUT visualizar.

displease [dɪs'pliːz] *t fml* disgustar.

displeasure [dɪs'pleʒəʳ] *n* disgusto.

disposable [dɪ'spəʊzəbəl] *adj* desechable.

disposal [dɪ'spəʊzəl] *n (removal)* eliminación. ◆*at sb.'s* ~, a la disposición de algn.

dispose [dɪ'spəʊz] *t* disponer. **2** *to* ~ *of, (rubbish)* tirar; *(object)* deshacerse de; *fig* echar por tierra.

disposition [dɪspə'zɪʃən] *n fml* carácter *m*.

dispossess [dɪspə'zes] *t* desposeer.

disproportionate [dɪsprə'pɔːʃənət] *adj* desproporcionado,-a.

disprove [dɪs'pruːv] *t* refutar.

dispute ['dɪspjuːt] *n* discusión, controversia; *(quarrel)* disputa. — **2** *t (doubt)* refutar. — **3** *t-i (argue)* disputar, discutir. ●*beyond* ~, indiscutiblemente. ■ *industrial* ~, conflicto laboral. ▲ *En 2 y 3 (verbo)* [dɪ'spjuːt].

disqualification [dɪskwɒlɪfɪ'keɪʃən] *n* descalificación.

disqualify [dɪs'kwɒlɪfaɪ] *t* SP descalificar. **2** *(make unfit)* incapacitar.

disquiet [dɪs'kwaɪət] *n* inquietud, desasosiego. — **2** *t* inquietar, desasosegar.

disregard [dɪsrɪ'gɑːd] *n* indiferencia, despreocupación. — **2** *t* no hacer caso de.

disrepair [dɪsrɪ'peəʳ] *n* mal estado. ●*to fall into* ~, deteriorarse.

disreputable [dɪs'repjʊtəbəl] *adj (person, place)* de mala reputación. **2** *(behaviour)* vergonzoso,-a.

disrepute [dɪsrɪ'pjuːt] *n* mala reputación, oprobio.

disrespect [dɪsrɪ'spekt] *n* falta de respeto, desacato.

disrespectful [dɪsrɪ'spektfʊl] *adj* irrespetuoso,-a.

disrupt [dɪs'rʌpt] *t* trastornar.

disruption [dɪs'rʌpʃən] *n* trastorno.

disruptive [dɪs'rʌptɪv] *adj* perjudicial.

dissatisfaction [dɪssætɪs'fækʃən] *n* insatisfacción, descontento.

dissatisfied [dɪs'sætɪsfaɪd] *adj* descontento,-a.

dissect [dɪ'sekt, daɪ'sekt] *t* disecar.

disseminate [dɪ'semɪneɪt] *t fml* diseminar.

dissension [dɪ'senʃən] *n* disensión.

dissent [dɪ'sent] *n* disensión. — **2** *i* disentir.

dissertation [dɪsə'teɪʃən] *n* disertación. **2** EDUC tesina.

disservice [dɪs'sɜːvɪs] *n to do a* ~, perjudicar.

dissident ['dɪsɪdənt] *adj-n* disidente *(mf)*.

dissimilar [dɪ'sɪmɪləʳ] *adj* diferente.

dissimulation [dɪsɪmjʊ'leɪʃən] *n fml* disimulo, disimulación.

dissipate ['dɪsɪpeɪt] *t-i* disipar(se), dispersar(se). — **2** *t (waste)* derrochar.

dissociate [dɪ'səʊʃɪeɪt] *t* disociar, separar.

dissolute ['dɪsəluːt] *adj* disoluto,-a.

dissolution [dɪsə'luːʃən] *n* disolución; *(of agreement)* rescisión.

dissolve [dɪ'zɒlv] *t-i* disolver(se). — **2** *i fig* deshacerse: *to* ~ *into tears/laughter,* deshacerse en lágrimas/risa.

dissuade [dɪ'sweɪd] *t* disuadir *(from,* de).

dissuasion [dɪ'sweɪʒən] *n* disuasión.

distance ['dɪstəns] *n* distancia. — **2** *t* distanciar. ●*in the* ~, a lo lejos; *to keep one's* ~, mantenerse alejado,-a.

distant ['dɪstənt] *adj* lejano,-a. **2** *(cold)* distante, frío,-a.

distaste [dɪs'teɪst] *n* aversión.

distasteful [dɪs'teɪstfʊl] *adj* desagradable, de mal gusto.

distemper [dɪs'tempəʳ] *n (paint)* temple *m*. **2** *(disease)* moquillo.

distend [dɪ'stend] *t-i* dilatar(se).

distil [dɪs'tɪl] *t* destilar.

distillation [dɪstɪ'leɪʃən] *n* destilación.

distillery [dɪ'stɪlərɪ] *n* destilería.

distinct [dɪ'stɪŋkt] *adj* distinto,-a. **2** *(clear)* marcado,-a, inconfundible.

distinction [dɪ'stɪŋkʃən] *n (difference)* diferencia. **2** *(worth)* distinción. **3** EDUC sobresaliente *m*.

distinctive [dɪ'stɪŋktɪv] *adj* distintivo,-a.

distinguish [dɪ'stɪŋgwɪʃ] *t-i* distinguir(se).

distort [dɪ'stɔːt] *t* deformar; *fig* distorsionar.

distortion [dɪ'stɔːʃən] *n* deformación; *fig* distorsión.

distract [dɪ'strækt] *t* distraer *(from,* de).

distracted [dɪ'stræktɪd] *adj* distraído,-a.

distraction [dɪ'strækʃən] *n* distracción. **2** *(confusion)* confusión. ●*to drive sb. to* ~, sacar a algn. de quicio.

distraught [dɪ'strɔːt] *adj* afligido,-a, turbado,-a.

distress [dɪ'stres] *n* aflicción. — **2** *t* afligir. ■ ~ *call/signal,* señal *f* de socorro.

distressing [dɪ'stresɪŋ] *adj* penoso,-a.

distribute [dɪ'strɪbjuːt] *t* distribuir, repartir.

distribution [dɪstrɪ'bjuːʃən] *n* distribución.

district ['dɪstrɪkt] *n (of town)* distrito, barrio; *(of country)* región. ■ ~ *council,* municipio; *postal* ~, distrito postal.

distrust [dɪs'trʌst] *n* desconfianza, recelo. — **2** *t* desconfiar, recelar.

disturb [dɪ'stɜːb] *t* molestar. **2** *(interrupt)* interrumpir. **3** *(worry)* perturbar, inquietar. **4** *(stir)* mover.

disturbance [dɪ'stɜːbəns] *n (public)* disturbio, alboroto. **2** *(nuisance)* molestia.

disturbed [dɪ'stɜːbd] *adj* desequilibrado,-a.

disuse [dɪs'juːs] *n* desuso.

ditch [dɪtʃ] *n* zanja, foso, cuneta; *(for water)* acequia. — **2** *t fam* dejar tirado,-a.

dither ['dɪðəʳ] *i* vacilar, titubear.

ditto ['dɪtəʊ] *n inv* ídem *m*.

divan [dɪ'væn] *n* diván *m*. ■ ~ *(bed)*, cama turca.

dive [daɪv] *n (into water)* zambullida, inmersión; *(of diver)* buceo. **2** *(birds, planes)* picado. **3** SP salto. **4** *fam* antro. — **5** *i (into water)* zambullirse, tirarse (de cabeza); *(diver)* bucear. **6** *(birds, planes)* bajar en picado. **7** SP saltar. **8** *(dash)* moverse rápidamente: *she dived for the phone,* se precipitó hacia el teléfono. ▲ US *pt* dove.

diver ['daɪvəʳ] *n* buceador,-ra; *(professional)* buzo.

diverge [daɪ'vɜːdʒ] *i* divergir; *(roads)* bifurcarse.

divergent [daɪ'vɜːdʒənt] *adj* divergente.

diverse [daɪ'vɜːs] *adj fml* diverso,-a.

diversify [daɪ'vɜːsɪfaɪ] *t-i* diversificar(se).

diversion [daɪ'vɜːʃən] *n (detour)* desvío, desviación. **2** *(distraction)* distracción.

diversity [daɪ'vɜːsɪtɪ] *n* diversidad.

divert [daɪ'vɜːt] *t* desviar. **2** *(distract)* distraer.

divide [dɪ'vaɪd] *t-i* dividir(se), separar(se). — **2** *t (share)* repartir (*among/between,* entre). — **3** *i (road, stream)* bifurcarse. — **4** *n* división.

dividend ['dɪvɪdend] *n* dividendo. **2** *fig* beneficio.

divine [dɪ'vaɪn] *adj* divino,-a. — **2** *t-i* adivinar.

diving ['daɪvɪŋ] *n* buceo. ■ ~ *board,* trampolín *m*.

divinity [dɪ'vɪnɪtɪ] *n* divinidad. **2** *(subject)* teología.

division [dɪ'vɪʒən] *n* división.

divisor [dɪ'vaɪzəʳ] *n* divisor *m*.

divorce [dɪ'vɔːs] *n* divorcio. — **2** *t-i* divorciar(se): *he divorced her,* se divorció de ella.

divorcé [dɪ'vɔːseɪ] divorciado.

divorcée [dɪvɔː'siː] *n* divorciada.

divulge [daɪ'vʌldʒ] *t* divulgar.

dizziness ['dɪzɪnəs] *n* mareo; *(of heights)* vértigo.

dizzy ['dɪzɪ] *adj* mareado,-a.

do [duː] *aux (not translated) (in interrog and negatives)* ~ *you smoke?,* ¿fumas?; *I don't want to come,* no quiero venir. **2** *(emphatic)* ~ *come with us!,* ¡ánimo, vente con nosotros! **3** *(substituting main verb)* *he likes them, and so* ~ *I,* a él le gustan, y a mí también; *who went?,* --*I did,* ¿quién asistió?, --yo. **4** *(in question tags)* *you don't drive,* ~ *you?,* no fumas, ¿verdad? — **5** *t* hacer, realizar: *what are you doing?,* ¿qué haces? **6** *(suffice)* ser suficiente: *ten will* ~ *us,* con diez tenemos suficiente. — **7** *i (act)* hacer: ~ *as I tell you,* haz lo que te digo. **8** *(proceed)* *how are you doing?,* ¿cómo te van las cosas?; *she did badly in the exams,* le fueron mal los exámenes. **9** *(suffice)* bastar, servir: *that will* ~, (así) basta; *this cushion will* ~ *as/for a pillow,* este cojín servirá de almohada. — **10** *n fam (party)* fiesta, guateque *m*. ◆*to* ~ *away with t* abolir. **2** *fam* eliminar. ◆*to* ~ *in t fam (kill)* matar, cargarse. **2** *(tire)* agotar: *I'm done in,* estoy hecho,-a polvo. ◆*to* ~ *up t fam (fasten) (belt)* abrochar(se); *(laces)* atar. **2** *(wrap)* envolver. **3** *(dress up)* arreglar; *(decorate)* renovar. ◆*to* ~ *with t (need) I could* ~ *with a rest,* un descanso me vendría muy bien. ◆*to* ~ *without t* pasar sin. ■*how* ~ *you* ~*?,* *(greeting)* ¿cómo está usted?; *(answer)* mucho gusto, encantado,-a; *to* ~ *one's best,* hacer lo mejor posible; *to* ~ *one's hair,* peinarse; *to* ~ *the cleaning/ cooking,* cocinar/limpiar; *fam well done!,* ¡enhorabuena! ■ *do's and don'ts,* reglas *fpl* de conducta. ▲ *3ª pers sing pres* does; *pt* did; *pp* done.

docile ['dəʊsaɪl] *adj* dócil; *(animal)* manso,-a.

dock [dɒk] *n* MAR muelle *m*; *(for cargo)* dársena. **2** JUR banquillo (de los acusados). — **3** *t-i* MAR atracar (*at,* a). — **4** *t* cortar la cola a; *fig* recortar.

docker ['dɒkəʳ] *n* estibador *m*.

dockyard ['dɒkjɑːd] *n* astillero.

doctor ['dɒktəʳ] *n* médico,-a, doctor,-ra. **2** EDUC doctor,-ra (*of,* en). — **3** *t pej* falsificar, amañar. **4** *(animal)* esterilizar. ■ *family* ~, médico,-a de cabecera.

doctorate ['dɒktərət] *n* doctorado.

doctrine ['dɒktrɪn] *n* doctrina.

document ['dɒkjʊmənt] *n* documento. — **2** *t* documentar.

documentary [dɒkjʊ'mentərɪ] *adj-n* documental *(m)*.

doddering ['dɒdərɪŋ] *adj fam* tembloroso,-a.

doddle ['dɒdəl] *n fam* pan comido.

dodge [dɒdʒ] *n* regate *m*, evasión. **2** *fam* truco, astucia. — **3** *t-i (blow etc.)* esquivar. — **4** *t (pursuer)* despistar, dar esquinazo a. **5** *(tax)* evadir.

dodgy ['dɒdʒɪ] *adj* de poco fiar.

doe [dəʊ] *n (deer)* gama. **2** *(rabbit)* coneja.

does [dʌz] *3ª pers sing pres* → do.

dog [dɒg] *n* perro,-a. — **2** *t* acosar.

dogged ['dɒgɪd] *adj* terco,-a, obstinado,-a.

doggy ['dɒgɪ] *n* perrito,-a.

dogma ['dɒgmə] *n* dogma *m*.

dogmatic [dɒg'mætɪk] *adj* dogmático,-a.

dogsbody ['dɒgzbɒdɪ] *n* GB *fam* burro de carga.

do-it-yourself [du:ɪtjɔ:'self] *n* bricolaje *m*.

doldrums ['dɒldrəmz] *npl in the ~*, abatido,-a, deprimido,-a.

dole [dəʊl] *n* GB *fam* (subsidio de) desempleo/paro. ◆*to ~ out t* repartir.

doll [dɒl] *n* muñeca. ◆*to ~ up t fam* poner guapo,-a.

dollar ['dɒləʳ] *n* dólar *m*.

dolly ['dɒlɪ] *n* muñeca.

dolphin ['dɒlfɪn] *n* delfín *m*.

domain [də'meɪn] *n (land)* dominio. **2** *(sphere)* campo, esfera.

dome [dəʊm] *n* ARCH cúpula.

domestic [də'mestɪk] *adj* doméstico,-a. **2** *(home-loving)* hogareño,-a, casero,-a. **3** POL nacional. **– 4** *n* criado,-a.

domesticate [də'mestɪkeɪt] *t* domesticar.

dominant ['dɒmɪnənt] *adj* dominante.

dominate ['dɒmɪneɪt] *t-i* dominar.

domination [dɒmɪ'neɪʃən] *n* dominación.

domineering [dɒmɪ'nɪərɪŋ] *adj pej* dominante.

domino ['dɒmɪnəʊ] *n* ficha de dominó. **2** *pl (game)* dominó *m sing*. ▲ *pl* **dominoes**.

donate [dəʊ'neɪt] *t* donar; *(money)* hacer un donativo de.

donation [dəʊ'neɪʃən] *n (act)* donación. **2** *(gift)* donativo.

done [dʌn] *pp* → **do**. **– 2** *adj (finished)* terminado,-a, acabado,-a: *the job is ~*, el trabajo está terminado. **3** *fam (tired)* agotado,-a. **4** *(cooked)* cocido,-a; *(meat)* hecho,-a. **– 5** *interj fam* ¡trato hecho! ●*it isn't ~ to ...*, es de mal gusto ... .

donkey ['dɒŋkɪ] *n* burro,-a.

donor ['dəʊnəʳ] *n* donante *m*.

don't [dəʊnt] *contracción de do + not*.

doodle ['du:dəl] *i* garabatear, garrapatear. **– 2** *n* garabato.

doom [du:m] *n (fate)* destino; *(ruin)* perdición. **– 2** *t* condenar.

door [dɔ:ʳ] *n* puerta. **2** *(doorway)* portal *m*. ●*(from) ~ to ~*, de puerta en puerta; *next ~ (to)*, (en) la casa de al lado (de); *fig by the back ~*, por la puerta falsa; *fam to be on the ~*, hacer de portero,-a.

doorman ['dɔ:mən] *n* portero.

doorstep ['dɔ:step] *n* peldaño.

door-to-door [dɔ:tə'dɔ:] *adj* a domicilio.

doorway ['dɔ:weɪ] *n* entrada, portal *m*.

dopey ['dəʊpɪ] *adj sl (with drugs, sleep)* grogui. **2** *(silly)* estúpido,-a.

dope [dəʊp] *n sl* droga. **2** *fam (person)* imbécil *mf*. **– 3** *t fam (food, drink)* adulterar con drogas. **4** SP dopar.

dormant ['dɔ:mənt] *adj* inactivo,-a. **2** *fig* latente.

dormitory ['dɔ:mɪtərɪ] *n (room)* dormitorio. **2** US colegio mayor.

dosage ['dəʊsɪdʒ] *n* dosificación.

dose [dəʊs] *n* dosis *f inv*.

doss [dɒs] *i* GB *sl to ~ (down)*, echarse a dormir, acostarse.

dossier ['dɒsɪeɪ] *n* expediente *m*, dossier *m*.

dot [dɒt] *n* punto. **– 2** *t* poner el punto a. **3** *(scatter)* esparcir. ●*fam on the ~*, en punto.

dote [dəʊt] *i to ~ on/upon*, adorar.

double ['dʌbəl] *adj-adv* doble: *~ meaning*, doble sentido. **– 2** *n (amount)* doble *m*: *to earn ~*, ganar el doble. **3** *(person)* imagen *f* viva. **4** *pl (tennis)* partido *m sing* de dobles. **– 5** *t-i* doblar(se), duplicar(se). ◆*to ~ up t* retorcer. **– 2** *i* doblarse. **3** *(share)* compartir. ●*to ~ as*, hacer las veces de; *fam on the ~*, enseguida. ■ *~ agent*, agente *mf* doble; *~ bass*, contrabajo; *~ bed*, cama de matrimonio; *~ chin*, papada; *~ room*, habitación doble; *~ talk*, palabras *fpl* ambiguas.

double-cross [dʌbəl'krɒs] *t fam* engañar, traicionar.

double-decker [dʌbəl'dekəʳ] *n* GB *~ (bus)*, autobús *m* de dos pisos.

doubly ['dʌblɪ] *adv* doblemente.

doubt [daʊt] *n* duda, incertidumbre *f*. **– 2** *t (distrust)* dudar/desconfiar de. **3** *(not be sure)* dudar: *I ~ if she'll come*, dudo que venga. ●*beyond ~*, sin duda alguna; *no ~*, sin duda.

doubtful ['daʊtfʊl] *adj (uncertain)* dudoso,-a; *(look etc.)* de duda. **2** *(unlikely)* improbable.

doubtless ['daʊtləs] *adv* sin duda.

dough [dəʊ] *n* CULIN masa. **2** *sl (money)* pasta.

doughnut ['dəʊnʌt] *n* rosquilla, dónut® *m*.

douse [daʊs] *t (fire)* apagar. **2** *(wet)* mojar.

dove [dʌv] *n* paloma. **– 2** *pt* US → **dive**. ▲ *En 2 (verbo)* [dəʊv].

dowdy ['daʊdɪ] *adj pej (dress)* sin gracia; *(person)* mal vestido,-a.

down [daʊn] *prep* (hacia) abajo: ~ *the street,* calle abajo. **2** *(along)* por: *cut it ~ the middle,* córtalo por la mitad. — **3** *adv* (hacia) abajo; *(to the floor)* al suelo; *(to the ground)* a tierra: *to fall ~,* caerse (al suelo). **4** *(at lower level)* abajo: ~ *here/there,* aquí/allí abajo. **5** *(less)* **sales are ~ this year,** las ventas han bajado este año. **6** *(on paper)* **to write sth.** ~, apuntar algo. — **7** *interj* ~ *with ...!,* ¡abajo ...! — **8** *adj fam* **to feel** ~, estar deprimido,-a. — **9** *t* derribar. **10** *fam (drink)* tomarse de un trago. — **11** *n (on bird)* plumón *m; (hair)* pelusa, pelusilla. ●*face ~,* boca abajo. ■ ~ *payment,* entrada.

downcast [ˈdaʊnkɑːst] *adj* abatido,-a.

downfall [ˈdaʊnfɔːl] *n fig* perdición.

downgrade [daʊnˈgreɪd] *t* degradar.

downhearted [daʊnˈhɑːtɪd] *adj* desanimado,-a.

downhill [daʊnˈhɪl] *adv* cuesta abajo. — **2** *adj* en pendiente; *(skiing)* de descenso. ●*to go ~,* empeorar.

downpour [ˈdaʊnpɔːʳ] *n* chaparrón *m.*

downright [ˈdaʊnraɪt] *fam adj* total.

downstairs [daʊnˈsteəz] *adv* abajo: *to go ~,* bajar la escalera. **2** *(on ground floor)* en la planta baja. — **3** *adj* en la planta baja.

downstream [daʊnˈstriːm] *adv* río abajo.

downtown [daʊnˈtaʊn] *adv* US al/en el centro (de la ciudad).

downward [ˈdaʊnwəd] *adj* descendente. **2** FIN a la baja.

downward(s) [ˈdaʊnwədz] *adv* hacia abajo: *face ~,* boca abajo.

dowry [ˈdaʊərɪ] *n* dote *f.*

dowse [daʊs] *t* → **douse.**

doze [dəʊz] *n* cabezada. — **2** *i* dormitar, echar una cabezada. ●*to ~ off i* quedarse dormido,-a.

dozen [ˈdʌzən] *n* docena.

dozy [ˈdəʊzɪ] *adj* soñoliento,-a.

drab [dræb] *adj (colour)* pardo,-a. **2** *(dreary)* monótono,-a, gris.

draft [drɑːft] *n (rough copy)* borrador *m; (sketch)* esbozo. **2** *(bill)* letra de cambio, giro. **3** US MIL servicio militar obligatorio. **4** US → **draught.** — **5** *t (letter)* hacer un borrador de; *(plan)* redactar. **6** US MIL reclutar.

draftsman [ˈdrɑːftsmən] *n* US → **draughtsman.**

drafty [ˈdrɑːftɪ] *adj* US → **draughty.**

drag [dræg] *n (act)* arrastre *m.* **2** *(resistance)* resistencia; *fig* estorbo. **3** *fam (bore)* lata, rollo. **4** *fam (puff)* calada,

chupada. — **5** *t* arrastrar. **6** *(trawl)* rastrear, dragar. — **7** *i* arrastrarse. **8** *(go slowly)* rezagarse. ●*to ~ on i* prolongarse. ●*to ~ out t* alargar, prolongar. ◆*to ~ up t fam (revive)* sacar a relucir. ●*(man) in ~,* vestido de mujer.

dragon [ˈdrægən] *n* dragón *m.*

drain [dreɪn] *n (pipe)* desagüe *m; (for sewage)* alcantarilla. **2** *fig* desgaste *m,* agotamiento: *the boys are a ~ on her,* los niños le dejan agotada. — **3** *t (dry out)* desecar, desaguar. **4** *(glass)* apurar. **5** *fig* agotar. — **6** *t-i to ~ (off),* escurrir(se). **7** *(empty)* vaciar(se). ●*to go down the ~,* *(money)* esfumarse.

drainage [ˈdreɪnɪdʒ] *n (of marsh)* avenamiento; *(of region, building)* desagüe *m; (of town)* alcantarillado.

drainpipe [ˈdreɪnpaɪp] *n* tubo de desagüe.

drama [ˈdrɑːmə] *n (play)* obra de teatro, drama *m.* **2** *(subject)* teatro. **3** *fig* drama.

dramatic [drəˈmætɪk] *adj* THEAT dramático,-a. **2** *(exciting)* emocionante. **3** *(sharp)* notable.

dramatics [drəˈmætɪks] *n* teatro.

dramatist [ˈdræmətɪst] *n* dramaturgo,-a.

dramatization [dræmətaɪˈzeɪʃən] *n* adaptación teatral, dramatización.

drank [dræŋk] *pt* → **drink.**

drape [dreɪp] *t* cubrir *(with/in,* con). **2** *(part of body)* dejar colgado,-a. — **3** *n* US cortina.

drapery [ˈdreɪpərɪ] *n* GB pañería.

drastic [ˈdræstɪk] *adj* drástico,-a.

draught [drɑːft] *n* corriente *f* (de aire). **2** *(drink)* trago. **3** GB *pl* damas *fpl.* ■ *on ~,* a presión, de barril.

draughtsman [ˈdrɑːftsmən] *n* delineante *mf.*

draw [drɔː] *n (raffle)* sorteo. **2** *(score)* empate *m.* **3** *(attraction)* atracción. — **4** *t (picture)* dibujar; *(line, circle)* trazar. **5** *(pull)* arrastrar, tirar de. **6** *(curtains) (open)* descorrer; *(close)* correr. **7** *(take out)* sacar; *(sword)* desenvainar. **8** *(salary)* cobrar; *(cheque)* librar, extender. **9** *(attract)* atraer. **10** *(breath)* aspirar. **11** *(conclusion)* sacar. — **12** *i (sketch)* dibujar. **13** *(move)* moverse: *the train drew into/out of the station,* el tren entró en/salió de la estación. **14** SP empatar. **15** *(chimney)* tirar. ◆*to ~ back i* retroceder. **2** *(pull out)* echarse para atrás. ◆*to ~ in i* apartarse, echarse a un lado. ◆*to ~ on t* recurrir a. ◆*to ~ out t-i (lengthen)* alargar(se). ◆*to ~ up t (contract)* preparar; *(plan)* esbozar. — **2** *i (arrive)* llegar. ●*to*

~ *apart,* separarse (*from,* de); *to* ~ *attention to,* llamar la atención sobre; *to* ~ *blood,* hacer sangrar; *to* ~ *near,* acercarse; *fig the luck of the* ~, toca a quien toca; *fig to* ~ *the line (at sth.),* decir basta (a algo). ▲ *pt* **drew***; pp* **drawn**.

drawback ['drɔ:bæk] *n* inconveniente *m,* desventaja.

drawbridge ['drɔ:brɪdʒ] *n* puente levadizo.

drawer ['drɔ:əʳ] *n* cajón *m.*

drawing ['drɔ:ɪŋ] *n* dibujo. ■ GB ~ *pin,* chincheta; ~ *room,* sala de estar, salón *m.*

drawl [drɔ:l] *n* voz cansina. – **2** *i* hablar arrastrando las palabras.

drawn [drɔ:n] *pp* → **draw**. – **2** *adj (face)* ojeroso,-a.

dread [dred] *n* temor *m,* pavor *m.* – **2** *t-i* temer, tener pavor a.

dreadful ['dredful] *adj* terrible, espantoso,-a. **2** *fam* fatal, horrible. – **3** *dreadfully adv fam* muy.

dream [dri:m] *n* sueño. **2** *(while awake)* ensueño. **3** *fam* maravilla. – **4** *t-i* soñar. ◆*to* ~ *up t fam pej* inventarse. ▲ *pt & pp* **dreamed** o **dreamt**.

dreamer ['dri:məʳ] *n* soñador,-ra.

dreamt [dremt] *pt & pp* → **dream**.

dreary ['drɪərɪ] *adj* triste, deprimente. **2** *fam* pesado,-a.

dredge [dredʒ] *t-i* dragar, rastrear.

dredger ['dredʒəʳ] *n* draga.

dregs [dregz] *npl* heces *fpl,* sedimento *m sing.*

drench [drentʃ] *t* mojar, empapar.

dress [dres] *n (frock)* vestido. **2** *(clothing)* ropa, vestimenta. – **3** *t* vestir. **4** *(wound)* vendar. **5** CULIN aderezar; *(salad)* aliñar. – **6** *i* vestirse. ◆*to* ~ *down t (scold)* regañar. ◆*to* ~ *up i (child)* disfrazarse (*as,* de); *(formal)* ponerse de tiros largos. – **2** *t fig* disfrazar. ■ THEAT ~ *rehearsal,* ensayo general.

dresser ['dresəʳ] *n* GB aparador *m.* **2** US tocador *m.*

dressing ['dresɪŋ] *n (bandage)* vendaje *m.* **2** *(salad)* ~, aliño. ■ ~ *gown,* bata; ~ *table,* tocador *m.*

drew [dru:] *pt* → **draw**.

dribble ['drɪbəl] *n (of liquid)* gotas *fpl,* hilo. **2** *(of saliva)* baba. – **3** *i (liquid)* gotear. **4** *(baby)* babear. – **5** *t* dejar caer. **6** SP driblar.

drier ['draɪəʳ] *n* → **dryer**.

drift [drɪft] *n (flow)* flujo. **2** *(of snow)* ventisquero; *(of sand)* montón *m.* **3** *fig (meaning)* significado. – **4** *t-i (snow etc.)*

amontonar(se). – **5** *i (boat)* ir a la deriva. **6** *fig (person)* vagar.

drill [drɪl] *n (tool)* taladro. **2** MIL instrucción. **3** *(exercise)* ejercicio. **4** *(material)* dril *m.* **5** *(dentist's)* fresa. – **6** *t* taladrar. **7** MIL instruir. – **8** *i* taladrar. **9** MIL entrenarse. ■ *safety* ~, instrucciones *fpl* de seguridad.

drink [drɪŋk] *n* bebida; *(alcoholic)* copa. – **2** *t-i* beber. ◆*to* ~ *in t (scene etc.)* apreciar. ●*to* ~ *to sth./sb.,* brindar por algo/algn.; *to have sth. to* ~, tomar algo. ▲ *pt* **drank***; pp* **drunk**.

drinking ['drɪŋkɪŋ] *n* ~ *fountain,* fuente *f* de agua potable; ~ *water,* agua potable.

drip [drɪp] *n* goteo. **2** MED gota a gota *m inv.* **3** *fam* necio,-a. – **4** *i* gotear. – **5** *t* dejar caer gota a gota.

drive [draɪv] *n* paseo en coche. **2** *(road)* calle *f; (to house)* camino de entrada. **3** SP *(golf)* golpe *m* inicial; *(tennis)* golpe fuerte. **4** *(energy)* energía, ímpetu *m.* **5** *(need)* necesidad. **6** MECH transmisión; AUTO tracción. – **7** *t (vehicle)* conducir. **8** *(take)* llevar (en coche): *I'll* ~ *you home,* te llevaré a casa. **9** *(power)* impulsar. **10** *(force) (cattle)* arrear; *(ball)* mandar. **11** *(strike in)* clavar. **12** *(force)* forzar: *to* ~ *sb. mad/crazy,* volver loco,-a a algn. ◆*to* ~ *at t fam* insinuar. ▲ *pt* **drove***; pp* **driven**.

drivel ['drɪvəl] *n* tonterías *fpl.*

driven ['drɪvən] *pp* → **drive**.

driver ['draɪvəʳ] *n (of bus, car)* conductor,-ra. **2** *(of taxi)* taxista *mf.* **3** *(of lorry)* camionero,-a. **4** *(of racing car)* piloto *mf.*

driving ['draɪvɪŋ] *adj* ~ *licence,* carnet *m/* permiso de conducir; ~ *school,* autoescuela.

drizzle ['drɪzəl] *n* llovizna. – **2** *i* lloviznar.

droll [drəul] *adj* gracioso,-a, curioso,-a.

dromedary ['drɒmədərɪ] *n* dromedario.

drone [drəun] *n (bee)* zángano. **2** *(noise)* zumbido. – **3** *i* zumbar.

drool [dru:l] *n* baba. – **2** *i* babear.

droop [dru:p] *n* caída, inclinación. – **2** *i* inclinarse, caerse. **3** *(flower)* marchitarse.

drop [drɒp] *n* gota. **2** *(sweet)* pastilla. **3** *(descent)* pendiente *f,* desnivel *m.* **4** *(fall)* caída. – **5** *t* dejar caer: *he dropped the glass,* se le cayó el vaso. **6** *fam (leave)* dejar. **7** *(abandon)* abandonar. **8** *(omit) (in speaking)* comerse; *(in writing)* omitir. **9** SP echar. **10** *(knitting)* soltar. – **11** *i (fall)* caerse. **12** *(voice, price, etc.)* bajar, caer. **13** *(wind)* amainar. ◆*to* ~ *away i* disminuir. ◆*to* ~ *by/in/round i* dejarse caer, pasar. ◆*to* ~ *off i fam* quedarse dormido,-a. 2 *(lessen)* disminuir. ◆*to* ~ *out i (of school)* dejar los estudios; *(match)* retirarse. ●*to* ~ *sb. a line,* escribir cuatro líneas a algn.

dropper ['drɒpəʳ] *n* cuentagotas *m inv.*

droppings ['drɒpɪŋz] *npl* excrementos *mpl,* cagadas *fpl.*

dross [drɒs] *n* escoria.

drought [draʊt] *n* sequía.

drove [drəʊv] *pt* → **drive.** − 2 *n (of cattle)* manada. 3 *(of people)* multitud *f.*

drown [draʊn] *t-i* ahogar(se). − 2 *t (flood)* inundar.

drowse [draʊz] *i to* ~ *(off),* dormitar.

drowsiness ['draʊzɪnəs] *n* somnolencia.

drowsy ['draʊzɪ] *adj* soñoliento,-a. 2 *(scene etc.)* soporífero,-a.

drudge [drʌdʒ] *n* machaca *mf.*

drudgery ['drʌdʒərɪ] *n* trabajo duro.

drug [drʌg] *n (medicine)* medicamento, medicina. 2 *(narcotic)* droga, estupefaciente *m,* narcótico. − 3 *t* drogar. ●*to be on/take drugs,* drogarse. ■ ~ *addict,* drogadicto,-a; ~ *pusher,* traficante *mf* de drogas; ~ *squad,* brigada de estupefacientes.

drugstore ['drʌgstɔ:ʳ] *n* US *establecimiento donde se compran medicamentos, periódicos, etc.*

drum [drʌm] *n* tambor *m.* 2 *(container)* bidón *m.* 3 TECH tambor. − 4 *i (noise)* tabalear.

drummer ['drʌməʳ] *n (in band)* tambor *mf; (in pop group)* batería *mf.*

drumstick ['drʌmstɪk] *n* MUS baqueta. 2 CULIN muslo.

drunk [drʌŋk] *pp* → **drink.** − 2 *adj-n* borracho,-a. ●*to get* ~, emborracharse.

drunkard ['drʌŋkəd] *n* borracho,-a.

drunken ['drʌŋkən] *adj* borracho,-a.

dry [draɪ] *adj* seco,-a. 2 *(dull)* aburrido,-a. − 3 *t-i to* ~ *(off),* secar(se).

dry-clean [draɪ'kli:n] *t* limpiar en seco.

dryer ['draɪəʳ] *n* secadora.

dryness ['draɪnəs] *n* sequedad.

dual ['dju:əl] *adj* dual, doble. ■ ~ *carriageway,* autovía de doble calzada.

dub [dʌb] *t (subtitle)* doblar (*into,* a). 2 *(nickname)* apodar.

dubious ['dju:bɪəs] *adj* dudoso,-a.

duchess ['dʌtʃəs] *n* duquesa.

duck [dʌk] *n* pato,-a. 2 CULIN pato. − 3 *t-i (lower)* agachar(se). 4 *(go under water)* zambullir(se).

duckling ['dʌklɪŋ] *n* patito.

duct [dʌkt] *n* conducto.

dud [dʌd] *n fam (object)* trasto inútil, engañifa. 2 *(person)* desastre *m.*

due [dju:] *adj fml* debido,-a. 2 *(payable)* pagadero,-a. 3 *(expected)* esperado,-a: *I'm* ~ *for a rise,* me toca una subida de sueldo; *she's* ~ *to arrive tomorrow,* está previsto que llegue mañana; *the train is* ~ *at five,* el tren debe llegar a las cinco. − 4 *n* merecido: *to give sb. his/her* ~, dar a algn. su merecido. 5 *pl* cuota *f sing.* − 6 *adv* derecho hacia. ●*in* ~ *course/time,* a su debido tiempo; *to be* ~ *to,* deberse a. ■ ~ *date,* plazo, vencimiento.

duel ['dju:əl] *n* duelo. − 2 *i* batirse en duelo.

duet [dju:'et] *n* dúo.

duffel ['dʌfəl] *n* ~ *coat,* trenca.

dug [dʌg] *pt & pp* → **dig.**

duke [dju:k] *n* duque *m.*

dull [dʌl] *adj (not bright)* apagado,-a; *(weather)* gris. 2 *(sound, pain)* sordo,-a. 3 *(slow)* torpe. 4 *(uninteresting)* monótono,-a, pesado,-a. − 5 *t (pain)* aliviar; *(sound)* amortiguar.

duly ['dju:lɪ] *adv fml (properly)* debidamente. 2 *(as expected)* como era de esperar.

dumb [dʌm] *adj* mudo,-a. 2 *fam (stupid)* tonto,-a. − 3 *dumbly adv* sin decir nada.

dum(b)found [dʌm'faʊnd] *t* pasmar.

dummy ['dʌmɪ] *n (sham)* imitación. 2 *(model)* maniquí *m.* 3 GB *(for baby)* chupete *m.* 4 *fam* imbécil *mf.*

dump [dʌmp] *n (tip)* vertedero; *(for cars)* cementerio (de coches). 2 *fam pej (town)* poblacho; *(dwelling)* tugurio. − 3 *t* verter; *fam (leave)* dejar. ●*fam (down) in the dumps,* pocho,-a, depre.

dumpling ['dʌmplɪŋ] *n (in stew)* bola de masa *hervida para acompañar carnes etc.* 2 *(as dessert)* tipo de budín relleno.

dumpy ['dʌmpɪ] *adj fam* rechoncho,-a.

dune [dju:n] *n (sand)* ~, duna.

dung [dʌŋ] *n* estiércol *m.*

dungarees [dʌngə'ri:z] *n* pantalones *mpl* con peto.

dungeon ['dʌndʒən] *n* mazmorra.

duo ['dju:əʊ] *n* dúo.

dupe [dju:p] *n* ingenuo,-a. − 2 *t* embaucar.

duplicate ['dju:plɪkət] *adj-n* duplicado,-a *(m).* − 2 *t* duplicar. ▲ *En 2 (verbo)* ['dju:plɪkeɪt].

durability [djʊərə'bɪlɪtɪ] *n* durabilidad.

durable ['djʊərəbəl] *adj* duradero,-a.

duration [djʊə'reɪʃən] *n* duración.

during [ˈdjʊərɪŋ] *prep* durante.
dusk [dʌsk] *n* anochecer *m*.
dust [dʌst] *n* polvo. − 2 *t* desempolvar, quitar el polvo a. 3 *(sprinkle)* espolvorear.
dustbin [ˈdʌstbɪn] *n* GB cubo de la basura.
duster [ˈdʌstəʳ] *n* paño, trapo. 2 *(for blackboard)* borrador *m*.
dustman [ˈdʌstmən] *n* GB basurero.
dustpan [ˈdʌstpæn] *n* (re)cogedor *m*.
dusty [ˈdʌstɪ] *adj* polvoriento,-a, lleno,-a de polvo.
duty [ˈdjuːtɪ] *n* deber *m*, obligación. 2 *(task)* cometido. 3 *(tax)* impuesto. 4 *(availability)* guardia. ●*to be on/off* ∼, estar/no estar de servicio/guardia; *to do one's* ∼, cumplir con su deber. ■ *customs duties,* derechos *mpl* de aduana, aranceles *mpl*.
duty-free [ˈdjuːtɪfriː] *adj* libre de impuestos. − 2 *adv* sin pagar impuestos. − 3 *n* duty-free *m*.
duvet [ˈduːveɪ] *n* edredón *m*.

dwarf [dwɔːf] *n* enano,-a. − 2 *t* achicar.
dwell [dwel] *i fml* habitar, morar. ◆*to* ∼ *on/upon t* insistir en. ▲ *pt & pp* **dwelt**.
dweller [ˈdweləʳ] *n* habitante *mf*.
dwelling [ˈdwelɪŋ] *n* morada.
dwelt [dwelt] *pt & pp* → **dwell**.
dwindle [ˈdwɪndəl] *i* menguar, disminuir.
dye [daɪ] *n* tinte *m*, colorante *m*. − 2 *t-i* teñir(se).
dyed-in-the-wool [daɪdɪnðəˈwʊl] *adj pej* acérrimo,-a, inflexible, intransigente.
dyke [daɪk] *n (bank)* dique *m*, barrera. 2 *(causeway)* terraplén *m*. 3 *sl pej (lesbian)* tortillera.
dynamic [daɪˈnæmɪk] *adj* dinámico,-a.
dynamics [daɪˈnæmɪks] *n* dinámica.
dynamite [ˈdaɪnəmaɪt] *n* dinamita.
dynamo [ˈdaɪnəməʊ] *n* dinamo.
dynasty [ˈdɪnəstɪ] *n* dinastía.
dysentery [ˈdɪsəntrɪ] *n* disentería.
dyslexia [dɪsˈleksɪə] *n* dislexia.

E

each [i:tʃ] *adj* cada: ~ *day,* todos los días. — **2** *pron* cada uno,-a: ~ *with his wife,* cada uno con su esposa. — **3** *adv* cada uno,-a. ●~ *other,* el/la uno,-a al/a la otro,-a: *we love* ~ *other,* nos queremos.

eager ['i:gə^r] *adj* ávido,-a, ansioso,-a, impaciente. — **2** *eagerly adv* ávidamente, con afán.

eagerness ['i:gənəs] *n* avidez *f,* ansia, afán *m,* ardor *m.*

eagle ['i:gəl] *n* águila.

ear [ɪə^r] *n* oreja. **2** *(sense)* oído. **3** *(of corn)* espiga.

ear-ache ['ɪəreɪk] *n* dolor *m* de oídos.

eardrum ['ɪədrʌm] *n* tímpano.

earl [ɜ:l] *n* conde *m.*

earlobe ['ɪələʊb] *n* lóbulo.

early ['ɜ:lɪ] *adj* temprano,-a: ~ *in the morning/afternoon,* a primera hora de la mañana/tarde. — **2** *adv* temprano. ●*in the* ~ *morning,* de madrugada.

earmark ['ɪəmɑ:k] *t* destinar *(for,* a).

earn [ɜ:n] *t gen* ganar. **2** *(interest)* devengar.

earnest ['ɜ:nɪst] *adj* serio,-a, formal. ●*in* ~, en serio.

earnings ['ɜ:nɪŋz] *npl* ganancias *fpl.*

earpiece ['ɪəpi:s] *n* auricular *m.*

earplug ['ɪəplʌg] *n* tapón *m* (para los oídos).

earring ['ɪərɪŋ] *n* pendiente *m.*

earth [ɜ:θ] *n* tierra. **2** *(fox's)* madriguera. ●*fam what/where on* ~ *...?,* ¿qué/dónde demonios ...?

earthenware ['ɜ:θənweə^r] *n* loza de barro.

earthly ['ɜ:θlɪ] *adj* terrenal. ●*not to have an* ~ *(chance),* no tener la más mínima posibilidad.

earthquake ['ɜ:θkweɪk] *n* terremoto.

earthworm ['ɜ:θwɜ:m] *n* lombriz *f.*

earthy ['ɜ:θɪ] *adj* terroso,-a. **2** *(coarse)* grosero,-a.

earwig ['ɪəwɪg] *n* tijereta.

ease [i:z] *n (lack of difficulty)* facilidad. **2** *(lack of worry)* tranquilidad. **3** *(comfort)* comodidad. — **4** *t (pain)* aliviar. — **5** *i (tension)* disminuir. ◆*to* ~ *off i* disminuir. ●*at* ~, relajado,-a; *to set sb.'s mind at* ~, tranquilizar a algn.

easel ['i:zəl] *n* caballete *m.*

easiness ['i:zɪnəs] *n* facilidad.

east [i:st] *n* este *m,* oriente *m.* — **2** *adj* (del) este, oriental. — **3** *adv* hacia el este.

Easter ['i:stə^r] *n* REL Pascua (de Resurrección). **2** *(holiday)* Semana Santa.

easterly ['i:stəlɪ] *adj (to the east)* al este, hacia el este. **2** *(from the east)* del este.

eastern ['i:stən] *adj* oriental.

eastward ['i:stwəd] *adj* hacia el este.

eastwards ['i:stwədz] *adv* hacia el este.

easy ['i:zɪ] *adj* fácil, sencillo,-a. **2** *(comfortable)* cómodo,-a, holgado,-a. — **3** *easily adv* fácilmente. **4** *(by a long way)* con mucho. ●*take it* ~!, ¡tranquilo,-a!; *to take things* ~, tomar(se) las cosas con calma; *fam I'm* ~, me es igual. ■ ~ *chair,* sillón *m.*

easy-going ['i:zɪgəʊɪŋ] *adj* calmado,-a, tranquilo,-a.

eat [i:t] *t-i* comer. ◆*to* ~ *away t* desgastar; *(metal)* corroer. ◆*to* ~ *into t fig* consumir. ◆*to* ~ *out i* comer fuera. ◆*to* ~ *up t* comerse. ▲ *pt* ate; *pp* eaten.

eatable ['i:təbəl] *adj* comestible.

eaten ['i:tən] *pp* → **eat**.

eau-de-Cologne [əʊdəkə'ləʊn] *n* colonia.

eaves [i:vz] *npl* alero *m sing.*

eavesdrop ['i:vzdrɒp] *i* escuchar a escondidas.

ebb [eb] *n* reflujo. — **2** *i* bajar, menguar. ●*at a low* ~, en un punto bajo. ■ ~ *and* *flow,* flujo y reflujo; ~*-tide,* marea menguante.

ebony ['ebənɪ] *n* ébano.

ebullient [ɪ'bʌljənt] *adj* eufórico,-a, exaltado,-a.

eccentric [ɪk'sentrɪk] *adj-n* excéntrico,-a.

eccentricity [eksen'trɪsɪtɪ] *n* excentricidad.

ecclesiastic [ɪkli:zi'æstɪk] *adj-n* eclesiástico,-a *(m).*

ecclesiastical [ɪkli:zɪ'æstɪkəl] *adj* eclesiástico,-a.

echo ['ekəʊ] *n* eco. – **2** *t* repetir. – **3** *i* hacer eco, resonar.

éclair [ɪ'kleəʳ] *n* palo de nata.

eclipse [ɪ'klɪps] *n* eclipse *m.* – **2** *t* eclipsar.

ecological [i:kə'lɒdʒɪkəl] *adj* ecológico,-a.

ecologist [ɪ'kɒlədʒɪst] *n* ecólogo,-a, ecologista *mf.*

ecology [ɪ'kɒlədʒɪ] *n* ecología.

economic [i:kə'nɒmɪk] *adj* económico,-a. **2** *(profitable)* rentable.

economical [i:kə'nɒmɪkəl] *adj* barato,-a, económico,-a.

economics [i:kə'nɒmɪks] *n* economía, ciencias *fpl* económicas.

economist [ɪ'kɒnəmɪst] *n* economista *mf.*

economize [iː'kɒnəmaɪz] *i* economizar, ahorrar.

economy [ɪ'kɒnəmɪ] *n* economía.

ecosystem ['iːkɒsɪstɪm] *n* ecosistema *m.*

ecstasy ['ekstəsɪ] *n* éxtasis *m inv.*

ecstatic [ek'stætɪk] *adj* extático,-a.

eczema ['eksɪmə] n eccema *m.*

edge [edʒ] *n* borde *m.* **2** *(of coin, step, etc.)* canto. **3** *(of knife)* filo. **4** *(of water)* orilla. **5** *(of town)* afueras *fpl.* – **6** *t* ribetear. ◆*to* ~ *forward i* avanzar lentamente. ●*on* ~, impaciente; *to have the* ~ *on/over sb.,* llevar ventaja a algn.

edgeways ['edʒweɪz] *adv* de lado.

edging ['edʒɪŋ] *n* ribete *m,* orla.

edgy ['edʒɪ] *adj* nervioso,-a.

edible ['edɪbəl] *adj* comestible.

edict ['iːdɪkt] *n* edicto.

edifice ['edɪfɪs] *n* (gran) edificio.

edify ['edɪfaɪ] *t* edificar, dar ejemplo a.

edit ['edɪt] *t* *(prepare for printing)* preparar para la imprenta. **2** *(correct)* corregir. **3** *(newspaper etc.)* dirigir. **4** CINEM TV montar, editar; *(cut)* cortar.

edition [ɪ'dɪʃən] *n* edición.

editor ['edɪtəʳ] *n* *(of book)* editor,-ra; *(writer)* redactor,-ra. **2** *(of newspaper etc.)* director,-ra. **3** CINEM TV montador,-ra.

editorial [edɪ'tɔːrɪəl] *adj* editorial. – **2** *n* editorial *m.* ■ ~ *staff,* redacción.

educate ['edjʊkeɪt] *t* educar.

educated ['edjʊkeɪtɪd] *adj* culto,-a.

education [edjʊ'keɪʃən] *n gen* educación. **2** *(instruction)* enseñanza. **3** *(studies)* estudios *mpl.* **4** *(field of study)* pedagogía.

educational [edjʊ'keɪʃənəl] *adj* educativo,-a.

eel [iːl] *n* anguila.

eerie ['ɪərɪ] *adj* misterioso,-a.

efface [ɪ'feɪs] *t fml* borrar.

effect [ɪ'fekt] *n* efecto. **2** *pl* *(property)* efectos *mpl.* – **3** *t* efectuar. ●*in* ~, de hecho; *to come into* ~, entrar en vigor; *to take* ~, *(drug etc.)* surtir/hacer efecto; *(law)* entrar en vigor; *to the* ~ *that,* en el sentido de que.

effective [ɪ'fektɪv] *adj* eficaz. **2** *(real)* efectivo,-a. **3** *(impressive)* impresionante.

effectuate [ɪ'fektjʊeɪt] *t* efectuar, realizar.

effeminacy [ɪ'femɪnəsɪ] *n* afeminación.

effeminate [ɪ'femɪnət] *adj* afeminado,-a.

effervescence [efə'vesəns] *n* efervescencia.

effervescent [efə'vesənt] *adj* efervescente.

effete [e'fiːt] *adj* débil, agotado,-a.

efficacious [efɪ'keɪʃəs] *adj* eficaz.

efficacy ['efɪkəsɪ] *n* eficacia.

efficiency [ɪ'fɪʃənsɪ] *n* *(of person)* eficiencia, competencia. **2** *(of product)* eficacia. **3** *(of machine)* rendimiento.

efficient [ɪ'fɪʃənt] *adj* *(person)* eficiente, competente. **2** *(product)* eficaz. **3** *(machine)* de buen rendimiento.

effigy ['efɪdʒɪ] *n* efigie *f.*

effort ['efət] *n* esfuerzo. **2** *(attempt)* intento.

effortless ['efətləs] *adj* fácil, sin esfuerzo.

effrontery [e'frʌntərɪ] *n* descaro, desfachatez *f.*

effusive [ɪ'fjuːsɪv] *adj* efusivo,-a.

egalitarian [ɪgælɪ'teərɪən] *adj* igualitario,-a.

egg [eg] *n* huevo. ◆*to* ~ *on t* animar. ■ *boiled* ~, huevo pasado por agua; ~ *cup,* huevera; *fried* ~, huevo frito; *hard-boiled* ~, huevo duro.

eggplant ['egplɑːnt] *n* berenjena.

ego ['iːgəʊ] *n* *(in psychology)* yo. **2** *fam* amor *m* propio.

egocentric(al) [iːgəʊ'sentrɪk(əl)] *adj* egocéntrico,-a.

egoism ['iːgəʊɪzəm] *n* egoísmo.

egoist ['iːgəʊɪst] *n* egoísta *mf.*

egotism ['iːgətɪzəm] *n* egotismo.

egotist ['iːgətɪst] *n* egoísta *mf.*

egotistic(al) [iːgə'tɪstɪk(əl)] *adj* egoísta.

eiderdown ['aɪdədaʊn] *n* edredón *m.*

eight [eɪt] *adj-n* ocho.

eighteen [eɪ'tiːn] *adj-n* dieciocho.

eighteenth [eɪ'tiːnθ] *adj-n* decimoctavo,-a. – **2** *n (fraction)* decimoctavo, decimoctava parte.

eighth [eɪtθ] *adj-n* octavo,-a. – **2** *n (fraction)* octavo, octava parte.

eightieth ['eɪtɪɪθ] *adj-n* octogésimo,-a. – **2** *n (fraction)* octogésimo, octogésima parte.

eighty ['eɪtɪ] *adj-n* ochenta *(m).*

either ['aɪðə', 'iːðə'] *adj (affirmative)* cualquiera: ~ *of them,* cualquiera de los dos. **2** *(negative)* ni el uno/la una ni el otro/la otra, ninguno,-a: *I don't like* ~ *of them,* no me gusta ninguno de los dos. – **3** *adj* cada, los/las dos, ambos,-as: *with a gun in* ~ *hand,* con una pistola en cada mano. – **4** *conj* o: ~ *red or green,* o rojo o verde. – **5** *adv* tampoco: *Ann didn't come* ~, tampoco vino Ana.

ejaculate [ɪ'dʒækjʊleɪt] *i* eyacular. **2** *(exclaim)* exclamar.

eject [iː'dʒekt] *t* expulsar. – **2** *i* AV eyectar(se).

elaborate [ɪ'læbərət] *adj (detailed)* detallado,-a. **2** *(complex)* complicado,-a. – **3** *t (embellish)* adornar. – **4** *i (say more)* extenderse. ▲ *En 3 y 4 (verbo)* [ɪ'læbəreɪt].

elapse [ɪ'læps] *i* transcurrir.

elastic [ɪ'læstɪk] *adj-n* elástico,-a *(m).* ■ ~ *band,* goma elástica.

elated [ɪ'leɪtɪd] *adj* eufórico,-a.

elation [ɪ'leɪʃən] *n* euforia, júbilo.

elbow ['elbəʊ] *n* codo. **2** *(bend)* recodo. – **3** *t* dar un codazo a.

elder ['eldə'] *adj* mayor. – **2** *n* mayor *m.* **3** BOT saúco.

elderly ['eldəlɪ] *adj* mayor, anciano,-a.

eldest ['eldɪst] *adj* mayor.

elect [ɪ'lekt] *adj* electo,-a. – **2** *t* elegir.

election [ɪ'lekʃən] *n* elección.

elector [ɪ'lektə'] *n* elector,-ra.

electoral [ɪ'lektərəl] *adj* electoral.

electorate [ɪ'lektərət] *n* electorado.

electric [ɪ'lektrɪk] *adj* eléctrico,-a. **2** *fig* electrizante. ■ ~ *chair,* silla eléctrica; ~ *shock,* electrochoque *m,* descarga eléctrica.

electrical [ɪ'lektrɪkəl] *adj* eléctrico,-a.

electrician [ɪlek'trɪʃən] *n* electricista *mf.*

electricity [ɪlek'trɪsɪtɪ] *n* electricidad.

electrify [ɪ'lektrɪfaɪ] *t* electrificar. **2** *fig* electrizar.

electrocute [ɪ'lektrəkjuːt] *t* electrocutar.

electrode [ɪ'lektrəʊd] *n* electrodo.

electron [ɪ'lektrɒn] *n* electrón *m.*

electronic [ɪlek'trɒnɪk] *adj* electrónico,-a.

electronics [ɪlek'trɒnɪks] *n* electrónica.

elegance ['elɪgəns] *n* elegancia.

elegant ['elɪgənt] *adj* elegante.

element ['elɪmənt] *n gen* elemento. **2** *(component)* componente *m.* **3** ELEC resistencia. **4** *pl* rudimentos *mpl.*

elementary [elɪ'mentərɪ] *adj* elemental. ■ ~ *education,* enseñanza primaria.

elephant ['elɪfənt] *n* elefante *m.*

elevate ['elɪveɪt] *t* elevar. **2** *(in rank)* ascender.

elevation [elɪ'veɪʃən] *n* elevación. **2** *(in rank)* ascenso. **3** *(height)* altitud.

elevator ['elɪveɪtə'] *n* US ascensor *m.* **2** GB escalera mecánica.

eleven [ɪ'levən] *adj-n* once *(m).* – **2** *n* SP equipo, once *m.*

eleventh [ɪ'levənθ] *adj-n* undécimo,-a. – **2** *n (fraction)* onceavo, onceava parte.

elf [elf] *n* elfo.

elicit [ɪ'lɪsɪt] *t* sonsacar, obtener.

eligible ['elɪdʒəbəl] *adj* elegible.

eliminate [ɪ'lɪmɪneɪt] *t* eliminar.

elimination [ɪlɪmɪ'neɪʃən] *n* eliminación.

elite [eɪ'liːt] *n* elite *f.*

elixir [ɪ'lɪksə'] *n* elixir *m.*

elk [elk] *n* alce *m.*

elliptical [ɪ'lɪptɪkəl] *adj* elíptico,-a.

elm [elm] *n* olmo.

elocution [elə'kjuːʃən] *n* elocución.

elongate ['iːlɒŋgeɪt] *t* alargar, extender.

elope [ɪ'ləʊp] *i* fugarse (para casarse).

eloquence ['eləkwəns] *n* elocuencia.

eloquent ['eləkwənt] *adj* elocuente.

else [els] *adv* más: *anything* ~?, ¿algo más?; *nobody* ~, nadie más; *someone* ~, otra persona más. ●*or* ~, si no: *behave yourself or* ~, pórtate bien, si no (ya verás).

elsewhere [els'weə'] *adv* en otro sitio.

elude [ɪ'luːd] *t* eludir, escapar(se).

elusive [ɪ'luːsɪv] *adj* huidizo,-a, esquivo,-a.

emaciated [ɪ'meɪʃɪeɪtɪd] *adj* enflaquecido,-a; *(face)* demacrado,-a.

emanate ['eməneɪt] *i* emanar.

emancipate [ɪ'mænsɪpeɪt] *t* emancipar.

embalm [ɪm'bɑːm] *t* embalsamar.

embankment [ɪmˈbæŋkmənt] n terraplén m. 2 (river bank) dique m.

embargo [emˈbɑːgəʊ] n embargo. – 2 t (prohibit) prohibir. 3 (seize) embargar.

embark [ɪmˈbɑːk] t-i embarcar(se). •to ~ on sth., emprender algo.

embarkation [ˌembɑːˈkeɪʃən] n embarque m.

embarrass [ɪmˈbærəs] t turbar, azorar, desconcertar.

embarrassing [ɪmˈbærəsɪŋ] adj embarazoso,-a, violento,-a.

embarrassment [ɪmˈbærəsmənt] n (state) turbación, desconcierto. 2 (object) embarazo, estorbo.

embassy [ˈembəsɪ] n embajada.

embed [ɪmˈbed] t empotrar, incrustar.

embellish [ɪmˈbelɪʃ] t adornar.

embellishment [ɪmˈbelɪʃmənt] n adorno.

ember [ˈembər] n ascua, rescoldo.

embezzle [ɪmˈbezəl] t desfalcar.

embezzlement [ɪmˈbezəlmənt] n desfalco.

emblem [ˈembləm] n emblema m.

embody [ɪmˈbɒdɪ] t encarnar. 2 (include) incorporar, incluir.

emboss [ɪmˈbɒs] t estampar en relieve.

embrace [ɪmˈbreɪs] n abrazo. – 2 t-i abrazar(se). – 3 t (include) abarcar. 4 (religion etc.) abrazar.

embroider [ɪmˈbrɔɪdər] t bordar. 2 fig adornar.

embroidery [ɪmˈbrɔɪdərɪ] n bordado. 2 fig adorno.

embroil [ɪmˈbrɔɪl] t enredar.

embryo [ˈembrɪəʊ] n embrión m.

embryonic [ˌembrɪˈɒnɪk] adj embrionario,-a.

emend [ɪˈmend] t enmendar.

emendation [ˌiːmenˈdeɪʃən] n enmienda.

emerald [ˈemərəld] n (stone) esmeralda f. 2 (colour) esmeralda m. – 3 adj (de color) esmeralda.

emerge [ɪˈmɜːdʒ] i emerger, aparecer: it emerged that ..., resultó que ... .

emergence [ɪˈmɜːdʒəns] n aparición.

emergency [ɪˈmɜːdʒənsɪ] n emergencia. 2 MED (caso de) urgencia. ■ ~ exit, salida de emergencia.

emergent [ɪˈmɜːdʒənt] adj emergente.

emery [ˈemərɪ] n esmeril m. ■ ~ board, lima de uñas.

emigrant [ˈemɪgrənt] n emigrante mf.

emigrate [ˈemɪgreɪt] i emigrar.

emigration [ˌemɪˈgreɪʃən] n emigración.

eminence [ˈemɪnəns] n eminencia.

eminent [ˈemɪnənt] adj eminente.

emir [eˈmɪər] n emir m.

emirate [ˈemɪrət] n emirato.

emissary [ˈemɪsərɪ] n emisario.

emission [ɪˈmɪʃən] n emisión.

emit [ɪˈmɪt] t emitir.

emotion [ɪˈməʊʃən] n emoción.

emotional [ɪˈməʊʃənəl] adj emocional. 2 (moving) emotivo,-a.

emotive [ɪˈməʊtɪv] adj emotivo,-a.

emperor [ˈempərər] n emperador m.

emphasis [ˈemfəsɪs] n énfasis m inv. •to place ~ on, hacer hincapié en.

emphasize [ˈemfəsaɪz] t enfatizar, hacer hincapié en, subrayar.

emphatic [emˈfætɪk] adj enfático,-a, enérgico,-a.

empire [ˈempaɪər] n imperio.

empirical [emˈpɪrɪkəl] adj empírico,-a.

employ [ɪmˈplɔɪ] n empleo. – 2 t emplear.

employee [emˈplɔɪiː, emplɔˈiː] n empleado,-a.

employer [emˈplɔɪər] n patrón,-ona.

employment [emˈplɔɪmənt] n empleo.

empower [ɪmˈpaʊər] t autorizar, facultar.

empress [ˈempres] n emperatriz f.

emptiness [ˈemptɪnəs] n vacío.

empty [ˈemptɪ] adj vacío,-a. – 2 t-i vaciar(se).

emulate [ˈemjʊleɪt] t emular.

emulsion [ɪˈmʌlʃən] n emulsión.

enable [ɪˈneɪbəl] t permitir.

enact [ɪˈnækt] t (law) promulgar. 2 (play) representar.

enamel [ɪˈnæməl] n esmalte. – 2 t esmaltar.

encapsulate [ɪŋˈkæpsjʊleɪt] t encapsular.

enchant [ɪnˈtʃɑːnt] t encantar, hechizar.

enchanting [ɪnˈtʃɑːntɪŋ] adj encantador,-ra.

enchantment [ɪnˈtʃɑːntmənt] n encanto, hechizo.

encircle [ɪnˈsɜːkəl] t rodear, cercar.

enclave [ˈenkleɪv] n enclave m.

enclose [ɪnˈkləʊz] t cercar, rodear. 2 (with letter) adjuntar.

enclosure [ɪnˈkləʊʒər] n (area) cercado. 2 (with letter) anexo.

encompass [ɪnˈkʌmpəs] t abarcar.

encore [ˈɒŋkɔːr] interj ¡otra! – 2 n repetición.

encounter [ɪnˈkaʊntər] n encuentro. – 2 t encontrar, encontrarse con.

encourage [ɪnˈkʌrɪdʒ] t (cheer) animar. 2 (develop) fomentar.

encouragement [ɪnˈkʌrɪdʒmənt] *n* aliento, ánimo. 2 *(development)* fomento.

encouraging [ɪnˈkʌrɪdʒɪŋ] *adj* alentador,-ra. 2 *(promising)* prometedor,-ra.

encroach [ɪnˈkrəʊtʃ] *i* pasar los límites de, invadir.

encrusted [ɪnˈkrʌstɪd] *adj* incrustado,-a.

encumber [ɪnˈkʌmbəʳ] *t* estorbar.

encyclop(a)edia [ensaɪkləʊˈpiːdjə] *n* enciclopedia.

encyclop(a)edic [ensaɪkləʊˈpiːdɪk] *adj* enciclopédico,-a.

end [end] *n (of rope)* cabo; *(of street)* final *m*; *(of table)* extremo; *(point)* punta. 2 *(time)* fin *m*, final, conclusión. 3 *(aim)* objeto, objetivo. – 4 *t-i* acabar(se), terminar(se). ◆*to ~ up i* acabar, terminar. ●*at the ~ of,* al final de; *in the ~,* al fin; *to come/draw to àn ~,* acabarse.

endanger [ɪnˈdeɪndʒəʳ] *t* poner en peligro.

endearing [ɪnˈdɪərɪŋ] *adj* simpático,-a.

endearment [ɪnˈdɪəmənt] *n* expresión cariñosa.

endeavour [ɪnˈdevəʳ] *n* esfuerzo, empeño. – 2 *i* esforzarse.

endemic [enˈdemɪk] *adj* endémico,-a.

ending [ˈendɪŋ] *n* final *m*. 2 GRAM terminación.

endive [ˈendaɪv] *n* endibia.

endless [ˈendləs] *adj* sin fin, interminable.

endocrine [ˈendəʊkrɪn] *adj* endocrino,-a.

endorse [ɪnˈdɔːs] *t* endosar. 2 *(approve)* aprobar.

endorsement [ɪnˈdɔːsmənt] *n* endoso. 2 *(approval)* aprobación. 3 AUTO nota de sanción.

endow [ɪnˈdaʊ] *t* dotar.

endurance [ɪnˈdjʊərəns] *n* resistencia, aguante *m*.

endure [ɪnˈdjʊəʳ] *t* soportar, resistir. – 2 *i* durar.

enduring [ɪnˈdjʊərɪŋ] *adj* duradero,-a.

enema [ˈenɪmə] *n* enema *m*.

enemy [ˈenəmɪ] *n* enemigo,-a.

energetic [enəˈdʒetɪk] *adj* enérgico,-a.

energy [ˈenədʒɪ] *n* energía.

enforce [ɪnˈfɔːs] *t (law)* hacer cumplir.

enforcement [ɪnˈfɔːsmənt] *n* aplicación, imposición.

engage [ɪnˈgeɪdʒ] *(hire)* contratar. 2 *(attention)* atraer. 3 TECH engranar con. ●*to ~ sb. in conversation,* trabar conversación con algn.

engaged [ɪnˈgeɪdʒd] *adj (to be married)* prometido,-a. 2 *(busy)* ocupado,-a; *(phone)* comunicando. ●*to get ~,* prometerse.

engagement [ɪnˈgeɪdʒmənt] *n (to be married)* petición de mano; *(period)* noviazgo. 2 *(appointment)* compromiso, cita. 3 MIL combate *m*.

engaging [ɪnˈgeɪdʒɪŋ] *adj* atractivo,-a, simpático,-a.

engine [ˈendʒɪn] *n* motor *m*. 2 *(of train)* máquina, locomotora. ■ *~ driver,* maquinista *mf*; *~ room,* sala de máquinas.

engineer [endʒɪˈnɪəʳ] *n* ingeniero,-a. 2 US maquinista *mf*. – 3 *t fig* maquinar.

engineering [endʒɪˈnɪərɪŋ] *n* ingeniería.

engrave [ɪnˈgreɪv] *t* grabar.

engraving [ɪnˈgreɪvɪŋ] *n* grabado.

engrossed [ɪnˈgrəʊst] *adj* absorto,-a.

engrossing [ɪnˈgrəʊsɪŋ] *adj* absorbente.

engulf [ɪnˈgʌlf] *t* sumergir, sumir.

enhance [ɪnˈhɑːns] *t* realzar.

enigma [ɪˈnɪgmə] *n* enigma *m*.

enigmatic [enɪgˈmætɪk] *adj* enigmático,-a.

enjoy [ɪnˈdʒɔɪ] *t* gozar de, disfrutar de: *did you ~ the show?,* ¿te gustó el espectáculo? ●*to ~ o.s.,* divertirse, pasarlo bien.

enjoyable [ɪnˈdʒɔɪəbəl] *adj* agradable.

enjoyment [ɪnˈdʒɔɪmənt] *n* placer *m*, goce *m*, disfrute *m*, gusto.

enlarge [ɪnˈlɑːdʒ] *t-i* aumentar(se), ampliar(se); *(photograph)* ampliar(se). ◆*to ~ upon t* extenderse sobre.

enlargement [ɪnˈlɑːdʒmənt] *n (photograph)* ampliación.

enlighten [ɪnˈlaɪtən] *t* iluminar. ●*to ~ sb. on sth.,* aclararle algo a algn.

enlightened [ɪnˈlaɪtənd] *adj* culto,-a.

enlightenment [ɪnˈlaɪtənmənt] *n* aclaración.

enlist [ɪnˈlɪst] *t-i* MIL alistar(se).

enliven [ɪnˈlaɪvən] *t* avivar, animar.

enmity [ˈenmɪtɪ] *n* enemistad.

enormity [ɪˈnɔːmɪtɪ] *n* enormidad.

enormous [ɪˈnɔːməs] *adj* enorme.

enough [ɪˈnʌf] *adj* bastante, suficiente. – 2 *adv* bastante. – 3 *n* lo suficiente.

enquire [ɪŋˈkwaɪəʳ] *i* preguntar. 2 JUR investigar.

enquiry [ɪŋˈkwaɪərɪ] *n* pregunta. 2 JUR investigación. ●*to make an ~,* preguntar.

enrage [ɪnˈreɪdʒ] *t* enfurecer.

enrich [ɪnˈrɪtʃ] *t* enriquecer.

enrol [ɪnˈrəʊl] *t-i* matricular(se), inscribir(se).

enrolment [ɪnˈrəʊlmənt] *n* matrícula, inscripción.
ensemble [ɒnˈsɒmbəl] *n* conjunto.
ensign [ˈensaɪn] *n* bandera.
enslave [ɪnˈsleɪv] *t* esclavizar.
ensue [ɪnˈsjuː] *i* seguir. **2** *(result)* resultar.
ensuing [ɪnˈsjuːɪŋ] *adj* consiguiente.
ensure [ɪnˈʃʊəʳ] *t* asegurar.
entail [ɪnˈteɪl] *t* suponer, implicar, acarrear. **2** JUR vincular.
entangle [ɪnˈtæŋgəl] *t* enredar, enmarañar.
enter [ˈentəʳ] *t gen* entrar en. **2** *(join)* ingresar en; *(competition)* inscribirse a. **3** *(write down)* anotar, apuntar. **– 4** *i* entrar. ◆*to ~ into* *t (negotiations)* iniciar. **2** *(contract)* firmar. **3** *(conversation)* entablar.
enterprise [ˈentəpraɪz] *n* empresa. **2** *(spirit)* energía, iniciativa, espíritu *m* emprendedor.
enterprising [ˈentəpraɪzɪŋ] *adj* emprendedor,-ra.
entertain [entəˈteɪn] *t (amuse)* entretener, divertir. **2** *(act as host)* agasajar. **3** *(consider)* considerar.
entertainer [entəˈteɪnəʳ] *n* artista *mf.*
entertaining [entəˈteɪnɪŋ] *adj* divertido,-a.
entertainment [entəˈteɪnmənt] *n* entretenimiento, diversión. **2** THEAT espectáculo.
enthral [ɪnˈθrɔːl] *t* cautivar.
enthralling [ɪnˈθrɔːlɪŋ] *adj* cautivador,-ra.
enthrone [ɪnˈθrəʊn] *t* entronizar.
enthronement [ɪnˈθrəʊnmənt] *n* entronización.
enthuse [ɪnˈθjuːz] *i fam* *to ~ over*, entusiasmarse por.
enthusiasm [ɪnˈθjuːzɪæzəm] *n* entusiasmo.
enthusiast [ɪnˈθjuːzɪæst] *n* entusiasta *mf.*
enthusiastic [ɪnθjuːzɪˈæstɪk] *adj* entusiástico,-a. **2** *(person)* entusiasta. **– 3** *enthusiastically adv* con entusiasmo.
entice [ɪnˈtaɪs] *t* atraer.
enticing [ɪnˈtaɪsɪŋ] *adj* tentador,-ra.
entire [ɪnˈtaɪəʳ] *adj* entero,-a, completo,-a, íntegro,-a. **– 2** *entirely adv* enteramente, totalmente.
entirety [ɪnˈtaɪrəti] *n* totalidad.
entitle [ɪnˈtaɪtəl] *t* dar derecho a. ◆*to be entitled, (book)* titularse; *(person)* tener derecho *(to,* a).
entity [ˈentɪti] *n* entidad.

entomology [entəˈmɒlədʒɪ] *n* entomología.
entourage [ɒntʊˈrɑːʒ] *n* séquito.
entrails [ˈentreɪlz] *npl* entrañas *fpl*, vísceras *fpl.*
entrance [ˈentrəns] *n* entrada. **2** THEAT entrada en escena. **– 3** *t* encantar, hechizar. ◆*'no ~',* 'se prohíbe la entrada'. ■ *~ examination,* examen *m* de ingreso. ▲ *En 3 (verbo)* [enˈtrɑːns].
entrancing [ɪnˈtrɑːnsɪŋ] *adj* fascinante, encantador,-ra.
entrant [ˈentrənt] *n* participante *mf.*
entreat [ɪnˈtriːt] *t-i* suplicar, rogar.
entrench [ɪnˈtrentʃ] *t* atrincherar.
entrepreneur [ɒntrəprəˈnɜːʳ] *n* empresario,-a *m,f.*
entrust [ɪnˈtrʌst] *t* confiar.
entry [ˈentrɪ] *n* entrada. **2** *(competition)* participante *mf.* ◆AUTO *'no ~',* 'prohibida la entrada'.
enumerate [ɪˈnjuːməreɪt] *t* enumerar.
enunciate [ɪˈnʌnsɪeɪt] *t* pronunciar. **2** *(express)* expresar.
envelop [ɪnˈveləp] *t* envolver.
envelope [ˈenvələʊp] *n* sobre *m.*
enviable [ˈenvɪəbəl] *adj* envidiable.
envious [ˈenvɪəs] *adj* envidioso,-a.
environment [ɪnˈvaɪrənmənt] *n* medio ambiente. **2** *fig* contexto.
environs [ɪnˈvaɪrənz] *npl* alrededores *mpl.*
envisage [ɪnˈvɪzɪdʒ] *t* prever. **2** *(imagine)* concebir.
envoy [ˈenvɔɪ] *n* enviado,-a.
envy [ˈenvɪ] *n* envidia. **– 2** *t* envidiar.
enzyme [ˈenzaɪm] *n* enzima *m & f.*
epaulet(te) [epəˈlet] *n* charretera.
ephemeral [ɪˈfemərəl] *adj* efímero,-a.
epic [ˈepɪk] *adj* épico,-a. **– 2** epopeya.
epicure [ˈepɪkjʊəʳ] *n* epicúreo,-a.
epidemic [epɪˈdemɪk] *n* epidemia.
epigram [ˈepɪgræm] *n* epigrama *m.*
epilepsy [ˈepɪlepsɪ] *n* epilepsia.
epileptic [epɪˈleptɪk] *adj-n* epiléptico,-a.
epilogue [ˈepɪlɒg] *n* epílogo.
episcopal [ɪˈpɪskəpəl] *adj* episcopal.
episode [ˈepɪsəʊd] *n* episodio.
epistle [ɪˈpɪsəl] *n* epístola.
epitaph [ˈepɪtɑːf] *n* epitafio.
epithet [ˈepɪθet] *n* epíteto.
epitome [ɪˈpɪtəmɪ] *n* epítome *m*, personificación.
epitomize [ɪˈpɪtəmaɪz] *t* epitomar, personificar.
epoch [ˈiːpɒk] *n* época.

equable ['ekwebəl] *adj (climate)* uniforme. 2 *(person)* ecuánime.

equal ['i:kwəl] *adj-n* igual *(mf)*. — 2 *t* MATH ser igual a, equivaler a. 3 *(match)* igualar. — 4 *equally adv* igualmente, por igual. ●*all things being* ~, en igualdad de circunstancias; *to be* ~ *to, (occasion)* estar a la altura de; *(task)* sentirse con fuerzas para. ■ ~ *rights,* igualdad de derechos.

equality [ɪ'kwɒlɪtɪ] *n* igualdad.

equalize ['i:kwəlaɪz] *i* SP igualar el marcador.

equanimity [i:kwə'nɪmɪtɪ] *n* ecuanimidad.

equate [ɪ'kweɪt] *t* equiparar.

equation [ɪ'kweɪʒən] *n* ecuación.

equator [ɪ'kweɪtəʳ] *n* ecuador *m*.

equatorial [ekwə'tɔːrɪəl] *adj* ecuatorial.

equestrian [ɪ'kwestrɪən] *adj* ecuestre.

equilateral [i:kwɪ'lætərəl] *adj* equilátero,-a.

equilibrium [i:kwɪ'lɪbrɪəm] *n* equilibrio.

equinox ['i:kwɪnɒks] *n* equinoccio.

equip [ɪ'kwɪp] *t* equipar.

equipment [ɪ'kwɪpmənt] *n* equipo. 2 *(act of equipping)* equipamiento.

equitable ['ekwɪtəbəl] *adj* equitativo,-a.

equivalence [ɪ'kwɪvələns] *n* equivalencia.

equivalent [ɪ'kwɪvələnt] *adj-n* equivalente *(m)*. ●*to be* ~ *to,* equivaler a.

equivocal [ɪ'kwɪvəkəl] *adj* equívoco,-a.

era ['ɪərə] *n* era.

eradicate [ɪ'rædɪkeɪt] *t* erradicar, extirpar, desarraigar.

eradication [ɪrædɪ'keɪʃən] *n* erradicación, extirpación.

erase [ɪ'reɪz] *t* borrar.

eraser [ɪ'reɪzəʳ] *n* goma de borrar.

erasure [ɪ'reɪʒə] *n* borradura.

erect [ɪ'rekt] *adj* derecho,-a, erguido,-a. 2 *(penis)* erecto,-a. — 3 *t* erigir.

erection [ɪ'rekʃən] *n (penis)* erección. 2 *(building)* construcción.

ermine ['ɜ:mɪn] *n* armiño.

erode [ɪ'rəʊd] *t (rock)* erosionar. 2 *(metal)* corroer, desgastar. 3 *fig (power)* mermar.

erosion [ɪ'rəʊʒən] *n (of rock)* erosión. 2 *(of metal)* corrosión, desgaste *m*.

erotic [ɪ'rɒtɪk] *adj* erótico,-a.

err [ɜ:ʳ] *i* errar, equivocarse.

errand ['erənd] *n* encargo, recado.

errata [ɪ'rɑːtə] *npl* fe *f sing* de erratas.

erratic [ɪ'rætɪk] *adj* irregular, inconstante.

erratum [ɪ'rɑːtəm] *n* errata. ▲ *pl* **errata**.

erroneous [ɪ'rəʊnjəs] *adj* erróneo,-a.

error ['erəʳ] *n* error *m*.

erudite ['erʊdaɪt] *adj* erudito,-a.

erudition [erʊ'dɪʃən] *n* erudición.

erupt [ɪ'rʌpt] *i (volcano)* entrar en erupción. 2 *(violence)* estallar.

eruption [ɪ'rʌpʃən] *n (volcano)* erupción. 2 *(violence)* estallido. 3 MED erupción.

escalate ['eskəleɪt] *(war)* intensificarse. 2 *(prices)* aumentarse.

escalation [eskə'leɪʃən] *n (war)* escalada. 2 *(prices)* subida, aumento.

escalator ['eskəleɪtəʳ] *n* escalera mecánica.

escapade [eskə'peɪd] *n* aventura.

escape [ɪ'skeɪp] *n* fuga, huída. 2 *(gas)* fuga, escape *m*. — 3 *i* escaparse, fugarse, huir. 4 *(gas)* escapar. — 5 *t (avoid)* evitar, librarse de. ●*to make one's* ~, escaparse.

escort ['eskɔ:t] *n* acompañante *mf*. 2 MIL escolta. — 3 *t* acompañar. 4 MIL escoltar. ▲ *En 3 y 4 (verbo)* [ɪ'skɔ:t].

esoteric [esəʊ'terɪk] *adj* esotérico,-a.

especial [ɪ'speʃəl] *adj* especial, particular. — 2 *especially adv* especialmente, sobre todo.

espionage ['espɪənɑːʒ] *n* espionaje *m*.

esplanade [esplə'neɪd] *n* paseo marítimo.

esquire [ɪ'skwaɪəʳ] *n* GB señor *m* don.

essay ['eseɪ] *n (school)* redacción; *(university)* trabajo. 2 *(literary)* ensayo.

essence ['esəns] *n* esencia.

essential [ɪ'senʃəl] *adj (central)* esencial. 2 *(vital)* vital, indispensable. — 3 *n* elemento esencial. — 4 *essentially adv* esencialmente.

establish [ɪ'stæblɪʃ] *t* establecer, fundar, crear. 2 *(proof)* demostrar. 3 *(facts)* constatar. 4 *(precedent)* sentar. 5 *(fame)* consolidar.

establishment [ɪ'stæblɪʃmənt] *n* establecimiento. 2 GB *the Establishment,* el poder.

estate [ɪ'steɪt] *n (in country)* finca. 2 *(with houses)* urbanización. 3 *(goods)* bienes *mpl*. ■ ~ *agent,* agente *mf* inmobiliario,-a; ~ *agent's,* agencia inmobiliaria; GB ~ *car,* coche *m* familiar; *housing* ~, urbanización; *industrial* ~, polígono industrial.

esteem [ɪ'sti:m] *t* apreciar. 2 *(regard)* juzgar, considerar. — 3 *n* aprecio. ●*to hold sb. in high* ~, apreciar mucho a algn.

estimate ['estɪmət] *n (calculation)* cálculo. 2 *(for work)* presupuesto. — 3 *t* calcular. ▲ *En 3 (verbo)* ['estɪmeɪt].

estimation [estɪ'meɪʃən] *n* opinión, juicio.

estuary ['estjuərɪ] *n* estuario.

etch [etʃ] *t* grabar al aguafuerte.

etching ['etʃɪŋ] *n* aguafuerte *m & f*.

eternal [ɪ'tɜ:nəl] *adj* eterno,-a.

eternity [ɪ'tɜ:nɪtɪ] *n* eternidad.

ether ['i:θəʳ] *n* éter *m*.

ethereal [ɪ'θɪərɪəl] *adj* etéreo,-a.

ethic ['eθɪk] *n* ética.

ethical ['eθɪkəl] *adj* ético,-a.

ethnic ['eθnɪk] *adj* étnico,-a.

ethyl ['i:θaɪl] *n* CHEM etilo. ■ ~ *alcohol,* alcohol etílico.

etiquette ['etɪket] *n* protocolo, etiqueta.

etymological [etɪmə'lɒdʒɪkəl] *adj* etimológico,-a.

etymology [etɪ'mɒlədʒɪ] *n* etimología.

eucalyptus [ju:kə'lɪptəs] *n* eucalipto.

Eucharist ['ju:kərɪst] *n* Eucaristía.

eulogize ['ju:lədʒaɪz] *t* elogiar.

eulogy ['ju:lədʒɪ] *n* elogio.

eunuch ['ju:nək] *n* eunuco.

euphemism ['ju:fɪmɪzəm] *n* eufemismo.

euphemistic [ju:fɪ'mɪstɪk] *adj* eufemístico,-a.

euphoria [ju:'fɔ:rɪə] *n* euforia.

euphoric [ju:'fɒrɪk] *adj* eufórico,-a.

euthanasia [ju:θə'neɪzɪə] *n* eutanasia.

evacuate [ɪ'vækjʊeɪt] *t (people)* evacuar. 2 *(place)* desalojar, desocupar.

evacuation [ɪvækjʊ'eɪʃən] *n* evacuación.

evade [ɪ'veɪd] *t* evadir, eludir, evitar.

evaluate [ɪ'væljʊeɪt] *t* evaluar. 2 MATH calcular.

evangelical [i:væn'dʒelɪkəl] *adj* evangélico,-a.

evangelism [ɪ'vændʒɪlɪzəm] *n* evangelismo.

evangelist [ɪ'vændʒɪlɪst] *n* evangelista *mf*.

evaporate [ɪ'væpəreɪt] *t-i* evaporar(se).

evaporation [ɪvæpə'reɪʃən] *n* evaporación.

evasion [ɪ'veɪʒən] *n* evasión.

evasive [ɪ'veɪsɪv] *adj* evasivo,-a.

eve [i:v] *n* víspera, vigilia.

even ['i:vən] *adj (level)* llano,-a. 2 *(smooth)* liso,-a. 3 *(uniform)* uniforme, regular. 4 *(evenly matched)* igual, igualado,-a. 5 *(number)* par. – 6 *adv* hasta, incluso: ~ *John was there,* hasta John estaba allí. 7 *(with negative)* siquiera: *not* ~ *John was there,* ni siquiera John estaba allí. – 8 *t-i* igualar(se), nivelar(se). – 9 *evenly adv (uniformly)* uniformemente. 10 *(fairly)* equitativamente. ◆*to* ~ *out t-i* igualar. ●~ *as,* mientras; ~ *if,* aun si; ~ *so,* incluso/aun así; ~ *though,* aunque, aun cuando; *to break* ~, cubrir gastos; *to get* ~ *with sb.,* desquitarse con algn.

evening ['i:vnɪŋ] *n (early)* tarde *f*; *(late)* noche *f*: *yesterday/tomorrow* ~, ayer/mañana por la tarde. ●*good* ~!, ¡buenas tardes!; ¡buenas noches! ■ ~ *dress, (woman)* vestido de noche; *(man)* traje *m* de etiqueta.

event [ɪ'vent] *n* suceso, acontecimiento. 2 *(case)* caso. 3 SP prueba. ●*at all events,* en todo caso; *in any* ~, pase lo que pase; *in the* ~ *of,* en caso de.

eventful [ɪ'ventfʊl] *adj* lleno,-a de acontecimientos, memorable.

eventual [ɪ'ventʃʊəl] *adj (final)* final. 2 *(resulting)* consiguiente. – 3 *eventually adv* finalmente.

eventuality [ɪventʃʊ'ælɪtɪ] *n* eventualidad.

ever ['evəʳ] *adv (never)* nunca, jamás: *nobody* ~ *comes,* no viene nunca nadie. 2 *(at some time)* alguna vez: *have you* ~ *seen her?,* ¿la has visto alguna vez? 3 *(always)* siempre: ~ *since the war,* desde la guerra. 4 *(at any time) better than* ~, mejor que nunca; *the best* ~, el mejor que nunca se ha visto. 5 *(with questions) what* ~ *shall I do?,* ¿qué demonios hago? ●~ *so ...,* muy ...; *for* ~ *(and* ~*),* para siempre; *hardly* ~, casi nunca.

evergreen ['evəgri:n] *adj* BOT de hoja perenne. ■ ~ *oak,* encina.

everlasting [evə'lɑ:stɪŋ] *adj* eterno,-a, sempiterno,-a.

every ['evrɪ] *adj* cada, todos,-as: ~ *day,* cada día, todos los días; ~ *other day,* un día sí un día no. ●~ *now and then,* de vez en cuando.

everybody ['evrɪbɒdɪ] *pron* todos,-as, todo el mundo.

everyday ['evrɪdeɪ] *adj* diario,-a, de todos los días.

everyone ['evrɪwʌn] *pron* → **everybody**.

everything ['evrɪθɪŋ] *pron* todo.

everywhere ['evrɪweəʳ] *adv (situation)* en/por todas partes. 2 *(movement)* a todas partes.

evict [ɪ'vɪkt] *t* desahuciar.

eviction [ɪ'vɪkʃən] *n* desahucio.

evidence ['evɪdəns] *n (proof)* pruebas *fpl*. 2 *(signs)* indicios *mpl*. 3 JUR testimonio. ●*to give* ~, prestar declaración.

evident ['evɪdənt] *adj* evidente, patente. – 2 *evidently adv* evidentemente. 3 *(apparently)* por lo visto.

evil ['i:vəl] *adj (person)* malo,-a, malvado,-a. **2** *(thing)* malo,-a, pernicioso,-a. — **3** *n* mal *m*.

evocative [ɪ'vɒkətɪv] *adj* evocador,-ra.

evoke [ɪ'vəuk] *t* evocar.

evolution [i:və'lu:ʃən] *n* evolución.

evolve [ɪ'vɒlv] *t* desarrollar. — **2** *i* evolucionnnar, desarrollarse.

ewe [ju:] *n* oveja.

exacerbate [ɪg'zæsɜ:beɪt] *t* exacerbar.

exact [ɪg'zækt] *adj* exacto,-a. **2** *(thorough)* preciso,-a. — **3** *t* exigir, imponer. — **4** *exactly adv* exactamente.

exacting [ɪg'zæktɪŋ] *adj* exigente.

exactitude [ɪg'zæktɪtju:d], **exactness** [ɪg'zæktnəs] *n* exactitud.

exaggerate [ɪg'zædʒəreɪt] *t-i* exagerar.

exaggeration [ɪgzædʒə'reɪʃən] *n* exageración.

exalt [ɪg'zɔ:lt] *t* exaltar.

exam [ɪg'zæm] *n fam* examen *m*.

examination [ɪgzæmɪ'neɪʃən] *n* EDUC examen *m*. **2** MED reconocimiento. **3** JUR interrogatorio.

examine [ɪg'zæmɪn] *t (inspect)* inspeccionar. **2** EDUC examinar. **3** MED hacer un reconocimiento a. **4** JUR interrogar.

examinee [ɪgzæmɪ'ni:] *n* examinando,-a.

examiner [ɪg'zæmɪnər] *n* examinador,-ra.

example [ɪg'zɑ:mpəl] *n* ejemplo. **2** *(specimen)* ejemplar *m*. •*for ~,* por ejemplo.

exasperate [ɪg'zɑ:spəreɪt] *t* exasperar, irritar.

excavate ['ekskəveɪt] *t* excavar.

excavation [ekskə'veɪʃən] *n* excavación.

excavator ['ekskəveɪtər] *n (person)* excavador,-ra. **2** *(machine)* excavadora.

exceed [ɪk'si:d] *t* exceder, sobrepasar.

exceedingly [ɪk'si:dɪŋli] *adv* extremadamente, sumamente.

excel [ɪk'sel] *t* aventajar, superar. — **2** *i* sobresalir. •*to ~ o.s.,* superarse.

excellence ['eksələns] *n* excelencia.

Excellency ['eksələnsɪ] *n* Excelencia.

excellent ['eksələnt] *adj* excelente.

except [ɪk'sept] *prep* excepto, salvo, a excepción de. — **2** *t* excluir, exceptuar.

exception [ɪk'sepʃən] *n* excepción. •*to take ~ to sth.,* ofenderse por algo.

exceptional [ɪk'sepʃənəl] *adj* excepcional.

excerpt ['eksɜ:pt] *n* extracto.

excess [ɪk'ses] *n* exceso. **2** COM excedente *m*. •*in ~ of,* superior a.

excessive [ɪk'sesɪv] *adj* excesivo,-a.

exchange [ɪks'tʃeɪndʒ] *n gen* cambio. **2** *(of ideas etc.)* intercambio. **3** *(of prisoners, documents, etc.)* canjeo. **4** FIN cambio. **5** *(building)* lonja. **6** *(telephone)* central telefónica. — **7** *t* cambiar; *(ideas)* intercambiar. **8** *(prisoners, documents, etc.)* canjear. •*in ~ for,* a cambio de. ■ *bill of ~,* letra de cambio; *~ rate,* tipo de cambio; *foreign ~,* divisas *fpl*; *stock* ‖*~,* bolsa.

exchequer [ɪks'tʃekər] *n* tesoro público.

excitable [ɪk'saɪtəbəl] *adj* excitable.

excite [ɪk'saɪt] *t* emocionar, entusiasmar. **2** *(give rise to)* provocar, despertar.

excited [ɪk'saɪtɪd] *adj* emocionado,-a, entusiasmado,-a.

excitement [ɪk'saɪtmənt] *n* emoción. **2** *(commotion)* agitación, alboroto.

exciting [ɪk'saɪtɪŋ] *adj* emocionante, apasionante.

exclaim [ɪks'kleɪm] *t-i* exclamar.

exclamation [eksklə'meɪʃən] *n* exclamación. ■ *~ mark,* signo de admiración.

exclude [ɪks'klu:d] *t* excluir.

excluding [ɪk'slu:dɪŋ] *prep* excepto.

exclusion [ɪks'klu:ʒən] *n* exclusión.

exclusive [ɪks'klu:sɪv] *adj* exclusivo,-a. **2** *(select)* selecto,-a. — **3** *exclusively adv* exclusivamente. •*~ of,* con exclusión de.

excommunicate [ekskə'mju:nɪkeɪt] *t* excomulgar.

excommunication [ekskəmju:nɪ'keɪʃən] *n* excomunión.

excrement ['ekskrɪmənt] *n* excremento.

excrete [ɪk'skri:t] *t* excretar.

excretion [ɪk'skri:ʃən] *n* excreción.

excruciating [ɪk'skru:ʃɪeɪtɪŋ] *adj* insoportable.

excursion [ɪk'skɜ:ʃən] *n* excursión.

excusable [ɪk'skju:zəbəl] *adj* excusable.

excuse [ɪk'skju:s] *n* disculpa. **2** *(pretext)* excusa. — **3** *t* perdonar, disculpar. **4** *(justify)* justificar. •*~ me, (interrupting)* perdone, por favor; *(leaving)* disculpe; *to ~ sb. from doing sth.,* dispensar/eximir a algn. de hacer algo. ▲ *En 3 y 4 (verbo)* [ɪk'skju:z].

execute ['eksɪkju:t] *t (put to death)* ejecutar, ajusticiar. **2** *(perform)* ejecutar. **3** *(order)* cumplir. **4** *(music etc.)* interpretar. **5** JUR *(will)* cumplir.

execution [eksɪ'kju:ʃən] *n gen* ejecución. **2** *(of order)* cumplimiento. **3** *(of music etc.)* interpretación.

executioner [eksɪ'kju:ʃənər] *n* verdugo.

executive [ɪg'zekjʊtɪv] *adj-n* ejecutivo,-a.

executor [ɪg'zekjʊtər] *n* JUR albacea.

exemplify [ɪgˈzemplɪfaɪ] *t* ejemplificar.
exempt [ɪgˈzempt] *adj* exento,-a, libre. –
2 *t* eximir.
exemption [ɪgˈzempʃən] *n* exención.
exercise [ˈeksəsaɪz] *n* ejercicio. – 2 *t* ejercer. 3 *(dog)* sacar de paseo. – 4 *i* hacer ejercicio. ■ ~ *book,* cuaderno.
exert [ɪgˈzɜːt] *t* ejercer. ●*to* ~ *o.s.,* esforzarse.
exertion [ɪgˈzeːʃən] *n* esfuerzo.
exhale [eksˈheɪl] *t-i* espirar.
exhaust [ɪgˈzɔːst] *n (pipe)* (tubo de) escape *m.* 2 *(fumes)* gases *mpl* de combustión. – 3 *t* agotar.
exhausted [ɪgˈzɔːstɪd] *adj* agotado,-a.
exhausting [ɪgˈzɔːstɪŋ] *adj* agotador,-ra.
exhaustion [ɪgˈzɔːstʃən] *n* agotamiento.
exhibit [ɪgˈzɪbɪt] *n* objeto expuesto. 2 JUR prueba instrumental. – 3 *t (art etc.)* exponer. 4 *(manifest)* mostrar, dar muestras de.
exhibition [eksɪˈbɪʃən] *n (art etc.)* exposición. 2 *(display)* demostración. ●*to make an* ~ *of o.s.,* ponerse en ridículo.
exhibitionist [eksɪˈbɪʃənɪst] *adj-n* exhibicionista *(mf).*
exhibitor [ɪgˈzɪbɪtəʳ] *n* expositor,-ra.
exhilarate [ɪgˈzɪləreɪt] *t* alegrar, animar.
exhilarating [ɪgˈzɪləreɪtɪŋ] *adj* estimulante.
exhilaration [ɪgzɪləˈreɪʃən] *n* alegría, regocijo.
exhort [ɪgˈzɔːt] *t* exhortar.
exhume [eksˈhjuːm] *t* exhumar, desenterrar.
exile [ˈeksaɪl] *n (action)* destierro, exilio. 2 *(person)* desterrado,-a, exiliado,-a. – 3 *t* desterrar, exiliar.
exist [ɪgˈzɪst] *i* existir. 2 *(subsist)* subsistir.
existence [ɪgˈzɪstəns] *n* existencia. ●*to come into* ~, nacer.
existential [egzɪˈstenʃəl] *adj* existencial.
existing [egzɪˈstɪŋ] *adj* existente, actual.
exit [ˈeksɪt] *n* salida. 2 THEAT mutis *m.* – 3 *i* THEAT hacer mutis, salir de escena.
exodus [ˈeksədəs] *n* éxodo.
exonerate [ɪgˈzɒnəreɪt] *t* exonerar, exculpar.
exoneration [ɪgzɒnəˈreɪʃən] *n* exoneración, exculpación.
exorbitant [ɪgˈzɔːbɪtənt] *adj* exorbitante, desorbitado,-a.
exorcise [ˈeksɔːsaɪz] *t* exorcizar.
exorcism [ˈeksɔːsɪzəm] *n* exorcismo.
exorcist [ˈeksɔːsɪst] *n* exorcista *mf.*
exotic [egˈzɒtɪk] *adj* exótico,-a.

expand [ɪkˈspænd] *t-i* ampliar(se). 2 *(gas, metal)* dilatar(se). 3 *(trade)* desarrollar(se). ●*to* ~ *on t* ampliar.
expanse [ɪkˈspæns] *n* extensión.
expansion [ɪkˈspænʃən] *n* ampliación, expansión. 2 *(gas, metal)* dilatación. 3 *(trade)* desarrollo.
expatriate [ekˈspætrɪət] *adj-n* expatriado,-a. – 2 *t* desterrar, expatriar. ▲ *En* 2 *(verbo)* [eksˈpætrɪeɪt].
expect [ɪkˈspekt] *t* esperar. 2 *(suppose)* suponer, imaginar. ●*fam to be expecting,* estar embarazada.
expectancy [ɪkˈspektənsɪ] *n* expectación.
expectant [ɪkˈspektənt] *adj* ilusionado,-a. ■ ~ *mother,* futura madre.
expectation [ekspekˈteɪʃən] *n* expectativa. ●*contrary to expectations,* contrariamente a lo que se esperaba.
expedient [ɪkˈspiːdjənt] *adj* conveniente. – 2 *n* expediente *m,* recurso.
expedition [ekspɪˈdɪʃən] *n* expedición.
expel [ɪkˈspel] *t* expulsar.
expend [ɪkˈspend] *t* gastar, expender.
expendable [ɪkˈspendəbəl] *adj* prescindible.
expenditure [ɪkˈspendɪtʃəʳ] *n* gasto, desembolso.
expense [ɪkˈspens] *n* gasto, desembolso. 2 *pl* COM gastos *mpl* de representación. ●*to spare no* ~, no escatimar gastos; *fig at the* ~ *of,* a expensas/costa de.
expensive [ɪkˈspensɪv] *adj* caro,-a, costoso,-a.
experience [ɪkˈspɪərɪəns] *n* experiencia. – 2 *t* experimentar; *(difficulty)* tener.
experienced [ɪkˈspɪərɪənst] *adj* experimentado,-a, con experiencia.
experiment [ɪkˈsperɪmənt] *n* experimento. – 2 *i* experimentar.
experimental [ɪksperɪˈmentəl] *adj* experimental.
expert [ˈekspɜːt] *adj-n* experto,-a.
expertise [ekspɜːˈtiːz] *n* pericia.
expire [ɪkˈspaɪəʳ] *i (die)* expirar, morir. 2 *(contract)* vencer; *(passport)* caducar.
expiry [ɪkˈspaɪərɪ] *n* expiración. 2 *(of contract)* vencimiento. ■ ~ *date,* fecha de caducidad.
explain [ɪkˈspleɪn] *t-i* explicar. 2 *(clarify)* aclarar. ●*to* ~ *o.s.,* explicarse.
explanation [ekspləˈneɪʃən] *n* explicación. 2 *(clarification)* aclaración.
explanatory [ɪkˈsplænətərɪ] *adj* explicativo,-a.
explicit [ɪkˈsplɪsɪt] *adj* explícito,-a.

explode [ɪk'spləʊd] *t* hacer estallar, hacer explotar. – **2** *i* estallar, explotar, hacer explosión.

exploit ['eksplɔɪt] *n* hazaña, proeza. – **2** *t* explotar. ▲ *En 2 (verbo)* [ɪk'splɔɪt].

exploitation [eksplɔɪ'teɪʃən] *n* explotación.

exploration [eksplə'reɪʃən] *n* exploración.

exploratory [ɪk'splɒrətərɪ] *adj* exploratorio,-a.

explore [ɪk'splɔːʳ] *t* explorar.

explorer [ɪk'splɔːrəʳ] *n* explorador,-ra.

explosion [ɪk'spləʊʒən] *n* explosión, estallido.

explosive [ɪk'spləʊsɪv] *adj-n* explosivo,-a *(m)*.

exponent [ɪk'spəʊnənt] *n* exponente *m*. **2** *(supporter)* defensor,-ra.

export ['ekspɔːt] *n (trade)* exportación. **2** *(article)* artículo de exportación. – **3** *t* exportar. ▲ *En 3 (verbo)* [ɪk'spɔːt].

exportation [ekspɔː'teɪʃən] *n* exportación.

exporter [ek'spɔːtəʳ] *n* exportador,-ra.

expose [ɪk'spəʊz] *t gen* exponer. **2** *(reveal truth about)* descubrir.

exposition [ekspə'zɪʃən] *n (exhibition)* exposición. **2** *(account)* explicación.

exposure [ɪk'spəʊʒəʳ] *n gen* exposición. **2** *(revelation of truth)* descubrimiento. **3** *(photo)* fotografía. ●*to die of* ~, morir de frío.

expound [ɪk'spaʊnd] *t* exponer.

express [ɪk'spres] *adj* expreso,-a. **2** *(mail)* urgente. – **3** *n* (tren *m*) expreso. – **4** *t* expresar. **5** *(juice)* exprimir. – **6** *adv* urgente.

expressive [ɪk'spresɪv] *adj* expresivo,-a.

expression [ɪk'spreʃən] *n* expresión.

expulsion [ɪk'spʌlʃən] *n* expulsión.

expurgate ['ekspɜːgeɪt] *t* expurgar.

exquisite ['ekskwɪzɪt] *adj* exquisito,-a.

extend [ɪk'stend] *t* extender. **2** *(enlarge)* ampliar. **3** *(lengthen)* alargar. **4** *(prolong)* alargar; *(visa etc.)* prorrogar. **4** *(limb)* alargar. **5** *(give)* dar. – **6** *i (stretch)* alargarse, extenderse. **7** *(stick out)* sobresalir. ●*to* ~ *an invitation to sb.*, invitar a algn.

extension [ɪk'stenʃən] *n gen* extensión. **2** *(time)* prórroga.

extensive [ɪk'stensɪv] *adj* extenso,-a. – **2** *extensively adv* extensamente.

extent [ɪk'stent] *n* extensión. **2** *(limit)* límite *m*. ●*to a certain* ~, hasta cierto punto; *to a greater or lesser* ~, en mayor o menor grado; *to a large* ~, en

gran parte; *to what* ~?, ¿hasta qué punto?

extenuate [ɪk'stenjʊeɪt] *t* atenuar.

exterior [ɪk'stɪərɪəʳ] *adj-n* exterior *(m)*.

exterminate [ɪk'stɜːmɪneɪt] *t* exterminar.

extermination [ɪkstɜːmɪ'neɪʃən] *n* exterminio.

external [ek'stɜːnəl] *adj* externo,-a, exterior.

extinct [ɪk'stɪŋkt] *adj (volcano)* extinto,-a. **2** *(animal)* extinguido,-a.

extinction [ɪk'stɪŋkʃən] *n* extinción.

extinguish [ɪk'stɪŋgwɪʃ] *t* extinguir, apagar.

extort [ɪk'stɔːt] *t* arrancar (por fuerza).

extortion [ɪk'stɔːʃən] *n* extorsión.

extortionate [ɪk'stɔːʃənət] *adj* desorbitado,-a.

extra ['ekstrə] *adj* extra, adicional, más: *two* ~ *plates,* dos platos más. **2** *(spare)* de sobra: *have you got an* ~ *pen?,* ¿tienes un boli de sobra? – **3** *adv* extra: *we paid* ~, pagamos un suplemento. – **4** *n* extra *m*. **5** *(charge)* suplemento. **6** CINEM extra *mf*. ■ ~ *charge,* suplemento.

extract ['ekstrækt] *n* extracto. – **2** *t* extraer. ▲ *En 2 (verbo)* [ɪk'strækt].

extractor [ɪk'stræktəʳ] *n* extractor *m*.

extradition [ekstrə'dɪʃən] *n* extradición.

extramarital [ekstrə'mærɪtəl] *adj* extramatrimonial.

extraneous [ek'streɪnjəs] *adj* extraño,-a, ajeno,-a.

extraordinary [ɪk'strɔːdənrɪ] *adj* extraordinario,-a. **2** *(strange)* raro,-a.

extraterrestrial [ekstrətə'restrɪəl] *adj-n* extraterrestre *(mf)*.

extravagance [ɪk'strævəgəns] *n* despilfarro, derroche *m*.

extravagant [ɪk'strævəgənt] *adj (wasteful)* derrochador,-ra. **2** *(exaggerated)* exagerado,-a, excesivo,-a.

extreme [ɪk'striːm] *adj* extremo,-a; *(case)* excepcional. – **2** *n* extremo. – **3** *extremely adv* sumamente, extremadamente.

extremist [ɪk'striːmɪst] *n* extremista *mf*.

extremity [ɪk'stremɪtɪ] *n* extremidad.

extricate ['ekstrɪkeɪt] *t* librar.

extrovert ['ekstrəvɜːt] *adj-n* extrovertido,-a.

exuberant [ɪg'zjuːbərənt] *adj (person)* eufórico,-a.

exude [ɪg'zjuːd] *t-i* exudar, rezumar. – **2** *t fig* rebosar de.

exult [ɪg'zʌlt] *i* exultar, regocijarse.

exultant [ɪgˈzʌltənt] *adj* exultante, triunfante.

eye [aɪ] *n gen* ojo. − **2** *t* mirar. ●*to turn a blind ~ to,* hacer la vista gorda a.

eyeball [ˈaɪbɔːl] *n* globo del ojo.

eyebrow [ˈaɪbraʊ] *n* ceja.

eyelash [ˈaɪlæʃ] *n* pestaña.

eyelid [ˈaɪlɪd] *n* párpado.

eyeshadow [ˈaɪʃædəʊ] *n* sombra de ojos.

eyesight [ˈaɪsaɪt] *n* vista.

eyesore [ˈaɪsɔːʳ] *n* monstruosidad.

eyewitness [ˈaɪˈwɪtnəs] *n* testigo *mf* presencial.

F

fable ['feɪbəl] *n* fábula.

fabric ['fæbrɪk] *n* tela, tejido. **2** *fig* estructura.

fabricate ['fæbrɪkeɪt] *t (story)* fraguar.

fabrication [fæbrɪ'keɪʃən] *n* invención.

fabulous ['fæbjʊləs] *adj* fabuloso,-a.

façade, facade [fə'sɑːd] *n* fachada.

face [feɪs] *n* cara, rostro, semblante *m*. **2** *(surface)* superficie *f*. **3** *(of card, coin)* cara. **4** *(of dial)* cuadrante *m*. **5** *(of watch)* esfera. **6** *fig (of earth)* faz *f*. **7** *(look)* apariencia. — **8** *t (look onto)* dar a, mirar hacia. **9** *(confront)* hallarse frente a, encontrarse ante. **10** *(deal with)* afrontar, enfrentarse con. **11** *(tolerate)* soportar. **12** *(cover)* revestir **(with,** de). — **13** *i* mirar hacia. ◆*to ~ up to t* hacer cara a, afrontar. ●*in the ~ of,* ante; *to lose ~,* desprestigiarse; *to pull faces,* hacer muecas; *to save ~,* salvar las apariencias. ■ *~ cream,* crema de belleza; *~ value,* valor *m* nominal.

faceless ['feɪsləs] *adj* anónimo,-a.

facelift ['feɪslɪft] *n* operación de cirugía estética. **2** *fig* renovación.

facet ['fæsɪt] *n* faceta.

facial ['feɪʃəl] *adj* facial.

facile ['fæsaɪl] *adj pej* superficial.

facilitate [fə'sɪlɪteɪt] *t* facilitar.

facility [fə'sɪlɪtɪ] *n* facilidad. **2** *pl* instalaciones *fpl*, servicios *mpl*.

facsimile [fæk'sɪmɪlɪ] *n* facsímil(e) *m*.

fact [fækt] *n* hecho. **2** *(truth)* realidad: *in ~,* de hecho, en realidad. ●*as a matter of ~,* en realidad. ■ *euph* **the facts of life,** los misterios de la vida.

faction ['fækʃən] *n (group)* facción.

factor ['fæktə'] *n* factor *m*.

factory ['fæktərɪ] *n* fábrica.

factual ['fækʃʊəl] *adj* factual.

faculty ['fækəltɪ] *n* facultad. **2** US UNIV profesorado.

fad [fæd] *n* capricho. **2** *(fashion)* moda.

fade [feɪd] *t-i* descolorar(se), desteñir(se). — **2** *i (light)* apagarse. ◆*to ~ away i* desvanecerse.

faeces ['fiːsiːz] *npl* heces *fpl*.

fag [fæg] *n sl (drag)* lata, rollo. **2** GB *(cig)* pitillo. **3** US *(gay)* marica *m*.

fail [feɪl] *n* EDUC suspenso. — **2** *t-i* fallar. **3** EDUC suspender. — **4** *i* fracasar. **5** COM quebrar. ●*to ~ to, (be unable to)* no lograr; *(neglect)* dejar de; *without ~,* sin falta.

failing ['feɪlɪŋ] *n* defecto, fallo. — **2** *prep* a falta de.

failure ['feɪljə'] *n* fracaso, malogro. **2** COM quiebra. **3** EDUC suspenso. **4** *(breakdown)* fallo, avería. **5** *(inability)* negativa: *her ~ to answer,* el hecho de que no contesta.

faint [feɪnt] *adj* débil. **2** *(colour)* pálido,-a. **3** *(slight)* vago,-a. — **4** *i* desmayarse.

fair [feə'] *adj (just)* justo,-a, equitativo,-a. **2** *(considerable)* considerable. **3** *(weather)* bueno,-a. **4** *(hair)* rubio,-a; *(skin)* blanco,-a. **5** *fml* bello,-a. — **6** *n (market)* mercado. **7** *(show)* feria. — **8** *fairly adv* justamente. **9** *(quite)* bastante. ●*~ and square, (honestly)* merecidamente; *~ enough,* de acuerdo. ■ *~ play,* juego limpio.

fairground ['feəgraʊnd] *n* recinto ferial.

fairness ['feənəs] *n* justicia. **2** *(of hair)* color rubio; *(of skin)* palidez *f*, blancura.

fairy ['feərɪ] *n* hada. **2** *fam* marica *m*. ■ *~ tale,* cuento de hadas.

faith [feɪθ] *n* fe *f*. ●*in good/bad ~,* de buena/mala fe.

faithful ['feɪθfʊl] *adj* fiel **(to,** a/con). — **2** *faithfully adv* fielmente. **3** *(in letter)* *yours faithfully,* le saluda atentamente.

faithfulness ['feɪθfʊlnəs] *n* fidelidad.

fake [feɪk] *n* falsificación. 2 *(person)* impostor,-ra, farsante. – 3 *adj* falso,-a, falsificado,-a. – 4 *t* falsificar. 5 *(pretend)* fingir.

falcon ['fɔːlkən] *n* halcón *m*.

fall [fɔːl] *n* caída. 2 *(of rock)* desprendimiento: ~ *of snow,* nevada. 3 *(decrease)* baja, descenso. 4 US otoño. 5 *pl* cascada *f sing.* – 6 *i* caer(se). 7 *fml (be killed)* caer, perecer. 8 *(decrease)* bajar. ◆*to* ~ *back i* retroceder. ◆*to* ~ *back on t* recurrir a, echar mano de. ◆*to* ~ *behind i* retrasarse. ◆*to* ~ *for t (be tricked)* dejarse engañar por. 2 *fam (in love)* enamorarse de. ◆*to* ~ *off i* bajar, flojear. ◆*to* ~ *out i* reñir *(with,* con). ◆*to* ~ *through i* fracasar. ●*to* ~ *asleep,* dormirse; *to* ~ *in love,* enamorarse; *to* ~ *short,* no alcanzar *(of,* -); *fig to* ~ *flat,* salir mal. ▲ *pt fell; pp fallen.*

fallacy ['fæləsɪ] *n* falacia.

fallen ['fɔːlən] *pp* → **fall**.

fallible ['fælɪbəl] *adj* falible.

fall-out ['fɔːlaʊt] *n (radioactive)* ~, lluvia radioactiva. ■ ~ *shelter,* refugio atómico.

fallow ['fæləʊ] *adj* en barbecho.

false [fɔːls] *adj* falso,-a. – 2 *falsely adv* falsamente. ■ ~ *alarm,* falsa alarma; ~ *bottom,* doble fondo; ~ *start,* salida nula; ~ *teeth,* dentadura postiza.

falsehood ['fɔːlshʊd] *n* falsedad.

falsify ['fɔːlsɪfaɪ] *t* falsificar. 2 *(misrepresent)* falsear.

falter ['fɔːltəʳ] *i* vacilar, titubear; *(voice)* fallar.

fame [feɪm] *n* fama.

familiar [fə'mɪlɪəʳ] *adj* familiar. 2 *(aware)* al corriente *(with,* de). 3 *(intimate)* íntimo,-a.

familiarity [fəmɪlɪ'ærɪtɪ] *n* familiaridad.

familiarize [fə'mɪljəraɪz] *t* familiarizar. 2 *(divulge)* popularizar.

family ['fæmɪlɪ] *n* familia. ●*to run in the* ~, venir de familia. ■ ~ *film,* película apta para todos los públicos; US ~ *name,* apellido; ~ *planning,* planificación familiar; ~ *tree,* árbol genealógico.

famine ['fæmɪn] *n* hambre *f.*

famished ['fæmɪʃt] *adj* muerto,-a de hambre.

famous ['feɪməs] *adj* famoso,-a, célebre. – 2 *famously adv fam* estupendamente.

fan [fæn] *n* abanico. 2 ELEC ventilador *m.* 3 *(follower)* aficionado,-a; *(of pop star etc.)* admirador,-ra, fan *mf.* 4 *(of football)* hincha *mf.* – 5 *t* abanicar; ELEC ventilar.

fanatic [fə'nætɪk] *adj-n* fanático,-a.

fanciful ['fænsɪfʊl] *adj (idea)* imaginario,-a. 2 *(extravagant)* caprichoso,-a, rebuscado,-a.

fancy ['fænsɪ] *n* fantasía, imaginación. 2 *(whim)* capricho, antojo. – 3 *adj* de fantasía. – 4 *t* imaginarse, figurarse. 5 *(like)* apetecer. ●~ *that!,* ¡figúratelo!; *to take a* ~ *to sth.,* encapricharse con algo. ■ ~ *dress,* disfraz *m.*

fancy-free [fænsɪ'friː] *adj* sin compromiso.

fanfare ['fænfeəʳ] *n* fanfarria.

fang [fæŋ] *n* colmillo.

fantastic [fæn'tæstɪk] *adj* fantástico,-a.

fantasy ['fæntəsɪ] *n* fantasía.

far [fɑːʳ] *adj* lejano,-a. 2 *(more distant)* opuesto,-a, extremo,-a. – 3 *adv* lejos *(from,* de): *how* ~ *is it?,* ¿a qué distancia está? 4 *(with comp)* mucho: ~ *better,* mucho mejor. ●*as/so* ~ *as I know,* que yo sepa; *by* ~, con mucho; ~ *and wide,* por todas partes; ~ *away,* lejos; *in so* ~ *as ...,* en la medida en que ...; *so* ~, *(until now)* hasta ahora; *(to a point)* hasta cierto punto. ▲ *comp* **farther** *o* **further***; superl* **farthest** *o* **furthest**.

faraway ['fɑːrəweɪ] *adj* lejano,-a, remoto,-a; *(look)* distraído,-a.

farce [fɑːs] *n* farsa.

farcical ['fɑːsɪkəl] *adj* absurdo,-a.

fare [feəʳ] *n (price)* tarifa, precio del billete/viaje; *(boat)* pasaje *m.* 2 *(passenger)* viajero,-a, pasajero,-a. 3 *(food)* comida. – 4 *i* desenvolverse: *he fared well in the exam,* le fue bien el examen.

farewell [feə'wel] *interj* ¡adiós! – 2 *n* despedida.

far-fetched [fɑː'fetʃt] *adj* rebuscado,-a, inverosímil.

farm [fɑːm] *n* granja, AM hacienda. – 2 *t* cultivar, labrar. – 3 *i* cultivar la tierra.

farmer ['fɑːməʳ] *n* granjero,-a, agricultor,-ra, AM hacendado,-a.

farmhouse ['fɑːmhaʊs] *n* granja, AM hacienda.

farming ['fɑːmɪŋ] *n* agricultura. ■ ~ *industry,* industria agropecuaria.

farmyard ['fɑːmjɑːd] *n* corral *m.*

far-reaching [fɑː'riːtʃɪŋ] *adj* de gran alcance.

far-sighted [fɑː'saɪtɪd] *adj* previsor,-ra.

fart * [fɑːt] *n* pedo*. – 2 *i* tirarse un pedo*.

farther ['fɑːðəʳ] *adj-adv comp* → **far**.

farthest ['fɑːðɪst] *adj-adv superl* → **far**.

fascinate ['fæsɪneɪt] *t* fascinar.

fascinating ['fæsɪneɪtɪŋ] *adj* fascinante.

fascination [fæsɪ'neɪʃən] *n* fascinación.

fascism ['fæʃɪzəm] *n* fascismo.

fascist ['fæʃɪst] *adj-n* fascista *(mf)*.

fashion ['fæʃən] *n (style)* moda. **2** *(way)* modo. – **3** *t (clay)* formar; *(metal)* labrar. ●*in/out of* ~, de/pasado,-a de moda.

fashionable ['fæʃənəbəl] *adj* de moda. – **2 fashionably** *adv* a la moda.

fast [fɑːst] *adj (quick)* rápido,-a. **2** *(tight etc.)* firme, seguro,-a. **3** *(colour)* sólido,-a. **4** *(clock)* adelantado,-a. – **5** *adv* rápidamente, deprisa: *how* ~?, ¿a qué velocidad?; *to drive* ~, correr. **6** *(securely)* firmemente: ~ *asleep*, profundamente dormido,-a. – **7** *i* ayunar. – **8** *n* ayuno. ●*to stand* ~, mantenerse firme; *fam not so* ~!, ¡un momento!

fasten ['fɑːsən] *t (attach)* fijar, sujetar. **2** *(tie)* atar. – **3** *t-i (door)* cerrar(se); *(belt, dress)* abrochar(se).

fastener ['fɑːsənə^r] *n* cierre *m*.

fastidious · [fæ'stɪdɪəs] *adj* quisquilloso,-a.

fat [fæt] *adj* gordo,-a. **2** *(thick)* grueso,-a. – **3** *n* grasa. ●*to get* ~, engordar.

fatal ['feɪtəl] *adj* fatal.

fatality [fə'tælɪtɪ] *n* víctima *f* mortal.

fate [feɪt] *n* destino. **2** *(end)* suerte *f*.

fated ['feɪtɪd] *adj* predestinado,-a.

fateful ['feɪtful] *adj* fatídico,-a.

father ['fɑːðə^r] *n* padre *m*. – **2** *t* engendrar. ■ REL *Our Father*, Padre Nuestro; *Father Christmas*, Papá *m* Noel.

father-in-law ['fɑːðərɪnlɔː] *n* suegro.

fatherland ['fɑːðəlænd] *n* patria.

fatherly ['fɑːðəlɪ] *adj* paternal.

fathom ['fæðəm] *n* brazo. – **2** *t* penetrar en, comprender.

fatigue [fə'tiːg] *n* fatiga, cansancio. **2** TECH fatiga. **3** MIL faena. – **4** *t fml* fatigar, cansar.

fatten ['fætən] *t (animal)* cebar. **2** *(person)* engordar.

fatty ['fætɪ] *adj* graso,-a.

fatuous ['fætjʊəs] *adj* fatuo,-a.

faucet ['fɔːsɪt] *n* US grifo.

fault [fɔːlt] *n (defect)* defecto; *(in merchandise)* defecto, desperfecto. **2** *(blame)* culpa: *it's his* ~, es culpa suya. **3** *(mistake)* error *m*, falta. **4** *(in earth)* falla. **5** *(tennis)* falta. – **6** *t* criticar. ●*to be at* ~, tener la culpa; *to find* ~ *with sb./sth.*, poner reparos a algn./algo.

fault-finding ['fɔːltfaɪndɪŋ] *adj* criticón,-ona.

faultless ['fɔːltləs] *adj* perfecto,-a.

faulty ['fɔːltɪ] *adj* defectuoso,-a.

fauna ['fɔːnə] *n* fauna.

faux pas [fəʊ'pɑː] *n inv* metedura de pata.

favour ['feɪvə^r] *n* favor *m*. – **2** *t* favorecer. **3** *(approve)* estar a favor de. ●*in* ~ *of*, partidario,-a de.

favourable ['feɪvərəbəl] *adj* favorable.

favourite ['feɪvərɪt] *adj-n* preferido,-a.

favouritism ['feɪvərɪtɪzəm] *n* favoritismo.

fawn [fɔːn] *n* ZOOL cervato. – **2** *adj-n (colour)* (de) color *(m)* café con leche. ◆*to* ~ *on/upon* *t* adular, lisonjear.

fear [fɪə^r] *n* miedo, temor *m*. – **2** *t-i* temer, tener miedo (a). ●*I* ~ *(that)* ..., me temo que ... .

fearful ['fɪəful] *adj (frightened)* temeroso,-a. **2** *(terrible)* terrible, espantoso,-a, tremendo,-a.

fearless ['fɪələs] *adj* intrépido,-a.

fearsome ['fɪəsəm] *adj* temible.

feasible ['fiːzəbəl] *adj* factible, viable.

feast [fiːst] *n* festín *m*, banquete *m*. **2** *fam* comilona. **3** REL fiesta de guardar. – **4** *i* banquetear. ●*fig to* ~ *on sth.*, regalarse con algo.

feat [fiːt] *n* proeza, hazaña.

feather ['feðə^r] *n* pluma.

feature ['fiːtʃə^r] *n (of face)* rasgo, facción. **2** *(characteristic)* rasgo, característica. **3** *(press)* crónica especial. – **4** *t* poner de relieve. **5** *(in film etc.)* tener como protagonista. – **6** *i* figurar, constar. ■ ~ *(film)*, largometraje *m*.

February ['februərɪ] *n* febrero.

fed [fed] *pt & pp* → **feed**. – **2** *adj fam* ~ *up*, harto,-a *(with,* de).

federal ['fedərəl] *adj* federal.

federation [fedə'reɪʃən] *n* federación.

fee [fiː] *n (doctor's etc.)* honorarios *mpl*; *(membership)* cuota.

feeble ['fiːbəl] *adj* débil.

feed [fiːd] *n* comida. **2** *(for cattle)* pienso. – **3** *t* alimentar, dar de comer a; *fig* cebar. **4** *(insert)* introducir. – **5** *i* alimentarse *(on,* de). ▲ *pt & pp* **fed**.

feedback ['fiːdbæk] *n* realimentación. **2** *fig* reacción.

feel [fiːl] *n* tacto. – **2** *t* tocar, palpar. **3** *(search)* tantear. **4** *(sense)* sentir; *(notice)* notar, apreciar. **5** *(believe)* creer. – **6** *i* sentir(se), encontrarse. **7** *(seem)* parecer: *it feels like leather*, parece piel. **8** *(opinion)* opinar. ◆*to* ~ *for* *t (have sympathy for)* compadecer a, compadecerse de. ●*to* ~ *like*, apetecer: *I* ~ *like an ice cream*, me apetece un helado; *to* ~ *like* *doing sth.,* tener ganas de hacer algo. ▲ *pt & pp* felt.

feeler ['fi:lə^r] *n* antena.

feeling ['fi:lɪŋ] *n (emotion)* sentimiento, emoción. **2** *(concern)* compasión. **3** *(impression)* impresión. **4** *(artistic)* sensibilidad, talento. **5** *(opinion)* sentir *m*, opinión. – **6** *adj* sensible, compasivo,-a. ●*fam* **no hard feelings,** no nos guardemos rencor.

feet [fi:t] *npl* → **foot**.

feign [feɪn] *t* fingir, aparentar.

feint [feɪnt] *n fml (fencing)* finta.

feline ['fi:laɪn] *adj-n* felino,-a.

fell [fel] *pt* → **fall**. – **2** *adj* feroz. – **3** *t (tree)* talar. **4** *(enemy)* derribar.

fellow ['feləʊ] *n fam* tipo, tío. **2** *(member)* socio,-a. – **3** *adj* con-: ~ *citizen,* conciudadano,-a; ~ *student/worker,* compañero,-a de estudios/trabajo.

fellowship ['feləʊʃɪp] *n (group)* asociación, sociedad. **2** *(companionship)* compañerismo. **3** EDUC beca.

felony ['felənɪ] *n* crimen *m*, delito mayor.

felt [felt] *pt & pp* → **feel**. – **2** *n* fieltro.

felt-tip ['felttɪp] *adj* ~ *pen,* rotulador *m*.

female ['fi:meɪl] *n* hembra. **2** *(woman)* mujer *f*; *(girl)* chica. – **3** *adj* femenino,-a. **4** ZOOL hembra.

feminine ['femɪnɪn] *adj-n* femenino,-a *(m)*.

feminism ['femɪnɪzəm] *n* feminismo.

fence [fens] *n* valla, cerca. **2** *fam* perista *mf*. – **3** *i* practicar la esgrima. **4** *to* ~ *(in),* cercar. **5** *fig* hablar con evasivas. ◆*to* ~ *off t* separar mediante cercas. ●*to sit on the* ~, ver los toros desde la barrera.

fencing ['fensɪŋ] *n* SP esgrima. **2** *(fences)* cercado. **3** *(material)* material *m* para cercas.

fend [fend] *t to* ~ *for o.s.,* valerse por sí mismo,-a. ◆*to* ~ *off t* parar, desviar; *fig* esquivar.

fender ['fendə^r] *n* pantalla. **2** US parachoques *m inv*.

fennel ['fenəl] *n* hinojo.

ferment ['fɜ:mənt] *n* fermento. – **2** *t-i* fermentar. ▲ *En* **2** *(verbo)* [fə'ment].

fermentation [fɜ:men'teɪʃən] *n* fermentación.

fern [fɜ:n] *n* helecho.

ferocious [fə'rəʊʃəs] *adj* feroz.

ferocity [fə'rɒsɪtɪ] *n* ferocidad.

ferret ['ferɪt] *n* hurón *m*. – **2** *i* huronear. ◆*to* ~ *out t* descubrir.

ferrous ['ferəs] *adj* ferroso,-a.

ferry ['ferɪ] *n* barca de pasaje; *(large)* transbordador *m*, ferry *m*. – **2** *t-i* transportar.

fertile ['fɜ:taɪl] *adj* fértil, fecundo,-a.

fertility [fə'tɪlɪtɪ] *n* fertilidad.

fertilize ['fɜ:tɪlaɪz] *t* fertilizar, abonar. **2** *(egg)* fecundar.

fertilizer ['fɜ:tɪlaɪzə^r] *n* fertilizante *m*, abono.

fervent ['fɜ:vənt] *adj* fervoroso,-a.

fervour ['fɜ:və^r] *n* fervor *m*.

fester ['festə^r] *i* supurar.

festival ['festɪvəl] *n* festival *m*. **2** *(feast)* fiesta.

fetch [fetʃ] *t (go and get)* ir por, ir a buscar, buscar. **2** *fam (sell for)* venderse por, alcanzar.

fête [feɪt] *n* fiesta. – **2** *t* festejar.

fetid ['fetɪd] *adj* fétido,-a.

fetish ['fetɪʃ] *n* fetiche *m*.

fetishist ['fetɪʃɪst] *n* fetichista *mf*.

fetter ['fetə^r] *t* encadenar. – **2** *npl* grillo *m sing*, grilletes *mpl*, cadenas *fpl*.

feud [fju:d] *n* enemistad (duradera).

feudal ['fju:dəl] *adj* feudal.

feudalism ['fju:dəlɪzəm] *n* feudalismo.

fever ['fi:və^r] *n* fiebre *f*.

feverish ['fi:vərɪʃ] *adj* febril.

few [fju:] *adj-pron (not many)* pocos,-as. **2** *a* ~, unos,-as cuantos,-as, algunos,-as: *a* ~ *of them,* algunos de ellos. ●*as* ~ *as,* solamente; **no fewer than,** no menos de; *quite a* ~, un buen número (de).

fiancé [fɪ'ænseɪ] *n* prometido.

fiancée [fɪ'ænseɪ] *n* prometida.

fiasco [fɪ'æskəʊ] *n* fiasco, fracaso.

fib [fɪb] *fam n* bola. – **2** *i* contar bolas.

fibre ['faɪbə^r] *n* fibra.

fibreglass ['faɪbəglɑ:s] *n* fibra de vidrio.

fibrous ['faɪbrəs] *adj* fibroso,-a.

fickle ['fɪkəl] *adj* inconstante, voluble.

fiction ['fɪkʃən] *n (novels)* novela, narrativa. **2** *(invention)* ficción.

fictional ['fɪkʃənəl], **fictitious** [fɪk'tɪʃəs] *adj* ficticio,-a.

fiddle ['fɪdəl] *fam n* violín *m*. **2** *(shady deal)* estafa, trampa. – **3** *i* juguetear *(with,* con). – **4** *t* falsificar. ◆*to* ~ *about/around i* perder el tiempo.

fiddler ['fɪdlə^r] *n fam* violinista *mf*.

fidelity [fɪ'delɪtɪ] *n* fidelidad.

fidget ['fɪdʒɪt] *n* persona inquieta. – **2** *i* moverse, no poder estar(se) quieto,-a. ●*to* ~ *with,* jugar con.

fidgety ['fɪdʒɪtɪ] *adj* inquieto,-a.

field [fi:ld] *n* campo. **2** *(for mining)* yacimiento. **3** *(subject, area)* campo, terreno.

fiend 98

fiend [fi:nd] *n* demonio, diablo. **2** *fam* fanático,-a.
fiendish ['fi:ndɪʃ] *adj* diabólico,-a.
fierce [fɪəs] *adj* feroz. **2** *fig* fuerte, intenso,-a.
fiery ['faɪərɪ] *adj (colour)* encendido,-a. **2** *fig* fogoso,-a.
fifteen [fɪf'ti:n] *adj-n* quince *(m)*.
fifteenth [fɪf'ti:nθ] *adj-n* decimoquinto,-a. – **2** *n (fraction)* decimoquinto, decimoquinta parte.
fifth [fɪfθ] *adj-n* quinto,-a. – **2** *n (fraction)* quinto, quinta parte.
fiftieth ['fɪftɪəθ] *adj-n* quincuagésimo,-a. – **2** *n (fraction)* quincuagésimo, quincuagésima parte.
fifty ['fɪftɪ] *adj-n* cincuenta *(m)*.
fig [fɪg] *n* higo. ■ ~ *tree,* higuera.
fight [faɪt] *n* lucha. **2** *(physical violence)* pelea. **3** *(boxing)* combate *m.* – **4** *i (quarrel)* pelearse, discutir. – **5** *t (bull)* lidiar. **6** *(battle)* librar. – **7** *t-i (with physical violence)* pelearse, luchar. **8** *fig* luchar *(against/for,* contra/por), combatir. ◆*to* ~ *back i* resistir. ◆*to* ~ *off t* rechazar. **2** *fig (illness)* librarse de, cortar. ▲ *pt & pp* **fought**.
fighter ['faɪtər] *n* combatiente *mf.* **2** *(boxing)* boxeador,-ra, púgil *m.* **3** *fig* luchador,-ra. ■ AV ~ *(plane),* (avión *m* de) caza *m.*
figurative ['fɪgərətɪv] *adj* figurado,-a.
figure ['fɪgər, US 'fɪgjər] *n (shape)* forma. **2** *(of body)* figura, tipo. **3** *(personality)* figura, personaje *m.* **4** MATH cifra, número. – **5** *i (appear)* figurar, constar. – **6** *t US* suponer. ◆*to* ~ *out t fam* comprender, explicarse. ●*that figures!,* ¡ya me parecía a mí! ■ ~ *of speech,* figura retórica; ~ *skating,* patinaje artístico.
figurehead ['fɪgəhed] *n* MAR mascarón *m* de proa. **2** *fig* figura decorativa.
filament ['fɪləmənt] *n* filamento.
file [faɪl] *n (tool)* lima. **2** *(folder)* carpeta. **3** *(archive)* archivo, expediente *m.* **4** COMPUT archivo. **5** *(line)* fila. – **6** *t (smooth)* limar. **7** *(put away)* archivar; *(in card-index)* fichar. **8** JUR presentar. – **9** *i* desfilar. ●*to be on* ~, estar archivado,-a. ■ *single* ~, fila india.
filigree ['fɪlɪgri:] *n* filigrana.
filing ['faɪlɪŋ] *n* clasificación. **2** *pl* limaduras *fpl.* ■ ~ *cabinet,* archivador *m.*
fill [fɪl] *n* saciedad. – **2** *t-i* llenar(se) *(with,* de). – **3** *t (cover)* cubrir. **4** CULIN rellenar. **5** *(tooth)* empastar. ◆*to* ~ *in t (space, form)* rellenar. **2** *(inform)* poner al corriente *(on,* de). ◆*to* ~ *in for t*

su(b)stituir a. ◆*to* ~ *out i* engordar. ◆*to* ~ *up t-i* llenar(se). ●*fam* **to have had one's** ~ *of sth./sb.,* estar harto,-a de algo/algn.
fillet ['fɪlɪt] *n* filete *m.* – **2** *t* cortar a filetes.
filling ['fɪlɪŋ] *n (in tooth)* empaste *m.* **2** CULIN relleno. ■ ~ *station,* gasolinera.
filly ['fɪlɪ] *n* potra.
film [fɪlm] *n* película, film(e) *m.* **2** *(of dust etc.)* capa. **3** *(roll)* película. – **4** *t* rodar, filmar.
filter ['fɪltər] *n* filtro. – **2** *t-i* filtrar(se).
filth [fɪlθ] *n* suciedad, porquería. **2** *fig (obscenity)* obscenidades *fpl.*
filthy ['fɪlθɪ] *adj* sucio,-a, asqueroso,-a.
fin [fɪn] *n* aleta.
final ['faɪnəl] *adj* final, último,-a. **2** *(definitive)* definitivo,-a. – **3** *n* SP final *f.* **4** *pl* UNIV exámenes *mpl* finales. – **5** *finally adv (at last)* por fin. **6** *(definitively)* definitivamente.
finalist ['faɪnəlɪst] *n* finalista *mf.*
finalize ['faɪnəlaɪz] *t* ultimar.
finance ['faɪnæns] *n* finanzas *fpl.* **2** *pl* fondos *mpl.* – **3** *t* financiar.
financial [faɪ'nænʃəl] *adj* financiero,-a.
financier [faɪ'nænsɪər] *n* financiero,-a.
find [faɪnd] *n* hallazgo. – **2** *t* encontrar, hallar. **3** *(end up)* venir a parar. **4** *(discover)* descubrir. **5** JUR declarar. ◆*to* ~ *out t-i* averiguar. **2** *(discover)* enterarse *(about,* de). ●*to* ~ *one's way,* encontrar el camino. ▲ *pt & pp* **found**.
findings ['faɪndɪŋz] *npl* conclusiones *fpl,* resultados *mpl.*
fine [faɪn] *n* multa. – **2** *t* multar, poner una multa. – **3** *adj (thin)* fino,-a. **4** *(subtle)* sutil. **5** *(excellent)* excelente. **6** *(weather)* bueno,-a. **7** *iron* menudo,-a. – **8** *adv (finely)* fino, finamente. **9** *fam (very well)* muy bien.
finger ['fɪŋgər] *n* dedo. – **2** *t* tocar; *pej* manosear.
fingernail ['fɪŋgəneɪl] *n* uña.
fingerprint ['fɪŋgəprɪnt] *n* huella digital/dactilar.
fingertip ['fɪŋgətɪp] *n* punta/yema del dedo. ●*fig* **to have sth. at one's fingertips,** saberse algo al dedillo.
finicky ['fɪnɪkɪ] *adj* remilgado,-a.
finish ['fɪnɪʃ] *n* fin *m,* final *m.* **2** SP llegada. **3** *(surface)* acabado. – **4** *t-i (end)* acabar, terminar. – **5** *t (consume)* acabar, agotar: ~ *(up) your potatoes,* termínate las patatas. **6** *fam to* ~ *(off),* agotar. ◆*to* ~ *with t* acabar con. **2** *(person)* romper con. ●SP *a close* ~, un final muy reñido; *to the* ~, hasta el final.

finishing ['fınıʃıŋ] *adj* final. ■ ~ *line,* (línea de) meta.

finite ['faınaıt] *adj* finito,-a.

fir [fɜːʳ] *n* abeto.

fire ['faıəʳ] *n* fuego. **2** *(blaze)* incendio, fuego. **3** *(heater)* estufa. **4** MIL fuego. – **5** *t (weapon)* disparar; *(rocket)* lanzar. **6** *(pottery)* cocer. **7** *fig* inflamar, enardecer. **8** *fam (dismiss)* despedir. – **9** *i (shoot)* disparar *(at,* sobre). – **10** *interj* ¡fuego! ●*to be on ~,* estar ardiendo/en llamas; *to catch ~,* incendiarse; *to set ~ to sth.,* prender fuego a algo, incendiar algo. ■ ~ *engine,* camión *m* de bomberos; ~ *escape,* escalera de incendios; ~ *extinguisher,* extintor *m;* ~ *station,* parque *m* de bomberos.

firearm ['faıərɑːm] *n* arma de fuego.

fireman ['faıəmən] *n* bombero.

fireplace ['faıəpleıs] *n* chimenea. **2** *(hearth)* hogar *m.*

fireproof ['faıəpruːf] *adj* incombustible.

firewood ['faıəwʊd] *n* leña.

fireworks ['faıəwɜːks] *npl* fuegos *mpl* artificiales.

firing ['faıərıŋ] *n* tiroteo. ■ ~ *squad,* pelotón *m* de fusilamiento.

firm [fɜːm] *adj* firme. – **2** *n* empresa, firma. – **3** *firmly adv* firmemente.

firmness ['fɜːmnəs] *n* firmeza.

first [fɜːst] *adj* primero,-a. – **2** *adv* primero. – **3** *n* primero,-a. **4** *(beginning)* principio. **5** UNIV sobresaliente *m.* – **6** *firstly adv* en primer lugar, ante todo. ●*at ~,* al principio; *at ~ sight,* a primera vista; ~ *of all,* en primer lugar. ■ ~ *aid,* primeros auxilios *mpl;* ~ *floor,* GB primer piso, US planta baja; ~ *name,* nombre *m* de pila.

first-class ['fɜːstklɑːs] *adj* de primera clase. **2** *fig* excelente. – **3** *adv* en primera.

first-rate ['fɜːstreıt] *adj* excelente.

fiscal ['fıskəl] *adj* fiscal.

fish [fıʃ] *n* pez *m.* **2** CULIN pescado. – **3** *i* pescar *(for,* -). ■ ~ *shop,* pescadería.

fisherman ['fıʃəmən] *n* pescador *m.*

fishing ['fıʃıŋ] *n* pesca. ●*to go ~,* ir de pesca. ■ ~ *rod,* caña de pescar.

fishmonger ['fıʃmʌŋgəʳ] *n* GB pescadero,-a. ■ *fishmonger's (shop),* pescadería.

fishy ['fıʃı] *adj (taste, smell)* a pescado. **2** *(suspicious)* sospechoso,-a.

fission ['fıʃən] *n* fisión.

fissure ['fıʃəʳ] *n* fisura, grieta.

fist [fıst] *n* puño.

fistful ['fıstfʊl] *n* puñado.

fit [fıt] *n* MED ataque *m,* acceso. **2** *fig* arranque *m,* arrebato. **3** SEW corte *m.* – **4** *t* ir bien a. **5** *(slot)* encajar en. **6** *(install)* poner, colocar. **7** *(correspond)* encajar con. – **8** *i* caber. **9** *(match)* cuadrar. – **10** *adj (suitable)* apto,-a, adecuado,-a: *he isn't ~ to drive,* no está en condiciones de conducir. **11** *(healthy)* en (plena) forma. ◆*to ~ in i (adapt)* encajar. **2** *(match)* cuadrar. – **3** *t* encontrar un hueco para. ◆*to ~ out t* equipar. ●*by fits and starts,* a trompicones; *to see/think sth. ~,* estimar algo oportuno.

fitness ['fıtnəs] *n (health)* buena forma (física).

fitted ['fıtıd] *adj* empotrado,-a.

fitting ['fıtıŋ] *adj fml* apropiado,-a. – **2** *n* SEW prueba. **3** *pl* accesorios *mpl.*

five [faıv] *adj-n* cinco *(m).*

fix [fıks] *n fam* apuro, aprieto. **2** *sl (drugs)* pico. – **3** *t* fijar. **4** *(arrange)* arreglar. **5** *(dishonestly)* amañar. **6** *(repair)* arreglar. **7** US *(prepare)* preparar. ◆*to ~ on t* decidir, optar por. ◆*to ~ up t* proveer *(with,* de). ●*to ~ one's eyes on sth.,* fijar los ojos en algo.

fixation [fık'seıʃən] *n* obsesión.

fixed [fıkst] *adj* fijo,-a.

fixture ['fıkstʃəʳ] *n* SP encuentro. **2** *pl* muebles *mpl* empotrados.

fizz [fız] *n* burbujeo. – **2** *i* burbujear.

fizzle ['fızəl] *i to ~ out,* desvanecer(se).

fizzy ['fızı] *adj* gaseoso,-a, con gas; *(wine)* espumoso,-a.

flabbergasted ['flæbəgɑːstıd] *adj* pasmado,-a, atónito,-a.

flabby ['flæbı] *adj* fofo,-a.

flaccid ['flæksıd] *adj* fláccido,-a.

flag [flæg] *n* bandera. **2** MAR pabellón *m.* **3** *(for charity)* banderita. – **4** *i* decaer.

flagship ['flægʃıp] *n* buque *m* insignia.

flagstone ['flægstəun] *n* losa.

flair [fleəʳ] *n* talento, don *m.*

flake [fleık] *n (of snow, oats)* copo. **2** *(of skin, soap)* escama. **3** *(of paint)* desconchón *m.* – **4** *i gen* descamarse. **5** *(paint)* desconcharse.

flamboyant [flæm'bɔıənt] *adj* llamativo,-a, extravagante.

flame [fleım] *n* llama.

flamingo [flə'mıŋgəu] *n* flamenco.

flan [flæn] *n* CULIN tarta rellena.

flange [flændʒ] *n* brida, reborde *m.*

flank [flæŋk] *n* ijada, ijar *m.* **2** MIL flanco. – **3** *t* flanquear, bordear.

flannel ['flænəl] *n* franela.

flap [flæp] *n (of envelope, pocket)* solapa. **2** *(of tent)* faldón *m*. — **3** *t* batir. — **4** *i (wings)* aletear. **5** *(flag)* ondear.

flare [fleəʳ] *n (flame)* llamarada. **2** *(signal)* bengala. — **3** *i* llamear. ◆*to* ~ *up i* estallar.

flared [fleəd] *adj* acampanado,-a.

flash [flæʃ] *n* destello: *like a* ~, como un rayo. **2** *(burst)* ráfaga. **3** *(photography)* flash *m*. — **4** *i* destellar. **5** *(dash)* pasar como un rayo. — **6** *t (light)* despedir, lanzar; *(torch)* encender. **7** *(send)* enviar. ■ ~ *of lightning,* relámpago; *(news)* ~, flash *m*, noticia de última hora.

flashback ['flæʃbæk] *n* escena retrospectiva.

flashlight ['flæʃlaɪt] *n* linterna.

flashy ['flæʃɪ] *adj* llamativo,-a.

flask [flæsk] *n* frasco. **2** CHEM matraz *m*. ■ *(thermos)* ~, termo.

flat [flæt] *adj (surface)* llano,-a, plano,-a. **2** *(tyre)* desinflado,-a. **3** *(battery)* descargado,-a. **4** *(drink)* sin gas. **5** *fig (dull)* monótono,-a, soso,-a. **6** *(firm)* rotundo,-a. **7** MUS bemol. — **8** *n (plain)* superficie *f* plana, llanura. **9** *(of hand)* palma. **10** GB *(apartment)* piso. — **11** *adv (exactly)* *in ten seconds* ~, en diez segundos justos. **12** *flatly adv* rotundamente. ■ ~ *rate,* precio fijo.

flatten ['flætən] *t-i* allanar(se), aplanar(se). — **2** *t (crush)* aplastar.

flatter ['flætəʳ] *t* adular, halagar. **2** *(suit)* favorecer.

flattering ['flætərɪŋ] *adj* lisonjero,-a, halagüeño,-a. **2** *(attractive)* favorecedor,-ra.

flattery ['flætərɪ] *n* adulación, halago.

flatulence ['flætjʊlens] *n fml* flatulencia.

flaunt [flɔːnt] *t* hacer alarde de.

flautist ['flɔːtɪst] *n* flautista *mf*.

flavour ['fleɪvəʳ] *n* sabor *m*. **2** *fig* atmósfera. — **3** *t* sazonar, condimentar.

flavouring ['fleɪvərɪŋ] *n* condimento. ■ *artificial* ~, aroma *m* artificial.

flaw [flɔː] *n (failing)* defecto. **2** *(fault)* desperfecto.

flawless ['flɔːləs] *adj* sin defecto/tacha.

flea [fliː] *n* pulga.

fleck [flek] *n* mota, punto.

flee [fliː] *t-i* huir (de). ▲ *pt & pp* **fled** [fled].

fleece [fliːs] *n (coat)* lana. **2** *(sheared)* vellón *m*. — **3** *t fam* desplumar, robar.

fleet [fliːt] *n* MAR armada. **2** *(of cars)* escuadra.

fleeting ['fliːtɪŋ] *adj* fugaz, efímero,-a.

flesh [fleʃ] *n* carne *f*.

fleshy ['fleʃɪ] *adj* gordo,-a.

flew [fluː] *pt* → **fly**.

flex [fleks] *n* GB cable *m*. — **2** *t (body, joints)* doblar; *(muscles)* flexionar.

flexible ['fleksɪbəl] *adj* flexible.

flick [flɪk] *n (jerk)* movimiento rápido/ brusco. — **2** *t (switch)* dar. **3** *(whip)* chasquear.

flicker ['flɪkəʳ] *n* parpadeo; *(of light)* titileo. **2** *fig (trace)* indicio. — **3** *i (eyes)* parpadear; *(flame)* vaacilar.

flight [flaɪt] *n* vuelo. **2** *(flock of birds)* bandada. **3** *(of stairs)* tramo. **4** *(escape)* huida, fuga. ●*to take* ~, darse a la fuga.

flighty ['flaɪtɪ] *adj fig* frívolo,-a.

flimsy ['flɪmzɪ] *adj (thin)* fino,-a. **2** *(structure)* poco sólido,-a. **3** *fig (excuse)* flojo,-a.

flinch [flɪntʃ] *i (wince)* estremecerse. **2** *(shun)* retroceder.

fling [flɪŋ] *n (throw)* lanzamiento. **2** *(wild time)* juerga. **3** *(affair)* lío *(amoroso)*. — **4** *t* arrojar, tirar, lanzar. ●*to have a* ~, echar una cana al aire. ▲ *pt & pp* **flung**.

flint [flɪnt] *n* pedernal *m*. **2** *(of lighter)* piedra *(de mechero)*.

flip [flɪp] *n* capirotazo. — **2** *interj fam* ¡ostras! — **3** *t (toss)* echar (al aire). **4** *(turn over)* dar la vuelta a. — **5** *i fam (freak out)* perder los estribos.

flippant ['flɪpənt] *adj* frívolo,-a.

flipper ['flɪpəʳ] *n* aleta.

flirt [flɜːt] *n* coqueto,-a. — **2** *i* flirtear, coquetear.

flirtation [flɜːˈteɪʃən] *n* coqueteo.

float [fləʊt] *n (fishing)* flotador *m*. **2** *(swimming)* flotador *m*. **3** *(vehicle)* carroza. — **4** *i* flotar. — **5** *t* hacer flotar. **6** FIN *(shares)* emitir.

flock [flɒk] *n (of sheep, goats)* rebaño; *(of birds)* bandada. **2** *fam (crowd)* tropel *m*. **3** REL grey *f*. — **4** *i* acudir en masa. ●*to* ~ *together,* congregarse.

flog [flɒg] *t (beat)* azotar. **2** GB *fam* vender.

flood [flʌd] *n* inundación. **2** *(of river)* riada. **3** *fig* torrente *m*, avalancha. — **4** *t* inundar. — **5** *i* desbordarse.

floodlight ['flʌdlaɪt] *n* foco.

floor [flɔːʳ] *n* suelo, piso. **2** GEOG fondo. **3** *(storey)* piso. — **4** *t (knock down)* derribar. **5** *fig* apabullar.

flop [flɒp] *n fam* fracaso. — **2** *i (fall heavily)* dejarse caer. **3** *fam* fracasar.

floppy ['flɒpɪ] *adj* blando,-a, flexible. ■ COMPUT ~ *disk,* disco flexible, disquete *m*.

flora ['flɔːrə] *n* flora.

floral ['flɔːrəl] *adj* floral.

florid ['flɒrɪd] *adj pey (style)* florido,-a, recargado,-a.

florist ['flɒrɪst] *n* florista *mf*. ■ **florist's (shop),** floristería.

flounce [flaʊns] *n* SEW volante *m*. ◆*to* ~ *in/out i* entrar/salir airadamente.

flounder ['flaʊndəʳ] *n (fish)* platija. – 2 *i (energetically)* forcejear. 3 *fig (dither)* vacilar.

flour ['flaʊəʳ] *n* harina.

flourish ['flʌrɪʃ] *n (gesture)* ademán *m*, gesto. – 2 *t (wave)* ondear, agitar. – 3 *i* florecer.

flourishing ['flʌrɪʃɪŋ] *adj* floreciente.

flow [fləʊ] *n gen* flujo. 2 *(of river)* corriente *f*. 3 *(of traffic)* circulación. – 4 *i* fluir, manar. 5 *(traffic)* circular. 6 *fig (ideas etc.)* correr. ●*to* ~ *into,* desembocar en. ■ ~ *chart,* organigrama *m*.

flower ['flaʊəʳ] *n* flor *f*. – 2 *i* florecer. ■ ~ *bed,* parterre *m*.

flowerpot ['flaʊəpɒt] *n* maceta, tiesto.

flowery ['flaʊərɪ] *adj (pattern)* de flores. 2 *(style)* florido,-a.

flowing ['fləʊɪŋ] *adj (liquid)* que fluye. 2 *(style)* fluido,-a, suelto,-a.

flown [fləʊn] *pp* → **fly**.

flu [fluː] *n* gripe *f*.

fluctuate ['flʌktjʊeɪt] *i* fluctuar.

fluency ['fluːənsɪ] *n* fluidez. 2 *(of language)* dominio *(in,* de).

fluent ['fluːənt] *adj* fluido,-a. – 2 *fluently adv* con soltura.

fluff [flʌf] *n* pelusa, lanilla. – 2 *t fam* hacer mal/a destiempo. ◆*to* ~ *out/up t-i (hair etc.)* encrespar(se), erizar(se).

fluffy ['flʌfɪ] *adj* mullido,-a.

fluid ['fluːɪd] *adj-n* fluido,-a *(m)*.

fluke [fluːk] *n fam* chiripa.

flung [flʌŋ] *pt & pp* → **fling**.

fluorescent [flʊə'resənt] *adj* fluorescente. ■ ~ *light,* fluorescente *m*.

flurry ['flʌrɪ] *n (of wind)* ráfaga. 2 *fig (burst)* oleada. – 3 *t* poner nervioso,-a. ■ ~ *of snow,* nevisca.

flush [flʌʃ] *adj (level)* ~ *with,* a ras de. – 2 *n (blush)* rubor *m*. – 3 *t (clean)* limpiar con agua. 4 *fig (enemy)* hacer salir. – 5 *i (blush)* ruborizarse. ●*to* ~ *the lavatory/ toilet,* tirar de la cadena (del wáter); *fam to be/feel* ~, andar bien de dinero.

fluster ['flʌstəʳ] *t* poner nervioso,-a. ●*to get in a* ~, ponerse nervioso,-a.

flute [fluːt] *n* flauta.

flutter ['flʌtəʳ] *n* agitación. 2 *(of wings)* aleteo. 3 *fam (bet)* apuesta. – 4 *t-i (wave)* ondear. 5 *(birds)* aletear. – 6 *i* revolo-

tear. ●*fig to be in a* ~, estar nervioso,-a; *to* ~ *one's eyelashes,* parpadear.

fly [flaɪ] *n (insect)* mosca. 2 *pl (zip)* bragueta *f sing*. – 3 *i* volar. 4 *(go by plane)* ir en avión. 5 *(flag)* estar izado,-a. 6 *(sparks)* saltar. 7 *(leave quickly)* irse volando. – 8 *t* AV pilotar. 9 *(send by plane)* enviar por avión. 10 *(travel over)* sobrevolar. 11 *(kite)* hacer volar. 12 *(flag)* enarbolar. ▲ *pt* **flew**; *pp* **flown**.

flying ['flaɪɪŋ] *n* AV aviación. 2 *(action)* vuelo. – 3 *adj (soaring)* volante. 4 *(quick)* rápido,-a. ●*to pass (an exam) with* ~ *colours,* salir airoso,-a (de un examen). ■ ~ *saucer,* platillo volante; ~ *visit,* visita relámpago.

flyover ['flaɪəʊvəʳ] *n* GB paso elevado.

foal [fəʊl] *n* potro,-a.

foam [fəʊm] *n* espuma. – 2 *i (bubble)* hacer espuma. ■ ~ *rubber,* gomaespuma.

foamy ['fəʊmɪ] *adj* espumoso,-a.

fob [fɒb] *t to* ~ *off,* embaucar. ●*to* ~ *sb. off with excuses,* darle largas a algn.

focus ['fəʊkəs] *n* foco. – 2 *t* enfocar. – 3 *i* centrarse *(on,* en). ●*in/out of* ~, enfocado,-a/desenfocado,-a. ▲ *pt & pp* **focus(s)ed**.

foetus ['fiːtəs] *n* feto.

fog [fɒg] *n* niebla. – 2 *t-i to* ~ *(up),* empañar(se).

foggy ['fɒgɪ] *adj* de niebla: *it's* ~, hay niebla.

foglamp ['fɒglæmp] *n* faro antiniebla.

foible ['fɔɪbəl] *n (habit)* manía.

foil [fɔɪl] *n (metal paper)* papel *m* de aluminio. 2 *(contrast)* contraste *m*. – 3 *t fml* frustrar.

fold [fəʊld] *n (crease)* pliegue *m*, doblez *m*. 2 *(for sheep)* redil *m*, aprisco. – 3 *t-i* doblar(se), plegar(se). ●*to* ~ *one's arms,* cruzar los brazos.

folder ['fəʊldəʳ] *n* carpeta.

folding ['fəʊldɪŋ] *adj* plegable.

foliage ['fəʊlɪɪdʒ] *n fml* follaje *m*.

folk [fəʊk] *npl* gente *f sing*. 2 **folks,** *fam (family)* familia *f sing*. – 3 *adj* popular. ■ ~ *music,* música folk; ~ *song,* canción tradicional/folk.

folklore ['fəʊklɔː] *n* folclor(e) *m*.

follow ['fɒləʊ] *t-i* seguir. 2 *(understand)* entender, seguir: *I don't* ~ *(you),* no (te) entiendo. – 3 *t (pursue)* perseguir. – 4 *i (be logical)* resultar, derivarse. ◆*to* ~ *out t* ejecutar. ◆*to* ~ *through t* llevar a cabo. ◆*to* ~ *up t* seguir de cerca, profundizar en.

follower ['fɒləʊəʳ] *n* seguidor,-ra.

following [ˈfɒləʊɪŋ] *adj* siguiente. − **2** *n* seguidores *mpl*.

follow-up [ˈfɒləʊʌp] *n* continuación.

folly [ˈfɒlɪ] *n fml* locura, desatino.

fond [fɒnd] *adj* (*loving*) cariñoso,-a. **2** (*partial*) ser aficionado,-a (*of*, a). − **3** *fondly adv* (*lovingly*) cariñosamente. **4** (*naively*) ingenuamente. ●*to be ~ of sb.*, tenerle cariño a algn.

fondle [ˈfɒndəl] *t* acariciar.

fondness [ˈfɒndnəs] *n* cariño. **2** (*liking*) afición (*for*, a/por).

font [fɒnt] *n* pila (bautismal).

food [fuːd] *n* comida, alimento. ■ *~ poisoning*, intoxicación alimenticia.

foodstuffs [ˈfuːdstʌfs] *npl* alimentos *mpl*, productos *mpl* alimenticios.

fool [fuːl] *n* tonto,-a, imbécil *mf*: *don't be a ~*, no seas tonto,-a. **2** (*jester*) bufón,-ona. − **3** *t* engañar. − **4** *i* bromear. ◆*to ~ about/around i* hacer el tonto. ●*to make a ~ of*, poner en ridículo a; *to play the ~*, hacer el tonto.

foolhardy [ˈfuːlhɑːdɪ] *adj* (*risky*) temerario,-a. **2** (*person*) intrépido,-a.

foolish [ˈfuːlɪʃ] *adj* estúpido,-a.

foolishness [ˈfuːlɪʃnəs] *n* estupidez *f*.

foolproof [ˈfuːlpruːf] *adj* infalible.

foot [fʊt] *n gen* pie *m*. **2** (*of animal*) pata. − **3** *t fam* (*pay*) pagar. ●*on ~*, a pie; *to set ~ in*, entrar en; *fam to get off on the wrong ~*, empezar con mal pie; *fam to put one's ~ down*, imponerse. ▲ *pl* feet.

football [ˈfʊtbɔːl] *n* fútbol *m*. **2** (*ball*) balón *m*. ■ *~ pools*, quinielas *fpl*.

footballer [ˈfʊtbɔːləʳ] *n* futbolista *mf*.

footlights [ˈfʊtlaɪts] *npl* candilejas *fpl*.

footnote [ˈfʊtnəʊt] *n* nota a pie de página.

footpath [ˈfʊtpɑːθ] *n* sendero, camino.

footprint [ˈfʊtprɪnt] *n* huella, pisada.

footstep [ˈfʊtstep] *n* paso, pisada.

footwear [ˈfʊtweəʳ] *n* calzado.

for [fɔːʳ] *prep* (*intended*) para: *it's ~ you*, es para ti. **2** (*purpose*) para: *what's this ~?*, ¿para qué sirve esto? **3** (*in lieu of*) por: *do it ~ me*, hazlo por mí. **4** (*because of*) por. **5** (*during*) por, durante: *~ two weeks*, durante dos semanas. **6** (*distance*) *I walked ~ five miles*, caminé cinco millas. **7** (*destination*) para, hacia. **8** (*price*) por: *I got it ~ £500*, lo conseguí por quinientas libras. **9** (*in favour of*) a favor de. **10** (*despite*) a pesar de. **11** (*as*) como: *what do they use ~ fuel?*, ¿qué utilizan como combustible? **12** (*+ object + inf*) *it's time ~ you to go*, es hora de que te marches. − **13** *conj* ya que. ●*as ~ me*, por mi parte, en cuanto a mí; *~ all I know*, que yo sepa; *~ good*, para siempre; *~ one thing*, para empezar; *what ~?*, ¿para qué?

forage [ˈfɒrɪdʒ] *n* forraje *m*. − **2** *t* hurgar, fisgar.

forbade [fɔːˈbeɪd] *pt* → **forbid**.

forbear [fɔːˈbeəʳ] *i fml* abstenerse (*from*, de). ▲ *pt* **forbore**; *pp* **forborne**.

forbid [fəˈbɪd] *t* prohibir. ▲ *pt* **forbade**; *pp* **forbidden** [fəˈbɪdən].

forbidding [fəˈbɪdɪŋ] *adj* severo,-a.

forbore [fɔːˈbɔːʳ] *pt* → **forbear**.

forborne [fɔːˈbɔːn] *pp* → **forbear**.

force [fɔːs] *n* fuerza. **2** MIL cuerpo. − **3** *t* forzar. ●*by ~*, a/por la fuerza; *to come into ~*, entrar en vigor.

forceful [ˈfɔːsfʊl] *adj* enérgico,-a.

forceps [ˈfɔːseps] *npl* fórceps *m inv*.

ford [fɔːd] *n* vado. − **2** *t* vadear.

forearm [ˈfɔːrɑːm] *n* antebrazo.

foreboding [fɔːˈbəʊdɪŋ] *n* presentimiento.

forecast [ˈfɔːkɑːst] *n* pronóstico, previsión. − **2** *t* pronosticar. ▲ *pt & pp* **forecast** *o* **forecasted** [ˈfɔːkɑːstɪd].

forefathers [ˈfɔːfɑːðəz] *npl* antepasados *mpl*.

forefinger [ˈfɔːfɪŋgəʳ] *n* (dedo) índice *m*.

forefront [ˈfɔːfrʌnt] *n* vanguardia.

forego [fɔːˈgəʊ] *t* renunciar a, sacrificar. ▲ *pt* **forewent**; *pp* **foregone**.

foregoing [fɔːˈgəʊɪŋ] *adj* precedente.

foregone [fɔːˈgɒn] *pp* → **forego**.

foreground [ˈfɔːgraʊnd] *n* primer plano.

forehead [ˈfɒrɪd, ˈfɔːhed] *n* frente *f*.

foreign [ˈfɒrɪn] *adj* extranjero,-a. **2** (*policy etc.*) exterior. **3** (*strange*) ajeno,-a. ■ FIN *~ exchange*, divisas *fpl*; GB *Foreign Office*, Ministerio de Asuntos Exteriores.

foreigner [ˈfɒrɪnəʳ] *n* extranjero,-a.

foreman [ˈfɔːmən] *n* capataz *m*.

foremost [ˈfɔːməʊst] *adj* principal.

forensic [fəˈrensɪk] *adj* forense.

forerunner [ˈfɔːrʌnəʳ] *n* precursor,-ra.

foresee [fɔːˈsiː] *t* prever. ▲ *pt* **foresaw** [fɔːˈsɔː]; *pp* **foreseen** [fɔːˈsiːn].

foresight [ˈfɔːsaɪt] *n* previsión.

foreskin [ˈfɔːskɪn] *n* prepucio.

forest [ˈfɒrɪst] *n* (*small*) bosque *m*; (*large*) selva. ■ *~ fire*, incendio forestal.

forestall [fɔːˈstɔːl] *t* anticiparse a.

forestry [ˈfɒrɪstrɪ] *n* silvicultura.

foretell [fɔːˈtel] *t* presagiar, pronosticar. ▲ *pt & pp* **foretold**.

forethought [ˈfɔːθɔːt] *n* previsión. **2** JUR premeditación.

foretold [fɔː'təʊld] *pt & pp* → **foretell**.
forever [fə'revər] *adv* siempre. 2 *(for good)* para siempre.
forewarn [fɔː'wɔːn] *t* prevenir.
forewent [fɔː'went] *pp* → **forego**.
foreword ['fɔːwɜːd] *n* prólogo.
forfeit ['fɔːfɪt] *n* pena, multa. 2 *(in games)* prenda. – 3 *t* perder, renunciar a.
forgave [fə'ɡeɪv] *pt* → **forgive**.
forge [fɔːdʒ] *n (apparatus)* fragua. 2 *(blacksmith's)* herrería. – 3 *t (counterfeit)* falsificar. 4 *(metal)* forjar, fraguar. 5 *fig* forjar.
forgery ['fɔːdʒərɪ] *n* falsificación.
forget [fə'ɡet] *t* olvidar, olvidarse de. ●~ *it!,* ¡olvídalo!, ¡déjalo!; *fig to ~ o.s.,* perder los estribos. ▲ *pt* **forgot**; *pp* **forgotten**.
forgetful [fə'ɡetfʊl] *adj* despistado,-a.
forgive [fə'ɡɪv] *t* perdonar. ▲ *pt* **forgave**; *pp* **forgiven** [fə'ɡɪvən].
forgiveness [fə'ɡɪvnəs] *n* perdón *m*.
forgo [fɔː'ɡəʊ] *t* → **forego**.
forgone [fɔː'ɡɒn] *pp* → **forego**.
forgot [fə'ɡɒt] *pt* → **forget**.
forgotten [fə'ɡɒtən] *pp* → **forget**.
fork [fɔːk] *n* tenedor *m*. 2 AGR horca, horquilla. 3 *(in road)* bifurcación. – 4 *i* bifurcarse. ◆*to ~ out t fam (money)* soltar, aflojar.
forlorn [fə'lɔːn] *adj* abandonado,-a. 2 *(desolate)* triste. 3 *(hopeless)* desesperado,-a.
form [fɔːm] *n gen* forma. 2 *(kind)* clase *f*, tipo. 3 *(formality)* formas *fpl*. 4 *(document)* formulario. 5 EDUC curso. – 6 *t-i* formar(se). ●*on/off ~,* en forma/en baja forma.
formal ['fɔːməl] *adj* formal. 2 *(dress)* de etiqueta. 3 *(person, language)* ceremonioso,-a.
formality [fɔː'mælɪtɪ] *n* formalidad.
format ['fɔːmæt] *n* formato.
formation [fɔː'meɪʃən] *n* formación.
former ['fɔːmər] *adj* anterior. 2 *(one-time)* antiguo,-a. 3 *(person)* ex-: *the ~ champion,* el excampeón. – 4 *pron the ~,* aquél, aquélla. – 5 *formerly adv* antiguamente.
formidable ['fɔːmɪdəbəl] *adj* formidable. 2 *(daunting)* temible.
formula ['fɔːmjʊlə] *n* fórmula. ▲ *pl* **formulas** o **formulae** ['fɔːmjʊliː].
formulate ['fɔːmjʊleɪt] *t* formular.
fornicate ['fɔːnɪkeɪt] *i fml* fornicar.
forsake [fə'seɪk] *t fml* abandonar. 2 *(give up)* renunciar a. ▲ *pt* **forsook** [fə'sʊk]; *pp* **forsaken** [fə'seɪkən].

fort [fɔːt] *n* fuerte *m*, fortaleza.
forte ['fɔːteɪ] *n* fuerte *m*.
forth [fɔːθ] *adv and so ~,* y así sucesivamente.
forthcoming [fɔːθ'kʌmɪŋ] *adj fml* próximo,-a. 2 *(available)* disponible.
fortieth ['fɔːtɪəθ] *adj-n* cuadragésimo,-a. – 2 *n* cuadragésimo, cuadragésima parte.
fortification [fɔːtɪfɪ'keɪʃən] *n* fortificación.
fortify ['fɔːtɪfaɪ] *t* MIL fortificar. 2 *fig* fortalecer.
fortnight ['fɔːtnaɪt] *n* GB quincena.
fortnightly ['fɔːtnaɪtlɪ] *adj* quincenal. – 2 *adv* cada quince días.
fortress ['fɔːtrəs] *n* fortaleza.
fortunate ['fɔːtʃənət] *adj* afortunado,-a. – 2 **fortunately** *adv* afortunadamente.
fortune ['fɔːtʃən] *n gen* fortuna. 2 *(luck)* suerte *f*.
fortune-teller ['fɔːtʃəntelər] *n* adivino,-a.
forty ['fɔːtɪ] *adj-n* cuarenta *(m)*.
forward ['fɔːwəd] *adv gen* hacia adelante: *to go ~,* ir hacia adelante. 2 *(time)* en adelante: *from this day ~,* de ahora/aquí en adelante. – 3 *adj* hacia adelante. 4 *(position)* delantero,-a, frontal. 5 *(advanced)* adelantado,-a. 6 *(person)* atrevido,-a, descarado,-a. – 7 *n* SP delantero,-a. – 8 *t (send on)* remitir. 9 *fml (further)* adelantar. ●*to bring sth. ~,* adelantar algo; *to put the clock ~,* adelantar el reloj. ▲ *En 1 también puede ser* **forwards**.
forwent [fɔː'went] *pt* → **forego**.
fossil ['fɒsəl] *n* fósil *m*.
foster ['fɒstər] *t (child)* criar. – 2 *adj* adoptivo,-a. ■ *~ child,* hijo,-a adoptivo,-a; *~ mother,* madre adoptiva.
fought [fɔːt] *pt & pp* → **fight**.
foul [faʊl] *adj* asqueroso,-a. 2 *(smell)* fétido,-a. 3 *fml (evil)* vil, atroz. – 4 *n* SP falta. – 5 *t-i (dirty)* ensuciar(se). – 6 *t* SP cometer una falta contra. ◆*to ~ up t fam* estropear.
foul-mouthed [faʊl'maʊðd] *adj* malhablado,-a.
found [faʊnd] *pt & pp* → **find**. – 2 *t (establish)* fundar. 3 TECH fundir.
foundation [faʊn'deɪʃən] *n (act, organization)* fundación. 2 *(basis)* fundamento, base *f*. 3 *pl* cimientos *mpl*.
founder ['faʊndər] *n (person)* fundador,-ra. – 2 *i* irse a pique.
foundry ['faʊndrɪ] *n* fundición.
fountain ['faʊntən] *n* fuente *f*. 2 *(jet)* surtidor *m*. ■ *~ pen,* pluma estilográfica.

four

104

four [fɔːʳ] *adj-n* cuatro. •*on all fours,* a gatas.

fourteen [fɔːˈtiːn] *adj-n* catorce *(m)*.

fourteenth [fɔːˈtiːnθ] *adj-n* decimocuarto,-a. − 2 *n (fraction)* decimocuarto, decimocuarta parte.

fourth [fɔːθ] *adj-n* cuarto,-a. − 2 *n* cuarto, cuarta parte.

fowl [faʊl] *n inv* ave(s) *m(pl)* de corral.

fox [fɒks] *n* zorro,-a. − 2 *t fam (trick)* engañar.

foxy [ˈfɒksɪ] *adj fam* astuto,-a.

foyer [ˈfɔɪeɪ, ˈfɔɪəʳ] *n* vestíbulo.

fraction [ˈfrækʃən] *n* fracción.

fracture [ˈfræktʃəʳ] *n* fractura. − 2 *t-i* fracturar(se), romper(se).

fragile [ˈfrædʒaɪl] *adj* frágil. 2 *fig (health)* delicado,-a.

fragility [frəˈdʒɪlɪtɪ] *n* fragilidad.

fragment [ˈfrægmənt] *n* fragmento. − 2 *i* fragmentarse. ▲ *En 2 (verbo)* [frægˈment].

fragrance [ˈfreɪgrəns] *n* fragancia.

frail [freɪl] *adj* frágil, delicado,-a.

frame [freɪm] *n (of building, machine)* armazón *f.* 2 *(of bed)* armadura. 3 *(of bicycle)* cuadro. 4 *(of spectacles)* montura. 5 *(of human, animal)* cuerpo. 6 *(of window, door, etc.)* marco. − 7 *t (picture)* enmarcar. 8 *(door)* encuadrar. 9 *fam (set up)* tender una trampa a *para que parezca culpable.* 10 *fml (question)* formular. ■ ~ *of mind,* estado de ánimo.

framework [ˈfreɪmwɜːk] *n* armazón *f.* 2 *fig* estructura.

franc [fræŋk] *n* franco.

franchise [ˈfræntʃaɪz] *n* COM concesión, licencia. 2 *(vote)* derecho de voto.

frank [fræŋk] *adj* franco,-a.

frankness [ˈfræŋknəs] *n* franqueza.

frantic [ˈfræntɪk] *adj (hectic)* frenético,-a. 2 *(anxious)* desesperado,-a.

fraternal [frəˈtɜːnəl] *adj* fraternal.

fraternity [frəˈtɜːnɪtɪ] *n (society)* asociación; REL hermandad, cofradía. 2 US *(university)* club *m* de estudiantes.

fraternize [ˈfrætənaɪz] *i* fraternizar.

fraud [frɔːd] *n (act)* fraude *m.* 2 *(person)* impostor,-ra.

fraught [frɔːt] *adj (full)* lleno,-a/cargado,-a *(with,* de). 2 *fam (anxious)* nervioso,-a, alterado,-a.

fray [freɪ] *n (fight)* combate *m.* − 2 *i (cloth)* deshilacharse; *(become worn)* raerse. 3 *fig (nerves)* crisparse.

freak [friːk] *n (monster)* monstruo. 2 *sl (fan)* fanático,-a. − 3 *adj (unusual)* insólito,-a. ◆*to ~ out t-i sl* flipar, alucinar.

freakish [ˈfriːkɪʃ] *adj* insólito,-a.

freckle [ˈfrekəl] *n* peca.

freckled [ˈfrekəld] *adj* pecoso,-a.

free [friː] *adj gen* libre. 2 *(without cost)* gratuito,-a. 3 *(generous)* generoso,-a. − *adv (gratis)* gratis. 5 *(loose)* suelto,-a. − 6 *t (liberate)* poner en libertad. 7 *(release)* liberar. 8 *(let loose, disengage)* soltar. − 9 *freely adv* libremente. 10 *(without cost)* gratis. •*feel ~!,* ¡tú mismo,-a!; ~ *and easy,* despreocupado,-a; *to run ~,* andar suelto,-a; *to set sb. ~,* liberar a/poner en libertad a algn. ■ ~ *speech,* libertad de expresión; ~ *trade,* librecambio; ~ *will,* libre albedrío.

freedom [ˈfriːdəm] *n* libertad.

free-for-all [ˈfriːfərɔːl] *n fam* pelea.

freelance [ˈfriːlɑːns] *adj* independiente. − 2 *n* persona que trabaja por cuenta propia.

freemason [ˈfriːmeɪsən] *n* (franc)masón,-ona.

free-style [ˈfriːstaɪl] *n* estilo libre.

freeway [ˈfriːweɪ] *n* US autopista.

freeze [friːz] *n* helada. 2 COM congelación. − 3 *t* congelar. − 4 *i (liquid)* helarse; *(food)* congelarse. 5 *fig (become still)* quedarse inmóvil. ▲ *pt* froze; *pp* frozen.

freezer [ˈfriːzəʳ] *n* congelador *m.*

freezing [ˈfriːzɪŋ] *adj* glacial. − 2 *n* congelación. ■ ~ *point,* punto de congelación.

freight [freɪt] *n (transport)* transporte *m.* 2 *(goods)* carga, flete *m.* ■ ~ *train,* tren *m* de mercancías.

frenzy [ˈfrenzɪ] *n* frenesí *m.*

frequency [ˈfriːkwənsɪ] *n* frecuencia.

frequent [ˈfriːkwənt] *adj* frecuente. − 2 *t* frecuentar. − 3 *frequently adv* frecuentemente. ▲ *En 2 (verbo)* [frɪˈkwent].

fresco [ˈfreskəʊ] *n* fresco.

fresh [freʃ] *adj gen* fresco,-a. 2 *(water)* dulce. 3 *(air)* puro,-a. 4 *(complexion)* sano,-a. 5 *fig (new)* nuevo,-a. − 6 *freshly adv* recién. •*in the ~ air,* al aire libre. ■ ~ *water,* agua dulce.

freshen [ˈfreʃən] *t-i* refrescar(se). ◆*to ~ up t-i* asear(se).

fresher [ˈfreʃəʳ], **freshman** [ˈfreʃmən] *n* estudiante *mf* de primer año/curso (de universidad).

freshness [ˈfreʃnəs] *n (brightness)* frescura. 2 *(cool)* frescor *m.* 3 *(newness)* novedad. 4 *fam (cheek)* descaro.

fret [fret] *n (on guitar)* traste *m.* − 2 *i* preocuparse. ◆*to ~ for t* añorar.

fretful [ˈfretfʊl] *adj* preocupado,-a.

friar [ˈfraɪəʳ] *n* fraile *m.*

friction ['frɪkʃən] *n* fricción.
Friday ['fraɪdɪ] *n* viernes *m inv*.
fridge [frɪdʒ] *n* nevera, frigorífico.
fried [fraɪd] *adj* frito,-a.
friend [frend] *n* amigo,-a. ●*to make friends (with sb.),* trabar amistad (con algn.).
friendly ['frendlɪ] *adj (person)* simpático,-a. **2** *(atmosphere)* acogedor,-ra. ●*to become* ~, hacerse amigos,-as. ■ SP ~ *game/match,* partido amistoso.
friendship ['frendʃɪp] *n* amistad.
frieze [friːz] *n* friso.
frigate ['frɪgət] *n* fragata.
fright [fraɪt] *n (shock)* susto. **2** *(fear)* miedo. ●*to get a* ~, pegarse un susto; *to take* ~, asustarse; *fam to look a* ~, estar hecho,-a un adefesio.
frighten ['fraɪtən] *t* asustar, espantar. ◆*to* ~ *away/off t* ahuyentar.
frightening ['fraɪtənɪŋ] *adj* espantoso,-a.
frightful ['fraɪtfʊl] *adj* espantoso,-a, horroroso,-a. – **2** *frightfully adv fam* muchísimo.
frigid ['frɪdʒɪd] *adj* MED frígido,-a. **2** *(icy)* glacial.
frill [frɪl] *n (on dress)* volante *m*. **2** *(decoration)* adorno. ●*with no frills,* sencillo,-a.
fringe [frɪndʒ] *n (decorative)* fleco. **2** *(of hair)* flequillo. **3** *(edge)* borde *m*.
frisk [frɪsk] *t* registrar, cachear.
frisky ['frɪskɪ] *adj (child, animal)* retozón,-ona, juguetón,-ona. **2** *(adult)* vivo,-a.
fritter ['frɪtər] *n* CULIN buñuelo. ◆*to* ~ *away i pej* malgastar.
frivolous ['frɪvələs] *adj* frívolo,-a.
frizzy ['frɪzɪ] *adj* crespo,-a, rizado,-a.
fro [frəʊ] *adv* *to and* ~, de un lado para otro.
frog [frɒg] *n* rana.
frogman ['frɒgmən] *n* hombre *m* rana.
frolic ['frɒlɪk] *i* juguetear, retozar.
from [frɒm] *prep gen* de. **2** *(number, position)* de, desde. **3** *(time)* desde, a partir de. **4** *(train, plane)* procedente de. **5** *(according to)* según, por: ~ *experience,* por experiencia. ●~ *now on,* de ahora en adelante, a partir de ahora.
front [frʌnt] *n (forward part)* parte delantera, frente *m & f*. **2** METEOR frente *m & f*. **3** *(facade)* fachada. **4** MIL frente *m*. **5** *fig (business etc.)* tapadera. – **6** *adj* delantero,-a, de delante. – **7** *i* dar *(on/onto,* a). ●*in* ~ *(of),* delante (de); *from the* ~, por delante, de frente. ■ ~ *door,* puerta principal/de entrada.

frontal ['frʌntəl] *adj* frontal.
frontier ['frʌntɪər] *n* frontera.
frost [frɒst] *n (covering)* escarcha. **2** *(freezing)* helada. – **3** *i to* ~ *(over),* helarse.
frostbite ['frɒstbaɪt] *n* congelación.
frosted ['frɒstɪd] *adj (glass)* esmerilado,-a.
frosty ['frɒstɪ] *adj* helado,-a.
froth [frɒθ] *n gen* espuma. **2** *(from mouth)* espumarajos *mpl*. – **3** *i* espumar.
frothy ['frɒθɪ] *adj* espumoso,-a.
frown [fraʊn] *n* ceño. – **2** *i* fruncir el ceño. ◆*to* ~ *upon t fig* desaprobar, censurar.
froze [frəʊz] *pt* → **freeze**.
frozen ['frəʊzən] *pp* → **freeze**.
frugal ['fruːgəl] *adj* frugal.
fruit [fruːt] *n* fruta. **2** BOT fruto. – **3** *i* dar fruto. ■ ~ *dish,* frutero; ~ *machine,* máquina tragaperras; ~ *salad,* macedonia (de frutas).
fruitful ['fruːtfʊl] *adj* fructuoso,-a.
fruitless ['fruːtləs] *adj* infructuoso,-a.
frustrate [frʌ'streɪt] *t* frustrar.
frustration [frʌ'streɪʃən] *n* frustración.
fry [fraɪ] *npl (fish)* alevines *mpl*. – **2** *t-i* freír(se). ■ *small* ~, gente *f sing* de poca monta.
frying ['fraɪɪŋ] *n* ~ *pan,* sartén *f*.
fuchsia ['fjuːʃə] *n* fucsia.
fuck* [fʌk] *t-i* joder*, follar*. ●~ *(it)!*,* ¡joder!*; ~ *off!*,* ¡vete al carajo!*
fucking* ['fʌkɪŋ] *adj* jodidò,-a*: *you're a* ~ *idiot!*,* ¡eres un gilipollas!*
fudge [fʌdʒ] *n* dulce *hecho con azúcar, leche y mantequilla*.
fuel [fjʊəl] *n* combustible *m*. **2** *(for motors)* carburante *m*. – **3** *t-i (plane)* abastecer(se) de combustible. – **4** *t fig* empeorar.
fugitive ['fjuːdʒɪtɪv] *adj-n* fugitivo,-a.
fulfil [fʊl'fɪl] *t (promise)* cumplir. **2** *(task)* realizar, efectuar. **3** *(need)* satisfacer.
fulfilment [fʊl'fɪlmənt] *n* realización. **2** *(of duty)* cumplimiento.
full [fʊl] *adj gen* lleno,-a. **2** *(entire, complete)* completo,-a. **3** *(clothing)* holgado,-a. – **4** *adv (directly)* justo, de lleno. – **5** *fully adv* completamente, enteramente. ●*at* ~ *speed,* a toda velocidad; ~ *well,* perfectamente; *in* ~, en su totalidad; *to be* ~ *of o.s.,* ser un/una engreído,-a; *fam in* ~ *swing,* en pleno auge. ■ ~ *board,* pensión completa; ~ *moon,* luna llena; ~ *stop,* punto (y seguido/aparte).

full-grown [fʊl'grəʊn] *adj (plant)* creci-do,-a. 2 *(person, animal)* adulto,-a.

full-length [fʊl'leŋθ] *adj (image, portrait)* de cuerpo entero. 2 *(garment)* largo,-a. 3 *(film)* de largo metraje.

full-scale [fʌl'skeɪl] *adj (model)* de tama-ño natural. 2 *(total)* completo,-a, total.

full-time [fʊl'taɪm] *adj* a tiempo comple-to.

fumble ['fʌmbəl] *i* revolver torpemente.

fume [fjuːm] *i* echar humo. 2 *fig (person)* subirse por las paredes. — 3 *npl* humos *mpl*, vapores *mpl*.

fumigate ['fjuːmɪgeɪt] *t* fumigar.

fun [fʌn] *n* diversión. — 2 *adj* divertido,-a. ●*in/for* ~, en broma; *to be (great)* ~, ser (muy) divertido,-a; *to have* ~, di-vertirse; pasarlo bien; *to make* ~ *of,* reírse de.

function ['fʌŋkʃən] *n (purpose)* función. 2 *(ceremony)* acto, ceremonia. — 3 *i* fun-cionar.

functional ['fʌŋkʃənəl] *adj* funcional.

fund [fʌnd] *n* fondo. — 2 *t* patrocinar.

fundamental [fʌndə'mentəl] *adj* funda-mental. — 2 *npl* fundamentos *mpl*.

funeral ['fjuːnərəl] *n* entierro, funerales *mpl*. ■ ~ *procession,* cortejo fúnebre; US ~ *parlor,* funeraria.

funfair ['fʌnfeəʳ] *n* GB feria, parque *m* de atracciones.

fungus ['fʌŋgəs] *n* hongo. ▲ *pl funguses* o *fungi* ['fʌndʒaɪ].

funnel ['fʌnəl] *n (for liquid)* embudo. 2 *(chimney)* chimenea. — 3 *t-i* verter(se) por un embudo. — 4 *t fig* encauzar.

funny ['fʌnɪ] *adj (amusing)* gracioso,-a, di-vertido,-a. 2 *(strange)* raro,-a, extra-ño,-a, curioso,-a.

fur [fɜːʳ] *n (of living animal)* pelo, pelaje *m*. 2 *(of dead animal)* piel *f*. 3 *(on appliance, tongue)* sarro. ■ ~ *coat,* abrigo de pieles.

furious ['fjʊərɪəs] *adj* furioso,-a.

furnace ['fɜːnəs] *n* horno.

furnish ['fɜːnɪʃ] *t (house etc.)* amueblar. 2 *fml (supply)* suministrar.

furnishings ['fɜːnɪʃɪŋz] *npl* muebles *mpl*, mobiliario *m sing*. 2 *(fittings)* accesorios *mpl*.

furniture ['fɜːnɪtʃəʳ] *n* mobiliario, mue-bles *mpl*. ●*a piece of* ~, un mueble. ■ ~ *van,* camión *m* de mudanzas.

furrow ['fʌrəʊ] *n* surco. 2 *(wrinkle)* arru-ga. — 3 *t* surcar. 4 *(forehead)* arrugar.

furry ['fɜːrɪ] *adj* peludo,-a.

further ['fɜːðəʳ] *adj-adv comp* → *far*. — 2 *adj (new)* nuevo,-a. 3 *(additional)* adicio-nal. 4 *(later)* ulterior, posterior. — 5 *adv* más: ~ *along,* más adelante. 6 *fml (be-sides)* además. — 7 *t* fomentar, promo-ver.

furthermore [fɜːðə'mɔːʳ] *adv fml* ade-más.

furthest ['fɜːðɪst] *adj-adv superl* → *far*.

furtive ['fɜːtɪv] *adj* furtivo,-a.

fury ['fjʊərɪ] *n* furia, furor *m*.

fuse [fjuːz] *n* ELEC fusible *m*, plomo. 2 *(of bomb)* mecha; *(detonator)* espoleta. — 3 *i gen* fundir(se). 4 *fig (merge)* fusio-nar(se). ■ ~ *box,* caja de fusibles.

fusion ['fjuːʒən] *n* fusión.

fuss [fʌs] *n* alboroto, jaleo. — 2 *i* preo-cuparse *(over,* de). ●*to kick up a* ~, ar-mar un escándalo; *to make a* ~, que-jarse.

fussy ['fʌsɪ] *adj* quisquilloso,-a.

fusty ['fʌstɪ] *adj (musty)* mohoso,-a. 2 *(old-fashioned)* chapado,-a a la antigua.

futile ['fjuːtaɪl] *adj* vano,-a, inútil.

future ['fjuːtʃəʳ] *adj* futuro,-a. — 2 *n* fu-turo, porvenir *m*. 3 GRAM futuro. ●*in the* ~, en el futuro; *in the near* ~, en un futuro próximo.

fuzz [fʌz] *n* pelusa. — 2 *t* rizar. ●*sl the* ~, la bofia.

fuzzy ['fʌzɪ] *adj (hair)* rizado,-a, crespo,-a. 2 *(blurred)* borroso,-a.

G

gab [gæb] *n* labia. — **2** *i* charlar.
gabardine ['gæbədi:n] *n* gabardina.
gabble ['gæbəl] *n* farfulla. — **2** *t* farfullar.
gad [gæd] *i to ~ about/around,* callejear.
gadget ['gædʒɪt] *n* aparato, chisme *m*.
gaffe [gæf] *n* metedura de pata.
gag [gæg] *n* mordaza. **2** *(joke)* chiste *m*. — **3** *t* amordazar.
gaga ['gɑ:gɑ:] *adj fam* choco,-a.
gage [geɪdʒ] *n* US → **gauge.**
gaiety ['geɪətɪ] *n* alegría, diversión.
gaily ['geɪlɪ] *adv* alegremente.
gain [geɪn] *n (achievement)* logro. **2** *(profit)* ganancia, beneficio. **3** *(increase)* aumento. — **4** *t (achieve)* lograr, conseguir. **5** *(obtain)* ganar. **6** *(increase)* aumentar. — **7** *t-i (clock)* adelantarse (en). — **8** *i (shares)* subir. ●*to ~ ground,* ganar terreno.
gait [geɪt] *n* andares *mpl*.
gala ['gɑ:lə] *n* gala.
galactic [gə'læktɪk] *adj* galáctico,-a.
galaxy ['gæləksɪ] *n* galaxia.
gale [geɪl] *n* vendaval *m*.
gall [gɔ:l] *n fig* descaro. — **2** *t* irritar.
gallant ['gælənt] *adj (brave)* valiente. **2** *(chivalrous)* galante.
gallantry ['gæləntrɪ] *n (bravery)* valentía. **2** *(chivalry)* galantería.
galleon ['gælɪən] *n* galeón *m*.
gallery ['gælərɪ] *n* galería. **2** THEAT gallinero.
galley ['gælɪ] *n (ship)* galera. **2** *(kitchen)* cocina.
gallivant [gælɪ'vænt] *i* callejear.
gallon ['gælən] *n* galón *m*.
gallop ['gæləp] *n* galope *m*. — **2** *i* galopar.
gallows ['gæləuz] *n* horca, patíbulo.
galore [gə'lɔ:ʳ] *adv* en abundancia.
galvanize ['gælvənaɪz] *t* galvanizar.
gambit ['gæmbɪt] *n* gambito; *fig* táctica.

gamble ['gæmbəl] *n* jugada, empresa arriesgada. **2** *(risk)* riesgo. — **3** *i* jugar(se). — **4** *t (bet)* apostar, jugar.
gambler ['gæmbləʳ] *n* jugador,-ra.
gambling ['gæmblɪŋ] *n* juego. ■ *~ house/den,* casa de juego.
gambol ['gæmbəl] *i* brincar, retozar.
game [geɪm] *n* juego. **2** *(match)* partido. **3** *(of cards, chess, etc.)* partida. **4** *(hunting)* caza; *fig* presa. **5** *pl* EDUC educación *f sing* física. — **6** *adj* dispuesto,-a, listo,-a. ■ *big ~,* caza mayor; *~ reserve,* coto de caza.
gamekeeper ['geɪmki:pəʳ] *n* guardabosque *mf*.
gammon ['gæmən] *n* jamón *m*.
gamut ['gæmət] *n* gama.
gander ['gændəʳ] *n* ganso.
gang [gæŋ] *n (criminals)* banda. **2** *(youths)* pandilla. **3** *(workers)* cuadrilla, brigada. **4** *(friends)* pandilla. ◆*to ~ up on t* unirse contra.
gangplank ['gæŋplæŋk] *n* plancha.
gangrene ['gæŋgri:n] *n* gangrena.
gangster ['gæŋstəʳ] *n* gángster *m*.
gangway ['gæŋweɪ] *n (passage)* pasillo. **2** MAR pasarela.
gaol [dʒeɪl] *n* cárcel *f*.
gap [gæp] *n (hole)* abertura, hueco. **2** *(empty space)* espacio. **3** *(blank)* blanco. **4** *(time)* intervalo. **5** *(deficiency)* laguna.
gape [geɪp] *i* abrirse. **2** *(stare)* mirar boquiabierto,-a.
garage ['gærɑ:ʒ, 'gærɪdʒ] *n* garaje *m*. **2** *(for repairs)* taller mecánico. **3** *(for petrol etc.)* gasolinera.
garbage ['gɑ:bɪdʒ] *n* basura.
garbled ['gɑ:bəld] *adj* confuso,-a, incomprensible.
garden ['gɑ:dən] *n* jardín *m*. — **2** *i* cuidar el jardín.
gardener ['gɑ:dnəʳ] *n* jardinero,-a.

gardening ['gɑ:dnɪŋ] n jardinería.
gargle ['gɑ:gəl] i hacer gárgaras.
garish ['geərɪʃ] adj chillón,-ona.
garlic ['gɑ:lɪk] n ajo.
garment ['gɑ:mənt] n prenda.
garnish ['gɑ:nɪʃ] n guarnición. – 2 t guarnecer.
garrison ['gærɪsən] n guarnición. – 2 t MIL guarnecer.
garrulous ['gærələs] adj locuaz.
garter ['gɑ:tə'] n liga.
gas [gæs] n gas m. 2 US gasolina. – 3 t asfixiar con gas. – 4 i fam charlotear. ■ ~ mask, careta/máscara antigás.
gaseous ['gæsɪəs] adj gaseoso,-a.
gash [gæʃ] n raja. – 2 t rajar.
gasoline ['gæsəli:n] n US gasolina.
gasp [gɑ:sp] i abrir la boca con asombro/miedo. ●to ~ for air, hacer esfuerzos por respirar.
gassy ['gæsɪ] adj gaseoso,-a.
gastric ['gæstrɪk] adj gástrico,-a.
gastronomy [gæs'trɒnəmɪ] n gastronomía.
gate [geɪt] n puerta, verja. 2 (at airport) puerta.
gateau ['gætəʊ] n pastel m. ▲ pl gateaux ['gætəʊz].
gatecrash ['geɪtkræʃ] t-i fam colarse.
gateway ['geɪtweɪ] n puerta.
gather ['gæðə'] t (collect) juntar. 2 (call together) reunir. 3 (pick up) recoger. 4 (fruit, flowers) coger. 5 (taxes) recaudar. 6 (speed) ganar, cobrar. 7 SEW fruncir. 8 (deduce) deducir, inferir. – 9 i (come together) reunirse. 10 (build up) acumularse.
gathering ['gæðərɪŋ] n reunión.
gauche [gəʊʃ] adj torpe.
gaudy ['gɔ:dɪ] adj chillón,-ona.
gauge [geɪdʒ] n (device) indicador m. 2 (measure) medida estándar. 3 (railways) ancho de vía. – 4 t medir. 5 fig juzgar.
gaunt [gɔ:nt] adj demacrado,-a.
gauze [gɔ:z] n gasa.
gave [geɪv] pt → give.
gawky ['gɔ:kɪ] adj desgarbado,-a.
gawp [gɔ:p] i to ~ at, mirar boquiabierto,-a.
gay [geɪ] adj fam gai, homosexual. 2 (happy, lively) alegre. 3 (bright) vistoso,-a. – 4 fam n (man) gai m, homosexual m. 5 (woman) lesbiana.
gaze [geɪz] n mirada fija. – 2 i mirar fijamente.
gazelle [gə'zel] n gacela.
gazette [gə'zet] n gaceta.

gear [gɪə'] n TECH engranaje m. 2 AUTO marcha, velocidad. 3 (equipment) equipo. 4 fam cosas fpl, efectos mpl personales; (clothes) ropa. ■ ~ lever, palanca de cambio.
gearbox ['gɪəbɒks] n caja de cambios.
gee [dʒi:] interj US ¡caramba!
geese [gi:s] npl → goose.
gelatine [dʒelə'ti:n] n gelatina.
gem [dʒem] n gema, piedra preciosa. 2 fig joya.
Gemini ['dʒemɪnaɪ] n Géminis m.
gen [dʒen] n fam información.
gender ['dʒendə'] n género.
gene [dʒi:n] n gen m.
genealogy [dʒi:nɪ'ælədʒɪ] n genealogía.
general ['dʒenərəl] adj general. – 2 n MIL general m. – 3 generally adv generalmente, por lo general. ●in ~, por lo general. ■ ~ practitioner, médico,-a de cabecera.
generality [dʒenə'rælɪtɪ] n generalidad.
generalization [dʒenərəlaɪ'zeɪʃən] n generalización.
generalize ['dʒenərəlaɪz] t-i generalizar.
generate ['dʒenəreɪt] t generar; fig producir.
generation [dʒenə'reɪʃən] n generación.
generator ['dʒenəreɪtə'] n generador m.
generic [dʒɪ'nerɪk] adj genérico,-a.
generosity [dʒenə'rɒsɪtɪ] n generosidad.
generous ['dʒenərəs] adj generoso,-a. 2 (abundant) abundante, copioso,-a.
genetic [dʒə'netɪk] adj genético,-a.
genetics [dʒə'netɪks] n genética.
genial ['dʒi:nɪəl] adj simpático,-a.
genital ['dʒenɪtəl] adj genital.
genitals ['dʒenɪtəlz] npl (órganos) genitales mpl.
genitive ['dʒenɪtɪv] adj-n genitivo,-a (m).
genius ['dʒi:nɪəs] n (person) genio. 2 (gift) don m.
genocide ['dʒenəsaɪd] n genocidio.
gent [dʒent] n fam caballero.
genteel [dʒen'ti:l] adj fino,-a. 2 pej cursi.
gentile ['dʒentaɪl] adj-n no judío,-a.
gentle ['dʒentəl] adj (person) tierno,-a. 2 (breeze, movement, touch, etc.) suave. 3 (hint) discreto,-a.
gentleman ['dʒentəlmən] n caballero.
gently ['dʒentlɪ] adv suavemente. 2 (slowly) despacio.
gents [dʒents] n fam servicio de caballeros.
genuine ['dʒenjuɪn] adj genuino,-a, auténtico,-a. 2 (sincere) sincero,-a. – 3

genuinely *adv* verdaderamente, realmente.

genus ['dʒiːnəs] *n* género. ▲ *pl* **genera** ['dʒenərə].

geographic(al) [dʒɪə'græfɪk(əl)] *adj* geográfico,-a.

geography [dʒɪ'ɒgrəfɪ] *n* geografía.

geologic(al) [dʒɪə'lɒdʒɪk(əl)] *adj* geológico,-a.

geology [dʒɪ'ɒlədʒɪ] *n* geología.

geometric(al) [dʒɪə'metrɪk(əl)] *adj* geométrico,-a.

geometry [dʒɪ'ɒmɪtrɪ] *n* geometría.

geranium [dʒɪ'reɪnɪəm] *n* geranio.

geriatric [dʒerɪ'ætrɪk] *adj* geriátrico,-a.

germ [dʒɜːm] *n* germen *m*.

germinate ['dʒɜːmɪneɪt] *t-i* germinar.

gerund ['dʒerənd] *n* gerundio.

gesticulate [dʒes'tɪkjʊleɪt] *i* gesticular.

gesticulation [dʒestɪkjʊ'leɪʃən] *n* gesticulación.

gesture ['dʒestʃəʳ] *n* ademán *m*, gesto. 2 *(token)* muestra. – 3 *i* hacer un ademán. ●*as a ~ of,* en señal de.

get [get] *t (obtain)* obtener, conseguir: *I want to ~ a job,* quiero conseguir un trabajo; *she got £1,000 for her car,* le dieron mil libras por su coche. 2 *(receive)* recibir: *I got a bike for my birthday,* me regalaron una bici para mi cumpleaños. 3 *(fetch)* traer. 4 *(catch)* coger. 5 *(persuade)* persuadir, convencer: *can you ~ him to help us?,* ¿puedes convencerlo para que nos ayude? 6 *(meals, drinks)* preparar. 7 *fam (jokes)* entender: *I don't ~ it,* no lo entiendo. 8 *(annoy)* poner nervioso,-a. – 9 *i (become)* ponerse, volverse: *to ~ better/dirty/tired/wet,* mejorar/ensuciarse/cansarse/mojarse. 10 *(go)* ir: *how do you ~ there?,* ¿cómo se va hasta allí? 11 *(arrive)* llegar. 12 *(come to)* llegar a: *you'll ~ to like it in the end,* acabará gustándote. ◆*to ~ about i* moverse; *(travel)* viajar. ◆*to ~ across t (cross)* cruzar. 2 *(communicate)* comunicar. ◆*to ~ ahead i (manage)* adelantar, progresar. ◆*to ~ along i (manage)* arreglárselas. 2 *(leave)* marcharse. ◆*to ~ along with t* llevarse (bien) con. ◆*to ~ around i* moverse; *(travel)* viajar. ◆*to ~ around to t* encontrar el tiempo para. ◆*to ~ at t (reach)* alcanzar, llegar a. 2 *(insinuate)* insinuar. 3 *(criticize)* meterse con. ◆*to ~ away i* escaparse. ◆*to ~ away with t* salir impune de. ◆*to ~ back i (return)* volver, regresar. – 2 *t (recover)* recuperar. ◆*to ~ behind i* atrasarse. ◆*to ~ by i (manage)* arreglárselas.

2 *(pass)* pasar. ◆*to ~ down t (depress)* deprimir. – 2 *i (descend)* bajarse. ◆*to ~ down to t* ponerse a. ◆*to ~ in i (arrive)* llegar. 2 *(enter)* entrar; *(car)* subir. ◆*to ~ into t (arrive)* llegar a. 2 *(enter)* entrar en; *(car)* subir a. ◆*to ~ off t (remove)* quitar. 2 *(vehicle, horse, etc.)* bajarse de. – 3 *i* bajarse. 4 *(leave)* salir. 5 *(begin)* comenzar. 6 *(escape)* escaparse. ◆*to ~ off with t* ligar. ◆*to ~ on t (vehicle)* subir(se) a; *(bicycle, horse, etc.)* montar. – 2 *i (make progress)* progresar, avanzar. 3 *(succeed)* tener éxito. 4 *(be friendly)* llevarse bien, avenirse. 5 *(continue)* seguir. 6 *(grow old)* envejecerse. ◆*to ~ on for t* ser casi: *it's getting on for 5 o'clock,* son· casi las cinco. ◆*to ~ onto t (person)* ponerse en contacto con. 2 *(subject)* empezar a hablar de. ◆*to ~ out t (thing)* sacar; *(stain)* quitar. – 2 *i (leave)* salir. 3 *(escape)* escapar. ◆*to ~ out of t (avoid)* librarse de. ◆*to ~ over t (illness)* recuperarse de. 2 *(loss)* sobreponerse a. 3 *(obstacle)* salvar; *(difficulty)* vencer. 4 *(idea)* comunicar. ◆*to ~ over with t* acabar con. ◆*to ~ round t (obstacle)* salvar. 2 *(law)* soslayar. 3 *(person)* convencer. ◆*to ~ round to t* encontrar el tiempo para. ◆*to ~ through i (on 'phone)* conseguir hablar *(to,* con). 2 *(arrive)* llegar. – 3 *t (finish)* acabar. 4 *(consume)* consumir; *(money)* gastar; *(drink)* beber. 5 *(exam)* aprobar. 6 *(make understand)* hacer comprender. ◆*to ~ together t-i* reunir(se), juntar(se). ◆*to ~ up t-i* levantar(se). ◆*to ~ up to t* hacer. ●*to ~ on one's nerves,* irritar, poner nervioso,-a; *to ~ ready,* preparar(se); *to ~ rid of,* deshacerse de; *to ~ to know sb.,* llegar a conocer a algn. ▲ *pt* **got**; *pp* **got,** US **gotten.**

getaway ['getəweɪ] *n fam* fuga.

get-together ['gettəgeðəʳ] *n fam* reunión.

getup ['getʌp] *n fam* atavío.

ghastly ['gɑːstlɪ] *adj* horrible, horroroso,-a. 2 *(pale)* lívido,-a.

gherkin ['gɜːkɪn] *n* pepinillo.

ghetto ['getəʊ] *n* ghetto, gueto.

ghost [gəʊst] *n* fantasma *m*.

ghoul [guːl] *n* persona de gustos macabros.

giant ['dʒaɪənt] *n* gigante,-a. – 2 *adj* gigante, gigantesco,-a.

gibberish ['dʒɪbərɪʃ] *n* galimatías *m inv*.

gibbet ['dʒɪbɪt] *n* horca, patíbulo.

gibe [dʒaɪb] *n* mofa. – 2 *i* mofarse *(at,* de).

giddy ['gɪdɪ] *adj* mareado,-a.

gift [gɪft] n (present) regalo. 2 (talent) don m.

gifted ['gɪftɪd] adj dotado,-a.

gigantic [dʒaɪ'gæntɪk] adj gigantesco,-a.

giggle ['gɪgəl] n risita tonta. — 2 i reírse tontamente.

gild [gɪld] t dorar.

gill [gɪl] n (of fish) agalla.

gilt [gɪlt] adj-n dorado,-a (m).

gimmick ['gɪmɪk] n reclamo.

gin [dʒɪn] n ginebra.

ginger ['dʒɪndʒəʳ] n (spice) jengibre m. — 2 adj (hair) rojo,-a; (person) pelirrojo,-a.

gingerly ['dʒɪndʒəlɪ] adv cautelosamente.

gipsy ['dʒɪpsɪ] n gitano,-a.

giraffe [dʒɪ'rɑːf] n jirafa.

girdle ['gɜːdəl] n faja.

girl [gɜːl] n chica, muchacha, joven f; (small) niña.

girlfriend ['gɜːlfrend] n novia. 2 us amiga, compañera.

girlish ['gɜːlɪʃ] adj de niña.

giro ['dʒaɪrəʊ] n giro.

gist [dʒɪst] n lo esencial.

give [gɪv] n elasticidad. — 2 t dar. 3 (as a gift) dar, regalar, donar. 4 (pay) pagar. 5 (yield) ceder. — 6 i dar de sí, ceder. ◆to ~ away t regalar. 2 (betray) delatar, traicionar. ◆to ~ back t devolver. ◆to ~ in i ceder, rendirse. — 2 t entregar. ◆to ~ off t desprender. ◆to ~ out t repartir. 2 (announce) anunciar. — 3 i acabarse, agotarse. ◆to ~ over i parar. ◆to ~ up t dejar: to ~ up smoking, dejar de fumar. — 2 i (surrender) rendirse; (to police etc.) entregarse. ●to ~ sb. to understand that, dar a entender a algn. que; to ~ sb. up for dead, dar por muerto,-a algn.; to ~ the game away, descubrir el pastel; to ~ way, ceder, AUTO ceder el paso. ▲ pt gave; pp given ['gɪvən].

glacial ['gleɪsɪəl] adj glacial.

glacier ['glæsɪəʳ] n glaciar m.

glad [glæd] adj contento,-a. — 2 gladly adv de buena gana, con mucho gusto. ●to be ~ of, agradecer.

gladden ['glædən] t alegrar.

glamorize ['glæməraɪz] t hacer más atractivo,-a.

glamorous ['glæmərəs] adj atractivo,-a. 2 (charming) encantador,-ra.

glamour ['glæməʳ] n atractivo. 2 (charm) encanto.

glance [glɑːns] n mirada, vistazo. — 2 i dar una mirada, echar un vistazo (at, a). ●at first ~, a primera vista.

gland [glænd] n glándula.

glare [gleəʳ] n luz f deslumbrante. 2 AUTO deslumbramiento. 3 (look) mirada feroz. — 4 i deslumbrar. 5 (look) mirar ferozmente (at, -).

glaring ['gleərɪŋ] adj deslumbrador,-ra. 2 (blatant) patente, evidente.

glass [glɑːs] n (material) vidrio, cristal m. 2 (for drinking) vaso; (with stem) copa. 3 pl gafas fpl.

glassware ['glɑːsweəʳ] n cristalería.

glassy ['glɑːsɪ] adj (eyes) vidrioso,-a.

glaze [gleɪz] n vidriado. — 2 t (pottery) vidriar. 3 (windows) poner cristales a. 4 CULIN glasear.

gleam [gliːm] n destello. — 2 i relucir, brillar. ●a ~ of hope, un rayo de esperanza.

glean [gliːn] t espigar. 2 fig recoger.

glee [gliː] n regocijo.

glen [glen] n cañada.

glib [glɪb] adj charlatán,-ana.

glide [glaɪd] n deslizamiento. 2 AV planeo. — 3 i deslizarse. 4 AV planear.

glider ['glaɪdəʳ] n planeador m.

glimmer ['glɪməʳ] n luz f tenue. — 2 i brillar con luz ténue. ●a ~ of hope, un rayo de esperanza.

glimpse [glɪmps] n visión f fugaz. — 2 t vislumbrar. ●to catch a ~ of, vislumbrar.

glint [glɪnt] n destello, centelleo. — 2 i destellar, centellear.

glisten ['glɪsən] i brillar, relucir.

glitter ['glɪtəʳ] n brillo. — 2 i brillar, relucir.

gloat [gləʊt] i regocijarse/recrearse (over, con).

global ['gləʊbəl] adj mundial. 2 (total) global.

globe [gləʊb] n globo. 2 (map) globo terrestre.

globule ['glɒbjuːl] n glóbulo.

gloom [gluːm] n penumbra. 2 (sadness) tristeza. 3 (of place) desolación.

gloomy ['gluːmɪ] adj lóbrego,-a. 2 (sad) triste. 3 (pessimistic) pesimista.

glorify ['glɔːrɪfaɪ] t glorificar.

glorious ['glɔːrɪəs] adj glorioso,-a. 2 (wonderful) espléndido,-a, magnífico,-a.

glory ['glɔːrɪ] n gloria. 2 fig esplendor m. — 3 i gloriarse (in, de).

gloss [glɒs] n lustre m, brillo. 2 (explanation) glosa. — 3 t glosar. ■ ~ paint, esmalte m brillante.

glossary ['glɒsərɪ] n glosario.

glossy ['glɒsɪ] adj brillante, lustroso,-a.

glove [glʌv] *n* guante *m*.
glow [gləʊ] *n* luz *f*, brillo. **2** *fig* sensación de bienestar/satisfacción. − **3** *i* brillar.
glower ['glaʊəʳ] *i* mirar con ceño.
glowing ['gləʊɪŋ] *adj fig* entusiasta.
glucose ['gluːkəʊz] *n* glucosa.
glue [gluː] *n* cola. − **2** *t* encolar, pegar.
glum [glʌm] *adj* desanimado,-a.
glut [glʌt] *n* superabundancia. − **2** *t* (*market*) inundar, saturar. ●*to* ~ *o.s.*, hartarse.
glutton ['glʌtn] *n* glotón,-ona.
gluttony ['glʌtənɪ] *n* glotonería.
glycerine [glɪsə'riːn] *n* glicerina.
gnarled [nɑːld] *adj* nudoso,-a.
gnash [næʃ] *i* hacer rechinar.
gnat [næt] *n* mosquito.
gnaw [nɔː] *t* roer.
go [gəʊ] *n* (*energy*) energía, empuje *m*. **2** (*turn*) turno: *it's my* ~, me toca a mí. **3** (*try*) intento. − **4** *i* ir. **5** (*leave*) marcharse, irse; (*bus, train, etc.*) salir. **6** (*vanish*) desaparecer. **7** (*function*) funcionar. **8** (*become*) volverse, ponerse, quedarse. **9** (*fit*) entrar, caber. **10** (*break*) romperse, estropearse. **11** (*be kept*) guardarse. − **12** *t* (*make a noise*) hacer: *it goes ticktock*, hace tic-tac. ◆*to* ~ *after* *t* perseguir. ◆*to* ~ *along with* *t* estar de acuerdo con. **2** (*accompany*) acompañar. ◆*to* ~ *around* *i* (*be enough*) bastar, ser suficiente. ◆*to* ~ *away* *i* marcharse. ◆*to* ~ *back* *i* volver. ◆*to* ~ *back on* *t* romper. ◆*to* ~ *by* *i* pasar. ◆*to* ~ *down* *i* bajar; (*tyre*) deshincharse. **2** (*be received*) ser acogido,-a. ◆*to* ~ *down with* *t* coger. ◆*to* ~ *for* *t* (*attack*) atacar. **2** (*fetch*) ir a buscar. **3** *fam* (*like*) gustar. **4** *fam* (*be valid*) valer para. ◆*to* ~ *in for* *t* dedicarse a: *I don't* ~ *in for that*, eso no me va. **2** (*exam*) presentarse para. ◆*to* ~ *into* *t* (*investigate*) investigar. **2** (*crash*) chocar contra. ◆*to* ~ *off* *i* (*bomb*) estallar; (*alarm*) sonar; (*gun*) dispararse. **2** (*food*) estropearse. − **3** *t* perder el gusto/interés por. ◆*to* ~ *on* *i* (*continue*) seguir. **2** (*happen*) pasar. **3** (*complain*) quejarse (*about,* de). ◆*to* ~ *out* *i* salir. **2** (*fire, light*) apagarse. ◆*to* ~ *over* *t* (*check, revise*) revisar. ◆*to* ~ *over to* *t* pasarse a. ◆*to* ~ *round* *i* dar vueltas, girar. ◆*to* ~ *through* *t* (*undergo*) sufrir, padecer. **2** (*examine*) examinar; (*search*) registrar. − **3** *i* ser aprobado,-a. ◆*to* ~ *through with* *t* llevar a cabo. ◆*to* ~ *under* *i* hundirse; *fig* fracasar. ◆*to* ~ *up* *i* subir. **2** (*explode*) estallar. ◆*to* ~ *without* *t* pasar sin, prescindir de. ●*to be all the* ~, estar muy de

moda; *to* ~ *about one's business*, ocuparse de sus asuntos; *to* ~ *to sleep*, dormirse; *to have a* ~ *at sb.*, criticar a algn.; *to make a* ~ *of sth.*, tener éxito en algo. ▲ *pt went; pp gone*.
goal [gəʊl] *n* SP meta, portería. **2** SP (*point*) gol *m*, tanto. **3** (*aim*) fin *m*, objeto. ●*to score a* ~, marcar un tanto.
goalkeeper ['gəʊlkiːpəʳ] *n* portero, guardameta *m*.
goat [gəʊt] *n* (*female*) cabra; (*male*) macho cabrío.
gobble ['gɒbəl] *t* engullir.
go-between ['gəʊbɪtwiːn] *n* intermediario,-a. **2** (*between lovers*) alcahueta.
goblet ['gɒblət] *n* copa.
god [gɒd] *n* dios *m*.
godchild ['gɒdtʃaɪld] *n* ahijado,-a.
goddaughter ['gɒddɔːtəʳ] *n* ahijada.
goddess ['gɒdəs] *n* diosa.
godfather ['gɒdfɑːðəʳ] *n* padrino.
godforsaken ['gɒdfəseɪkən] *adj* dejado,-a de la mano de Dios.
godmother ['gɒdmʌðəʳ] *n* madrina.
godparents ['gɒdpeərənts] *npl* padrinos *mpl*.
godsend ['gɒdsend] *n* regalo caído del cielo.
godson ['gɒdsʌn] *n* ahijado.
goggle ['gɒgəl] *i* quedarse atónito,-a. − **2** *npl* gafas *fpl* protectoras.
going ['gəʊɪŋ] *n* (*leaving*) ida. **2** (*pace*) paso, ritmo. **3** (*conditions*) estado del camino. − **4** *adj* (*current*) actual. **5** (*business*) que marcha bien.
going-over [gəʊɪŋ'əʊvəʳ] *n fam* inspección. **2** (*beating*) paliza.
goings-on [gəʊɪŋz'ɒn] *npl fam* tejemanejes *mpl*.
gold [gəʊld] *n* (*metal*) oro. **2** (*colour*) dorado. ■ ~ *leaf*, pan *m* de oro.
golden ['gəʊldən] *adj* de oro. **2** (*colour*) dorado,-a.
goldfish ['gəʊldfɪʃ] *n inv* pez *m* de colores.
goldsmith ['gəʊldsmɪθ] *n* orfebre *m*.
golf [gɒlf] *n* golf *m*. ■ ~ *club*, (*stick*) palo de golf; (*place*) club *m* de golf; ~ *course*, campo de golf.
golfer ['gɒlfəʳ] *n* jugador,-a de golf.
gone [gɒn] *pp* → **go**.
gong [gɒŋ] *n* gong *m*, batintín *m*.
good [gʊd] *adj* bueno,-a; (*before m sing noun*) buen. **2** (*healthy*) sano,-a. − **3** *n* bien *m*. **4** *pl* bienes *mpl*. **5** *pl* COM género *m sing*, artículos *mpl*. − **6** *interj* ¡bien! ●*as* ~ *as*, prácticamente; *a* ~ *deal (of)*,

goodbye

112

bastante; *for* ~, para siempre; ~ *after-noon/evening,* buenas tardes; *Good Friday,* Viernes Santo; ~ *morning,* buenos días; ~ *night,* buenas noches; *to do* ~, hacer bien. ▲ *comp better; superl best.*

goodbye [gʊd'baɪ] *n* adiós *m.* − 2 *interj* ¡adiós! ●*to say* ~ *to,* despedirse de.

good-for-nothing ['gʊdfənʌθɪŋ] *adj-n* inútil *(mf).*

good-humoured [gʊd'hjuːməd] *adj* de buen humor.

good-looking [gʊd'lʊkɪŋ] *adj* guapo,-a.

good-natured [gʊd'neɪtʃɪd] *adj* bondadoso,-a.

goodness ['gʊdnəs] *n (virtue)* bondad. 2 *(in food)* lo nutritivo. ●*for* ~ *sake!,* ¡por Dios!; *my* ~*!,* ¡Dios mío!

goodwill [gʊd'wɪl] *n* buena voluntad.

goody ['gʊdɪ] *n fam* el bueno. 2 *pl* golosinas *fpl.*

goody-goody ['gʊdɪgʊdɪ] *adj-n fam* santurrón,-ona.

goose [guːs] *n* ganso, oca. ■ ~ *pimples,* piel *f sing* de gallina. ▲ *pl geese.*

gooseflesh ['guːsfleʃ] *n* piel *f* de gallina.

gore [gɔːʳ] *n* sangre *f* derramada. − 2 *t* cornear.

gorge [gɔːdʒ] *n* desfiladero. ●*to* ~ *o.s. on,* atiborrarse/hartarse de.

gorgeous ['gɔːdʒəs] *adj* magnífico,-a, espléndido,-a. 2 *(person)* guapo,-a.

gorilla [gə'rɪlə] *n* gorila *m.*

gory ['gɔːrɪ] *adj* sangriento,-a.

gosh [gɒʃ] *interj fam* ¡cielos!

go-slow [gəu'sləu] *n* huelga de celo.

gospel ['gɒspəl] *n* evangelio.

gossip ['gɒsɪp] *n (talk)* cotilleo, chismorreo. 2 *(person)* cotilla *mf.* − 3 *i* cotillear, chismorrear. ■ ~ *column,* crónica de sociedad.

gossipy ['gɒsɪpɪ] *adj fam (style)* informal.

got [gɒt] *pt & pp* → **get.**

gourmet ['gʊəmeɪ] *n* gastrónomo,-a.

gout [gaʊt] *n* MED gota.

govern ['gʌvən] *t* gobernar. 2 GRAM regir. 3 *(determine)* dictar.

governess ['gʌvənəs] *n* institutriz *f.*

government ['gʌvənmənt] *n* gobierno.

governmental [gʌvən'mentəl] *adj* gubernamental.

governor ['gʌvənəʳ] *n* gobernador,-ra. 2 *(prison)* director,-ra. 3 *(school)* administrador,-ra.

gown [gaʊn] *n* vestido largo. 2 *(judge's etc.)* toga.

grab [græb] *t* asir, coger. 2 *fam* entusiasmar: *how does that* ~ *you?,* ¿qué te parece eso?

grace [greɪs] *n* gracia. 2 *(blessing)* bendición. 3 *(courtesy)* delicadeza, cortesía. 4 *(delay)* plazo. − 5 *t (adorn)* adornar. 6 *(honour)* honrar.

graceful ['greɪsfʊl] *adj* elegante.

gracious ['greɪʃəs] *adj* gracioso. 2 *(polite)* cortés. 3 *(kind)* amable. 4 *(monarch)* gracioso,-a. − 5 *interj* ¡Dios mío!

grade [greɪd] *n* grado. 2 *(of quality)* clase *f,* calidad. 3 US *(gradient)* pendiente *f.* 4 US *(mark)* nota. 5 US *(form)* clase *f.* − 6 *t* clasificar. ●*to make the* ~, tener éxito.

gradient ['greɪdɪənt] *n* pendiente *f.*

gradual ['grædjʊəl] *adj* gradual. − 2 *gradually adv* poco a poco, gradualmente.

graduate ['grædjʊət] *n* graduado,-a, licenciado,-a. − 2 *t* graduar. ▲ *En 2 (verbo)* ['grædjʊeɪt].

graduation [grædjʊ'eɪʃən] *n* graduación.

graffiti [grə'fiːtɪ] *npl* grafiti *mpl.*

graft [grɑːft] *n* AGR MED injerto. 2 GB *fam* trabajo duro. 3 US corrupción. − 4 *t* AGR MED injertar. 5 GB *fam* currar. 6 US hacer trampas.

grain [greɪn] *n* gen grano. 2 *(cereals)* cereales *mpl.* 3 *(in wood)* fibra.

gram [græm] *n* gramo.

grammar ['græməʳ] *n* gramática. ■ GB ~ *school,* instituto de segunda enseñanza.

grammatical [grə'mætɪkəl] *adj* gramatical. 2 *(correct)* correcto,-a.

gramme [græm] *n* gramo.

granary ['grænərɪ] *n* granero.

grand [grænd] *adj (splendid)* grandioso,-a, espléndido,-a. 2 *(impressive)* impresionante. 3 *(person)* distinguido,-a. 4 *fam (great)* fenomenal. ■ ~ *piano,* piano de cola; ~ *total,* total *m.*

grandchild ['græntʃaɪld] *n* nieto,-a.

granddad ['grændæd] *n fam* abuelo.

granddaughter ['grændɔːtəʳ] *n* nieta.

grandeur ['grændʒəʳ] *n* grandeza.

grandfather ['grænfɑːðəʳ] *n* abuelo. ■ ~ *clock,* reloj *m* de caja.

grandiose ['grændɪəus] *adj* grandioso,-a.

grandma ['grænmɑː] *n fam* abuela.

grandmother ['grænmʌðəʳ] *n* abuela.

grandpa ['grænpɑː] *n fam* abuelo.

grandparents ['grænpeərənts] *npl* abuelos *mpl.*

grandson ['grænsʌn] *n* nieto.

grandstand ['grændstænd] *n* tribuna.

granite ['grænɪt] *n* granito.

granny ['grænɪ] *n fam* abuela.
grant [grɑːnt] *n* EDUC beca. **2** *(subsidy)* subvención. − **3** *t* conceder. **4** *(admit)* reconocer. ●*to take sth. for granted,* dar algo por sentado.
granulated ['grænjʊleɪtɪd] *adj* granulado,-a.
grape [greɪp] *n* uva.
grapefruit ['greɪpfruːt] *n* pomelo.
grapevine ['greɪpvaɪn] *n* vid *f; (climbing)* parra. ●*to hear sth. on the* ~, enterarse de algo por ahí.
graph [grɑːf] *n* gráfica. ■ ~ *paper,* papel cuadriculado.
graphic ['græfɪk] *adj* gráfico,-a.
graphite ['græfaɪt] *n* grafito.
grapple ['græpəl] *i* forcejear. ●*to* ~ *with,* luchar con; *(problem)* esforzarse por resolver.
grasp [grɑːsp] *n* asimiento. **2** *(of hands)* apretón *m.* **3** *(understanding)* comprensión. − **4** *t* asir, agarrar. **5** *(understand)* comprender. ●*to have a good* ~ *of,* dominar.
grass [grɑːs] *n* hierba. **2** *(lawn)* césped *m.* **3** *(pasture)* pasto. **4** *sl (drug)* hierba. − **5** *i* chivar *(on,* a). ■ POL ~ *roots,* base *f.*
grasshopper ['grɑːshɒpəʳ] *n* saltamontes *m inv.*
grassland ['grɑːslænd] *n* prado, tierra de pasto.
grassy ['grɑːsɪ] *adj* cubierto,-a de hierba.
grate [greɪt] *n (in fireplace)* rejilla. **2** *(fireplace)* chimenea. − **3** *t* CULIN rallar. − **4** *t-i* (hacer) rechinar.
grateful ['greɪtfʊl] *adj* agradecido,-a. ●*to be* ~ *for,* agradecer.
gratification [grætɪfɪ'keɪʃən] *n (pleasure)* placer *m,* satisfacción. **2** *(reward)* gratificación.
gratify ['grætɪfaɪ] *t* complacer, satisfacer.
gratifying ['grætɪfaɪɪŋ] *adj* grato,-a, gratificante.
grating ['greɪtɪŋ] *n* rejilla, reja. − **2** *adj (noise)* chirriante. **3** *(voice)* irritante.
gratis ['grætɪs] *adv* gratis, de balde.
gratitude ['grætɪtjuːd] *n* gratitud, agradecimiento.
gratuitous [grə'tjuːɪtəs] *adj* gratuito,-a.
gratuity [grə'tjuːɪtɪ] *n* gratificación. **2** *(tip)* propina.
grave [greɪv] *n* tumba. − **2** *adj (serious)* grave, serio,-a. **3** GRAM *(accent)* grave. ▲ *En 3* [grɑːv].
gravedigger ['greɪvdɪgəʳ] *n* sepulturero,-a, enterrador,-ra.
gravel ['grævəl] *n* grava, gravilla.

gravestone ['greɪvstəʊn] *n* lápida.
graveyard ['greɪvjɑːd] *n* cementerio.
gravitate ['grævɪteɪt] *i* gravitar. ●*to* ~ *towards* *t* sentirse atraido,-a por.
gravity ['grævɪtɪ] *n* gravedad.
gravy ['greɪvɪ] *n* CULIN salsa, jugo.
gray [greɪ] *adj* US → **grey**.
graze [greɪz] *n* roce *m,* rasguño. − **2** *t (scrape)* rozar, rascar. − **3** *i* pacer, pastar.
grease [griːs] *n* grasa. − **2** *t* engrasar.
greasy ['griːsɪ] *adj* grasiento,-a; *(hair, food)* graso,-a. **2** *(slippery)* resbaladizo,-a.
great [greɪt] *adj* grande; *(before sing noun)* gran. **2** *fam (excellent)* estupendo,-a, fantástico,-a. − **3** *greatly adv* muy, mucho.
great-aunt [greɪt'ɑːnt] *n* tía abuela.
great-grandchild [greɪt'græntʃaɪld] *n* bisnieto,-a.
great-granddaughter [greɪt'grændɔːtəʳ] *n* bisnieta.
great-grandfather [greɪt'grænfɑːðəʳ] *n* bisabuelo.
great-grandmother [greɪt'grænmʌðəʳ] *n* bisabuela.
great-grandson [greɪt'grænsʌn] *n* bisnieto.
great-great-grandfather [greɪtgreɪt'grænfɑːðəʳ] *n* tatarabuelo.
great-great-grandmother [greɪtgreɪt'grænmʌðəʳ] *n* tatarabuela.
greatness ['greɪtnəs] *n* grandeza.
greed [griːd], **greediness** ['griːdɪnəs] *n* codicia, avaricia. **2** *(food)* gula.
greedy ['griːdɪ] *adj* codicioso,-a, avaro,-a. **2** *(food)* glotón,-ona.
green [griːn] *adj* verde. **2** *(inexperienced)* novato,-a; *(gullible)* ingenuo,-a. **3** *(pale)* pálido,-a. − **4** *n (colour)* verde *m.* **5** *(in golf)* green *m.* **6** *pl* verduras *fpl.*
greenery ['griːnərɪ] *n* follaje *m.*
greengrocer ['griːngrəʊsəʳ] *n* verdulero,-a.
greenhouse ['griːnhaʊs] *n* invernadero.
greet [griːt] *t* saludar. **2** *(welcome)* dar la bienvenida a. **3** *(receive)* recibir.
greeting ['griːtɪŋ] *n* saludo. **2** *(welcome)* bienvenida. ■ *greetings card,* tarjeta de felicitación.
gregarious [gre'geərɪəs] *adj* gregario,-a.
gremlin ['gremlɪn] *n* duende *m.*
grenade [grɪ'neɪd] *n* granada.
grew [gruː] *pt* → **grow**.
grey [greɪ] *adj gen* gris. **2** *(hair)* cano,-a. **3** *(gloomy)* triste. − **4** *n* gris *m.*
greyhound ['greɪhaʊnd] *n* galgo.

grid [grɪd] *n* reja, parrilla. **2** ELEC red *f* nacional. **3** *(on map)* cuadrícula.

griddle ['grɪdəl] *n* CULIN plancha.

grief [griːf] *n* dolor *m*, pena. ●*to come to* ~, sufrir un percance; *(fail)* fracasar; *fam good* ~!, ¡Dios mío!

grievance [griːvəns] *n* agravio.

grieve [griːv] *t-i* afligir(se).

grievous ['griːvəs] *adj* doloroso,-a, penoso,-a. **2** *(serious)* muy grave.

grill [grɪl] *n* CULIN parrilla. **2** CULIN *(dish)* parrillada. – **3** CULIN *t* asar a la parrilla. **4** *fam* interrogar.

grille [grɪl] *n* rejilla.

grim [grɪm] *adj* terrible. **2** *(place)* lúgubre, deprimente. **3** *(person)* severo,-a, muy serio,-a; *(expression)* ceñudo,-a. **4** *fam* malísimo,-a.

grimace ['grɪməs] *n* mueca. – **2** *i* hacer una mueca.

grime [graɪm] *n* mugre *f*, suciedad.

grimy ['graɪmɪ] *adj* mugriento,-a, sucio,-a.

grin [grɪn] *n* sonrisa. – **2** sonreír.

grind [graɪnd] *t (coffee, corn, etc.)* moler; *(stone)* pulverizar. **2** *(sharpen)* afilar. **3** *(teeth)* hacer rechinar. – **4** *n fam* rutina. ▲ *pt & pp* **ground**.

grinder ['graɪndə'] *n (for coffee etc.)* molinillo.

grindstone ['graɪnstəʊn] *n* muela, piedra de afilar.

grip [grɪp] *n* asimiento; *(handshake)* apretón *m*; *(of tyre)* adherencia. **2** *(control)* dominio. – **3** *t* asir, agarrar; *(hand)* apretar. ●*to lose one's* ~, perder el control.

gripe [graɪp] *fam i* quejarse. – **2** *n* queja.

gripping ['grɪpɪŋ] *adj* apasionante.

grisly ['grɪzlɪ] *adj* espeluznante.

grit [grɪt] *n (fine)* arena; *(coarse)* gravilla. **2** *fam* valor *m*. ●*to* ~ *one's teeth,* apretar los dientes.

grizzly bear [grɪzlɪ'beə'] *n* oso pardo.

groan [grəʊn] *n* gemido, quejido. **2** *fam (of disapproval)* gruñido. – **3** *i* gemir. **4** *(creak)* crujir. **5** *fam (complain)* quejarse.

grocer ['grəʊsə'] *n* tendero,-a. ■ *grocer's (shop),* tienda de comestibles.

groceries ['grəʊsərɪz] *npl* comestibles *mpl*.

groggy ['grɒgɪ] *adj fam* grogui, atontado,-a. **2** *(weak)* débil.

groin [grɔɪn] *n* ingle *f*.

groom [gruːm] *n (bridegroom)* novio. **2** *(for horses)* mozo de cuadra. – **3** *t (take care of) (horse)* almohazar; *(person)* cuidar, arreglar, asear. **4** *(prepare)* praparar.

groove [gruːv] *n* ranura. **2** *(on record)* surco.

grope [grəʊp] *i* andar a tientas. – **2** *t sl* sobar. ●*to* ~ *for,* buscar a tientas.

gross [grəʊs] *adj (fat)* obeso,-a. **2** *(coarse)* grosero,-a, tosco,-a, basto,-a. **3** *(injustice)* flagrante. **4** *(error)* craso,-a. **5** COM ECON bruto,-a. – **6** *n* COM gruesa. – **7** *t* ganar en bruto. – **8** *grossly adv* enormemente.

grotesque [grəʊ'tesk] *adj* grotesco,-a.

grotty ['grɒtɪ] *adj* GB *sl* asqueroso,-a, malísimo,-a.

grouch [graʊtʃ] *fam n* gruñón,-ona. – **2** *i* refunfuñar, quejarse.

grouchy ['graʊtʃɪ] *adj* refunfuñón,-ona.

ground [graʊnd] *pt & pp* → **grind**. – **2** *adj* molido,-a. – **3** *n (floor)* tierra, suelo. **4** *(terrain)* terreno. **5** *(for football, battle, etc.)* campo. **6** *pl (reasons)* razón *f sing*, motivo *m sing*. **7** *pl (of coffee)* poso *m sing*. **8** *pl (gardens)* jardines *mpl*. – **9** *t* AV obligar a quedarse en tierra. **10** *(base)* fundamentar. – **11** *i* MAR encallar. ■ ~ *floor,* planta baja.

grounding ['graʊndɪŋ] *n* base *f*.

groundnut ['graʊndnʌt] *n* GB cacahuete *m*.

group [gruːp] *n* grupo, conjunto. – **2** *t-i* agrupar(se), juntar(se).

grouse [graʊs] *n (bird)* urogallo. – **2** *i fam (complain)* quejarse.

grove [grəʊv] *n* arboleda.

grovel ['grɒvəl] *i* arrastrarse.

grow [grəʊ] *i* crecer. **2** *(increase)* aumentarse. **3** *(become)* hacerse, volverse. – **4** *t (crops)* cultivar. **5** *(beard)* dejarse (crecer). ◆*to* ~ *into t* convertirse en. ◆*to* ~ *on t* llegar a gustar. ◆*to* ~ *up i* hacerse mayor. ▲ *pt* **grew**; *pp* **grown**.

grower ['grəʊə'] *n* cultivador,-ra.

growl [graʊl] *n* gruñido. – **2** *i* gruñir.

grown [grəʊn] *pp* → **grow**.

grown-up ['grəʊnʌp] *adj-n* adulto,-a.

growth [grəʊθ] *n (process)* crecimiento; *(increase)* aumento. **2** *(tumour)* bulto, tumor *m*.

grub [grʌb] *n* larva, gusano. **2** *fam* manduca.

grubby ['grʌbɪ] *adj* sucio,-a.

grudge [grʌdʒ] *n* resentimiento, rencor *m*. – **2** *t* dar/hacer a regañadientes. **3** *(envy)* envidiar.

grudgingly ['grʌdʒɪŋlɪ] *adv* de mala gana.

gruelling ['gruːəlɪŋ] *adj* agotador,-ra.

gruesome ['gruːsəm] *adj* horrible, horripilante.

gruff [grʌf] *adj (manner)* rudo,-a, malhumorado,-a. **2** *(voice)* bronco,-a.

gruffness ['grʌfnəs] n (of manner) mal-humor m. 2 (of voice) bronquedad.
grumble ['grʌmbəl] n queja. – 2 i refunfuñar.
grumbler ['grʌmbləʳ] n refunfuñón,-ona.
grumpy ['grʌmpɪ] adj gruñón,-ona. – 2 **grumpily** adv de mal humor.
grunt [grʌnt] n gruñido. – 2 i gruñir.
guarantee [gærən'tiː] n garantía. – 2 t garantizar. 3 (assure) asegurar.
guarantor [gærən'tɔːʳ] n garante mf.
guard [gɑːd] n MIL (duty) guardia f; (sentry) guardia mf; (group of sentries) guardia f. 2 (on train) jefe m de tren. 3 (on machine) dispositivo de seguridad. – 4 t guardar, proteger, defender. – 5 i guardarse. ●off one's ~, desprevenido,-a; on ~, de guardia; on one's ~, en guardia. ■ ~ dog, perro guardián.
guarded ['gɑːdɪd] adj cauteloso,-a .
guardian ['gɑːdɪən] n guardián,-ana. 2 JUR tutor,-ra. ■ ~ angel, ángel m de la guarda.
guer(r)illa [gə'rɪlə] n guerrillero,-a. ■ ~ warfare, guerra de guerrillas.
guess [ges] n conjetura, suposición. 2 (estimate) cálculo. – 3 t-i adivinar, imaginarse. 4 fam (suppose) suponer.
guesswork ['geswɜːk] n conjetura.
guest [gest] n huésped,-a, invitado,-a. 2 (in hotel) cliente,-a, huésped,-a.
guesthouse ['gesthaus] n casa de huéspedes.
guffaw [gʌ'fɔː] n carcajada. – 2 i reír(se) a carcajadas.
guidance ['gaɪdəns] n orientación.
guide [gaɪd] n (person) guía mf. 2 (book, device) guía f. – 3 t guiar, orientar.
guidebook ['gaɪdbʊk] n guía f.
guideline ['gaɪdlaɪn] n pauta, directriz f.
guild [gɪld] n gremio, cofradía.
guile [gaɪl] n astucia.
guileless ['gaɪlləs] adj ingenuo,-a.
guillotine ['gɪlətiːn] n guillotina. – 2 t guillotinar.
guilt [gɪlt] n culpa. 2 JUR culpabilidad.
guilty ['gɪltɪ] adj culpable.
guinea ['gɪnɪ] n guinea. ■ ~ pig, conejillo de Indias.
guise [gaɪz] n apariencia.
guitar [gɪ'tɑːʳ] n guitarra.
guitarist [gɪ'tɑːrɪst] n guitarrista mf.
gulf [gʌlf] n golfo. 2 fig abismo.
gull [gʌl] n gaviota.
gullible ['gʌlɪbəl] adj crédulo,-a.
gully ['gʌlɪ] n torrentera.

gulp [gʌlp] n trago. – 2 t tragar. – 3 i tragar aire; (with fear) tragar saliva.
gum [gʌm] n ANAT encía. 2 (substance) goma; (glue) goma, pegamento. – 3 t engomar, pegar con goma.
gumption ['gʌmpʃən] n sentido común.
gun [gʌn] n gen arma de fuego. 2 (handgun) pistola, revólver m. 3 (rifle) rifle m, fusil m. 4 (shotgun) escopeta. 5 (cannon) cañón m. ◆to ~ down t matar a tiros. ■ ~ dog, perro de caza.
gunfire ['gʌnfaɪəʳ] n fuego, disparos mpl. 2 (shooting) tiroteo.
gunman ['gʌnmən] n pistolero.
gunner ['gʌnəʳ] n artillero.
gunpowder ['gʌnpaʊdəʳ] n pólvora.
gunrunner ['gʌnrʌnəʳ] n traficante mf de armas.
gunrunning ['gʌnrʌnɪŋ] n tráfico de armas.
gunshot ['gʌnʃɒt] n disparo.
gurgle ['gɜːgəl] n (water) gorgoteo. 2 (baby) gorjeo. – 3 i (water) gorgotear. 4 (baby) gorjear.
guru ['gʊruː] n gurú m.
gush [gʌʃ] n chorro. – 2 i brotar/manar a borbotones. 3 (person) ser efusivo,-a.
gushing ['gʌʃɪŋ] adj (water) que sale a borbotones. 2 (person) efusivo,-a.
gust [gʌst] n ráfaga, racha.
gusto ['gʌstəʊ] n entusiasmo.
gusty ['gʌstɪ] adj (wind) racheado,-a.
gut [gʌt] n ANAT intestino, tripa. 2 (catgut) cuerda de tripa. 3 pl (entrails) entrañas fpl, vísceras fpl. 4 pl sl agallas fpl. – 5 t (fish) destripar. 6 (building) destruir el interior de.
gutter ['gʌtəʳ] n (in street) arroyo, canalón m. 2 (on roof) canal m. ■ ~ press, prensa amarilla.
guy [gaɪ] n fam tipo, tío, individuo.
guzzle ['gʌzəl] t zamparse, engullirse.
gym [dʒɪm] n fam (place) gimnasio. 2 (sport) gimnasia. ■ ~ shoes, zapatillas fpl de deporte.
gymkhana [dʒɪm'kɑːnə] n gymkhana.
gymnasium [dʒɪm'neɪzɪəm] n gimnasio.
gymnast ['dʒɪmnæst] n gimnasta mf.
gymnastics [dʒɪm'næstɪks] n gimnasia.
gynaecological [gaɪnɪkə'lɒdʒɪkəl] adj ginecológico,-a.
gynaecologist [gaɪnɪ'kɒlədʒɪst] n ginecólogo,-a.
gynaecology [gaɪnɪ'kɒlədʒɪ] n ginecología.
gypsum ['dʒɪpsəm] n yeso.
gypsy ['dʒɪpsɪ] adj-n gitano,-a.
gyrate [dʒaɪ'reɪt] i girar, dar vueltas.

H

habit ['hæbɪt] *n* hábito, costumbre *f*. **2** *(garment)* hábito.

habitable ['hæbɪtəbəl] *adj* habitable.

habitat ['hæbɪtæt] *n* hábitat *m*.

habitual [hə'bɪtjʊəl] *adj (usual)* habitual, acostumbrado,-a. **2** *(liar etc.)* empedernido,-a, inveterado,-a.

hack [hæk] *n* machaca *mf*. — **2** *t* tajar, cortar.

hackneyed ['hæknɪd] *adj* gastado,-a.

hacksaw ['hæksɔ:] *n* sierra para metales.

had [hæd] *pt & pp* → **have**.

haddock ['hædək] *n* eglefino.

haemorrhage ['hemərɪdʒ] *n* hemorragia.

haemorrhoids ['hemərɔɪdz] *npl* hemorroides *fpl*.

hag [hæg] *n* bruja.

haggard ['hægəd] *adj* ojeroso,-a.

haggle ['hægəl] *i* regatear.

hail [heɪl] *n* METEOR granizo, pedrisco. — **2** *i* METEOR granizar. **3** *(call)* llamar. **4** *(acclaim)* aclamar. ●*to* ~ *from,* ser de.

hailstone ['heɪlstəʊn] *n* granizo.

hailstorm ['heɪlstɔ:m] *n* granizada.

hair [heə^r] *n (on head)* cabello, pelo. **2** *(on body)* vello.

hairbrush ['heəbrʌʃ] *n* cepillo para el pelo.

haircut ['heəkʌt] *n* corte *m* de pelo.

hairdo ['heədu:] *n fam* peinado.

hairdresser ['heədresə^r] *n* peluquero,-a. ■ *hairdresser's (shop),* peluquería.

hairdryer ['heədraɪə^r] *n* secador *m* (de pelo).

hairpiece ['heəpi:s] *n* peluquín *m*.

hairpin ['heəpɪn] *n* horquilla.

hair-raising ['heəreɪzɪŋ] *adj* espeluznante.

hairspray ['heəspreɪ] *n* laca para el pelo.

hairstyle ['heəstaɪl] *n* peinado.

hairy ['heərɪ] *adj* peludo,-a. **2** *fig* espeluznante.

hake [heɪk] *n* merluza.

half [hɑ:f] *n* mitad *f*: *a kilo and a* ~, un kilo y medio. — **2** *adv* medio,-a: ~ *a dozen,* media docena. — **3** *adv* medio, a medias: ~ *dead,* medio muerto,-a. ●*to go halves on,* pagar a medias. ■ *better* ~, media naranja. ▲ *pl* **halves**.

half-brother ['hɑ:fbrʌðə^r] *n* hermanastro.

half-caste ['hɑ:fkɑ:st] *adj-n* mestizo,-a.

half-hearted [hɑ:f'hɑ:tɪd] *adj* poco entusiasta.

halfpenny ['heɪpnɪ] *n* medio penique.

half-sister ['hɑ:fsɪstə^r] *n* hermanastra.

half-time [hɑ:f'taɪm] *n* SP descanso *m*.

half-way ['hɑ:fweɪ] *adj* intermedio,-a. — **2** *adv* a medio camino.

half-wit ['hɑ:fwɪt] *n* imbécil *mf*.

hall [hɔ:l] *n (entrance)* vestíbulo. **2** *(for concerts)* sala. **3** *(mansion)* casa solariega. ■ ~ *of residence,* colegio mayor.

hallmark ['hɔ:lmɑ:k] *n (on gold etc.)* contraste *m*. **2** *fig* sello.

hallo! [hə'ləʊ] *interj* → **hello**.

Halloween [hæləʊ'i:n] *n* víspera de Todos los Santos.

hallucination [həlu:sɪ'neɪʃən] *n* alucinación.

halo ['heɪləʊ] *n* halo.

halt [hɔ:lt] *n* alto, parada. — **2** *t-i* parar(se), detener(se).

halter ['hɔ:ltə^r] *n* cabestro.

halting ['hɔ:ltɪŋ] *adj* vacilante.

halve [hɑ:v] *t* partir en dos. **2** *(reduce)* reducir a la mitad.

ham [hæm] *n* jamón *m*. ●*to* ~ *it up,* exagerar.

hamburger ['hæmbɜ:gə^r] *n* hamburguesa.

hammer ['hæmə'] *n* martillo. − **2** *t-i* martillar. − **3** *t fam* dar una paliza a.

hammock ['hæmək] *n* hamaca.

hamper ['hæmpə'] *n* cesta. − **2** *t* estorbar.

hamster ['hæmstə'] *n* hámster *m*.

hand [hænd] *n* mano *f*. **2** *(worker)* trabajador,-ra, operario,-a; MAR tripulante *mf*. **3** *(of clock)* manecilla. **4** *(handwriting)* letra. **5** *(of cards)* mano. **6** *(applause)* aplauso. − **7** *t* dar, entregar. ◆*to ~ back* *t* devolver. ◆*to ~ in* *t* entregar, presentar. ◆*to ~ out* *t* repartir. ◆*to ~ over* *t* entregar. ◆*to ~ round* *t* ofrecer. ●*at first ~*, de primera mano; *at ~*, a mano; *by ~*, a mano; *hands up!*, ¡manos arriba!; *on ~*, disponible; *on the one/other ~*, por una/otra parte; *to have the upper ~*, llevar ventaja; *to hold hands,* estar cogidos,-as de la mano; *to lend a ~,* echar una mano.

handbag ['hændbæg] *n* bolso.

handball ['hændbɔːl] *n* balonmano.

handbrake ['hændbreɪk] *n* freno de mano.

handcuff ['hændkʌf] *t* esposar. − **2** *npl* esposas *fpl*.

handful ['hændfʊl] *n* puñado.

handicap ['hændɪkæp] *n* MED incapacitación, invalidez *f*. **2** SP hándicap *m*. − **3** *t* obstaculizar.

handicapped ['hændɪkæpt] *adj (physically)* minusválido,-a; *(mentally)* retrasado,-a. **2** *fig* desfavorecido,-a.

handicraft ['hændɪkrɑːft] *n* artesanía.

handkerchief ['hæŋkətʃiːf] *n* pañuelo.

handle ['hændəl] *n (of door)* manilla. **2** *(of drawer)* tirador *m*. **3** *(of cup)* asa. **4** *(of knife)* mango. − **5** *t* manejar. **6** *(people)* tratar. **7** *(tolerate)* aguantar. − **8** *i (car)* comportarse.

handlebar ['hændəlbɑː'] *n* manillar *m*.

handmade [hænd'meɪd] *adj* hecho,-a a mano.

handout ['hændaʊt] *n (leaflet)* folleto. **2** EDUC material *m*. **3** *(press)* nota de prensa. **4** *(charity)* limosna.

handshake ['hændʃeɪk] *n* apretón *m* de manos.

handsome ['hænsəm] *adj (man)* guapo,-a, de buen ver. **2** *(generous)* generoso,-a.

handwriting ['hændraɪtɪŋ] *n* letra.

handwritten [hænd'rɪtən] *adj* escrito,-a a mano.

handy ['hændɪ] *adj (person)* hábil. **2** *(useful)* práctico,-a, útil. **3** *(near)* a mano.

hang [hæŋ] *t gen* colgar. **2** *(wallpaper)* colocar. **3** JUR ahorcar. − **4** *i* colgar, pen-

der; *(float)* flotar. **5** JUR ser ahorcado,-a. **6** *(dress etc.)* caer. − **7** *n (of dress etc.)* caída. ◆*to ~ about/around* *i* esperar. **2** *(waste time)* perder el tiempo. ◆*to ~ back* *i* quedarse atrás. ◆*to ~ out* *t* tender. − **2** *i fam* frecuentar. ◆*to ~ up* *t-i* colgar. ●*to get the ~ of,* cogerle el truquillo a. ▲ *pt & pp* **hung**, excepto en **3** y **5** que son regulares.

hangar ['hæŋə'] *n* hangar *m*.

hanger ['hæŋə'] *n* percha.

hang-glider ['hæŋglaɪdə'] *n* ala delta.

hang-gliding ['hæŋglaɪdɪŋ] *n* vuelo libre.

hanging ['hæŋɪŋ] *adj* colgante. − **2** *n* ejecución en la horca. **3** *(on wall)* colgadura.

hangman ['hæŋmæn] *n* verdugo. **2** *(game)* el ahorcado.

hangout ['hæŋaʊt] *n fam* guarida.

hangover ['hæŋəʊvə'] *n* resaca.

hang-up ['hæŋʌp] *n fam* problema *m*. **2** *(complex)* complejo.

hanker ['hæŋkə'] *i to ~ after,* ansiar, anhelar.

hanky-panky [hæŋkɪ'pæŋkɪ] *n fam* tejemaneje *m*.

haphazard [hæp'hæzəd] *adj* desordenado,-a. **2** *(plans etc.)* improvisado,-a.

happen ['hæpən] *i* ocurrir, pasar, suceder: *if you ~ to ...,* si por casualidad ...

happening ['hæpənɪŋ] *n* acontecimiento.

happily ['hæpɪlɪ] *adv* felizmente. **2** *(luckily)* afortunadamente.

happiness ['hæpɪnəs] *n* felicidad.

happy ['hæpɪ] *adj (cheerful)* feliz, alegre. **2** *(glad)* contento,-a.

harass ['hærəs] *t* acosar, hostigar.

harassment ['hærəsmənt] *n* acoso.

harbour ['hɑːbə'] *n* puerto. − **2** *t (criminal)* encubrir. **3** *(doubts)* abrigar.

hard [hɑːd] *adj gen* duro,-a. **2** *(difficult)* difícil. **3** *(harsh)* severo,-a. − **4** *adv* fuerte. ●*~ of hearing,* duro,-a de oído; *to work ~,* trabajar mucho; *fam to be ~ up,* estar sin blanca. ■ *~ labour,* trabajos *mpl* forzados; *~ shoulder,* arcén *m*.

harden ['hɑːdən] *t-i* endurecer(se).

hard-headed ['hɑːdhedɪd] *adj* frío,-a, cerebral.

hard-hearted ['hɑːdhɑːtɪd] *adj* cruel, duro,-a.

hardly ['hɑːdlɪ] *adv* apenas.

hardness ['hɑːdnəs] *n* dureza. **2** *(difficulty)* dificultad.

hardship ['hɑːdʃɪp] *n* privación.

hardware ['hɑːdweəʳ] *n* ferretería. — 2 COMPUT hardware *m*.

hardworking ['hɑːdwɜːkɪŋ] *adj* trabajador,-ra.

hardy ['hɑːdɪ] *adj* fuerte, robusto. 2 *(plant)* resistente.

hare [heəʳ] *n* liebre *f*.

harebrained ['heəbreɪnd] *adj* irreflexivo,-a.

harem [hɑːˈriːm] *n* harén *m*.

haricot bean [hærɪkəʊˈbiːn] *n* alubia.

harlequin ['hɑːlɪkwɪn] *n* arlequín *m*.

harlot ['hɑːlət] *n* ramera.

harm [hɑːm] *n* mal, daño, perjuicio. — 2 *t* dañar, perjudicar.

harmful ['hɑːmfʊl] *adj* dañino,-a, nocivo,-a, perjudicial.

harmless ['hɑːmləs] *adj* inofensivo,-a.

harmonic [hɑːˈmɒnɪk] *adj-n* armónico,-a *(m)*.

harmonica [hɑːˈmɒnɪkæ] *n* armónica.

harmonious [hɑːˈməʊnɪəs] *adj* armonioso,-a.

harmonize ['hɑːmənaɪz] *t-i* armonizar.

harmony ['hɑːmənɪ] *n* armonía.

harness ['hɑːnəs] *n* arreos *mpl*. — 2 *t* *(horse)* poner los arreos a. 3 *(resources)* aprovechar.

harp [hɑːp] *n* arpa. ◆*to* ~ *on about* ·*t* insistir en.

harpoon [hɑːˈpuːn] *n* arpón *m*. — 2 *t* arponear.

harpsichord ['hɑːpsɪkɔːd] *n* clavicordio.

harrowing ['hærəʊɪŋ] *adj* angustioso,-a.

harry ['hærɪ] *t* acosar.

harsh [hɑːʃ] *adj* *(cruel)* cruel, severo,-a. 2 *(dazzling)* deslumbrante. 3 *(rough)* áspero,-a.

harvest ['hɑːvɪst] *n* cosecha. 2 *(grapes)* vendimia. — 3 *t* cosechar. 4 *(grapes)* vendimiar.

harvester ['hɑːvɪstəʳ] *n* segador,-ra. 2 *(machine)* segadora.

has [hæz] *3rd pers sing pres* → **have**.

hash [hæʃ] *n* CULIN picadillo. 2 *fam* hachís *m*. ◆*to make a* ~ *of sth.*, estropear algo.

hashish ['hæʃiːʃ] *n* hachís *m*.

hassle ['hæsəl] *fam* rollo, problema *m*, lío. 2 *(argument)* discusión. — 3 *t* molestar, fastidiar.

haste [heɪst] *n* prisa, precipitación.

hasten ['heɪsən] *t-i* apresurar(se).

hasty ['heɪstɪ] *adj* apresurado,-a. 2 *(rash)* precipitado,-a.

hat [hæt] *n* sombrero.

hatch [hætʃ] *n* escotilla. — 2 *t* empollar, incubar. 3 *fig* idear, tramar. — 4 *i* salir del cascarón.

hatchet ['hætʃɪt] *n* hacha.

hate [heɪt] *n* odio. — 2 *t* odiar, detestar. 3 *(regret)* lamentar.

hateful ['heɪtfʊl] *adj* odioso,-a.

hatred ['heɪtrɪd] *n* odio.

haughty ['hɔːtɪ] *adj* arrogante.

haul [hɔːl] *n* *(pull)* tirón *m*. 2 *(fish)* redada. 3 *(loot)* botín *m*. — 4 *t* tirar de, arrastrar. ●*a long* ~, un largo camino.

haulage ['hɔːlɪdʒ] *n* transporte *m*.

haulier ['hɔːljəʳ] *n* transportista *mf*.

haunch [hɔːntʃ] *n* cadera y muslo. 2 CULIN pierna.

haunt [hɔːnt] *n* sitio preferido. — 2 *t* frecuentar. 3 *(thought)* obsesionar. 4 *(ghost)* *(place)* rondar por; *(person)* atormentar.

haunted ['hɔːntɪd] *adj* encantado,-a.

have [hæv] *t* *(possess)* tener, poseer. 2 *(food)* comer; *(drink)* beber: *to* ~ *breakfast/lunch/tea/dinner,* desayunar/comer/merendar/cenar. 3 *(cigarette)* fumar. 4 *(shower, bath)* tomar: *to* ~ *a bath/shower,* bañarse/ducharse. 5 *(illness)* tener. 6 *(party)* hacer. 7 *(meeting)* hacer, celebrar. 8 *(baby)* tener, dar a luz. 9 *(cause to happen)* hacer, mandar: *he had the house painted,* hizo pintar la casa. 10 *(allow)* permitir, consentir. 11 *fam* *(cheat)* timar. — 12 *aux* haber: *I* ~ *seen,* he visto; *I had seen,* había visto. ◆*to* ~ *on t* llevar puesto,-a. ◆*to* ~ *out t (tooth)* sacarse; *(appendix)* operarse de. ●*had better,* más vale que: *you'd better come alone,* más vale que vengas solo,-a; GB ~ *got,* tener; *to* ~ *done with,* acabar con; *to* ~ *had it, (broken)* estar hecho,-a polvo; *(in trouble)* cargarlo; *to* ~ *just,* acabar de; *to* ~ *sb. on,* tomarle el pelo a algn.; *to* ~ *sth. on,* tener algo planeado, tener algo que hacer; *to* ~ *it in for sb.,* tenerla tomada con algn.; *to* ~ *it out with sb.,* ajustar las cuentas con algn.; *to* ~ *to,* tener que, haber de; *to* ~ *to do with,* tener que ver con; *to* ~ *it away/off*, echar un polvo*. ▲*3rd pers pres sing* **has**; *pt & pp* **had**. GB *en 1 y 5 también* ~ *got.*

haven ['heɪvən] *n fig* refugio.

haversack ['hævəsæk] *n* mochila.

havoc ['hævək] *n* estragos *mpl*.

hawk [hɔːk] *n* halcón *m*.

hay [heɪ] *n* heno.

hay-fever ['heɪfiːvəʳ] *n* fiebre *f* del heno.

haywire ['heɪwaɪəʳ] *adj to go* ~, descontrolarse.

held

hazard ['hæzəd] *n* riesgo. − 2 *t* arriesgar, poner en peligro.

hazardous ['hæzədəs] *adj* arriesgado,-a, peligroso,-a.

haze [heɪz] *n* neblina.

hazel ['heɪzəl] *n* avellano. − 2 *adj* (de color de) avellana.

hazelnut ['heɪzəlnʌt] *n* avellana.

hazy ['heɪzɪ] *adj* brumoso,-a. 2 *fig* vago,-a.

he [hiː] *pers pron* él: ~ *came yesterday,* (él) vino ayer. − 2 *adj* macho.

head [hed] *n gen* cabeza. 2 *(on tape recorder)* cabezal *m*. 3 *(of bed, table)* cabecera. 4 *(of page)* principio. 5 *(on beer)* espuma. 6 *(cape)* cabo. 7 *(of school, company)* director,-ra. 8 *(cattle)* res *f*. − 9 *t* encabezar. 10 *(ball)* rematar de cabeza. ◆*to* ~ *for t* dirigirse hacia. ●*heads or tails?,* ¿cara o cruz?

headache ['hedeɪk] *n* dolor *m* de cabeza.

heading ['hedɪŋ] *n* encabezamiento. 2 *(letterhead)* membrete *m*.

header ['hedə'] *n* çabezazo.

headlamp ['hedlæmp] *n* faro.

headland ['hedlənd] *n* cabo.

headlight ['hedlaɪt] *n* faro.

headline ['hedlaɪn] *n* titular *m*.

headlong ['hedlɒŋ] *adj* de cabeza.

headmaster ['hedmɑːstə'] *n* director *m*.

headmistress [hed'mɪstrəs] *n* directora.

headphones ['hedfəunz] *npl* auriculares *mpl*.

headquarters ['hedkwɔːtəz] *npl* sede *f sing*. 2 MIL cuartel *m sing* general.

headstrong ['hedstrɒŋ] *adj* obstinado,-a, testarudo,-a.

headway ['hedweɪ] *n to make* ~, avanzar.

headword ['hedwɜːd] *n* entrada.

heal [hiːl] *t-i* curar(se).

health [helθ] *n* salud *f*. 2 *(service)* sanidad. ■ ~ *centre,* ambulatorio.

healthy ['helθɪ] *adj* sano,-a. 2 *(good for health)* saludable.

heap [hiːp] *n* montón *m*. − 2 *t* amontonar.

hear [hɪə'] *t-i* oír. ●*to* ~ *from,* tener noticias de; *to* ~ *of,* oír hablar de. ▲ *pt & pp* **heard** [hɜːd].

hearer ['hɪərə'] *n* oyente *mf*.

hearing ['hɪərɪŋ] *n* oído. 2 JUR audiencia.

hearsay ['hɪəseɪ] *n* rumores *mpl*.

hearse [hɜːs] *n* coche *m* fúnebre.

heart [hɑːt] *n* corazón *m*. 2 *(courage)* valor *m*. 3 *(of lettuce etc.)* cogollo. 3 *pl (cards)*

copas *fpl*. ●*by* ~, de memoria. ■ ~ *attack,* infarto de miocardio.

heartbeat ['hɑːtbiːt] *n* latido (del corazón).

heartbreaking ['hɑːtbreɪkɪŋ] *n* desgarrador,-ora.

heartbroken ['hɑːtbrəukən] *adj* que tiene el corazón destrozado,-a.

hearten ['hɑːtən] *t* animar.

hearth [hɑːθ] *n* hogar *m*, chimenea.

heartless ['hɑːtləs] *adj* cruel.

heartthrob ['hɑːtθrɒb] *n* ídolo.

hearty ['hɑːtɪ] *adj (person)* campechano,-a. 2 *(welcome)* cordial. 3 *(meal)* abundante.

heat [hiːt] *n* calor *m*. 2 *(heating)* calefacción. 3 SP eliminatoria. − 4 *t-i* calentar(se). ●*on* ~, en celo.

heated ['hiːtɪd] *adj fig (argument)* acalorado,-a.

heater ['hiːtə'] *n* calentador *m*.

heath [hiːθ] *n (land)* brezal *m*. 2 *(plant)* brezo.

heathen ['hiːðən] *adj-n* pagano,-a.

heather ['heðə'] *n* brezo.

heating ['hiːtɪŋ] *n* calefacción.

heatwave ['hiːtweɪv] *n* ola de calor.

heave [hiːv] *n (pull)* tirón *m*. − 2 *t (pull)* tirar. 3 *fam (throw)* lanzar. − 4 *i* subir y bajar; *(chest)* jadear.

heaven ['hevən] *n* cielo. 2 *fam* gloria.

heavenly ['hevənlɪ] *adj* celestial. 2 *fig* divino,-a. 3 ASTRON celeste.

heavy ['hevɪ] *adj gen* pesado,-a. 2 *(rain, blow)* fuerte. 3 *(traffic)* denso,-a. 4 *(sleep)* profundo,-a. 5 *(crop)* abundante.

heavyweight ['hevɪweɪt] *n* peso pesado.

heckle ['hekəl] *t* interrumpir.

hectare ['hektɑː'] *n* hectárea.

hectic ['hektɪk] *adj* agitado,-a, ajetreado,-a.

hedge [hedʒ] *n* seto vivo. 2 *fig* protección. − 3 *i* contestar con evasivas.

hedgehog ['hedʒhɒg] *n* erizo.

heed [hiːd] *n* atención. − 2 *t* prestar atención a.

heel [hiːl] *n* talón *m*. 2 *(on shoe)* tacón *m*.

hefty ['heftɪ] *adj* fuerte.

heifer ['hefə'] *n* vaquilla.

height [haɪt] *n* altura. 2 *(altitude)* altitud. 3 *(of person)* estatura.

heighten ['haɪtən] *t fig* intensificar.

heinous ['heɪnəs] *adj* atroz.

heir [eə'] *n* heredero.

heiress ['eərəs] *n* heredera.

heirloom ['eəluːm] *n* reliquia de familia.

held [held] *pt & pp* → **hold.**

helicopter ['helikɒptə'] *n* helicóptero.
helium ['hi:liəm] *n* helio.
hell [hel] *n* infierno. ●*fam a ~ of a, (good)* estupendo,-a, fantástico,-a; *(bad)* fatal, horrible.
hellish ['heliʃ] *adj fam* infernal.
hello! [he'ləʊ] *interj* ¡hola! **2** *(on 'phone)* ¡diga!
helm [helm] *n* timón *m.*
helmet ['helmət] *n* casco.
help [help] *n* ayuda. – **2** *interj* ¡socorro! – **3** *t* ayudar. **4** *(avoid)* evitar. ●*~ yourself,* sírvete tú mismo,-a; *I can't ~ it,* no es culpa mía; *it can't be helped,* no hay nada que hacer.
helpful ['helpfʊl] *adj (thing)* útil. **2** *(person)* amable.
helping ['helpɪŋ] *n* ración.
helpless ['helpləs] *adj* indefenso,-a. **2** *(powerless)* impotente.
helter-skelter [heltə'skeltə'] *adv* atropelladamente. – **2** *n (at fair)* tobogán *m.*
hem [hem] *n* dobladillo. – **2** *t* hacer un dobladillo en. ◆*to ~ in t* cercar, rodear.
he-man ['hi:mæn] *n* machote *m.*
hemisphere ['hemisfiə'] *n* hemisferio.
hemp [hemp] *n* cáñamo.
hen [hen] *f* gallina.
hence [hens] *adv (so)* por eso. **2** *(from now)* de aquí a.
henceforth [hens'fɔ:θ] *adv* de ahora en adelante.
henchman ['hentʃmən] *n* secuaz *m.*
hepatitis [hepə'taitis] *n* hepatitis *f inv.*
her [hɜ:'] *pron (direct object)* la: *I love ~,* la quiero. **2** *(indirect object)* le; *(with other pronouns)* se: *give ~ the money,* dale el dinero; *give it to ~,* dáselo. **3** *(after preposition)* ella: *go with ~,* vete con ella. – **4** *poss adj* su, sus; *(emphatic)* de ella.
herald ['herəld] *n* heraldo. – **2** *t* anunciar.
heraldry ['herəldrɪ] *n* heráldica.
herb [hɜ:b] *n* hierba.
herbal ['hɜ:bəl] *adj* herbario,-a.
herbalist ['hɜ:bəlist] *n* herbolario,-a.
herbivorous ['hɜ:bivərəs] *adj* herbívoro,-a.
herd [hɜ:d] *n (cattle)* manada; *(goats)* rebaño; *(pigs)* piara. – **2** *t-i* juntar(se) en manada/rebaño.
here [hiə'] *adv* aquí.
hereafter [hiər'ɑ:ftə'] *adv* de ahora en adelante.
hereby [hiə'bai] *adv* por el/la presente.
hereditary [hi'redɪtəri] *adj* hereditario,-a.
heredity [hi'redɪtɪ] *n* herencia.
heresy ['herəsi] *n* herejía.

heretic ['herətɪk] *n* hereje *mf.*
heritage ['herɪtɪdʒ] *n* herencia, patrimonio.
hermaphrodite [hɜ:'mæfrədait] *adj-n* hermafrodita *(mf).*
hermetic [hɜ:'metɪk] *adj* hermético,-a.
hermit ['hɜ:mɪt] *n* ermitaño.
hernia ['hɜ:nɪə] *n* hernia.
hero ['hiərəʊ] *n* héroe.
heroic [hi'rəʊkɪk] *adj* heroico,-a.
heroin ['herəʊin] *n (drug)* heroína.
heroine ['herəʊin] *n* heroína.
heroism ['herəʊizəm] *n* heroísmo.
herring ['herɪŋ] *n* arenque *m.*
hers [hɜ:z] *poss pron* (el) suyo, (la) suya; (los) suyos, (las) suyas.
herself [hɜ:'self] *pers pron* se. **2** *(emphatic)* ella/sí misma.
hesitate ['heziteit] *i* vacilar, dudar.
hesitant ['hezitənt] *adj* indeciso,-a.
hesitation [hezi'teiʃən] *n* duda.
heterogeneous [hetərəʊ'dʒi:nɪəs] *adj* heterogéneo,-a.
heterosexual [hetərəʊ'seksjuːəl] *adj-n* heterosexual *(mf).*
hexagon ['heksəgən] *n* hexágono.
hey! [hei] *interj* ¡oye!, ¡oiga!
heyday ['heidei] *n* auge *m,* apogeo.
hi! [hai] *interj* ¡hola!
hibernate ['haibəneit] *i* hibernar.
hibernation [haibə'neiʃən] *n* hibernación.
hiccough, hiccup ['hikʌp] *n* hipo. – **2** *i* tener hipo.
hid [hid] *pt & pp →* **hide.**
hidden ['hidən] *pp →* **hide.** – **2** *adj* escondido,-a, oculto,-a.
hide [haid] *n* piel *f,* cuero. – **2** *t-i* esconder(se). ▲ *pt* **hid;** *pp* **hid** o **hidden.**
hide-and-seek [haidən'si:k] *n* escondite *m.*
hideous ['hidiəs] *adj* horroroso,-a. **2** *(ugly)* horrendo,-a.
hiding ['haidɪŋ] *n* paliza. ●*to go into ~ ,* esconderse.
hierarchy ['haiərɑːkɪ] *n* jerarquía.
hieroglyph ['haiərəglif] *n* jeroglífico.
high [hai] *adj* alto,-a. **2** *(food)* pasado,-a. **3** *(game)* manido,-a. **4** *sl (on drugs)* flipado,-a. – **5** *n* punto máximo. – **6** *highly adv* muy; *(favourably)* muy bien. ●*~ and low,* por todas partes. ■ *~ chair,* trona; *~ fidelity,* alta fidelidad.
highbrow ['haibrau] *adj* intelectual.
higher ['haiə'] *adj* superior.
high-heeled ['haihi:ld] *adj* de tacón alto.
highlands ['hailəndz] *npl* tierras *fpl* altas.

highlight ['haɪlaɪt] *t* hacer resaltar.
Highness ['haɪnəs] *n* Alteza *mf*.
high-pitched ['haɪpɪtʃt] *adj* agudo,-a.
high-speed ['haɪspiːd] *adj* de gran velocidad.
highway ['haɪweɪ] *n* US autovía. ▪ GB *Highway Code*, código de la circulación.
highwayman ['haɪweɪmən] *n* salteador *m* de caminos.
hijack ['haɪdʒæk] *n* secuestro. – 2 *t* secuestrar.
hijacker ['haɪdʒækəʳ] *n* secuestrador,-ra.
hike [haɪk] *n* *(walk)* excursión. – 2 *i* ir de excursión.
hiker ['haɪkəʳ] *n* excursionista *mf*.
hilarious [hɪ'leərɪəs] *adj* graciosísimo,-a.
hill [hɪl] *n* colina. 2 *(slope)* cuesta.
hillside ['hɪlsaɪd] *n* ladera.
hilly ['hɪlɪ] *adj* montañoso,-a.
hilt [hɪlt] *n* empuñadura. ●*up to the ~,* al máximo.
him [hɪm] *pers pron (direct object)* lo: *I love ~,* lo quiero. 2 *(indirect object)* le; *(with other pronouns)* se: *give ~ the money,* dale el dinero; *give it to ~,* dáselo. 3 *(after preposition)* él: *we went with ~,* fuimos con él.
himself [hɪm'self] *pers pron* se. 2 *(emphatic)* él/sí mismo.
hind [haɪnd] *adj* trasero,-a.
hinder ['hɪndəʳ] *t-i* entorpecer, estorbar.
hindrance ['hɪndrəns] *n* estorbo, obstáculo.
hindsight ['haɪndsaɪt] *n* retrospectiva.
hinge [hɪndʒ] *n* gozne *m*, bisagra. ●*to ~ on,* depender de.
hint [hɪnt] *n* insinuación, indirecta. 2 *(advice)* consejo. 3 *(clue)* pista. – 4 *t* insinuar. – 5 *i* lanzar indirectas.
hinterland ['hɪntəlænd] *n* interior *m*.
hip [hɪp] *n* cadera. ●*~ ~ hooray!,* ¡hurra!
hippopotamus [hɪpə'pɒtəməs] *n* hipopótamo.
hippie, hippy ['hɪpɪ] *adj-n* *fam* hippie *(mf)*.
hire ['haɪəʳ] *n* alquiler *m*. – 2 *t* alquilar. ▪ *on ~ purchase,* a plazos.
his [hɪz] *poss adj* su, sus: *~ dog,* su perro. 2 *(emphatic)* de él. – 3 *poss pron* (el) suyo, (la) suya; (los) suyos, (las) suyas.
hiss [hɪs] *n* siseo, silbido. 2 *(protest)* silbido. – 3 *i* sisear, silbar. 4 *(in protest)* silbar.
historian [hɪs'tɔːrɪən] *n* historiador,-ra.
historic(al) [hɪs'tɒrɪk(əl)] *adj* histórico,-a.
history ['hɪstərɪ] *n* historia.

hit [hɪt] *n* golpe *m*. 2 *(success)* éxito. – 3 *t* golpear, pegar: *he ~ his head on the door,* dio con la cabeza contra la puerta. 4 *(crash into)* chocar contra. 5 *(affect)* afectar. 6 *(reach)* alcanzar. ●*to ~ it off with,* llevarse bien con; *to score a direct ~,* dar en el blanco. ▲ *pt & pp* **hit**.
hit-and-miss ['hɪtənmɪs] *adj* a la buena de Dios.
hitch [hɪtʃ] *n* tropiezo, dificultad. – 2 *t* enganchar, atar. – 3 *i fam* hacer autoestop.
hitch-hike ['hɪtʃhaɪk] *i* hacer autoestop.
hitch-hiker ['hɪtʃhaɪkəʳ] *n* autoestopista *mf*.
hitherto [hɪðə'tuː] *adv* hasta ahora.
hive [haɪv] *n* colmena.
hoard [hɔːd] *n* provisión. 2 *(money)* tesoro. – 3 *t* acumular. 4 *(money)* atesorar.
hoarding ['hɔːdɪŋ] *n* valla.
hoarse [hɔːs] *adj* ronco,-a, áspero,-a.
hoax [həʊks] *n* trampa, engaño. – 2 *t* engañar.
hobble ['hɒbəl] *i* cojear.
hobby ['hɒbɪ] *n* afición, hobby *m*.
hockey ['hɒkɪ] *n* hockey *m*.
hog [hɒg] *n* cerdo. – 2 *t* acaparar.
hoist [hɔɪst] *n* grúa. 2 *(lift)* montacargas *m inv*. – 3 *t* levantar. 4 *(flag)* izar.
hold [həʊld] *n (grip)* agarro, asimiento. 2 *(place to grip)* asidero. 3 AV MAR bodega. – 4 *t* aguantar, sostener; *(tightly)* agarrar. 5 *(contain)* dar cabida a, tener capacidad para. 6 *(meeting)* celebrar; *(conversation)* mantener. 7 *(think)* creer, considerar. 8 *(keep)* guardar. – 9 *i* resistir; *fig* seguir siendo válido,-a. ◆*to ~ back t* retener. 2 *(information)* ocultar. ◆*to ~ forth i* hablar largamente. ◆*to ~ on i* agarrar(se) fuerte. 2 *(wait)* esperar; *(on 'phone)* no colgar. ◆*to ~ out t (hand)* tender. – 2 *i* durar; *(person)* resistir. ◆*to ~ over t* aplazar. ◆*to ~ up t (rob)* atracar, asaltar. 2 *(delay)* retrasar. 3 *(raise)* levantar. 4 *(support)* aguantar, sostener. ◆*to ~ with t* estar de acuerdo con. ●*to get ~ of,* asir; *(obtain)* hacerse con. ▲ *pt & pp* **held**.
holder ['həʊldəʳ] *n* poseedor,-ra; *(of passport)* titular *mf*. 2 *(container)* recipiente *m*, receptáculo.
holding ['həʊldɪŋ] *n* posesión. 2 COM holding *m*.
hold-up ['həʊldʌp] *n* atraco. 2 *(delay)* retraso. 3 AUTO atasco.
hole [həʊl] *n* agujero; *(in ground)* hoyo. 2 *(golf)* hoyo. 3 *(in road)* bache *m*.

holiday [ˈhɒlɪdeɪ] *n (one day)* fiesta. **2** *(period)* vacaciones *fpl*.

holiday-maker [ˈhɒlɪdeɪmeɪkəʳ] *n* turista *mf*.

holiness [ˈhəʊlɪnəs] *n* santidad.

hollow [ˈhɒləʊ] *adj* hueco,-a. **2** *fig* falso,-a. **– 3** *n* hueco. **4** GEOG hondonada.

holly [ˈhɒlɪ] *n* acebo.

holocaust [ˈhɒləkɔːst] *n* holocausto.

holster [ˈhəʊlstəʳ] *n* pistolera.

holy [ˈhəʊlɪ] *adj* santo,-a, sagrado,-a. **2** *(blessed)* bendito,-a.

homage [ˈhɒmɪdʒ] *n* homenaje *m*.

home [həʊm] *n* hogar *m*, casa. **2** *(institution)* asilo. **– 3** *adj* casero,-a. **4** POL (del) interior. ●*at ~*, en casa; *make yourself at ~*, póngase cómodo,-a. ■ *Home Office,* Ministerio del Interior.

homeland [ˈhəʊmlænd] *n* patria.

homeless [ˈhəʊmləs] *adj* sin hogar.

homely [ˈhəʊmlɪ] *adj* sencillo,-a, casero,-a. **2** US feo,-a.

homemade [həʊmˈmeɪd] *adj* de fabricación casera.

homesick [ˈhəʊmsɪk] *adj* nostálgico,-a. ●*to be ~*, tener morriña.

homesickness [ˈhəʊmsɪknəs] *n* añoranza, morriña.

homework [ˈhəʊmwɜːk] *n* deberes *mpl*.

homicidal [hɒmɪˈsaɪdəl] *adj* homicida.

homicide [ˈhɒmɪsaɪd] *n (crime)* homicidio. **2** *(criminal)* homicida *mf*.

homogeneous [hɒməˈdʒiːnɪəs] *adj* homogéneo,-a.

homosexual [həʊməʊˈseksjʊəl] *adj-n* homosexual *(mf)*.

honest [ˈɒnɪst] *adj* honrado,-a, honesto,-a. **2** *(frank)* sincero,-a, franco,-a. **– 3** *honestly adv* honradamente. **4** *(frankly)* con franqueza.

honesty [ˈɒnɪstɪ] *n* honradez *f*, rectitud.

honey [ˈhʌnɪ] *n* miel *f*. **2** US *(dear)* cariño.

honeymoon [ˈhʌnɪmuːn] *n* luna de miel.

honk [hɒŋk] *n (goose)* graznido. **2** *(car horn)* bocinazo *m*. **– 3** *i (goose)* graznar. **4** *(car)* tocar la bocina.

honour [ˈɒnəʳ] *n* honor *m*, honra. **– 2** *t* honrar. **3** *(cheque)* pagar; *(promise)* cumplir. ■ *Your Honour,* Su Señoría.

honourable [ˈɒnərəbəl] *adj (person)* honrado,-a; *(title)* honorable. **2** *(actions)* honroso,-a.

hood [hʊd] *n* capucha. **2** *(on pram etc.)* capota. **3** US AUTO *(bonnet)* capó *m*.

hoof [huːf] *n* pezuña. **2** *(of horse)* casco.

hook [hʊk] *n* gancho. **2** *(for fishing)* anzuelo. **3** *(boxing)* gancho. **– 4** *t* enganchar.

hooked [hʊkt] *adj (nose)* aquilino,-a. **2** *(on drug etc.)* enganchado,-a.

hooligan [ˈhuːlɪgən] *n* gamberro,-a.

hooliganism [ˈhuːlɪgənɪzəm] *n* gamberrismo.

hoop [huːp] *n* aro.

hoorah! [huːˈrɑː], **hooray!** [huːˈreɪ] *interj* ¡hurra!

hoot [huːt] *n (of owl)* ululato, grito. **2** *(of car)* bocinazo. **– 3** *i (owl)* ulular, gritar. **4** *(car)* dar un bocinazo; *(driver)* tocar la bocina.

hooter [ˈhuːtəʳ] *n* sirena. **2** *(on car)* bocina. **3** *fam* napias *fpl*.

hop [hɒp] *n* salto. **2** BOT lúpulo. **– 3** *i* saltar (con un solo pie).

hope [həʊp] *n* esperanza. **– 2** *t-i* esperar.

hopeful [ˈhəʊpfʊl] *adj* esperanzado,-a. **2** *(promising)* prometedor,-ra. **– 3** *hopefully adv* con esperanza/ilusión. **4** *fam (all being well)* se espera que.

hopeless [ˈhəʊpləs] *adj* desesperado,-a. **2** *fam (useless)* inútil.

horizon [həˈraɪzən] *n* horizonte *m*.

horizontal [hɒrɪˈzɒntəl] *adj* horizontal.

hormone [ˈhɔːməʊn] *n* hormona.

horn [hɔːn] *n* ZOOL asta, cuerno. **2** AUTO bocina. **3** MUS trompa.

horny [ˈhɔːnɪ] *adj* calloso,-a. **2** *fam (sexually)* cachondo,-a.

horoscope [ˈhɒrəskəʊp] *n* horóscopo.

horrible [ˈhɒrɪbəl] *adj* horrible.

horrid [ˈhɒrɪd] *adj* horroroso,-a.

horrific [həˈrɪfɪk] *adj* horrendo,-a.

horrify [ˈhɒrɪfaɪ] *t* horrorizar.

horror [ˈhɒrəʳ] *n* horror *m*. ■ *~ film,* película de terror.

hors d'oeuvre [ɔːˈdɜːvrə] *n* entremés *m*.

horse [hɔːs] *n* caballo. **2** *(in gym)* potro.

horseman [ˈhɔːsmən] *n* jinete *m*.

horsemanship [ˈhɔːsmənʃɪp] *n* equitación.

horsepower [ˈhɔːspaʊəʳ] *n* caballo (de vapor).

horseshoe [ˈhɔːsʃuː] *n* herradura.

horsewoman [ˈhɔːswʊmən] *n* amazona.

horticultural [hɔːtɪˈkʌltʃərəl] *adj* hortícola.

horticulture [ˈhɔːtɪkʌltʃəʳ] *n* horticultura.

hose [həʊz] *n (pipe)* manguera. **2** *pl (socks)* calcetines *mpl*; *(stockings)* medias *fpl*.

hospitable [hɒˈspɪtəbəl] *adj* hospitalario,-a.

hospital [ˈhɒspɪtəl] *n* hospital *m*.

hospitality [hɒspɪˈtælɪtɪ] *n* hospitalidad.

host [həʊst] *n* anfitrión *m*. **2** TV presentador *m*. **3** *(large number)* multitud *f*. **4** REL hostia. – **5** *t* TV presentar.

hostage [ˈhɒstɪdʒ] *n* rehén *mf*.

hostel [ˈhɒstəl] *n* residencia, hostal *m*.

hostess [ˈhəʊstəs] *n* anfitriona. **2** *(on plane etc.)* azafata. **3** *(in club)* camarera. **4** TV presentadora.

hostile [ˈhɒstaɪl] *adj* hostil.

hostility [hɒˈstɪlɪtɪ] *n* hostilidad.

hot [hɒt] *adj* caliente. **2** METEOR caluroso,-a, cálido,-a. **3** CULIN picante. **4** *(news)* de última hora. ●*to be* ~, *(person)* tener calor; *(weather)* hacer calor. ■ ~ *dog,* perrito caliente.

hotch-potch [ˈhɒtʃpɒtʃ] *n fam* revoltijo.

hotel [həʊˈtel] *n* hotel *m*.

hotelier [həʊˈtelɪeɪ] *n* hotelero,-a.

hot-headed [ˈhɒthedɪd] *adj* impetuoso,-a.

hothouse [ˈhɒthaʊs] *n* invernadero.

hotplate [ˈhɒtpleɪt] *n* placa de cocina.

hound [haʊnd] *n* perro de caza. – **2** *t* acosar.

hour [ˈaʊəʳ] *n* hora. ■ ~ *hand,* aguja horaria.

hourly [ˈaʊəlɪ] *adj* cada hora. – **2** *adv* a cada hora.

house [haʊs] *n* casa. **2** POL cámara. **3** THEAT sala. – **4** *t* alojar. ■ *House of Commons,* Cámara de los Comunes. ▲ *En 4 (verbo)* [haʊz].

housebreaking [ˈhaʊsbreɪkɪŋ] *n* JUR allanamiento de morada.

household [ˈhaʊshəʊld] *n* casa, familia.

householder [ˈhaʊshəʊldəʳ] *n* dueño,-a de la casa.

housekeeper [ˈhæʊskiːpəʳ] *n* ama de llaves.

housekeeping [ˈhaʊskiːpɪŋ] *n* administración de la casa. **2** ~ *(money),* dinero para los gastos de la casa.

house-trained [ˈhaʊstreɪnd] *adj (pet)* adiestrado,-a.

housewife [ˈhaʊswaɪf] *n* ama de casa.

housework [ˈhaʊswɜːk] *n* quehaceres *mpl* domésticos.

housing [ˈhaʊzɪŋ] *n* vivienda. **2** TECH caja. ■ ~ *estate,* urbanización.

hovel [ˈhɒvəl] *n* cuchitril *m*.

hover [ˈhɒvəʳ] *i* permanecer inmóvil (en el aire). **2** *(bird)* cernerse.

hovercraft [ˈhɒvəkrɑːft] *n* hovercraft *m*.

how [haʊ] *adv* cómo. **2** *(in exclamations)* qué. ●~ *do you do?,* ¿cómo está usted?; ~ *much,* cuánto,-a; ~ *many,* cuántos,-as.

however [haʊˈevəʳ] *conj* sin embargo, no obstante. – **2** *adv* ~ *much,* por más que, por mucho que.

howl [haʊl] *n* aullido. – **2** *i* aullar.

hub [hʌb] *n* AUTO cubo. **2** *fig* centro, eje *m*.

hubbub [ˈhʌbʌb] *n* bullicio.

hubby [ˈhʌbɪ] *n fam* marido.

huddle [ˈhʌdəl] *n* montón *m*. – **2** *i (crouch)* acurrucarse. **3** *(cluster)* apiñarse.

hue [hjuː] *n* matiz *m*, tinte *m*. ●~ *and cry,* protesta.

huff [hʌf] *n* enfado, enojo.

hug [hʌg] *n* abrazo. – **2** *t* abrazar.

huge [hjuːdʒ] *adj* enorme, inmenso,-a.

hulk [hʌlk] *n (ship)* buque viejo. **2** *(mass)* mole *f*.

hull [hʌl] *n (of ship)* casco. – **2** *t* desvainar.

hullabaloo [hʌləbəˈluː] *n* griterío.

hullo [hʌˈləʊ] *interj* → **hello**.

hum [hʌm] *n* zumbido. – **2** *i* zumbar. – **3** *t-i (sing)* tararear, canturrear.

human [ˈhjuːmən] *adj* humano,-a. – **2** *n* ~ *(being),* (ser) humano.

humane [hjuːˈmeɪn] *adj* humano,-a.

humanism [ˈhjuːmənɪzəm] *n* humanismo.

humanitarian [hjuːmænɪˈteərɪən] *adj* humanitario,-a.

humanity [hjuːˈmænɪtɪ] *n* humanidad. **2** *(mankind)* género humano.

humble [ˈhʌmbəl] *adj* humilde. – **2** *t* humillar.

humbleness [ˈhʌmbəlnəs] *n* humildad.

humdrum [ˈhʌmdrʌm] *adj* monótono,-a, aburrido,-a.

humid [ˈhjuːmɪd] *adj* húmedo,-a.

humidity [hjuːˈmɪdɪtɪ] *n* humedad.

humiliate [hjuːˈmɪlɪeɪt] *t* humillar.

humiliation [hjuːmɪlɪˈeɪʃən] *n* humillación.

humility [hjuːˈmɪlɪtɪ] *n* humildad.

humming-bird [ˈhʌmɪŋbɜːd] *n* colibrí *m*.

humorist [ˈhjuːmərɪst] *n* humorista *mf*.

humour [ˈhjuːməʳ] *n* humor *m*. – **2** *t* complacer.

humorous [ˈhjuːmərəs] *adj (funny)* gracioso,-a.

hump [hʌmp] *n* jiba, joroba. – **2** *t (carry)* cargar.

hunch [hʌntʃ] *n* presentimiento. – **2** *t* encorvar.

hundred ['hʌndrəd] *adj* cien, ciento. — **2** *n* cien *m*, ciento.

hundredth ['hʌndrədθ] *adj-n* centésimo,-a. — **2** *n (fraction)* centésimo, centésima parte.

hundredweight ['hʌndrədweɪt] *n* quintal *m*. ▲ GB = *50,8 kg;* US = *45,4 kg.*

hung [hʌŋ] *pt & pp* → **hang.**

hunger ['hʌŋgəʳ] *n* hambre *f.* — **2** *i* tener hambre. ●*to ~ for,* ansiar.

hungry ['hʌŋgrɪ] *adj* hambriento,-a. ●*to be ~,* tener hambre.

hunk [hʌŋk] *n fam* pedazo (grande). **2** *fam* machote *m.*

hunt [hʌnt] *n* caza. **2** *(search)* búsqueda. — **3** *t-i* cazar. ●*to ~ for,* buscar.

hunter ['hʌntəʳ] *n* cazador *m.*

hunting ['hʌntɪŋ] *n* caza, montería. ●*to go ~,* ir de caza.

huntress ['hʌntrəs] *n* cazadora.

hurdle ['hɜːdəl] *n* SP valla. **2** *fig* obstáculo.

hurl [hɜːl] *t* lanzar, arrojar.

hurly-burly ['hɜːlɪbɜːlɪ] *n* bullicio.

hurrah [hʊˈrɑː], **hurray** [hʊˈreɪ] *interj* ¡hurra!

hurricane ['hʌrɪkən] *n* huracán *m.*

hurried ['hʌrɪd] *adj* apresurado,-a, hecho,-a de prisa.

hurry ['hʌrɪ] *n* prisa. — **2** *t* dar prisa a, apresurar. — **3** *i* apresurarse, darse prisa. ●*to be in a ~,* tener prisa.

hurt [hɜːt] *n* daño, dolor *m*, mal *m.* — **2** *adj (physically)* herido,-a. **3** *(offended)* dolido,-a. — **4** *t (physically)* lastimar, hacer daño. **5** *(offend)* herir, ofender. — **6** *i* doler. ▲ *pt & pp* **hurt.**

hurtful ['hɜːtfʊl] *adj* hiriente.

hurtle ['hɜːtəl] *i* precipitarse.

husband ['hʌzbənd] *n* marido, esposo.

hush [hʌʃ] *n* quietud, silencio. — **2** *t* callar, silenciar.

hush-hush ['hʌʃhʌʃ] *adj fam* confidencial.

husk [hʌsk] *n* cáscara.

huskiness ['hʌskɪnəs] *n* ronquera.

husky ['hʌskɪ] *adj* ronco,-a. — **2** *n* perro esquimal.

hustle ['hʌsəl] *n* bullicio. — **2** *t* dar prisa a. — **3** *i* apresurarse.

hustler ['hʌsləʳ] *n (cheat)* estafador,-ra. **2** US *sl* puta*.

hut [hʌt] *n* cabaña. **2** *(in garden)* cobertizo.

hutch [hʌtʃ] *n* conejera.

hyaena [haɪˈiːnə] *n* hiena.

hybrid ['haɪbrɪd] *adj-n* híbrido,-a *(m).*

hydrant ['haɪdrənt] *n* boca de riego. ■ *fire ~,* boca de incendio.

hydraulic [haɪˈdrɔːlɪk] *adj* hidráulico,-a.

hydrochloric [haɪdrəʊˈklɒrɪk] *adj* clorhídrico,-a.

hydroelectric [haɪdrəʊɪˈlektrɪk] *adj* hidroeléctrico,-a.

hydrofoil ['haɪdrəfɔɪl] *n* hidroala.

hydrogen ['haɪdrɪdʒən] *n* hidrógeno.

hydroplane ['haɪdrəʊpleɪn] *n* hidroavión *m.*

hyena [haɪˈiːnə] *n* hiena.

hygiene ['haɪdʒiːn] *n* higiene.

hygienic [haɪˈdʒiːnɪk] *adj* higiénico,-a.

hymen ['haɪmen] *n* himen *m.*

hymn [hɪm] *n* himno. ■ *~ book,* cantoral *m.*

hyperbola [haɪˈpɜːbələ] *n* hipérbola.

hyperbole [haɪˈpɜːbəlɪ] *n* hipérbole *f.*

hypermarket ['haɪpəmɑːkɪt] *n* hipermercado.

hyphen ['haɪfən] *n* guión *m.*

hyphenate ['haɪfəneɪt] *t* escribir con guión.

hypnosis [hɪpˈnəʊsɪs] *n* hipnosis *f inv.*

hypnotic [hɪpˈnɒtɪk] *adj* hipnótico,-a.

hypnotism ['hɪpnətɪzəm] *n* hipnotismo.

hypnotist ['hɪpnətɪst] *n* hipnotizador,-a.

hypnotize ['hɪpnətaɪz] *t* hipnotizar.

hypochondriac [haɪpəʊˈkɒndriæk] *n* hipocondríaco,-a.

hypocrisy [hɪˈpɒkrɪsɪ] *n* hipocresía.

hypocrite ['hɪpəkrɪt] *n* hipócrita *mf.*

hypocritical [hɪpəˈkrɪtɪkəl] *adj* hipócrita.

hypodermic [haɪpəʊˈdɜːmɪk] *adj* hipodérmico,-a.

hypotenuse [haɪˈpɒtɪnjuːz] *n* hipotenusa.

hypothesis [haɪˈpɒθɪsɪs] *n* hipótesis *f inv.*

hypothetic(al) [haɪpəˈθetɪk(əl)] *adj* hipotético,-a.

hysterectomy [hɪstəˈrektəmɪ] *n* histerectomía.

hysteria [hɪˈstɪərɪə] *n* histeria.

hysterical [hɪˈsterɪkəl] *adj* histérico,-a.

hysterics [hɪˈsterɪks] *n* ataque *m* de histeria.

I

I [aɪ] *pers pron* yo.

ice [aɪs] *n* hielo. **2** *(ice-cream)* helado. **— 3** *t (cake)* glasear. ◆*to ~ over/up* i helarse. ■ *~ cube,* cubito (de hielo).

iceberg [ˈaɪsbɜːg] *n* iceberg *m*.

icebox [ˈaɪsbɒks] *n* nevera.

icebreaker [ˈaɪsbreɪkəʳ] *n* rompehielos *m inv*.

icecap [ˈaɪskæp] *n* casquete *m* glaciar.

ice-cream [aɪsˈkriːm] *n* helado.

ice-skate [ˈaɪsskeɪt] *i* patinar sobre hielo.

ice-skating [ˈaɪsskeɪtɪŋ] *n* patinaje *m* sobre hielo.

icicle [ˈaɪsɪkəl] *n* carámbano.

icing [ˈaɪsɪŋ] *n* alcorza. ■ *~ sugar,* azúcar *m & f* glas/lustre.

icon [ˈaɪkən] *n* icono.

icy [ˈaɪsɪ] *adj* helado,-a. **2** *(wind)* glacial.

idea [aɪˈdɪə] *n gen* idea. **2** *(opinion)* opinión. **3** *(concept)* concepto.

ideal [aɪˈdiːl] *adj-n* ideal *(m)*. **— 2** *ideally adv* idealmente.

idealism [aɪˈdɪəlɪzəm] *n* idealismo.

idealist [aɪˈdɪəlɪst] *n* idealista *mf*.

idealistic [aɪdɪəˈlɪstɪk] *adj* idealista.

idealize [aɪˈdɪəlaɪz] *t* idealizar.

identical [aɪˈdəntɪkəl] *adj* idéntico,-a.

identification [aɪdentɪfɪˈkeɪʃən] *n* identificación. **2** *(papers)* documentación. ■ *~ parade,* rueda de identificación.

identify [aɪˈdentɪfaɪ] *t* identificar.

identity [aɪˈdentɪtɪ] *n* identidad. ■ *~ card,* carnet *m* de identidad.

ideological [aɪdɪəˈlɒdʒɪkəl] *adj* ideológico,-a.

ideology [aɪdɪˈɒlədʒɪ] *n* ideología.

idiom [ˈɪdɪəm] *n (phrase)* locución, modismo. **2** *(language)* lenguaje *m*.

idiomatic [ɪdɪəˈmætɪk] *adj* idiomático,-a.

idiosyncrasy [ɪdɪəˈsɪŋkrəsɪ] *n* idiosincrasia.

idiot [ˈɪdɪət] *n* idiota *mf*.

idiotic [ɪdɪˈɒtɪk] *adj* idiota.

idle [ˈaɪdəl] *adj (lazy)* perezoso,-a. **2** *(not working)* parado,-a. **3** *(gossip etc.)* frívolo,-a; *(threat)* futil. ◆*to ~ away* t desperdiciar.

idleness [ˈaɪdəlnəs] *n (laziness)* pereza. **2** *(inactivity)* inactividad. **3** *(gossip)* frivolidad; *(threat)* futilidad.

idol [ˈaɪdəl] *n* ídolo.

idolize [ˈaɪdəlaɪz] *t* idolatrar.

idyll [ˈɪdɪl] *n* idilio.

idyllic [ɪˈdɪlɪk] *adj* idílico,-a.

if [ɪf] *conj gen* si: *~ I were you,* yo de ti; *~ you want,* si quieres. **2** *(although)* aunque: *a clever ~ rather talkative child,* un niño inteligente aunque demasiado hablador. ●*as ~,* como si; *~ so,* de ser así.

igloo [ˈɪgluː] *n* iglú *m*.

ignite [ɪgˈnaɪt] *t-i* encender(se).

ignition [ɪgˈnɪʃən] *n* ignición. **2** AUTO encendido. ■ *~ key,* llave *f* de contacto.

ignominious [ɪgnəˈmɪnɪəs] *n* ignominioso,-a.

ignoramus [ɪgnəˈreɪməs] *n* ignorante *mf*.

ignorance [ˈɪgnərəns] *n* ignorancia.

ignorant [ˈɪgnərənt] *adj* ignorante. ●*to be ~ of,* desconocer, ignorar.

ignore [ɪgˈnɔːʳ] *t gen* ignorar. **2** *(order, warning)* no hacer caso de. **3** *(behaviour)* pasar lor alto. **4** *(person)* hacer como si no existiese.

ill [ɪl] *adj (sick)* enfermo,-a. **2** *(bad)* malo,-a; *(before masc sing noun)* mal. **— 3** *n* mal *m*. **— 4** *adv* mal: *I can ~ afford it,* mal me lo puedo permitir. ■ *~ health,* mala salud; *~ will,* rencor *m*.

ill-advised [ɪlædˈvaɪzd] *adj* imprudente.

illegal [ɪˈliːgəl] *adj* ilegal.

illegality [ɪlɪˈgælɪtɪ] *n* ilegalidad.

illegible [ɪˈledʒɪbəl] *adj* ilegible.

illegitimate [ɪlɪˈdʒɪtɪmət] *adj* ilegítimo,-a.

ill-equipped [ɪlɪˈkwɪpt] *adj* mal equipado,-a; *fig* mal preparado,-a.

illicit [ɪˈlɪsɪt] *adj* ilícito,-a.

illiteracy [ɪˈlɪtərəsɪ] *n* analfabetismo.

illiterate [ɪˈlɪtərət] *adj-n* analfabeto,-a. **2** *(uneducated)* inculto,-a.

illness [ˈɪlnəs] *n* enfermedad.

illogical [ɪˈlɒdʒɪkəl] *adj* ilógico,-a.

ill-timed [ɪlˈtaɪmd] *adj* inoportuno,-a.

ill-treat [ɪlˈtriːt] *t* maltratar.

ill-treatment [ɪlˈtriːtmənt] *n* malos tratos *mpl*.

illuminate [ɪˈluːmɪneɪt] *t* iluminar.

illumination [ɪluːmɪˈneɪʃən] *n* iluminación. **2** *(clarification)* aclaración.

illusion [ɪˈluːʒən] *n* ilusión. ●*to be under the ~ that ...,* engañarse pensando que ... .

illustrate [ˈɪləstreɪt] *t* ilustrar.

illustration [ɪləsˈtreɪʃən] *n* ilustración. **2** *(example)* ejemplo.

illustrative [ˈɪləstrətɪv] *adj gen* ilustrativo,-a. **2** *(example)* aclaratorio,-a.

illustrious [ɪˈlʌstrɪəs] *adj* ilustre.

image [ˈɪmɪdʒ] *n gen* imagen *f*.

imaginable [ɪˈmædʒɪnəbəl] *adj* imaginable.

imaginary [ɪˈmædʒɪnərɪ] *adj* imaginario,-a.

imagination [ɪmædʒɪˈneɪʃən] *n* imaginación.

imaginative [ɪˈmædʒɪnətɪv] *adj* imaginativo,-a.

imagine [ɪˈmædʒɪn] *t* imaginar. **2** *(suppose)* suponer, imaginar(se).

imbalance [ɪmˈbæləns] *n* desequilibrio.

imbecile [ˈɪmbɪsiːl] *n* imbécil *mf*.

imbue [ɪmˈbjuː] *t* imbuir (*with,* de).

imitate [ˈɪmɪteɪt] *t* imitar.

imitation [ɪmɪˈteɪʃən] *n* imitación.

immaculate [ɪˈmækjʊlət] *adj* inmaculado,-a; *(clothes)* impecable.

immaterial [ɪməˈtɪərɪəl] *adj* irrelevante.

immature [ɪməˈtjʊər] *adj* inmaduro,-a.

immeasurable [ɪˈmeʒərəbəl] *adj* inconmensurable.

immediacy [ɪˈmiːdɪəsɪ] *n (urgency)* urgencia. **2** *(nearness)* proximidad.

immediate [ɪˈmiːdɪət] *adj* inmediato,-a. **2** *(near)* próximo,-a, cercano,-a. **– 3** *immediately adv* inmediatamente, de inmediato, en seguida. **4** *(directly)* directamente. **– 5** *immediately conj* en cuanto.

immense [ɪˈmens] *adj* inmenso,-a.

immemorial [ɪməˈmɔːrɪəl] *adj* inmemorial.

immerse [ɪˈmɜːs] *t* sumergir.

immersion [ɪˈmɜːʃən] *n* inmersión.

immigrant [ˈɪmɪgrənt] *adj-n* inmigrante *(mf)*.

immigration [ɪmɪˈgreɪʃən] *n* inmigración.

imminent [ˈɪmɪnənt] *adj* inminente.

immobile [ɪˈməʊbaɪl] *adj* inmóvil.

immobilize [ɪˈməʊbɪlaɪz] *t* inmovilizar.

immoderate [ɪˈmɒdərət] *adj* desmedido,-a.

immodest [ɪˈmɒdɪst] *adj (not modest)* presumido,-a, engreído,-a. **2** *(indecent)* indecente.

immoral [ɪˈmɒrəl] *adj* inmoral.

immortal [ɪˈmɔːtəl] *adj* inmortal. **2** *fig* imperecedero,-a.

immortality [ɪmɔːˈtælɪtɪ] *n* inmortalidad.

immovable [ɪˈmuːvəbəl] *adj* inamovible. **2** *(person)* inconmovible.

immune [ɪˈmjuːn] *adj* inmune.

immunity [ɪˈmjuːnɪtɪ] *n* inmunidad.

immunize [ˈɪmjʊnaɪz] *t* inmunizar.

imp [ɪmp] *n* diablillo. **2** *fig (child)* pillo.

impact [ˈɪmpækt] *n* impacto. **2** *(crash)* choque *m*.

impair [ɪmˈpeər] *t* perjudicar. **2** *(weaken)* debilitar.

impale [ɪmˈpeɪl] *t* empalar.

impart [ɪmˈpɑːt] *t* impartir.

impartial [ɪmˈpɑːʃəl] *adj* imparcial.

impassable [ɪmˈpɑːsəbəl] *adj* intransitable.

impasse [æmˈpæːs] *n* punto muerto.

impassioned [ɪmˈpæʃənd] *adj* apasionado,-a.

impassive [ɪmˈpæsɪv] *adj* impasible, imperturbable.

impatience [ɪmˈpeɪʃəns] *n* impaciencia.

impatient [ɪmˈpeɪʃənt] *adj* impaciente.

impeach [ɪmˈpiːtʃ] *t* JUR acusar. **2** *(try)* procesar.

impeccable [ɪmˈpəkəbəl] *adj* impecable.

impede [ɪmˈpiːd] *t* estorbar, dificultar.

impediment [ɪmˈpedɪmənt] *n* impedimento, estorbo.

impel [ɪmˈpel] *t* impeler, impulsar.

impending [ɪmˈpendɪŋ] *adj* inminente.

impenetrable [ɪmˈpenɪtrəbəl] *adj* impenetrable.

imperative [ɪmˈperætɪv] *adj (vital)* esencial. **2** LING imperativo,-a. **– 3** *n* LING imperativo.

imperceptible [ɪmpəˈseptəbəl] *adj* imperceptible.

imperfect [ɪmˈpɜːfekt] *adj* LING imperfecto,-a. **2** *(faulty)* defectuoso,-a. − **3** *n* LING imperfecto.

imperfection [ɪmpəˈfekʃən] *n* imperfección.

imperial [ɪmˈpɪərɪəl] *adj* imperial.

imperialism [ɪmˈpɪərɪəlɪzəm] *n* imperialismo.

imperious [ɪmˈpɪərɪəs] *adj* imperioso,-a.

impermeable [ɪmˈpɜːmɪəbəl] *adj* impermeable.

impersonal [ɪmˈpɜːsənəl] *adj* impersonal.

impersonate [ɪmˈpɜːsəneɪt] *t* hacerse pasar por. **2** *(actor)* imitar.

impersonation [ɪmpɜːsəˈneɪʃən] *n* imitación.

impersonator [ɪmˈpɜːsəneɪtər] *n* imitador,-ra.

impertinence [ɪmˈpɜːtɪnəns] *n* impertinencia.

impertinent [ɪmˈpɜːtɪnənt] *adj* impertinente.

impervious [ɪmˈpɜːvɪəs] *adj* insensible.

impetuous [ɪmˈpetjʊəs] *adj* impetuoso,-a.

impetus [ˈɪmpɪtəs] *n* ímpetu *m*, impulso.

impinge [ɪmˈpɪndʒ] *i* **to ~ on**, afectar a.

implacable [ɪmˈplækəbəl] *adj* implacable.

implant [ˈɪmplɑːnt] *t* implantar.

implausible [ɪmˈplɔːzəbəl] *adj* poco probable.

implement [ˈɪmplɪmənt] *n* instrumento, utensilio; *(tool)* herramienta. − **2** *t* llevar a cabo, poner en práctica. **3** *(law)* aplicar. ▲ *En 2 y 3 (verbo)* [ˈɪmplɪment].

implicate [ˈɪmplɪkeɪt] *t* implicar.

implication [ɪmplɪˈkeɪʃən] *n* implicación.

implicit [ɪmˈplɪsɪt] *adj* implícito,-a. **2** *(complete)* absoluto,-a, incondicional.

implied [ɪmˈplaɪd] *adj* implícito,-a.

implore [ɪmˈplɔːr] *t* implorar.

imply [ɪmˈplaɪ] *t* *(involve)* implicar. **2** *(mean)* significar. **3** *(hint)* insinuar.

impolite [ɪmpəˈlaɪt] *adj* maleducado,-a.

import [ˈɪmpɔːt] *n* COM *(article)* artículo de importación. **2** COM *(activity)* importación. **3** *fml (meaning)* significado. **4** *fml (importance)* importancia. − **5** *t* COM importar.

importance [ɪmˈpɔːtəns] *n* importancia.

important [ɪmˈpɔːtənt] *adj* importante.

importer [ɪmˈpɔːtər] *n* importador,-ra.

impose [ɪmˈpəʊz] *t* imponer. ◆**to ~ on**, abusar de.

imposing [ɪmˈpəʊzɪŋ] *adj* imponente, impresionante.

imposition [ɪmpəˈzɪʃən] *n* imposición.

impossibility [ɪmpɒsəˈbɪlɪtɪ] *n* imposibilidad.

impossible [ɪmˈpɒsəbəl] *adj* imposible.

impostor [ɪmˈpɒstər] *n* impostor,-ra.

impotence [ˈɪmpətəns] *n* impotencia.

impotent [ˈɪmpətənt] *adj* impotente.

impound [ɪmˈpaʊnd] *t* confiscar, incautarse.

impoverish [ɪmˈpɒvərɪʃ] *t* empobrecer.

impracticable [ɪmˈpræktɪkəbəl] *adj* irrealizable, impracticable.

impractical [ɪmˈpræktɪkəl] *adj* poco práctico,-a.

imprecise [ɪmprɪˈsaɪs] *adj* impreciso,-a.

imprecision [ɪmprɪˈsɪʒən] *n* imprecisión.

impregnable [ɪmˈpregnəbəl] *adj* inexpugnable.

impregnate [ˈɪmpregneɪt] *t* impregnar.

impresario [ɪmprəˈsɑːrɪəʊ] *n* empresario,-a.

impress [ɪmˈpres] *t* impresionar; *I was favourably/unfavourably impressed,* me causó una buena/mala impresión. **2** *(stress)* subrayar.

impression [ɪmˈpreʃən] *n gen* impresión. **2** *(imitation)* imitación.

impressionist [ɪmˈpreʃənɪst] *adj-n* impresionista *(mf)*.

impressive [ɪmˈpresɪv] *adj* impresionante.

imprinted [ɪmˈprɪntɪd] *adj fig* grabado,-a.

imprisonment [ɪmˈprɪzənmənt] *n* encarcelamiento. ■ *life ~,* cadena perpetua.

improbability [ɪmprɒbəˈbɪlɪtɪ] *n* improbabilidad. **2** *(of story)* inverosimilitud.

improbable [ɪmˈprɒbəbəl] *adj* improbable. **2** *(story)* inverosímil.

impromptu [ɪmˈprɒmptjuː] *adj* improvisado,-a. − **2** *adv* improvisadamente.

improper [ɪmˈprɒpər] *adj* impropio,-a. **2** *(indecent)* indecoroso,-a.

improve [ɪmˈpruːv] *t gen* mejorar. **2** *(knowledge)* perfeccionar. − **3** *i* mejorar(se). ◆*to ~ on* *t* mejorar respecto a.

improvement [ɪmˈpruːvmənt] *n* mejora. **2** *(in knowledge)* perfeccionamiento. ◆*to be an ~ on,* ser mejor que.

improvisation [ɪmprəvaɪˈzeɪʃən] *n* improvisación.

improvise [ˈɪmprəvaɪz] *t-i* improvisar.

imprudent [ɪmˈpruːdənt] *adj* imprudente.

impudence [ˈɪmpjʊdəns] *n* descaro.

impudent [ˈɪmpjʊdənt] *adj* descarado,-a.

impulse ['ımpʌls] *n* impulso.
impulsive [ım'pʌlsıv] *adj* impulsivo,-a.
impunity [ım'pju:nıtı] *n* impunidad.
impure [ım'pjʊər] *adj (contaminated)* contaminado,-a; *(adulterated)* adulterado,-a. 2 *(morally)* deshonesto,-a, impuro,-a.
impurity [ım'pjʊərıtı] *n* impureza.
impute [ım'pju:t] *t* imputar, atribuir.

in [ın] *prep (within, inside)* en, dentro de: ~ *May,* en mayo; ~ *the box,* en la caja; ~ *the morning,* por la mañana; *we'll be back* ~ *twenty minutes,* estaremos de vuelta dentro de veinte minutos. 2 *(motion)* en: *put it* ~ *your pocket,* métetelo en el bolsillo; *we arrived* ~ *Bonn,* llegamos a Bonn. 3 *(wearing)* en, vestido,-a de: *the man* ~ *black,* el hombre vestido de negro. 4 *(manner)* en: ~ *public,* en público; *written* ~ *Greek/pencil,* escrito en griego/lápiz. – 5 *adv* dentro. 6 *(at home)* en casa. 7 *(fashionable)* de moda. 8 *(in power)* en el poder. 9 *(with pres p)* al: ~ *doing that,* al hacer eso. 10 *(with superlative)* de: *the biggest* ~ *the world,* el más grande del mundo. ●~ *so far as,* en lo que, hasta donde; ~ *the sun/shade,* al sol/a la sombra; *to be* ~ *for sth.,* estar a punto de recibir/ tener algo; *to be* ~ *on sth.,* estar enterado,-a de algo; *to be (well)* ~ *with sb.,* llevarse (muy) bien con algn. ■ *ins and outs,* detalles *mpl,* pormenores *mpl.*
inability [ınə'bılıtı] *n* incapacidad.
inaccessible [ınæk'sesəbəl] *adj* inaccesible.
inaccurate [ın'ækjʊrət] *adj* inexacto,-a, incorrecto,-a.
inactive [ın'æktıv] *adj* inactivo,-a.
inadequacy [ın'ædıkwəsı] *n* insuficiencia. 2 *(personal)* incapacidad.
inadequate [ın'ædıkwət] *adj* insuficiente. 2 *(person)* incapaz.
inadmissible [ınəd'mısıbəl] *adj* inadmisible.
inadvertent [ınəd'vɜ:tənt] *adj* inadvertido,-a. – 2 *inadvertently adv* inadvertidamente.
inadvisable [ınəd'vaızəbəl] *adj* poco aconsejable.
inane [ı'neın] *adj* fatuo,-a, necio,-a.
inanimate [ın'ænımıt] *adj* inanimado,-a.
inapplicable [ın'æplıkəbəl] *adj* inaplicable.
inappropriate [ınə'prəuprıət] *adj* poco apropiado,-a. 2 *(inopportune)* inoportuno,-a.

inarticulate [ınɑ:'tıkjʊlət] *adj (person)* incapaz de expresarse. 2 *(sound)* inarticulado,-a.
inasmuch as [ınəz'mʌtʃəz] *conj fml* puesto que, ya que.
inattentive [ınə'tentıv] *adj* desatento,-a.
inaudible [ın'ɔ:dıbəl] *adj* inaudible.
inaugural [ı'nɔ:gjʊrəl] *adj* inaugural.
inaugurate [ı'nɔ:gjʊreıt] *t* inaugurar. 2 *(as president)* investir.
inauguration [ınɔ:gjʊ'reıʃən] *n* inauguración. 2 *(president)* investidura.
inauspicious [ınɔ:'spıʃəs] *adj* poco propicio, desfavorable.
inborn ['ınbɔ:n], **inbred** ['ınbred] *adj* innato,-a.
incalculable [ın'kælkjʊləbəl] *adj* incalculable.
incandescent [ınkæn'desənt] *adj* incandescente.
incantation [ınkæn'teıʃən] *n* conjuro.
incapable [ın'keıpəbəl] *adj* incapaz.
incapacitate [ınkə'pæsıteıt] *t* incapacitar.
incapacity [ınkə'pæsıtı] *n* incapacidad.
incarcerate [ın'kɑ:səreıt] *t* encarcelar.
incarnate [ın'kɑ:nət] *adj* encarnado,-a.
incarnation [ınkɑ:'neıʃən] *n* encarnación.
incendiary [ın'sendıərı] *adj* incendiario,-a.
incense ['ınsens] *n* incienso. – 2 *t* enfurecer. ▲ *En 2 (verbo)* [ın'sens].
incentive [ın'sentıv] *n* incentivo.
inception [ın'sepʃən] *n fml* principio.
incessant [ın'sesənt] *adj* incesante. – 2 *incessantly adv* sin cesar.
incest ['ınsest] *n* incesto.
incestuous [ın'sestjʊəs] *adj* incestuoso,-a.
inch [ıntʃ] *n* pulgada.
incidence ['ınsıdəns] *n* frecuencia.
incident ['ınsıdənt] *n* incidente.
incidental [ınsı'dentəl] *adj* incidental, incidente. – 2 *incidentally adv* a propósito.
incinerate [ın'sınəreıt] *t* incinerar.
incinerator [ın'sınəreıtər] *n* incinerador *m.*
incision [ın'sıʒən] *n* incisión.
incisive [ın'saısıv] *adj* incisivo,-a. 2 *(mind)* penetrante.
incisor [ın'saızər] *n* (diente) incisivo.
incite [ın'saıt] *t* incitar.
incitement [ın'saıtmənt] *n* incitación.
inclement [ın'klemənt] *adj fml* inclemente.

inclination [ɪnklɪ'neɪʃən] *n* inclinación.
incline ['ɪnklaɪn] *n* pendiente *f*, cuesta. — 2 *t* inclinar. — 3 *i (tend)* tender (*to*, a). 4 *(slope)* inclinarse. ▲ *En 2, 3 y 4 (verbo)* [ɪn'klaɪn].
include [ɪn'kluːd] *t* incluir.
including [ɪn'kluːdɪŋ] *prep* incluso, inclusive.
inclusion [ɪn'kluːʒən] *n* inclusión.
inclusive [ɪn'kluːsɪv] *adj* inclusivo,-a. ●*to be ~ of,* incluir.
incognito [ɪnkɒg'niːtəʊ] *adv* de incógnito.
incoherence [ɪnkəʊ'hɪərəns] *n* incoherencia.
incoherent [ɪnkəʊ'hɪərənt] *adj* incoherente.
income ['ɪnkʌm] *n* ingresos *mpl*, renta. ■ *~ tax,* impuesto sobre la renta.
incoming ['ɪnkʌmɪŋ] *adj* entrante, nuevo,-a.
incommunicado [ɪnkəmjuːnɪ'kɑːdəʊ] *adj* incomunicado,-a.
incomparable [ɪn'kɒmpərəbəl] *adj* incomparable, inigualable.
incompatibility [ɪnkəmpætɪ'bɪlɪtɪ] *n* incompatibilidad.
incompatible [ɪnkəm'pætɪbəl] *adj* incompatible.
incompetence [ɪn'kɒmpɪtəns] *n* incompetencia, ineptitud.
incompetent [ɪn'kɒmpɪtənt] *adj* incompetente, inepto,-a.
incomplete [ɪnkəm'pliːt] *adj* incompleto,-a. 2 *(unfinished)* inacabado,-a.
incomprehensible [ɪnkɒmprɪ'hensɪbəl] *adj* incomprensible.
inconceivable [ɪnkən'siːvəbəl] *adj* inconcebible.
inconclusive [ɪnkən'kluːsɪv] *adj (discussion etc.)* no decisivo,-a. 2 *(proof)* no concluyente.
incongruous [ɪn'kɒŋgrʊəs] *adj* incongruente, incongruo,-a.
inconsequential [ɪnkɒnsɪ'kwenʃəl] *adj* de poca importancia.
inconsiderate [ɪnkən'sɪdərət] *adj* desconsiderado,-a.
inconsistent [ɪnkən'sɪstənt] *adj* inconsecuente, incongruo,-a: *it's ~ with the facts,* no concuerda con los hechos.
inconspicuous [ɪnkən'spɪkjʊəs] *adj* que pasa desapercibido,-a, que no llama la atención.
incontinent [ɪn'kɒntɪnənt] *adj* incontinente.

inconvenience [ɪnkən'viːnɪəns] *n* inconveniente *f*, molestia. — 2 *t* causar molestia a, molestar.
inconvenient [ɪnkən'viːnɪənt] *adj gen* molesto,-a; *(place)* mal situado,-a; *(time)* inoportuno,-a.
incorporate [ɪn'kɔːpəreɪt] *t* incorporar.
incorrect [ɪnkə'rekt] *adj* incorrecto,-a.
increase ['ɪnkriːs] *n* aumento, incremento. — 2 *t-i* aumentar; *(price)* subir. ●*to be on the ~,* ir en aumento. ▲*En 2 (verbo)* [ɪn'kriːs].
increasing [ɪn'kriːsɪŋ] *adj* creciente. — 2 *increasingly adv* cada vez más.
incredible [ɪn'kredɪbəl] *adj* increíble.
incredulous [ɪn'kredjʊləs] *adj* incrédulo,-a.
increment ['ɪnkrɪmənt] *n* incremento.
incriminate [ɪn'krɪmɪneɪt] *t* incriminar.
incriminating [ɪn'krɪmɪneɪtɪŋ] *adj* icriminatorio,-a.
incubate ['ɪnkjʊbeɪt] *t-i* incubar.
incubator ['ɪnkjʊbeɪtəʳ] *n* incubadora.
inculcate ['ɪnkʌlkeɪt] *t* inculcar.
incumbent [ɪn'kʌmbənt] *n* titular *mf*. ●*to be ~ on,* incumbir a.
incur [ɪn'kɜːʳ] *t* incurrir en. 2 *(debt)* contraer.
incurable [ɪn'kjʊərəbəl] *adj* incurable.
indebted [ɪn'detɪd] *adj* endeudado,-a. 2 *fig* agradecido,-a.
indecent [ɪn'diːsənt] *adj* indecente.
indecisive [ɪndɪ'saɪsɪv] *adj* indeciso,-a.
indeed [ɪn'diːd] *adv* en efecto, efectivamente. 2 *(intensifier)* realmente, de veras: *thank you very much ~,* muchísimas gracias.
indefinable [ɪndɪ'faɪnəbəl] *adj* indefinible.
indefinite [ɪn'defɪnət] *adj* indefinido,-a. — 2 *indefinitely adv* indefinidamente.
indelible [ɪn'delɪbəl] *adj* indeleble.
indelicate [ɪn'delɪkət] *adj* poco delicado,-a.
indemnity [ɪn'demnɪtɪ] *n* indemnidad. 2 *(compensation)* indemnización.
indent [ɪn'dent] *t* sangrar.
independence [ɪndɪ'pendəns] *n* independencia.
independent [ɪndɪ'pendənt] *adj* independiente. ●*to become ~,* independizarse.
in-depth [ɪn'depθ] *adj* exhaustivo,-a, a fondo.
indescribable [ɪndɪ'skraɪbəbəl] *adj* indescriptible.

indestructible [ɪndɪ'strʌktəbəl] *adj* indestructible.

index ['ɪndeks] *n* índice *m.* — 2 *t (book)* poner un índice a; *(collection)* catalogar.

indicate ['ɪndɪkeɪt] *t* indicar. — 2 *i* AUTO poner el intermitente.

indication [ɪndɪ'keɪʃən] *n* indicio, señal *f.*

indicative [ɪn'dɪkətɪv] *adj-n* indicativo,-a *(m).*

indict [ɪn'daɪt] *t* encausar *(for,* de).

indictment [ɪn'daɪtmənt] *n* (acta de) acusación. 2 *fig* crítica feroz.

indifference [ɪn'dɪfərəns] *n* indiferencia.

indifferent [ɪn'dɪfərənt] *adj* indiferente. 2 *(mediocre)* mediocre, regular.

indigenous [ɪn'dɪdʒɪnəs] *adj* indígena.

indigestible [ɪndɪ'dʒestəbəl] *adj* indigesto,-a.

indigestion [ɪndɪ'dʒestʃən] *n* indigestión.

indignant [ɪn'dɪgnənt] *adj (person)* indignado,-a; *(look etc.)* de indignación.

indignation [ɪndɪg'neɪʃən] *n* indignación.

indigo ['ɪndɪgəʊ] *n* añil *m.* — 2 *adj* de color añil.

indirect [ɪndɪ'rekt] *adj* indirecto,-a.

indiscreet [ɪndɪ'skriːt] *adj* indiscreto,-a.

indiscretion [ɪndɪ'skreʃən] *n* indiscreción.

indiscriminate [ɪndɪ'skrɪmɪnət] *adj* indiscriminado,-a.

indispensable [ɪndɪ'spensəbəl] *adj* indispensable, imprescindible.

indisposed [ɪndɪ'spəʊzd] *adj* indispuesto,-a.

indisputable [ɪndɪ'spjuːtəbəl] *adj* indiscutible.

indistinct [ɪndɪ'stɪŋkt] *adj (memory)* vago,-a; *(shape)* borroso,-a.

indistinguishable [ɪndɪ'stɪŋgwɪʃəbəl] *adj* indistinguible.

individual [ɪndɪ'vɪdjuəl] *adj (separate)* individual. 2 *(different)* particular, personal. — 3 *n* individuo.

indoctrination [ɪndɒktrɪ'neɪʃən] *n* adoctrinamiento.

indoor ['ɪndɔːʳ] *adj* interior; *(clothes etc.)* de estar por casa. ■ ~ *football,* fútbol *m* sala; ~ *pool,* piscina cubierta.

indoors [ɪn'dɔːz] *adv* dentro (de casa). ●*to stay* ~, quedarse en casa.

induce [ɪn'djuːs] *t gen* inducir. 2 *(cause)* causar, producir.

inducement [ɪn'djuːsmənt] *n* incentivo.

indulge [ɪn'dʌldʒ] *t* satisfacer. 2 *(person)* complacer; *(child)* mimar. ●*to* ~ *in,* permitirse, darse el lujo de.

indulgence [ɪn'dʌlʒəns] *n* indulgencia. 2 *(luxury)* (pequeño) lujo.

indulgent [ɪn'dʌldʒənt] *adj* indulgente.

industrial [ɪn'dʌstrɪəl] *adj* industrial. ■ ~ *accident,* accidente *m* laboral; ~ *action,* huelga; ~ *estate,* polígono industrial.

industrialist [ɪn'dʌstrɪəlɪst] *n* industrial *mf,* empresario,-a.

industrialize [ɪn'dʌstrɪəlaɪz] *t-i* industrializar(se).

industrious [ɪn'dʌstrɪəs] *adj* trabajador,-ra.

industry ['ɪndəstrɪ] *n* industria. 2 *(hard work)* diligencia.

inebriated [ɪn'iːbrɪeɪtɪd] *adj* ebrio,-a.

inedible [ɪn'edɪbəl] *adj* incom(est)ible.

ineffective [ɪnɪ'fektɪv], **ineffectual** [ɪnɪ'fektʃuəl] *adj* ineficaz, inútil. 2 *(person)* incompetente, inepto,-a.

inefficiency [ɪnɪ'fɪʃənsɪ] *n* ineficacia. 2 *(of person)* incompetencia, ineptitud.

inefficient [ɪnɪ'fɪʃənt] *adj* ineficaz, ineficiente. 2 *(person)* incompetente, inepto,-a.

inept [ɪ'nept] *adj* inepto,-a.

inequality [ɪnɪ'kwɒlɪtɪ] *n* desigualdad.

inert [ɪ'nɜːt] *adj* inerte.

inertia [ɪ'nɜːʃə] *n* inercia.

inescapable [ɪnɪ'skeɪpəbəl] *adj* ineludible.

inestimable [ɪn'estɪməbəl] *adj* inestimable.

inevitable [ɪn'evɪtəbəl] *adj* inevitable.

inexact [ɪnɪg'zækt] *adj* inexacto,-a.

inexcusable [ɪnɪk'skjuːzəbəl] *adj* inexcusable, imperdonable.

inexhaustible [ɪnɪg'zɔːstəbəl] *adj* inagotable.

inexorable [ɪn'eksərəbəl] *adj* inexorable.

inexpensive [ɪnɪk'spensɪv] *adj* barato,-a.

inexperience [ɪnɪk'spɪərɪəns] *n* inexperiencia.

inexperienced [ɪnɪk'spɪərɪənst], **inexpert** [ɪn'ekspɜːt] *adj* inexperto,-a.

inexplicable [ɪnɪk'splɪkəbəl] *adj* inexplicable.

inexpressive [ɪnɪk'spresɪv] *adj* inexpresivo,-a.

inextricable [ɪn'ekstrɪkəbəl] *adj* inseparable.

infallible [ɪn'fæləbəl] *adj* infalible.

infamous ['ɪnfəməs] *adj* infame.

infancy ['ɪnfənsɪ] *n* infancia.

infant ['ɪnfənt] *n* niño,-a.

infantile ['ɪnfəntaɪl] *adj* infantil.
infantry ['ɪnfəntrɪ] *n* infantería.
infatuated [ɪn'fætjʊeɪtɪd] *adj* encapricha-do,-a.
infect [ɪn'fekt] *t* infectar. **2** *(person)* contagiar.
infection [ɪn'fekʃən] *n* infección.
infectious [ɪn'fekʃəs] *adj* infeccioso,-a, contagioso,-a.
infer [ɪn'fɜː'] *t* inferir.
inference ['ɪnfərəns] *n* inferencia.
inferior [ɪn'fɪərɪə'] *adj-n* inferior *(mf)*.
inferiority [ɪnfɪərɪ'ɒrɪtɪ] *n* inferioridad.
infernal [ɪn'fɜːnəl] *adj* infernal.
inferno [ɪn'fɜːnəʊ] *n* infierno.
infertile [ɪn'fɜːtaɪl] *adl* estéril.
infest [ɪn'fest] *t* infestar.
infidelity [ɪnfɪ'delɪtɪ] *n* infidelidad.
infiltrate ['ɪnfɪltreɪt] *t* infiltrarse en.
infiltrator [ɪnfɪl'treɪtə'] *n* infiltrado,-a.
infinite ['ɪnfɪnət] *adj* infinito,-a.
infinitive [ɪn'fɪnɪtɪv] *n* infinitivo.
infinity [ɪn'fɪnɪtɪ] *n* MATH infinito. **2** *fig* infinidad.
infirm [ɪn'fɜːm] *adj* débil, enfermizo,-a.
infirmary [ɪn'fɜːmərɪ] *n* hospital *m*. **2** *(in school etc.)* enfermería.
infirmity [ɪn'fɜːmɪtɪ] *n* debilidad. **2** *(illness)* enfermedad.
inflame [ɪn'fleɪm] *t* inflamar.
inflammable [ɪn'flæməbəl] *adj* inflamable; *fig* explosivo,-a.
inflammation [ɪnflə'meɪʃən] *n* inflamación.
inflammatory [ɪn'flæmətərɪ] *adj* incendiario,-a.
inflate [ɪn'fleɪt] *t-i* inflar(se), hinchar(se).
inflation [ɪn'fleɪʃən] *n* inflación.
inflationary [ɪn'fleɪʃənərɪ] *adj* inflacionista, inflacionario,-a.
inflect [ɪn'flekt] *t-i (verb)* conjugar(se); *(noun)* declinar(se).
inflection [ɪn'flekʃən] *n* inflexión.
inflexible [ɪn'fleksɪbəl] *adj* inflexible.
inflict [ɪn'flɪkt] *t* infligir. **2** *fig (views etc.)* imponer.
influence ['ɪnflʊəns] *n* influencia. **– 2** *t* influir en.
influential [ɪnflʊ'enʃəl] *adj* influyente.
influenza [ɪnflʊ'enzə] *n* gripe *f*.
influx ['ɪnflʌks] *n* afluencia.
info ['ɪnfəʊ] *n fam* información.
inform [ɪn'fɔːm] *t* informar. ●*to ~ on sb.,* delatar/denunciar a algn.
informal [ɪn'fɔːməl] *adj gen* informal; *(language)* coloquial.

informality [ɪnfɔː'mælɪtɪ] *n* sencillez *f*.
informant [ɪn'fɔːmənt] *n* informante *mf*.
information [ɪnfə'meɪʃən] *n* información. **2** *(knowledge)* conocimientos *mpl*.
informative [ɪn'fɔːmətɪv] *adj* informativo,-a.
informer [ɪn'fɔːmə'] *n* delator,-ra. **2** *(to police)* informador,-ra, chivato,-a.
infrared [ɪnfrə'red] *adj* infrarrojo,-a.
infrastructure ['ɪnfrəstrʌktʃə'] *n* infraestructura.
infrequent [ɪn'friːkwənt] *adj* infrecuente.
infringe [ɪn'frɪndʒ] *t* infringir, transgredir. ●*to ~ on/upon,* usurpar, invadir.
infuriate [ɪn'fjʊərɪeɪt] *t* enfurecer.
infuriating [ɪn'fjʊərɪeɪtɪŋ] *adj* exasperante.
infusion [ɪn'fjuːʒən] *n* infusión.
ingenious [ɪn'dʒiːnɪəs] *adj* ingenioso,-a.
ingenuity [ɪndʒɪ'njuːɪtɪ] *n* ingenio, inventiva.
ingenuous [ɪn'dʒenjʊəs] *adj* ingenuo,-a.
ingot ['ɪŋgət] *n* lingote *m*.
ingrained [ɪn'greɪnd] *adj (dirt)* incrustado,-a. **2** *(habit)* arraigado,-a.
ingratiate [ɪn'greɪʃɪeɪt] *t to ~ o.s. with sb.,* congraciarse con algn.
ingratitude [ɪn'grætɪtjuːd] *n* ingratitud.
ingredient [ɪn'griːdɪənt] *n* ingrediente *m*. **2** *fig* componente *m*.
inhabit [ɪn'hæbɪt] *t* habitar, vivir en.
inhabitant [ɪn'hæbɪtənt] *n* habitante *mf*.
inhale [ɪn'heɪl] *t* aspirar; MED inhalar. **– 2** *i (smoker)* tragar(se) el humo.
inherent [ɪn'hɪərənt] *adj* inherente.
inherit [ɪn'herɪt] *t* heredar.
inheritance [ɪn'herɪtəns] *n* herencia.
inhibit [ɪn'hɪbɪt] *t* inhibir.
inhibition [ɪnhɪ'bɪʃən] *n* inhibición.
inhospitable [ɪn'hɒspɪtəbəl] *adj* inhospitalario,-a. **2** *(place)* inhóspito,-a.
inhuman [ɪn'hjuːmən], **inhumane** [ɪnhjuː'meɪn] *adj* inhumano,-a.
inimitable [ɪ'nɪmɪtəbəl] *adj* inimitable.
initial [ɪ'nɪʃəl] *adj-n* inicial *(f)*. **– 2** *t* firmar con las iniciales.
initiate ['ɪnɪʃɪeɪt] *t* iniciar.
initiation [ɪnɪʃɪ'eɪʃən] *n* iniciación.
initiative [ɪ'nɪʃɪətɪv] *n* iniciativa.
inject [ɪn'dʒekt] *t* inyectar.
injection [ɪn'dʒekʃən] *n* inyección.
injunction [ɪn'dʒʌŋkʃən] *n* entredicho.
injure ['ɪndʒə'] *t* herir.
injured ['ɪndʒəd] *adj* herido,-a; *(look etc.)* ofendido,-a.

injurious [ɪn'dʒʊərɪəs] *adj* perjudicial.

injury ['ɪndʒərɪ] *n* herida. ■ SP ~ *time,* tiempo de descuento.

injustice [ɪn'dʒʌstɪs] *n* injusticia.

ink [ɪŋk] *n* tinta.

inkling ['ɪŋklɪŋ] *n* noción, (vaga) idea. **2** *(suspicion)* sospecha. **3** *(hint)* indicio.

inlaid [ɪn'leɪd] *adj gen* taraceado,-a; *(gems)* incrustado,-a.

inland ['ɪnlənd] *adj* de tierra adentro. **— 2** *adv (travel)* tierra adentro; *(live)* en el interior. ▲ *En* **2** *(adv)* [ɪn'lænd].

inlay ['ɪnleɪ] *n gen* taracea; *(gems)* incrustación. **— 2** *t gen* taracear; *(gems)* incrustar. ▲ *En* **2** *(verbo)* [ɪn'leɪ].

inlet ['ɪnlet] *n (in coast)* cala, ensenada. **2** TECH entrada.

inmate ['ɪnmeɪt] *n gen* residente *mf.* **2** *(of prison)* preso,-a. **3** *(of hospital)* enfermo,-a. **4** *(of asylum)* interno,-a.

inmost ['ɪnməʊst] *adj* → **innermost**.

inn [ɪn] *n* posada, fonda, mesón *m.* **2** *(pub)* taberna.

innate [ɪ'neɪt] *adj* innato,-a.

inner ['ɪnəʳ] *adj* interior. ■ ~ *tube,* cámara.

innermost ['ɪnəməʊst] *adj* más interior. **2** *(thoughts)* más íntimo,-a.

innocence ['ɪnəsəns] *n* inocencia.

innocent ['ɪnəsənt] *adj-n* inocente *(mf).*

innocuous [ɪ'nɒkjʊəs] *adj* inocuo,-a.

innovation [ɪnə'veɪʃən] *n* innovación.

innovative ['ɪnəvətɪv] *adj* innovador,-ra.

innuendo [ɪnjʊ'endəʊ] *n* insinuación.

innumerable [ɪ'njuːmərəbəl] *adj* innumerable.

inoculate [ɪ'nɒkjʊleɪt] *t* inocular.

inoffensive [ɪnə'fensɪv] *adj* inofensivo,-a.

inoperative [ɪn'ɒpərətɪv] *adj* inoperante.

inopportune [ɪn'ɒpətjuːn] *adj* inoportuno,-a.

inorganic [ɪnɔː'gænɪk] *adj* inorgánico,-a.

in-patient ['ɪnpeɪʃənt] *n* (paciente) interno,-a.

input ['ɪnpʊt] *n* entrada; *(of money)* inversión; *(of data)* input *m.* **— 2** *t* COMPUT entrar, introducir. ▲ *pt & pp* **input**.

inquest ['ɪnkwest] *n* investigación judicial. **2** *fam fig* investigación.

inquire [ɪn'kwaɪəʳ] *t* preguntar. ●*"~ within",* "razón aquí"; *to* ~ *about sth.,* preguntar por algo: *to* ~ *into sth.,* investigar algo.

inquiring [ɪn'kwaɪərɪŋ] *adj (mind)* curioso,-a.

inquiry [ɪn'kwaɪərɪ] *n* pregunta. **2** *(investigation)* investigación. ●*"inquiries",* "información".

inquisition [ɪnkwɪ'zɪʃən] *n* inquisición.

inquisitive [ɪn'kwɪzɪtɪv] *adj* curioso,-a.

inroads ['ɪnrəʊds] *npl* incursión *f sing.* ●*to make* ~ *into,* reducir, hacer bajar.

insane [ɪn'seɪn] *adj* demente.

insanitary [ɪn'sænɪtərɪ] *adj* insalubre.

insanity [ɪn'sænɪtɪ] *n* locura, demencia.

insatiable [ɪn'seɪʃəbəl] *adj* insaciable.

inscribe [ɪn'skraɪb] *t* inscribir.

inscription [ɪn'skrɪpʃən] *n* inscripción.

insect ['ɪnsekt] *n* insecto.

insecticide [ɪn'sektɪsaɪd] *n* insecticida *m.*

insecure [ɪnsɪ'kjʊəʳ] *adj* inseguro,-a.

insecurity [ɪnsɪ'kjʊərɪtɪ] *n* inseguridad.

inseminate [ɪn'semɪneɪt] *t* inseminar.

insensitive [ɪn'sensɪtɪv] *adj* insensible.

inseparable [ɪn'sepərəbəl] *adj* inseparable.

insert [ɪn'sɜːt] *t* insertar, introducir.

insertion [ɪn'sɜːʃən] *n* inserción.

inside [ɪn'saɪd] *n* interior *m.* **2** *pl* tripas *fpl,* entrañas *fpl.* **— 3** *adj* interior, interno,-a. **— 4** *adv (position)* dentro; *(movement)* adentro. **— 5** *prep* dentro de. ●~ *out,* de dentro afuera, al revés.

insider [ɪn'saɪdəʳ] *n* persona enterada.

insight ['ɪnsaɪt] *n (faculty)* perspicacia, penetración. **2** *(idea)* idea.

insignificance [ɪnsɪg'nɪfɪkəns] *n* insignificancia.

insignificant [ɪnsɪg'nɪfɪkənt] *adj* insignificante.

insincere [ɪnsɪn'sɪəʳ] *adj* falso,-a.

insincerity [ɪnsɪn'serɪtɪ] *n* falsedad.

insinuate [ɪn'sɪnjʊeɪt] *t* insinuar.

insinuation [ɪnsɪnjʊ'eɪʃən] *n* indirecta.

insipid [ɪn'sɪpɪd] *adj* insípido,-a, soso,-a.

insist [ɪn'sɪst] *i* insistir *(on,* en).

insistence [ɪn'sɪstəns] *n* insistencia.

insistent [ɪn'sɪstənt] *adj* insistente.

insofar as [ɪnsəʊ'fɑːrəz] *adv* en la medida en que.

insolence ['ɪnsələns] *n* insolencia.

insolent ['ɪnsələnt] *adj* insolente.

insoluble [ɪn'sɒljʊbəl] *adj* insoluble.

insolvent [ɪn'sɒlvənt] *adj* insolvente.

insomnia [ɪn'sɒmnɪə] *n* insomnio.

insomniac [ɪn'sɒmnɪæk] *n* insomne *mf.*

inspect [ɪn'spekt] *t gen* inspeccionar. **2** *(luggage)* registrar. **3** *(troops)* pasar revista a.

inspection [ɪn'spekʃən] *n gen* inspección. **2** *(of luggage)* registro. **3** *(of troops)* revista.

inspector [ɪn'spektər] *n gen* inspector,-ra. **2** *(on train)* revisor,-ra.

inspiration [ɪnspɪ'reɪʃən] *n* inspiración.

inspire [ɪn'spaɪər] *t gen* inspirar. **2** *(encourage)* animar.

instability [ɪnstə'bɪlɪti] *n* inestabilidad.

install [ɪn'stɔ:l] *t* instalar.

installation [ɪnstə'leɪʃən] *n* instalación.

instalment [ɪn'stɔ:lmənt] *n (of payment)* plazo. **2** *(of book etc.)* entrega.

instance ['ɪnstəns] *n* ejemplo, caso. ●*for* ~, por ejemplo; *in the first* ~, en primer lugar.

instant ['ɪnstənt] *n* instante *m*, momento. – **2** *adj* inmediato,-a. **3** *(coffee etc.)* instantáneo,-a. – **4** *instantly adv* al instante, inmediatamente.

instantaneous [ɪnstən'teɪnɪəs] *adj* instantáneo,-a.

instead [ɪn'sted] *adv* en cambio. ●~ *of,* en lugar de, en vez de.

instep ['ɪnstep] *n* empeine *m*.

instigate ['ɪnstɪgeɪt] *t* instigar.

instigation [ɪnstɪ'geɪʃən] *n* instigación.

instigator ['ɪnstɪgeɪtər] *n* instigador,-ra.

instil [ɪn'stɪl] *t* inculcar.

instinct ['ɪnstɪŋkt] *n* instinto.

instinctive [ɪn'stɪŋktɪv] *adj* instintivo,-a.

institute ['ɪnstɪtju:t] *n* instituto. **2** *(of professionals)* colegio, asociación. – **3** *t* instituir.

institution [ɪnstɪ'tju:ʃən] *n* institución. **2** *(home)* asilo.

institutional [ɪnstɪ'tju:ʃənəl] *adj* institucional.

instruct [ɪn'strʌkt] *t* instruir. **2** *(order)* ordenar, mandar.

instruction [ɪn'strʌkʃən] *n* instrucción. **2** *pl* instrucciones *fpl*, indicaciones *fpl*.

instructor [ɪn'strʌktər] *n gen* instructor,-ra. **2** *(of driving)* profesor,-ra. **3** SP monitor,-ra.

instrument ['ɪnstrumənt] *n* instrumento.

instrumental [ɪnstrə'mentəl] *adj* instrumental. ●*to be* ~ *in,* contribuir decisivamente a.

insubordinate [ɪnsə'bɔ:dɪnət] *adj* insubordinado,-a.

insubordination [ɪnsəbɔ:dɪ'neɪʃən] *n* insubordinación.

insufficient [ɪnsə'fɪʃənt] *adj* insuficiente.

insular ['ɪnsjulər] *adj* insular.

insulate ['ɪnsjuleɪt] *t* aislar.

insulation [ɪnsju'leɪʃən] *n* aislamiento.

insulin ['ɪnsjulɪn] *n* insulina.

insult ['ɪnsʌlt] *n (words)* insulto. **2** *(action)* afrenta. – **3** *t* insultar. ▲ *En 3 (verbo)* [ɪn'sʌlt].

insurance [ɪn'ʃuərəns] *n* seguro.

insure [ɪn'ʃuər] *t* asegurar.

insurgent [ɪn'sɜ:dʒənt] *adj-n* insurgente *(mf)*, insurrecto,-a.

insurmountable [ɪnsə'maʊntəbəl] *adj* insuperable.

insurrection [ɪnsə'rekʃən] *n* insurrección.

intact [ɪn'tækt] *adj* intacto,-a.

intake ['ɪnteɪk] *n (of food etc.)* consumo. **2** *(of students etc.)* número de admitidos.

intangible [ɪn'tændʒɪbəl] *adj* intangible.

integral ['ɪntɪgrəl] *adj* integrante. **2** *(whole)* íntegro,-a, entero,-a. – **3** *adj-n* MATH integral *(f)*.

integrate ['ɪntɪgreɪt] *t-i* integrar(se).

integration [ɪntɪ'greɪʃən] *n* integración.

integrity [ɪn'tegrɪti] *n* integridad.

intellect ['ɪntɪlekt] *n* intelecto, inteligencia.

intellectual [ɪntɪ'lektjuəl] *adj-n* intelectual *(mf)*.

intelligence [ɪn'telɪdʒəns] *n* inteligencia. **2** *(information)* información.

intelligent [ɪn'telɪʒənt] *adj* inteligente.

intend [ɪn'tend] *t* tener la intención de, proponerse.

intended [ɪn'tendɪd] *adj (desired)* deseado,-a. **2** *(intentional)* intencionado,-a. ●~ *for,* para, dirigido,-a a.

intense [ɪn'tens] *adj* intenso,-a. **2** *(person)* muy serio,-a.

intensify [ɪn'tensɪfaɪ] *t-i* intensificar(se).

intensity [ɪn'tensɪti] *n* intensidad.

intensive [ɪn'tensɪv] *adj* intensivo,-a.

intent [ɪn'tent] *adj (look etc.)* fijo,-a. – **2** *n* intención. ●*to be* ~ *on,* estar decidido,-a a/empeñado,-a en; *with* ~ *to,* con la intención de.

intention [ɪn'tenʃən] *n* intención.

intentional [ɪn'tenʃənəl] *adj* intencional. – **2** *intentionally adv* adrede.

inter [ɪn'tɜ:r] *t fml* enterrar, sepultar.

interact [ɪntər'ækt] *i* actuar recíprocamente.

interactive [ɪntər'æktɪv] *adj* interactivo,-a.

intercede [ɪntə'si:d] *i* interceder.

intercept [ɪntə'sept] *t* interceptar.

interchange ['ɪntətʃeɪndʒ] *n* intercambio. **2** AUTO enlace *m*.

intercom ['ɪntəkɒm] *n* interfono.

intercontinental [ɪntəkɒntɪ'nentəl] *adj* intercontinental.

intercourse ['ɪntəkɔːs] *n* trato. **2** *(sexual)* coito, relaciones *fpl* sexuales.

interest ['ɪntrɪst] *n gen* interés *m*. **2** *(in business)* participación. – **3** *t* interesar. ●*in the interests of ...,* en pro de ...; *to be of ~,* interesar; *to take an ~ in,* interesarse por. ■ *~ rate,* tipo de interés.

interested ['ɪntrɪstɪd] *adj* interesado,-a.

interesting ['ɪntrɪstɪŋ] *adj* interesante.

interface ['ɪntəfeɪs] *n* COMPUT interface *f*.

interfere [ɪntə'fɪə'] *i (meddle)* entrometerse. **2** PHYS interferir. ●*to ~ with, (hinder)* dificultar, estorbar; *(block)* obstaculizar.

interference [ɪntə'fɪərəns] *n (meddling)* intromisión. **2** *(hindrance)* dificultad, estorbo. **3** PHYS interferencia.

interfering [ɪntə'fɪərɪŋ] *adj* entrometido,-a.

interim ['ɪntərɪm] *adj* interino,-a. – **2** *n* ínterin *m*.

interior [ɪn'tɪərɪə'] *adj-n* interior *(m)*.

interjection [ɪntə'dʒekʃən] *n* GRAM interjección. **2** *(comment)* interposición.

interlock [ɪntə'lɒk] *t-i* entrelazar(se).

interloper ['ɪntələupə'] *n* intruso,-a.

interlude ['ɪntəluːd] *n* intermedio. **2** *(in music)* interludio.

intermediary [ɪntə'miːdɪərɪ] *n* intermediario,-a.

intermediate [ɪntə'miːdɪət] *adj* intermedio,-a.

interminable [ɪn'tɜːmɪnəbəl] *adj* interminable.

intermingle [ɪntə'mɪŋgəl] *i* entremezclarse.

intermission [ɪntə'mɪʃən] *n* intermedio.

intermittent [ɪntə'mɪtənt] *adj* intermitente.

intern ['ɪntɜːn] *n* US MED interno,-a. – **2** *t* internar. ▲*En 2 (verbo)* [ɪn'tɜːn].

internal [ɪn'tɜːnəl] *adj* interior; *(in group, body, organization)* interno,-a.

international [ɪntə'næʃənəl] *adj-n* internacional *(mf)*.

internee [ɪntɜː'niː] *n* interno,-a.

internment [ɪn'tɜːnmənt] *n* internamiento.

interplay ['ɪntəpleɪ] *n* interacción.

interpret [ɪn'tɜːprət] *t* interpretar. – **2** *i* actuar de intérprete.

interpretation [ɪntɜːprɪ'teɪʃən] *n* interpretación.

interpreter [ɪn'tɜːprɪtə'] *n* intérprete *mf*.

interrogate [ɪn'terəgeɪt] *t* interrogar.

interrogation [ɪnterə'geɪʃən] *n* interrogatorio.

interrogative [ɪntə'rɒgəætɪv] *adj* interrogativo,-a. – **2** *n (word)* palabra interrogativa; *(phrase)* oración interrogativa.

interrupt [ɪntə'rʌpt] *t-i* interrumpir.

interruption [ɪntə'rʌpʃən] *n* interrupción.

intersect [ɪntə'sekt] *t-i* cruzar(se). **2** *(in geometry)* intersecar(se).

intersection [ɪntə'sekʃən] *n (of roads)* cruce *m*. **2** *(in geometry)* intersección.

intersperse [ɪntə'spɜːs] *t* entremezclar.

interstate [ɪntə'steɪt] *adj* interestatal.

interval ['ɪntəvəl] *n* intervalo. **2** *(in play etc.)* descanso.

intervene [ɪntə'viːn] *i* intervenir. **2** *(event)* sobrevenir, ocurrir. **3** *(time)* transcurrir.

intervention [ɪntə'venʃən] *n* intervención.

interview ['ɪntəvjuː] *n* entrevista, interviú *m*. – **2** *t* entrevistar.

interviewee [ɪntəvjuː'iː] *n* entrevistado,-a.

interviewer ['ɪntəvjuːə'] *n* entrevistador,-ra.

intestine [ɪn'testɪn] *n* intestino.

intimacy ['ɪntɪməsɪ] *n* intimidad.

intimate ['ɪntɪmət] *adj* íntimo,-a. – **2** *t* dar a entender, insinuar. ▲ *En 2 (verbo)* ['ɪntɪmeɪt].

intimation [ɪntɪ'meɪʃən] *n (sign)* indicio. **2** *(feeling)* presentimiento.

intimidate [ɪn'tɪmɪdeɪt] *t* intimidar.

intimidating [ɪn'tɪmɪdeɪtɪŋ] *adj* amenazador,-ra.

intimidation [ɪntɪmɪ'deɪʃən] *n* intimidación.

into ['ɪntu] *prep* en, dentro de. ●*fam to be ~ sth.,* apetecerle algo a algn.; *(hobby)* ser aficionado,-a a.

intolerable [ɪn'tɒlərəbəl] *adj* intolerable.

intolerance [ɪn'tɒlərəns] *n* intolerancia.

intolerant [ɪn'tɒlərənt] *adj* intolerante.

intonation [ɪntə'neɪʃən] *n* entonación.

intoxicated [ɪn'tɒksɪkeɪt] *adj* ebrio,-a.

intoxication [ɪntɒksɪ'keɪʃən] *n* embriaguez *f*.

intransigence [ɪn'trænsɪdʒəns] *n* intransigencia.

intransigent [ɪn'trænsɪdʒent] *adj* intransigente.

intransitive [ɪn'trænsɪtɪv] *adj* intransitivo,-a.

intrepid [ɪn'trepɪd] *adj* intrépido,-a.

intricacy ['ɪntrɪkəsɪ] *n* complejidad.

intricate ['ɪntrɪkət] *adj* complejo,-a.

intrigue [ɪn'tri:g] *n* intriga. – **2** *t-i* intrigar.

intriguing [ɪn'tri:gɪŋ] *adj* intrigante.

intrinsic [ɪn'trɪnsɪk] *adj* intrínseco,-a.

introduce [ɪntrə'dju:s] *t* introducir. **2** *(person)* presentar. **3** *(law)* promulgar.

introduction [ɪntrə'dʌkʃən] *n* introducción. **2** *(of person)* presentación. **3** *(of law)* promulgación.

introductory [ɪntrə'dʌktərɪ] *adj* introductorio,-a; *(words)* preliminar.

introvert ['ɪntrəvɜ:t] *n* introvertido,-a.

introverted ['ɪntrəvɜ:tɪd] *adj* introvertido,-a.

intrude [ɪn'tru:d] *i* entrometerse. **2** *(disturb)* molestar, estorbar.

intruder [ɪn'tru:dəʳ] *n* intruso,-a.

intrusion [ɪn'tru:ʒən] *n* intrusion. **2** *(on privacy)* invasión.

intuition [ɪntju:ɪ'ʃən] *n* intuición.

intuitive [ɪn'tju:ɪtɪv] *adj* intuitivo,-a.

inundate ['ɪnʌndeɪt] *t* inundar.

invade [ɪn'veɪd] *t* invadir.

invader [ɪn'veɪdəʳ] *n* invasor,-ra.

invalid [ɪn'vælɪd] *adj* inválido,-a, nulo,-a. – **2** *n (person) (disabled)* inválido,-a; *(ill)* enfermo,-a.

invalidate [ɪn'vælɪdeɪt] *t* invalidar, anular.

invaluable [ɪn'væljʊəbəl] *adj* inestimable.

invariable [ɪn'veərɪəbəl] *adj* invariable.

invasion [ɪn'veɪʒən] *n* invasión.

invective [ɪn'vektɪv] *n* invectiva.

invent [ɪn'vent] *t* inventar.

invention [ɪn'venʃən] *n (thing)* invento. **2** *(action)* invención.

inventiveness [ɪn'ventɪvnəs] *n* inventiva.

inventor [ɪn'ventəʳ] *n* inventor,-ra.

inventory ['ɪnventrɪ] *n* inventario.

inversion [ɪn'vɜ:ʃən] *n* inversión.

invert [ɪn'vɜ:t] *t* invertir.

invertebrate [ɪn'vɜ:tɪbrət] *adj-n* invertebrado,-a.

inverted [ɪn'vɜ:tɪd] *adj* invertido,-a. ■ ~ *commas,* comillas.

invest [ɪn'vest] *t (money)* invertir. – **2** *i* invertir dinero en; *(buy)* comprar.

investigate [ɪn'vestɪgeɪt] *t* investigar.

investigation [ɪnvestɪ'geɪʃən] *n* investigación.

investigator [ɪn'vestɪgeɪtəʳ] *n* investigador,-ra.

investment [ɪn'vestmənt] *n (money)* inversión.

investor [ɪn'vestəʳ] *n* inversor,-ra.

inveterate [ɪn'vetərət] *adj* empedernido,-a.

invigilate [ɪn'vɪdʒɪleɪt] *t-i* vigilar.

invigilator [ɪn'vɪdʒɪleɪtəʳ] *n* vigilante *mf.*

invigorate [ɪn'vɪgəreɪt] *t* vigorizar.

invigorating [ɪn'vɪgəreɪtɪŋ] *adj* vigorizante.

invincible [ɪn'vɪnsɪbəl] *adj* invencible.

inviolable [ɪn'vaɪələbəl] *adj* inviolable.

invisible [ɪn'vɪzəbəl] *adj* invisible. ■ ~ *ink,* tinta simpática.

invitation [ɪnvɪ'teɪʃən] *n* invitación.

invite [ɪn'vaɪt] *t* invitar. **2** *(comments etc.)* solicitar; *(problems etc.)* provocar.

inviting [ɪn'vaɪtɪŋ] *adj* tentador,-ra.

invoice ['ɪnvɔɪs] *n* factura. – **2** *t* facturar.

invoke [ɪn'vəʊk] *t* invocar.

involuntary [ɪn'vɒləntərɪ] *adj* involuntario,-a.

involve [ɪn'vɒlv] *t* involucrar, comprometer. **2** *(affect)* tener que ver con, afectar a. **3** *(entail)* suponer, implicar.

involved [ɪn'vɒlvd] *adj* complicado,-a. ●*to get ~ in,* meterse/enredarse en.

involvement [ɪn'vɒlvmənt] *n* participación. **2** *(in crime)* complicidad.

inward ['ɪnwəd] *adj* interior.

inward(s) ['ɪnwəd(z)] *adv* hacia adentro.

iodine ['aɪədi:n] *n* yodo.

irascible [ɪ'ræsɪbəl] *adj* irascible.

irate [aɪ'reɪt] *adj* airado,-a.

iris ['aɪərɪs] *n (of eye)* iris *m inv.* **2** BOT lirio.

irk [ɜ:k] *t* fastidiar.

iron ['aɪən] *n* hierro. **2** *(appliance)* plancha. – **3** *t (clothes)* planchar. ■ *Iron Age,* Edad de Hierro.

ironic [aɪ'rɒnɪk] *adj* irónico,-a.

ironing ['aɪənɪŋ] *n (not ironed)* ropa por planchar; *(ironed)* ropa planchada. ●*to do the ~,* planchar. ■ ~ *board,* tabla de planchar.

ironmonger ['aɪənmʌŋgəʳ] *n* ferretero,-a. ■ *ironmonger's (shop),* ferretería.

irony ['aɪrənɪ] *n* ironía.

irrational [ɪ'ræʃənəl] *adj* irracional.

irregular [ɪ'regjʊləʳ] *adj* irregular.

irregularity [ɪregjʊ'lærɪtɪ] *n* irregularidad.

irrelevant [ɪ'relɪvənt] *adj* irrelevante.

irreligious [ɪrɪ'lɪdʒəs] *adj* irreligioso,-a.

irreparable [ɪ'repərəbəl] *adj* irreparable.

irreplaceable [ɪrɪ'pleɪsəbəl] *adj* insustituible.

irresistible [ɪrɪ'zɪstəbəl] *adj* irresistible.

irresolute [ɪ'rezəlu:t] *adj* indeciso,-a.

irrespective of [ɪrɪ'spektɪvəv] *prep* sin tener en cuenta.

irresponsible [ɪrɪ'spɒnsəbəl] *adj* irresponsable.

irreverent [ɪ'revərənt] *adj* irreverente.

irreversible [ɪrɪ'vɜ:səbəl] *adj* irreversible.

irrevocable [ɪ'revəkəbəl] *adj* irrevocable.

irrigate ['ɪrɪgeɪt] *t* regar.

irrigation [ɪrɪ'geɪʃən] *n* riego.

irritable ['ɪrɪtəbəl] *adj* irritable.

irritate ['ɪrɪteɪt] *t* irritar.

irritating ['ɪrɪteɪtɪŋ] *adj* irritante.

irritation [ɪrɪ'teɪʃən] *n* irritación.

is [ɪz] *3rd pers sing pres* → **be**.

Islam ['ɪzlɑ:m] *n* islam *m*.

Islamic [ɪz'læmɪk] *adj* islámico,-a.

island ['aɪlənd] *n* isla.

islander ['aɪləndəʳ] *n* isleño,-a.

isle [aɪl] *n* isla.

isolate ['aɪsəleɪt] *t* aislar.

isolation [aɪsə'leɪʃən] *n* aislamiento.

issue ['ɪʃu:] *n (topic)* asunto, tema *m*. 2 *(of book)* edición; *(of newspaper)* número. 3 *(of stamps, shares, etc.)* emisión. 4 *(of passport)* expedición. 5 *fml (children)* descendencia. − 6 *t (book)* publicar. 7 *(stamps, shares, etc.)* emitir. 8 *(passport)* expedir. 9 *(order)* dar; *(decree)* promulgar.

isthmus ['ɪsməs] *n* istmo.

it [ɪt] *pers pron (subject)* él, ella, ello. 2 *(object) (direct)* lo, la; *(indirect)* le. 3 *(after prep)* él, ella, ello.

italics [ɪ'tælɪks] *n* cursiva.

itch [ɪtʃ] *n* picazón *f*, picor *m*. − *i* picar.
•*to be itching to do sth.*, estar impaciente por hacer algo.

itchy [ɪtʃ] *adj* que pica.

item ['aɪtəm] *n* artículo, cosa. 2 *(on agenda)* asunto. 3 *(on bill)* partida. 4 *(piece of news)* noticia.

itemize ['aɪtəmaɪz] *t* hacer una lista de. 2 *(specify)* detallar.

itinerant [ɪ'tɪnərənt] *adj* itinerante.

itinerary [aɪ'tɪnərərɪ] *n* itinerario.

its [ɪts] *poss adj* su, sus.

itself [ɪt'self] *pers pron (reflexive)* se. 2 *(emphatic)* él/ello mismo, ella misma. 3 *(after prep)* sí (mismo,-a).

ivory ['aɪvərɪ] *n* marfil *m*.

ivy ['aɪvɪ] *n* hiedra.

J

jab [dʒæb] *n* pinchazo; *(with elbow)* codazo. **2** *fam* inyección. – **3** *t* pinchar; dar un codazo a.

jabber [ˈdʒæbəʳ] *n* farfulla. – **2** *i-t* farfullar.

jack [dʒæk] *n* AUTO gato. **2** *(in cards)* jota; *(Spanish pack)* sota.

jackal [ˈdʒækɔːl] *n* chacal *m*.

jackass [ˈdʒækæs] *n* burro.

jackdaw [ˈdʒækdɔː] *n* grajilla.

jacket [ˈdʒækɪt] *n* chaqueta; *(of suit)* americana. **2** *(leather etc.)* cazadora. **3** *(of book)* sobrecubierta.

jack-knife [ˈdʒæknaɪf] *n* navaja. – **2** *i (lorry)* colear.

jack-of-all-trades [ˈdʒækəvɔːltreɪdz] *n* persona de muchos oficios.

jackpot [ˈdʒækpɒt] *n* (premio) gordo.

jade [dʒeɪd] *n* jade *m*.

jaded [ˈdʒeɪdɪd] *adj* agotado,-a, cansado,-a.

jagged [ˈdʒægɪd] *adj* dentado,-a.

jaguar [ˈdʒægjʊəʳ] *n* jaguar *m*.

jail [dʒeɪl] *n* cárcel *f*, prisión. – **2** *t* encarcelar.

jailer [ˈdʒeɪləʳ] *n* carcelero,-a.

jam [dʒæm] *n* confitura, mermelada. **2** *(tight spot)* aprieto. **3** *fam (luck)* churra. – **4** *t (block)* atascar. **5** *(crowd)* atestar, apiñar. **6** *(cram)* embutir, meter. **7** RAD interferir con. – **8** *i (door)* atrancarse. **9** *(machine parts)* agarrotarse. ■ *traffic ~,* atasco, embotellamiento.

jamboree [dʒæmbəˈriː] *n* juerga. **2** *(scout meeting)* reunión de muchachos exploradores.

jammy [ˈdʒæmɪ] *adj fam* suertudo,-a.

jam-packed [dʒæmˈpækt] *adj fam* atestado,-a.

jangle [ˈdʒæŋgəl] *t-i* (hacer) sonar de un modo discordante.

janitor [ˈdʒænɪtəʳ] *n* portero.

January [ˈdʒænjʊərɪ] *n* enero.

jar [dʒɑːʳ] *n (glass)* tarro, pote *m*. – **2** *t* hacer mover, sacudir. – **3** *i (sounds)* chirriar. **4** *(colours)* chocar.

jargon [ˈdʒɑːgən] *n* jerga, jerigonza.

jasmin [ˈdʒæzmɪn] *n* jazmín *m*.

jaundice [ˈdʒɔːndɪs] *n* ictericia.

jaundiced [ˈdʒɔːndɪst] *adj fig* amargado,-a.

jaunt [dʒɔːnt] *n* excursión, viaje *m*. – **2** *i* ir de excursión/viaje.

jaunty [ˈdʒɔːntɪ] *adj* garboso,-a.

javelin [ˈdʒævəlɪn] *n* jabalina.

jaw [dʒɔː] *n* mandíbula.

jay [dʒeɪ] *n* arrendajo (común).

jaywalker [ˈdʒeɪwɔːkəʳ] *n* peatón *m* imprudente.

jazz [dʒæz] *n* jazz *m*. ◆*to ~ up t* animar, alegrar.

jazzy [ˈdʒæzɪ] *adj fam fig* llamativo,-a.

jealous [ˈdʒeləs] *adj* celoso,-a. **2** *(envious)* envidioso,-a.

jealousy [ˈdʒeləsɪ] *n* celos *mpl*. **2** *(envy)* envidia.

jeans [dʒiːnz] *npl* tejanos *mpl*, vaqueros *mpl*.

jeep [dʒiːp] *n* jeep *m*.

jeer [dʒɪəʳ] *n* burla. **2** *(boo)* abucheo. **3** *pl* insultos *mpl*. – **4** *i* burlarse *(at,* de). **5** *(boo)* abuchear.

Jehovah [dʒɪˈhəʊvə] *n* REL Jehová *m*. ■ *Jehova's Witness,* testigo de Jehová.

jelly [ˈdʒelɪ] *n* jalea. **2** *(fruit)* gelatina.

jellyfish [ˈdʒelɪfɪʃ] *n* medusa.

jeopardize [ˈdʒepədaɪz] *t* poner en peligro.

jeopardy [ˈdʒepədɪ] *n* peligro.

jerk [dʒɜːk] *n* tirón *m*, sacudida. **2** *fam* imbécil *mf*. – **3** *t* sacudir, tirar de. – **4** *i* dar una sacudida. ◆*to ~ off* *i* hacer una paja*.

jerkin [ˈdʒɜːkɪn] *n* chaleco.

jerry-built [ˈdʒerɪbɪlt] *adj* mal construido,-a.

jersey [ˈdʒɜːzɪ] *n* jersey *m*, suéter *m*.

jest [dʒest] *n* broma. – **2** *i* bromear.

Jesuit [ˈdʒezjʊɪt] *n* jesuita *m*.

jet [dʒet] *n* AV reactor *m*. **2** *(mineral)* azabache *m*. **3** *(stream)* chorro. **4** *(outlet)*
mechero. – **5** *i* salir a chorro. **6** *fam* viajar en avión.

jetsam [ˈdʒetsəm] *n* MAR echazón *m*.

jet-set [ˈdʒetset] *n the* ~, la jetset.

jettison [ˈdʒetɪsən] *t fig* deshacerse de. **2**
(idea) olvidarse de.

jetty [ˈdʒetɪ] *n* malecón *m*.

jewel [ˈdʒuːəl] *n* joya, alhaja. **2** *(stone)*
piedra preciosa.

jeweller [ˈdʒuːələ^r] *n* joyero,-a. ▪ *jeweller's (shop)*, joyería.

jewellery [ˈdʒuːəlrɪ] *n* joyas *fpl*.

jibe [dʒaɪb] *n-i* → **gibe**.

jiffy [ˈdʒɪfɪ] *n fam* instante *m*. ●*in a* ~, en
un santiamén.

jig [dʒɪg] *n* giga.

jiggle [ˈdʒɪgəl] *t* zangolotear.

jigsaw [ˈdʒɪgsɔː] *n (saw)* sierra de vaivén.
2 *(puzzle)* rompecabezas *m inv*.

jilt [dʒɪlt] *i* dejar plantado,-a a.

jingle [ˈdʒɪŋgəl] *n* tintineo. **2** TV canción
publicitaria. – **3** *i* tintinear. – **4** *t* hacer
sonar.

jingoism [ˈdʒɪŋgəʊɪzəm] *n* patriotería.

jinx [dʒɪŋks] *n (person)* gafe *mf*. **2** *(bad
luck)* mala suerte.

jitters [ˈdʒɪtəz] *npl fam* nervios *mpl*. ●*to
get the* ~, ponerse nervioso,-a.

jittery [ˈdʒɪtərɪ] *adj* nervioso,-a.

job [dʒɒb] *n (piece of work)* trabajo. **2**
(task) tarea. **3** *(employment)* empleo,
(puesto de) trabajo. **4** *(duty)* deber *m*.
●*it's a good* ~ *that ...*, menos mal que
...; *out of a* ~, parado,-a.

jobless [ˈdʒɒbləs] *adj* parado,-a.

jockey [ˈdʒɒkɪ] *n* jockey *m*.

jockstrap [ˈdʒɒkstræp] *n* suspensorio.

jocular [ˈdʒɒkjʊlə^r] *adj* jocoso,-a.

jodhpurs [ˈdʒɒdpəz] *npl* pantalones *mpl*
de montar.

jog [dʒɒg] *n (push)* empujoncito, sacudida. **2** *(pace)* trote *m*. – **3** *t* empujar, sacudir. **4** *(memory)* refrescar. – **5** *i* hacer
footing.

jogging [ˈdʒɒgɪŋ] *n* footing *m*.

join [dʒɔɪn] *t (bring together)* juntar, unir.
2 *(company etc.)* unirse a, incorporarse a.
3 *(army)* alistarse en. **4** *(club)* hacerse socio,-a de. **5** *(party)* afiliarse a. – **6** *i* jun-

tarse. **7** *(roads, rivers)* confluir. ◆*to* ~ *in*
i participar.

joiner [ˈdʒɔɪnə^r] *n* carpintero.

joinery [ˈdʒɔɪnərɪ] *n* carpintería.

joint [dʒɔɪnt] *n* junta, juntura, unión;
(wood) ensambladura. **2** ANAT articulación. **3** CULIN corte *m* de carne. **4** *sl
(drugs)* porro. **5** *sl (place)* antro. – **6** *adj*
colectivo,-a, mutuo,-a. – **7** *t* CULIN descuartizar. – **8** *jointly adv* conjuntamente.

joke [dʒəʊk] *n* chiste *m*. **2** *(practical)* broma. – **3** *i* bromear. ●*to play a* ~ *on*, gastar una broma a.

joker [ˈdʒəʊkə^r] *n* bromista *mf*. **2** *(card)*
comodín *m*.

jolly [ˈdʒɒlɪ] *adj* alegre. – **2** *adv* muy.

jolt [dʒəʊlt] *n* sacudida. **2** *(fright)* susto. –
3 *t* sacudir. – **4** *i* dar tumbos.

jostle [ˈdʒɒsəl] *t* empujar. – **2** *i* dar empujones.

jot [dʒɒt] *n* pizca. – **2** *t* apuntar, anotar.

jotter [ˈdʒɒtə^r] *n* GB bloc *m*.

joule [dʒuːl] *n* julio.

journal [ˈdʒɜːnəl] *n (magazine)* revista. **2**
(diary) diario.

journalism [ˈdʒɜːnəlɪzəm] *n* periodismo.

journalist [ˈdʒɜːnəlɪst] *n* periodista *mf*.

journey [ˈdʒɜːnɪ] *n* viaje *m*. **2** *(distance)*
trayecto.

jovial [ˈdʒəʊvɪəl] *adj* jovial, alegre.

jowl [dʒaʊl] *n (cheek)* carrillo.

joy [dʒɔɪ] *n* gozo, júbilo, alegría.

joyful [ˈdʒɔɪfʊl] *adj* jubiloso,-a, alegre.

joyous [ˈdʒɔɪəs] *adj lit* alegre.

joyride [ˈdʒɔɪraɪd] *n fam* paseo en un coche robado.

joystick [ˈdʒɔɪstɪk] *n* AV palanca de mando. **2** COMPUT joystick *m*.

jubilant [ˈdʒuːbɪlənt] *adj* jubiloso,-a.

jubilation [dʒuːbɪˈleɪʃən] *n* júbilo.

jubilee [ˈdʒuːbɪliː] *n* festejos *mpl*. **2** *(anniversary)* aniversario. ▪ *golden/silver*
~, quincuagésimo/veinticinco aniversario.

judder [ˈdʒʌdə^r] *i* dar sacudidas/botes.

judge [dʒʌdʒ] *n* juez *mf*, jueza *f*. – **2** *t-i*
juzgar. – **3** *t (calculate)* calcular.

judgement [ˈdʒʌdʒment] *n (ability)*
(buen) juicio/criterio. **2** *(opinion)* juicio,
opinión. **3** *(decision)* fallo. ▪ ~ *day*, día
m del juicio.

judicial [dʒuːˈdɪʃəl] *adj* judicial.

judicious [dʒuːˈdɪʃəs] *adj* juicioso,-a.

judo [ˈdʒuːdəʊ] *n* judo.

jug [dʒʌg] *n* jarro.

juggernaut [ˈdʒʌgənɔːt] *n* GB camión pesado.

juggle [ˈdʒʌgəl] *i* hacer juegos malabares.

juggler [ˈdʒʌgləʳ] *n* malabarista *mf*.

juice [dʒuːs] *n gen* jugo. **2** *(of fruit)* zumo.

juicy [ˈdʒuːsɪ] *adj* jugoso,-a. **2** *fam* picante.

July [dʒuːˈlaɪ] *n* julio.

jukebox [ˈdʒuːkbɒks] *n* máquina de discos.

jumble [ˈdʒʌmbəl] *n* revoltijo, confusión. − **2** *t* mezclar.

jumbo [ˈdʒʌmbəʊ] *adj* gigante. − **2** *n* AV jumbo *m*.

jump [dʒʌmp] *n* salto. − **2** *t-i* saltar. − **3** *i (rise sharply)* dar un salto. ◆*to* ~ *at t* aceptar sin pensarlo.

jumper [ˈdʒʌmpəʳ] *n* GB jersey *m*. **2** US *(skirt)* pichi *m*.

jump-suit [ˈdʒʌmpsuːt] *n* mono.

jumpy [ˈdʒʌmpɪ] *adj* nervioso,-a.

junction [ˈdʒʌŋkʃən] *n (railways)* empalme *m*. **2** *(roads)* cruce m.

juncture [ˈdʒʌŋktʃəʳ] *n* coyuntura.

June [dʒuːn] *n* junio.

jungle [ˈdʒʌŋgəl] *n* jungla, selva.

junior [ˈdʒuːnɪəʳ] *adj (in age)* menor, más joven. **2** *(in rank)* subalterno,-a. − **3** *n (in age)* menor *mf*. **4** *(in rank)* subalterno,-a. **5** GB alumno,-a de EGB. **6** US hijo,-a.

juniper [ˈdʒuːnɪpəʳ] *n* enebro.

junk [dʒʌnk] *n* trastos *mpl*. **2** *(boat)* junco.

junkie [ˈdʒʌŋkɪ] *n sl* yonqui *mf*.

junta [ˈdʒʌntə] *n* POL junta (militar).

Jupiter [ˈdʒuːpɪtəʳ] *n* Júpiter *m*.

jurisdiction [dʒʊərɪsˈdɪkʃən] *n* jurisdicción.

juror [ˈdʒʊərəʳ] *n* jurado.

jury [ˈdʒʊərɪ] *n* jurado.

just [dʒʌst] *adj (fair)* justo,-a. **2** *(deserved)* merecido,-a. − **3** *adv (exactly)* exactamente, precisamente, justo. **4** *(only)* solamente. **5** *(right now)* en este momento. ●~ *about,* prácticamente; ~ *in case,* por si acaso; ~ *now,* ahora mismo; *to have* ~, acabar de.

justice [ˈdʒʌstɪs] *n* justicia. **2** *(judge)* juez *mf*, jueza.

justifiable [dʒʌstɪˈfaɪəbəl] *adj* justificable.

justification [dʒʌstɪfɪˈkeɪʃən] *n* justificación.

justified [ˈdʒʌstɪfaɪd] *adj* justificado,-a.

justify [ˈdʒʌstɪfaɪ] *t* justificar.

justness [ˈdʒʌstnəs] *n* justicia.

jut [dʒʌt] *i* sobresalir.

jute [dʒuːt] *n* yute *m*.

juvenile [ˈdʒuːvɪnaɪl] *adj* juvenil. **2** *(childish)* infantil. − **3** *n* menor *mf*.

juxtapose [ˈdʒʌkstəpəʊz] *t* yuxtaponer.

juxtaposition [dʒʌkstəpəˈzɪʃən] *n* yuxtaposición.

K

kaftan ['kæftæn] *n* caftán *m*.

kaleidoscope [kə'laɪdəskəʊp] *n* calidoscopio.

kamikaze [kæmɪ'kɑːzɪ] *adj-n* kamikaze *(mf)*.

kangaroo [kæŋgə'ruː] *n* canguro.

kaput [kə'pʊt] *adj fam* roto,-a, estropeado,-a.

karate [kə'rɑːtɪ] *n* kárate *m*.

kayak ['kaɪæk] *n* kayac *m*.

kebab [kɪ'bæb] *n* pincho moruno, broqueta.

keel [kiːl] *n* quilla. ◆*to ~ over i (ship)* zozobrar; *(person)* desplomarse.

keen [kiːn] *adj (eager)* entusiasta, muy aficionado,-a. 2 *(sharp) (mind etc.)* agudo,-a; *(look)* penetrante; *(wind)* cortante. 3 *(competition)* fuerte. 4 *(price)* competitivo,-a. ●*~ on,* aficionado,-a a; *I'm not very ~ on it,* no me gusta demasiado; *to take a ~ interest in,* mostrar un gran interés por.

keenness ['kiːnnəs] *n (eagerness)* entusiasmo, interés *m*, afición. 2 *(sharpness)* agudeza.

keep [kiːp] *n (board)* sustento, mantenimiento. 2 *(of castle)* torreón *m*, torre *f* del homenaje. — 3 *t (not give back)* guardar. 4 *(put away, save)* guardar, tener guardado,-a. 5 *(detain)* retener, detener; *(hold up)* entretener: *sorry to ~ you waiting,* discúlpeme por hacerlo esperar. 6 *(shop etc.)* dirigir, tener. 7 *(things for sale)* tener, vender. 8 *(accounts)* llevar. 9 *(diary)* escribir. 10 *(order)* mantener. 11 *(promise)* cumplir. 12 *(secret)* guardar. 13 *(appointment)* acudir a, no faltar a. 14 *(person)* mantener. 15 *(chickens, pigs, etc.)* criar. — 16 *i (do continually)* no dejar de. 17 *(food)* conservarse (bien). ◆*to ~ away t-i* mantener(se) a distancia. ◆*to ~ back t* reservar, retener; *(information)* ocultar. 2 *(enemy)* tener a raya. ◆*to ~ down t (oppress)* oprimir. ◆*to ~ in t* no dejar salir. ◆*to ~ on i* seguir, continuar. — 2 *t (clothes)* no quitarse. ◆*to ~ out t* no dejar entrar. — 2 *i* no entrar. ◆*to ~ up t* mantener. 2 *(from sleeping)* mantener despierto,-a, tener en vela. ●*~ the change,* quédese con la vuelta; *to ~ going,* seguir (adelante); *to ~ one's head,* no perder la cabeza; *to ~ quiet,* callarse, no hacer ruido; *to ~ sb. company,* hacerle compañía a algn.; *to ~ sth. clean,* conservar algo limpio,-a; *to ~ sth. to o.s.,* guardar algo para sí. ▲ *pt & pp* **kept**.

keeper ['kiːpə'] *n (in zoo)* guardián,-ana. 2 *(in park)* guarda *mf*.

keeping ['kiːpɪŋ] *n* cuidado, custodia. ●*in ~ with,* en consonancia con.

keg [keg] *n* barril *m*.

kennel ['kenəl] *n* perrera, caseta para perros. 2 *pl (boarding)* residencia *f sing* canina.

kept [kept] *pt & pp* → **keep**.

kerb [kɜːb] *n* bordillo.

kerfuffle [kə'fʌfəl] *n fam* jaleo.

kernel ['kɜːnəl] *n (of fruit, nut)* semilla, almendra. 2 *fig* núcleo.

ketchup ['ketʃəp] *n* ketchup *m*, catsup *m*.

kettle ['ketəl] *n* hervidor *m*.

key [kiː] *n (of lock)* llave *f*. 2 *(to mystery)* clave *f*. 3 *(on keyboard)* tecla. 4 MUS tono. 5 GEOG cayo, isleta. — 6 *adj* clave. ■ *~ ring,* llavero.

keyboard ['kiːbɔːd] *n* teclado.

keyed up [kiːd'ʌp] *adj* nervioso,-a, excitado,-a.

keyhole ['kiːhəʊl] *n* ojo de la cerradura.

khaki ['kɑːkɪ] *adj-n* caqui *(m)*.

kick [kɪk] *n (by person)* puntapié *m*, patada. 2 *(by animal)* coz *f*. 3 *(thrill)* emoción. — 4 *t (person)* dar un puntapié/una patada a. 5 *(animal)* dar coces a. ◆*to ~*

out *t* echar. ●*fam to ~ the bucket,* estirar la pata; *fam to ~ up a fuss,* armar un jaleo.

kick-off ['kɪkɒf] *n* sp saque *m* inicial.

kid [kɪd] *n (animal)* cabrito. **2** *(leather)* cabritilla. **3** *fam* niño,-a; chico,-a. – **4** *t* tomar el pelo a. – **5** *i* estar de broma.

kidnap ['kɪdnæp] *t* secuestrar.

kidnapper ['kɪdnæpəʳ] *n* secuestrador,-ra.

kidnapping ['kɪdnæpɪŋ] *n* secuestro.

kidney ['kɪdnɪ] *n* riñón *m*.

kill [kɪl] *t* matar. ◆*to ~ off t* exterminar. ●*to ~ two birds with one stone,* matar dos pájaros de un tiro.

killer ['kɪləʳ] *n* asesino,-a.

killing ['kɪlɪŋ] *n* matanza; *(of person)* asesinato. ●*to make a ~,* hacer su agosto.

killjoy ['kɪldʒɔɪ] *n* aguafiestas *mf inv*.

kiln [kɪln] *n* horno.

kilogram(me) ['kɪləgræm] *n* kilogramo.

kilometre [kɪ'lɒmɪtəʳ] *n* kilómetro.

kilowatt ['kɪləwɒt] *n* kilowatt, kilovatio.

kilt [kɪlt] *n* falda escocesa.

kin [kɪn] *n* parientes *mpl*, familia. ■ *next of ~,* pariente(s) más cercano(s).

kind [kaɪnd] *adj* simpático,-a, amable. – **2** *n (sort)* tipo, género, clase *f*. ●*in ~, (payment)* en especie; *(treatment)* con la misma moneda; **to be so ~ as to,** tener la bondad de.

kindergarten ['kɪndəgæːtən] *n* parvulario, guardería.

kind-hearted [kaɪnd'hɑːtɪd] *adj* bondadoso,-a.

kindle ['kɪndəl] *t* encender.

kindliness ['kaɪndlɪnəs] *n* bondad, amabilidad.

kindly ['kaɪndlɪ] *adj* bondadoso,-a, amable. – **2** *adv* bondadosamente. **3** *(please)* por favor.

kindness ['kaɪndnəs] *n* bondad, amabilidad. **2** *(favour)* favor.

kinetic [kɪ'netɪk] *adj* cinético,-a.

kinetics [kɪ'netɪks] *n* cinética.

king [kɪŋ] *n* rey *m*.

kingdom ['kɪŋdəm] *n* reino.

kink [kɪŋk] *n* coca; *(in hair)* rizo; *fig* manía.

kinky ['kɪŋkɪ] *adj fam* peculiar; *(sexually)* pervertido, -a.

kinship ['kɪnʃɪp] *n* parentesco.

kiosk ['kiːɒsk] *n* quiosco. **2** *(telephone)* cabina telefónica.

kip [kɪp] *i fam* dormir. ●*to have a ~,* dormir.

kipper ['kɪpəʳ] *n* arenque ahumado.

kiss [kɪs] *n* beso. – **2** *t-i* besar(se).

kit [kɪt] *n (equipment)* equipo. **2** MIL avíos *mpl*. **3** *(model)* maqueta, kit *m*.

kitchen ['kɪtʃɪn] *n* cocina.

kite [kaɪt] *n* cometa.

kitten ['kɪtən] *n* gatito,-a.

kitty ['kɪtɪ] *n fam* minino,-a. **2** *(money)* bote *m*.

kiwi ['kiːwiː] *n* kiwi *m*.

kleptomania [kleptə'meɪnɪə] *n* cleptomanía.

kleptomaniac [kleptə'meɪnɪæk] *n* cleptómano,-a.

knack [næk] *n* maña, truquillo.

knacker ['nækəʳ] *n* matarife *m*. **2*** *pl* cojones* *mpl*.

knackered ['nækəd] *adj fam* reventado,-a, agotado,-a.

knapsack ['næpsæk] *n* mochila.

knave [neɪv] *n (cards)* jota; *(Spanish pack)* sota.

knead [niːd] *t* amasar.

knee [niː] *n* ANAT rodilla. **2** *(of trousers)* rodillera. ●*on one's knees,* de rodillas.

kneecap ['niːkæp] *n* rótula.

kneel [niːl] *i* arrodillarse. ▲ *pt & pp* **knelt**.

knell [nel] *n* toque *m* de difuntos.

knelt [nelt] *pt & pp* → **kneel**.

knew [njuː] *pt* → **know**.

knickers ['nɪkəz] *npl* bragas *fpl*.

knick-knack ['nɪknæk] *n* chuchería.

knife [naɪf] *n* cuchillo. – **2** *t* apuñalar.

knight [naɪt] *n* caballero. **2** *(chess)* caballo. – **3** *t* armar caballero.

knit [nɪt] *t* tejer. – **2** *i* hacer punto/calceta, tricotar. **3** MED soldarse. ▲ *pt & pp* **knit** *o* **knitted**.

knitting ['nɪtɪŋ] *n* punto, ˙calceta. ■ *~ needle,* aguja de tejer.

knob [nɒb] *n (on door) (large)* pomo; *(small)* tirador *m*. **2** *(on stick)* puño. **3** *(natural)* bulto, protuberancia. **4** *(on radio etc.)* botón *m*.

knobbly ['nɒblɪ] *adj* nudoso, -a.

knock [nɒk] *n* golpe *m*. **2** *fig (bad luck)* revés *m*. – **3** *t* golpear. **4** *(criticize)* criticar. – **5** *i (at door)* llamar. ◆*to ~ back t* beber (de un trago). ◆*to ~ down t (building)* derribar. **2** *(with a car)* atropellar. ◆*to ~ off t* tirar. **2** *fam (steal)* birlar, mangar. **3** *sl (kill)* liquidar a. **4** *(price)* rebajar. – **5** *i (stop work)* acabar, salir del trabajo. ◆*to ~ out t* dejar sin conocimiento; *(boxing)* poner fuera de combate. ◆*to ~ over t* volcar; *(with a car)* atropellar. ◆*to ~ up t* GB *fam* despertar. **2** US *sl* dejar preñada. – **3** *i (tennis etc.)* pelotear.

knocker ['nɒkəʳ] *n* aldaba. **2*** *pl* tetas *fpl*.

knock-kneed [nɒk'niːd] *adj* estevado,-a.

knockout ['nɒkaʊt] *n* knock-out *m*, fuera *m* de combate. **2** SP eliminatoria. **3** *fam* maravilla.

knot [nɒt] *n* nudo. – **2** *t* anudar. .

knotty ['nɒtɪ] *adj* nudoso,-a. **2** *(problem)* difícil, espinoso,-a.

know [nəʊ] *t-i (be acquainted with)* conocer: *do you ~ Colin?,* ¿conoces a Colin? **2** *(have knowledge of)* saber: *I don't ~ the answer,* no sé la respuesta. ●*as far as I ~,* que yo sepa; *to ~ by sight,* conocer de vista; *to ~ how to do sth.,* saber hacer algo. ▲ *pt knew; pp known.*

know-all ['nəʊɔːl] *n* sabelotodo *mf.*

know-how ['nəʊhaʊ] *n* conocimiento práctico.

knowing ['nəʊɪŋ] *adj (smile, look)* de complicidad. – **2** *knowingly adv (intentionally)* intencionadamente, a sabiendas, adrede.

knowledge ['nɒlɪdʒ] *n* conocimiento. **2** *(learning)* conocimientos *mpl.* ●*to have a good ~ of,* conocer bien.

knowledgeable ['nɒlɪdʒəbəl] *adj* erudito, -a, entendido,-a.

known [nəʊn] *pp* → **know.**

knuckle ['nʌkəl] *n* nudillo. ◆*to ~ down i fam* ponerse a trabajar en serio. ◆*to ~ under i* pasar por el aro.

koala [kəʊ'ɑːlə] *n* koala *m.*

Koran [kɔ'rɑːn] *n* Corán *m.*

L

label ['leɪbəl] *n* etiqueta. — **2** *t* etiquetar.
laboratory [ləˈbɒrətərɪ] *n* laboratorio.
laborious [leˈbɔ:rɪəs] *adj* laborioso,-a.
labour ['leɪbəʳ] *n* trabajo. **2** *(task)* tarea, faena. **3** *(workforce)* mano *f* de obra. — **4** *t* insistir en. ●*Labour Party*, partido laborista.
labourer ['leɪbərəʳ] *n* peón *m*. ■ *farm* ~, peón agrícola.
labyrinth ['læbərɪnθ] *n* laberinto.
lace [leɪs] *n (of shoe)* cordón *m*. **2** *(material)* encaje *m*. — **3** *t (shoes)* atar.
lacerate ['læsəreɪt] *t fml* lacerar.
lack [læk] *n* falta, carencia. — **2** *t* carecer de.
lacking ['lækɪŋ] *adj* carente de.
laconic [ləˈkɒnɪk] *adj* lacónico,-a.
lacquer ['lækəʳ] *n* laca. — **2** *t (paint)* lacar; *(hair)* poner laca a.
lad [læd] *n* muchacho, chaval *m*.
ladder ['lædəʳ] *n* escalera. **2** *(in stocking)* carrera.
laden ['leɪdən] *adj* cargado,-a.
lading ['leɪdɪŋ] *n* embarque *m*. ■ *bill of* ~, conocimiento de embarque.
ladle ['leɪdəl] *n* cucharón *m*.
lady ['leɪdɪ] *n* señora, dama.
ladybird ['leɪdɪbɜ:d] *n* mariquita.
lady-killer ['leɪdɪkɪləʳ] *n* donjuán *m*.
ladylike ['leɪdɪlaɪk] *adj* delicado,-a, elegante.
lag [læg] *n* retraso. — **2** *t* TECH revestir. ●*to* ~ *behind,* rezagarse.
lager ['lɑ:gəʳ] *n* cerveza rubia.
lagoon [ləˈgu:n] *n* laguna.
laid [leɪd] *pt & pp* → **lay**.
lain [leɪn] *pp* → **lie**.
lair [leəʳ] *n* guarida.
lake [leɪk] *n* lago.
lamb [læm] *n* cordero. **2** *(meat)* carne *f* de cordero.

lame [leɪm] *adj* cojo,-a.
lameness ['leɪmnəs] *n* cojera.
lament [ləˈment] *n* lamento. — **2** *t-i* lamentar(se).
lamentable ['læmentəbəl] *adj* lamentable.
laminate ['læmɪnət] *n* laminado. — **2** *t* laminar. ▲ *En 2 (verbo)* ['læmɪneɪt].
lamp [læmp] *n* lámpara. **2** AUTO faro. ■ *street* ~, farol *m*.
lampooon [læmˈpu:n] *n* pasquín *m*. — **2** *t* satirizar.
lamp-post ['læmppəʊst] *n* poste *m* de farol.
lampshade ['læmpʃeɪd] *n* pantalla (de lámpara).
lance [lɑ:ns] *n (spear)* lanza. **2** MED lanceta. — **3** *t* MED abrir con lanceta.
land [lænd] *n gen* tierra. **2** *(soil)* suelo, tierra. **3** *(property)* terreno, finca. — **4** *i (plane)* aterrizar, tomar tierra. — **5** *t (fish)* sacar del agua. **6** *fig* conseguir. — **7** *t-i (from ship)* desembarcar.
landing ['lændɪŋ] *n (plane)* aterrizaje *m*. **2** *(on stairs)* descansillo, rellano. **3** *(of people)* desembarco.
landlady ['lændleɪdɪ] *n (of flat)* propietaria, casera. **2** *(of boarding house)* patrona.
landlocked ['lændlɒkt] *adj (country)* sin salida al mar.
landlord ['lænlɔ:d] *n (of flat)* propietario, casero. **2** *(of boarding house)* patrón *m*.
landmark ['lændmɑ:k] *n* lugar/edificio muy conocido. **2** *fig* hito.
landowner ['lændəʊnəʳ] *n* propietario,-a, terrateniente *mf*.
landscape ['lændskeɪp] *n* paisaje *m*.
landslide ['lændslaɪd] *n* desprendimiento de tierras.
lane [leɪn] *n* camino. **2** AUTO carril *m*. **3** SP calle *f*. **3** AV MAR ruta.

language ['læŋgwɪdʒ] *n (faculty, way of speaking)* lenguaje *m.* **2** *(tongue)* lengua, idioma *m.*

languid ['læŋgwɪd] *adj* lánguido,-a.

languish ['læŋgwɪʃ] *i* languidecer.

lank [læŋk] *adj* lacio,-a.

lanky ['læŋkɪ] *adj* larguirucho,-a.

lanolin(e) ['lænəlɪn] *n* lanolina.

lantern ['læntən] *n* linterna, farol *m.*

lap [læp] *n* regazo; *(knees)* rodillas *fpl.* **2** SP vuelta; *fig* etapa. − **3** *t* SP doblar. **4** *(drink)* lamer, beber lamiendo. − **5** *i (waves)* chapalear.

lapel [lə'pel] *n* solapa.

lapse [læps] *n (in time)* transcurso, lapso. **2** *(slip)* desliz *m; (speaking)* lapsus *m inv.* − **3** *i (err)* cometer un desliz. **4** *(contract)* caducar. **5** *(custom)* desaparecer.

larceny ['lɑːsənɪ] *n* latrocinio.

lard [lɑːd] *n* manteca de cerdo.

larder ['lɑːdər] *n* despensa.

large [lɑːdʒ] *adj* grande; *(before sing noun)* gran. **2** *(sum)* importante. − **3** *largely adv* en gran parte. ●*at ~,* suelto,-a, en libertad.

large-scale ['lɑːdʒskeɪl] *adj* de gran escala. **2** *(map)* a gran escala.

lark [lɑːk] *n (bird)* alondra. **2** *(joke)* broma. ◆*to ~ about/around i* hacer tonterías/ el indio.

laryngitis [lærɪn'dʒaɪtɪs] *n* laringitis *f inv.*

larynx ['lærɪŋks] *n* laringe *f.*

lascivious [lə'sɪvɪəs] *adj* lascivo,-a.

laser ['leɪzər] *n* láser *m.*

lash [læʃ] *n* latigazo, azote *m.* **2** *(thong)* tralla. **3** *(eyelash)* pestaña. − **4** *t gen* azotar. **5** *(tie)* atar. ◆*to ~ out i* repartir golpes a diestro y siniestro. **2** *(spend)* despilfarrar. ◆*to ~ out at t* criticar. ◆*to ~ out on t* gastar mucho dinero en.

lass [læs] *n* chica, chavala, muchacha.

lasso [læ'suː] *n* lazo.

last [lɑːst] *adj (final)* último,-a, final. **2** *(latest)* último,-a. **3** *(days)* pasado,-a; *~ Monday,* el lunes pasado; *~ night,* anoche. − **4** *adv* por última vez. **5** *(at the end)* en último lugar; *(in race)* en última posición. − **6** *n (person)* el/la último,-a. **7** *(for shoes)* horma. − **8** *t-i* durar. − **9** *lastly adv* finalmente. ●*at ~,* al/por fin; *~ but one,* penúltimo,-a; *to the ~,* hasta el final.

lasting ['lɑːstɪŋ] *adj* duradero,-a, perdurable.

latch [lætʃ] *n* picaporte *m,* pestillo.

late [leɪt] *adj* tardío,-a. **2** *(in period)* tarde: *in ~ May,* a finales de Mayo. **3** *euf* difunto,-a. − **4** *adv* tarde. − **5** *lately adv*

últimamente. ●*to arrive/be ~,* llegar tarde.

latent ['leɪtənt] *adj* latente.

later ['leɪtər] *adj* más tardío,-a. **2** *(more recent)* más reciente. **3** *(in series)* posterior. − **4** *adv* más tarde. **5** *(afterwards)* después, luego.

latest ['leɪtɪst] *adj* último,-a. ●*at the ~,* a más tardar.

lateral ['lætərəl] *adj* lateral.

latex ['leɪteks] *n* látex *m.*

lathe [leɪð] *n* torno.

lather ['lɑːðər] *n (of soap)* espuma. − **2** *t* enjabonar(se). − **3** *i* hacer espuma.

Latin ['lætɪn] *adj-n* latino,-a. − **2** *n (language)* latín *m.*

latitude ['lætɪtjuːd] *n* latitud *f.*

latter ['lætər] *adj* último,-a. − **2** *pron the ~,* éste,-a, este,-a último,-a.

lattice ['lætɪs] *n* celosía, enrejado.

laudable ['lɔːdəbəl] *adj* laudable.

laugh [lɑːf] *n* risa. − **2** *i* reír(se). ●*to ~ at,* reírse de.

laughable ['lɑːfəbəl] *adj* ridículo,-a.

laughing ['lɑːfɪŋ] *adj* risueño,-a. − **2** *n* risas *fpl.* ■ *~ gas,* gas *m* hilarante.

laughing-stock ['lɑːfɪŋstɒk] *n* hazmerreír *m inv.*

laughter ['lɑːftər] *n* risas *fpl.*

launch [lɔːntʃ] *n (action) gen* lanzamiento; *(of boat)* botadura; *(of film)* estreno. **2** *(boat)* lancha. − **3** *t gen* lanzar; *(boat)* botar; *(film)* estrenar.

launder ['lɔːndər] *t (clothes)* lavar y planchar. **2** *(money)* blanquear.

launderette [lɔːndə'ret] *n* lavandería automática.

laundry ['lɔːndrɪ] *n (place)* lavandería. **2** *(clothes)* colada; *(clean)* ropa lavada.

laurel ['lɒrəl] *n* laurel *m.*

lava ['lɑːvə] *n* lava.

lavatory ['lævətərɪ] *n* wáter *m.* **2** *(room)* lavabo, baño. **3** *(public)* servicios *mpl.*

lavender ['lævɪndər] *n* espliego, lavanda.

lavish ['lævɪʃ] *adj (generous)* pródigo,-a, generoso,-a. **2** *(abundant)* abundante. **3** *(luxurious)* lujoso,-a. − **4** *t* prodigar.

law [lɔː] *n ley f.* **2** *(subject)* derecho. **3** *fam the ~,* la pasma.

law-abiding ['lɔːəbaɪdɪŋ] *adj* observante de la ley.

law-breaker ['lɔːbreɪkər] *n* infractor,-ra de la ley.

lawful ['lɔːfʊl] *adj* legal, legítimo,-a, lícito,-a.

lawless ['lɔːləs] *adj* sin ley. **2** *(person)* rebelde.

lawn [lɔːn] *n* césped *m*.

lawnmower ['lɔːnməʊəʳ] *n* cortacésped *m & f*.

lawsuit ['lɔːsjuːt] *n* pleito.

lawyer ['lɔːjəʳ] *n* abogado,-a.

lax [læks] *adj* laxo,-a. **2** *(careless)* descuidado,-a.

laxative ['læksətɪv] *adj-n* laxante *(m)*.

lay [leɪ] *pt →* lie. **– 2** *t gen* poner. **3** *(cable, pipe)* tender. **4** *(foundations)* echar. **5** *(eggs)* poner. **6*** follar*. **– 7** *adj* REL laico,-a, seglar. **8** *(not professional)* lego,-a, no profesional. **– 9** *n (ballad)* balada. ◆**to ~ down** *t (tools)* dejar; *(arms)* deponer. **2** *(wine)* guardar (en bodega). ◆**to ~ in** *t* proveerse de. ◆**to ~ into** *t* atacar. ◆**to ~ off** *t (worker)* despedir. **2** *fam* dejar en paz. ◆**to ~ on** *t* proveer. ◆**to ~ out** *t* tender, extender. **2** *(town etc.)* hacer el trazado de; *(garden)* diseñar. **3** *fam (knock down)* dejar fuera de combate. ◆**to ~ up** *t* almacenar. ●**to be laid up,** tener que guardar cama; **to ~ one's hands on sb.,** pillar a algn. ▲ *pt & pp* **laid**.

layabout ['leɪəbaʊt] *n fam* holgazán,-ana.

lay-by ['leɪbaɪ] *n* área de descanso.

layer ['leɪəʳ] *n* capa; *(of rock)* estrato.

layman ['leɪmən] *n* REL laico. **2** *(not expert)* profano.

layout ['leɪaʊt] *n* disposición. **2** *(of town)* trazado.

laziness ['leɪzɪnəs] *n* pereza.

lazy ['leɪzɪ] *adj* perezoso,-a.

lead [led] *n (metal)* plomo. **2** *(in pencil)* mina. **3** *(front position)* delantera; SP liderato; *(difference)* ventaja. **4** *(for dog)* correa. **5** THEAT primer papel *m*. **6** ELEC cable *m*. **7** *(clue)* pista. **– 8** *t (guide)* llevar, conducir. **9** *(be leader of)* liderar, dirigir. **10** *(be first in)* ocupar el primer puesto en. **– 11** *i (go first)* ir primero,-a; *(in race)* llevar la delantera. **12** *(command)* tener el mando. **13** *(road)* conducir *(to,* a). ●**to be in the ~,** ir en cabeza; **to ~ sb. on,** engañar a algn.; **to ~ sb. to believe sth.,** llevar a algn. a creer algo; **to ~ the way,** enseñar el camino; **to take the ~,** tomar la delantera. ▲ *De 3 a 13* [liːd]; *pt & pp* **lead** [led].

leader [liːdəʳ] *n* POL líder *mf*, dirigente *mf*. **2** *(in race)* líder *mf*. **3** *(in newspaper)* editorial *m*.

leadership ['liːdəʃɪp] *n (position)* liderato, liderazgo. **2** *(qualities)* dotes *mpl* de mando. **3** *(leaders)* dirección.

lead-free ['ledfriː] *adj* sin plomo.

leading ['liːdɪŋ] *adj* destacado,-a, principal.

leaf [liːf] *n* hoja.

leaflet ['liːflət] *n* folleto.

leafy ['liːfɪ] *adj* frondoso,-a.

league [liːg] *n* liga.

leak [liːk] *n (of gas, fluid)* escape *m*; *fig* filtración. **2** *(hole)* agujero. **3** *(in roof)* gotera. **4** *fam euph* meada. **– 5** *i (gas, fluid)* escaparse; *(information)* filtrarse. **6** *(container)* tener un agujero. **7** *(pipe)* tener un escape. **8** *(shoes)* dejar entrar agua. **9** *(roof)* gotear.

leaky ['liːkɪ] *adj (pipe)* que tiene escapes. **2** *(container)* que tiene agujeros. **3** *(shoe)* que deja entrar agua. **4** *(roof)* que tiene goteras.

lean [liːn] *adj (person)* delgado,-a, flaco,-a. **2** *(meat)* magro,-a. **– 3** *t-i (against sth.)* apoyar(se). **– 4** *i* inclinarse. ▲ *pt & pp* **leant** *o* **leaned**.

leaning ['liːnɪŋ] *adj* inclinado,-a. **– 2** *n* inclinación, tendencia.

leant [lent] *pt & pp →* lean.

leap [liːp] *n* salto, brinco. **– 2** *i* saltar, brincar. ■ **~ year,** año bisiesto. ▲ *pt & pp* **leapt** *o* **leaped**.

leapfrog ['liːpfrɒg] *n* pídola.

leapt [lept] *pt & pp →* leap.

learn [lɜːn] *t-i* aprender. **– 2** *t (find out about)* enterarse de. ▲ *pt & pp* **learnt** *o* **learned**.

learned ['lɜːnɪd] *adj* erudito,-a.

learner ['lɜːnəʳ] *n* estudiante *mf*. ■ **~ driver,** aprendiz,-za de conductor.

learning ['lɜːnɪŋ] *n* conocimientos *mpl*, saber *m*.

learnt [lɜːnt] *pt & pp →* learn.

lease [liːs] *n* contrato de arrendamiento. **– 2** *t* arrendar.

leash [liːʃ] *n* correa.

least [liːst] *adj* mínimo,-a, menor. **– 2** *adv* menos. **– 3** *n* lo menos. ●**at ~,** por lo menos; **not in the ~,** en lo más mínimo.

leather ['leðəʳ] *n* piel *f*, cuero.

leave [liːv] *n* permiso; *(holidays)* vacaciones *fpl*. **– 2** *t* dejar, abandonar; *(go out of)* salir de. **3** *(forget)* olvidarse. **– 4** *i* marcharse, irse, partir. ◆**to ~ out** *t (omit)* omitir. ●**to take one's ~ of,** despedirse de. ▲ *pt & pp* **left**.

lecherous ['letʃərəs] *adj* lujurioso,-a, lascivo,-a.

lectern ['lektən] *n* atril *m*. **2** *(in church)* facistol *m*.

lecture ['lektʃəʳ] *n* conferencia. **2** *(in university)* clase *f*. **3** *(reproof)* represión, sermón *m*. **– 4** *i* dar una conferencia. **5** *(in* *university)* dar clase. **6** *(scold)* sermonear. **– 7** *t* echar una reprimenda a.

lecturer ['lektʃərəʳ] *n* conferenciante *mf.* **2** *(in university)* profesor,-ra.

led [led] *pt & pp* → **lead**.

ledge [ledʒ] *n* repisa. **2** *(of rock)* saliente *m.*

ledger ['ledʒəʳ] *n* COM libro mayor.

leech [li:tʃ] *n* sanguijuela.

leek [li:k] *n* puerro.

leer [lɪəʳ] *i* mirar con lascivia. **– 2** *n* mirada lasciva.

lees [li:z] *npl* poso *m sing.*

left [left] *pt & pp* → **leave**. **– 2** *adj-n* izquierdo,-a *(f).* **– 3** *adj* POL de izquierdas. **– 4** *adv* a/hacia la izquierda. ●*on the ~,* a mano izquierda; *to be ~ over,* quedar, sobrar.

left-hand ['lefthænd] *adj* izquierdo,-a.

left-handed [left'hændɪd] *adj* zurdo,-a.

leftist ['leftɪst] *adj-n* izquierdista *(mf).*

left-luggage [left'lʌgɪdʒ] *n ~ office,* consigna.

left-wing ['leftwɪŋ] *adj* de izquierdas.

leg [leg] *n* ANAT pierna. **2** *(of animal, furniture)* pata. **3** CULIN *(lamb etc.)* pierna; *(chicken etc.)* muslo. **4** *(of trousers)* pernera. ●*to pull sb.'s ~,* tomar el pelo a algn.

legacy ['legəsɪ] *n* legado, herencia.

legal ['li:gəl] *adj* legal, legítimo,-a, lícito,-a. **2** *(relating to the law)* legal, jurídico,-a.

legalize ['li:gəlaɪz] *t* legalizar.

legend ['ledʒənd] *n* leyenda.

legendary ['ledʒəndərɪ] *adj* legendario,-a.

legible ['ledʒəbəl] *adj* legible.

legion ['li:dʒən] *n* legión.

legislate ['ledʒɪsleɪt] *i* legislar.

legislation [ledʒɪs'leɪʃən] *n* legislación.

legislature ['ledʒɪsleɪtʃəʳ] *n* cuerpo legislativo.

legitimate [lɪ'dʒɪtɪmət] *adj* legítimo,-a.

legitimize [lɪ'dʒɪtɪmaɪz] *t* legitimar.

leisure ['leʒəʳ] *n* ocio, tiempo libre.

leisurely ['leʒəlɪ] *adj* sin prisa.

lemon ['lemən] *n* limón *m.* ■ *~ tree,* limonero.

lemonade [lemə'neɪd] *n* limonada.

lend [lend] *t* dejar, prestar. ●*to ~ a hand,* echar una mano. ▲ *pt & pp* **lent**.

length [leŋθ] *n* longitud; *it's 5 metres in ~,* mide 5 metros de largo. **2** *(time)* duración. **3** *(piece)* trozo. **4** *(of road)* tramo; *(of swimming pool)* largo.

lengthen ['leŋθən] *t-i* alargar(se).

lengthy ['leŋθɪ] *adj* largo,-a.

lenient ['li:nɪənt] *adj* indulgente.

lens [lenz] *n* lente *f.* **2** *(of camera)* objetivo. **3** ANAT cristalino.

lent [lent] *pt & pp* → **lend**. **– 2 Lent** *n* REL Cuaresma.

lentil ['lentɪl] *n* lenteja.

Leo [li:əʊ] *n* Leo.

leopard ['lepəd] *n* leopardo.

leotard ['li:ətɑ:d] *n* malla.

leper ['lepəʳ] *n* leproso,-a.

leprosy ['leprəsɪ] *n* lepra.

lesbian ['lezbɪən] *adj-n* lesbiano,-a *(f).*

less [les] *adj-adv-prep* menos.

lessen ['lesən] *t-i* disminuir(se).

lesser ['lesəʳ] *adj* menor.

lesson ['lesən] *n* lección, clase *f.*

lest [lest] *conj fml* para que no.

let [let] *t* *(allow)* dejar, permitir. **2** *(rent)* arrendar, alquilar. **– 3** *aux* ~ *this be a warning,* que esto sirva de advertencia; *~ us pray,* oremos. ◆*to ~ down t (deflate)* deshinchar. **2** *(lengthen)* alargar. **3** *(disappoint)* defraudar. ◆*to ~ in t* dejar entrar/pasar. ◆*to ~ off t (bomb)* hacer explotar; *(firework)* hacer estallar. **2** *(forgive)* perdonar. ◆*to ~ on i fam* descubrir el pastel: *you won't ~ on, will you?,* no dirás nada, ¿verdad? ◆*to ~ out t* dejar salir; *(release)* soltar. **2** *(rent)* alquilar. **3** *(utter)* soltar. ◆*to ~ through t* dejar pasar. ◆*to ~ up i* cesar. ●*~ alone ...,* y mucho menos ...; *to ~ alone,* dejar en paz, no tocar; *to ~ go of,* soltar; *to ~ loose,* soltar, desatar; *to ~ off steam,* desfogarse; *to ~ sb. in on sth.,* revelar algo a algn.; *to ~ sb. know,* hacer saber a algn. ▲ *pt & pp* **let**.

letdown ['letdaʊn] *n* decepción.

lethal ['li:θəl] *adj* letal, mortal.

lethargic [lɪ'θɑ:dʒɪk] *adj* aletargado,-a.

lethargy ['leθədʒɪ] *n* letargo.

letter ['letəʳ] *n (of alphabet)* letra. **2** *(message)* carta. ■ *~ box,* buzón *m.*

lettuce ['letɪs] *n* lechuga.

leukaemia [lu:'ki:mɪə] *n* leucemia.

level ['levəl] *adj* llano,-a, plano,-a. **2** *(equal)* a nivel, nivelado,-a. **– 3** *n* nivel *m.* **– 4** *t* nivelar. **5** *(raze)* arrasar. ●*fam on the ~,* de fiar, honrado,-a, legal. ■ *~ crossing,* paso a nivel.

lever ['li:vəʳ] *n* palanca.

levitate ['levɪteɪt] *t-i* (hacer) levitar.

levy ['levɪ] *n* recaudación. **– 2** *t* recaudar.

lewd [lu:d] *adj* lascivo,-a. **2** *(obscene)* obsceno,-a.

lexicographer [leksɪ'kɒgrəfər] *n* lexicó-grafo,-a.

lexicography [leksɪ'kɒgrəfɪ] *n* lexicogra-fía.

liability [laɪə'bɪlɪtɪ] *n* JUR responsabilidad. **2** *pl* COM pasivo *m sing*.

liable ['laɪəbəl] *adj* JUR responsable. **2** *(to colds etc.)* propenso,-a. ●*to be ~ to do sth.*, tener tendencia a hacer algo.

liaise [lɪ'eɪz] *i* comunicarse.

liaison [lɪ'eɪzən] *n* enlace *m*. **2** *(love affair)* amorío.

liar ['laɪər] *n* mentiroso,-a.

libel ['laɪbəl] *n* libelo, difamación. **– 2** *t* difamar.

liberal ['lɪbərəl] *adj* liberal. **2** *(abundant)* abundante. **– 3** *n* POL liberal *mf*.

liberalize ['lɪbərəlaɪz] *t* liberalizar.

liberate ['lɪbəreɪt] *t* liberar.

liberation [lɪbə'reɪʃən] *n* liberación.

liberator ['lɪbəreɪtər] *n* libertador,-ra.

liberty ['lɪbətɪ] *n* libertad.

Libra ['liːbrə] *n* Libra.

librarian [laɪ'breərɪən] *n* bibliotecario,-a.

library ['laɪbrərɪ] *n* biblioteca.

lice [laɪs] *npl* → **louse**.

licence ['laɪsəns] *n* licencia, permiso.

license ['laɪsəns] *t* autorizar.

licensee [laɪsən'siː] *n* concesionario,-a. **2** *(of pub)* dueño,-a.

licentious [laɪ'senʃəs] *adj* licencioso,-a.

lichen ['laɪkən] *n* liquen *m*.

lick [lɪk] *n* lamedura. **– 2** *t* lamer.

licking ['lɪkɪŋ] *n fam* paliza.

licorice ['lɪkərɪs] *n* regaliz *m*.

lid [lɪd] *n* tapa, tapadera.

lie [laɪ] *n (untruth)* mentira. **– 2** *i (tell lies)* mentir. **3** *(in a flat position) (act)* acos-tarse, tumbarse; *(state)* estar acosta-do,-a/tumbado,-a. **4** *(be buried)* yacer. **5** *(be situated)* estar (situado,-a), encon-trarse. **6** *(remain)* quedarse, permanecer. ◆*to ~ back i* recostarse. ●*to ~ down i* acostarse, tumbarse. ●*to ~ low,* estar escondido,-a. ▲ *En 2 es regular; en 3, 4, 5 y 6 pt lay; pp lain.*

lie-down ['laɪdaʊn] *n* siesta *f*.

lieu [luː] *n in ~ of,* en lugar de.

lieutenant [lef'tenənt] *n* MIL teniente *m*.

life [laɪf] *n* vida. ■ *~ belt,* salvavidas *m inv*; *~ sentence,* cadena perpetua.

life-boat ['laɪfbəʊt] *n (on ship)* bote *m* sal-vavidas. **2** *(on shore)* lancha de socorro.

lifeguard ['laɪfgɑːd] *n* socorrista *mf*.

lifelong [laɪflɒŋ] *adj* de toda la vida.

lifelike ['laɪflaɪk] *adj* natural. **2** *(portrait)* fiel.

life-size(d) ['laɪfsaɪz(d)] *adj* (de) tamaño natural.

lifetime ['laɪftaɪm] *n* vida.

lift [lɪft] *n* GB ascensor *m*. **2** *fig (boost)* es-tímulo. **– 3** *t-i* levantar. **– 4** *t fam (steal)* afanar, birlar. ●*to give sb. a ~,* llevar a algn. en coche.

lift-off ['lɪftɒf] *n* despegue *m*.

ligament ['lɪgəmənt] *n* ligamento.

light [laɪt] *n gen* luz *f*. **2** *(lamp)* luz, lám-para. **3** *(for cigarette etc.)* fuego. **– 4** *t-i* encender(se). **– 5** *t (illuminate)* iluminar, alumbrar. **– 6** *adj (not heavy)* ligero,-a. **7** *(colour)* claro,-a. **8** *(room)* con mucha cla-ridad. **– 9** *lightly adv* ligeramente. **10** *(not seriously)* a la ligera. ●*in the ~ of,* en vista de; *to come to ~,* salir a luz; *to travel ~,* viajar con poco equipaje. ■ *~ bulb,* bombilla; *~ year,* año luz. ▲ *pt & pp lighted o lit.*

lighten ['laɪtən] *t-i (colour)* aclarar(se). **– 2** *t (illuminate)* iluminar. **3** *(make less heavy)* aligerar. **– 4** *i* relampaguear.

lighter ['laɪtər] *n (for cigarettes)* encende-dor *m*, mechero. **2** *(boat)* gabarra.

light-fingered ['laɪtfɪŋgəd] *adj* de uñas largas.

light-headed [laɪt'hedɪd] *adj (foolish)* li-gero,-a de cascos. **2** *(dizzy)* mareado,-a.

lighthouse ['laɪthaʊs] *n* faro.

lighting ['laɪtɪŋ] *n (act)* iluminación. **2** *(system)* alumbrado.

lightning ['laɪtnɪŋ] *n* rayo; *(flash only)* relámpago.

like [laɪk] *adj (similar)* semejante, pareci-do,-a. **2** *(equal)* igual. **– 3** *prep* como. **– 4** *t* gustar: *I ~ wine,* me gusta el vino; *do you ~ him?,* ¿te gusta?; *would you like me to leave?,* ¿quieres que me vaya? **– 5** *n* cosa parecida. **6** *pl* gustos *mpl*. ●*~ father, ~ son,* de tal palo tal astilla; *~ this,* así; *to be/look ~,* pare-cerse a; *to feel ~,* tener ganas de.

likeable ['laɪkəbəl] *adj* simpático,-a.

likelihood ['laɪklɪhʊd] *n* probabilidad.

likely ['laɪklɪ] *adj* probable. **– 2** *adv* pro-bablemente.

liken ['laɪkən] *t* comparar.

likeness ['laɪknəs] *n* semejanza, pareci-do. **2** *(portrait)* retrato.

likewise ['laɪkwaɪz] *adv* también. **2** *(the same)* lo mismo.

liking ['laɪkɪŋ] *n* gusto, preferencia. ●*to be to sb.'s ~,* gustarle a algn.

Lilo® ['laɪləʊ] *n* colchoneta.

lilt [lɪlt] *n* melodía.

lily ['lɪlɪ] *n* lirio, azucena. ■ *water ~,* ne-núfar *m*.

limb [lɪmb] *n* miembro.
limber up [lɪmbər'ʌp] *i* precalentarse.
lime [laɪm] *n* CHEM cal *f*. **2** *(citrus fruit)* lima. **3** *(tree)* tilo.
limelight ['laɪmlaɪt] *n to be in the* ~, ser el centro de atención.
limestone ['laɪmstəʊn] *n* piedra caliza.
limit ['lɪmɪt] *n* límite *m*. − **2** *t* limitar.
limitation [lɪmɪ'teɪʃən] *n* limitación.
limited ['lɪmɪtɪd] *adj* limitado,-a. ■ ~ *company,* sociedad anónima.
limousine [lɪmə'ziːn] *n* limusina.
limp [lɪmp] *n* cojera. − **2** *i* cojear. − **3** *adj* flojo,-a, fláccido,-a. **4** *(weak)* débil.
limpet ['lɪmpɪt] *n* lapa.
limpid ['lɪmpɪd] *adj* límpido,-a.
linchpin ['lɪntʃpɪn] *n fig* pieza clave.
linden ['lɪndən] *n* tilo.
line [laɪn] *n gen* línea. **2** *(drawn on paper)* raya. **3** *(of text)* línea. **4** *(cord)* cuerda, cordel *m*; *(fishing)* sedal *m*. **5** US *(queue)* cola. **6** *(wrinkle)* arruga. − **7** *t (clothes)* forrar. **8** TECH revestir. ◆*to* ~ *up* *t-i* poner(se) en fila. − **2** *t fam* preparar, organizar.
linear ['lɪnɪə'] *adj* lineal.
lined [laɪnd] *adj (paper)* rayado,-a. **2** *(face)* arrugado,-a. **3** *(garment)* forrado,-a.
linen ['lɪnɪn] *n* lino. **2** *(sheets etc.)* ropa blanca.
liner ['laɪnə'] *n* transatlántico.
linesman ['laɪnzmən] *n* juez *mf* de línea.
linger ['lɪŋgə'] *i (stay)* quedarse. **2** *(persist)* persistir.
lingerie ['lɑːnʒəriː] *n fml* lencería.
lingering ['lɪŋgərɪŋ] *adj (slow)* lento,-a. **2** *(persistent)* persistente.
linguist ['lɪŋgwɪst] *n* lingüista *mf*. **2** *(polyglot)* políglota *mf*.
linguistic [lɪŋ'gwɪstɪk] *adj* lingüístico,-a.
linguistics [lɪŋ'gwɪstɪks] *n* lingüística.
liniment ['lɪnɪmənt] *n* linimento.
lining ['laɪnɪŋ] *n* forro. **2** TECH revestimiento.
link [lɪŋk] *n (in chain)* eslabón *m*. **2** *(connection)* enlace *m*. **3** *fig* vínculo. **4** *pl* campo *m sing* de golf. − **5** *t* unir, conectar. **6** *fig* vincular, relacionar.
linkage ['lɪŋkɪdʒ] *n* conexión.
linoleum [lɪ'nəʊlɪəm] *n* linóleo.
lint [lɪnt] *n* hilas *fpl*.
lintel ['lɪntəl] *n* dintel *m*.
lion ['laɪən] *n* león *m*.
lioness ['laɪənəs] *n* leona.
lip [lɪp] *n* labio. **2** *(of cup etc.)* borde *m*. **3** *fam (cheek)* impertinencia.
lip-read ['lɪpriːd] *t-i* leer en los labios.

lipstick ['lɪpstɪk] *n* pintalabios *m inv*.
liquefy ['lɪkwɪfaɪ] *t-i* licuar(se).
liqueur [lɪ'kjʊə'] *n* licor *m*.
liquid ['lɪkwɪd] *adj-n* líquido,-a *(m)*.
liquidate ['lɪkwɪdeɪt] *t* liquidar.
liquidize ['lɪkwɪdaɪz] *t* licuar.
liquor ['lɪkə'] *n* bebidas *fpl* alcohólicas.
liquorice ['lɪkərɪs] *n* regaliz *m*.
lisp [lɪsp] *n* ceceo. − **2** *i* cecear.
list [lɪst] *n* lista. **2** MAR escora. − **3** *t* hacer una lista de. − **4** *i* MAR escorar.
listen ['lɪsən] *i* escuchar. **2** *(pay attention)* prestar atención.
listener ['lɪsənə'] *n* oyente *mf*. **2** RAD radioyente *mf*.
listless ['lɪstləs] *adj* decaído,-a.
lit [lɪt] *pt & pp* → **light**.
literacy ['lɪtərəsɪ] *n* alfabetización.
literal ['lɪtərəl] *adj* literal. − **2** *literally adv (really)* materialmente.
literary ['lɪtərərɪ] *adj* literario,-a.
literate ['lɪtərət] *adj* alfabetizado,-a.
literature ['lɪtərɪtʃə'] *n* literatura. **2** *(booklets etc.)* información.
lithe [laɪð] *adj* ágil.
lithography [lɪ'θɒgrəfɪ] *n* litografía.
litigate ['lɪtɪgeɪt] *i* litigar.
litigation [lɪtɪ'geɪʃən] *n* litigio.
litmus ['lɪtməs] *n* tornasol *m*.
litre ['liːtə'] *n* litro.
litter ['lɪtə'] *n* basura; *(paper)* papeles *mpl*. **2** *(of young)* camada. − **3** *t* ensuciar, dejar en desorden: *littered with books,* lleno,-a/cubierto,-a de libros.
little ['lɪtəl] *adj (small)* pequeño,-a. **2** *(not much)* poco,-a. − **3** *pron* poco. − **4** *adv* poco. ◆~ *by* ~, poco a poco.
liturgy ['lɪtədʒɪ] *n* liturgia.
live [laɪv] *adj (not dead)* vivo,-a. **2** TV RAD en directo. **3** ELEC con corriente. **4** *(ammunition)* real. − **5** *t-i* vivir. ◆*to* ~ *down* *t* lograr que se olvide. ●*to* ~ *it up,* pasárselo bomba. ▲ *En 5 (verbo)* [lɪv].
livelihood ['laɪvlɪhʊd] *n* sustento.
liveliness ['laɪvlɪnəs] *n* vivacidad, animación.
lively ['laɪvlɪ] *adj (person)* vivo,-a. **2** *(event, place)* animado,-a.
liven up [laɪvən'ʌp] *t-i* animar(se).
liver ['lɪvə'] *n* hígado.
livestock ['laɪvstɒk] *n* ganado.
livid ['lɪvɪd] *adj* lívido. **2** *fam* furioso,-a.
living ['lɪvɪŋ] *adj* vivo,-a, viviente. − **2** *n* vida. ■ ~ *room,* sala de estar.
lizard ['lɪzəd] *n* lagarto; *(small)* lagartija.
llama ['lɑːmə] *n* ZOOL llama.

load [ləʊd] *n* carga. **2** *(weight)* peso. − **3** *t-i* cargar. ●*loads of ...,* montones de ... .

loaded ['ləʊdɪd] *adj* cargado,-a. **2** *(question)* tendencioso,-a. **3** *fam (rich)* forrado,-a.

loaf [ləʊf] *n* pan *m*; *(French)* barra. **2** *fam (head)* mollera. − **3** *i* holgazanear.

loafer ['ləʊfəʳ] *n* holgazán,-ana.

loan [ləʊn] *n* préstamo. − 2 *t* prestar.

loath [ləʊθ] *adj* reacio,-a.

loathe [ləʊð] *t* detestar, odiar.

loathing ['ləʊðɪŋ] *n* odio.

loathsome ['ləʊðsəm] *adj* odioso,-a.

lob [lɒb] *n (tennis)* lob *m*, globo. − **2** *i* hacer un lob. **3** *fam* tirar.

lobby ['lɒbɪ] *n* vestíbulo. **2** POL grupo de presión. − **3** *t* POL presionar, ejercer presión sobre.

lobe [ləʊb] *n* lóbulo.

lobster ['lɒbstəʳ] *n* bogavante *m*. ■ *spiny* ∼, langosta.

local ['ləʊkəl] *adj gen* local. **2** *(person)* del barrio/pueblo, de la ciudad. **3** *(government)* municipal, regional. − **4** *n* vecino,-a. **5** GB *fam* bar *m* del barrio.

locale [ləʊ'kɑːl] *n* lugar *m*.

locality [ləʊ'kælɪtɪ] *n* localidad.

locate [ləʊ'keɪt] *t (find)* localizar. **2** *(situate)* situar, ubicar.

location [ləʊ'keɪʃən] *n (place)* lugar *m*. **2** *(act of placing)* ubicación. **3** *(finding)* localización.

loch [lɒk] *n (in Scotland)* lago.

lock [lɒk] *n (on door etc.)* cerradura. **2** *(in canal)* esclusa. **3** *(of hair)* mecha, mechón *m*. − **4** *t* cerrar con llave.

locker ['lɒkəʳ] *n* taquilla, armario.

locket ['lɒkɪt] *n* guardapelo, medallón *m*.

lockout ['lɒkaʊt] *n* locaut *m*, cierre *m* patronal.

locksmith ['lɒksmɪθ] *n* cerrajero.

locomotive [ləʊkə'məʊtɪv] *adj-n* locomotor,-ra *(f)*.

locum ['ləʊkəm] *n* suplente *mf*.

locust ['ləʊkəst] *n* langosta.

locution [lə'kjuːʃən] *n* locución.

lodge [lɒdʒ] *n* casita. **2** *(porter's)* portería. **3** *(masonic)* logia. − **4** *i (as guest)* alojarse, hospedarse. **5** *(fix)* quedarse, fijarse. − **6** *t (complaint)* presentar.

lodger ['lɒdʒəʳ] *n* huésped,-da.

lodging ['lɒdʒɪŋ] *n* alojamiento.

loft [lɒft] *n* desván *m*.

log [lɒg] *n* tronco; *(for fire)* leño. **2** MAR cuaderno de bitácora. **3** AV diario de vuelo. − **4** *t* registrar. ●*to* ∼ *in i* COMPUT

entrar (en el sistema). ●*to* ∼ *out i* COMPUT salir (del sistema).

logarithm ['lɒgərɪðəm] *n* logaritmo.

loggerheads ['lɒgəhedz] *npl* **to be at** ∼, tener malas relaciones.

logic ['lɒdʒɪk] *n* lógica.

logical ['lɒdʒɪkəl] *adj* lógico,-a.

logistic [lə'dʒɪstɪk] *adj* logístico,-a.

loin [lɔɪn] *n* ijada. **2** CULIN *(pork)* lomo; *(beef)* solomillo.

loincloth ['lɔɪnklɒθ] *n* taparrabo(s).

loiter ['lɔɪtəʳ] *i* holgazanear. **2** *(lag behind)* rezagarse. **3** *(suspiciously)* merodear.

loll [lɒl] *i (sit)* repantigarse.

lollipop ['lɒlɪpɒp] *n* pirulí *m*, chupachup® *m*. **2** *(iced)* polo.

lolly ['lɒlɪ] *fam n* pirulí *m*, chupachup® *m*. **2** *(iced)* polo. **3** *(money)* pasta.

lone [ləʊn] *adj* solo,-a. **2** *(solitary)* solitario,-a.

loneliness ['ləʊnlɪnəs] *n* soledad.

lonely ['ləʊnlɪ] *adj* solo,-a, solitario,-a. **2** *(place)* aislado,-a.

long [lɒŋ] *adj* largo,-a: *how* ∼ *is the film?,* ¿cuánto dura la película?; *the garden is 30 metres* ∼, el jardín hace 30 metros de largo. − **2** *adv* mucho tiempo: *how have you had this problem?,* ¿desde cuándo tienes este problema? − **3** *i to* ∼ *for,* anhelar. **4** *to* ∼ *to,* tener muchas ganas de. ●*as* ∼ *as,* mientras, con tal que; *in the* ∼ *run,* a la larga; ∼ *ago,* hace mucho tiempo; *so* ∼, hasta la vista. ■ ∼ *jump,* salto de longitud.

longbow ['lɒŋbəʊ] *n* arco.

long-distance [lɒŋ'dɪstəns] *adj* de larga distancia. **2** *(phone call)* interurbano,-a. **3** *(runner)* de fondo.

longhand ['lɒŋhænd] *n* escritura a mano.

longing ['lɒŋɪŋ] *n* ansia, anhelo. **2** *(nostalgia)* nostalgia.

longitude ['lɒŋdʒɪtjuːd] *n* longitud.

long-playing [lɒŋ'pleɪɪŋ] *adj* de larga duración.

long-range [lɒŋ'reɪndʒ] *adj (distance)* de largo alcance. **2** *(time)* de largo plazo.

long-sighted [lɒŋ'saɪtɪd] *adj* MED présbita.

long-standing [lɒŋ'stændɪŋ] *adj* antiguo,-a.

long-suffering [lɒŋ'sʌfərɪŋ] *adj* sufrido,-a.

long-term [lɒŋ'tɜːm] *adj* a largo plazo.

longways ['lɒŋweɪz] *adv* a lo largo.

loo [luː] *n fam* wáter *m*.

look [lʊk] *n* mirada. **2** *(appearance)* aspecto, apariencia. **3** *(expression)* expresión.

4 *pl* belleza *f sing.* — 5 *i* mirar. 6 *(seem)* parecer. ◆*to ~ after t (deal with)* ocuparse de. 2 *(take care of)* cuidar. ◆*to ~ ahead i* mirar al futuro. ◆*to ~ at t* mirar. ◆*to ~ down on t* despreciar. ◆*to ~ for t* buscar. ◆*to ~ forward to t* esperar (con ansia). ◆*to ~ into t* investigar. ◆*to ~ on t* considerar. — 2 *i* mirar. ◆*to ~ onto t* dar a. ◆*to ~ out i* vigilar, ir con cuidado. ◆*to ~ round i* volver la cabeza. 2 *(in shop)* mirar. — 3 *t (town)* visitar. ◆*to ~ through t* examinar, revisar; *(book, quickly)* hojear. ◆*to ~ up i* mejorar. — 2 *t* buscar. 3 *(visit)* ir a visitar.

lookalike ['lʊkəlaɪk] *n* doble *mf,* sosia *m.*

lookout ['lʊkaʊt] *n (person)* vigía *mf.* 2 *(place)* atalaya. ●*to be on the ~ for,* estar al acecho de.

loom [lu:m] *n* telar *m.* — 2 *i* vislumbrarse.

loony ['lu:nɪ] *adj fam* chalado,-a.

loop [lu:p] *n (in string)* lazo.

loophole ['lu:phəʊl] *n fig* escapatoria.

loose [lu:s] *adj gen* suelto,-a. 2 *(not tight)* flojo,-a; *(clothes)* holgado,-a. 3 *(not tied)* desatado,-a. — 4 *t* soltar. ●*on the ~,* suelto,-a.

loosen ['lu:sən] *t-i* soltar(se), aflojar(se).

loot [lu:t] *n* botín *m.* 2 *fam (money)* pasta.- 3 *t-i* saquear.

lop [lɒp] *t* podar.

lope [ləʊp] *i* andar con paso largo.

lopsided [lɒp'saɪdɪd] *adj* desequilibrado,-a.

loquacious [lə'kweɪʃəs] *adj* locuaz.

lord [lɔ:d] *n* señor *m.* 2 *(title)* lord *m.* ■ *the Lord,* el Señor; *the Lord's Prayer,* el padrenuestro.

lordship ['lɔ:dʃɪp] *n (title)* señoría.

lore [lɔ:ʳ] *n* saber *m* popular.

lorry ['lɒrɪ] *n* camión *m.*

lose [lu:z] *t-i gen* perder. 2 *(clock)* atrasarse. ●*to ~ one's way,* perderse. ▲ *pt & pp* lost.

loser ['lu:zəʳ] *n* perdedor,-a. ●*to be a good/bad ~,* saber/no saber perder.

loss [lɒs] *n* pérdida.

lost [lɒst] *pt & pp* → lose. — 2 *adj* perdido,-a. ●*to get ~,* perderse.

lot [lɒt] *n (fate)* suerte *f.* 2 us *(land)* solar *m.* 3 *(in auction)* lote *m.* 4 *(large number)* cantidad: *a ~,* mucho, muchísimo; *a ~ of ...,* muchísimo,-a, muchísimos,-as; *lots of ...,* cantidad de ... . ●*to cast lots,* echar suertes.

lotion ['ləʊʃən] *n* loción.

lottery ['lɒtərɪ] *n* lotería.

loud [laʊd] *adj (sound)* fuerte. 2 *(voice)* alto,-a. 3 *(colour)* chillón,-ona. 4 *(behav-*iour)* vulgar, ordinario,-a. — 5 *adv* fuerte, alto.

loudmouth ['laʊdmaʊθ] *n pej* voceras *mf inv,* bocazas *mf inv.*

loudspeaker [laʊd'spi:kəʳ] *n* altavoz *m.*

lounge [laʊndʒ] *n* salón *m.* — 2 *i* holgazanear. 3 *(on sofa etc.)* repantigarse.

louse [laʊs] *n* piojo. 2 *fam* canalla *mf.* ▲ *En 1 pl* lice.

lousy ['laʊzɪ] *adj* piojoso,-a. 2 *fam* fatal, malísimo,-a; *(vile)* asqueroso,-a.

lout [laʊt] *n* patán *m.*

loutish ['laʊtɪʃ] *adj* bruto,-a.

lovable ['lʌvəbəl] *adj* adorable.

love [lʌv] *n* amor *m.* 2 *(tennis)* cero. — 3 *t* amar a, querer a. 4 *(like a lot)* tener afición a: *I ~ fish,* me encanta el pescado. ●*not for ~ or money,* por nada del mundo; *to be in ~ with,* estar enamorado,-a de. ■ *~ affair,* aventura amorosa; *~ at first sight,* amor a primera vista.

lovely ['lʌvlɪ] *adj* maravilloso,-a; *(beautiful)* hermoso,-a, precioso,-a; *(charming)* encantador,-ra.

lover ['lʌvəʳ] *n* amante *mf.*

loving ['lʌvɪŋ] *adj* afectuoso,-a.

low [ləʊ] *adj gen* bajo,-a. 2 *(depressed)* abatido,-a. — 3 *adv* bajo. — 4 *i* mugir.

lowdown ['ləʊdaʊn] *n fam* detalles *mpl.*

lower ['ləʊəʳ] *adj* inferior. — 2 *t gen* bajar. 3 *(flag)* arriar.

lower-class [ləʊə'klɑ:s] *adj* de clase baja.

low-necked [ləʊ'nekt] *adj* escotado,-a.

lowly ['ləʊlɪ] *adj* humilde, modesto,-a.

loyal ['lɔɪəl] *adj* leal, fiel.

loyalty ['lɔɪəltɪ] *n* lealtad, fidelidad.

lozenge ['lɒzɪndʒ] *n* pastilla.

lubricant ['lu:brɪkənt] *n* lubricante *m.*

lubricate ['lu:brɪkeɪt] *t* lubricar.

lubrication [lu:brɪ'keɪʃən] *n* lubricación.

lucid ['lu:sɪd] *adj* lúcido,-a.

luck [lʌk] *n* suerte *f.*

luckily ['lʌkɪlɪ] *adv* afortunadamente.

luckless ['lʌkləs] *adj* desafortunado,-a.

lucky ['lʌkɪ] *adj* afortunado,-a.

lucrative ['lu:krətɪv] *adj* lucrativo,-a.

ludicrous ['lu:dɪkrəs] *adj* ridículo,-a.

lug [lʌg] *t fam* arrastrar.

luggage ['lʌgɪdʒ] *n* equipaje *m.*

lugubrious [lə'gju:brɪəs] *adj* lúgubre.

lukewarm ['lu:kwɔ:m] *adj* templado,-a.

lull [lʌl] *n* momento de calma, recalmón *m.* — 2 *t* adormecer.

lullaby ['lʌləbaɪ] *n* canción de cuna, nana.

lumbago [lʌm'beɪgəʊ] *n* lumbago.

lumber ['lʌmbəʳ] *n (wood)* madera. **2** *(junk)* trastos *mpl* viejos. − **3** *i* moverse pesadamente.
lumberjack ['lʌmbədʒæk] *n* leñador *m*.
luminous ['lu:mɪnəs] *adj* luminoso,-a.
lump [lʌmp] *n* pedazo, trozo. **2** *(sugar)* terrón *m*. **3** *(swelling)* bulto. **4** *(in sauce)* grumo. ◆*to ~ together t* juntar. ●*fam to ~ it,* apechugar. ■ *~ sum,* suma global.
lumpy ['lʌmpɪ] *adj* lleno,-a de bultos. **2** *(sauce)* grumoso,-a.
lunacy ['lu:nəsɪ] *n* locura.
lunar ['lu:nəʳ] *adj* lunar.
lunatic ['lu:nətɪk] *adj-n* loco,-a.
lunch [lʌntʃ] *n* comida, almuerzo. − **2** *i* comer, almorzar.
luncheon ['lʌntʃən] *n fml* almuerzo.
lunchtime ['lʌntʃtaɪm] *n* hora de comer/almorzar.
lung [lʌŋ] *n* pulmón *m*.
lunge [lʌndʒ] *n* arremetida, embestida. − **2** *i* arremeter, embestir.
lurch [lɜːtʃ] *n* sacudida, tumbo, bandazo. − **2** *i* dar sacudidas/bandazos. **3** *(person)* tambalear(se). ●*to leave in the ~,* dejar en la estacada.
lure [ljʊəʳ] *n* señuelo. **2** *fig* atractivo. − **3** *t* atraer.

lurid ['ljuərɪd] *adj (colours etc.)* chillón,-ona. **2** *(details)* horripilante, espeluznante.
lurk [lɜːk] *i* estar al acecho.
luscious ['lʌʃəs] *adj* delicioso,-a, exquisito,-a.
lush [lʌʃ] *adj* exuberante.
lust [lʌst] *n* codicia. **2** *(sexual)* lujuria. ◆*to ~ after t* codiciar.
lustful ['lʌstfʊl] *adj* lujurioso,-a.
lustre ['lʌstəʳ] *n* lustre *m*, brillo.
lusty ['lʌstɪ] *adj* fuerte, robusto,-a.
lute [lu:t] *n* laúd *m*.
luxurious [lʌgˈzjuərɪəs] *adj* lujoso,-a.
luxury ['lʌkʃərɪ] *n* lujo.
lying ['laɪɪŋ] *adj* mentiroso,-a. − **2** *n* mentiras *fpl*.
lymphatic [lɪmˈfætɪk] *adj* linfático,-a.
lynch [lɪntʃ] *t* linchar.
lynching ['lɪntʃɪŋ] *n* linchamiento.
lynx [lɪŋks] *n* lince *m*.
lyre ['laɪəʳ] *n* MUS lira.
lyric ['lɪrɪk] *adj* lírico,-a. − **2** *npl (of song)* letra *f* sing.
lyrical ['lɪrɪkəl] *adj* lírico,-a.
lyricist ['lɪrɪsɪst] *n* letrista *mf*.

M

ma'am [mæm, mɑːm] *n fml* señora.
macabre [məˈkɑːbrə] *adj* macabro,-a.
mac(c)aroni [mækəˈrəʊnɪ] *n* macarrones *mpl*.
mace [meɪs] *n* maza.
machine [məˈʃiːn] *n* máquina, aparato. ■ ~ **gun,** ametralladora.
machinery [məˈʃiːnərɪ] *n* maquinaria. **2** *(workings)* mecanismo.
mackerel [ˈmækrəl] *n* caballa.
mac(k)intosh [ˈmækɪntɒʃ] *n* impermeable *m*.
mad [mæd] *adj* loco,-a. **2** *(idea, plan)* disparatado,-a, insensato,-a. **3** *(uncontrolled)* desenfrenado,-a. – **4 madly** *adv* locamente. **5** *(hurriedly)* precipitadamente. **6** *fam (very)* terriblemente. ●*to be ~ about,* estar loco,-a por; *to be ~ at/with sb.,* estar enfadado,-a con algn.; *to go ~,* volverse loco,-a.
madam [ˈmædəm] *n fml* señora.
madden [ˈmædən] *t* enfurecer.
made [meɪd] *pt & pp* → **make.**
made-up [ˈmeɪdʌp] *adj (face)* maquillado,-a; *(eyes)* pintado,-a. **2** *(invented)* inventado,-a.
madhouse [ˈmædhaʊs] *n fam* casa de locos, manicomio.
madman [ˈmædmən] *n* loco.
madness [ˈmædnəs] *n* locura.
magazine [mægəˈziːn] *n* revista. **2** *(in gun)* recámara.
magic [ˈmædʒɪk] *n* magia. – **2** *adj* mágico,-a. ●*as if by ~,* como por arte de magia.
magical [ˈmædʒɪkəl] *adj* mágico,-a.
magician [məˈdʒɪʃən] *n* prestidigitador,-ra, mago,-a.
magistrate [ˈmædʒɪstreɪt] *n* magistrado,-a, juez *mf*.
magnanimous [mægˈnænɪməs] *adj* magnánimo,-a.

magnate [ˈmægneɪt] *n* magnate *m*.
magnet [ˈmægnət] *n* imán *m*.
magnetic [mægˈnetɪk] *adj* magnético,-a. ■ ~ **field,** campo magnético; ~ **tape,** cinta magnetofónica.
magnificent [mægˈnɪfɪsənt] *adj* magnífico,-a, espléndido,-a.
magnify [ˈmægnɪfaɪ] *t* aumentar, ampliar. **2** *fig* exagerar.
magnifying glass [ˈmægnɪfaɪɪŋglɑːs] *n* lupa.
magnitude [ˈmægnɪtjuːd] *n* magnitud.
mahogany [məˈhɒgənɪ] *n* caoba.
maid [meɪd] *n* criada, sirvienta. **2** *(in hotel)* camarera. ■ ~ **of honour,** dama de honor.
maiden [ˈmeɪdən] *n* doncella. – **2** *adj (unmarried)* soltera. **3** *(voyage)* inaugural. ■ ~ **name,** apellido de soltera.
mail [meɪl] *n* correo. – **2** *t US (post)* echar al buzón. **3** *(send)* enviar por correo. ■ ~ **order,** venta por correo; ~ **train,** tren *m* correo.
mailbox [ˈmeɪlbɒks] *n US* buzón *m*.
maim [meɪm] *t* mutilar, lisiar.
main [meɪn] *adj* principal. **2** *(essential)* esencial. – **3** *n (pipe, wire)* conducto principal. **4** ELEC corriente eléctrica. – **5 mainly** *adv (chiefly)* principalmente. **6** *(mostly)* en su mayoría. ■ ARCH ~ **beam,** viga maestra; ~ **course,** plato principal; ~ **office,** oficina central; ~ **street,** calle *f* mayor. ▲ **3** *y* **4** *gen pl*.
mainland [ˈmeɪnlənd] *n* continente *m*.
mainstream [ˈmeɪnstriːm] *n* corriente *f* principal.
maintain [meɪnˈteɪn] *t* mantener.
maintenance [ˈmeɪntənəns] *n* mantenimiento. **2** JUR pensión.
maisonette [meɪzəˈnet] *n* dúplex *m*.
maize [meɪz] *n* maíz *m*.
majestic [məˈdʒestɪk] *adj* majestuoso,-a.

majesty ['mædʒəstɪ] *n* majestad.
major ['meɪdʒəʳ] *adj* mayor, principal. 2 *(important)* importante, considerable. 3 MUS mayor. – 4 *n* MIL comandante *m*.
majority [mə'dʒɒrɪtɪ] *n* mayoría. ■ ~ *rule,* gobierno mayoritario.
make [meɪk] *n* marca. – 2 *t gen* hacer. 3 *(speech)* pronunciar. 4 *(decision)* tomar. 5 *(compel)* obligar: *to ~ sb. do sth.,* obligar a algn. a hacer algo. 6 *(earn)* ganar. 7 *(achieve)* conseguir: *I made it!,* ¡lo conseguí! ◆*to ~ for t (move towards)* dirigirse hacia. 2 *(result in)* contribuir a. ◆*to ~ out t (write)* hacer; *(cheque)* extender. 2 *(see)* distinguir; *(writing)* descifrar. 3 *(understand)* entender. 4 *fam (pretend)* pretender. – 5 *i (manage)* arreglárselas. ◆*to ~ up t (invent)* inventar. 2 *(put together)* hacer; *(package)* empaquetar. 3 *(complete)* completar. 4 *(constitute)* componer, formar. – 5 *t-i (cosmetics)* maquillar(se). ◆*to ~ up for t* compensar. ●*to be made of,* ser/estar hecho,-a de; *to ~ a fresh start,* volver a empezar; *to ~ a living,* ganarse la vida; *to ~ a mistake,* equivocarse; *to ~ believe,* hacer ver; *to ~ do (with sth.),* arreglárselas (con algo); *to ~ fun of,* burlarse de; *to ~ it up with sb.,* hacer las paces; *to ~ sense,* tener sentido; *to ~ sb. angry,* (hacer) enfadar a algn.; *to ~ sth. clear,* aclarar algo; *to ~ sth. known,* dar a conocer algo; *to ~ sure (of sth.),* asegurarse (de algo); *to ~ the best/most of sth.,* sacar partido de algo; *to ~ up one's mind,* decidirse. ▲ *pt & pp* made.
make-believe ['meɪkbɪliːv] *n* fantasía, invención.
maker ['meɪkəʳ] *n (manufacturer)* fabricante *mf*.
makeshift ['meɪkʃɪft] *adj* provisional.
make-up ['meɪkʌp] *n (cosmetics)* maquillaje *m*. 2 *(composition)* composición. 3 *(of person)* carácter *m*. 4 *(of book, page)* compaginación. ■ ~ *remover,* desmaquillador *m*.
making ['meɪkɪŋ] *n (manufacture)* fabricación. 2 *(construction)* construcción. 3 *(creation)* creación. ●*to have the makings of sth.,* tener madera de algo.
maladjusted [mælə'dʒʌstɪd] *adj* inadaptado,-a.
malaria [mə'leərɪə] *n* malaria, paludismo.
male [meɪl] *adj-n (animal, plant)* macho. 2 *(person)* varón *(m)*. – 3 *adj (sex)* masculino,-a. ■ ~ *chauvinism,* machismo.
malevolent [mə'levələnt] *adj* malévolo,-a.

malformation [mælfɔː'meɪʃən] *n* malformación.
malfunction [mæl'fʌnkʃən] *n* funcionamiento defectuoso.
malice ['mælɪs] *n* malicia, maldad. ●*to bear sb. ~,* guardar rencor a algn.
malicious [mə'lɪʃəs] *adj* malévolo,-a. 2 *(bitter)* rencoroso,-a.
malignant [mə'lɪgnənt] *adj (person)* malvado,-a. 2 MED maligno,-a.
mallet ['mælət] *n* mazo.
malnutrition [mælnjuː'trɪʃən] *n* desnutrición.
malpractice [mæl'præktɪs] *n* MED negligencia. 2 JUR procedimiento ilegal.
malt [mɔːlt] *n* malta.
mammal ['mæməl] *n* mamífero.
mammoth ['mæməθ] *n* mamut *m*. – 2 *adj* gigantesco,-a, descomunal.
man [mæn] *n* hombre *m*. 2 *(humanity)* Man, el hombre. 3 *(chess)* pieza; *(draughts)* ficha. – 4 *t (boat, plane)* tripular. 5 *(post)* servir. ●~ *and wife,* marido y mujer; *the ~ in the street,* el hombre de la calle. ▲ *pl* men.
manacle ['mænəkəl] *n* esposa. – 2 *t* esposar. ▲ *1 gen pl*.
manage ['mænɪdʒ] *t (business)* dirigir, llevar. 2 *(household)* llevar. 3 *(affairs, child)* manejar. 4 *(succeed)* conseguir: *can you ~ (to do) it?,* ¿puedes con eso? – 5 *i* poder. 6 *(financially)* arreglárselas, apañarse.
manageable ['mænɪdʒəbəl] *adj* manejable.
management ['mænɪdʒmənt] *n (of business etc.)* dirección, administración. 2 *(board of directors)* junta directiva, consejo de administración.
manager ['mænɪdʒəʳ] *n (of company)* director,-ra, gerente *mf*. 2 *(of restaurant etc.)* encargado. 3 THEAT empresario,-a. 4 *(of actor)* representante *mf*, mánager *mf*. 5 *(sports)* entrenador *m*, mánager *mf*.
manageress [mænɪdʒə'res] *n (of company)* directora, gerente *f*. 2 *(of shop etc.)* encargada, jefa.
mandate ['mændeɪt] *n* mandato.
mane [meɪn] *n (of horse)* crin *f*; *(of lion)* melena.
manger ['meɪndʒəʳ] *n* pesebre *m*.
mangle ['mæŋgəl] *n* escurridor *m*, rodillo. – 2 *t (cut to pieces)* destrozar. 3 *(crush)* aplastar.
mango ['mæŋgəu] *n* mango.
manhandle ['mænhændəl] *t (person)* maltratar.
manhole ['mænhəul] *n* boca de acceso.

manhood ['mænhʊd] *n* madurez *f*. ●*to reach ~,* llegar a la edad viril.

mania ['meɪnɪə] *n* manía.

maniac ['meɪnɪæk] *n* maníaco,-a. 2 *fam* loco,-a.

manic ['mænɪk] *adj* maníaco,-a.

manicure ['mænɪkjʊəʳ] *n* manicura.

manifest ['mænɪfest] *fml adj* manifiesto,-a, patente. − 2 *t* manifestar.

manifesto [mænɪ'festəʊ] *n* manifiesto.

manifold ['mænɪfəʊld] *adj fml* múltiples, varios,-as. − 2 *n* colector *m* de escape.

manipulate [mə'nɪpjʊleɪt] *t* manipular.

mankind [mæn'kaɪnd] *n* la humanidad, el género humano.

manly ['mænlɪ] *adj* varonil, viril, macho.

man-made [mæn'meɪd] *adj (lake)* artificial. 2 *(fabric etc.)* sintético,-a.

manner ['mænəʳ] *n* manera, modo. 2 *(way of behaving)* forma de ser, comportamiento. 3 *pl* maneras *fpl*, modales *mpl*. ●*in a ~ (of speaking),* por decirlo así; *in this ~,* de esta manera, así.

mannerism ['mænərɪzəm] *n* peculiaridad.

manoeuvre [mə'nu:vəʳ] *n* maniobra. − 2 *t-i* maniobrar. − 3 *t (person)* manipular.

manor ['mænəʳ] *n* señorío. ■ *~ house,* casa solariega.

manpower ['mænpaʊəʳ] *n* mano *f* de obra.

mansion ['mænʃən] *n* casa grande; *(country)* casa solariega.

manslaughter ['mænslɔːtəʳ] *n* homicidio involuntario.

mantelpiece ['mæntəlpiːs] *n* repisa de chimenea.

manual ['mænjʊəl] *adj-n* manual *(m)*. − 2 *manually adv* a mano.

manufacture [mænjʊ'fæktʃəʳ] *n gen* fabricación. 2 *(of clothing)* confección. 3 *(of foodstuffs)* elaboración. − 4 *t gen* fabricar. 5 *(clothing)* confeccionar. 6 *(foodstuffs)* elaborar.

manufacturer [mænjʊ'fæktʃərəʳ] *n* fabricante *mf*.

manure [mə'njʊəʳ] *n* abono, estiércol *m*. − 2 *t* abonar, estercolar.

manuscript ['mænjʊskrɪpt] *n* manuscrito.

many ['menɪ] *adj-pron* muchos,-as. ●*as ~ ... as,* tantos,-as ... como; *how ~?,* ¿cuántos,-as?; *~ people,* mucha gente; *not ~,* pocos,-as; *too ~,* demasiados,-as. ▲ *comp* **more**; *superl* **most**.

map [mæp] *n (of country, region)* mapa *m*. 2 *(of town, transport)* plano. ◆*to ~ out t*

(plan) proyectar, planear. ■ *~ of the world,* mapamundi *m*.

maple ['meɪpəl] *n* arce *m*.

mar [mɑːʳ] *t* estropear, echar a perder.

marathon ['mærəθən] *n* maratón . − 2 *adj* maratoniano,-a.

marble ['mɑːbəl] *n* mármol *m*. 2 *(glass ball)* canica. − 3 *adj* de mármol.

March [mɑːtʃ] *n* marzo.

march [mɑːtʃ] *n* MIL marcha; *(walk)* caminata. 2 *(demonstration)* manifestación. 3 *fig (of time)* marcha, paso. − 4 *i* MIL marchar, hacer una marcha; *(walk)* caminar. ◆*to ~ in/out i* entrar/salir enfadado,-a. ◆*to ~ past i* desfilar. ●*to ~ sb. off,* llevarse a algn. (a la fuerza).

mare [meəʳ] *n* yegua.

margarine [mɑːdʒə'riːn] *n* margarina.

margin ['mɑːdʒɪn] *n* margen *m*.

marginal ['mɑːdʒɪnəl] *adj* marginal. 2 *(small)* insignificante.

marigold ['mærɪgəʊld] *n* maravilla, caléndula.

marinate ['mærɪneɪt] *t* adobar.

marine [mə'riːn] *n* marino,-a, marítimo,-a. − 2 *n* soldado de infantería de marina.

marionette [mærɪə'net] *n* marioneta, títere *m*.

marital ['mærɪtəl] *adj* matrimonial. ■ *~ status,* estado civil.

maritime ['mærɪtaɪm] *adj* marítimo,-a.

mark [mɑːk] *n (imprint)* huella; *(from blow)* señal *f*. 2 *(stain)* mancha. 3 *(sign)* señal, marca. 4 EDUC nota, calificación. 5 SP tanto. 6 *(target)* blanco. 7 TECH *(type)* serie *f*. 8 FIN marco (alemán). − 9 *t* marcar. 10 *(stain)* manchar. 11 *(indicate)* señalar. 12 EDUC *(correct)* corregir; *(give mark to)* puntuar, calificar. ◆*to ~ down t (lower)* rebajar. ◆*to ~ out t (area)* delimitar. 2 *(person)* destinar *(for,* a). ●*~ my words!,* ¡verás cómo tengo razón!; *on your marks!,* ¡preparados!; *to hit the ~,* dar en el blanco; *to make one's ~,* distinguirse; *fig to ~ time,* hacer (el) tiempo.

marked [mɑːkt] *adj* marcado,-a, apreciable.

marker ['mɑːkəʳ] *n (stake)* jalón *m*. 2 *(pen)* rotulador *m*.

market ['mɑːkɪt] *n* mercado. − 2 *t* vender, poner en venta. ●*to be on the ~,* estar a la/en venta.

marketing ['mɑːkɪtɪŋ] *n* márketing *m*.

marksman ['mɑːksmən] *n* tirador *m*.

marmalade ['mɑːməleɪd] *n* mermelada (de cítricos).

maroon [mə'ruːn] *adj-n* granate *(m)*. – 2 *t* aislar, abandonar.

marquee [mɑːˈkiː] *n* carpa, entoldado.

marquis ['mɑːkwɪs] *n* marqués *m*.

marriage ['mærɪdʒ] *n* matrimonio. 2 *(wedding)* boda.

married ['mærɪd] *adj* casado,-a *(to,* con). ●*to get* ~, casarse. ■ ~ *name,* apellido de casada.

marrow ['mærəʊ] *n (of bone)* tuétano, médula. 2 BOT calabacín *m*.

marry ['mærɪ] *t (take in marriage)* casarse con. 2 *(unite in marriage)* casar. ●*to* ~ *into money,* emparentar con una familia adinerada.

marsh [mɑːʃ] *n* pantano. 2 *(area)* pantanal *m*.

marshal ['mɑːʃəl] *n* MIL mariscal. 2 *(at event)* maestro de ceremonias.

martial ['mɑːʃəl] *adj* marcial. ■ ~ *law,* ley *f* marcial.

martyr ['mɑːtəʳ] *n* mártir *mf*. – 2 *t* martirizar.

martyrdom ['mɑːtədəm] *n* martirio.

marvel ['mɑːvəl] *n* maravilla. – 2 *i* maravillarse.

marvellous ['mɑːvələs] *adj* maravilloso,-a, estupendo,-a.

Marxism ['mɑːksɪzəm] *n* marxismo.

marzipan ['mɑːzɪpæn] *n* mazapán *m*.

mascara [mæˈskɑːrə] *n* rímel *m*.

mascot ['mæskɒt] *n* mascota.

masculine ['mɑːskjʊlɪn] *adj-n* masculino,-a *(m)*.

mash [mæʃ] *n fam* puré *m* de patatas. – 2 *t* triturar. 3 CULIN hacer un puré de.

mask [mɑːsk] *n* máscara. 2 MED mascarilla. – 3 *t* enmascarar. ■ *masked ball,* baile *m* de disfraces.

masochism ['mæsəkɪzəm] *n* masoquismo.

mason ['meɪsən] *n* albañil *m*.

masonry ['meɪsənrɪ] *n* albañilería.

masquerade [mæskəˈreɪd] *n* farsa, mascarada. – 2 *i* disfrazarse *(as,* de).

mass [mæs] *n* masa. 2 *(large quantity)* montón *m*. 3 REL misa. – 4 *i* congregarse. ■ ~ *media,* medios *mpl* de comunicación (de masas); ~ *production,* fabricación en serie; *the masses,* la masa.

massacre ['mæsəkəʳ] *n* masacre *f*, carnicería, matanza. – 2 *t* masacrar.

massage ['mæsɑːʒ] *n* masaje *m*. – 2 *t* dar masajes a.

massive ['mæsɪv] *adj (solid)* macizo,-a. 2 *(huge)* enorme, descomunal.

mast [mɑːst] *n* mástil *m*, palo.

master ['mɑːstəʳ] *n* amo. 2 *(owner)* dueño. 3 *(teacher)* maestro, profesor *m* de instituto. 4 *(expert)* maestro. 5 EDUC *master's,* tesina, máster *m*. – 6 *t (control)* dominar. 7 *(learn)* llegar a dominar. ■ ~ *builder,* maestro de obras, contratista *mf*; ~ *key,* llave maestra; ~ *of ceremonies,* maestro de ceremonias.

masterpiece ['mɑːstəpiːs] *n* obra maestra.

mastery ['mɑːstərɪ] *n (control)* dominio. 2 *(skill)* maestría.

masturbate ['mæstəbeɪt] *t-i* masturbar(se).

mat [mæt] *n (rug)* alfombrilla. 2 *(doormat)* felpudo. 3 *(tablemat)* salvamanteles *m inv*. 4 SP colchoneta. – 5 *adj* mate.

match [mætʃ] *n* fósforo, cerilla. 2 *(equal)* igual *mf*. 3 SP partido, encuentro. – 4 *t* igualar. 5 *(compare)* equiparar. – 6 *t-i (clothes, colours)* hacer juego (con), combinar (con). ●*to be a good* ~, *(clothes etc.)* hacer juego; *(people)* hacer buena pareja; *to meet one's* ~, encontrar uno la horma de su zapato.

matchbox ['mætʃbɒks] *n* caja de cerillas.

matching ['mætʃɪŋ] *adj* que hace juego.

mate [meɪt] *n (companion)* compañero,-a, colega *mf*. 2 ZOOL pareja; *(male)* macho; *(female)* hembra. 3 MAR piloto. 4 *(chess)* mate *m*. – 5 *t-i* aparear(se), acoplar(se).

material [məˈtɪərɪəl] *n (substance)* materia. 2 *(cloth)* tela, tejido. 3 *(information, ideas, etc.)* material *m*. 4 *pl* material *m sing,* materiales *mpl*. – 5 *adj* material. 6 *(important)* importante, substancial.

materialism [məˈtɪərɪəlɪzəm] *n* materialismo.

materialize [məˈtɪərɪəlaɪz] *i* realizarse.

maternity [məˈtɜːnɪtɪ] *n* maternidad. ■ ~ *hospital,* maternidad; ~ *leave,* baja por maternidad.

mathematics [mæθəˈmætɪks] *n* matemáticas *fpl*.

maths [mæθs] *n fam* mates *fpl*.

matriarch ['meɪtrɪɑːk] *n* matriarca.

matriculate [məˈtrɪkjʊleɪt] *t-i* matricular(se).

matron ['meɪtrən] *n (in hospital)* enfermera jefe/jefa. 2 *(in school)* ama de llaves.

matronly ['meɪtrənlɪ] *adj* madura y recia.

matter ['mætəʳ] *n (substance)* materia. 2 *(affair, subject)* asunto, cuestión. – 3 *i* importar: *it doesn't* ~, no importa, da igual. ●*as a* ~ *of fact,* en realidad; *it's a* ~ *of ten minutes,* es cuestión/cosa de diez minutos; *no* ~ *how,* como sea; *no*

~ *where you go,* dondequiera que vayas; *there's nothing the* ~ *with him,* no le pasa nada; *to make matters worse,* para colmo de desgracias; *what's the* ~*?,* ¿qué pasa/ocurre?; *what's the* ~ *with you?,* ¿qué te pasa?

matter-of-fact [mætərəvˈfækt] *adj* práctico,-a, realista.

mattress [ˈmætrəs] *n* colchón *m.*

mature [məˈtʃʊəʳ] *adj* maduro,-a. 2 FIN vencido,-a. − 3 *t-i* madurar. − 4 *i* FIN vencer.

maturity [məˈtʃʊərɪtɪ] *n* madurez *f.*

maul [mɔːl] *t* herir, agredir.

mauve [məʊv] *adj-n* malva *(m).*

maximum [ˈmæksɪməm] *adj-n* máximo,-a *(m).* ●*as a* ~, como máximo; *to the* ~, al máximo.

May [meɪ] *n* mayo.

may [meɪ] *aux* poder, ser posible: *he* ~ *come,* es posible que venga, puede que venga. 2 *(permission)* poder: ~ *I go?,* ¿puedo irme? 3 *(wish)* ojalá: ~ *it be so,* ojalá sea así. ●*come what* ~, pase lo que pase; *I* ~*/might as well stay,* más vale que me quede. ▲ *pt* **might.**

maybe [ˈmeɪbiː] *adv* quizá(s), tal vez: ~ *it'll rain,* tal vez llueva.

mayonnaise [meɪəˈneɪz] *n* mayonesa, mahonesa.

mayor [meəʳ] *n* alcalde *m.*

maze [meɪz] *n* laberinto.

me [miː] *pers pron* me; *(with prep)* mí: *follow* ~, sígueme; *it's for* ~, es para mí. 2 *(emphatic)* yo: *it's* ~*!,* ¡soy yo! ●*with* ~, conmigo.

meadow [ˈmedəʊ] *n* prado, pradera.

meagre [ˈmiːgəʳ] *adj* escaso,-a.

meal [miːl] *n* comida. 2 *(flour)* harina. ●*to have a* ~, comer.

mean [miːn] *adj (miserly)* tacaño,-a. 2 *(unkind)* malo,-a. 3 US *(nasty)* antipático,-a. 4 *(humble)* humilde. 5 *(average)* medio,-a: ~ *temperature,* temperatura media. − 6 *n* media. − 7 *t (signify)* querer decir. 8 *(be important)* significar: *this means a lot to me,* esto significa mucho para mí. 9 *(intend)* tener intención de: *I didn't* ~ *to do it,* lo hice sin querer. 10 *(entail)* suponer, implicar. 11 *(destine)* destinar *(for,* para). ●*to* ~ *it,* decirlo en serio; *to* ~ *well,* tener buenas intenciones; *what do you* ~ *(by that)?,* ¿qué quiere(s) decir (con eso)? ▲ *pt & pp* **meant.**

meander [mɪˈændəʳ] *i (river)* serpentear. 2 *(person)* vagar.

meaning [ˈmiːnɪŋ] *n* sentido, significado.

meaningful [ˈmiːnɪŋfʊl] *adj* significativo,-a.

means [miːnz] *n inv (way)* medio, manera. 2 *pl (resources)* medios *mpl,* recursos *mpl* (económicos). ●*a man of* ~, un hombre acaudalado; *by all* ~*!,* ¡naturalmente!; *by* ~ *of,* por medio de, mediante; *by no* ~, de ninguna manera, de ningún modo.

meant [ment] *pt & pp* → **mean.**

meantime [ˈmiːntaɪm] *n in the* ~, mientras tanto, entretanto.

meanwhile [ˈmiːnwaɪl] *adv* mientras tanto, entretanto.

measles [ˈmiːzəlz] *n* sarampión *m.* ■ *German* ~, rubeola.

measure [ˈmeʒəʳ] *n gen* medida. 2 MUS compás *m.* − 3 *t (area etc.)* medir. 4 *(person)* tomar las medidas de. ◆*to* ~ *up i* estar a la altura *(to,* de). ●*in some* ~, hasta cierto punto; *to take measures,* tomar medidas.

measurement [ˈmeʒəmənt] *n (act)* medición. 2 *(length)* medida.

meat [miːt] *n* carne *f.* 2 *fig* esencia. ■ ~ *pie,* empanada de carne.

meatball [ˈmiːtbɔːl] *n* albóndiga.

mechanic [mɪˈkænɪk] *n* mecánico,-a.

mechanical [mɪˈkænɪkəl] *adj* mecánico,-a.

mechanics [mɪˈkænɪks] *n* mecánica. 2 *(ways)* mecanismos *mpl.*

mechanism [ˈmekənɪzəm] *n* mecanismo.

mechanize [ˈmekənaɪz] *t* mecanizar.

medal [ˈmedəl] *n* medalla.

medallion [mɪˈdælɪən] *n* medallón *m.*

meddle [ˈmedəl] *i* entrometerse *(in,* en).

meddlesome [ˈmedəlsəm] *adj* entrometido,-a.

media [ˈmiːdɪə] *npl* medios *mpl* de comunicación. ▲ → **medium.**

mediate [ˈmiːdɪeɪt] *i* mediar *(between,* entre).

mediator [ˈmiːdɪeɪtəʳ] *n* mediador,-ra.

medi(a)eval [medɪˈiːvəl] *adj* medieval.

medical [ˈmedɪkəl] *adj* médico,-a. − 2 *fam* chequeo, reconocimiento médico.

medication [medɪˈkeɪʃən] *n* medicación.

medicine [ˈmedsɪn] *n* medicina.

mediocre [miːdɪˈəʊkəʳ] *adj* mediocre.

meditate [ˈmedɪteɪt] *i* meditar, reflexionar.

meditation [medɪˈteɪʃən] *n* meditación.

medium [ˈmiːdɪəm] *n* medio. 2 *(TV, radio, etc.)* medio de comunicación. 3 *(environment)* medio ambiente. 4 *(person)*

médium *mf.* — **5** *adj* mediano,-a. ▲ *En 1 y 2 pl* **media**.

medley ['medlɪ] *n* MUS popurrí *m*. **2** *(mixture)* mezcla.

meek [miːk] *adj* manso,-a, dócil.

meet [miːt] *t (by chance)* encontrar, encontrarse con. **2** *(by arrangement)* reunirse con. **3** *(get to know)* conocer. **4** *(collect)* ir/venir a buscar: *he'll ~ me at the station,* me vendrá a buscar a la estación. **5** *(danger, death)* encontrar. **6** *(requirements)* satisfacer. **7** *(expenses)* cubrir. — **8** *i (by chance)* encontrarse. **9** *(by arrangement)* reunirse, verse. **10** *(get acquainted)* conocerse. **11** SP enfrentarse. **12** *(join)* unirse; *(rivers)* confluir; *(roads)* empalmar. — **13** *n* SP encuentro. **14** *(hunting)* partida de caza. ◆*to ~ up i fam (by arrangement)* quedar. ◆*to ~ with t (difficulty)* tropezar con; *(success)* tener. ●*pleased to ~ you!,* ¡encantado,-a (de conocerle)!; *to ~ with,* encontrarse con; *fam to make ends ~,* llegar a fin de mes. ▲ *pt & pp* **met**.

meeting ['miːtɪŋ] *n gen* reunión. **2** FIN junta. **3** POL mitin *m*. **4** *(chance encounter)* encuentro. **5** *(by arrangement)* cita. **6** SP encuentro.

megaphone ['megəfəʊn] *n* megáfono, altavoz *m*.

melancholy ['melənkəlɪ] *n* melancolía. — **2** *adj* melancólico,-a.

mellow ['meləʊ] *adj (fruit)* maduro,-a; *(wine)* añejo,-a. **2** *(colour, voice)* suave. **3** *(person)* sereno,-a. — **4** *t-i* madurar. **5** *(colour, voice)* suavizar(se). **6** *(person)* serenar(se).

melodrama ['melədrɑːmə] *n* melodrama *m*.

melody ['melədɪ] *n* melodía.

melon ['melən] *n* melón *m*.

melt [melt] *t-i (ice, snow)* derretir(se). **2** *(metal)* fundir(se). **3** *fig (anger etc.)* atenuar(se), disipar(se). ◆*to ~ away i (ice, snow)* derretirse. **2** *fig* desvanecerse. ●*to ~ into tears,* deshacerse en lágrimas.

member ['membəʳ] *n gen* miembro. **2** *(of club)* socio,-a. **3** POL afiliado,-a. **4** ANAT miembro. ■ POL *Member of Parliament,* diputado,-a; *~ of staff,* empleado,-a.

membership ['membəʃɪp] *n* calidad de miembro,-a/socio,-a. **2** *(members)* número de miembros/socios. ■ *~ (fee),* cuota de socio.

memento [mə'mentəʊ] *n* recuerdo, recordatorio. ▲ *pl* **mementos** *o* **mementoes**.

memo ['meməʊ] *n* → **memorandum**.

memoir ['memwɑːʳ] *n* memoria.

memorable ['memərəbəl] *adj* memorable.

memorandum [memə'rændəm] *n* memorándum *m*. **2** *(personal note)* nota, apunte *m*. ▲ *pl* **memorandums** *o* **memoranda** [memə'rændə].

memorial [mə'mɔːrɪəl] *adj* conmemorativo,-a. — **2** *n* monumento conmemorativo.

memorize ['meməraɪz] *t* memorizar, aprender de memoria.

memory ['memərɪ] *n (ability)* memoria. **2** *(recollection)* recuerdo. ●*from ~,* de memoria.

men [men] *npl* → **man**.

menace ['menəs] *n* amenaza. **2** *fam (person)* pesado,-a. — **3** *t* amenazar.

menacing ['menəsɪŋ] *adj* amenazador,-ra.

mend [mend] *n* remiendo. — **2** *t (repair)* reparar, arreglar. **3** *(clothes)* remendar. — **4** *i (health)* mejorar(se). ●*to ~ one's ways,* reformarse.

menopause ['menəpɔːz] *n* menopausia.

menstruation [menstrʊ'eɪʃən] *n* menstruación, regla.

mental ['mentəl] *adj* mental. **2** *fam* chalado,-a, tocado,-a. ■ *~ home/hospital,* hospital *m* psiquiátrico.

mention ['menʃən] *n* mención. — **2** *t* mencionar, hacer mención de. ●*don't ~ it!,* ¡de nada!, ¡no hay de qué!

menu ['menjuː] *n (list)* carta. **2** *(fixed meal)* menú *m*. **3** COMPUT menú.

mercenary ['mɜːsənərɪ] *adj-n* mercenario,-a.

merchandise ['mɜːtʃəndaɪz] *n* mercancías *fpl*, géneros *mpl*.

merchant ['mɜːtʃənt] *n* comerciante *mf*. ■ *~ navy,* marina mercante.

merciless ['mɜːsɪləs] *adj* despiadado,-a.

mercury ['mɜːkjʊrɪ] *n* mercurio.

mercy ['mɜːsɪ] *n* misericordia, clemencia, compasión. ●*at the ~ of,* a la merced de.

mere [mɪəʳ] *adj* mero,-a, simple. — **2** *merely adv* solamente, simplemente.

merge [mɜːdʒ] *t-i* unir(se), combinar(se); *(roads)* empalmar(se). **2** COM fusionar(se).

merger ['mɜːdʒəʳ] *n* fusión.

merit ['merɪt] *n* mérito. — **2** *t* merecer.

mermaid ['mɜːmeɪd] *n* sirena.

merry ['merɪ] *adj* alegre. ●*~ Christmas!,* ¡felices Navidades!

merry-go-round ['merɪɡəʊraʊnd] *n* tiovivo, caballitos *mpl*.

mesh [meʃ] *n* malla. **2** TECH engranaje *m*. − **3** *i* engranar.

mesmerize ['mezməraɪz] *t* hipnotizar.

mess [mes] *n (disorder)* desorden *m*. **2** *(confusion)* lío, follón *m*. **3** MIL comedor *m*. ◆*to* ∼ *about/around* *i (idle)* gandulear. **2** *(act the fool)* hacer el primo. − **3** *t* fastidiar. ◆*to* ∼ *up* *t fam (untidy)* desordenar. **2** *(spoil)* estropear. ●*fam to look a* ∼, estar horrible, tener mal aspecto; *fam to make a* ∼ *of*, estropear.

message ['mesɪdʒ] *n* mensaje *m*. ●*fam to get the* ∼, darse por enterado,-a.

messenger ['mesɪndʒəʳ] *n* mensajero,-a.

messy ['mesɪ] *adj (untidy)* desordenado,-a. **2** *(dirty)* sucio,-a.

met [met] *pt & pp* → **meet**.

metabolism [me'tæbəlɪzəm] *n* metabolismo.

metal ['metəl] *n* metal *m*. − **2** *adj* metálico,-a, de metal.

metallic [mə'tælɪk] *adj* metálico,-a.

metaphor ['metəfɔːʳ] *n* metáfora.

meteor ['miːtɪəʳ] *n* meteorito, aerolito.

meteorite ['miːtɪəraɪt] *n* bólido.

meter ['miːtəʳ] *n* contador *m*. **2** US → **metre**.

method ['meθəd] *n* método. **2** *(technique)* técnica.

methodical [mə'θɒdɪkəl] *adj* metódico,-a.

meticulous [mə'tɪkjʊləs] *adj* meticuloso,-a.

metre ['miːtəʳ] *n* metro.

metric ['metrɪk] *adj* métrico,-a.

metropolitan [metrə'pɒlɪtən] *adj* metropolitano,-a.

mew [mjuː] *i* maullar.

mezzanine ['mezəniːn] *n* entresuelo.

mice [maɪs] *npl* → **mouse**.

microbe ['maɪkrəʊb] *n* microbio.

microphone ['maɪkrəfəʊn] *n* micrófono.

microscope ['maɪkrəskəʊp] *n* microscopio.

microwave ['maɪkrəʊweɪv] *n* microonda. ■ ∼ *oven,* (horno de) microondas *m inv*.

midday [mɪd'deɪ] *n* mediodía *m*. ●*at* ∼, al mediodía.

middle ['mɪdəl] *adj (central)* de en medio, central. **2** *(medium)* mediano,-a. − **3** *n* medio, centro. **4** *(halfway point)* mitad *f*. **5** *fam* cintura. ●*in the* ∼ *of*, en medio de; *(activity)* metido,-a en. ■ ∼ *age,* mediana edad; ∼ *class,* clase media; *the Middle Ages,* la Edad Media.

middleman ['mɪdəlmæn] *n* intermediario.

middle-of-the-road [mɪdələvðə'rəʊd] *adj fig* moderado,-a.

midget ['mɪdʒɪt] *n* enano,-a. − **2** *adj* diminuto,-a. **3** *(miniature)* en miniatura.

midnight ['mɪdnaɪt] *n* medianoche *f*.

midway ['mɪdweɪ] *adv* a medio camino. − **2** *adj* intermedio,-a.

midweek ['mɪdwiːk] *adj* de entre semana.

midwife ['mɪdwaɪf] *n* comadrona.

might [maɪt] *aux* → **may**. − **2** *n* poder *m*, fuerza. ●*with all one's* ∼, con todas sus fuerzas.

mighty ['maɪtɪ] *adj* fuerte, poderoso,-a.

migraine ['maɪɡreɪn] *n* jaqueca, migraña.

migrant ['maɪɡrənt] *adj (animal)* migratorio,-a. **2** *(person)* emigrante.

migrate [maɪ'ɡreɪt] *i* emigrar.

mike [maɪk] *n fam* micro *m*.

mild [maɪld] *adj (gentle)* suave. **2** *(person)* apacible. − **3** *mildly adv (softly)* suavemente. **4** *(slightly)* ligeramente.

mildew ['mɪldjuː] *n (on leather etc.)* moho. **2** *(on plants)* añublo.

mile [maɪl] *n* milla. ●*fam it's miles away,* está lejísimos.

milestone ['maɪlstəʊn] *n* hito.

militant ['mɪlɪtənt] *adj* combativo,-a.

military ['mɪlɪtərɪ] *adj* militar. − **2** *n the* ∼, los militares, las fuerzas armadas.

milk [mɪlk] *n* leche *f*. − **2** *t* ordeñar. ●*fam to* ∼ *sb. of sth.,* quitarle algo a algn. ■ ∼ *chocolate,* chocolate *m* con leche; ∼ *products,* productos *mpl* lácteos; ∼ *shake,* batido (de leche).

milkman ['mɪlkmən] *n* lechero, repartidor *m* de la leche.

milky ['mɪlkɪ] *adj* lechoso,-a; *(coffee)* con mucha leche. **2** *(colour)* pálido,-a. ■ *Milky Way,* Vía Láctea.

mill [mɪl] *n* molino. **2** *(for coffee etc.)* molinillo. **3** *(factory)* fábrica. − **4** *t* moler. ◆*to* ∼ *about/around* *i* arremolinarse.

millimetre ['mɪlɪmiːtəʳ] *n* milímetro.

million ['mɪljən] *n* millón *m*: *one* ∼ *dollars,* un millón de dólares.

millionaire [mɪljə'neəʳ] *n* millonario,-a.

millionth ['mɪljənθ] *adj-n* millonésimo,-a.

mime [maɪm] *n (art)* mímica. **2** *(person)* mimo. − **3** *t* imitar.

mimic ['mɪmɪk] *n* mimo. − **2** *adj* mímico,-a. − **3** *t* imitar. ▲ *pt & pp* **mimicked**.

mince [mɪns] *n* GB carne picada. — **2** *t* picar. ●*not to* ~ *one's words*, no tener pelos en la lengua.

mincemeat ['mɪnsmiːt] *n* conserva de picadillo de fruta.

mind [maɪnd] *n* (*intellect*) mente *f*. **2** (*mentality*) mentalidad. — **3** *t* (*heed*) hacer caso de. **4** (*look after*) cuidar. — **5** *t-i* (*object*) importar: *do you* ~ *if I close the window?*, ¿le importa que cierre la ventana?; *I don't* ~ *staying*, no tengo inconveniente en quedarme. ●~ (*out*)!, ¡ojo!; ~ *you* ..., ten en cuenta que ...; ~ *your own business*, no te metas en lo que no te importa; *never* ~, no importa, da igual; *to bear sth. in* ~, tener algo en cuenta; *to change one's* ~, cambiar de opinión/parecer; *to have sth. in* ~, estar pensando en algo; *to lose one's* ~, perder el juicio; *to make up one's* ~, decidirse; *to speak one's* ~, hablar sin rodeos.

mindless ['maɪndləs] *adj* absurdo,-a, estúpido,-a.

mine [maɪn] *pos pron* (el) mío, (la) mía, (los) míos, (las) mías: *a friend of* ~, un/una amigo,-a mío,-a; *these keys are* ~, estas llaves son mías. — **2** *n* mina. — **3** *t* extraer. **4** (*road*) sembrar minas en; (*ship*) volar con minas.

miner ['maɪnə'] *n* minero,-a.

mineral ['mɪnərəl] *adj-n* mineral (*m*). ■ ~ *water*, agua mineral.

mingle ['mɪŋgəl] *t-i* mezclar(se).

miniature ['mɪnɪtʃə'] *n* miniatura. — **2** *adj* en miniatura. **3** (*tiny*) diminuto,-a.

minimal ['mɪnɪməl] *adj* mínimo,-a.

minimum ['mɪnɪməm] *adj-n* mínimo,-a (*m*).

mining ['maɪnɪŋ] *n* minería, explotación de minas.

minister ['mɪnɪstə'] *n* ministro,-a. **2** REL pastor,-ra.

ministry ['mɪnɪstrɪ] *n* ministerio. **2** REL sacerdocio.

mink [mɪŋk] *n* visón *m*.

minor ['maɪnə'] *adj-n* menor (*mf*).

minority [maɪ'nɒrɪtɪ] *n* minoría. — **2** *adj* minoritario,-a.

minstrel ['mɪnstrəl] *n* trovador *m*, juglar *m*.

mint [mɪnt] *n* BOT menta. **2** (*sweet*) pastilla de menta. — **3** *t* acuñar. ●*in* ~ *condition*, en perfecto estado. ■ FIN *the Mint*, la Casa de la Moneda.

minus ['maɪnəs] *prep* menos: *four* ~ *three*, cuatro menos tres; ~ *five degrees*, cinco grados bajo cero. — **2** *adj* negativo,-a. ■ ~ (*sign*), signo menos.

minute ['mɪnɪt] *n* minuto. **2** *pl* (*notes*) actas *fpl*. — **3** *adj* (*tiny*) diminuto,-a. **4** (*exact*) minucioso,-a. ●*at the last* ~, al último momento; *the* ~ (*that*), en el momento que, en seguida que. ■ ~ *hand*, minutero. ▲ *En* **3** *y* **4** (*adj*) [maɪ'njuːt].

miracle ['mɪrəkəl] *n* milagro.

miraculous [mɪ'rækjʊləs] *adj* milagroso,-a. — **2** *miraculously adv* de milagro.

mirage [mɪ'rɑːʒ] *n* espejismo.

mirror ['mɪrə'] *n* espejo. — **2** *t* reflejar.

misappropriate [mɪsə'prəʊprɪeɪt] *t* malversar.

misbehave [mɪsbɪ'heɪv] *i* (com)portarse mal.

miscalculate [mɪs'kælkjʊleɪt] *t-i* calcular mal.

miscarriage [mɪs'kærɪdʒ] *n* aborto (espontáneo).

miscellaneous [mɪsɪ'leɪnɪəs] *adj* misceláneo,-a, diverso,-a.

mischance [mɪs'tʃɑːns] *n* desgracia.

mischief ['mɪstʃɪf] *n* travesura. ●*to get into/up to* ~, hacer travesuras.

mischievous ['mɪstʃɪvəs] *adj* travieso,-a.

misconception [mɪskən'sepʃən] *n* idea equivocada.

misconduct [mɪs'kɒndʌkt] *n* mala conducta.

misdemeanour [mɪsdɪ'miːnə'] *n* fechoría. **2** JUR delito menor.

miser ['maɪzə'] *n* avaro,-a.

miserable ['mɪzərəbəl] *adj* (*unhappy*) desgraciado,-a. **2** (*bad*) desagradable. **3** (*paltry*) miserable.

misery ['mɪzərɪ] *n* (*wretchedness*) desgracia, desdicha. **2** (*suffering*) sufrimiento. **3** (*poverty*) miseria.

misfire [mɪs'faɪə'] *i* fallar.

misfortune [mɪs'fɔːtʃən] *n* infortunio, desgracia.

misgiving [mɪs'gɪvɪŋ] *n* recelo.

misguided [mɪs'gaɪdɪd] *adj* desacertado,-a, desencaminado,-a.

mishandle [mɪs'hændəl] *t* llevar mal.

mishap ['mɪshæp] *n* percance *m*, contratiempo.

misinterpret [mɪsɪn'tɜːprət] *t* interpretar mal.

misjudge [mɪs'dʒʌdʒ] *t* juzgar mal.

mislay [mɪs'leɪ] *t* extraviar, perder.

mislead [mɪs'liːd] *t* despistar, desorientar. ▲ *pt & pp misled* [mɪs'led].

mismanagement [mɪs'mænɪdʒmənt] *n* mala administración.

misplace [mɪs'pleɪs] *t (trust etc.)* encauzar mal. **2** *(lose)* perder, extraviar.

misprint ['mɪsprɪnt] *n* errata, error *m* de imprenta.

misread [mɪs'ri:d] *t* leer mal; *fig* interpretar mal. ▲ *pt & pp* **misread** [mɪs'red].

misrepresent [mɪsreprɪ'zent] *t* desvirtuar.

miss [mɪs] *n* señorita: *Miss Brown,* la señorita Brown. **2** *(wrong throw etc.)* fallo; *(shot)* tiro errado. − **3** *t-i (throw etc.)* fallar; *(shot)* errar. − **4** *t (fail to catch)* perder: *he missed the train,* perdió el tren. **5** *(fail to see, hear, etc.)* no entender. **6** *(long for) (person)* echar de menos; *(place)* añorar. **7** *(not find)* echar en falta. − **8** *i (be lacking)* faltar: *nobody is missing,* no falta nadie. ◆*to ~ out t (omit)* saltarse. − **2** *i to ~ out on,* dejar pasar, perderse. ●*to ~ class,* faltar a clase; *fig* *to ~ the boat,* perder el tren; *fam* *to give sth. a ~,* pasar de.

misshapen [mɪs'ʃeɪpən] *adj* deforme.

missile ['mɪsaɪl] *n* misil *m,* mísil *m.* ■ *~ launcher,* lanzamisiles *m inv.*

missing ['mɪsɪŋ] *adj (object)* perdido,-a, extraviado,-a; *(person)* desaparecido,-a.

mission ['mɪʃən] *n* misión.

missionary ['mɪʃənəri] *n* misionero,-a.

misspell [mɪs'spel] *t (write)* escribir mal; *(say)* deletrear mal. ▲ *pt & pp* **misspelled** o **misspelt** [mɪs'spelt].

misspend [mɪs'spend] *t* malgastar.

mist [mɪst] *n (fog)* niebla. **2** *(on window)* vaho. ◆*to ~ over/up i* empañarse.

mistake [mɪs'teɪk] *n* equivocación, error *m; (in test)* falta. − **2** *t (misunderstand)* entender mal. **3** *(confuse)* confundir *(for,* con). ●*by ~,* por error/descuido; *to make a ~,* equivocarse. ▲ *pt* **mistook**; *pp* **mistaken** [mɪs'teɪkən].

mister ['mɪstə'] *n* señor *m.*

mistook [mɪs'tʊk] *pt →* **mistake.**

mistress ['mɪstrəs] *n (of house)* ama, señora. **2** *(lover)* amante *f.*

mistrust [mɪs'trʌst] *n* desconfianza, recelo. − **2** *t* desconfiar de.

misunderstanding [mɪsʌndə'stændɪŋ] *n* malentendido.

misuse [mɪs'ju:s] *n* mal uso. **2** *(of power)* abuso. − **3** *t* emplear mal. **4** *(of power)* abusar de. ▲ *En 3 y 4 (verbo)* [mɪs'ju:z].

mitten ['mɪtən] *n* manopla.

mix [mɪks] *n* mezcla. − **2** *t-i gen* mezclar(se). − **3** *i (person)* llevarse bien *(with,* con). ◆*to ~ up t* mezclar. **2** *(confuse)* confundir. **3** *(mess up)* revolver.

mixed [mɪkst] *adj* variado,-a. **2** *(feelings)* contradictorio,-a. **3** *(sexes)* mixto,-a.

mixer ['mɪksə'] *n* batidora.

mixture ['mɪkstʃə'] *n* mezcla.

mix-up ['mɪksʌp] *n fam* lío, confusión.

moan [məun] *n* gemido, quejido. − **2** *i* gemir. **3** *pej (complain)* quejarse.

moat [məut] *n* foso.

mob [mɒb] *n* muchedumbre *f,* gentío; *pej* chusma. − **2** *t* acosar, rodear.

mobile ['məubaɪl] *adj-n* móvil *(m).* ■ *~ home,* caravana, remolque *m.*

mobilize ['məubɪlaɪz] *t* movilizar.

moccasin ['mɒkəsɪn] *n* mocasín *m.*

mock [mɒk] *adj (object)* de imitación. **2** *(event)* de prueba, simulado,-a. − **3** *t-i* burlarse (de).

mockery ['mɒkəri] *n (ridicule)* burla, mofa. **2** *(farce)* farsa.

model ['mɒdəl] *n gen* modelo. **2** *(of fashion)* modelo *mf.* − **3** *adj (plane etc.)* en miniatura. **4** *(exemplary)* ejemplar. − **5** *t* modelar. **6** *(clothes)* presentar. ■ *~ home,* casa piloto.

moderate ['mɒdərət] *adj* moderado,-a; *(price)* módico,-a. **2** *(average)* mediano,-a, regular. − **3** *adj-n* POL centrista *(mf).* − **4** *t-i* moderar(se). − **5** *moderately adv* medianamente.

moderation [mɒdə'reɪʃən] *n* moderación. ●*in ~,* con moderación.

modern ['mɒdən] *adj* moderno,-a. **2** *(literature etc.)* contemporáneo,-a.

modernism ['mɒdənɪzəm] *n* modernismo.

modernize ['mɒdənaɪz] *t* modernizar, actualizar.

modest ['mɒdɪst] *adj* modesto,-a. **2** *(rise, success)* discreto,-a.

modesty ['mɒdɪsti] *n* modestia.

modify ['mɒdɪfaɪ] *t* modificar.

modulate ['mɒdjuleɪt] *t* modular.

module ['mɒdju:l] *n* módulo.

moist [mɔɪst] *adj (damp)* húmedo,-a. **2** *(slightly wet)* ligeramente mojado,-a.

moisten ['mɔɪsən] *t* humedecer. **2** *(wet)* mojar ligeramente.

moisture ['mɔɪstʃə'] *n* humedad.

moisturizer ['mɔɪstʃəraɪzə'] *n* hidratante *m.*

molar ['məulə'] *n* muela.

mold [məuld] *n* US *→* **mould.**

moldy ['məuldi] *adj* US *→* **mouldy.**

mole [məul] *n* ZOOL topo. **2** *(spot)* lunar *m.*

molecule ['mɒləkju:l] *n* molécula.

molest [mə'lest] *t* acosar.

mollify ['mɒlɪfaɪ] *t* aplacar, apaciguar.

molt [məʊlt] *i* US → **moult**.

molten ['məʊltən] *adj* fundido,-a.

mom [mɒm] *n* US *fam* mamá *f*.

moment ['məʊmənt] *n* momento. ●*at any ~*, de un momento a otro; *at the ~*, en este momento; *at the last ~*, a última hora; *for the ~*, de momento.

momentarily [məʊmən'terɪlɪ] *adv* momentáneamente.

momentum [məʊ'mentəm] *n* PHYS momento. **2** *fig* ímpetu *m*, velocidad.

monarch ['mɒnək] *n* monarca *m*.

monarchy ['mɒnəkɪ] *n* monarquía.

monastery ['mɒnəstərɪ] *n* monasterio.

Monday ['mʌndɪ] *n* lunes *m inv*.

monetary ['mʌnɪtərɪ] *adj* monetario,-a.

money ['mʌnɪ] *n* dinero. **2** *(currency)* moneda. ●*to get one's money's worth*, sacar partido del dinero; *to make ~*, *(person)* ganar dinero; *(business)* rendir; *fam to be in the ~*, andar bien de dinero. ■ *~ order*, giro postal.

moneyed ['mʌnɪd] *adj* adinerado,-a.

mongrel ['mʌŋgrəl] *n (dog)* perro mestizo.

monitor ['mɒnɪtəʳ] *n (screen)* monitor *m*. **2** *(pupil)* responsable *mf*. − **3** *(listen to)* escuchar. **4** *(follow)* seguir de cerca.

monk [mʌŋk] *n* monje *m*.

monkey ['mʌŋkɪ] *n* mono. **2** *fam (child)* diablillo. ■ *~ wrench,* llave inglesa.

monogram ['mɒnəgræm] *n* monograma *m*.

monolith ['mɒnəlɪθ] *n* monolito.

monologue ['mɒnəlɒg] *n* monólogo.

monopolize [mə'nɒpəlaɪz] *t* monopolizar. **2** *fig* acaparar.

monopoly [mə'nɒpəlɪ] *n* monopolio.

monotonous [mə'nɒtənəs] *adj* monótono,-a.

monotony [mə'nɒtənɪ] *n* monotonía.

monster ['mɒnstəʳ] *n* monstruo. − **2** *adj* enorme.

monstrosity [mɒn'strɒsɪtɪ] *n* monstruosidad.

monstrous ['mɒnstrəs] *adj* enorme, monstruoso,-a. **2** *(shocking)* escandaloso,-a.

month [mʌnθ] *n* mes *m*.

monthly ['mʌnθlɪ] *adj* mensual. − **2** *adv* mensualmente, cada mes. ■ *~ instalment/payment,* mensualidad.

monument ['mɒnjʊmənt] *n* monumento.

monumental [mɒnjʊ'mentəl] *adj* monumental.

moo [mu:] *n* mugido. − **2** *i* mugir.

mood [mu:d] *n* humor *m*. **2** GRAM modo. ●*to be in a good/bad ~*, estar de buen/ mal humor; *to be in the ~ for*, tener ganas de.

moody ['mu:dɪ] *adj* malhumorado,-a.

moon [mu:n] *n* luna. ●*to be over the ~*, estar en el séptimo cielo. ■ *~ landing,* alunizaje *m*.

moonlight ['mu:nlaɪt] *n* claro/luz *f* de la luna. − **2** *i fam* estar pluriempleado,-a.

moor [mʊəʳ] *n* páramo, brezal *m*. − **2** *t* amarrar; *(with anchor)* anclar.

mop [mɒp] *n* fregona. **2** *fam (of hair)* mata de pelo. − **3** *t* fregar. ◆*to ~ up t* enjuagar.

mope [məʊp] *i* estar deprimido,-a/abatido,-a.

moped ['məʊped] *n* ciclomotor *m*, vespa®.

moral ['mɒrəl] *adj* moral. − **2** *n* moraleja. **3** *pl* moral *f sing*.

morale [mə'rɑ:l] *n* moral *f*.

moralize ['mɒrəlaɪz] *i* moralizar.

moratorium [mɒrə'tɔ:rɪəm] *n* moratoria. ▲ *pl moratoria* [mɒrə'tɔ:rɪə].

morbid ['mɔ:bɪd] *adj* morboso,-a.

more [mɔ:ʳ] *adj-adv-pron* más: *~ than twenty people,* más de veinte personas. ●*... any ~*, ya no ...: *I don't live here any ~*, ya no vivo aquí; *~ and ~ expensive,* cada vez más caro,-a; *~ or less,* más o menos; *once ~*, una vez más; *the ~ he has, the ~ he wants, cuanto más tiene más quiere; would you like some ~?*, ¿quieres más? ▲ → many *y* much.

moreover [mɔ:'rəʊvəʳ] *adv fml* además, por otra parte.

morgue [mɔ:g] *n* depósito de cadáveres.

morning ['mɔ:nɪŋ] *n* mañana. − **2** *adj* matutino,-a, de la mañana. ●*good ~!,* ¡buenos días!; *in the ~*, por la mañana; *tomorrow ~*, mañana por la mañana.

moron ['mɔ:rɒn] *n pej* imbécil *mf*, idiota *mf*.

morphine ['mɔ:fi:n] *n* morfina.

morsel ['mɔ:səl] *n* bocado. **2** *fig* pizca.

mortal ['mɔ:təl] *adj-n* mortal *(mf)*. − **2** *mortally adv* mortalmente, de muerte.

mortality [mɔ:'tælɪtɪ] *n* mortalidad.

mortar ['mɔ:təʳ] *n* mortero.

mortgage ['mɔ:gɪdʒ] *n* hipoteca. − **2** *t* hipotecar.

mortify ['mɔ:tɪfaɪ] *t* mortificar.

mortuary ['mɔ:tʃʊərɪ] *n* depósito de cadáveres.

mosaic [mə'zeɪɪk] *adj* mosaico.
mosque [mɒsk] *n* mezquita.
mosquito [məs'ki:təʊ] *n* mosquito. ■ ~
net, mosquitero.
moss [mɒs] *n* musgo.
most [məʊst] *adj* más: *he's got (the)* ~
points, él tiene más puntos. **2** *(majority)*
la mayoría: ~ *people live in flats,* la mayoría de la gente vive en pisos. — **3** *adv*
más: *the* ~ *difficult question,* la pregunta más difícil. — **4** *pron* la mayor parte.
5 *(people)* la mayoría. — **6** *mostly adv*
principalmente. ●*at the (very)* ~, como
máximo; *for the* ~ *part,* por lo general;
~ *likely,* muy probablemente; *to make*
the ~ *of sth.,* aprovechar algo al máximo. ▲ → **many** *y* **much.**
motel [məʊ'tel] *n* motel *m.*
moth [mɒθ] *n* mariposa nocturna. **2** *(of*
clothes) polilla.
mother ['mʌðər] *n* madre *f.* — **2** *t* cuidar
como una madre; *pej* mimar. ■ ~ *coun-*
try, (madre) patria; ~ *tongue,* lengua
materna.
motherhood ['mʌðəhʊd] *n* maternidad.
mother-in-law ['mʌðərɪnlɔ:] *n* suegra. ▲
pl **mothers-in-law.**
motherly ['mʌðəlɪ] *adj* maternal.
motif [məʊ'ti:f] *n* ART motivo. **2** *(subject)*
tema.
motion ['məʊʃən] *n* movimiento. **2** *(ges-*
ture) gesto, ademán *m.* **3** POL moción. —
4 *i-t* hacer señas. ●*in* ~, en marcha; CI-
NEM *in slow* ~, a cámara lenta. ■ ~ *pic-*
tures, el cine.
motionless ['məʊʃənləs] *adj* inmóvil.
motivation [məʊtɪ'veɪʃən] *n* motivación.
motive ['məʊtɪv] *n* motivo. **2** JUR móvil
m.
motor ['məʊtər] *n* motor *m.* **2** *fam (car)*
coche *m.* ■ ~ *racing,* carreras *fpl* de coches; ~ *show,* salón *m* del automóvil.
motorbike ['məʊtəbaɪk] *n fam* moto *f.*
motorcycle ['məʊtəsaɪkəl] *n* motocicleta, moto *f.*
motorist ['məʊtərɪst] *n* automovilista *mf.*
motorway ['məʊtəweɪ] *n* GB autopista.
motto ['mɒtəʊ] *n* lema *m.* ▲ *pl* **mottos** o
mottoes.
mould [məʊld] *n (growth)* moho. **2** *(cast)*
molde *m.* — **3** *t* moldear; *(clay)* modelar.
mouldy ['məʊldɪ] *adj* mohoso,-a, enmo-
hecido,-a.
moult [məʊlt] *i* mudar.
mound [maʊnd] *n* montón *m.*
mount [maʊnt] *n (mountain)* monte *m.* **2**
(horse) montura. **3** *(base)* montura, marco. — **4** *t (horse)* subirse a; *(bicycle)* mon-

tar en. **5** *fml* subir. **6** *(photo)* enmarcar.
7 *(jewel)* montar. ◆*to* ~ *up i* subir, aumentar.
mountain ['maʊntən] *n* montaña. — **2** *adj*
de montaña, montañés,-esa. ■ ~
range, cordillera, sierra.
mountaineer [maʊntə'nɪər] *n* montañe-
ro,-a.
mountainous ['maʊntənəs] *adj* montañoso,-a.
mourn [mɔ:n] *t-i to* ~ *(for/over) sb.,* llorar la muerte de algn.
mourning ['mɔ:nɪŋ] *n* luto, duelo. ●*to be*
in ~, estar de luto.
mouse [maʊs] *n* ratón *m.* ▲ *pl* **mice.**
mousetrap ['maʊstræp] *n* ratonera.
moustache [məs'tɑ:ʃ] *n* bigote *m.*
mouth [maʊθ] *n* boca. **2** *(of river)* desembocadura. — **3** *t (words)* articular. **4** *(in-*
sults) proferir. ●*by word of* ~, de palabra; *down in the* ~, deprimido,-a; *to*
keep one's ~ *shut,* no decir esta boca es
mía. ■ ~ *organ,* armónica. ▲ *En 3 y 4*
(verbo) [maʊð].
mouthful ['maʊθfʊl] *n (of food)* bocado;
(of drink) sorbo.
mouth-organ ['maʊθɔ:gən] *n* armónica.
mouthpiece ['maʊθpi:s] *n* MUS boquilla.
2 *(of phone)* micrófono.
movable ['mu:vəbəl] *adj* movible, móvil.
move [mu:v] *n* movimiento. **2** *(in game)*
turno, jugada. **3** *(to new home)* mudanza.
— **4** *t gen* mover. **5** *(emotionally)* conmover. **6** *(propose)* proponer. — **7** *i* moverse. **8** *(travel, go)* ir. **9** *(game)* jugar.
◆*to* ~ *along i* avanzar. ◆*to* ~ *away i*
apartarse. **2** *(change house)* mudarse (de
casa). ◆*to* ~ *forward t-i* avanzar. — **2** *t*
(clock) adelantar. ◆*to* ~ *in i* instalarse.
◆*to* ~ *on i (people, cars)* circular. ◆*to* ~
over t-i correr(se), mover(se). ●*to make*
a ~, dar un paso; *to* ~ *house,* mudarse (de casa); *fam* *to get a* ~ *on,* darse
prisa.
movement ['mu:vmənt] *n* movimiento. **2** *(of goods)* traslado; *(of troops)*
desplazamiento. **3** *(mechanism)* mecanismo.
movie ['mu:vɪ] *n* US película. ●*to go to the*
movies, ir al cine.
moving ['mu:vɪŋ] *adj (that moves)* móvil.
2 *(causing motion)* motor,-ra, motriz. **3**
(emotional) conmovedor,-ra. ■ ~ *stair-*
case, escalera mecánica.
mow [məʊ] *t* segar. ▲ *pp* **mowed** o **mown**
[məʊn].
much [mʌtʃ] *adj* mucho,-a. — **2** *adv-pron*
mucho. ●*as* ~ *... as,* tanto,-a ... como;

how ~?, ¿cuánto?; *so* ~, tanto; *very* ~, muchísimo; *to make* ~ *of sth.*, dar mucha importancia a algo. ▲ *comp more*; *superl most*.

muck [mʌk] *n (dirt)* suciedad. 2 *(manure)* estiércol *m*. ◆*to* ~ *about/around* i perder el tiempo. ◆*to* ~ *in* i fam echar una mano. ◆*to* ~ *up* t ensuciar. 2 *fig* echar a perder.

mucus ['mju:kəs] *n* mocosidad.

mud [mʌd] *n* barro, lodo.

muddle ['mʌdəl] *n (mess)* desorden *m*. 2 *(mix-up)* embrollo, lío. – 3 *t to* ~ *(up)*, confundir. ◆*to* ~ *through* i ingeniárselas. ●*to be in a* ~, *(person)* estar hecho,-a un lío.

muddy ['mʌdɪ] *adj (path etc.)* fangoso,-a, lodoso,-a. 2 *(person)* cubierto,-a/lleno,-a de barro. 3 *(water)* turbio,-a.

mudguard ['mʌdgɑ:d] *n* guardabarros *m inv*.

muffle ['mʌfəl] *t* amortiguar.

muffler ['mʌflə^r] *n (scarf)* bufanda. 2 us AUTO silenciador *m*.

mug [mʌg] *n (cup)* tazón *m*. 2 *(tankard)* jarra. 3 GB *fam* ingenuo,-a. – 4 *t* asaltar, atacar.

muggy ['mʌgɪ] *adj* bochornoso,-a.

mule [mju:l] *n* mulo,-a.

multinational [mʌltɪ'næʃənəl] *adj-n* multinacional *(f)*.

multiple ['mʌltɪpəl] *adj* múltiple. – 2 *n* múltiplo.

multiplication [mʌltɪplɪ'keɪʃən] *n* multiplicación.

multiply ['mʌltɪplaɪ] *t-i* multiplicar(se).

multitude ['mʌltɪtju:d] *n* multitud *f*, muchedumbre *f*.

mum [mʌm] *n* GB *fam* mamá *f*.

mumble ['mʌmbəl] *t-i* murmurar, musitar.

mummy ['mʌmɪ] *n* momia. 2 GB *fam* mamá *f*.

mumps [mʌmps] *n* paperas *fpl*.

munch [mʌntʃ] *t-i* mascar.

mundane [mʌn'deɪn] *adj* mundano,-a.

municipal [mju:'nɪsɪpəl] *adj* municipal.

municipality [mju:nɪsɪ'pælɪtɪ] *n* municipio.

munitions [mju:'nɪʃənz] *npl* municiones *fpl*.

murder ['mɜ:də^r] *n* asesinato, homicidio. – 2 *t* asesinar, matar.

murderer ['mɜ:dərə^r] *n* asesino,-a, homicida *mf*.

murky ['mɜ:kɪ] *adj* o(b)scuro,-a, tenebroso,-a. 2 *fig* turbio,-a.

murmur ['mɜ:mə^r] *n* murmullo; *(of traffic)* rumor *m*. – 2 *t-i* murmurar. ●*without a* ~, sin rechistar.

muscle ['mʌsəl] *n* músculo. ●*she didn't move a* ~, ni se inmutó.

muscular ['mʌskjʊlə^r] *adj* muscular. 2 *(person)* musculoso,-a.

muse [mju:z] *i* meditar, reflexionar *(on/over*, sobre). – 2 *n* musa.

museum [mju:'zɪəm] *n* museo.

mushroom ['mʌʃrʊm] *n* BOT seta, hongo. 2 CULIN champiñón *m*. – 3 *i* crecer rápidamente.

music ['mju:zɪk] *n* música. ●*to face the* ~, dar la cara. ■ ~ *hall*, teatro de variedades; ~ *score*, partitura; ~ *stand*, atril *m*.

musical ['mju:zɪkəl] *adj* musical. 2 *(person) (gifted)* dotado,-a para la música; *(fond of music)* aficionado,-a a la música. – 2 *n* comedia musical.

musician [mju:'zɪʃən] *n* músico,-a.

musk [mʌsk] *n* almizcle *m*.

musketeer [mʌskə'tɪə^r] *n* mosquetero.

Muslim ['mʌzlɪm] *adj-n* musulmán,-ana.

mussel ['mʌsəl] *n* mejillón *m*.

must [mʌst] *aux (obligation)* deber, tener que: *I* ~ *leave*, debo marcharme. 2 *(probability)* deber de: *she* ~ *be ill*, debe de estar enferma. – 3 *n (mould)* moho. – 4 *fam (need)* necesidad. ●*you mustn't do that again*, no lo vuelvas a hacer.

mustard ['mʌstəd] *n* mostaza.

musty ['mʌstɪ] *adj* que huele a cerrado/a humedad.

mute [mju:t] *adj-n* mudo,-a.

muted ['mju:tɪd] *adj* apagado,-a, sordo,-a.

mutilate ['mju:tɪleɪt] *t* mutilar.

mutineer [mju:tɪ'nɪə^r] *n* amotinado,-a.

mutiny ['mju:tɪnɪ] *n* motín *m*. – 2 *i* amotinarse.

mutter ['mʌtə^r] *n* refunfuño. – 2 *t* decir entre dientes. – 3 *i* refunfuñar.

mutton ['mʌtən] *n* (carne *f* de) cordero.

mutual ['mju:tʃʊəl] *adj* mutuo,-a, recíproco,-a. – 2 *mutually adv* mutuamente. ●*by* ~ *consent*, de común acuerdo.

muzzle ['mʌzəl] *n (snout)* hocico. 2 *(device)* bozal *m*. 3 *(of gun)* boca. – 4 *t (dog)* poner bozal a. 5 *fig* amordazar.

my [maɪ] *pos adj* mi, mis: ~ *book*, mi libro; ~ *friends*, mis amigos. – 2 *interj* ¡caramba!

myopia [maɪ'əʊpɪə] *n* miopía.

myself [maɪˈself] *pron (reflexive)* me: *I cut ~*, me corté. **2** *(after preposition)* mí: *I kept it for ~*, lo guardé para mí. ●*by ~*, yo mismo,-a: *I did it by ~*, lo hice yo mismo,-a.

mysterious [mɪˈstɪərɪəs] *adj* misterioso,-a.

mystery [ˈmɪstərɪ] *n* misterio.

mystic [ˈmɪstɪk] *adj-n* místico,-a.

mystify [ˈmɪstɪfaɪ] *t* dejar perplejo,-a, desconcertar.

mystique [mɪsˈtiːk] *n* misterio.

myth [mɪθ] *n* mito.

mythology [mɪˈθɒlədʒɪ] *n* mitología.

N

nab [næb] *t fam* pescar, pillar.

nag [næg] *t (worry)* molestar. **2** *(complain)* dar la tabarra a. **- 3** *i* quejarse.

nail [neɪl] *n* ANAT uña. **2** *(metal)* clavo. **- 3** *t* clavar. ■ ~ *file,* lima de uñas; ~ *varnish,* esmalte *m* de uñas.

naive [naɪˈiːv] *adj* ingenuo,-a.

naked [ˈneɪkɪd] *adj* desnudo,-a. ●*with the* ~ *eye,* a simple vista.

name [neɪm] *n* nombre *m.* **2** *(surname)* apellido. **3** *(fame)* fama, reputación. **- 4** *t* llamar. **5** *(appoint)* nombrar. ●*what's your* ~?, ¿cómo te llamas?

nameless [ˈneɪmləs] *adj* anónimo,-a.

namely [ˈneɪmlɪ] *adv* a saber.

namesake [ˈneɪmseɪk] *n* tocayo,-a.

nanny [ˈnænɪ] *n* niñera.

nap [næp] *n* siesta. **- 2** *i* dormir la siesta. ●*to catch napping,* coger desprevenido,-a.

nape [neɪp] *n* nuca, cogote *m.*

napkin [ˈnæpkɪn] *n* servilleta.

nappy [ˈnæpɪ] *n* pañal *m.*

narcissist [ˈnɑːsɪsɪst] *n* narcisista *mf.*

narcissus [nɑːˈsɪsəs] *n* narciso.

narcotic [nɑːˈkɒtɪk] *adj-n* narcótico,-a *(m).*

narrate [nəˈreɪt] *t* narrar.

narration [nəˈreɪʃən] *n* narración.

narrative [ˈnærətɪv] *adj* narrativo,-a. **- 2** *n* narración. **3** *(genre)* narrativa.

narrow [ˈnærəʊ] *adj* estrecho,-a. **2** *(restricted)* reducido,-a, restringido,-a. **- 3** *t-i* estrechar(se). **- 4** *narrowly adv* por poco. ◆*to* ~ *down t* reducir.

narrow-minded [nærəʊˈmaɪndɪd] *adj* de miras estrechas.

narrowness [ˈnærəʊnəs] *n* estrechez *f.*

nasal [ˈneɪzəl] *adj* nasal.

nasty [ˈnɑːstɪ] *adj* desagradable, repugnante. **2** *(dirty)* sucio,-a, asqueroso,-a, **3** *(obscene)* obsceno,-a. **4** *(unfriendly)* antipático,-a. **5** *(dangerous)* peligroso,-a. **6** *(serious)* grave.

nation [ˈneɪʃən] *n* nación.

national [ˈnæʃnəl] *adj* nacional. **- 2** *n* súbdito,-a.

nationalism [ˈnæʃnəlɪzəm] *n* nacionalismo.

nationalist [ˈnæʃnəlɪst] *adj-n* nacionalista *(mf).*

nationality [næʃəˈnælɪtɪ] *n* nacionalidad.

nationalize [ˈnæʃnəˈlaɪz] *t* nacionalizar.

native [ˈneɪtɪv] *adj* natal. **2** *(plant animal)* originario,-a. **- 3** *n* natural *mf,* nativo,-a. **4** *(original inhabitant)* indígena *mf.*

Nativity [nəˈtɪvɪtɪ] *n* Natividad.

natter [ˈnætəʳ] *i fam* charlar.

natty [ˈnætɪ] *adj (smart)* elegante.

natural [ˈnætʃərəl] *adj* natural. **2** *(born)* nato,-a. **- 3** *naturally adv* naturalmente.

naturalist [ˈnætʃərəlɪst] *n* naturalista *mf.*

nature [ˈneɪtʃəʳ] *n* naturaleza. **2** *(type)* índole *f.*

naturist [ˈneɪtʃərɪst] *n* naturista *mf.*

naught [nɔːt] *n* nada.

naughty [ˈnɔːtɪ] *adj* travieso,-a. **2** *(risqué)* atrevido,-a.

nausea [ˈnɔːzɪə] *n* náusea.

nauseating [ˈnɔːzɪeɪtɪŋ] *adj* nauseabundo,-a.

nautical [ˈnɔːtɪkəl] *adj* náutico,-a.

naval [ˈneɪvəl] *adj* naval.

nave [neɪv] *n* nave *f.*

navel [ˈneɪvəl] *n* ombligo.

navigate [ˈnævɪgeɪt] *t (river)* navegar por. **2** *(ship)* gobernar. **- 3** *i* navegar.

navigation [nævɪˈgeɪʃən] *n* navegación.

navigator [ˈnævɪgeɪtəʳ] *n* MAR navegante *mf.*

navy [ˈneɪvɪ] *n* marina de guerra, armada. ■ ~ *blue,* azul marino.

Nazi ['nɑːtsɪ] *adj-n* nazi *(mf)*.

near [nɪə'] *adj* cercano,-a. **2** *(time)* próximo,-a. − **3** *adv* cerca. − **4** *prep* cerca de. − **5** *t* acercarse a. − **6** *nearly adv* casi.

nearby ['nɪəbaɪ] *adj* cercano,-a. − **2** *adv* cerca.

neat [niːt] *adj (room)* ordenado,-a; *(garden)* bien arreglado,-a. **2** *(person)* pulcro,-a; *(in habits)* ordenado,-a. **3** *(writing)* claro,-a. **4** *(clever)* ingenioso,-a. **5** *(drinks)* solo,-a.

neatness ['niːtnəs] *n* esmero.

nebulous ['nebjʊləs] *adj* nebuloso,-a.

necessarily [nesə'serɪlɪ] *adv* necesariamente.

necessary ['nesɪsərɪ] *adj* necesario,-a.

necessitate [nɪ'sesɪteɪt] *t* necesitar.

necessity [nɪ'sesɪtɪ] *n* necesidad. **2** *(item)* requisito indispensable.

neck [nek] *n* cuello. − **2** *i fam* besuquearse.

necklace ['nekləs] *n* collar *m*.

neckline ['neklaɪn] *n* escote *m*.

nectar ['nektə'] *n* néctar *m*.

née [neɪ] *adj* de soltera.

need [niːd] *n* necesidad. − **2** *t* necesitar. − **3** *aux* tener que, deber.

needful ['niːdfʊl] *adj* necesario,-a.

needle ['niːdəl] *n* aguja. − **2** *t fam* pinchar.

needless ['niːdləs] *adj* innecesario,-a.

needy ['niːdɪ] *adj* necesitado,-a.

negation [nɪ'geɪʃən] *n* negación.

negative ['negətɪv] *adj* negativo,-a. − **2** *n* LING negación. **3** *(answer)* negativa. **4** *(photograph)* negativo.

neglect [nɪ'glekt] *n* descuido, negligencia. − **2** *t* descuidar.

neglectful [nɪ'glektfʊl] *adj* negligente.

negligée ['neglɪdʒeɪ] *n* salto de cama.

negligence ['neglɪdʒəns] *n* negligencia.

negligent ['neglɪdʒənt] *adj* negligente.

negligible ['neglɪdʒɪbəl] *adj* insignificante.

negotiate [nɪ'gəʊʃɪeɪt] *t-i* negociar. − **2** *t (obstacle)* salvar.

negotiation [nɪgəʊʃɪ'eɪʃən] *n* negociación.

negro ['niːgrəʊ] *adj-n* negro,-a.

neigh [neɪ] *n* relincho. − **2** *i* relinchar.

neighbour ['neɪbə'] *n* vecino,-a. **2** REL prójimo,-a.

neighbourhood ['neɪbəhʊd] *n* vecindad. **2** *(people)* vecindario.

neighbouring ['neɪbərɪŋ] *adj* vecino,-a.

neighbourly ['neɪbəlɪ] *adj* amable.

neither ['naɪðə', 'niːðə'] *adj-pron* ninguno,-a de los dos/las dos. − **2** *adv-conj* ni. **3** tampoco. ●~ *... nor...,* ni ... ni ... .

neolithic [niːəʊ'lɪθɪk] *adj* neolítico,-a.

neon ['niːən] *n* neón *m*.

nephew ['nevjuː] *n* sobrino.

nerve [nɜːv] *n* nervio. **2** *(daring)* valor *m*. **3** *(cheek)* descaro.

nervous ['nɜːvəs] *adj* nervioso,-a. **2** *(afraid)* miedoso,-a, tímido,-a.

nervousness ['nɜːvəsnəs] *n* nerviosismo, nerviosidad. **2** *(fear)* miedo.

nest [nest] *n* nido; *(hen's)* nidal *m*. − **2** *i* anidar.

nestle ['nesəl] *t* recostar. − **2** *i* acomodarse.

net [net] *n* red *f*. − **2** *adj* neto,-a. − **3** *t* coger con red. **4** *(earn)* ganar neto,-a.

netball ['netbɔːl] *n* baloncesto (femenino).

netting ['netɪŋ] *n* malla.

nettle ['netəl] *n* ortiga. − **2** *t* irritar.

network ['netwɜːk] *n* red *f*.

neurotic [njʊ'rɒtɪk] *adj-n* neurótico,-a.

neuter ['njuːtə'] *adj* neutro,-a. − **2** *n* LING neutro. − **3** *t* castrar.

neutral ['njuːtrəl] *adj* neutro,-a. **2** POL neutral. − **3** *n* AUTO punto muerto.

neutralize ['njuːtrəlaɪz] *t* neutralizar.

never ['nevə'] *adv* nunca, jamás.

never-ending [nevə'rendɪŋ] *adj* interminable.

nevertheless [nevəðə'les] *adv* sin embargo.

new [njuː] *adj* nuevo,-a. − **2** *newly adv* recién, recientemente.

newborn ['njuːbɔːn] *adj* recién nacido,-a.

newcomer ['njuːkʌmə'] *n* recién llegado,-a.

newlywed ['njuːlɪwed] *n* recién casado,-a.

news [njuːz] *n* noticias *fpl*. ■ *a piece of* ~, una noticia.

newsagent ['njuːzeɪdʒənt] *n* vendedor,-ra de periódicos. ■ *newsagent's (shop)*, tienda/puesto de periódicos.

newsflash ['njuːzflæʃ] *n* noticia de última hora.

newsletter ['njuːzletə'] *n* hoja informativa.

newspaper ['njuːspeɪpə'] *n* diario, periódico.

newsreader ['njuːzriːdə'] *n* TV RAD presentador,-ra del informativo.

newsworthy ['njuːzwɜːðɪ] *adj* de interés periodístico.

newt [njuːt] *n* tritón *m*.

next [nekst] *adj (following)* próximo,-a, siguiente. **2** *(time)* próximo,-a. **3** *(room, house, etc.)* de al lado. — **4** *adv* luego, después, a continuación. ●~ *to*, al lado de.

nib [nɪb] *n* plumilla.

nibble ['nɪbəl] *n* mordisco. **2** *(piece)* bocadito. — **3** *t-i* mordisquear.

nice [naɪs] *n (person)* amable, simpático,-a, majo,-a. **2** *(thing)* bueno,-a, agradable. **3** *(food)* delicioso,-a, exquisito,-a. **4** *(pretty)* bonito,-a, mono,-a, guapo,-a. **5** *(subtle)* sutil. — **6** *nicely adv* muy bien.

niche [niːʃ] *n* nicho, hornacina.

nick [nɪk] *n* mella, muesca. **2** GB *sl (gaol)* chirona. — **3** *t* mellar. **4** *fam (steal)* birlar, mangar. **5** *fam (arrest)* pillar. ●*in the ~ of time*, en el momento crítico; *sl in good ~*, en buenas condiciones.

nickel ['nɪkəl] *n* níquel *m*. **2** US moneda de cinco centavos.

nickname ['nɪkneɪm] *n* apodo. — **2** *t* apodar.

niece [niːs] *n* sobrina.

niggle ['nɪgəl] *n (doubt)* duda. **2** *(worry)* preocupación. — **3** *i (worry)* preocupar. **4** *(fuss)* reparar en nimiedades.

night [naɪt] *n* noche *f*. ●*at/by ~*, de noche; *last ~*, anoche.

nightclub ['naɪtklʌb] *n* club *m* nocturno.

nightgown ['naɪtgaʊn] *n* camisón *m*.

nightingale ['naɪtɪŋgeɪl] *n* ruiseñor *m*.

nightlife ['naɪtlaɪf] *n* ambiente nocturno.

nightly ['naɪtlɪ] *adv* cada noche.

nightmare ['naɪtmeəʳ] *n* pesadilla.

nil [nɪl] *n* nada. **2** SP cero.

nimble ['nɪmbəl] *adj* ágil.

nine [naɪn] *adj-n* nueve *(m)*.

ninepins ['naɪnpɪnz] *n* juego de bolos.

nineteen [naɪn'tiːn] *adj-n* diecinueve *m*.

nineteenth [naɪn'tiːnθ] *adj-n* decimonono,-a. — **2** *n (fraction)* decimonono, decimonona parte.

ninetieth ['naɪntɪəθ] *adj-n* nonagésimo,-a. — **2** *n (fraction)* nonagésimo, nonagésima parte.

ninety ['naɪntɪ] *adj-n* noventa *(m)*.

ninth [naɪnθ] *adj-n* nono,-a, noveno,-a. — **2** *n (fraction)* noveno, novena parte.

nip [nɪp] *n* pellizco. **2** *(bite)* mordisco. **3** *(drink)* trago. — **4** *t-i* pellizcar. **5** *(bite)* mordiscar. — **6** *i (go quickly)* ir (en un momento). ●*to ~ in the bud*, cortar de raíz.

nipper ['nɪpəʳ] *n fam* chaval,-la.

nipple ['nɪpəl] *n (female)* pezón *m*. **2** *(male)* tetilla. **3** *(teat)* boquilla.

nippy ['nɪpɪ] *adj fam (quick)* rápido,-a. **2** *(cold)* fresquito,-a.

nit [nɪt] *n* liendre *f*. **2** *fam* imbécil *mf*.

nitrogen ['naɪtrɪdʒən] *n* nitrógeno.

no [nəʊ] *adv* no. — **2** *adj* ninguno,-a; *(before masc sing)* ningún: *I have ~ time*, no tengo tiempo.

nobility [nəʊ'bɪlɪtɪ] *n* nobleza.

noble ['nəʊbəl] *adj-n* noble *(mf)*.

nobleman ['nəʊbəlmən] *n* noble *m*.

noblewoman ['nəʊbəlwʊmən] *n* noble *f*.

nobody ['nəʊbədɪ] *pron* nadie. — **2** *n* nadie *m*.

nocturnal [nɒk'tɜːnəl] *adj* nocturno,-a.

nod [nɒd] *n* saludo (con la cabeza). **2** *(in agreement)* señal *f* de asentimiento. — **3** *i* saludar (con la cabeza). **4** *(agree)* asentir (con la cabeza). ◆*to ~ off i* dormirse.

nohow ['nəʊhaʊ] *adv* de ninguna manera.

noise [nɔɪz] *n* ruido, sonido.

noiseless ['nɔɪzləs] *adj* silencioso,-a.

noisy ['nɔɪzɪ] *adj* ruidoso,-a.

nomad ['nəʊməd] *adj-n* nómada *(mf)*.

nominal ['nɒmɪnəl] *adj* nominal. **2** *(price)* simbólico,-a.

nominate ['nɒmɪneɪt] *t* nombrar. **2** *(propose)* proponer.

nomination [nɒmɪ'neɪʃən] *n* nombramiento. **2** *(proposal)* propuesta.

nonchalant ['nɒnʃələnt] *adj* impasible.

noncommittal [nɒnkə'mɪtəl] *adj* no comprometedor,-ra.

nonconformist [nɒnkən'fɔːmɪst] *adj-n* disidente *(mf)*.

nondescript ['nɒndɪskrɪpt] *adj* aburrido,-a.

none [nʌn] *pron* ninguno,-a: *~ of this is mine*, nada de esto es mío. — **2** *adv* de ningún modo.

nonentity [nɒ'nentɪtɪ] *n* nulidad.

nonetheless [nʌnðə'les] *adv* no obstante.

nonexistent [nɒnɪg'zɪstənt] *adj* inexistente.

nonplussed [nɒn'plʌst] *adj* perplejo,-a.

nonsense ['nɒnsəns] *n* tonterías *fpl*.

nonsmoker [nɒn'sməʊkəʳ] *n* no fumador,-ra.

nonstick [nɒn'stɪk] *adj* antiadherente.

nonstop [nɒn'stɒp] *adj* directo,-a. — **2** *adv* sin parar.

noodle ['nuːdəl] *n* fideo.

nook [nʊk] *n* rincón *m*.

noon [nuːn] *n* mediodía *m*.

no-one ['nəʊwʌn] *pron* nadie.

noose [nu:s] *n* lazo. 2 *(hangman's)* dogal *m*.

nor [nɔːʳ] *conj* ni: *neither you ~ I*, ni tú ni yo. 2 tampoco: *~ do I*, yo tampoco.

norm [nɔːm] *n* norma.

normal [ˈnɔːməl] *adj* normal. — 2 *normally adv* normalmente.

normality [nɔːˈmælɪtɪ] *n* normalidad.

north [nɔːθ] *n* norte *m*. — 2 *adj* del norte. — 3 *adv* al norte.

northeast [nɔːθˈiːst] *n* nor(d)este *m*.

northerly [ˈnɔːðəlɪ], **northern** [ˈnɔːðən] *adj* del norte, septentrional.

northerner [ˈnɔːðənəʳ] *n* norteño,-a.

northwest [nɔːθˈwest] *n* noroeste *m*.

nose [nəʊz] *n* nariz *f*. 2 *(sense)* olfato. 3 *(of car)* morro.

nosebleed [ˈnəʊzbliːd] *n* hemorragia nasal.

nosey [ˈnəʊzɪ] *adj fam* curioso,-a, entrometido,-a.

nosey-parker [nəʊzɪˈpɑːkəʳ] *n fam* entrometido,-a, metomentodo *mf*.

nosh [nɒʃ] *n sl* papeo.

nostalgia [nɒˈstældʒɪə] *n* nostalgia.

nostril [ˈnɒstrɪl] *n* fosa nasal.

not [nɒt] *adv* no. •*thanks, — ~ at all*, gracias, — de nada.

notable [ˈnəʊtəbəl] *adj* notable.

notation [nəʊˈteɪʃən] *n* notación.

notch [nɒtʃ] *n* muesca. — 2 *t* hacer muescas en.

note [nəʊt] *n* MUS nota; *(key)* tecla. 2 *(message)* nota. 3 *(money)* billete *m*. 4 *pl* apuntes *mpl*. — 5 *t (notice)* notar, observar. 6 *(write down)* apuntar, anotar.

notebook [ˈnəʊtbʊk] *n* libreta, cuaderno.

noted [ˈnəʊtɪd] *adj* conocido,-a, célebre.

notepaper [ˈnəʊtpeɪpəʳ] *n* papel *m* de cartas.

noteworthy [ˈnəʊtwɜːðɪ] *adj* digno,-a de mención.

nothing [ˈnʌθɪŋ] *n* nada. — 2 *adv* de ningún modo.

notice [ˈnəʊtɪs] *n (sign)* letrero. 2 *(announcement)* anuncio. 3 *(attention)* atención. 4 *(warning)* aviso. — 5 *t* notar, fijarse en, darse cuenta de. •*to take no ~ of*, no hacer caso de; *until further ~*, hasta nuevo aviso.

noticeable [ˈnəʊtɪsəbəl] *adj* que se nota, evidente.

noticeboard [ˈnəʊtɪsbɔːd] *n* tablón *m* de anuncios.

notify [ˈnəʊtɪfaɪ] *t* notificar, avisar.

notion [ˈnəʊʃən] *n* noción, idea, concepto. 2 *pl* US mercería *f sing*.

notorious [nəʊˈtɔːrɪəs] *adj pej* célebre.

notwithstanding [nɒtwɪθˈstændɪŋ] *adv* no obstante. — 2 *prep* a pesar de.

nougat [ˈnuːgɑː] *n* turrón blando.

nought [nɔːt] *n* cero: *~ point six six*, cero coma sesenta y seis.

noun [naʊn] *n* nombre *m*, sustantivo.

nourish [ˈnʌrɪʃ] *t* nutrir, alimentar.

nourishing [ˈnʌrɪʃɪŋ] *adj* nutritivo,-a.

nourishment [ˈnʌrɪʃmənt] *n* nutrición.

novel [ˈnɒvəl] *adj* original. — 2 *n* novela.

novelist [ˈnɒvəlɪst] *n* novelista *mf*.

novelty [ˈnɒvəltɪ] *n* novedad.

November [nəʊˈvembəʳ] *n* noviembre *m*.

novice [ˈnɒvɪs] *n* novato,-a. 2 REL novicio,-a.

now [naʊ] *adv* ahora. 2 *(these days)* hoy en día, actualmente. 3 *(in past)* ya. •*from ~ on*, de ahora en adelante; *~ and then*, de vez en cuando; *~ that*, ahora que, ya que.

nowadays [ˈnaʊədeɪz] *adv* hoy (en) día.

nowhere [ˈnəʊweəʳ] *adv* en ninguna parte.

noxious [ˈnɒkʃəs] *adj* nocivo,-a.

nozzle [ˈnɒzəl] *n* boca, boquilla.

nuance [njuˈɑːns] *n* matiz *m*.

nuclear [ˈnjuːklɪəʳ] *adj* nuclear.

nucleus [ˈnjuːklɪəs] *n* núcleo.

nude [njuːd] *adj-n* desnudo,-a *(m)*.

nudge [nʌdʒ] *n* codazo. — 2 *t* dar un codazo a.

nudist [ˈnjuːdɪst] *adj-n* nudista *(mf)*.

nudity [ˈnjuːdɪtɪ] *n* desnudez *f*.

nugget [ˈnʌgɪt] *n* pepita.

nuisance [ˈnjuːsəns] *n* molestia, fastidio, lata. 2 *(person)* pesado,-a.

null [nʌl] *adj* nulo,-a.

numb [nʌm] *adj* entumecido,-a. — 2 *t* entumecer.

number [ˈnʌmbəʳ] *n* número. — 2 *t* numerar. 3 *(count)* contar.

numberplate [ˈnʌmbəpleɪt] *n* GB placa de la matrícula.

numbness [ˈnʌmnəs] *n* entumecimiento.

numeral [ˈnjuːmərəl] *n* número, cifra.

numerate [ˈnjuːmərət] *adj* que tiene conocimientos de matemáticas.

numerical [njuːˈmerɪkəl] *adj* numérico,-a.

numerous [ˈnjuːmərəs] *adj* numeroso,-a.

numismatics [njuːmɪzˈmætɪks] *n* numismática.

nun [nʌn] *n* monja, religiosa.

nuncio [ˈnʌnʃɪəʊ] *n* nuncio apostólico.

nunnery [ˈnʌnərɪ] *n* convento (de monjas).

nuptial [ˈnʌpʃəl] *adj* nupcial.

nurse [nɜːs] *n* enfermero,-a. **2** *(children's)* niñera. **– 3** *t (look after)* cuidar. **4** *(suckle)* amamantar. **5** *(feeling)* guardar.

nursery [ˈnɜːsrɪ] *n (in house)* cuarto de los niños. **2** *(kindergarten)* guardería, parvulario. **3** *(for plants)* vivero.

nursing [ˈnɜːsɪŋ] *n* profesión de enfermera. ■ ~ *home,* clínica.

nurture [ˈnɜːtʃəʳ] *t* nutrir.

nut [nʌt] *n* BOT fruto seco. **2** TECH tuerca. **3** *fam (head)* coco. **4** *fam (nutcase)* chalado,-a.

nutcase [ˈnʌtkeɪs] *n fam* chalado,-a.

nutcracker [ˈnʌtkrækəʳ] *n* cascanueces *m inv.*

nutmeg [ˈnʌtmeg] *n* nuez moscada.

nutrient [ˈnjuːtrɪənt] *n* sustancia nutritiva.

nutrition [njuːˈtrɪʃən] *n* nutrición.

nutritious [njuːˈtrɪʃəs] *adj* nutritivo,-a.

nutshell [ˈnʌtʃel] *n* cáscara. ●*in a ~,* en pocas palabras.

nutter [ˈnʌtəʳ] *n fam* chalado,-a.

nutty [ˈnʌtɪ] *adj* CULIN que sabe a nuez.

nuzzle [ˈnʌzəl] *i to ~ up to,* arrimarse a.

nylon [ˈnaɪlɒn] *n* nilón *m.* **2** *pl* medias *fpl* de nilón.

nymph [nɪmf] *n* ninfa.

nymphomaniac [nɪmfəˈmeɪnɪæk] *n* ninfómana.

O [əʊ] *n (as number)* cero.

oaf [əʊf] *n* palurdo,-a, zoquete *mf*.

oak [əʊk] *n* roble *m*.

oar [ɔːʳ] *n* remo.

oarsman ['ɔːzmən] *n* remero.

oasis [əʊ'eɪsɪs] *n* oasis *m inv*.

oath [əʊθ] *n* juramento. **2** *(swearword)* palabrota.

oats [əʊt] *npl* avena *f sing*.

obdurate ['ɒbdjʊrət] *n* obstinado,-a.

obedience [ə'biːdɪəns] *n* obediencia.

obedient [ə'biːdɪənt] *adj* obediente.

obelisk ['ɒbɪlɪsk] *n* obelisco.

obese [əʊ'biːs] *adj* obeso,-a.

obesity [əʊ'biːsɪtɪ] *n* obesidad.

obey [ə'beɪ] *t* obedecer. **2** *(law)* cumplir.

obituary [ə'bɪtjʊərɪ] *n* necrología, obituario.

object ['ɒbdʒɪkt] *n* objeto. **2** *(aim)* objetivo *m*. **3** GRAM complemento. − **4** *t* objetar. − **5** *i* oponerse. ●*money is no ~*, el dinero no importa. ▲ *En 4 y 5 (verbo)* [əb'dʒekt].

objection [əb'dʒekʃən] *n* objeción, reparo.

objectionable [əb'dʒekʃənəbəl] *adj* desagradable.

objective [əb'dʒektɪv] *adj-n* objetivo,-a *(m)*.

objector [əb'dʒektəʳ] *n* objetor,-ra.

obligation [ɒblɪ'geɪʃən] *n* obligación.

obligatory [ɒ'blɪgətərɪ] *adj* obligatorio,-a.

oblige [ə'blaɪdʒ] *t (compel)* obligar. **2** *(do a favour)* hacer un favor a. ●*much obliged*, muy agradecido,-a.

obliging [ə'blaɪdʒɪŋ] *adj* complaciente.

oblique [ə'bliːk] *adj* oblicuo,-a. **2** *fig* indirecto,-a.

obliterate [ə'blɪtəreɪt] *t* borrar, destruir.

oblivion [ə'blɪvɪən] *n* olvido.

oblivious [ə'blɪvɪəs] *adj* inconsciente.

oblong ['ɒblɒŋ] *adj* oblongo,-a. − **2** *n* rectángulo.

obnoxious [əb'nɒkʃəs] *adj* repugnante.

oboe ['əʊbəʊ] *n* oboe *m*.

obscene [ɒb'siːn] *adj* obsceno,-a.

obscenity [əb'senɪtɪ] *n* obscenidad.

obscure [əbs'kjʊəʳ] *adj* o(b)scuro,-a, recóndito,-a. **2** *(unknown)* desconocido,-a. − **3** *t* obscurecer.

obscurity [əb'skjʊərɪtɪ] *n* obscuridad.

obsequious [əb'siːkwɪəs] *adj* servil.

observance [əb'zɜːvəns] *n* observancia.

observant [əb'zɜːvənt] *adj* observador,-ra.

observation [ɒbzə'veɪʃən] *n* observación.

observatory [əb'zɜːvətrɪ] *n* observatorio.

observe [əb'zɜːv] *t gen* observar. **2** *(law)* cumplir.

observer [əb'zɜːvəʳ] *n* observador,-ra.

obsess [əb'ses] *t* obsesionar.

obsession [əb'seʃən] *n* obsesión.

obsessive [əb'sesɪv] *adj* obsesivo,-a.

obsolete ['ɒbsəliːt] *adj* obsoleto,-a.

obstacle ['ɒbstəkəl] *n* obstáculo.

obstetrics [ɒb'stetrɪks] *n* obstetricia.

obstinacy ['ɒbstɪnəsɪ] *n* obstinación.

obstinate ['ɒbstɪnət] *adj* obstinado,-a.

obstruct [əb'strʌkt] *t* obstruir. **2** *(hinder)* obstaculizar.

obstruction [əb'strʌkʃən] *n* obstrucción. **2** *(hindrance)* obstáculo.

obtain [əb'teɪn] *t* obtener, conseguir.

obtrusive [əb'truːsɪv] *adj* molesto,-a.

obtuse [əb'tjuːs] *adj* obtuso,-a.

obverse ['ɒbvɜːs] *n* anverso.

obviate ['ɒbvɪeɪt] *t* obviar, evitar.

obvious ['ɒbvɪəs] *adj* obvio,-a, evidente.

occasion [ə'keɪʒən] *n* ocasión. — 2 *t* ocasionar. ●*on the ~ of*, con motivo de.

occasional [ə'keɪʒənəl] *adj* esporádico,-a. — 2 *occasionally adv* de vez en cuando, ocasionalmente.

occult ['ɒkʌlt] *adj* oculto,-a. ●*the ~*, las ciencias ocultas.

occupant ['ɒkjʊpənt] *n* ocupante *mf*. 2 *(of flat)* inquilino,-a.

occupation [ɒkjʊ'peɪʃən] *n* ocupación. 2 *(job)* profesión.

occupier ['ɒkjʊpaɪəʳ] *n* → **occupant**.

occupy ['ɒkjʊpaɪ] *t* ocupar.

occur [ə'kɜːʳ] *i* ocurrir, suceder. 2 *(come to mind)* ocurrir(se).

occurrence [ə'kʌrəns] *n* suceso: *a common ~*, un caso frecuente.

ocean ['əʊʃən] *n* océano.

oceanic [əʊʃɪ'ænɪk] *adj* oceánico,-a.

ochre ['əʊkəʳ] *adj-n* ocre *(m)*.

o'clock [ə'klɒk] *adv (it's) one ~*, (es) la una; *(it's) two ~*, (son) las dos.

octave ['ɒktɪv] *n* octava.

October [ɒk'təʊbəʳ] *n* octubre *m*.

octopus ['ɒktəpəs] *n* pulpo.

oculist ['ɒkjʊlɪst] *n* oculista *mf*.

odd [ɒd] *adj (strange)* extraño,-a, raro,-a. 2 *(number)* impar. 3 *(after numbers)* y pico: *thirty ~*, treinta y pico. 4 *(sock etc.)* suelto,-a, desparejado,-a. 5 *(occasional)* ocasional, esporádico,-a.

oddity ['ɒdɪtɪ] *n* rareza.

odds [ɒdz] *npl* probabilidades *fpl*: *the ~ are that ...*, lo más probable es que ... . ●*it makes no ~*, lo mismo da; *to be at ~*, estar reñidos,-as; *to fight against the ~*, luchar contra fuerzas superiores. ■ *~ and ends*, cositas *fpl*, cosas *fpl* sueltas.

ode [əʊd] *n* oda.

odious ['əʊdɪəs] *adj* odioso,-a.

odontology [ɒdɒn'tɒlədʒɪ] *n* odontología.

odour ['əʊdəʳ] *n* olor *m*.

odourless ['əʊdələs] *adj* inodoro,-a.

oesophagus [iː'sɒfəgəs] *n* esófago.

of [ɒv, *unstressed* əv] *prep* de.

off [ɒf] *prep (from)* de; *it fell ~ the wall*, se cayó de la pared. 2 *(not wanting)* I'm *~ coffee*, he perdido el gusto por el café. — 3 *adv (away) he ran ~*, se fue corriendo. 4 *(on holiday) two days ~*, dos días libres. 5 *(ill) ~ (sick)*, *(from school)* ausente; *(from work)* de baja (por enfermedad). 6 *(machinery)* conectado,-a. 7 *(gas, electricity)* apagado,-a. 8 *(water, tap)* cerrado,-a. 9 *(event)* suspendido,-a. 10 *(bad)* malo,-a, pasado,-a; *(milk)* agrio,-a.

offal ['ɒfəl] *n* asaduras *fpl*; *(chicken)* menudillos *mpl*.

off-colour ['ɒfkʌləʳ] *adj (ill)* indispuesto,-a.

offence [ə'fens] *n* ofensa. 2 JUR infracción, delito.

offend [ə'fend] *t* ofender.

offender [ə'fendəʳ] *n* delincuente *mf*.

offensive [ə'fensɪv] *adj-n* ofensivo,-a *(f)*.

offer ['ɒfəʳ] *n* oferta. — 2 *t* ofrecer. ●*to ~ to ...*, ofrecerse para ... .

offering ['ɒfərɪŋ] *n* ofrecimiento. 2 REL ofrenda.

offhand [ɒf'hænd] *adv* de improviso. — 2 *adj* descortés, brusco,-a.

office ['ɒfɪs] *n (room)* despacho, oficina. 2 *(post)* cargo. 3 POL ministerio. ●*in ~*, en el poder. ■ *~ hours*, horas *fpl* de oficina; *~ worker*, oficinista *mf*.

officer ['ɒfɪsəʳ] *n* oficial *m*.

official [ə'fɪʃəl] *adj* oficial. — 2 *n* funcionario,-a, oficial *mf*. — 3 *officially adv* oficialmente.

officiate [ə'fɪʃɪeɪt] *i* REL oficiar.

officious [ə'fɪʃəs] *adj* oficioso,-a, entrometido,-a.

offing ['ɒfɪŋ] *n in the ~*, en perspectiva.

off-key [ɒf'kiː] *adj* MUS desafinado,-a.

off-licence ['ɒflaɪsəns] *n* GB ≈ bodega.

off-peak ['ɒfpiːk] *adj (period)* de consumo reducido.

offset [ɒf'set] *t* compensar. ▲ *pt & pp off-set*.

offshoot ['ɒfʃuːt] *n* BOT renuevo, vástago. 2 *fig* retoño.

offside [ɒf'saɪd] *adj-adv* SP fuera de juego.

offspring ['ɒfsprɪŋ] *n inv* descendiente *mf*.

often ['ɒf(t)ən] *adv* a menudo, frecuentemente. ●*every so ~*, de vez en cuando.

ogle ['əʊgəl] *t-i* comerse con los ojos.

ogre ['əʊgəʳ] *n* ogro.

oh [əʊ] *interj* ¡oh!

ohm [əʊm] *n* ohmio, ohm *m*.

oil [ɔɪl] *n* aceite *m*. 2 *(petroleum)* petróleo. 3 *(paint)* (pintura al) óleo. — 4 *t* engrasar, lubri(fi)car. ■ *~ industry*, industria petrolera; *~ slick*, marea negra; *~ tanker*, petrolero.

oilcan ['ɔɪlkæn] *n* aceitera.

oilcloth ['ɔɪlklɒθ] *n* hule *m*.

oilfield ['ɔɪlfiːld] *n* yacimiento petrolífero.

oily ['ɔɪlɪ] *adj* aceitoso,-a, grasiento,-a. **2** *(skin)* graso,-a.

ointment ['ɔɪntmənt] *n* ungüento.

okay [əʊ'keɪ] *interj* ¡vale!, ¡de acuerdo! – **2** *adj-adv* bien. – **3** *n* visto bueno. – **4** *t* dar el visto bueno a.

old [əʊld] *adj gen* viejo,-a. **2** *(person)* mayor, viejo,-a. **3** *(wine)* añejo,-a. **4** *(clothes)* usado,-a. **5** *(former)* antiguo,-a. ●*how ~ are you?*, ¿cuántos años tienes? ■ ~ *boy/girl,* antiguo,-a alumno,-a; *Old Testament,* Antiguo Testamento.

olden ['əʊldən] *adj* antiguo,-a.

old-fashioned [əʊld'fæʃənd] *adj* anticuado,-a.

oligarchy ['ɒlɪɡɑːkɪ] *adj* oligarquía.

olive ['ɒlɪv] *n (tree)* olivo. **2** *(fruit)* aceituna, oliva. ■ ~ *oil,* aceite *m* de oliva: ~ *tree,* olivo.

Olympiad [ə'lɪmpɪæd] *n* Olimpíada, Olimpiada.

Olympic [ə'lɪmpɪk] *adj* olímpico,-a. ■ ~ *Games,* Juegos *mpl* Olímpicos.

omelet(te) ['ɒmlət] *n* tortilla.

omen ['əʊmən] *n* agüero, presagio.

ominous ['ɒmɪnəs] *adj* de mal agüero, amenazador,-ra.

omission [əʊ'mɪʃən] *n* omisión. **2** *fig* olvido.

omit [əʊ'mɪt] *t* omitir. **2** *(not do)* pasar por alto. **3** *(forget)* olvidar.

omnibus ['ɒmnɪbəs] *n (bus)* ómnibus *m.* **2** *(collection)* antología.

omnipotent [ɒm'nɪpətənt] *adj* omnipotente.

omniscient [ɒm'nɪsɪənt] *adj* omnisciente.

omnivorous [ɒm'nɪvərəs] *adj* omnívoro,-a.

on [ɒn] *prep gen* en. **2** *(on top of)* sobre, encima de, en: ~ *the floor,* en el suelo; ~ *the table,* sobre la mesa. **3** *(about)* sobre: *a talk* ~ *birds,* una charla sobre las aves. **4** *(time expressions)* ~ *my birthday,* el día de mi cumpleaños; ~ *Sunday,* el domingo; ~ *Sundays,* los domingos. – **5** *adv (machinery)* conectado,-a, puesto,-a. **6** *(gas, electricity)* encendido,-a. **7** *(water, tap)* abierto,-a. **8** *(clothes)* puesto,-a. **9** *(event) the match is* ~ *after all,* el partido se celebra según lo previsto. ●*and so* ~, y así sucesivamente.

once [wʌns] *adv* una vez: ~ *a week,* una vez por semana. **2** *(before)* antes, anteriormente. – **3** *conj* una vez que. ●*all at* ~, repentinamente; *at* ~, a la vez, de una vez; *(immediately)* en seguida; ~

and for all, de una vez para siempre; ~ *upon a time,* érase una vez.

once-over [wʌns'əʊvəʳ] *n fam* vistazo.

oncoming ['ɒnkʌmɪŋ] *adj* que viene de frente.

one [wʌn] *adj* un, una. **2** *(only)* único,-a. – **3** *pron* uno,-a: *a red* ~, uno,-a rojo,-a; ~ *has to be careful,* hay que ir con cuidado; *the* ~ *who,* el/la que; *this* ~, éste,-a. ●~ *another,* el uno al otro, mutuamente.

one-armed ['wʌnɑːmd] *adj* manco,-a. ■ ~ *bandit,* máquina tragaperras.

one-eyed ['wʌnaɪd] *adj* tuerto,-a.

one-off ['wʌnɒf] *adj fam* único,-a.

onerous ['ɒnərəs] *adj* oneroso,-a.

oneself [wʌn'self] *pron* uno,-a mismo,-a, sí mismo,-a. **2** *(alone)* uno,-a mismo,-a.

one-sided ['wʌnsaɪdɪd] *adj* desigual. **2** *(view)* parcial.

one-time ['wʌntaɪm] *adj* antiguo,-a.

one-way ['wʌnweɪ] *adj (street)* de sentido único. **2** *(ticket)* sólo de ida.

ongoing ['ɒnɡəʊɪŋ] *adj* que sigue, continuo,-a.

onion ['ʌnɪən] *n* cebolla.

onlooker ['ɒnlʊkəʳ] *n* espectador,-ra.

only ['əʊnlɪ] *adj* único,-a. – **2** *adv* sólo, solamente, únicamente. – **3** *conj* pero. ●*if* ~, ojalá.

onrush ['ɒnrʌʃ] *n* arremetida, avalancha.

onset ['ɒnset] *n* asalto. **2** *(start)* principio.

onslaught ['ɒnslɔːt] *n* ataque violento.

onto ['ɒntʊ] *prep* sobre.

onus ['əʊnəs] *n* responsabilidad.

onwards ['ɒnwədz] *adj* hacia adelante. – **2** *onward(s) adv* en adelante.

onyx ['ɒnɪks] *n* ónice *m.*

oops [uːps] *interj* ¡ay!

ooze [uːz] *n* fango, cieno. – **2** *i* rezumar. – **3** *t (charm etc.)* desprender.

opal ['əʊpəl] *n* ópalo.

opaque [əʊ'peɪk] *adj* opaco,-a.

open ['əʊpən] *adj* abierto,-a. **2** *(sincere)* sincero,-a. – **3** *t-i* abrir(se). – **4** *openly adv* abiertamente. ●*in the* ~ *air*, al aire libre.

open-air ['əʊpəneəʳ] *adj* al aire libre.

opener ['əʊpənəʳ] *n* abridor *m.*

opening ['əʊpənɪŋ] *n (act)* apertura. **2** *(hole)* abertura, brecha. **3** *(chance)* oportunidad. **4** *(vacancy)* vacante *f.* ■ ~ *night,* noche *f* de estreno.

open-minded [əʊpən'maɪndɪd] *adj* tolerante.

opera ['ɒpərə] *n* ópera. ■ ~ *house,* ópera.

operate ['ɒpəreɪt] *t* hacer funcionar. **2** *(switch)* accionar. **3** *(business)* dirigir. − **4** *i* funcionar. **5** MED operar *(on,* a).

operation [ɒpə'reɪʃən] *n* operación. **2** *(of machine)* funcionamiento; *(by person)* manejo.

operational [ɒpə'reɪʃənəl] *adj (ready for use)* operativo,-a. **2** *(in use)* en funcionamiento.

operative ['ɒpərətɪv] *adj* JUR vigente. − **2** *n* operario,-a. •*the ~ word,* la palabra clave.

operator ['ɒpəreɪtə^r] *n* operario,-a. ■ *telephone ~,* operador,-ra, telefonista *mf.*

opinion [ə'pɪnɪən] *n* opinión. •*in my ~,* a mi juicio/parecer; *to have a high/low ~ of sb.,* tener buen/mal concepto de algn.

opinionated [ə'pɪnɪəneɪtɪd] *adj* dogmático,-a.

opium ['əupɪəm] *n* opio.

opossum [ə'pɒsəm] *n* zarigüeya.

opponent [ə'pəunənt] *n* adversario,-a.

opportune ['ɒpətjuːn] *adj* oportuno,-a.

opportunity [ɒpə'tjuːnɪti] *n* oportunidad.

oppose [ə'pəuz] *t* oponerse a.

opposed [ə'pəuzd] *adj* opuesto,-a, contrario,-a.

opposing [ə'pəuzɪŋ] *adj* contrario,-a, adversario,-a.

opposite ['ɒpəzɪt] *adj (facing)* de enfrente. **2** *(contrary)* opuesto,-a, contrario,-a. − **3** *prep* enfrente de, frente a. − **4** *adv* enfrente. − **5** *n* antítesis *f inv.*

opposition [ɒpə'zɪʃən] *n* oposición.

oppress [ə'pres] *t* oprimir.

oppression [ə'preʃən] *n* opresión.

oppressor [ə'presə^r] *n* opresor,-ra.

opt [ɒpt] *i* optar.

optative ['ɒptətɪv] *adj* optativo,-a.

optic(al) ['ɒptɪk(əl)] *adj* óptico,-a.

optician [ɒp'tɪʃən] *n* óptico,-a. ■ *optician's,* óptica.

optimism ['ɒptɪmɪzəm] *n* optimismo.

optimist ['ɒptɪmɪst] *n* optimista *mf.*

optimistic [ɒptɪ'mɪstɪk] *adj* optimista.

optimize ['ɒptɪmaɪz] *t* optimizar.

optimum ['ɒptɪməm] *adj* óptimo,-a. − **2** *n* grado óptimo.

option ['ɒpʃən] *n* opción.

optional ['ɒpʃənəl] *adj* opcional, optativo,-a.

opulence ['ɒpjuləns] *n* opulencia.

opulent ['ɒpjulənt] *adj* opulento,-a.

or [ɔː^r] *conj* o. **2** *(with negative)* ni.

oracle ['ɒrəkəl] *n* oráculo.

oral ['ɔːrəl] *adj* oral. − **2** *n* examen *m* oral.

orange ['ɒrɪndʒ] *n* BOT naranja. **2** *(colour)* naranja *m.* − **3** *adj* (de color) naranja. ■ *~ blossom,* azahar *m; ~ tree,* naranjo.

orang-utan [ɔːræŋuː'tæn] *n* orangután *m.*

oration [ɔː'reɪʃən] *n* oración.

orator ['ɒrətə^r] *n* orador,-ra.

oratory ['ɒrətəri] *n* oratoria. **2** *(chapel)* oratorio, capilla.

orb [ɔːb] *n* orbe *m.*

orbit ['ɔːbɪt] *n* órbita. − **2** *t* girar alrededor de. − **3** *i* orbitar.

orchard ['ɔːtʃəd] *n* huerto.

orchestra ['ɔːkɪstrə] *n* orquesta.

orchestral [ɔː'kestrəl] *adj* orquestal.

orchid ['ɔːkɪd] *n* orquídea.

ordain [ɔː'deɪn] *t* ordenar.

ordeal [ɔː'diːl] *n fig* mala experiencia, sufrimiento.

order ['ɔːdə^r] *n (command)* orden *f.* **2** COM pedido. **3** *(series)* orden *m,* serie *f.* **4** *(condition)* condiciones *fpl.* **5** *(tidiness, peace)* orden *m.* **6** *(class, type)* orden *m.* **7** REL orden *f.* **8** *(medal)* orden *f.* − **9** *t (command)* ordenar, mandar. **10** *(organize)* ordenar. **11** *(ask for)* pedir. •*in ~,* en orden; *(acceptable)* bien; *in ~ to,* para, a fin de; *law and ~,* orden público; "*out of ~*", "no funciona". ■ *~ form,* hoja de pedido.

orderly ['ɔːdəli] *adj* ordenado,-a, metódico,-a. **2** *(not rowdy)* disciplinado,-a. − **3** *n* MIL ordenanza *m.* **4** MED auxiliar *mf,* ayudante *mf.*

ordinal ['ɔːdɪnəl] *adj-n* ordinal *(m).*

ordinance ['ɔːdɪnəns] *n fml* ordenanza.

ordinary ['ɔːdɪnəri] *adj* normal, corriente. •*out of the ~,* fuera de lo común.

ordination [ɔːdɪ'neɪʃən] *n* ordenación.

ore [ɔː^r] *n* mineral *m,* mena.

oregano [ɒrɪ'gɑːnəu] *n* orégano.

organ ['ɔːgən] *n* órgano.

organic [ɔː'gænɪk] *adj* orgánico,-a.

organism ['ɔːgənɪzəm] *n* organismo.

organist ['ɔːgənɪst] *n* organista *mf.*

organization [ɔːgənaɪ'zeɪʃən] *n* organización.

organize ['ɔːgənaɪz] *t-i* organizar(se).

orgasm ['ɔːgæzəm] *n* orgasmo.

orgy ['ɔːdʒi] *n* orgía.

Orient ['ɔːrɪənt] *n* oriente *m.*

Oriental [ɔːrɪ'entəl] *adj-n* oriental *(mf).*

orientate ['ɔːrɪənteɪt] *t* orientar.

orientation [ɔːrɪen'teɪʃən] *n* orientación.

orifice ['ɒrɪfɪs] *n* orificio.

origin ['ɒrɪdʒɪn] *n* origen *m.*

original [ə'rɪdʒɪnəl] *adj-n* original *(m)*. ●*in the* ~, en versión original.

originality [ərɪdʒɪ'nælɪtɪ] *n* originalidad.

originate [ə'rɪdʒɪneɪt] *t* originar, crear. — 2 *i* tener su origen (*in/from,* en).

ornament ['ɔːnəmənt] *n* ornamento, adorno. — 2 *t* adornar, decorar.

ornamental [ɔːnə'mentəl] *adj* ornamental, decorativo,-a.

ornate [ɔː'neɪt] *adj* recargado,-a.

ornithology [ɔːnɪ'θɒlədʒɪ] *n* ornitología.

orphan ['ɔːfən] *n* huérfano,-a. ●*to be orphaned,* quedar huérfano,-a.

orphanage ['ɔːfənɪdʒ] *n* orfanato.

orthodox ['ɔːθədɒks] *adj* ortodoxo,-a.

orthodoxy ['ɔːθədɒksɪ] *n* ortodoxia.

orthography [ɔː'θɒgrəfɪ] *n* ortografía.

orthopaedic [ɔːθəʊ'piːdɪk] *adj* ortopédico,-a.

oscillate ['ɒsɪleɪt] *i* oscilar.

ostensible [ɒ'stensɪbəl] *adj* aparente. — 2 **ostensibly** *adv* aparentemente.

ostentation [ɒsten'teɪʃən] *n* ostentación.

ostentatious [ɒsten'teɪʃəs] *adj* ostentoso,-a.

ostracize ['ɒstrəsaɪz] *t* condenar al ostracismo.

ostrich ['ɒstrɪtʃ] *n* avestruz *m*.

other ['ʌðəʳ] *adj-pron* otro,-a. ●*every* ~ *day,* días alternos; ~ *than, (except)* aparte de, salvo; *(not)* sino.

otherwise ['ʌðəwaɪz] *adv* de otra manera, de manera distinta. 2 *(apart from that)* por lo demás. — 3 *conj* si no, de lo contrario. — 4 *adj* distinto,-a.

otter ['ɒtəʳ] *n* nutria.

ought [ɔːt] *aux* ~ *to,* deber: *I* ~ *to write,* debería escribir. 2 *(expectation) you* ~ *to get the job,* seguramente conseguirás el trabajo.

ounce [aʊns] *n* onza. ▲ = 28.35 g.

our ['aʊəʳ] *adj* nuestro,-a.

ours ['aʊəz] *poss pron* (el) nuestro, (la) nuestra, (los) nuestros, (las) nuestras.

ourselves [aʊə'selvz] *pers pron* nos. 2 *(emphatic)* nosotros,-as mismos,-as.

oust [aʊst] *t* echar.

out [aʊt] *adv* fuera, afuera: *he ran* ~, salió corriendo. 2 *(absent)* fuera: *he's* ~ *at the moment,* ha salido un momento. 3 *(wrong)* equivocado,-a: *my calculation was* ~ *by £50,* mi cálculo tenía un error de 50 libras. 4 *(not fashionable) white socks are* ~, los calcetines blancos ya no se llevan. 5 *(unconscious)* inconsciente. 6 *(on strike)* en huelga. 7 *(light, fire,*

etc.) apagado,-a. 8 SP *(ball)* fuera; *(player)* eliminado,-a. 9 *(published)* publicado,-a. 10 *(completely)* totalmente. 11 *(finished)* acabado,-a. — 12 *out of prep* fuera de. 13 *(using)* de: *made* ~ *of wood,* hecho,-a de madera. 14 *(from)* de: ~ *of a tin,* de una lata. 15 *(showing motive)* por: ~ *of spite,* por despecho. 16 *(lacking)* sin: *we're* ~ *of tea,* se nos ha acabado el te. 17 *(mark)* sobre: *five* ~ *of ten in French,* (un) cinco sobre diez en francés. 18 *(proportion)* (de) entre (cada): *eight (smokers)* ~ *of ten,* ocho de cada diez (fumadores). ●~ *of favour,* en desgracia; ~ *of print,* fuera de catálogo; ~ *of sorts,* indispuesto,-a; ~ *of this world,* extraordinario,-a; ~ *of work,* parado,-a; ~ *to win,* decidido,-a a vencer.

outboard ['aʊtbɔːd] *adj* fueraborda.

outbreak ['aʊtbreɪk] *n (of violence)* estallido. 2 *(of war)* comienzo. 3 *(of disease)* brote *m*.

outbuilding ['aʊtbɪldɪŋ] *n* dependencia.

outburst ['aʊtbɜːst] *n* explosión, arranque *m*.

outcast ['aʊtkɑːst] *n* marginado,-a.

outcome ['aʊtkʌm] *n* resultado.

outcry ['aʊtkraɪ] *n* protesta.

outdated [aʊt'deɪtɪd] *adj* anticuado,-a.

outdo [aʊt'duː] *t* exceder. ●*not to be outdone,* para no ser menos. ▲ *pt* **outdid** [aʊt'dɪd]; *pp* **outdone** [aʊt'dʌn].

outdoor [aʊt'dɔːʳ] *adj* al aire libre. — 2 **outdoors** *adv* fuera, al aire libre.

outer ['aʊtəʳ] *adj* exterior, externo,-a. ■ ~ *space,* espacio exterior.

outfit ['aʊtfɪt] *n* equipo. 2 *(clothes)* conjunto. 3 *(of tools)* juego. 4 *fam* grupo.

outflow ['aʊtfləʊ] *n* efusión, flujo, salida.

outgoing [aʊt'gəʊɪŋ] *adj (departing)* saliente. 2 *(sociable)* sociable. — 3 *npl* gastos *mpl*.

outing ['aʊtɪŋ] *n* salida, excursión.

outgrow [aʊt'grəʊ] *t he's outgrown his shoes,* se le han quedado pequeños los zapatos. ▲ *pt* **outgrew** [aʊt'gruː]; *pp* **outgrown** [aʊt'grəʊn].

outlandish [aʊt'lændɪʃ] *adj* extravagante.

outlaw ['aʊtlɔː] *n* forajido,-a, proscrito,-a. — 2 *t* prohibir.

outlay ['aʊtleɪ] *n* desembolso.

outlet ['aʊtlet] *n* salida. 2 *(for water)* desagüe *m*.

outline ['aʊtlaɪn] *n* contorno, perfil *m*. 2 *(general idea)* idea general. 3 *(summary)* resumen *m*. — 4 *t* perfilar. 5 *(describe)* dar una idea general de. **6** *(summarize)* resumir.

outlive [aʊt'lɪv] *t* sobrevivir a.

outlook ['aʊtlʊk] *n (view)* vista. **2** *(point of view)* punto de vista. **3** *(prospect)* perspectiva.

outlying ['aʊtlaɪɪŋ] *adj* alejado,-a. **2** *(suburb)* periférico,-a.

outnumber [aʊt'nʌmbəʳ] *t* exceder en número, ser más que.

out-of-date [aʊtəv'deɪt] *adj* anticuado,-a.

outpatient ['aʊtpeɪʃənt] *n* paciente externo,-a.

outpost ['aʊtpəʊst] *n* MIL avanzada.

output ['aʊtpʊt] *n* producción.

outrage ['aʊtreɪdʒ] *n* atropello, ultraje *m*. − **2** *t* ultrajar.

outrageous [aʊt'reɪdʒəs] *adj* escandaloso,-a, indignante.

outright [aʊt'raɪt] *adv (openly)* directamente. **2** *(instantly)* instantáneamente. **3** *(clearly)* claramente. − **4** *adj (absolute)* absoluto,-a, total. ▲ *En 4 (adjetivo)* ['aʊtraɪt].

outset ['aʊtset] *n* principio.

outside [aʊt'saɪd] *n* exterior *m*, parte *f* exterior. − **2** *prep* fuera de. − **3** *adv* (a)fuera. − **4** *adj* exterior. ●*at the* ∼, como máximo. ▲ *En 4 (adjetivo)* ['aʊtsaɪd].

outsider [aʊt'saɪdəʳ] *n* forastero,-a.

outskirts ['aʊtskɜːts] *npl* afueras *fpl*.

outspoken [aʊt'spəʊkən] *adj* sincero,-a: *to be* ∼, no tener pelos en la lengua.

outstanding [aʊt'stændɪŋ] *adj* destacado,-a, sobresaliente. **2** *(payment, question)* pendiente.

outstretched [aʊt'stretʃt] *adj* extendido,-a.

outstrip [aʊt'strɪp] *t* dejar atrás.

outward ['aʊtwəd] *adj* exterior, externo,-a. **2** *(journey)* de ida. − **3** *outwards adv* hacia (a)fuera.

outweigh [aʊt'weɪ] *t* pesar más que.

outwit [aʊt'wɪt] *t* ser más listo,-a que.

oval ['əʊvəl] *adj* oval, ovalado,-a. − **2** *n* óvalo.

ovary ['əʊvərɪ] *n* ovario.

ovation [əʊ'veɪʃən] *n* ovación.

oven ['ʌvən] *n* horno.

over ['əʊvəʳ] *adv (down) to fall* ∼, caerse. **2** *(across)* **come** ∼ **to see me**, ven a verme. **3** *(too much)* de más. **4** *(more)* más. **5** *(left)* sin usar/gastar. **6** *(finished)* acabado,-a. − **7** *prep* (por) encima de. **8** *(covering)* cubriendo; *he put his hand* ∼ *his mouth*, se tapó la boca con la mano. **9** *(more than)* más de. **10** *(across)* al otro lado de. **11** *(during)* durante. **12** *(because of)* a causa de, por. **13** *(recovered from)* recuperado,-a de. **14** *(by means of)* por: ∼ *the phone*, por teléfono. ●*all* ∼, en todas partes, *all* ∼ *the world*, en todo el mundo; ∼ *again*, otra vez.

overall ['əʊvərɔːl] *adj* global, total. **2** *(general)* general. − **3** *adv* en total. **4** *(in general)* en conjunto. − **5** *npl* mono *m sing*. ▲ *En 3 y 4 (adverbio)* [əʊvər'ɔːl].

overbearing [əʊvə'beərɪŋ] *adj* dominante, despótico,-a.

overboard ['əʊvəbɔːd] *adv* por la borda. ●*fam to go* ∼, pasarse.

overcame [əʊvə'keɪm] *pt* → **overcome**.

overcast ['əʊvəkɑːst] *adj* cubierto,-a.

overcharge [əʊvə'tʃɑːdʒ] *t* sobrecargar. **2** *(charge too much)* cobrar demasiado.

overcoat ['əʊvəkəʊt] *n* abrigo.

overcome [əʊvə'kʌm] *t* vencer, superar. **2** *(overwhelm)* abrumar. ▲ *pt* **overcame**; *pp* **overcome**.

overcrowded [əʊvə'kraʊdɪd] *adj* atestado,-a.

overdo [əʊvə'duː] *t* exagerar. **2** CULIN cocer demasiado. ▲ *pt* **overdid** [əʊvə'dɪd]; *pp* **overdone** [əʊvə'dʌn].

overdose ['əʊvədəʊs] *n* sobredosis *f inv*.

overdraft ['əʊvədrɑːft] *n* saldo deudor.

overdue [əʊvə'djuː] *adj (train etc.)* atrasado,-a. **2** COM vencido,-a y sin pagar.

overexposed [əʊvərɪk'spəʊzd] *adj* sobreexpuesto,-a.

overflow ['əʊvəfləʊ] *n* desbordamiento. **2** *(in bath etc.)* desagüe *m*. − **3** *i* desbordarse. ▲ *En 3 (verbo)* [əʊvə'fləʊ].

overgrown [əʊvə'grəʊn] *adj* cubierto,-a de plantas/hierbas. **2** *(too big)* demasiado,-a grande.

overhaul ['əʊvəhɔːl] *n* revisión general. − **2** *t* repasar, revisar. ▲ *En 2 (verbo)* [əʊvə'hɔːl].

overheads ['əʊvəhedz] *npl* gastos *mpl* generales/fijos.

overhear [əʊvə'hɪəʳ] *t* oír por casualidad. ▲ *pt & pp* **overheard** [əʊvə'hɜːd].

overheat [əʊvə'hiːt] *i* recalentarse.

overjoyed [əʊvə'dʒɔɪd] *adj* encantadísimo,-a.

overland ['əʊvəlænd] *adj-adv* por tierra.

overlap [əʊvə'læp] *i* superponerse.

overleaf [əʊvə'liːf] *adv* al dorso.

overlook [əʊvə'lʊk] *t (not see)* pasar por alto. **2** *(ignore)* hacer la vista gorda a. **3** *(have a view)* dar a, tener vistas a.

overnight [əuvə'naɪt] *adv to stay* ~, pasar la noche.

overpower [əuvə'pauə^r] *t* dominar. **2** *fig* abrumar.

overran [əuvə'ræn] *pt* → **overrun**.

overrate [əuvə'reɪt] *t* sobrevalorar.

override [əuvə'raɪd] *t* no tener en cuenta. ▲ *pt* **overrode** [əuvə'rəud]; *pp* **overridden** [əuvə'rɪdən].

overrule [əuvə'ru:l] *t* denegar, invalidar. **2** *(person)* desautorizar.

overrun [əuvə'rʌn] *t* invadir. – **2** *i* durar más de lo previsto. ▲ *pt* **overran**; *pp* **overrun**.

overseas [əuvə'si:z] *adj* de ultramar. – **2** *adv* en ultramar.

oversee [əuvə'si:] *t* supervisar. ▲ *pt* **oversaw** [əuvə'sɔ:]; *pp* **overseen** [əuvə'si:n].

overseer ['əuvəsɪə^r] *n* supervisor,-ra.

overshadow [əuvə'ʃædəu] *t fig* eclipsar.

oversight ['əuvəsaɪt] *n* descuido.

oversleep [əuvə'sli:p] *i* dormirse. ▲ *pt & pp* **overslept** [əuvə'slept]

overstep [əuvə'step] *t to* ~ *the mark,* pasarse de la raya.

overt ['əuvɜ:t, əu'vɜ:t] *adj* público,-a.

overtake [əuvə'teɪk] *t* AUTO adelantar a. ▲ *pt* **overtook** [əuvə'tuk]; *pp* **overtaken** [əuvə'teɪkən].

overthrow [əuvə'θrəu] *t* derribar, derrocar. ▲ *pt* **overthrew** [əuvə'θru:]; *pp* **overthrown** [əuvə'θrəun].

overtime ['əuvətaɪm] *n* horas *fpl* extra(ordinaria)s.

overture ['əuvətjuə^r] *n* MUS obertura.

overturn [əuvə'tɜ:n] *t-i* volcar.

overwhelm [əuvə'welm] *t* arrollar. **2** *fig (overcome)* abrumar.

overwhelming [əuvə'welmɪŋ] *adj* aplastante, arrollador,-ra.

overwork [əuvə'wɜ:k] *t-i* (hacer) trabajar demasiado.

overwrought [əuvə'rɔ:t] *adj* muy nervioso,-a.

ovulation [ɒvju'leɪʃən] *n* ovulación.

ovum ['əuvəm] *n* óvulo. ▲ *pl* **ova** ['əuvə].

owe [əu] *t* deber.

owing to ['əuɪŋtu] *prep* debido a.

owl [aul] *n* búho, mochuelo, lechuza.

own [əun] *adj* propio,-a. – **2** *pron my/your/his* ~, lo mío/tuyo/suyo. – **3** *t* poseer, ser dueño,-a de, tener. ◆*to* ~ *up i* confesar.

owner ['əunə^r] *n* dueño,-a, propietario,-a, poseedor,-ra.

ownership ['əunəʃɪp] *n* propiedad, posesión.

ox [ɒks] *n* buey *m.* ▲ *pl* **oxen** ['ɒksən].

oxide ['ɒksaɪd] *n* óxido.

oxidize ['ɒksɪdaɪz] *t-i* oxidar(se).

oxygen ['ɒksɪdʒən] *n* oxígeno.

oyster ['ɔɪstə^r] *n* ostra.

ozone ['əuzəun] *n* ozono. ■ ~ *layer,* capa del ozono.

P

pace [peɪs] *n* paso. **2** *(rhythm)* marcha, ritmo. – **3** *t-i* ir de un lado a otro (de).
pacemaker [ˈpeɪsmeɪkəʳ] *n* SP liebre *f*. **2** MED marcapasos *m inv*.
pacific [pəˈsɪfɪk] *adj* pacífico,-a.
pacifist [ˈpæsɪfɪst] *adj-n* pacifista *(mf)*.
pacify [ˈpæsɪfaɪ] *t* pacificar, apaciguar.
pack [pæk] *n* paquete *m*. **2** *(of cards)* baraja. **3** *(of thieves)* banda. **4** *(of wolves)* manada. **5** *(of hounds)* jauría. **6** *(of lies)* sarta. – **7** *t* empaquetar. **8** *(suitcase)* hacer. **9** *(fill)* atestar, abarrotar. **10** *(compress)* apretar. – **11** *i* hacer las maletas. ◆*to ~ up i* terminar. **2** *(machine)* estropearse.
package [ˈpækɪdʒ] *n* paquete *m*. ■ ~ *tour,* viaje organizado.
packaging [ˈpækɪdʒɪŋ] *n* embalaje *m*.
packet [ˈpækɪt] *n* paquete *m*. **2** *(envelope)* sobre *m*. **3** *(of cigarettes)* cajetilla, paquete. ◆*to cost a ~,* costar un ojo de la cara.
packing [ˈpækɪŋ] *n* embalaje *m*.
pact [pækt] *n* pacto.
pad [pæd] *n* almohadilla. **2** *(of brake)* zapata. **3** *(inkpad)* tampón *m*. **4** *(of paper)* taco, bloc *m*. **5** *fam* casa, piso. – **6** *t* acolchar.
padded [ˈpædɪd] *adj* acolchado,-a.
padding [ˈpædɪŋ] *n* relleno, acolchado. **2** *(in writing etc.)* paja.
paddle [ˈpædəl] *n* pala. – **2** *t-i* remar con pala. – **3** *i* chapotear.
paddock [ˈpædək] *n* *(field)* cercado.
paddy [ˈpædɪ] *n* arrozal *m*.
padlock [ˈpædlɒk] *n* candado. – **2** *t* cerrar con candado.
pagan [ˈpeɪgən] *adj-n* pagano,-a.
page [peɪdʒ] *n* página. **2** → **pageboy.** – **3** *t* llamar por altavoz.
pageant [ˈpædʒənt] *n* espectáculo; *(with horses)* cabalgata.

pageboy [ˈpeɪdʒbɔɪ] *n* *(at wedding)* paje *m*. **2** *(in hotel)* botones *m inv*.
pagoda [pəˈgəudə] *n* pagoda.
paid [peɪd] *pt & pp* → **pay.**
pail [peɪl] *n* cubo.
pain [peɪn] *n* dolor *m*. – **2** *t* doler. ◆*on ~ of,* so pena de; *to take pains to,* esforzarse en.
painful [ˈpeɪnfʊl] *adj* doloroso,-a.
painkiller [ˈpeɪnkɪləʳ] *n* calmante *m*.
painless [ˈpeɪnləs] *adj* indoloro,-a
painstaking [ˈpeɪnzteɪkɪŋ] *adj* meticuloso,-a, minucioso,-a.
paint [peɪnt] *n* pintura. – **2** *t-i* pintar.
paintbrush [ˈpeɪntbrʌʃ] *n* brocha. **2** *(artist's)* pincel *m*.
painter [ˈpeɪntəʳ] *n* pintor,-ra.
painting [ˈpeɪntɪŋ] *n* pintura.
paint-stripper [ˈpeɪntstrɪpəʳ] *n* quitapinturas *f inv*.
pair [peəʳ] *n* *(of shoes, socks, etc.)* par *m*. **2** *(of people)* pareja. – **3** *t-i* *(people)* emparejar(se). **4** *(animals)* aparear(se). ■ *a ~ of scissors,* unas tijeras; *a ~ of trousers,* unos pantalones.
pal [pæl] *n* *fam* camarada *mf*, colega *mf*.
palace [ˈpæləs] *n* palacio.
palatable [ˈpælətəbəl] *adj* sabroso,-a. **2** *(acceptable)* aceptable.
palate [ˈpælət] *n* paladar *m*.
pale [peɪl] *adj* pálido,-a. **2** *(colour)* claro,-a. – **3** *i* palidecer.
paleness [ˈpeɪlnəs] *n* palidez *f*.
palette [ˈpælət] *n* paleta.
pall [pɔːl] *n* paño mortuorio. **2** *(of smoke)* cortina. – **3** *i* aburrir, cansar.
pallet [ˈpælət] *n* pallet *m*. **2** *(bed)* jergón de paja.
pallid [ˈpælɪd] *adj* pálido,-a.
palm [pɑːm] *n* ANAT palma. **2** *(tree)* palmera. ◆*to ~ sth. off on sb.,* endosar

algo a algn. ■ *Palm Sunday,* Domingo de Ramos.

palmist ['pɑ:mɪst] *n* quiromántico,-a.

palmistry ['pɑ:mɪstrɪ] *n* quiromancia.

palpable ['pælpəbəl] *adj* palpable.

palpitate ['pælpɪteɪt] *i* palpitar.

palpitation [pælpɪ'teɪʃən] *n* palpitación.

paltry ['pɔ:ltrɪ] *adj* insignificante.

pampas ['pæmpəs] *npl* pampa *f sing.*

pamper ['pæmpər] *t* mimar.

pamphlet ['pæmflət] *n* folleto.

pan [pæn] *n* cazo, olla. ■ *frying* ~, sartén *f.*

panacea [pænə'sɪə] *n* panacea.

panache [pə'næʃ] *n* garbo, gracia.

pancake ['pænkeɪk] *n* crepe *f.*

pancreas ['pæŋkrɪəs] *n* páncreas *m inv.*

panda ['pændə] *n* (oso) panda *m.* ■ ~ *car,* coche *m* patrulla.

pandemonium [pændə'məʊnɪəm] *n* jaleo *m.*

pander ['pændər] *t to* ~ *to,* satisfacer.

pane [peɪn] *n* cristal *m*, vidrio.

panel ['pænəl] *n gen* panel *m.* 2 *(on ceiling)* artesón *m.* 3 *(of instruments)* tablero, cuadro. 4 *(jury)* jurado.

panelling ['pænəlɪŋ] *n* paneles *mpl.* 2 *(on ceiling)* artesonado.

panellist ['pænəlɪst] *n* miembro del jurado.

pang [pæŋ] *n* punzada, dolor *m* agudo.

panic ['pænɪk] *n* pánico. – 2 *i* entrar el pánico, tener miedo.

panic-striken ['pænɪkstrɪkən] *adj* preso,-a de pánico.

pannier ['pænɪər] *n* serón *m.* 2 *(on horse)* alforja. 3 *(on cycle)* bolsa.

panorama [pænə'rɑ:mə] *n* panorama *m.*

panoramic [pænə'ræmɪk] *adj* panorámico,-a.

pansy ['pænzɪ] *n* BOT pensamiento. 2 *fam* mariquita *m.*

pant [pænt] *n* jadeo, resuello. 2 *pl (men's)* calzoncillos *mpl*; *(women's)* bragas *fpl.* 3 US pantalones *mpl.* – 4 *i* jadear, resollar.

pantechnicon [pæn'teknɪkən] *n* camión *m* de mudanzas.

panther ['pænθər] *n* pantera.

panties ['pæntɪz] *npl* bragas *fpl.*

pantomime ['pæntəmaɪm] *n* pantomima. 2 GB representación teatral navideña *basada en cuentos infantiles.*

pantry ['pæntrɪ] *n* despensa.

papa [pæ'pɑ:] *n fam* papá *m.*

papacy ['peɪpəsɪ] *n* papado, pontificado.

papal ['peɪpəl] *adj* papal, pontificio.

paper ['peɪpər] *n* papel *m.* 2 *(newspaper)* diario, periódico. 3 *(examination)* examen *m.* – 4 *t* empapelar.

paperback ['peɪpəbæk] *n* libro en rústica.

paperclip ['peɪpəklɪp] *n* clip *m.*

paperweight ['peɪpəweɪt] *n* pisapapeles *m inv.*

paperwork ['peɪpəwɜ:k] *n* papeleo.

papier-mâché [pæpɪeɪ'mæʃeɪ] *n* cartón *m* piedra.

paprika ['pæprɪkə] *n* paprika.

par [pɑ:r] *n* igualdad. 2 *(in golf)* par *m.*

parable ['pærəbəl] *n* parábola.

parabolic [pærə'bɒlɪk] *adj* parabólico,-a.

parachute ['pærəʃu:t] *n* paracaídas *m inv.* – 2 *t-i* lanzar(se) en paracaídas.

parachutist ['pærəʃu:tɪst] *n* paracaidista *mf.*

parade [pə'reɪd] *n* desfile *m.* 2 MIL revista. – 3 *i* desfilar. 4 MIL pasar revista. – 5 *t (show off)* hacer alarde de.

paradise ['pærədaɪs] *n* paraíso.

paradox ['pærədɒks] *n* paradoja.

paradoxical [pærə'dɒksɪkəl] *adj* paradójico,-a.

paraffin ['pærəfɪn] *n* parafina.

paragon ['pærəgən] *n* dechado.

paragraph ['pærəgrɑ:f] *n* párrafo.

parakeet ['pærəki:t] *n* periquito.

parallel ['pærəlel] *adj* paralelo,-a. – 2 *n* GEOG paralelo. 3 *(similarity)* paralelismo. 4 *(equal)* par, igual. – 5 *t* ser análogo,-a a.

parallelogram [pærə'leləgræm] *n* paralelogramo.

paralysis [pə'rælɪsɪs] *n* parálisis *f inv.*

paralytic [pærə'lɪtɪk] *adj-n* paralítico,-a.

paralyse ['pærəlaɪz] *t* paralizar.

parameter [pə'ræmɪtər] *n* parámetro.

paramilitary [pærə'mɪlɪtərɪ] *adj* paramilitar.

paramount ['pærəmaʊnt] *adj* supremo,-a.

paranoia [pærə'nɔɪə] *n* paranoia.

paranoic [pærə'nɔɪk], **paranoid** ['pærənɔɪd] *adj-n* paranoico,-a.

parapet ['pærəpɪt] *n* parapeto.

paraphrase ['pærəfreɪz] *n* paráfrasis *f inv.* – 2 *t* parafrasear.

parasite ['pærəsaɪt] *n* parásito,-a.

parasitic [pærə'sɪtɪk] *adj* parasitario,-a.

parasol [pærə'sɒl] *n* sombrilla.

paratrooper ['pærətru:pər] *n* paracaidista *mf.*

parcel ['pɑ:səl] *n* paquete *m.* ◆*to* ~ *out t* repartir. ◆*to* ~ *up t* empaquetar.

parched [pɑːtʃt] *adj* abrasado,-a, reseco,-a. **2** *(thirsty)* muerto,-a de sed.

parchment [ˈpɑːtʃmənt] *n* pergamino.

pardon [ˈpɑːdən] *n* perdón *m*. **2** JUR indulto, amnistía. − **3** *t* perdonar. **4** JUR indultar. ●~ *me!,* ¡perdone!

pare [peəʳ] *t (fruit)* pelar. **2** *(nails)* cortar.

parent [ˈpeərənt] *n (father)* padre *m*; *(mother)* madre *f*. **2** *pl* padres *mpl*.

parentage [ˈpeərəntɪdʒ] *n* origen *m*, linaje *m*.

parenthesis [pəˈrenθəsɪs] *n* paréntesis *m inv*.

pariah [pəˈraɪə] *n* paria *m*.

parish [ˈpærɪʃ] *n* parroquia.

parishioner [pəˈrɪʃənəʳ] *n* feligrés,-esa.

parity [ˈpærɪtɪ] *n* igualdad.

park [pɑːk] *n* parque *m*. − **2** *t-i* aparcar. ■ *car* ~, aparcamiento.

parking [ˈpɑːkɪŋ] *n* aparcamiento. ■ ~ *meter,* parquímetro; ~ *place,* sitio para aparcar.

parlance [ˈpɑːləns] *n* lenguaje *m*.

parliament [ˈpɑːləmənt] *n* parlamento.

parliamentary [pɑːləˈmentərɪ] *adj* parlamentario,-a.

parlour [ˈpɑːləʳ] *n* salón *m*. ■ *beauty* ~, salón de belleza.

parochial [pəˈrəukɪəl] *adj* parroquial. **2** *fig* pueblerino,-a.

parody [ˈpærədɪ] *n* parodia. − **2** *t* parodiar.

parole [pəˈrəul] *n* libertad condicional.

paroxysm [ˈpærəksɪzəm] *n* paroxismo.

parquet [ˈpɑːkeɪ] *n* parqué *m*.

parrot [ˈpærət] *n* loro.

parry [ˈpærɪ] *t* parar, desviar. **2** *(question)* evitar, esquivar.

parsimonious [pɑːsɪˈməuɪəs] *adj* tacaño,-a.

parsley [ˈpɑːslɪ] *n* perejil *m*.

parsnip [ˈpɑːsnɪp] *n* chirivía.

parson [ˈpɑːsən] *n* párroco, cura *m*.

parsonage [ˈpɑːsənɪdʒ] *n* casa del párroco.

part [pɑːt] *n gen* parte *f*. **2** TECH pieza. **3** THEAT papel *m*. − **4** *t-i* separar(se). − **5** *partly adv* parcialmente. ◆*to* ~ *with t* separarse de. ●*for my* ~, por mi parte; *to take* ~ *in,* participar en.

partial [ˈpɑːʃəl] *adj* parcial. − **2** *partially adv* parcialmente. ●*to be* ~ *to,* ser aficionado,-a a.

partiality [pɑːʃɪˈælɪtɪ] *n* parcialidad. **2** *(liking)* afición.

participate [pɑːˈtɪsɪpeɪt] *i* participar.

participation [pɑːtɪsɪˈpeɪʃən] *n* participación.

participle [ˈpɑːtɪsɪpəl] *n* participio.

particle [ˈpɑːtɪkəl] *n* partícula.

particular [pəˈtɪkjuləʳ] *adj* particular. **2** *(fussy)* exigente. − **3** *npl* detalles *mpl*. − **4** *particularly adv* especialmente. ●*in* ~, en particular.

parting [ˈpɑːtɪŋ] *n (in hair)* raya. **2** *(separation)* separación, división. **3** *(goodbye)* despedida.

partisan [pɑːtɪˈzæn] *n* partidiario,-a. **2** MIL partidista *mf*.

partition [pɑːˈtɪʃən] *n* partición. **2** *(wall)* tabique *m*. − **3** *t* partir, dividir.

partner [ˈpɑːtnəʳ] *n* compañero,-a. **2** COM socio,-a. **3** SP pareja *f*. **4** *(spouse)* cónyuge *mf*.

partridge [ˈpɑːtrɪdʒ] *n* perdiz *f* (pardilla).

part-time [pɑːtˈtaɪm] *adj* de media jornada. − **2** *adv* a tiempo parcial.

party [ˈpɑːtɪ] *n* fiesta. **2** POL partido. **3** *(group)* grupo. **4** *(in contract)* parte *f*.

pass [pɑːs] *n* GEOG puerto. **2** *(document)* pase *m*. **3** *(in exam)* aprobado. **4** SP pase *m*. − **5** *t-i gen* pasar. **6** *(overtake)* adelantar. **7** *(exam)* aprobar. **8** *(approve)* aprobar. ◆*to* ~ *away i* pasar a mejor vida. ◆*to* ~ *by i* pasar (cerca). − **2** *t* hacer caso omiso de. ◆*to* ~ *off i* transcurrir. **2** *(stop)* parar. − **3** *t* hacer pasar por. ◆*to* ~ *on t* pasar. − **2** *i* pasar a mejor vida. ◆*to* ~ *out i* desmayarse. ◆*to* ~ *over t* hacer caso omiso de. ◆*to* ~ *through i* estar de paso. ◆*to* ~ *up t* dejar pasar. ●*to* ~ *judgment on,* juzgar; *to* ~ *water,* orinar.

passable [ˈpɑːsəbəl] *adj* pasable. **2** *(road)* transitable.

passage [ˈpæsɪdʒ] *n (street)* pasaje *m*. **2** *(in building)* pasillo. **3** *(of traffic)* tránsito, paso. **4** MAR pasaje. **5** *(extract)* pasaje.

passageway [ˈpæsɪdʒweɪ] *n* pasillo.

passé [pæˈseɪ] *adj* pasado,-a de moda.

passenger [ˈpæsɪndʒəʳ] *n* viajero,-a, pasajero,-a.

passer-by [pɑːsəˈbaɪ] *n* transeúnte *mf*.

passing [ˈpɑːsɪŋ] *adj* pasajero,-a. ●*to say sth. in* ~, decir algo de pasada.

passion [ˈpæʃən] *n* pasión.

passionate [ˈpæʃənət] *adj* apasionado,-a.

passive [ˈpæsɪv] *adj* pasivo,-a. − **2** *n* GRAM voz pasiva.

passover [ˈpɑːsəuvəʳ] *n* Pascua judía.

passport [ˈpɑːspɔːt] *n* pasaporte *m*.

password [ˈpɑːswɜːd] *n* contraseña.

past [pɑ:st] *adj* pasado,-a. **2** *(last)* últi-mo,-a: *the ~ few days,* los últimos días. **3** *(over)* acabado,-a, terminado,-a. **4** *(former)* antiguo,-a. **– 5** *n* pasado. **– 6** *prep* más allá de: *it's just ~ the cinema,* es un poco más allá del cine; *she ran ~ me,* pasó cerca de mí/cerca de mí/por mi lado corriendo. **7** *(time)* y: *five ~ six,* las seis y cinco. ●*I'm/he's ~ caring,* me/le trae sin cuidado.

pasta ['pæstə] *n* pasta.

paste [peist] *n gen* pasta. **2** *(glue)* engru-do. **– 3** *t* pegar (con engrudo).

pasteboard ['peistbɔ:d] *n* cartón *m*.

pastel ['pæstəl] *n* pastel *m*.

pasteurized ['pɑ:stʃəraizd] *adj* pasteu-rizado,-a.

pastille ['pæstil] *n* pastilla.

pastime ['pɑ:staim] *n* pasatiempo.

pastor ['pɑ:stə'] *n* pastor *m*.

pastoral ['pɑ:stərəl] *adj (rustic)* pastoril. **2** REL pastoral.

pastry ['peistri] *n* pasta. **2** *(cake)* pastel *m*.

pasture ['pɑ:stʃə'] *n* pasto.

pasty ['pæsti] *n* CULIN empanada. **– 2** *adj (pale)* pálido,-a.

pat [pæt] *n* golpecito, palmadita. **2** *(of butter)* porción. **– 3** *t* dar golpecitos/pal-maditas a. ●*to know sth. off ~,* saberse algo al dedillo.

patch [pætʃ] *n (mend)* remiendo. **2** *(over eye)* parche *m*. **3** *(of ground)* trozo. **4** *(of colour, damp, etc.)* mancha. **– 5** *t* remen-dar. ●*not to be a ~ on,* no tener ni pun-to de comparación con. ■ *a bad ~,* una mala racha.

pâté ['pætei] *n* paté *m*.

patent ['peitənt] *adj (obvious)* patente, evidente. **2** COM patentado. **– 3** *n* pa-tente *f*. **– 4** *t* patentar.

paternal [pə'tɜ:nəl] *adj (fatherly)* pater-nal. **2** *(side of family)* paterno,-a.

paternalistic [pətɜ:nə'listik] *adj* pater-nalista.

paternity [pə'tɜ:niti] *n* paternidad.

path [pɑ:θ] *n* camino, sendero. **2** *(of bul-let)* trayectoria. ●*on the right ~,* bien encaminado,-a.

pathetic [pə'θetik] *adj* patético,-a. **2** *(aw-ful)* malísimo,-a.

pathologist [pə'θɒlədʒist] *n* patólogo,-a.

pathology [pə'θɒlədʒi] *n* patología.

pathos ['peiθɒs] *n* patetismo.

pathway ['pɑ:θwei] *n* camino, sendero.

patience ['peiʃəns] *n* paciencia. **2** *(card game)* solitario.

patient ['peiʃənt] *adj* paciente. **– 2** *n* pa-ciente *mf*, enfermo,-a.

patio ['pætiəu] *n* patio.

patriarch ['peitriɑ:k] *n* patriarca *m*.

patrimony ['pætriməni] *n* patrimonio.

patriot ['peitriət] *n* patriota *mf*.

patriotic [pætri'ɒtik] *adj* patriótico,-a.

patriotism ['pætriətizəm] *n* patriotismo.

patrol [pə'trəul] *n* patrulla. **– 2** *i-t* patru-llar (por).

patron ['peitrən] *adj (customer)* cliente,-a habitual. **2** *(sponsor)* patrocinador,-ra. **3** *(of arts)* mecenas *m inv*. ■ *~ saint,* (san-to,-a) patrón,-ona.

patronage ['pætrənidʒ] *n* patrocinio. **2** *(protection)* protección.

patronize ['pætrənaiz] *t (shop etc.)* ser cliente,-a habitual de. **2** *(sponsor)* patro-cinar. **3** *(arts)* proteger. **4** *pej* tratar con condescendencia.

patter ['pætə'] *n (of rain)* tamborileo. **2** *(of feet)* ruido. **3** *fam (talk)* labia. **– 4** *t (rain)* golpear. **5** *(feet)* corretear.

pattern ['pætən] *n* modelo. **2** *(for clothes)* patrón *m*. **3** *(design)* dibujo, diseño. **4** *fig* pauta.

paunch [pɔ:ntʃ] *n* panza, barriga.

pauper ['pɔ:pə'] *n* pobre *mf*.

pause [pɔ:z] *n* pausa. **– 2** *i* hacer una pausa. **3** *(speaker)* detenerse.

pave [peiv] *t* pavimentar, adoquinar. ●*fig to ~ the way,* preparar el terreno.

pavement ['peivmənt] *n* acera.

pavillion [pə'viliən] *n* pabellón *m*.

paw [pɔ:] *n* pata. **– 2** *t* manosear, sobar.

pawn [pɔ:n] *n (in chess)* peón *m*. **– 2** *t* em-peñar.

pawnbroker ['pɔ:nbrəukə'] *n* prestamis-ta *mf*.

pawnshop ['pɔ:nʃɒp] *n* casa de empe-ños.

pay [pei] *n* paga, sueldo. **– 2** *t-i* pagar. **3** *i (be profitable)* ser rentable. ◆*to ~ back t* devolver. ◆*to ~ in t* ingresar. ◆*to ~ off t (debt)* saldar. **2** *(mortgage)* acabar de pagar. **3** *(worker)* dar el fini-quito a. **– 4** *i (be successful)* dar resulta-do. ●*to ~ attention,* prestar atención; *to ~ a visit,* hacer una visita. ■ *~ packet,* sobre *m* del sueldo. ▲ *pt & pp* **paid**.

payable ['peiəbəl] *adj* pagadero,-a.

payday ['peidei] *n* día *m* de pago.

payee [pei'i:] *n* beneficiario,-a.

payment ['peimənt] *n* pago.

payroll ['peirəul] *n* nómina.

payslip ['peislip] *n* hoja de nómina.

pea [pi:] *n* guisante *m*.

peace [pi:s] *n* paz *f*. **2** *(calm)* tranquilidad. •*at/in* ~, en paz.

peaceable ['pi:səbəl] *adj* pacífico,-a.

peaceful ['pi:sfʊl] *adj* pacífico,-a. **2** *(calm)* tranquilo,-a.

peace-keeping ['pi:ski:pɪŋ] *adj* de pacificación.

peach [pi:tʃ] *n* melocotón *m*. ■ ~ *tree,* melocotonero.

peacock ['pi:kɒk] *n* pavo real.

peahen ['pi:hen] *n* pava real.

peak [pi:k] *n (mountain)* pico. **2** *fig* cumbre *f*. **3** *(of cap)* visera. – **4** *i* culminar.

peal [pi:l] *n* repique *m*. **2** *(of thunder)* estrépito, estruendo. – **3** *t-i (bells)* repicar.

peanut ['pi:nʌt] *n* cacahuete *m*.

pear [peəʳ] *n* pera. ■ ~ *tree,* peral *m*.

pearl [pɜ:l] *n* perla.

pearly ['pɜ:lɪ] *adj* perlino,-a, nacarado,-a.

peasant ['pezənt] *n* campesino,-a. **2** *pej* inculto,-a.

peat [pi:t] *n* turba.

pebble ['pebəl] *n* guija, guijarro, china.

pebbly ['peblɪ] *adj* guijarroso,-a.

peck [pek] *n* picotazo. – **2** *t* picotear.

peckish ['pekɪʃ] *adj* algo hambriento,-a.

pectoral ['pektərəl] *adj-n* pectoral *(m)*.

peculiar [pɪ'kju:lɪəʳ] *adj (strange)* extraño,-a, raro,-a. **2** *(particular)* peculiar, propio,-a.

peculiarity [pɪkju:lɪ'ærɪtɪ] *n* cosa rara. **2** *(feature)* característica, peculiaridad.

pecuniary [pɪ'kju:nɪərɪ] *adj* pecuniario,-a.

pedagogical [pedə'gɒdzɪkəl] *adj* pedagógico,-a.

pedagogy ['pedəgɒdzɪ] *n* pedagogía.

pedal ['pedəl] *n* pedal *m*. – **2** *i* pedalear.

pedant ['pedənt] *n* pedante *mf*.

pedantic [pe'dæntɪk] *adj* pedante.

peddle ['pedəl] *t-i* vender (de puerta en puerta). **2** *(drugs)* traficar con.

peddler ['pedləʳ] *n* traficante *mf* de drogas.

pederast ['pedəræst] *n* pederasta *m*.

pedestal ['pedɪstəl] *n* pedestal *m*.

pedestrian [pɪ'destrɪən] *n* peatón *m*. – **2** *adj* pedestre. ■ ~ *crossing,* paso de peatones; ~ *precinct,* zona peatonal.

pediatrician [pi:dɪə'trɪʃən] *n* pediatra *mf*.

pediatrics [pi:dɪ'ætrɪks] *n* pediatría.

pedigree ['pedɪgri:] *n (of animals)* pedigrí *m*. – **2** *adj* de raza.

pedlar ['pedləʳ] *n* buhonero,-a.

pee [pi:] *fam n* pis *m*. – **2** *i* hacer pis.

peek [pi:k] *n* ojeada. – **2** *i* mirar, espiar. •*to (have a)* ~ *at,* echar una ojeada a.

peel [pi:l] *n* piel *f*. **2** *(of orange etc.)* corteza. – **3** *t-i* pelar(se).

peep [pi:p] *n* ojeada. **2** *(noise)* pío. •*to (have a)* ~ *at,* echar una ojeada a.

peep-hole ['pi:phəʊl] *n* mirilla.

peeping Tom [pi:pɪŋ'tɒm] *n* mirón *m*.

peer [pɪəʳ] *n* par *m*. **2** *(noble)* par *m*. – **3** *i* mirar (atentamente).

peerage ['pɪərɪdʒ] *n* título de par.

peerless ['pɪələs] *adj* sin par.

peeved ['pi:vd] *adj fam* fastidiado,-a.

peevish ['pi:vɪʃ] *adj* malhumorado,-a.

peg [peg] *n* clavija. **2** *(for clothes)* percha, colgador *m*. – **3** *t (prices)* fijar. ■ *clothes* ~, pinza.

pejorative [pə'dʒɒrətɪv] *adj* peyorativo,-a, despectivo,-a.

pelican ['pelɪkən] *n* pelícano.

pellet ['pelɪt] *n* pelotilla, bolita. **2** *(shot)* perdigón *m*.

pelt [pelt] *n* pellejo. – **2** *t* atacar: *they pelted him with eggs,* le tiraron huevos. – **3** *i (rain)* llover a cántaros. **4** *(run)* correr.

pelvis ['pelvɪs] *n* pelvis *f inv*.

pen [pen] *n* pluma. **2** *(ballpoint)* bolígrafo. **3** *(for animals)* corral *m*; *(for sheep)* aprisco. – **4** *t (write)* escribir. **5** *(shut up)* acorralar.

penal ['pi:nəl] *adj* penal.

penalize ['pi:nəlaɪz] *t* castigar. **2** SP penalizar.

penalty ['penəltɪ] *n* pena, castigo. **2** SP castigo; *(football)* penalti *m*.

penance ['penəns] *n* penitencia.

pence [pens] *npl* → **penny**.

penchant ['pɒnʃɒn] *n* predilección.

pencil ['pensəl] *n* lápiz *m*. ■ ~ *case,* plumier *m*; ~ *sharpener,* sacapuntas *m inv*.

pendant ['pendənt] colgante *m*.

pending ['pendɪŋ] *adj* pendiente. – **2** *prep* hasta.

pendulum ['pendjʊləm] *n* péndulo.

penetrate ['penɪtreɪt] *t* penetrar (por).

penetrating ['penɪtreɪtɪŋ] *adj* penetrante. **2** *(mind)* perspicaz.

penetration [penɪ'treɪʃən] *n* penetración.

penfriend ['penfrend] *n* amigo,-a por correspondencia.

penguin ['peŋgwɪn] *n* pingüino.

penicillin [penɪ'sɪlɪn] *n* penicilina.

peninsula [pə'nɪnsjʊlə] *n* península.

peninsular [pə'nɪnsjʊləʳ] *adj* peninsular.

penis ['pi:nɪs] *n* pene *m*.

penitence ['penɪtəns] *n* REL penitencia. **2** *(sorrow)* arrepentimiento.

penitent ['penɪtent] *adj-n* REL penitente *(mf)*. — **2** *adj (sorry)* arrepentido,-a.

penitentiary [penɪ'tenʃərɪ] *n* US penitenciaría.

penknife ['pennaɪf] *n* cortaplumas *m inv*.

pennant ['penənt] *n* flámula, gallardete *m*. **2** MAR insignia.

penniless ['penɪləs] *adj* sin dinero.

penny ['penɪ] *n* penique *m*. ●*fam to spend a ~*, ir al servicio. ▲ *pl pence*.

pension ['penʃən] *n* pensión. ●*to ~ sb. off*, jubilar a algn.

pensioner ['penʃənəʳ] *n* jubilado,-a, pensionista *mf*.

pensive ['pensɪv] *adj* pensativo,-a.

pentagon ['pentəgən] *n* pentágono.

pentathlon [pen'tæθlən] *n* pentatlón *m*.

Pentecost ['pentɪkɒst] *n* Pentecostés *m*.

penthouse ['penthaʊs] *n* (sobre)ático.

penultimate [pɪ'nʌltɪmət] *adj* penúltimo,-a.

penury ['penjʊrɪ] *n* penuria, miseria.

people ['pi:pəl] *npl gen* gente *f sing*, personas *fpl*: *over 100 ~*, más de cien personas. **2** *sing* pueblo. — **3** *t* poblar. ▲ *En 1 funciona como si fuese el plural de person; concuerda con el verbo en plural*.

pep [pep] *n fam* energía, brío, empuje *m*.

pepper ['pepəʳ] *n (spice)* pimienta. **2** *(vegetable)* pimiento. — **3** *t* CULIN sazonar con pimienta.

peppermint ['pepəmɪnt] *n* menta.

peppery ['pepərɪ] *adj* picante.

per [pɜ:ʳ] *prep* por. ● *as ~*, según; *~ cent*, por ciento.

perceive [pə'si:v] *t* percibir, ver, distinguir.

percentage [pə'sentɪdʒ] *n* porcentaje *m*.

perceptible [pə'septɪbəl] *adj* perceptible.

perception [pə'sepʃən] *n* percepción.

perch [pɜ:tʃ] *n (fish)* perca. **2** *(for bird)* percha. — **3** *t-i* encaramar(se). — **4** *i (bird)* posarse.

percolate ['pɜ:kəleɪt] *t-i* filtrar(se).

percolator ['pɜ:kəleɪtəʳ] *n* cafetera de filtro.

percussion [pɜ:'kʌʃən] *n* percusión.

peregrination [perɪgrɪ'neɪʃən] *n* peregrinación, viaje *m*.

peremptory [pə'remptərɪ] *adj* perentorio,-a.

perennial [pə'renɪəl] *adj* perenne.

perfect ['pɜ:fɪkt] *adj* perfecto,-a. **2** *(total)* total, absoluto,-a, completo,-a. — **3** *t* perfeccionar. — **4** *perfectly adv* perfectamente, a la perfección. ▲ *En 3 (verbo)* [pə'fekt].

perfection [pə'fekʃən] *n* perfección.

perfectionist [pə'fekʃənɪst] *n* perfeccionista *mf*.

perforate ['pɜ:fəreɪt] *t* perforar.

perform [pə'fɔ:m] *t* hacer, ejecutar, realizar. **2** *(piece of music)* interpretar. **3** *(play)* representar. — **4** *i (actor)* actuar. **5** *(machine)* funcionar.

performance [pə'fɔ:məns] *n* ejecución, cumplimiento. **2** MUS interpretación. **3** THEAT representación. **4** *(of machine)* funcionamiento. **5** *(of car)* prestaciones *fpl*. **6** *(fuss)* lío.

performer [pə'fɔ:məʳ] *n* artista *mf*. **2** MUS intérprete *mf*.

perfume ['pɜ:fju:m] *n* perfume *m*. — **2** *t* perfumar.

perfunctory [pə'fʌŋktərɪ] *adj* hecho,-a sin interés.

perhaps [pə'hæps] *adv* quizá(s), tal vez.

peril ['perɪl] *n* peligro.

perilous ['perɪləs] *adj* peligroso,-a.

perimeter [pə'rɪmɪtəʳ] *n* perímetro.

period ['pɪərɪəd] *n* período, periodo. **2** *(class)* clase *f*. **3** *(menstruation)* regla. **4** *(full stop)* punto final. — **5** *adj* de época.

periodic [pɪərɪ'ɒdɪk] *adj* periódico,-a.

periodical [pɪərɪ'ɒdɪkəl] *adj* periódico,-a. — **2** *n* revista.

peripheral [pə'rɪfərəl] *adj* periférico,-a.

periphery [pə'rɪfərɪ] *n* periferia.

periscope ['perɪskəʊp] *n* periscopio.

perish ['perɪʃ] *i (die)* perecer, fenecer. — **2** *t-i (decay)* estropear(se).

perishable ['perɪʃəbəl] *adj* perecedero,-a.

perjure ['pɜ:dʒəʳ] *i* jurar en falso.

perjury ['pɜ:dʒərɪ] *n* perjurio.

perk [pɜ:k] *n fam* beneficio. — **2** *t-i to ~ up*, reanimar(se).

perky ['pɜ:kɪ] *adj* animado,-a.

perm [pɜ:m] *fam n* permanente *f*. — **2** *t* hacer la permanente a algn.

permanence ['pɜ:mənəns] *n* permanencia.

permanent ['pɜ:mənənt] *adj* permanente. **2** *(job, address)* fijo,-a.

permeate ['pɜ:mɪeɪt] *t-i* penetrar.

permission [pə'mɪʃən] *n* permiso.

permissive [pə'mɪsɪv] *adj* permisivo,-a.

permit ['pɜ:mɪt] *n* permiso. **2** *(pass)* pase *m*. — **3** *t* permitir. ▲ *En 3 (verbo)* [pə'mɪt].

pernicious [pɜ:'nɪsəs] *adj* pernicioso,-a.

pernickety [pɜ:'nɪkətɪ] *adj fam* quisquilloso,-a.

perpendicular [pɜ:pən'dɪkjʊləʳ] *adj-n* perpendicular *(f)*.

perpetrate [ˈpɜːpɪtreɪt] *t* perpetrar.
perpetual [pəˈpetjʊəl] *adj* perpetuo,-a. **2** *(continual)* continuo,-a, incesante.
perpetuate [pəˈpetjʊeɪt] *t* perpetuar.
perplex [pəˈpleks] *t* dejar perplejo,-a.
perplexity [pəˈpleksɪtɪ] *n* perplejidad.
persecute [ˈpɜːsɪkjuːt] *t* perseguir.
persecution [pɜːsɪˈkjuːʃən] *n* persecución.
perseverance [pɜːsɪˈvɪərəns] *n* perseverancia.
persevere [pɜːsɪˈvɪəʳ] *i* perseverar.
persist [pəˈsɪst] *i* persistir. ●*to ~ in doing sth.,* empeñarse en hacer algo.
persistence [pəˈsɪstəns] *n* persistencia. **2** *(insistence)* empeño.
persistent [pəˈsɪstənt] *adj* persistente.
person [ˈpɜːsən] *n* persona. ▲ *El plural suele ser* **people**.
personable [ˈpɜːsənəbəl] *adj* bien parecido,-a. **2** *(in character)* amable.
personage [ˈpɜːsənɪdʒ] *n* personaje *m*.
personal [ˈpɜːsənəl] *adj gen* personal. **2** *(private)* particular, privado,-a. **3** *(in person)* en persona.
personality [pɜːsəˈnælɪtɪ] *n* personalidad.
personify [pɜːˈsɒnɪfaɪ] *t* personificar.
personnel [pɜːsəˈnel] *n* personal *m*.
perspective [pəˈspektɪv] *n* perspectiva.
perspicacious [pɜːspɪˈkeɪʃəs] *adj* perspicaz.
perspicacity [pɜːspɪˈkæsɪtɪ] *n* perspicacia.
perspiration [pɜːspɪˈreɪʃən] *n* transpiración, sudor *m*.
perspire [pəˈspaɪəʳ] *t-i* transpirar, sudar.
persuade [pəˈsweɪd] *t* persuadir, convencer. ●*to ~ sb. to do sth.,* convencer a algn. para que haga algo.
persuasion [pəˈsweɪʒən] *n* *(act)* persuasión. **2** *(ability)* persuasiva. **3** *(belief)* credo.
persuasive [pəˈsweɪsɪəv] *adj* persuasivo,-a, convincente.
pert [pɜːt] *adj* coqueto,-a. **2** *(cheeky)* fresco,-a.
pertain [pɜːˈteɪn] *i* tener que ver con.
pertinacious [pɜːtɪˈneɪʃəs] *adj* pertinaz.
pertinent [ˈpɜːtɪnənt] *adj* pertinente, oportuno,-a.
perturb [pəˈtɜːb] *t* perturbar, inquietar.
perusal [pəˈruːzəl] *n* lectura (atenta).
peruse [pəˈruːz] *t* leer (con cuidado).
pervade [pɜːˈveɪd] *t* extenderse/difundirse por.

perverse [pəvɜːs] *adj* perverso,-a. **2** *(stubborn)* terco,-a.
perversion [pəˈvɜːʃən] *n* perversión. **2** *(of truth etc.)* tergiversación.
perverseness [pəˈvɜːsnəs], **perversity** [pəˈvɜːsɪtɪ] *n* perversidad. **2** *(stubbornness)* terquedad.
pervert [ˈpɜːvɜːt] *n* pervertido,-a. – **2** *t* pervertir. **3** *(truth etc.)* tergiversar. ▲ *En* **2** *y* **3** *(verbo)* [pəˈvɜːt].
pessimism [ˈpesɪmɪzəm] *n* pesimismo.
pessimist [ˈpesɪmɪst] *n* pesimista *mf*.
pessimistic [pesɪˈmɪstɪk] *adj* pesimista.
pest [pest] *n* insecto/animal nocivo. **2** *(person) fam* pelma *mf*.
pester [ˈpestəʳ] *t* molestar.
pesticide [ˈpestɪsaɪd] *n* pesticida.
pestilence [ˈpestɪləns] *n* pestilencia.
pestle [ˈpesəl] *n* mano *f* de mortero.
pet [pet] *n* animal doméstico. **2** *(person)* favorito,-a. – **3** *adj (tame)* domesticado,-a. **4** *(favourite)* favorito,-a. – **5** *t* acariciar. – **6** *i fam (sexually)* besuquearse.
petal [ˈpetəl] *n* pétalo.
peter out [piːtərˈaʊt] *i* acabarse, agotarse.
petition [pəˈtɪʃən] *n* petición, solicitud. – **2** *t* presentar una solicitud a.
petrify [ˈpetrɪfaɪ] *t-i* petrificar(se). – **2** *i fig* horrorizar.
petrol [ˈpetrəl] *n* gasolina. ■ ~ *station,* gasolinera; ~ *tank,* depósito de gasolina.
petroleum [pəˈtrəʊlɪəm] *n* petróleo.
petticoat [ˈpetɪkəʊt] *n* enaguas *fpl*. **2** *(slip)* combinación.
petty [ˈpetɪ] *adj* insignificante. **2** *(mean)* mezquino,-a. ■ ~ *cash,* gastos *mpl* menores; ~ *officer,* suboficial *m* de marina.
petulance [ˈpetjʊləns] *n* malhumor *m*.
petulant [ˈpetjʊlənt] *adj* malhumorado,-a.
pew [pjuː] *n* banco (de iglesia).
pewter [ˈpjuːtəʳ] *n* peltre *m*.
phallic [ˈfælɪk] *adj* fálico,-a.
phallus [ˈfæləs] *n* falo.
phantom [ˈfæntəm] *n* fantasma *m*.
pharaoh [ˈfeərəʊ] *n* faraón *m*.
pharmaceutical [fɑːməˈsjuːtɪkəl] *adj* farmacéutico,-a.
pharmacist [ˈfɑːməsɪst] *n* farmacéutico,-a.
pharmacy [ˈfɑːməsɪ] *n* farmacia.
pharyngitis [færɪnˈdʒaɪtɪs] *n* faringitis *f inv*.
phase [feɪz] *n* fase *f*.

pheasant ['fezənt] *n* faisán *m*. ◆*to ~ in/ out t* introducir/retirar progresivamente.

phenomenon [fɪ'nɒmɪnən] *n* fenómeno.

philanthropic [fɪlən'θrɒpɪk] *adj* filantrópico,-a.

philanthropist [fɪ'lænθrəpɪst] *n* filántropo,-a.

philanthropy [fɪ'lænθrəpɪ] *n* filantropía.

philharmonic [fɪlæːˈmɒnɪk] *adj* filarmónico,-a.

philately [fɪ'lætəlɪ] *n* filatelía.

philologist [fɪ'lɒlədʒɪst] *n* filólogo,-a.

philology [fɪ'lɒlədʒɪ] *n* filología.

philosopher [fɪ'lɒsəfəʳ] *n* filósofo,-a.

philosophy [fɪ'lɒsəfɪ] *n* filosofía.

phlegm [flem] *n* flema.

phlegmatic [fleg'mætɪk] *adj* flemático,-a.

phone [fəʊn] *n-t-i fam* → **telephone**.

phonetic [fə'netɪk] *adj* fonético,-a.

phonetics [fə'netɪks] *n* fonética.

phon(e)y ['fəʊnɪ] *adj fam* falso,-a.

phosphate ['fɒsfeɪt] *n* fosfato.

phosphorus ['fɒsfərəs] *n* fósforo.

photo ['fəʊtəʊ] *n fam* foto *f*.

photocopier ['fəʊtəʊkɒpɪəʳ] *n* fotocopiadora.

photocopy ['fəʊtəʊkɒpɪ] *n* fotocopia *f*. – 2 *t* fotocopiar.

photograph ['fəʊtəgrɑːf] *n* fotografía. – 2 *t-i* fotografiar.

photographer [fə'tɒgrəfəʳ] *n* fotógrafo,-a.

photographic [fəʊtə'græfɪk] *adj* fotográfico,-a.

photography [fə'tɒgrəfɪ] *n* fotografía.

phrasal verb [freɪzəl'vɜːb] *n* verbo compuesto.

phrase [freɪz] *n* frase *f*. – 2 *t* expresar.

phrasebook ['freɪzbʊk] *n* libro de frases.

phraseology [freɪzɪ'ɒlədʒɪ] *n* fraseología.

physical ['fɪzɪkəl] *adj* físico,-a.

physician [fɪ'zɪʃən] *n* médico,-a.

physicist ['fɪzɪsɪst] *n* físico,-a.

physics ['fɪzɪks] *n* física.

physiological [fɪzɪə'lɒdʒɪkəl] *adj* fisiológico,-a.

physiology [fɪzɪ'ɒlədʒɪ] *n* fisiología.

physiotherapy [fɪzɪəʊ'θerəpɪ] *n* fisioterapía.

physique [fɪ'ziːk] *n* físico.

pianist ['pɪənɪst] *n* pianista *mf*.

piano [pɪ'ænəʊ] *n* piano.

pick [pɪk] *n (tool)* pico. – 2 *t* escoger. 3 *(flowers, fruit)* coger. 4 *(pocket)* robar. 5

(lock) forzar. 6 *(teeth)* mondarse. ◆*to ~ off t* matar uno a uno. ◆*to ~ on t* meterse con. ◆*to ~ out t* escoger. 2 *(see)* distinguir. ◆*to ~ up t* coger; *(from floor)* recoger. 2 *(acquire)* conseguir. 3 *(go and get)* ir a buscar. 4 *fam (sexual object)* ligar con. 5 *(on radio)* captar. ●*take your ~,* escoge el/la que quieras; *the ~ of,* la flor y nata de; *to ~ a fight with,* buscar camorra con; *to ~ holes in,* encontrar defectos en; *to ~ one's nose,* hurgarse la nariz.

pickaxe ['pɪkæks] *n* pico.

picket ['pɪkɪt] *n* piquete *m*. – 2 *t* piquetear. – 3 *i* hacer de piquete.

pickle ['pɪkəl] *n* CULIN escabeche *m*. 2 *(mess)* aprieto. – 3 *t* escabechar.

pick-me-up ['pɪkmiːʌp] *n* tónico.

pickpocket ['pɪkpɒkɪt] *n* carterista *mf*.

pick-up ['pɪkʌp] *n* ELEC fonocaptor *m*. 2 *(vehicle)* furgoneta.

picnic ['pɪknɪk] *n* merienda, picnic *m*. – 2 *i* hacer un picnic.

pictorial [pɪk'tɔːrɪəl] *adj* ilustrado,-a.

picture ['pɪktʃəʳ] *n (painting)* pintura, cuadro. 2 *(portrait)* retrato. 3 *(drawing)* dibujo. 4 *(photo)* fotografía. 5 *(illustration)* lámina. 6 *(film)* película. 7 TV imagen *f*. – 8 *t* pintar, retratar. 9 *(imagine)* imaginar(se).

picturesque [pɪktʃə'resk] *adj* pintoresco,-a.

piddling ['pɪdəlɪŋ] *adj fam* insignificante.

pidgin ['pɪdʒɪn] *n* lengua franca.

pie [paɪ] *n (sweet)* pastel *m*, tarta. 2 *(savoury)* pastel, empanada.

piece [piːs] *n (bit)* trozo. 2 *(part)* pieza. 3 *(coin)* moneda. 4 MUS pieza. ◆*to ~ together t* reconstruir. ●*to take to pieces,* desmontar; *fam it's a ~ of cake,* es pan comido. ▲ *Sirve para individualizar los nombres incontables: news, noticias; a ~ of news,* una noticia.

piecemeal ['piːsmiːl] *adv* poco a poco.

piecework ['piːswɜːk] *n* trabajo a destajo.

pier [pɪəʳ] *n* muelle *m*, embarcadero. 2 *(pillar)* pilar.

pierce [pɪəs] *t* perforar, agujerear.

piercing ['pɪəsɪŋ] *adj* penetrante.

piety ['paɪətɪ] *n* piedad.

pig [pɪg] *n* cerdo,-a. 2 *(glutton)* glotón,-ona. 3 *sl (copper)* madero. ■ *farm,* granja porcina.

pigeon ['pɪdʒɪn] *n* paloma.

pigeonhole ['pɪdʒɪnhəʊl] *n* casilla.

pig-headed [pɪg'hedɪd] *adj* testarudo,-a.

piglet ['pɪglət] *n* cochinillo, lechón *m*.

pigment ['pɪgmənt] *n* pigmento.

pigsty ['pɪgstaɪ] *n* pocilga.

pigtail ['pɪgteɪl] *n* trenza.

pike [paɪk] *n* MIL pica. **2** *(fish)* lucio.

pile [paɪl] *n (heap)* montón *m*. **2** ARCH pilote *m*. **3** *fam (fortune)* fortuna. **4** *pl* MED almorranas *fpl*. **– 5** *t* amontonar, apilar. ◆*to ~ up t-i* amontonarse.

pile-up ['paɪlʌp] *n* choque *m* en cadena.

pilfer ['pɪlfəʳ] *t-i* hurtar.

pilgrim ['pɪlgrɪm] *n* peregrino,-a.

pilgrimage ['pɪlgrɪmɪdʒ] *n* peregrinación.

pill [pɪl] *n* píldora, pastilla.

pillage ['pɪlɪdʒ] *n* pillaje *m*, saqueo. **– 2** *t-i* pillar, saquear.

pillar ['pɪləʳ] *n* pilar *m*, columna.

pillion ['pɪlɪən] *n* asiento trasero.

pillory ['pɪlərɪ] *n* picota.

pillow ['pɪləʊ] *n* almohada.

pilot ['paɪlət] *n* piloto. **– 2** *adj* piloto. **– 3** *t* pilotar.

pimento [pɪ'mentəʊ] *n* pimiento morrón.

pimp [pɪmp] *n* chulo, macarra *m*.

pimple ['pɪmpəl] *n* grano.

pin [pɪn] *n* alfiler *m*. **2** TECH clavija. **3** *(wooden)* espiga. **– 4** *t* prender (con alfileres). **5** *(notice)* clavar.

pinafore ['pɪnəfɔːʳ] *n* delantal *m*.

pincers ['pɪnsəz] *npl (tool)* tenazas *fpl*. **2** *(crab's etc.)* pinzas *fpl*.

pinch [pɪntʃ] *n (nip)* pellizco. **2** *(bit)* pizca. **– 3** *t (nip)* pellizcar. **4** *(shoes)* apretar. **5** *fam* birlar, afanar.

pine [paɪn] *n* pino. **– 2** *i to ~ (away)*, consumirse. ■ *~ cone*, piña; *~ nut*, piñón *m*.

pineapple ['paɪnæpəl] *n* piña (tropical).

ping [pɪŋ] *n* sonido metálico. **– 2** *i* hacer un sonido metálico.

ping-pong ['pɪŋpɒŋ] *n* tenis *m* de mesa, pimpón *m*.

pinion ['pɪnɪən] *n* TECH piñón *m*. **– 2** *t* maniatar.

pink [pɪŋk] *adj* (de color) rosa, rosado,-a. **– 2** *n (colour)* rosa *m*. **3** BOT clavel *m*, clavellina.

pinnacle ['pɪnəkəl] *n* pináculo. **2** *(of mountain)* cima, cumbre *f*. **3** *fig* cumbre.

pinpoint ['pɪnpɔɪnt] *t* señalar.

pint [paɪnt] *n* pinta. ▲ GB = *0,57 litros;* US = *0,47 litros.*

pioneer [paɪə'nɪəʳ] *n* pionero,-a. **– 2** *t* iniciar.

pious ['paɪəs] *adj* piadoso,-a.

pip [pɪp] *n* pepita. **2** *(sound)* bip *m*. ◆*to be pipped at the post*, perder por los pelos.

pipe [paɪp] *n* tubería, cañería. **2** MUS caramillo. **3** *(for smoking)* pipa. **– 4** *t* llevar/conducir por tubería. **– 5** *t-i* MUS tocar (el caramillo). ◆*to ~ down i* callarse.

pipeline ['paɪplaɪn] *n* tubería. **2** *(gas)* gasoducto. **3** *(oil)* oleoducto. ●*in the ~*, en trámite.

piper ['paɪpəʳ] *n* gaitero,-a.

piping ['paɪpɪŋ] *n* tubería(s). **– 2** *adv ~ hot*, muy caliente.

piquant ['piːkənt] *adj* picante. **2** *fig* estimulante.

pique [piːk] *n* resentimiento. **– 2** *t* picar(se).

piracy ['paɪərəsɪ] *n* piratería.

piranha [pɪ'rɑːnə] *n (fish)* piraña.

pirate ['paɪərət] *n* pirata *m*. **– 2** *t* piratear.

pirouette [pɪrʊ'et] *n* pirueta. **– 2** *i* hacer piruetas.

Pisces ['paɪsiːz] *n* Piscis *m inv*.

piss* [pɪs] *n* meada*. **– 2** *i* mear*. **3** *(rain)* llover a cántaros. ◆*to ~ off sl i* largarse. **– 2** *t* cabrear*, poner de mala leche*. ●*to take the ~ out of*, cachondearse de.

pissed* [pɪst] *adj (drunk)* trompa.

pistachio [pɪs'tɑːʃɪəʊ] *n* pistacho.

pistol ['pɪstəl] *n* pistola.

piston ['pɪstən] *n* TECH pistón *m*, émbolo.

pit [pɪt] *n (hole)* hoyo, foso. **2** *(mine)* mina. **3** *(mark)* hoyo. **4** US *(stone)* hueso. **– 5** *t (mark)* picar. ●*to ~ one's strength/wits against*, medirse con. ■ *orchestra ~*, foso de la orquesta.

pitch [pɪtʃ] *n (tar)* pez *f*, brea. **2** MUS tono. **3** SP campo, terreno. **4** *(degree)* grado, nivel *m*. **5** *(slope)* pendiente *f*. **6** *(throw)* lanzamiento. **– 7** *t (throw)* tirar, arrojar, lanzar. **8** *(set)* fijar. **9** *(tent)* plantar, armar. **– 10** *i (fall)* caerse. ◆*to ~ into t* atacar. ■ *pitched battle*, batalla campal.

pitcher ['pɪtʃəʳ] *n* cántaro. **2** US jarro. **3** SP lanzador,-ra; *(baseball)* pícher *m*.

pitchfork ['pɪtʃfɔːk] *n* AGR horca.

piteous ['pɪtɪəs] *adj* lastimoso,-a.

pitfall ['pɪtfɔːl] *n* escollo.

pith [pɪθ] *n* médula. **2** *(of orange etc.)* piel blanca.

pitiable ['pɪtɪəbəl] *adj* lastimoso,-a.

pitiful ['pɪtɪfʊl] *adj* lastimoso,-a. **2** *(bad)* miserable.

pitiless ['pɪtɪləs] *adj* despiadado,-a.

pittance ['pɪtəns] *n* miseria.

pity ['pɪtɪ] *n* piedad. **– 2** compadecerse de. ●*what a ~!*, ¡qué lástima!

pivot ['pɪvət] *n* pivote *m*. **– 2** *i* girar.

pixie, pixy ['pɪksɪ] *n* duendecillo.

pizza ['pi:tsə] *n* pizza. ■ ~ *parlour,* pizzería.

placard ['plækɑ:d] *n* pancarta.

placate [plə'keɪt] *t* aplacar, apaciguar.

place [pleɪs] *n* lugar *m,* sitio. **2** *(seat)* asiento, sitio. **3** *(in school etc.)* plaza. **4** *(in race etc.)* posición. **5** *fam* casa, piso. **− 6** *t* colocar, poner, situar. **7** *(remember)* recordar. ●*in the first* ~, en primer lugar; *out of* ~, fuera de lugar; *to* ~ *an order,* hacer un pedido; *to take* ~, tener lugar; *to take the* ~ *of,* su(b)stituir. ■ *decimal* ~, punto decimal; ~ *name,* topónimo.

placenta [plə'sentə] *n* placenta.

placid ['plæsɪd] *adj* plácido,-a, apacible.

plagiarize ['pleɪdʒəraɪz] *t* plagiar.

plague [pleɪg] *n* plaga. **2** MED peste *f.* **− 3** *t* plagar. **4** *fig* acosar, importunar.

plaice [pleɪs] *n inv (fish)* solla.

plaid [plæd] *n* tejido escocés.

plain [pleɪn] *adj (clear)* claro,-a, evidente. **2** *(simple)* sencillo,-a. **3** *(unattractive)* sin atractivo. **4** *(frank)* franco,-a, directo,-a. **5** *(without pattern)* liso,-a. **6** *(chocolate)* sin leche. **− 8** *n* llanura. ●*in* ~ *clothes,* vestido,-a de paisano.

plain-spoken [pleɪn'spəʊkən] *adj* franco,-a.

plaintiff ['pleɪntɪf] *n* demandante *mf.*

plaintive ['pleɪntɪv] *adj* lastimero,-a, triste.

plait [plæt] *n* trenza. **− 2** *t* trenzar.

plan [plæn] *n (project)* plan *m.* **2** *(map, drawing)* plano. **− 3** *t* planear, planificar. **− 4** *i* hacer planes.

plane [pleɪn] *n (surface)* plano. **2** AV aeroplano, avión *m.* **3** *(for wood)* cepillo, garlopa. **− 4** *t* cepillar. ■ ~ *tree,* plátano.

planet ['plænət] *n* planeta *m.*

planetary ['plænɪtərɪ] *adj* planetario,-a.

plank [plæŋk] *n* tablón *m,* tabla.

plankton ['plæŋktən] *n* plancton *m.*

planning ['plænɪŋ] *n* planificación. ■ *town* ~, urbanismo.

plant [plɑ:nt] *n* BOT planta. **2** *(equipment)* equipo. **3** *(factory)* fábrica, planta. **− 4** *t* plantar. **5** *(seed)* sembrar. **6** *(bomb)* colocar. ■ ~ *pot,* maceta, tiesto.

plantation [plæn'teɪʃən] *n* plantación.

plaque [plæk] *n* placa.

plasma ['plæzmə] *n* plasma *m.*

plaster ['plɑ:stər] *n* yeso. **2** MED escayola. **3** *(dressing)* tirita®. **− 4** *t* enyesar. **5** *fig* cubrir.

plastic ['plæstɪk] *adj-n* plástico,-a *(m).*

plasticine® ['plæstɪsi:n] *n* plastilina.

plate [pleɪt] *n* plato. **2** *(sheet)* placa. **3** *(illustration)* grabado, lámina. **− 4** *t* chapar.

plateau ['plætəʊ] *n* meseta.

platform ['plætfɔ:m] *n* plataforma. **2** *(stage)* tarima, tribuna, estrado. **3** *(railway)* andén *m.* **4** POL programa *m.*

platinum ['plætɪnəm] *n* platino.

platitude ['plætɪtju:d] *n* tópico, lugar *m* común.

platonic [plə'tɒnɪk] *adj* platónico,-a.

platoon [plə'tu:n] *n* pelotón *m.*

plausible ['plɔ:zɪbəl] *adj* plausible.

play [pleɪ] *n gen* juego. **2** THEAT obra (de teatro). **3** TECH *(movement)* juego. **− 4** *t-i gen* jugar. **5** MUS tocar. **− 6** *t* THEAT *(part)* hacer el papel de. **7** SP *(sport)* jugar a. **8** SP *(opponent)* jugar contra. **9** *(record, song)* poner. ◆*to* ~ *down* *t* quitar importancia a. ◆*to* ~ *on* *t* aprovecharse de. ◆*to* ~ *up* *t* causar problemas a. **− 2** *i (machine)* no funcionar bien. **3** *(child)* portarse mal. ●*to* ~ *a trick on,* hacer una mala jugada a; *to* ~ *for time,* tratar de ganar tiempo; *to* ~ *hard to get,* hacerse (de) rogar; *to* ~ *the fool,* hacer el indio; *to* ~ *truant,* hacer novillos/campana; *fam to* ~ *it by ear,* decidir sobre la marcha.

playboy ['pleɪbɔɪ] *n* play-boy *m.*

player ['pleɪər] *n* jugador,-ra. **2** THEAT actor *m,* actriz *f.* ■ *tennis* ~, tenista *mf; trumpet* ~, trompetista *mf.*

playful ['pleɪfʊl] *adj* juguetón,-ona.

playground ['pleɪgraʊnd] *n* patio de recreo.

playhouse ['pleɪhaʊs] *n* teatro.

playmate ['pleɪmeɪt] *n* compañero,-a de juego.

play-off ['pleɪɒf] *n* partido de desempate.

plaything ['pleɪθɪŋ] *n* juguete *m.*

playtime ['pleɪtaɪm] *n* recreo.

playwright ['pleɪraɪt] *n* dramaturgo,-a.

plea [pli:] *n* súplica. **2** *(excuse)* excusa. **3** JUR alegato, declaración.

plead [pli:d] *i* suplicar *(with,* -). **− 2** *t (give as excuse)* alegar. ●*to* ~ *guilty/not guilty,* declararse culpable/inocente.

pleasant ['plezənt] *adj* agradable. **2** *(person)* simpático,-a, amable.

please [pli:z] *t-i* agradar, gustar, placer, complacer. **− 2** *interj* por favor. ●~ *yourself,* haz lo que tú quieras.

pleased [pli:zd] *adj* contento,-a. **2** *(satisfied)* satisfecho,-a. ●~ *to meet you!,* ¡encantado,-a!, ¡mucho gusto!

pleasing ['pli:zɪŋ] *adj* agradable.

pleasurable ['pleʒərəbəl] *adj* agradable.

pleasure [ˈpleʒəʳ] *n* placer *m*. ●*it gives me great ~ to ...*, me complace ... .

pleat [pliːt] *n* pliegue. – **2** *t* plisar.

pledge [pledʒ] *n* (*promise*) promesa. **2** (*guarantee*) prenda. – **3** *t-i* prometer.

plentiful [ˈplentɪfʊl] *adj* abundante.

plenty [ˈplentɪ] *n* abundancia. ●*~ of*, de sobra, en abundancia.

pliable [ˈplaɪəbəl] *adj* flexible.

pliers [ˈplaɪəz] *npl* alicates *mpl*.

plight [plaɪt] *n* situación (grave).

plimsolls [ˈplɪmsəlz] *npl* GB playeras *fpl*.

plod [plɒd] *i* andar pesadamente. **2** *fig* hacer laboriosamente.

plonk [plɒŋk] *t* dejar caer. – **2** *n* golpe/ruido seco. **3** *fam* vinazo.

plot [plɒt] *n* conspiración, complot *m*. **2** (*of land*) parcela, terreno. **3** (*of book, film, etc.*) trama, argumento. – **4** *t* trazar. – **5** *i* conspirar.

plough [plaʊ] *n* arado. – **2** *t-i* arar, labrar.

ploughman [ˈplaʊmən] *n* arador, labrador.

plow [plaʊ] *n-t-i* US → **plough**.

pluck [plʌk] *n* valor *m*. – **2** *t* arrancar. **3** (*bird*) desplumar. ●*to ~ up courage*, cobrar ánimo.

plug [plʌg] *n* (*for sink etc.*) tapón *m*. **2** ELEC (*on cable*) enchufe *m*, clavija; (*socket*) enchufe *m*, toma. **3** AUTO bujía. – **4** *t* tapar. ◆*to ~ in* *t-i* enchufar(se).

plughole [ˈplʌghəʊl] *n* desagüe *m*.

plum [plʌm] *n* ciruela. ■ *~ tree*, ciruelo.

plumage [ˈpluːmɪdʒ] *n* plumaje *m*.

plumb [plʌm] *n* plomada. – **2** *adj-adv* a plomo. – **3** *adv* US completamente. **4** US (*exactly*) justo. – **5** *t* sond(e)ar.

plumber [ˈplʌməʳ] *n* fontanero,-a.

plumbing [ˈplʌmɪŋ] *n* fontanería.

plume [pluːm] *n* penacho.

plummet [ˈplʌmət] *i* caer en picado.

plump [plʌmp] *adj* rechoncho,-a, rollizo,-a. ◆*to ~ for* *t* optar por.

plunder [ˈplʌndəʳ] *n* pillaje *m*, saqueo. **2** (*loot*) botín *m*. – **3** *t* saquear.

plunge [plʌndʒ] *n* zambullida. – **2** *i* (*dive*) zambullirse, tirarse de cabeza. **3** (*fall*) caer(se). – **4** *t* (*immerse*) sumergir. **5** (*thrust*) hundir. ●*to take the ~*, dar el paso decisivo.

plunger [ˈplʌndʒəʳ] *n* (*for sink etc.*) desatascador *m*.

pluperfect [pluːˈpɜːfekt] *n* pluscuamperfecto.

plural [ˈplʊərəl] *adj-n* plural (*m*).

plus [plʌs] *prep* más. – **2** *adj* MATH positivo,-a. – **3** *n* MATH *~ (sign)*, signo de más.

plush [plʌʃ] *adj fam* lujoso,-a.

ply [plaɪ] *i* (*ship*) *to ~ between*, hacer el servicio entre, cubrir la línea entre. **2** (*trade*) ejercer. ◆*to ~ with* *t* no parar de ofrecer.

plywood [ˈplaɪwʊd] *n* contrachapado.

pneumatic [njuːˈmætɪk] *adj* neumático,-a.

pneumonia [njuːˈməʊnɪə] *n* pulmonía.

poach [pəʊtʃ] *i* cazar/pescar en vedado. – **2** *t* CULIN hervir; (*eggs*) escalfar.

poacher [ˈpəʊtʃəʳ] *n* cazador,-ora/pescador,-ra furtivo,-a.

pocket [ˈpɒkɪt] *n* bolsillo. – **2** *t* embolsar.

pocketbook [ˈpɒkɪtbʊk] *n* US bolso.

pod [pɒd] *n* vaina.

podgy [ˈpɒdʒɪ] *adj* regordete,-a.

podium [ˈpəʊdɪəm] *n* podio.

poem [ˈpəʊəm] *n* poema *m*, poesía.

poet [ˈpəʊət] *n* poeta *mf*.

poetic [pəʊˈetɪk] *adj* poético,-a.

poetry [ˈpəʊətrɪ] *n* poesía.

poignant [ˈpɔɪnjənt] *adj* conmovedor,-ra.

point [pɔɪnt] *n* gen punto. **2** (*sharp end*) punta. **3** (*in time*) punto, momento. **4** (*in space, on scale*) punto. **5** (*in score*) punto, tanto. **6** GEOG punta. **7** (*railway*) aguja. **8** (*in decimals*) coma: *5 ~ 66*, cinco coma sesenta y seis. **9** ELEC (*power*) *~*, toma de corriente. – **10** *i* señalar; *fig* indicar. – **11** *t-i* (*with weapon*) apuntar: *to ~ a gun at sb.*, apuntar a algn. con una pistola. ●*beside the ~*, fuera de propósito; *on the ~ of*, a punto de; *there's no ~ in ...*, no vale la pena ...; *to come to the ~*, ir al grano. ■ *~ of view*, punto de vista.

point-blank [pɔɪntˈblæŋk] *adj* (*refusal*) categórico,-a. **2** (*shot*) a quemarropa. – **3** *adv* categóricamente. **4** (*shoot*) a quemarropa.

pointed [ˈpɔɪntɪd] *adj* puntiagudo,-a. **2** (*comment*) intencionado,-a.

pointer [ˈpɔɪntəʳ] *n* indicador *m*. **2** (*dog*) perro de muestra.

pointless [ˈpɔɪntləs] *adj* sin sentido.

poise [pɔɪz] *n* equilibrio. **2** (*of body*) porte *m*, elegancia. – **3** *t* equilibrar, balancear.

poison [ˈpɔɪzən] *n* veneno. – **2** *t* envenenar.

poisonous [ˈpɔɪzənəs] *adj* venenoso,-a.

poke [pəʊk] *n* empujón *m*, golpe *m*. – **2** *t* empujar. **3** (*fire*) atizar.

poker ['pǝukǝʳ] *n* atizador *m*. 2 *(game)* póquer *m*.

polar ['pǝulǝʳ] *adj* polar. ■ ~ *bear,* oso polar.

polarize ['pǝulǝraɪz] *t-i* polarizar(se).

pole [pǝul] *n* polo. 2 *(stick)* pértiga. ■ ~ *star,* estrella polar; ~ *vault,* salto con pértiga.

polemic [pǝ'lemɪk] *adj-n* polémico,-a *(f)*.

police [pǝ'li:s] *npl* policía *f sing.* — 2 *t* vigilar.

policeman [pǝ'li:smǝn] *n* policía *m*, guardia *m*.

policewoman [pǝ'li:swʊmǝn] *n* mujer *f* policía.

policy ['pɒlɪsɪ] *n* política. 2 *(insurance)* póliza.

polish ['pɒlɪʃ] *n* pulimento; *(wax)* cera; *(for shoes)* betún *m*. 2 *(shine)* lustre *m*, brillo. — 3 *t* abrillantar, sacar brillo a. 4 *fig* pulir. ◆*to* ~ *off t* despachar. 2 *(food)* zamparse.

polite [pǝ'laɪt] *adj* cortés, (bien) educado,-a.

politeness [pǝ'laɪtnǝs] *n* cortesía, educación.

politic ['pɒlɪtɪk] *adj* prudente.

political [pǝ'lɪtɪkǝl] *adj* político,-a.

politician [pɒlɪ'tɪʃǝn] *n* político,-a.

politics ['pɒlɪtɪks] *n* política. 2 *pl* opiniones *fpl* políticas.

poll [pǝul] *n* votación. 2 *(opinion)* ~, encuesta, sondeo. — 3 *t (votes)* obtener.

pollen ['pɒlǝn] *n* polen *m*.

pollutant [pǝ'lu:tǝnt] *n* contaminante *m*.

pollute [pɒ'lu:t] *t* contaminar.

pollution [pɒ'lu:ʃǝn] *n* contaminación.

polo ['pǝulǝu] *n* polo. ■ ~ *neck,* cuello cisne; *water* ~, water-polo.

poltergeist ['pɒltǝgaɪst] *n* duende *m* travieso.

polyester [pɒlɪ'estǝʳ] *n* poliéster *m*.

polygamy [pɒ'lɪgǝmɪ] *n* poligamia.

polyglot ['pɒlɪglɒt] *adj-n* políglota,-a.

polystyrene [pɒlɪ'staɪri:n] *n* poliestireno *m*.

polytechinic [pɒlɪ'teknɪk] *n* escuela politécnica.

polyurethane [pɒlɪ'jʊǝrǝθeɪn] *n* poliuretano.

pomegranate ['pɒmɪgrænǝt] *n* BOT granada.

pomp [pɒmp] *n* pompa.

pompom ['pɒmpɒm] *n* pompón *m*.

pompous ['pɒmpǝs] *adj* pomposo,-a.

poncho ['pɒntʃǝu] *n* poncho.

pond [pɒnd] *n* estanque *m*.

ponder ['pɒndǝʳ] *t* ponderar, considerar.

pong [pɒŋ] *fam n* tufo. — 2 *t* apestar.

pontiff ['pɒntɪf] *n* pontífice *m*.

pontificate [pɒn'tɪfɪkeɪt] *i* pontificar.

pontoon [pɒn'tu:n] *n* pontón *m*. 2 *(game)* veintiuna.

pony ['pǝunɪ] *n* poni *m*.

ponytail ['pǝunɪteɪl] *n* cola de caballo.

poodle ['pu:dǝl] *n* caniche *m*.

poof [pʊf] *n sl* marica *m*.

pooh-pooh [pu:'pu:] *t* despreciar.

pool [pu:l] *n* charco. 2 *(pond)* estanque *m*. 3 *(money)* fondo común. 4 *(game)* billar *m* americano. — 5 *t* reunir. ■ *football pools,* quinielas *fpl*.

poor [pʊǝʳ] *adj* pobre. 2 *(bad quality)* malo,-a, de mala calidad.

poorly ['pʊǝlɪ] *adj (ill)* mal, malo,-a. — 2 *adv* mal.

pop [pɒp] *n* estallido. 2 *(of cork)* taponazo. 3 *fam (drink)* gaseosa. 4 *fam (music)* música pop. 5 *fam (dad)* papá. — 6 *t-i* (hacer) saltar. 7 *(burst)* (hacer) reventar/estallar. — 8 *t (put)* poner. ◆*to* ~ *in/out i* entrar/salir un momento.

popcorn ['pɒpkɔ:n] *n* palomitas *fpl*, rosetas *fpl* de maíz.

pope [pǝup] *n* papa *m*, pontífice *m*.

poplar ['pɒplǝʳ] *n* álamo, chopo.

poppy ['pɒpɪ] *n* amapola.

popular ['pɒpjulǝʳ] *adj* popular.

popularity [pɒpju'lærɪtɪ] *n* popularidad.

popularize ['pɒpjulǝraɪz] *t* popularizar.

populate ['pɒpjuleɪt] *t* poblar.

population [pɒpju'leɪʃǝn] *n* población, habitantes *mpl*.

porcelain ['pɔ:sǝlɪn] *n* porcelana.

porch [pɔ:tʃ] *n* pórtico, entrada.

porcupine ['pɔ:kjupaɪn] *n* puerco espín.

pore [pɔ:ʳ] *n* poro. ◆*to* ~ *over t* leer detenidamente.

pork [pɔ:k] *n* carne *f* de cerdo.

pornographic [pɔ:nǝ'græfɪk] *adj* pornográfico,-a.

pornography [pɔ:'nɒgrǝfɪ] *n* pornografía.

porous ['pɔ:rǝs] *adj* poroso,-a.

porpoise ['pɔ:pǝs] *n* marsopa.

porridge ['pɒrɪdʒ] *n* gachas *fpl* de avena.

port [pɔ:t] *n (place)* puerto. 2 MAR babor *m*. 3 *(wine)* vino de Oporto.

portable ['pɔ:tǝbǝl] *adj* portátil.

portend [pɔ:'tend] *t* presagiar.

portent ['pɔ:tent] *n* presagio.

portentous [pɔ:'tentǝs] *adj* trascendente.

porter [ˈpɔːtəʳ] *n* portero,-a. **2** *(at station)* mozo de estación.

portfolio [pɔːtˈfəʊlɪəʊ] *n* carpeta. **2** POL cartera.

portion [ˈpɔːʃən] *n* porción, parte *f*. **2** *(helping)* ración. — **3** *t to* ~ *(out),* repartir.

porthole [ˈpɔːthəʊl] *n* portilla.

portly [ˈpɔːtlɪ] *adj* corpulento,-a.

portrait [ˈpɔːtreɪt] *n* retrato.

portray [pɔːˈtreɪ] *t* retratar. **2** *fig* describir.

pose [pəʊz] *n* actitud, postura. **2** *pej* afectación. — **3** *t* *(problem etc.)* plantear. **4** *(threat)* representar. — **5** *i* presumir. **6** *(as model)* posar. ●*to* ~ *as,* hacerse pasar por.

posh [pɒʃ] GB *fam adj* elegante. **2** *pej (person)* presumido,-a.

position [pəˈzɪʃən] *n gen* posición. **2** *(posture)* postura, actitud. **3** *(job)* puesto, empleo. **4** *(state)* situación. — **5** *t* colocar.

positive [ˈpɒzɪtɪv] *adj* positivo,-a. **2** *(definite)* seguro,-a. **3** *fam (total)* auténtico,-a.

possess [pəˈzes] *t* poseer, tener.

possession [pəˈzeʃən] *n* posesión.

possessive [pəˈzesɪv] *adj* posesivo,-a.

possibility [pɒsɪˈbɪlɪtɪ] *n* posibilidad.

possible [ˈpɒsɪbəl] *adj* posible. — **2** *possibly adv* posiblemente. ●*as soon as* ~, cuanto antes.

post [pəʊst] *n* *(wooden)* poste *m*. **2** *(job)* puesto, cargo. **3** MIL puesto. **4** *(mail)* correo. — **5** *t (letter)* echar al correo. **6** *(notice)* poner. **7** *(send)* enviar, destinar. ■ ~ *office,* oficina de correos; ~ *office box,* apartado de correos.

postage [ˈpəʊstɪdʒ] *n* franqueo, porte *m*. ■ ~ *stamp,* sello de correos.

postal [ˈpəʊstəl] *adj* postal. ■ ~ *order,* giro postal.

postbox [ˈpəʊstbɒks] *n* buzón *m*.

postcard [ˈpəʊstkɑːd] *n* (tarjeta) postal.

postcode [ˈpəʊstkəʊd] *n* código postal.

poster [ˈpəʊstəʳ] *n* póster *m*, cartel *m*.

posterior [pɒˈstɪərɪəʳ] *adj* posterior. — **2** *n fam* trasero.

posterity [pɒsˈterɪtɪ] *n* posteridad.

postgraduate [pəʊstˈɡrædjʊət] *n* postgraduado,-a.

posthumous [ˈpɒstjʊməs] *adj* póstumo,-a.

postman [ˈpəʊstmən] *n* cartero.

postmark [ˈpəʊstmɑːk] *n* matasellos *m inv*.

postmortem [pəʊstˈmɔːtəm] *n* autopsia.

postpone [pəsˈpəʊn] *t* aplazar, posponer.

postponement [pəsˈpəʊnmənt] *n* aplazamiento.

postscript [ˈpəʊstskrɪpt] *n* posdata *f*.

posture [ˈpɒstʃəʳ] *n* postura.

posy [ˈpəʊzɪ] *n* ramillete *m*.

pot [pɒt] *n* pote *m*, tarro. **2** *(teapot)* tetera. **3** *(coffee* ~*)* cafetera. **4** *(of paint)* bote *m*. **5** *(flower* ~*)* maceta, tiesto. **6** *(chamber* ~*)* orinal *m*. **7** *sl* hachís *m*. ●*fam to go to* ~, irse al traste.

potassium [pəˈtæsɪəm] *n* potasio.

potato [pəˈteɪtəʊ] *n* patata. ■ *sweet* ~, boniato.

potent [ˈpəʊtənt] *adj* potente.

potential [pəˈtenʃəl] *adj-n* potencial *(m)*.

pothole [ˈpɒthəʊl] *n* *(cave)* cueva. **2** *(in road)* bache *m*.

potluck [pɒtˈlʌk] *n to take* ~, comer de lo que haya.

potted [ˈpɒtɪd] *adj (food)* en conserva. **2** *(plant)* en maceta/tiesto.

potter [ˈpɒtəʳ] *n* alfarero,-a. — **2** *i to* ~ *about/around,* entretenerse.

pottery [ˈpɒtərɪ] *n* *(craft, place)* alfarería. **2** *(objects)* cerámica.

potty [ˈpɒtɪ] *fam adj* chiflado,-a. — **2** *n* orinal *m*.

pouch [paʊtʃ] *n* bolsa. **2** *(for tobacco)* petaca.

pouf(fe) [puːf] *n* puf *m*.

poultice [ˈpəʊltɪs] *n* cataplasma *m*.

poultry [ˈpəʊltrɪ] *n* aves *fpl* de corral.

pounce [paʊns] *n* salto súbito. — **2** *i* abalanzarse *(on,* sobre).

pound [paʊnd] *n* libra. **2** *(for dogs)* perrera. **3** *(for cars)* depósito de coches. — **4** *t* machacar. **5** *(beat)* golpear. — **6** *i (heart)* palpitar.

pour [pɔːʳ] *t* verter, echar. — **2** *i* fluir, correr. **3** *to* ~ *(down),* llover a cántaros.

pout [paʊt] *n* puchero. — **2** *i* hacer pucheros.

poverty [ˈpɒvətɪ] *n* pobreza.

powder [ˈpaʊdəʳ] *n* polvo. — **2** *t* poner polvos a.

power [ˈpaʊəʳ] *n* *(strength)* fuerza. **2** *(ability)* poder *m*, capacidad. **3** *(faculty)* facultad. **4** ELEC fuerza, corriente *f*. **5** *(authority)* poder *m*. **6** *(nation)* potencia. **7** MATH TECH potencia. — **8** *t* mover, propulsar. ●*in* ~, en el poder. ■ ~ *station,* central eléctrica.

powerful [ˈpaʊəfʊl] *adj (influential)* poderoso,-a. **2** *(strong)* fuerte. **3** *(medicine etc.)* potente, eficaz.

powerless ['pauələs] *adj* impotente.
practicable ['præktıkəbəl] *adj* factible.
practical ['præktıkəl] *adj* práctico,-a. − 2 *practically adv* casi, prácticamente.
practice ['præktıs] *n* práctica. 2 *(training)* entrenamiento. 3 *(habit)* costumbre *f.* 4 *(of profession)* ejercicio. 5 *(doctor's, lawyer's, etc.)* clientela. ●*in* ~, en la práctica; *to put into* ~, poner en práctica.
practise, us **practice** ['præktıs] *t-i* practicar. 2 *(profession)* ejercer. − 3 *i* sp entrenar. 4 theat ensayar.
practitioner [præk'tıʃənəʳ] *n* médico,-a.
pragmatic [præg'mætık] *adj* pragmático,-a.
prairie ['preərı] *n* pradera, llanura.
praise [preız] *n* alabanza, elogio. − 2 *t* alabar.
praiseworthy ['preızwɜːðı] *adj* loable.
pram [præm] *n* gb cochecito de niño.
prance [prɑːns] *i* *(horse)* hacer cabriolas. 2 *(person)* saltar, brincar.
prank [præŋk] *n* travesura, broma.
prattle ['prætəl] *n* charla, parloteo. − 2 *i* charlar, parlotear.
prawn [prɔːn] *n* gamba.
pray [preı] *i* orar, rezar.
prayer [preəʳ] *n* rel oración. 2 *(entreaty)* ruego, súplica.
preach [priːtʃ] *t-i* predicar.
preacher ['priːtʃəʳ] *n* predicador,-ra.
preamble [priː'æmbəl] *n* preámbulo.
precarious [prı'keərıəs] *adj* precario,-a, inseguro,-a.
precaution [prı'kɔːʃən] *n* precaución.
precede [prı'siːd] *t-i* preceder.
precedence ['presıdəns] *n* precedencia.
precedent ['presıdənt] *adj* precedente.
precept ['priːsept] *n* precepto.
precinct ['priːsıŋkt] *n* recinto. 2 *(area)* distrito, zona.
precious ['preʃəs] *adj* precioso,-a. − 2 *adv* muy.
precipice ['precıpıs] *n* precipicio.
precipitate [prı'sıpıtət] *adj-n* precipitado,-a *(m)*. − 2 *t* precipitar. ▲ *En 2 (verbo)* [prı'sıpıteıt].
precipitation [prısıpı'teıʃən] *n* precipitación.
precipitous [prı'sıpıtəs] *adj* escarpado,-a.
precise [prı'saıs] *adj* preciso,-a, exacto,-a. 2 *(meticulous)* meticuloso,-a. − 3 *precisely adv* precisamente.
precision [prı'sıʒən] *n* precisión, exactitud.
preclude [prı'kluːd] *t* excluir.

precocious [prı'kəuʃəs] *adj* precoz.
preconceived [priːkən'siːvd] *adj* preconcebido,-a.
precooked [priː'kukt] *t* precocinado,-a.
precursor [prı'kɜːsəʳ] *n* precursor,-ra.
predator ['predətəʳ] *n* (de)predador *m.*
predecessor ['priːdısesəʳ] *n* predecesor,-ra.
predestination [priːdestı'neıʃən] *n* predestinación.
predestine [priː'destın] *t* predestinar.
predetermine [priːdı'tɜːmın] *t* predeterminar.
predicament [prı'dıkəmənt] *n* apuro, aprieto.
predicate ['predıkət] *n* predicado.
predict [prı'dıkt] *t* predecir, vaticinar.
predictable [prı'dıktəbəl] *adj* previsible.
prediction [prı'dıkʃən] *n* predicción, vaticinio.
predilection [priːdı'lekʃən] *n* predilección.
predispose [priːdıs'pəuz] *t* predisponer.
predominance [prı'dɒmınəns] *n* predominio.
predominant [prı'dɒmınənt] *adj* predominante.
predominate [prı'dɒmıneıt] *i* predominar.
pre-eminent [priː'emınənt] *adj* preeminente.
pre-empt [priː'empt] *t* adelantarse a.
preen [priːn] *t* arreglar.
prefabricated [priː'fæbrıkeıtıd] *adj* prefabricado,-a.
preface ['prefəs] *n* prefacio, prólogo.
prefect ['priːfekt] *n* prefecto. 2 gb *(school)* monitor,-ra.
prefer [prı'fɜːʳ] *t* preferir. 2 jur *(charge)* presentar.
preferable ['prefərəbəl] *adj* preferible.
preference ['prefərəns] *n* preferencia.
preferential [prefə'renʃəl] *adj* preferente.
prefix ['priːfıks] *n* prefijo.
pregnancy ['pregnənsı] *n* embarazo.
pregnant ['pregnənt] *adj* *n* *(animal)* preñado,-a. 2 *(woman)* embarazado,-a.
prehistoric [priːhı'stɒrık] *n* prehistórico,-a.
prejudge [priː'dʒʌdʒ] *t* prejuzgar.
prejudice ['predʒədıs] *n* prejuicio. − 2 *t* predisponer. 3 *(harm)* perjudicar, dañar.
prejudicial [predʒə'dıʃəl] *adj* perjudicial.
prelate ['prelət] *n* prelado.
preliminary [prı'lımınərı] *adj-n* preliminar *(m)*.

prelude ['prelju:d] *n* preludio.

premature [premə'tjʊərⁱ] *adj* prematuro,-a.

premeditated [pri:'medɪteɪtɪd] *adj* premeditado,-a.

premier ['premɪərⁱ] *adj* primero,-a, principal. – **2** *n* primer,-ra ministro,-a.

première ['premɪeərⁱ] *n* estreno.

premise ['premɪs] *n* premisa. **2** *pl* local *m sing*.

premium ['pri:mɪəm] *n* prima.

premonition [pri:mə'nɪʃən] *n* premonición.

preoccupation [pri:ɒkjʊ'peɪʃən] *n* preocupación.

preoccupy [pri:'ɒkjʊpaɪ] *t* preocupar.

prepaid [pri:'peɪd] *adj* pagado,-a por adelantado.

preparation [prepə'reɪʃən] *n (action)* preparación. **2** CHEM preparado. **3** *pl* preparativos *mpl*.

preparatory [prɪ'pærətərɪ] *adj* preparatorio,-a, preliminar.

prepare [prɪ'peərⁱ] *t-i* preparar(se).

prepared [prɪ'peəd] *adj* listo,-a, preparado,-a. **2** *(willing)* dispuesto,-a.

preponderance [prɪ'pɒndərəns] *n* preponderancia.

preposition [prepə'zɪʃən] *n* preposición.

prepossessing [pri:pə'zesɪŋ] *adj* atractivo,-a.

preposterous [prɪ'pɒstərəs] *adj* absurdo,-a, descabellado,-a.

prerequisite [pri:'rekwɪzɪt] *n* requisito previo.

prerogative [prɪ'rɒgətɪv] *n* prerrogativa.

Presbyterian [prezbɪ'tɪərɪən] *adj-n* presbiteriano,-a.

preschool [pri:'sku:l] *adj* preescolar.

prescribe [prɪs'kraɪb] *t* prescribir. **2** *(medicine)* recetar.

prescription [prɪs'krɪpʃən] *n* receta (médica).

presence ['prezəns] *n* presencia. **2** *(attendance)* asistencia.

present ['prezənt] *adj (attending)* presente. **2** *(current)* actual. **3** GRAM presente. – **4** *n (now)* presente *m*, actualidad. **5** GRAM presente *m*. **6** *(gift)* regalo. – **7** *t (introduce)* presentar. **8** *(give)* entregar, presentar, dar. **9** *(play)* representar. **10** TV RAD presentar. – **11** *presently adv* GB pronto. **12** US ahora. ●*for the* ~, por ahora; *to be* ~, estar presente, asistir; *to* ~ *a problem*, plantear un problema. ▲ *De 7 a 10 (verbo)* [prɪ'zent].

presentable [prɪ'zentəbəl] *adj* presentable. ●*to make o.s.* ~, arreglarse.

presentation [prezən'teɪʃən] *n* presentación.

presenter [prɪ'zentərⁱ] *n* RAD locutor,-ra. **2** TV presentador,-ra.

presentiment [prɪ'zentɪmənt] *n* presentimiento.

preservation [prezə'veɪʃən] *n* conservación, preservación.

preservative [prɪ'zɜ:vətɪv] *n* conservante *m*.

preserve [prɪ'zɜ:v] *n* CULIN conserva, confitura. **2** *(hunting)* coto, vedado. – **3** *t* conservar.

preside [prɪ'zaɪd] *i* presidir.

president ['prezɪdənt] *n* presidente,-a.

press [pres] *n (newspapers)* prensa. **2** *(machine)* prensa. **3** *(printing business)* imprenta. – **4** *t (button)* pulsar, apretar. **5** *(grapes, olives, etc.)* prensar. **6** *(clothes)* planchar. **7** *(urge)* presionar. – **8** *i* apretar. ●*to* ~ *ahead/on i* seguir adelante.

pressing ['presɪŋ] *adj* urgente, apremiante.

pressure ['preʃərⁱ] *n* presión. **2** *(tension)* tensión. ●*to put* ~ *on*, presionar a. ■ ~ *cooker*, olla a presión; ~ *group*, grupo de presión.

pressurize ['preʃəraɪz] *t* presurizar. **2** *fig* presionar.

prestige [pres'ti:ʒ] *n* prestigio.

prestigious [pres'tɪdʒəs] *adj* prestigioso,-a.

presumably [prɪ'zju:məblɪ] *adv* se supone que.

presume [prɪ'zju:m] *t-i* suponer. – **2** *i (dare)* atreverse a.

presumption [prɪ'zʌmpʃən] *n* suposición. **2** *(arrogance)* presunción.

presumptuous [prɪ'zʌmptjʊəs] *adj* presuntuoso,-a.

presuppose [pri:sə'pəʊz] *t* presuponer.

pretence [prɪ'tens] *n (make-believe)* fingimiento, apariencia. **2** *(pretext)* pretexto. ●*under false pretences*, con engaño, fraudulentemente.

pretend [prɪ'tend] *t-i* aparentar, fingir. – **2** *i (claim)* pretender.

pretentious [prɪ'tenʃəs] *adj* pretencioso,-a, presumido,-a.

pretext ['pri:tekst] *n* pretexto.

pretty ['prɪtɪ] *adj* bonito,-a, guapo,-a, mono,-a. – **2** *adv* bastante.

prevail [prɪ'veɪl] *i (be usual)* predominar. **2** *(win)* prevalecer. ●*to* ~ *upon*, convencer, persuadir.

prevailing [prɪ'veɪlɪŋ], **prevalent** ['prevələnt] *adj* predominante.

prevaricate [prɪ'værɪkeɪt] *i* buscar evasivas.

prevent [prɪ'vent] *t (stop)* impedir. 2 *(avoid)* evitar.

prevention [prɪ'venʃən] *n* prevención.

preventive [prɪ'ventɪv] *adj* preventivo,-a.

preview ['pri:vju:] *n* preestreno.

previous ['pri:vɪəs] *adj* previo,-a, anterior. – 2 *previously adv* previamente, con anterioridad. ●~ *to,* antes de. ■ ~ *convictions,* antecedentes *mpl* penales.

prey [preɪ] *n* presa. 2 *fig* víctima. – 3 *t to* ~ *on,* alimentarse de.

price [praɪs] *n* precio, importe *m.* – 2 *t* poner un precio a. 3 *(ask ~ of)* preguntar el precio de. ●*at any ~,* a toda costa. ■ *set ~,* precio fijo.

priceless ['praɪsləs] *adj* que no tiene precio.

pric(e)y ['praɪsɪ] *adj fam* caro,-a.

prick [prɪk] *n* pinchazo. 2* *(penis)* polla*. 3* *(person)* gilipollas* *mf inv.* – 4 *t* pinchar. ●*to* ~ *up one's ears,* aguzar el oído.

prickle ['prɪkəl] *n* pincho, púa, espina. – 2 *t-i* pinchar, picar.

prickly ['prɪklɪ] *adj* espinoso,-a. 2 *(which prickles)* que pica.

pride [praɪd] *n* orgullo. 2 *(self respect)* amor propio. – 3 *t to* ~ *o.s. on,* enorgullecerse de. ●*to take* ~ *in,* enorgullecerse de.

priest [pri:st] *n* sacerdote *m.*

priestess ['pri:stes] *n* sacerdotisa.

prig [prɪg] *n* presuntuoso,-a.

prim [prɪm] *adj* remilgado,-a.

prim(a)eval [praɪ'mi:vəl] *adj* primitivo,-a.

primarily [praɪ'merɪlɪ] *adv* ante todo.

primary ['praɪmərɪ] *adj (main)* principal. 2 *(school)* primario,-a.

primate ['praɪmət] *n* REL primado. 2 ZOOL primate *m.* ▲ *En* 2 ['praɪmeɪt].

prime [praɪm] *adj* primero,-a, principal. 2 MATH primo. 3 *(best quality)* selecto,-a, de primera. – 4 *t (pump)* cebar. 5 *(wood)* imprimar. ■ *Prime Minister,* primer ministro; *the* ~ *of life,* la flor de la vida.

primer ['praɪmər] *n (paint)* imprimación.

primitive ['prɪmɪtɪv] *adj* primitivo,-a.

primrose ['prɪmrəʊz] *n* primavera.

prince [prɪns] *n* príncipe *m.*

princess ['prɪnses] *n* princesa.

principal ['prɪnsɪpəl] *adj* principal. – 2 *n (of school)* director,-ra. 3 FIN capital *m.*

principality [prɪnsɪ'pælɪtɪ] *n* principado.

principle ['prɪnsɪpəl] *n* principio. ●*on* ~, por principio.

print [prɪnt] *n (mark)* impresión, huella. 2 *(type size)* letra. 3 *(photo)* copia. 4 *(picture)* grabado. – 5 *t* imprimir. 6 *(publish)* publicar. 7 *(photo)* sacar una copia de. 8 *(write)* escribir con letra de imprenta. ●*in* ~, impreso,-a; *out of* ~, agotado,-a.

printer ['prɪntər] *n (person)* impresor,-ra. 2 *(machine)* impresora.

printing ['prɪntɪŋ] *n (action)* impresión. 2 *(art)* imprenta.

prior ['praɪər] *adj* anterior, previo,-a. – 2 *n* REL prior *m.* ●~ *to,* antes de.

priority [praɪ'ɒrɪtɪ] *n* prioridad.

prise [praɪz] *t* abrir/levantar/quitar *etc.* con palanca.

prism ['prɪzəm] *n* prisma.

prison ['prɪzən] *n* prisión, cárcel *f.*

prisoner ['prɪzənər] *n* preso,-a. 2 MIL prisionero,-a.

privacy ['praɪvəsɪ] *n* intimidad.

private ['praɪvət] *adj* privado,-a. 2 *(personal)* personal. 3 *(confidential)* confidencial. 4 *(class)* particular. 5 *(school)* de pago. – 6 *n* MIL soldado raso. – 7 *privately adv* en privado.

privation [praɪ'veɪʃən] *n* privación.

privilege ['prɪvɪlɪdʒ] *n* privilegio.

privileged ['prɪvɪlɪdʒd] *adj* privilegiado,-a.

privy ['prɪvɪ] *adj* ~ *to,* enterado,-a, de.

prize [praɪz] *n* premio. – 2 *adj* selecto,-a. – 3 *t* apreciar. 4 → **prise.**

probability [prɒbə'bɪlɪtɪ] *n* probabilidad.

probable ['prɒbəbəl] *adj* probable. – 2 *probably adv* probablemente.

probation [prə'beɪʃən] *n* JUR libertad condicional.

probe [prəʊb] *n* sonda. 2 *(investigation)* investigación. – 3 *t* sond(e)ar. 4 *(investigate)* investigar.

problem ['prɒbləm] *n* problema *m.*

problematic(al) [prɒblə'mætɪk(əl)] *adj* problemático,-a.

procedure [prə'si:dʒər] *n* procedimiento.

proceed [prə'si:d] *i* (pro)seguir.

proceedings [prə'si:dɪŋz] *npl* actas *fpl.* ●*JUR to take* ~ *against sb.,* proceder contra algn.

proceeds ['prəʊsi:dz] *npl* beneficios *mpl.*

process ['prəʊses] *n* proceso. – 2 *t* procesar. 3 *(photo)* revelar.

procession [prə'seʃən] *n* desfile *m,* procesión.

proclaim [prə'kleɪm] *t* proclamar.

proclamation [prɒklə'meɪʃən] *n* proclamación.

procrastinate [prə'kræstɪneɪt] *i* aplazar una decisión.

procreation [prəʊkrɪ'eɪʃən] *n* procreación.

procure [prə'kjʊəʳ] *t* conseguir, obtener. — **2** *i* alcahuetear.

prod [prɒd] *n* golpe *m*. — **2** *t* golpear.

prodigal ['prɒdɪgəl] *adj* pródigo,-a.

prodigious [prə'dɪdʒəs] *adj* prodigioso,-a.

prodigy ['prɒdɪdʒɪ] *n* prodigio.

produce ['prɒdjuːs] *n* productos *mpl* (agrícolas). — **2** *t gen* producir. **3** *(show)* enseñar. **4** *(cause)* causar. **5** RAD TV realizar. **6** CINEM producir. **7** THEAT dirigir. ▲ *De 2 a 7 (verbo)* [prə'djuːs].

producer [prə'djuːsəʳ] *n* productor,-ra. **2** RAD TV realizador,-ra. **3** CINEM director,-ra.

product ['prɒdəkt] *n gen* producto. **2** *(result)* resultado, fruto.

production [prə'dʌkʃən] *n gen* producción. **2** *(showing)* presentación. **3** RAD TV realización. **4** CINEM producción. **5** THEAT representación.

productive [prə'dʌktɪv] *adj* productivo,-a. **2** *(fertile)* fértil.

productivity [prɒdʌk'tɪvɪtɪ] *n* productividad.

profane [prə'feɪn] *adj* sacrílego,-a. — **2** *t* profanar.

profess [prə'fes] *t* profesar, declarar. **2** *(claim)* pretender.

profession [prə'feʃən] *n* profesión.

professional [prə'feʃənəl] *adj-n* profesional *(mf)*.

professor [prə'fəsəʳ] *n* catedrático,-a.

proffer ['prɒfəʳ] *t* ofrecer.

proficiency [prə'fɪʃənsɪ] *n* pericia, habilidad.

proficient [prə'fɪʃənt] *adj* hábil, perito,-a: *he/she's ~ in French,* tiene un buen nivel de/en francés.

profile ['prəʊfaɪl] *n* perfil *m*. ●*in ~,* de perfil.

profit ['prɒfɪt] *n* FIN ganancia, beneficio. **2** *fig* provecho. — **3** *i* ganar. **4** *fig* sacar provecho de. ■ *~ and loss,* ganancias y pérdidas.

profitable ['prɒfɪtəbəl] *adj* FIN rentable. **2** *fig* provechoso,-a.

profound [prə'faʊnd] *adj* profundo,-a.

profuse [prə'fjuːs] *adj* profuso,-a. — **2** *profusely adv* con profusión.

profusion [prə'fjuːʒən] *n* profusión.

progeny ['prɒdʒənɪ] *n* prole *f*.

prognosticate [prɒg'nɒstɪkeɪt] *t* pronosticar.

programme ['prəʊgræm] *n* programa *m*. — **2** *t* programar. ▲ US *y* COMPUT *se escribe* **program**.

programmer, US **programer** ['prəʊgræməʳ] *n* programador,-ra.

progress ['prəʊgres] *n* progreso, avance *m*. — **2** *i* progresar, avanzar. ●*to make ~,* avanzar; *(improve)* mejorar. ▲ *En 2 (verbo)* [prəʊ'gres].

progressive [prə'gresɪv] *adj* progresivo,-a. — **2** *adj-n* POL progresista *(mf)*.

prohibit [prə'hɪbɪt] *t* prohibir.

prohibition [prəʊɪ'bɪʃən] *n* prohibición.

project ['prɒdʒekt] *n* proyecto. — **2** *t* proyectar. — **3** *i* sobresalir. ▲ *En 2 y 3 (verbo)* [prə'dʒekt].

projectile [prə'dʒektaɪl] *n* proyectil *m*.

projector [prə'dʒektəʳ] *n* proyector *m*.

proletarian [prəʊlə'tɜərɪən] *adj* proletario,-a.

proletariat [prəʊlə'teərɪət] *n* proletariado.

proliferate [prə'lɪfəreɪt] *i* proliferar.

proliferation [prəlɪfə'reɪʃən] *n* proliferación.

prolific [prə'lɪfɪk] *adj* prolífico,-a.

prologue ['prəʊlɒg] *n* prólogo.

prolong [prə'lɒŋ] *t* prolongar, alargar.

promenade [prɒmə'nɑːd] *n* paseo (marítimo).

prominence ['prɒmɪnəns] *n* prominencia. **2** *fig* importancia.

prominent ['prɒmɪnənt] *adj* prominente. **2** *fig* importante.

promiscuous [prə'mɪskjʊəs] *adj* promiscuo,-a.

promise ['prɒmɪs] *n* promesa. — **2** *t-i* prometer.

promising ['prɒmɪsɪŋ] *adj* prometedor,-ra.

promontory ['prɒməntərɪ] *n* promontorio.

promote [prə'məʊt] *t (in rank)* promover, ascender. **2** *(encourage)* promover, fomentar. **3** COM promocionar. ●SP *to be promoted,* subir de categoría.

promotion [prə'məʊʃən] *n* promoción. **2** *(encouragement)* fomento.

prompt [prɒmpt] *adj* pronto,-a, rápido,-a. **2** *(punctual)* puntual. — **3** *adv* en punto. — **4** *t (move)* motivar. **5** THEAT apuntar.

prompter ['prɒmptəʳ] *n* apuntador,-ra.

prone [prəʊn] *adj* boca abajo. ●~ *to,* propenso,-a a.

prong [prɒŋ] *n* púa.

pronoun ['prəʊnaʊn] *n* pronombre *m*.

pronounce [prə'naʊns] *t* pronunciar. **2** *(declare)* declarar. ●*to* ~ *sentence,* dictar sentencia.

pronounced [prə'naʊnst] *adj* pronunciado,-a, marcado,-a.

pronunciation [prənʌnsɪ'eɪʃən] *n* pronunciación.

proof [pru:f] *n gen* prueba. **2** *(alcohol)* graduación. ●~ *against,* a prueba de.

prop [prɒp] *n* puntual. **2** *fig* apoyo. **3** THEAT accesorio. – **4** *t to* ~ *(up),* apuntalar. **5** *fig* apoyar, sostener.

propaganda [prɒpə'gændə] *n* propaganda.

propagate ['prɒpəgeɪt] *t-i* propagar(se).

propagation [prɒpə'geɪʃən] *n* propagación.

propel [prə'pel] *t* propulsar, impulsar.

propeller [prə'pelə^r] *n* hélice *f*.

propensity [prə'pensɪtɪ] *n* propensión.

proper ['prɒpə^r] *adj (suitable)* adecuado,-a. **2** *(right)* correcto,-a. **3** *(decent)* decente. **4** *(after noun)* propiamente dicho,-a. **5** *fam (real)* auténtico,-a; *(as it should be)* como Dios manda, en condiciones. – **7** *properly adv* bien, correctamente. ■ ~ *noun,* nombre propio.

property ['prɒpətɪ] *n gen* propiedad. **2** THEAT accesorios *mpl*. ■ *personal* ~, bienes *mpl* personales.

prophecy ['prɒfəsɪ] *n* profecía.

prophesy ['prɒfəsaɪ] *t-i* predecir. **2** REL profetizar.

prophet ['prɒfɪt] *n* profeta *m*.

prophetic [prə'fetɪk] *adj* profético,-a.

propitiate [prə'pɪʃɪeɪt] *i* propiciar.

propitious [prə'pɪʃəs] *adj* propicio,-a.

proportion [prə'pɔ:ʃən] *n* proporción.

proportional [prə'pɔ:ʃənəl] proporcional.

proportionate [prə'pɔ:ʃənət] *adj* proporcionado,-a.

proposal [prə'pəʊzəl] *n* propuesta.

propose [prə'pəʊz] *t* proponer(se). – **2** *i* declararse *(to,* a).

proposition [prɒpə'zɪʃən] *n* proposición. **2** *(business)* negocio.

propound [prə'paʊnd] *t* exponer.

proprietor [prə'praɪətə^r] *n* propietario,-a, dueño,-a.

propriety [prə'praɪətɪ] *n* corrección, decencia. **2** *(suitability)* conveniencia.

propulsion [prə'pʌlʃən] *n* propulsión.

prose [prəʊz] *n* prosa.

prosecute ['prɒsɪkju:t] *t* procesar, enjuiciar.

prosecution [prɒsɪ'kju:ʃən] *n (action)* proceso, juicio. **2** *(person)* parte acusadora.

prosecutor ['prɒsɪkju:tə^r] *n* acusador,-ra. ■ *public* ~, fiscal *(mf)*.

prospect ['prɒspekt] *n* perspectiva. **2** *(probability)* probabilidad. – **3** *t* explorar. – **4** *i to* ~ *for,* buscar. ▲ *En 3 y 4 (verbo)* [prə'spekt].

prospective [prə'spektɪv] *adj* futuro,-a. **2** *(possible)* posible.

prospectus [prə'spektəs] *n* prospecto.

prosper ['prɒspə^r] *i* prosperar.

prosperity [prɒ'sperɪtɪ] *n* prosperidad.

prosperous ['prɒspərəs] *adj* próspero,-a.

prostate ['prɒsteɪt] *n* próstata.

prostitute ['prɒstɪtju:t] *n* prostituta.

prostitution [prɒstɪ'tju:ʃən] *n* prostitución.

prostrate ['prɒstreɪt] *adj* postrado,-a. – **2** *t* postrar. ▲ *En 2 (verbo)* [prɒ'streɪt].

protagonist [prəʊ'tægənɪst] *n* protagonista *mf*.

protect [prə'tekt] *t* proteger.

protection [prə'tekʃən] *n* protección.

protective [prə'tektɪv] *adj* protector,-ra.

protector [prə'tektə^r] *n (person)* protector,-ra. **2** *(thing)* protector *m*.

protégé(e) ['prəʊtəʒeɪ] *n* protegido,-a.

protein ['prəʊti:n] *n* proteína.

protest ['prəʊtest] *n* protesta. – **2** *t-i* protestar. ▲ *En 2 (verbo)* [prə'test].

Protestant ['prɒtɪstənt] *adj-n* protestante *(mf)*.

protocol ['prəʊtəkɒl] *n* protocolo.

prototype ['prəʊtətaɪp] *n* prototipo.

protracted [prə'træktɪd] *t* prolongado,-a.

protractor [prə'træktə^r] *n* transportador *m*.

protrude [prə'tru:d] *i* sobresalir.

protruding [prə'tru:dɪŋ] *adj* saliente, prominente.

protuberance [prə'tju:bərəns] *n* protuberancia.

proud [praʊd] *adj* orgulloso,-a. ●*to be* ~ *of,* enorgullecerse de; *to be* ~ *to,* tener el honor de.

prove [pru:v] *t* probar, demostrar. – **2** *i (turn out to be)* resultar. ▲ *pp* **proved** o **proven** ['pru:vən].

proverb ['prɒvɜ:b] *n* proverbio, refrán *m*.

proverbial [prə'vɜ:bɪəl] *adj* proverbial.

provide [prə'vaɪd] *t* proporcionar, facilitar, suministrar. **2** *(law)* estipular.

provided [prə'vaɪdɪd] *conj* ~ *(that),* siempre que, con tal que.
providence ['prɒvɪdəns] *n* providencia.
provident ['prɒvɪdənt] *adj* previsor,-ra.
provindential [prɒvɪ'denʃəl] *adj* providencial.
providing [prə'vaɪdɪŋ] *conj* → **provided**.
province ['prɒvɪns] *n* provincia. ●*fig it's not my* ~, no es de mi competencia/incumbencia.
provincial [prə'vɪnʃəl] *adj* provincial. 2 *pej* provinciano,-a,
provision [prə'vɪʒən] *n* provisión. 2 JUR disposición. ●*to make* ~ *for,* prever.
provisional [prə'vɪʒənəl] *adj* provisional.
proviso [prə'vaɪzəʊ] *n* condición.
provocative [prə'vɒkətɪv] *adj* provocativo,-a.
provoke [prə'vəʊk] *t* provocar.
provoking [prə'vəʊkɪŋ] *adj* provocador,-ra.
prow [praʊ] *n* proa.
prowess ['praʊəs] *n* destreza, habilidad.
prowl [praʊl] *i* merodear.
proximity ['prɒksɪmɪtɪ] *n* proximidad.
proxy ['prɒksɪ] *n* poder *m.* 2 *(person)* apoderado,-a. ●*by* ~, por poder(es).
prude [pruːd] *n* remilgado,-a, mojigato,-a.
prudence ['pruːdəns] *n* prudencia.
prudent ['pruːdənt] *adj* prudente.
prudish ['pruːdɪʃ] *adj* remilgado,-a.
prune [pruːn] *n* ciruela pasa. – 2 *t* podar.
pry [praɪ] *i* husmear. – 2 *t* → **pise**.
psalm [sɑːm] *n* salmo.
pseudonym ['suːdənɪm] *n* seudónimo.
psyche ['saɪkɪ] *n* psique *f.*
psychiatrist [saɪ'kaɪətrɪst] *n* psiquiatra *mf.*
psychoanalysis [saɪkəʊə'nælɪsɪs] *n* psicoanálisis *m inv.*
psychoanalyst [saɪkəʊ'ænəlɪst] *n* psicoanalista *mf.*
psychological [saɪkə'lɒdʒɪkəl] *adj* psicológico,-a.
psychologist [saɪ'kɒlədʒɪst] *n* psicólogo,-a.
psychology [saɪ'kɒlədʒɪ] *n* psicología.
psychopath ['saɪkəʊpæθ] *n* psicópata *mf.*
psychosis [saɪ'kəʊsɪs] *n* psicosis *f inv.*
pub [pʌb] *n* bar *m,* pub *m,* taberna.
puberty ['pjuːbətɪ] *n* pubertad.
pubic ['pjuːbɪk] *adj* púbico,-a.
public ['pʌblɪk] *adj-n* público,-a *(m).* ■ ~ *house,* bar *m,* pub *m.*
publication [pʌblɪ'keɪʃən] *n* publicación.

publicity [pʌ'blɪsɪtɪ] *n* publicidad.
publicize [pʌblɪ'saɪz] *t* divulgar, hacer público,-a. 2 *(advertise)* promocionar.
publish ['pʌblɪʃ] *t* publicar, editar.
publisher ['pʌblɪʃər] *n* editor,-ra. 2 *(company)* editorial *f.*
pucker ['pʌkər] *n* arruga, pliegue *m.* – 2 *t* arrugar, plegar.
pudding ['pʊdɪŋ] *n* budín *m,* pudín *m.* 2 *fam* postre *m.*
puddle ['pʌdəl] *n* charco.
puerile ['pjʊəraɪl] *adj* pueril.
puff [pʌf] *n* soplo, bufido. 2 *(at cigarette)* fumada; *(of smoke)* humareda. – 3 *i* soplar. 4 *(pant)* jadear. ◆*to* ~ *up* *t-i* hinchar(se). ■ ~ *pastry,* hojaldre *m.*
puke ['pjuːk] *i fam* vomitar.
pull [pʊl] *n* tirón *m,* sacudida. 2 *(on drawer etc.)* tirador *m.* 3 *(attraction)* atracción. 4 *fam (influence)* influencia. – 5 *t* tirar de, dar un tirón a. 6 *(drag)* arrastrar. 7 *fam (attract)* atraer. – 8 *i* tirar. ◆*to* ~ *away* *i* salir. ◆*to* ~ *down* *t* derribar. ◆*to* ~ *in* *t* atraer. – 2 *i (train)* entrar en la estación. ◆*to* ~ *off* *t* llevar a cabo. ◆*to* ~ *out* *t* arrancar. – 2 *i (train)* salir de la estación. 3 *(withdraw)* retirarse. ◆*to* ~ *through* *i* reponerse. ◆*to* ~ *together* *i* trabajar como equipo. – 2 *t* to ~ *o.s. together,* serenarse. ◆*to* ~ *up* *t* arrancar. – 2 *i* detenerse. ●*to* ~ *a face,* hacer una mueca; *to* ~ *a gun on sb.,* amenazar a algn. con una pistola; *to* ~ *sb.'s leg,* tomar el pelo a algn.; *to* ~ *sth. to pieces,* hacer algo a pedazos; *to* ~ *strings,* tocar teclas; *fam to* ~ *a fast one on sb.,* hacer una mala jugada a algn.
pulley ['pʊlɪ] *n* polea.
pullover ['pʊləʊvər] *n* pullover *m.*
pulp [pʌlp] *n* pulpa. 2 *(wood)* pasta.
pulpit ['pʊlpɪt] *n* púlpito.
pulsate [pʌl'seɪt] *i* pulsar, latir.
pulse [pʌls] *n* pulsación. 2 ANAT pulso. 3 BOT legumbre *f.* – 4 *i* pulsar, latir.
pulverize ['pʌlvəraɪz] *t* pulverizar.
puma ['pjuːmə] *n* puma *m.*
pumice stone ['pʌmɪsstəʊn] *n* piedra pómez.
pump [pʌmp] *n* bomba. 2 *(shoe)* zapatilla. – 3 *t* bombear. 4 *fam (for information)* sonsacar. ■ *petrol* ~, surtidor de gasolina.
pumpkin ['pʌmpkɪn] *n* calabaza.
pun [pʌn] *n* juego de palabras.
Punch [pʌntʃ] *n* polichinela *m.*
punch [pʌntʃ] *n (blow)* puñetazo. 2 *(drink)* ponche *m.* 3 *(tool)* punzón *m;* *(for tickets)* taladro. 4 *fig* empuje *m.* – 5 *t* dar

un puñetazo a. **6** *(make a hole in)* taladrar; *(ticket)* picar.

punch-up [ˈpʌntʃʌp] *n fam* riña, pelea.

punctilious [pʌŋkˈtɪlɪəs] *adj* puntilloso,-a.

punctual [ˈpʌŋktjʊəl] *adj* puntual.

punctuality [pʌŋktjʊˈælɪtɪ] *n* puntualidad.

punctuate [ˈpʌŋktjʊeɪt] *t* puntuar.

punctuation [pʌŋktjʊˈeɪʃən] *n* puntuación.

puncture [ˈpʌŋktʃəʳ] *n* pinchazo. **– 2** *t-i* pinchar(se).

pungent [ˈpʌndʒənt] *adj (smell)* acre. **2** *(taste)* picante. **3** *fig* mordaz.

punish [ˈpʌnɪʃ] *t* castigar.

punishment [ˈpʌnɪʃmənt] *n* castigo.

punk [pʌŋk] *n fam* punk *mf*.

punnet [ˈpʌnɪt] *n* cestita.

punt [pʌnt] *n* batea. **– 2** *i* ir en batea. **3** GB *fam* apostar.

punter [ˈpʌntəʳ] *n fam* apostante *mf*. **2** *(customer)* cliente,-a *m,f*.

puny [ˈpjuːnɪ] *adj* endeble, canijo,-a.

pup [pʌp] *n* cachorro,-a.

pupil [ˈpjuːpɪl] *n* alumno,-a. **2** ANAT pupila.

puppet [ˈpʌpɪt] *n* títere *m*, marioneta. **2** *fig* títere.

puppy [ˈpʌpɪ] *n* cachorro,-a.

purchase [ˈpɜːtʃəs] *n* compra. **2** *(hold)* agarre *m*. **– 3** *t* comprar, adquirir. ■ *purchasing power*, poder *m* adquisitivo.

purchaser [ˈpɜːtʃəsəʳ] *n* comprador,-ra.

pure [pjʊəʳ] *adj* puro,-a. **– 2** *purely adv* simplemente.

purée [ˈpjʊəreɪ] *n* puré *m*. **– 2** *t* hacer un puré de.

purgative [ˈpɜːgətɪv] *n* purgante *m*.

purgatory [ˈpɜːgətərɪ] *n* purgatorio.

purge [pɜːdʒ] *n* purga. **– 2** *t* purgar.

purification [pjʊərɪfɪˈkeɪʃən] *n* purificación. **2** *(of water)* depuración.

purifier [ˈpjʊərɪfaɪəʳ] *n* purificador *m*.

Puritan [ˈpjʊərɪtən] *adj-n* puritano,-a.

purity [ˈpjʊərɪtɪ] *n* pureza.

purple [ˈpɜːpəl] *adj* purpúreo,-a, morado,-a. **– 2** *n* púrpura, color *m* morado.

purport [pɜːˈpɔːt] *n* significado. **– 2** *t* pretender, dar a entender.

purpose [ˈpɜːpəs] *n* propósito. **2** *(use)* utilidad. **– 3** *purposely adv* a propósito. ●*on ~*, de propósito.

purposeful [ˈpɜːpəsfʊl] *adj* decidido,-a.

purr [pɜːʳ] *n* ronroneo. **– 2** *i* ronronear.

purse [pɜːs] *n* GB monedero. **2** US bolso. **3** *(prize)* premio. **– 4** *t* apretar.

pursue [pəˈsjuː] *t* perseguir. **2** *(studies)* seguir.

pursuer [pəˈsjuːəʳ] *n* perseguidor,-ra.

pursuit [pəˈsjuːt] *n* persecución. **2** *(occupation)* actividad, pasatiempo.

purveyor [pɜːˈveɪəʳ] *n* proveedor,-ra.

pus [pʌs] *n* pus *m*.

push [pʊʃ] *n* empujón *m*, empuje *m*. **– 2** *t-i gen* empujar. **– 3** *t (button)* pulsar, apretar. **4** *fam (try to sell)* promocionar. **5** *fam (person)* presionar. ◆*to ~ around* *t* dar órdenes a. ◆*to ~ off* *i fam* largarse. ◆*to ~ on* *i* seguir, continuar. ●*to give sb. the ~*, poner a algn. de patitas en la calle; *to ~ one's luck*, arriesgarse demasiado.

pushchair [ˈpʊʃtʃeəʳ] *n* sillita (de ruedas).

pusher [ˈpʊʃəʳ] *n fam (of drugs)* camello.

pushover [ˈpʊʃəʊvəʳ] *n fam it's a ~*, está chupado.

pushy [ˈpʊʃɪ] *adj fam* insistente.

pussy [ˈpʊsɪ] *n* minino.

put [pʊt] *t gen* poner, colocar. **2** *(express)* expresar. **3** *(write)* escribir. **4** SP *(shot)* lanzar. ◆*to ~ across* *t* comunicar. ◆*to ~ aside* *t* guardar. ◆*to ~ away* *t* guardar. ◆*to ~ back* *t* atrasar. **2** *(replace)* devolver a su sitio. ◆*to ~ down* *t* dejar. **2** *(rebellion)* sofocar. **3** *(animal)* sacrificar. **4** *(write)* apuntar, escribir. **5** *fam (humble)* humillar. ◆*to ~ down to* *t* atribuir a. ◆*to ~ forward* *t* proponer. ◆*to ~ in* *i (ship)* hacer escala. ◆*to ~ in for* *t* solicitar. ◆*to ~ off* *t (postpone)* aplazar. **2** *(distract)* distraer. **3** *(discourage)* desanimar, quitar las ganas a uno. ◆*to ~ on* *t gen* poner. **2** *(clothes, glasses, etc.)* ponerse. **3** *(weight, speed)* ganar. **4** *(play, show)* montar. ◆*to ~ out* *t (fire, light)* apagar. **2** *(cause trouble to)* molestar. ◆*to ~ over* *t* comunicar. ◆*to ~ through* *t (on 'phone)* conectar (*to*, con). ◆*to ~ to* *t* proponer. ◆*to ~ together* *t (gather)* reunir, juntar. **2** *(assemble)* montar. ◆*to ~ up* *t (lodge)* alojar. **2** *(tent)* armar. **3** *(building)* construir. **4** *(things on wall)* colocar. **5** *(prices, taxes)* aumentar, subir. ◆*to ~ up with* *t* soportar, aguantar. ●*~ together*, juntos,-as; *to be hard ~ to do sth.*, hacérsele a uno cuesta arriba hacer algo; *to ~ an end to*, acabar con; *to ~ a question to sb.*, hacerle una pregunta a algn.; *to ~ it about that*, hacer correr la voz que; *to ~ one over on sb.*, engañar a algn.; *to ~ right*, arreglar; *to ~ sb. up to sth.*, incitar a algn. a hacer algo; *to ~ the blame on*, echar la culpa a; *to ~ the clocks back/forward*, retrasar/adelantar la hora; *to ~ to bed*, acostar; *to ~ to death,* ejecutar; *to ~ to sea,* zarpar; *to ~ to the vote,* someter a votación; *to ~ two and two together,* atar cabos; *to ~ up a fight,* ofrecer resistencia; *to ~ up for sale,* poner en venta; *fam to ~ paid to,* acabar con; *fam to stay ~,* quedarse quieto,-a.

putrefy ['pjuːtrɪfaɪ] *i* pudrirse.

putsch [pʊtʃ] *n* golpe *m* de estado.

putrid ['pjuːtrɪd] *adj* pútrido,-a.

putt [pʌt] *n* tiro al hoyo. − **2** *t-i* tirar al hoyo.

putty ['pʌtɪ] *n* masilla.

puzzle ['pʌzəl] *n* rompecabezas *m inv,* puzle *m.* **2** *(mystery)* misterio. − **3** *t* dejar perplejo,-a. ◆*to ~ out t* descifrar, resolver. ●*to ~ about/over sth.,* dar vueltas a algo (en la cabeza).

puzzled ['pʌzəld] *adj* perplejo,-a.

puzzling ['pʌzəlɪŋ] *adj* extraño,-a.

pygmy ['pɪgmɪ] *adj-n* pigmeo,-a, enano,-a.

pyjamas [pəˈdʒɑːməz] *npl* pijama *m sing.*

pylon ['paɪlən] *n* torre *f* (de tendido eléctrico).

pyramid ['pɪrəmɪd] *n* pirámide *f.*

pyre ['paɪəʳ] *n* pira, hoguera.

pyromaniac [paɪrəʊˈmeɪnɪæk] *n* pirómano,-a.

python ['paɪθən] *n* pitón *m.*

Q

quack [kwæk] *n* graznido. **2** *(doctor)* curandero,-a. — **3** *i* graznar.

quad [kwɒd] *n* GB patio interior. **2** *fam (quadruplet)* cuatrillizo,-a.

quadrangle [ˈkwɒdræŋgəl] *n* patio interior.

quadrant [ˈkwɒdrənt] *n* cuadrante *m.*

quadraphonic [kwɒdrəˈfɒnɪk] *adj* cuadrafónico,-a.

quadruped [ˈkwɒdrʊped] *n* cuadrúpedo.

quadruple [ˈkwɒdrʊpəl] *n* cuádruplo. — **2** *adj* cuádruple. — **3** *t-i* cuadruplicar(se).

quadruplet [ˈkwɒdrʊplət] *n* cuatrillizo,-a.

quagmire [ˈkwɒgmaɪəʳ] *n* cenagal *m.*

quail [kweɪl] *n* codorniz *f.* — **2** *i* acobardarse.

quaint [kweɪnt] *adj* pintoresco,-a, típico,-a. **2** *(odd)* singular, original.

quake [kweɪk] *n* *fam* terremoto. — **2** *i* temblar.

Quaker [ˈkweɪkəʳ] *adj-n* cuáquero,-a.

qualification [kwɒlɪfɪˈkeɪʃən] *n* *(for job)* requisito. **2** *(paper)* diploma *m,* título. **3** *(reservation)* reserva, salvedad.

qualified [ˈkwɒlɪfaɪd] *adj* *(for job)* capacitado,-a.

qualify [ˈkwɒlɪfaɪ] *t* *(entitle)* capacitar. **2** *(modify)* modificar, matizar. — **3** *i* reunir las condiciones necesarias. **4** *(obtain degree)* obtener el título (*as,* de). **5** SP calificarse.

qualitative [ˈkwɒlɪtətɪv] *adj* cualitativo,-a.

quality [ˈkwɒlɪtɪ] *n* calidad. **2** *(attribute)* cualidad.

qualm [kwɑːm] *n* duda, inquietud. ●*to have no qualms about doing sth.,* no tener escrúpulos en hacer algo.

quandary [ˈkwɒndərɪ] *n* dilema *m.*

quantify [ˈkwɒntɪfaɪ] *t* cuantificar.

quantity [ˈkwɒntɪtɪ] *n* cantidad.

quarantine [ˈkwɒrənti:n] *n* cuarentena. — **2** *t* poner en cuarentena.

quarrel [ˈkwɒrəl] *n* riña, disputa. — **2** *i* reñir, pelear, disputar.

quarrelsome [ˈkwɒrəlsəm] *adj* pendenciero,-a.

quarry [ˈkwɒrɪ] *n* cantera. **2** *(in hunting)* presa. — **3** *t* extraer.

quart [kwɔ:t] *n* cuarto de galón. ▲ GB = 1,14 *litros;* US = *0,95 litros.*

quarter [ˈkwɔ:təʳ] *n* cuarto. **2** *(area)* barrio. **3** *(three months)* trimestre *m.* **4** US *(moneda de)* veinticinco centavos. **5** *pl* alojamiento *m sing.* — **6** *t* dividir en cuatro. **7** *(reduce)* reducir a la cuarta parte. **8** *(lodge)* alojar. ●*from all quarters,* de todas partes; *to give no* ~, no dar cuartel.

quarterfinal [kwɔ:təˈfaɪnəl] *n* cuarto de final.

quarterly [ˈkwɔ:təlɪ] *adj* trimestral. — **2** *adv* trimestralmente. — **3** *n* revista trimestral.

quartermaster [ˈkwɔ:təmɑ:stəʳ] *n* oficial *m* de intendencia.

quartet [kwɔ:ˈtet] *n* cuarteto.

quartz [kwɔ:ts] *n* cuarzo.

quash [kwɒʃ] *t* sofocar. **2** JUR anular.

quaver [ˈkweɪvəʳ] *n* *(note)* corchea. **2** *(voice)* trémolo. — **3** *i* temblar.

quay [ki:] *n* muelle *m.*

queasy [ˈkwi:zɪ] *adj* mareado,-a.

queen [kwi:n] *n* reina. **2** *sl* loca. ■ ~ *bee,* abeja reina; ~ *mother,* reina madre.

queer [kwɪəʳ] *adj* raro,-a, extraño.-a. **2** *(ill)* malucho,-a. **3** *fam* gay. — **4** *n* *fam* gay *m.*

quell [kwel] *t* reprimir, sofocar.

quench [kwentʃ] *t* saciar. **2** *(fire)* apagar.

querulous [ˈkwerjʊləs] *adj* quejumbroso,-a.

query ['kwɪərɪ] *n* pregunta, duda. − **2** *t* poner en duda.

quest [kwest] *n* búsqueda.

question ['kwestʃən] *n* pregunta. **2** *(matter)* cuestión. **3** *(topic)* cuestión, problema, asunto. − **4** *t* hacer preguntas a, interrogar. **5** *(cast doubt on)* cuestionar, poner en duda. ●*out of the ~,* imposible; *to call into ~,* poner en duda. ■ *~ mark,* interrogante *m.*

questionable ['kwestʃənəbəl] *adj* cuestionable, discutible. **2** *(doubtful)* dudoso,-a, sospechoso,-a.

questionnaire [kwestʃə'neər] *n* cuestionario.

queue [kju:] *n* cola. − **2** *i* hacer cola.

quibble ['kwɪbəl] *n* pega. − **2** *i* poner pegas.

quick [kwɪk] *adj* rápido,-a. **2** *(clever)* espabilado,-a, despierto,-a. − **3** *quickly adv* rápido, rápidamente. ●*to cut to the ~,* herir en lo vivo; *to have a ~ temper,* tener un genio vivo.

quicken ['kwɪkən] *t-i* acelerar(se).

quickie ['kwɪkɪ] *n fam* uno,-a rápido,-a.

quicksand ['kwɪksænd] *n* arenas *fpl* movedizas.

quick-tempered [kwɪk'tempəd] *adj* de genio vivo.

quick-witted [kwɪk wɪtɪd] *adj* agudo,-a, listo,-a.

quid [kwɪd] *n inv fam* GB libra.

quiet ['kwaɪət] *adj (silent)* callado,-a, silencioso,-a. **2** *(peaceful)* tranquilo,-a. − **3** *n (silence)* silencio. **4** *(calm)* tranquilidad, calma. − **5** *t-i* US → **quieten.** − **6** *quietly adv* silenciosamente, sin hacer ruido. ●*on the ~,* a la chita callando.

quieten ['kwaɪətən] *t-i* callar(se). **2** *(calm down)* tranquilizar(se).

quietness ['kwaɪətnəs] *n (silence)* silencio. **2** *(calm)* tranquilidad .

quill [kwɪl] *n (feather)* pluma. **2** *(spine)* púa.

quilt [kwɪlt] *n* colcha, edredón *m.* − **2** *t* acolchar.

quince [kwɪns] *n* membrillo.

quinine ['kwɪniːn] *n* quinina.

quintessence [kwɪn'tesəns] *n* quintaesencia.

quintet [kwɪn'tet] *n* quinteto.

quintuplet [kwɪn'tjʊplət] *n* quintillizo,-a.

quip [kwɪp] *n* ocurrencia, chiste *m.* − **2** *i* bromear.

quirk [kwɜːk] *n* manía. **2** *(of fate)* avatar *m.*

quirky ['kwɜːkɪ] *adj* raro,-a.

quit [kwɪt] *t* dejar, abandonar. **2** *(stop)* dejar de. − **3** *i* marcharse. ●*to call it quits,* hacer las paces.

quite [kwaɪt] *adv (rather)* bastante. **2** *(totally)* completamente, realmente, verdaderamente: *I ~ understand,* lo entiendo perfectamente.

quiver ['kwɪvər] *n (for arrows)* carcaj *m.* **2** *(tremble)* temblor *m.* − **3** *i* temblar, estremecerse.

quiz [kwɪz] *n* RAD TV concurso. − **2** *t* preguntar.

quoit [kwɔɪt] *n* tejo.

quorum ['kwɔːrəm] *n* quórum *m.*

quota ['kwəʊtə] *n (share)* cuota. **2** *(fixed limit)* cupo.

quotation [kwəʊ'teɪʃən] *n* cita. **2** FIN cotización. **3** COM presupuesto. ■ *~ marks,* comillas *fpl.*

quote [kwəʊt] *n* cita. − **2** *t* citar. **3** COM dar el precio de. **4** FIN cotizar.

quotient ['kwəʊʃənt] *n* cociente *m.*

R

rabbi ['ræbaɪ] *n* rabí *m*, rabino.
rabbit ['ræbɪt] *n* conejo. ●*to ~ on,* no parar de hablar.
rabble ['ræbəl] *n* populacho.
rabble-rouser ['ræbəlrauzə^r] *n pej* demagogo,-a.
rabid ['ræbɪd] *adj* rabioso,-a. **2** *fig* furioso,-a.
rabies ['reɪbiːz] *n* rabia.
rac(c)oon [rə'kuːn] *n* mapache *m*.
race [reɪs] *n (people)* raza. **2** SP carrera. – **3** *i* correr, competir.
racecourse ['reɪskɔːs] *n* GB hipódromo.
racehorse ['reɪhɔːs] *n* caballo de carreras.
racial ['reɪʃəl] *adj* racial.
racing ['reɪsɪŋ] *n* carreras *fpl*.
racism ['reɪsɪzəm] *n* racismo.
racist ['reɪsɪst] *adj-n* racista *(mf)*.
rack [ræk] *n* estante *m*. **2** AUTO baca. **3** *(on train)* rejilla. **4** *(for plates)* escurreplatos *m inv*. **5** *(for torture)* potro. – **6** *t* atormentar. ●*to ~ one's brains,* devanarse los sesos.
racket ['rækɪt] *n* SP raqueta. **2** *(din)* alboroto, ruido. **3** *fam (fraud)* timo.
racketeer [rækə'tɪə^r] *n* timador,-ra.
raconteur [rækɒn'tɜː^r] *n* anecdotista *mf*.
racy ['reɪsɪ] *adj* atrevido,-a.
radar ['reɪdɑː^r] *n* radar *m*.
radial ['reɪdɪəl] *adj* radial.
radiance ['reɪdɪəns] *n* resplandor *m*.
radiant ['reɪdɪənt] *adj* radiante.
radiate ['reɪdɪeɪt] *t-i* irradiar.
radiation [reɪdɪ'eɪʃən] *n* radiación.
radiator ['reɪdɪeɪtə^r] *n* radiador *m*.
radical ['rædɪkəl] *adj-n* radical *(mf)*.
radio ['reɪdɪəʊ] *n* radio *f*.
radioactive [reɪdɪəʊ'æktɪv] *adj* radiactivo,-a.
radioactivity [reɪdɪəʊæk'tɪvɪtɪ] *n* radiactividad.

radio-controlled [reɪdɪəʊkɒn'trəʊld] *adj* teledirigido,-a.
radish ['rædɪʃ] *n* rábano.
radium ['reɪdɪəm] *n* radio.
radius ['reɪdɪəs] *n* radio. ▲ *pl* **radii** ['reɪdɪaɪ].
raffle ['ræfəl] *n* rifa. – **2** *t-i* rifar, sortear.
raft [rɑːft] *n* balsa.
rafter ['rɑːftə^r] *n* viga.
rag [ræg] *n* harapo, andrajo, pingajo. **2** *(for cleaning)* trapo. **3** *(joke)* broma pesada. **4** *fam (newspaper)* periódico malo. **5** GB función benéfica universitaria. – **6** *t* gastar bromas a. ●*in rags,* harapiento,-a, andrajoso,-a.
ragamuffin ['rægəmʌfɪn] *n* pilluelo,-a.
ragbag ['rægbæg] *n fam* mezcolanza.
rage [reɪdʒ] *n* rabia, furor *m*, cólera. – **2** *i (person)* rabiar. **3** *(fire etc.)* hacer estragos. ●*to be all the ~,* hacer furor; *to fly into a ~,* montar en cólera.
ragged ['rægɪd] *adj (person)* andrajoso,-a, harapiento,-a. **2** *(clothes)* roto,-a, deshilachado,-a.
raid [reɪd] *n* MIL incursión, ataque *m*. **2** *(by police)* redada. **3** *(robbery)* atraco. – **4** *t* MIL hacer una incursión en. **5** *(police)* hacer una redada en. **6** *(rob)* atracar, asaltar.
raider ['reɪdə^r] *n* MIL invasor,-ra. **2** *(robber)* atracador,-ra, asaltante *mf*.
rail [reɪl] *n* barra. **2** *(handrail)* pasamano, barand(ill)a. **3** *(for train)* raíl *m*, carril *m*, riel *m*. ●*to ~ against,* despotricar contra. ■ *~ strike,* huelga de ferroviarios.
railings ['reɪlɪŋz] *npl* verja *f sing*.
railway ['reɪlweɪ], US **railroad** ['reɪlrəʊd] *n* ferrocarril *m*.
rain [reɪn] *n* lluvia. – **2** *i* llover.
rainbow ['reɪnbəʊ] *n* arco iris.
raincoat ['reɪnkəʊt] *n* impermeable *m*.

rainfall ['reɪnfɔ:l] *n* precipitación. **2** *(quantity)* pluviosidad.

rainy ['reɪnɪ] *adj* lluvioso,-a.

raise [reɪz] *n* US → **rise**. – **2** *t (lift up)* levantar. **3** *(increase)* subir, aumentar. **4** *(laugh etc.)* provocar. **5** *(children)* criar, educar. **6** *(matter)* plantear.

raisin ['reɪzən] *n* pasa.

raja(h) ['rɑ:dʒə] *n* rajá *m*.

rake [reɪk] *n (tool)* rastrillo. **2** *(man)* libertino. – **3** *t* rastrillar. ●*to be raking it in,* estar forrándose; *to ~ up the past,* desenterrar el pasado.

rake-off ['reɪkɒf] *n sl* tajada.

rally ['rælɪ] *n*·reunión. **2** POL mitin *m*. **3** AUTO rally *m*. **4** *(tennis)* intercambio (de golpes). – **5** *i* reponerse. ◆*to ~ round i* unirse.

ram [ræm] *n* ZOOL carnero. **2** TECH pisón *m*. – **3** *t* TECH apisonar. **4** *(cram)* apretar, embutir. **5** *(crash into)* chocar contra. ■ *battering ~,* ariete *m*.

ramble ['ræmbəl] *n* excursión. – **2** *i* ir de excursión. **3** *(digress)* divagar.

rambler ['ræmblər] *n* excursionista *mf*.

rambling ['ræmblɪŋ] *adj (speech etc.)* enmarañado,-a. **2** *(house etc.)* laberíntico,-a.

ramp [ræmp] *n* rampa.

rampage [ræm'peɪdʒ] *i* comportarse como un loco.

rampant ['ræmpənt] *adj* incontrolado,-a.

rampart ['ræmpɑ:t] *n* muralla.

ramshackle ['ræmʃækəl] *adj* destartalado,-a.

ran [ræn] *pt* → **run**.

ranch [rænt∫] *n* rancho, hacienda.

rancher ['rænt∫ər] *n* ranchero,-a.

rancid ['rænsɪd] *adj* rancio,-a.

rancorous ['ræŋkərəs] *adj* rencoroso,-a.

rancour ['ræŋkər] *n* rencor *m*.

random ['rændəm] *adj* fortuito,-a. ●*at ~,* al azar.

randy ['rændɪ] *adj fam* cachondo,-a.

rang [ræŋ] *pp* → **ring**.

range [reɪndʒ] *n (choice)* gama, surtido. **2** *(reach)* alcance *m*. **3** *(of mountains)* cordillera, sierra. – **4** *i* variar, oscilar: *they ~ from ... to...,* van desde ... hasta ... . **5** *(wander)* vagar *(over,* por). ■ *firing ~,* campo de tiro.

rank [ræŋk] *n (line)* fila. **2** MIL *(position)* graduación. – **3** *i (be)* figurar, estar. – **4** *adj (plants)* exuberante. **5** *(smelly)* fétido,-a. **6** *(complete)* total, completo,-a.

ranking ['ræŋkɪŋ] *n* clasificación, ranking *m*.

rankle ['ræŋkəl] *i* doler.

ransack ['rænsæk] *t* saquear, desvalijar. **2** *(search)* registrar.

ransom ['rænsəm] *n* rescate *m*. **2** *t* rescatar. ●*to hold to ~,* pedir rescate por.

rant [rænt] *i* vociferar.

rap [ræp] *n* golpe *m* seco. **2** MUS rap *m*. – **3** *i* golpear. ●*to take the~,* pagar el pato.

rape [reɪp] *n* violación. **2** BOT colza. – **3** *t* violar.

rapid ['ræpɪd] *adj* rápido,-a. – **2** *npl* rápidos *mpl*.

rapidity [rə'pɪdɪtɪ] *n* rapidez *f*.

rapier ['reɪpɪər] *n* estoque *m*.

rapist ['reɪpɪst] *n* violador,-ra.

rapport [ræ'pɔːr] *n* compenetración.

rapt [ræpt] *adj* arrebatado,-a, absorto,-a.

rapture ['ræpt∫ər] *n* éxtasis *m inv*.

rapturous ['ræpt∫ərəs] *adj* entusiasta.

rare [reər] *adj (uncommom)* poco común, raro,-a. **2** *(air)* enrarecido,-a. **3** CULIN poco hecho,-a. – **4** *rarely adv* raras veces.

rarefied ['reərɪfaɪd] *adj* enrarececido,-a.

rarity ['reərɪtɪ] *n* rareza.

raring ['reərɪŋ] *adj fam* con unas ganas locas de.

rascal ['rɑːskəl] *n* bribón *m*, pillo.

rash [ræ∫] *adj* imprudente. – **2** *n* MED sarpullido. **3** *(series)* sucesión.

rasher ['ræ∫ər] *n (of bacon)* loncha.

rasp [rɑːsp] *n* escofina. – **2** *t* raspar. **3** *(say)* decir con voz áspera.

raspberry ['rɑːzbərɪ] *n* frambuesa. **2** *fam (noise)* pedorreta.

rasping ['rɑːspɪŋ] *adj (voice)* áspero,-a.

rat [ræt] *n* rata. **2** *fam* canalla *m*. ●*to ~ on sb./a promise,* chivar a algn./romper una promesa; *to smell a ~,* olerse algo raro.

ratchet ['ræt∫ɪt] *n* trinquete *m*.

rate [reɪt] *n* tasa, índice *m*. **2** *(speed)* velocidad. **3** *(price)* tarifa, precio. **4** *pl* GB contribución *f sing* urbana. – **5** *t* considerar. **6** *(fix value)* tasar. ●*at any ~,* de todos modos; *at the ~ of,* a razón de; *first/second ~,* de primera/segunda (categoría). ■ *exchange/interest ~,* tipo de cambio/interés.

ratepayer ['reɪtpeɪər] *n* GB contribuyente *mf*.

rather ['rɑːðər] *adv* bastante, algo, un tanto. ●*I would ~,* preferiría; *or ~,* o mejor dicho; *~ than,* en vez de, mejor que.

ratify ['rætɪfaɪ] *t* ratificar.

rating ['reɪtɪŋ] *n* valoración. **2** MAR marinero. **3** *pl* TV índice *m* *sing* de audiencia.
ratio ['reɪʃɪəʊ] *n* razón *f*, relación, proporción.
ration ['ræʃən] *n* ración. – **2** *t* racionar.
rational ['ræʃənəl] *adj* racional.
rationale [ræʃə'nɑ:l] *n* fundamento.
rationalize ['ræʃənəlaɪz] *t* racionalizar.
rationing ['ræʃənɪŋ] *n* racionamiento.
rattle ['rætəl] *n* (*baby's*) sonajero. **2** (*instrument*) carraca, matraca. **3** (*noise*) traqueteo. – **4** *t-i* (hacer) sonar. – **5** *t* *fam* poner nervioso,-a. ◆**to** ~ **off** *t* decir/escribir a toda prisa. ◆**to** ~ **on** *i* hablar sin parar. ◆**to** ~ **through** *t* despachar rápidamente.
rattlesnake ['rætəlsneɪk] *n* serpiente *f* de cascabel.
ratty ['rætɪ] *adj* *fam* malhumorado,-a.
raucous ['rɔ:kəs] *adj* estridente.
raunchy ['rɔ:ntʃɪ] *adj* *fam* lujurioso,-a.
ravage ['rævɪdʒ] *n* estrago. – **2** *t* devastar.
rave [reɪv] *i* delirar. **2** (*rage*) enfurecerse. **3** *fam* entusiasmarse.
raven ['reɪvən] *n* cuervo.
ravenous ['rævənəs] *adj* voraz.
rave-up ['reɪvʌp] *n* *fam* juerga.
ravine [rə'vi:n] *n* barranco.
raving ['reɪvɪŋ] *adj-adv* de atar. ● ~ **mad**, loco,-a de atar.
ravish ['rævɪʃ] *t* extasiar. **2** (*rape*) violar.
ravishing ['rævɪʃɪŋ] *adj* encantador,-ra.
raw [rɔ:] *adj* (*uncooked*) crudo,-a. **2** (*unprocessed*) bruto,-a. **3** (*inexperienced*) novato,-a. **4** (*weather*) crudo,-a. ■ ~ **material(s)**, materia prima.
ray [reɪ] *n* rayo. **2** (*fish*) raya.
rayon ['reɪɒn] *n* rayón *m*.
raze [reɪz] *t* arrasar.
razor ['reɪzəʳ] *n* navaja de afeitar. **2** (*electric*) maquinilla de afeitar.
re [ri:] *prep* respecto a, con referencia a.
reach [ri:tʃ] *n* alcance *m*. – **2** *t-i* (*arrive*) llegar (a). **3** (*be able to touch*) alcanzar, llegar (a). – **4** *t* (*contact*) contactar. **5** (*pass*) alcanzar. ●**within** ~ **of**, al alcance de.
react [rɪ'ækt] *i* reaccionar.
reaction [rɪ'ækʃən] *n* reacción.
reactionary [rɪ'ækʃənərɪ] *adj-n* reaccionario,-a.
read [ri:d] *t* leer. **2** (*decipher*) descifrar. **3** (*interpret*) interpretar. **4** (*at university*) estudiar, cursar. – **5** *i* (*instrument*) indicar, marcar. **6** (*sign, notice*) decir, poner. ◆**to** ~ **up on** *t* investigar, buscar datos sobre. ▲ *pt & pp* **read** [red].

reader ['ri:dəʳ] *n* lector,-ra.
readily ['redɪlɪ] *adv* (*easily*) fácilmente. **2** (*willingly*) de buena gana.
readiness ['redɪnəs] *n* (*willingness*) disposición, buena voluntad. ●**in** ~ **for**, preparado,-a para.
reading ['ri:dɪŋ] *n* lectura. **2** (*of instrument*) indicación.
readjust [ri:ə'dʒʌst] *t* reajustar.
ready ['redɪ] *n* preparado,-a, listo,-a. **2** (*willing*) dispuesto,-a. **3** (*quick*) rápido,-a.
ready-made [redɪ'meɪd] *adj* hecho,-a, confeccionado,-a.
real [rɪəl] *adj* real, verdadero,-a. **2** (*genuine*) genuino,-a, auténtico,-a. – **3** *adv* *fam* muy. – **4** *really adv* realmente, verdaderamente. ■ ~ **estate**, bienes *mpl* inmuebles.
realism ['rɪəlɪzəm] *n* realismo.
realistic [rɪə'lɪstɪk] *adj* realista.
reality [rɪ'ælɪtɪ] *n* realidad.
realization [rɪəlaɪ'zeɪʃən] *n* realización. **2** comprensión.
realize ['rɪəlaɪz] *t* darse cuenta de. **2** (*carry out*) realizar. **3** COM realizar.
realm [relm] *n* reino. **2** (*field*) campo, terreno.
reap [ri:p] *t* cosechar.
reaper ['ri:pəʳ] *n* (*person*) segador,-ra. **2** (*machine*) segadora.
reappear [ri:ə'pɪəʳ] *i* reaparecer.
reappearance [ri:əpɪərəns] *n* reaparición.
reappraisal [ri:ə'preɪzəl] *n* revaluación.
reappraise [ri:ə'preɪz] *t* revaluar.
rear [rɪəʳ] *adj* trasero,-a, último,-a, posterior. – **2** *n* parte *f* de atrás. **3** (*of room*) fondo. **4** *fam* (*of person*) trasero. – **5** *t* (*raise*) criar. **6** (*lift up*) levantar. – **7** *i* to ~ (*up*), encabritarse.
rearmament [ri:'ɑ:məment] *n* rearme *m*.
rearrange [ri:ə'reɪndʒ] *t* (*objects*) colocar de otra manera. **2** (*event*) cambiar la fecha/hora de.
rear-view ['rɪəvju:] *adj* ~ **mirror**, retrovisor *m*.
reason ['ri:zən] *n* razón *f*. – **2** *i* razonar. ●**it stands to** ~, es lógico.
reasonable ['ri:zənəbəl] *adj* razonable.
reasoning ['ri:zənɪŋ] *n* razonamiento.
reassurance [ri:ə'ʃʊərəns] *n* tranquilidad, consuelo.
reassure [ri:ə'ʃʊəʳ] *t* tranquilizar, dar confianza a.
reassuring [ri:ə'ʃʊərɪŋ] *adj* tranquilizador,-ra.

rebate ['riːbeɪt] *n* FIN devolución.

rebel ['rebəl] *adj-n* rebelde *(mf).* – **2** *i* rebelarse. ▲ *En* **2** *(verbo)* [rɪ'bel].

rebellion [rɪ'beljən] *n* rebelión.

rebellious [rɪ'beljəs] *adj* rebelde.

rebound ['riːbaʊnd] *n* rebote *m.* – **2** *i* rebotar. ●*on the* ~, de rebote. ▲ *En* **2** *(verbo)* [rɪ'baʊnd].

rebuff [rɪ'bʌf] *n* repulsa, desaire. – **2** *t* repulsar, desairar.

rebuild [riː'bɪld] *t* reconstruir. ▲ *pt & pp* **rebuilt** [riː'bɪlt].

rebuke [rɪ'bjuːk] *n* reproche *m.* – **2** *t* reprender.

rebut [rɪ'bʌt] *t* refutar.

recalcitrant [rɪ'kælsɪtrənt] *adj* recalcitrante.

recall [rɪ'kɔːl] *n* llamada. **2** *(memory)* memoria. – **3** *t* llamar. **4** *(withdraw)* retirar. **5** *(remember)* recordar.

recant [rɪ'kænt] *i* retractarse.

recap ['riːkæp] *fam,* **recapitulate** [riːkə'pɪtjʊleɪt] *t-i* recapitular, resumir.

recapitulation [riːkəpɪtjʊ'leɪʃən] *n* recapitulación, resumen *m.*

recapture [riː'kæptʃəʳ] *t* volver a capturar. **2** *fig* hacer revivir.

recede [rɪ'siːd] *i* retroceder.

receipt [rɪ'siːt] *n* recibo. **2** *pl* COM entradas *fpl.*

receive [rɪ'siːv] *t* recibir.

receiver [rɪ'siːvəʳ] *n (person)* receptor,-ra. **2** RAD TV receptor *m.* **3** *(telephone)* auricular *m.*

recent ['riːsənt] *adj* reciente.

receptacle [rɪ'septəkəl] *n* receptáculo, recipiente *m.*

reception [rɪ'sepʃən] *n gen* recepción. **2** *(welcome)* acogida. **3** *(at wedding)* banquete *m.*

receptionist [rɪ'sepʃənɪst] *n* recepcionista *mf.*

recess ['riːses] *n (in wall)* hueco. **2** *(rest)* descanso. **3** POL período de vacaciones.

recharge [riː'tʃɑːdʒ] *t* recargar.

rechargeable [riː'tʃɑːdʒəbəl] *adj* recargable.

recherché [rə'ʃeəʃeɪ] *adj* rebuscado,-a.

recipe ['resəpɪ] *n* receta.

recipient [rɪ'sɪpɪənt] *n* receptor,-ra.

reciprocal [rɪ'sɪprəkəl] *adj* recíproco,-a.

reciprocate [rɪ'sɪprəkeɪt] *i* corresponder. – **2** *t (invitation)* devolver.

recital [rɪ'saɪtəl] *n* recital *m.*

recite [rɪ'saɪt] *t-i* recitar.

reckless ['rekləs] *adj (hasty)* precipitado,-a. **2** *(careless)* temerario,-a.

recklessness ['rekləsnəs] *n (haste)* imprudencia. **2** *(carelessness)* temeridad.

reckon ['rekən] *t-i (count)* contar. **2** *(calculate)* calcular. – **3** *t (think)* creer, considerar. ●*to* ~ *on t* contar con. ●*to* ~ *with t* tener en cuenta. **2** *(deal with)* vérselas con.

reckoning ['rekənɪŋ] *n* cuenta. ●*by my* ~, según mis cálculos.

reclaim [rɪ'kleɪm] *t (money, right, etc.)* reclamar. **2** *(land)* ganar (al mar). **3** *(recycle)* reciclar.

recline [rɪ'klaɪn] *t-i* reclinar(se).

recluse [rɪ'kluːs] *adj* recluso,-a.

recognition [rekəg'nɪʃən] *n* reconocimiento.

recognize ['rekəgnaɪz] *t* reconocer.

recoil ['riːkɔɪl] *n (of guns)* retroceso. – **2** *i* retroceder. ▲ *En* **2** *(verbo)* [rɪ'kɔɪl].

recollect [rekə'lekt] *t-i* recordar.

recollection [rekə'lekʃən] *n* recuerdo.

recommend [rekə'mend] *t* recomendar.

recommendation [rekəmen'deɪʃən] *n* recomendación.

recompense ['rekəmpens] *n* recompensa. **2** JUR indemnización. – **3** *t* recompensar. **4** JUR indemnizar.

reconcile ['rekənsaɪl] *t (people)* reconciliar. **2** *(ideas)* conciliar. ●*to* ~ *o.s. to,* resignarse a.

reconciliation [rekənsɪlɪ'eɪʃən] *n* reconciliación.

recondite ['rekəndaɪt] *adj* recóndito,-a.

recondition [riːkən'dɪʃən] *t* rectificar.

reconnaissance [rɪ'kɒnɪsəns] *n* reconocimiento.

reconnoitre [rekə'nɔɪtəʳ] *t* reconocer.

reconsider [riːkən'sɪdəʳ] *t* reconsiderar.

reconstitute [riː'kɒnstɪtjuːt] *t* reconstituir.

reconstruct [riːkəns'trʌkt] *t* reconstruir.

record ['rekɔːd] *n* constancia (escrita). **2** *(facts about a person)* historial *m.* **3** MUS disco. **4** SP récord *m,* marca. – **5** *t* hacer constar. **6** *(write down)* anotar. **7** *(voice, music)* grabar. ●*off the* ~, confidencialmente. ■ *criminal* ~, antecedentes *mpl* penales; *medical* ~, historial *m* médico. ▲ *De 5 a 7 (verbo)* [rɪ'kɔːd].

recorder [rɪ'kɔːdəʳ] *n* MUS flauta. ■ *cassette* ~, casete *m; tape* ~, magnetófono.

recording [rɪ'kɔːdɪŋ] *n* grabación.

recount [rɪ'kaʊnt] *t* contar, relatar. **2** *(count again)* volver a contar. – **3** *n* recuento. ▲ *En* **2** [riː'kaʊnt]; *en* **3** ['riːkaʊnt].

recoup [rɪ'kuːp] *t* recuperar.

recourse [rɪ'kɔːs] *n* recurso. ●*to have ~ to,* recurrir a.
recover [rɪ'kʌvə^r] *t-i* recuperar(se).
re-cover [riː'kʌvə^r] *t* recubrir.
recovery [rɪ'kʌvərɪ] *n* recuperación.
recreate [riːkrɪ'eɪt] *t* recrear.
recreation [rekrɪ'eɪʃən] *n* diversión.
recriminate [rɪ'krɪmɪneɪt] *t* recriminar.
recruit [rɪ'kruːt] *n* recluta *m.* − **2** *t* reclutar.
rectangle ['rektæŋgəl] *n* rectángulo.
rectangular [rekt'æŋgjʊlə^r] *adj* rectangular.
rectify ['rektɪfaɪ] *t* rectificar, corregir.
rectitude ['rektɪtjuːd] *n* rectitud.
rector ['rektə^r] *n* REL párroco.
rectory ['rektərɪ] *n* rectoría.
rectum ['rektəm] *n* recto.
recumbent [rɪ'kʌmbənt] *adj* recostado,-a, yacente.
recuperate [rɪk'uːpəreɪt] *i* recuperar(se).
recuperation [rɪkuːpər'eɪʃən] *n* recuperación.
recur [rɪ'kɜː^r] *i* repetirse, reproducirse.
recurrence [rɪ'kʌrəns] *n* repetición, reaparición.
recycle [riː'saɪkəl] *t* reciclar.
recycling [riː'saɪkəlɪŋ] *n* reciclaje *m.*
red [red] *adj-n* rojo,-a *(m).* − **2** *adj (hair)* pelirrojo,-a. ●*to be in the ~,* estar en descubierto; *to turn ~,* ponerse colorado,-a, sonrojarse. ■ *~ corpuscle,* glóbulo rojo; *Red Cross,* Cruz *f* Roja; *~ tape,* papeleo burocrático; *~ wine,* vino tinto.
redden ['redən] *t-i* enrojecer(se).
reddish ['redɪʃ] *adj* rojizo,-a.
redeem [rɪ'diːm] *t* rescatar, recuperar. **2** REL redimir. **3** *(promise)* cumplir.
redeemer [rɪ'diːmə^r] *n* redentor,-ra. ■ *The Redeemer,* el Redentor.
redemption [rɪ'dempʃən] *n* rescate *m.* **2** REL redención.
red-handed [red'hændɪd] *adj* con las manos en la masa, in fraganti.
redhead ['redhed] *n* pelirrojo,-a.
red-hot [red'hɒt] *adj* al rojo vivo.
redness ['rednəs] *n* rojez *f.*
redouble [riː'dʌbəl] *t* redoblar, reduplicar.
redoubtable [rɪ'dautəbəl] *adj* temible.
redress [rɪ'dres] *n* reparación, desagravio. − **2** *t* reparar, corregir.
redskin ['redskɪn] *n* piel roja *m.*
reduce [rɪ'djuːs] *t-i* reducir(se).
reduction [rɪ'dʌkʃən] *n* reducción.
redundancy [rɪ'dʌndənsɪ] *n* despido.

redundant [rɪ'dʌndənt] *adj* redundante. **2** *(worker)* despedido,-a. ●*to be made ~,* perder el empleo, ser despedido,-a.
reed [riːd] *n* caña, junco. **2** MUS lengüeta.
reef [riːf] *n* arrecife *m.*
reefer ['riːfə^r] *n sl* porro *m.*
reek [riːk] *n* tufo. − **2** *i* apestar.
reel [riːl] *n* carrete *m.* **2** CINEM bobina. − **3** *i* tambalear(se). **4** *(head)* dar vueltas.
re-entry [riː'entrɪ] *n* reingreso.
refer [rɪ'fɜː^r] *t* remitir, enviar. − **2** *i (mention)* referirse (*to,* a). **3** *(consult)* consultar (*to,* -).
referee [refə'riː] *n* SP árbitro. **2** *(for job)* garante *m,* avalador,-ra. − **3** *t* arbitrar.
reference ['refərəns] *n* referencia. ●*with ~ to,* referente a. ■ *~ book,* libro de consulta.
referendum [refə'rendəm] *n* referéndum *m.* ▲ *pl* **referendums** *o* **referenda** [refə'rendə].
refill ['riːfɪl] *n* recambio. − **2** *t* rellenar. ▲ *En 2 (verbo)* [riː'fɪl].
refine [rɪ'faɪn] *t* refinar.
refined [rɪ'faɪnd] *adj* refinado,-a.
refinement [rɪ'faɪnmənt] *n* refinamiento.
refinery [rɪ'faɪnərɪ] *n* refinería.
reflect [rɪ'flekt] *t* reflejar. − **2** *i (think)* reflexionar. ●*~ on* *t* perjudicar.
reflection [rɪ'flekʃən] *n (image)* reflejo. **2** *(thought)* reflexión. **3** *(aspersion)* descrédito.
reflector [rɪ'flektə^r] *n* AUTO catafaro.
reflex ['riːfleks] *adj* reflejo.
reflexive [rɪ'fleksɪv] *adj* reflexivo,-a.
reform [rɪ'fɔːm] *n* reforma. − **2** *t* reformar.
reformation [refə'meɪʃən] *n* reforma.
reformatory [rɪ'fɔːmətərɪ] *n* reformatorio.
reformer [rɪ'fɔːmə^r] *n* reforamador,-ra.
refrain [rɪ'freɪn] *n* MUS estribillo. − **2** *i* abstenerse.
refresh [rɪ'freʃ] *t* refrescar.
refreshing [rɪ'freʃɪŋ] *adj* refrescante.
refreshment [rɪ'freʃmənt] *n* refresco, refrigerio.
refrigerate [rɪ'frɪdʒəreɪt] *t* refrigerar.
refrigeration [rɪfrɪdʒə'reɪʃən] *n* refrigeración.
refrigerator [rɪ'frɪdʒəreɪtə^r] *n* frigorífico, nevera.
refuel [riː'fjʊəl] *t-i* repostar (combustible).
refuge ['refjuːdʒ] *n* refugio.
refugee [refjuː'dʒiː] *n* refugiado,-a.

refund ['ri:fʌnd] *n* reembolso. − 2 *t* reembolsar. ▲ *En* 2 *(verbo)* [ri:'fʌnd].

refusal [rɪ'fju:zəl] *n* negativa. ■ *first* ~, primera opción.

refuse ['refju:s] *n* basura. − 2 *t* rehusar, rechazar. − 3 *i* negarse. ▲ *En* 2 *y* 3 *(verbo)* [rɪ'fju:z].

refute [rɪ'fju:t] *t* refutar.

regain [rɪ'geɪn] *t* recobrar, recuperar.

regal ['ri:gəl] *adj* real, regio,-a.

regard [rɪ'gɑ:d] *n* respeto, consideración. 2 *pl* recuerdos *mpl*. − 3 *t* considerar. ●*with* ~ *to*, con respecto a; *without* ~ *to*, sin hacer caso de.

regarding [rɪ'gɑ:dɪŋ] *prep* tocante a, respecto a.

regardless [rɪ'gɑ:dləs] *fam adv* a pesar de todo. − 2 *prep* ~ *of*, sin tener en cuenta.

regenerate [rɪ'dʒenəreɪt] *t-i* regenerar(se).

regency ['ri:dʒensɪ] *n* regencia.

regent ['ri:dʒənt] *n* regente *mf*.

regime [reɪ'ʒi:m] *n* régimen *m*.

regiment ['redʒɪmənt] *n* regimiento. − 2 *t* regimentar.

region ['ri:dʒən] *n* región.

register ['redʒɪstə'] *n* registro. − 2 *t-i* registrar(se), inscribir(se). − 3 *t (letter)* certificar. 4 *(luggage)* facturar. − 5 *i (for classes)* matricularse. ■ *cash* ~, caja registradora.

registrar [redʒɪs'trɑ:'] *n* registrador,-ra.

registration [redʒɪs'treɪʃən] *n* registro. 2 *(of luggage)* facturación. 3 *(for classes)* matrícula. ■ AUTO ~ *number*, matrícula.

registry ['redʒɪstrɪ] *n* registro. ■ ~ *office*, registro civil.

regress [rɪ'gres] *i* retroceder.

regression [rɪ'greʃən] *n* regresión.

regret [rɪ'gret] *n* remordimiento. 2 *(sadness)* pesar *m*. − 3 *t* lamentar, arrepentirse de.

regretful [rɪ'gretfʊl] *adj* arrepentido,-a.

regrettable [rɪ'gretəbəl] *adj* lamentable.

regular ['regjʊlə'] *adj* regular. 2 *(methodical)* metódico,-a. 3 *(normal)* normal. − 4 *n fam* cliente *mf* habitual.

regularity [regjʊ'lærətɪ] *n* regularidad.

regulate ['regjʊleɪt] *t* regular.

regulation [regjʊ'leɪʃən] *n* regulación. 2 *(rule)* regla.

rehabilitate [ri:hə'bɪlɪteɪt] *t* rehabilitar.

rehash ['ri:hæʃ] *n* refrito. − 2 *t* refundir.

rehearsal [rɪ'hɜ:səl] *n* ensayo.

rehearse [rɪ'hɜ:s] *t* ensayar.

reign [reɪn] *n* reinado. − 2 *i* reinar.

reimburse [ri:ɪm'bɜ:s] *t* reembolsar.

rein [reɪn] *n* rienda. 2 *pl (child's)* andadores *mpl*.

reincarnation [ri:ɪnkɑ:'neɪʃən] *n* reencarnación.

reindeer ['reɪndɪə'] *n* reno.

reinforce [ri:ɪn'fɔ:s] *t* reforzar. ■ *reinforced concrete,* hormigón *m* armado.

reinforcement [ri:ɪn'fɔ:smənt] *n* refuerzo.

reinstate [ri:ɪn'steɪt] *t (to job)* readmitir.

reiterate [ri:'ɪtəreɪt] *t* reiterar.

reject ['ri:dʒekt] *n* desecho. − 2 *t* rechazar, rehusar. ▲ *En* 2 *(verbo)* [rɪ'dʒekt].

rejection [rɪ'dʒekʃən] *n* rechazo.

rejoice [rɪ'dʒɔɪs] *i* alegrarse, regocijarse.

rejoicing [rɪ'dʒɔɪsɪŋ] *n* alegría, regocijo. 2 *(public)* fiestas *fpl*.

rejoinder [rɪ'dʒɔɪndə'] *n* réplica.

rejuvenate [rɪ'dʒu:vəneɪt] *t* rejuvenecer.

relapse [rɪ'læps] *n* MED recaída. 2 *(crime)* reincidencia. − 3 *i* MED recaer. 4 *(crime)* reincidir.

relate [rɪ'leɪt] *t (tell)* relatar, contar. − 2 *t-i (connect)* relacionar(se).

related [rɪ'leɪtɪd] *adj* relacionado,-a. 2 *(family)* emparentado,-a.

relation [rɪ'leɪʃən] *n (connection)* relación. 2 *(family)* pariente,-a.

relationship [rɪ'leɪʃənʃɪp] *n* relación. 2 *(between people)* relaciones *fpl*.

relative ['relətɪv] *adj* relativo,-a. − 2 *n* pariente,-a.

relax [rɪ'læks] *t-i* relajar(se).

relaxation [ri:læk'seɪʃən] *n* relajación. 2 *(rest)* descanso. 3 *(pastime)* diversion.

relaxed [rɪ'lækst] *adj* relajado,-a.

relaxing [rɪ'læksɪŋ] *adj* relajante.

relay ['ri:leɪ] *n* relevo. 2 ELEC relé *m*. − 3 *t* RAD TV retransmitir.

release [rɪ'li:s] *n* liberación, puesta en libertad. 2 CINEM estreno. 3 *(record)* disco recién salido. − 4 *t* liberar, poner en libertad. 5 CINEM estrenar. 6 *(record)* sacar. 7 *(let go of)* soltar.

relegate ['relɪgeɪt] *t* relegar. ●SP *to be relegated,* descender.

relegation [relɪ'geɪʃən] *n* SP descenso.

relent [rɪ'lent] *i* ablandarse, apiadarse.

relentless [rɪ'lentləs] *adj* implacable, inexorable.

relevance ['reləvəns] *n* pertinencia.

relevant ['reləvənt] *adj* pertinente.

reliable [rɪ'laɪəbəl] *adj (person)* fiable, de fiar. 2 *(news etc.)* fidedigno,-a. 3 *(machine)* seguro,-a.

reliance [rɪ'laɪəns] *n* dependencia.

relic ['relɪk] *n* vestigio. 2 REL reliquia.

relief [rɪ'liːf] *n* alivio. **2** *(help)* auxilio, socorro. **3** *(person)* relevo. **4** GEOG relieve *m.*

relieve [rɪ'liːv] *t* aliviar. **2** *(brighten up)* alegrar. **3** *(take over from)* relevar.

religion [rɪ'lɪdʒən] *n* religión.

religious [rɪ'lɪdʒəs] *adj* religioso,-a.

relinquish [rɪ'lɪŋkwɪʃ] *t* renunciar a.

relish ['relɪʃ] *n* gusto, deleite *m.* **2** CULIN condimento. − **3** *t* disfrutar de: *I don't ~ the idea,* no me gusta la idea.

reluctance [rɪ'lʌktəns] *n* renuencia.

reluctant [rɪ'lʌktənt] *adj* reacio,-a.

rely [rɪ'laɪ] *i to ~ on,* confiar en, contar con.

remain [rɪ'meɪn] *i (stay)* quedarse, permanecer. **2** *(be left)* quedar, sobrar. − **3** *npl* restos *mpl.*

remainder [rɪ'meɪndə^r] *n* resto.

remaining [rɪ'meɪnɪŋ] *adj* restante.

remark [rɪ'mɑːk] *n* observación, comentario. − **2** *t* observar, comentar.

remarkable [rɪ'mɑːkəbəl] *adj* notable, extraordinario,-a.

remedy ['remədɪ] *n* remedio. − **2** *t* remediar.

remember [rɪ'membə^r] *t* recordar, acordarse de. **2** *(commemorate)* conmemorar. •~ *me to Katherine,* (dale) recuerdos a Katherine de mi parte.

remembrance [rɪ'membrəns] *n* conmemoración. **2** *(keepsake)* recuerdo. •*in ~ of,* para conmemorar.

remind [rɪ'maɪnd] *t* recordar: *~ her to phone me,* recuérdale que me llame.

reminder [rɪ'maɪndə^r] *n* recordatorio.

reminisce [remɪ'nɪs] *t-i* rememorar.

reminiscent [remɪ'nɪsənt] *adj* lleno,-a de recuerdos. •~ *of ...,* que recuerda ... .

remiss [rɪ'mɪs] *adj* negligente.

remission [rɪ'mɪʃən] *n* remisión.

remit [rɪ'mɪt] *t* remitir.

remittance [rɪ'mɪtəns] *n (money)* giro.

remnant ['remnənt] *n* resto. **2** *(cloth)* retal *m.*

remonstrate [rɪ'mɒnstreɪt] *i* protestar, quejarse.

remorse [rɪ'mɔːs] *n* remordimiento.

remorseful [rɪ'mɔːsful] *adj* arrepentido,-a.

remorseless [rɪ'mɔːsləs] *adj* implacable.

remote [rɪ'məʊt] *adj* remoto,-a. •*not the remotest idea,* ni la más mínima idea. ■ ~ *control,* mando a distancia.

removal [rɪ'muːvəl] *n* eliminación. **2** *(house)* traslado, mudanza.

remove [rɪ'muːv] *t* quitar, eliminar. **2** *(dismiss)* despedir. − **3** *i* trasladarse.

remuneration [rɪ'mjuːnəreɪʃən] *t* remuneración.

remunerative [rɪ'mjuːnərətɪv] *adj* remunerador,-ra.

Renaissance [rə'neɪsəns] *n* Renacimiento.

rend [rend] *t* rasgar. ▲ *pt & pp* **rent.**

render ['rendə^r] *t (give)* dar, prestar. **2** *(make)* hacer, convertir en. **3** *(song)* cantar; *(music)* interpretar.

rendezvous ['rɒndɪvuː] *n inv* cita. **2** *(place)* punto/lugar *m* de reunión.

rendition ['rendɪʃən] *n* interpretación.

renegade ['renɪgeɪd] *n* renegado,-a.

renew [rɪ'njuː] *t* renovar. **2** *(start again)* reanudar.

renewable [rɪ'njuːəbəl] *adj* renovable.

renewal [rɪ'njuːəl] *n* renovación. **2** *(new start)* reanudación.

renounce [rɪ'naʊns] *t* renunciar.

renovate ['renəveɪt] *t (building)* restaurar.

renovation [renə'veɪʃən] *n* restauración.

renown [rɪ'naʊn] *n* renombre *m,* fama.

renowned [rɪ'naʊnd] *adj* renombrado,-a, famoso,-a.

rent [rent] *n (for flat etc.)* alquiler *m.* **2** *(for land)* arriendo. − **3** *t* alquilar, arrendar. − **4** *pt & pp →* **rend.**

rental ['rentəl] *n* alquiler *m.*

renunciation [rɪnʌnsɪ'eɪʃən] *n* renuncia.

reorganization [riːɔːgənaɪ'zeɪʃən] *n* reorganización.

reorganize [riːˈɔːgənaɪz] *t* reorganizar.

repair [rɪ'peə^r] *n* reparación. − **2** *t* reparar, arreglar. •*in good ~,* en buen estado.

reparation [repə'reɪʃən] *n* compensación, indemnización.

repatriate [riːˈpætrɪeɪt] *t* repatriar.

repay [riːˈpeɪ] *t* devolver.

repayment [riːˈpeɪmənt] *n* devolución, reembolso.

repeal [rɪ'piːl] *n* abrogación, revocación. − **2** *t* abrogar, revocar.

repeat [rɪ'piːt] *n* repetición. − **2** *t* repetir.

repeatedly [rɪ'piːtɪdlɪ] *adv* repetidamente.

repel [rɪ'pel] *t gen* repeler. **2** *(disgust)* repugnar.

repellent [rɪ'pelənt] *adj* repelente. − **2** *n* loción anti-insectos.

repent [rɪ'pent] *i* arrepentirse. − **2** *t* arrepentirse de.

repentance [rɪ'pentəns] *n* arrepentimiento.

repentant [rɪ'pentənt] *adj* arrepentido,-a.

repercussion [ri:pə'kʌʃən] *n* repercusión.

repertoire ['repətwɑ:ʳ] *n* repertorio.

repetition [repə'tıʃən] *n* repetición.

repetitive [rı'petıtıv] *adj* reiterativo,-a.

replace [rı'pleıs] *t* devolver a su sitio. 2 *(substitute)* reemplazar, substituir.

replacement [rı'pleısmənt] *n* su(b)stitución. 2 *(person)* su(b)stituto,-a. 3 *(part)* pieza de cambio.

replay ['ri:pleı] *n* TV repetición. 2 SP partido de desempate. − 3 *t* TV repetir. ▲ *En 3 (verbo)* [ri:'pleı].

replenish [rı'plenıʃ] *t* rellenar, llenar de nuevo. 2 *(stocks)* reponer.

replete [rı'pli:t] *adj* repleto,-a.

reply [rı'plaı] *n* respuesta, contestación. − 2 *i* responder *(to,* a), contestar *(to,* a).

report [rı'pɔ:t] *n* informe *m*. 2 *(news)* noticia. 3 RAD TV reportaje *m*. 4 *(rumour)* rumor *m*. − 5 *t* informar sobre, dar parte de. 6 *(to authority)* denunciar. 7 *(for work)* presentarse.

reporter [rı'pɔ:təʳ] *n* reportero,-a, periodista *mf*.

repose [rı'pəuz] *n* reposo. − 2 *t-i* reposar, descansar.

reprehensible [reprı'hensıbəl] *adj* reprensible.

represent [reprı'zent] *t* representar.

representation [reprızen'teıʃən] *n* representación.

representative [reprı'zentətıv] *adj* representativo,-a. − 2 *n* representante *mf*. 3 US POL diputado,-a.

repress [rı'pres] *t* reprimir.

repression [rı'preʃən] *n* represión.

repressive [rı'presıv] *adj* represivo,-a.

reprieve [rı'pri:v] *n* indulto. 2 *fig* respiro, tregua. − 3 *t* indultar.

reprimand ['reprımɑ:nd] *n* reprimenda, reprensión. − 2 *t* reprender.

reprint ['ri:prınt] *n* reimpresión. − 2 *t* reimprimir. ▲ *En 2 (verbo)* [ri:'prınt].

reprisal [rı'praızəl] *n* represalia.

reproach [rı'prəutʃ] *n* reproche *m*. − 2 *t* reprochar.

reprobate ['reprəbeıt] *adj-n* réprobo,-a.

reproduce [ri:prə'dju:s] *t-i* reproducir(se).

reproduction [ri:prə'dʌkʃən] *n* reproducción.

reproductive [ri:prə'dʌktıv] *adj* reproductor,-ra.

reproof [rı'pru:f] *n* reprobación, reprensión.

reprove [rı'pru:v] *t* reprobar, reprender.

reptile ['reptaıl] *n* reptil *m*.

republic [rı'pʌblık] *n* república.

republican [rı'pʌblıkən] *adj-n* republicano,-a.

repudiate [rı'pju:dıeıt] *t* rechazar.

repugnance [rı'pʌgnəns] *n* repugnancia.

repugnant [rı'pʌgnənt] *adj* repugnante.

repulse [rı'pʌls] *t* rechazar.

repulsive [rı'pʌlsıv] *adj* repulsivo,-a.

reputable ['repjutəbəl] *adj* acreditado,-a. 2 *(person)* de confianza.

reputation [repju'teıʃən] *n* reputación, fama.

repute [rı'pju:t] *n* reputación, fama.

reputed [rı'pju:tıd] *adj* considerado,-a. − 2 *reputedly adv* según se dice.

request [rı'kwest] *n* solicitud, petición. − 2 *t* pedir, solicitar.

require [rı'kwaıəʳ] *t-i* requerir, exigir. 2 *(need)* necesitar.

requirement [rı'kwaıəmənt] *n* requisito, condición. 2 *(need)* necesidad.

requisite ['rekwızıt] *adj* requerido,-a, necesario,-a. − 2 *n* requisito.

requisition [rekwı'zıʃən] MIL *n* requisa. − 2 *t* requisar.

rescind [rı'sınd] *t* rescindir.

rescue ['reskju:] *n* rescate *m*. − 2 *t* rescatar.

rescuer ['reskjuəʳ] *n* salvador,-ra.

research [rı'sɜ:tʃ] *n* investigación. − 2 *t-i* investigar.

researcher [rı'sɜ:tʃəʳ] *n* investigador,-ra.

resemblance [rı'zembləns] *n* parecido, semejanza.

resemble [rı'zembəl] *t* parecerse a.

resent [rı'zent] *t* ofenderse por, tomar a mal.

resentful [rı'zentful] *adj* resentido,-a, ofendido,-a.

resentment [rı'zentmənt] *n* resentimiento, rencor *m*.

reservation [rezə'veıʃən] *n* reserva.

reserve [rı'zɜ:v] *n* reserva. − 2 *t* reservar.

reserved [rı'zɜ:vd] *adj* reservado,-a.

reservoir ['rezəvwɑ:ʳ] *n* embalse *m*.

reshuffle [ri:'ʃʌfəl] *n* POL reorganización. − 2 *t* POL reorganizar. 3 *(cards)* volver a barajar.

reside [rı'zaıd] *i* residir.

residence ['rezıdəns] *n* residencia.

resident ['rezıdənt] *adj-n* residente *(mf)*.

residential [rezı'denʃəl] *adj* residencial.

residual [rı'zıdjuəl] *adj* residual.

residue ['rezıdju:] *n* residuo.

resign [rı'zaın] *t-i* dimitir *(from,* de). ●*to* ~ *o.s. to sth.,* resignarse a algo.

resignation [rezɪg'neɪʃən] *n* dimisión. 2 *(acceptance)* resignación.

resilience [rɪ'zɪlɪəns] *n* elasticidad. 2 *(strength)* fuerza, resistencia.

resilient [rɪ'zɪlɪənt] *adj* elástico,-a. 2 *(strong)* fuerte, resistente.

resin ['rezɪn] *n* resina.

resist [rɪ'zɪst] *t* resistir (a). 2 *(fight)* oponer resistencia a.

resistance [rɪ'zɪstəns] *n* resistencia.

resistant [rɪ'zɪstənt] *adj* resistente.

resolute ['rezəluːt] *adj* resuelto,-a.

resolution [rezə'luːʃən] *n* resolución.

resolve [rɪ'zɒlv] *n* resolución. — 2 *t-i* resolver(se).

resonance ['rezənəns] *n* resonancia.

resort [rɪ'zɔːt] *n (place)* lugar *m* de vacaciones. 2 *(recourse)* recurso. — 3 *i* recurrir *(to,* a).

resound [rɪ'zaʊnd] *i* resonar.

resounding [rɪ'zaʊndɪŋ] *adj* resonante. 2 *fig* enorme, importante.

resource [rɪ'zɔːs] *n* recurso.

resourceful [rɪ'zɔːsfʊl] *adj* ingenioso,-a.

respect [rɪ'spekt] *n* respeto. — 2 *t* respetar. ♦*with ~ to,* con respeto a.

respectable [rɪ'spektəbəl] *adj* respetable. 2 *(decent)* decente, presentable.

respectful [rɪ'spektfʊl] *adj* respetuoso,-a.

respective [rɪ'spektɪv] *adj* respectivo,-a.

respiration [respɪ'reɪʃən] *n* respiración.

respiratory ['respərətərɪ] *adj* respiratorio,-a.

respite ['respaɪt] *n* respiro, alivio.

resplendent [rɪ'splendənt] *adj* resplandeciente.

respond [rɪ'spɒnd] *i* responder.

response [rɪ'spɒns] *n* respuesta.

responsibility [rɪspɒnsɪ'bɪlɪtɪ] *n* responsabilidad.

responsible [rɪ'spɒnsəbəl] *adj* responsable.

responsive [rɪ'spɒnsɪv] *adj* que reacciona/muestra interés.

rest [rest] *n* descanso, reposo. 2 *(peace)* paz *f*, tranquilidad. 3 *(support)* soporte *m*. 4 *(remainder)* resto: *the ~,* lo/los demás. — 5 *t-i* descansar. — 6 *i (be calm)* quedarse tranquilo,-a. — 7 *t (lean)* apoyar. ♦*to ~ with i* corresponder a, depender de.

restaurant ['restərɒnt] *n* restaurante *m*.

restful ['restfʊl] *adj* tranquilo,-a.

restive ['restɪv], **restless** ['restləs] *adj* inquieto,-a

restoration [restə'reɪʃən] *n* restauración. 2 *(return)* devolución.

restore [rɪ'stɔːʳ] *t* restaurar. 2 *(return)* devolver. 3 *(order)* restablecer.

restrain [rɪ'streɪn] *t* contener, reprimir.

restraint [rɪ'streɪnt] *n* limitación. 2 *(moderation)* moderación.

restrict [rɪ'strɪkt] *t* restringir.

restriction [rɪ'strɪkʃən] *n* restricción.

restrictive [rɪ'strɪktɪv] *adj* restrictivo,-a.

result [rɪ'zʌlt] *n* resultado. 2 *(consequence)* consecuencia. — 3 *i to ~ from,* resultar de. ♦*to ~ in t* producir, causar.

resume [rɪ'zjuːm] *t-i* reanudar(se). ♦*to ~ one's seat,* volver a sentarse.

résumé ['rezjuːmeɪ] *n* resumen *m*.

resumption [rɪ'zʌmpʃən] *n* reanudación.

resurgence [rɪ'sɜːdʒəns] *n* resurgimiento.

resurrect [rezə'rekt] *t* resucitar.

resurrection [rezə'rekʃən] *n* resurrección.

resuscitate [rɪ'sʌsɪteɪt] *t-i* resucitar.

resuscitation [rɪsʌsɪ'teɪʃən] *n* resucitación.

retail ['riːteɪl] *n* venta al detall/al por menor. — 2 *t-i* vender(se) (al por menor).

retailer ['riːteɪləʳ] *n* detallista *mf*.

retain [rɪ'teɪn] *t* retener, conservar. 2 *(in possession)* guardar.

retaliate [rɪ'tælɪeɪt] *i* vengarse, tomar represalias.

retaliation [rɪtælɪ'eɪʃən] *n* venganza, represalias *fpl*.

retard [rɪ'tɑːd] *t* retardar, retrasar.

retarded [rɪ'tɑːdɪd] *adj* retrasado, -a.

retch [retʃ] *i* tener arcadas/náuseas.

retention [rɪ'tenʃən] *n* retención.

reticence ['retɪsəns] *n* reticencia, reserva.

reticent ['retɪsənt] *adj* reservado,-a.

retina ['retɪnə] *n* retina.

retinue ['retɪnjuː] *n* séquito.

retire [rɪ'taɪəʳ] *t-i (from work)* jubilar(se). — 2 *i* retirarse. 3 *(to bed)* acostarse.

retired [rɪ'taɪəd] *adj* jubilado,-a.

retirement [rɪ'taɪəmənt] *n* jubilación.

retiring [rɪ'taɪərɪŋ] *adj (shy)* retraído,-a, tímido,-a. 2 *(from post)* saliente.

retort [rɪ'tɔːt] *n* réplica. 2 CHEM retorta. — 3 *t* replicar.

retrace [rɪ'treɪs] *t* desandar, volver sobre. ♦*to ~ one's steps,* volver sobre sus pasos.

retract [rɪ'trækt] *t-i* retractarse (de). — 2 *t* retraer.

retreat [rɪ'triːt] *n* retirada. 2 *(place)* retiro, refugio. — 3 *i* retirarse.

retrial [riː'traɪəl] *n* nuevo juicio.

retribution [retrɪ'bju:ʃən] *n* justo castigo.
retrieval [rɪ'tri:vəl] *n* recuperación.
retrieve [rɪ'tri:v] *t* recuperar.
retrograde ['retrəgreɪd] *adj* retrógrado,-a.
retrospect ['retrəspekt] *n in* ~, retros-
pectivamente.
retrospective [retrə'spektɪv] *adj* retrospectivo,-a. **2** *(law)* retroactivo,-a.
return [rɪ'tɜ:n] *n* vuelta, regreso, retorno.
2 *(giving back)* devolución. **3** *(profit)* be-
neficio.ʼ − **4** *i* volver, regresar. − **5** *t (give
back)* devolver. **6** POL elegir. **7** *(verdict)*
pronunciar. ●*in* ~ *for*, a cambio de;
many happy returns (of the day)!, ¡feliz
cumpleaños! ■ *income tax* ~, declaración de la renta; ~ *ticket*, billete de ida
y vuelta.
reunion [ri:'ju:nɪən] *n* reunión, encuentro.
reunite [ri:ju:'naɪt] *t-i* reunir(se). **2** *(reconcile)* reconciliar(se).
revalue [ri:'vælju:] *t* revalorizar.
reveal [rɪ'vi:l] *t* revelar, descubrir.
reveille [rɪ'vælɪ] *n* MIL diana.
revel ['revəl] *i to* ~ *in*, disfrutar mucho
con.
revelry ['revəlrɪ] *n* juerga.
revelation [revə'leɪʃən] *n* revelación.
revenge [rɪ'vendʒ] *n* venganza. − **2** *t* vengar. ●*to* ~ *o.s.*, vengarse.
revenue ['revənju:] *n* renta. ■ GB *Inland
Revenue*, US *Internal Revenue*, Hacienda Pública.
reverberate [rɪ'vɜ:bəreɪt] *t* resonar, retumbar.
reverberation [rɪvɜ:bə'reɪʃən] *n* resonancia, retumbo.
revere [rɪ'vɪər] *t* reverenciar.
reverence ['revərəns] *n* reverencia.
reverend ['revərənd] *adj* reverendo,-a.
reverent ['revərənt] *adj* reverente.
reverie ['revərɪ] *n* ensueño.
reversal [rɪ'vɜ:səl] *n (in order)* inversión.
2 *(change)* cambio completo.
reverse [rɪ'vɜ:s] *adj* inverso,-a, contrario,-a. − **2** *n* lo contrario. **3** *(of coin)* reverso. **4** *(of cloth)* revés *m*. **5** AUTO marcha atrás. **6** *(setback)* revés *m*. − **7** *t* invertir. **8** *(turn round)* volver al revés. − **9**
i AUTO poner/dar marcha atrás. ●*to* ~
the charges, llamar a cobro revertido.
revert [rɪ'vɜ:t] *i* volver *(to, a)*.
review [rɪ'vju:] *n* revista. **2** *(examination)*
examen *m*. **3** *(of film, book, etc.)* crítica.
− **4** *t (troops)* pasar revista a. **5** *(examine)*

examinar. **6** *(film, book, etc.)* hacer una
crítica.
reviewer [rɪ'vju:ər] *n* crítico,-a.
revile [rɪ'vaɪl] *t* injuriar, vilipendiar.
revise [rɪ'vaɪz] *t* revisar. **2** *(correct)* corregir. **3** *(change)* modificar. − **4** *t-i (for
exam)* repasar.
revision [rɪ'vɪʒən] *n* revisión. **2** *(correction)* corrección. **3** *(change)* modificación. **4** *(for exam)* repaso.
revitalize [ri:'vaɪtəlaɪz] *t* revivificar.
revival [rɪ'vaɪvəl] *n (rebirth)* renacimiento.
2 *(of economy)* reactivación. **3** *(of play)*
reestreno.
revive [rɪ'vaɪv] *t* reanimar, reavivar, despertar. **2** *(economy)* reactivar. **3** *(play)*
reestrenar. − **4** *t-i* MED (hacer) volver en
sí.
revoke [rɪ'vəuk] *t* revocar.
revolt [rɪ'vəult] *n* revuelta, rebelión. − **2**
i sublevarse, rebelarse. − **3** *t* repugnar.
revolting [rɪ'vəultɪŋ] *adj* repugnante.
revolution [revə'lu:ʃən] *n* revolución.
revolutionary [revəl'u:ʃənərɪ] *adj-n* revolucionario,-a.
revolve [rɪ'vɒlv] *t-i* (hacer) girar.
revolver [rɪ'vɒlvər] *n* revólver *m*.
revolving [rɪ'vɒlvɪŋ] *adj* giratorio,-a.
revue [rɪ'vju:] *n* revista.
revulsion [rɪ'vʌlʃən] *n* revulsión.
reward [rɪ'wɔ:d] *n* recompensa. − **2** *t* recompensar.
rewarding [rɪ'wɔ:dɪŋ] *adj* gratifica-
dor,-ra.
rhapsody ['ræpsədɪ] *n* rapsodia.
rhetoric ['retərɪk] *n* retórica.
rheumatic [ru:'mætɪk] *adj* reumático,-a.
rheumatism ['ru:mətɪzəm] *n* reumatismo, reuma *m*.
rhinoceros [raɪ'nɒsərəs] *n* rinoceronte *m*.
rhubarb ['ru:bɑ:b] *n* ruibarbo.
rhyme [raɪm] *n* rima. − **2** *t-i* rimar. ●*without* ~ *or reason*, sin ton ni son.
rhythm ['rɪðəm] *n* ritmo.
rhythmic ['rɪðmɪk] *adj* rítmico,-a.
rib [rɪb] *n* costilla.
ribald ['rɪbəld] *adj* grosero,-a, obsceno,-a.
ribbon ['rɪbən] *n* cinta. **2** *(for hair)* lazo.
rice [raɪs] *n* arroz *m*. ■ ~ *field*, arrozal *m*.
rich [rɪtʃ] *adj* rico,-a. **2** *(luxurious)* suntuoso,-a, lujoso,-a. **3** *(fertile)* fértil. **4** *(food)*
fuerte, pesado,-a. **5** *(voice)* sonoro,-a.
riches ['rɪtʃɪz] *npl* riqueza *f sing*.
rickets ['rɪkɪts] *npl* raquitismo *m sing*.
rickety ['rɪkətɪ] *adj* desvencijado,-a. **2**
(unsteady) tambaleante.

ricochet ['rɪkəʃeɪ] *n* rebote *m*. − 2 *i* rebotar.

rid [rɪd] *t* librar. ●*to get ~ of,* deshacerse/desembarazarse de. ▲ *pt & pp* **rid** *o* **ridded** ['rɪdɪd].

ridden ['rɪdən] *pp* → **ride**.

riddle ['rɪdəl] *n* acertijo, adivinanza. 2 *(sieve)* criba. − 3 *t* cribar. 4 *(with bullets)* acribillar.

ride [raɪd] *n* paseo, viaje *m*, vuelta. − 2 *i (horse)* montar a caballo. 3 *(in vehicle)* viajar. − 4 *t (horse)* montar. 5 *(bicycle)* montar/andar en. ●*to ~ on t* depender de. ●*to ~ out t* aguantar hasta el final de. ●*to take sb. for a ~,* tomar el pelo a algn. ▲ *pt* **rode**; *pp* **ridden**.

rider ['raɪdə'] *n (on horse)* jinete *m*, amazona. 2 *(on bicycle)* ciclista *mf*. 3 *(on motorcycle)* motorista *mf*.

ridge [rɪdʒ] *n* GEOG cresta. 2 *(of roof)* caballete *m*.

ridicule ['rɪdɪkju:l] *n* ridículo. − 2 *t* ridiculizar, poner en ridículo.

ridiculous [rɪ'dɪkjʊləs] *adj* ridículo,-a.

riding ['raɪdɪŋ] *n* equitación.

rife [raɪf] *adj* abundante. ●*to be ~,* abundar.

riffraff ['rɪfræf] *n* chusma.

rifle ['raɪfəl] *n* rifle *m*, fusil *m*. − 2 *t* robar.

rift [rɪft] *n* hendedura, grieta. 2 *fig* ruptura, desavenencia.

rig [rɪg] *n (oil) ~,* plataforma petrolífera. − 2 *t* MAR aparejar. 3 *fam (fix)* amañar. ●*to ~ up t* improvisar.

rigging ['rɪgɪŋ] *n* MAR aparejo, jarcia.

right [raɪt] *adj (not left)* derecho,-a. 2 *(correct)* correcto,-a. 3 *(just)* justo,-a. 4 *(suitable)* apropiado,-a, adecuado,-a. 5 *fam (total)* auténtico,-a, total. − 6 *adv* a/hacia la derecha. 7 *(correctly)* bien, correctamente. 8 *(immediately)* inmediatamente. 9 *(very)* muy. − 10 *n (not left)* derecha. 11 *(entitlement)* derecho. − 12 *t* corregir. 13 MAR enderezar. − 14 *rightly adv* con razón, correctamente. ●*all ~!,* ¡bien!, ¡conforme!, ¡vale!; *it serves you/him ~,* te/le está bien empleado; *~ away,* en seguida; *~ now,* ahora mismo; *to be ~,* tener razón; *to put ~,* arreglar. ■ *~ and wrong,* el bien y el mal; *~ angle,* ángulo recto; *~ of way,* JUR derecho de paso; AUTO prioridad; POL *~ wing,* derecha.

righteous ['raɪtʃəs] *adj* recto,-a, justo,-a. 2 *(justified)* justificado,-a.

rightful ['raɪtfʊl] *adj* legítimo,-a.

right-hand ['raɪthænd] *adj* derecho,-a.

right-wing ['raɪtwɪŋ] *adj* POL de derechas.

rigid ['rɪdʒɪd] *adj* rígido,-a.

rigmarole ['rɪgmərəʊl] *n* galimatías *m inv*.

rigorous ['rɪgərəs] *adj* riguroso,-a.

rigour ['rɪgə'] *n* rigor *m*.

rile [raɪl] *t fam* poner nervioso,-a, irritar.

rim [rɪm] *n* borde *m*, canto. 2 *(of wheel)* llanta.

rind [raɪnd] *n* corteza.

ring [rɪŋ] *n (for finger)* anillo, sortija. 2 *(hoop)* anilla, aro. 3 *(circle)* círculo; *(of people)* corro. 4 *(circus)* pista, arena. 5 *(boxing)* ring *m*, cuadrilátero. 6 *(of bell)* tañido, toque *m*; *(of doorbell)* llamada. 7 *(phonecall)* llamada. − 8 *i (bell)* sonar. 9 *(ears)* zumbar. − 10 *t (call)* llamar. 11 *(bell)* tocar. 12 *(bird)* anillar. 13 *(encircle)* rodear. ■ *~ road,* cinturón *m* de ronda. ▲ *pt* **rang**; *pp* **rung**.

ringing ['rɪŋɪŋ] *n* campaneo, repique *m*. 2 *(in ears)* zumbido.

ringleader ['rɪŋli:də'] *n* cabecilla *mf*.

ringlet ['rɪŋlət] *n* rizo.

ringside ['rɪŋsaɪd] *adj-n* (de) primera fila.

rink [rɪŋk] *n* pista de patinaje.

rinse [rɪns] *t* aclarar. 2 *(dishes, mouth)* enjuagar.

riot ['raɪət] *n* disturbio. 2 *(in prison)* motín *m*. − 3 *i* amotinarse.

rioter ['raɪətə'] *n* amotinado,-a.

riotous ['raɪətəs] *adj* amotinado,-a. 2 *(unrestrained)* desenfrenado,-a.

rip [rɪp] *n* rasgadura. − 2 *t-i* rasgar(se). ●*to ~ off t* arrancar. 2 *fam* timar.

ripe [raɪp] *adj* maduro,-a.

ripen ['raɪpən] *t-i* madurar.

ripeness ['raɪpnəs] *n* madurez *f*.

rip-off ['rɪpɒf] *n fam* timo.

ripple ['rɪpəl] *n* onda. 2 *(sound)* murmullo. − 3 *t-i* rizar(se). − 4 *i* murmurar.

rise [raɪz] *n* ascenso, subida. 2 *(increase)* aumento. 3 *(slope)* subida, cuesta. − 4 *i* ascender, subir. 5 *(increase)* aumentar. 6 *(stand up)* ponerse de pie. 7 *(get up)* levantarse. 8 *(sun)* salir. 9 *(river)* nacer. 10 *(level of river)* crecer. 11 *(mountains)* elevarse. ●*to give ~ to,* dar origen a; *to ~ to the occasion,* ponerse a la altura de las circunstancias. ▲ *pt* **rose**; *pp* **risen** ['rɪzən].

rising ['raɪzɪŋ] *n (rebellion)* levantamiento.

risk [rɪsk] *n* riesgo, peligro. − 2 *t* arriesgar. ●*to ~ doing sth.,* exponerse a hacer algo.

risky ['rɪskɪ] *adj* arriesgado,-a.

risqué ['rɪskeɪ] *adj* atrevido,-a.
rite [raɪt] *n* rito.
ritual ['rɪtjʊəl] *adj-n* ritual *(m)*.
rival ['raɪvəl] *adj-n* competidor,-ra, rival *(mf)*. − **2** *t* competir/rivalizar con.
rivalry ['raɪvəlrɪ] *n* rivalidad.
river ['rɪvə^r] *n* río.
river-bank ['rɪvəbæŋk] *n* ribera, orilla.
river-bed ['rɪvəbed] *n* lecho.
riverside ['rɪvəsaɪd] *n* ribera, orilla.
rivet ['rɪvɪt] *n* remache *m*. − **2** *t* remachar. **3** *fig* fijar, absorber.
riveting ['rɪvɪtɪŋ] *adj fig* fascinante.
road [rəʊd] *n* carretera. **2** *(way)* camino. ●*fam in the road,* estorbando el paso. ■ ~ *safety,* seguridad vial; ~ *sign,* señal *f* de tráfico.
roadblock ['rəʊdblɒk] *n* control *m* policial.
roadway ['rəʊdweɪ] *n* calzada.
roadworthy ['rəʊdwɜ:ðɪ] *adj* AUTO en buen estado.
roam [rəʊm] *t-i* vagar (por).
roar [rɔ:^r] *n* bramido. **2** *(of lion)* rugido. **3** *(of crowd)* griterío, clamor *m*. − **4** *i* rugir, bramar.
roaring ['rɔ:rɪŋ] *n fig* tremendo,-a, enorme.
roast [rəʊst] *adj-n* asado,-a *(m)*. − **2** *t-i* asar(se). − **3** *t (coffee, nuts, etc.)* tostar.
roasting ['rəʊstɪŋ] *adj* abrasador,-ra.
rob [rɒb] *t* robar. **2** *(bank)* atracar.
robber ['rɒbə^r] *n* ladrón,-ona. **2** *(of bank)* atracador,-ra.
robbery ['rɒbərɪ] *n* robo. **2** *(of bank)* atraco.
robe [rəʊb] *n* bata. **2** *(ceremonial)* vestidura, toga.
robin ['rɒbɪn] *n* petirrojo.
robot ['rəʊbɒt] *n* robot *m*.
robust [rəʊ'bʌst] *adj* robusto,-a, fuerte.
rock [rɒk] *n* roca. **2** MUS rock *m*. − **3** *t-i (chair)* mecer(se). − **4** *t (baby)* acunar. **5** *(upset)* sacudir. ●*on the rocks,* arruinado,-a; *(drink)* con hielo.
rock-climbing ['rɒkklaɪmɪŋ] *n* alpinismo.
rocker ['rɒkə^r] *n* balancín *m*. ● *fam off one's* ~, mal de la cabeza.
rocket ['rɒkɪt] *n* cohete *m*. − **2** *i (rise)* dispararse.
rocking-chair ['rɒkɪŋtʃeə^r] *n* mecedora.
rocky ['rɒkɪ] *adj* rocoso,-a.
rod [rɒd] *n* vara. **2** *(thick)* barra. ■ *fishing* ~ , caña de pescar.
rode [rəʊd] *pt* → **ride**.
rodent ['rəʊdənt] *n* roedor *m*.
rodeo ['rəʊdɪəʊ] *n* rodeo.

roe [rəʊ] *n* hueva.
rogue [rəʊg] *n* pícaro, bribón *m*.
role, rôle [rəʊl] *n* papel *m*.
roll [rəʊl] *n* rollo. **2** *(list)* lista. **3** *(of bread)* bollo, panecillo. − **4** *t-i* (hacer) rodar. **5** *(move)* mover (lentamente). **6** *(into a ball)* enroscar(se). **7** *(paper)* enrollar(se). − **8** *t (flatten)* allanar. ◆*to* ~ *out t (pastry)* extender. ◆*to* ~ *up t-i* enrollar(se). **2** *(into a ball)* enroscar(se). ●*to* ~ *up one's sleeves,* arremangarse; *fam* **to be rolling in it,** estar forrado,-a.
roller ['rəʊlə^r] *n* rodillo. **2** *(wave)* ola grande. **3** *(for hair)* rulo. ■ ~ *skating,* patinaje *m* sobre ruedas.
roller-skate ['rəʊləskeɪt] *i* patinar sobre ruedas.
rolling ['rəʊlɪŋ] *adj* ondulante. ■ ~ *stock,* material *m* rodante; ~ *pin,* rodillo.
Roman ['rəʊmən] *adj-n* romano,-a.
Romance [rəʊ'mæns] *adj* románico,-a.
romance [rəʊ'mæns] *n* romance *m*. **2** *(novel)* novela romántica. **3** *(quality)* lo romántico. **4** *(affair)* idilio.
romantic [rəʊ'mæntɪk] *adj* romántico,-a.
romanticize [rəʊ'mæntɪsaɪz] *i* fantasear.
romp [rɒmp] *i* jugar, retozar.
rompers ['rɒmpəz] *npl* pelele *m sing*.
roof [ru:f] *n* tejado; *(tiled)* techado. **2** *(of mouth)* cielo. **3** AUTO techo. − **4** *t* techar. ■ *flat* ~, azotea.
roof-rack ['ru:fræk] *n* baca.
rook [rʊk] *n (bird)* grajo. **2** *(in chess)* torre *f*.
room [ru:m] *n* cuarto, habitación. **2** *(space)* espacio, sitio.
roomy ['ru:mɪ] *adj* espacioso,-a, amplio,-a.
roost [ru:st] *n* percha. − **2** *i* dormir (en una percha).
rooster ['ru:stə^r] *n* gallo.
root [ru:t] *n* raíz *f*. − **2** *t-i* arraigar. − **3** *i (search)* buscar. ●*to take* ~, arraigar.
rope [rəʊp] *n* cuerda. − **2** *t* atar, amarrar. ◆*to* ~ *in t fam* enganchar.
rosary ['rəʊzərɪ] *n* rosario.
rose [rəʊz] *n (flower)* rosa. **2** *(bush)* rosal. − **3** *pt* → **rise**.
rosé ['rəʊzeɪ] *n (vino)* rosado.
rosemary ['rəʊzmərɪ] *n* romero.
rosette [rəʊ'zet] *n* escarapela.
roster ['rɒstə^r] *n* lista.
rostrum ['rɒstrəm] *n* tribuna. ▲ *pl ros-trums o rostra.*
rosy ['rəʊzɪ] *adj* (son)rosado,-a. **2** *(future)* prometedor,-ra.
rot [rɒt] *n* putrefacción. − **2** *t-i* pudrir(se).

rota [ˈrəutə] *n* → **roster**.
rotary [ˈrəutərɪ] *adj* rotatorio,-a.
rotate [rəuˈteɪt] *t-i* (hacer) girar/dar vueltas. **2** *fig* alternar.
rotation [rəuˈteɪʃən] *n* rotación.
rotten [ˈrɒtən] *adj* podrido,-a. **2** *(tooth)* picado,-a. **3** *fam* malísimo,-a.
rotter [ˈrɒtəʳ] *n fam* sinvergüenza *mf*.
rotund [rəˈtʌnd] *adj (fat)* regordete,-a.
rouble [ˈruːbəl] *n* rublo.
rouge [ruːʒ] *n* colorete *m*.
rough [rʌf] *adj* áspero,-a, basto,-a. **2** *(road)* lleno,-a de baches. **3** *(edge)* desigual. **4** *(terrain)* escabroso,-a. **5** *(sea)* agitado,-a. **6** *(weather)* tempestuoso,-a. **7** *(wine)* áspero,-a. **8** *(rude)* rudo,-a. **9** *(violent)* violento,-a. **10** *(approximate)* aproximado,-a. **11** *fam (bad)* fatal. − **12** *roughly adv (about)* aproximadamente. **13** *(not gently)* bruscamente. ●*to ~ it,* vivir sin comodidades; *to sleep ~,* dormir al raso. ■ *~ copy/version,* borrador *m*.
roughen [ˈrʌfən] *t* poner áspero,-a.
roughness [ˈrʌfnəs] *n* aspereza. **2** *(violence)* violencia.
roulette [ruːˈlet] *n* ruleta.
round [raund] *adj* redondo,-a. − **2** *n (circle)* círculo. **3** *(series)* serie *f*, tanda; *(one of a series)* ronda. **4** SP ronda; *(boxing)* asalto. **5** *(of drinks)* ronda. **6** *(of policeman etc.)* ronda. **7** *(shot)* disparo. − **8** *adv (about)* por ahí. **9** *(to visit)* *they came ~ to see me,* vinieron (a casa) a verme. − **10** *prep* alrededor de. − **11** *t* dar la vuelta a. ◆*to ~ off t* completar, acabar. ◆*to ~ up t (number)* redondear. **2** *(cattle)* acorralar. **3** *(people)* reunir. ●*all the year ~,* durante todo el año; *~ the clock,* día y noche; *~ the corner,* a la vuelta de la esquina; *the other way ~,* al revés; *to go ~,* dar vueltas; *to turn ~,* hacer girar alrededor de.
roundabout [ˈraundəbaut] *adj* indirecto,-a. − **2** *n* tiovivo. **3** AUTO plaza circular.
rounders [ˈraundəz] *n especie de béisbol m infantil*.
round-up [ˈraundʌp] *n (cattle)* rodeo. **2** *(by police)* redada. **3** *(summary)* resumen *m*.
rouse [rauz] *t-i* despertar(se). − **2** *t (provoke)* provocar.
rousing [ˈrauzɪŋ] *adj* apasionante. **2** *(moving)* conmovedor,-ra.
rout [raut] *n* derrota. − **2** *t* derrotar.
route [ruːt] *n* ruta, camino, vía. **2** *(of bus)* línea, trayecto.
routine [ruːˈtiːn] *n* rutina. − **2** *adj* rutinario,-a.

rove [rəuv] *i* vagar, errar.
row [rau] *n* riña, pelea. **2** *(noise)* jaleo, ruido. **3** *(line)* fila, hilera. **4** *(in a boat)* paseo en bote. − **5** *i* pelearse. **6** *(in a boat)* remar. − **7** *t* impeler mediante remos. ▲ *En 3, 4, 6, y 7* [rəu].
rowdy [ˈraudɪ] *adj* alborotador,-ra. **2** *(noisy)* ruidoso,-a.
rowing [ˈrəuɪŋ] *n* remo. ■ *~ boat,* bote *m* de remos.
royal [ˈrɔɪəl] *adj* real.
royalist [ˈrɔɪəlɪst] *adj-n* monárquico,-a.
royalty [ˈrɔɪəltɪ] *n* realeza. **2** *(people)* miembros de la familia real. **3** *pl* derechos *mpl* (de autor).
rub [rʌb] *n* friega. − **2** *t* frotar; *(hard)* restregar. − **3** *i* rozar. ◆*to ~ out t* borrar. ●*fam to ~ it in,* insistir.
rubber [ˈrʌbəʳ] *n* caucho, goma. **2** *(eraser)* goma de borrar. **3** US *fam* goma. ■ *~ band,* goma elástica.
rubbish [ˈrʌbɪʃ] *n (refuse)* basura. **2** *fam (thing)* birria, porquería. **3** *(nonsense)* tonterías *fpl*.
rubble [ˈrʌbəl] *n* escombros *mpl*.
rubella [ruːˈbelə] *n* rubéola.
ruby [ˈruːbɪ] *n* rubí *m*.
rucksack [ˈrʌksæk] *n* mochila.
ructions [ˈrʌkʃənz] *npl fam* follón *m sing*.
rudder [ˈrʌdəʳ] *n* timón *m*.
ruddy [ˈrʌdɪ] *adj* colorado,-a. **2** GB *fam* maldito,-a.
rude [ruːd] *adj* maleducado,-a, descortés. **2** *(simple)* rudo,-a, tosco,-a. **3** *(improper)* grosero,-a.
rudeness [ˈruːdnəs] *n* falta de educación. **2** *(simplicity)* rudeza, tosquedad. **3** *(impropriety)* grosería.
rudimentary [ruːdɪˈmentrɪ] *adj* rudimentario,-a.
rudiment [ˈruːdɪmənt] *n* rudimento.
rue [ruː] *t* lamentàr, arrepentirse de.
rueful [ˈruːful] *adj* arrepentido,-a, afligido,-a.
ruff [rʌf] *n* gorguera. **2** ZOOL collarín *m*.
ruffian [ˈrʌfɪən] *adj* rufián *m*.
ruffle [ˈrʌfəl] *n* chorrera. − **3** *t* agitar. **4** *(feathers)* erizar. **5** *(hair)* despeinar. **6** *(annoy)* irritar.
rug [rʌg] *n* alfombra, alfombrilla.
rugby [ˈrʌgbɪ] *n* rugby *m*.
rugged [ˈrʌgɪd] *adj (terrain)* escabroso,-a.
ruin [ˈruːɪn] *n* ruina. − **2** *t* arruinar. **3** *(spoil)* estropear.
ruined [ˈruːɪnd] *adj* arruinado,-a. **2** *(spoilt)* estropeado,-a. **3** *(building)* en ruinas.

rule [ru:l] *n* regla, norma. **2** *(control)* dominio. **3** *(of monarch)* reinado. **4** *(measure)* regla. – **5** *t-i* gobernar, mandar. **6** *(monarch)* reinar. **7** *(decree)* decretar. ◆*to* ~ *out* *t* excluir, descartar. ●*as a* ~, por regla general.

ruler [ˈruːləʳ] *n* gobernante *mf*, dirigente *mf*. **2** *(monarch)* soberano,-a. **3** *(instrument)* regla.

ruling [ˈruːlɪŋ] *adj* dirigente. – **2** *n* JUR fallo.

rum [rʌm] *n* ron *m*.

rumble [ˈrʌmbəl] *n* retumbo, ruido sordo. **2** *(stomach)* borborigmo. – **3** *i* retumbar, hacer un ruido sordo. **4** *(stomach)* hacer ruidos.

ruminant [ˈruːmɪnənt] *adj-n* rumiante *(m)*.

ruminate [ˈruːmɪneɪt] *t-i* rumiar.

rummage [ˈrʌmɪdʒ] *t-i* revolver (buscando).

rumour [ˈruːməʳ] *n* rumor *m*. – **2** *t* rumorear.

rump [rʌmp] *n* ancas *fpl*. **2** *(of person)* trasero.

rumple [ˈrʌmpəl] *t* arrugar. **2** *(hair)* despeinar.

rumpus [ˈrʌmpəs] *n fam* jaleo.

run [rʌn] *n* carrera. **2** *(trip)* viaje *m*; *(for pleasure)* paseo. **3** *(sequence)* racha. **4** *(ski* ~*)* pista. **5** *(in stocking)* carrera. **6** *(demand)* gran demanda. – **7** *i gen* correr. **8** *(flow)* correr, discurrir. **9** *(drip)* gotear. **10** *(operate)* funcionar. **11** *(in election)* presentarse. **12** *(last)* durar. **13** *(bus, train)* circular. **14** *(colour)* desteñirse. – **15** *t (race)* correr en. **16** *(take by car)* llevar. **17** *(manage)* llevar, dirigir, regentar. **18** *(organize)* organizar, montar. **19** *(operate)* hacer funcionar. **20** *(publish)* publicar. ◆*to* ~ *after* *t* perseguir. ◆*to* ~ *along* *i* irse. ◆*to* ~ *away* *i* escaparse. ◆*to* ~ *down* *t (knock down)* atropellar. **2** *(criticize)* criticar. – **3** *t-i (battery)* agotar(se). **4** *(clock)* pararse. ◆*to* ~ *in* *t (car)* rodar. **2** *(criminal)* detener. ◆*to* ~ *into* *t (car)* chocar con. **2** *(meet)* tropezar con. ◆*to* ~ *off with* *t* escaparse con. ◆*to* ~ *out* *i* acabarse: *I've* ~ *out of sugar,* se

me ha acabado el azúcar. ◆*to* ~ *over* *t (knock down)* atropellar. – **2** *i (overflow)* rebosar. **3** *(spill)* derramar. ◆*to* ~ *through* *t* ensayar. **2** *(read)* echar un vistazo a. ◆*to* ~ *up* *t (debts)* acumular. **2** *(flag)* izar. ●*in the long* ~, a la larga. ▲ *pt ran; pp run*.

runaway [ˈrʌnəweɪ] *adj-n* fugitivo,-a. – **2** *adj (out of control)* incontrolado,-a. **3** *(tremendous)* aplastante.

rung [rʌŋ] *n* escalón *m*. – **2** *pp* → **ring**.

runner [ˈrʌnəʳ] *n* corredor,-ra. **2** *(of sledge)* patín *m*.

runner-up [rʌnərˈʌp] *n* subcampeón, -ona. ▲ *pl runners-up*.

running [ˈrʌnɪŋ] *n* el correr. – **2** *adj* corriente. **3** *(continuous)* contínuo,-a. – **4** *adv* seguido,-a. ●*out of/in the* ~, sin/con posibilidades de ganar. ■ ~ *costs,* gastos de mantenimiento.

runny [ˈrʌnɪ] *adj* blando,-a, líquido,-a. **2** *(nose)* que moquea.

run-of-the-mill [rʌnəvðəˈmɪl] *adj* corriente y moliente.

runway [ˈrʌnweɪ] *n* pista de aterrizaje.

run-up [ˈrʌnʌp] *n* etapa preliminar.

rupee [ruːˈpiː] *n* rupia.

rupture [ˈrʌptʃəʳ] *n* hernia. **2** *fig* ruptura. – **3** *t* romper. ●*to* ~ *o.s.,* herniarse.

rural [ˈrʊərəl] *adj* rural.

ruse [ruːz] *n* ardid *m*, astucia.

rush [rʌʃ] *n* prisa, precipitación. **2** *(movement)* movimiento/avance impetuoso. BOT junco. – **4** *t-i* precipitar(se), apresurar(se). – **5** *t (job etc.)* hacer de prisa. **6** *fam* cobrar. ●*to be rushed off one's feet,* ir de culo. ■ ~ *hour,* hora punta.

rusk [rʌsk] *n* galleta.

rust [rʌst] *n* óxido. – **2** *t-i* oxidar(se).

rustic [ˈrʌstɪk] *adj* rústico,-a.

rustle [ˈrʌsəl] *n* crujido. – **2** *t-i* (hacer) crujir. – **3** *i* robar ganado.

rustler [ˈrʌsələʳ] *n* cuatrero,-a.

rusty [ˈrʌstɪ] *adj* oxidado,-a.

rut [rʌt] *n* surco. **2** ZOOL celo. ●*in a* ~, esclavo,-a de la rutina.

ruthless [ˈruːθləs] *adj* cruel, despiadado,-a.

rye [raɪ] *n* centeno.

S

sabbatical [səˈbætɪkəl] *n* año sabático.
sabotage [ˈsæbətɑːʒ] *n* sabotaje *m*. – 2 *t* sabotear.
sack [sæk] *n* saco. – 2 *t* MIL saquear. 3 *fam* despedir a, echar del trabajo a. ●*fam to get the* ~, ser despedido,-a; *fam to hit the* ~, irse al catre.
sacrament [ˈsækrəmənt] *n* sacramento.
sacred [ˈseɪkrəd] *adj* sagrado,-a. ■ ~ *music*, música religiosa.
sacrifice [ˈsækrɪfaɪs] *n* sacrificio. 2 *(offering)* ofrenda. – 3 *t* sacrificar.
sacrilege [ˈsækrɪlɪdʒ] *n* sacrilegio.
sad [sæd] *adj* triste. 2 *(deplorable)* lamentable.
sadden [ˈsædən] *t-i* entristecer(se).
saddle [ˈsædəl] *n (for horse)* silla (de montar). 2 *(of bicycle)* sillín *m*. – 3 *t* ensillar.
sadism [ˈseɪdɪzəm] *n* sadismo.
sadness [ˈsædnəs] *n* tristeza.
safe [seɪf] *adj (unharmed)* ileso,-a. 2 *(out of danger)* a salvo, fuera de peligro. 3 *(not harmful)* inocuo,-a. 4 *(secure)* seguro,-a. – 5 *n* caja fuerte. – 6 *safely adv (surely)* con toda seguridad. 7 *(without mishap)* sin contratiempos. ●~ *and sound*, sano,-a y salvo,-a; ~ *from*, a salvo de; *to be on the* ~ *side*, para mayor seguridad.
safe-conduct [seɪfˈkɒndəkt] *n* salvoconducto.
safeguard [ˈseɪfgɑːd] *n* salvaguarda. – 2 *t* salvaguardar.
safety [ˈseɪftɪ] *n* seguridad. ■ ~ *belt*, cinturón *m* de seguridad; ~ *pin*, imperdible *m*.
saffron [ˈsæfrɒn] *n* azafrán *m*.
sag [sæg] *i (wood, iron)* combarse. 2 *(roof)* hundirse. 3 *(wall)* pandear. 4 *fig* flaquear.
saga [ˈsɑːgə] *n* saga.
sage [seɪdʒ] *adj-n* sabio,-a. 2 BOT salvia.

Sagittarius [sædʒɪˈteərɪəs] *n* Sagitario.
said [sed] *pt & pp* → say.
sail [seɪl] *n (canvas)* vela. 2 *(trip)* paseo en barco. – 3 *t* navegar. 4 *(cross)* cruzar en barco. – 5 *i* ir en barco. 6 *(leave)* zarpar. ●*to set* ~, zarpar; *fig to* ~ *through sth.*, encontrar algo muy fácil.
sailing [ˈseɪlɪŋ] *n gen* navegación. 2 *(yachting)* vela. ■ ~ *boat/ship*, velero, barco de vela.
sailor [ˈseɪləʳ] *n* marinero.
saint [seɪnt] *n* san, santo,-a.
saintly [ˈseɪntlɪ] *adj* santo,-a.
sake [seɪk] *n* bien *m*. ●*for old times'* ~, por los viejos tiempos; *for the* ~ *of*, por (el bien de); *fam for God's/goodness'* ~!, ¡por el amor de Dios!
salad [ˈsæləd] *n* ensalada. ■ ~ *dressing*, aliño, aderezo.
salamander [ˈsæləmændəʳ] *n* salamandra.
salary [ˈsælərɪ] *n* salario, sueldo.
sale [seɪl] *n gen* venta. 2 *(special offering)* liquidación, rebajas *fpl*. 3 *(auction)* subasta. ●*for/on* ~, en venta. ■ *sales manager*, jefe,-a de ventas, director,-a comercial.
salesclerk [ˈseɪlzklɑːk] *n* dependiente,-a.
salesman [ˈseɪlzmən] *n* vendedor *m*. 2 *(in shop)* dependiente. 3 *(travelling)* representante *m*.
saleswoman [ˈseɪlzwʊmən] *n* vendedora. 2 *(in shop)* dependienta. 3 *(travelling)* representante *f*.
saliva [səˈlaɪvə] *n* saliva.
sallow [ˈsæləʊ] *adj* cetrino,-a.
salmon [ˈsæmən] *n* salmón *m*.
salon [ˈsælɒn] *n* salón *m*.
saloon [səˈluːn] *n* US taberna, bar *m*. ■ GB ~ *(bar)*, bar *m* de lujo; GB ~ *(car)*, turismo.

salt [sɔːlt] *n* sal *f*. – **2** *adj* salado,-a. – **3** *t* *(cure)* curar. **4** *(season)* salar. ●*fig the* ~ *of the earth,* la sal de la tierra. ■ ~ *beef,* cecina; ~ *pork,* tocino.

saltcellar [ˈsɔːltselə^r] *n* salero.

saltpetre [sɔːltˈpiːtə^r] *n* salitre *m*.

saltwater [ˈsɔːltwɔːtə^r] *adj* de agua salada.

salty [ˈsɔːltɪ] *adj* salado,-a.

salutary [ˈsæljʊtərɪ] *adj* beneficioso,-a.

salute [səˈluːt] *n* saludo. – **2** *t-i* saludar.

salvage [ˈsælvɪdʒ] *n* salvamento, rescate *m*. **2** *(property)* objetos *mpl* recuperados. – **3** *t* salvar, rescatar.

salvation [sælˈveɪʃən] *n* salvación.

salve [sælv] *n* pomada. – **2** *t fml* aliviar.

same [seɪm] *adj* mismo,-a. – **2** *pron the* ~, lo mismo. – **3** *adv* igual, del mismo modo. ●*all the* ~, a pesar de todo; *at the* ~ *time,* a la vez, al mismo tiempo; *fam* ~ *here,* yo también; *fam the* ~ *to you!,* ¡igualmente!

sample [ˈsɑːmpəl] *n* muestra. – **2** *t gen* probar; *(wine)* catar.

sanatorium [sænəˈtɔːrɪəm] *n* sanatorio. ▲ *pl* **sanatoriums** *o* **sanatoria** [sænəˈtɔːrɪə].

sanctimonious [sæŋktɪˈməʊnɪəs] *adj pej* santurrón,-ona.

sanction [ˈsæŋkʃən] *n* sanción. **2** *fml (permission)* autorización, permiso. – **3** *t fml* autorizar.

sanctuary [ˈsæŋktjʊərɪ] *n* santuario. **2** *(asylum)* asilo. **3** *(for animals)* refugio.

sand [sænd] *n* arena. ■ ~ *dune,* duna.

sandal [ˈsændəl] *n* sandalia.

sandbank [ˈsændbæŋk] *n* banco de arena.

sandpaper [ˈsændpeɪpə^r] *n* papel *m* de lija. – **2** *t* lijar.

sandstone [ˈsændstəʊn] *n* arenisca.

sandwich [ˈsænwɪdʒ] *n* sandwich *m*, bocadillo. – **2** *t* intercalar, encajonar.

sandy [ˈsændɪ] *adj* arenoso,-a. **2** *(hair)* rubio,-a oscuro,-a.

sane [seɪn] *adj* cuerdo,-a. **2** *(sensible)* sensato,-a.

sang [sæŋ] *pt* → **sing**.

sanitary [ˈsænɪtərɪ] *adj* sanitario,-a, de sanidad. **2** *(clean)* higiénico,-a. ■ ~ *towel,* compresa.

sanitation [sænɪˈteɪʃən] *n (public health)* sanidad (pública). **2** *(plumbing)* sistema *m* de saneamiento.

sanity [ˈsænɪtɪ] *n* cordura, juicio. **2** *(sense)* sensatez *f*.

sank [sæŋk] *pt* → **sink**.

sap [sæp] *n* savia. – **2** *t fig* minar, debilitar.

sapphire [ˈsæfaɪə^r] *n* zafiro.

sarcasm [ˈsɑːkæzəm] *n* sarcasmo, sorna.

sarcastic [sɑːˈkæstɪk] *adj* sarcástico,-a.

sardine [sɑːˈdiːn] *n* sardina.

sardonic [sɑːˈdɒnɪk] *adj* sardónico,-a.

sash [sæʃ] *n (waistband)* faja. **2** *(frame)* marco (de ventana). ■ ~ *window,* ventana de guillotina.

sat [sæt] *pt & pp* → **sit**.

satanic [səˈtænɪk] *adj* satánico,-a.

satchel [ˈsætʃəl] *n* mochila (de colegial).

satellite [ˈsætəlaɪt] *n* satélite *m*. ■ ~ *dish aerial,* antena parabólica.

satiate [ˈseɪʃɪeɪt] *t* saciar.

satin [ˈsætɪn] *n* satén *m*, raso.

satire [ˈsætaɪə^r] *n* sátira.

satirical [səˈtɪrɪkəl] *adj* satírico,-a.

satirize [ˈsætəraɪz] *t* satirizar.

satisfaction [sætɪsˈfækʃən] *n* satisfacción.

satisfactory [sætɪsˈfæktərɪ] *adj* satisfactorio,-a.

satisfy [ˈsætɪsfaɪ] *t* satisfacer. **2** *(requirements)* cumplir. **3** *(convince)* convencer.

saturate [ˈsætʃəreɪt] *t* saturar. **2** *(soak)* empapar.

Saturday [ˈsætədɪ] *n* sábado.

sauce [sɔːs] *n* salsa. **2** *fam (cheek)* frescura, descaro. ■ ~ *boat,* salsera.

saucepan [ˈsɔːspən] *n* cazo, cacerola. **2** *(large)* olla.

saucer [ˈsɔːsə^r] *n* platillo. ■ *flying* ~, platillo volante.

saucy [ˈsɔːsɪ] *adj fam* descarado,-a, fresco,-a.

sauna [ˈsɔːnə] *n* sauna.

saunter [ˈsɔːntə^r] *i* pasearse.

sausage [ˈsɒsɪdʒ] *n (uncooked)* salchicha. **2** *(cooked)* embutido.

sauté [ˈsəʊteɪ] *t* saltear.

savage [ˈsævɪdʒ] *adj (fierce)* feroz. **2** *(cruel)* salvaje, cruel. **3** *(uncivilized)* salvaje. – **4** *n* salvaje *mf*. – **5** *t* embestir.

save [seɪv] *t* salvar. **2** *(keep)* guardar. **3** *(money, time, energy)* ahorrar(se). – **4** *i to* ~ *(up),* ahorrar. – **5** *prep fml* salvo. ◆*to* ~ *on t* ahorrar.

saving [ˈseɪvɪŋ] *n* ahorro, economía. **2** *pl* ahorros *mpl*. ■ *savings account/bank,* cuenta/caja de ahorros.

saviour [ˈseɪvɪə^r] *n* salvador,-ra.

savour [ˈseɪvə^r] *n* sabor *m*. – **2** *t* saborear.

savoury [ˈseɪvərɪ] *adj* salado,-a. – **2** *n* canapé *m*, entremés *m*.

saw [sɔ:] *pt* → **see**. – **2** *n (tool)* sierra. – **3** *t-i* (a)serrar. ▲ *pp* **sawed** *o* **sawn** [sɔ:n].

sawdust ['sɔ:dʌst] *n* serrín *m*.

sawn [sɔ:n] *pp* → **saw**.

saxophone ['sæksəfəʊn] *n* saxofón *m*.

say [seɪ] *t* decir: *he says (that) he's innocent,* dice que es inocente. **2** *(clock, meter)* marcar. **3** *(suppose)* (su)poner: *let's ̀ ~ it costs about £20,* pongamos que cuesta unas veinte libras. – **4** *n* opinión. ●*it is said that ...,* dicen que ...; se dice que ...; *that is to ~,* es decir; *to have one's ~,* dar su opinión; *to ~ the least,* como mínimo; *fam you don't ~!,* ¡no me digas! ▲ *pt & pp* **said**.

saying ['seɪɪŋ] *n* dicho, decir *m*.

scab [skæb] *n* costra, postilla. **2** *pej (blackleg)* esquirol *m*.

scaffold ['skæfəʊld] *n* andamio. **2** *(for criminals)* patíbulo.

scaffolding ['skæfəldɪŋ] *n* andamio.

scald [skɔ:ld] *n* escaldadura. – **2** *t (burn)* escaldar. **3** *(liquid)* calentar.

scale [skeɪl] *n gen* escala. **2** *(of fish etc.)* escama. **3** *(on pipes etc.)* incrustaciones *fpl*. **4** *pl (for weighing)* balanza *f sing*; *(in bathroom)* báscula *f sing*. – **5** *t (climb up)* escalar. **6** *(fish)* escamar. ◆*to ~ down/up t* reducir/aumentar proporcionalmente. ●*on a large ~,* a gran escala; *to ~,* a escala. ■ *~ drawing,* dibujo (hecho) a escala; *~ model,* maqueta.

scalp [skælp] *n* cuero cabelludo.

scalpel ['skælpəl] *n* bisturí *m*.

scaly ['skeɪlɪ] *adj* escamoso,-a.

scamp [skæmp] *n* diablillo,-a, pícaro,-a.

scamper ['skæmpəʳ] *i* corretear.

scampi ['skæmpɪ] *n* cigalas *fpl* empanadas/rebozadas.

scan [skæn] *t (examine)* escrutar. **2** *(glance over)* echar un vistazo a. – **3** *n* exploración ultrasónica, ecografía.

scandal ['skændəl] *n* escándalo. **2** *(gossip)* chismes *mpl*.

scandalize ['skændəlaɪz] *t* escandalizar.

scandalous ['skændələs] *adj* escandaloso,-a.

scant [skænt] *adj* escaso,-a.

scanty ['skæntɪ] *adj* escaso,-a; *(meal)* insuficiente.

scapegoat ['skeɪpgəʊt] *n fig* cabeza de turco, chivo expiatorio.

scar [skɑ:ʳ] *n* cicatriz *f*. **2** *fig* huella. – **3** *t* dejar cicatriz.

scarce [skeəs] *adj* escaso,-a. – **2** *scarcely adv* apenas. ●*scarcely ever,* casi nunca; *to be ~,* escasear.

scarcity ['skeəsɪtɪ] *n* escasez *f*.

scare [skeəʳ] *n (fright)* susto. **2** *(widespread)* alarma, pánico. – **3** *t-i* asustar(se), espantar(se). ◆*to ~ away/off t* espantar, ahuyentar.

scarecrow ['skeəkrəʊ] *n* espantapájaros *m inv*, espantajo.

scarf [skɑ:f] *n (small)* pañuelo. **2** *(long, woolen)* bufanda. ▲ *pl* **scarfs** *o* **scarves** [skɑ:vz].

scarlet ['skɑ:lət] *adj-n* escarlata *(m)*. ■ *~ fever,* escarlatina.

scary ['skeərɪ] *adj fam* espantoso,-a. **2** *(film, story)* de miedo/terror.

scatter ['skætəʳ] *t-i (disperse)* dispersar(se). **2** *(spread)* esparcir, derramar.

scatterbrain ['skætəbreɪn] *n* cabeza de chorlito.

scattering ['skætərɪŋ] *n a ~ of,* unos,-as cuantos,-as, algunos,-as.

scavenge ['skævɪndʒ] *i* rebuscar. – **2** *t* encontrar en la basura.

scavenger ['skævɪndʒəʳ] *n (animal)* animal carroñero. **2** *(person)* rebuscador,-ra, trapero,-ra.

scenario [sɪ'nɑ:rɪəʊ] *n* CINEM guión *m*. **2** *(situation)* (posible) situación, circunstancias *fpl*.

scene [si:n] *n gen* escena. **2** *(place)* escenario. **3** *(view)* vista, panorama *m*. ●*behind the scenes,* entre bastidores; *the ~ of the crime,* el lugar del crimen; *to make a ~,* armar un escándalo.

scenery ['si:nərɪ] *n* paisaje *m*. **2** THEAT decorado.

scent [sent] *n* olor *m*. **2** *(perfume)* perfume *m*. **3** *(track)* pista, rastro. – **4** *t (smell)* olfatear; *fig* presentir. **5** *(add perfume to)* perfumar.

sceptre ['septəʳ] *n* cetro.

schedule ['ʃedju:l, 'skedju:l] *n (programme)* programa *m*. **2** *(list)* lista. **3** US *(timetable)* horario. – **4** *t* programar, fijar. ●*on ~,* a la hora (prevista); *to be ahead of/behind ~,* ir adelantado,-a/retrasado,-a.

scheme [ski:m] *n (plan)* plan *m*, programa *m*; *(system)* sistema *m*. **2** *(plot)* intriga; *(trick)* ardid *m*. – **3** *i* conspirar, tramar.

schism ['skɪzəm] *n* cisma *m*.

schizophrenia [skɪtsəʊ'fri:nɪə] *n* esquizofrenia.

scholar ['skɒləʳ] *n (learned person)* erudito,-a. **2** *(holder of scholarship)* becario,-a.

scholarship ['skɒləʃɪp] *n (grant)* beca. **2** *(learning)* erudición.

school [sku:l] *n* escuela. **2** *(students)* alumnos *mpl*, alumnado. **3** *(of university)* facultad *f.* **4** *(of fish)* banco. – **5** *t (teach)* enseñar; *(train)* educar, formar. ■ ~ *of thought,* corriente *f* de opinión; ~ *year,* año escolar.

schoolchild ['skuːltʃaɪld] *n* alumno,-a. ▲ *pl* **schoolchildren** ['skuːltʃɪldrən].

schooling ['skuːlɪŋ] *n* estudios *mpl.*

schoolmaster ['skuːlmɑːstə^r] *n* profesor *m.* **2** *(primary education)* maestro.

schoolmistress ['skuːlmɪstrəs] *n* profesora. **2** *(primary education)* maestra.

science ['saɪəns] *n* ciencia. **2** *(subject)* ciencias *fpl.* ■ ~ *fiction,* ciencia-ficción.

scientific [saɪən'tɪfɪk] *adj* científico,-a.

scientist ['saɪəntɪst] *n* científico,-a.

scissors ['sɪzəz] *npl* tijeras *fpl.* ●*a pair of* ~, unas tijeras.

scoff [skɒf] *i (mock)* mofarse/burlarse *(at,* de). **2** *fam (eat fast)* zamparse.

scold [skəʊld] *t* reñir, regañar.

scoop [skuːp] *n gen* pala; *(for ice-cream)* cucharón *m.* **2** *(amount)* cucharada. **3** *(exclusive)* exclusiva. ◆*to* ~ *out t* sacar con pala/cucharón.

scooter ['skuːtə^r] *n (adult's)* Vespa®. **2** *(child's)* patinete *m.*

scope [skəʊp] *n (range)* alcance *m*; *(of undertaking)* ámbito. **2** *(chance)* oportunidad.

scorch [skɔːtʃ] *t (singe)* chamuscar. **2** *(burn)* abrasar.

scorching ['skɔːtʃɪŋ] *adj* abrasador,-ra.

score [skɔː^r] *n* SP tanteo; *(golf, cards)* puntuación. **2** *(result)* resultado. **3** *(notch)* muesca. **4** MUS partitura; *(of film)* música. – **5** *t-i* SP marcar (un tanto); *(football)* marcar (un gol). **6** *fig (have success)* tener (éxito). – **7** *t (notch)* hacer una muesca en; *(paper)* rayar. ●*on that* ~, a ese respecto; *to keep the* ~, seguir el marcador; *what's the* ~?, ¿cómo van?

scoreboard ['skɔːbɔːd] *n* marcador *m.*

scorn [skɔːn] *n* desdén *m*, desprecio. – **2** *t* desdeñar, despreciar.

Scorpio ['skɔːpɪəʊ] *n* Escorpión *m.*

scorpion ['skɔːpɪən] *n* escorpión *m.*

scoundrel ['skaʊndrəl] *n* canalla *m.*

scour ['skaʊə^r] *t (search)* recorrer. **2** *(clean)* fregar, restregar.

scout [skaʊt] *n* explorador,-ra. – **2** *i* reconocer el terreno.

scowl [skaʊl] *i* fruncir el ceño.

scramble ['skræmbəl] *n (climb)* subida. **2** *(struggle)* lucha. – **3** *i (climb)* trepar. **4** *(struggle)* pelearse: *to* ~ *for seats,* pelearse por encontrar asiento. – **5** *t* revolver. ■ *scrambled eggs,* huevos *mpl* revueltos.

scrap [skræp] *n* trozo, pedazo. **2** *pl* restos *mpl*; *(of food)* sobras *fpl.* **3** *fam (fight)* pelea. – **4** *t* desechar. – **5** *i fam* pelearse. ■ ~ *(metal),* chatarra; ~ *paper,* papel *m* borrador.

scrape [skreɪp] *n (act)* raspado. **2** *(mark)* rasguño. – **3** *t (paint)* raspar. **4** *(skin)* hacerse un rasguño en. ◆*to* ~ *along i* ir tirando. ◆*to* ~ *through t (exam)* aprobar de chiripa/por los pelos.

scratch [skrætʃ] *n* arañazo; *(on record, photo)* raya. **2** *(noise)* chirrido. – **3** *t-i* arañar, rasguñar; *(paintwork etc.)* rayar. **4** *(itch)* rascarse. – **5** *t* SP cancelar. ●*fam to be/come up to* ~, dar la talla; *fam to start from* ~, partir de cero. ■ SP ~ *team,* equipo improvisado.

scrawny ['skrɔːnɪ] *adj pej* flacucho,-a.

scream [skriːm] *n* grito, chillido. – **2** *t-i* gritar. ●*fam it was a* ~, fue la monda.

screech [skriːtʃ] *n (of person)* chillido. **2** *(of tyres etc.)* chirrido. – **3** *i (person)* chillar. **4** *(tyres etc.)* chirriar.

screen [skriːn] *n (partition)* biombo. **2** *(cinema, TV, etc.)* pantalla. **3** *fig* cortina. – **4** *t (protect)* proteger. **5** *(hide)* ocultar, tapar. **6** *(test)* examinar. **7** *(film)* proyectar. ■ CINEM ~ *test,* prueba.

screw [skruː] *n* tornillo. **2** *(propeller)* hélice *f.* – **3** *t* atornillar. – **4*** *t-i (have sex with)* joder*. ◆*to* ~ *up t (twist)* arrugar; *(face)* torcer. **2** *sl (ruin)* jorobar, fastidiar. ●*sl to* ~ *money out of sb.,* sacarle dinero a algn.

screwdriver ['skruːdraɪvə^r] *n* destornillador *m.*

scribble ['skrɪbəl] *n* garabatos *mpl.* – **2** *t-i* garabatear.

script [skrɪpt] *n (handwriting)* letra. **2** *(writing)* escritura. **3** CINEM guión *m.*

scrounge [skraʊndʒ] *i* gorrear, vivir de gorra. – **2** *t* gorrear *(from,* de/a). ●*to* ~ *off sb.,* vivir a costa de algn.

scrub [skrʌb] *n (undergrowth)* maleza. **2** *(cleaning)* fregado. – **3** *t gen* fregar; *(clothes)* lavar.

scruff [skrʌf] *n* cogote *m.*

scruffy ['skrʌfɪ] *adj* desaliñado,-a.

scruple ['skruːpəl] *n* escrúpulo.

scrupulous ['skruːpjʊləs] *adj* escrupuloso,-a.

scrutinize ['skruːtɪnaɪz] *t* escudriñar, examinar a fondo.

sculptor ['skʌlptə^r] *n* escultor *m.*

sculptress ['skʌlptrəs] *n* escultora.

sculpture ['skʌlptʃə^r] *n* escultura. – **2** *t* esculpir.

scum [skʌm] *n* espuma. **2** *fig* escoria.

scurry ['skʌrɪ] *i* correr. ◆*to* ~ *away/off i* escabullirse.

scuttle ['skʌtəl] *t* MAR hundir. – 2 *i (run)* corretear.

sea [si:] *n* mar *m & f.* ●*at* ~, en el mar; *fam fig* desorientado,-a; *by the* ~, a orillas del mar. ■ *rough* ~, marejada; ~ *level,* nivel *m* del mar; ~ *lion,* león marino; ~ *trout,* trucha de mar, reo.

seafood ['si:fu:d] *n* mariscos *mpl.*

seagull ['si:gʌl] *n* gaviota.

sea-horse ['si:hɔ:s] *n* caballito de mar.

seal [si:l] *n* ZOOL foca. 2 *(stamp)* sello. – 3 *t* sellar; *(bottle)* precintar. ◆*to* ~ *off t (close)* cerrar. 2 *(block)* cerrar el acceso a.

seam [si:m] *n* costura. 2 TECH juntura, junta. 3 MED sutura. 4 *(of mineral)* veta.

seamstress ['semstrəs] *n* costurera.

search [sɜ:tʃ] *n* búsqueda. 2 *(of building)* registro. – 3 *t-i* buscar (en). – 4 *t (building, suitcase)* registrar. 5 *(person)* cachear. ●*in* ~ *of,* en busca de. ■ ~ *party,* equipo de salvamento.

searchlight ['sɜ:tʃlaɪt] *n* reflector *m*, proyector *m.*

seasick ['si:sɪk] *adj* mareado,-a.

seaside ['si:saɪd] *n* playa, costa. ■ ~ *resort,* lugar *m*/complejo turístico de veraneo.

season ['si:zən] *n (of year)* estación. 2 *(time)* época. 3 *(for sport etc.)* temporada. – 4 *t (food)* sazonar. 5 *(person)* avezar. ●*in* ~, *(fruit)* en sazón; *(animal)* en celo. ■ ~ *ticket,* abono.

seat [si:t] *n* asiento. 2 *(at theatre etc.)* localidad. 3 *(of cycle)* sillín *m.* 4 *(centre)* sede *f*, centro. 5 *(in parliament)* escaño. – 6 *t* sentar. 7 *(accomodate)* tener cabida para. ●*to take a* ~, sentarse, tomar asiento.

secession [sɪ'seʃən] *n* secesión.

secluded [sɪ'klu:dɪd] *adj* aislado,-a, apartado,-a.

seclusion [sɪ'klu:ʒən] *n* aislamiento.

second ['sekənd] *adj-n* segundo,-a. – 2 *n (time)* segundo. 3 *pl* COM artículos *mpl* defectuosos. – 4 *adv* segundo, en segundo lugar. – 5 *t (support)* apoyar, secundar. 6 GB *(transfer)* trasladar temporalmente. – 7 *secondly adv* en segundo lugar. ●*to have* ~ *thoughts about sth.,* dudar de algo. ■ ~ *hand, (of watch)* segundero. ▲ *En 6 (verbo)* [sɪ'kɒnd].

secondary ['sekəndərɪ] *adj* secundario,-a.

second-hand ['sekəndhænd] *adj* de segunda mano.

secrecy ['si:krəsɪ] *n* secreto. 2 *(practice)* discreción.

secret ['si:krət] *adj* secreto,-a. – 2 *n* secreto. – 3 *secretly adv* en secreto. ●*in* ~, en secreto. ■ ~ *service,* servicio secreto.

secretary ['sekrətərɪ] *n* secretario,-a. ■ *Secretary of State,* GB ministro,-a con cartera, US ministro,-a de Asuntos Exteriores.

secrete [sɪ'kri:t] *t* secretar, segregar.

sect [sekt] *n* secta.

section ['sekʃən] *n gen* sección. 2 *(of road, track)* tramo. 3 *(of law)* apartado. – 4 *t* cortar, seccionar.

sector ['sektə] *n* sector *m.*

secular ['sekjʊlə] *adj (education)* laico,-a. 2 *(art, music)* profano,-a.

secure [sɪ'kjʊə] *adj* seguro,-a. – 2 *t* asegurar. 3 *(fasten)* sujetar, fijar; *(window etc.)* asegurar. 4 *(obtain)* obtener, conseguir.

security [sɪ'kjʊərɪtɪ] *n (safety)* seguridad. 2 *(property)* fianza, aval *m.* 3 *pl* COM valores *mpl.*

sedative ['sedətɪv] *adj-n* sedativo,-a, sedante *(m).*

sedentary ['sedəntərɪ] *adj* sedentario,-a.

sediment ['sedɪmənt] *n* sedimento. 2 *(of wine)* hez *f*, poso.

sedition [sɪ'dɪʃən] *n* sedición.

seduce [sɪ'dju:s] *t* seducir.

see [si:] *t-i* ver. 2 *(ensure)* procurar: ~ *that you arrive on time,* procura llegar a la hora. 3 *(accompany)* acompañar *(to,* a). – 4 *n* sede *f.* ◆*to* ~ *about t* ocuparse de. ◆*to* ~ *off t* despedirse de. ◆*to* ~ *out t (last)* durar. 2 *(go to door with)* acompañar hasta la puerta. ◆*to* ~ *through t* calar a, verle el plumero a. ◆*to* ~ *to t* ocuparse de. ●~ *you later/Monday!,* ¡hasta luego/el lunes!; *to be seeing things,* ver visiones; *to* ~ *red,* ponerse negro,-a; *we'll* ~, ya veremos. ▲ *pt saw; pp seen.*

seed [si:d] *n* semilla; *(of fruit)* pepita. 2 SP cabeza *m* de serie. – 3 *t* sembrar.

seedy ['si:dɪ] *adj* sórdido,-a. 2 *(unwell)* pachucho,-a.

seek [si:k] *t (look for)* buscar. 2 *(ask for)* solicitar. ◆*to* ~ *after/out t* buscar. ▲ *pt & pp sought.*

seem [si:m] *i* parecer: *it seems to me that ...,* me parece que ... . ●*so it seems,* eso parece.

seeming ['si:mɪŋ] *adj* aparente. – 2 *seemingly adv* aparentemente, al parecer.

seen [si:n] *pp* → **see.**

seep [si:p] *i* rezumarse. ●*to* ~ *into/out sth.*, filtrarse en/de algo.

seesaw ['si:sɔ:] *n* subibaja *m*.

seethe [si:ð] *i* hervir. **2** *fig (with anger)* rabiar.

segment ['segmənt] *n* segmento.

segregate ['segrɪgeɪt] *t* segregar.

segregation [segrɪ'geɪʃən] *n* segregación.

seismic ['saɪzmɪk] *adj* sísmico,-a.

seize [si:z] *t* asir, agarrar, coger. **2** JUR incautar, embargar. **3** MIL tomar, apoderarse de. ◆*to* ~ *up i* agarrotarse.

seizure ['si:ʒər] *n* JUR incautación, embargo. **2** MED ataque *m* (de apoplejía).

seldom ['seldəm] *adv* raramente, rara vez.

select [sɪ'lekt] *t* escoger, elegir. **2** SP seleccionar. – **3** *adj* selecto,-a, escogido,-a.

selection [sɪ'lekʃən] *n* selección. **2** *(choosing)* elección. **3** *(range)* surtido.

selective [sɪ'lektɪv] *adj* selectivo,-a.

self [self] *n* yo, identidad propia: *my other* ~, mi otro yo. ▲ *pl* **selves** [selvz].

self-assured [selfə'ʃʊəd] *adj* seguro,-a de sí mismo,-a.

self-centred [self'sentəd] *adj* egocéntrico,-a.

self-confidence [self'kɒnfɪdəns] *n* seguridad/confianza en sí mismo,-a.

self-conscious [self'kɒnʃəs] *adj* cohibido,-a, tímido,-a.

self-defence [selfdɪ'fens] *n* defensa personal, autodefensa.

self-employed [selfɪm'plɔɪd] *adj* autónomo,-a, que trabaja por cuenta propia.

self-government [self'gʌvənmənt] *n* autonomía, autogobierno.

selfish ['selfɪʃ] *adj* egoísta.

selfishness ['selfɪʃnəs] *n* egoísmo.

selfless ['selfləs] *adj* desinteresado,-a.

self-respect [selfrɪ'spekt] *n* amor *m* propio, dignidad.

self-righteous [self'raɪtʃəs] *adj* altivo,-a.

self-service [self'sɜ:vɪs] *adj-n* (de) autoservicio.

sell [sel] *t-i* vender(se). ◆*to* ~ *off t (cheaply)* liquidar. ◆*to* ~ *out i (be disloyal)* claudicar, venderse. – **2** *t* agotarse: *the tickets are sold out,* las localidades están agotadas. ◆*to* ~ *up i* venderlo todo. ●*fam to be sold on sth.,* entusiasmarse por algo. ▲ *pt & pp* **sold**.

seller ['selər] *n* vendedor,-ra.

sellotape® ['seləteɪp] *n* celo®, cinta adhesiva.

semantics [sɪ'mæntɪks] *n* semántica.

semen ['si:mən] *n* semen *m*.

semester [sɪ'mestər] *n* semestre *m*.

semicircle ['semɪsɜ:kəl] *n* semicírculo.

semicolon [semɪ'kəʊlən] *n* punto y coma.

semidetached [semɪdɪ'tætʃt] *adj* adosado,-a. – **2** *n* casa adosada.

semifinal [semɪ'faɪnəl] *n* semifinal *f*.

seminar ['semɪnɑ:r] *n* seminario.

senate ['senət] *n* senado.

senator ['senətər] *n* senador,-ra.

send [send] *t gen* enviar, mandar: ~ *me the results,* envíeme los resultados. **2** *(cause to become)* volver: *the noise sent her mad,* el ruido la volvió loca. – **3** *i to* ~ *for sb./sth.,* mandar llamar a algn./ pedir algo (por correo). ◆*to* ~ *away t* despachar. – **2** *i to* ~ *away for sth.,* pedir algo por correo. ◆*to* ~ *back t (goods etc.)* devolver. **2** *(person)* hacer volver. ◆*to* ~ *in t (post)* mandar, enviar. **2** *(visitor)* hacer pasar. ◆*to* ~ *off t (post)* enviar. **2** *(footbal)* expulsar. ◆*to* ~ *on t (letter)* hacer seguir. **2** *(luggage)* facturar. ●*to* ~ *sth. flying,* tirar algo (al aire); *to* ~ *word,* mandar recado. ▲ *pt & pp* **sent**.

sender ['sendər] *n* remitente *mf*.

send-off ['sendɒf] *n fam* despedida.

senile ['si:naɪl] *adj* senil.

senior ['si:nɪər] *adj (in age)* mayor; *(in rank)* superior. **2** *(with longer service)* de más antigüedad. – **3** *n (in age)* mayor *mf*; *(in rank)* superior *m*. ■ ~ *citizen,* jubilado,-a, persona de la tercera edad.

seniority [si:nɪ'ɒrɪtɪ] *n* antigüedad.

sensation [sen'seɪʃən] *n* sensación. ●*to be a* ~, ser (todo) un éxito.

sensational [sen'seɪʃənəl] *adj* sensacional. **2** *(exaggerated)* sensacionalista.

sense [sens] *n gen* sentido. **2** *(feeling)* sensación. – **3** *t* sentir, percibir. ●*in a* ~, hasta cierto punto; *there's no* ~ *in ...,* ¿de qué sirve ...?; *to come to one's senses,* recobrar el juicio; *to make* ~, tener sentido.

senseless ['sensləs] *adj (unconscious)* inconsciente. **2** *(foolish)* absurdo,-a, insensato,-a.

sensibility [sensɪ'bɪlɪtɪ] *n* sensibilidad.

sensible ['sensɪbəl] *adj* sensato,-a, razonable.

sensitive ['sensɪtɪv] *adj* sensible (*to,* a). **2** *(touchy)* susceptible. **3** *(document)* confidencial.

sensual ['sensjʊəl] *adj* sensual.

sent [sent] *pt & pp* → **send**.

sentence ['sentəns] *n* frase *f*, oración. 2 JUR sentencia, fallo, condena. − 3 *t* JUR condenar. ●*to pass ~ on sb.*, imponer una pena a algn.

sentimental [sentɪ'mentəl] *adj* sentimental.

sentry ['sentrɪ] *n* centinela *m & f*.

separable ['sepərəbəl] *adj* separable.

separate ['sepərət] *t-i* separar(se). − 2 *t* (*divide*) dividir. − 3 *adj* separado,-a. 4 (*individual*) individual. 5 (*different*) distinto,-a. − 6 *separately adv* por separado. ▲ *De 3 a 5* (*adjetivo*) ['sepərət].

separation [sepə'reɪʃən] *n* separación.

separatist ['sepərətɪst] *n* separatista *mf*.

September [səp'tembə^r] *n* septiembre *m*.

septic ['septɪk] *adj* séptico,-a.

sepulchre ['sepəlkə^r] *n* sepulcro.

sequel ['si:kwəl] *n* secuela.

sequence ['si:kwəns] *n* secuencia.

sequin ['si:kwɪn] *n* lentejuela.

serenade [serə'neɪd] *n* serenata. − 2 *t* dar una serenata a.

serene [sə'ri:n] *adj* sereno,-a, tranquilo,-a.

serenity [sə'renɪtɪ] *n* serenidad.

sergeant ['sɑːdʒənt] *n* MIL sargento. 2 (*of police*) cabo. ■ *~ major*, sargento mayor, brigada *m*.

serial ['sɪərɪəl] *adj* de serie. − 2 *n* serial *m*; (*book*) novela por entregas.

series ['sɪəri:z] *n inv* serie *f*. 2 (*of films, lectures*) ciclo.

serious ['sɪərɪəs] *adj* serio,-a. 2 (*causing concern*) grave. − 3 *seriously adv* (*in earnest*) en serio. 4 (*severely*) seriamente, gravemente. ●*seriously wounded*, herido,-a de gravedad; *to be ~*, (*person*) hablar en serio.

seriousness ['sɪərɪəsnəs] *n* seriedad, gravedad.

sermon ['sɜːmən] *n* sermón *m*.

servant ['sɜːvənt] *n* criado,-a.

serve [sɜːv] *t-i* servir (*as/for*, de). − 2 *t* (*provide*) equipar (*with*, de). 3 (*sentence*) cumplir. 4 (*tennis etc.*) sacar, servir. ●*to ~ time*, cumplir una condena; *fam it serves him/you right*, lo tiene(s) bien merecido.

server ['sɜːvə^r] *n* (*cutlery*) cubierto de servir. 2 SP jugador,-ra al servicio.

service ['sɜːvɪs] *n* servicio. 2 (*maintenance*) revisión; (*of car*) puesta a punto. 3 REL oficio. 4 (*of dishes*) juego, servicio. 5 (*tennis*) saque *m*, servicio. ●*at your ~*, a su disposición. ■ *~ station*, estación de servicio.

serviceman ['sɜːvɪsmən] *n* militar *m*.

serviette [sɜːvɪ'et] *n* GB servilleta.

session ['seʃən] *n* sesión.

set [set] *n* juego. 2 (*books, poems*) colección. 3 MATH conjunto. 4 (*tennis*) set *m*. 5 CINEM THEAT escenario, decorado. 6 (*equipment*) aparato. − 7 *adj* (*fixed*) fijo,-a. 8 (*rigid*) rígido,-a; (*opinion*) inflexible. 9 (*ready*) listo,-a (*for/to*, para). − 10 *t* (*put, place*) poner, colocar; (*trap*) tender. 11 (*establish*) fijar. 12 (*adjust*) ajustar; (*clock, alarm*) poner. 13 (*give, assign*) poner. 14 (*precious stone*) montar. 15 (*hair*) marcar. − 16 *i* (*sun*) ponerse. 17 (*liquid, jelly*) cuajar; (*cement*) endurecerse. ◆*to ~ about t* empezar a. ◆*to ~ aside t* (*save*) guardar, reservar. 2 (*disregard*) dejar de lado. ◆*to ~ back t* (*at a distance*) apartar. 2 (*make late*) retrasar. 3 *fam* (*cost*) costar. ◆*to ~ down t* (*write*) poner por escrito. 2 GB (*leave off*) dejar. ◆*to ~ in i* (*bad weather*) comenzar; (*problems etc.*) surgir. ◆*to ~ off i* salir, ponerse en camino. − 2 *t* (*bomb*) hacer estallar; (*alarm*) hacer sonar/saltar. 3 (*enhance*) hacer resaltar. ◆*to ~ out i* partir, salir (*for*, para). 2 (*intend*) proponerse (*to*, -). − 3 *t* disponer. ◆*to ~ up t* (*raise*) levantar; (*tent, stall*) montar. 2 (*establish*) crear. 3 *to ~* (*o.s.*) *up*, establecerse (*as*, como). ●*to be ~ on doing sth.*, estar empeñado,-a en hacer algo; *to ~ sb. free*, poner a algn. en libertad; *to ~ the pace*, marcar el paso; *to ~ the table*, poner la mesa; *to ~ to work*, ponerse a trabajar. ■ *~ lunch*, menú del día; *~ phrase*, frase hecha. ▲ *pt & pp set*.

setback ['setbæk] *n* revés *m*, contratiempo.

settee [se'ti:] *n* sofá *m*.

setting ['setɪŋ] *n* (*of sun*) puesta. 2 (*of jewel*) engaste *m*. 3 (*background*) marco; (*of film etc.*) escenario. 4 (*of machine etc.*) ajuste *m*.

settle ['setəl] *t* (*place*) colocar, asentar. 2 (*decide on*) acordar. 3 (*sort out*) resolver. 4 (*calm*) calmar. 5 (*debt*) pagar. 6 (*colonize*) colonizar, poblar. − 7 *i* (*bird*) posarse; (*sediment*) precipitarse; (*liquid*) asentarse. 8 (*sit down*) acomodarse (*into*, en). 9 (*go and live*) afincarse. 10 (*calm down*) calmarse; (*weather*) estabilizarse. ◆*to ~ down i* instalarse, afincarse. 2 (*live a quiet life*) sentar la cabeza. 3 (*adapt*) adaptarse. ◆*to ~ for t* conformarse con. ◆*to ~ in i* (*adapt*) acostumbrarse. ◆*to ~ on t* decidirse por. ●JUR *to ~ out of court*, llegar a un acuerdo amistoso.

settlement ['setəlmənt] *n (village)* poblado; *(colony)* colonia. **2** *(agreement)* acuerdo. **3** *(of bill, debt)* pago.
settler ['setlə'] *n* poblador,-ra, colono.
setup ['setʌp] *n* situación. **2** *sl* montaje *m*.
seven ['sevən] *adj-n* siete *(m)*.
seventeen [sevən'ti:n] *adj-n* diecisiete
(m).
seventeenth [sevən'ti:nθ] *adj-n* decimoséptimo,-a. **– 2** *n (fraction)* decimoséptimo, decimoséptima parte.
seventh ['sevənθ] *adj-n* séptimo,-a. **– 2**
n (fraction) séptimo, séptima parte.
seventieth ['sevəntɪəθ] *adj-n* septuagésimo,-a. **– 2** *n (fraction)* septuagésimo,
septuagésima parte.
seventy ['sevəntɪ] *adj-n* setenta *(m)*.
sever ['sevə'] *t* cortar. **– 2** *i* romperse.
several ['sevərəl] *adj-pron (a few)* varios,-as. **– 2** *adj (respective)* respectivos,-as.
severe [sɪ'vɪə'] *adj (strict)* severo,-a. **2**
(pain) agudo,-a; *(illness)* grave; *(climate)*
duro,-a. **– 3** *severely adv* severamente,
gravemente.
severity [sɪ'verɪtɪ] *n (strictness)* severidad.
2 *(of pain)* agudeza; *(of illness)* gravedad;
(of climate) rigor *m*.
sew [səʊ] *t-i* coser *(on,* a). **▲** *pp* sewed *o*
sewn.
sewage ['sɪu:ɪdʒ] *n* aguas *fpl* residuales.
■ *~ system,* alcantarillado.
sewer [sjʊə'] *n* alcantarilla, cloaca.
sewing ['səʊɪŋ] *n* costura. **■** *~ machine,*
máquina de coser.
sewn [səʊn] *pp* → **sew**.
sex [seks] *n* sexo. **●***to have ~ with,* tener
relaciones sexuales con.
sexist ['seksɪst] *adj-n* sexista *(mf)*.
sexual ['seksjʊəl] *adj* sexual.
sexuality [seksjʊ'ælɪtɪ] *n* sexualidad.
sexy ['seksɪ] *adj* sexi.
shabby ['ʃæbɪ] *adj (clothes)* raído,-a, desharrapado,-a. **2** *(person)* mal vestido,-a.
3 *(mean)* mezquino,-a.
shack [ʃæk] *n* choza.
shackle ['ʃækəl] *n* grillete *m*, grillo. **2** *fig*
traba. **– 3** *t* poner grilletes a. **4** *fig* poner
trabas a. **▲ 1** *gen pl.*
shade [ʃeɪd] *n (shadow)* sombra. **2** *(of*
lamp) pantalla. **3** *(of colour)* matiz *m*. **4**
(small bit) poquito. **5** *fig* matiz *m*. **– 6** *t*
proteger contra el sol/la luz.
shadow ['ʃædəʊ] *n* sombra. **– 2** *t fig* seguir la pista a. **●***without a ~ of doubt,*
sin lugar a dudas.
shadowy ['ʃædəʊɪ] *adj* oscuro,-a.

shady ['ʃeɪdɪ] *adj (place)* a la sombra. **2**
fam (suspicious) sospechoso,-a.
shaft [ʃɑ:ft] *n (of axe, tool)* manga; *(of ar-*
row) astil *m*. **2** TECH eje *m*. **3** *(of mine)*
pozo; *(of lift)* hueco. **4** *(of light)* rayo.
shaggy ['ʃægɪ] *adj* desgreñado,-a.
shake [ʃeɪk] *n* sacudida. **2** *(milkshake)* batido. **– 3** *t* sacudir, agitar; *(building etc.)*
hacer temblar. **– 4** *i* temblar. **5** *(hands)*
estrecharse la mano. **●***to ~ off t* sacu-
dirse. **2** *fig* quitarse de encima. **●***to ~*
up t (liquid) agitar. **2** *fig (stun)* conmocionar. **3** *fig (rearrange)* reorganizar. **●***to*
~ hands, darse/estrecharse la mano; *to*
~ one's head, negar con la cabeza; *to ~*
with cold/fear, tiritar de frío/temblar de
miedo. **▲** *pt shook; pp shaken* ['ʃeɪkən].
shake-up ['ʃeɪkʌp] *n fig* reorganización.
shaky ['ʃeɪkɪ] *adj gen* tembloroso,-a;
(writing) temblón,-ona; *(ladder etc.)* inestable. **2** *(health)* débil. **3** *fig (argument*
etc.) sin fundamento.
shall [ʃæl, *unstressed* ʃəl] *aux (future)* I ~
go tomorrow, iré mañana; *we ~ see*
them on Sunday, los veremos el domin-
go. **2** *(offers)* ~ *I close the window?,* ¿cie-
rro la ventana? **3** *(emphatic, command)*
you ~ leave immediately, debes irte enseguida. **▲** *En 1 y 2 se emplea sólo para*
la 1ª pers del sing y pl.
shallow ['ʃæləʊ] *adj* poco profundo,-a. **2**
fig superficial.
sham [ʃæm] *n* farsa. **– 2** *adj* falso,-a. **– 3**
t-i fingir(se).
shambles ['ʃæmbəlz] *n* desorden *m*,
confusión.
shame [ʃeɪm] *n* vergüenza. **– 2** *t* deshonrar. **●***to put sb./sth. to ~,* humillar a
algn./aplastar algo; *what a ~!,* ¡qué
pena!, ¡qué lástima!
shameful ['ʃeɪmfʊl] *adj* vergonzoso,-a.
shameless ['ʃeɪmləs] *adj* desvergonzado,-a.
shampoo [ʃæm'pu:] *n* champú *m*. **– 2** *t*
lavar con champú.
shandy ['ʃændɪ] *n* GB clara, cerveza con
gaseosa.
shape [ʃeɪp] *n gen* forma; *(shadow)* figura,
silueta. **2** *(condition)* estado. **– 3** *t gen* dar
forma a; *(clay)* modelar. **4** *fig* formar. **–**
5 *i to ~ (up),* evolucionar. **●***out of ~,* en
baja forma; *to get (o.s.) into ~,* ponerse
en forma.
shapeless ['ʃeɪpləs] *adj* informe, sin forma.
share [ʃeə'] *n* parte *f*. **2** FIN acción. **– 3** *t-*
i compartir. **– 4** *t (divide)* repartir. **●***to do*
one's ~, hacer uno su parte.

shareholder [ˈʃeəhəʊldəʳ] *n* accionista *mf*.

shark [ʃɑːk] *n* tiburón *m*. **2** *fam* estafador,-ra, timador,-ra.

sharp [ʃɑːp] *adj (knife)* afilado,-a; *(pointed object)* puntiagudo,-a. **2** *(alert)* avispado,-a, (d)espabilado,-a. **3** *(intense)* fuerte; *(pain, cry)* agudo,-a. **4** *(sudden)* brusco,-a. **5** *(distinct)* definido,-a, nítido,-a. **6** *(criticism)* mordaz; *(scolding)* severo,-a. **7** MUS sostenido,-a: *F ~*, fa sostenido. **− 8** *adv* en punto: *at ten o'clock ~*, a las diez en punto.

sharpen [ˈʃɑːpən] *t (knife)* afilar; *(pencil)* sacar punta a. **2** *fig* agudizar.

sharpener [ˈʃɑːpənəʳ] *n (for knife)* afilador *m*; *(for pencil)* sacapuntas *m inv*.

shatter [ˈʃætəʳ] *t-i* romper(se), hacer(se) añicos/pedazos. **− 2** *t fig* destrozar, quebrantar.

shave [ʃeɪv] *n* afeitado. **− 2** *t-i (person)* afeitar(se). **− 3** *t (wood)* cepillar. •*fig to have a close/narrow ~*, salvarse por los pelos.

shaver [ˈʃeɪvəʳ] *n (electric) ~*, máquina de afeitar.

shaving [ˈʃeɪvɪŋ] *n* afeitado. **2** *(wood)* viruta. ■ *~ brush*, brocha de afeitar.

shawl [ʃɔːl] *n* chal *m*.

she [ʃiː] *pers pron* ella.

sheaf [ʃiːf] *n* gavilla, haz *m*. **2** *(of notes etc.)* fajo.

shear [ʃɪəʳ] *t* esquilar. **− 2** *npl* tijeras *fpl* (grandes). ▲ *pp* sheared o shorn.

sheath [ʃiːθ] *n (for sword)* vaina; *(for knife)* funda. **2** *(condom)* preservativo. ▲ *pl* sheaths [ʃiːðz].

shed [ʃed] *n (in garden)* cobertizo; *(workman's)* barraca. **− 2** *t (pour forth)* derramar. **3** *(throw off)* despojarse de; *(get rid of)* deshacerse de. •*to ~ its skin, (animal)* mudar de piel. ▲ *pt & pp* shed.

sheep [ʃiːp] *n inv* oveja.

sheer [ʃɪəʳ] *adj (total)* total, absoluto,-a. **2** *(cliff)* escarpado,-a. **3** *(stockings etc.)* fino,-a.

sheet [ʃiːt] *n (on bed)* sábana. **2** *(of paper)* hoja; *(of metal, glass, etc.)* lámina; *(of ice)* capa. ■ *~ metal*, chapa de metal; *~ music*, papel pautado.

shelf [ʃelf] *n (on wall)* estante *m*. **2** *(in rock)* promontorio. ■ *(set of) shelves*, estantería.

shell [ʃel] *n (of egg, nut)* cáscara. **2** *(of pea)* vaina. **3** *(of tortoise, lobster)* caparazón *m*. **4** *(of snail, oyster)* concha. **5** *(of building)* armazón *m*, esqueleto. **6** MIL proyectil *m*. **− 7** *t (nuts)* descascarar; *(peas)* des-

vainar. **8** MIL bombardear. ◆*to ~ out t fam* soltar, pagar.

shellfish [ˈʃelfɪʃ] *n inv* marisco(s) *m(pl)*.

shelter [ˈʃeltəʳ] *n* abrigo, protección. **2** *fig* refugio, cobijo. **3** *(for homeless)* asilo. **− 4** *t* abrigar, amparar. **− 5** *i* refugiarse. •*to take ~*, refugiarse *(from,* de).

shelve [ʃelv] *t (put on shelf)* poner en la estantería. **2** *fig (postpone)* dejar de lado.

shepherd [ˈʃepəd] *n* pastor *m*.

sherry [ˈʃerɪ] *n* (vino de) jerez *m*.

shield [ʃiːld] *n* MIL escudo; *(of police)* placa. **2** TECH pantalla protectora. **− 3** *t* proteger *(from,* de).

shift [ʃɪft] *n (change)* cambio. **2** *(of work, workers)* turno, tanda. **− 3** *t-i (change)* cambiar; *(move)* cambiar de sitio, desplazar(se).

shilling [ˈʃɪlɪŋ] *n* chelín *m*.

shimmer [ˈʃɪməʳ] *n* luz trémula. **− 2** *i* relucir, rielar.

shin [ʃɪn] *n* espinilla.

shine [ʃaɪn] *n* brillo, lustre *m*. **− 2** *i* brillar; *(metal)* relucir. **3** *fig (excel)* sobresalir *(at,* en). **− 4** *t (light)* dirigir. **5** *(shoes)* sacar brillo a. ▲ *pt & pp* shone; en **5** *pt & pp* shined.

shingle [ˈʃɪŋgəl] *n (pebbles)* guijarros *mpl*. **2** *pl* MED herpes *m inv*.

shining [ˈʃaɪnɪŋ] *adj* brillante, reluciente. **2** *fig* destacado,-a.

shiny [ˈʃaɪnɪ] *adj* brillante.

ship [ʃɪp] *n* barco, buque *m*. **− 2** *t (send)* enviar; *(by ship)* transportar (en barco). •*on board ~*, a bordo.

shipment [ˈʃɪpmənt] *n* transporte *m*, embarque *m*. **2** *(load)* consignación, remesa.

shipping [ˈʃɪpɪŋ] *n (ships)* barcos *mpl*. **2** *(sending)* envío; *(transporting)* transporte *m*.

shipwreck [ˈʃɪprek] *n* naufragio. **− 2** *t to be shipwrecked*, naufragar.

shipyard [ˈʃɪpjɑːd] *n* astillero.

shirk [ʃɜːk] *t* eludir, esquivar.

shirt [ʃɜːt] *n* camisa. •*in ~ sleeves*, en mangas de camisa.

shit* [ʃɪt] *n* mierda*. **− 2** *i* cagar*. ▲ *pt & pp* shitted o shit.

shitty* [ˈʃɪtɪ] *adj* de mierda*: *a ~ book**, una porquería de libro.

shiver [ˈʃɪvəʳ] *n* escalofrío. **− 2** *i* tiritar, estremecerse.

shock [ʃɒk] *n (jolt)* choque *m*, sacudida. **2** *(upset)* golpe *m*. **3** *(scare)* susto. **4** MED shock *m*. **− 5** *t (upset)* conmocionar. **6** *(startle)* asustar.

shocking ['ʃɒkɪŋ] *adj (horrific)* espantoso,-a, horroroso,-a. **2** *(disgraceful)* chocante. **3** *(colour)* chillón: ~ *pink,* rosa chillón.
shod [ʃɒd] *pt & pp* → **shoe**.
shoddy ['ʃɒdɪ] *adj* chapucero,-a.
shoe [ʃuː] *n* zapato. **2** *(for horse)* herradura. – **3** *t (horse)* herrar. ■ ~ *polish,* betún *m;* ~ *shop,* zapatería. ▲ *pt & pp* **shod**.
shoehorn ['ʃuːhɔːn] *n* calzador *m.*
shoemaker ['ʃuːmeɪkəʳ] *n* zapatero,-a.
shone [ʃɒn] *pt & pp* → **shine**.
shoo [ʃuː] *interj* ¡fuera! – **2** *t to* ~ *(away),* ahuyentar.
shook [ʃʊk] *pt* → **shake**.
shoot [ʃuːt] *n* BOT brote *m,* retoño. **2** GB *(shooting party)* cacería. – **3** *t* pegar un tiro a. **4** *(missile)* lanzar; *(arrow, bullet)* disparar. **5** *(film)* rodar; *(photo)* fotografiar. – **6** *i* disparar *(at,* a/sobre). ◆*to* ~ *down t (aircraft)* derribar. ◆*to* ~ *out i* salir disparado,-a; *(liquid)* brollar. ◆*to* ~ *past i* pasar volando. ◆*to* ~ *up i (flames)* salir; *(prices)* dispararse; *(plant, child)* crecer rápidamente. **2** *sl (heroin etc.)* chutarse. ▲ *pt & pp* **shot**.
shooting ['ʃuːtɪŋ] *n* ~ *star,* estrella fugaz.
shop [ʃɒp] *n gen* tienda; *(large)* almacén *m.* **2** *(business)* comercio, negocio. **3** *(workshop)* taller *m.* – **4** *i* hacer compras. ◆*to go shopping,* ir de compras; *to set up* ~, abrir un negocio; *to talk* ~, hablar del trabajo. ■ ~ *assistant,* dependiente,-a; ~ *floor,* planta; ~ *window,* escaparate *m.*
shoplifting ['ʃɒplɪftɪŋ] *n* ratería, hurto.
shopper ['ʃɒpəʳ] *n* comprador,-ra.
shore [ʃɔːʳ] *n (of sea, lake)* orilla; *(coast)* costa. **2** US playa. – **3** *t to* ~ *(up),* apuntalar; *fig* consolidar. ◆*on* ~, en tierra.
shorn [ʃɔːn] *pp* → **shear**.
short [ʃɔːt] *adj* corto,-a. **2** *(person)* bajo,-a. **3** *(brief)* breve, corto,-a. **4** *(curt)* seco,-a, brusco,-a. – **5** *adv* bruscamente. – **6** *n (drink)* bebida corta, copa. **7** CINEM cortometraje *m.* **8** ELEC cortocircuito. **9** *pl* pantalones *mpl* cortos. – **10** *shortly adv* dentro de poco, en breve. ◆*at* ~ *notice,* con poca antelación; *in* ~, en pocas palabras; *for* ~, para abreviar; *shortly after,* poco después; *to be* ~ *of,* andar escaso,-a/mal de; *to cut* ~, interrumpir. ■ ~ *circuit,* cortocircuito; ~ *cut,* atajo.
shortage ['ʃɔːtɪdʒ] *n* falta, escasez *f.*
shortbread ['ʃɔːtbred] *n* mantecado.

shortcomings ['ʃɔːtkʌmɪŋz] *npl* defectos *mpl.*
shorten ['ʃɔːtən] *t* acortar, abreviar, reducir.
shortfall ['ʃɔːtfɔːl] *n* déficit *m.*
shorthand ['ʃɔːthænd] *n* taquigrafía. ■ ~ *typing,* taquimecanografía.
short-sighted [ʃɔːt'saɪtɪd] *adj* corto,-a de vista.
short-term [ʃɔːt'tɜːm] *adj* a corto plazo.
shot [ʃɒt] *pt & pp* → **shoot**. – **2** *n* tiro, disparo, balazo. **3** *(projectile)* bala. **4** *(person)* tirador,-ra. **5** *(kick)* tiro (a gol), chut *m.* **6** *(try)* intento. **7** *(injection)* inyección, pinchazo. **8** *(drink)* trago. **9** *(photo)* foto *f;* CINEM toma. ◆*to be off like a* ~, salir disparado,-a; *to have a* ~ *at sth.,* intentar hacer algo; *fig not by a long* ~, ni mucho menos.
shotgun ['ʃɒtgʌn] *n* escopeta.
should [ʃʊd] *aux verb (duty)* deber: *you* ~ *see the dentist,* deberías ir al dentista. **2** *(probability)* deber de: *the clothes* ~ *be dry now,* la ropa ya debe de estar seca. ◆*I* ~ *like to ask a question,* quisiera hacer una pregunta; *I* ~ *think so,* me imagino que sí.
shoulder ['ʃəʊldəʳ] *n* hombro. **2** *(of meat)* espalda. **3** *(slope)* lomo. – **4** *t* cargar con. ◆~ *to* ~, hombro con hombro; *to give sb. the cold* ~, volver la espalda a algn. ■ ~ *bag,* bolso (de bandolera).
shout [ʃaʊt] *n* grito. – **2** *t-i* gritar. ◆*to* ~ *down t* abuchear.
shouting ['ʃaʊtɪŋ] *n* gritos *mpl,* vocerío.
shove [ʃʌv] *n* empujón *m.* – **2** *t-i* empujar. ◆*to* ~ *off i fam* largarse.
shovel ['ʃʌvəl] *n* pala. – **2** *t* mover/quitar con pala.
show [ʃəʊ] *n* THEAT *(entertainment)* espectáculo; *(performance)* función. **2** RAD TV programa *m.* **3** *(exhibition)* exposición. **4** *(display)* demostración. **5** *(outward appearance)* apariencia. **6** *fam (organization)* negocio, tinglado. – **7** *t gen* mostrar, enseñar. **8** *(teach)* enseñar. **9** *(indicate)* indicar. **10** *(demonstrate)* demostrar. **11** *(at exhibition)* exponer. **12** *(guide)* llevar, acompañar. – **13** *t-i* CINEM TV poner: *what's showing?,* ¿qué ponen? – **14** *i* verse: *the stain doesn't* ~, no se ve la mancha. ◆*to* ~ *off i* fardar, fanfarronear. ◆*to* ~ *up t (reveal)* hacer resaltar, destacar. **2** *(embarrass)* dejar en ridículo. – **3** *i fam (arrive)* presentarse, aparecer. ◆*time will* ~, el tiempo lo dirá; *to be on* ~, estar expuesto,-a; *to make a* ~ *of,* hacer gala/alarde de; *to* ~

sb. how to do sth., enseñar a algn. a hacer algo; *to ~ sb. in,* hacer pasar a algn.; *to steal the ~,* llevarse la palma. ■ *horse ~,* concurso hípico; *motor ~,* salón *m* del automóvil; *~ business,* el mundo del espectáculo; *~ of hands,* votación a mano alzada. ▲ *pp* **showed** *o* **shown.**

showdown ['ʃəʊdaʊn] *n* enfrentamiento.

shower ['ʃaʊə'] *n* METEOR chubasco, chaparrón *m.* 2 *(fall)* lluvia. 3 *(bath)* ducha. – 4 *t fig* inundar, colmar. – 5 *i (fall)* caer. 6 *(in bath)* ducharse. ●*to have/take a ~,* ducharse.

showground ['ʃəʊgraʊnd] *n* recinto ferial.

showjumping ['ʃəʊdʒʌmpɪŋ] *n* concurso hípico.

shown [ʃəʊn] *pp* → **show.**

show-off ['ʃəʊɒf] *n fam* fanfarrón,-ona.

showroom ['ʃəʊrʊm] *n* COM exposición. 2 ART sala de exposiciones.

showy ['ʃəʊɪ] *adj* ostentoso,-a, llamativo,-a.

shrank [ʃræŋk] *pt* → **shrink.**

shrapnel ['ʃræpnəl] *n* metralla.

shred [ʃred] *n gen* triza; *(of cloth)* jirón *m; (of paper)* tira. 2 *fig (bit)* pizca. – 3 *t* hacer trizas/jirones; *(vegetables)* rallar. ●*to tear sth. to shreds,* hacer algo trizas.

shrew [ʃruː] *n* ZOOL musaraña. 2 *fig* arpía, bruja.

shrewd [ʃruːd] *adj* astuto,-a, perspicaz. 2 *(decision etc.)* acertado,-a, razonable.

shriek [ʃriːk] *n* chillido. – 2 *i* chillar, gritar.

shrill [ʃrɪl] *adj* agudo,-a, chillón,-ona.

shrimp [ʃrɪmp] *n* camarón *m,* gamba. 2 *pej* enano,-a.

shrine [ʃraɪn] *n (holy place)* santuario. 2 *(chapel)* capilla; *(remote)* ermita.

shrink [ʃrɪŋk] *t-i* encoger(se). – 2 *i (move back)* retroceder. ●*to ~ from doing sth.,* no tener valor para hacer algo. ▲ *pt* **shrank***; pp* **shrunk.**

shrinkage ['ʃrɪŋkɪdʒ] *n* encogimiento.

shrivel ['ʃrɪvəl] *t-i* encoger(se); *(plant)* secar(se); *(skin)* arrugar(se).

shroud [ʃraʊd] *n* mortaja, sudario. 2 *fig* velo. – 3 *t fig* envolver.

shrub [ʃrʌb] *n* arbusto.

shrug [ʃrʌg] *t-i to ~ (one's shoulders),* encogerse de hombros. – 2 *n* encogimiento de hombros. ●*to ~ off t* quitar importancia a.

shrunk [ʃrʌŋk] *pp* → **shrink.**

shudder ['ʃʌdə'] *n* escalofrío, estremecimiento. – 2 *i* estremecerse, temblar *(with,* de).

shuffle ['ʃʌfəl] *n* arrastre *m.* 2 *(shake-up)* reajuste *m.* – 3 *t (cards)* barajar; *(papers)* revolver. – 4 *i* andar arrastrando los pies.

shush! [ʃʊʃ] *interj* ¡chis!, ¡chitón!

shut [ʃʌt] *t-i* cerrar(se). ◆*to ~ away t* encerrar. ◆*to ~ down t-i* cerrar(se). ◆*to ~ off t* cortar, cerrar. 2 *(isolate)* aislar *(from,* de). ◆*to ~ up t (close)* cerrar. 2 *fam (quieten)* callar(se). ▲ *pt & pp* **shut.**

shutdown ['ʃʌtdaʊn] *n* cierre *m.*

shutter ['ʃʌtə'] *n* postigo, contraventana. 2 *(of camera)* obturador *m.*

shuttle ['ʃʌtəl] *n* AV puente *m* aéreo; *(bus, train)* servicio regular. – 2 *t* transportar. ■ *(space) ~,* transbordador *m* espacial.

shy [ʃaɪ] *adj* tímido,-a. – 2 *i* espantarse *(at,* de). ●*to be ~ to do sth.,* no atreverse a hacer algo.

shyness ['ʃaɪnəs] *n* timidez *f.*

sick [sɪk] *adj (ill)* enfermo,-a. 2 *(nauseated)* mareado,-a. 3 *(morbid)* morboso,-a. ●*to be ~,* vomitar; *to be ~ of sb./sth.,* estar harto,-a de algn./algo; *fam it makes me ~,* me revienta. ■ *~ leave,* baja por enfermedad; *~ pay,* subsidio por enfermedad.

sicken ['sɪkən] *t* poner enfermo,-a. 2 *(revolt)* dar asco. – 3 *i* caer/ponerse enfermo,-a.

sickening ['sɪkənɪŋ] *adj* repugnante, asqueroso,-a.

sickly ['sɪklɪ] *adj* enfermizo,-a. 2 *(pale)* pálido,-a. 3 *(smell, taste)* empalagoso,-a.

sickness ['sɪknəs] *n* enfermedad. 2 *(nausea)* náusea.

sickroom ['sɪkrʊm] *n* enfermería.

side [saɪd] *n gen* lado. 2 *(of animal)* ijar *m,* ijada. 3 *(edge)* borde *m; (of lake etc.)* orilla. 4 SP equipo. – 5 *i* unirse *(with,* a). ●*by his/my ~,* a su/mi lado; *~ by ~,* juntos,-as, uno,-a al lado de otro,-a; *to look on the bright ~,* ver el lado bueno de las cosas; *to put sth. on/to one ~,* guardar algo; *to take sides with sb.,* ponerse de parte de algn. ■ *~ dish,* guarnición; *~ door/entrance,* puerta/entrada lateral; *~ effect,* efecto secundario.

sideboard ['saɪdbɔːd] *n* aparador *m.* 2 *pl* patillas *fpl.*

sidelight ['saɪdlaɪt] *n* piloto, luz *f* lateral.

sideline ['saɪdlaɪn] *n* SP línea de banda. 2 *(extra job)* empleo suplementario.

sidelong ['saɪdlɒŋ] *adj* de soslayo. – 2 *adv* de lado.

sidetrack ['saɪdtræk] *t* despistar, distraer.

sidewalk ['saɪdwɔːk] *n* US acera.

sideways ['saɪdweɪz] *adj (movement)* lateral; *(look)* de soslayo. – 2 *adv* de lado.

siege [siːdʒ] *n* sitio, cerco. ●*to lay* ~ *to*, sitiar, cercar.

sieve [sɪv] *n (fine)* tamiz *m; (coarse)* criba. – 2 *t* tamizar, cribar.

sift [sɪft] *t* tamizar, cribar. ●*to* ~ *through*, examinar cuidadosamente.

sigh [saɪ] *n* suspiro. – 2 *i* suspirar.

sight [saɪt] *n gen* vista. 2 *(spectacle)* espectáculo. 3 *(on gun)* mira. 4 *pl (of city)* atracciones *fpl*, monumentos *mpl*. 5 *fam a* ~, mucho: *a* ~ *cheaper*, mucho más barato,-a. – 6 *t* observar, ver; *(land)* divisar. ●*at first* ~, a primera vista; *by* ~, de vista; *to catch* ~ *of*, ver, divisar; *to come into* ~, aparecer; *to lose* ~ *of*, perder de vista; *to see the sights*, visitar la ciudad.

sightseeing ['saɪtsiːɪŋ] *n* visita turística, turismo.

sign [saɪn] *n (symbol)* signo. 2 *(signal, indication)* señal *f*. 3 *(gesture)* gesto. 4 *(board)* letrero; *(notice)* anuncio, aviso. 5 *(trace)* rastro, huella. – 6 *t-i (name)* firmar. ◆*to* ~ *away t* ceder. ◆*to* ~ *in i* firmar el registro. ◆*to* ~ *on/up t (worker)* contratar; *(player)* fichar. ●*as a* ~ *of*, como muestra de.

signal ['sɪgnəl] *n* señal *f*. 2 RAD TV sintonía. – 3 *i (with hands)* hacer señales; *(in car)* señalar. – 4 *t* indicar, señalar.

signatory ['sɪgnətəri] *n fml* signatario,-a.

signature ['sɪgnɪtʃəʳ] *n* firma.

significance [sɪg'nɪfɪkəns] *n* significado. 2 *(importance)* importancia.

significant [sɪg'nɪfɪkənt] *adj* significativo,-a.

signify ['sɪgnɪfaɪ] *t fml* significar. 2 *(show)* mostrar.

signpost ['saɪnpəʊst] *n* poste *m* indicador.

silence ['saɪləns] *n* silencio. – 2 *t* acallar, hacer callar. ●*in* ~, en silencio.

silencer ['saɪlənsəʳ] *n* silenciador *m*.

silent ['saɪlənt] *adj gen* silencioso,-a. 2 *(not talking)* callado,-a. 3 *(film, letter)* mudo,-a. – 4 *silently adv* silenciosamente, en silencio. ●*to be* ~, callarse.

silhouette [sɪluːˈet] *n* silueta.

silk [sɪlk] *n* seda.

silkworm ['sɪlkwɜːm] *n* gusano de la seda.

silky ['sɪlkɪ] *adj* sedoso,-a.

sill [sɪl] *n* alféizar *m*, antepecho.

silliness ['sɪlɪnəs] *n (quality)* estupidez *f*. 2 *(act)* tontería.

silly ['sɪlɪ] *adj* tonto,-a, necio,-a. 2 *(absurd)* absurdo,-a. ●*to do sth.* ~, hacer una tontería.

silo ['saɪləʊ] *n* silo.

silver ['sɪlvəʳ] *n* plata. 2 *(coins)* monedas *fpl* (de plata). 3 *(tableware)* vajilla de) plata. – 4 *adj* de plata. ■ ~ *foil/paper*, papel *m* de plata/aluminio; ~ *wedding*, bodas *fpl* de plata.

silversmith ['sɪlvəsmɪθ] *n* platero,-a.

silverware ['sɪlvəweəʳ] *n* (vajilla de) plata.

similar ['sɪmɪləʳ] *adj* parecido,-a, similar, semejante. – 2 *similarly adv* igualmente, del mismo modo.

similarity [sɪmɪˈlærɪtɪ] *n* semejanza, parecido.

simmer ['sɪməʳ] *t-i* cocer(se)/hervir a fuego lento.

simple ['sɪmpəl] *adj gen* sencillo,-a. 2 *(foolish)* simple, tonto,-a. – 3 *simply adv* simplemente.

simplicity [sɪmˈplɪsɪtɪ] *n gen* sencillez *f*. 2 *(foolishness)* simpleza.

simplify ['sɪmplɪfaɪ] *t* simplificar.

simplistic [sɪmˈplɪstɪk] *adj* simplista.

simulate ['sɪmjʊleɪt] *t* simular, imitar.

simultaneous [sɪməlˈteɪnɪəs] *adj* simultáneo,-a. – 2 *simultaneously adv* simultáneamente, a la vez.

sin [sɪn] *n* pecado. – 2 *i* pecar.

since [sɪns] *adv* desde entonces. – 2 *prep* desde: *I've been here* ~ *four o'clock*, llevo aquí desde las cuatro. – 3 *conj (time)* desde que. 4 *(because)* ya/puesto que.

sincere [sɪnˈsɪəʳ] *adj* sincero,-a. – 2 *sincerely adv* sinceramente; *(in letter)* *yours sincerely*, (le saluda) atentamente.

sincerity [sɪnˈserɪtɪ] *n* sinceridad.

sinecure ['saɪnɪkjʊəʳ] *n* sinecura, prebenda.

sinful ['sɪnfʊl] *adj (person)* pecador,-ra. 2 *(thought, act)* pecaminoso,-a.

sing [sɪŋ] *t-i* cantar. ▲ *pt* sang; *pp* sung.

singe [sɪndʒ] *t* chamuscar.

singer ['sɪŋəʳ] *n* cantante *mf*.

singing ['sɪŋɪŋ] *n* canto, cantar *m*.

single ['sɪŋgəl] *adj (solitary)* solo,-a. 2 *(only one)* único,-a. 3 *(not double)* individual. 4 *(unmarried)* soltero,-a. – 5 *n* GB *(ticket)* billete sencillo/de ida. 6 *(record)* single *m*. 7 *pl* SP individuales *mpl*. – 8 *singly adv (separately)* por separado; *(one by one)* uno por uno. ◆*to* ~ *out t (choose)* escoger. 2 *(distinguish)* destacar. ●*every* ~ *day/month*, todos los días/

meses; *in* ~ *file,* en fila india. ■ ~ *bed/ room,* cama/habitación individual.

single-handed [sɪŋgəl'hændɪd] *adj & adv* sin ayuda, solo,-a.

sing-song ['sɪŋsɒŋ] *adj* cantarín,-ina. – 2 *n* sonsonete *m.*

singular ['sɪŋgjʊləʳ] *adj-n* GRAM singular *(m).* – 2 *adj fml* excepcional.

sinister ['sɪnɪstəʳ] *adj* siniestro,-a.

sink [sɪŋk] *n* fregadero. 2 US lavabo. – 3 *t (ship)* hundir, echar a pique. 4 *fig* acabar con. 5 *(hole, shaft)* cavar; *(well)* abrir. 6 *(teeth)* hincar *(into,* en). 7 *(invest)* invertir. – 8 *i gen* hundirse. 9 *(sun, moon)* ponerse. 10 *(decrease)* bajar. ◆*to* ~ *in i* penetrar. 2 *fig* causar impresión. ▲ *pt sank; pp sunk.*

sinner ['sɪnəʳ] *n* pecador,-ra.

sip [sɪp] *n* sorbo. – 2 *t* beber a sorbos.

siphon ['saɪfən] *n* sifón *m.*

sir [sɜːʳ] *n fml* señor *m: yes,* ~, sí, señor. 2 *(title)* **Sir Winston Churchill,** Sir Winston Churchill. ●*Dear Sir,* muy señor mío, estimado señor.

siren ['saɪərən] *n* sirena.

sirloin ['sɜːlɔɪn] *n* solomillo.

sister ['sɪstəʳ] *n* hermana. 2 GB enfermera jefe. 3 REL hermana, monja; *(before name)* sor. ■ ~ *ship,* barco gemelo.

sister-in-law ['sɪstərɪnlɔː] *n* cuñada. ▲ *pl sisters-in-law.*

sit [sɪt] *t-i* sentar(se): *he's sitting in my chair,* está sentado en mi silla. – 2 *i (lie, rest)* yacer. 3 *(be situated)* hallarse, estar. 4 *(stay)* quedarse. 5 *(animal)* posar. 6 *(be a member)* ser miembro: *he sits on a jury,* es miembro de un jurado. 7 *(have meeting)* reunirse. – 8 *t* GB *(exam)* presentarse a. ◆*to* ~ *about/around i fam* hacer el vago. ◆*to* ~ *in for t* sustituir a. ◆*to* ~ *on t fam (delay)* dejar dormir, aplazar. ◆*to* ~ *out/through t* aguantar (hasta el final). ◆*to* ~ *up t-i (in bed)* incorporar(se) (en la cama). – 2 *i (stay up late)* quedarse levantado,-a. ◆*to* ~ *down,* sentarse. ▲ *pt & pp sat.*

site [saɪt] *n (location)* emplazamiento, zona. 2 *(area)* terreno. ■ *building* ~, solar *m.*

sit-in ['sɪtɪn] *n* huelga de brazos cruzados.

sitting ['sɪtɪŋ] *n (of meal)* turno. 2 *(meeting)* sesión. ■ POL ~ *member,* miembro activo; ~ *room,* sala de estar, salón *m.*

situated ['sɪtjʊeɪtɪd] *adj* situado,-a, ubicado,-a.

situation [sɪtjʊ'eɪʃən] *n* situación. ■ *"situations vacant",* "bolsa de trabajo".

six [sɪks] *adj-n* seis *(m).*

sixteen [sɪks'tiːn] *adj-n* dieciséis *(m).*

sixteenth [sɪks'tiːnθ] *adj-n* decimosexto,-a. – 2 *n (fraction)* decimosexto, decimosexta parte.

sixth [sɪksθ] *adj-n* sexto,-a. – 2 *n (fraction)* sexto, sexta parte.

sixtieth ['sɪkstɪəθ] *adj-n* sexagésimo,-a. – 2 *n (fraction)* sexagésimo, sexagésima parte.

sixty ['sɪkstɪ] *adj-n* sesenta *(m).*

size [saɪz] *n* tamaño. 2 *(of garment, person)* talla; *(of shoes)* número. 3 *(magnitude)* magnitud *f.* ◆*to* ~ *up t* evaluar. ●*fig to cut sb. down to* ~, bajarle los humos a algn.

sizzle ['sɪzəl] *i* chisporrotear.

skate [skeɪt] *n* patín *m.* – 2 *i* patinar.

skateboard ['skeɪtbɔːd] *n* monopatín *m.*

skating ['skeɪtɪŋ] *n* patinaje *m.* ■ ~ *rink,* pista de patinaje.

skeleton ['skelɪtən] *n (of person, animal)* esqueleto. 2 *(of building, ship)* armazón *m.* – 3 *adj* reducido,-a. ■ ~ *key,* llave maestra. –

sketch [sketʃ] *n (rough drawing)* croquis *m;* *(preliminary)* bosquejo, esbozo. 2 *(outline)* esquema *m.* 3 THEAT TV sketch *m.* – 4 *t (rough drawing)* hacer un croquis de; *(preliminary)* bosquejar, esbozar.

ski [skiː] *n* esquí *m.* – 2 *i* esquiar. ■ ~ *lift,* telesquí *m;* *(with seats)* telesilla *m;* ~ *resort,* estación de esquí.

skid [skɪd] *n* patinazo, resbalón *m.* – 2 *i* patinar, derrapar.

skier ['skɪəʳ] *n* esquiador,-ra.

skiing ['skiːɪŋ] *n* esquí *m.*

skilful ['skɪlfʊl] *adj* diestro,-a, hábil. – 2 *skilfully adv* hábilmente, con destreza.

skill [skɪl] *n (ability)* habilidad, destreza. 2 *(technique)* técnica, arte *m.*

skilled [skɪld] *adj* cualificado,-a, especializado,-a.

skim [skɪm] *t (milk)* desnatar, descremar. 2 *(brush against)* rozar.

skimp [skɪmp] *t-i* escatimar *(on,* -).

skin [skɪn] *n gen* piel *f;* *(of face)* cutis *m;* *(complexion)* tez *f.* 2 *(of animal, sausage)* pellejo. 3 *(peeling)* monda, mondadura. 4 *(on paint)* telilla. 5 *(on milk)* nata. – 6 *t (animal)* desollar, despellejar. 7 *(fruit, vegetable)* pelar. 8 *(elbow, knee)* hacer un rasguño en. ●*fig to get under one's* ~, irritarle a uno; *fam to save one's own* ~, salvar el pellejo.

skin-deep [skɪn'diːp] *adj* superficial.

skin-diving ['skɪndaɪvɪŋ] *n* buceo, submarinismo.

skinny [ˈskɪnɪ] *adj fam* flaco,-a, delgadu-cho,-a.

skip [skɪp] *n* salto, brinco. **2** *(container)* contenedor *m,* container *m.* − **3** *i* saltar. − **4** *t fig* saltarse.

skirmish [ˈskɜːmɪʃ] *n* MIL escaramuza; *(fight)* refriega, pelea.

skirt [skɜːt] *n* falda. **2** *(cover)* cubierta. − **3** *t* bordear, rodear. **4** *fig* esquivar. ■ GB **skirting (board),** zócalo, rodapié *m.*

skittle [ˈskɪtəl] *n* bolo. **2** *pl* bolos *mpl,* boliche *m sing.*

skull [skʌl] *n* cráneo, calavera. **2** *fam* coco, crisma.

skunk [skʌŋk] *n* mofeta, AM zorrillo.

sky [skaɪ] *n* cielo.

sky-diving [ˈskaɪdaɪvɪŋ] *n* paracaidismo.

skylight [ˈskaɪlaɪt] *n* tragaluz *m,* claraboya.

skyscraper [ˈskaɪskreɪpəʳ] *n* rascacielos *m inv.*

slab [slæb] *n (of stone)* losa. **2** *(of cake)* trozo.

slack [slæk] *adj (not taut, strict)* flojo,-a. **2** *(careless)* descuidado,-a. **3** *(sluggish)* flojo,-a; *(season)* bajo,-a. − **4** *n* parte floja. − **5** *i pej* gandulear.

slacken [ˈslækən] *t (loosen)* aflojar. **2** *(reduce)* reducir. − **3** *i* aflojar(se).

slag [slæg] *n* escoria. **2** GB *sl* fulana.

slain [sleɪn] *pp* → **slay.**

slam [slæm] *n* golpe *m;* *(of door)* portazo. − **2** *t-i* cerrar(se) de golpe. − **3** *t fig (attack)* criticar duramente. ●AUTO *to* ∼ *on the brakes,* dar un frenazo; *to* ∼ *the door,* dar un portazo.

slander [ˈslɑːndəʳ] *n* difamación. **2** JUR calumnia. − **3** *t* difamar. **4** JUR calumniar.

slanderous [ˈslɑːndərəs] *adj* difamatorio,-a. **2** JUR calumnioso,-a.

slang [slæŋ] *n* argot *m,* jerga.

slant [slɑːnt] *n (slope)* inclinación; *(slope)* declive *m.* **2** *(point of view)* punto de vista. − **3** *t-i* inclinar(se). − **4** *t pej* enfocar subjetivamente.

slap [slæp] *n gen* palmada; *(smack)* cachete *m;* *(in face)* bofetada. − **2** *adv fam* justo, de lleno. − **3** *t* pegar (con la mano); *(in face)* abofetear, dar una bofetada a. ●*fam to* ∼ *paint on a wall,* dar un poco de pintura a la pared.

slapdash [ˈslæpdæʃ] *adj* descuidado,-a; *(work)* chapucero,-a.

slash [slæʃ] *n (with sword)* tajo; *(with knife)* cuchillada; *(with razor)* navajazo. **2*** *sl* meada*. **3** *fam (mark)* barra oblicua. − **4** *t (with sword)* dar un tajo a; *(with*

knife) acuchillar. **5** *fig (lower)* rebajar, reducir. ●*to have a* ∼*, mear*.

slate [sleɪt] *n* pizarra. − **2** *t* GB *(attack)* criticar duramente.

slaughter [ˈslɔːtəʳ] *n (of animals)* matanza; *(of people)* carnicería. − **2** *t (animals)* matar; *(many people)* masacrar. **3** *fam* dar una paliza a.

slaughterhouse [ˈslɔːtəhaʊs] *n* matadero.

slave [sleɪv] *n* esclavo,-a. − **2** *i to* ∼ *(away) at sth.,* trabajar como un negro en algo. ■ ∼ *trade,* trata de esclavos.

slavery [ˈsleɪvərɪ] *n* esclavitud *f.*

slay [sleɪ] *t* matar, asesinar. ▲ *pt* **slew;** *pp* **slain.**

sledge [sledʒ] *n* trineo.

sleek [sliːk] *adj (hair)* liso,-a, lustroso,-a. **2** *(appearance)* impecable, elegante.

sleep [sliːp] *n* sueño. − **2** *t-i* dormir. − **3** *i fam (numb)* entumecerse. − **4** *t (accomodate)* tener camas para. ◆*to* ∼ *in i* quedarse en la cama. ◆*to* ∼ *through t* no oír. ●*to go to* ∼, irse a dormir; *fig to* ∼ *on sth.,* consultar algo con la almohada; *fam to* ∼ *it off,* dormir la mona; *fam to* ∼ *like a log/top,* dormir como un tronco. ▲ *pt & pp* **slept.**

sleeping [ˈsliːpɪŋ] *adj* durmiente, dormido,-a. ■ ∼ *bag,* saco de dormir; ∼ *car,* coche-cama *m;* ∼ *pill,* somnífero.

sleepwalker [ˈsliːpwɔːkəʳ] *n* sonámbulo,-a.

sleepy [ˈsliːpɪ] *adj* soñoliento,-a. ●*to be* ∼, tener sueño; *to make* ∼, dar sueño.

sleet [sliːt] *n* aguanieve *f.* − **2** *i* caer aguanieve.

sleeve [sliːv] *n (of garment)* manga. **2** *(of record)* funda. ●*to have sth. up one's* ∼, guardar una carta en la manga.

slender [ˈslendəʳ] *adj* delgado,-a, esbelto,-a. **2** *fig (slight)* ligero,-a.

slept [slept] *pt & pp* → **sleep.**

slew [sluː] *pt* → **slay.**

slice [slaɪs] *n (of bread)* rebanada; *(of ham)* lonja, loncha; *(of beef etc.)* tajada; *(of salami, lemon)* rodaja; *(of cake)* porción, trozo. **2** *fig (share)* parte *f.* **3** *(tool)* pala, paleta. − **4** *t* cortar a rebanadas/lonjas etc. − **5** *i* SP dar efecto a la pelota. ◆*to* ∼ *off/through t* cortar.

slick [slɪk] *adj (skilful)* mañoso,-a, hábil. **2** *pej (glib)* despabilado,-a. − **3** *n* marea negra.

slide [slaɪd] *n (movement)* deslizamiento, desliz *m;* *(slip)* resbalón *m.* **2** *(in playground)* tobogán *m.* **3** *fig (fall)* baja. **4** *(film)* diapositiva. **5** *(of microscope)* platina. — **6** *i-t* deslizar(se). — **7** *i (slip)* resbalar. •*to let sth.* ~, no ocuparse de algo. ■ ~ *rule,* regla de cálculo; *sliding door,* puerta corredera. ▲ *pt & pp* **slid** [slɪd].

slight [slaɪt] *adj (small)* ligero,-a. **2** *(person)* delicado,-a. **3** *(trivial)* leve. — **4** *n* desaire *m.* — **5** *t* despreciar. — **6** **slightly** *adv* ligeramente, un poco.

slim [slɪm] *adj* delgado,-a, esbelto,-a. **2** *fig* remoto,-a. — **3** *i* adelgazar.

slime [slaɪm] *n (mud)* lodo, cieno. **2** *(of snail)* baba.

sling [slɪŋ] *n* MED cabestrillo. **2** *(catapult)* honda. **3** *(child's)* tirador *m.* — **4** *t* tirar, arrojar. ▲ *pt & pp* **slung**.

slink [slɪŋk] *i* desplazarse sigilosamente. ◆*to* ~ *away/off i* escabullirse. ▲ *pt & pp* **slunk**.

slip [slɪp] *n (slide)* resbalón *m; (trip)* traspié *m.* **2** *fig* error *m; (moral)* desliz *m.* **3** *(women's)* combinación. **4** *(of paper)* trocito (de papel). — **5** *i* resbalar. **6** *(move quickly)* escabullirse. **7** *(decline)* empeorar. — **8** *t (give)* dar a escondidas. ◆*to* ~ *away/by i* pasar volando. ◆*to* ~ *into/on t* ponerse rápidamente. ◆*to* ~ *off t* quitarse. ◆*to* ~ *up i* cometer un desliz, equivocarse. •*a* ~ *of the pen/tongue,* un lapsus; *to let a chance* ~, dejar escapar una oportunidad; *to* ~ *one's memory/mind,* írsele a uno de la memoria.

slipknot [ˈslɪpnɒt] *n* nudo corredizo.

slipper [ˈslɪpəʳ] *n* zapatilla. **2** TECH zapata, patín *m.*

slippery [ˈslɪpərɪ] *adj* resbaladizo,-a. **2** *(viscous)* escurridizo,-a. **3** *fig* astuto,-a.

slit [slɪt] *n (opening)* abertura, hendedura; *(cut)* corte *m.* — **2** *t* cortar, rajar, hender. ▲ *pt & pp* **slit**.

sliver [ˈslɪvəʳ] *n* astilla.

slob [slɒb] *n fam* palurdo,-a.

slobber [ˈslɒbəʳ] *i* babear.

slog [slɒg] GB *fam n* paliza. — **2** *i* currar.

slogan [ˈsləugən] *n* (e)slogan *m,* lema *m.*

slop [slɒp] *t-i* derramar(se), verter(se). — **2** *npl (food)* gachas *fpl; (left-over)* bazofia *f sing.*

slope [sləup] *n (incline)* cuesta, pendiente *f.* **2** *(of mountain)* vertiente *f.* — **3** *i* inclinarse.

sloppy [ˈslɒpɪ] *adj (loose)* muy ancho,-a. **2** *(careless)* descuidado,-a.

sloshed [slɒʃt] *adj fam* **to get** ~, pillar/ coger una trompa.

slot [slɒt] *n gen* abertura; *(for coin)* ranura; *(groove)* muesca. **2** *fig* hueco. — **3** *t* meter, introducir. ■ ~ *machine,* GB distribuidor automático; US (máquina) tragaperras *f inv.*

slouch [slautʃ] *i* andar/sentarse con los hombros caídos.

slovenly [ˈslʌvənlɪ] *adj* descuidado,-a, desaseado,-a.

slow [sləu] *adj gen* lento,-a; *(clock)* atrasado,-a. **2** *(dull)* aburrido,-a, pesado,-a. **3** *(person)* lento,-a, torpe. — **4** *slow(ly) adv* despacio, lentamente. — **5** *i* **to** ~ *(down/up),* ir más despacio; *(vehicle)* reducir la velocidad. •*in* ~ *motion,* a cámara lenta.

slowness [ˈsləunəs] *n* lentitud *f.* **2** *(dullness)* pesadez *f.* **3** *(of person)* torpeza.

slug [slʌg] *n* babosa.

sluggish [ˈslʌgɪʃ] *adj* lento,-a. **2** COM inactivo,-a.

slum [slʌm] *n fam (area)* barrio bajo/de chabolas. **2** *(place)* chabola.

slump [slʌmp] *n (crisis)* crisis *f* económica; *(drop)* bajón *m.* — **2** *i (decline)* hundirse; *fig* desplomarse. **3** *(fall)* caer: **to** ~ **to the floor,** caer desmayado,-a al suelo.

slung [slʌŋ] *pt & pp →* **sling**.

slunk [slʌŋk] *pt & pp →* **slink**.

slur [slɜːʳ] *n* mala pronunciación. **2** *(remark)* calumnia, difamación. — **3** *t (letters, syllables)* comerse, pronunciar mal.

slurp [slɜːp] *t-i* sorber/beber ruidosamente.

slush [slʌʃ] *n (snow)* aguanieve *f.* **2** *(mud)* lodo. **3** *fam* sentimentalismo.

slut [slʌt] *n pej* fulana, ramera.

sly [slaɪ] *adj* astuto,-a, taimado,-a. **2** *(secretive)* furtivo,-a. •*on the* ~, a escondidas/hurtadillas.

smack [smæk] *n (slap)* bofetada, cachete *m.* **2** *sl (heroin)* caballo. — **3** *t (slap)* dar una bofetada a, abofetear; *(hit)* golpear. ◆*to* ~ *of t fig* oler a. •*fig* **to** ~ **one's lips,** relamerse.

small [smɔːl] *adj gen* pequeño,-a. **2** *(scant)* escaso,-a. **3** *(minor)* insignificante. •*a* ~ *table,* una mesita; *(it's)* ~ *wonder that* ..., no me extraña que ...; *in the* ~ *hours,* a altas horas de la noche. ■ ~ *change,* cambio, suelto.

smallish [ˈsmɔːlɪʃ] *adj* más bien pequeño,-a.

small-minded [smɔːlˈmaɪndɪd] *adj* de miras estrechas.

smallness [ˈsmɔːlnəs] *n* pequeñez *f.*

smallpox [ˈsmɔːlpɒks] *n* viruela.

smart [smɑːt] *adj (elegant)* elegante, fino,-a. **2** US listo,-a, inteligente. **3** *(quick)* rápido,-a. — **4** *i* picar, escocer. ■ *the* ~ *set,* la gente bien.

smash [smæʃ] *n (breaking)* rotura. **2** *(noise)* estrépito. **3** *(collision)* choque violento. **4** *(tennis)* smash *m*, mate *m*. – **5** *t-i gen* romper(se), hacer(se) pedazos. **6** *(car)* estrellar(se) *(into,* contra*)*. – **7** *t, (crush)* aplastar. **8** *fig* aplastar, derrotar. ■ ~ *hit,* gran éxito, exitazo.

smashing ['smæʃɪŋ] *adj* GB *fam* estupendo,-a, fenomenal.

smattering ['smætərɪŋ] *n* nociones *fpl: he has a ~ of French,* tiene nociones de francés.

smear [smɪəʳ] *n* mancha. **2** *fig* calumnia. – **3** *t (spread)* untar. **4** *(stain)* manchar. **5** *fig* calumniar, difamar.

smell [smel] *n (sense)* olfato. **2** *(odour)* olor *m*. – **3** *t* oler. **4** *fig* olfatear. – **5** *i* oler (a): *it smells good/like orange,* huele bien/a naranja. ▲ *pt & pp* **smelled** *o* **smelt**.

smelly ['smelɪ] *adj* apestoso,-a, pestilente.

smelt [smelt] *t* fundir. – **2** *pt & pp* → **smell**.

smile [smaɪl] *n* sonrisa. – **2** *i* sonreír.

smirk [smɜːk] *n* sonrisa boba. – **2** *i* sonreír tontamente.

smock [smɒk] *n (blouse)* blusón *m*. **2** *(overall)* bata, guardapolvo.

smog [smɒg] *n* niebla tóxica, smog *m*.

smoke [sməʊk] *n* humo. – **2** *t-i (cigarettes etc.)* fumar. – **3** *t (meat etc.)* ahumar. – **4** *i* echar humo. *"no smoking",* "prohibido fumar"; *fam* **to have a ~,** fumarse un pitillo. ■ ~ *screen,* cortina de humo.

smoked [sməʊkt] *adj* ahumado,-a.

smoker ['sməʊkəʳ] *n* fumador,-ra.

smoky ['sməʊkɪ] *adj (fire etc.)* humeante. **2** *(room)* lleno,-a de humo. **3** *(food, colour)* ahumado,-a.

smooth [smuːð] *adj gen* liso,-a. **2** *(road)* llano,-a. **3** *(liquid)* sin grumos. **4** *(wine etc.)* suave. **5** *fig (pleasant)* agradable, tranquilo,-a. **6** *pej* zalamero,-a, meloso,-a. – **7** *t* alisar. – **8** *smoothly adv fig* tranquilamente. ◆*to ~ back/down/out t* alisar. ◆*to ~ over t fig* limar.

smother ['smʌðəʳ] *t-i* asfixiar(se). – **2** *t (cover)* cubrir *(with,* de*)*.

smoulder ['sməʊldəʳ] *i (fire)* arder sin llama. **2** *fig* arder.

smudge [smʌdʒ] *n* borrón *m*. – **2** *i* emborronar.

smug [smʌg] *adj* engreído,-a, satisfecho,-a. – **2** *smugly adv* con engreimiento.

smuggle ['smʌgəl] *t* pasar de contrabando.

smuggler ['smʌgləʳ] *n* contrabandista *mf*.

smut [smʌt] *n (of soot)* hollín *m*; *(stain)* tizón *m*. **2** *fam* obscenidades *fpl*.

snack [snæk] *n* bocado, tentempié *m*; *(afternoon)* merienda. ■ ~ *bar,* cafetería, bar *m*.

snag [snæg] *n (thread)* enganchón *m*. **2** *fig* pega, problema *m*.

snail [sneɪl] *n* caracol *m*.

snake [sneɪk] *n* serpiente *f*; *(small)* culebra. – **2** *i fig* serpentear.

snap [snæp] *n (sharp noise)* ruido seco; *(of fingers)* chasquido. – **2** *adj* instantáneo,-a, repentino,-a. – **3** *t-i (break)* romper(se) (en dos). **4** *(make sharp noise)* chasquear. – **5** *i (speak angrily)* regañar *(at,* a*)*. ◆*to ~ up t* llevarse, agarrar. ●*to ~ shut,* cerrarse de golpe; *fam* **to ~ out of it,** olvidarlo.

snappy ['snæpɪ] *adj (quick)* rápido,-a. **2** *(stylish)* elegante. **3** *(short-tempered)* irascible.

snapshot ['snæpʃɒt] *n* foto *f* instantánea.

snarl [snɑːl] *n (growl)* gruñido. **2** *(tangle)* enredo, maraña. – **3** *i (growl)* gruñir. – **4** *t-i (entangle)* enredar(se).

snatch [snætʃ] *n* arrebatamiento. **2** *fam* robo, hurto. **3** *(bit)* trocito. – **4** *t* arrebatar. **5** *fam (steal)* robar; *(kidnap)* secuestrar. ●*to ~ an opportunity,* aprovechar una ocasión.

sneak [sniːk] *n fam* chivato,-a, soplón,-ona. – **2** *t* sacar (a escondidas). ◆*to ~ away/off i* escabullirse. ◆*to ~ in/out i* entrar/salir a hurtadillas. ●*to ~ up on sb.,* sorprender a algn.

sneer [snɪəʳ] *n (look)* mueca de desprecio. **2** *(remark)* comentario desdeñoso. – **3** *i* burlarse *(at,* de*)*.

sneeze [sniːz] *n* estornudo. – **2** *i* estornudar.

sniff [snɪf] *n (inhaling)* inhalación; *(by dog)* olfateo, husmeo. – **2** *t-i* **to ~ (at),** oler; *(suspiciously)* olfatear, husmear.

sniffle ['snɪfəl] *n* resfriado. – **2** *i* sorberse los mocos. **3** *fig* lloriquear.

snip [snɪp] *n* tijeretazo. **2** *(small piece)* recorte *m*. **3** GB *fam* ganga, chollo. – **4** *t* tijeretear. ◆*to ~ off t* cortar con tijeras.

sniper ['snaɪpəʳ] *n* francotirador,-ra.

snob [snɒb] *n* (e)snob *mf*.

snobbery ['snɒbərɪ] *n* (e)snobismo.

snobbish ['snɒbɪʃ] *adj* (e)snob.

snooze [snuːz] *fam n* cabezada. – **2** *i* dormitar. ●*to have a ~,* echar una cabezada.

snore [snɔːʳ] *n* ronquido. – **2** *i* roncar.

snorkel [ˈsnɔːkəl] *n* tubo respiratorio.

snort [snɔːt] *i* resoplar.

snout [snaut] *n* hocico.

snow [snəʊ] *n* nieve *f*. – **2** *i* nevar. ●*to be snowed in/up,* quedar aislado,-a por la nieve; *fig* **to be snowed under with work,** estar agobiado,-a de trabajo.

snowfall [ˈsnəʊfɔːl] *n* nevada.

snowflake [ˈsnəʊfleɪk] *n* copo de nieve.

snub [snʌb] *n* desaire *m.* – **2** *t (person)* desairar; *(offer)* rechazar.

snuff [snʌf] *n* rapé *m.* ◆*to* ~ *out t* sofocar.

snug [snʌg] *adj (cosy)* cómodo,-a; *(warm)* calentito,-a. **2** *(tight)* ajustado,-a, ceñido,-a.

so [səʊ] *adv* tan: *she's* ~ *tired that ...,* está tan cansada que ... . – **2** *conj (result)* así que, por lo tanto. **3** *(purpose)* para que. ●*and* ~ *forth/on,* y así sucesivamente; *an hour or* ~, una hora más o menos; *if* ~, en ese caso; *I hope/think* ~, espero/creo que sí; ~ *... as ...,* tan ... como ...; ~ *many,* tantos,-as; ~ *much,* tanto,-a; ~ *(that) ...,* para que ...; *fam* ~ *what?,* ¿y qué?

soak [səʊk] *t* poner en remojo, remojar. – **2** *i* estar en remojo. ◆*to* ~ *through i* penetrar. ◆*to* ~ *up t* absorber. ●*soaked to the skin,* calado,-a hasta los huesos; *to get soaked,* empaparse.

soap [səʊp] *n* jabón *m.* – **2** *t* (en)jabonar. ■ ~ *opera,* TV telenovela; RAD radionovela; ~ *powder,* jabón en polvo.

soapy [ˈsəʊpɪ] *adj* jabonoso,-a.

soar [sɔːʳ] *i* remontar el vuelo. **2** *fig* crecer, aumentar.

sob [sɒb] *n* sollozo. – **2** *i* sollozar.

sober [ˈsəʊbəʳ] *adj* sobrio,-a. **2** *(thoughtful)* sensato,-a, serio,-a. **3** *(colour)* discreto,-a. ◆*to* ~ *up i* pasársele a uno la borrachera.

sobriety [səˈbraɪətɪ] *n* sobriedad. **2** *(sense)* sensatez *f.*

so-called [ˈsəʊkɔːld] *adj* supuesto,-a, llamado,-a.

soccer [ˈsɒkəʳ] *n* fútbol *m.*

sociable [ˈsəʊʃəbəl] *adj* sociable.

social [ˈsəʊʃəl] *adj gen* social. **2** *(sociable)* sociable. ■ *Social Democrat,* socialdemócrata *mf*; ~ *science,* ciencias *fpl* sociales; ~ *security,* seguro/seguridad social; ~ *worker,* asistente,-a social.

socialism [ˈsəʊʃəlɪzəm] *n* socialismo.

socialist [ˈsəʊʃəlɪst] *adj-n* socialista *(mf).*

socialize [ˈsəʊʃəlaɪz] *i* relacionarse, alternar.

society [səˈsaɪətɪ] *n gen* sociedad. **2** *(company)* compañía. ■ ~ *column,* ecos *mpl* de sociedad.

sociology [səʊsɪˈɒlədʒɪ] *n* sociología.

sock [sɒk] *n* calcetín *m.*

socket [ˈsɒkɪt] *n (of eye)* cuenca. **2** ELEC enchufe *m.*

sod [sɒd] *n (turf)* terrón *m.* **2*** *(bastard)* cabrón,-ona*. **3*** *(wretch)* desgraciado,-a. ●~ *it!**, ¡maldito,-a sea!

soda [ˈsəʊdə] *n* sosa. **2** US gaseosa. ■ ~ *water,* soda, sifón *m.*

sofa [ˈsəʊfə] *n* sofá *m.* ■ ~ *bed,* sofá cama *m.*

soft [sɒft] *adj (not hard)* blando,-a. **2** *(smooth, quiet)* suave. **3** *(weak)* débil. – **4** *softly adv* suavemente. ■ ~ *drink,* refresco.

soften [ˈsɒfən] *t-i (make less tough)* ablandar(se). **2** *(smooth)* suavizar(se).

softness [ˈsɒftnəs] *n gen* blandura. **2** *(smoothness)* dulzura. **3** *(weakness)* debilidad.

soggy [ˈsɒgɪ] *adj (wet)* empapado,-a. **2** *(too soft)* pastoso,-a.

soil [sɔɪl] *n* tierra. – **2** *t* ensuciar; *fig* manchar.

solar [ˈsəʊləʳ] *adj* solar.

sold [səʊld] *pt & pp* → **sell.**

solder [ˈsɒldəʳ] *n* soldadura. – **2** *t* soldar.

soldier [ˈsəʊldʒəʳ] *n* soldado. **2** *(military man)* militar *m.*

sole [səʊl] *n (of foot)* planta. **2** *(of shoe)* suela. **3** *(fish)* lenguado. – **4** *adj* único,-a. – **5** *solely adv* solamente, únicamente. – **6** *t* poner suela a.

solemn [ˈsɒləm] *adj* solemne.

solemnity [səˈlemnɪtɪ] *n* solemnidad.

solicit [səˈlɪsɪt] *t-i* pedir, solicitar. – **2** *i (prostitute etc.)* ejercer la prostitución.

solicitor [səˈlɪsɪtəʳ] *n* JUR abogado,-a, procurador,-ra. **2** *(for wills)* notario,-a.

solid [ˈsɒlɪd] *adj gen* sólido,-a. **2** *(not hollow)* macizo,-a. **3** *(firm, strong)* fuerte, macizo,-a. **4** *(continuous)* entero,-a: *we waited for two* ~ *hours,* esperamos dos horas enteras. **5** *(pure)* puro,-a. – **6** *n* sólido.

solidarity [sɒlɪˈdærɪtɪ] *n* solidaridad.

solidify [səˈlɪdɪfaɪ] *t-i* solidificar(se).

solidity [səˈlɪdɪtɪ] *n* solidez *f.*

solitary [ˈsɒlɪtərɪ] *adj (alone)* solitario,-a. **2** *(only, sole)* solo,-a. **3** *(secluded)* apartado,-a.

solitude [ˈsɒlɪtjuːd] *n* soledad.

solo [ˈsəʊləʊ] *n* solo. – **2** *adj* en solitario. – **3** *adv* solo,-a, a solas.

solution [sə'lu:ʃən] *n* solución.

solve [sɒlv] *t* resolver, solucionar.

sombre ['sɒmbəʳ] *adj (dark)* sombrío,-a; *(gloomy)* lúgubre, umbrío,-a.

some [sʌm] *adj (with pl nouns)* unos,-as, algunos,-as: *there were ~ flowers,* había unas/algunas flores. **2** *(with sing nouns)* un poco (de): *would you like ~ coffee?,* ¿quieres (un poco de) café? **3** *(certain)* cierto,-a. **4** *(unspecified)* algún,-una: *~ day,* algún día. **5** *(quite a lot of)* bastante. — **6** *pron (unspecified)* algunos,-as, unos,-as; *(quite a few)* unos,-as cuantos,-as. **7** *(a little)* algo, un poco. ●*in ~ ways,* en cierto modo/sentido; *~ ... or other,* algún,-una ... que otro,-a; *~ other time,* en otro momento.

somebody ['sʌmbədɪ] *pron* alguien. ●*~ else,* otro,-a, otra persona.

somehow ['sʌmhaʊ] *adv (in some way)* de algún modo. **2** *(for some reason)* por alguna razón.

someone ['sʌmwʌn] *pron* → **somebody**.

somersault ['sʌməsɔ:lt] *n (acrobatics)* salto mortal; *(by child etc.)* voltereta; *(by car)* vuelta de campana.

something ['sʌmθɪŋ] *n* algo. ●*~ else,* otra cosa.

sometime ['sʌmtaɪm] *adv* un/algún día. — **2** *adj* antiguo,-a, ex-. ●*~ or other,* un día de éstos.

sometimes ['sʌmtaɪmz] *adv* a veces, de vez en cuando.

somewhat ['sʌmwɒt] *n* algo, un tanto.

somewhere ['sʌmweəʳ] *adv* en/a alguna parte. ●*~ else,* en otra parte.

son [sʌn] *n* hijo.

song [sɒŋ] *n* canción. **2** *(singing)* canto. ●*to burst into ~,* ponerse a cantar.

songbook ['sɒŋbʊk] *n* cancionero.

son-in-law ['sʌnɪnlɔ:] *n* yerno, hijo político. ▲ *pl* **sons-in-law**.

soon [su:n] *adv (within a short time)* pronto, dentro de poco. **2** *(early)* pronto, temprano. ●*as ~ as,* en cuanto; *as ~ as possible,* cuanto antes; *I would (just) as ~ ...,* prefiero/preferiría ...; *~ afterwards,* poco después.

sooner ['su:nəʳ] *adv* más temprano. ●*I would ~,* preferiría; *no ~ ...,* nada más ... .

soot [sʊt] *n* hollín *m*.

soothe [su:ð] *t (calm)* calmar. **2** *(pain)* aliviar.

sophisticated [sə'fɪstɪkeɪtɪd] *adj* sofisticado,-a.

soprano [sə'prɑ:nəʊ] *n* soprano *mf*.

sorcerer ['sɔ:sərəʳ] *n* hechicero, brujo.

sordid ['sɔ:dɪd] *adj* sórdido,-a.

sore [sɔ:ʳ] *adj* dolorido,-a, inflamado,-a. **2** *fam (angry)* enfadado,-a (*at,* con). — **3** *n* llaga, úlcera. — **4** *sorely adv* profundamente, muy. ●*to have a ~ throat,* tener dolor de garganta. ■ *~ point,* asunto delicado.

soreness ['sɔ:nəs] *n* dolor *m*.

sorrow ['sɒrəʊ] *n* pena, pesar *m*, dolor *m*.

sorry ['sɒrɪ] *adj (pitiful)* triste, lamentable. — **2** *interj* ¡perdón!, ¡disculpe! ●*to be ~ (about sth.),* sentir (algo): *I'm ~,* lo siento; *I'm ~ I'm late,* siento haber llegado tarde; *to feel ~ for sb.,* compadecer a algn.

sort [sɔ:t] *n (type)* clase *f*, tipo. **2** *fam (person)* tipo. — **3** *t* clasificar. ◆*to ~ out t* clasificar, ordenar. **2** *(solve)* arreglar, solucionar. ●*of sorts,* de alguna clase; *out of sorts, (unwell)* pachucho,-a; *(moody)* de mal humor; *~ of,* un poco; *fam to be ~ of ...,* estar como ... .

so-so ['səʊsəʊ] *adv fam* así así, regular.

sought [sɔ:t] *pt & pp* → **seek**.

soul [səʊl] *n gen* alma. **2** *(feeling)* ánimo. ●*not a ~,* ni un alma.

soulful ['səʊlfʊl] *adj* conmovedor,-a, emotivo,-a.

sound [saʊnd] *n gen* sonido. **2** *(noise)* ruido. **3** GEOG estrecho. — **4** *t* tocar, hacer sonar. **5** MAR MED sondar. — **6** *i* sonar: *it sounds like Mozart,* (me) suena a Mozart. **7** *fig (give impression)* parecer. — **8** *adj (healthy)* sano,-a. **9** *(in good condition)* en buen estado. **10** *(reasonable)* razonable. **11** *(robust)* fuerte, robusto,-a. **12** *(sleep)* profundo,-a. ●*to be ~ asleep,* estar profundamente dormido,-a.

sounding ['saʊndɪŋ] *n* sondeo.

soundproof ['saʊndpru:f] *adj* insonorizado,-a. — **2** *t* insonorizar.

soundtrack ['saʊndtræk] *n* banda sonora.

soup [su:p] *n* sopa. **2** *(clear, thin)* caldo, consomé *m*. ■ *~ spoon,* cuchara sopera.

sour ['saʊəʳ] *adj* ácido,-a, agrio,-a. **2** *(milk)* cortado,-a. **3** *fig (bitter)* amargado,-a.

source [sɔ:s] *n* fuente *f*. **2** *(of infection)* foco.

sourness ['saʊənəs] *n* acidez *f*. **2** *(of milk)* agrura. **3** *fig* amargura, acritud.

south [saʊθ] *n* sur *m*. — **2** *adj* del sur. — **3** *adv* hacia el sur, al sur.

southeast [saʊθ'i:st] *n* sudeste *m*. — **2** *adj* (del) sudeste. — **3** *adv* hacia el sudeste, al sudeste.

southern [ˈsʌðən] *adj* del sur, meridional.

souvenir [suːvəˈnɪəʳ] *n* recuerdo.

sovereign [ˈsɒvrɪn] *adj-n* soberano,-a.

sow [saʊ] *n* cerda, puerca. – **2** *t* sembrar.
▲ *En* **2** *(verbo)* [səʊ]; *pp* **sowed** *o* **sown**.

space [speɪs] *n gen* espacio. **2** *(room)* sitio, lugar *m*. – **3** *t* espaciar. ■ ~ *age,* era espacial.

spacecraft [ˈspeɪskrɑːft] *n* nave *f* espacial.

spacious [ˈspeɪʃəs] *adj* espacioso,-a, amplio,-a.

spade [speɪd] *n* pala. **2** *(cards)* pica; *(Spanish pack)* espada.

span [spæn] *n (of wing)* envergadura; *(of arch etc.)* luz *f*, ojo. **2** *(of time)* lapso, espacio. – **3** *t (bridge etc.)* atravesar. **4** *(life etc.)* abarcar.

spangle [ˈspæŋgəl] *n* lentejuela.

spank [spæŋk] *t* zurrar, pegar.

spanner [ˈspænəʳ] *n* llave *f* de tuerca.

spar [spɑːʳ] *n* palo, verga. – **2** *i (boxing)* entrenarse. **3** *(argue)* discutir.

spare [speəʳ] *adj (extra)* de sobra/más; *(left over)* sobrante, que sobra. – **2** *n* AUTO (pieza de) recambio/repuesto. – **3** *t (do without)* prescindir de, pasar sin. **4** *(begrudge)* escatimar. ●*can you ~ five minutes?,* ¿tienes cinco minutos? ■ ~ *wheel,* rueda de recambio.

sparing [ˈspeərɪŋ] *adj (frugal)* frugal. **2** *(economical)* económico,-a. – **3** *sparingly adv* en poca cantidad.

spark [spɑːk] *n* chispa. – **2** *i* echar chispas. ●*to ~ off t* provocar. ■ ~ *plug,* bujía.

sparkle [ˈspɑːkəl] *n* centelleo, brillo. **2** *fig* viveza. – **3** *i* centellear, destellar. **4** *fig* brillar.

sparkler [ˈspɑːkələʳ] *n* bengala.

sparrow [ˈspærəʊ] *n* gorrión *m*.

sparse [spɑːs] *adj (thin)* escaso,-a. **2** *(scattered)* disperso,-a. **3** *(hair)* ralo,-a.

spasm [ˈspæzəm] *n* MED espasmo. **2** *(of anger, coughing)* acceso.

spat [spæt] *pt & pp* → **spit**. – **2** *n* polaina.

spate [speɪt] *n (of letters)* avalancha; *(of accidents)* racha.

spatter [ˈspætəʳ] *t* salpicar, rociar.

speak [spiːk] *i gen* hablar. **2** *(give speech)* pronunciar un discurso. – **3** *t (utter)* decir: *he spoke the truth,* dijo la verdad. **4** *(language)* hablar. ●*to ~ out i* hablar claro. ●*to ~ up i* hablar más fuerte. ●*generally speaking,* en términos generales; *so to ~,* por así decirlo; *to be nothing to ~ of,* no ser nada especial; *to*

~ *one's mind,* hablar claro/sin rodeos. ▲ *pt* **spoke**; *pp* **spoken**.

speaker [ˈspiːkəʳ] *n* persona que habla, el/la que habla. **2** *(in dialogue)* interlocutor,-ra. **3** *(lecturer)* conferenciante *mf*. **4** *(of language)* hablante *mf*. **5** *(loudspeaker)* altavoz *m*.

spear [spɪəʳ] *n gen* lanza. **2** *(harpoon)* arpón *m*.

special [ˈspeʃəl] *adj* especial. **2** *(specific, unusual)* particular. – **3** *n (train)* tren *m* especial. **4** RAD TV programa *m* especial. – **5** *specially adv* especialmente. ■ ~ *delivery,* express *m*; ~ *offer,* oferta.

specialist [ˈspeʃəlɪst] *n* especialista *mf*.

speciality [speʃɪˈælɪtɪ] *n* especialidad.

specialize [ˈspeʃəlaɪz] *i* especializarse.

species [ˈspiːʃiːz] *n inv* especie *f*.

specific [spəˈsɪfɪk] *adj* específico,-a. **2** *(exact)* preciso,-a. – **3** *npl* datos *mpl* (concretos). – **4** *specifically adv* concretamente, en concreto.

specifications [spesɪfɪˈkeɪʃənz] *npl* datos *mpl* específicos.

specify [ˈspesɪfaɪ] *t* especificar, precisar.

specimen [ˈspesɪmən] *n* espécimen *m*, muestra, ejemplar *m*.

speck [spek] *n (of dust, soot)* mota. **2** *(trace)* pizca. **3** *(dot)* punto negro.

speckled [ˈspekəld] *adj* moteado,-a, con puntitos.

spectacle [ˈspektəkəl] *n* espectáculo. – **2** *npl* gafas *fpl*.

spectacular [spekˈtækjʊləʳ] *adj* espectacular. – **2** *n* superproducción.

spectator [spekˈteɪtəʳ] *n* espectador,-ra.

spectre [ˈspektəʳ] *n* espectro, fantasma *m*.

speculate [ˈspekjʊleɪt] *i* especular *(on/about,* sobre).

speculation [spekjʊˈleɪʃən] *n* especulación.

sped [sped] *pt & pp* → **speed**.

speech [spiːtʃ] *n (faculty)* habla. **2** *(pronunciation)* pronunciación. **3** *(address)* discurso. **4** GRAM oración. ●*to give/make a ~,* pronunciar un discurso.

speechless [ˈspiːtʃləs] *adj* mudo,-a, boquiabierto,-a.

speed [spiːd] *n* velocidad. – **2** *i (go fast)* ir corriendo/a toda prisa. ●*to ~ past i* pasar volando. ●*to ~ up t-i* acelerar; *(person)* apresurar(se). ▲ *pt & pp* **speeded** *o* **sped**.

speedometer [spɪˈdɒmɪtəʳ] *n* velocímetro.

speedy [ˈspiːdɪ] *adj* rápido,-a, veloz.

spell [spel] *n (magical)* hechizo, encanto.
2 *(period)* período, temporada; *(short)*
racha. **3** *(shift)* tanda. **– 4** *t-i (letter by letter)* deletrear. **5** *(write)* escribir correctamente. **– 6** *t fig (denote)* representar.
▲ *pt & pp* **spelled** *o* **spelt.**

spelling ['spelıŋ] *n* ortografía.

spelt [spelt] *pt & pp* → **spell.**

spend [spend] *t (money)* gastar (**on,** en). **2**
(time) pasar: *we spent two days there,*
pasamos allí dos días. **3** *(devote)* dedicar.
▲ *pt & pp* **spent.**

spending ['spendıŋ] *n* gasto(s) *m(pl).*

spendthrift ['spendθrıft] *n* derrochador,-ra.

spent [spent] *pt & pp* → **spend.**

sperm [spɜ:m] *n* esperma *mf.*

sphere [sfıə[r]] *n* esfera.

sphinx [sfıŋks] *n* esfinge *f.*

spice [spaıs] *n* especia. **2** *fig* sazón *m,* sal
f. **– 3** *t* sazonar, condimentar.

spicy ['spaısı] *adj* sazonado,-a; *(hot)* picante. **2** *fig* picante.

spider ['spaıdə[r]] *n* araña. ■ *spider's web,*
telaraña.

spike [spaık] *n (stake)* estaca. **2** *(metal rod)*
pincho. **3** *(sharp point)* punta. **4** *(on shoes)* clavo. **5** BOT espiga.

spiky ['spaıkı] *adj* puntiagudo,-a. **2** *fam
(hair)* de punta.

spill [spıl] *n* derrame *m.* **– 2** *t-i* derramar(se); *(pour)* verter(se). ◆*to ~ over t*
desbordarse. ●*fam to ~ the beans,* descubrir el pastel. ▲ *pt & pp* **spilled** *o* **spilt.**

spin [spın] *n* vuelta, giro. **2** *(of washing
machine)* centrifugado. **3** *(of ball)* efecto.
– 4 *t-i (turn)* (hacer) girar, dar vueltas
(a). **5** *(cotton, wool, etc.)* hilar. ◆*to ~ out
t* prolongar. ●*to go for a ~,* dar una
vuelta (en coche/moto); *fam to ~ sb. a
yarn,* pegarle un rollo a algn. ▲ *pt* **spun**
o **span;** *pp* **spun.**

spinach ['spınıdʒ] *n* espinacas *fpl.*

spinal ['spaınəl] *adj* espinal, vertebral.
■ *~ column,* columna vertebral.

spin-dryer [spın'draıə[r]] *n* secador,-ra
centrífugo,-a.

spine [spaın] *n* ANAT columna vertebral,
espina dorsal. **2** *(of book)* lomo. **3** ZOOL
púa.

spineless ['spaınləs] *adj* invertebrado,-a.
2 *fig* débil.

spinning ['spınıŋ] *n (act)* hilado; *(art)* hilandería. ■ *~ top,* peonza, trompo; *~
wheel,* rueca, torno de hilar.

spinster ['spınstə[r]] *n* soltera. ●*pej to be
an old ~,* ser una vieja solterona.

spiral ['spaıərəl] *adj-n* espiral *(f).* **– 2** *i*
moverse en espiral. ■ *~ staircase,* escalera de caracol.

spire [spaıə[r]] *n* aguja.

spirit ['spırıt] *n gen* espíritu *m.* **2** *(ghost)*
fantasma *m.* **3** *(force, vitality)* vigor *m,*
ánimo; *(personality)* carácter *m.* **4** CHEM
alcohol *m.* **5** *pl (mood)* moral *f sing.* **6** *pl
(drink)* licores *mpl.* ◆*to ~ away/off t* llevarse como por arte de magia. ●*to be in
high/low spirits,* estar animado,-a/desanimado,-a. ■ *~ level,* nivel *m* de aire;
the Holy Spirit, el Espíritu Santo.

spirited ['spırıtıd] *adj* enérgico,-a, vigoroso,-a.

spiritual ['spırıtjuəl] *adj* espiritual. **– 2** *n*
espiritual *m* negro.

spit [spıt] *n* saliva, esputo. **2** CULIN asador
m. **3** GEOG punta. **– 4** *t-i* escupir. ◆*to ~
out t* escupir. **2** *fig* soltar. ▲ *pt & pp* **spat.**

spite [spaıt] *n* rencor *m,* ojeriza. **– 2** *t* fastidiar. ●*in ~ of,* a pesar de, pese a; *out
of ~,* por despecho.

spiteful ['spaıtful] *adj* rencoroso,-a, malévolo,-a. **– 2** *spitefully adv* con rencor.

splash [splæʃ] *n (noise)* chapoteo. **2**
(spray) salpicadura, rociada. **3** *fig (of
light etc.)* mancha. **– 4** *t* salpicar, rociar
(**with,** de). **– 5** *i* chapotear. **– 6** *interj*
¡plaf! ◆*to ~ out i fam* derrochar dinero.
●*to make a ~,* causar sensación.

splendid ['splendıd] *adj* espléndido,-a,
maravilloso,-a.

splendour ['splendə[r]] *n* esplendor *m.*

splice [splaıs] *t* empalmar. **2** CINEM montar.

splint [splınt] *n* tablilla.

splinter ['splıntə[r]] *n (of wood)* astilla; *(of
metal, bone)* esquirla; *(of glass)* fragmento. **– 2** *t-i* astillar(se), hacer(se) astillas.
■ POL *~ group,* grupo disidente, facción.

split [splıt] *n* grieta, hendidura. **2** *(tear)*
desgarrón *m.* **3** *fig* división, ruptura. **4**
fig POL escisión. **– 5** *adj* partido,-a, hendido,-a. **– 6** *t-i (crack)* agrietar(se), hender(se). **7** *(in two)* partir(se). **8** *(tear)* rajar(se). **9** *(divide)* dividir(se). **– 10** *i* POL
escindirse. **11** *sl* largarse. ◆*to ~ up t*
partir, dividir. **– 2** *i* dispersarse; *(couple)*
separarse. ●*in a ~ second,* en una fracción de segundo. ▲ *pt & pp* **split.**

spoil [spɔıl] *t-i* estropear(se), echar(se) a
perder. **– 2** *t (child etc.)* mimar. **– 3** *npl
botín m sing.* ▲ *pt & pp* **spoiled** *o* **spoilt**
[spɔılt].

spoke [spəuk] *pt* → **speak.** **– 2** *n* radio,
rayo.

spoken ['spəʊkən] *pp* → **speak**.

spokesman ['spəʊksmən] *n* portavoz *mf*.

sponge [spʌndʒ] *n* esponja. – 2 *t* lavar/limpiar con esponja. – 3 *i pej* vivir de gorra, gorrear. ◆*to* ~ *off/on t pej* vivir a costa de. ∎ ~ *cake*, bizcocho.

sponger ['spʌndʒəʳ] *n pej* gorrón,-ona, sablista *mf*.

spongy ['spʌndʒɪ] *adj* esponjoso,-a.

sponsor ['spɒnsəʳ] *n gen* patrocinador,-ra. 2 FIN avalador,-ra, garante *mf*. 3 REL *m* padrino, *f* padrina. – 4 *t gen* patrocinar. 5 FIN avalar. 6 REL apadrinar.

spontaneous [spɒn'teɪnɪəs] *adj* espontáneo,-a.

spoof [spu:f] *n* parodia.

spooky ['spu:kɪ] *adj fam* escalofriante.

spool [spu:l] *n* carrete *m*, bobina.

spoon [spu:n] *n* cuchara. 2 *(small)* cucharilla, cucharita.

spoonful ['spu:nfʊl] *n* cucharada. ▲ *pl* **spoonfuls** *o* **spoonsful**.

sporadic [spə'rædɪk] *adj* esporádico,-a.

sport [spɔ:t] *n* deporte *m*. – 2 *t* lucir. ◆*fam* **to be a (good)** ~, ser buena persona. ∎ **sports car**, coche deportivo; **sports jacket**, chaqueta (de) sport.

sporting ['spɔ:tɪŋ] *adj* deportivo,-a.

sportsman ['spɔ:tsmən] *m* deportista *m*.

sportsmanship ['spɔ:tsmənʃɪp] *n* deportividad.

sportswoman ['spɔ:tswʊmən] *n* deportista.

spot [spɒt] *n (dot)* punto; *(on fabric)* lunar *m*. 2 *(stain)* mancha. 3 *(on face)* grano. 4 *(place)* sitio, lugar *m*. 5 *(fix)* aprieto, apuro. 6 *(advert)* spot (publicitario). 7 *fam (bit)* poquito. – 8 *t (pick out)* reconocer, encontrar. 9 *(notice)* darse cuenta de. 10 *(mark with spots)* motear. ◆**to be on the** ~, estar allí/presente; **to put sb. on the** ~, poner a algn. en un aprieto.

spotless ['spɒtləs] *adj* limpísimo,-a, impecable. 2 *fig* intachable.

spotlight ['spɒtlaɪt] *n* foco. ◆*fig* **to be in the** ~, ser objeto de la atención pública.

spouse [spaʊz] *n* cónyuge *mf*.

spout [spaʊt] *n (of jug)* pico; *(of fountain)* surtidor *m*; *(of roof-gutter)* canalón *m*. 2 *(of water)* chorro. – 3 *t* echar, arrojar. – 4 *i* salir a chorros.

sprain [spreɪn] *n* torcedura. – 2 *t* torcer: *she sprained her ankle,* se torció el tobillo.

sprang [spræŋ] *pt* → **spring**.

sprawl [sprɔ:l] *i (person)* tumbarse, repantigarse. 2 *(city etc.)* extenderse.

spray [spreɪ] *n (of water)* rociada; *(from sea)* espuma. 2 *(from can)* pulverización. 3 *(aerosol)* spray *m*, atomizador *m*. 4 *(of flowers)* ramita. – 5 *t (water)* rociar; *(perfume)* atomizar; *(insecticide)* pulverizar. ∎ ~ *can,* aerosol *m*; ~ *paint,* pintura spray.

spread [spred] *n gen* extensión. 2 *(of ideas, news)* difusión. 3 *(of disease, fire)* propagación. 4 *(of wings, sails)* envergadura. 5 CULIN pasta (para untar). 6 *fam (meal)* comilona. – 7 *t-i gen* extender(se). 8 *(unfold)* desplegar(se). 9 *(news etc.)* difundir(se). 10 *(disease, fire)* propagar(se). – 11 *t (butter etc.)* untar. ∎ *two-page* ~, doble página. ▲ *pt & pp* **spread**.

spree [spri:] *n* juerga, parranda. ◆*to go on a* ~, ir de juerga.

sprig [sprɪg] *n* ramita, ramito.

spring [sprɪŋ] *n (season)* primavera. 2 *(source)* manantial *m*, fuente *f*. 3 *(of furniture etc.)* muelle *m*; *(of watch, lock, etc.)* resorte *m*; *(of car)* ballesta. 4 *(elasticity)* elasticidad. – 5 *i* saltar. – 6 *t fig* espetar *(on,* a): *he sprang the news on me,* me espetó la noticia. ◆*to* ~ *up i* aparecer, surgir. ◆*to* ~ *a leak,* hacer agua; *to* ~ *to one's feet,* levantarse de un salto. ∎ ~ *onion,* cebolleta. ▲ *pt* **sprang**; *pp* **sprung**.

springboard ['sprɪŋbɔ:d] *n* trampolín *m*.

springtime ['sprɪŋtaɪm] *n* primavera.

sprinkle ['sprɪŋkəl] *t (with water)* rociar, salpicar *(with,* de). 2 *(with flour etc.)* espolvorear *(with,* de).

sprinkler ['sprɪŋkələʳ] *n* aspersor *m*.

sprint [sprɪnt] *n* carrera corta; SP (e)sprint *m*. – 2 *i* correr a toda velocidad; SP (e)sprintar.

sprout [spraʊt] *n* brote *m*, retoño. – 2 *i* brotar. 3 *fig* crecer rápidamente. ∎ *(Brussels) sprouts,* coles *fpl* de Bruselas.

spruce [spru:s] *n inv* BOT picea. – 2 *adj* acicalado,-a, apuesto,-a. ◆*to* ~ *up t* acicalar, arreglar.

sprung [sprʌŋ] *pp* → **spring**.

spun [spʌn] *pt & pp* → **spin**.

spur [spɜ:ʳ] *n (rider's)* espuela. 2 ZOOL espolón *m*. 3 *fig* aguijón *m*. – 4 *t* espolear. 5 *fig* estimular, incitar. ◆*on the* ~ *of the moment,* sin pensarlo.

spurn [spɜ:n] *t fml* desdeñar.

spurt [spɜ:t] *n (of liquid)* chorro. 2 *fig* racha, ataque *m*. 3 SP esfuerzo. – 4 *i* chorrear, salir a chorro. **5** *fig* hacer un último esfuerzo.

sputter [ˈspʌtəʳ] *i (fire, fat)* chisporrotear. **2** *(engine)* petardear.

spy [spaɪ] *n* espía *mf.* − **2** *i* espiar *(on,* a).

spyhole [ˈspaɪhəʊl] *n* mirilla.

squabble [ˈskwɒbəl] *n* disputa, riña. − **2** *i* disputar, reñir *(over,* por).

squad [skwɒd] *n* MIL pelotón *m.* **2** *(of police)* brigada. ■ ~ *car,* coche *m* patrulla.

squadron [ˈskwɒdrən] *n* MIL escuadrón *m.* **2** AV escuadrilla.

squalid [ˈskwɒlɪd] *adj* sucio,-a, mugriento,-a. **2** *(poor)* miserable.

squalor [ˈskɒləʳ] *n* suciedad, mugre *f.* **2** *(poverty)* miseria.

squander [ˈskwɒndəʳ] *t* derrochar, malgastar.

square [skweəʳ] *n (shape)* cuadrado; *(on fabric)* cuadro. **2** *(on chessboard, paper)* casilla. **3** *(in town)* plaza. **4** MATH cuadrado. **5** *fam (person)* carroza *mf.* − **6** *adj* cuadrado,-a. **7** *(meal)* bueno,-a, decente. **8** *fam (fair)* justo,-a. − **9** *adv* justo, exactamente. − **10** *t-i* cuadrar. − **11** *t* MATH elevar al cuadrado. **12** *(settle)* ajustar, arreglar. ◆*to* ~ *up i fam* ajustar las cuentas. ●*to get a* ~ *deal,* recibir un trato justo. ■ ~ *brackets,* corchetes *mpl; squared paper,* papel cuadriculado; ~ *metre,* metro cuadrado.

squash [skɒʃ] *n (crowd)* apiñamiento, agolpamiento. **2** *(drink)* zumo. **3** BOT calabaza. **4** SP squash *m.* − **5** *t-i* aplastar(se), chafar(se). − **6** *t fig (person)* apabullar, hacer callar.

squat [skwɒt] *adj* rechoncho,-a, achaparrado,-a. − **2** *i (crouch)* agacharse, sentarse en cuclillas. **3** *(in building)* vivir ilegalmente.

squatter [ˈskwɒtəʳ] *n* ocupante *mf* ilegal.

squawk [skwɔːk] *n* graznido, chillido. − **2** *i* graznar, chillar.

squeak [skwiːk] *n (of animal)* chillido. **2** *(of wheel etc.)* chirrido, rechinamiento. − **3** *i (animal)* chillar; *(wheel etc.)* chirriar, rechinar.

squeaky [ˈskwiːkɪ] *adj* chirriante; *(voice)* chillón,-ona.

squeal [skwiːl] *n* chillido. − **2** *i* chillar. **3** *fam* cantar, chivarse *(on,* de).

squeamish [ˈskwiːmɪʃ] *adj* muy sensible, remilgado,-a.

squeeze [skwiːz] *n* estrujón *m.* **2** *(of hand)* apretón *m.* **3** *(crowd)* apretujón *m.* − **4** *t gen* apretar. **5** *(lemon etc.)* exprimir. **6** *(sponge)* estrujar. ◆*to* ~ *in/out i* meterse/salir con dificultad.

squelch [skweltʃ] *i* chapotear.

squid [skwɪd] *n* calamar *m; (small)* chipirón *m.*

squint [skwɪnt] *n* MED bizquera. **2** *fam (look)* vistazo, ojeada. − **3** *i* MED bizquear, ser bizco,-a. **4** *(in sunlight)* entrecerrar los ojos.

squirm [skwɜːm] *i* retorcerse.

squirrel [ˈskwɪrəl] *n* ardilla.

squirt [skwɜːt] *n* chorro. **2** *fam pej (person)* mequetrefe *mf.* − **3** *t* lanzar a chorro. ◆*to* ~ *out i* salir a chorro.

stab [stæb] *n* puñalada, navajazo. − **2** *t-i* apuñalar, acuchillar. ■ ~ *of pain,* punzada.

stability [stəˈbɪlɪtɪ] *n* estabilidad.

stabilize [ˈsteɪbəlaɪz] *t-i* estabilizar(se).

stable [ˈsteɪbəl] *adj* estable. − **2** *n* cuadra, caballeriza, establo.

stack [stæk] *n* montón *m.* − **2** *t* apilar, amontonar.

stadium [ˈsteɪdɪəm] *n* estadio.

staff [stɑːf] *n (personnel)* personal *m,* empleados *mpl.* **2** *(stick)* bastón *m;* REL báculo. **3** MUS pentagrama *m.* − **4** *t* proveer de personal. ■ *editorial* ~, redacción; *teaching* ~, cuerpo docente, profesorado.

stag [stæg] *n* ciervo, venado. ■ ~ *party,* despedida de soltero.

stage [steɪdʒ] *n (period)* etapa, fase *f.* **2** *(of road)* tramo. **3** THEAT escenario, escena. **4** *(platform)* estrado, plataforma. − **5** *t* THEAT poner en escena, representar. **6** *(carry out)* llevar a cabo. ●*by/in stages,* por etapas; *to go on* ~, salir al escenario. ■ ~ *manager,* director,-ra de escena.

stagecoach [ˈsteɪdʒkəʊtʃ] *n* diligencia.

stagger [ˈstægəʳ] *i* tambalearse.- **2** *t (hours, work)* escalonar.

stagnant [ˈstægnənt] *adj* estancado,-a.

stagnate [stægˈneɪt] *i* estancarse.

stain [steɪn] *n* mancha. **2** *(dye)* tinte *m.* − **3** *t-i* manchar(se). − **4** *t* teñir. ■ *stained glass,* vidrio de colores.

stainless [ˈsteɪnləs] *adj* ~ *steel,* acero inoxidable.

stair [steəʳ] *n* escalón *m,* peldaño. **2** *pl* escalera *f sing.*

staircase [ˈsteəkeɪs] *n* escalera.

stake [steɪk] *n (stick)* estaca, palo. **2** *(post)* poste *m.* **3** *(bet)* (a)puesta. **4** *(interest)* intereses *mpl.* − **5** *t (bet)* apostar. **6** *(invest)* invertir. ◆*to* ~ *out t* cercar con estacas. ●*at* ~, *(at risk)* en juego; *(in danger)* en peligro.

stalactite [ˈstæləktaɪt] *n* estalactita.

stale [steɪl] *adj (bread)* duro,-a; *(food)* pasado,-a. **2** *(smell)* a cerrado. **3** *fig (joke)* gastado,-a.

stalemate [ˈsteɪlmeɪt] *n (chess)* tablas *fpl.* **2** *fig* punto muerto.

stalk [stɔːk] *n (of plant)* tallo. **2** *(of fruit)* rabo. – **3** *t* cazar al acecho. – **4** *i* andar con paso majestuoso.

stall [stɔːl] *n (in market)* puesto; *(at fair)* caseta. **2** *(stable compartment)* casilla (de establo). **3** *pl* platea *f sing.* – **4** *t-i* AUTO calar(se), parar(se). – **5** *i fam (delay)* andarse con rodeos.

stallion [ˈstælɪən] *n* semental *m.*

stalwart [ˈstɔːlwət] *adj* fuerte, fornido,-a. – **2** *n* partidario,-a incondicional.

stammer [ˈstæmər] *n* tartamudeo. – **2** *i* tartamudear.

stamp [stæmp] *n (postage)* sello; *(fiscal)* timbre *m.* **2** *(of rubber)* sello de goma, tampón *m.* **3** *(of foot)* patada. – **4** *t (post)* poner sello a. **5** *(with rubber stamp)* sellar. – **6** *i* patear, patalear; *(in dancing)* zapatear. ◆*to ~ out t fig* acabar con. ◆*to ~ one's feet,* patalear; *(in dancing)* zapatear. ■ *~ collecting,* filatelia.

stampede [stæmˈpiːd] *n* estampida, desbandada. – **2** *i* desbandarse.

stance [stæns] *n* postura.

stand [stænd] *n* posición, postura. **2** *(of lamp etc.)* pie *m.* **3** *(market stall)* puesto; *(at exhibition)* stand *m,* pabellón *m.* **4** *(platform)* plataforma. **5** SP tribuna. – **6** *i (be upright)* estar de pie; *(get up)* ponerse de pie, levantarse; *(stay upright)* quedarse de pie. **7** *(measure)* medir. **8** *(be situated)* encontrarse. **9** *(remain valid)* seguir en pie. **10** *(be)* estar. – **11** *t* poner, colocar. **12** *fam (bear)* aguantar: *I can't ~ him,* no lo aguanto. ◆*to ~ back i* abrir paso. ◆*to ~ by i* quedarse sin hacer nada. **2** *(be ready)* estar preparado,-a. – **3** *t (person)* respaldar a; *(decision etc.)* atenerse a. ◆*to ~ for t* significar. **2** *(put up with)* tolerar. ◆*to ~ in for t* sustituir a. ◆*to ~ out i* destacar(se). ◆*to ~ up i* ponerse de pie. – **2** *t fam* dejar plantado,-a. ◆*to ~ up for t fig* defender. ●*as things ~,* tal como están las cosas; *to ~ to reason,* ser lógico,-a; *fig to ~ up to sb.,* hacer frente a algn. ▲ *pt & pp* **stood.**

standard [ˈstændəd] *n* nivel *m.* **2** *(principle)* criterio, valor *m.* **3** *(norm)* norma. **4** *(flag)* estandarte *m.* **5** *(measure)* patrón *m.* – **6** *adj* normal, corriente, estándar. ●*to be up to/below ~,* satisfacer/no satisfacer los requisitos. ■ *~ of living,* nivel de vida; *~ time,* hora oficial.

standardize [ˈstændədaɪz] *t* normalizar, estandarizar.

standby [ˈstændbaɪ] *n (person)* suplente *mf.* ●*to be on ~,* *(passenger)* estar en la lista de espera; MIL estar de retén.

standing [ˈstændɪŋ] *adj (not sitting)* de pie. **2** *(vertical)* derecho,-a. **3** *(committee)* permanente. – **4** *n (position)* rango, estatus *m.* **5** *(reputation)* fama, reputación. **6** *(duration)* duración. ■ *~ invitation,* invitación abierta; FIN *~ order,* pago fijo; *~ ovation,* ovación calurosa; SP *~ start,* salida parada.

stand-offish [stændˈɒfɪʃ] *adj fam* estirado,-a, altivo,-a.

standpoint [ˈstændpɔɪnt] *n* punto de vista.

standstill [ˈstændstɪl] *n* paralización. ●*at a ~,* *(traffic etc.)* parado,-a; *(industry)* paralizado,-a.

stank [stæŋk] *pt* → **stink.**

stanza [ˈstænzə] *n* estrofa.

staple [ˈsteɪpəl] *n (fastener)* grapa. **2** *(product)* producto principal. – **3** *adj (food, diet)* básico,-a. – **4** *t* grapar.

stapler [ˈsteɪplər] *n* grapadora.

star [stɑːr] *n* estrella. – **2** *adj* estelar. – **3** *i* protagonizar *(in, -).* – **4** *t* tener como protagonista a.

starboard [ˈstɑːbəd] *n* estribor *m.*

starch [stɑːtʃ] *n* almidón *m;* *(of potatoes)* fécula. – **2** *t* almidonar.

stardom [ˈstɑːdəm] *n* estrellato.

stare [steər] *n* mirada fija. – **2** *i* mirar fijamente, clavar la vista/los ojos *(at,* en). ●*to ~ into space,* mirar al vacío.

starfish [ˈstɑːfɪʃ] *n* estrella de mar.

stark [stɑːk] *adj (landscape)* desolado,-a. **2** *(décor, colour)* sobrio,-a, austero,-a. **3** *fig (truth etc.)* desnudo,-a. – **4** *adv* completamente. ●*~ mad,* loco,-a de remate; *fam ~ naked,* en cueros.

starlight [ˈstɑːlaɪt] *n* luz *f* de estrellas.

starry [ˈstɑːrɪ] *adj* estrellado,-a.

starry-eyed [stɑːrɪˈaɪd] *adj* idealista, ilusionado,-a.

start [stɑːt] *n (beginning)* principio, comienzo. **2** *(of race)* salida. **3** *(advantage)* ventaja. **4** *(fright)* susto, sobresalto. – **5** *t-i gen* empezar, comenzar. **6** *(car, engine)* arrancar, poner(se) en marcha. – **7** *t (cause)* causar. ◆*to ~ back i* emprender la vuelta. ◆*to ~ off/out i (begin)* empezar. **2** *(leave)* salir, partir. ◆*to ~ up i (car etc.)* arrancar. ●*for a ~,* para empezar; *from the ~,* desde el principio; *starting point,* punto de partida; *to make an early ~,* salir a primera hora;

to ~ *doing/to do sth.,* empezar a hacer algo.

starter ['stɑːtə^r] *n* SP *(official)* juez *mf* de salida. **2** AUTO motor *m* de arranque. **3** *fam (dish)* primer plato. ●*fig for starters,* para empezar.

startle [stɑːtəl] *t* asustar, sobresaltar.

startling ['stɑːtəlɪŋ] *adj (frightening)* alarmante. **2** *(amazing)* sorprendente.

starvation [stɑːˈveɪʃən] *n* hambre *f*, inanición.

starve [stɑːv] *i* pasar hambre. – **2** *t* matar de hambre, hacer pasar hambre. ●*to* ~ *to death,* morirse de hambre.

starving ['stɑːvɪŋ] *adj* hambriento,-a, muerto,-a de hambre.

state [steɪt] *n gen* estado. – **2** *adj* POL estatal, del Estado. **3** *(solemn)* solemne. – **4** *t (express)* expresar; *(say)* afirmar. **5** *(date etc.)* fijar. ●*to lie in* ~, estar de cuerpo presente. ■ ~ *education,* enseñanza pública; ~ *of mind,* estado de ánimo; ~ *visit,* visita oficial.

stated ['steɪtɪd] *adj* indicado,-a, señalado,-a.

stately ['steɪtlɪ] *adj* majestuoso,-a.

statement ['steɪtmənt] *n gen* exposición, afirmación. **2** *(official, formal)* comunicado. **3** FIN extracto de cuentas. ●JUR *to make a* ~, prestar declaración.

statesman ['steɪtsmən] *n* estadista *m*, hombre *m* de estado.

station ['steɪʃən] *n (railway, bus)* estación. **2** RAD emisora; TV canal *m*. **3** *(position)* puesto. – **4** *t* MIL estacionar, apostar.

stationary ['steɪʃənərɪ] *adj (still)* inmóvil. **2** *(unchanging)* estacionario,-a.

stationery ['steɪʃənərɪ] *n (paper)* papel *m* de carta. **2** *(other materials)* artículos de escritorio.

statistical [stəˈtɪstɪkəl] *adj* estadístico,-a.

statistics [stəˈtɪstɪks] *n (science)* estadística. **2** *pl (numbers)* estadísticas *fpl*.

statue ['stætjuː] *n* estatua.

stature ['stætʃə^r] *n* estatura. **2** *fig* talla.

status ['steɪtəs] *n* estado, condición. **2** *(recognition)* estatus *m*. ■ ~ *quo,* statu quo *m*.

statute ['stætjuːt] *n* estatuto.

staunch [stɔːntʃ] *adj* fiel, leal.

stave [steɪv] *n (of barrel)* duela. **2** MUS pentagrama *m*. ◆*to* ~ *off t (avoid)* evitar. **2** *(delay)* aplazar.

stay [steɪ] *n* estancia. **2** JUR aplazamiento. – **3** *i gen* quedarse, permanecer. **4** *(in hotel etc.)* alojarse. – **5** *t* resistir. ◆*to* ~ *in i* quedarse en casa, no salir. ◆*to* ~ *on i*

quedarse. ◆*to* ~ *out i* quedarse fuera. ◆*to* ~ *up i* no acostarse: *to* ~ *up late,* acostarse tarde. ●*to* ~ *away from sth.,* no acercarse a algo;

steadfast ['stedfɑːst] *adj* firme, resuelto,-a.

steadiness ['stedɪnəs] *n* firmeza. **2** *fig* estabilidad.

steady ['stedɪ] *adj gen* firme, seguro,-a; *(table etc.)* estable. **2** *(job, gaze)* fijo,-a. **3** *(regular)* regular. **4** *(student, worker)* aplicado,-a. – **5** *t-i* estabilizar(se). – **6** *steadily adv* constantemente. ●*to* ~ *sb.'s nerves,* calmarle a algn. los nervios.

steak [steɪk] *n* bistec *m*, filete *m* de buey.

steal [stiːl] *t-i* robar, hurtar. ◆*to* ~ *away i* escabullirse. ●*to* ~ *into a room,* colarse en una habitación; *to* ~ *the show,* acaparar la atención de todos. ▲ *pt* **stole;** *pp* **stolen.**

stealthy ['stelθɪ] *adj* sigiloso,-a.

steam [stiːm] *n* vapor *m*. – **2** *t* cocer al vapor. – **3** *i* echar vapor; *(soup etc.)* humear. ◆*to* ~ *up i* empañarse. ■ ~ *engine,* máquina de vapor.

steamer ['stiːmə^r] *n* → **steamship.**

steamroller ['stiːmrəʊlə^r] *n* apisonadora.

steamship ['stiːmʃɪp] *n (buque m de)* vapor *m*.

steel [stiːl] *n* acero. ●*fig to* ~ *o.s.,* armarse de valor. ■ ~ *industry,* industria siderúrgica; ~ *wool,* estropajo de acero.

steep [stiːp] *adj* empinado,-a, escarpado,-a. **2** *fig (price etc.)* excesivo,-a. – **3** *t* remojar.

steeple ['stiːpəl] *n* aguja, chapitel *m*.

steer [stɪə^r] *n* buey *m*. – **2** *t gen* dirigir. **3** *(vehicle)* conducir. **4** *(ship)* gobernar. **5** *fig (conversation)* llevar.

steering ['stɪərɪŋ] *n* dirección. ■ ~ *wheel,* volante *m*.

stem [stem] *n* BOT tallo. **2** *(of glass)* pie *m*. **3** GRAM raíz *f*. – **4** *t* contener, detener. ◆*to* ~ *from t* derivarse de.

stench [stentʃ] *n* hedor *m*, peste *f*.

step [step] *n gen* paso. **2** *(stair)* escalón *m*, peldaño. **3** *(formality)* gestión, trámite *m*. **4** *pl (outdoor)* escalinata *f sing; (indoor)* escalera *f sing.* – **5** *i* dar un paso, andar. ◆*to* ~ *aside i* apartarse. ◆*to* ~ *down i* renunciar *(from,* a). ◆*to* ~ *in i* intervenir. ◆*to* ~ *out i* salir. ◆*to* ~ *up t fam* aumentar. ●~ *by* ~, paso a paso, poco a poco; *to* ~ *on sth.,* pisar algo; *to take steps,* tomar medidas; *fig to watch one's* ~, ir con cuidado.

stepchild ['steptʃaɪld] *n* hijastro,-a.

stepfather ['stepfɑːðə^r] *n* padrastro.

stepladder ['steplædə'] *n* escalera de tijera.

stepmother ['stepmʌðə'] *n* madrastra.

stepping-stone ['stepɪŋstəʊn] *n* pasadera. 2 *fig* trampolín *m*.

stereo ['steriəʊ] *n (set)* equipo estereofónico. 2 *(sound)* estéreo. — 3 *adj* estereofónico,-a.

stereotype ['steriətaɪp] *n* estereotipo. — 2 *t* estereotipar.

sterile ['steraɪl] *adj (barren)* estéril. 2 *(germ-free)* esterilizado,-a.

sterilize ['sterəlaɪz] *t* esterilizar.

sterling ['stɜ:lɪŋ] *n inv* libra esterlina. — 2 *adj* puro,-a, de ley: ~ *silver,* plata de ley.

stern [stɜ:n] *adj* austero,-a, severo,-a. — 2 *n* popa.

sternness ['stɜ:nnəs] *n* severidad, austeridad.

stevedore ['sti:vədɔ:'] *n* estibador *m*.

stew [stju:] *n* estofado, guisado. — 2 *t (meat)* estofar, guisar; *(fruit)* cocer.

steward ['stju:əd] *n (on ship)* camarero; *(on plane)* auxiliar *m* de vuelo.

stewardess ['stju:ədes] *n (on ship)* camarera; *(on plane)* azafata.

stick [stɪk] *n (piece of wood)* (trozo de) madera. 2 *(rod)* palo. 3 *(for walking)* bastón *m*. 4 MUS batuta. 5 *(of celery etc.)* rama. — 6 *t (pointed object)* clavar, hincar. 7 *fam* poner, meter. 8 *(fix, glue)* pegar. 9 *fam (bear)* aguantar. — 10 *i (become attached)* pegarse. 11 *(get caught)* atrancarse; *(machine part)* encasquillarse. ◆*to ~ around i fam* quedarse. ◆*to ~ at t* seguir con. ◆*to ~ by t fam (friend)* apoyar; *(promise)* cumplir con. ◆*to ~ out i (protrude)* sobresalir. 2 *fam (be obvious)* saltar a la vista. — 3 *t* sacar. ◆*to ~ to t (keep to)* atenerse a. 2 *(carry out)* cumplir con. ◆*to ~ up i (sobre)*salir; *(hair)* estar de punta. — 3 *t (raise)* levantar. ◆*to ~ up for t fam* defender. ●*fig to ~ one's neck out,* jugarse el tipo; *fam* to get hold of the wrong end of the ~, coger el rábano por las hojas. ▲ *pt & pp* **stuck**.

sticker ['stɪkə'] *n (label)* etiqueta adhesiva. 2 *(with message, picture)* pegatina.

sticky ['stɪkɪ] *adj* pegajoso,-a. 2 *(weather)* bochornoso,-a. 3 *fam (situation)* difícil.

stiff [stɪf] *adj (rigid)* rígido,-a, tieso,-a. 2 *(joint)* entumecido,-a. 3 *(firm)* espeso,-a. 4 *(manner)* frío,-a, estirado,-a. 5 *fig (difficult)* difícil, duro,-a. 6 *fam (drink)* fuerte, cargado,-a. ●*to feel ~,* tener agujetas; *fig* to keep a ~ upper lip, poner a

mal tiempo buena cara; *fam* to be scared ~, estar muerto,-a de miedo.

stiffen ['stɪfən] *t (fabric)* reforzar; *(collar)* almidonar. 2 *(paste)* endurecer. — 3 *i (person)* ponerse rígido,-a; *(joint)* entumecerse. — 4 *t-i fig* fortalecer(se).

stiffness ['stɪfnəs] *n* rigidez *f*.

stifle ['staɪfəl] *t-i* ahogar(se), sofocar(se).

stifling ['staɪfəlɪŋ] *adj* sofocante.

stigma ['stɪgmə] *n* estigma *m*.

still [stɪl] *adj (not moving)* quieto,-a. 2 *(calm)* tranquilo,-a. 3 *(silent)* silencioso,-a. 4 *(drink)* sin gas. — 5 *adv* todavía, aún: *I can ~ hear it,* todavía lo oigo. 6 *(even so)* a pesar de todo. 7 *(however)* sin embargo. — 8 *n fml* silencio. 9 CINEM vista fija. — 10 *t fml* acallar. ●*to keep ~,* estarse quieto,-a; *to stand ~,* no moverse. ■ ART ~ *life,* naturaleza muerta.

stillborn ['stɪlbɔ:n] *adj* nacido,-a muerto,-a.

stillness ['stɪlnəs] *n (calm)* calma, quietud *f*. 2 *(silence)* silencio.

stilt [stɪlt] *n* zanco.

stilted ['stɪltɪd] *adj* afectado,-a.

stimulant ['stɪmjʊlənt] *n* estimulante *m*.

stimulate ['stɪmjʊleɪt] *t* estimular.

stimulus ['stɪmjʊləs] *n* estímulo. ▲ *pl* **stimuli** ['stɪmjʊli:].

sting [stɪŋ] *n (organ)* aguijón *m*. 2 *(wound)* picadura. 3 *(burning)* escozor *m*, picazón *f*. 4 *fig (of remorse)* punzada. — 5 *t-i* picar. — 6 *t fig (remark)* herir en lo más hondo. ▲ *pt & pp* **stung**.

stinginess ['stɪndʒɪnəs] *n* tacañería.

stingy ['stɪndʒɪ] *n* tacaño,-a, roñoso,-a.

stink [stɪŋk] *n* peste *f*, hedor *m*. — 2 *i* apestar/heder *(of,* a). ▲ *pt* **stank** o **stunk**; *pp* **stunk**.

stint [stɪnt] *n* período, temporada. — 2 *t* escatimar.

stipulate ['stɪpjʊleɪt] *t* estipular.

stir [stɜ:'] *n* acción de agitar. 2 *fig* revuelo, conmoción. — 3 *t (mixture)* remover. 4 *fig (curiosity etc.)* despertar, estimular. — 5 *t-i (move)* mover(se). ◆*to ~ up t fig* provocar.

stirrup ['stɪrəp] *n* estribo.

stitch [stɪtʃ] *n (sewing)* puntada. 2 *(knitting)* punto. 3 MED punto de sutura. — 4 *t* coser *(on,* a). 5 MED suturar. ●*fam* to be in stitches, troncharse de risa.

stock [stɒk] *n (supply)* reserva. 2 COM existencias *fpl,* stock *m*. 3 FIN *(capital)* capital *m* social. 4 *(livestock)* ganado. 5 CULIN caldo. 6 *(descent)* linaje *m*. — 7 *adj pej* consabido,-a, muy visto,-a. 8 COM normal, de serie. — 9 *t (have in stock)* tener (en el almacén). **10** *(provide)* surtir *(with,* de). **11** *(fill up)* llenar *(with,* de). ◆*to ~ up* i abastecerse *(on/with,* de). ●*to be out of ~,* estar agotado,-a; *fig to take ~ of,* evaluar. ■ *~ exchange/market,* bolsa (de valores).

stockade [stɒˈkeɪd] *n* empalizada, estacada.

stockbreeder [ˈstɒkbriːdəʳ] *n* ganadero,-a.

stockbroker [ˈstɒkbrəʊkəʳ] *n* corredor,-ra de bolsa.

stocking [ˈstɒkɪŋ] *n* media.

stocky [ˈstɒkɪ] *adj* robusto,-a, fornido,-a.

stoical [ˈstəʊɪkəl] *adj* estoico,-a.

stoke [stəʊk] *t* atizar, avivar. ◆*to ~ up* i *fig* atiborrarse *(on,* de).

stole [stəʊl] *pt →* **steal**. **– 2** *n* estola.

stolen [ˈstəʊlən] *pp →* **steal**.

stolid [ˈstɒlɪd] *adj* impasible.

stomach [ˈstʌmək] *n* estómago. **– 2** *t fig* aguantar, tragar. ●*on an empty ~,* en ayunas. ■ *~ ache,* dolor *m* de estómago.

stomp [stɒmp] *i fam* caminar pisando fuerte.

stone [stəʊn] *n* piedra. **2** *(of fruit)* hueso. **3** *(weight)* = 6,348 kg: *she weighs 9 ~,* pesa 57 kilos. **– 4** *adj* de piedra. **– 5** *t (person)* apedrear. **6** *(fruit)* deshuesar. ●*fig at a stone's throw,* a tiro de piedra. ■ *Stone Age,* Edad *f* de Piedra.

stone-cold [stəʊnˈkəʊld] *adj* helado,-a.

stoned [stəʊnd] *adj sl (on drugs)* flipado,-a, colocado,-a. **2** *(drunk)* trompa.

stonewall [ˈstəʊnwɔːl] *i* andarse con evasivas.

stony [ˈstəʊnɪ] *adj* pedregoso,-a. **2** *fig* frío,-a, glacial.

stood [stʊd] *pt & pp →* **stand**.

stool [stuːl] *n* taburete *m*. **2** MED deposición, heces *fpl*.

stoop [stuːp] *n* encorvamiento. **– 2** *i (bend)* inclinarse, agacharse. **3** *(habitually)* ser cargado,-a de espaldas. ◆*to ~ to* *t fig* rebajarse a.

stop [stɒp] *n (halt)* parada, alto. **2** *(break)* descanso; AV escala. **3** *(overnight)* estancia. **4** *(for bus etc.)* parada. **5** MUS *(on organ)* registro. **– 6** *t-i* parar(se), detener(se). **– 7** *t (prevent)* impedir, evitar. **8** *(production)* paralizar. **9** *(put an end to)* poner fin/término a, acabar con. **10** *(suspend)* suspender. **11** *(habit)* dejar de. **– 12** *i (cease)* terminar. **13** *fam (stay)* quedarse. **– 14** *interj* ¡pare!, ¡alto! ◆*to ~ by* i *fam* pasar *(at,* por). ◆*to ~ off* i hacer una parada *(at/in,* en). ◆*to ~ up*

t tapar, taponar. ●*to come to a ~,* pararse. ■ *~ sign,* stop *m*.

stopover [ˈstɒpəʊvəʳ] *n* parada; AV escala.

stoppage [ˈstɒpɪdʒ] *n (of work)* paro; *(strike)* huelga. **2** *(deduction)* deducción. **3** *(blockage)* obstrucción.

stopper [ˈstɒpəʳ] *n* tapón *m*.

stopwatch [ˈstɒpwɒtʃ] *n* cronómetro.

storage [ˈstɔːrɪdʒ] *n* almacenaje *m*, almacenamiento. ■ *~ heater,* placa acumuladora; *~ unit,* armario.

store [stɔːʳ] *n (supply)* provisión, reserva. **2** *pl* MIL pertrechos *mpl*. **3** *(warehouse)* almacén *m*. **4** US tienda. **– 5** *t (put in storage)* almacenar; *(keep)* guardar. ◆*to ~ up* *t* acumular.

storey [ˈstɔːrɪ] *n* piso.

stork [stɔːk] *n* cigüeña.

storm [stɔːm] *n gen* tormenta; *(at sea)* tempestad *f*; *(with wind)* borrasca. **2** *fig (uproar)* revuelo. **3** *fig (of missiles, insults)* lluvia. **– 4** *t* asaltar. **– 5** *i* echar pestes, vociferar.

stormy [ˈstɔːmɪ] *adj* tormentoso,-a. **2** *fig* acalorado,-a, tempestuoso,-a.

story [ˈstɔːrɪ] *n gen* historia. **2** *(tale)* cuento. **3** *(account)* relato. **4** *(article)* artículo. **5** *(plot)* argumento.

stout [staʊt] *adj (fat)* gordo,-a, robusto,-a. **2** *(strong)* sólido,-a. **3** *(determined)* firme, resuelto,-a. **– 4** *n* cerveza negra.

stove [stəʊv] *n (for heating)* estufa. **2** *(cooker)* cocina; *(ring)* hornillo.

stow [stəʊ] *t* guardar. **2** MAR estibar.

stowaway [ˈstəʊəweɪ] *n* polizón *mf*.

straddle [ˈstrædəl] *t* sentarse a horcajadas sobre.

straggle [ˈstrægəl] *i (spread)* desparramarse. **2** *(lag behind)* rezagarse.

straggly [ˈstrægəlɪ] *adj* desparramado,-a.

straight [streɪt] *adj* recto,-a, derecho,-a. **2** *(hair)* liso,-a. **3** *(successive)* seguido,-a: *eight hours ~,* ocho horas seguidas. **4** *(honest)* honrado,-a, de confianza. **5** *(answer etc.)* sincero,-a. **6** THEAT serio,-a. **7** *(drink)* solo,-a. **8** *sl (conventional)* carca. **– 9** *adv (in a line)* en línea recta. **10** *(directly)* directamente: *he went ~ to the office,* fue directamente al despacho. **11** *(immediately)* en seguida. **12** *(frankly)* francamente. **– 13** *n (line)* línea recta. **14** *(in race)* recta. ●*~ off,* sin pensarlo; *to get things ~,* hablar claro; *to keep a ~ face,* contener la risa.

straightaway [streɪtəˈweɪ] *adv* en seguida.

straighten ['streɪtən] *t gen* enderezar, poner bien, arreglar. **2** *(hair)* estirar. ◆*to ~ out t-i* resolver(se). ◆*to ~ up t (tidy)* ordenar. − **2** *t-i* poner(se) derecho,-a.

straightforward [streɪt'fɔ:wəd] *adj* franco,-a, honrado,-a.

strain [streɪn] *n gen* tensión. **2** *(on metal)* deformación. **3** MED torcedura. **4** *(breed)* raza. **5** *(streak)* vena. − **6** *t (stretch)* estirar, tensar. **7** MED torcer(se); *(voice, eyes)* forzar. **8** *(filter)* colar. − **9** *i* tirar *(at, de)*.

strainer ['streɪnə'] *n* colador *m*.

strait [streɪt] *n* GEOG estrecho. **2** *(difficulty)* aprieto. ●*in dire straits,* en un gran aprieto.

straitjacket ['streɪtdʒækɪt] *n* camisa de fuerza.

strait-laced [streɪt'leɪst] *adj pej* mojigato,-a.

strand [strænd] *n (of thread)* hebra, hilo. **2** *(of rope)* ramal *m*. **3** *(of hair)* pelo. **4** *(of pearls)* sarta. − **5** *t* MAR varar. **6** *fig* abandonar: **he was left stranded,** le dejaron plantado.

strange [streɪndʒ] *adj (bizarre)* extraño,-a, raro,-a. **2** *(unknown)* desconocido,-a. − **3** *strangely adv* extrañamente.

strangeness ['streɪndʒnəs] *n* rareza.

stranger ['streɪndʒə'] *n* extraño,-a, desconocido,-a.

strangle ['stræŋgəl] *t* estrangular.

strangulation [stræŋgjʊ'leɪʃən] *n* estrangulación.

strap [stræp] *n gen* correa. **2** *(on dress)* tirante *m*. − **3** *t* atar/sujetar con correa.

strapping ['stræpɪŋ] *adj* fornido,-a.

strata ['strɑ:tə] *npl* → **stratum**.

strategic(al) [strə'ti:dʒɪk(əl)] *adj* estratégico,-a.

strategy ['strætədʒɪ] *n* estrategia.

stratify ['strætɪfaɪ] *t* estratificar.

stratum ['strɑ:təm] *n* estrato. ▲ *pl* **strata**.

straw [strɔ:] *n* paja. **2** *(for drinking)* paja, pajita. ●*fam that's the last ~!,* ¡es el colmo! ■ *~ hat,* sombrero de paja.

strawberry ['strɔ:bərɪ] *n* fresa; *(large)* fresón *m*.

stray [streɪ] *adj* perdido,-a. − **2** *n* animal extraviado. − **3** *i* extraviarse, perderse.

streak [stri:k] *n (line)* raya, lista. **2** *(in hair)* mecha, mechón *m*. **3** *fig (of madness etc.)* vena; *(of luck)* racha. − **4** *t* rayar *(with, de)*.

streaky ['stri:kɪ] *adj (hair)* con mechas. **2** *(bacon)* entreverado,-a.

stream [stri:m] *n (brook)* arroyo, riachuelo. **2** *(current)* corriente *f*. **3** *(of water)* flujo; *(of blood)* chorro. **4** *fig (of people)* oleada. − **5** *i* manar, correr, chorrear. **6** *fig (people etc.)* desfilar.

streamer ['stri:mə'] *n* serpentina.

streamline ['stri:mlaɪn] *n* línea aerodinámica. − **2** *t* aerodinamizar. **3** *fig* racionalizar.

street [stri:t] *n* calle *f*.

streetlamp ['stri:tlæmp] *n* farol *m*.

strength [streŋθ] *n gen* fuerza. **2** *(of currency)* valor *m*. **3** *(of emotion, colour)* intensidad. **4** *(power)* poder *m*, potencia. ●*in ~,* en gran número; *on the ~ of,* en base a.

strengthen ['streŋθən] *t-i gen* fortalecer(se), reforzar(se). **2** *(colour)* intensificar(se).

strenuous ['strenjʊəs] *adj (energetic)* enérgico,-a. **2** *(exhausting)* fatigoso,-a.

stress [stres] *n* tensión (nerviosa), estrés *m*. **2** TECH tensión. **3** *(emphasis)* hincapié *m*, énfasis *m*. **4** GRAM acento. − **5** *t* recalcar, subrayar. **6** GRAM acentuar. ●*to lay great ~ on sth.,* hacer hincapié/poner énfasis en algo.

stressful ['stresfʊl] *adj* estresante.

stretch [stretʃ] *n gen* extensión. **2** *(elasticity)* elasticidad. **3** *(length)* trecho, tramo. **4** *(of time)* período, intervalo. − **5** *t-i (spread)* extender(se). **6** *(elastic)* estirar(se); *(shoes)* ensanchar(se). ◆*to ~ out t-i* estirar(se); *(lie down)* tumbar(se). **2** *(lengthen)* alargar(se). ●*to ~ one's legs,* estirar las piernas; *fig at a ~,* de un tirón.

stretcher ['stretʃə'] *n* camilla.

stretchy ['stretʃɪ] *adj* elástico,-a.

strew [stru:] *t* esparcir. ▲ *pp* **strewed** *o* **strewn** [stru:n].

stricken ['strɪkən] *adj (with grief)* afligido,-a; *(by disaster)* afectado,-a.

strict [strɪkt] *adj* estricto,-a. − **2** *adv* estrictamente. **3** *(exclusively)* exclusivamente. ●*in the strictest confidence,* en el más absoluto secreto; *strictly speaking,* en sentido estricto.

strictness ['strɪktnəs] *n* severidad. **2** *(precision)* exactitud.

stride [straɪd] *n* zancada, trancada. − **2** *i* andar a zancadas. ●*fig to take sth. in one's ~,* tomarse las cosas con calma. ▲ *pt* **strode**; *pp* **stridden** ['strɪdən].

strident ['straɪdənt] *adj* estridente.

strife [straɪf] *n* conflictos *mpl*, luchas *fpl*.

strike [straɪk] *n (by workers etc.)* huelga. **2** *(blow)* golpe *m*. **3** *(find)* hallazgo. **4** MIL ataque *m*. − **5** *t (hit)* pegar, golpear. **6** *(collide with)* dar/chocar contra; *(light-*

ning, bullet) alcanzar. **7** *(gold, oil)* descubrir. **8** *(coin)* acuñar. **9** *(match)* encender. **10** *(clock)* dar, tocar. **11** *(deal)* cerrar. − **12** *i (attack)* atacar. **13** *(workers etc.)* hacer huelga. **14** *(clock)* dar/tocar la hora. ◆*to ~ back i* devolver el golpe. ◆*to ~ down t* abatir. ◆*to ~ off t* tachar. **2** JUR suspender. ◆*to ~ up t* entablar. •*it strikes me that ...,* se me ocurre que ...; *to be/go on ~,* estar/declararse en huelga; *to be struck dumb,* quedarse mudo,-a; *to ~ out on one's own,* volar con sus propias alas; *fam to ~ it rich,* hacerse rico,-a. ▲ *pt & pp struck.*

striker ['straɪkə'] *n* huelguista *mf.* **2** SP marcador,-ra.

striking ['straɪkɪŋ] *adj* llamativo,-a, impresionante. **2** *(on strike)* en huelga.

string [strɪŋ] *n gen* cuerda; *(lace)* cordón *m.* **2** *(of garlic, lies)* ristra. **3** *(of hotels, events)* cadena. − **4** *t (beads)* ensartar. **5** *(racket etc.)* encordar. •*fig to pull strings for sb.,* enchufar a algn. ◆*to ~ along i* seguir la corriente *(with,* a). ▲ *pt & pp strung.*

stringent ['strɪndʒənt] *adj* severo,-a, estricto,-a.

strip [strɪp] *n (of paper, leather)* tira. **2** *(of land)* franja. **3** *(of metal)* fleje *m.* **4** *(cartoon)* historieta. − **5** *t (tear up)* hacer tiras. **6** *(paint etc.)* quitar; *(room)* vaciar. − **7** *t-i (undress)* desnudar(se). ◆*to ~ down t* desmontar. ◆*to ~ off i* desnudarse. •*to ~ sb. of sth.,* despojar a algn. de algo.

stripe [straɪp] *n* raya, lista. **2** MIL galón *m.* − **3** *t* pintar/dibujar a rayas.

striped [straɪpt] *adj* a rayas.

striptease ['strɪptiːz] *n* strip-tease *m.*

strive [straɪv] *i* esforzarse *(after/for,* por). ▲ *pt strove; pp striven* ['strɪvən].

strode [strəʊd] *pt →* **stride.**

stroke [strəʊk] *n gen* golpe *m.* **2** *(swimming)* brazada; *(billiards)* tacada. **3** *(of bell)* campanada. **4** *(of engine)* tiempo. **5** *(of brush)* pincelada. **6** MED apoplejía. − **7** *t* acariciar. ■ *~ of luck,* golpe *m* de suerte.

stroll [strəʊl] *n* paseo. − **2** *i* pasear, dar un paseo. •*to take a ~,* dar una vuelta.

strong [strɒŋ] *adj gen* fuerte. **2** *(firm)* firme, acérrimo,-a. **3** *(severe)* severo,-a. − **4** *adv* fuerte. − **5 strongly** *adv* fuertemente. •*to be ~ ~,* contar con ... miembros. ■ *~ room,* cámara acorazada.

stronghold ['strɒŋhəʊld] *n* fortaleza. **2** *fig* baluarte *m.*

strong-minded [strɒŋ'maɪndɪd] *adj* resuelto,-a, decidido,-a.

stroppy ['strɒpɪ] *adj* GB *fam* de mala uva.

strove [strəʊv] *pt →* **strive.**

struck [strʌk] *pt & pp →* **strike.**

structural ['strʌktʃərəl] *adj* estructural. ■ *~ fault,* fallo de armazón.

structure ['strʌktʃə'] *n* estructura. **2** *(thing constructed)* construcción. − **3** *t* estructurar.

struggle ['strʌgəl] *n* lucha. **2** *(physical)* pelea, forcej(e)o. − **3** *i* luchar. **4** *(physically)* forcejear.

strung [strʌŋ] *pt & pp →* **string.**

strut [strʌt] *n* ARCH puntal *m*, riostra. − **2** *i* pavonearse.

stub [stʌb] *n (of cigarette)* colilla. **2** *(of pencil, candle)* cabo. **3** *(of cheque)* matriz *f.*

stubble ['stʌbəl] *n (in field)* rastrojo. **2** *(on chin)* barba incipiente.

stubborn ['stʌbən] *adj* terco,-a, testarudo,-a, obstinado,-a.

stubbornness ['stʌbənnəs] *n* testarudez *f.*

stubby ['stʌbɪ] *adj* rechoncho,-a.

stuck [stʌk] *pt & pp →* **stick.**

stuck-up [stʌk'ʌp] *adj fam* creído,-a.

stud [stʌd] *n (on clothing)* tachón *m*; *(on shirt)* botonadura. **2** *(on furniture)* tachuela. **3** *(animal)* semental *m.* − **4** *t* tachonar *(with,* de).

student ['stjuːdənt] *n* estudiante *mf.* ■ *~ teacher,* profesor,-ra en prácticas.

studied ['stʌdɪd] *adj* estudiado,-a, pensado,-a. **2** *pej* afectado,-a.

studio ['stjuːdɪəʊ] *n* estudio; *(artist's)* taller *m.* ■ *~ flat,* estudio.

studious ['stjuːdɪəs] *adj* estudioso,-a, aplicado,-a.

study ['stʌdɪ] *n* estudio. − **2** *t-i gen* estudiar. − **3** *t (examine)* investigar.

stuff [stʌf] *n* materia, material *m.* **2** *fam (things)* cosas *fpl*, trastos *mpl.* **3** *(fabric)* tela, género. − **4** *t (fill)* rellenar *(with,* de). **5** *(animal)* disecar. **6** *(cram)* atiborrar *(with,* de). •*fam to do one's ~,* hacer uno lo suyo; *fam to ~ o.s.,* hartarse de comida. ■ *stuffed toy,* muñeco de peluche; *fam stuffed shirt,* persona estirada.

stuffing ['stʌfɪŋ] *n* relleno.

stuffy ['stʌfɪ] *adj* cargado,-a, mal ventilado,-a. **2** *(person)* estirado,-a.

stumble ['stʌmbəl] *n* tropezón *m*, traspié *m.* − **2** *i* tropezar *(across/on,* con), dar un traspié. ■ *stumbling block,* escollo, tropiezo.

stump [stʌmp] *n (of tree)* tocón *m.* **2** *(of pencil, candle)* cabo. **3** *(of arm, leg)* muñón *m,* chueca. **4** *(cricket)* estaca. — **5** *t fam* desconcertar. — **6** *i* pisar fuerte.

stun [stʌn] *t* aturdir, atontar. **2** *fig* sorprender.

stung [stʌŋ] *pt & pp* → **sting.**

stunk [stʌŋk] *pt & pp* → **stink.**

stunning [ˈstʌnɪŋ] *adj* aturdidor,-ra. **2** *fig* estupendo,-a, impresionante.

stunt [stʌnt] *n* CINEM escena peligrosa. **2** *(trick)* truco. — **3** *t* atrofiar. ■ ~ *man/ woman,* doble *mf,* especialista *mf.*

stunted [ˈstʌntɪd] *adj* enano,-a, raquítico,-a.

stupefy [ˈstjuːpɪfaɪ] *t* atontar, aletargar. **2** *fig* dejar pasmado,-a.

stupid [ˈstjuːpɪd] *adj-n* tonto,-a, imbécil *(mf).*

stupidity [stjuːˈpɪdɪtɪ] *n* estupidez *f.*

stupor [ˈstjuːpəʳ] *n* estupor *m.*

sturdy [ˈstɜːdɪ] *adj* robusto,-a, fuerte.

stutter [ˈstʌtəʳ] *n* tartamudeo. — **2** *i* tartamudear.

stutterer [ˈstʌtərəʳ] *n* tartamudo,-a.

sty [staɪ] *n* pocilga.

style [staɪl] *n gen* estilo. **2** *(of hair)* peinado. **3** *(fashion)* moda.

stylish [ˈstaɪlɪʃ] *adj* elegante. **2** *(fashionable)* a la moda.

suave [swɑːv] *adj* afable.

subconscious [sʌbˈkɒnʃəs] *adj-n* subconsciente *(m).*

subdivide [sʌbdɪˈvaɪd] *t* subdividir.

subdue [səbˈdjuː] *t (conquer)* someter, dominar. **2** *(feelings etc.)* contener. **3** *(colour)* atenuar, suavizar.

subheading [sʌbˈhedɪŋ] *n* subtítulo.

subject [ˈsʌbdʒekt] *n (topic)* tema *m.* **2** *(at school)* asignatura. **3** *(citizen)* súbdito. — **4** *adj gen* sujeto,-a *(to,* a). **5** *(fine)* expuesto,-a *(to,* a). **6** *(delay)* susceptible *(to,* de). — **7** *t* someter. ●~ *to approval,* previa aprobación. ▲ *En 7 (verbo)* [səbˈdʒekt].

subjective [səbˈdʒektɪv] *adj* subjetivo,-a.

subjugate [ˈsʌbdʒʊɡeɪt] *t* sojuzgar.

subjunctive [səbˈdʒʌŋktɪv] *adj-n* subjuntivo,-a *(m).*

sublet [sʌbˈlet] *t-i* realquilar, subarrendar. ▲ *pt & pp* **sublet.**

sublime [səˈblaɪm] *adj* sublime.

submarine [sʌbməˈriːn] *n* submarino.

submerge [səbˈmɜːdʒ] *t-i* sumergir(se). — **2** *t (flood)* inundar.

submission [səbˈmɪʃən] *n* sumisión. **2** *(of documents)* presentación.

submissive [səbˈmɪsɪv] *adj* sumiso,-a.

submit [səbˈmɪt] *t-i* someter(se). — **2** *t (application etc.)* presentar.

subnormal [sʌbˈnɔːməl] *adj* subnormal.

subordinate [səˈbɔːdɪnət] *adj-n* subordinado,-a. — **2** *t* subordinar *(to,* a). ▲ *En 2 (verbo)* [səˈbɔːdɪneɪt].

subordination [səbɔːdɪˈneɪʃən] *n* subordinación.

subscribe [səbˈskraɪb] *i* su(b)scribirse *(to,* a). **2** *(opinion)* estar de acuerdo *(to,* con).

subscriber [səbˈscraɪbəʳ] *n* su(b)scriptor,-ra, abonado,-a.

subscription [səbˈskɪpʃən] *n* su(b)scripción, abono.

subsequent [ˈsʌbsɪkwənt] *adj* subsiguiente, posterior *(to,* a). — **2** *subsequently adv* posteriormente.

subservient [səbˈsɜːvɪənt] *adj* servil.

subside [səbˈsaɪd] *i (sink)* hundirse. **2** *(weather, anger)* amainar.

subsidiary [səbˈsɪdɪərɪ] *adj* secundario,-a. — **2** *n* filial *f,* sucursal *f.*

subsidize [ˈsʌbsɪdaɪz] *t* subvencionar.

subsidy [ˈsʌbsɪdɪ] *n* subvención, subsidio.

subsist [səbˈsɪst] *i* subsistir. ●*to ~ on ...,* sustentarse a base de ... .

subsistence [səbˈsɪstəns] *n* subsistencia. **2** *(sustenance)* sustento. ■ ~ *wage,* sueldo miserable.

substance [ˈsʌbstəns] *n* su(b)stancia. **2** *fig* esencia. **3** *(wealth)* riqueza.

substandard [sʌbˈstændəd] *adj* inferior (a la media).

substantial [səbˈstænʃəl] *adj (solid)* sólido,-a. **2** *(considerable)* importante, substancial. **3** *(meal)* abundante.

substantiate [səbˈstænʃɪeɪt] *t* justificar.

substantive [ˈsʌbstəntɪv] *n* su(b)stantivo.

substitute [ˈsʌbstɪtjuːt] *n (person)* su(b)stituto,-a, suplente *mf.* **2** *(food)* sucedáneo. — **3** *t* su(b)stituir.

substitution [sʌbstɪˈtjuːʃən] *n gen* su(b)stitución. **2** *(in job)* suplencia.

subterfuge [ˈsʌbtəfjuːdʒ] *n* subterfugio.

subterranean [sʌbtəˈreɪnɪən] *adj* subterráneo,-a.

subtitle [ˈsʌbtaɪtəl] *n* subtítulo. — **2** *t* subtitular.

subtle [ˈsʌtəl] *adj gen* sutil. **2** *(taste etc.)* delicado,-a. **3** *(remark)* agudo,-a. — **4** *subtly adv* sutilmente.

subtlety [ˈsʌtəltɪ] *n gen* sutileza. **2** *(of taste)* delicadeza. **3** *(of remark)* agudeza.

subtract [səbˈtrækt] *t* restar *(from,* de).

subtraction [səb'trækʃən] *n* resta.
suburb ['sʌbɜːb] *n* barrio periférico/residencial. ■ *the suburbs,* las afueras.
subversion [sʌb'vɜːʃən] *n* subversión.
subversive [sʌb'vɜːsɪv] *adj-n* subversivo,-a.
subway ['sʌbweɪ] *n* GB paso subterráneo.
2 US metro.
succeed [sək'siːd] *i gen* tener éxito, triunfar; *(plan)* salir bien. − 2 *t* suceder a. ●*to ~ in doing sth.,* conseguir hacer algo.
success [sək'ses] *n* éxito.
successful [sək'sesfʊl] *adj* que tiene éxito, de éxito, afortunado,-a; *(plan)* acertado,-a. 2 *(business)* próspero,-a; *(marriage)* feliz. − 3 *successfully adv* con éxito.
succession [sək'seʃən] *n* sucesión.
successive [sək'sesɪv] *adj* sucesivo,-a.
successor [sək'səsəʳ] *n* sucesor,-ra.
succinct [sək'sɪŋkt] *adj* sucinto,-a.
succulent ['sʌkjʊlənt] *adj* suculento,-a.
succumb [sə'kʌm] *i* sucumbir (*to,* a).
such [sʌtʃ] *adj (of that sort)* tal, semejante: *there's no ~ thing,* no existe tal cosa. 2 *(so much, so great)* tanto,-a: *he's always in ~ a hurry,* siempre anda con tanta prisa; *there were ~ a lot of books,* había tantos libros. − 3 *adv* tan: *she's ~ a clever woman,* es una mujer tan inteligente. ●*at ~ and ~ a time,* a tal hora; *in ~ a way that ...,* de tal manera que ... .
suchlike ['sʌtʃlaɪk] *adj* tal, semejante. − 2 *n* cosas *fpl* por el estilo.
suck [sʌk] *n* chupada. − 2 *t-i gen* chupar; *(baby)* mamar. − 3 *t (vacuum cleaner)* aspirar. 4 *(whirlpool)* tragar. ●*fam to ~ up to sb.,* dar coba a algn.
sucker ['sʌkəʳ] *n* ZOOL ventosa. 2 BOT chupón *m.* 3 *fam (mug)* primo,-a.
suckle ['sʌkəl] *t* amamantar. − 2 *i* mamar.
suction ['sʌkʃən] *n* succión. ■ *~ pump,* bomba de aspiración.
sudden ['sʌdən] *adj (quick)* repentino,-a. 2 *(unexpected)* inesperado,-a, imprevisto,-a. − 3 *suddenly adv* de repente/pronto. ●*all of a ~,* de repente/pronto.
suds [sʌdz] *npl* jabonaduras *fpl,* espuma *f sing* (de jabón).
sue [suː] *t-i* demandar.
suede [sweɪd] *n* ante *m,* gamuza. − 2 *adj* de ante/gamuza.
suffer ['sʌfəʳ] *t-i* sufrir (*from,* de). − 2 *t (bear)* aguantar, soportar.
suffering ['sʌfərɪŋ] *n* sufrimiento. 2 *(pain)* dolor *m.*

suffice [sə'faɪs] *t-i fml* bastar, ser suficiente.
sufficient [sə'fɪʃənt] *adj* suficiente, bastante. − 2 *sufficiently adv* suficientemente.
suffix ['sʌfɪks] *n* sufijo.
suffocate ['sʌfəkeɪt] *t-i* asfixiar(se), ahogar(se).
suffrage ['sʌfrɪdʒ] *n* sufragio.
sugar ['ʃʊgəʳ] *n* azúcar *m & f.* − 2 *t* azucarar. ■ *~ bowl,* azucarero; *~ cane,* caña de azúcar.
sugarbeet ['ʃʊgəbiːt] *n* remolacha (azucarera).
sugary ['ʃʊgərɪ] *adj* azucarado,-a. 2 *fig* almibarado,-a.
suggest [sə'dʒest] *t* sugerir. 2 *(advise)* aconsejar. 3 *(imply)* implicar.
suggestion [sə'dʒestʃən] *n (proposal)* sugerencia. 2 *(insinuation)* insinuación. 3 *(hint)* sombra, traza.
suggestive [sə'dʒestɪv] *adj* sugestivo,-a. 2 *(indecent)* provocativo,-a.
suicidal [sjuː'saɪdəl] *adj* suicida.
suicide ['sjuːɪsaɪd] *n* suicidio. ●*to commit ~,* suicidarse.
suit [sjuːt] *n (man's)* traje *m; (woman's)* traje de chaqueta. 2 JUR pleito. 3 *(cards)* palo. − 4 *t (be convenient for)* convenir a, venir bien a. 5 *(be appropriate)* ir/sentar bien (a), favorecer: *red suits you,* el rojo te favorece mucho. 6 *(please)* satisfacer. ●*~ yourself!,* ¡como quieras!; *fig to follow ~,* seguir el ejemplo.
suitable ['sjuːtəbəl] *adj* conveniente. 2 *(appropriate)* adecuado,-a, apto,-a: *~ for children,* apto,-a para niños.
suitcase ['suːtkeɪs] *n* maleta.
suite [swiːt] *n (of furniture)* juego. 2 *(musical, in hotel)* suite *f.*
suitor ['sjuːtəʳ] *n (wooer)* pretendiente *mf.* 2 JUR demandante *mf.*
sulk [sʌlk] *i* enfurruñarse, estar de mal humor.
sulky ['sʌlkɪ] *adj* malhumorado,-a.
sullen ['sʌlən] *adj* hosco,-a, huraño,-a.
sulphur ['sʌlfəʳ] *n* azufre *m.*
sultana [sʌl'tɑːnə] *n (raisin)* pasa de Esmirna.
sultry ['sʌltrɪ] *adj (muggy)* bochornoso,-a, sofocante. 2 *(seductive)* sensual.
sum [sʌm] *n gen* suma. 2 *(of invoice, money)* importe *m.* ◆*to ~ up* resumir. ●*in ~,* en suma/resumen. ■ *~ total,* (suma) total *m.*
summarize ['sʌməraɪz] *t* resumir.
summary ['sʌmərɪ] *n* resumen *m.*

summer ['sʌmə^r] n verano. – 2 adj gen de verano. 3 (weather) veraniego,-a. 4 (resort) de veraneo.

summertime ['sʌmətaɪm] n verano.

summit ['sʌmɪt] n cumbre f.

summon ['sʌmən] t to ~ up one's strength, armarse de valor.

summons ['sʌmənz] n llamamiento. 2 JUR citación. – 3 t JUR citar.

sumptuous ['sʌmptjʊəs] adj suntuoso,-a.

sun [sʌn] n sol m. •in the ~, al sol; to ~ o.s., tomar el sol.

sunbathe ['sʌnbeɪð] i tomar el sol.

sunburnt ['sʌnbɜːnt] adj quemado,-a por el sol.

Sunday ['sʌndeɪ] n domingo. ■ ~ school, catequesis f inv.

sundial ['sʌndaɪəl] n reloj m de sol.

sunflower ['sʌnflaʊə^r] n girasol m.

sung [sʌŋ] pp → sing.

sunglasses ['sʌnglɑːsɪz] npl gafas fpl de sol.

sunk [sʌŋk] pp → sink.

sunlight ['sʌnlaɪt] n (luz f del) sol m.

sunny ['sʌnɪ] adj soleado,-a. 2 fig alegre. •to be ~, hacer sol.

sunrise ['sʌnraɪz] n salida del sol, amanecer m.

sunset ['sʌnset] n puesta del sol, ocaso.

sunshade ['sʌnʃeɪd] n (parasol) sombrilla. 2 (awning) toldo.

sunshine ['sʌnʃaɪn] n (luz f de) sol m.

sunstroke ['sʌnstrəʊk] n insolación.

suntan ['sʌntæn] n bronceado.

super ['suːpə^r] adj fam fenomenal, de primera.

superb [suːˈpɜːb] adj estupendo,-a, magnífico,-a.

supercilious [suːpəˈsɪlɪəs] adj altanero,-a, desdeñoso,-a.

superficial [suːpəˈfɪʃəl] adj superficial.

superfluous [suːˈpɜːfluəs] adj superfluo,-a.

superhuman [suːpəˈhjuːmən] adj sobrehumano,-a.

superintendent [suːpərɪnˈtendənt] n inspector,-ra, supervisor,-ra.

superior [suːˈpɪərɪə^r] adj gen superior. 2 (haughty) altanero,-a. – 3 n superior,-ra.

superiority [suːpɪərɪˈɒrɪtɪ] n superioridad.

superlative [suːˈpɜːlətɪv] adj-n superlativo,-a (m).

supermarket [suːpəˈmɑːkɪt] n supermercado.

supernatural [suːpəˈnætʃərəl] adj sobrenatural.

superpower ['suːpəpaʊə^r] n superpotencia.

supersede [suːpəˈsiːd] t fml reemplazar, substituir.

supersonic [suːpəˈsɒnɪk] adj supersónico,-a.

superstition [suːpəˈstɪʃən] n superstición.

superstitious [sjuːpəˈstɪʃəs] adj supersticioso,-a.

supervise ['suːpəvaɪz] t (watch over) vigilar. 2 (run) supervisar.

supervision [suːpəˈvɪʒən] n inspección, vigilancia.

supervisor ['suːpəvaɪzə^r] n supervisor,-ra.

supper ['sʌpə^r] n cena. •to have ~, cenar.

supplant [səˈplɑːnt] t suplantar.

supple ['sʌpəl] adj flexible.

supplement ['sʌplɪmənt] n suplemento. – 2 t complementar. ▲ En 2 (verbo) ['sʌplɪment].

supplementary [sʌplɪˈmentərɪ] adj suplementario,-a.

supplier [səˈplaɪə^r] n suministrador,-ra. 2 COM proveedor,-ra.

supply [səˈplaɪ] n (provision) suministro; COM provisión. 2 (stock) surtido, existencias fpl. 3 pl (food) víveres mpl; MIL pertrechos mpl. – 4 t suministrar; COM surtir. 5 MIL aprovisionar. 6 (information) facilitar. •~ and demand, la oferta y la demanda.

support [səˈpɔːt] n gen apoyo. 2 (financial) ayuda económica. – 3 t (weight etc.) sostener. 4 fig apoyar, respaldar. 5 SP seguir. 6 (keep) mantener. •to ~ o.s., ganarse la vida.

supporter [səˈpɔːtə^r] n POL partidario,-a. 2 SP seguidor,-ra; (fan) hincha mf, forofo,-a.

supportive [səˈpɔːtɪv] adj comprensivo,-a.

suppose [səˈpəʊz] t suponer. 2 (suggestion) ~ we leave now?, ¿y si nos fuéramos ya? •I ~ so/not, supongo que sí/no; to be supposed to ..., (supposition) se dice/supone que ...; (obligation) deber ...; you're supposed to be in bed, deberías estar en la cama.

supposed [səˈpəʊzd] adj supuesto,-a. – 2 supposedly adv aparentemente.

suppository [səˈpɒzɪtərɪ] n supositorio.

suppress [səˈpres] t suprimir. 2 (feelings, revolt, etc.) reprimir.

suppression [sə'preʃən] *n* supresión. 2 *(of feelings, revolt, etc.)* represión.

supremacy [su:'preməsɪ] *n* supremacía.

supreme [su:'pri:m] *adj* supremo,-a. – 2 *supremely adv* sumamente, sin duda. 6 ■ JUR ~ *court*, tribunal supremo.

surcharge ['sɜ:tʃɑ:dʒ] *n* recargo.

sure [ʃʊər] *adj* seguro,-a. – 2 *adv* claro. 3 *(certainly)* seguro. 4 US *(really) he ~ is handsome,* ¡qué guapo es! – 5 *surely adv (no doubt)* seguramente, sin duda. 6 *(in a sure manner)* con seguridad. ●~ *enough,* efectivamente; *to be ~ to ...,* no olvidarse de ...; *to make ~,* asegurarse *(of,* de).

surf [sɜ:f] *n (waves)* oleaje *m.* 2 *(foam)* espuma. – 3 *i* hacer surf.

surface ['sɜ:fəs] *n gen* superficie. 2 *(of road)* firme *m.* – 3 *t* revestir. – 4 *i* salir a la superficie; *fig* asomarse.

surge [sɜ:dʒ] *n (of sea)* oleaje *m.* 2 *(growth)* alza, aumento. 3 *fig* oleada. – 4 *i* agitarse, encresparse.

surgeon ['sɜ:dʒən] *n* cirujano,-a.

surgery ['sɜ:dʒərɪ] *n* cirugía. 2 GB *(consulting room)* consultorio.

surgical ['sɜ:dʒɪkəl] *adj* quirúrgico,-a.

surly ['sɜ:lɪ] *adj* hosco,-a, arisco,-a.

surmise [sɜ:'maɪz] *n* conjetura. – 2 *t* conjeturar, suponer.

surname ['sɜ:neɪm] *n* apellido.

surpass [sɜ:'pɑ:s] *t* superar, sobrepasar.

surplus ['sɜ:pləs] *adj-n* sobrante *(m),* excedente *(m).* – 2 *n (of budget)* superávit *m.*

surprise [sə'praɪz] *n* sorpresa. – 2 *adj* inesperado,-a; *(attack)* sorpresa. – 3 *t* sorprender. ●*to take sb. by ~,* coger desprevenido,-a a algn.

surprising [sə'praɪzɪŋ] *adj* sorprendente.

surreal [sə'rɪəl] *adj* surrealista.

surrealism [sə'rɪəlɪzəm] *n* surrealismo.

surrender [sə'rendər] *n* MIL rendición; *(of weapons)* entrega. – 2 *t-i* rendir(se), entregar(se).

surround [sə'raʊnd] *t* rodear *(with,* de).

surrounding [sə'raʊndɪŋ] *adj* circundante. – 2 *npl* alrededores *mpl.* 3 *(environment)* entorno *m sing.*

surveillance [sɜ:'veɪləns] *n* vigilancia.

survey ['sɜ:veɪ] *n (of opinion)* sondeo; *(of trends etc.)* encuesta, estudio. 2 *(of building, land)* reconocimiento; *(in topography)* medición. 3 *(view)* panorama. – 4 *t (look at)* contemplar. 5 *(study)* estudiar. 6 *(building, land)* inspeccionar. ▲ *De 4 a 6 (verbo)* [sə'veɪ].

surveyor [sə'veɪər] *n* agrimensor,-ra, topógrafo,-a. ■ *quantity ~,* aparejador,-ra.

survival [sə'vaɪvəl] *n* supervivencia. 2 *(relic)* vestigio.

survive [sə'vaɪv] *t-i* sobrevivir (a).

survivor [sə'vaɪvər] *n* superviviente *mf.*

susceptible [sə'septɪbəl] *adj (to attack etc.)* susceptible. 2 *(to illness)* propenso,-a. 3 *(to flattery etc.)* sensible.

suspect ['sʌspekt] *adj-n* sospechoso,-a. – 2 *t gen* sospechar. 3 *(imagine)* imaginar. ▲ *En 2 y 3 (verbo)* [sə'spekt].

suspend [sə'spend] *t* suspender. 2 *(pupil)* expulsar. 3 SP *(player)* sancionar. ■ JUR *suspended sentence,* condena condicional.

suspender [sə'spendər] *n* liga. 2 *pl* tirantes *mpl.*

suspense [səs'spens] *n (anticipation)* incertidumbre *f.* 2 *(intrigue)* suspense *m.*

suspension [sə'spenʃən] *n gen* suspensión. 2 *(of pupil)* expulsión. 3 SP *(of player)* sanción. ■ *~ bridge,* puente *m* colgante.

suspicion [sə'spɪʃən] *n* sospecha. 2 *(mistrust)* recelo, desconfianza.

suspicious [sə'spɪʃəs] *adj* sospechoso,-a. 2 *(wary)* desconfiado,-a. – 3 *suspiciously adv* de modo sospechoso. 4 *(warily)* con recelo.

sustain [sə'steɪn] *t gen* sostener. 2 *(nourish)* sustentar. 3 *(suffer)* sufrir.

sustenance ['sʌstɪnəns] *n* sustento.

swagger ['swægər] *i* contonearse.

swallow ['swɒləʊ] *n (of drink, food)* trago. 2 *(bird)* golondrina. – 3 *t-i* tragar. – 4 *t fig (believe)* tragarse.

swam [swæm] *pt* → **swim**.

swamp [swɒmp] *n* pantano, ciénaga. – 2 *t (flood)* inundar *(by/with,* de). 3 *(sink)* hundir. 4 *fig* abrumar *(with,* de).

swan [swɒn] *n* cisne *m.*

swank [swæŋk] *fam n* farol *m.* – 2 *i* fanfarronear, fardar.

swap [swɒp] *t-i fam* (inter)cambiar. ◆*to ~ round t* cambiar de sitio.

swarm [swɔ:m] *n* enjambre *m.* – 2 *i* enjambrar. 3 *fig* rebosar *(with,* de).

swarthy ['swɔ:ðɪ] *adj* moreno,-a, atezado,-a.

swat [swɒt] *t* aplastar.

sway [sweɪ] *n (movement)* balanceo, vaivén *m.* 2 *fig (influence)* dominio. – 3 *t-i* balancear(se). 4 *(totter)* tambalear(se). – 5 *t fig* convencer.

swear [sweər] *t-i (vow)* jurar. – 2 *i (curse)* decir palabrotas; *(blaspheme)* jurar, blasfemar. ◆*to* ~ *by* t *fam* tener entera confianza en. ●*to be sworn in,* jurar el cargo. ▲ *pt swore; pp sworn.*

swear-word [ˈsweəwɜ:d] n palabrota, taco.

sweat [swet] n sudor m. 2 *fam (hard work)* trabajo duro. − 3 t-i sudar. ●*fam to* ~ *it out,* aguantar.

sweater [ˈswetəʳ] n suéter m, jersey m.

sweatshirt [ˈswetʃɜ:t] n sudadera.

sweep [swi:p] n barrido. 2 *(of arm)* movimiento/gesto amplio. 3 *(range)* abanico. 4 *(curve)* curva. 5 *(police)* redada. 6 *fam (person)* deshollinador,-ra. − 7 t-i *(with broom)* barrer. − 8 t *(wind, waves)* barrer. 9 *(spread)* recorrer, extenderse por. 10 *(carry away)* arrastrar. ◆*to* ~ *aside* t *fig* rechazar. ●*to* ~ *in/out/past,* entrar/salir/pasar rápidamente; *to* ~ *sb. off his/her feet,* hacerle a algn. perder la cabeza; *fig* **to make a clean** ~ **of things,** hacer tabla rasa. ▲ *pt & pp swept.*

sweeper [ˈswi:pəʳ] n *(person)* barrendero,-a. 2 *(machine)* barredora.

sweeping [ˈswi:pɪŋ] adj *(broad)* amplio,-a. 2 *(victory etc.)* arrollador,-ra.

sweet [swi:t] adj dulce. 2 *(pleasant)* agradable; *(smell)* fragante. 3 *(charming)* encantador,-ra. − 4 n *(candy)* caramelo, golosina. 5 *(dessert)* postre m. ●*to have a* ~ *tooth,* ser goloso,-a. ■ ~ *pea,* guisante m de olor; ~ *potato,* boniato, batata.

sweeten [ˈswi:tən] t endulzar, azucarar. 2 *fig* ablandar.

sweetener [ˈswi:tənəʳ] n edulcorante m.

sweetheart [ˈswi:thɑ:t] n *(dear)* cariño. 2 *(loved one)* novio,-a.

swell [swel] n marejada, oleaje m. − 2 adj us *fam* fenomenal. − 3 i *(sea)* levantarse; *(river, sales)* crecer. 4 *(body)* hincharse. ▲ *pp swollen.*

swelling [ˈswelɪŋ] n hinchazón f.

swelter [ˈsweltəʳ] i achicharrarse.

swept [swept] pt & pp → **sweep.**

swerve [swɜ:v] n viraje m (brusco). − 2 t-i desviar(se) bruscamente.

swift [swɪft] adj *fml* rápido,-a, veloz. − 2 n vencejo común.

swiftness [ˈswɪftnəs] n velocidad, rapidez f.

swim [swɪm] n baño. − 2 i nadar. − 3 t pasar/cruzar a nado. ●*to go for a* ~, ir a nadar/bañarse. ▲ *pt swam; pp swum.*

swimming [ˈswɪmɪŋ] n natación. ■ ~ *baths,* piscina f *sing* (interior); ~ *costume/trunks,* bañador m *sing;* ~ *pool,* piscina.

swindle [ˈswɪndəl] n estafa, timo. − 2 t estafar, timar.

swindler [ˈswɪndləʳ] n estafador,-ra, timador,-ra.

swine [swaɪn] n inv cerdo. 2 *fam (person)* cerdo,-a, canalla mf.

swing [swɪŋ] n *(movement)* balanceo, oscilación. 2 *(plaything)* columpio. 3 *fig (change)* giro. 4 sp mus swing m. − 5 t-i *(to and fro)* balancear(se). 6 *(arms etc.)* menear(se). 7 *(on plaything)* columpiar(se). 8 *fig* girar, virar. − 9 t *(turn)* hacer girar. ●*in full* ~, en plena marcha; *to* ~ *open/shut,* *(door)* abrirse/cerrarse de golpe. ▲ *pt & pp swung.*

swipe [swaɪp] n golpe m. − 2 t golpear, pegar. 3 *fam (pinch)* birlar, mangar.

swirl [swɜ:l] n gen remolino. 2 *(of smoke)* voluta. 3 *(of skirt)* vuelo. − 4 i arremolinarse. 5 *(person)* dar vueltas.

switch [swɪtʃ] n ELEC interruptor m, llave f. 2 *(change)* cambio repentino. 3 *(exchange)* canje m. 4 *(stick)* vara. − 5 t gen cambiar de. 6 *(train, attention, support)* desviar. ◆*to* ~ *off* t *(radio, TV, etc.)* apagar; *(current)* cortar. ◆*to* ~ *on* t *(light)* encender; *(radio, TV)* poner. ◆*to* ~ *over* i cambiar.

switchboard [ˈswɪtʃbɔ:d] n centralita.

swivel [ˈswɪvəl] t-i girar(se).

swollen [ˈswəʊlən] pp → **swell.**

swoop [swu:p] i *(bird)* abalanzarse. 2 *(plane)* bajar en picado. 3 *(police)* hacer una redada.

sword [sɔ:d] n espada.

swordfish [ˈsɔ:dfɪʃ] n pez m espada.

swore [swɔ:ʳ] pt → **swear.**

sworn [swɔ:n] pp → **swear.**

swot [swɒt] *fam* n empollón,-ona. − 2 i empollar.

swum [swʌm] pp → **swim.**

swung [swʌŋ] pt & pp → **swing.**

sycamore [ˈsɪkəmɔ:ʳ] n sicomoro.

syllable [ˈsɪləbəl] n sílaba.

syllabus [ˈsɪləbəs] n programa m de estudios.

symbol [ˈsɪmbəl] n símbolo.

symbolic(al) [sɪmˈbɒlɪk(əl)] adj simbólico,-a.

simbolize [ˈsɪmbəlaɪz] t simbolizar.

symmetric(al) [sɪˈmetrɪk(əl)] adj simétrico,-a.

symmetry [ˈsɪmɪtrɪ] n simetría.

sympathetic [sɪmpəˈθetɪk] adj *(showing pity)* compasivo,-a. 2 *(understanding)* comprensivo,-a (*to,* con).

sympathize [ˈsɪmpəθaɪz] *i (show pity)* compadecerse (*with,* de). 2 *(understand)* comprender (*with,* -).

sympathizer [ˈsɪmpəθaɪzəʳ] *n* simpatizante *mf.*

sympathy [ˈsɪmpəθɪ] *n (pity)* compasión, lástima. 2 *(condolences)* condolencia, pésame *m.* 3 *(understanding)* comprensión.
●*to express one's* ~, dar el pésame.

symphony [ˈsɪmfənɪ] *n* sinfonía.

symptom [ˈsɪmptəm] *n* síntoma *m.*

synagogue [ˈsɪnəgɒg] *n* sinagoga.

synchronize [ˈsɪŋkrənaɪz] *t* sincronizar.

syndicate [ˈsɪndɪkət] *n* corporación, empresa. 2 *(agency)* agencia (de prensa).

syndrome [ˈsɪndrəʊm] *n* síndrome *m.*

synonym [ˈsɪnənɪm] *n* sinónimo.

synonymous [sɪˈnɒnɪməs] *adj* sinónimo,-a (*with,* de).

syntax [ˈsɪntæks] *n* sintaxis *f inv.*

synthesis [ˈsɪnθəsɪs] *n* síntesis *f inv.*

synthesize [ˈsɪnθəsaɪz] *t* sintetizar.

synthetic [sɪnˈθetɪk] *adj-n* sintético,-a *(m).*

syringe [sɪˈrɪndʒ] *n* jeringa, jeringuilla.

syrup [ˈsɪrəp] *n* MED jarabe *m.* 2 CULIN almíbar *m.*

system [ˈsɪstəm] *n* sistema *m.*

systematic [sɪstəˈmætɪk] *adj* sistemático,-a.

systematize [ˈsɪstɪmətaɪz] *t* sistematizar.

T

ta [tɑ:] *interj* GB *fam* ¡gracias!
tab [tæb] *n* lengüeta. **2** *(label)* etiqueta.
table ['teɪbəl] *n* mesa. **2** *(grid)* tabla, cuadro. – **3** *t* presentar. ■ ~ **tennis,** tenis *m* de mesa.
tablecloth ['teɪbəlklɒθ] *n* mantel *m*.
tablespoon ['teɪbəlspu:n] *n* cucharón *m*.
tablet ['tæblət] *n* MED pastilla. **2** *(stone)* lápida.
tabloid ['tæblɔɪd] *n* periódico de formato pequeño.
taboo [tə'bu:] *adj-n* tabú *(m)*.
tabulate ['tæbjʊleɪt] *t* tabular.
tacit ['tæsɪt] *adj* tácito,-a.
taciturn ['tæsɪtɜ:n] *adj* taciturno,-a.
tack [tæk] *n (nail)* tachuela. – **2** *t* clavar con tachuelas. **3** SEW hilvanar. ●*to change* ~, cambiar de rumbo.
tackle ['tækəl] *n* equipo, aparejos *mpl*. **2** *(pulleys etc.)* polea. **3** SP *(football)* entrada; *(rugby)* placaje *m*. – **4** *t (deal with)* abordar. **5** SP *(football)* atajar; *(rugby)* placar.
tacky ['tækɪ] *adj* pegajoso,-a. **2** *(bad)* de pacotilla.
tact [tækt] *n* tacto.
tactful ['tæktfʊl] *adj* diplomático,-a.
tactics ['tæktɪks] *npl* táctica *f sing*.
tactless ['tæktləs] *adj* falto,-a de tacto.
tadpole ['tædpəʊl] *n* renacuajo.
tag [tæg] *n* etiqueta. **2** *(phrase)* coletilla. **3** *(game)* marro. – **4** *t* etiquetar. ●*to* ~ *on t* añadir.
tail [teɪl] *n* cola. **2** *pl (of coin)* cruz *f sing*. – **3** *t* seguir.
tailback ['teɪlbæk] *n (holdup)* caravana.
tailor ['teɪlə'] *n* sastre,-a. – **2** *fig* adaptar.
tailor-made [teɪlə'meɪd] *adj* hecho,-a a la medida.
taint [teɪnt] *t* corromper.
take [teɪk] *t* tomar, coger, AM agarrar. **2** *(meals, drink, etc.)* tomar. **3** *(accept)* acep-

tar. **4** *(transport, carry)* llevar. **5** *(need)* requerir, necesitar. **6** *(write down)* apuntar. **7** *(occupy)* ocupar. **8** *(stand)* aguantar. **9** *(suppose)* suponer. – **10** *n* CINEM toma. ◆*to* ~ *after t* parecerse a. ◆*to* ~ *away t* llevarse. **2** *(remove)* quitar. **3** MATH restar. ◆*to* ~ *back t* recibir otra vez. **2** *(one's word)* retractar. ◆*to* ~ *down t (remove)* desmontar. **2** *(coat etc.)* descolgar. **3** *(write)* apuntar. ◆*to* ~ *in t (shelter)* dar cobijo a. **2** *(deceive)* engañar. **3** *(grasp)* asimilar. **4** *(include)* incluir. **5** *(clothes)* meter. ◆*to* ~ *off t (clothes)* quitarse. **2** *(imitate)* imitar. – **3** *i (plane)* despegar. ◆*to* ~ *on t (job)* hacerse cargo de, aceptar. **2** *(worker)* contratar. ◆*to* ~ *out t* sacar. **2** *(person)* invitar a salir. **3** *(insurance)* hacer. ◆*to* ~ *over t* tomar posesión de. ◆*to* ~ *over from t* relevar. ◆*to* ~ *to t (person)* tomar cariño a. **2** *(vice)* darse a. **3** *(start to do)* empezar a. ◆*to* ~ *up t* ocupar. **2** *(continue)* continuar. **3** *(offer)* aceptar. **4** *(start to do)* dedicarse a. ●*to* ~ *it out on sb.,* desquitarse con algn; *to* ~ *sth. up with sb.,* consultar algo con algn.; *to* ~ *to one's heels,* darse a la fuga. ▲ *pt took; pp taken.*
takeaway ['teɪkəweɪ] *n* restaurante *m* que vende comida para llevar.
taken ['teɪkən] *pp* → **take.**
takeoff ['teɪkɒf] *n* AV despegue *m*. **2** *(imitation)* imitación.
takeover ['teɪkəʊvə'] *n* toma de posesión. **2** COM adquisición. ■ *military* ~, golpe *m* de estado.
takings ['teɪkɪŋz] *npl* recaudación *f sing*.
talcum powder ['tælkəmpaʊdə'] *n* polvos *mpl* de talco.
tale [teɪl] *n* cuento. ●*to tell tales,* contar cuentos.
talent ['tælənt] *n* talento.
talisman ['tælɪzmən] *n* talismán *m*.

talk [tɔːk] *t-i* hablar. – 2 *n* conversación, charla. 3 *(romour)* rumor *m.* ◆*to ~ over t* discutir. ◆*to ~ round t* convencer. ●*to ~ sb. into sth.,* convencer a algn. para que haga algo; *to ~ sb. out of sth.,* disuadir a algn. de hacer algo.

talkative ['tɔːkətɪv] *adj* hablador,-ra.

talker ['tɔːkəʳ] *n* hablador,-ra.

talking-to ['tɔːkɪŋtuː] *n fam* bronca.

tall [tɔːl] *adj* alto,-a; *how ~ are you?,* ¿cuánto mides?; *it's 5 metres ~,* mide 5 metros de alto. ■ *~ story,* cuento chino.

tally ['tælɪ] *n* cuenta. – 2 *i* concordar *(with,* con).

talon ['tælən] *n* garra.

tambourine [tæmbə'riːn] *n* pandereta.

tame [teɪm] *adj (by nature)* manso,-a, dócil. 2 *(tamed)* domesticado,-a. 3 *fig* soso,-a. – 4 *t* domar, domesticar.

tamer ['teɪməʳ] *n* domador,-ra.

tamper ['tæmpəʳ] *i to ~ with,* interferir en. 2 *(document)* falsificar.

tampon ['tæmpɒn] *n* tampón *m.*

tan [tæn] *n* color *m* canela. 2 *(suntan)* bronceado. – 3 *t (leather)* curtir. – 4 *t-i (skin)* broncear(se), poner(se) moreno,-a.

tang [tæŋ] *n* sabor *m*/olor *m* fuerte.

tangent ['tændʒənt] *n* tangente *f.*

tangerine [tændʒəˈriːn] *n* clementina.

tangible ['tændʒəbəl] *adj* tangible.

tangle ['tæŋgəl] *n* enredo. – 2 *t-i* enredar(se), enmarañar(se). ◆*to ~ with t* meterse con.

tango ['tæŋgəʊ] *n* tango.

tank [tæŋk] *n* depósito, tanque *m.* 2 MIL tanque.

tankard ['tæŋkəd] *n* bock *m.*

tanker ['tæŋkəʳ] *n (ship)* buque *m* cisterna. 2 *(for oil)* petrolero. 3 *(lorry)* camión *m* cisterna.

tantamount ['tæntəmaʊnt] *adj ~ to,* equivalente a.

tantrum ['tæntrəm] *n* berrinche *m,* rabieta.

tap [tæp] *n* grifo. 2 *(blow)* golpecito. – 3 *t* golpear suavemente. 4 *fig* explotar. 5 *(phone)* pinchar, intervenir. ■ *~ dance,* claqué *m.*

tape [teɪp] *n* cinta. – 2 *t* pegar con cinta. 3 *(record)* grabar. ■ *~ measure,* cinta métrica; *~ recorder,* magnetófono.

taper ['teɪpəʳ] *t-i* ahusar(se).

tapestry ['tæpəstrɪ] *n* tapiz *m.*

tapeworm ['teɪpwɜːm] *n* tenia, solitaria.

tar [tɑːʳ] *n* alquitrán *m.* – 2 *t* alquitranar.

tarantula [təˈræntjʊlə] *n* tarántula.

target ['tɑːgɪt] *n* blanco. 2 *(aim)* meta.

tariff ['tærɪf] *n* tarifa, arancel *m.*

tarmac ['tɑːmæk] *n* alquitrán *m.* – 2 *t* alquitranar.

tarnish ['tɑːnɪʃ] *t-i* deslustrar(se).

tarot ['tærəʊ] *n* tarot *m.*

tarpaulin [tɑːˈpɔːlɪn] *n* lona.

tarragon ['tærəgən] *n* estragón *m.*

tart [tɑːt] *adj* acre, agrio,-a. 2 *(reply)* mordaz. – 3 *n* tarta, pastel *m.* 4 *sl* fulana.

tartan ['tɑːtən] *n* tartán *m.*

task [tɑːsk] *n* tarea, labor *f.*

tassel ['tæsəl] *n* borla.

taste [teɪst] *n (sense)* gusto. 2 *(flavour)* sabor. – 3 *t (food)* probar. 4 *(wine)* catar. – 5 *i* saber *(of,* a). ●*in bad ~,* de mal gusto.

tasteful ['teɪstfʊl] *adj* de buen gusto.

tasteless ['teɪstləs] *adj* de mal gusto. 2 *(insipid)* insípido,-a, soso,-a.

tasty ['teɪstɪ] *adj* sabroso,-a.

ta-ta [tæˈtɑː] *interj* GB *fam* ¡adiós!

tattered ['tætəd] harapiento,-a, andrajoso,-a.

tatters ['tætəz] *npl* harapos *mpl,* andrajos *mpl.*

tattoo [təˈtuː] *n* MIL retreta. 2 *(show)* espectáculo militar. 3 *(on skin)* tatuaje *m.* – 4 *t* tatuar.

tatty ['tætɪ] *adj* en mal estado. 2 *(clothes)* raído,-a.

taught [tɔːt] *pt & pp →* **teach.**

taunt [tɔːnt] *n* mofa, pulla. – 2 *t* mofarse de.

Taurus ['tɔːrəs] *n* Tauro.

taut [tɔːt] *adj* tirante, tieso,-a.

tavern ['tævən] *n* taberna, mesón *m.*

tawdry ['tɔːdrɪ] *adj* hortera, charro,-a.

tawny ['tɔːnɪ] *adj* leonado,-a.

tax [tæks] *n* impuesto, contribución. – 2 *t (thing)* gravar. 3 *(person)* imponer contribuciones a.

taxation [tækˈseɪʃən] *n* impuestos *mpl.*

taxi ['tæksɪ] *n* taxi *m.* ■ *~ driver,* taxista *mf.*

taxidermist ['tæksɪdɜːmɪst] *n* taxidermista *mf.*

taximeter ['tæksɪmiːtəʳ] *n* taxímetro.

taxpayer ['tækspeɪəʳ] *n* contribuyente *mf.*

tea [tiː] *n* té *m.* 2 *(light meal)* merienda. 3 *(full meal)* cena. ■ *~ set,* juego de té; *~ spoon,* cucharilla.

teach [tiːtʃ] *t* enseñar. 2 *(subject)* dar clases de. – 3 *i* dar clases. ▲ *pt & pp* **taught.**

teacher [ˈtiːtʃəʳ] *n* maestro,-a, profesor,-ra.

teaching [ˈtiːtʃɪŋ] *n* enseñanza.

teacloth [ˈtiːklɒθ] *n* paño (de cocina).

teacup [ˈtiːkʌp] *n* taza para té.

teak [tiːk] *n* teca.

team [tiːm] *n* equipo.

teapot [ˈtiːpɒt] *n* tetera.

tear [tɪəʳ] *n* lágrima. **2** *(rip)* rasgón *m*, desgarrón *m*. — **3** *t (rip)* rasgar, desgarrar. ◆*to* ~ *down* *t* derribar. ◆*to* ~ *into* *t* arremeter contra. ◆*to* ~ *up* *t* romper en pedazos. ●*to burst into tears,* romper a llorar. ■ ~ *gas,* gas *m* lacrimógeno; *wear and* ~, desgaste *m*. ▲ *pt* **tore**; *pp* **torn**.

tearaway [ˈteərəweɪ] *n* GB gamberro,-a.

teardrop [ˈtɪədrɒp] *n* lágrima.

tearful [ˈtɪəfʊl] *adj* lloroso,-a.

tease [tiːz] *t* tomar el pelo a.

teaspoon [ˈtiːspuːn] *n* cucharilla.

teaspoonful [ˈtiːspuːnfʊl] *n* cucharadita.

teat [tiːt] *n* ZOOL teta. **2** *(on bottle)* tetina.

technical [ˈteknɪkəl] *adj* técnico,-a.

technician [tekˈnɪʃən] *n* técnico,-a.

technique [tekˈniːk] *n* técnica.

technological [teknəˈlɒdʒɪkəl] *adj* tecnológico,-a.

technology [tekˈnɒlədʒɪ] *n* tecnología.

teddy bear [ˈtedɪbeəʳ] *n* osito de peluche.

tedious [ˈtiːdɪəs] *adj* tedioso,-a, aburrido,-a.

tediousness [ˈtiːdɪəsnəs] *n* tedio, aburrimiento.

teem [tiːm] *i to* ~ *with,* abundar en, estar lleno,-a de.

teenage [ˈtiːneɪdʒ] *adj* adolescente.

teenager [ˈtiːneɪdʒəʳ] *n* adolescente *mf* de 13 a 19 años.

teeny(-weeny) [ˈtiːnɪ(ˈwiːnɪ)] *adj fam* chiquitín,-ina.

tee-shirt [ˈtiːʃɜːt] *n* camiseta.

teeter [ˈtiːtəʳ] *i* balancearse.

teeth [tiːθ] *npl* → **tooth**.

teethe [tiːð] *i* endentecer, echar los dientes.

teetotaller [tiːˈtəʊtləʳ] *n* abstemio,-a.

telecommunications [ˈtelɪkəmjuːnɪˈkeɪʃənz] *npl* telecomunicaciones *fpl.*

telegram [ˈtelɪɡræm] *n* telegrama *m.*

telegraph [ˈtelɪɡrɑːf] *n* telégrafo. — **2** *i* telegrafiar. ■ ~ *pole,* poste *m* telegráfico.

telepathy [tɪˈlepəθɪ] *n* telepatía.

telephone [ˈtelɪfəʊn] *n* teléfono. — **2** *t-i* telefonear, llamar por teléfono. ■ ~

box, cabina telefónica; ~ *number,* número de teléfono.

telephonist [təˈlefənɪst] *n* telefonista *mf.*

telephoto lens [telɪfəʊtəʊˈlenz] *n* teleobjetivo.

telescope [ˈtelɪskəʊp] *n* telescopio. — **2** *t-i* plegar(se).

televise [ˈtelɪvaɪz] *t* televisar.

television [ˈtelɪvɪʒən] *n* televisión. **2** *(set)* televisor *m.*

telex [ˈteleks] *n* télex *m.* — **2** *t-i* enviar un télex (a).

tell [tel] *t* decir. **2** *(story)* contar. **3** *(order)* mandar, ordenar. **4** *(one fron another)* distinguir. **5** *(know)* saber. ◆*to* ~ *off* *t* echar una bronca a. ◆*to* ~ *on* *t* (have effect) afectar a. **2** *(tell tales)* chivar.

teller [ˈteləʳ] *n (in bank)* cajero,-a.

telling-off [telɪŋˈɒf] *n fam* bronca.

telltale [ˈtelteɪl] *n* chivato,-a, acusica *mf.*

telly [ˈtelɪ] *n fam* tele *f.*

temerity [təˈmerɪtɪ] *n* temeridad.

temper [ˈtempəʳ] *n* humor *m.* **2** *(bad* ~*)* mal genio. **3** *(nature)* temperamento. — **4** *t* templar. — **5** *fig* moderar. ●*to lose one's* ~, enfadarse.

temperament [ˈtempərəmənt] *n* temperamento.

temperance [ˈtempərəns] *n* moderación. **2** *(from alcohol)* abstinencia.

temperate [ˈtempərət] *adj* moderado,-a. **2** *(climate)* templado,-a.

temperature [ˈtempərətʃəʳ] *n* temperatura. ●*to have a* ~, tener fiebre.

tempest [ˈtempəst] *n* tempestad.

tempestuous [temˈpestjʊəs] *adj* tempestuoso,-a.

temple [ˈtempəl] *n* templo. **2** ANAT sien *f.*

tempo [ˈtempəʊ] *n* MUS tempo. **2** *fig* ritmo.

temporary [ˈtempərərɪ] *adj* temporal, provisional.

tempt [tempt] *t* tentar.

temptation [tempˈteɪʃən] *n* tentación.

tempter [ˈtemptəʳ] *n* tentador,-ra.

ten [ten] *adj-n* diez *(m).*

tenable [ˈtenəbəl] *adj* sostenible.

tenacious [təˈneɪʃəs] *adj* tenaz.

tenacity [təˈnæsɪtɪ] *n* tenacidad.

tenant [ˈtenənt] *n* inquilino,-a, arrendatario,-a.

tend [tend] *t* cuidar. — **2** *i* tender a, tener tendencia a.

tendency [ˈtendənsɪ] *n* tendencia.

tender [ˈtendəʳ] *adj (meat etc.)* tierno,-a. **2** *(loving)* tierno,-a, cariñoso,-a. **3** *(sore)* dolorido,-a. — **5** *n (of train)* ténder *m.* **6**

MAR lancha (auxiliar). **6** COM oferta. **– 7** *t* presentar. ■ *legal* ~, moneda de curso legal.

tenderhearted ['tendəhɑːtɪd] *adj* compasivo,-a, bondadoso,-a.

tenderness ['tendənəs] *n* ternura.

tendon ['tendən] *n* tendón *m*.

tendril ['tendrəl] *n* zarcillo.

tenement ['tenəmənt] *n* casa de vecindad.

tenet ['tenət] *n* principio, dogma *m*.

tennis ['tenɪs] *n* tenis *m*. ■ ~ *court*, pista de tenis.

tenor ['tenəʳ] *n* MUS tenor *m*. **2** *(meaning)* significado.

tense [tens] *adj* tenso,-a. **– 2** *n* GRAM tiempo.

tension ['tenʃən] *n* tensión.

tent [tent] *n* tienda de campaña.

tentacle ['tentəkəl] *n* tentáculo.

tentative ['tentətɪv] *adj* de prueba/ensayo, provisional. **2** *(person)* indeciso,-a.

tenterhooks ['tentəhʊks] *npl on* ~, sobre ascuas.

tenth [tenθ] *adj-n* décimo,-a. **– 2** *n* décimo, décima parte *f*.

tenuous ['tenjʊəs] *adj* tenue, sutil.

tenure ['tenjəʳ] *n* tenencia, posesión.

tepid ['tepɪd] *adj* tibio,-a.

term [tɜːm] *n* EDUC trimestre *m*. **2** *(period)* período. **3** *(expression, word)* término. **4** *pl* COM condiciones *fpl*. **5** *pl (relations)* relaciones *fpl*. **– 6** *t* calificar de, llamar. ●*to be on good terms with,* tener buenas relaciones con; *to come to terms,* llegar a un arreglo. ■ *easy terms,* facilidades *fpl* de pago.

terminal ['tɜːmɪnəl] *adj* terminal. **– 2** *n* ELEC borne *m*. **3** COMPUT terminal *m*. **4** *(at airport etc.)* terminal *f*.

terminate ['tɜːmɪneɪt] *t-i* terminar.

termination [tɜːmɪ'neɪʃən] *n* terminación.

terminology [tɜːmɪ'nɒlədʒɪ] *n* terminología.

terminus ['tɜːmɪnəs] *n* término. ▲ *pl terminuses o termini* ['tɜːmɪnaɪ].

termite ['tɜːmaɪt] *n* termita.

terrace ['terəs] *n (of houses)* hilera. **2** AGR terraza. **3** *(patio)* terraza. **4** *pl* SP gradas *fpl*.

terrain [tə'reɪn] *n* terreno.

terrestrial [tə'restrɪəl] *adj* terrestre.

terrible ['terɪbəl] *adj* terrible. **2** *fam* fatal. **– 3** *terribly adv* terriblemente. **4** *(very)* muy.

terrific [tə'rɪfɪk] *adj* fabuloso,-a, estupendo,-a.

terrify ['terɪfaɪ] *t* aterrar, aterrorizar.

terrifying ['terɪfaɪɪŋ] *adj* aterrador,-ra.

territory ['terɪtərɪ] *n* territorio.

terror ['terəʳ] *n* terror *m*, espanto.

terrorism ['terərɪzəm] *n* terrorismo.

terrorist ['terərɪst] *adj-n* terrorista *(mf)*.

terrorize ['terəraɪz] *t* aterrorizar.

terse [tɜːs] *adj* lacónico,-a.

test [test] *n* prueba. **2** EDUC examen *m*, test *m*. **3** MED análisis *m*. **– 4** *t* probar, poner a prueba. ■ ~ *tube*, probeta.

testament ['testəmənt] *n* testamento.

testicle ['testɪkəl] *n* testículo.

testify ['testɪfaɪ] *t* atestiguar. **– 2** *i* declarar.

testimonial [testɪ'məʊnɪəl] *n* recomendación.

testimony ['testɪmənɪ] *n* testimonio.

testy ['testɪ] *adj* irritable.

tetanus ['tetənəs] *n* tétanos *m inv*.

tetchy ['tetʃɪ] *adj* → **testy**.

tête-à-tête [teɪtə'teɪt] *n* conversación privada.

tether ['teðəʳ] *n* cuerda. **– 2** *t* atar. ●*at the end of one's* ~, hasta la coronilla.

text [tekst] *n* texto.

textbook ['tekstbʊk] *n* libro de texto.

textile ['tekstaɪl] *adj* textil. **– 2** *n* textil *m*, tejido.

texture ['tekstʃəʳ] *n* textura.

than [ðæn, *unstressed* ðən] *conj* que: *he is taller* ~ *you,* él es más alto que tú. **2** *(with numbers)* de: *more* ~ *once,* más de una vez.

thank [θæŋk] *t* dar las gracias a, agradecer. **– 2** *npl* gracias *fpl*. ●~ *you,* gracias.

thankful ['θæŋkfʊl] *adj* agradecido,-a.

thankless ['θæŋkləs] *adj* ingrato,-a.

thanksgiving [θæŋks'gɪvɪŋ] *n* acción de gracias.

that [ðæt] *adj* ese, esa; *(remote)* aquel, aquella: *look at* ~ *cow,* mira esa/aquella vaca. **– 2** *pron* ése *m*, ésa; *(remote)* aquél *m*, aquélla: *this is mine,* ~ *is yours,* esta es mía, ésa/aquélla es tuya. **3** *(indefinite)* eso; *(remote)* aquello: *what's* ~?, ¿qué es eso/aquello? **– 4** *conj* que: *I know (*~*) it's true,* sé que es verdad. **– 5** *pron (relative)* que: *the car (*~*) he drives,* el coche que tiene. **6** *(with preposition)* que, el/la que, el/la cual: *the door (*~*) he went through,* la puerta por la que/cual pasó. **– 7** *adv fam* tan: *it's not* ~ *dear,* no es tan caro. ●~ *much,* tanto,-a;

that's right, eso es. ▲ *En 1, 2 y 3 pl those. En 4 y 5 también se pronuncia* [ðət].

thatch [θætʃ] *n* paja. — **2** *t* poner techo de paja a.

thaw [θɔː] *n* deshielo. — **2** *t-i* deshelar(se).

the [ðə] *art* el, la; *pl* los, las. — **2** *adv* ~ *more you have* ~ *more you want,* cuanto más se tiene más se quiere; ~ *sooner,* ~ *better,* cuanto antes mejor. ▲ *Delante de una vocal* [ði]; *con enfasis* [ðiː].

theatre ['θɪətəʳ] *n* teatro. **2** MED quirófano.

theatrical [θɪ'ætrɪkəl] *adj* teatral.

theft [θeft] *n* robo, hurto.

their [ðeəʳ] *poss adj* su; *pl* sus.

theirs [ðeəz] *pron* (el) suyo, (la) suya; *pl* (los) suyos, (las) suyas.

them [ðem, *unstressed* ðəm] *m pron (direct object)* los, las; *(indirect object)* les. **2** *(with preposition, stressed)* ellos, ellas.

theme [θiːm] *n* tema *m.*

themselves [ðəm'selvz] *pers pron (subject)* ellos mismos, ellas mismas. **2** *(object)* se. **3** *(after preposition)* sí mismos/ mismas.

then [ðen] *adv* entonces. **2** *(next)* entonces, luego, después. **3** *(in that case)* pues, en ese caso. — **4** *adj* (de) entonces. ●*now and* ~, de vez en cuando; *now* ~, pues bien.

theological [θɪə'lɒdʒɪkəl] *adj* teológico,-a.

theology [θɪ'ɒlədʒɪ] *n* teología.

theorem ['θɪərəm] *n* teorema *m.*

theoretic(al) [θɪə'retɪk(əl)] *adj* teórico,-a.

theorize ['θɪəraɪz] *i* teorizar.

theory ['θɪərɪ] *n* teoría.

therapeutic [θerə'pjuːtɪk] *adj* terapéutico,-a.

therapy ['θerəpɪ] *n* terapia, terapéutica.

there [ðeəʳ] *adv* allí, allá, ahí. ●~ *is/are,* hay; ~ *was/were,* había.

thereabouts [ðeərə'baʊts] *adv* por ahí.

thereafter [ðeə'ræftəʳ] *adv* a partir de entonces.

thereby ['ðeəbaɪ] *adv* por eso/ello.

therefore ['ðeəfɔːʳ] *adv* por lo tanto.

thermal ['θɜːməl] *adj* termal. **2** PHYS térmico,-a.

thermometer [θe'mɒmɪtəʳ] *n* termómetro.

thermos® ['θɜːmɒs] *n* ~ *(flask),* termo.

thermostat ['θɜːməstæt] *n* termostato.

thesaurus [θɪ'sɔːrəs] *n* diccionario de sinónimos.

these [ðiːz] *adj pl* estos,-as. — **2** *pron pl* éstos,-as.

thesis ['θiːsɪs] *n* tesis *f.* ▲ *pl* **theses** ['θiːsiːz].

they [ðeɪ] *pers pron* ellos,-as. ●~ *say that,* dicen/se dice que.

thick [θɪk] *adj* grueso,-a: *two inches* ~, de dos pulgadas de grueso. **2** *(liquid, gas, forest, etc.)* espeso,-a. **3** *(beard)* poblado,-a, tupido,-a. **4** *fam* corto,-a de alcances, de pocas luces.

thicken ['θɪkən] *t-i* espesar(se).

thicket ['θɪkɪt] *n* espesura, matorral *m.*

thickness ['θɪknəs] *n* espesor *m,* grueso, grosor *m.*

thief [θiːf] *n* ladrón,-ona.

thieve [θiːv] *t-i* robar, hurtar.

thigh [θaɪ] *n* muslo.

thimble ['θɪmbəl] *n* dedal *m.*

thin [θɪn] *n (person)* delgado,-a, flaco,-a. **2** *(slice, material)* fino,-a. **3** *(hair, vegetation, etc.)* ralo,-a. **4** *(liquid)* líquido,-a, poco espeso,-a. — **5** *t.(liquid)* diluir.

thing [θɪŋ] *n* cosa. ●*for one* ~, entre otras cosas; *poor* ~!, ¡pobrecito,-a!

think [θɪŋk] *t-i gen* pensar. **2** *(imagine)* pensar, imaginar. — **3** *t (believe)* pensar, creer. **4** *(remember)* acordarse. ◆*to* ~ *over t* considerar. ◆*to* ~ *up t* inventar. ●~ *nothing of it,* no tiene importancia; *to* ~ *better of it,* pensárselo mejor. ▲ *pt & pp* **thought.**

thinker ['θɪŋkəʳ] *n* pensador,-ra.

thinking ['θɪŋkɪŋ] *n* opinión, parecer *m.*

thinness ['θɪnnəs] *n* delgadez *f.*

third [θɜːd] *adj* tercero,-a. — **2** *n (in series)* tercero,-a. **3** *(fraction)* tercio, tercera parte *f.* ■ ~ *party,* tercera persona; ~ *party insurance,* seguro a terceros.

thirst [θɜːst] *n* sed *f.*

thirsty ['θɜːstɪ] *adj* sediento,-a. ●*to be* ~, tener sed.

thirteen [θɜː'tiːn] *adj-n* trece *(m).*

thirteenth [θɜː'tiːnθ] *adj-n* decimotercero,-a. — **2** *n* decimotercero, decimotercera parte.

thirtieth ['θɜːtɪəθ] *adj-n* trigésimo,-a. — **2** *n* trigésimo, trigésima parte.

thirty ['θɜːtɪ] *adj-n* treinta *(m).*

this [ðɪs] *adj* este, esta. — **2** *pron* éste, ésta; *(indefinite)* esto. — **3** *adv* tan. ●*like* ~, así.

thistle ['θɪsəl] *n* cardo.

thong [θɒŋ] *n* correa.

thorax ['θɔːræks] *n* tórax *m.*

thorn [θɔːn] *n* espina, pincho.

thorny ['θɔːnɪ] *adj* espinoso,-a.

thorough ['θʌrə] *adj (deep)* profundo,-a. **2** *(careful)* cuidadoso,-a, minucioso,-a. **3**

(total) total. — **4 thoroughly** *adv* a fondo. **5** *(totally)* totalmente.

thoroughbred ['θʌrəbred] *adj-n* (de) pura sangre.

thoroughfare ['θʌrəfeəʳ] *n* vía pública.

those [ðəuz] *adj* esos,-as; *(remote)* aquellos,-as. — **2** *pron* ésos,-as; *(remote)* aquéllos,-as.

though [ðəu] *conj* aunque, si bien. — **2** *adv* sin embargo. •*as* ~, como si

thought [θɔ:t] *pt & pp* → **think**. — **2** *n* pensamiento. **3** *(consideration)* consideración.

thoughtful ['θɔ:tful] *adj* pensativo,-a, meditabundo,-a. **2** *(considerate)* considerado,-a, atento,-a.

thoughtfulness ['θɔ:tfulnəs] *n* meditación. **2** *(consideration)* consideración, atención.

thoughtless ['θɔ:tləs] *adj* irreflexivo,-a. **2** *(person)* desconsiderado,-a.

thoughtlessness ['θɔ:tləsnəs] *n* irreflexión, falta de consideración.

thousand ['θauzənd] *adj-n* mil *(m)*.

thousandth ['θauzənθ] *adj-n* milésimo,-a. — **2** *n* *(fraction)* milésimo, milésima parte *f*.

thrash [θræʃ] *t* azotar. **2** *(defeat)* derrotar. — **3** *i* revolcarse, agitarse.

thrashing ['θræʃiŋ] *n* zurra, paliza.

thread [θred] *n* hilo. **2** *(of screw)* rosca. — **3** *t* enhebrar. **4** *(beads)* ensartar.

threat [θret] *n* amenaza.

threaten ['θretən] *t-i* amenazar.

threatening ['θretəniŋ] *adj* amenazador,-ra.

three [θri:] *adj-n* tres *(m)*.

three-dimensional [θri:di'menʃənəl] *adj* tridimensional.

thresh [θreʃ] *t-i* trillar.

threshold ['θreʃ(h)əuld] *n* umbral *m*.

threw [θru:] *pt* → **throw**.

thrift [θrift] *n* economía, frugalidad.

thrifty ['θrifti] *adj* económico,-a, frugal.

thrill [θril] *n* emoción. — **2** *t-i* emocionar(se).

thriller ['θrilər] *n* novela/película/obra de suspense.

thrilling ['θriliŋ] *adj* emocionante.

thrive [θraiv] *i* *(grow)* crecer. **2** *(prosper)* prosperar. ▲ *pt* **throve** o **thrived**; *pp* **thrived** o **thriven** ['θrivən].

thriving ['θraiviŋ] *adj* próspero,-a, floreciente.

throat [θrəut] *n* garganta. ■ *sore* ~, dolor *m* de garganta.

throb [θrɒb] *n* latido, palpitación. — **2** *i* latir, palpitar.

throes [θrəuz] *n* agonía *f sing*. •*in the* ~ *of*, en medio de.

thrombosis [θrɒm'bəusis] *n* trombosis *f*.

throne [θrəun] *n* trono.

throng [θrɒŋ] *n* muchedumbre *f*, tropel *m*. — **2** *i* apiñarse, agolparse. — **3** *t* atestar.

throttle ['θrɒtəl] *n* válvula reguladora. — **2** *t* estrangular.

through [θru:] *prep* por, a través de: ~ *the door*, por la puerta. **2** *(because of)* por, a causa de: *off work* ~ *illness*, de baja por enfermedad. **3** *(time)* durante todo,-a: *we danced* ~ *the night*, bailamos durante toda la noche. **4** *(to the end)* hasta el final de: *he read* ~ *the book*, leyó todo el libro. — **5** *adv* de un lado a otro: *he let me* ~, me dejó pasar. **6** *(to the end)* hasta el final: *he read the book* ~, leyó todo el libro. — **7** *adj* *(train)* directo,-a. •*to be* ~ *with*, haber acabado con.

throughout [θru:'aut] *prep* por/en todo,-a: ~ *the world*, en todo el mundo. **2** *(time)* durante todo,-a, a lo largo de: ~ *the year*, durante todo el año. — **3** *adv* *(all over)* por/en todas partes. **4** *(completely)* completamente. **5** *(from start to end)* desde el principio hasta el fin.

throve [θrəuv] *pt* → **thrive**.

throw [θrəu] *n* lanzamiento, tiro. **2** *(of dice)* tirada. — **3** *t* tirar, arrojar, lanzar. **4** *fam (party)* organizar. ◆*to* ~ *away* *t* tirar. **2** *(chance)* desaprovechar. ◆*to* ~ *in* *t* *fam* incluir (gratis). ◆*to* ~ *off* *t* librarse de. ◆*to* ~ *out* *t* echar. **2** *(reject)* rechazar. ◆*to* ~ *up* *i* vomitar. — **2** *t* dejar. ▲ *pt* **threw**; *pp* **thrown** [θrəun].

thru [θru:] *prep-adv* US → **through**: *Monday* ~ *Friday*, de lunes a viernes.

thrush [θrʌʃ] *n* *(bird)* tordo.

thrust [θrʌst] *n* PHYS empuje *m*. **2** *(with sword)* estocada. — **3** *t* empujar. **4** *(sword)* clavar.

thud [θʌd] *n* ruido sordo. — **2** *t* hacer un ruido sordo.

thug [θʌg] *n* matón *m*. **2** *(criminal)* gángster *m*.

thumb [θʌm] *n* pulgar *m*.

thumbtack ['θʌmtæk] *n* US chincheta.

thump [θʌmp] *n* golpe *m*. — **2** *t* golpear.

thunder ['θʌndəʳ] *n* trueno. — **2** *i* tronar.

thunderbolt ['θʌndəbəult] *n* rayo.

thunderous ['θʌndərəs] *adj fig* ensordecedor,-ra.

thunderstorm ['θʌndəstɔːm] *n* tormenta.

Thursday ['θɜːzdɪ] *n* jueves *m inv.*

thus [ðʌs] *adv* así, de este modo.

thwart [θwɔːt] *t* desbaratar, frustrar.

thyme [taɪm] *n* tomillo.

tiara [tɪ'ɑːrə] *n* diadema.

tic [tɪk] *n* tic *m.*

tick [tɪk] *n* ZOOL garrapata. **2** *(noise)* tictac *m.* **3** *(mark)* marca, señal *f.* **4** *fam* momento, instante *m.* **5** *fam* crédito. — **6** *i (clock)* hacer tictac. — **7** *t* señalar, marcar. ◆*to ~ off t* marcar. **2** *(scold)* regañar.

ticket ['tɪkɪt] *n* billete *m.* **2** *(for zoo, cinema, etc.)* entrada. **3** *(label)* etiqueta. **4** *fam (fine)* multa. ■ *return ~,* billete de ida y vuelta; *~ office,* taquilla.

ticking-off [tɪkɪŋ'ɒf] *n fam* rapapolvo.

tickle ['tɪkəl] *t* hacer cosquillas a. — **2** *i* hacer cosquillas, picar.

ticklish ['tɪkəlɪʃ] *adj to be ~,* tener cosquillas. **2** *fig* delicado.

tick-tock ['tɪktɒk] *n* tic-tac *m.*

tiddly ['tɪdlɪ] *adj* GB *fam* achispado,-a.

tide [taɪd] *n* marea. **2** *fig* corriente *f.* **3** *(progress)* marcha. ◆*to ~ over t* ayudar, sacar de un apuro. ■ *high/low ~,* pleamar *f*/bajamar *f.*

tidings ['taɪdɪŋz] *n* noticias *fpl,* nuevas *fpl.*

tidy ['taɪdɪ] *adj* ordenado,-a. **2** *(appearance)* arreglado,-a. — **3** *t to ~ (up),* poner en orden. — **4** *i to ~ (up),* poner las cosas en orden. ◆*to ~ o.s. up,* arreglarse.

tie [taɪ] *n (man's)* corbata. **2** *fig* lazo, vínculo. **3** SP *(draw)* empate *m.* **4** *(hindrance)* atadura. — **5** *t* atar; *(knot)* hacer. — **6** *i* empatar. ◆*to ~ down t* sujetar. ◆*to ~ up t* atar. **2** *(connect)* conectar.

tier [tɪə^r] *n* grada, fila. **2** *(of cake)* piso.

tiff [tɪf] *n fam* desavenencia.

tiger ['taɪgə^r] *n* tigre *m.*

tight [taɪt] *adj* apretado,-a. **2** *(rope)* tensado,-a. **3** *(clothes)* ajustado,-a, ceñido,-a. **4** *fam (stingy)* agarrado,-a. **5** *fam (scarce)* escaso,-a. ■ *~ spot,* aprieto.

tighten ['taɪtən] *t-i* apretar(se). **2** *(rope)* tensar(se).

tightfisted [taɪt'fɪstɪd] *adj* tacaño,-a.

tightrope ['taɪtrəʊp] *n* cuerda floja. ■ *~ walker,* funámbulo,-a.

tights [taɪts] *npl* panties *mpl,* medias *fpl.* **2** *(thick)* leotardos *mpl.*

tigress ['taɪgrəs] *n* tigresa.

tile [taɪl] *n (wall)* azulejo. **2** *(floor)* baldosa. **3** *(roof)* teja. — **4** *t (wall)* alicatar, poner azulejos a. **5** *(floor)* embaldosar. **6** *(roof)* tejar.

till [tɪl] *prep* hasta. — **2** *conj* hasta que. — **3** *n (for cash)* caja. — **4** *t* labrar, cultivar.

tiller ['tɪlə^r] *n* caña del timón.

tilt [tɪlt] *n* inclinación, ladeo. — **2** *t-i* inclinar(se), ladear(se). ●*at full ~,* a toda velocidad.

timber ['tɪmbə^r] *n* madera (de construcción). **2** *(beam)* viga. **3** *(trees)* árboles *mpl* maderables.

time [taɪm] *n gen* tiempo: *~ flies,* el tiempo vuela. **2** *(short period)* rato: *we spoke for a ~,* hablamos durante un rato. **3** *(of day)* hora: *it's ~ to go,* es (la) hora de marchar; *what ~ is it?,* ¿qué hora es? **4** *(age, period, season)* época. **5** *(occasion)* vez *f: how many times?,* ¿cuántas veces?; *two at a ~,* de dos en dos. **6** MUS compás *m.* — **7** *t (measure ~)* medir la duración de; SP cronometrar. **8** *(set ~)* fijar la hora de. ●*at any ~,* en cualquier momento; *at no ~,* nunca; *at the same ~,* al mismo tiempo; *at times,* a veces; *behind the times,* anticuado; *from ~ to ~,* de vez en cuando; *in ~, (in the long run)* con el tiempo; *(not late)* con tiempo de sobra; *on ~,* puntual; *to have a good ~,* divertirse, pasarlo bien. ■ *~ bomb,* bomba de relojería.

time-honoured ['taɪmɒnəd] *adj* consagrado,-a.

timekeeper ['taɪmkiːpə^r] *n* cronometrador,-ra.

timely ['taɪmlɪ] *adj* oportuno,-a.

timepiece ['taɪmpiːs] *n* reloj *m.*

timer ['taɪmə^r] *n (machine)* temporizador *m.*

times [taɪmz] *prep* (multiplicado) por.

timetable ['taɪmteɪbəl] *n* horario.

timid ['tɪmɪd] *adj* tímido,-a.

timidity [tɪ'mɪdɪtɪ] *n* timidez *f.*

tin [tɪn] *n (metal)* estaño. **2** *(can)* lata, bote *m.* **3** *(for baking)* molde *m.* — **4** *t* enlatar. ■ *~ opener,* abrelatas *m inv.*

tinder ['tɪndə^r] *n* yesca.

tinfoil ['tɪnfɔɪl] *n* papel *m* de estaño.

tinge [tɪndʒ] *n* tinte *m,* matiz *f.* — **2** *t* teñir.

tingle ['tɪŋgəl] *n* hormigueo. — **2** *i* hormiguear.

tinker ['tɪŋkə^r] *n* hojalatero,-a. — **2** *i to ~ with,* tratar de arreglar; *(ruin)* estropear.

tinkle ['tɪŋkəl] *n* tintineo. — **2** *t-i* (hacer) tintinear. ●GB *fam to give sb. a ~,* llamar a algn. por teléfono.

tinny ['tɪnɪ] *adj* metálico,-a. **2** *(cheap)* de pacotilla.

tinsel ['tɪnsəl] *n* oropel *m.*

tint [tɪnt] *n* tinte *m*, matiz *f*. — **2** *t* teñir, matizar.

tiny ['taɪnɪ] *adj* diminuto,-a.

tip [tɪp] *n* extremo, punta. **2** *(money)* propina. **3** *(advice)* consejo. **4** *(for rubbish)* vertedero, basurero. — **5** *t-i* inclinar(se), ladear(se). — **6** *t* *(rubbish)* verter. **7** *(give money)* dar una propina a. ◆*to* ~ *off t* dar un soplo a. ◆*to* ~ *over/up t-i* volcar(se).

tip-off ['tɪpɒf] *n fam* soplo.

tipsy ['tɪpsɪ] *adj* achispado,-a.

tiptoe ['tɪptəʊ] *n on* ~, de puntillas.

tiptop ['tɪptɒp] *adj fam* de primera.

tirade [taɪ'reɪd] *n* invectiva.

tire ['taɪə'] *t-i* cansar(se), fatigar(se).

tired ['taɪəd] *adj* cansado,-a.

tiredness ['taɪədnəs] *n* cansancio.

tireless ['taɪələs] *adj* incansable.

tiresome ['taɪəsəm] *adj* molesto,-a, pesado,-a.

tiring ['taɪərɪŋ] *adj* cansado,-a, agotador,-ra.

tissue ['tɪʃuː] *n* tisú *m*. **2** *(handkerchief)* pañuelo de papel. **3** BIOL tejido. ■ ~ *paper*, papel *m* de seda.

tit [tɪt] *n sl* teta. ●~ *for tat*, donde las dan las toman.

titbit ['tɪtbɪt] *n* golosina.

tithe [taɪð] *n* diezmo.

titillate ['tɪtɪleɪt] *t* excitar.

titivate ['tɪtɪveɪt] *t* emperifollar.

title ['taɪtəl] *n* título. ■ ~ *deed*, escritura de propiedad; ~ *page*, portada.

titter ['tɪtə'] *n* risita. — **2** *i* reírse disimuladamente.

tizzy ['tɪzɪ] *n fam to get into a* ~, ponerse nervioso,-a.

tittle-tattle ['tɪtəltætəl] *n* chismes *mpl*.

to [tʊ, *unstressed* tə] *prep gen* a. **2** *(towards)* hacia. **3** *(as far as)* a, hasta. **4** *(telling time)* menos: **ten** ~ **two**, las dos menos diez. **5** *(in order* ~*)* para, a fin de. ●~ *and fro*, de acá para allá; *to come* ~, volver en sí. ▲ *Cuando se usa para formar el infinitivo del verbo no se traduce.*

toad [təʊd] *n* sapo.

toadstool ['təʊdstuːl] *n* hongo *venenoso*.

toast [təʊst] *n* pan *m* tostado: *a piece of* ~, una tostada. **2** *(drink)* brindis *m*. — **3** *t* tostar. **4** *(drink)* brindar por.

toaster ['təʊstə'] *n* tostador *m*.

tobacco [tə'bækəʊ] *n* tabaco.

tobacconist [tə'bækənɪst] *n* estanquero,-a. ■ *tobacconist's (shop)*, estanco.

toboggan [tə'bɒgən] *n* tobogán *(m)*. — **2** *i* ir en tobogán.

today [tə'deɪ] *n* hoy *m*. — **2** *adv* hoy. **3** *(nowadays)* hoy en día.

toddle ['tɒdəl] *i (child)* dar los primeros pasos.

toddler ['tɒdlə'] *n* niño,-a *que empieza a andar*.

to-do [tə'duː] *n* lío, jaleo.

toe [təʊ] *n* dedo del pie. **2** *(of shoe)* punta.

toenail ['təʊneɪl] *n* uña del dedo del pie.

toffee ['tɒfɪ] *n* caramelo.

together [tə'geðə'] *adv* junto, juntos,-as. ●*to come* ~, juntarse; ~ *with*, junto con.

toggle ['tɒgəl] *n* botón *m* de madera.

togs [tɒgz] *npl fam* ropa *f sing*.

toil [tɔɪl] *n* trabajo, esfuerzo. — **2** *i* afanarse, esforzarse.

toilet ['tɔɪlət] *n* wáter *m*, lavabo. **2** *(public)* servicios *mpl*. **3** *(washing)* aseo. ■ ~ *paper*, papel *m* higiénico.

token ['təʊkən] *n* señal *f*, prueba. **2** *(coupon)* vale *m*. **3** *(coin)* ficha. — **4** *adj* simbólico,-a.

told [təʊld] *pt & pp* → **tell**.

tolerance ['tɒlərəns] *n* tolerancia.

tolerant ['tɒlərənt] *adj* tolerante.

tolerate ['tɒləreɪt] *t* tolerar.

toll [təʊl] *n* peaje *m*. **2** *(of bell)* tañido. — **3** *t-i* tañer, doblar.

tomato [tə'mɑːtəʊ, US tə'meɪtəʊ] *n* tomate *m*.

tomb [tuːm] *n* tumba, sepulcro.

tomboy ['tɒmbɔɪ] *n* marimacho *f*.

tombstone ['tuːmstəʊn] *n* lápida (sepulcral).

tomcat ['tɒmkæt] *n* gato (macho).

tome [təʊm] *n* tomo.

tomfoolery [tɒm'fuːlərɪ] *n* tonterías *fpl*.

tomorrow [tə'mɒrəʊ] *adv-n* mañana *(m)*.

tom-tom ['tɒmtɒm] *n* tam-tam *m*.

ton [tʌn] *n* tonelada.

tone [təʊn] *n* tono. ◆*to* ~ *down t* atenuar, suavizar.

tone-deaf [təʊn'def] *adj* duro,-a de oído.

tongs [tɒŋz] *npl* tenacillas *fpl*.

tongue [tʌŋ] *n* lengua. ●*to hold one's* ~, callarse. ■ ~ *twister*, trabalenguas *m inv*.

tonic ['tɒnɪk] *adj-n* tónico,-a *(m)*.

tonight [tə'naɪt] *adv-n* esta noche *(f)*.

tonnage ['tʌnɪdʒ] *n* tonelaje *m*.

tonsil ['tɒnsəl] *n* amígdala.

tonsillitis [tɒnsə'laɪtəs] *n* amigdalitis *f*.

too [tuː] *adv* demasiado. **2** *(also)* también. **3** *(besides)* además. ●~ *many*, demasiados,-as; ~ *much*, demasiado,-a.

took [tʊk] *pt* → **take**.

tool [tuːl] *n* herramienta, instrumento.

toot [tuːt] AUTO *n* bocinazo. — **2** *t-i* tocar (la bocina).

tooth [tuːθ] *n* diente *m*; *(molar)* muela. **2** *(of comb)* púa. **3** *(of saw)* diente. ▲ *pl* **teeth**.

toothache ['tuːθeɪk] *n* dolor *m* de muelas.

toothbrush ['tuːθbrʌʃ] *n* cepillo de dientes.

toothless ['tuːθləs] *adj* desdentado,-a.

toothpaste ['tuːθpeɪst] *n* pasta de dientes.

toothpick ['tuːθpɪk] *n* mondadientes *m inv*, palillo.

top [tɒp] *n* parte *f* superior/de arriba. **2** *(of mountain)* cumbre *m*. **3** *(of tree)* copa. **4** *(surface)* superficie *f*. **5** *(of bottle)* tapón *m*, tapa. **6** *(of list)* cabeza. **7** *(toy)* peonza. **8** *(clothes)* blusa (corta), top *m*. — **9** *adj* de arriba, superior, más alto,-a. **10** *(best)* mejor. — **11** *t* cubrir, rematar. **12** *(better)* superar. ◆*to ~ up t* llenar hasta arriba. ●*at ~ speed,* a toda velocidad; *from ~ to bottom,* de arriba abajo; *on ~ of,* encima de. ■ *~ hat,* chistera.

topaz ['təʊpæz] *n* topacio.

topic ['tɒpɪk] *n* tema *m*.

topical ['tɒpɪkəl] *adj* de actualidad.

topless ['tɒpləs] *adj* desnudo,-a de cintura para arriba.

topple ['tɒpəl] *t-i* volcar(se). **2** *fig* derribar(se).

top-secret [tɒp'siːkrət] *adj* sumamente secreto,-a.

torch [tɔːtʃ] *n* antorcha. **2** *(electric)* linterna.

tore [tɔːʳ] *pt* → **tear**.

torment ['tɔːmənt] *n* tormento, tortura. — **2** *t* atormentar, torturar. ▲ *En 2 (verbo)* [tɔː'ment].

torn [tɔːn] *pp* → **tear**. — **2** *adj* rasgado,-a, roto,-a.

tornado [tɔː'neɪdəʊ] *n* tornado.

torpedo [tɔː'piːdəʊ] *n* torpedo. — **2** *t* torpedear.

torrent ['tɒrənt] *n* torrente *m*.

torrid ['tɒrɪd] *adj* tórrido,-a.

torso ['tɔːsəʊ] *n* torso.

tortoise ['tɔːtəs] *n* tortuga (de tierra).

tortuous ['tɔːtjʊəs] *adj* tortuoso,-a.

torture ['tɔːtʃə] *n* tortura, tormento. — **2** *t* torturar, atormentar.

Tory ['tɔːrɪ] *adj-n* GB POL conservador,-a.

toss [tɒs] *n* sacudida. **2** *(of coin)* sorteo a cara o cruz. — **3** *t* sacudir, menear. **4** *(ball)* arrojar, lanzar. — **5** *i* moverse, agitarse. ◆*to ~ up for t* echar a cara y cruz.

toss-up ['tɒsʌp] *n it's a ~,* tanto puede ser uno como otro.

tot [tɒt] *n* chiquitín,-na. **2** *fam (drink)* trago. ◆*to ~ up t* sumar.

total ['təʊtəl] *adj-n* total *(m)*. — **2** *t-i* sumar.

totalitarian [təʊtælɪ'teərɪən] *adj* totalitario,-a.

tote [təʊt] *t fam* acarrear.

totter ['tɒtəʳ] *i* tambalearse.

touch [tʌtʃ] *n* toque *m*. **2** *(sense)* tacto. **3** *(detail)* detalle *m*. **4** *fam* habilidad. — **5** *t-i* tocar(se). — **6** *t (move)* conmover. **7** *(equal)* igualar. ◆*to ~ down i (plane)* aterrizar. **2** SP hacer un ensayo. ◆*to ~ off t* provocar. ◆*to ~ up t* retocar. ●*to get in ~ with,* ponerse en contacto con.

touchdown ['tʌtʃdaʊn] *n (on land)* aterrizaje *m*. **2** *(on sea)* amerizaje *m*. **3** SP ensayo.

touched [tʌtʃt] *adj* conmovido,-a. **2** *(crazy)* tocado,-a.

touchiness ['tʌtʃɪnəs] *n* susceptibilidad.

touching ['tʌtʃɪŋ] *adj* conmovedor,-ra.

touchy ['tʌtʃɪ] *adj* susceptible.

tough [tʌf] *adj* fuerte, resistente. **2** *(difficult, severe)* duro,-a. **3** *(meat)* duro,-a.

toughen ['tʌfən] *t-i* endurecer(se).

toughness ['tʌfnəs] *n* dureza, resistencia. **2** *(difficulty)* dificultad. **3** *(severity)* severidad.

toupee ['tuːpeɪ] *n* peluquín *m*.

tour [tʊəʳ] *n* viaje *m*. **2** *(round building)* visita. **3** SP THEAT gira. — **4** *t* recorrer. **5** *(building)* visitar.

tourism ['tʊərɪzəm] *n* turismo.

tourist ['tʊərɪst] *n* turista *mf*.

tournament ['tʊənəmənt] *n* torneo.

tourniquet ['tʊənɪkeɪ] *n* torniquete *m*.

tousled ['taʊzəld] *adj* despeinado,-a.

tout [taʊt] *n* revendedor,-ra. — **2** *t* revender. — **3** *i* intentar captar clientes.

tow [təʊ] *t* remolcar. ●*on ~,* de remolque.

toward(s) [tə'wɔːd(z)] *prep* hacia. **2** *(attitude)* para con. **3** *(payment)* para.

towel ['taʊəl] *n* toalla.

tower ['taʊəʳ] *n* torre *f*. **2** *(of church)* campanario. — **3** *i* elevarse. ◆*to ~ above/ over t* dominar.

towering ['taʊərɪŋ] *adj* alto,-a.

town [taʊn] *n* ciudad. **2** *(small)* población, municipio, pueblo. ●*on the ~,* de juerga; *to paint the ~ red ,* ir de juerga. ■ *~ council/hall,* ayuntamiento.

toxic ['tɒksɪk] *n* tóxico,-a.
toxicology [tɒksɪ'kɒlədʒɪ] *n* toxicología.
toy [tɔɪ] *n* juguete *m*. – **2** *i* jugar.
toyshop ['tɔɪʃɒp] *n* juguetería.
trace [treɪs] *n* indicio, rastro. – **2** *t (draw)* trazar, esbozar. **3** *(copy)* calcar. **4** *(track)* seguir la pista de. **5** *(find origin)* buscar el origen de.
tracing ['treɪsɪŋ] *n* calco.
track [træk] *n (marks)* pista, huellas *fpl*. **2** *(path)* camino. **3** SP pista. **4** *(for motor-racing)* circuito. **5** *(of railway)* vía. – **6** *t* seguir la pista de. ◆*to* ~ *down t* localizar, encontrar.
tracksuit ['træksuːt] *n* chándal *m*.
tract [trækt] *n (land)* extensión. **2** *(treatise)* tratado. ■ *digestive* ~, aparato digestivo.
tractable ['træktəbəl] *adj* tratable.
traction ['trækʃən] *n* tracción.
tractor ['træktəʳ] *n* tractor *m*.
trade [treɪd] *n* oficio. **2** *(business)* negocio; *(industry)* industria. **3** *(commerce)* comercio. – **4** *i* comerciar. – **5** *t (exchange)* cambiar, trocar. ■ ~ *union*, sindicato obrero.
trader ['treɪdəʳ] *n* comerciante *mf*.
tradesman ['treɪdzmən] *n* comerciante *m*.
trading ['treɪdɪŋ] *n* comercio.
tradition [trə'dɪʃən] *n* tradición.
traditional [trə'dɪʃənəl] *adj* tradicional.
traffic ['træfɪk] *n* AUTO tráfico, tránsito, circulación. **2** *(trade)* tráfico. – **3** *i* traficar. ■ ~ *light*, semáforo.
trafficker ['træfɪkəʳ] *n* traficante *mf*.
tragedy ['trædʒədɪ] *n* tragedia.
tragic ['trædʒɪk] *adj* trágico,-a.
trail [treɪl] *n* rastro, pista. **2** *(path)* camino. **3** *(of comet, jet)* estela. – **4** *t (follow)* seguir (la pista de). – **5** *t-i (drag)* arrastrar(se). – **6** *i (lag behind)* rezagarse. **7** *(plant)* arrastrar(se).
trailer ['treɪləʳ] *n* AUTO remolque *m*. **2** CINEM tráiler *m*.
train [treɪn] *n* tren *m*. **2** *(of dress)* cola. **3** *(of mules)* recua. – **4** *t-i* SP entrenar(se). **5** *(teach)* formar(se). **6** *(gun)* apuntar *(on, a)*. – **7** *t (animal)* adiestrar.
trainee [treɪ'niː] *n* aprendiz,-za.
trainer ['treɪnəʳ] *n* SP entrenador,-ra. **2** *(of dogs)* amaestrador,-ra. **3** *(shoe)* zapatilla.
training ['treɪnɪŋ] *n* formación. **2** SP entrenamiento. **3** *(of dogs)* amaestramiento.
trait [treɪt] *n* rasgo.
traitor ['treɪtəʳ] *n* traidor,-ra.

trajectory [trə'dʒektərɪ] *n* trayectoria.
tram [træm] *n* tranvía *m*.
tramp [træmp] *n* vagabundo,-a. – **2** *i* caminar (con pasos pesados).
trample ['træmpəl] *t* pisotear.
trampoline ['træmpəliːn] *n* cama elástica.
trance [trɑːns] *n* trance *m*.
tranquil ['træŋkwɪl] *adj* tranquilo,-a.
tranquility [træŋ'kwɪlɪtɪ] *n* tranquilidad.
tranquillize ['træŋkwɪlaɪz] *t* tranquilizar.
tranquillizer ['træŋkwɪlaɪzəʳ] *n* tranquilizante *m*, calmante *m*.
transact [træn'zækt] *t* llevar a cabo, despachar.
transaction [træn'zækʃən] *n* operación, transacción.
transatlantic [trænzət'læntɪk] *adj* transatlántico,-a.
transcend [træn'send] *t* sobrepasar, trascender.
transcendental [trænsen'dentəl] *adj* trascendental.
transcribe [træn'skraɪb] *t* transcribir.
transcript ['trænskrɪpt] *n* transcripción.
transfer ['trænsfɜːʳ] *n* transferencia. **2** JUR traspaso. – **3** *t* transferir. **4** JUR traspasar. ▲ *En 3 y 4 (verbo)* [træns'fɜːʳ].
transform [træns'fɔːm] *t-i* transformar(se).
transformation [trænsfə'meɪʃən] *n* transformación.
transformer [træns'fɔːməʳ] *n* ELEC transformador *m*.
transfusion [træns'fjuːʒən] *n* transfusión (de sangre).
transgress [træns'gres] *t* transgredir.
transgression [træns'greʃən] *n* transgresión.
transient ['trænzɪənt] *adj* transitorio,-a.
transistor [træn'zɪstəʳ] *n* transistor *m*.
transit ['trænsɪt] *n* tránsito, paso.
transition [træn'zɪʃən] *n* transición.
transitive ['trænsɪtɪv] *adj* transitivo,-a.
transitory ['trænsɪtərɪ] *adj* transitorio,-a.
translate [træns'leɪt] *t* traducir.
translation [træns'leɪʃən] *n* traducción.
translator [træns'leɪtəʳ] *n* traductor,-ra.
translucent [trænz'luːsənt] *adj* translúcido,-a.
transmission [trænz'mɪʃən] *n* transmisión.
transmit [trænz'mɪt] *t* transmitir.
transmitter [trænz'mɪtəʳ] *n (apparatus)* transmisor *m*. **2** RAD TV emisora.

transparence [træns'peərəns] *n* transparencia.

transparency [træns'peərensɪ] *n* transparencia. **2** *(slide)* diapositiva.

transparent [træns'peərənt] *adj* transparente.

transpiration [trænspɪ'reɪʃən] *n* transpiración.

transpire [træns'paɪəʳ] *t-i* transpirar. **2** *fam (happen)* pasar, ocurrir.

transplant ['trænsplɑːnt] *n* transplante *m*. **− 2** *t* transplantar. ▲ *En* 2 *(verbo)* [træns'plɑːnt].

transport ['trænspɔːt] *n* transporte *m*. **− 2** *t* transportar. ▲ *En* 2 *(verbo)* [træns'pɔːt].

transportation [trænspɔː'teɪʃən] *n* transporte *m*.

transporter [træns'pɔːtəʳ] *n* transportador *m*.

transpose [træns'pəʊz] *t* transponer. **2** MUS transportar.

transversal [trænz'vɜːsəl] *adj* transversal.

transvestite [trænz'vestaɪt] *n* travestido,-a, travesti *m*, travestí *m*.

trap [træp] *n* trampa. **− 2** *t* atrapar. ●*to set a* ~, tender una trampa.

trapeze [trə'piːz] *n* trapecio.

trapper ['træpəʳ] *n* trampero,-a.

trappings ['træpɪŋz] *npl* adornos *mpl*, atavíos *mpl*.

trash [træʃ] *n* pacotilla. **2** US basura.

trashy ['træʃɪ] *adj* de pacotilla.

traumatic [trɔː'mætɪk] *adj* traumático,-a.

travel ['trævəl] *n* viajes *mpl*. **− 2** *i* viajar. ■ ~ *agency,* agencia de viajes.

traveller ['trævələʳ] *n* viajero,-a. **2** COM viajante *mf*. ■ *traveller's cheque,* cheque *m* de viaje.

travelling ['trævəlɪŋ] *adj* ambulante. **− 2** *n* viajar *m*. ■ ~ *expenses,* gastos *mpl* de viaje.

travel-sick ['trævəlsɪk] *adj* mareado,-a.

travel-sickness ['trævəlsɪknəs] *n* mareo.

traverse [trə'vɜːs] *t* cruzar, atravesar.

travesty ['trævəstɪ] *n* parodia. **− 2** *t* parodiar.

trawl [trɔːl] *n* red *f* barredera. **− 2** *i* pescar al arrastre.

trawler ['trɔːləʳ] *n* barco de arrastre.

tray [treɪ] *n* bandeja.

treacherous ['tretʃərəs] *adj* traidor,-ra, traicionero,-a. **2** *(dangerous)* muy peligroso,-a.

treachery ['tretʃərɪ] *n* traición.

treacle ['triːkəl] *n* GB melaza.

tread [tred] *n* paso. **2** *(on tyre)* dibujo. **− 3** *t-i* pisar. ▲ *pt* **trod**; *pp* **trodden** *o* **trod**.

treason ['triːzən] *n* traición.

treasure ['treʒəʳ] *n* tesoro. **− 2** *t (keep)* guardar como un tesoro. **3** *(value)* apreciar mucho.

treasurer ['treʒərəʳ] *n* tesorero,-a.

treasury ['treʒərɪ] *n* tesorería.

treat [triːt] *n* convite *m*. **2** *(present)* regalo. **3** *(pleasure)* placer *m*, deleite *m*. **− 4** *t* tratar. **5** *(invite)* convidar, invitar.

treatise ['triːtɪs] *n* tratado.

treatment ['triːtmənt] *n* tratamiento. **2** *(behaviour)* trato, conducta.

treaty ['triːtɪ] *n* tratado.

treble ['trebəl] *adj* triple. **2** MUS de tiple. **− 3** *t-i* triplicar(se).

tree [triː] *n* árbol *m*.

trek [trek] *n* viaje *m* (largo y difícil); *(on foot)* caminata. **− 2** *i* viajar; *(on foot)* caminar.

trellis ['trelɪs] *n* enrejado.

tremble ['trembəl] *n* temblor *m*, estremecimiento. **− 2** *i* temblar, estremecerse.

tremendous [trɪ'mendəs] *adj* tremendo,-a, inmenso,-a. **2** *fam (great)* fantástico,-a, estupendo,-a.

tremor ['tremoʳ] *n* temblor *m*.

trench [trentʃ] *n* zanja. **2** MIL trinchera.

trend [trend] *n* tendencia.

trendy ['trendɪ] *adj fam* moderno,-a.

trepidation [trepɪ'deɪʃən] *n* turbación.

trespass ['trespəs] *n* entrada ilegal. **− 2** *i* entrar ilegalmente.

trestle ['tresəl] *n* caballete *m*.

trial ['traɪəl] *n* JUR proceso, juicio. **2** *(test)* prueba. **2** *(suffering)* aflicción.

triangle ['traɪæŋgəl] *n* triángulo.

triangular [traɪ'æŋgjʊləʳ] *adj* triangular.

tribal ['traɪbəl] *adj* tribal.

tribe [traɪb] *n* tribu *f*.

tribulation [trɪbjʊ'leɪʃən] *n* tribulación.

tribunal [traɪ'bjuːnəl] *n* tribunal *m*.

tributary ['trɪbjʊtərɪ] *n* afluente *m*.

tribute ['trɪbjuːt] *n* homenaje *m*. **2** *(payment)* tributo.

trice [traɪs] *n in a* ~, en un santiamén.

trick [trɪk] *n (skill, magic)* truco. **2** *(deception)* ardid *m*, engaño. **3** *(joke)* broma. **4** *(cards won)* baza. **− 5** *t* engañar. **6** *(swindle)* timar, estafar. ●*to play a* ~ *on,* gastar una broma a.

trickery ['trɪkərɪ] *n* superchería, engaño.

trickle ['trɪkəl] *n* goteo, hilo. **− 2** *i* gotear.

tricky ['trɪkɪ] *adj* taimado,-a, astuto,-a. **2** *(difficult)* difícil, delicado,-a.

tricycle ['traɪsɪkəl] *n* triciclo.

trident ['traɪdənt] *n* tridente *m*.

trifle ['traɪfəl] *n* fruslería, bagatela, nimiedad. 2 CULIN GB postre *m de bizcocho borracho, fruta, gelatina, crema y nata*. — 3 *i* jugar (*with*, con).

trifling ['traɪfəlɪŋ] *adj* insignificante.

trigger ['trɪgər] *n* disparador *m*. 2 *(of gun)* gatillo. — 3 *t* desencadenar.

trigonometry [trɪgə'nɒmətrɪ] *n* trigonometría.

trill [trɪl] *n* trino. — 2 *t-i* trinar.

trillion ['trɪlɪən] *n* GB trillón *m*. 2 US billón *m*.

trilogy ['trɪlədʒɪ] *n* trilogía.

trim [trɪm] *adj* bien arreglado,-a. 2 *(person)* aseado,-a. — 3 *n (cut)* recorte *m*. 4 *(condition)* estado, condiciones *fpl*. — 5 *t* arreglar. 6 *(cut)* recortar. 7 *(decorate)* decorar. ●*in* ~, en forma.

trimmings ['trɪmɪŋs] *npl* adornos *mpl*, decoración *f sing*. 2 CULIN guarnición *f sing*.

trio ['triːəʊ] *n* trío.

trinket ['trɪŋkɪt] *n* baratija.

trip [trɪp] *n* viaje *m*. 2 *(excursion)* excursión. 3 *sl (drugs)* viaje. — 4 *i* tropezar. — 5 *t to* ~ *(up)*, zancadillear.

tripe [traɪp] *n* CULIN callos *mpl*. 2 *fam* bobadas *fpl*.

triple ['trɪpəl] *adj* triple. — 2 *t-i* triplicar(se).

triplet ['trɪplət] *n* trillizo,-a.

triplicate ['trɪplɪkət] *adj in* ~, por triplicado,-a.

tripod ['traɪpɒd] *n* trípode *m*.

trite [traɪt] *adj* gastado,-a, trillado,-a.

triumph ['traɪəmf] *n* triunfo. 2 *(joy)* júbilo. — 3 *i* triunfar.

triumphal [traɪ'ʌmfəl] *adj* triunfal.

triumphant [traɪ'ʌmfənt] *adj* triunfante.

trivial ['trɪvɪəl] *adj* trivial.

trod [trɒd] *pt & pp* → **tread**.

trodden ['trɒdən] *pp* → **tread**.

trolley ['trɒlɪ] *n* carro, carrito.

trombone [trɒm'bəʊn] *n* trombón *m*.

troop [truːp] *n* grupo, banda. 2 MIL tropa. — 3 *i* marchar/ir (en masa).

trooper ['truːpər] *n* soldado de caballería.

trophy ['trəʊfɪ] *n* trofeo.

tropic ['trɒpɪk] *n* trópico.

tropical ['trɒpɪkəl] *adj* tropical.

trot [trɒt] *n* trote *m*. — 2 *i* trotar. ●*on the* ~, seguidos,-as.

trotter ['trɒtər] *n (pig's)* mano *f*, pie *m*.

trouble ['trʌbəl] *n (problem)* problema *m*, dificultad. 2 *(worry)* preocupación. 3

(anxiety) ansiedad, pena. 4 *(inconvenience)* molestia. — 5 *t (worry)* preocupar. — 6 *t-i (bother)* molestar(se). ●*to be in* ~, estar en un apuro; *it's not worth the* ~, no vale la pena; *fam to get sb. into* ~, dejar embarazada a algn. ■ ~ *spot*, punto conflictivo.

trouble-free ['trʌbəlfriː] *adj* sin problemas.

troublemaker ['trʌbəlmeɪkər] *n* alborotador,-ra.

troubleshooter ['trʌbəlʃuːtər] *n* conciliador,-ra, mediador,-ra.

troublesome ['trʌbəlsəm] *adj* molesto,-a, fastidioso,-a.

trounce [traʊns] *t* zurrar.

trough [trɒf] *n (for water)* abrevadero. 2 *(for food)* comedero. 3 METEOR depresión.

troupe [truːp] *n* compañía.

trousers ['traʊzəz] *npl* pantalón *m sing*, pantalones *mpl*.

trousseau ['truːsəʊ] *n* ajuar *m* de novia. ▲ *pl* **trousseaus** *o* **trousseaux**.

trout [traʊt] *n* trucha.

trowel ['traʊəl] *n* paleta. 2 *(garden tool)* desplantador *m*.

truant ['truːənt] *n to play* ~, hacer novillos.

truce [truːs] *n* tregua.

truck [trʌk] *n* GB vagón *m*. 2 US camión *m*.

trucker ['trʌkər] *n* US camionero,-a.

truculent ['trʌkjʊlənt] *adj* agresivo,-a.

trudge [trʌdʒ] *i* andar penosamente.

true [truː] *adj* verdadero,-a, cierto,-a. 2 *(genuine)* auténtico,-a, genuino,-a. 3 *(faithful)* fiel, leal. 4 *(exact)* exacto,-a. ●*it's* ~, es verdad.

truffle ['trʌfəl] *n* trufa.

truism ['truːɪzəm] *n* perogrullada.

truly ['truːlɪ] *adv* verdaderamente. ●*yours* ~, atentamente.

trump [trʌmp] *n* triunfo. — 2 *t* matar con un triunfo. ◆*to* ~ *up t* inventar.

trumpet ['trʌmpɪt] *n* trompeta.

truncate [trʌŋ'keɪt] *t* truncar.

truncheon ['trʌntʃən] *n* porra.

trunk [trʌŋk] *n (of tree, body)* tronco. 2 *(box)* baúl *m*, mundo. 3 *(elephant's)* trompa. 4 US AUTO maletero. 5 *pl* bañador *m sing*. ■ ~ *call*, conferencia interurbana.

truss [trʌs] *t* atar. — 2 *n* MED braguero.

trust [trʌst] *n* confianza, fe *f*. 2 *(responsibility)* responsabilidad. 3 FIN trust *m*. 4

(care) custodia. **– 5** *t* confiar en, fiarse de. **6** *(hope)* esperar.

trustee [trʌs'tiː] *n* fideicomisario,-a, depositario,-a.

trustful ['trʌstfʊl], **trusting** ['trʌstɪŋ] *adj* confiado,-a.

trustworthy ['trʌstwɜːðɪ] *adj* digno,-a de confianza. **2** *(news etc.)* fidedigno,-a.

truth [truːθ] *n* verdad.

truthful ['truːθfʊl] *adj* verídico,-a. **2** *(person)* veraz.

truthfulness ['truːθfʊlnəs] *n* veracidad.

try [traɪ] *n* intento, tentativa. **2** *(rugby)* ensayo. **– 3** *t-i (attempt)* intentar. **– 4** *t* probar. **5** JUR juzgar. **6** *(test)* probar, poner a prueba. ◆*to* ~ *on t* probarse. ◆*to* ~ *out t* probar.

trying ['traɪɪŋ] *adj* molesto,-a.

tsar [zɑːʳ] *n* zar *m*.

tsarina [zɑː'riːnə] *n* zarina.

tsetse fly ['tsetsɪflaɪ] *n* mosca tsetsé.

tub [tʌb] *n* tina. **2** *(bath)* bañera, baño.

tuba ['tjuːbə] *n* tuba.

tubby ['tʌbɪ] *adj* rechoncho,-a.

tube [tjuːb] *n* tubo. **2** ANAT trompa. **3** *(underground)* metro.

tubeless ['tjuːbləs] *adj* sin cámara.

tuber ['tjuːbəʳ] *n* tubérculo.

tuberculosis [tjʊbɜːkjʊ'ləʊsɪs] *n* tuberculosis *f inv*.

tubular ['tjuːbjʊləʳ] *adj* tubular.

tuck [tʌk] *n* pliegue *m*. **– 2** *t to* ~ *(in/into etc.)*, meter: *to* ~ *in the bedclothes*, remeter la ropa de la cama. ◆*to* ~ *in i* comer con apetito.

Tuesday ['tjuːzdɪ] *n* martes *m inv*.

tuft [tʌft] *n (feathers)* copete *m*. **2** *(hair)* mechón *m*. **3** *(grass)* mata.

tug [tʌɡ] *n* tirón *m*, estirón *m*. **2** *(boat)* remolcador *m*. **– 3** *t* tirar de, arrastrar. **4** *(boat)* remolcar.

tugboat ['tʌɡbəʊt] *n* remolcador *m*.

tuition [tjʊ'ɪʃən] *n* enseñanza, instrucción.

tulip ['tjuːlɪp] *n* tulipán *m*.

tumble ['tʌmbəl] *n* caída, tumbo. **– 2** *i* caer(se). **■** ~ *dryer,* secadora.

tumbledown ['tʌmbəldaʊn] *adj* ruinoso,-a.

tumbler ['tʌmbələʳ] *n* vaso.

tummy ['tʌmɪ] *n fam* barriguita.

tumour ['tjuːməʳ] *n* tumor *m*.

tumult ['tjuːmʌlt] *n* tumulto.

tumultuous [tjuː'mʌltjʊəs] *adj* tumultuoso,-a.

tuna ['tjuːnə] *n inv* atún *m*, bonito.

tundra ['tʌndrə] *n* tundra.

tune [tjuːn] *n* melodía. **– 2** *t* MUS afinar. **3** *(engine)* poner a punto. ◆*to* ~ *in to t* RAD sintonizar. ●*in* ~, afinado,-a; *out of* ~, desafinado,-a; *to sing out of* ~, desafinar.

tuneful ['tjuːnfʊl] *adj* melodioso,-a.

tuner ['tjuːnəʳ] *n* afinador,-ra. **2** *(radio)* sintonizador *m*.

tungsten ['tʌŋstən] *n* tungsteno.

tunic ['tjuːnɪk] *n* túnica.

tuning fork ['tjuːnɪŋfɔːk] *n* diapasón *m*.

tunnel ['tʌnəl] *n* túnel *m*. **– 2** *t* abrir un túnel.

tunny ['tʌnɪ] *n* atún *m*, bonito.

turban ['tɜːbən] *n* turbante *m*.

turbine ['tɜːbaɪn] *n* turbina.

turbojet ['tɜːbəʊdʒet] *n* turborreactor *m*.

turbot ['tɜːbət] *n inv* rodaballo.

turbulence ['tɜːbjʊləns] *n* turbulencia.

turbulent ['tɜːbjʊlənt] *adj* turbulento,-a.

tureen [təˈriːn] *n* sopera.

turf [tɜːf] *n* césped *m*. ◆*to* ~ *out t fam* poner de patitas en la calle. **■** *the* ~, las carreras de caballos.

turkey ['tɜːkɪ] *n* pavo.

turmoil ['tɜːmɔɪl] *n* confusión, alboroto.

turn [tɜːn] *n* vuelta, giro, revolución. **2** *(bend)* recodo. **3** *(in game)* turno. **4** *(favour)* favor *m*. **5** *(turning)* bocacalle *f*. **6** *fam (shock)* susto. **– 7** *t* girar, dar la vuelta a: *to* ~ *the corner,* doblar la esquina. **8** *(page)* pasar. **9** *(change)* convertir, transformar. **– 10** *i* girar, dar vueltas. **11** *(person)* girarse, dar la vuelta. **12** *(direction)* torcer. **13** *(become)* hacerse, ponerse, volverse. ◆*to* ~ *away t* rechazar. **– 2** *i* volver la cabeza. ◆*to* ~ *back t-i* (hacer) retroceder. ◆*to* ~ *down t (reject)* rechazar. **2** *(radio etc.)* bajar. ◆*to* ~ *in t* entregar a la policía. **2** *i fam* acostarse. ◆*to* ~ *off t (electricity)* desconectar. **2** *(light, gas)* apagar. **3** *(water)* cerrar. **– 4** *t-i* desviarse (de). ◆*to* ~ *on t (electricity)* conectar. **2** *(light)* encender. **3** *(gas, tap)* abrir. **4** *(machine)* poner en marcha. **5** *(attack)* atacar. **6** *fam* chiflar. ◆*to* ~ *out t (gas, light)* apagar. **2** *(produce)* producir. **3** *(empty)* vaciar. **– 4** *i (prove to be)* salir, resultar. **5** *(attend)* acudir. **6** *(crowds)* salir a la calle. ◆*to* ~ *over t* dar la vuelta a. **2** *(idea)* dar vueltas a. **3** COM facturar. **– 4** *i* darse la vuelta, volcarse. ◆*to* ~ *to t (person)* acudir a. **2** *(page)* buscar. ◆*to* ~ *up i* aparecer. **2** *(arrive)* presentarse, llegar. **– 3** *t (light, gas, etc.)* subir.

turncoat ['tɜːnkəʊt] *n* tránsfuga *mf*.

turning ['tɜːnɪŋ] *n* bocacalle *f*, esquina. **■** ~ *point,* punto decisivo.

turnip ['tɜːnɪp] *n* nabo.
turnout ['tɜːnaʊt] *n* asistencia, concurrencia.
turnover ['tɜːnəʊvə^r] *n* COM facturación.
turnpike ['tɜːnpaɪk] *n* US autopista de peaje.
turnstile ['tɜːnstaɪl] *n* torniquete *m*.
turntable ['tɜːnteɪbəl] *n* plato giratorio.
turn-up ['tɜːnʌp] *n* GB vuelta.
turpentine ['tɜːpəntaɪn] *n* trementina, aguarrás *m*.
turquoise ['tɜːkwɔɪz] *n (gem)* turquesa. 2 *(colour)* azul *m* turquesa. – 3 *adj* de color turquesa.
turret ['tʌrət] *n* torrecilla.
turtle ['tɜːtəl] *n* tortuga.
turtleneck ['tɜːtəlnek] *n* cuello cisne/alto.
tusk [tʌsk] *n* colmillo.
tussle ['tʌsəl] *n* pelea. – 2 *i* pelearse.
tutor ['tjuːtə^r] *n* profesor,-ra particular. 2 *(at university)* tutor,-ra.
tutorial [tjuːˈtɔːriəl] *n clase con grupo reducido.*
tuxedo [tʌkˈsiːdəʊ] *n* US esmoquin *m*.
twaddle ['twɒdəl] *n fam* tonterías *fpl.*
twang [twæŋ] *n* sonido vibrante. 2 *(through nose)* gangueo.
tweak [twiːk] *t* pellizcar.
tweed [twiːd] *n* tweed *m*.
tweet [twiːt] *n* pío. – 2 *i* piar.
tweezers ['twiːzəz] *npl* pinzas *fpl.*
twelfth [twelfθ] *adj-n* duodécimo,-a. – 2 *n (fraction)* duodécimo, duodécima parte. ■ ~ **night,** noche *f* de reyes.
twelve [twelv] *adj-n* doce *(m).*
twentieth ['twentɪəθ] *adj-n* vigésimo,-a. – 2 *n* vigésimo, vigésima parte.
twenty ['twentɪ] *adj-n* veinte *(m).*
twice [twaɪs] *adv* dos veces. ~ **as big as this one,** el doble de grande que este.
twiddle ['twɪdəl] *t* dar vueltas a.

twig [twɪg] *n* ramita. – 2 *i* caer en la cuenta.
twilight ['twaɪlaɪt] *n* crepúsculo.
twin [twɪn] *n* gemelo,-a, mellizo,-a. – 2 *t* hermanar.
twine [twaɪn] *n* cordel *m*. – 2 *t* enroscar.
twinge [twɪndʒ] *n* punzada.
twinkle ['twɪŋkəl] *n* centelleo. 2 *(in eye)* brillo. – 3 *i* centellear. 4 *(eyes)* brillar.
twirl [twɜːl] *n* giro rápido. – 2 *t-i* girar rápidamente. 3 *(spin)* retorcer.
twist [twɪst] *n (in road)* recodo, vuelta. 2 *(action)* torsión. 3 MED torcedura. 4 *(dance)* twist *m*. – 5 *t-i* torcer(se), retorcer(se). – 6 *i (road)* serpentear. 7 *(dance)* bailar el twist.
twit [twɪt] *n fam* tonto,-a.
twitch [twɪtʃ] *n* tirón. 2 *(nervous)* tic *m* nervioso. – 3 *t* tirar de, dar un tirón a. – 4 *i* moverse nerviosamente.
twitter ['twɪtə^r] *n* gorjeo. – 2 *i* gorjear.
two [tuː] *adj-n* dos *(m).*
twofaced [tuːˈfeɪst] *adj* hipócrita.
two-piece ['tuːpiːs] *adj* de dos piezas.
tycoon [taɪˈkuːn] *n* magnate *m*.
type [taɪp] *n* tipo, clase *f*. 2 *(letter)* letra, carácter *m*. – 3 *t* pasar/escribir a máquina, mecanografiar.
typewriter ['taɪpraɪtə^r] *n* máquina de escribir.
typewritten ['taɪprɪtən] *adj* escrito,-a a máquina.
typhoid ['taɪfɔɪd] *n* fiebre *f* tifoidea.
typhoon [taɪˈfuːn] *n* tifón *m*.
typical ['tɪpɪkəl] *adj* típico,-a.
typify ['tɪpɪfaɪ] *t* tipificar.
typing ['taɪpɪŋ] *n* mecanografía.
typist ['taɪpɪst] *n* mecanógrafo,-a.
tyrannical [tɪˈrænɪkəl] *adj* tiránico,-a
tyrannize ['tɪrənaɪz] *t* tiranizar.
tyranny ['tɪrənɪ] *n* tiranía.
tyrant ['taɪərənt] *n* tirano,-a.
tyre ['taɪə^r] *n* neumático.

U

ubiquitous [juːˈbɪkwɪtəs] *adj* ubicuo,-a.
udder [ˈʌdəʳ] *n* ubre *f*.
ufo [ˈjuːfəʊ], **UFO** [juːefˈəʊ] *n fam* ovni *m*.
ugliness [ˈʌglɪnəs] *n* fealdad.
ugly [ˈʌglɪ] *adj* feo,-a. **2** *(situation etc.)* desagradable.
ulcer [ˈʌlsəʳ] *n* llaga. **2** *(in stomach)* úlcera.
ulcerate [ˈʌlsəreɪt] *t-i* ulcerar(se).
ulterior [ʌlˈtɪərɪəʳ] *adj* oculto,-a.
ultimate [ˈʌltɪmət] *adj* último,-a, final. — **2 ultimately** *adv* finalmente. **3** *(basically)* en el fondo.
ultimatum [ʌltɪˈmeɪtəm] *n* ultimátum *m*.
ultraviolet [ʌltrəˈvaɪələt] *adj* ultravioleta.
umbilical [ʌmˈbɪlɪkəl] *adj* umbilical. ■ ~ *cord,* cordón *m* umbilical.
umbrage [ˈʌmbrɪdʒ] *n* **to take** ~, ofenderse.
umbrella [ʌmˈbrelə] *n* paraguas *m inv*. ■ *beach* ~, sombrilla.
umpire [ˈʌmpaɪəʳ] *n* árbitro. — **2** *t* arbitrar.
umpteen [ʌmpˈtiːn] *adj fam* la tira de, un montón de.
umpteenth [ʌmpˈtiːnθ] *adj* enésimo,-a.
unabashed [ˈʌnəˈbæʃt] *adj* descarado,-a.
unable [ʌnˈeɪbəl] *adj* **to be** ~ **to**, no poder.
unabridged [ʌnəˈbrɪdʒd] *adj* íntegro,-a.
unacceptable [ʌnəkˈseptəbəl] *adj* inaceptable.
unaccompanied [ʌnəˈkʌmpənɪd] *adj* solo,-a. **2** MUS sin acompañamiento.
unaccountable [ʌnəˈkauntəbəl] *adj* inexplicable.
unadvisable [ʌnədˈvaɪzəbəl] *adj* poco aconsejable.
unadulterated [ʌnəˈdʌltəreɪtɪd] *adj* puro,-a.
unaffected [ʌnəˈfektɪd] *adj* no afectado,-a. **2** *(natural)* sencillo,-a, natural.
unafraid [ʌnəˈfreɪd] *adj* impertérrito,-a.

unanimity [juːnəˈnɪmɪtɪ] *n* unanimidad.
unanimous [juːˈnænɪməs] *adj* unánime.
unanswerable [ʌnˈɑːnsərəbəl] *adj* incontestable.
unapproachable [ʌnəˈprəʊtʃəbəl] *adj* inaccesible.
unarmed [ʌnˈɑːmd] *adj* desarmado,-a.
unassailable [ʌnəˈseɪləbəl] *adj* inexpugnable.
unassuming [ʌnəˈsjuːmɪŋ] *adj* modesto,-a.
unattached [ʌnəˈtætʃt] *adj* suelto,-a. **2** *(person)* sin compromiso.
unattainable [ʌnəˈteɪnəbəl] *adj* inasequible.
unattended [ʌnəˈtendɪd] *adj* sin vigilar.
unauthorized [ʌnˈɔːθəraɪzd] *adj* no autorizado,-a.
unavailable [ʌnəˈveɪləbəl] *adj* no disponible.
unavoidable [ʌnəˈvɔɪdəbəl] *adj* inevitable, ineludible.
unaware [ʌnəˈweəʳ] *adj* ignorante. ●**to be** ~ **of**, ignorar.
unawares [ʌnəˈweəz] *adv* desprevenido,-a. **2** *(unintentionally)* inconscientemente, sin darse cuenta.
unbalanced [ʌnˈbælənst] *adj* desequilibrado,-a.
unbearable [ʌnˈbeərəbəl] *adj* insoportable.
unbeatable [ʌnˈbiːtəbəl] *adj* sin rival/igual.
unbecoming [ʌnbɪˈkʌmɪŋ] *adj* impropio,-a.
unbelievable [ʌnbɪˈliːvəbəl] *adj* increíble.
unbias(s)ed [ʌnˈbaɪəst] *adj* imparcial.
unborn [ʌnˈbɔːn] *adj* aún no nacido,-a. **2** *fig* nonato,-a.
unbosom [ʌnˈbuzəm] *t* **to** ~ **o.s.**, desahogarse.

unbounded [ʌn'baʊndɪd] *adj* ilimitado,-a, infinito,-a.

unbreakable [ʌn'breɪkəbəl] *adj* irrompible.

unbridled [ʌn'braɪdld] *adj* desenfrenado,-a.

unbroken [ʌn'brəʊkən] *adj* entero,-a, intacto,-a. **2** *(uninterrupted)* ininterrumpido,-a. **3** *(record)* imbatido,-a.

unburden [ʌn'bɜːdən] *t* descargar. ●*to ~ o.s.,* desahogarse.

unbutton [ʌn'bʌtən] *t* desabrochar.

uncalled-for [ʌn'kɔːldfɔːʳ] *adj* injustificado,-a.

uncanny [ʌn'kænɪ] *adj* misterioso,-a, extraño,-a.

uncared-for [ʌn'keədfɔː] *adj* descuidado,-a.

unceasing [ʌn'siːsɪŋ] *adj* incesante.

uncertain [ʌn'sɜːtən] *adj* incierto,-a, dudoso,-a. **2** *(indecisive)* indeciso,-a.

uncertainty [ʌn'sɜːtəntɪ] *n* incertidumbre *f.*

unchangeable [ʌn'tʃeɪndʒəbəl] *adj* inmutable.

unchanged [ʌn'tʃeɪndʒd] *adj* igual.

uncharitable [ʌn'tʃærɪtəbəl] *adj* poco caritativo,-a.

unchecked [ʌn'tʃekt] *adj* no comprobado,-a. **2** *(unrestrained)* desenfrenado,-a.

uncivil [ʌn'sɪvəl] *adj* descortés.

uncivilized [ʌn'sɪvɪlaɪzd] *adj* incivilizado,-a.

uncle ['ʌŋkəl] *n* tío.

unclear [ʌn'klɪər] *adj* poco claro,-a.

uncoil [ʌn'kɔɪl] *t-i* desenrollar(se).

uncomfortable [ʌn'kʌmfətəbəl] *adj* incómodo,-a.

uncommon [ʌn'kɒmən] *adj* poco común. **2** *(strange)* insólito,-a. **– 3** *uncommonly adv* extraordinariamente.

uncommunicative [ʌnkə'mjuːnɪkətɪv] *adj* poco comunicativo,-a.

uncomplimentary [ʌnkɒmplɪ'mëntərɪ] *adj* poco halagüeño,-a.

uncompromising [ʌn'kɒmprəmaɪzɪŋ] *adj* inflexible, intransigente.

unconcerned [ʌnkən'sɜːnd] *adj* indiferente.

unconditional [ʌnkən'dɪʃənəl] *adj* incondicional.

unconscious [ʌn'kɒnʃəs] *adj* inconsciente.

unconsciousness [ʌn'kɒnʃəsnəs] *n* pérdida del conocimiento.

unconstitutional [ʌnkɒnstɪ'tjuːʃənəl] *adj* inconstitucional.

uncontrollable [ʌnkən'trəʊləbəl] *adj* incontrolable.

unconventional [ʌnkən'venʃənəl] *adj* poco convencional.

uncooperative [ʌnkəʊ'ɒpərətɪv] *adj* poco cooperativo,-a.

uncork [ʌn'kɔːk] *t* descorchar.

uncouth [ʌn'kuːθ] *adj* tosco,-a, inculto,-a.

uncover [ʌn'kʌvəʳ] *t* destapar. **2** *(secret)* revelar.

uncultivated [ʌn'kʌltɪveɪtɪd] *adj (land)* yermo,-a, baldío,-a. **2** *(person)* inculto,-a.

uncut [ʌn'kʌt] *adj* sin cortar. **2** *(gem)* sin tallar. **2** *(film)* íntegro,-a.

undaunted [ʌn'dɔːntɪd] *adj* impávido,-a.

undecided [ʌndɪ'saɪdɪd] *adj* indeciso,-a. **2** *(question)* no resuelto,-a.

undecipherable [ʌndɪ'saɪfrəbəl] *adj* indescifrable.

undefeated [ʌndɪ'fiːtɪd] *adj* invicto,-a.

undefended [ʌndɪ'fendɪd] *adj* indefenso,-a.

undefined [ʌndɪ'faɪnd] *adj* indefinido,-a.

undeniable [ʌndɪ'naɪəbəl] *adj* innegable, indiscutible.

under ['ʌndəʳ] *prep* bajo, debajo de. **2** *(less than)* menos de. **3** *(ruler)* bajo: ~ *Cromwell,* bajo Cromwell. **4** *(according to)* conforme a, según. **– 5** *adv* abajo, debajo.

underarm ['ʌndərɑːm] *adj-adv* SP por debajo del hombro. **– 2** *adj (of the armpit)* axilar.

undercarriage ['ʌndəkærɪdʒ] *n* tren *m* de aterrizaje.

undercharge [ʌndə'tʃɑːdʒ] *t* cobrar menos de lo debido.

underclothes ['ʌndəkləʊðz] *npl* ropa *f sing* interior.

undercoat ['ʌndəkəʊt] *n (of paint)* primera mano *f.*

undercover [ʌndə'kʌvəʳ] *adj* clandestino,-a.

undercurrent ['ʌndəkʌrənt] *n* corriente *f* submarina. **2** *fig* tendencia oculta.

undercut [ʌndə'kʌt] *t* vender más barato que. ▲ *pt & pp* **undercut.**

underdeveloped [ʌndədɪ'veləpt] *adj* subdesarrollado,-a.

underdog ['ʌndədɒg] *n* desvalido,-a, perdedor,-ra.

underdone [ʌndə'dʌn] *adj* CULIN poco hecho,-a.

underestimate [ʌndər'estɪmət] *n* infravaloración. **– 2** *t* subestimar. ▲ *En 2 (verbo)* [ʌndər'estɪmeɪt].

underexposure [ʌndərɪk'spəʊʒə'] *n* (*of photo*) subexposición.

undergo [ʌndə'gəʊ] *t* experimentar, sufrir. ▲ *pt* **underwent**; *pp* **undergone** [ʌndə'gɒn].

undergraduate [ʌndə'grædjʊət] *n* estudiante *mf* universitario,-a no licenciado,-a.

underground ['ʌndəgraʊnd] *adj* subterráneo. 2 *fig* clandestino,-a. – 3 *n* (*railway*) metro. 4 (*resistance*) resistencia. – 5 *adv* bajo tierra. 6 (*secretly*) en secreto. ▲ *En 5 y 6* (*adverbio*) [ʌndə'graʊnd].

undergrowth ['ʌndəgrəʊθ] *n* maleza.

underhand ['ʌndəhænd] *adj* ilícito,-a, deshonesto,-a.

underline [ʌndə'laɪn] *t* subrayar.

underlying [ʌndə'laɪɪŋ] *adj* subyacente. 2 *fig* fundamental.

undermine [ʌndə'maɪn] *t* minar, socavar.

underneath [ʌndə'ni:θ] *prep* debajo de. – 2 *adv* debajo. – 3 *n* parte *f* inferior.

underpaid [ʌndə'peɪd] *t* mal pagado,-a.

underpants ['ʌndəpænts] *npl* calzoncillos *mpl*, eslip *m sing*.

underpass ['ʌndəpæs] *n* paso subterráneo.

underrate [ʌndə'reɪt] *t* subestimar.

undersigned [ʌndə'saɪnd] *adj-n* abajo firmante (*mf*).

underskirt ['ʌndəskɜ:t] *n* combinación.

understaffed [ʌndə'stɑ:ft] *adj* falto,-a de personal.

understand [ʌndə'stænd] *t* entender, comprender. 2 (*believe*) tener entendido. ●*to give to ~,* dar a entender. ▲ *pt & pp* **understood**.

understandable [ʌndə'stændəbəl] *adj* comprensible.

understanding [ʌndə'stændɪŋ] *n* entendimiento. 2 (*agreement*) acuerdo. 3 (*condition*) condición. 4 (*interpretation*) interpretación. – 5 *adj* comprensivo,-a.

understatement [ʌndə'steɪtmənt] *n* atenuación; *it's an ~ to say that ...,* es quedarse corto decir... .

understood [ʌndə'stʊd] *pt & pp* → **understand**. ●*to make o.s. ~,* hacerse entender.

understudy ['ʌndəstʌdɪ] *n* THEAT suplente *mf*.

undertake [ʌndə'teɪk] *t* emprender; (*responsibility*) asumir. 2 (*promise*) comprometerse (*to,* a). ▲ *pt* **undertook**; *pp* **undertaken** [ʌndə'teɪkən].

undertaker ['ʌndəteɪkə'] *n* empresario,-a de pompas fúnebres.

undertaking [ʌndə'teɪkɪŋ] *n* empresa. 2 (*promise*) promesa.

undertone ['ʌndətəʊn] *n* voz *f* baja.

undertook [ʌndə'tʊk] *pt* → **undertake**.

undervalue [ʌndə'vælju:] *t* infravalorar.

underwater [ʌndə'wɔ:tə'] *adj* submarino,-a. – 2 *adv* bajo el agua.

underwear ['ʌndəwɛ:ə'] *n* ropa interior.

underwent [ʌndə'went] *pt* → **undergo**.

underworld ['ʌndəwɜ:ld] *n* hampa, bajos fondos *mpl*. 2 (*Hades*) el Hades.

underwrite [ʌndə'raɪt] *t* asegurar. 2 *fig* garantizar. ▲ *pt* **underwrote** [ʌndə'rəʊt]; *pp* **underwritten** [ʌndə'rɪtən].

underwriter ['ʌndəraɪtə'] *n* asegurador,-ra.

undeserved [ʌndɪ'zɜ:vd] *adj* inmerecido,-a.

undesirable [ʌndɪ'zaɪərəbəl] *adj-n* indeseable (*mf*).

undeveloped [ʌndɪ'veləpt] *adj* sin desarrollar. 2 (*land*) sin edificar.

undid [ʌn'dɪd] *pt* → **undo**.

undisciplined [ʌn'dɪsɪplɪnd] *adj* indisciplinado,-a.

undisputed [ʌndɪs'pju:tɪd] *adj* indiscutible.

undivided [ʌndɪ'vaɪdɪd] *adj* entero,-a.

undo [ʌn'du:] *t* deshacer. 2 (*button*) desabrochar. ●*to leave sth. undone,* dejar algo sin hacer. ▲ *pt* **undid**; *pp* **undone** [ʌn'dʌn].

undoubted [ʌn'daʊtɪd] *adj* indudable.

undreamed-of [ʌn'dri:mdɒv] *adj* nunca soñado,-a.

undress [ʌn'dres] *t-i* desnudar(se), desvestir(se).

undue [ʌn'dju:] *adj* indebido,-a, excesivo,-a.

undulate ['ʌndjʊleɪt] *i* ondular, ondear.

unduly [ʌn'dju:lɪ] *adv* indebidamente.

undying [ʌn'daɪɪŋ] *adj* imperecedero,-a.

unearned [ʌn'ɜ:nd] *adj* no ganado,-a. ■ *~ income,* renta.

unearth [ʌn'ɜ:θ] *t* desenterrar.

unearthly [ʌn'ɜ:θlɪ] *adj* sobrenatural. 2 (*hour*) intempestivo,-a.

uneasiness [ʌn'i:zɪnəs] *n* inquietud.

uneasy [ʌn'i:zɪ] *adj* intranquilo,-a, inquieto,-a.

uneconomic(al) [ʌni:kə'nɒmɪk(əl)] *adj* poco rentable.

uneducated [ʌn'edjʊkeɪtɪd] *adj* inculto,-a, ignorante.

unemployed [ʌnɪm'plɔɪd] *adj* parado,-a, sin trabajo.

unemployment [ʌnɪmˈplɔɪmənt] *n* paro, desempleo. ■ ~ *benefit,* subsidio de desempleo.

unending [ʌnˈendɪŋ] *adj* interminable.

unenviable [ʌnˈenvɪəbəl] *adj* poco envidiable.

unequal [ʌnˈiːkwəl] *adj* desigual.

unequalled [ʌnˈiːkwəld] *adj* sin par.

unequivocal [ʌnɪˈkwɪvəkəl] *adj* inequívoco,-a.

unerring [ʌnˈɜːrɪŋ] *adj* infalible.

uneven [ʌnˈiːvən] *adj* desigual. 2 *(varying)* irregular. 3 *(road)* lleno,-a de baches.

unevenness [ʌnˈiːvənnəs] *n* desigualdad.

uneventful [ʌnɪˈventful] *adj* sin acontecimientos, tranquilo,-a.

unexceptional [ʌnɪkˈsepʃənəl] *adj* corriente.

unexpected [ʌnɪkˈspektɪd] *adj* inesperado,-a.

unexplored [ʌnɪkˈsplɔːd] *adj* inexplorado,-a.

unexpurgated [ʌnˈekspɡeɪtɪd] *adj* íntegro,-a.

unfailing [ʌnˈfeɪlɪŋ] *adj* indefectible.

unfair [ʌnˈfeər] *adj* injusto,-a.

unfaithful [ʌnˈfeɪθful] *adj* infiel.

unfaithfulness [ʌnˈfeɪθfulnəs] *n* infidelidad.

unfamiliar [ʌnfəˈmɪlɪər] *adj* desconocido,-a. ●*to be* ~ *with,* desconocer.

unfashionable [ʌnˈfæʃənəbəl] *adj* pasado,-a de moda.

unfasten [ʌnˈfɑːsən] *t* desabrochar. 2 *(untie)* desatar. 3 *(open)* abrir.

unfavourable [ʌnˈfeɪvərəbəl] *adj* desfavorable, adverso,-a.

unfeeling [ʌnˈfiːlɪŋ] *adj* insensible.

unfinished [ʌnˈfɪnɪʃt] *adj* inacabado,-a, incompleto,-a.

unfit [ʌnˈfɪt] *adj* no apto,-a. 2 *(physically)* no en forma. 3 *(injured)* lesionado,-a. 4 *(incompetent)* incompetente.

unfold [ʌnˈfəuld] *t-i* desplegar(se), abrir(se).

unforeseeable [ʌnfɔːˈsiːəbəl] *adj* imprevisible.

unforeseen [ʌnfɔːˈsiːn] *adj* imprevisto,-a.

unforgettable [ʌnfəˈɡetəbəl] *adj* inolvidable.

unforgivable [ʌnfəˈɡɪvəbəl] *adj* imperdonable.

unforgiving [ʌnfəˈɡɪvɪŋ] *adj* implacable.

unfortunate [ʌnˈfɔːtjunət] *adj* desgraciado,-a. 2 *(remark)* desafortunado,-a. – 3 *unfortunately adv* degraciadamente, desafortunadamente.

unfounded [ʌnˈfaundɪd] *adj* infundado,-a, sin base.

unfrequented [ʌnfrɪˈkwentɪd] *adj* poco frecuentado,-a.

unfriendly [ʌnˈfrendlɪ] *adj* poco amistoso, antipático,-a.

unfurl [ʌnˈfɜːl] *t-i* desplegar(se).

unfurnished [ʌnˈfɜːnɪʃt] *adj* sin amueblar.

ungainly [ʌnˈɡeɪnlɪ] *adj* desgarbado,-a, torpe.

ungodly [ʌnˈɡɒdlɪ] *adj* impío,-a. 2 *(hour)* intempestivo,-a.

ungrateful [ʌnˈɡreɪtful] *adj* desagradecido,-a.

unhappily [ʌnˈhæpɪlɪ] *adv* desgraciadamente.

unhappiness [ʌnˈhæpɪnəs] *n* infelicidad, desdicha.

unhappy [ʌnˈhæpɪ] *adj* infeliz, triste. 2 *(unsuitable)* desafortunado,-a.

unharmed [ʌnˈhɑːmd] *adj* ileso,-a.

unhealthy [ʌnˈhelθɪ] *adj* malsano,-a. 2 *(ill)* enfermizo,-a. 3 *(unnatural)* morboso,-a.

unheard [ʌnˈhɜːd] *adj* no oído,-a.

unheard-of [ʌnˈhɜːdəv] *adj* inaudito,-a.

unheeded [ʌnˈhiːdɪd] *adj* desatendido,-a.

unhesitating [ʌnˈhezɪteɪtɪŋ] *adj* resuelto,-a. 2 *(answer)* pronto,-a.

unhinge [ʌnˈhɪndʒ] *t* desquiciar, sacar de quicio.

unhook [ʌnˈhuk] *t* desenganchar. 2 *(take down)* descolgar. 3 *(dress)* desabrochar.

unhurt [ʌnˈhɜːt] *adj* ileso,-a.

unicorn [ˈjuːnɪkɔːn] *n* unicornio.

unidentified [ʌnaɪˈdentɪfaɪd] *adj* no identificado,-a.

unification [juːnɪfɪˈkeɪʃən] *n* unificación.

uniform [ˈjuːnɪfɔːm] *adj-n* uniforme *(m)*.

unify [ˈjuːnɪfaɪ] *t* unificar.

unilateral [juːnɪˈlætərəl] *adj* unilateral.

unimaginable [ʌnɪˈmædʒɪnəbəl] *adj* inimaginable.

unimaginative [ʌnɪˈmædʒɪnətɪv] *adj* poco imaginativo,-a.

unimpaired [ʌnɪmˈpeəd] *adj* no disminuido,-a.

unimportant [ʌnɪmˈpɔːtənt] *adj* insignificante, sin importancia.

uninhabited [ʌnɪˈhæbɪtɪd] *adj* deshabitado,-a.

uninspired [ʌnɪnˈspaɪəd] *adj* soso,-a.

unintelligible [ˌʌnɪnˈtelɪdʒəbəl] *adj* ininteligible.

unintentional [ˌʌnɪnˈtenʃənəl] *adj* involuntario,-a.

uninterested [ʌnˈɪntrəstɪd] *adj* no interesado,-a.

uninteresting [ʌnˈɪntrəstɪŋ] *adj* sin interés.

uninterrupted [ˌʌnɪntəˈrʌptɪd] *adj* ininterrumpido,-a, continuo,-a.

union [ˈjuːnɪən] *n* unión. **2** *(of workers)* sindicato.

unique [juːˈniːk] *adj* único,-a.

unisex [ˈjuːnɪseks] *adj* unisex.

unison [ˈjuːnɪsən] *n in* ~, al unísono.

unit [ˈjuːnɪt] *n* unidad.

unite [juːˈnaɪt] *t-i* unir(se).

unity [ˈjuːnɪtɪ] *n* unidad.

universal [juːnɪˈvɜːsəl] *adj* universal.

universe [ˈjuːnɪvɜːs] *n* universo.

university [juːnɪˈvɜːsɪtɪ] *n* universidad. — **2** *adj* universitario,-a.

unjust [ʌnˈdʒʌst] *adj* injusto,-a.

unjustifiable [ʌndʒʌstɪˈfaɪəbəl] *adj* injustificable.

unjustified [ʌnˈdʒʌstɪfaɪd] *adj* injustificado,-a.

unkempt [ʌnˈkempt] *adj* descuidado,-a. **2** *(hair)* despeinado,-a.

unkind [ʌnˈkaɪnd] *adj* poco amable. **2** *(cruel)* cruel.

unkindness [ʌnˈkaɪndnəs] *n* falta de amabilidad, antipatía. **2** *(cruelty)* crueldad.

unknown [ʌnˈnəʊn] *adj* desconocido,-a. ■ ~ *quantity,* incógnita.

unlawful [ʌnˈlɔːfʊl] *adj* ilegal.

unleash [ʌnˈliːʃ] *t* soltar. **2** *fig* desatar.

unleavened [ʌnˈlevənd] *adj* ácimo,-a.

unless [ənˈles] *conj* a menos que, a no ser que.

unlike [ʌnˈlaɪk] *adj* diferente. — **2** *prep* a diferencia de.

unlikely [ʌnˈlaɪklɪ] *adj* improbable.

unlikelihood [ʌnˈlaɪklɪhʊd] *n* improbabilidad.

unlimited [ʌnˈlɪmɪtɪd] *adj* ilimitado,-a.

unlit [ʌnˈlɪt] *adj* sin luz.

unload [ʌnˈləʊd] *t* descargar.

unlock [ʌnˈlɒk] *t* abrir (con llave).

unlooked-for [ʌnˈlʊktfɔːʳ] *adj* inesperado,-a.

unloosen [ʌnˈluːsən] *t* aflojar. **2** *(set free)* soltar.

unlucky [ʌnˈlʌkɪ] *adj* desafortunado,-a, desgraciado,-a. ●*to be* ~, tener mala suerte.

unmade [ʌnˈmeɪd] *adj (bed)* sin hacer. **2** *(road)* sin asfaltar.

unmanageable [ʌnˈmænɪdʒəbəl] *adj* ingobernable, indomable.

unmanned [ʌnˈmænd] *adj (spacecraft)* no tripulado,-a.

unmarried [ʌnˈmærɪd] *adj* soltero,-a.

unmask [ʌnˈmɑːsk] *t* desenmascarar.

unmatched [ʌnˈmætʃt] *adj* sin par.

unmentionable [ʌnˈmenʃənəbəl] *adj* que no se debe mencionar.

unmerciful [ʌnˈmɜːsɪfʊl] *adj* despiadado,-a.

unmethodical [ʌnmeˈθɒdɪkəl] *adj* poco metódico,-a.

unmitigated [ʌnˈmɪtɪgeɪtɪd] *adj* absoluto,-a, total.

unmistakable [ʌnmɪsˈteɪkəbəl] *adj* inconfundible.

unmoved [ʌnˈmuːvd] *adj* impasible.

unnatural [ʌnˈnætʃərəl] *adj* poco natural. **2** *(perverse)* antinatural.

unnecessary [ʌnˈnesəsərɪ] *adj* innecesario,-a.

unnerve [ʌnˈnɜːv] *t* acobardar.

unnoticed [ʌnˈnəʊtɪst] *adj* inadvertido,-a.

unobserved [ʌnəbˈzɜːvd] *adj* inadvertido,-a.

unobtainable [ʌnəbˈteɪnəbəl] *adj* que no se puede conseguir.

unobtrusive [ʌnɒbˈtruːsɪv] *adj* discreto,-a.

unoccupied [ʌnˈɒkjʊpaɪd] *adj (house)* deshabitado,-a. **2** *(person)* desocupado,-a. **3** *(post)* vacante.

unofficial [ʌnəˈfɪʃəl] *adj* extraoficial, oficioso,-a.

unorthodox [ʌnˈɔːθədɒks] *adj* poco ortodoxo,-a. **2** REL heterodoxo,-a.

unpack [ʌnˈpæk] *t* desempaquetar. **2** *(suitcase)* deshacer. — **3** *i* deshacer las maletas.

unpaid [ʌnˈpeɪd] *adj* sin pagar. **2** *(work)* no retribuido,-a.

unpalatable [ʌmˈpælətəbəl] *adj* desagradable.

unparalleled [ʌnˈpærəleld] *adj* incomparable.

unpardonable [ʌnˈpɑːdənəbəl] *adj* imperdonable.

unperturbed [ʌnpəˈtɜːbd] *adj* impertérrito,-a.

unpick [ʌnˈpɪk] *t* descoser.

unpleasant [ʌnˈplezənt] *adj* desagradable.

unplug [ʌnˈplʌg] *t* desenchufar.

unpolluted [ʌnpə'luːtɪd] *adj* no contaminado,-a.

unpopular [ʌn'pɒpjʊləʳ] *adj* impopular.

unprecedented [ʌn'presɪdentɪd] *adj* sin precedente, inaudito,-a.

unpredictable [ʌnprɪ'dɪktəbəl] *adj* imprevisible.

unprejudiced [ʌn'predʒʊdɪst] *adj* imparcial.

unpretentious [ʌnprɪ'tenʃəs] *adj* modesto,-a, sin pretensiones.

unprincipled [ʌn'prɪnsɪpəld] *adj* sin escrúpulos.

unproductive [ʌnprə'dʌktɪv] *adj* improductivo,-a. **2** *fig* infructuoso,-a.

unprofessional [ʌnprə'feʃənəl] *adj* poco profesional, inexperto,-a.

unprofitable [ʌn'prɒfɪtəbəl] *adj* poco rentable.

unprotected [ʌnprə'tektɪd] *adj* indefenso,-a.

unprovoked [ʌnprə'vəʊkt] *adj* no provocado,-a.

unpublished [ʌn'pʌblɪʃt] *adj* inédito,-a.

unpunished [ʌn'pʌnɪʃt] *adj* impune, sin castigo.

unqualified [ʌn'kwɒlɪfaɪd] *adj* sin título. **2** *(absolute)* incondicional.

unquestionable [ʌn'kwestʃənəbəl] *adj* incuestionable, indiscutible.

unravel [ʌn'rævəl] *t-i* desenmarañar(se).

unreadable [ʌn'riːdəbəl] *adj* ilegible.

unreal [ʌn'rɪəl] *adj* irreal.

unreasonable [ʌn'riːzənəbəl] *adj* poco razonable. **2** *(excessive)* desmesurado,-a.

unrecognizable [ʌnrekəg'naɪzəbəl] *adj* irreconocible.

unrefined [ʌnrɪ'faɪnd] *adj* no refinado,-a. **2** *(person)* inculto,-a, rudo,-a.

unrehearsed [ʌnrɪ'hɜːst] *adj* improvisado,-a.

unrelenting [ʌnrɪ'lentɪŋ] *adj* inexorable.

unreliable [ʌnrɪ'laɪəbəl] *adj* *(person)* de poca confianza. **2** *(machine)* poco fiable. **3** *(news)* poco fidedigno,-a.

unrelieved [ʌnrɪ'liːvd] *adj* absoluto,-a, total.

unremitting [ʌnrɪ'mɪtɪŋ] *adj* incesante.

unrepentant [ʌnrɪ'pentənt] *adj* impenitente.

unrequited [ʌnrɪ'kwaɪtɪd] *adj* no correspondido,-a.

unreserved [ʌnrɪ'zɜːvd] *adj* *(not booked)* no reservado,-a. **2** *(unconditional)* incondicional.

unrest [ʌn'rest] *n* malestar *m*.

unrewarded [ʌnrɪ'wɔːdɪd] *adj* sin recompensa.

unripe [ʌn'raɪp] *adj* verde, inmaduro,-a.

unrivalled [ʌn'raɪvəld] *adj* sin par/rival.

unroll [ʌn'rəʊl] *t-i* desenrollar(se).

unruly [ʌn'ruːlɪ] *adj* revoltoso,-a. **2** *(hair)* rebelde.

unsafe [ʌn'seɪf] *adj* inseguro,-a. **2** *(dangerous)* peligroso,-a.

unsatisfactory [ʌnsætɪs'fæktərɪ] *adj* insatisfactorio,-a.

unsatisfied [ʌn'sætɪsfaɪd] *adj* insatisfecho,-a.

unsavoury [ʌn'seɪvərɪ] *adj* desagradable.

unscathed [ʌn'skeɪðd] *adj* indemne, ileso,-a.

unscrew [ʌn'skruː] *t* destornillar.

unscrupulous [ʌn'skruːpjʊləs] *adj* sin escrúpulos.

unseasonable [ʌn'siːzənəbəl] *adj* atípico,-a.

unseat [ʌn'siːt] *t* POL quitar el escaño a.

unseemly [ʌn'siːmlɪ] *adj* indecoroso,-a.

unselfish [ʌn'selfɪʃ] *adj* desinteresado,-a.

unselfishness [ʌn'selfɪʃnəs] *n* desinterés *m*.

unsettle [ʌn'setəl] *t* perturbar.

unsettled [ʌn'setəld] *adj* *(weather)* inestable.

unshak(e)able [ʌn'ʃeɪkəbəl] *adj* firme.

unshaven [ʌn'ʃeɪvən] *adj* sin afeitar.

unsightly [ʌn'saɪtlɪ] *adj* feo,-a.

unskilled [ʌn'skɪld] *adj* *(worker)* no cualificado,-a. **2** *(job)* no especializado,-a.

unsociable [ʌn'səʊʃəbəl] *adj* insociable.

unsophisticated [ʌnsə'fɪstɪkeɪtɪd] *adj* ingenuo,-a, sencillo,-a.

unsound [ʌn'saʊnd] *adj* defectuoso,-a. **2** *(idea)* erróneo,-a.

unsparing [ʌn'speərɪŋ] *adj* generoso,-a, pródigo,-a.

unspeakable [ʌn'spiːkəbəl] *adj* indecible.

unstable [ʌn'steɪbəl] *adj* inestable.

unsteady [ʌn'stedɪ] *adj* inseguro,-a, inestable.

unstressed [ʌn'strest] *adj* LING átono,-a.

unstuck [ʌn'stʌk] *adj* **to come ~**, despegarse; *fig* fracasar.

unsuccessful [ʌnsək'sesfʊl] *adj* fracasado,-a, sin éxito. ●*to be ~*, no tener éxito, fracasar.

unsuitable [ʌn'suːtəbəl] *adj* *(person)* no apto,-a. **2** *(thing)* inapropiado,-a, impropio,-a.

unsuited [ʌn'suːtɪd] *adj* no apto,-a. **2** *(people)* incompatible.

unsure [ʌnˈʃʊəʳ] *adj* inseguro,-a.

unsurmountable [ʌnsəˈmaʊntəbəl] *adj* insuperable.

unsurpassed [ʌnsəˈpɑːst] *adj* no superado,-a.

unsuspected [ʌnsəsˈpektɪd] *adj* insospechado,-a.

unsuspecting [ʌnsəsˈpektɪŋ] *adj* confiado,-a.

unswerving [ʌnˈswɜːvɪŋ] *adj* firme.

untangle [ʌnˈtæŋgəl] *t* desenmarañar.

untapped [ʌnˈtæpt] *adj* sin explotar.

untenable [ʌnˈtenəbəl] *adj* insostenible.

unthinkable [ʌnˈθɪŋkəbəl] *adj* impensable.

untidiness [ʌnˈtaɪdɪnəs] *n* desorden *m*. 2 *(scruffiness)* desaliño, desaseo.

untidy [ʌnˈtaɪdɪ] *adj* desordenado,-a. 2 *(scruffy)* desaliñado,-a, desaseado,-a.

untie [ʌnˈtaɪ] *t* desatar. 2 *(liberate)* soltar.

until [ənˈtɪl] *prep* hasta. – 2 *conj* hasta que.

untimely [ʌnˈtaɪmlɪ] *adj* inoportuno,-a. 2 *(premature)* prematuro,-a.

untiring [ʌnˈtaɪərɪŋ] *adj* incansable.

untold [ʌnˈtəʊld] *adj (not told)* no contado,-a. 2 *fig* incalculable; *pej* indecible.

untouchable [ʌnˈtʌtʃəbəl] *adj-n* intocable *(mf)*.

untoward [ʌnˈtəwɔːd] *adj* desafortunado,-a, adverso,-a.

untrained [ʌnˈtreɪnd] *adj* inexperto,-a. 2 *(unskilled)* sin formación (profesional).

untried [ʌnˈtraɪd] *adj* no probado,-a. 2 JUR no procesado,-a; *(case)* no visto,-a.

untrue [ʌnˈtruː] *adj* falso,-a. 2 *(unfaithful)* infiel.

untrustworthy [ʌnˈtrʌstwɜːðɪ] *adj* poco fiable.

untruth [ʌnˈtruːθ] *n* mentira.

untruthful [ʌnˈtruːθfʊl] *adj* mentiroso,-a.

unused [ʌnˈjuːzd] *adj* no usado,-a. 2 *(unaccustomed)* no acostumbrado,-a. ▲ *En 2* [ʌnˈjuːst].

unusual [ʌnˈjuːʒʊəl] *adj* raro,-a, insólito,-a. – 2 **unusually** *adv* excepcionalmente.

unveil [ʌnˈveɪl] *t* descubrir.

unwanted [ʌnˈwɒntɪd] *adj* indeseado,-a. 2 *(child)* no deseado,-a.

unwarranted [ʌnˈwɒrəntɪd] *adj* injustificado,-a.

unwary [ʌnˈweərɪ] *adj* incauto,-a.

unwelcome [ʌnˈwelkəm] *adj* inoportuno,-a, molesto,-a.

unwell [ʌnˈwel] *adj* indispuesto,-a.

unwieldy [ʌnˈwiːldɪ] *adj* difícil de manejar.

unwilling [ʌnˈwɪlɪŋ] *adj* reacio,-a, poco dispuesto,-a.

unwillingness [ʌnˈwɪlɪŋnəs] *n* desgana.

unwind [ʌnˈwaɪnd] *t-i* desenrollar(se). – 2 *i fam (relax)* relajarse. ▲ *pt & pp* **unwound**.

unwise [ʌnˈwaɪz] *adj* imprudente.

unwitting [ʌnˈwɪtɪŋ] *adj* inconsciente. – 2 **unwittingly** *adv* inconscientemente.

unworthy [ʌnˈwɜːðɪ] *adj* indigno,-a.

unwound [ʌnˈwaʊnd] *pt & pp* → **unwind**.

unwrap [ʌnˈræp] *t* desenvolver.

unyielding [ʌnˈjiːldɪŋ] *adj* inflexible.

up [ʌp] *adv* (hacia) arriba: *to sit ~ in bed,* incorporarse; *to walk ~,* subir andando. 2 *(out of bed)* levantado,-a: *he isn't ~ yet,* aún no se ha levantado. 3 *(towards)* hacia: *he came ~ and ...,* se acercó y ... . 4 *(northwards)* hacia el norte: *we went ~ to Scotland,* fuimos a Escocia. 5 *(louder)* más alto,-a: *turn the radio ~,* sube la radio. 6 *(totally finished)* acabado,-a: *eat it ~,* acábatelo, cómetelo todo. 7 *(into pieces)* a trozos/porciones/raciones: – 8 *prep (movement) to go ~ the stairs,* subir la escalera; *to run ~ the street,* ir corriendo calle arriba. 9 *(position)* en lo alto de: *~ a tree,* en lo alto de un árbol. – 10 *t fam* subir, aumentar. ●*close ~,* muy cerca; *to be ~ to sth.,* estar haciendo algo; *pej* estar tramando algo; *to feel ~ to doing sth.,* sentirse con fuerzas de hacer algo; *~ to,* hasta; *well ~ in sth.,* saber mucho de algo; *fam it's not ~ to much,* no vale gran cosa; *fam it's ~ to you,* es cosa tuya; *fam to be on the ~ and ~,* ir cada vez mejor; *fam to ~ and go,* coger e irse; *fam what's ~?,* ¿qué pasa?; *~ yours!*, ¡métetelo por el culo!* ■ *ups and downs,* altibajos *mpl*.

up-and-coming [ʌpənˈkʌmɪŋ] *adj* prometedor,-ra.

upbraid [ʌpˈbreɪd] *t* reprender.

upbringing [ˈʌpbrɪŋɪŋ] *n* educación.

update [ˈʌpdeɪt] *n* actualización. – 2 *t* actualizar. ▲ *En 2 (verbo)* [ˈʌpdeɪt].

upgrade [ʌpˈgreɪd] *t* subir de categoría.

upheaval [ʌpˈhiːvəl] *n* trastorno.

upheld [ʌpˈheld] *pt & pp* ↔ **uphold**.

uphill [ˈʌphɪl] *adj* ascendente. 2 *fig* difícil. – 3 *adv* cuesta arriba. ▲ *En 3 (adverbio)* [ʌpˈhɪl].

uphold [ʌpˈhəʊld] *t (defend)* defender. 2 *(confirm)* confirmar. ▲ *pt & pp* **upheld**.

upholster [ʌpˈhəʊlstəʳ] *t* tapizar.

upholstery [ʌp'həʊlstərɪ] *n* tapicería, tapizado.

upkeep ['ʌpkiːp] *n* mantenimiento.

uplift [ʌp'lɪft] *t* edificar, inspirar.

upon [ə'pɒn] *prep* → **on.**

upper ['ʌpəʳ] *adj* superior. − **2** *n (of shoe)* pala. ■ ~ *case,* caja alta; ~ *class,* clase *f* alta; ~ *house,* cámara alta.

uppermost ['ʌpəməʊst] *adj* más alto,-a. **2** *fig* principal.

upright ['ʌpraɪt] *adj* derecho,-a, vertical. **2** *(honest)* recto,-a, honrado,-a. − **3** *adv* derecho. − **4** *n* SP poste *m.*

uprising [ʌp'raɪzɪŋ] *n* sublevación.

uproar ['ʌprɔːʳ] *n* alboroto, tumulto.

uproarious [ʌp'rɔːrɪəs] *adj* tumultuoso,-a.

uproot [ʌp'ruːt] *t* desarraigar.

upset [ʌp'set] *adj* disgustado,-a, contrariado,-a. **2** *(stomach)* trastornado,-a. − **3** *n* revés *m,* contratiempo. − **4** *t (person)* contrariar; *(worry)* preocupar; *(displease)* disgustar. **5** *(stomach)* trastornar. **6** *(plans)* desbaratar. **7** *(overturn)* volcar. **8** *(spill)* derramar. ▲ *En* **3** *(sustantivo)* ['ʌpset]; *de* **4** *a* **8** *pt & pp* **upset.**

upshot ['ʌpʃɒt] *n* resultado.

upside down [ʌpsaɪd'daʊn] *n* al revés, patas arriba.

upstairs [ʌp'steəz] *adv* al/en el piso de arriba. − **2** *adj* de arriba. − **3** *n* piso de arriba. ▲ *En* **2** *(adjetivo)* ['ʌpsteəz].

upstanding [ʌp'stændɪŋ] *adj* honrado,-a.

upstart ['ʌpstɑːt] *n* advenedizo,-a.

upsurge ['ʌpsɜːdʒ] *n* subida.

up-to-date [ʌptə'deɪt] *adj* al día. **2** *(modern)* moderno,-a.

upward ['ʌpwəd] *adj* hacia arriba, ascendente.

upward(s) ['ʌpwəd(z)] *adv* hacia arriba.

uranium [jʊ'reɪnɪəm] *n* uranio.

urban ['ɜːbən] *adj* urbano,-a.

urbane [ɜː'beɪn] *adj* cortés, urbano,-a.

urbanize ['ɜːbənaɪz] *t* urbanizar.

urchin ['ɜːtʃɪn] *n* pilluelo,-a. **2** ZOOL erizo *(de mar).*

urge [ɜːdʒ] *n* impulso. − **2** *t* encarecer: *to* ~ *sb. to do sth.,* instar a algn. a hacer algo.

urgency ['ɜːdʒənsɪ] *n* urgencia.

urgent ['ɜːdʒənt] *adj* urgente.

urinate ['jʊərɪneɪt] *i* orinar.

urinal [jʊ'raɪnəl] *n* urinario.

urine ['jʊərɪn] *n* orina.

urn [ɜːn] *n* urna. **2** *(for tea)* tetera grande.

us [ʌs, *unstressed* əz] *pers pron* nos; *(with preposition)* nosotros,-as; *give* ~ *your gun,* danos tu pistola; *come with* ~, ven con nosotros; *it's* ~, somos nosotros,-as. **2** *fam* me: *give* ~ *a kiss,* dame un beso.

usage ['juːzɪdʒ] *n* uso.

use [juːs] *n* uso, empleo. **2** *(usefulness)* utilidad. − **3** *t* usar, utilizar, emplear, hacer servir. **4** *(consume)* gastar. **5** *(exploit unfairly)* aprovecharse de. − **6** *aux (past habits)* soler, acostumbrar: *he used to get up early,* solía levantarse temprano; *I used to be fat,* antes estaba gordo,-a. ●*in* ~, en uso; *"not in* ~", "no funciona"; *of* ~, útil; *out of* ~, desusado,-a; *what's the* ~ *of ...?,* ¿de qué sirve ... ? ▲ *En* **3**, **4** *y* **5** [juːz]. *In* **6**, *if no habit is involved, translate using the imperfect.*

used [juːst] *adj* usado,-a. **2** *(accustomed)* acostumbrado,-a.

useful ['juːsfʊl] *adj* útil, provechoso,-a.

usefulness ['juːsfʊlnəs] *n* utilidad.

useless ['juːsləs] *adj* inútil.

user ['juːzəʳ] *n* usuario,-a.

usher ['ʌʃəʳ] *n* ujier *m.* **2** CINEM THEAT acomodador,-ra. ◆*to* ~ *in t* hacer pasar.

usual ['juːʒʊəl] *adj* usual, habitual, normal. − **2** *usually adv* normalmente. ●*as* ~, como de costumbre, como siempre.

usurer ['juːʒərəʳ] *n* usurero,-a.

usurp [juː'zɜːp] *t* usurpar.

usurpation [juːzɜː'peɪʃən] *n* usurpación.

utensil [juː'tensəl] *n* utensilio.

uterus ['juːtərəs] *n* útero. ▲ *pl* **uteruses** *o* **uteri** ['juːtəraɪ].

utilitarian [juːtɪlɪ'teərɪən] *adj* utilitario,-a.

utility [juː'tɪlɪtɪ] *n* utilidad. **2** *(company)* empresa de servicio público.

utilize ['juːtɪlaɪz] *t* utilizar.

utmost ['ʌtməʊst] *adj* sumo,-a, extremo,-a. ●*to do one's* ~, hacer todo lo posible.

utopia [juː'təʊpɪə] *n* utopía.

utter ['ʌtəʳ] *adj* absoluto,-a, total. − **2** *t* pronunciar, articular. − **3** *utterly adv* totalmente, completamente.

utterance ['ʌtərəns] *n* declaración.

U-turn ['juːtɜːn] *n* cambio de sentido.

V

vacancy ['veɪkənsɪ] *n (job)* vacante *f.* **2** *(room)* habitación libre.

vacant ['veɪkənt] *adj* vacío. **2** *(job)* vacante. **3** *(room)* libre.

vacate [və'keɪt] *t (job)* dejar (vacante). **2** *(house)* desocupar.

vacation [və'keɪʃən] *n* vacaciones *fpl.*

vaccinate ['væksɪneɪt] *t* vacunar.

vaccine ['væksiːn] *n* vacuna.

vacillate ['væsɪleɪt] *t* vacilar.

vacuum ['vækjʊəm] *n* vacío. – **2** *t* pasar la aspiradora por. ■ ~ *cleaner,* aspiradora; ~ *flask,* termo.

vacuum-packed ['vækjʊəmpækt] *adj* envasado,-a al vacío.

vagabond ['vægəbɒnd] *n* vagabundo,-a.

vagary ['veɪgərɪ] *n* capricho.

vagina [və'dʒaɪnə] *n* vagina.

vaginal [və'dʒaɪnəl] *adj* vaginal.

vagrant ['veɪgrənt] *n* vagabundo,-a.

vague [veɪg] *adj* vago,-a, indefinido,-a.

vain [veɪn] *adj* vanidoso,-a. **2** *(useless)* vano,-a, fútil. ●*in* ~, en vano.

vale [veɪl] *n* valle *m.*

valency ['veɪlənɪ] *n* valencia.

valentine ['væləntaɪn] *n* tarjeta *enviada por San Valentín.* **2** *(person)* novio,-a.

valet ['væleɪ] *n* ayuda *m* de cámara.

valiant ['vælɪənt] *adj* valiente.

valid ['vælɪd] *adj* válido,-a. **2** *(ticket)* valedero,-a.

validity [və'lɪdɪtɪ] *n* validez *f.*

valley ['vælɪ] *n* valle *m.*

valour ['vælər] *n* valor *m,* valentía.

valuable ['væljʊəbəl] *adj* valioso,-a. – **2** *npl* objetos *mpl* de valor.

valuation [væljʊ'eɪʃən] *n* valoración.

value ['væljuː] *n* valor *m.* – **2** *t* valorar. ●*it's good* ~ *for money,* bien vale lo que cuesta.

valve [vælv] *n* válvula. **2** RAD lámpara.

vampire ['væmpaɪər] *n* vampiro.

van [væn] *n* camioneta, furgoneta. **2** GB *(on train)* furgón *m.*

vandal ['vændəl] *n* vándalo,-a.

vandalism ['vændəlɪzəm] *n* vandalismo.

vandalize ['vændəlaɪz] *t* destrozar.

vane [veɪn] *n* veleta. **2** *(of fan etc.)* aspa.

vanguard ['vængɑːd] *n* vanguardia.

vanilla [və'nɪlə] *n* vainilla.

vanish ['vænɪʃ] *i* desaparecer.

vanity ['vænɪtɪ] *n* vanidad.

vanquish ['væŋkwɪʃ] *t* vencer.

vaporize ['veɪpəraɪz] *t-i* vaporizar(se).

vapour ['veɪpər] *n* vapor *m,* vaho.

variable ['veərɪəbəl] *adj-n* variable *(f).*

variance ['veərɪəns] *n* discrepancia. ●*to be at* ~, no concordar; *(people)* estar en desacuerdo.

variant ['veərɪənt] *n* variante *f.*

variation [veərɪ'eɪʃən] *n* variación.

varicose ['værɪkəʊs] *adj* ~ *veins,* varices *fpl.*

varied ['veərɪd] *adj* variado,-a.

variegated ['veərɪgeɪtɪd] *adj* abigarrado,-a.

variety [və'raɪtɪ] *n* variedad. ■ ~ *show,* (espectáculo de) variedades *(fpl).*

various ['veərɪəs] *adj (different)* diverso,-a, distinto,-a. **2** *(various)* varios,-as.

varnish ['vɑːnɪʃ] *n* barniz *m.* – **2** *t* barnizar.

vary ['veərɪ] *t-i* variar.

vase [vɑːz] *n* jarrón *m,* florero.

vasectomy [væ'sektəmɪ] *n* vasectomía.

vassal ['væsəl] *n* vasallo,-a.

vast [vɑːst] *adj* vasto,-a, inmenso,-a, enorme.

vastness ['vɑːstnəs] *n* inmensidad.

vat [væt] *n* tina, cuba.

vault [vɔːlt] *n (ceiling)* bóveda. **2** *(in bank)* cámara acorazada. **3** *(for dead)* panteón

m; (in church) cripta. **4** *(gymnastisc)* salto.
– 5 *t-i* saltar.
vaunt [vɔ:nt] *i* jactarse de.
veal [vi:l] *n* ternera.
vector ['vektə'] *n* vector *m*.
veer [vɪə'] *i* virar, girar, desviarse.
vegetable ['vedʒɪtəbəl] *adj-n* vegetal *(m)*.
– **2** *n (as food)* hortaliza, verdura, legumbre *f*.
vegetarian [vedʒɪ'teərɪən] *adj-n* vegetariano,-a.
vegetate ['vedʒɪteɪt] *i* vegetar.
vegetation [vedʒɪ'teɪʃən] *n* vegetación.
vehemence ['vɪəməns] *n* vehemencia.
vehement ['vɪəmənt] *adj* vehemente.
vehicle ['vi:əkəl] *n* vehículo.
veil [veɪl] *n* velo. – **2** *t* velar.
vein [veɪn] *n* ANAT vena. **2** BOT vena, nervio. **3** *(of mineral)* veta. **4** *(mood)* humor *m*, veta.
velocity [və'lɒsɪtɪ] *n* velocidad.
velvet ['velvɪt] *n* terciopelo.
velvety ['velvɪtɪ] *adj* aterciopelado,-a.
venal ['vi:nəl] *adj* venal.
vendetta [ven'detə] *n* enemistad mortal.
vending machine ['vendɪŋməʃi:n] *n* máquina expendedora.
vendor ['vendə'] *n* vendedor,-ra.
veneer [və'nɪə'] *n* chapa. **2** *fig* apariencia. – **3** *t* chap(e)ar.
venerable ['venərəbəl] *adj* venerable.
venerate ['venəreɪt] *t* venerar, reverenciar.
veneration [venə'reɪʃən] *n* veneración.
venereal [və'nɪərɪəl] *adj* venéreo,-a.
vengeance ['vendʒəns] *n* venganza. ●*with a* ~, con furia.
vengeful ['vendʒfʊl] *adj* vengativo,-a.
venison ['venɪsən] *n* (carne *f* de) venado.
venom ['venəm] *n* veneno. **2** *fig* odio.
venomous ['venəməs] *adj* venenoso,-a.
vent [vent] *n (opening)* abertura. **2** *(hole)* orificio, respiradero. **3** *(grille)* rejilla de ventilación. – **4** *t* descargar. ●*to give* ~ *to, (feelings)* descargar.
ventilate ['ventɪleɪt] *t* ventilar.
ventilation [ventɪ'leɪʃən] *n* ventilación.
ventilator ['ventɪleɪtə'] *n* ventilador *m*.
ventriloquist [ven'trɪləkwɪst] *n* ventrílocuo,-a.
venture ['ventʃə'] *n* aventura, empresa arriesgada. – **2** *t* arriesgar, aventurar. – **3** *i* aventurarse.
venue ['venju:] *n* lugar *m*.
veranda(h) [və'rændə] *n* veranda, terraza.
verb [vɜ:b] *n* verbo.

verbal ['vɜ:bəl] *adj* verbal.
verbatim [vɜ:'beɪtɪm] *adj* textual. – **2** *adv* textualmente.
verbiage ['vɜ:bɪɪdʒ] *n* verborrea.
verbose [vɜ:'bəʊs] *adj* verboso,-a.
verbosity [vɜ:'bɒsɪtɪ] *n* verbosidad.
verdict ['vɜ:dɪkt] *n* veredicto. **2** *(opinion)* opinión *f*.
verge [vɜ:dʒ] *n* borde *m*, margen *m*. **2** *(of road)* arcén *m*. ●*to* ~ *on t* rayar en. ●*on the* ~ *of,* a punto de.
verification [verɪfɪ'keɪʃən] *n* verificación, comprobación.
verify ['verɪfaɪ] *t* verificar, comprobar.
verisimilitude [verɪsɪ'mɪlɪtju:d] *n* verosimilitud.
veritable ['verɪtəbəl] *adj* verdadero,-a.
vermicelli [vɜ:mɪ'selɪ] *n* fideos *mpl*.
vermilion [və'mɪlɪən] *n* bermellón *m*. – **2** *adj* bermejo,-a.
vermin ['vɜ:mɪn] *n inv* alimaña. **2** *(insects)* bichos *mpl*, sabandijas *fpl*.
vernacular [və'nækjʊlə'] *adj* vernáculo,-a. – **2** *n* lengua vernácula.
verruca [və'ru:kə] *n* verruga.
versatile ['vɜ:sətaɪl] *adj* versátil.
versatility [vɜ:sə'tɪlɪtɪ] *n* versatilidad.
verse [vɜ:s] *n* estrofa. **2** *(in Bible)* versículo. **3** *(genre)* verso, poesía.
versed [vɜ:st] *adj* versado,-a.
version ['vɜ:ʒən] *n* versión.
versus ['vɜ:səs] *prep* contra.
vertebra ['vɜ:tɪbrə] *n* vértebra. ▲ *pl* **vertebrae** ['vɜ:tɪbri:].
vertebrate ['vɜ:tɪbrət] *adj-n* vertebrado,-a *(m)*.
vertical ['vɜ:tɪkəl] *adj* vertical.
vertigo ['vɜ:tɪgəʊ] *n* vértigo.
verve [vɜ:v] *n* brío, empuje *m*.
very ['verɪ] *adv* muy. **2** *(emphatic) at the* ~ *latest,* a más tardar. – **3** *adj* mismo,-a, mismísimo,-a: *at that* ~ *moment,* en aquel mismo instante. **4** *(emphatic) at the* ~ *end,* al final de todo.
vespers ['vespəz] *npl* vísperas.
vessel ['vesəl] *n (ship)* nave *f*, buque *m*. **2** *(container)* recipiente *m*, vasija. **3** ANAT vaso.
vest [vest] *n* camiseta. **2** US chaleco. – **3** *t to* ~ *in,* conferir a. ■ *vested interests,* intereses *mpl* creados.
vestibule ['vestɪbju:l] *n* vestíbulo.
vestige ['vestɪdʒ] *n* vestigio.
vestment ['vestmənt] *n* vestidura.
vestry ['vestrɪ] *n* sacristía.
vet [vet] *n fam* veterinario,-a. – **2** *t* GB investigar, examinar.

veteran ['vetərən] *adj-n* veterano,-a.
veterinarian [vetəri'neəriən] *n* US veterinario,-a.
veterinary ['vetərinəri] *adj* veterinario,-a.
veto ['vi:təu] *n* veto. − **2** *t* vetar, prohibir.
vex [veks] *t* molestar, disgustar.
via ['vaiə] *prep* vía, por vía de, por.
viability [vaiə'biliti] *n* viabilidad.
viable ['vaiəbəl] *adj* viable, factible.
viaduct ['vaiədʌkt] *n* viaducto.
vibrant ['vaibrənt] *adj* vibrante.
vibrate [vai'breit] *t-i* (hacer) vibrar.
vibration [vai'breiʃən] *n* vibración.
vicar ['vikəʳ] *n* (Anglican) párroco. **2** (Catholic) vicario.
vicarage ['vikəridʒ] *n* casa del párroco.
vicarious [vi'keəriəs] *adj* experimentado,-a por otro.
vice [vais] *n* vicio. **2** (tool) torno/tornillo de banco. − **3** *pref* vice-: ~ *president,* vicepresidente.
viceroy ['vaisrɔi] *n* virrey *m.*
vice versa [vais'vɜ:sə] *adv* viceversa.
vicinity [vi'siniti] *n* vecindad, inmediaciones *fpl.* ●*in the* ~ *of,* cerca de.
vicious ['viʃəs] *adj* (cruel) cruel. **2** (violent) violento,-a. **3** (dangerous) peligroso,-a. ■ ~ *circle,* círculo vicioso.
victim ['viktim] *n* víctima.
victimize ['viktimaiz] *t* perseguir, tomar represalias contra.
victor ['viktəʳ] *n* vencedor,-ra.
Victorian [vik'tɔ:riən] *adj-n* victoriano,-a.
victorious [vik'tɔ:riəs] *adj* victorioso,-a.
victory ['viktəri] *n* victoria, triunfo.
victuals ['vitəlz] *npl* víveres *mpl.*
video ['vidiəu] *n* vídeo. ■ ~ *camera,* videocámara; ~ *cassette,* videocasete *f;* ~ *recorder,* vídeo; ~ *tape,* videocinta, cinta de vídeo.
videotape ['vidiəuteip] *t* grabar en vídeo.
vie [vai] *i* competir.
view [vju:] *n* vista, panorama *m.* **2** (opinion) parecer *m,* opinión, punto de vista. − **3** *t* (look at) mirar. **4** (see) ver. ●*in* ~ *of,* en vista de; *with a* ~ *to,* con el propósito de; *fam to take a dim/poor* ~ *of,* ver con malos ojos.
viewer ['vju:əʳ] *n* telespectador,-ra, televidente *mf.*
viewpoint ['vju:pɔint] *n* punto de vista.
vigil ['vidʒil] *n* vigilia. ●*to keep* ~, velar.
vigilance ['vidʒiləns] *n* vigilancia.
vigilant ['vidʒilənt] *adj* vigilante, atento,-a.

vigilante [vidʒi'lænti] *n* vigilante *mf.*
vigorous ['vigərəs] *adj* vigoroso,-a.
vigour ['vigəʳ] *n* vigor *m,* energía.
vile [vail] *adj* vil. **2** *fam* malísimo,-a.
vilify ['vilifai] *t* vilipendiar.
villa ['vilə] *n* villa. **2** (at coast) chalet *m.*
village ['vilidʒ] *n* pueblo; (small) aldea.
villager ['vilidʒəʳ] *n* aldeano,-a.
villain ['vilən] *n* CINEM malo,-a. **2** GB *fam* criminal *m,* delincuente *mf.*
villainous ['vilənəs] *adj* malvado,-a. **2** *fam (bad)* malísimo,-a.
villainy ['viləni] *n* vileza, maldad.
vinaigrette [vinə'gret] *n* vinagreta.
vindicate ['vindikeit] *t* vindicar, justificar.
vindication [vindi'keiʃən] *n* vindicación.
vindictive [vin'diktiv] *adj* vengativo,-a.
vine [vain] *n* vid *f.* **2** (climbing) parra.
vinegar ['vinigəʳ] *n* vinagre *m.*
vineyard ['vinja:d] *n* viña, viñedo.
vintage ['vintidʒ] *n* cosecha. ■ ~ *car,* coche *m* de época *construido entre 1919 y 1930;* ~ *wine,* vino añejo.
vinyl ['vainəl] *n* vinilo.
viola [vi'əulə] *n* viola.
violate ['vaiəleit] *t* violar.
violation [vaiə'leiʃən] *n* violación.
violence ['vaiələns] *n* violencia.
violent ['vaiələnt] *adj* violento,-a.
violet ['vaiələt] *n* BOT violeta *f.* **2** (colour) violeta *m.* − **3** *adj* (de color) violeta.
violin [vaiə'lin] *n* violín *m.*
violinist [vaiə'linist] *n* violinista *mf.*
violoncello [vaiələn'tʃeləu] *n* violoncelo.
viper ['vaipəʳ] *n* víbora.
viral ['vairəl] *adj* viral, vírico,-a.
virgin ['vɜ:dʒin] *adj-n* virgen (f).
virginity [vɜ:'dʒiniti] *n* virginidad.
Virgo ['vɜ:gəu] *n* Virgo *m inv.*
virile ['virail] *adj* viril, varonil.
virility [vi'riliti] *n* virilidad.
virtual ['vɜ:tjuəl] *adj* virtual. − **2** *virtually adv* casi, prácticamente.
virtue ['vɜ:tju:] *n* virtud. ●*by* ~ *of,* en virtud de.
virtuoso [vɜ:tju'əuzəu] *n* virtuoso,-a.
virtuous ['vɜ:tʃuəs] *adj* virtuoso,-a.
virulence ['viruləns] *n* virulencia.
virulent ['virulənt] *adj* virulento,-a.
virus ['vairəs] *n* virus *m.*
visa ['vi:zə] *n* visado.
visage ['vizidʒ] *n* rostro, semblante *m.*
vis-à-vis [vi:za:'vi:] *prep* respecto a.
viscose ['viskəus] *n* viscosa.
viscosity [vis'kɒsiti] *n* viscosidad.

viscount ['vaɪkaʊnt] *n* vizconde *m*.
viscountess ['vaɪkaʊntəs] vizcondesa.
viscous ['vɪskəs] *adj* viscoso.
vise [vaɪs] *n* US → **vice 2**.
visibility [vɪzɪ'bɪlɪtɪ] *n* visibilidad.
visible ['vɪzɪbəl] *adj* visible.
vision ['vɪʒən] *n gen* visión. **2** *(eyesight)* vista.
visionary ['vɪʒənərɪ] *n* visionario,-a.
visit ['vɪzɪt] *n* visita. − **2** *t* visitar.
visitor ['vɪzɪtər] *n (at home)* invitado,-a. **2** *(tourist)* visitante *mf*. **3** *(in hotel)* cliente,-a.
visor ['vaɪzər] *n* visera.
vista ['vɪstə] *n* vista, panorama *m*.
visual ['vɪzjʊəl] *adj* visual.
visualize ['vɪzjʊəlaɪz] *t* imaginar(se).
vital ['vaɪtəl] *adj* vital. **2** *(essential)* esencial, fundamental. − **3** *npl* órganos *mpl* vitales. − **4** *vitally adv* sumamente.
vitality [vaɪ'tælɪtɪ] *n* vitalidad.
vitamin ['vɪtəmɪn] *n* vitamina.
vitreous ['vɪtrɪəs] *adj* vítreo,-a.
vitriol ['vɪtrɪəl] *n* vitriolo.
vitriolic [vɪtrɪ'ɒlɪk] *adj* vitriólico,-a. **2** *fig* virulento,-a.
vivacious [vɪ'veɪʃəs] *adj* vivaz, animado,-a.
vivacity [vɪ'væsɪtɪ] *n* animación, vivacidad.
vivid ['vɪvɪd] *adj* vivo,-a. **2** *(description)* gráfico,-a.
vividness ['vɪvɪdnəs] *n* viveza.
vivisection [vɪvɪ'sekʃən] *n* vivisección.
vixen ['vɪksən] *n* zorra.
viz [vɪz] *adv* a saber.
vocabulary [və'kæbjʊlərɪ] *n* vocabulario, léxico.
vocal ['vəʊkəl] *adj* vocal. **2** *(noisy)* ruidoso,-a. ■ ~ *chords,* cuerdas *fpl* vocales.
vocalist ['vəʊkəlɪst] *n* cantante *mf*, vocalista *mf*.
vocation [vəʊ'keɪʃən] *n* vocación.
vocational [vəʊ'keɪʃənəl] *adj* profesional, vocacional.
vociferous [və'sɪfərəs] *adj* vociferante, vocinglero,-a.
vodka ['vɒdkə] *n* vodka *m & f*.
vogue [vəʊg] *n* boga, moda.
voice [vɔɪs] *n* voz *f*. − **2** *t* expresar.
voiced [vɔɪst] *adj* LING sonoro,-a.
voiceless ['vɔɪsləs] *adj* afónico,-a. **2** LING sordo,-a.

void [vɔɪd] *adj* vacío,-a. **2** JUR nulo,-a, inválido,-a. − **3** *n* vacío.
volatile ['vɒlətaɪl] *adj* volátil.
volcanic [vɒl'kænɪk] *adj* volcánico,-a.
volcano [vɒl'keɪnəʊ] *n* volcán *m*.
vole [vəʊl] *n* campañol *m*.
volition [və'lɪʃən] *n* volición, voluntad.
volley ['vɒlɪ] *n* descarga. **2** *(in tennis)* volea. − **3** *i* volear.
volleyball ['vɒlɪbɔːl] *n* balonvolea *m*, voleibol *m*.
volt [vəʊlt] *n* voltio.
voltage ['vəʊltɪdʒ] *n* voltaje *m*, tensión.
voluble ['vɒljubəl] *adj* locuaz, hablador,-ra.
volume ['vɒljuːm] *n* volumen *m*. **2** *(book)* tomo.
voluminous [və'ljuːmɪnəs] *adj* voluminoso,-a.
voluntary ['vɒləntərɪ] *adj* voluntario,-a.
volunteer [vɒlən'tɪər] *n* voluntario,-a. − **2** *t-i* ofrecer(se) voluntario,-a.
voluptuous [və'lʌptjʊəs] *adj* voluptuoso,-a.
voluptuousness [və'lʌptjʊəsnəs] *n* voluptuosidad.
vomit ['vɒmɪt] *n* vómito. − **2** *t-i* vomitar.
voodoo ['vuːduː] *n* vudú *m*.
voracious [və'reɪʃəs] *adj* voraz.
voracity [və'ræsɪtɪ] *n* voracidad.
vortex ['vɔːteks] *n* vórtice *m*. **2** *fig* vorágine *f*. ▲ *pl* **vortexes** o **vortices** ['vɔːtɪsiːz].
vote [vəʊt] *n* voto. **2** *(voting)* votación. **3** *(right to ~)* sufragio, derecho al voto. − **4** *t-i* votar [dær su vɒtɒ]. − **5** *t (elect)* elegir. **6** *fam* considerar.
voter ['vəʊtər] *n* votante *mf*.
vouch [vaʊtʃ] *i* to ~ *for sb./sth.,* responder de algn./algo.
voucher ['vaʊtʃər] *n* vale *m*, bono.
vow [vaʊ] *n* voto, promesa solemne. − **2** *t* jurar, prometer solemnemente.
vowel ['vaʊəl] *n* vocal *f*.
voyage ['vɔɪɪdʒ] *n* viaje *m*. − **2** *i* viajar.
voyager ['vɔɪədʒər] *n* viajero,-a.
vulgar ['vʌlgər] *adj* grosero,-a. **2** *(in bad taste)* de mal gusto. **3** LING vulgar.
vulgarity [vʌl'gærɪtɪ] *n* vulgaridad, ordinariez, grosería. **2** *(bad taste)* mal gusto.
vulnerable ['vʌlnərəbəl] *adj* vulnerable.
vulture ['vʌltʃər] *n* buitre *m*.
vulva ['vʌlvə] *n* vulva. ▲ *pl* **vulvas** or **vulvae** ['vʌlviː].

W

wad [wɒd] *n* taco, tapón *m*. **2** *(of notes)* fajo.

waddle ['wɒdəl] *i* anadear, andar como los patos.

wade [weɪd] *i* andar por el agua: *to ~ across a river,* vadear un río.

wafer ['weɪfə'] *n* barquillo, oblea. **2** REL hostia.

waffle ['wɒfəl] *n* CULIN gofre *m*. **2** GB *fam* palabrería. – **3** *i* GB *fam* hablar mucho sin decir nada.

waft [wɒft] *t* llevar por el aire. – **2** *i* moverse por el aire, flotar.

wag [wæg] *n (of tail)* meneo. – **2** *t-i* menear(se).

wage [weɪdʒ] *n* sueldo, salario. ●*to ~ war on,* hacer la guerra a.

wager ['weɪdʒə'] *n* apuesta. – **2** *t* apostar.

waggle ['wægəl] *t-i* menear(se).

wag(g)on ['wægən] *n* carro; *(covered)* carromato. **2** *(railway)* vagón *m*.

waif [weɪf] *n* niño,-a abandonado,-a.

wail [weɪl] *n* lamento, gemido. – **2** *i* lamentarse, gemir.

waist [weɪst] *n* cintura.

waistcoat ['weɪskəut] *n* chaleco.

waistline ['weɪstlaɪn] *n* cintura.

wait [weɪt] *n* espera. **2** *(delay)* demora. – **3** *i* esperar. **4** *(at table)* servir.

waiter ['weɪtə'] *n* camarero.

waiting ['weɪtɪŋ] *n* espera. ■ *~ list,* lista de espera; *~ room,* sala de espera.

waitress ['weɪtrəs] *n* camarera.

waive [weɪv] *t* renunciar a.

wake [weɪk] *n (of ship)* estela. **2** *(for dead)* velatorio. – **3** *t* despertar. ◆*to ~ up t-i* despartar(se). ●*in the ~ of,* tras. ▲ *pt* **woke**; *pp* **woken**.

waken ['weɪkən] *t-i* despertar(se).

walk [wɔːk] *n* paseo. **2** *(long)* caminata. **3** *(path)* paseo. **4** *(gait)* andares *mpl*. – **5** *i* andar, caminar: *I'll ~ there,* iré andan-do/a pie. – **6** *t (dog)* pasear. **7** *(person)* acompañar. ◆*to ~ away/off with t (win)* ganar con facilidad. **2** *fam (steal)* mangar, birlar. ◆*to ~ out i* marcharse. **2** *(strike)* ir a la huelga. ◆*to ~ out on t* abandonar a. ●*to go for a ~,* dar un paseo; *to ~ all over sb.,* tratar a algn. a patadas; *to ~ into a trap,* caer en una trampa. ■ *~ of life,* condición social.

walkie-talkie [wɔːkɪ'tɔːkɪ] *n* walkie-talkie *m*.

walking stick ['wɔːkɪŋstɪk] *n* bastón *m*.

Walkman® ['wɔːkmən] *n* walkman® *m*.

walkout ['wɔːkaut] *n* huelga.

walkover ['wɔːkəuvə'] *n fam* paseo.

wall [wɔːl] *n* muro. **2** *(interior)* pared *f*. **3** *(defensive)* muralla. **4** *(in garden)* tapia.

walled [wɔːld] *adj (city)* amurallado,-a.

wallet ['wɒlɪt] *n* cartera.

wallop ['wɒləp] *fam n* golpazo. – **2** *t* pegar fuerte.

wallow ['wɒləu] *i* revolcarse.

wallpaper ['wɔːlpeɪpə'] *n* papel *m* pintado. – **2** *t* empapelar.

wally ['wɒlɪ] *n fam* inútil *mf*.

walnut ['wɔːlnʌt] *n* nuez *f*. ■ *~ tree,* nogal *m*.

walrus ['wɔːlrəs] *n* morsa.

waltz [wɔːls] *n* vals *m*. – **2** *i* valsar.

wan [wɒn] *adj* pálido,-a. **2** *(sad)* triste, apagado,-a.

wand [wɒnd] *n* varita.

wander ['wɒndə'] *i* vagar, deambular. **2** *(from the point)* desviarse. – **3** *t* vagar por, recorrer.

wanderer ['wɒndərə'] *n* viajero,-a.

wandering ['wɒndərɪŋ] *adj* errante. – **2** *npl* viajes *mpl*.

wane [weɪn] *i* menguar. ●*on the ~,* menguando.

wangle ['wæŋgəl] *t fam* agenciarse.

wank* [wæŋk] *n* paja*. — **2** *i* hacerse una paja*.

wanker* ['wæŋkə^r] *n* gilipollas* *mf inv*.

want [wɒnt] *n (necessity)* necesidad. **2** *(lack)* falta, carencia. **3** *(poverty)* miseria. — **4** *t* querer, desear: *I ~ you to come with me,* quiero que me acompañes. **5** *fam (need)* necesitar. ●*for ~ of,* por falta de; *to be in ~,* estar necesitado.

wanted ['wɒntɪd] *adj* necesario,-a: *"boy ~",* "se busca chico". **2** *(by police)* buscado,-a: *"~",* "se busca".

wanton ['wɒntən] *adj* sin motivo. **2** *(wild)* desenfrenado,-a.

war [wɔ:^r] *n* guerra.

warble ['wɔ:bəl] *n* gorjeo. — **2** *t-i* gorjear.

ward [wɔ:d] *n (in hospital)* sala. **2** GB POL distrito electoral. **3** JUR pupilo,-a. ◆*to ~ off* *t* prevenir, evitar. **2** *(blow)* parar.

warden ['wɔ:dən] *n* vigilante *mf*, guardián,-ana. **2** US *(of prison)* alcaide *m*. ■ *traffic ~,* guardia *mf* urbano.

warder ['wɔ:də^r] *n* carcelero,-a.

wardrobe ['wɔ:drəʊb] *n* armario (ropero), guardarropa *m*. **2** *(clothes)* vestuario.

warehouse ['weəhaʊs] *n* almacén *m*.

wares [weəz] *npl* género *m sing*, mercancías *fpl*.

warfare ['wɔ:feə^r] *n* guerra.

warhead ['wɔ:hed] *n (nuclear) ~,* cabeza nuclear.

warily ['weərɪlɪ] *adv* cautamente.

warlike ['wɔ:laɪk] *adj* belicoso,-a.

warm [wɔ:m] *adj* caliente; *(tepid)* tibio,-a, templado,-a. **2** *(climate, colour)* cálido,-a. **3** *(day, welcome)* caluroso,-a. **4** *(clothes)* de abrigo. — **5** *t* calentar. **6** *(heart)* alegrar. ◆*to ~ up* *t-i* calentar(se). — **2** *i* SP hacer ejercicios de calentamiento. ●*to ~ to sb.,* coger simpatía a algn.

warm-blooded [wɔ:m'blʌdɪd] *adj* de sangre caliente.

warm-hearted [wɔ:m'hɑ:tɪd] *adj* afectuoso,-a.

warmth [wɔ:mθ] *n* calor moderado. **2** *fig* afecto.

warn [wɔ:n] *t* avisar, advertir, prevenir: *he warned me not to touch it,* me advirtió que no lo tocara. **2** *(instead of punishing)* amonestar.

warning ['wɔ:nɪŋ] *n* aviso, advertencia. **2** *(instead of punishment)* amonestación.

warp [wɔ:p] *n (thread)* urdimbre *f*. **2** *(in wood)* alabeo. — **3** *t-i* alabear(se), combar(se).

warped [wɔ:pt] *adj* combado,-a. **2** *fig* pervertido,-a, rertorcido,-a.

warrant ['wɒrənt] *n* JUR orden *f* judicial. — **2** *t* justificar. ■ *search ~,* orden de registro.

warranty ['wɒrəntɪ] *n* COM garantía.

warren ['wɒrən] *n* madriguera. **2** *fig* laberinto.

warrior ['wɒrɪə^r] *n* guerrero,-a.

warship ['wɔ:ʃɪp] *n* buque *m* de guerra.

wart [wɔ:t] *n* verruga.

wary ['weərɪ] *adj* cauto,-a, cauteloso,-a.

was [wɒz, *unstressed* wəz] *pt* → **be**.

wash [wɒʃ] *n* lavado. **2** *(dirty clothes)* ropa sucia; *(clean clothes)* colada. **3** *(of ship)* remolinos *mpl*. **4** MED enjuague *m*. — **5** *t-i* lavar(se). — **6** *t (dishes)* fregar. **7** *(carry away)* llevar, arrastrar. ◆*to ~ out* *t (stain)* quitar lavando. ◆*to ~ up* *t-i* fregar (los platos). — **2** *i* US lavarse las manos y la cara. ●*to have a ~,* lavarse. ■ *that won't ~!,* ¡eso no cuela!

washable ['wɒʃəbəl] *adj* lavable.

washbasin ['wɒʃbeɪsən], US **washbowl** ['wɒʃbəʊl] *n* lavabo.

washed-out [wɒʃt'aʊt] *adj* agotado,-a.

washer ['wɒʃə^r] *n (metal)* arandela. **2** *(rubber)* junta. **3** *(machine)* lavadora.

washing ['wɒʃɪŋ] *n (action)* lavado. **2** *(laundry)* colada. ■ *~ line,* tendedero; *~ machine,* lavadora.

washing-up [wɒʃɪŋ'ʌp] *n (action)* fregado. **2** *(dishes)* platos *mpl*. ■ *~ liquid,* lavavajillas *m inv*.

washout [wɒʃaʊt] *n fam* fracaso.

washroom ['wɒʃru:m] *n* US servicios *mpl*.

wasp [wɒsp] *n* avispa. ■ *wasp's nest,* avispero.

wastage ['weɪstɪdʒ] *n* desperdicio, pérdidas *fpl*.

waste [weɪst] *n* desperdicio. **2** *(of money)* derroche *m*, despilfarro. **3** *(products)* desechos *mpl*, desperdicios *mpl*. — **4** *adj* desechado,-a. **5** *(land)* yermo,-a, baldío,-a. — **6** *t* desperdiciar, malgastar. **7** *(money)* despilfarrar, derrochar. ●*it's a ~ of time,* es una pérdida de tiempo.

wasteful ['weɪstfʊl] *adj* pródigo,-a.

wastepaper basket [weɪst'peɪpəbɑːskɪt] *n* papelera.

watch [wɒtʃ] *n (timepiece)* reloj *m*. **2** *(vigilance)* vigilancia. **3** MIL MAR cuerpo de guardia. — **4** *t* mirar; *(television)* ver. **5** *(observe)* observar. **6** *(keep an eye on)* vigilar. **7** *(take care with)* tener cuidado con, prestar atención a. ●*~ out!,* ¡ojo!, ¡cuidado!

watchdog ['wɒtʃdɒg] *n* perro guardián. **2** *fig* guardián,-ana.

watchful ['wɒtʃful] *adj* vigilante, atento,-a.

watchfulness ['wɒtʃfulnəs] *n* vigilancia.

watchmaker ['wɒtʃmeɪkə'] *n* relojero,-a.

watchman ['wɒtʃmən] *n* vigilante *m*. 2 *(on street)* sereno.

watchword ['wɒtʃwɜːd] *n* santo y seña. 2 *(motto)* consigna, lema *m*.

water ['wɔːtə'] *n* agua. 2 *(urine)* orina. – 3 *t* regar. 4 *(animals)* abrevar. – 5 *i (eyes)* llorar. ◆*to ~ down t* aguar. 2 *fig* descafeinar. ●*to get into hot ~,* meterse en un buen lío; *to hold ~,* retener el agua; *fig* aguantarse; *to keep one's head above ~,* mantenerse a flote; *to pass ~,* orinar; *under ~,* inundado,-a. ■ *~ polo,* waterpolo.

watercolour ['wɔːtəkʌlə'] *n* acuarela.

watercress ['wɔːtkres] *n* berro.

waterfall ['wɔːtəfɔːl] *n* cascada, salto de agua.

watering ['wɔːtərɪŋ] *n* riego. ■ *~ can,* regadera.

waterlogged ['wɔːtəlɒgd] *adj* empapado,-a, anegado,-a.

watermark ['wɔːtəmɑːk] *n* filigrana.

watermelon ['wɔːtəmelən] *n* sandía.

watermill ['wɔːtəmɪl] *n* molino de agua.

waterproof ['wɔːtəpruːf] *adj* impermeable. 2 *(watch)* sumergible. – 3 *t* impermeabilizar.

watershed ['wɔːtəʃed] *n* GEOG línea divisoria de aguas. 2 *fig* punto decisivo.

water-ski ['wɔːtəskiː] *n* esquí *m* acuático. – 2 *i* hacer esquí acuático.

water-skiing ['wɔːtəskiːɪŋ] *n* esquí acuático.

watertight ['wɔːtətaɪt] *adj* estanco,-a. 2 *fig* irrecusable.

waterway ['wɔːtəweɪ] *n* vía fluvial.

watery ['wɔːtəri] *adj* acuoso,-a. 2 *(soup, drinks)* aguado,-a.

watt [wɒt] *n* watt *m*, vatio.

wave [weɪv] *n (in sea)* ola. 2 *(in hair)* onda. 3 PHYS onda. 4 *(of hand)* ademán *m*, movimiento. 5 *(of crime etc.)* ola, oleada. – 6 *i (greet)* saludar (con la mano). – 7 *(flag)* ondear. – 8 *t* agitar. 9 *(hair)* marcar, ondular.

wavelength ['weɪvleŋθ] *n* longitud de onda. ●*fam to be on different wavelengths,* no estar en la misma onda.

waver ['weɪvə'] *i (hesitate)* vacilar.

wavy ['weɪvi] *adj* ondulado,-a.

wax [wæks] *n* cera. – 2 *t* encerar. – 3 *i (grow)* crecer.

waxwork ['wækswɜːks] *n* museo de cera.

way [weɪ] *n (path)* camino: *which ~ did you go?,* ¿por dónde fuisteis? 2 *(direction)* dirección: *on the ~ to work,* yendo al trabajo; *which ~ is the harbour?,* ¿dónde cae el puerto? 3 *(manner, method)* manera, modo. – 4 *adv fam* muy: *~ back,* hace muchísimo. ●*a long ~ from,* lejos de; *by the ~,* a propósito; *by ~ of,* vía, por vía de; *fig* a modo de; *on the ~,* por el camino; *(coming)* en camino; *on the ~ down/up,* bajando/subiendo; *to get out of the ~,* apartarse del camino, quitarse de en medio; *to get under ~,* empezar, ponerse en marcha; *to give ~,* ceder; AUTO ceder el paso; *to lose one's ~,* perderse; *to stand in the ~ of,* obstaculizar; *fam in a bad ~,* mal.

waylay [weɪˈleɪ] *t* abordar. 2 *(attack)* atacar. ▲ *pt & pp* **waylaid** [weɪˈleɪd].

wayside ['weɪsaɪd] *n* borde *m* del camino.

wayward ['weɪwəd] *adj* voluntarioso,-a.

we [wiː, *unstressed* wɪ] *pers pron* nosotros,-as.

weak [wiːk] *adj* débil, flojo,-a.

weaken ['wiːkən] *t-i* debilitar(se).

weakness ['wiːknəs] *n* debilidad. 2 *(fault)* fallo.

weal [wiːl] *n* cardenal *m*.

wealth [welθ] *n* riqueza.

wealthy ['welθi] *adj* rico,-a.

wean [wiːn] *t* destetar.

weapon ['wepən] *n* arma.

wear [weə'] *n* ropa. 2 *(use)* uso. 3 *(~ and tear)* desgaste *m*, deterioro. – 4 *t* llevar puesto,-a, vestir. 5 *(shoes)* calzar. – 6 *t-i (erode)* desgastar(se). ◆*to ~ away t-i* erosionar(se). ◆*to ~ off i* desaparecer. ◆*to ~ out t-i* romper(se) con el uso. – 2 *t (person)* agotar. ▲ *pt* **wore**; *pp* **worn**.

weariness ['wɪərɪnəs] *n* cansancio.

weary ['wɪəri] *adj* cansado,-a. – 2 *t-i* cansar(se).

weasel ['wiːzəl] *n* comadreja.

weather ['weðə'] *n* tiempo: *what's the ~ like?,* ¿qué tiempo hace? – 2 *t* aguantar. 3 *(rocks)* erosionar. ●*to ~ the storm,* capear el temporal. ■ *~ forecast,* parte *m* meteorológico.

weather-beaten ['weðəbiːtən] *adj* deteriorado,-a por la intemperie. 2 *(person)* curtido,-a.

weathercock ['weðəkɒk] *n* veleta.

weave [wiːv] *n* tejido. – 2 *t-i* tejer. 3 *(zigzag)* serpentear, zigzaguear. – 4 *t fig* *(plot)* tramar. ▲ *En 2 y 4 pt* **wove;** *pp* **woven.**

weaver ['wiːvə^r] *n* tejedor,-ra.

web [web] *n* telaraña. **2** *fig* red *f*.

webbed [webd] *adj* palmeado,-a.

wed [wed] *t* casarse con. ▲ *pt & pp* **wedded** *o* **wed.**

wedding ['wedɪŋ] *n* boda. ■ ~ **cake,** tarta nupcial; ~ **day,** día *m* de la boda; ~ **dress,** vestido de novia; ~ **present,** regalo de boda; ~ **ring,** alianza, anillo de boda.

wedge [wedʒ] *n* cuña, calce *m*. – **2** *t* acuñar, calzar.

Wednesday ['wenzdɪ] *n* miércoles *m inv*.

wee [wiː] *adj* pequeñito,-a, – **2** *n fam* pipí *m*. – **3** *i* hacer pipí.

weed [wiːd] *n* mala hierba. **2** *fam* canijo,-a. – **3** *t-i* escardar.

weedkiller ['wiːdkɪlə^r] *n* herbicida *m*.

weedy ['wiːdɪ] *adj pej* debilucho,-a.

week [wiːk] *n* semana.

weekday ['wiːkdeɪ] *n* (día *m*) laborable *m*.

weekend ['wiːkend] *n* fin *m* de semana.

weekly ['wiːklɪ] *adj* semanal. – **2** *adv* semanalmente. – **3** *n* semanario.

weep [wiːp] *i* llorar. ▲ *pt & pp* **wept.**

weft [weft] *n* trama.

weigh [weɪ] *t* pesar. **2** *fig* sopesar. ◆*to ~ down t* sobrecargar. **2** *fig* abrumar, agobiar. ◆*to ~ up t* evaluar. ●*to ~ anchor,* levar anclas.

weight [weɪt] *n* peso. **2** *(piece of metal)* pesa. – **3** *t* cargar con peso. ●*to put on ~,* engordar.

weightless ['weɪtləs] *adj* ingrávido,-a.

weightlessness ['weɪtləsnəs] *n* ingravidez *f*.

weightlifting ['weɪtlɪftɪŋ] *n* halterofilia.

weighty ['weɪtɪ] *adj* pesado,-a. **2** *fig* de peso.

weir [wɪə^r] *n* presa.

weird [wɪəd] *adj* raro,-a, extraño,-a.

weirdo ['wɪədəʊ] *n fam* tipo raro.

welcome ['welkəm] *adj* bienvenido,-a. **2** *(pleasing)* grato,-a, agradable. – **3** *n* bienvenida, acogida. – **4** *t* acoger, recibir, dar la bienvenida a. **5** *(approve of)* aplaudir, acoger con agrado. ●*you're ~,* no hay de qué, de nada.

weld [weld] *n* soldadura. – **2** *t* soldar.

welder ['weldə^r] *n* soldador,-ra.

welfare ['welfeə^r] *n* bienestar *m*.

well [wel] *n* pozo. – **2** *adj-adv* bien. – **3** *i* manar, brotar. – **4** *interj* bueno, pues. **5** *(surprise)* ¡vaya! ●*as ~,* también; *as ~ as,* además de; *it would be as ~ to ...,* no estaría de más + *inf; just as ~,* menos mal; *pretty ~,* casi; *to do ~,* tener éxito, prosperar; *to get ~,* reponerse; ~ *done,* CULIN bien hecho,-a; *(congratulating)* ¡muy bien!

well-being [wel'biːɪŋ] *n* bienestar *m*.

well-built [wel'bɪlt] *adj* de construcción sólida. **2** *(person)* fornido,-a.

well-heeled [wel'hiːld] *adj fam* adinerado,-a.

wellington ['welɪŋtən] *n* bota de goma.

well-intentioned [welɪn'tenʃənd] *adj* bien intencionado,-a.

well-known [wel'nəʊn] *adj* (bien) conocido,-a.

well-meaning [wel'miːnɪŋ] *adj* bien intencionado,-a.

well-off [wel'ɒf] *adj* rico,-a.

well-timed [wel'taɪmd] *adj* oportuno,-a.

well-to-do [weltə'duː] *adj* acomodado,-a.

welt [welt] *n* verdugón *m*.

welter ['weltə^r] *n* mezcolanza.

wench [wentʃ] *n* moza, mozuela.

wend [wend] *t to ~ one's way,* encaminarse a/hacia.

went [went] *pt* → **go.**

wept [wept] *pt & pp* → **weep.**

were [wɜː^r] *pt* → **be.**

west [west] *n* oeste *m*, occidente *m*. – **2** *adj* occidental, del oeste. – **3** *adv* al/hacia el oeste.

westbound ['westbaʊnd] *adj* en dirección al oeste.

westerly ['westəlɪ] *adj* oeste. **2** *(wind)* del oeste.

westward ['westwəd] *adj* hacia el oeste.

westwards ['westwəds] *adv* hacia el oeste.

wet [wet] *adj* mojado,-a. **2** *(permanently, naturally)* húmedo,-a. **3** *(weather)* lluvioso,-a. **4** *(paint)* fresco,-a. **5** *fam (person)* soso,-a. – **6** *n* humedad. **7** *(rain)* lluvia. – **8** *t* mojar, humedecer. ●*to ~ o.s.,* orinarse. ■ ~ *blanket,* aguafiestas *mf inv*.

wetness ['wetnəs] *n* humedad.

whack [wæk] *n* golpe *m*. **2** *fam* parte *f*. – **3** *t* pegar, golpear.

whacked [wækt] *adj fam* agotado,-a.

whacking ['wækɪŋ] *adj fam* enorme.

whale [weɪl] *n* ballena.

wharf [wɔːf] *n* muelle *m*, embarcadero.

what [wɒt] *adj (questions)* qué: ~ *time is it?,* ¿qué hora es?; *I don't know ~ time it is,* no sé qué hora es. **2** *(exclamations)* qué: ~ *a (smart) car!,* ¡qué coche (más chulo)! 3 *(all)* ~ *oil we have is here,* todo el aceite que tenemos está aquí. — 4 *pron (questions)* qué: ~ *is it?,* ¿qué es?; *I dont know* ~ *it is,* no sé qué es. 5 lo que: *that's* ~ *he said,* eso es lo que dijo. — 6 *interj* ¡cómo!: ~*!, you've lost it!,* ¡cómo! ¡lo has perdido!

whatever [wɔt'evəʳ] *adj* cualquiera que: ~ *colour you like,* el color que tú quieras. 2 *(at all)* en absoluto: *with no money* ~, sin absolutamente nada de dinero. — 3 *pron* (todo) lo que: ~ *you like,* (todo) lo que tú quieras; ~ *you do,* hagas lo que hagas.

whatsoever [wɔtsəʊ'evəʳ] *adj* → **whatever 2.**

wheat [wiːt] *n* trigo.

wheedle ['wiːdəl] *t* engatusar.

wheel [wiːl] *n* rueda. 2 *(steering* ~*)* volante *m.* — 3 *t* empujar. — 4 *i* girar. 5 *(birds)* revolotear.

wheelbarrow ['wiːlbærəʊ] *n* carretilla de mano.

wheelchair ['wiːltʃeəʳ] *n* silla de ruedas.

wheeze [wiːz] *n* resuello. — 2 *i* resollar.

when [wen] *adv* cuándo: ~ *did it happen?,* ¿cuándo pasó?; *tell me* ~, dime cuándo. — 2 *conj* cuando: ~ *I arrived,* cuando llegué yo. — 3 *pron* cuando: *that was* ~ *it broke,* fue entonces cuando se rompió.

whence [wens] *adv* de dónde. 2 *fig* por lo cual.

whenever [wen'evəʳ] *conj* cuando quiera que, siempre que. — 2 *adv* cuándo (demonios).

where [weəʳ] *adv* dónde; *(direction)* adónde: ~ *is it?,* ¿dónde está?; ~ *did you go?,* ¿adónde fuiste?; *tell me* ~ *it is,* dime dónde está. — 2 *pron* donde: *this is* ~ *it all happened,* es aquí donde pasó todo.

whereabouts ['weərəbaʊts] *n* paradero. — 2 *adv* dónde; *(direction)* adónde. ▲ En 2 *(adverbio)* [weərə'baʊts].

whereas [weər'æz] *conj* mientras que.

whereby [weə'baɪ] *adv* por el/la/lo cual.

whereupon ['weərəpɔn] *adv* con lo cual.

wherever [weər'evəʳ] *adv* dónde (diablos/demonios); *(direction)* adónde (diablos/demonios): ~ *did you put it,* ¿dónde diablos lo pusiste? — 2 *conj* dondequiera que.

wherewithal ['weəwɪðɔːl] *n* medios *mpl,* recursos *mpl.*

whet [wet] *t (appetite)* despertar.

whether ['weðəʳ] *conj* si: ~ *it rains or not,* llueva o no llueva.

whey [weɪ] *n* suero.

which [wɪtʃ] *adj* qué: ~ *size do you want?,* ¿qué tamaño quieres?; *tell me* ~ *size you want,* dime qué tamaño quieres. — 2 *pron (questions)* cuál, cuáles: ~ *do you want?,* ¿cuál quieres?; *ask him* ~ *they are,* pregúntale cuáles son. 3 *(defining relative)* que; *(with preposition)* el/la/lo que, el/la/lo cual, los/las que, los/las cuales: *the shoes* ~ *I bought,* los zapatos que compré; *the shop in* ~ *...,* la tienda en la que/cual ... . 4 *(nondefining relative)* el/la cual, los/las cuales: *two glasses, one of* ~ *was dirty,* dos copas, una de las cuales estaba sucia. 5 *(referring to a clause)* lo que/cual: *he lost,* ~ *was sad,* perdió, lo cual era triste.

whichever [wɪtʃ'evəʳ] *adj* (no importa) el/la/los/las que: ~ *model you choose,* no importa el modelo que elijas. — 2 *pron* cualquiera, el/la/los/las que: *take* ~ *you want,* coge el que quieras.

whiff [wɪf] *n* soplo. 2 *(smell)* olor *m* fugaz.

while [waɪl] *n* rato, tiempo. — 2 *conj* mientras. 3 *(although)* aunque. 4 *(whereas)* mientras que. ●*to be worth one's* ~, valer la pena; *to* ~ *away the time,* pasar el rato.

whilst [waɪlst] *conj* → **while.**

whim [wɪm] *n* antojo, capricho.

whimper ['wɪmpəʳ] *n* gemido. — 2 *i* lloriquear, gemir.

whine [waɪn] *n* quejido; *(dog)* gemido. — 2 *i* quejarse; *(dog)* gemir.

whinny ['wɪnɪ] *n* relincho *m.* — 2 *i* relinchar.

whip [wɪp] *n* látigo. 2 *(for punishment)* azote *m.* 3 POL oficial *mf* encargado,-a de la disciplina de partido. — 4 *t* azotar, zurrar. 5 CULIN batir; *(cream, egg whites)* montar. 6 *fam* birlar. 7 *hacer algo de prisa o bruscamente: to* ~ *off/out/past,* quitar/sacar/pasar de prisa.

whipping ['wɪpɪŋ] *n* azotamiento. ■ ~ *cream,* nata para montar.

whip-round ['wɪpraʊnd] *n fam* colecta.

whirl [wɜːl] *n* giro, vuelta. 2 *fig* torbellino. — 3 *i* girar, dar vueltas rápidamente. — 4 *t* hacer girar, dar vueltas a.

whirlpool ['wɜːlpuːl] *n* torbellino, remolino.

whirlwind ['wɜːlwɪnd] *n* torbellino.

whirr [wɜːʳ] *n* zumbido. — 2 *i* zumbar.

whisk [wɪsk] *n* movimiento brusco. 2 CULIN batidor *m;* *(electric)* batidora. — 3 *t* sacudir. 4 CULIN batir. 5 *hacer algo rápidamente: to* ~ *off/out,* quitar/sacar rápidamente.

whisker ['wɪskə^r] n pelo. 2 pl patillas fpl. 3 pl (cat's etc.) bigotes mpl.

whisk(e)y ['wɪskɪ] n whisky m, güisqui m.

whisper ['wɪspə^r] n susurro. – 2 t-i susurrar.

whistle ['wɪsəl] n (instrument) silbato, pito. 2 (noise) silbido, pitido. – 3 t-i silbar.

white [waɪt] adj-n blanco,-a (m). – 2 n (of egg) clara. ■ White House, Casa Blanca; ~ lie, mentira piadosa.

whitebait ['waɪtbeɪt] n inv CULIN chanquetes mpl (fritos).

white-collar [waɪt'kɒlə^r] adj administrativo,-a.

whiten ['waɪtən] t blanquear.

whiteness ['waɪtnəs] n blancura.

whitewash ['waɪtwɒʃ] n jalbegue m. – 2 t enjalbegar, encalar. 3 fig encubrir.

Whitsun(tide) ['wɪtsʌn(taɪd)] n Pentecostés m inv.

whittle ['wɪtəl] t cortar pedazos a. 2 fig reducir.

whiz(z) [wɪz] n zumbido. – 2 i zumbar, silbar. ●to ~ past, pasar zumbando.

whiz(z)-kid ['wɪzkɪd] n fam lince m, hacha.

who [hu:] pron (questions) quién, quiénes: ~ did it?, ¿quién lo hizo?; I don't know ~ they are, no sé quiénes son. 2 (defining relative) que: those ~ want to go, los que quieran ir; fam the boy ~ she loves, el chico que/a quien ama. 3 (non-defining relative) quien, quienes, el/la cual, los/las cuales: the workers, ~ were on strike, ..., los trabajadores, quienes/los cuales estaban en huelga, ...

whoever [hu:'evə^r] pron (questions) quién (diablos/demonios). 2 (no matter who) quienquiera que, cualquiera que.

whole [həʊl] adj entero,-a: the ~ day, todo el día. 2 (intact) intacto,-a. – 3 n conjunto, todo. ●as a ~, en conjunto; on the ~, en general; the ~ of, toda,-a.

wholemeal ['həʊlmi:l] adj integral.

wholesale ['həʊlseɪl] adj-adv COM al por mayor. – 2 adv fig en masa. – 3 adj masivo,-a. – 4 n venta al por mayor.

wholesaler ['həʊlseɪlə^r] n mayorista mf.

wholesome ['həʊlsəm] adj sano,-a, saludable.

wholly ['həʊlɪ] adv enteramente.

whom [hu:m] pron fml (questions) a quién/quiénes: ~ did he kill?, ¿a quién mató?; with ~?, ¿con quién? 2 (relative) a quien/quienes: pupils ~ I have taught, alumnos a quienes he dado cla-

se; the man with ~ she was seen, el hombre con quien/con el que la vieron.

whoop [hu:p] n grito, alarido. – 2 i gritar.

whooping cough ['hu:pɪŋkɒf] n tos f ferina.

whopper ['wɒpə^r] n fam cosa enorme. 2 (lie) trola, bola.

whopping ['wɒpɪŋ] adj fam enorme.

whore [hɔː^r] n puta*.

whose [hu:z] pron (questions) de quién/ quiénes: ~ is this?, ¿de quién es esto?; I know ~ it is, yo sé de quién es. – 2 adj de quién/quiénes: ~ dog is this?, ¿de quién es este perro? 3 (relative) cuyo,-a, cuyos,-as: the woman ~ car was stolen, la mujer cuyo coche fue robado.

why [waɪ] adv por qué. – 2 interj ¡vaya!, ¡toma! – 3 n porqué m, causa.

wick [wɪk] n mecha.

wicked ['wɪkɪd] adj malo,-a.

wickedness ['wɪkɪdnəs] n maldad.

wicker ['wɪkə^r] n mimbre m. – 2 adj de mimbre.

wicket ['wɪkɪt] n (in Cricket) palos mpl. 2 (pitch) terreno.

wide [waɪd] adj ancho,-a: two feet ~, de dos pies de ancho. 2 fig amplio,-a, extenso,-a. – 3 widely adv extensamente; (generally) generalmente. ●~ open, abierto,-a de par en par.

widen ['waɪdən] t-i ensanchar(se). 2 fig extender(se).

widespread ['waɪdspred] adj generalizado,-a.

widow ['wɪdəʊ] n viuda.

widowed ['wɪdəʊd] adj enviudado,-a.

widower ['wɪdəʊə^r] n viudo.

width [wɪdθ] n anchura. 2 (material) ancho.

wield [wi:ld] t manejar, empuñar. 2 (power) ejercer.

wife [waɪf] n esposa, mujer f.

wig [wɪg] n peluca.

wiggle ['wɪgəl] t-i menear(se).

wigwam ['wɪgwæm] n tienda india.

wild [waɪld] adj gen salvaje. 2 (plant) silvestre, campestre. 3 (country) agreste. 4 (angry) furioso,-a. 5 (violent) violento,-a. 6 (uncontrolled) incontrolado,-a. 7 (guess) al azar. – 8 n tierra virgen. ●in the ~, en estado salvaje; to be ~ about, estar loco,-a por.

wildcat ['waɪldkæt] n gato,-a montés,-esa. ■ ~ strike, huelga salvaje.

wilderness ['wɪldənəs] n yermo, desierto.

wildfire ['waɪldfaɪə^r] n to spread like ~, correr como la pólvora.

wildfowl ['waɪldfaʊl] npl aves fpl de caza. **wildlife** ['waɪldlaɪf] n fauna.

wiles [waɪlz] npl artimañas fpl.

wilful ['wɪlfʊl] adj voluntarioso,-a, terco,-a. 2 JUR premeditado,-a.

will [wɪl] n voluntad. 2 JUR testamento. − 3 t desear, querer, ordenar, mandar. 4 JUR legar, dejar en testamento. − 5 aux (future) she ~ be here tomorrow, estará aquí mañana; we won't finish today, no acabaremos hoy; it won't rain, ~ it?, no lloverá, ¿verdad? 6 (be disposed to) ~ you help me?, − no I won't, ¿quieres ayudarme? −no quiero; he won't open the door, se niega a abrir la puerta; the car won't start, el coche no arranca. 7 (insistence) he ~ leave the door open, es que no hay manera de que cierre la puerta. 8 (can) poder; this 'phone ~ accept credit cards, este teléfono acepta las tarjetas de crédito. 9 (supposition) that ~ be John's house, aquélla será/ debe de ser la casa de John.

willing ['wɪlɪŋ] adj complaciente. − 2 willingly adv de buena gana. ●~ to do sth., dispuesto,-a a hacer algo.

willingness ['wɪlɪŋnəs] n buena voluntad.

willow ['wɪləʊ] n sauce m.

willowy ['wɪləʊɪ] adj esbelto -a.

willpower ['wɪlpaʊə^r] n fuerza de voluntad.

willy-nilly ['wɪlɪ'nɪlɪ] adv a la fuerza.

wilt [wɪlt] t-i marchitar(se).

wily ['waɪlɪ] adj astuto,-a.

win [wɪn] n victoria, éxito. − 2 t-i ganar. ◆to ~ over/round t convencer, persuadir. ▲ pt & pp won.

wince [wɪns] n mueca de dolor. − 2 i hacer una mueca de dolor.

winch [wɪntʃ] n torno, cabrestante m.

wind [wɪnd] n METEOR viento, aire m. 2 (breath) aliento. 3 (flatulence) gases mpl, flato. − 4 t dejar sin aliento. 5 (wrap) envolver. 6 (on reel) arrollar, devanar. 7 (clock) dar cuerda a. 8 (handle) dar vueltas a. − 9 i (road) serpentear. ◆to ~ down i (clock) quedarse sin cuerda. 2 (person) relajarse. − 3 t AUTO (window) bajar. ◆to ~ up t (clock) dar cuerda a. − 2 t-i concluir. − 3 i fam acabar: to ~ up in jail, dar con los huesos en la cárcel. ●to break ~, ventosear; to get ~ of, olerse; fam to get the ~ up, ponerse nervioso,-a. ■ ~ instrument, instrumento

de viento. ▲ De 5 en adelante [waɪnd]; pt & pp wound.

windbag ['wɪndbæg] n charlatán,-ana.

windbreak ['wɪndbreɪk] n abrigadero.

windfall ['wɪndfɔ:l] n fig suerte f inesperada.

winding ['waɪndɪŋ] adj sinuoso,-a, tortuoso,-a.

windmill ['wɪndmɪl] n molino de viento.

window ['wɪndəʊ] n ventana. 2 (in vehicle) ventanilla. 3 (in bank, office, etc.) ventanilla. 4 (of shop) escaparate m. ■ ~ cleaner, limpiacristales mf inv.

window-shopping ['wɪndəʊʃɒpɪŋ] n to go ~, ir a mirar escaparates.

windowsill ['wɪndəʊsɪl] n alféizar m.

windpipe ['wɪndpaɪp] n tráquea.

windscreen ['wɪndskri:n], US **windshield** ['wɪndʃi:ld] n AUTO parabrisas m inv. ■ ~ wiper, limpiaparabrisas m inv.

windswept ['wɪndswept] adj azotado,-a por el viento.

windy ['wɪndɪ] adj ventoso,-a. ●it's ~, hace viento.

wine [waɪn] n vino.

wing [wɪŋ] n ala. 2 AUTO aleta. 3 SP banda. 4 pl THEAT bastidores mpl.

wingspan ['wɪŋspæn] n envergadura.

wink [wɪŋk] n guiño. − 2 i guiñar el ojo.

winkle ['wɪŋkəl] n bígaro.

winner ['wɪnə^r] n ganador,-ra. 2 (in battle) vencedor,-ra.

winning ['wɪnɪŋ] adj ganador,-ra. 2 (ticket etc.) premiado,-a. 3 (attractive) atractivo,-a, encantador,-ra. − 4 npl ganancias fpl.

winter ['wɪntə^r] n invierno. − 2 i invernar.

wintry ['wɪntrɪ] adj invernal.

wipe [waɪp] t (clean) limpiar. 2 (dry) enjugar. ◆to ~ out t (destroy) aniquilar, exterminar. 2 (erase) borrar.

wiper ['waɪpə^r] n limpiaparabrisas m inv.

wire ['waɪə^r] n alambre m. 2 (cable) cable m. 3 US telegrama m. − 4 t (house) hacer la instalación eléctrica de. 5 US enviar un telegrama a.

wireless ['waɪələs] n radio f.

wiring ['waɪrɪŋ] n cableado.

wiry ['waɪrɪ] adj (person) nervudo,-a.

wisdom ['wɪzdəm] n sabiduría. 2 (sense) prudencia, juicio. ■ ~ tooth, muela del juicio.

wise [waɪz] adj sabio,-a. 2 (sensible) juicioso,-a, prudente. ■ the Three Wise Men, los Reyes Magos.

wish [wɪʃ] *n* deseo. − **2** *t-i* desear. **3** *(want)* querer. ■ *I ~ that,* ojalá; *I ~ to ...,* quisiera ...; *to ~ sb. good luck,* desear buena suerte a algn.

wishful ['wɪʃfʊl] *adj ~ thinking,* ilusiones *fpl.*

wishy-washy ['wɪʃɪwɒʃɪ] *adj fam* soso,-a, insípido,-a.

wisp [wɪsp] *n (of grass)* brizna. **2** *(of hair)* mechón *m.* **3** *(of smoke)* voluta.

wistful ['wɪstfʊl] *adj* pensativo,-a, melancólico,-a.

wit [wɪt] *n* agudeza, ingenio. **2** *(intelligence)* inteligencia. **3** *(person)* persona aguda/ingeniosa. ●*to be at one's wit's end,* estar para volverse loco,-a.

witch [wɪtʃ] *n* bruja. ■ *~ doctor,* hechicero.

witchcraft ['wɪtʃkrɑːft] *n* brujería.

with [wɪð] *prep* con.

withdraw [wɪð'drɔː] *t-i* retirar(se). − **2** *t (words)* retractar. ▲ *pt* **withdrew;** *pp* **withdrawn.**

withdrawal [wɪð'drɔːəl] *n* retirada. **2** *(of words)* retractación.

withdrawn [wɪð'drɔːn] *pp* → **withdraw.** − **2** *adj* introvertido,-a.

withdrew [wɪð'druː] *pt* → **withdraw.**

wither ['wɪðəʳ] *t* marchitar(se).

withering ['wɪðərɪŋ] *adj (look)* fulminante. **2** *(remark)* mordaz.

withhold [wɪð'həʊld] *t* retener. **2** *(information)* ocultar. ▲ *pt & pp* **withheld.**

within [wɪ'ðɪn] *prep* dentro de. **2** *(in range of)* al alcance de: *~ hearing,* al alcance del oído. **3** *(distance)* a menos de: *~ 3 miles of,* a menos de tres millas de. − **4** *adv* dentro, en el interior.

without [wɪ'ðaʊt] *prep* sin.

withstand [wɪð'stænd] *t* resistir, aguantar. ▲ *pt & pp* **withstood** [wɪð'stʊd].

witness ['wɪtnəs] *n* testigo *mf.* − **2** *t* presenciar. **3** *(document)* firmar como testigo. ●*to bear ~ to,* dar fe de, atestiguar. ■ *~ box,* barra de los testigos.

witticism ['wɪtɪsɪzəm] *n* agudeza, ocurrencia.

wittiness ['wɪtɪnəs] *n* ingenio, agudeza.

witty ['wɪtɪ] *adj* ingenioso,-a, agudo,-a.

wizard ['wɪzəd] *n* brujo, hechicero.

wizened ['wɪzənd] *adj (skin)* arrugado,-a.

wobble ['wɒbəl] *n* tambaleo, bamboleo. − **2** *i* tambalearse, bambolear.

woe [wəʊ] *n* mal *m,* aflicción, desgracia.

woebegone ['wəʊbɪgɒn] *adj* desconsolado,-a.

woeful ['wəʊfʊl] *adj* triste.

woke [wəʊk] *pt* → **wake.**

woken ['wəʊkən] *pp* → **wake.**

wolf [wʊlf] *n* lobo. ◆*to ~ down t* zamparse. ■ *~ cub,* lobezno.

woman ['wʊmən] *n* mujer *f.* ■ *old ~,* vieja, anciana; *fam women's lib,* movimiento feminista. ▲ *pl* **women** [wɪmɪn].

womanhood ['wʊmənhʊd] *n* edad adulta (de mujer).

womanly ['wʊmənlɪ] *adj* femenino,-a.

womb [wuːm] *n* útero, matriz *f.*

won [wʌn] *pt & pp* → **win.**

wonder ['wʌndəʳ] *n* maravilla. **2** *(surprise)* admiración, asombro. − **3** *i* preguntarse. − **4** *t-i (marvel)* asombrarse, maravillarse. ●*I shouldn't ~ if ...,* no me sorprendería que + *subj; it makes you ~,* te da en qué pensar; *no ~ (that),* no es de extrañar que; *to ~ about sth,* pensar en algo.

wonderful ['wʌndəfʊl] *adj* maravilloso,-a.

wonky ['wɒŋkɪ] *adj* GB *fam* poco firme. **2** *(twisted)* torcido,-a.

wont [wəʊnt] *n* costumbre *f,* hábito. ●*to be ~ to,* tener la costumbre de.

woo [wuː] *t-i* cortejar.

wood [wʊd] *n* madera. **2** *(for fire)* leña. **3** *(forest)* bosque *m.*

woodcut ['wʊdkʌt] *n* grabado en madera.

woodcutter ['wʊdkʌtəʳ] *n* leñador,-ra.

wooded ['wʊdɪd] *adj* arbolado,-a, cubierto,-a de bosques.

wooden ['wʊdən] *adj* de madera. **2** *fig* rígido,-a. ■ *~ spoon,* cuchara de palo.

woodland ['wʊdlənd] *n* bosque *m,* arbolado.

woodpecker ['wʊdpekəʳ] *n* pájaro carpintero.

woodwork ['wʊdwɜːk] *n* carpintería. **2** *(of building)* maderaje *m,* maderamen *m.*

woodworm ['wʊdwɜːm] *n* carcoma.

woody ['wʊdɪ] *adj* arbolado,-a. **2** *(like wood)* leñoso,-a.

woof! [wʊf] *interj* ¡guau!

wool [wʊl] *n* lana: *all ~,* pura lana.

woollen, US **woolen** ['wʊlən] *adj* de lana. **2** COM lanero,-a. − **3** *npl* géneros *mpl* de punto.

woolly ['wʊlɪ] *adj* de lana. **2** *(like wool)* lanoso,-a. **3** *fig* confuso,-a.

word [wɜːd] *n* palabra. − **2** *t* expresar. ●*by ~ of mouth,* oralmente; *from the ~ go,* desde el principio; *in other words,* o sea; *to have a ~ with,* hablar con; *to*

have words with sb., discutir con algn.; **to keep one's ~,** cumplir su palabra.

wording ['wɜ:dɪŋ] *n* términos *mpl.*

wordy ['wɜ:dɪ] *adj* prolijo,-a, verboso,-a.

wore [wɔ:ʳ] *pt* → **wear.**

work [wɜ:k] *n gen* trabajo. **2** *(employment)* empleo, trabajo. **3** *(results)* trabajo. **4** *(literary etc.)* obra. **5** *pl (factory)* fábrica *f sing.* **6** *pl (parts)* mecanismo *m sing.* — **7** *t-i gen* trabajar. — **8** *i (machine, plan etc.)* funcionar. **9** *(medicine)* surtir efecto. ◆*to* ~ *out* *t (calculate)* calcular. **2** *(plan)* planear, pensar. **3** *(solve)* solucionar, resolver. — **4** *i (calculation)* salir. **5** *(turn out well)* ir/salir bien. **6** SP hacer ejercicios. ◆*to* ~ *up* *t (excite)* exaltar. **2** *(develop)* hacer, desarrollar. ●*at* ~, trabajando; *out of* ~, sin trabajo, parado,-a; *to get worked up,* exaltarse, excitarse; *to have one's* ~ *cut out to do sth.,* vérselas y deseárselas para hacer algo; *to make short* ~ *of sth.,* despachar algo deprisa; *to set to* ~, ponerse a trabajar; *to* ~ *loose,* soltarse, aflojarse; *to* ~ *to rule,* hacer huelga de celo; *to* ~ *wonders,* hacer maravillas. ■ *public works,* obras *fpl* públicas.

workable ['wɜ:kəbəl] *adj* factible, viable.

workbench ['wɜ:kbentʃ] *n* banco de trabajo.

workbook ['wɜ:kbʊk] *n* cuaderno/libreta de ejercicios.

workday ['wɜ:kdeɪ] *n* día *m* laborable.

worker ['wɜ:kəʳ] *n* trabajador,-ra. **2** *(manual)* obrero,-a, operario,-a.

workforce ['wɜ:kfɔ:s] *n* mano *f* de obra.

working ['wɜ:kɪŋ] *adj* de trabajo. **2** *(person)* que trabaja. — **3** *npl* funcionamiento *m sing.* ■ ~ *class,* clase obrera; ~ *knowledge,* conocimientos *mpl* básicos; ~ *model,* modelo que funciona.

workman ['wɜ:kmən] *n* trabajador *m.* **2** *(manual)* obrero.

workmanlike ['wɜ:kmənlaɪk] bien hecho,-a.

workmanship ['wɜ:kmənʃɪp] *n* hechura, ejecución. **2** *(skill)* habilidad.

workmate ['wɜ:kmeɪt] *n* compañero,-a de trabajo.

workout ['wɜ:kaʊt] *n* entrenamiento.

workshop ['wɜ:kʃɒp] *n* taller *m.*

worktop ['wɜ:ktɒp] *n* encimera.

work-to-rule [wɜ:ktə'ru:l] *n* huelga de celo.

world [wɜ:ld] *n* mundo. ●*all over the* ~, en todo el mundo; *it's a small* ~, el mundo es un pañuelo; *out of this* ~, fenomenal, estupendo,-a; *to think the* ~ *of,* adorar.

world-class [wɜ:ld'klɑ:s] *adj* de categoría mundial.

worldly ['wɜ:ldlɪ] *adj* mundano,-a.

worldwide ['wɜ:ldwaɪd] *adj* mundial, universal.

worm [wɜ:m] *n* gusano. **2** *(earth)* ~, lombriz *f.*

worn [wɔ:n] *pp* → **wear.**

worn-out [wɔ:n'aʊt] *adj* gastado,-a. **2** *(person)* rendido,-a, agotado,-a.

worried ['wʌrɪd] *adj* inquieto,-a, preocupado,-a.

worry ['wʌrɪ] *n* inquietud, preocupación. — **2** *t-i* inquietar(se), preocupar(se). — **3** *t (dog)* atacar.

worse [wɜ:s] *adj-adv comp* peor. — **2** *n* lo peor. ●*to get* ~, empeorarse; *to get* ~ *and* ~, ir de mal en peor.

worsen ['wɜ:sən] *t-i* empeorar(se).

worship ['wɜ:ʃɪp] *n* adoración. **2** *(ceremony)* culto. — **3** *t* adorar, rendir culto a.

worst [wɜ:st] *adj-adv superl* peor. — **2** *n* lo peor. ●*at the* ~, en el peor de los casos.

worsted ['wʊstəd] *n* estambre *m.*

worth [wɜ:θ] *n* valor *m.* — **2** *adj* que vale, que tiene un valor de: *it's* ~ *£10, but I got it for £5,* vale diez libras pero me costó solo cinco; *it's* ~ *seeing,* vale la pena verlo. ●*to be* ~, valer; *to be* ~ *the trouble/it,* valer la pena.

worthless ['wɜ:θləs] *adj* sin valor. **2** *(useless)* inútil.

worthwhile [wɜ:θ'waɪl] *adj* que vale la pena.

worthy ['wɜ:ðɪ] *adj* digno,-a, merecedor,-ra.

would [wʊd] *aux (conditional)* *she* ~ *tell you if she knew,* te lo diría si lo supiese. **2** *(be disposed to)* *he wouldn't help me,* se negó a ayudarme, no quiso ayudarme. **3** *(supposition)* *that* ~ *have been Jim,* ese debió ser/sería Jim. **4** *(past habit)* *soler:* *we* ~ *often go out together,* a menudo salíamos juntos. **5** *(insistence)* *he* ~ *go by car,* insistió en que teníamos que ir en coche. ▲ *En 1, 3 y 4 puede contraerse a 'd.*

would-be ['wʊdbi:] *adj* supuesto,-a, aspirante a.

wound [wu:nd] *n* herida. — **2** *t* herir. — **3** *pt & pp* → **wind.** ▲ *En 3* [waʊnd].

wounded ['wu:ndɪd] *adj* herido,-a.

wounding ['wu:ndɪŋ] *adj* hiriente.

wove [wəʊv] *pt* → **weave.**

woven ['wəʊvən] *pp* → **weave.**

wow [waʊ] *interj fam* ¡caramba!

wrangle ['ræŋgəl] *n* riña. — **2** *i* reñir.

wrap [ræp] *t* envolver. ◆*to ~ up i* abrigarse. ●*fig to be wrapped up in,* estar absorto,-a en.

wrapper ['ræpəʳ] *n* envoltorio.

wrapping ['ræpɪŋ] *n* envoltorio. ■ *~ paper,* papel *m* de envolver; *(fancy)* papel de regalo.

wrath [rɒθ] *n* cólera, ira.

wreak [ri:k] *t (havoc)* causar. ●*to ~ vengeance on,* vengarse de.

wreath [ri:θ] *n* corona.

wreck [rek] *n* MAR *(action)* naufragio. 2 MAR *(ship)* barco naufragado. 3 *(of car etc.)* restos *mpl.* 4 *(of building)* ruinas *fpl.* 5 *fig (person)* ruina. − 6 *t* MAR hacer naufragar. 7 *(destroy)* destrozar, destruir, arruinar.

wreckage ['rekɪdʒ] *n (of car etc.)* restos *mpl.* 2 *(of building)* ruinas *fpl.*

wrench [rentʃ] *n* tirón *m.* 2 *fig* separación dolorosa. 3 *(tool)* GB llave inglesa; US llave. − 4 *t* arrancar (de un tirón).

wrest [rest] *t* arrancar, arrebatar.

wrestle ['resəl] *i* luchar.

wrestler ['resələʳ] *n* SP luchador,-ra.

wrestling ['reslɪŋ] *n* lucha.

wretch [retʃ] *n* desgraciado,-a.

wretched ['retʃɪd] *adj* desgraciado,-a. 2 *(unhappy)* infeliz, desdichado,-a. 3 *fam* horrible, malísimo,-a.

wriggle ['rɪɡəl] *t-i* retorcer(se), menear(se). ●*to ~ out of sth.,* escaparse de algo.

wring [rɪŋ] *t* torcer, retorcer. 2 *(clothes)* escurrir. ● *to ~ sb.'s neck,* torcer el pescuezo a algn.; *to ~ sth. out of sb.,* arrancarle algo a algn. ▲ *pt & pp* **wrung**.

wringing wet ['rɪŋɪŋwet] *adj* empapado,-a.

wrinkle ['rɪŋkəl] *n* arruga. − 2 *t-i* arrugar(se).

wrist [rɪst] *n* muñeca.

wristwatch ['rɪstwɒtʃ] *n* reloj *m* de pulsera.

writ [rɪt] *n* mandato/orden *f* judicial.

write [raɪt] *t-i* escribir. − 2 *t (cheque)* extender. ◆*to ~ back i* contestar (por carta). ◆*to ~ down t* poner por escrito. 2 *(note)* anotar, apuntar. ◆*to ~ off t (debt)* anular. 2 *fig* dar por perdido,-a. ◆*to ~ off for t* pedir por correo. ◆*to ~ out t* escribir (en su forma completa). 2 *(cheque etc.)* extender. ◆*to ~ up t* escribir. ▲ *pt* **wrote**; *pp* **written**.

write-off ['raɪtɒf] *n* siniestro total.

writer ['raɪtəʳ] *n* escritor,-ra, autor,-ra.

write-up ['raɪtʌp] *n fam* crítica, reseña.

writhe [raɪð] *t* retorcerse.

writing ['raɪtɪŋ] *n* escritura. 2 *(handwriting)* letra. 3 *(professsion)* profesión de autor. 4 *pl* obras *fpl.* ■ *~ desk,* escritorio; *~ paper,* papel *m* de escribir.

written ['rɪtən] *pp →* **write**. − 2 *adj* escrito,-a.

wrong [rɒŋ] *adj* erróneo,-a, equivocado,-a, incorrecto,-a. 2 *(evil)* malo,-a. 3 *(unfair)* injusto,-a. 4 *(unsuitable)* inadecuado,-a; *(time)* inoportuno,-a. − 5 *adv* mal, incorrectamente, equivocadamente. − 6 *n (evil)* mal *m.* 7 *(injustice)* injusticia. − 8 *t* ser injusto,-a con. − 9 *wrongly adv* mal. 10 *(mistakenly)* sin razón, equivocadamente. 12 *(unjustly)* injustamente. ●*to be in the ~,* no tener razón; *(be to blame)* tener la culpa; *to be ~,* estar equivocado,-a; *(person)* equivocarse; *to go ~,* equivocarse; *(machine)* estropearse; *(plan)* fallar.

wrong-doer ['rɒŋduəʳ] *n* malhechor,-ra.

wrongful ['rɒŋfʊl] *adj* injusto,-a. 2 *(illegal)* ilegal.

wrote [rəʊt] *pt →* **write**.

wrought [rɔ:t] *adj (iron)* forjado,-a.

wrung [rʌŋ] *pt & pp →* **wring**.

wry [raɪ] *adj* irónico,-a.

X

xenophobia [zenə'fəʊbɪə] *n* xenofobia.
xenophobic [zenə'fəʊbɪk] *adj* xenófobo,-a.
Xerox® ['zɪərɒks] *n* xerocopia. — **2** *t* xerocopiar.
Xmas ['eksməs, 'krɪsməs] *n* → **Christmas**.

X-ray ['eksreɪ] *n* rayo X. **2** *(photograph)* radiografía. — **3** *t* radiografiar.
xylophone ['zaɪləfəʊn] *n* xilófono.
xylophonist [zaɪ'lɒfənɪst] *n* xilofonista *mf*.

Y

yacht [jɒt] *n* yate *m*. **2** *(with sails)* velero, yate.

yachting [ˈjɒtɪŋ] *n* deporte *m* de la vela.

yachtsman [ˈjɒtsmən] *n* deportista *m* de vela.

yak [jæk] *n* yac *m*, yak *m*.

yam [jæm] *n* ñame *m*.

Yank [jæŋk] *n pej* yanqui *mf*.

yank [jæŋk] *fam n* tirón *m*. — **2** *t* tirar de.

Yankee [ˈjæŋkɪ] *adj-n pej* yanqui *(mf)*.

yap [jæp] *n* ladrido (agudo). — **2** *i* ladrar.

yard [jɑːd] *n* patio. **2** US jardín *m*. **3** *(measure)* yarda. ▲ **3** = 0,914 metros.

yardstick [ˈjɑːdstɪk] *n fig* criterio, norma.

yarn [jɑːn] *n* hilo. **2** *(story)* cuento.

yawn [jɔːn] *n* bostezo. — **2** *i* bostezar.

yeah [jeə] *adv fam* sí.

year [jɪəːʳ] *n* año. **2** EDUC curso.

yearling [ˈjɪəlɪŋ] *adj-n* primal,-la.

yearly [ˈjɪəlɪ] *adj* anual. — **2** *adv* anualmente.

yearn [jɜːn] *i* anhelar.

yearning [ˈjɜːnɪŋ] *n* anhelo.

yeast [jiːst] *n* levadura.

yell [jel] *n* grito, alarido. — **2** *i* gritar, dar alaridos.

yellow [ˈjeləʊ] *adj* amarillo,-a. **2** *(cowardly)* cobarde. — **3** *n* amarillo. — **4** *t* volver amarillo. — **5** *i* amarillear.

yelp [jelp] *n* gañido. — **2** *i* gañir.

yen [jen] *n* deseo. **2** FIN yen *m*.

yeoman [ˈjəʊmən] *n* HIST labrador *m* rico. ■ ~ *of the guard,* alabardero de la Torre de Londres.

yes [jes] *adv-n* sí *(m)*. **2** *(on 'phone)* ¿dígame? • *to say* ~, decir que sí.

yes-man [ˈjesmæn] *n* cobista *mf*.

yesterday [ˈjestədɪ] *adv-n* ayer *(m)*. ■ *the day before* ~, anteayer.

yet [jet] *adv* todavía, aún. — **2** *conj* no obstante, sin embargo.

yeti [ˈjetɪ] *n* yeti *m*.

yew [juː] *n* tejo.

yield [jiːld] *n* rendimiento. **2** AGR cosecha. **3** FIN rédito. — **4** *t* producir. **5** FIN rendir. — **6** *i* *(surrender)* rendirse, ceder. **7** *(break)* ceder.

yippee [jɪˈpiː] *interj fam* ¡yupi!

yob(bo) [ˈjɒb(əʊ)] *n fam* gamberro,-a.

yodel [ˈjəʊdəl] *i* cantar a la tirolesa.

yoga [ˈjəʊgə] *n* yoga *m*.

yog(h)urt [ˈjɒgət] *n* yogur *m*.

yoke [jəʊk] *n* yugo. — **2** *t* uncir.

yokel [ˈjəʊkəl] *n* paleto,-a.

yolk [jəʊk] *n* yema.

yon [jɒn], **yonder** [ˈjɒndəʳ] *adj* aquel, aquella, aquellos,-as. — **2** *adv* allá.

you [juː] *pers pron (subject) (familiar)* tú; *(plural)* vosotros,-as. **2** *(subject) (polite)* usted; *(plural)* ustedes. **3** *(subject) (impers)* se. **4** *(object) (familiar)* ti; *(before verb)* te; *(plural)* vosotros,-as; *(before verb)* os. **5** *(object) (polite)* usted; *(before verb)* le; *(plural)* ustedes; *(before verb)* les. **6** *(object) (impers)*: *cyanide kills* ~, el cianuro mata.

young [jʌŋ] *adj* joven. ■ *the* ~, los jóvenes.

youngster [ˈjʌŋstəʳ] *n* joven *mf*.

your [jɔːʳ] *poss adj (familiar)* tu, tus; *(plural)* vuestro,-a, vuestros,-as. **2** *(polite)* su, sus.

yours [jɔːz] *poss pron* (el) tuyo, (la) tuya, (los) tuyos, (las) tuyas; *(plural)* (el) vuestro, (la) vuestra, (los) vuestros, (las) vuestras. **2** *(polite)* (el) suyo, (la) suya, (los) suyos, (las) suyas.

yourself [jɔːˈself] *pers pron (familiar)* te; *(emphatic)* tú mismo,-a. **2** *(polite)* se; *(emphatic)* usted mismo,-a.

yourselves [jɔːˈselvz] *pers pron pl (familiar)* os; *(emphatic)* vosotros,-as mismos,-as. **2** *(polite)* se; *(emphatic)* ustedes mismos,-as.

youth [ju:θ] *n* juventud. **2** *(young person)* joven *mf.* ■ ~ *hostel,* albergue *m* de juventud.

youthful [ˈjuːθfʊl] *adj* joven, juvenil.

yo-yo ® [ˈɪəʊɪəʊ] *n* yoyo, yoyó.

yucky [ˈjʌkɪ] *adj fam* asqueroso,-a.

yule [juːl] *n* Navidad.

yummy [ˈjʌmɪ] *adj fam* de rechupete.

Z

zany [ˈzeɪnɪ] *adj fam* estrafalario,-a. **2** *(mad)* chiflado,-a.

zeal [ziːl] *n* celo, entusiasmo.

zealot [ˈzelət] *n* fanático,-a.

zealous [ˈzeləs] *adj* celoso,-a, entusiasta.

zebra [ˈziːbrə, zebrə] *n* cebra. ■ ~ *crossing,* paso de peatones/cebra.

zenith [ˈzenɪθ] *n* cenit *m*. **2** *fig* apogeo.

zephyr [ˈzefər] *n* céfiro.

zeppelin [ˈzepəlɪn] *n* AV zepelín *m*.

zero [ˈzɪərəʊ] *n* cero.

zest [zest] *n* entusiasmo.

zigzag [ˈzɪgzæg] *n* zigzag *m*. – **2** *t* zigzaguear.

zinc [zɪŋk] *n* cinc *m*, zinc *m*.

zip [zɪp] *n* ~ *(fastener),* cremallera. ◆*to* ~ *by/past t-i* pasar como un rayo. ◆*to* ~ *up t* cerrar con cremallera. ■ US ~ *code,* código postal.

zipper [ˈzɪpər] *n* US cremallera.

zodiac [ˈzəʊdɪæk] *n* zodiaco, zodíaco.

zombie [ˈzɒmbɪ] *n* zombi(e) *mf*.

zone [zəʊn] *n* zona.

zoo [zuː] *n* zoo *m*, (parque *m*) zoológico.

zoological [zʊəˈlɒdʒɪkəl] *adj* zoológico,-a.

zoology [zʊˈɒlədʒɪ] *n* zoología.

zoom [zuːm] *n* *(noise)* zumbido. **2** ~ *(lens),* (objetivo) zoom *m*. – **3** *i* zumbar. **4** AER empinarse. ◆*to* ~ *by/past t-i fam* pasar volando.

Nombres geográficos e idiomas

[1] inhabitant only - habitante sólo
[2] adjective refering to the country (language if it exists) but not inhabitant - adjetivo referente al país (y nombre del idioma si existe) pero no habitante.
[3] adjective, inhabitant and language (if it exists) - adjetivo, habitante e idioma (si existe)
[4] adjective and inhabitant but not language - adjetivo y habitante pero no idioma
[5] language only - idioma sólo

Adriatic Sea	mar Adriático	Asturias	Asturias
Aegean Sea	mar Egeo	Atlantic Ocean	océano Atlántico
Afghan[3]	afgano	Australia	Australia
Afghanistan	Afganistán	Australian[3]	australiano
Africa	África	Austria	Austria
African[3]	africano	Austrian[3]	austríaco
Albania	Albania	Azerbaijan	Azerbaiján
Albanian[3]	albano	Azerbaijani[3]	azerbaijano
Algeria	Argelia	Azores	Azores
Algerian[3]	argelino		
Algiers	Argel		
Alps	Alpes	Balearic[2]	balear, baleárico
Amazon	Amazonas	Balearic Islands	Islas Baleares
America	América	Balkans	Balcanes
American[3]	estadounidense	Baltic Sea	mar Báltico
Andalusia	Andalucía	Bangladesh	Bangladesh
Andalusian[3]	andaluz	Bangladeshi[3]	bangladesí
Andes	Andes	Basque[3]	vasco
Andorra	Andorra	Basque Country	País Vasco
Andorran[3]	andorrano	Bay of Biscay	Golfo de Vizcaya
Anglosaxon[3]	anglosajón	Belgian[3]	belga
Antarctica	Antártida	Belgium	Bélgica
Apennines	Apeninos	Belize	Belice
Arabia	Arabia	Black Sea	mar Negro
Arabian[4]	árabe	Bolivia	Bolivia
Arabic[5]	árabe	Bolivian[3]	boliviano
Aragon	Aragón	Bosnia-	Bosnia-
Aragonese[3]	aragonés	Herzegovina	Herzegovina
Armenia	Armenia	Bosnian[3]	bosnio
Armenian[3]	armenio	Brazil	Brasil
Arctic Ocean	océano Ártico	Brazilian[3]	brasileño
Argentine	Argentina	Britain	Gran Bretaña
Argentinian[3]	argentino	British[2]	británico
Asia	Asia	Briton[1]	británico
Asian[3]	asiático	Bulgaria	Bulgaria
Asturian[3]	asturiano	Bulgarian[3]	búlgaro

Byelorussia	Bielorrusia	Dubliner[1]	dublinés
Byelorussian[3]	bielorruso	Dutch[3]	holandés
Cambodia	Camboya		
Cambodian[3]	camboyano	Earth	Tierra
Cameroon	Camerún	Ecuador	Ecuador
Cameroonian[3]	camerunés	Ecuadorian[3]	ecuatoriano
Canada	Canadá	Egypt	Egipto
Canadian[3]	canadiense	Egyptian[3]	egipcio
Canary Islands	Islas Canarias	Eire	Eire, República de
Cantabria	Cantabria		Irlanda
Cantabrian[3]	cántabro	El Salvador	El Salvador
Caribbean	Caribe	England	Inglaterra
Caribbean[3]	caribeño	English[2]	inglés
Castile	Castilla	English Channel	Canal de La
Castilian[3]	castellano		Mancha
Catalan[3]	catalán	Estonia	Estonia
Catalonia	Cataluña	Estonian[3]	estonio
Catalonian[4]	catalán	Estremadura	Extremadura
Celt[1]	celta	Estremaduran[3]	extremeño
Celtic[4]	celta	Ethiopia	Etiopía
Ceuta	Ceuta	Ethiopian[3]	etíope
Ceylon	Ceilán	Europe	Europa
Ceylonese[2]	ceilanés	European[3]	europeo
Channel Islands	Islas		
	Anglonormandas		
Chile	Chile	Falkland Islands	Islas Malvinas
Chilean[3]	chileno	Far East	Lejano Oriente
China	China	Filipino[2]	filipino
Chinese[3]	chino	Finland	Finlandia
Colombia	Colombia	Finn[1]	finlandés
Colombian[3]	colombiano	Finnish[2]	finlandés
Corsica	Córcega	France	Francia
Corsican[3]	corso	French[2]	francés
Costa Rica	Costa Rica	Fuerteventura	Fuerteventura
Costa Rican[3]	costarricense		
Croat[3], Croatian	croata		
Croatia	Croacia		
Cuba	Cuba	Galicia	Galicia
Cuban[3]	cubano	Galician[3]	gallego
Cypriot(e)[3]	chipriota	Georgia	Georgia
Cyprus	Chipre	Georgian[3]	georgiano
Czech[3]	checo	German[3]	alemán
Czechoslovak(ian)[3]	checoslovaco	Germany	Alemania
Czechoslovakia	Checoslovaquia	Gibraltar	Gibraltar
		Gibraltarian[3]	gibraltareño
		Gran Canaria,	Gran Canaria
Dane[1]	danés	Grand Canary	
Danish[2]	danés	Great Britain	Gran Bretaña
Danube	Danubio	Greece	Grecia
Dead Sea	mar Muerto	Greek[3]	griego
Denmark	Dinamarca	Greenland	Groenlandia
Dominican[3]	dominicano	Guatemala	Guatemala
Dominican	República	Guatemalan[3]	guatemalteco
Republic	Dominicana	Gulf of Lions	Golfo de León

Haiti	Haití	Laos	Laos
Haitian[3]	haitiano	Laotian[3]	laosiano
Hebrew[3]	hebreo	Latin America	América Latina,
Himalayas	Himalaya		Latinoamérica
Holland	Holanda	Latin American[3]	latinoamericano
Honduran[3]	hondureño	Latvia	Letonia
Honduras	Honduras	Latvian[3]	letón
Hungarian[3]	húngaro	Lebanese[3]	libanés
Hungary	Hungría	Lebanon	Líbano
		Libya	Libia
		Libyan[3]	libio
Iberian Peninsula	Península Ibérica	Liechtenstein	Liechtenstein
Ibiza	Ibiza	Liechtensteiner[1]	liechtenstiense
Ibizan[3]	ibicenco	Lithuania	Lituania
Iceland	Islandia	Lithuanian[3]	lituano
Icelander[1]	islandés	Londoner[1]	londinense
Icelandic[2]	islandés	Luxembourg	Luxemburgo
India	India	Luxembourger[1]	luxemburgués
Indian[3]	indio, hindú		
Indian Ocean	océano Índico		
Indochina	Indochina	Macedonia	Macedonia
Indonesia	Indonesia	Macedonian[3]	macedonio
Indonesian[3]	indonesio	Majorca	Mallorca
Irak	Irak	Majorcan[3]	mallorquín
Iran	Irán	Malaysia	Malasia
Iranian[3]	iraní	Malaysian[3]	malayo
Iraq	Irak	Mars	Marte
Iraqi[3]	iraquí	Mediterranean Sea	mar Mediterráneo
Ireland	Irlanda	Melilla	Melilla
Irish[2]	irlandés	Mercury	Mercurio
Israel	Israel	Mexican[3]	mejicano
Israeli[4]	israelí	Mexico	Méjico, México
Israelite[3]	israelita	Middle East	Oriente Medio
Italian[3]	italiano	Minorca	Menorca
Italy	Italia	Minorcan[3]	menorquín
		Mississippi	Misisipí
		Moldavia	Moldavia
Jamaica	Jamaica	Moldavian[3]	moldavo
Jamaican[3]	jamaicano,	Monaco	Mónaco
	jamaiquino	Monegasque[3]	monegasco
Japan	Japón	Montenegro	Montenegro
Japanese[3]	japonés	Montenegrin[3]	montenegrino
Jordan	Jordania	Moroccan[3]	marroquí
Jordanian[3]	jordano	Morocco	Marruecos
Jupiter	Júpiter		
Kenya	Kenia, Kenya	Navarre	Navarra
Kenyan[3]	keniano	Navarrese[3]	navarro
Korea	Corea	Nepal	Nepal
Korean[3]	coreano	Nepalese[3]	nepalí
Kuwait	Kuwait	Neptune	Neptuno
Kuwaiti[3]	kuwaití	Netherlands, The	Países Bajos
		New Yorker[1]	neoyorquino
		New Zealand	Nueva Zelanda
Lanzarote	Lanzarote	New Zealander[1]	neocelandés

Nicaragua	Nicaragua	Russia	Rusia
Nicaraguan[3]	nicaragüense	Russian[3]	ruso
Nigeria	Nigeria		
Nigerian[3]	nigeriano	Salvador(i)an[3]	salvadoreño
Nile	Nilo	Sardinia	Cerdeña
North America	América del Norte	Sardinian[3]	sardo
North American[3]	norteamericano	Saturn	Saturno
Northern Ireland	Irlanda del Norte	Saudi (Arabian)[4]	saudí, saudita
North Pole	Polo Norte	Saudi Arabia	Arabia Saudí
North Sea	mar del Norte	Scandinavia	Escandinavia
Norway	Noruega	Scandinavian[3]	escandinavo
Norwegian[3]	noruego	Scot[1]	escocés
		Scotland	Escocia
		Scots[2], Scottish[2]	escocés
Oceania	Oceanía	Seine	Sena
		Serb[3], Serbian[3]	serbio
		Serbo-Croat[3]	serbocroata
Pacific Ocean	océano Pacífico	Serbo-Croatian[2]	serbocroata
Pakistan	Paquistán, Pakistán	Sicilian[3]	siciliano
Pakistani[3]	paquistaní, pakistaní	Sicily	Sicilia
		Singapore	Singapur
Palestine	Palestina	Slav	eslavo
Palestinian[3]	palestino	Slovene[3]	esloveno
Panama	Panamá	Slovenia	Eslovenia
Panamanian[3]	panameño	Slovenian[3]	esloveno
Paraguay	Paraguay	South Africa	Suráfrica
Paraguayan[3]	paraguayo	South African[3]	surafricano
Persian[3]	pérsico, persa	South America	Sudamérica, América del Sur
Peru	Perú	South American[3]	sudamericano
Peruvian[3]	peruano	South Pole	Polo Sur
Philippine[5]	filipino	Spain	España
Philippines	Filipinas	Spaniard[1]	español
Pluto	Plutón	Spanish[2]	español
Poland	Polonia	Spanish America	Hispanoamérica
Pole[1]	polaco	Spanish American[4]	hispanoamericano
Polish[2]	polaco	Surinam	Suriname
Polynesia	Polinesia	Surinamese[3]	surinamés
Polynesian[3]	polinesio	Swede[1]	sueco
Portugal	Portugal	Sweden	Suecia
Portuguese[3]	portugués, luso	Swedish[2]	sueco
Puerto Rican[3]	puertorriqueño, portorriqueño	Swiss	suizo
		Switzerland	Suiza
Puerto Rico	Puerto Rico	Syria	Siria
Pyrenees	Pirineos	Syrian[3]	sirio
Red Sea	mar Rojo	Taiwan	Taiwan
Rhine	Rin	Tenerife	Tenerife
Rhone	Ródano	Thai[3]	tailandés
Rocky Mountains	Montañas Rocosas	Thailand	Tailandia
Romania, Rumania	Rumanía	Thames	Támesis
		Tunisia	Túnez
Romanian[3], Rumanian[3]	rumano	Tunisian[3]	tunecino
		Turk[1]	turco

Turkey	Turquía	Venezuela	Venezuela
Turkish[2]	turco	Venezuelan[3]	venezolano
		Venus	Venus
		Vietnam	Vietnam
Ukraine	Ucrania	Vietnamese[3]	vietnamita
Ukrainian[3]	ucraniano		
United Arab	Emiratos Árabes		
Emirates	Unidos	Wales	Gales
United Kingdom	Reino Unido	Welsh[2]	galés
United States (of	Estados Unidos	West Indes	Antillas
America)	(de América)	West Indian[3]	antillano
Uranus	Urano		
Uruguay	Uruguay		
Uruguayan[3]	uruguayo	Yugoslav(ian)[3]	yugoslavo
		Yugoslavia	Yugoslavia
Valencia	Valencia		
Valencian[3]	valenciano	Zaire	Zaire
Vatican	Vaticano	Zairian[3]	zairense

IDIOMS AND EXPRESSIONS / MODISMOS Y EXPRESIONES

A

A boca llena
Openly, plainly

A bordo
On board

A buena hora
On time

A buen santo te encomiendas
To bark up the wrong tree

A buen seguro
Certainly, very probably

A cada momento
Continually, frequently

A cada paso
At every turn (or step)

A cada rato
Each time, all the time

A cambio de
In exchange for

A campo raso
In the open

A campo traviesa
Cross-country

A casa
Home

A causa de
On account of

A ciegas
Blindly

A (or de) ciencia cierta
With certainty

A contrapelo
Against the grain

¿A cuánto(s) estamos?
What is the date?

A deshora(s)
At all hours, unexpectedly; at an untimely moment

A despecho de
In spite of, despite

A duras penas
With great difficulty, hardly, scarcely

A escape
Rapidly, at full speed

A escondidas
On the sly, undercover

A escondidas de
Without the knowledge of

A eso de
At about

A espaldas de
Behind one's back

A estas alturas
At this point or juncture

A falta de
For want of, lacking

A fin de cuentas
After all, in the final analysis

A fin de que
In order that, so that

A fines de
Late, towards the end of a period (week, etc.)

A flor de
Flush with

A fondo
Fully, thoroughly

A fuerza de
By force of, by dint of

A gatas
On all fours, crawling

A guisa de
Like, in the manner of

A hurto
On the sly, stealthily

A instancias de
At the request of

A la antigüita
Old-fashioned

A la buena (mala)
Willingly (unwillingly)

A la buena de Dios
Without malice, without plan, at random

A la carrera
In haste, on the run

A la fuerza
By force

A la larga
In the long run

A la moda
Up to date, in the latest fashion

A la noche
Tonight, at night

A la postre
At last, when all is said and done

A la redonda (or en redondo)
All around, round about

A la sazón
Then, at that time

A la ventura
Aimlessly, haphazardly, at random

A la verdad
In truth, in earnest, truly

A la vez
Together, at the same time

A la vista de
In plain view of

A la voluntad
At will, as you like

A la vuelta de
Around the corner, on returning

A la vuelta de la esquina
Around the corner

A la vuelta de los años
Within a few years

A lado de
Beside

A las claras
Clearly, openly, frankly, publicly

A las mil maravillas
Beautifully, wonderfully well

A lo largo (de)
Along, alongside of, lengthwise, at full length

A lo lejos
In the distance

A lo más
At most, at worst

A lo mejor
Perhaps, maybe

A lo sumo
At most

A los cuatro vientos
In all directions

A los pocos meses
After a few months

A (la) manera de
Like, in the style of

A mano
By hand, at hand, handmade

A mar de
A lot of, lots of

A más no poder
To the utmost, full blast

A más tardar
At the very latest

A más ver (or hasta más ver)
Goodbye

A mediados de
About the middle of the (day, week, etc.), during the (week, etc.)

A medida que
As, in proportion to

A medio camino
Halfway (to a place)

A medio hacer
Incomplete, half-done

A menos que
Unless

A menudo
Often

A merced de
At the mercy (or expense) of

A mi entender
In my opinion, as I understand it

A mi modo de ver
In my opinion

¡A mí qué!
What's that to me? So what!

A montones
In abundance, heaps

A ninguna parte
Nowhere

A no ser que
Unless

A ojo
By sight, by guess

A ojos cerrados
Blindly

A ojos vistas
Visibly, clearly; before one's eyes

A oscuras (or a obscuras)
In the dark

A partir de
As of, beginning on

A partir de hoy
From today on

A pedir de boca
Exactly as desired, to one's heart's content

A pesar de (todo)
In spite of (everything)

A pesar de que
In spite of the fact that

A pie
On foot, by foot

A piedra y lodo
Shut tight

A pie(s) juntillas
With both feet together; believe strongly

A poco
Shortly after

A pocos pasos
At a short distance

A porfía
In competition

A primera luz
At dawn

A principios de
Towards, early in, about the first of (day, week, etc.)

A propósito
By the way, apropos; on purpose

A prueba de
—proof, safe against

A puerta cerrada
Secretly, behind closed doors

A punto fijo
With certainty

A pura fuerza
By sheer force

A puros gritos
By just shouting

A que
I bet...(not a real wager)

¡A que no!
I bet you don't!

¿A qué viene eso?
What is the point of that?

A quema ropa (or a quemarropa)
Very close, point blank, without warning

A raíz de
Soon after, close to

A ras de (or al ras con)
Flush (or even) with

A ratos
From time to time, at times

A ratos perdidos
In (at) odd or spare moments

A rienda suelta
Free rein, violently, swiftly

A saber
Namely, that is

A sabiendas
Knowingly, consciously

A salvo
Safe, unharmed

A sangre fría
In cold blood

A secas
Plain, alone, simply, to the point

A semejanza de
Like, as

A su (debido) tiempo
In due course or time

A tiempo
On time, in time

A tientas
Blindly

A toda costa
By all means, at whatever cost

A toda hora
At any time, at all times

A toda prisa
At greatest speed

A toda vela
Under full sail, at full speed

A todas luces
By all means, any way you look at it

A todo correr
At full speed

A todo trance
At all costs

A todo trapo
Under full sail, speedily

A traición
Deceitfully, treacherously

A través de, al través de
Across, through

A última hora
At the last moment

A una brazada
At arm's length

A una voz
Unanimously

A un tiempo
At one (the same) time

A veces
At times

A ver (si)
Let's see (if)

A vista de
Within view, in the presence of

A vistas
On approval

A voluntad
At will

A vuelo de pájaro
As the crow flies

Abrir paso
To make way, to clear the way

Acabar de
To have just (done something)

Acabar por
To end up by (doing something)

Acerca de
About, with regard to

Acordar con
To be on good terms with

Acostarse con las gallinas
To go to bed early

¿Adónde va?
Where are you going?

Adondequiera que
Wherever

Agachar las orejas
To hang one's head

Aguantar el chubasco
To weather the storm

Águila o pico
Heads or tails

Águila o sello
Heads or tails

Aguzar las orejas (los oídos)
To prick up one's ears

¡Ahí está el detalle!
That's the point!

Ahogarse en poca agua
To worry about nothing

Ahora bien
Now then, well now, however

Ahora es cuando
Now is the time; now is your chance

Ahora mismo
Right now, at once

Al aire libre
In the open air, outdoors

Al azar
By chance, at random

Al cabo (de)
Finally or after

Al caer de la noche
At nightfall

Al centavo
Just right, to the letter

Al contado
Cash

Al contrario
On the contrary

Al cuidado de
In care of

Al derecho
Right side out

Al (or en) derredor
Around

Al descubierto
Openly

Al día
Per day

Al día siguiente
On the following day

Al filo de (las cinco)
At about (5 o'clock)

Al fin
At the end, at last

Al fin de cuentas
In any case

Al fin y al cabo
In short, at last, anyway

Al frente de
In front of

Al habla
Within speaking distance;
speaking! (in answering a
telephone)

Al igual
Equally

Al instante
At once

Al lado (de)
At one's side, near at hand,
next to

Al menos (or a lo menos)
At least, at the least

Al menudeo (or al por menor)
At retail, in small quantities

Al mismo tiempo
At the same time

Al oído
Confidentially

Al otro día
On the following day

Al otro lado de
On the other side of

Al pan, pan y al vino, vino
Call a spade a spade

Al parecer
Apparently

Al pelo
Perfectly, agreed, just right

Al pie de la letra
Literally, to the letter

Al (or a) poco rato
In a short while, soon after

Al presente
Now, at present

Al principio
At first

Al punto
At once

Al raso
In the open air

Al (or en) rededor
Around, about

Al remo
At hard labor

Al revés
Backwards, wrong side out, in
the opposite way

Al sereno
In the night air

Al sesgo
On the bias, diagonally,
obliquely

Al soslayo
On the bias, slanting, obliquely

Al tanteo
Hit or miss, by guess

Al través de
Through, throughout

Al trote
Quickly

Algo por el estilo
Similar, something of the sort

Algo sordo
Hard of hearing

Algo tarde
Rather late

Algún otro
Somebody else, some other

Alrededor de
Around about, more or less

Alzar el codo
To drink too much

Allá a las quinientas
Once in a blue moon

¡Allí está el toque!
There is the heart of the matter!

Amante de
Fond of

Amigo de
Fond of (friend of)

Amor propio
Self-esteem, pride, vanity

Andar a gatas
To creep, crawl

Andar agitado
To be out of sorts

Andar bien
To keep good time (e.g., a
watch), to work well, to be right

**Andar (or ir) de parranda (or de
fiesta en fiesta)**
To go on a spree

Andarse con rodeos
To beat around the bush

Andarse el tiempo
Meantime, as time goes on

Andarse por las ramas
To beat around the bush

Ante todo
Especially, first of all, above all

Antes de que
Before

Antes hoy que mañana
The sooner the better

Antes que
Rather than

Año antepasado
Year before last

Año entrante
Next year

Año bisiesto
Leap year

Aparte de eso
Besides that, aside from that

Aprender de memoria
To learn by heart

**Aprendiz de todo y oficial
de nada**
Jack of all trades

Aprovechar la ocasión
To take advantage of the
situation

Aquí cerca
Around (near) here

Aquí mismo
Right here

Arranque de cólera
Fit of anger

Así así
So-so

Así como
Just as, the same as, as well as

Así de largo
That long

Así es que
So that, as soon as

Así está bien
This will do (be OK)

Así nada más
Just plain, just as is

Así pues
So then, therefore

Así que
So that, as soon as, so,
therefore

¡Así se hace!
Well done!, Bully for you!

Así y todo
In spite of that, even so,
anyhow

Atrás de
Behind, in back of

Aun así
Even so

Aun cuando
Even if, even though

Aún no
Not yet

Ayer mismo
Just yesterday

Ayer por la tarde
Yesterday afternoon

Azotar el aire
To work in vain

B

Bailar a secas
To dance without music

Baja el radio
Turn down the radio

Bajo techo
Indoors

Barrios bajos
Slums

Beber a pulso
To gulp down

Bien arreglado
Neatly dressed

Bien asado
Well-done (well-cooked)

Bien cocido
Well-done (well-cooked)

Bien me lo merezco
It serves me right

Bien parecido
Good-looking

Bien peinado
Well-groomed, trim

Bien que
Although

Boca abajo
Face down, prone

Boca arriba
Face up, supine

Bromas aparte
All joking aside

Buen mozo
Handsome man

¡Buen provecho!
Good appetite! Enjoy your meal!

Buen rato
Pleasant (or long) time

Buen tipo
Good fellow

Burlarse de
To make fun of

Buscarle tres (cuatro) pies al gato
To look for trouble

Buscar una aguja en un pajar
To look for a needle in a haystack

C

Cada cual (or cada uno)
Each one

¿Cada cuánto tiempo?
How often?

Cada dos días
Every other day

Cada uno
Apiece

Cada vez menos
Less and less

Caer bien
To fit well, to be becoming, to please

Caer enfermo
To fall ill

Caer en gracia
To please

Caer en la cuenta
To realize, to get the point

Caer mal
To fit badly, displease

Caliente de cascos
Hot-headed

¡Cállate la trompa!
Shut up!

Calle abajo
Down the street

Calle arriba
Up the street

Callejón sin salida
Blind alley, dead end

Cambiar de tema
To change the subject

Caminar con pies de plomo
To go cautiously

Camino de
On the way to, on the road to

Camino trillado
Beaten path

Cara a cara
Face to face

Cara o cruz
Heads or tails

Cargar con
To carry away, assume responsibility

Cargar con el muerto
To get the blame unjustly

Carne de gallina
Goosebumps

Casarse con
To marry (someone)

Casi nunca
Hardly ever

Castañetear con los dedos
To snap one's fingers

Cerca de
Near to, close to

Cerrarse el cielo
To become overcast, cloudy

Cifrar la esperanza en
To place one's hope in

Claro que no
Of course not, certainly not

Claro que sí
Of course, naturally

Colmo de la locura
Height of folly

Como a costumbre
At about

Como de costumbre
As usual

Como dijo el otro
As someone said, as the saying goes

Como Dios manda
According to Hoyle (the rules)

Como en
In about

Como mínimo
At least

Como no
Unless

¡Cómo no!
Of course, why not!

Como por ensalmo
As if by magic, in a jiffy

Como que
Since, inasmuch as

Como quiera que
Since, inasmuch as

Como quiera que sea
At any rate

Como si
As if

Como si fuera
As if it were

Como siempre
As usual, like always

Como sigue
As follows

Como último recurso
As a last resort

Como una seda
As smooth as silk, soft as silk

Como visita de obispo
Once in a blue moon

Con anticipación
In advance

Con delirio
Madly

Con el propósito de
With the aim of

Con (or en or por) extremo
Very much, extremely

Con fuerzas para...(la tarea)
Equal to...(the task)

Con la lengua de corbata (or con la lengua de pechera)
Out of breath, with tongue hanging out

Con motivo de
With the idea of, because of, on the occasion of, on account of

¿Con qué cara?
How can I (one) have the nerve?

¡Con razón!
No wonder!

Con respecto a
With regard to

Con rumbo a
In the direction of

Con tal (de) que
Provided that, so that

Con tiempo
In advance, in good time

Con todo (or con todos) los obstáculos
In spite of that

Conciliar el sueño
To get to sleep

Confiar en
To trust, rely on

Conforme a
In accordance with

Conocer de vista
To know by sight

Consigo mismo
To oneself

Conspirar contra una persona
To frame someone

Consultar con la almohada
To sleep on it

Contar con
To reckon with, rely on, count on

Contra viento y marea
Against all odds, come hell or high water, come what may

Convenirle a uno
To be to one's advantage

Correr por cuenta de uno
To be one's own affair, to be up to oneself

Correr riesgo
To take a chance, to risk

Corrida del tiempo
Swiftness of time

Cortar el hilo
To break the thread of a story, to interrupt

Corto de oído
Hard of hearing

Corto de vista
Nearsighted

Cosa de
Approximately, about

Costar trabajo
To be very difficult

Costar un ojo de la cara
To cost an arm and a leg, be very expensive

Cruzarse con
To meet

Cualquier cosa
Anything at all

Cualquiera (or cualesquiera) de los dos
Either of the two

Cuando más tarde
At the latest

Cuando menos
At least

Cuando quiera
Whenever

Cuanto antes
As soon as possible

Cuatro letras
A few lines

Cuatro palabras
A few words

Cuento alegre
Spicy story

Cuento chino
Cock and bull story

Cueste lo que cueste
At any cost

Cumplir años
To have a birthday

Cumplir su palabra
To keep one's word

CH

Chueco o derecho
Hit or miss, happy-go-lucky

D

Dado caso
Supposing

Dado el caso que
Provided that

Dar a
To face, look towards, give to

Dar a conocer
To make known

Dar a entender
To pretend

Dar alas a
To embolden, give courage

Dar aliento
To encourage

Dar al traste con
To ruin, destroy

Dar al través con
To ruin, destroy

Dar ánimo
To cheer up

Dar atención
To pay attention

Dar batería
To raise a rumpus, to work hard

Dar calabazas
To reject, to jilt

Dar caza
To pursue, track down

Dar cima
To complete, carry out

Dar coba
To flatter, play up to, softsoap

Dar cuenta de
To give a report on

Dar de comer
To feed, be fed

Dar disgustos a
To cause distress or grief to

Dar el pésame por
To extend condolences to or for

Dar el visto bueno
To approve, OK

Dar en
To hit or to hit upon

Dar en cara
To reproach, blame

Dar en el clavo
To hit the nail on the head

Dar en (or dar con) el chiste
To guess right, hit the nail on the head

Dar en tierra con alguien
To overthrow someone

Dar esquinazo
To "ditch," avoid meeting someone

Dar fe de
To vouch for

Dar fin (a)
To complete

Dar gato por liebre
To cheat or swindle

Dar grasa
To polish (shoes)

Dar guerra
To make trouble

Dar la hora
To strike the hour

Dar la lata
To annoy

Dar la mano
To help, shake hands

Dar la noticia
To break the news

Dar la razón
To agree, to be of same opinion

Dar la razón a una persona
To admit a person is right

Dar (or darse) la vuelta
To turn (to turn around)

Dar largas
To postpone or delay, or give someone the run around

Dar las espaldas a
To turn one's back on

Dar las gracias
To give thanks, to thank

Dar lástima (de)
To arouse pity or sorrow

Dar lo mismo
To make no difference

Dar los recuerdos
To give regards

Dar lugar a
To give cause for

Dar lustre
To polish

Dar marcha atrás
To back up

Dar mucha pena
To cause sorrow, to be disconcerting

Dar parte
To inform

Dar pie
To give opportunity (or occasion to)

Dar por
To consider as

Dar por descontado
To take for granted

Dar por hecho
To take for granted, to consider as done

Dar por sabido
To take for granted

Dar por sentado
To take for granted

Dar por supuesto
To take for granted

Dar prestado
To lend

Dar propina
To tip (give a gratuity)

Dar que hacer
To cause extra work

Dar rabia
To anger

Dar razón
To inform, give account

Dar realce
To enhance, emphasize

Dar sepultura
To bury

Dar un paseo
To take a walk or ride

Dar un paseo en barco
To go for a sail

Dar un paso
To take a step

Dar un pisotón
To step hard upon

Dar un portazo
To slam the door

Dar un salto (or dar saltos)
To leap, jump

Dar un traspié
To trip, stumble

Dar un vistazo a
To glance over, peruse

Dar una cita
To make an appointment

Dar una fiesta
To give (throw) a party

Dar una pasada por
To pass by, walk by

Dar una pisada
To step (stomp) on (upon)

Dar una satisfacción
To apologize

Dar una vuelta
To take a stroll

Dar uno en la tecla
To hit the nail on the head, find the right way to do something

Darle a uno mala espina
To arouse one's suspicion

Darle lo mismo
It makes no difference

Darse aires a
To put on airs

Darse cuenta de (que)
To realize (that), to notice

Darse de baja
To drop out

Darse farol
To show off, put on airs

Darse la mano
To shake hands

Darse por vencido (or me doy)
To give up (or I give up)

Darse prisa
To hurry

Darse tono
To put on airs

Darse un tropezón
To trip, stumble

Darse un encontrón
To collide with, bump into each other

Darse un resbalón
To slip

Dárselas de
To pose as

De acuerdo con
In accordance with

De ahí en adelante
From then on

De ahí que
Hence

De ahora en adelante
From now on, in the future

De algún modo
Somehow

De algún tiempo para acá
For some time now

De alguna manera
Somehow

De arriba abajo
From top to bottom

De aquel tiempo en adelante
From that time on

De aquí en adelante
From now on

De aquí para allá
To and fro, back and forth

De broma
Jokingly, in jest

De buen tomo y lomo
Bulky, important

De buen tono
In good taste, stylish

De buen ver
Good-looking

De buena cepa
Of good stock or quality

De buena fe
In good faith

De buena gana (or de buen grado)
Willingly, gladly

De buena ley
Of good quality

De buenas a primeras
All of a sudden, unexpectedly, on the spur of the moment

De burla
In jest

De cabo a rabo
From beginning to end

De camino (or de camino real)
On the way

De canto
On edge

De copete
High rank, important, proud

De corrida
Without stopping

De cualquier modo
At any rate

De cuando en cuando
Sometimes, occasionally

De día
By day, before dark

De dientes afuera
Insincerely

¡De dónde!
Nonsense!

De dos caras
Two-faced

De dos en dos
By twos, two by two

De dos sentidos
Two-way

De ese modo (or de esa manera)
In that way

De espaldas
On one's back, supine

De este modo (or de esta manera)
In this way

De etiqueta
Formal

De golpe
Suddenly

De gorra
At another's expense

De grado en grado
By degrees

De hecho
In fact

De hilo
Without stopping

De hoy en adelante
From now on

De hoy en ocho días
One week from today

De hoy en quince días
Two weeks from today

De improviso
Unexpectedly

De lado
Tilted, oblique, sideways

De la noche a la mañana
Overnight

De lejos
From a distance

De lo contrario
If not, otherwise

De lo lindo
Wonderfully, very much, to the utmost

De mal en peor
From bad to worse

De mal grado
Reluctantly, unwillingly

De mal gusto
In poor taste

De mal temple
In a bad humor

De mala fe
In bad faith, deceitfully

De mala gana
Unwillingly

De mala suerte
Unlucky

De manera que
So that

De marca
Of excellent quality

De memoria
By heart

De moda
In vogue, stylish

De modo que
So what?, so that, and so

De momento
For the time being

De nada
Don't mention it; you're welcome

De ningún modo
By no means

¡De ninguna manera!
By no means!, I should say not!

De noche
By (at) night

De nuevo
Again, once again

De ocasión
Reduced price, a bargain

De (or al) oído
By ear

De oídos
Rumor, hearsay

De ordinario
Ordinary, usual

De otro modo
Otherwise

De palabra
By word of mouth

De par en par
Wide open

De parte a parte
Through, from one side to the other

De parte de
On behalf of, in favor of

De paso
In passing, at the same time, by the way, in transit

De pie
Standing

De pilón
To boot, besides, in addition

De poca monta
Of little value or importance

De poquito
In small amounts

De por sí
Separately, by itself

De prisa
Quickly

De pronto
At once, suddenly

De propósito
On purpose

De punta
On end

De puntillas (or de puntas)
On tiptoes

De punto
By the minute

De pura casualidad
By pure chance

De rebote
On the rebound, indirectly

De relieve
In relief, outstanding, prominent

De remate
Absolutely, without remedy

De repente
Suddenly, all of a sudden

De repuesto
Spare, extra

De resultas
As a result, consequently

De rigor
A "must," it must

De rodillas
On one's knees

De seguida
Continuously, without interruption

De segunda mano
Secondhand

De seguro
For certain, for sure

De sobra
More than enough, unnecessary

De sol a sol
Sunrise to sunset

De soslayo
Slanting, sideways

De subida
On the way up

De súbito
Suddenly

De suerte que
So that, and so, in such a way

De su (propia) cosecha
Of one's own making or invention

De suyo
Naturally, by nature

De tarde en tarde
From time to time, now and then, once in a blue moon

De tejas abajo
Here below, in this world

De todas maneras
Anyway, at any rate

De todos modos
At any rate, in any case, anyhow, by all means

De tránsito
In transit, on the way, passing through

De través
Across

De un golpe
All at once

De un modo u otro
Somehow, in some way or other

De un momento a otro
At any moment

De un salto
Quickly

De un solo sentido
One way (e.g., one-way street)

De un tirón
All at once

De una pieza
Solid, of one piece

De una tirada
All at once, in one fell swoop

De una vez
At once, at one time, at one stroke, once and for all

De una vez por todas
Once and for all

De uno en uno
One at a time

De unos
Of about

De uso
Secondhand

De veras (¿De veras?)
Really, in truth, in earnest
(really?, is that so?)

De verdad (¿De verdad?)
Truly, truthfully (really?, is
that so?)

De vez en cuando
Now and then, occasionally

De vicio
As a (bad) habit

De viva voz
By word of mouth

De (buena) voluntad
Willingly, with pleasure

De vuelta
Again

Debajo de
Under, beneath

Debe de ser
It must be, it probably is

Decir para sí
To say to one's self

Decir para su coleto (or capote)
To say to one's self

Dejar a uno plantado
To ''stand someone up,'' leave
someone in the lurch

Dejar caer
To drop

Dejar de
To stop

Dejar de asistir
To drop out

Dejar de la mano
To leave, abandon

Dejar dicho
To leave word

Dejar en las astas del toro
To leave in the lurch

Dejar en paz
To let be, to leave alone

Dejar saber
To let on, pretend

Dejar tranquilo
To leave alone

Dejarse de cuentos
Come to the point, stop beating
around the bush

Dejarse de rodeos
Stop the excuses, stop beating
around the bush

Del mismo modo
Of the same sort, in the
same way

Del próximo pasado
Of last month

Del todo
Wholly, at all

Delante de
In front of

Dentro de
Inside of, within

Dentro de poco
In a little while

Dentro de un momento
In a short time

Dentro de una semana
Within a week

Desayunarse con la noticia
To hear a piece of news early or
for the first time

Descabezar el sueño
To take a nap

Desde ahora
From now on

Desde el principio
All along, from the beginning

Desde entonces
Since then, ever since

Desde hace
Dating from, over a period of...

Desde lejos
From a distance, from afar

Desde luego
Actually, of course, at once

Desde que
Since

Desde un principio
From the beginning

Desempeñar un papel
To play a part

Despedirse de
To say goodbye to

Después de eso
Thereafter

Después de todo
After all

Detrás de
Behind, in back of

Devanarse los sesos
To rack one's brain

Día de raya
Payday

**Día de semana (or día de
trabajo)**
Weekday

Día hábil
Weekday, workday

Día tras día
Day after day

Días de antaño
Days of old

Días de semana
Weekdays

Dicho y hecho
Sure enough, no sooner said
than done

Dificultar el paso
To obstruct, impede

Digno de
Well worth it

Digno de confianza
Reliable, trustworthy

Dinero contante y sonante
Ready (or hard) cash

Dinero menudo
Change (re money)

Doblar a la esquina
To turn the corner

Dolerle a uno la garganta
To have a sore throat

Dolor de cabeza
Headache

Donde no
Otherwise, if not

**Dondequiera que (or por
dondequiera que)**
Wherever

Dormir a pierna suelta
To sleep soundly

Dormir la mona
To sleep it off

Dormir la siesta
To take an afternoon nap

E

**Echar a correr (or echarse a
correr)**
To begin running (to run away)

Echar(se) a perder
To spoil, to ruin

Echar a pique
To sink

Echar al olvido
To forget on purpose

Echar de menos
To miss

Echar de ver
To notice, to observe

Echar en cara
To reproach, blame

Echar espumarajos
To froth at the mouth, to be
very angry

Echar flores
To throw bouquets, to flatter,
to compliment

Echar la casa por la ventana
To spare no expense, squander
everything

Echar la culpa a
To blame

Echar la garra
To arrest, grab

Echar la llave
To lock the door

Echar la uña
To steal

Echar la zarpa
To grasp, to seize

Echar leña al fuego
To add fuel to the fire

Echar mano
To seize

Echar pajas
To draw lots

Echar papas
To fib

Echar por tierra
To knock down, demolish

Echar raíces
To take root, become firmly fixed

Echar suertes
To draw lots

Echar un piropo
To compliment, flatter

Echar un sueño
To take a nap

Echar (or soltar) un terno
To say a bad word, to swear, curse

Echar un trago
To take a drink

Echar una cana al aire
To go out for a good time or fling

Echar (una carta) al correo
To mail (a letter)

Echar una siesta
To take a nap

Echarle la bendición a una cosa
To give something up for lost

Echarse a
To begin to (do something)

Echarse al coleto
To drink down, devour

Echarse para atrás
To back out, go back on one's word

El caso es
The fact is

El común de las gentes
The majority of the people, the average person

El cuento del tío
Deceitful story told to get money

El de
The one with

El día menos pensado
When least expected, unexpectedly

El gusto es mío
The pleasure is mine

El más reciente
The latter

El mismísimo hombre
The very man

El mismo que (or lo mismo que)
The same as

El pro y el contra
Pro and con

El que
The one who, the one which

El sol poniente
The setting sun

El tren llegó con (x) minutos de retraso
The train was (x) minutes late

El uno al otro
Each other

El uno o el otro (or uno u otro)
Either, one or the other

Empeñar la palabra
To promise, pledge

Empinar el codo
To drink (too much)

En abonos
On installments

En absoluto
Absolutely (not)

En adelante
In the future, from now on

En alguna otra parte
Somewhere else

En alguna parte
Somewhere

En ambos casos
In either case

En aquel tiempo (en aquel entonces)
At that time, in those days

En balde
In vain

En breve
Shortly

En broma
In jest, as a joke

En buen romance
In plain language

En cambio
On the other hand

En casa
At home, indoors

En caso afirmativo
If so

En caso de
In the event of

En caso de que
In case of (that)

En concreto
Concretely, to sum up

En conformidad con
In compliance with

En conjunto
As a whole

En contra de
Against, opposed to

En cualquier caso
Anyway

En cuanto
As soon as

En cuanto a
As for, with regard to

En curso
In progress

En descubierto
Uncovered, unpaid

En días pasados
In days gone by

En efecto
In fact, indeed, really

En el acto
Right away, at once

En el extranjero
Abroad, out of the country

En el fondo
At bottom, at heart, in substance

En el momento preciso
In the nick of time

En el quinto infierno (or los quintos infiernos)
Very far away

En el sigilo (or silencio) de la noche
In the dead of the night

En especial
Especially, in particular

En espera de
Awaiting

En fecha a próxima
At an early date

En fin
In short, finally, in conclusion

En fragante
In the act

En grande
On a large scale

En grueso
In bulk, by wholesale

En junto (or en conjunto)
All together, in all

En la actualidad
At the present time

En libertad
Free

En lo futuro
In the future

En lo más crudo del invierno
In the dead of winter

En lo sucesivo
Hereafter, in future

En lontananza
In the distance, in the background

En lugar de
Instead of, in place of

En manga de camisa
In shirtsleeves

En marcha
In progress

En muchos puntos
In many respects

En (or al) ninguna parte
Nowhere

En obsequio de
In honor of, for the sake of

En otros términos
In other words

En parte
Partly

En particular
Especially

En pleno día
In broad daylight

En pleno rostro (or en plena cara)
Right on the face

En poder de
In the hands of

En prenda de
As proof of, as a pledge

En pro de
On behalf of

En pro y en contra
For and against

En punto
On the dot, sharp

En rama
Crude, raw

En realidad
As a matter of fact

En regla
In order

En resolución
In brief

En resumen
Summing up, in brief

En resumidas cuentas
In short, after all

En rigor
In fact, in reality

En rueda
In turn, in a circle

En salvo
In safety, out of danger

En sazón
Ripe, in season

En secreto
Secretly

En seguida
At once, right now

En señal de
In proof of, in token of

En serio
Seriously

En sueños
In one's sleep

En tal caso
In such a case

En tanto que
While

En todas partes
Everywhere

En todo caso
In any event

En un credo
In a jiffy, in a minute

En un chiflido
In a jiffy, in a second

En un improviso
In a moment

En un salto
Quickly

En un santiamén
Instantly, in the twinkling of an eye

En un soplo
In a jiffy, in a second

En vela
On watch, without sleep

En verdad
Really, truly

En vez de
Instead of

En vigor
In force, in effect

En vista de que
Since, in view of

En voz alta
Aloud, loud voice

En voz baja
In a low voice, whispering

Encargarse de
To take charge of

Encima de
On, upon

Encogerse de hombros
To shrug one's shoulders

Encontrarse con
To come across, to meet

Enfrentarse con
To confront, meet face to face

Enredarse con
To have an affair with

Entablar una conversación
To start a conversation

Entre azul y buenas noches
Undecided, on the fence

Entre bastidores
Behind the scenes, offstage

Entre la espada y la pared
Between the devil and the deep blue sea

Entre paréntesis
By the way

Entre semana
During the week

Entre tanto
Meanwhile, all the while, at the same time

Es cierto
It's true

Es decir
That is to say, in other words

Es (la) hora de (partir)
It is time for, it is time to (go)

Es lo de menos
It makes no difference, that's the least of the trouble

Eso corre prisa
That is urgent

Eso es
That is it, that's right

¡Eso es el colmo!
That is the limit!

Eso es harina de otro costal
That's a horse of a different color

Eso estriba en que
The basis for it is that

Eso no tiene quite
That can't be helped

Eso sí
That was (or is) true

Esperar en alguien
To place hope (or confidence) in someone

Esperar todo el santo día
To wait the whole blessed day

Está de más
It is unnecessary, superfluous

Está por hacer
It is yet to be done

Estamos a mano
We are even, quits

Estar a buen recaudo
To be safe

Estar a cargo de
To be in charge of

Estar a gusto
To be contented or comfortable

Estar a la altura de
To be equal to (a task)

Estar a la mira de
To be alert for, on the lookout for

Estar a punto de
To be about to

Estar al cabo de
To be well-informed, up-to-date

Estar al corriente de
To be informed, to be up-to-date

Estar afecto a
To be fond of

Estar afilando con (or afilar con)
To flirt with

Estar (or ponerse) ancho
To swell with pride

Estar arreglado
To be in order

Estar bien
To be all right, OK. Ex.: **Está bien.** (It is) all right, (it's) OK

Estar bien de salud
To be in good health

Estar bruja
To be broke

Estar con el agua al cuello
To be in big trouble

Estar de acuerdo
To agree

Estar de bote en bote
To be crowded, be completely filled up

Estar de buen humor (or de buen genio)
To be in a good mood

Estar de conformidad con
To be in compliance with

Estar de duelo
To mourn, be in mourning

Estar de luto
To be in mourning

Estar de malas
To be out of luck

Estar de mal humor (or de mal genio)
To be in a bad mood

Estar (or quedar) de non
To be left alone, without a partner or companion

Estar de paso
To be passing through

Estar de prisa
To be in a hurry

Estar de regreso
To be back

Estar de sobra
To be in the way

Estar de turno
To be on duty

Estar de vacaciones
To be on vacation

Estar de (or estar en) vena (para)
To be in the mood (for)

Estar de venta
To be on sale

Estar de viaje
To be traveling, on the road

Estar de vuelta
To be back

Estar desahogado
To be well off

Estar dispuesto
To be willing

Estar en buen uso
To be in good condition (re a thing)

Estar en camino
To be on the way

Estar en curso
To be going on, be under way

Estar en las mismas
To be in the same boat

Estar en las nubes
To daydream

Estar en las últimas
To be on one's last legs, to be at the end of one's rope, out of resources

Estar en pañales
To be in infancy, to possess scant knowledge

Estar en peligro
To be in danger

Estar en pugna con
To be opposed to, to be in conflict with, to be against

Estar en todo
To have a finger in everything

Estar en un aprieto
To be in a jam, to be in trouble

Estar en un error
To be wrong, to be mistaken

Estar encargado de
To have charge of, to be in charge of

Estar entre la espada y la pared
To be between the devil and the deep blue sea

Estar (or andar) escaso de dinero
To be just about out of money, be short of money

Estar fuera de la casa
To be out of the house, away from home

Estar fuera de la ley
To be against the law

Estar harto de
To be fed up with

Estar hasta los topes
To be filled up

Estar hecho un costal de huesos
To be very thin, nothing but skin and bones

Estar hecho una sopa
To be sopping wet, soaked through

Estar mal templado
To be in a bad humor

Estar muy metido en
To be deeply involved in

Estar para
To be about to

Estar peor que antes
To be worse off

Estar por
To be in favor of

Estar ras con ras
To be flush, perfectly even

Estar regular
To feel OK

Estar salado
To be unlucky; to be witty, salty

Estar sobre sí (...sobre aviso)
To be on the alert, cautious

Estar torcido con
To be on unfriendly terms with

Estar uno en sus cabales
To be in one's right mind

Estar uno hasta el copete
To be stuffed, fed up

Estar uno hasta la coronilla
To be fed up, satisfied

Estarse parado
To stand still

Estirar la pata
To die

Estrechar la mano (a)
To shake hands, grasp (or squeeze) a hand

Explicar una cátedra
To teach a course

F

Falta de conocimientos
Lack of instructions

Falta de saber
Lack of instructions

Faltar a clase
To cut class

Faltar a su palabra
To break one's word

Faltar poco
To be almost time

Faltarle a uno un tornillo
To have little sense, "to have a screw loose"

Fijarse en
To notice, pay attention to

Formar parte de
To be a part (or member) of

Forzar la entrada
To break into

Frente a
In front of

Fruncir el ceño
To frown, scowl

Fruncir el entrecejo
To wrinkle one's brow

Fruncir las cejas
To frown, knit the eyebrows

Fuera de broma
All joking aside

Fuera de lo corriente
Unusual, out of the ordinary

Fuera de propósito
Irrelevant

Fuera de sí
Beside oneself

G

Ganar para comer
To earn a living

Ganar tiempo
To save time

Ganarse la vida
To make one's living

Gente de baja estofa
Low-class people, rabble

Guardar cama
To stay in bed, to be confined in bed

Guardar rencor
To bear or hold a grudge

Guardar silencio
To keep silent

Gusano de la conciencia
Remorse

H

Había una vez (or érase que se era; érase una vez; y va de cuento)
Once upon a time

Hablar al alma
To speak frankly

Hablar al caso
To speak to the point, or in plain language

Hablar alto (or en voz alta)
To speak loudly

Hablar en secreto
To whisper

Hablar para sus adentros
To talk to oneself

Hablar por los codos
To talk too much, chatter constantly

Hace (dos, tres, etc.) años
(Two, three, etc.) years ago

Hace buen (mal) tiempo
It is good (bad) weather

Hace caso omiso
It (he, etc.) ignores

Hace mucho que no (juego, etc.)
It's been a long time since (I played, etc.)

Hace mucho tiempo
Long ago

Hacer alto
To stop

Hacer arreglos
To make arrangements

Hacer buen papel
To make a good showing

Hacer burla de
To make fun of

Hacer caso a (or hacer caso de)
To take into account, pay attention to

Hacer caso omiso de
To ignore

Hacer cocos
To make eyes at, flirt

Hacer cola
To form a line, wait in line

Hacer como si
To act as if

Hacer cuco a
To fool, make fun of

Hacer de
To act as

Hacer de nuevo
To do again, to do over

Hacer deducciones precipitadas
To jump to conclusions

Hacer destacar
To emphasize

Hacer ejercicio
To take exercise

Hacer el favor de
Please

Hacer el (or hacer un) papel
To play a role

Hacer el ridículo
To be ridiculous, act a fool

Hacer escala (en)
To stop over at

Hacer falta
To lack, be in need of

Hacer favoritismos en prejuicio de
To discriminate against

Hacer frente (a)
To face

Hacer gala de
To boast of

Hacer garras
To tear to pieces

Hacer gestos
To make faces at

Hacer gracia
To amuse, to make laugh

Hacer juego
To match

Hacer la corte
To court, woo

Hacer la zanguanga
To feign illness

Hacer las maletas
To pack, get ready to leave

Hacer las paces
To make up after a quarrel

Hacer lo posible
To do one's best

Hacer mal papel
To make a poor showing

Hacer mala obra
To hinder, interfere

Hacer mella
To make a dent or impression, to cause pain or worry

Hacer memoria
To remember, recollect

Hacer muecas
To make faces

Hacer otra vez
To do over

Hacer pedazos
To break into pieces

Hacer pinta
To play hooky, cut class

Hacer por escrito
To put in writing

Hacer preguntas (or hacer una pregunta)
To ask questions, to ask a question

Hacer presa
To seize

Hacer puente
To take a long weekend

Hacer rajas
To slice, to tear or cut into strips

Hacer rostro
To face

Hacer rumbo a
To head (or sail) towards

Hacer sombra
To shade, cast a shadow

Hacer su agosto
To make hay while the sun shines

Hacer teatro
To show off

Hacer trizas
To tear to pieces, to shred

Hacer un pedido
To place an order

Hacer un trato
To make a deal

Hacer un viaje
To go on a journey

Hacer una mala jugada
To play a mean trick

Hacer una perrada
To play a mean trick

Hacer una plancha
To make a ridiculous blunder

Hacer una visita
To pay a visit

Hacer vida
To live together

Hacerle daño a uno
To hurt or harm someone

Hacerse a
To get used to

Hacerse a la derecha
To pull over to the right

Hacerse a un lado
To step aside, move over

Hacerse amigo
To make friends with

Hacerse cargo
To take charge, to be responsible for

Hacerse de rogar
To be coaxed, to let oneself (or want to) be coaxed

Hacerse duro
To resist stubbornly

Hacerse el desentendido
To pretend not to notice

Hacerse el sordo
To pretend not to hear, turn a deaf ear

Hacerse el tonto
To play dumb, to act the fool

Hacerse entender
To make oneself understood

Hacerse ilusiones
To fool oneself

Hacerse noche
To grow late, get late in the evening

Hacerse tarde
To get late

Hacerse un lío
To get tangled up, become confused

Hacerse uno rajas
To wear oneself out

Hacia adelante
Forward

Hacia atrás
Backward

Hasta aquí (or hasta ahí)
Up to now, so far

Hasta cierto punto
In a way, up to a point

¿Hasta dónde?
How far?

Hasta más no poder
To the limit, utmost

Hasta el tope
Up to the top

Hasta la fecha
Up to date, up to now

Hasta que
Until

Hasta que se llene
Until full

Hay gato encerrado
There is more than meets the eye

Hay moros en la costa
Something is wrong; the coast is not clear; little pitchers have big ears

Hay que
One must, it is necessary to

He aquí
Behold, here is…

Hecho y derecho
Mature, full-fledged, grown up

Hincarse de rodillas
To kneel down

Hoy (en) día
Nowadays

I

Ida y vuelta
Round trip

Idas y venidas
Comings and goings

Igual que
The same as

Impedir el paso
To block the door, to obstruct the way

Ímpetu de ira
Fit of anger

Inaplicable al caso
Irrelevant

Incurrir en el odio de
To incur the hatred of

Incurrir en un error
To fall into (or commit) an error

Ingresar en
To join (a club, etc.)

Ir a caballo
To ride horseback

Ir a medias (or ir a la mitad)
To go halves (50-50)

Ir a pie
To walk, to go on foot

Ir al centro
To go downtown

Ir al grano
To get down to cases, come to the point

Ir corriendo
To be running

Ir de compras
To go shopping

Ir de jarana
To go on a spree

Ir de pesca
To go fishing

Ir de vacaciones
To go on vacation

Ir del brazo
To go arm in arm

Ir entendiendo
To begin to understand

Ir para atrás
To back up

Irse (or andar) a la deriva
To drift, be adrift

Irse abajo
To fall down

J

Juego de palabras
Pun, play on words

Juego limpio
Fair play

Juego sucio
Foul play

Jugar limpio
To play fair

Jugarle una mala partida
To play a bad trick on one

Junto a
Near to, or next to

Junto con
With, along with

L

La comidilla de la vecindad
The talk of the town

La cosa no cuajó
The thing did not jell (or work well)

La cuestión palpitante
The burning question

La gota que derrama el vaso
The last straw, the straw that broke the camel's back

La mayoría (de)
The majority (of), most of

La mayor parte (de)
The majority (of), most of

La mera idea de
The very thought of

La mera verdad
The real truth

La rutina diaria
The daily grind

La verdad clara y desnuda
The whole truth, the plain and simple truth

Lado flaco
Weak side

Largas uñas
A thief

¡Largo de aquí!
Get out of here!

Largos años
A long time, many years

Lavarse las manos de
To wash one's hands of

Levantar a pulso
To lift (something heavy) with the hand

Levantar la mesa
To clear the table

Levantarse de malas (or levantarse con las malas, or levantarse con el santo de espaldas)
To get up on (or out of) the wrong side of the bed

Ligero de cascos (or alegre de cascos)
Featherbrained

Limpio de polvo y paja
Net, entirely free, clear profit

Lo antes posible
The earliest possible

Lo de menos
Of little importance, the least of it

Lo expuesto
What has been said

Lo más pronto posible
As soon as possible

Lo menos posible
As little as possible

Lo mismo da
It makes no difference

Lo que
That which

Lo que hizo
Which caused

Lo recién llegado
A new arrival

Lo siento mucho
I'm very sorry

Loco de remate
Stark raving mad

Los (las) demás
The others, the rest of them

Los que
Those which, those who, the ones

Luego que
As soon as

LL

Llamar al pan pan, y al vino vino
Call a spade a spade

Llamar por teléfono
To call on the telephone

Llegar a saber
To come to know

Llegar a ser
To become, to get to be

Llenar un vacío
To bridge a gap

Lleno de bote en bote
Full to the brim

Llevar a cabo
To carry through, to accomplish

Llevar a efecto
To carry out

Llevar cuentas
To keep accounts

Llevar el compás
To beat time

Llevar la contra
To oppose, to object to

Llevar la cuenta (or llevar cuenta de)
To keep track of

Llevar puesto
To wear

Llevar ventaja
To have the lead, to be ahead

Llevarse adelante
To carry out

Llevarse bien (con)
To get along well with

Llevarse un chasco
To be disappointed

Llover a cántaros
To rain cats and dogs (pitchforks)

Llover sobre mojado
To come one after another (bad luck, misfortune)

M

Mal genio
Bad temper

Mal mandado (or muy mandado)
Ill-behaved

Mal sufrido
Impatient

Malas tretas
Bad tricks, bad habits

Mandar una bofetada
To slap

Mandar una pedrada
To throw a stone

Mañana Dios dirá
Tomorrow is another day

Mañana por la mañana (temprano)
Tomorrow morning (early)

Mañana por la noche
Tomorrow night

Mañana por la tarde
Tomorrow afternoon

Más acá
Closer

Más acá de
This side of, before you get to

Más adelante
Farther on, later on

Más ahorita
Right now

Más allá (de)
Beyond, farther away

Más aún
Furthermore, what is more

Más bien
Rather

Más bien que
Rather than

Más de
More than

Más de una vez
More than once

Más pesado que una mosca
Pesky as a fly

Más que
More than

Más que nadie
More than anyone

Más que nunca
More than ever

Más vale...
It is better...

Más vale tarde que nunca
Better late than never

Matar dos pájaros de un tiro
To kill two birds with one stone

Matar el gusano
To satisfy a need or desire (hunger, etc.)

Me entró miedo
I became afraid

Me hace falta
I need it

Me lloran los ojos
My eyes water

Media cuchara
A mediocre person

Medio sordo
Hard of hearing

Medir las calles
To walk the streets, be out of a job

Mejor dicho
Better yet, rather

Memoria de gallo
Poor memory

Menor de edad
A minor (person)

Menos de (or menos que)
Less than

Menos mal
At least

Merecer la pena
To be worthwhile

Meter la pata
To put one's foot in one's mouth

Meterse con
To pick a quarrel or fight with

Meterse de por medio
To intervene, meddle in a dispute

Meterse en un lío
To get oneself in a mess

Mientras más...menos
The more...the less...

Mientras tanto
Meanwhile

Mil gracias
A thousand thanks

Mirada de soslayo
Side glance

Mirar con el rabo del ojo
To look out of the corner of one's eye

Mirar por alguien
To take care of someone

Mirar por encima
To glance at

Mirar por encima del hombro
To look down on; despise

Molestarse en (con)
To bother about

Muchas subidas y bajadas
Many ups and downs, much going up and down

Mudar de casa
To move (change residence)

Muy a menudo
Very often

Muy de mañana
Very early in the morning

Muy trabajador
Hard-working

N

Nacer de pie (or pies)
To be born lucky

Nada de eso
Nothing like that

Nada de particular
Nothing unusual

Nada en absoluto
Nothing at all

Nada más
Just, only

Negarse a (contestar)
To refuse to (answer)

Ni con mucho
Not by far, not by a long shot,
far from

Ni esto ni aquello
Neither this nor that

Ni mucho menos
Not by any means, not anything
like it

Ni siquiera
Not even, even though

Ni yo tampoco
Nor I either

Ningún otro
Nobody else

No cabe duda (que)
There is no doubt (that)

No caer bien
To displease, (with direct
object) not to fit well

No da abasto a
To be unable to cope with

No dar pie con bola
To make a mistake, not to get
things right

No darse cuenta
Not to realize

No despegar los labios
Not to say a word, not to open
one's mouth

¡No diga!
Is that so? You don't say!

No es asunto mío (suyo, etc.)
It's none of my (your, etc.)
business

No es mucho que
It is no wonder that

No estar de humor
To be out of sorts, not in a
laughing mood

No estoy de acuerdo
I disagree

¡No faltaba más!
That's the last straw! Why, the
very idea!

No hallar vado
To find no way out

No hay de que
You're welcome; don't mention
it

No hay más remedio que
There's no other way but to;
there's nothing to do except

No hay para que
There's no need to

No hay prisa
There's no hurry

No hay que darle vueltas
There's no way around it; there
are no two ways about it

¡No importa!
Never mind!

No irle ni venirle a uno
To make no difference to one

No le hace
It doesn't matter, it makes no
difference

No más que
Only

No le haga caso
Pay no attention to him

No me da la gana
I don't want to

No nos debemos nada
We are even (quits)

No obstante
Notwithstanding, nevertheless

No pararse en pelillos
Not to bother about trifles

No poder con
Not to be able to stand, endure,
control, carry

No poder con la carga
Not to be able to lift the load,
not equal to the burden

No poder más
To be exhausted, ''all in''

No poder menos de
Not to be able to help... Ex.: No
puede menos de hacerlo;
he can't help doing it

No quedar otro recurso
No way out, no alternative

No querer hacerlo
To be unwilling to do it

No saber ni papa (de eso)
To know absolutely nothing
(about that)

No saber una (or ni) jota
Not to know anything

No se dé usted prisa
Don't hurry

¡No se ocupe!
Never mind! Don't worry!

¡No se preocupe usted!
Don't worry!

No se trata de eso
That's not the point; that's not
the question

No sea que
Or else, because

No ser cosa de juego
Not to be a laughing matter

No ser ni chicha ni limonada
To be worthless, neither fish nor
fowl

No servir para nada
To be good for nothing

No sólo...sino también
Not only...but also

No tan a menudo
Not so often

No tener alternativa (or elección)
To have no alternative, no way
out

No tener entrañas
To be cruel

No tener nada que ver con
To have nothing to do with

No tener pelillos en la lengua
To speak frankly

No tener razón
To be wrong

No tener remedio
To be beyond help or repair

No tener sal en la mollera
To be dull, stupid

No tenga usted cuidado
Don't worry about it; forget it

No tiene remedio
It can't be helped; it is hopeless

No tiene vuelta de hoja
There's no two ways about it

No vale la pena
It's not worthwhile

No vale un pito
Not worth a straw

No vale una cuartilla
Not worth a penny

No ver la hora de
To be anxious to

No viene al cuento (or no viene al caso)
It is not opportune, or to the
point

O

O sea que
That is to say

O si no...
Or else...

Oír decir que
To hear that

Oír hablar de
To hear about

Oler a
To smell like

Optar por
To choose, decide upon

¡Otra, otra!
Encore!

Otra vez
Again

P

Pagado de sí mismo
To be pleased with oneself

Pagar el pato
To be the scapegoat, get the
blame

Pagarse de
To be proud of, or boast of

¡Palabrita de honor!
Word of honor, honestly; no kidding?

Para mis adentros
To myself

Para que
In order that

¿Para qué?
What for? For what use?

Para (or por) siempre (+ jamás)
Forever (forever and ever)

Para todos lados
To right and left, on all sides

Para unos fines u otros
For one purpose or another

Para variar
For a change

Parar en seco
To stop short or suddenly

Parar mientes en
To consider, reflect on

Pararse en pelillos
To split hairs

Parece mentira
It seems to be impossible

Parecido a
Like, similar to

Pasado de moda
Out of style, out of date

Pasado mañana
Day after tomorrow

Pasar a mejor vida
To die

Pasar como un relámpago
To flash by

Pasar de la raya
To overstep bounds, take undue liberties

Pasar de moda
To go out of style

Pasar el rato
To while away time

Pasar la noche en claro (or en blanco)
Not to sleep a wink

Pasar lista
To call the roll

Pasar por alto
To omit, overlook

Pasar revista a
To review, to go over carefully

Pasar un buen rato
To have a good time

Pasarse sin
To do without

Pasear a pie
To take a walk

Pasear en coche
To go for a drive (by auto)

Pata de gallo
Crow's foot wrinkles

Patas arriba
Upside down

Pecar de bueno
To be too good

Pecar de oscuro
To be very unclear, too complicated

Pedir prestado
To borrow

Pegar de soslayo
To glance, to hit at a slant

Pegar fuego
To set afire

Pegar un chasco
To play a trick, surprise, disappoint

Pegar un salto
To take a jump

Pegar un susto
To give a scare

Pensar en
To intend, to think about

Peor que
Worse than

Peor que peor
That is even worse

Perder cuidado
Not to worry

Perder de vista
To lose sight of

Perder el juicio
To lose one's mind, go crazy

Perder el tiempo
To lose time

Perder la razón
To lose one's mind

Perder la vista
To go blind

Perder prestigio
To lose face

Perderse de vista
To vanish, to be lost from view, to drop out of sight

Pesarle a uno
To be sorry for someone, to regret

Picar en
To dabble in

Picar muy alto
To aim very high

(X) Pies de altura (or de alto)
(X) Feet tall

(X) Pies de largo
(X) Feet long

Pillar una mona
To get drunk

Pintar venado
To play hooky

Pintarle un violín
To break one's word

Planchar el asiento
To be a wallflower

Poca cosa
Not much

Poco a poco
Gradually, little by little

Poco después (de)
Shortly thereafter

Poco para las (tres)
To be nearly (3) o'clock

Poco rato
Very soon

Poner a buen recaudo
To place in safety

Poner adelantado
To set forward (e.g., a clock)

Poner al corriente
To inform, to bring up to date

Poner casa
To set up housekeeping

Poner defectos
To find fault with

Poner el grito en el cielo
To complain loudly, to "hit the ceiling"

Poner en claro
To clear up, to clarify

Poner en conocimiento
To inform

Poner en duda
To question, to doubt

Poner en el cielo
To praise, extol

Poner en juego
To set in motion, to coordinate

Poner en limpio
To make a clean copy, to recopy

Poner en marcha
To get going

Poner en razón
To pacify

Poner en ridículo
To humiliate, make a fool of

Poner faltas
To find fault with

Poner la luz, (el radio, etc.)
To turn on the light (radio, etc.)

Poner la mesa
To set the table

Poner la mira
To fix one's eyes on, aim at

Poner por las nubes
To praise to the skies

Poner por obra
To undertake, put into practice

Poner todo de su parte
To do one's best

Poner una queja
To file a complaint

Ponerse a
To begin, start

Ponerse bien
To get well

Ponerse colorado
To blush

Ponerse de acuerdo
To come to an agreement

Ponerse de pie
To get to one's feet

Ponerse de rodillas
To kneel

Ponerse duro
To resist stubbornly

Ponerse en
To reach

Ponerse en camino
To set out (on a trip, etc.)

Ponerse en contra de
To oppose, be against

Ponerse en marcha
To start, start out

Ponerse en pie
To get up, or rise

Por acá (or por aquí)
This way, over here

Por accidente
By accident

Por adelantado
In advance

Por ahí (or por allá)
Over there, about that

Por ahora
For the time being, for now

Por algo
For some reason; that's why

Por allí
That way

Por amor de
For the sake of

Por aquí
This way

Por aquí cerca
Around here, in this vicinity

Por arriba
Above

Por casualidad
By chance, by accident

Por completo
Completely

Por (or en) consecuencia de
Therefore, consequently

Por consiguiente
Consequently, therefore

Por de (or por lo) pronto
For the present

Por delante
Ahead

Por dentro
On the inside

Por desgracia
Unfortunately

Por despecho
Out of spite

Por detrás
From the rear

Por día
By the day

¿Por dónde?
Where, through, which? Which way?

Por el estilo
Such as that, of that kind

Por el (or por la or por lo) presente
For the present

Por encima de
On top of

Por encima de todo
Above all

Por ende
Hence, therefore

Por entre
Among, between

Por esa razón
For that reason, that is why

Por escrito
In writing

Por eso
For that reason, therefore

Por extenso
In detail, at length

Por favor
Please

Por fin
At last, finally

Por fuera
From the outside, on the outside

Por hoy
At present

Por instantes
Continually, moment to moment

Por la mañana (or por la tarde, etc.)
In the morning (afternoon, etc.)

Por la mitad
In half, in the middle

Por la noche (or en la noche)
At night, in the evening

Por las buenas o por las malas
Whether one likes it or not

Por las nubes
Sky-high

Por lo común
Generally

Por lo cual
Therefore

Por lo demás
Moreover, as for the rest (of us), aside from this

Por lo general
Usually, generally

Por lo menos
At least

Por lo pronto
For the time being

Por lo regular
Usually, as a rule

Por lo que
Because of which

Por lo que pueda tronar
Just in case

Por lo tanto
Therefore

Por lo visto
Apparently, by the looks of, evidently

Por más que
However much

Por medio de
By means of

Por menudo
In detail, retail

Por mi parte
As far as I'm concerned

Por motivo
On account of

Por mucho que
No matter how much

Por ningún lado
Nowhere

Por ningún motivo
Under no circumstances, no matter what

Por otra parte
On the other hand

Por otro lado
On the other hand (or side)

Por poco
Almost, nearly. Ex.: **Por poco se muere**; he almost died

Por primera vez
For the first time

¿Por qué?
Why?

Por rareza
Seldom

Por regla general
As a general rule, usually

Por separado
Separately

Por si acaso
In case, just in case

Por sí solo
By oneself

Por su cuenta
All by himself (oneself)

Por su mano
By oneself

Por supuesto
Of course

Por término medio
On an average

Por (or a or en) todas partes
All over, everywhere

Por toda suerte de penalidades
Through thick and thin

Por todo el mundo
All over the world

Por todo lo alto
Not sparing expense

Por todos lados
All over, everywhere, all sides

Por última vez
For the last time, finally

Por último
Finally, at last

Porque si no
Otherwise

Preguntar por
To ask about

Prender el fuego
To start the fire

Prender fuego a
To set fire to

Preocuparse de
To take care of

Preocuparse por
To worry about, to be
concerned about or for

Presencia de ánimo
Presence of mind, serenity

Prestar atención
To pay attention

Profundamente dormido
Fast asleep

Prohibida la entrada
No trespassing

Prohibido el paso
No trespassing, keep out

Prohibido estacionarse
No parking

Puede ser que
It may be that

Pues bien
Now then, well then, all right
then

Pues mire
Well, look

Pues que(?)
Since, so what?

Puesta del sol
Sunset

Puesto que
Although, since

Q

¡Qué barbaridad!
What nonsense! What an
atrocity!

¡Qué batingue!
What a mess!

¡Qué de!
What a lot! How much!

¡Qué desgracia!
How unfortunate!

¡Qué divino!
What a beauty!

¡Qué gusto!
What a pleasure! I am
delighted!

¿Qué haces?
What's the matter? What is it?

¿Qué hay?
What's the matter?

¿Qué hay de malo con eso?
What's wrong with that? So,
what's so bad about that?

¿Qué hay de nuevo?
What's new(s)?

¿Qué hora es? (or ¿qué horas son?)
What time is it?

¡Qué horror!
How awful!

¿Qué hubo?
How goes it? What's up?

¡Qué lástima!
Too bad! What a pity!

¿Qué le pasa (a Ud.)?
What's the matter with you?

Que le vaya bien
Good luck

Que lo pase bien
Have a good day, etc.

¿Qué mosca te ha picado?
What's eating you?

¡Qué nombrecito!
What a tonguetwister!

¿Qué pasa?
What's up? What's going on?

¿Qué pasó?
What happened?

¿Qué quiere decir?
What does it mean?

¡Que se divierta!
Have a good time

¿Qué tal?
Hello! How are you?

¿Qué tiene de malo?
What's wrong with...?

Quebrarse uno la cabeza
To rack one's brain

Quedar bien (con)
To come out well, to get along
well (with)

Quedar contento con
To be pleased with

Quedar en
To agree (to)

Quedar entendido que
To be understood, agreed to

Quedarle bien
To be becoming

Quedarse con (re una cosa)
To keep, to take (e.g., I'll take
it.)

Quedarse en la casa
To stay in

Quejarse de
To complain of

Quemarse hasta el suelo
To burn down

Quemarse las pestañas (or las cejas)
To burn the midnight oil, study
hard

Querer decir
To mean, signify

¿Quién sabe?
Who knows? I don't know

¿Quién te mete, Juan Copete?
Mind your own business.
What's it to you?

Quieras que no
Whether you wish or not

Quiere llover
It is trying (is about) to rain

Quince días
Two weeks

¡Quita allá!
Don't tell me that!

Quitar la mesa
To clear the table

Quitar uno un peso de encima
To be relieved of, to be a load
off one's mind

Quitarse de una cosa
To give up (or get rid of)
something

¡Quítese de aquí!
Get out of here!

R

Rabiar por
To be very eager to (or for)

Rara vez (or raras veces)
Seldom

Ratos perdidos
Leisure hours

Recibir noticias (de)
To hear from

Recuerdos a
Regards to...

Rechinar los dientes
To gnash one's teeth

Reírse para sus adentros
To laugh up one's sleeve

Remolino de gente
Throng, crowd

Repetidas veces
Over and over again, various
times

Repetir de carretilla
To rattle off, repeat
mechanically

Resarcirse de
To make up for

Respecto a
With regard to, concerning,
about

Reunión de confianza
Informal gathering or party

Reventar de risa
To burst with laughter

Romper a
To start to

Romper el alba
To dawn

Romperse los cascos
To rack one's brain

Rosario de desdichas
Chain of misfortunes

Rozarse con alguien
To have connections (or dealings) with someone

S

Saber a
To taste like

Saber de memoria
To know by heart

Sacar a bailar
To ask to dance

Sacar a uno de quicio
To exasperate someone

Sacar el cuerpo
To dodge

Sacar en claro (or en limpio)
To deduce, conclude

Salida de pie de banco
Silly remark, nonsense

Salida del sol
Sunrise

Salir a
To resemble, take after

Salir a gatas
To crawl out of a difficulty

Salir al encuentro de
To go out to meet, to oppose, take a stand against

Salir bien
To be successful, to come out well

Salir de
To leave, depart

Salir del paso
To get out of a difficulty

Salir fiador de
To vouch for

Salir ganando
To win, to come out ahead

Salir mal
To fail, to come out poorly

Salirse con la suya
To have one's own way

Saltar a la vista
To be obvious

Saltar a tierra
To disembark, to land

Saltar las trancas
To lose patience, lose one's head

Salvar el pellejo
To save one's skin

Sano y salvo
Safe and sound

Santo y bueno
Well and good

Se aguó la fiesta
The party was spoiled

Se conoce (que)
It is obvious

Se dice
It is said, they say

Se ha acabado
It is all over

Se prohíbe (fumar)
It is forbidden (to smoke); no (smoking)

Se solicita
Wanted

Se suena que
It is rumored that

Se ve que
It is obvious that

Se venció el plazo
The time limit expired

Seguir las pisadas
To follow in the footsteps (of), emulate

Según y conforme (or según y como)
Exactly as, just as, that depends

Seguro que están
I bet they are

Seguro que sí
Of course

Sentar bien a
To fit well

Sentarle bien
To be becoming

Sentarse en cuclillas
To squat

Sentir en el alma
To be terribly sorry, to regret very much

Sentirse destemplado
Not to feel well, to feel feverish

Ser aficionado a
To be a fan, a buff

Ser como un puño
To be close-fisted

Ser conocedor
To be a judge of

Ser de carne y hueso
To be only human

Ser de rigor
To be indispensable, to be required by custom

Ser de (or ser para) ver
Worth seeing

Ser duro de mollera
To be stubborn

Ser fuerza
To be necessary

Ser gente
To be cultured, socially important

Ser huésped en su casa
To be seldom at home

Ser oriundo de
To hail from, come from

Ser piedra de escándalo
To be the object of scandal

Ser plato de segunda mesa
To play second fiddle

Ser tan fuerte como un león
To be as strong as a horse

Ser tempranero
To be an early riser

Ser un cero a la izquierda
To be of no account

Ser un erizo
To be irritable; a grouchy person

Servir de
To serve, act as, be used as

Servir la mesa
To wait table

Servir para
To be good for, used for

Si acaso
If at all

Si alguna vez
If even

Si bien
Although

Si mal no recuerdo
If I remember correctly

Si me hace el favor
If you would do me the favor

Si no
Or else

Si no fuera por
Except for

Si no fuera porque
Except for

Siempre que
Whenever, provided that, as long as

Siempre y cuando
Provided

Sin ceremonia
Informal

Sin comentarios
No comment

Sin contar
Exclusive of

Sin disputa
Without question

Sin embargo
However, nevertheless

Sin falta
By all means, without fail, without fault

Sin fin
An infinite quantity

Sin hacer caso de
Regardless of

Sin igual
Unequaled

Sin novedad
As usual (to be well, in good health)

Sin par
Peerless, without equal

Sin que
Without

Sin qué ni para qué
Without rhyme or reason

Sin querer
Unwillingly

Sin rebozo
Openly, frankly

Sin recurso
Without remedy, without appeal

Sin remedio
Unavoidable, without help

Sin reserva
Unreserved, frankly

Sin sentir
Without realizing, inadvertently, unnoticed

Sin ton ni son
Without rhyme or reason

Sino que
But

Sobradas veces
Repeatedly, many times

Sobre manera
Excessively

Sobre mi palabra
Upon my honor

Sobre que
Besides, in addition to

Sobre seguro
Without risk

Sobre todo
Especially, above all

Soltar el hervor
To come to a boil

Soltar la rienda
To let loose, act without restraint

Sonar a
To sound like, seem like

Soñar con (or soñar en)
To dream of

Soñar despierto
To daydream

Su punto flaco
His weakness, her weak side

Subidas y bajadas
Ups and downs

Subir al tren
To get on the train

Subir de punto
To increase, get worse

Subirse de tono
To put on airs

Suceda lo que suceda
Come what may, no matter what

Sudar la gota gorda
To sweat profusely, work hard, sweat blood, have a bad time

Suerte negra
Very bad luck

Suma atención
Close attention

Supuesto que
Supposing that, since

Surtir efecto
To come out as desired or expected, to give good results

T

Tal como (or tales como)
Such as

Tal cual
Such as, so-so, fair

Tal para cual
Two of a kind

Tal vez
Maybe, perhaps

Tal vez sea que
It may be that

Tan pronto como
As soon as

Tanto...como
As much...as

Tanto mejor
So much the better

Tanto peor
So much the worse

Tardar en
To be long in, take a long time (in doing)

Tarde o temprano
Sooner or later

Tener a la vista
To have in sight

Tener a raya
To keep in bounds, hold in check

Tener al corriente
To keep up-to-date (informed, posted)

Tener...años
To be...years old

Tener buena cara
To look well

Tener cabida con alguien
To have influence with someone

Tener calor
To be hot

Tener celos
To be jealous

Tener confianza con
To be on intimate terms with

Tener cosquillas
To be ticklish

Tener cuidado (con)
To take care, watch out (for)

Tener deseos de
To want to, to be eager to

Tener el pico de oro
To be eloquent

Tener en cuenta
To consider, to take into account

Tener en la mente
To have in mind

Tener en la punta de la lengua
To have on the tip of one's tongue

Tener en mucho
To esteem highly

Tener en poco a
To hold in low esteem

Tener entendido que
To understand that...

Tener éxito
To be successful

Tener frío
To be cold

Tener gana(s) de
To feel like

Tener gancho
To be attractive, alluring

Tener gracia
To be funny

Tener gusto en
To be glad to

Tener hambre
To be hungry

Tener la bondad de
To be good enough to

Tener la costumbre de
To be used (accustomed) to...

Tener la culpa
To be to blame

Tener la intención de
To intend or mean to

Tener la lengua larga
To have a big mouth

Tener la pena de
To have the misfortune to

Tener la vida en un hilo
To be in great danger

Tener lástima de
To feel sorry for, take pity on

Tener lugar
To take place

Tener miedo
To be afraid

Tener mucho copete
To be arrogant, haughty

Tener murria
To be sulky, to have the blues

Tener para sí
To think, to be of the opinion

Tener por
To believe, judge, consider, to take for a...

Tener presente (de or que)
To bear in mind

Tener prisa
To be in a hurry

Tener probabilidad
To stand a chance

Tener que
To have to (do something)

Tener que ver (con)
To have to do with

Tener razón
To be right

Tener roce con
To have contact with a person

Tener sed
To be thirsty

Tener sueño
To be sleepy

Tener suerte
To be lucky

Tener tiempo libre
To have time off

Tener vergüenza
To be ashamed

Tenerle tirria a una persona
To have a dislike for (or grudge against) a person

Tenerse en pie
To keep one's feet

Tirar de
To pull

Tirar las riendas
To restrain, tighten the reins

Tirarse una plancha
To put oneself in a ridiculous situation

Tocar de oído
To play by ear

Tocar en lo vivo
To hurt to the quick, hit a nerve, touch a sore spot

Tocar por fantasía
To play by ear

Tocarle a uno
To be one's turn

Tocarle a uno la suerte
To be one's turn, to fall to one's lot, to be lucky

Tocarse el sombrero
To tip one's hat

Toda clase de
All kinds of

Todas las veces (que)
Every time, whenever

Todavía no
Not yet

Todo el año
All year round

Todo el día
All day

Todo el mundo
Everybody

Todo el que
Everybody who

Todo el tiempo
All the time

Todo hombre
Everyone

Todo lo contrario
Exactly the opposite

Todo lo demás
Everything else

Todo lo posible
All that is possible

Todo sigue bien
All goes well

Todos los días
Every day

Tomar a broma
To take as a joke

Tomar a pecho(s)
To take to heart, to take seriously

Tomar a risa
To laugh off, take lightly

Tomarle el pelo
To tease, pull one's leg

Tomar el rábano por las hojas
To put the cart before the horse, to misinterpret or misconstrue

Tomar el sol
To sunbathe

Tomar en cuenta
To consider, take into account

Tomar en serio
To take to heart

Tomar la delantera
To take the lead

Tomar por cierto
To take for granted

Tomar por su cuenta
To attend to personally

Tomar tiempo libre
To take time off

Tomarlo con calma
To take it easy

Tonto de capirote
Dunce, plain fool

Traer puesto
To wear, to have on

Transporte de locura
Fit of madness

Tras de
Behind, after, beside

Tratar con
To have dealings with

Tratar de
To try to; to treat, to deal with

Tratar en
To deal in

Tratarse de
To be a question of

¡Trato hecho!
It's a deal!

Tronar los dedos
To snap one's fingers

Tropezar con
To meet, come across, encounter

U

Un buen pasar
Enough to live on

Un día sí y otro no
Every other day

Un día sí y un día no
Every other day

Un hervidero de gente
A swarm of people

Un no sé qué
Something indefinable

Un nudo en la garganta
A lump in the throat

Un rato desagradable
A hard time

Un tanto
Somewhat

Una buena carcajada
A hearty laugh

Una infinidad de
A large number of

Una mala pasada
A mean trick

Una negativa rotunda
A flat denial

Una negativa terminante
A flat denial

Una que otra vez
Once in a while

Una y otra vez
More than once, over and over again

Unas cuantas (or unos cuantos)
A few

Uno a la vez
One at a time

Uno por uno
One by one

Unos a otros
Each other

Unos pocos
A few

V

Valer la pena
To be worthwhile. Ex.: No vale la pena, it's not worth the trouble

Valer más
To be better

Valer por
To be worth

Valerse de
To make use of

Varias veces
Several times

Venir a las manos
To come to blows

Venir a menos
To decline

Venir a parar
To turn out to be, to end up (as)

Venir a (or al) pelo
To come at the right moment, to suit perfectly, to be opportune

Venir a ser
To turn out to be

Venir bien
To suit

Venir en
To agree to

Venir sobre
To fall upon

Venirse abajo
To fall down, collapse, fail

Ver de (or ver que)
To try to, see to it that

Verse obligado a
To be obliged to or forced to

Visto que
Whereas, considering that

Vivir de sus uñas
To live by stealing

Voltear la espalda
To turn one's back

Volver a
To do…again

Volver a las andadas
To fall back into old habits

Volver corriendo
To hurry back

Volver en sí
To come to, regain consciousness

Volver loco
To drive crazy

Volver por
To return for, to defend

Volverse atrás
To go back, back out, go back on one's word

Volverse loco
To go crazy

Y

Y así sucesivamente
And so on, et cetera

Y pico
(A) little more

¿Y qué?
So what?

¿Y si?
What if…?

Ya es hora de
It's time to

Ya es tarde
It's too late now

Ya mero
Very soon, just about to…

¡Ya lo creo!
I should say so! Yes, of course

Ya no
No longer

Ya no sopla
To be no good, of no use as…

Ya que
Since, although

Ya se acabó
It is all over

Ya se ve
Of course; it is clear

Ya voy
I am coming

MODISMOS Y EXPRESIONES / IDIOMS AND EXPRESSIONS

A

About
Acerca de, al (or en) rededor de, alrededor de, cosa de, respecto a

About that
Por ahí, por allá

About the first of...
A principios de...

About the middle of...
A mediados de

Above
Por arriba

Above all
Ante todo, por encima de todo, sobre todo

Abroad
En el extranjero

Absolutely
De remate

Absolutely (not)
En absoluto

Accomplish
Llevar a cabo

According to Hoyle; according to the rules
Como Dios manda

Across
A través de, de través

Act a fool
Hacer el ridículo, hacerse el tonto

Act as
Hacer de, servir de

Act as if
Hacer como si

Actually
Desde luego

Act without restraint
Soltar la rienda

Add fuel to the fire
Echar leña al fuego

Admit a person is right
Dar la razón a una persona

After (in position)
Tras de

After a few months (etc.)
A los pocos meses

After all
A fin de cuentas, después de todo, en resumidas cuentas

Again
De nuevo, de vuelta, otra vez

Against
En contra de

Against all odds
Contra viento y marea

Against the grain
A contrapelo

Agree
Dar la razón, estar de acuerdo, quedar en

Agree to
Quedar en, venir en

Ahead
Por delante

Aim at
Poner la mira

Aimlessly
A la ventura

Aim very high
Picar muy alto

A little more
Y pico

All along
Desde el principio

All around
A la redonda, en redondo

All at once
De un golpe, de un tirón, de una tirada

All by oneself (himself)
Por su cuenta

All day
Todo el día

All goes well
Todo sigue bien

All joking aside
Bromas a un lado, fuera de broma

All kinds of
Toda clase de

All of a sudden
De buenas a primeras, de repente

All over
En todas partes, por todas partes, por todos lados

All that is possible
Todo lo posible

All the time
A cada rato, todo el tiempo

All the while
Entre tanto

All together
En conjunto, en junto

All year round
Todo el año

Almost
Por poco

Alone
A secas

Along, alongside of
A lo largo (de)

Along with
Junto con

Aloud
En voz alta, voz alta

Although
Bien que, puesto que, si bien, ya que

Among
Por entre

Amuse
Hacer gracia

And so
De modo que, de suerte que

And so on
Y así sucesivamente

Anger, to make angry
Dar rabia

Annoy
Dar la lata

Anyhow
Así y todo, de todos modos

Anything at all
Cualquier cosa

Anyway
Al fin y al cabo, de todas maneras, en cualquier caso

Any way you look at it
A todas luces

Apiece
Cada uno

Apologize
Dar una satisfacción

Apparently
Al parecer, por lo visto

Approve
Dar el visto bueno

Approximately
Cosa de

Apropos
A propósito

Around (about)
Al derredor, en derredor, al rededor, en rededor, alrededor de

Around here
Aquí cerca, por aquí cerca

Around the corner
A la vuelta de, a la vuelta de la esquina

Arouse one's suspicions
Darle a uno mala espina

Arouse pity (or sorrow)
Dar lástima (de)

Arrest
Echar la garra

As
A medida que, a semejanza de, según y conforme, según y como

As a general rule
Por regla general; por lo general

As a last resort
Como último recurso

As a matter of fact
En realidad

As a result (of)
A consecuencia de, de resultas

As a rule
Por lo regular

As a whole
En conjunto

As far as I'm concerned
Por mi parte

As follows
A continuación, como sigue

As for
En cuanto a

As for the rest (of us)
Por lo demás

Aside from that
Aparte de eso

Aside from this
Por lo demás

As if
Como si

As if by magic
Como por ensalmo

As if it were
Como si fuera

As I understand it
A mi entender

Ask about
Preguntar por

Ask a question (or questions)
Hacer una pregunta (preguntas)

Ask to dance
Sacar a bailar

As little as possible
Lo menos posible

As long as
Siempre que

As much as
Tanto como

As of
A partir de

As proof of
En prenda de

As smooth as silk
Como una seda

As soon as
Así es que, así que, en cuanto,
luego que, tan pronto como

As soon as possible
Cuanto antes, lo más pronto
posible

Assume responsibility
Cargar con

As the crow flies
A vuelo de pájaro

As the saying goes
Como dijo el otro

As time goes on
Andarse el tiempo

As usual
Como de costumbre, como
siempre, sin novedad

As well as
Así como

As you like
A la voluntad

At about
A eso de, como a costumbre

At about...(time)
Al filo de...

At all
Del todo

At all costs
A toda costa, a todo trance

At all hours
A deshora(s)

At all times
A toda hora

At an early date
En fecha a próxima

At another's expense
De gorra

At an untimely moment
A deshora(s)

At any cost
Cueste lo que cueste

At any moment
De un momento a otro

At any rate
Como quiera que sea, de
cualquier modo, de todas
maneras, de todos modos

At any time
A toda hora

At arm's length
A una brazada

At a short distance
A pocos pasos

At bottom
En el fondo

At every turn
A cada paso

At first
Al principio

At full length
A lo largo (de)

At full speed (or greatest speed)
A escape, a toda prisa, a toda
vela, a todo correr

At hand
A mano

At hard labor
Al remo

At heart
En el fondo

At home
En casa

At last
A la postre, al fin, al fin y al
cabo, por fin, por último

At (the) least
Al menos, a lo menos, como
mínimo, menos mal, por lo
menos

At length
Por extenso

At most
A lo más, a lo sumo

At once
Ahora mismo, al instante, al
punto, de pronto, de una vez,
desde luego, en el acto, en
seguida

At one stroke
De una vez

At one time
A un tiempo, de una vez

At present
Al presente, por hoy

At random
A la buena de Dios, a la
ventura, al azar

Attend to personally
Tomar por su cuenta

At that time
A la sazón, en aquel tiempo

At the end
Al fin

At the last moment
A última hora

At the mercy of
A merced de

At the most
A lo sumo

At the present time
En la actualidad

At the request of
A instancias de

At the same time
A la vez, al mismo tiempo, de
paso, entre tanto

At the very latest
A más tardar

At this point or juncture
A estas alturas

At times
A ratos, a veces

At whatever cost
A toda costa

At will
A la voluntad, a voluntad

At worst
A lo más

At your service
A sus órdenes, servidor de usted

Average person
El común de las gentes

Avoid someone
Dar esquinazo

Awaiting
En espera de

B

Back and forth
De aquí para allá

Back out
Echarse para atrás, volverse atrás

Back up
Dar marcha atrás, ir para atrás

Backward(s)
Al revés, hacia atrás

Bad habits
Malas tretas

Bad temper
Mal genio

Bark up the wrong tree
A buen santo te encomiendas

Be a buff
Ser aficionado a

Be about to
Estar a punto de, estar para

Be a fan of
Ser aficionado a

Be afraid
Tener miedo

Be against
Estar en pugna con, ponerse en contra de

Be agreed to
Quedar entendido que

Be ahead
Llevar ventaja

Be alert
Estar a la mira de, ponerse chango

Be all right, OK
Estar bien

Be alluring
Tener gancho

Be a load off one's mind
Quitarse uno un peso de encima

Be an early riser
Ser tempranero

Be anxious to
No ver la hora de

Be a part of
Formar parte de

Be a question of
Tratarse de

Bear or hold a grudge
Guardar rencor

Bear in mind
Tener presente (de lo que)

Be arrogant
Tener mucho copete

Be ashamed
Tener vergüenza

Be as strong as a horse
Ser tan fuerte como un león

Beat around the bush
Andarse con rodeos, andarse por las ramas

Beaten path
Camino trillado

Be at the end of one's rope or resources
Estar en las últimas

Beat (or mark) time
Llevar el compás

Be attractive
Tener gancho

Beautifully
A las mil maravillas

Be a wallflower
Planchar el asiento

Be away from home
Estar fuera de casa

Be back
Estar de regreso, estar de vuelta

Be becoming
Caer bien, quedarle bien, sentarle bien

Be beyond help or repair
No tener remedio

Be born lucky
Nacer de pie (...de pies)

Be broke
Estar bruja

Because
No sea que

Because of
Con motivo de

Because of which
Por lo que

Be cautious
Estar sobre sí, estar sobre aviso

Be close-fisted
Ser como un puño

Be coaxed
Hacerse del rogar

Become
Llegar a ser

Become confused
Hacerse un lío

Become effective
Entrar en vigor (e.g., a law)

Be contented
Estar a gusto

Be courageous
Tener puños

Be crowded
Estar de bote en bote

Be cruel
No tener entrañas

Be cultured
Ser gente

Be deeply involved in
Estar muy metido en

Be disappointed
Llevarse un chasco

Be disconcerting
Dar mucha pena

Be dull
No tener sal en la mollera

Be eager to
Tener deseos de

Be eloquent
Tener el pico de oro

Be equal to (a task)
Estar a la altura de

Be exhausted
No poder más

Be fed
Dar de comer

Be fed up
Estar uno hasta el copete, estar uno hasta la coronilla

Be fed up with
Estar harto de

Be filled up
Estar hasta los topes

Be flush (even with)
Estar ras con ras

Be fond of
Estar afecto a

Be forced to
Verse obligado a

Before
Antes de que

Before dark
De día

Beforehand
Con tiempo

Before one's (very) eyes
A ojos vistas

Be funny
Tener gracia

Begin
Echarse a, ponerse a, romper a

Beginning on
A partir de

Begin running
Echar(se) a correr

Begin to understand
Ir entendiendo

Be glad to
Tener gusto en

Be good for
Servir para

Be good for nothing
No servir para nada

Be haughty
Tener mucho copete

Behind
Atrás de, detrás de, tras de

Behind closed doors
A puerta cerrada

Behind one's back
A espaldas de

Behind the scenes
Entre bastidores

Behold
He aquí

Be in a bad mood
Estar mal templado, estar de mal humor, mal genio

Be in a good mood
Estar de buen humor, buen genio

Be in a hurry
Estar (or andar) de prisa, tener prisa

Be in a jam
Estar en un aprieto

Be in big trouble
Estar con el agua al cuello

Be in charge of
Estar a cargo de, estar encargado de

Be indebted to
Estar en deuda con

Be indispensable
Ser de rigor

Be in favor of
Estar por

Be in good condition (a thing)
Estar en buen uso

Be in good health
Estar bien de salud, sin novedad

Be in great danger
Tener la vida en un hilo

Be in infancy
Estar en pañales

Be in mourning
Estar de duelo, estar de luto

Be in need of
Hacer falta

Be in one's right mind
Estar uno en sus cabales

Be in order
Estar arreglado

Be in the mood (for)
Estar de (o en) vena (para)

Be in the same boat
Estar en las mismas

Be in the way
Estar de sobra

Be in trouble
Estar en un aprieto

Be irritable (or a grouchy person)
Ser un erizo

Be jealous
Tener celos

Be a judge of
Ser conocedor

Be just about out of money
Estar (or andar) escaso de dinero

Be left alone
Estar de non, quedar de non

Believe
Tener por

Believe strongly
A pie(s) juntillas

Be long (in doing)
Tardar en

Below
A continuación

Be lucky
Tener suerte, tocarle a uno la suerte

Be mistaken
Estar en un error

Be nearly...(o'clock)
Faltar un poco para las...(horas)

Beneath
Debajo de

Be necessary
Ser fuerza

Be obliged to
Verse obligado a

Be obvious
Saltar a la vista

Be of no account
Ser un cero a la izquierda

Be of no use
Ya no sopla

Be of the opinion
Dar la razón, tener para sí

Be on duty
Estar de turno

Be one's own affair
Correr por cuenta de uno

Be one's turn
Tocarle a uno, tocarle a uno la suerte

Be on good terms with
Acordar con

Be on intimate terms with
Tener confianza con

Be only human
Ser de carne y hueso

Be on one's last legs
Estar en las últimas

Be on the alert for
Estar a la mira de, estar sobre sí, estar sobre aviso

Be on the lookout for
Estar a la mira de

Be on unfriendly terms with
Estar torcido con

Be on vacation
Estar de vacaciones

Be opportune
Venir a (or al) pelo

Be opposed to
Estar en pugna con

Be out of a job
Medir las calles

Be out of luck
Andar de malas, estar de malas, tener la de malas

Be out of resources
Estar en las últimas

Be out of sorts
Andar agitado, no estar de humor

Be out of the house
Estar fuera de la casa

Be passing through
Estar de paso

Be perfectly even
Estar ras con ras

Be pleased with
Quedar contento con

Be pleased with oneself
Pagado de sí mismo

Be proud of (or vain about) something
Pagarse de algo

Be a question of
Tratarse de

Be relieved of
Quitarse uno un peso de encima

Be required by custom
Ser de rigor

Be responsible for
Hacerse cargo de

Be ridiculous
Hacer el ridículo

Be right
Andar bien; tener razón

Be safe
Estar a buen recaudo

Be satisfied
Estar uno hasta la coronilla

Be seldom at home
Ser huésped en su casa

Be short of money
Estar (or andar) escaso de dinero

Beside
A lado de, tras de

Beside oneself
Fuera de sí

Besides (to boot)
Además de, de pilón, sobre que

Beside that
Aparte de eso

Be sleepy
Tener sueño

Be soaked through
Estar hecho una sopa

Be sorry for someone
Pesarle a uno

Be stubborn
Ser duro de mollera

Be stuffed
Estar uno hasta el copete

Be stupid
No tener sal en la mollera

Be successful
Salir bien, tener éxito

Be sulky
Tener murria

Be terribly sorry
Sentir en el alma

Be the scapegoat
Pagar el pato

Be the object of scandal
Ser piedra de escándalo

Be thirsty
Tener sed

Be ticklish
Tener cosquillas

Be to blame
Tener la culpa

Be too complicated
Pecar de oscuro

Be too good
Pecar de bueno

Be to one's advantage
Convenirle a uno

Better late than never
Más vale tarde que nunca

Better yet
Mejor dicho

Between
Por entre

Between the devil and the deep blue sea
Entre la espada y la pared

Be unable to cope with
No da abasto a

Be understood
Quedar entendido que

Be unlucky
Estar salado

Be unwilling to do it
No querer hacerlo

Be up to date
Estar al cabo de, estar al corriente de, estar en corriente

Be up to oneself
Correr por cuenta de uno

Be used as
Servir de

Be used for
Servir para

Be used (or accustomed) to...
Tener la costumbre de...

Be very angry
Echar espumarajos

Be very eager to (or for)
Rabiar por

Be very difficult
Costar trabajo

Be very thin
Estar hecho un costal de huesos

Be very unclear
Pecar de oscuro

Be a wallflower
Planchar el asiento

Be well
Sin novedad

Be well-informed
Estar al cabo de, estar al corriente de, estar en corriente

Be well off
Estar desahogado

Be willing
Estar dispuesto

Be witty or salty
Estar salado

Be worse off
Estar peor que antes

Be worth
Valer por

Be worthless
No ser ni chicha ni limonada

Be worthwhile
Merecer la pena, valer la pena

Be wrong
Estar en un error, no tener razón

Be...years old
Tener...años

Beyond
Más allá (de)

Blame
Dar en cara, echar en cara, echar la culpa a

Blindly
A ciegas, a ojos cerrados, a tientas

Block the door
Impedir el paso

Blush
Ponerse colorado

Boast of
Hacer gala de, pagarse de

Borrow
Pedir prestado

Bother about
Molestarse en

Brand as (or accuse)
Motejar de

Break into
Forzar la entrada

Break into pieces
Hacer pedazos

Break one's word
Faltar a su palabra, pintarle un violín

Break the news
Dar la noticia

Break the thread of a story
Cortar el hilo

Bridge a gap
Llenar un vacío

Bring up to date
Poner al corriente

Bulky
De buen tomo y lomo

Bully for you!
¡Así se hace!

Bump into each other
Darse un encontrón

Burn down
Quemarse hasta el suelo

Burning question
La cuestión palpitante

Burn the midnight oil
Quemarse las pestañas (or las cejas)

Burst with laughter
Reventar de risa

Bury
Dar sepultura

But
Sino que

By all means
A toda costa, a todas luces, de todos modos, sin falta

By chance
Al azar, por casualidad

By dint of
A fuerza de

By ear
Al oído, de oído

By foot
A pie

By force (of)
A fuerza (de), a la fuerza

By guess
A ojo, al tanteo

By hand
A mano

By heart
De memoria

By itself
De por sí

By just shouting
A puros gritos

By means of
Por medio de

By mistake
Por equivocación, por descuido

By no means
De ningún modo, de ninguna manera, ni modo

By oneself
Por sí solo, por su mano

By pure chance
De pura casualidad

By sheer force
A pura fuerza

By sight
A ojo

By the looks of
Por lo visto

By the minute
De punto

By the roots
De raíz

By the way
A propósito, de paso, entre paréntesis

By twos
De dos en dos

By word of mouth
De palabra, de viva voz

C

Call a spade a spade
Al pan, pan y al vino, vino;
llamar al pan pan y al vino vino

Call on the phone (telephone)
Llamar por teléfono

Call the roll
Pasar lista

Carry away
Cargar con

Carry out
Dar cima, llevar a efecto,
llevarse adelante

Carry through
Llevar a cabo

Cast a shadow
Hacer sombra

Catch cold
Coger catarro, coger un
resfriado

Catch fire
Coger fuego

Cause distress or grief to
Dar disgustos a

Cause extra work
Dar que hacer

Cause pain or worry
Hacer mella

Cause sorrow
Dar mucha pena

Cents off
Rebaja de...centavos

Certainly
A buen seguro

Certainly not
Claro que no

Chain of misfortunes
Rosario de desdichas

Change one's mind
Cambiar de idea (...opinión,
...pensamiento)

Change the subject
Cambiar de tema

Chatter constantly
Hablar por los codos, hablar a
chorros

Cheat (in a bargain or exchange)
Dar gato por liebre

Cheer up
Dar ánimo

Choose
Optar por

Clarify
Poner en claro

Clearly
A las claras, a ojos vistas

Clear the table
Levantar la mesa, quitar la
mesa

Clear the way
Abrir paso

Clear up
Poner en claro

Close attention
Suma atención

Closer
Más acá

Close to
A raíz de, cerca de

Coast is not clear, the
Hay moros en la costa

Cock and bull story
Cuento chino

Collide with
Darse un encontrón

Collapse
Venirse abajo

Come across (someone or something)
Encontrarse con, tropezar con

Come at the right moment
Venir a (o al) pelo

Come from
Ser oriundo de

Come hell or high water
Contra viento y marea

Come one after another (bad luck or misfortunes)
Llover sobre mojado

Come out ahead
Salir ganando

Come out as desired
Surtir efecto

Come out poorly
Salir mal

Come out well
Quedar bien, salir bien, surtir
efecto

Come to (regain consciousness)
Volver en sí

Come to a boil
Soltar (o alzar) el hervor

Come to an agreement
Ponerse de acuerdo

Come to blows
Venir a las manos

Come to know
Llegar a saber

Come to pass
Llegar a suceder, ocurrir

Come to the point
Dejarse de cuentos, ir al grano

Come what may
Contra viento y marea, suceda
lo que suceda

Comings and goings
Idas y venidas

Complain loudly
Poner el grito en el cielo

Complain of
Quejarse de

Complete
Dar cima, dar fin (a)

Completely
De raíz, por completo

Compliment
Echar flores, echar un
piropo

Concerning
Respecto a

Confidentially
Al oído

Confront
Enfrentarse con

Consciously
A sabiendas

Consequently
De resultas, en consecuencia
de, por consecuencia de, por
consiguiente

Consider
Parar mientes en, tener en
cuenta, tener por, tomar en
cuenta

Consider as
Dar por

Consider as done
Dar por hecho

Considering that
Visto que

Continually
A cada momento, por instante

Continuously
De seguida

Coordinate
Poner en juego

Cost an arm and a leg
Costar un ojo de la cara

Count on
Contar con

Crawl (or creep)
Andar a gatas

Crawling
A gatas

Crawl out of a difficulty
Salir a gatas

Cross-country
A campo traviesa

Crowd
Hervidero de gente, remolino
de gente

Crowded
De bote en bote

Crow's feet (wrinkles)
Pata de gallo

Crude
En rama

Curse
Echar ternos, soltar un terno

Cut class
Faltar a (la) clase, hacer
pinta

Cut into strips
Hacer rajas

D

Dabble in
Picar en

Daily grind
La rutina diaria

Dance without music
Bailar a secas

Dating from
Desde hace

Day after day
Día tras día

Daydream
Estar en las nubes, soñar
despierto

Days of old
Días de antaño

Dead end
Callejón sin salida

Deal in
Tratar en

Deal with
Tratar de

Deceitfully
A traición, de mala fe

Deceitful story told to get money
El cuento del tío

Decide upon
Optar por

Decline
Venir a menos

Delay
Dar largas

Demolish
Echar por tierra

Depart
Salir de

Despite
A despecho de

Destroy
Dar al traste con, dar al través
con

Devour (eat up or drink down)
Echarse al coleto

Diagonally
Al sesgo

Die
Estirar la pata, pasar a mejor
vida

Disappoint
Pegar un chasco

Displease
Caer mal, no caer bien

Ditch (avoid)
Dar esquinazo

Do...again
Hacer...de nuevo, volver a...

Dodge the issue
Evadir el tema

Don't worry
¡No se ocupe!, ¡No se preocupe
usted!

Don't worry about it
No tenga usted cuidado

Do one's best
Hacer lo posible, poner todo de
su parte

Do over
Hacer de nuevo, hacer otra vez,
volver a hacer

Doubt
Poner en duda

Do without
Pasarse sin, prescindir de

Draw lots
Echar pajas, echar suertes

Dream of
Soñar con (or en)

Drift
Andar a la deriva, irse a la
deriva

Drink too much
Alzar el codo, empinar el codo

Drive someone crazy
Volver loco a uno

Drop
Dejar caer

Drop out (of)
Darse de baja, dejar de asistir,
retirarse (de)

Drop out of sight
Perderse de vista

Dunce
Tonto de capirote, zopenco

During the week
A mediados de la semana, entre
semana

E

Each one
Cada cual, cada uno

Each other
El uno al otro, unos a otros

Each time
A cada rato, cada vez

Earliest possible, the
Lo antes posible

Early in (a period of time)
A principios de

Earn a living
Ganar para comer, ganarse la
vida

Either
El uno o el otro, uno u otro

Either of the two
Cualesquiera (or cualquiera) de
los dos

Emphasize
Dar realce, hacer destacar

Encore!
¡Otra, otra!

Encounter
Tropezar con

Encourage
Dar aliento, dar alas a

Endanger
Poner al tablero, poner en
peligro

End up as
Venir a parar

End up by (doing something)
Acabar por

Enhance
Dar realce

Enjoy your meal!
¡Buen provecho!

Equally
Al igual

Equal to or up to
Con fuerzas para, estar a la
altura de

Especially
Ante todo, en especial, en
particular, sobre todo

Esteem highly
Tener en mucho, poner en (or
sobre) las nubes

Et cetera
Y así sucesivamente

Even if
Aun cuando

Even so
Así y todo

Even though
Aun cuando, ni siquiera

Even with (flush)
Al ras con, a ras de

Ever since
Desde entonces

Everybody
Todo el mundo

Everybody who
Todo el que

Every day
Todos los días

Everyone
Todo hombre

Every other day
Cada dos días, un día sí y otro
no, un día sí y un día no

Everything else
Todo lo demás

Every time
Todas las veces (que)

Everywhere
A todas partes, en todas partes,
por todas partes, por todos
lados

Evidently
Por lo visto

Exactly as
Según y como, según y
conforme

Exactly as desired
A pedir de boca

Exactly the opposite
Todo lo contrario

Exasperate (someone)
Sacar (a uno) de quicio

Except for
Si no fuera por, si no fuera porque

Excessively
Sobre manera

Exclusive of
Sin contar

Extend condolences to or for
Dar el pésame por

Extra
De repuesto

Extremely
Con (or en or por) extremo

F

Face
Dar a, hacer frente (a), hacer rostro

Face to face
Cara a cara

Fail
Dejar de, salir mal, venirse abajo

Fair (or such as it is)
Tal cual

Fair play
Juego limpio

Fall back into old habits
Volver a las andadas

Fall down
Irse abajo, venirse abajo

Fall ill
Caer enfermo, ponerse enfermo

Fall to one's lot
Tocarle a uno la suerte

Fall upon
Venir sobre

Far from
Ni con mucho

Farther away
Más allá de

Farther on
Más adelante

Fast asleep
Profundamente dormido

Featherbrained
Alegre de cascos, ligero de cascos

Feed
Dar de comer

Feel feverish
Sentirse destemplado

Feel like
Tener gana(s) de

Feel OK
Estar regular

Feel sorry for
Tener lástima de

Feign illness, to
Hacer la zanguanga

Few, a
Unas cuantas, unos cuantos

Few lines, a
Cuatro letras

Few words, a
Cuatro palabras

Fib
Echar papas

Finally
Al cabo, en fin, por fin, por última vez, por último

Find fault with
Poner defectos, poner faltas

Find no way out
No hallar vado

First of all
Ante todo

Fit badly
Caer mal

Fit of anger
Arranque de cólera, ímpetu de ira

Fit of madness
Transporte de locura

Fit well
Caer bien, sentar bien a

Fix one's eyes on
Poner la mira

Flash by
Pasar como un relámpago

Flat denial
Una negativa rotunda, una negativa terminante

Flatter
Dar coba, dar jabón (a), echar flores, echar un piropo

Flirt (with)
Afilar con, coquetear, hacer cocos

Flush with
A flor de, al ras con, a ras de

Follow in the footsteps (of)
Seguir las pisadas

Fond of
Amante de, amigo de

Fool, to
Hacer cuco a

Fool oneself
Hacerse ilusiones

Foot the bill
Pagar los gastos

For a change
Para variar

For and against
En pro y en contra

For certain
De seguro

Forever
Para siempre, por siempre

For example
Por ejemplo

Form a line
Hacer cola

For now
Por ahora

For one purpose or another
Para unos fines u otros

For some reason
Por algo

For some time now
De algún tiempo para acá

For sure
De seguro

For that reason
Por esa razón, por eso

For the first time
Por primera vez

For the last time
Por última vez

For the present
Por de pronto, por lo pronto, por el (or la or lo) presente

For the sake of
En obsequio de, por amor de

For the time being
De momento, por ahora, por el momento, por lo pronto

For want of
A falta de

Forward
Hacia adelante

Foul play
Juego sucio

Frame someone
Conspirar contra una persona

Frankly
A las claras, sin rebozo, sin reserva

Free
En libertad

Free rein
A rienda suelta

Frequently
A cada momento, a menudo, con mucha frecuencia

Frighten
Dar horror

From a distance
De lejos, desde lejos

From afar
Desde lejos

From bad to worse
De mal en peor

From beginning to end
De cabo a rabo

From now on
De ahora en adelante, de aquí en adelante, de hoy en adelante, desde ahora, en adelante

From one side to the other
De parte a parte

From that time on
De aquel tiempo en adelante, de aquel entonces

From the beginning
Desde el principio

From then on
De ahí en adelante

From the outside
Por fuera

From the rear
Por detrás

From time to time
A ratos, de tarde en tarde

From today on
A partir de hoy

From top to bottom
De arriba abajo

Full-fledged
Hecho y derecho

Full to the brim
Lleno de bote en bote

Fully
A fondo

Furthermore
Más aún

G

Generally
Por lo común, por lo general

Get along well with
Llevarse bien con, quedar bien con

Get down to cases
Ir al grano

Get drunk
Pillar una mona

Get going
Poner en marcha

Get late
Hacerse tarde

Get late in the evening
Hacerse noche

Get lost!
¡Vete a bañar!

Get married
Contraer matrimonio

Get oneself in a mess
Meterse en un lío

Get out of a difficulty
Salir del paso

Get out of here!
¡Largo de aquí!, ¡Quítese de aquí!

Get ready to leave
Hacer las maletas

Get tangled up
Hacerse un lío

Get the blame
Pagar el pato

Get the blame unjustly
Cargar con el muerto

Get the point
Caer en la cuenta

Get to one's feet
Ponerse de pie

Get to sleep
Conciliar el sueño

Get up
Ponerse de pie, ponerse en pie

Get up on the wrong side of the bed
Levantarse de malas, levantarse con las malas, levantarse con el santo de espaldas

Get well
Ponerse bien

Get worse
Subir de punto

Give account
Dar razón

Give a party
Dar una fiesta

Give a report on
Dar cuenta de

Give a scare
Pegar un susto

Give cause for
Dar lugar a

Give courage
Dar alas a

Give good results
Surtir efecto

Give it up
Darlo por abandonado

Given name
Nombre de bautismo, nombre de pila

Give opportunity (or occasion) to
Dar pie

Give regards
Dar los recuerdos

Give someone the run around
Dar largas

Give something up for lost
Echarle la bendición a una cosa

Give thanks
Dar las gracias

Give to
Dar a

Give up
Darse por vencido

Give up (or get rid of) something
Quitarse de una cosa

Gladly
Con mucho gusto, de buena gana, de buen grado, de (buena) voluntad

Glance at
Mirar por encima

Glance off
Pegar de soslayo

Glance over
Dar un vistazo a

Gnash one's teeth
Rechinar los dientes

Go arm in arm
Ir del brazo

Go back
Volverse atrás

Go back on one's word
Echarse para atrás, volverse atrás

Go blind
Perder la vista

Go cautiously
Caminar con pies de plomo

Go crazy
Perder el juicio, volverse loco

Go halves
Ir a medias, ir a la mitad

Go jump in the lake!
¡Vete a bañar!

Good-looking
Bien parecido, de buen ver

Good luck
Que le vaya bien

Go on a journey
Hacer un viaje

Go on a spree
Andar (or ir) de parranda, andar (or ir) de fiesta en fiesta, ir de jarana

Go on foot
Ir a pie

Go on vacation
Ir de vacaciones

Goosebumps
Carne de gallina

Go out for a good time or fling
Echar una cana al aire

Go out of style
Pasar de moda

Go out to meet
Salir al encuentro de

Go over carefully
Pasar revista a

Go over like a lead balloon
Caer mal, caer gordo

Go shopping
Ir de compras

Go to bed early
Acostarse con las gallinas

Grab
Echar la garra

Gradually
Poco a poco

Grasp
Echar la zarpa

Grow late
Hacerse noche

Grown up
Hecho y derecho

Guess right
Dar en (or con) el chiste

H

Hail from
Ser oriundo de

Half done
A medio hacer

Halfway (to a place)
A medio camino

Hang one's head
Agachar las orejas

Haphazardly
A la ventura

Happy-go-lucky
Chueco o derecho

Hard cash
Dinero contante y sonante

Hardly
A duras penas

Hardly ever
Casi nunca

Hard of hearing
Algo sordo, corto de oído,
medio sordo

Hard time
Un rato desagradable

Hard-working
Muy trabajador

Have a bad time
Sudar la gota gorda

Have a big mouth
Tener la lengua larga

Have a birthday
Cumplir años

Have a finger in everything
Estar en todo

Have a good day
Que lo pase bien

Have a good time
Pasar un buen rato

Have (an illness)
Estar con (una enfermedad)

Have a screw loose
Faltarle a uno un tornillo

**Have contact (or a lot to do) with
a person**
Tener roce con alguien

Have dealings with
Tratar con

Have a dislike for someone
Tenerle tirria a una persona

Have influence with someone
Tener cabida con alguien

Have in mind
Tener en la mente

Have in sight
Tener a la vista

Have just (done something)
Acabar de

Have little sense
Faltarle a uno un tornillo

Have nothing to do with
No tener nada que ver con

Have no way out
No tener alternativa (or
elección)

Have on
Traer puesto

Have one's own way
Salirse con la suya

Have on the tip of one's tongue
Tener en la punta de la lengua

Have the blues
Tener murria

Have the lead
Llevar ventaja

Have the misfortune to
Tener la pena de

Have time off
Tener tiempo libre

Have to (do something)
Tener que...

Have to do with
Tener que ver con

Heads or tails
Águila o pico, águila o sello,
cara o cruz

Head toward
Hacer rumbo a

Heaps
A montones

Hear about
Oír hablar de

**Hear news early or for the
first time**
Desayunarse con la noticia

Hear from
Recibir noticias de

Hearsay
De oídos

Hear that
Oír decir que

Hearty laugh
Una buena carcajada

Height of folly
El colmo de la locura

Help
Dar la mano

Help yourself
Sírvase usted

Hence
De ahí que, por ende

Here!
A sus órdenes

Hereafter
En lo sucesivo

Here below
De tejas abajo

Hinder
Hacer mala obra

Hit (upon)
Dar en

Hit a nerve
Tocar en lo vivo

Hit at a slant
Pegar de soslayo

Hit or miss
Al tanteo, chueco o derecho

Hit the ceiling
Poner el grito en el cielo

Hit the nail on the head
Dar en el clavo, dar en (or con)
el chiste, dar uno en la tecla

Hold in check
Tener a raya

Hold in low esteem
Tener en poco a

Honestly!
¡Palabrita de honor!

Horrify
Dar horror

Hot-headed
Caliente de cascos

How awful!
¡Qué horror!

How can I (one) have the nerve?
¿Con qué cara?

How do you like...?
¿Qué le parece...?

How do you say...?
¿Cómo se dice...?

However
Ahora bien, sin embargo

However much
Por más que

How far?
¿Hasta dónde?

How goes it? (or how is it going?)
¿Qué hubo?

How often?
¿Cada cuánto tiempo?

How should I know?
¿Qué sé yo?

How unfortunate!
¡Qué desgracia!

Humiliate
Poner en ridículo

Hurry
Darse prisa

Hurry back
Volver corriendo

Hurt or harm someone
Hacerle daño a uno

Hurt to the quick
Tocar en lo vivo

I

I bet... (not a real wager)
A que...

I bet they are...
Seguro que están

I bet you don't!
¡A que no!

If at all
Si acaso

If even
Si alguna vez

If I remember correctly
Si mal no recuerdo

If not
De lo contrario, donde no

I forgot to tell you
Se me pasó decirte

If so
En caso afirmativo

Ignore
Hacer caso omiso de

Ill-behaved
Mal mandado, muy mandado

Impatient
Mal sufrido

Impede
Dificultar el paso

Important
De buen tomo y lomo, de copete

In a bad humor
De mal temple

In about
Como en

In abundance
A montones

In accordance with
Conforme a, de acuerdo con

In addition to
Además de, a más de, sobre que

In advance
Con anticipación, con tiempo, de antemano, por adelantado

Inadvertently
Sin sentir

In a jiffy
Como por ensalmo, en un credo, en un chiflido, en un soplo

In a little while
Dentro de poco

In all
En junto, en conjunto

In all directions
A los cuatro vientos

In a loud voice
En voz alta

In a low voice
En voz baja

In a minute
En un credo

In a moment
En un improviso

In a month of Sundays
Como visita de obispo

In any case
Al fin de cuentas, de todos modos

In any event
En todo caso

In a second
En un chiflido, en un soplo

In a short time
Dentro de un momento

In a short while
A (or al) poco rato, dentro de poco

Inasmuch as
Como que, como quiera que

In a way
Hasta cierto punto

In back of
Atrás de, detrás de

In bad faith
De mala fe

In brief
En resolución, en resumen

In broad daylight
En pleno día

In case
Por si acaso

In case of (that)
En caso de (que)

In cold blood
En sangre fría

In competition
A porfía

Incomplete
A medio hacer

In compliance with
En conformidad con, estar de conformidad con

In conclusion
En fin

In conflict with
Estar en pugna con

Increase
Subir de punto

In days gone by
En días pasados

Indeed
En efecto

In detail
Por extenso, por menudo

Indirectly
De rebote

Indoors
Bajo techo, en casa

In due course or time
A su (debido) tiempo

In earnest
A la verdad, de veras

In either case
En ambos casos

In exchange for
A cambio de

In fact
De hecho, en efecto, en rigor

In favor of
De parte de

Inform
Dar parte, dar razón, poner al corriente, poner en conocimiento

Informal
Sin ceremonia

Informal gathering or party
Reunión de confianza

In front of
Al frente de, delante de, frente a

In good faith
De buena fe

In good taste
De buen tono, de buen gusto

In good time
Con tiempo

In half
Por la mitad

In haste
A la carrera

In honor of
En obsequio de

In jest
De broma, de burla, en broma

In many respects
En muchos puntos

In my opinion
A mi entender, a mi modo de ver

In (at) odd moments
A ratos perdidos

In one fell swoop
De una tirada

In one's sleep
En sueños

In order
En regla

In order that
A fin de que, para que

In other words
En otros términos, es decir

In particular
En especial

In passing
De paso

In place of
En lugar de

In plain language
En buen romance

In plain view (of)
A la vista (de)

In poor taste
De mal gusto

In the presence of
A vista de

In progress
En curso, en marcha

In proof of
En señal de

In proportion to
A medida que

In safety
En salvo

In season
En sazón

In shirtsleeves
En mangas de camisa

In short
Al fin y al cabo, en fin, en resumidas cuentas

Inside of
Dentro de

Insincerely
De dientes afuera

In small quantities
Al menudeo, al por menor, de poquito

In some way or other
De un modo u otro

In (at) spare moments
A ratos perdidos

In spite of
A despecho de, a pesar de

In spite of everything
A pesar de todo

In spite of that
Así y todo, con todo, con todos los obstáculos

In spite of the fact that
A pesar de que

Instantly
En un santiamén

Instead of
En lugar de, en vez de

In such a case
En tal caso

In such a way
De suerte que

Intend or mean to
Pensar en, tener la intención de

Interfere
Hacer mala obra

Interrupt
Cortar el hilo

Intervene
Meterse de por medio

In that way
De esa manera, de ese modo

In the act
En fragante

In the background
En lontananza

In the dark
A oscuras, a obscuras

In the dead of the night
En el sigilo (or silencio) de la noche, en las altas horas

In the dead of winter
En lo más crudo del invierno

In the direction of
Con rumbo a

In the distance
A lo lejos, en lontananza

In the evening
En la noche, por la noche

In the event of
En caso de

In the final analysis
A fin de cuentas

In the future
De ahora en adelante, en adelante, en lo futuro, en lo sucesivo

In the hands of
En poder de

In the latest fashion
A la moda

In the long run
A la larga

In the manner of
A guisa de

In the middle
Por la mitad

In the morning (afternoon, etc.)
Por la mañana (la tarde, etc.)

In the nick of time
En el momento preciso

In the night air
Al sereno

In the open
A campo raso

In the open air
Al aire libre, al raso

In the opposite way
Al revés

In the same way
Del mismo modo

In the style of
A (la) manera de

In the twinkling of an eye
En un abrir y cerrar de ojos, en un santiamén

In this vicinity
Por aquí cerca

In this way
De esta manera, de este modo

In this world
De tejas abajo

In those days
En aquel tiempo, en aquel entonces

In time
A tiempo

In transit
De paso, de tránsito

In truth
A la verdad, de veras

In turn
En rueda

In vain
En balde

In view of
En vista de que

In vogue
De moda

In writing
Por escrito

Irrelevant
Fuera de propósito, inaplicable al caso

I should say not!
¡De ninguna manera!

I should say so!
¡Ya lo creo!

Is that so?
¿De veras?, ¿de verdad?, ¡no diga!

It can't be helped
No hay remedio, no tiene remedio

It doesn't matter
No le hace, no tiene importancia

It is all over
Ha pasado, ha terminado, se ha acabado, ya se acabó

It is all right
Está bien

It is better…
Más vale…

It is clear
Ya se ve

It is forbidden
Se prohibe

It is good (bad) weather
Hace buen (mal) clima

It is hopeless
No tiene remedio

It is necessary to
Hay que

It is not worth the trouble
No vale la pena

It is no wonder that
No es mucho que

It is obvious
Se conoce (que)

It is obvious that
Se ve que

It is rumored that
Se suena que

It is said
Se dice

It is time for
Es (la) hora de

It is time to go
Es (la) hora de partir

It is unnecessary (superfluous)
Está de más

It is yet to be done
Está por hacer

It makes no difference
Darle lo mismo, es lo de menos, lo mismo da, no le hace

It may be that
Puede ser que, tal vez sea que

It must
De rigor

It must be
Debe de ser

It must be true
Ha de ser verdad

It probably is
Debe de ser

It's a deal!
¡Trato hecho!

It's almost time
Falta poco

It's been a long time since (I played)
Hace mucho que no (juego)

It seems to be impossible
Parece mentira

It seems to me that
Me parece que

It serves me right
Bien me lo merezco

It's none of your (my) business
No es asunto suyo (mío)

It's not important
No tiene importancia

It's not opportune (not to the point)
No viene al caso, no viene al cuento

It's not worthwhile
No vale la pena

It's time to...
Ya es hora de...

It's too late now
Ya es tarde

It's true
Es cierto

It won't be long now
Ya mero, ya merito

J

Jack of all trades
Aprendiz de todo y oficial de nada

Jilt
Dar calabazas

Join (a club, etc.)
Ingresar en

Jokingly
De broma

Judge
Tener por

Jump
Dar un salto, dar saltos

Jump to conclusions
Hacer deducciones precipitadas

Just
Nada más

Just about to
Ya mero

Just as
Así como, según y como, según y conforme

Just as is
Así nada más

Just in case
Por lo que pueda tronar, por si acaso

Just plain
Así nada más

Just right
Al centavo, al pelo

Just yesterday
Ayer mismo

K

Keep (something)
Quedarse con (una cosa)

Keep accounts
Llevar cuentas

Keep good time (a watch)
Andar bien

Keep in bounds
Tener a raya

Keep one's feet
Tenerse en pie

Keep one's word
Cumplir (con) su palabra

Keep out!
¡Prohibido el paso!

Keep silent
Guardar silencio

Keep track of
Llevar la cuenta, llevar cuenta de

Keep up to date, informed, posted
Tener al corriente

Kick out
Dar de baja

Kill two birds with one stone
Matar dos pájaros de un tiro

Kneel
Ponerse de rodillas

Kneel down
Hincarse de rodillas

Knit the eyebrows
Fruncir las cejas

Knock down
Echar por tierra

Know absolutely nothing (about that)
No saber ni papa (de eso)

Know by heart
Saber de memoria

Know by sight
Conocer de vista

Know how to (sew, dance, etc.)
Saber (coser, bailar, etc.)

Knowingly
A sabiendas

L

Lack
Hacer falta

Lacking
A falta de

Lame excuse
Disculpa pobre

Large number of
Una infinidad de

Last month
El mes pasado

Last straw
La gota que derrama el vaso

Last week
La semana pasada

Last year
El año pasado

Late
A fines de

Later on
Más adelante

Latter
El más reciente

Laugh at
Reírse de

Laugh off
Tomar a risa

Laugh up one's sleeve
Reírse para sus adentros

Leap year
Año bisiesto

Learn by heart
Aprender de memoria

Least of it
Lo de menos

Leave
Dejar de la mano; salir de

Leave alone
Dejar en paz, dejar tranquilo

Leave (someone) in the lurch
Dejar (a uno) plantado, dejar en las astas del toro

Leave word
Dejar dicho

Leisure hours
Ratos perdidos

Lend
Dar prestado

Lengthwise
A lo largo (de)

Less and less
Cada vez menos

Less than
Menos de, menos que

Let be
Dejar en paz

Let loose
Soltar la rienda

Let on
Dejar saber

Let oneself be coaxed
Hacerse del rogar

Let's see (if)
A ver (si)

Like
A guisa de, a (la) manera de, a semejanza de, parecido a

Like always
Como siempre

Literally
Al pie de la letra

Little by little
Poco a poco

Little more
Y pico

Little pitchers have big ears
Hay moros en la costa

Live by stealing
Vivir de sus uñas

Live together
Hacer vida

Long ago
Hace mucho tiempo

Long time
Largos años

Look
Pues, mire

Look down on
Mirar por encima del hombro

Look for a needle in a haystack
Buscar una aguja en un pajar

Look for trouble
Buscarle tres (or cuatro) pies al gato

Look out of the corner of one's eye
Mirar con el rabo del ojo

Look towards
Dar a

Look well
Tener buena cara

Lose face
Perder prestigio

Lose one's head
Saltar las trancas

Lose one's mind
Perder el juicio, perder la razón

Lose patience
Saltar las trancas

Lose sight of
Perder de vista

Lose time
Perder el tiempo

Lots of
A mar de

Loud voice
En voz alta

Lump in the throat
Un nudo en la garganta

M

Madly
Con delirio

Mail (a letter)
Echar (una carta) al correo

Majority of
La mayoría (de), la mayor parte (de)

Majority of the people
El común de las gentes

Make a deal
Hacer un trato

Make a dent
Hacer mella

Make a fool of
Poner en ridículo

Make a good showing
Hacer buen papel

Make a mistake
No dar pie con bola

Make an appointment
Dar una cita

Make a poor showing
Hacer mal papel

Make a ridiculous blunder
Hacer una plancha

Make arrangements
Hacer arreglos

Make eyes at
Hacer cocos

Make faces
Hacer gestos, hacer muecas

Make friends with
Hacerse amigo de

Make fun of
Burlarse de, hacer cuco a, hacer burla de

Make good
Tener buen éxito

Make hay while the sun shines
Hacer su agosto

Make known
Dar a conocer

Make laugh
Hacer gracia

Make no difference
Dar lo mismo, no irle ni venirle a uno

Make oneself understood
Hacerse entender

Make one's living
Ganarse la vida

Make trouble
Dar guerra

Make up
Inventar, imaginar

Make up (after a quarrel)
Hacer las paces

Make up for
Resarcirse de

Make use of
Valerse de

Make way for
Abrir paso para

Many years
Largos años

Match, to
Hacer juego

Mature
Hecho y derecho

Maybe
A lo mejor, tal vez

Mean (intend)
Querer decir

Meantime
Andarse el tiempo

Mean trick
Una mala pasada

Meanwhile
Entre tanto, mientras tanto

Measure
Tomar una providencia

Meddle
Meterse de por medio

Mediocre person
Media cuchara

Meet
Cruzarse con, encontrarse con, tropezar con

Meet face to face
Enfrentarse con

Mind your own business!
¿Quién te mete, Juan Copete?

Minor (in age)
Menor de edad

Misconstrue or misinterpret
Tomar el rábano por las hojas

Miss
Echar de menos

Moment to moment
Por instante

More or less
Alrededor de

Moreover
Por lo demás

More than
Más de, más que

More than anyone
Más que nadie

More than enough
De sobra

More than ever
Más que nunca

More than once
Más de una vez, una y otra vez

Most of
La mayoría de, la mayor parte de

Mourn
Estar de duelo

Move over
Hacerse a un lado

N

Namely
A saber

Naturally
Claro que sí

Near at hand
Al lado (de)

Nearly
Por poco

Neatly dressed
Bien arreglado(a)

Neither fish nor fowl
No ser ni chicha ni limonada

Neither this nor that
Ni esto ni aquello

Never mind
¡No importa!, ¡no se ocupe!

Nevertheless
No obstante, sin embargo

Next to
Al lado de, junto a

No...(smoking, eating, etc.)
Se prohibe...(fumar, comer, etc.)

Nobody else
Ningún otro

No comment
Sin comentarios

No kidding!
¡Palabrita de honor!

No longer
Ya no

No matter how much
Por mucho que

No matter what
Por ningún motivo, suceda lo que suceda

Nonsense
¡De dónde!; salida de pie de banco

No parking
Prohibido estacionarse

Nor I either
Ni yo tampoco

No sooner said than done
Dicho y hecho

Not by a long shot
Ni con mucho

Not by any means
Ni mucho menos

Not by far
Ni con mucho

Not equal to the burden
No poder con la carga

Not even
Ni siquiera

Nothing at all
Nada en absoluto

Nothing like that
Nada de eso

Nothing unusual
Nada de particular

Notice
Darse cuenta de, echar de ver, fijarse en

Not in a laughing mood
No estar de humor

Not much
Poca cosa

Not only...but also
No sólo...sino también

No trespassing
Prohibida la entrada, prohibido el paso, se prohibe entrar (pasar)

Not so often
No tan a menudo

Not to be a laughing matter
No ser cosa de juego

Not to bother about trifles
No pararse en pelillos

Not to feel well
Sentirse destemplado

Not to fit well
No caer bien

Not to get things right
No dar pie con bola

Not to know anything
No saber una (or ni) jota

Not to my knowledge
No que yo sepa

Not to open one's mouth
No despegar los labios

Not to realize
No darse cuenta

Not to say a word
No despegar los labios

Not to sleep a wink
Pasar la noche en claro (or en blanco)

Not to worry
Perder cuidado

Notwithstanding
No obstante

Not worth a red cent
No vale una cuartilla

Not worth a straw
No vale un pito

Not yet
Aún no, todavía no

Now
Al presente

Nowadays
Hoy (en) día

Now and then
De tarde en tarde, de vez en cuando

No way out
No quedar otro

No way out of it
No hay tu tía

Nowhere
A ninguna parte, en (or a) ninguna parte, por ningún lado

No wonder!
¡Con razón!

Now then
Ahora bien, pues bien

O

Object to
Levantar la contra

Obstruct (the way)
Dificultar (el paso), impedir (el paso)

Occasionally
De cuando en cuando, de vez en cuando

Of about
De unos

Of age
Mayor de edad

Of course
Claro que sí, ¿cómo no?, desde luego, por supuesto, seguro que sí, ya se ve

Of course not
Claro que no

Of last month
Del próximo pasado

Of little value or importance
De poca monta, lo de menos

Of one piece
De una pieza

Of one's own making or invention
De su (propia) cosecha

Often
A menudo

Of that kind
Por el estilo

Of the same sort
Del mismo modo

OK (to approve)
Dar el visto bueno

Omit
Pasar por alto

On (upon)
Encima de

On account of
A causa de, con motivo de, por motivo

On a large scale
En grande

On all fours
A gatas

On all sides
Para todos lados

On an average
Por término medio

On approval
A vistas

On behalf of
De parte de, en pro de

Once again
De nuevo

Once and for all
De una vez, de una vez por todas

Once in a blue moon
Allá a las quinientas, como visita de obispo, de tarde en tarde

Once in a while
Una que otra vez

Once upon a time
Había una vez, érase que se era, érase una vez, y va de cuento

One at a time
De uno en uno, uno a la vez

One by one
Uno por uno

On edge
De canto

One must
Hay que

On end
De punta

One of these (fine) days
Un día de estos

One or the other
El uno o el otro, uno u otro

One way
De un solo sentido

One week from today
De hoy en ocho días

On foot
A pie

Only
Nada más, no más que

Only yesterday
Ayer mismo

On one's back
De espaldas

On one's knees
De rodillas

On purpose
A propósito, de propósito

On returning
A la vuelta de

On the contrary
Al contrario, por el contrario

On the dot
En punto

On the fence
Entre azul y buenas noches

On the following day
Al día siguiente, al otro día

On the inside
Por dentro

On the lookout for
Estar a la mira de

On the occasion of
Con motivo de

On the other hand
En cambio, por otra parte, por otro lado

On the other side of
Al otro lado de

On the outside
Por fuera

On the rebound
De rebote

On the road to
Camino de

On the run
A la carrera

On the sly
A escondidas, a hurto

On the spur of the moment
De buenas a primeras

On the way
De camino, de tránsito, (estar) en camino

On time
A buena hora, a tiempo

On tiptoes
De puntillas, de puntas

On top of
Por encima de

On vacation
De vacaciones

On watch
En vela

Openly
A boca llena, a las claras, al descubierto, sin rebozo

Oppose
Llevar la contra, ponerse en contra de, salir al encuentro de

Opposed to
En contra de

Ordinary
De ordinario

Or else
No sea que, o si no, si no

Others
Los (las) demás

Otherwise
De lo contrario, de otro modo, donde no, porque si no

Out of breath
Con la lengua de corbata, con la lengua de pechera

Out of danger
En salvo

Out of date
Pasado de moda

Out of sorts
No estar de humor

Out of spite
Por despecho

Out of style
Pasado de moda

Out of the country
En el extranjero

Out of the ordinary
Fuera de lo corriente

Over and over again
Repetidas veces, una y otra vez

Over a period of (time)
Desde hace

Over here
Por acá, por aquí

Overlook
Pasar por alto

Overnight
De la noche a la mañana

Overstep the bounds
Pasar de la raya

Over there
Por ahí, por allá

Overthrow someone
Dar en tierra con alguien

P

Pacify
Poner en razón

Pack
Hacer las maletas

Partly
En parte

Pass by
Dar una pasada por

Passing through
De tránsito

Pay attention (to)
Dar atención, fijarse en, hacer caso (a or de), prestar atención

Pay a visit
Hacer una visita

Pay by cash
Pagar al contado

Payday
Día de raya

Peerless
Sin par

Perchance
Por ventura

Per day
Al día

Perhaps
A lo mejor, tal vez

Pesky as a fly
Más pesado que una mosca

Pick a fight or quarrel with
Meterse con

Place hope in someone
Esperar en alguien

Place in safety
Poner a buen recaudo

Place one's hope in
Cifrar la esperanza en

Plain
A secas

Plain and simple truth
La verdad clara y desnuda

Plain fool
Tonto de capirote

Plainly
A boca llena

Play a bad (or mean) trick (on someone)
Hacer una mala jugada, hacer una perrada, jugarle una mala partida

Play a part
Desempeñar un papel

Play a role
Hacer el (or un) papel

Play a trick
Pegar un chasco

Play by ear
Tocar de oído, tocar por fantasía

Play dumb
Hacerse el tonto

Play fair
Jugar limpio

Play hooky
Hacer pinta, pintar venado

Play on words
Juego de palabras

Play second fiddle
Ser plato de segunda mesa

Play up to (someone)
Dar coba a (alguien)

Please (make contented)
Caer bien, caer en gracia, dar gusto

Pledge
Empeñar la palabra

Point blank
A quema ropa, a quemarropa

Poor memory
Memoria de gallo

Pose as
Dárselas de

Praise (to the skies)
Poner en el cielo, poner por las nubes

Presence of mind
Presencia de ánimo

Present!
¡A sus órdenes!

Pretend
Dar a entender, dejar saber

Pretend not to hear
Hacerse el sordo

Pretend not to notice
Hacerse el desentendido

Pretend to be dead
Hacerse muerto

Prick up one's ears
Aguzar las orejas (or los oídos)

Pride
Amor propio

Proud
De copete

Provided
Siempre y cuando

Provided that
Con tal (de) que, dado el caso que, siempre que

Publicly
A las claras

Pull
Tirar de

Pull one's leg
Tomarle el pelo

Pull over to the right
Desviarse hacia la derecha, hacerse a la derecha

Pun
Juego de palabras

Pursue
Dar caza

Put into practice
Poner por obra

Put in writing
Hacer por escrito

Put on airs
Darse aires a, darse farol, darse tono, subirse de tono

Put oneself in a ridiculous situation
Tirarse una plancha

Put one's foot in one's mouth
Meter la pata

Put the cart before the horse
Tomar el rábano por las hojas

Q

Quarrel with
Meterse con

Question
Poner en duda

Quickly
Al trote, de prisa, de un salto, en un salto

R

Rabble
Gente de baja estofa

Rack one's brain
Devanarse los sesos, quebrarse uno la cabeza, romperse los cascos

Rain cats and dogs
Llover a cántaros

Rain or shine
Que llueva o no

Raise a rumpus
Dar batería

Rapidly
A escape

Rather
Más bien, mejor dicho

Rather late
Algo tarde

Rather than
Antes que, más bien que

Rattle off
Repetir de carretilla

Reach
Ponerse en

Realize (that)
Caer en la cuenta, darse cuenta de (que)

Really
De veras, en efecto, en verdad

Real truth, the
La mera verdad

Reckon with
Contar con

Reflect on (think about)
Parar mientes en

Regardless of
Sin hacer caso de

Regards to
Recuerdos a

Regret
Pesarle a uno

Regret very much
Sentir en el alma

Reject
Dar calabazas

Reliable
Digno de confianza

Reluctantly
De mal grado

Rely on
Confiar en, contar con

Remember (or recollect)
Hacer memoria

Remorse
Gusano de la conciencia

Repeatedly
Sobradas veces

Repeat mechanically
Repetir de carretilla

Reproach
Dar en cara, echar en cara

Resemble
Salir a

Resist stubbornly
Hacerse duro, ponerse duro

Rest of them, the
Los (las) demás

Restrain
Tirar las riendas

Return for
Volver por

Right away
En el acto

Right here
Aquí mismo

Right now
Ahora mismo, en seguida, más ahorita

Right side out
Al derecho

Ripe
En sazón

Rise
Ponerse en pie

Risk
Correr riesgo, poner al tablero

Round about
A la redonda, en redondo

Ruin
Dar al traste con, dar al través con, echar(se) a perder

Rumor
De oídos

Run away
Echar(se) a correr

S

Safe
A salvo

Safe against
A prueba de

Safe and sound
Sano y salvo

Same as, the
El (o lo) mismo que, igual que

Satisfy a need or desire
Matar el gusano

Save one's skin
Salvar el pellejo

Save time
Ganar tiempo

Say a bad word
Echar (or saltar) un terno

Say goodbye to
Despedirse de

Say to oneself
Decir para sí

Scarcely
A duras penas

Scowl
Fruncir el ceño

Secondhand
De segunda mano, de uso

Secretly
A puerta cerrada, en secreto

Seem like
Sonar a

See to it that
Ver de, ver que

Seize
Echar la zarpa, echar mano, hacer presa

Seldom
Por rareza, rara vez, raras veces

Self-esteem
Amor propio

Separately
De por sí, por separado

Serenity
Presencia de ánimo

Seriously
En serio

Serve
Servir de

Serve as
Oficiar de

Set forward (e.g., a clock)
Poner adelantado

Set in motion
Poner en juego

Set out (on a trip, etc.)
Ponerse en camino

Set the table
Poner la mesa

Set up housekeeping
Poner casa

Several times
Varias veces

Shake hands (with)
Dar la mano, darse la mano, estrechar la mano (a)

Sharp (on time)
En punto

Shortly
En breve

Shortly after
A poco

Shortly thereafter
Poco después de

Show off
Darse farol, hacer teatro

Shred
Hacer trizas

Shrug one's shoulders
Encogerse de hombros

Shut tight
A piedra y lodo

Sideways
De lado, de soslayo

Signify
Querer decir

Silly remark
Salida de pie de banco

Similar
Algo por el estilo, parecido a

Simply
A secas

Since
Como que, como quiera que, desde que, en vista de que, pues que, puesto que, supuesto que, ya que

Since then
Desde entonces

Sky high
Por las nubes

Slam the door
Dar un portazo

Slanting
Al soslayo, de soslayo

Slap
Mandar una bofetada

Sleep it off
Dormir la mona

Sleep on it
Consultar con la almohada

Sleep soundly
Dormir a pierna suelta

Slice
Hacer rajas

Slip
Darse un resbalón

Slowly
A la larga

Smell like
Oler a

Snap one's fingers
Castañetear con los dedos, tronar los dedos

So
Así que

So far
Hasta aquí, hasta ahí

Soft (or smooth) as silk
Como una seda

Softsoap or flatter (someone)
Dar coba a, dar jabón a

Somebody else
Algún otro

Someday
Algún día

Somehow
De algún modo, de alguna manera, de un modo u otro

Something indefinable
Un no sé qué

Something is wrong
Hay moros en la costa

Something of the sort
Algo por el estilo

Sometime
Algún día, algún tiempo, alguna vez

Sometimes
Algunas veces, de cuando en cuando

Somewhat
Un tanto

Somewhere
En alguna parte

Somewhere else
En alguna otra parte

So much the better
Tanto mejor

So much the worse
Tanto peor

Soon after
A raíz de, al (or a) poco rato

Sooner or later
A la corta o a la larga, tarde o temprano

Sooner the better, the
Antes hoy que mañana

So-so
Así así, tal cual

So that
A fin de que, así es que, así que, con tal (de) que, de manera que, de modo que, de suerte que

So then
Así pues

Sound like
Sonar a

So what?
¡A mí que!, ¿de modo que?, ¿pues que?, ¿y que?

Spare (extra)
De repuesto

Spare no expense
Echar la casa por la ventana

Speak frankly
Hablar al alma, no tener pelillos en la lengua

Speaking! (in answering a telephone)
Al habla

Speak loudly
Hablar alto, hablar en voz alta

Speak to the point
Hablar al caso

Speedily
A todo trapo

Spicy story
Un cuento alegre

Split hairs
Pararse en pelillos

Spoil
Echar(se) a perder

Stand a chance
Tener probabilidad

Standing
De pie

Stand someone up
Dejar a uno plantado

Stand still
Estarse parado

Stark raving mad
Loco de remate

Start to
Ponerse a, ponerse en marcha, romper a

Start a conversation
Entablar una conversación

Start a fire
Prender el fuego

Start out
Ponerse en marcha

Stay in
Quedarse en la casa

Stay in bed
Guardar (la) cama

Stealthily
A hurto

Step aside
Hacerse a un lado

Step hard upon
Dar un pisotón

Stomp or step on
Dar una pisada

Stop (smoking, etc.)
Dejar de (fumar, etc.)

Stop beating around the bush
Dejarse de cuentos, dejarse de rodeos

Stop over at
Hacer escala en

Stop short (or suddenly)
Parar en seco

Stop the excuses
Dejarse de rodeos

Straw that broke the camel's back
La gota que derrama el vaso

Strike the hour
Dar la hora

Study hard
Quemarse las pestañas (or las cejas)

Stumble
Dar un traspié, darse un tropezón

Stylish
De buen tono, de moda

Succeed
Tener éxito

Such as
Tal como, tales como, tal cual

Such as that
Por el estilo

Suddenly
De golpe, de pronto, de repente, de súbito

Suit
Venir bien

Suit perfectly
Venir a (or al) pelo

Summing up
En resumen

Superfluous
Está de más

Supposing
Dado caso, supuesto que

Sure enough
Dicho y hecho

Surprise
Pegar un chasco

Swarm of people
Un hervidero de gente, un remolino de gente

Swear (curse)
Echar un terno, soltar un terno

Sweat blood
Sudar la gota gorda

Sweat profusely
Sudar la gota gorda

Swell with pride
Estar (or ponerse) ancho

Swiftly
A rienda suelta

Swiftness of time
Corrida del tiempo

Swindle
Dar gato por liebre

T

Take (something)
Quedarse con (una cosa)

Take a chance
Correr riesgo

Take a drink
Echar un trago

Take advantage of the situation
Aprovechar la ocasión

Take after (someone)
Salir a

Take a jump
Pegar un salto

Take a long time (in doing something)
Tardar en (hacer algo)

Take a long weekend
Hacer puente

Take an afternoon nap
Dormir la siesta

Take a nap
Descabezar el sueño, echar un sueño, echar una siesta

Take a stand against
Salir al encuentro de

Take a step
Dar un paso, tomar una providencia

Take a stroll
Dar una vuelta

Take a walk
Pasear a pie

Take a walk or ride
Dar un paseo

Take care
Tener cuidado (con)

Take care of
Preocuparse de

Take care of someone
Mirar por alguien

Take charge (of)
Encargarse (de), hacerse cargo (de)

Take exercise
Hacer ejercicios

Take for a...
Tener por...

Take for granted
Dar por descontado, dar por hecho, dar por sabido (or sentado or supuesto), tomar por cierto

Take into account
Hacer caso a (or de), tener en cuenta, tomar en cuenta

Take it easy
Tomarlo con calma

Take lightly
Tomar a risa

Take pity on
Tener lástima de

Take place
Tener lugar

Take root
Echar raíces

Take seriously
Tomar a pechos(s)

Take the lead
Tomar la delantera

Take time off
Tomar tiempo libre

Take to heart
Tomar a (or en) pecho(s), tomar en serio

Take undue liberties
Pasar de la raya

Talk of the town
La comidilla de la vecindad

Talk too much
Hablar por los codos

Talk to oneself
Hablar para sus adentros

Tear into strips
Hacer rajas

Tear to pieces
Hacer garras, hacer trizas

Tease
Tomarle el pelo

Thank (or give thanks)
Dar las gracias

That can't be helped
Eso no tiene quite

That depends
Según y conforme, según y como

That is
A saber

That is a horse of a different color
Eso es harina de otro costal

That is even worse
Peor que peor

That is it
Eso es

That is the limit!
¡Eso es el colmo!

That is to say
Es decir, o sea que

That is urgent
Eso corre prisa

That is why
Por algo, por esa razón

That long
Así de largo

That's not the point (or the question)
No se trata de eso

That's right
Eso es

That's the last straw!
¡No faltaba más!

That's the least of the trouble
Es lo de menos

That's the point
¡Ahí está el detalle!

That was (is) true
Eso sí

That way
Por allí

That which
Lo que

The coast is not clear
Hay moros en la costa

The fact is
El caso es

The more...the less
Mientras más...mientras menos

Then
A la sazón

The ones
Los que

Thereafter
Después de eso

There are no two ways about it
No hay que darle vueltas, no tiene vuelta de hoja

Therefore
Así pues, así que, por (or en) consecuencia de, por consiguiente, por ende, por eso, por lo cual, por lo tanto

There is more than meets the eye
Hay gato encerrado

There is no doubt (that)
No cabe duda (que)

There is no way around it
No hay que darle vueltas

There is the heart of the matter!
¡Allí está el toque!

There's no hurry
No hay prisa

There's no need to
No hay para qué

There's no other way but to...
No hay más remedio que...

There's nothing to do except...
No hay más remedio que...

The same as
Así como, el (or lo) mismo que

They say
Se dice

Think (be of the opinion)
Tener para sí

Think about
Pensar en

Think not
Creer que no

Think so
Creer que sí

This side of
Más acá de

This way
Por acá, por aquí

This will do
Así está bien

Thoroughly
Por completo

Those which (or those who)
Los (or las) que

Thousand thanks, a
Mil gracias

Throng (of people)
Remolino de gente

Through or throughout
A través de, al través de, de parte a parte, por conducto de, por donde

Through thick and thin
Por toda suerte de penalidades

Throw a party
Dar una fiesta

Throw a stone
Mandar una pedrada

Tilted
De lado

Tip (give a gratuity)
Dar propina

Tip one's hat
Tocarse el sombrero

To and fro
De aquí para allá

To boot
De pilón

Together
A la vez

Tomorrow afternoon
Mañana por la tarde

Tomorrow is another day
Mañana Dios dirá

Tomorrow morning
Mañana por la mañana, mañana temprano

Tomorrow night
Mañana por la noche

To myself
Para mis adentros

Tonight
A la noche, por la noche

Too bad!
¡Qué lástima!

To oneself
Consigo mismo

To one's heart's content
A pedir de boca

To the letter (just right)
Al centavo, al pie de la letra

To the limit
Hasta más no poder

To the point
A secas, de perlas

To the utmost
A más no poder, de lo lindo, hasta más no poder

Touch a sore spot
Tocar en lo vivo

Towards (a period of time)
A principios de

Towards the end of (a period of time)
A fines de

Track down
Dar caza

Train was *x* minutes late
El tren llegó con *x* minutos de retraso

Treacherously
A traición

Treat (deal with)
Tratar de

Trip (or stumble)
Dar un traspié, darse un tropezón

Truly or truthfully
A la verdad, de veras, de verdad, en verdad

Trust
Confiar en

Trustworthy
Digno de confianza

Try to (attempt)
Tratar de, ver de, ver que

Turn (around)
Dar(se) la vuelta

Turn a deaf ear
Hacerse el sordo

Turn one's back (on)
Dar las espaldas (a), voltear la espalda

Turn out to be
Venir a parar, venir a ser

Turn the corner
Doblar a la esquina

Turn the page
Darle vuelta a la hoja

Two by two
De dos en dos

Two-faced
De dos caras

Two of a kind
Tal para cual

Two-way
De dos sentidos

Two weeks from today
De hoy en quince días

U

Unanimously
A una vez

Unavoidable
Sin remedio

Uncovered
En descubierto

Undecided
Entre azul y buenas noches

Under
Debajo de

Undercover
A escondidas

Understand that...
Tener entendido que...

Undertake
Poner por obra

Under the table (underhanded)
Bajo cuerda

Unequaled
Sin igual

Unexpectedly
A deshora(s), de buenas a primeras, de improviso, el día menos pensado

Unfortunately
Por desgracia

Unharmed
A salvo

Unless
A menos que, a no ser que, como no

Unlucky
De mala suerte

Unnecessary
De sobra

Unnoticed
Sin sentir

Unpaid
En descubierto

Unreserved
Sin reserva

Until
Hasta que

Unusual
Fuera de lo corriente

Unwillingly
A la mala, de mal grado, de mala gana, sin querer

Upon
Encima de

Upon my honor
Sobre mi palabra

Ups and downs
Subidas y bajadas

Upside down
Patas arriba

Up to a point
Hasta cierto punto

Up to date
A la moda, hasta la fecha

Up to now
Hasta aquí, hasta ahí, hasta la fecha

Up to the top
Hasta el tope

Usual
De ordinario

Usually
Por lo general, por lo regular, por regla general

V

Vanish
Perderse de vista

Vanity
Amor propio

Various times
Repetidas veces

Very bad luck
Suerte negra

Very close
A quema ropa, a quemarropa

Very early in the morning
Muy de mañana

Very far away
En el quinto infierno

Very much
Con (or en or por) extremo, de lo lindo

Very often
Con mucha frecuencia, muy a menudo

Very probably
A buen seguro

Very soon
Poco rato, ya mero

Very thought of, the
La mera idea de

Violently
A rienda suelta

Visibly
A ojos vistas

Vouch for
Dar fe de, salir fiador de

W

Wait in line
Hacer cola

Wait table
Servir la mesa

Wait the whole blessed day
Esperar todo el santo día

Walk
Ir a pie

Walk by
Dar una pasada por

Walk the streets
Medir las calles

Wanted
Se solicita

Want to
Tener deseos de

Wash one's hands of
Lavarse las manos de

Watch out (for)
Tener cuidado (con)

Weakness (or weak side)
Lado flaco, punto flaco

Wear
Llevar puesto, traer puesto

Wear oneself out
Hacerse uno rajas

Weather the storm
Aguantar el chubasco

Week before last
La semana antepasada

Weekday(s)
Día(s) de semana, día de trabajo, día hábil

Weekend
El fin de semana

Welcome
Dar la bienvenida

Well and good
Santo y bueno

Well done!
¡Así se hace!

Well-done (well-cooked)
Bien asado, bien cocido

Well-groomed
Bien peinado

Well now
Ahora bien

Well then
Pues bien

Well worth it
Digno de

What a mess!
¡Qué batingue!

What an atrocity!
¡Qué barbaridad!

What a pleasure!
¡Qué gusto!

What does it mean?
¿Qué quiere decir?, ¿qué
significa?

What do you think of it?
¿Qué le parece?

What for?
¿Para qué?

What happened?
¿Qué pasó?

What has been said
Lo expuesto

What if...?
¿Y si...?

What is it?
¿Qué haces?

What is it about?
¿De qué se trata?

What is it good for?
¿Para qué sirve?

What is more
Más aún

What is the date?
¿A cuánto(s) estamos?

What is the point of that?
¿A qué viene eso?

What is the use of it?
¿Qué ventaja tiene?

What nonsense!
¡Qué barbaridad!

What's eating you?
¿Qué mosca te ha picado?

What's it to you?
¿Quién te mete, Juan Copete?

What's going on?
¿Qué pasa?

What's new?
¿Qué hay de nuevo?

What's so bad about that?
¿Qué hay de malo con eso?

What's that to me?
¿A mí qué?

What's the difference?
¡Qué más da!

What's the matter with you?
¿Qué le (or te) pasa?

What's up?
¿Qué hubo?, ¿qué pasa?

What's wrong with...?
¿Qué tiene de malo...?

What's wrong with that?
¿Qué hay de malo con eso?

What time is it?
¿Qué hora es?, ¿qué horas son?

When all is said and done
A la postre

Whenever
Cuando quiera, siempre que,
todas las veces (que)

When least expected
El día menos pensado

Whereas
Visto que

Wherever
Adondequiera que,
dondequiera que, por
dondequiera que

Whether one likes it or not
Por las buenas o por las malas

Whether you wish or not
Quieras que no, quiera o no

While
En tanto que

While away the time
Pasar el rato

Whisper
Hablar en secreto

Whispering
En voz baja

Whole truth, the
La verdad clara y desnuda

Wholly
Del todo

Wide open
De par en par

Willingly
A la buena, con mucho gusto,
de buena gana, de buen grado,
de (buena) voluntad

Win
Salir ganando

With
Junto con

**With both feet together (or on
the ground)**
A pie(s) juntillas

With certainty
A (or de) ciencia cierta, a punto
fijo

With great difficulty
A duras penas

Within
Dentro de

Within a few years
A la vuelta de los años

Within a week
Dentro de una semana

Within speaking distance
Al habla

Within view
A vista de

With no confidence
De mala fe

Without
Sin que

Without a plan
A la buena de Dios

Without equal
Sin par

Without fail
Sin falta

Without help
Sin remedio

Without interruption
De seguida

Without question
Sin disputa

Without realizing
Sin sentir

Without remedy
De remate, sin recurso

Without rhyme or reason
Sin qué ni para qué, sin ton
ni son

Without risk
Sobre seguro

Without sleep
En vela

Without stopping
De corrida, de hilo

Without the knowledge of
A escondidas de

Without warning
A quema ropa, a quemarropa

With pleasure
De (buena) voluntad

With regard to
Acerca de, con respecto a, en
cuanto a, respecto a

With the aim of
Con el propósito de

With the idea of
Con motivo de

With tongue hanging out
Con la lengua de corbata, con
la lengua de pechera

With your permission
Con permiso

Wonderfully
De lo lindo

Wonderfully well
A las mil maravillas

Word of honor!
¡Palabrita de honor!

Workday
Día hábil

Work hard
Dar batería, sudar la gota gorda

Work in vain
Azotar el aire

Work well
Andar bien

Worry about
Preocuparse por

Worry about nothing
Ahogarse en poca agua

Worse than
Peor que

Worth seeing
Ser de ver, ser para ver

Wrinkle one's brow
Fruncir el entrecejo

Wrong side out
Al revés

Y

Year before last
Año antepasado

Years ago
Hace años

Yes, of course
Ya lo creo

Yesterday afternoon
Ayer por la tarde

You don't say!
¡No diga!

You're welcome
De nada, no hay de que

SPANISH-ENGLISH
ESPAÑOL-INGLÉS

REMARKS

For ease of reference, the reader should note the following:

- Within each entry, the word or group of words corresponding to each of the meanings of the Spanish word constitutes a separate numbered subentry.

- Examples of usage, phrases, and idioms are included in each entry immediately following the meaning of the word to which they correspond.

- Examples of usage, phrases, and idioms are given in a fixed sequence within each item of the entry: word groups not containing a verb; expressions containing a verb; phrases or locutions (adverbial, prepositional, etc.).

- Expressions, phrases, etc. that do not directly correspond to a specific meaning of the word are numbered separately within the entry.

- Words given as equivalents of the main entry are clarified further, when necessary, by synonyms and definitions enclosed in brackets.

- Abbreviations indicate meaning and usage in specific subject areas and geographical regions, as well as in grammar. See "Abbreviations Used in This Dictionary."

- The letters *ch* and *ll*, which are distinct letters in the Spanish alphabet, are listed as such.

In addition to the explanations of grammar within individual entries, certain points of grammar have been explained in greater detail in an overview preceding the lexicon. These summaries treat specific instances of Spanish grammar that have proven most troublesome to English-speaking readers (e.g., direct and indirect object pronouns, the subjunctive).

- An asterisk in the body of an entry indicates that the word it precedes is used only in the Americas.

In order to assist the reader, reference sections on a variety of topics are included in this dictionary. Idioms and expressions—both Spanish-to-English and English-to-Spanish —can be found in the center of the dictionary.

The appendices include:

- False Cognates and "Part-Time" Cognates
- Monetary Units / Unidades monetarias
- Weights and Measures / Pesas y medidas
- Numbers / Numerales
- Temperature / La temperatura
- Maps/Mapas

ABBREVIATIONS USED
IN THIS DICTIONARY

abbr	abbreviation		*interj*	interjection
adj	adjective		*interrog*	interrogative
adv	adverb		*inv*	invariable
AER	aeronautics		*iron*	irony
AGR	agriculture		*irreg*	irregular
algn	*alguien* someone		JUR	jurisprudence
A.M	American		LING	linguistics
ANAT	anatomy		*lit*	literary
arg	argot; slang		*loc*	locution
ARQ	*arquitectura* architecture		*m*	masculine
art	article		*m & f*	either gender
ASTROL	astrology		MAR	maritime
ASTRON	astronomy		MAT	mathematics
AUTO	automobiles		MED	medicina
aux	auxiliary verb		METEOR	meteorology
AV	aviation		*mf*	common gender
BIOL	biology		MIL	military
BOT	botany		MUS	music
CINEM	cinema		*n*	noun
COM	commerce		*neŭt*	neuter
comp	comparative		*npr*	*nombre propio* proper noun
cond	conditional		*o.s.*	oneself
conj	conjunction		*p*	pronominal verb
COST	*costura* sewing		*pers*	personas; personal
CULIN	culinary		*pey*	*peyorativo* pejorative
def	definite		*pl*	plural
DEP	*deporte* sports		POL	politics
ECON	economics		*pos*	possessive
EDUC	education		*pp*	past participle
ELEC	electricity		*prep*	preposition
esp	especially		*pres*	present
etc	et cetera		*pron*	pronoun
euf	*eufemismo* euphemism		*pt*	preterite; past
f	feminine		QUÍM	*química* chemistry
fam	familiar		®	trademark
fig	figurative		RAD	radio
FIN	finances		*rel*	relative
FÍS	*física* physics		REL	religion
fml	formal		sb.	somebody
fut	future		*sing*	singular
GB	Great Britain		sth.	*something*
gen	generally		*subj*	subjunctive
GEOG	geography		*superl*	superlative
GRAM	grammar		*t*	transitive verb
HIST	history		TEAT	*teatro* theater
i	intransitive verb		TÉC	*técnico* technical
imp	imperative		TV	television

IND	industry	US	United States
indef	indefinite	ZOOL	zoology
indic	indicative	*	taboo
inf	infinitive	≈	approximately equivalent to
INFORM	*informática* computers	→	see

KEY TO PRONUNCIATION
IN SPANISH

VOWELS

Letter	Approximate sound
a	Like *a* in English *far, father,* e.g., **casa, mano.**
e	When stressed, like *a* in English *pay,* e.g., **dedo, cerca.** When unstressed, it has a shorter sound like in English *bet, net,* e.g., **estado, decidir.**
i	Like *i* in English *machine* or *ee* in *feet,* e.g., **fin, salí.**
o	Like *o* in English *obey,* e.g., **mona, poner.**
u	Like *u* in English *rule* or *oo* in *boot,* e.g., **atún, luna.** It is silent in **gue** and **gui,** e.g., **guerra, guisado.** If it carries a diaeresis (**ü**), it is pronounced (see Diphthongs), e.g., **bilingüe, bilingüismo.** It is also silent in **que** and **qui,** e.g., **querer, quinto.**
y	When used as a vowel, it sounds like the Spanish **i,** e.g., **y, rey.**

DIPHTHONGS

Diphthong	Approximate sound
ai, ay	Like *i* in English *light,* e.g., **caigo, hay.**
au	Like *ou* in English *sound,* e.g., **cauto, paular.**
ei, ey	Like *ey* in English *they* or *a* in *ale,* e.g., **reina, ley.**
eu	Like the *a* in English *pay* combined with the sound of *ew* in English *knew,* e.g., **deuda, feudal.**
oi, oy	Like *oy* in English *toy,* e.g., **oiga, soy.**
ia, ya	Like *ya* in English *yarn,* e.g., **rabia, raya.**
ua	Like *wa* in English *wand,* e.g., **cuatro, cual.**
ie, ye	Like *ye* in English *yet,* e.g., **bien, yeso.**
ue	Like *wa* in English *wake,* e.g., **buena, fue, bilingüe.**
io, yo	Like *yo* in English *yoke,* without the following sound of *w* in this word, e.g., **región, yodo.**
uo	Like *uo* in English *quote,* e.g., **cuota, oblicuo.**
iu, yu	Like *yu* in English *Yule,* e.g., **ciudad, triunfo, yunta.**
ui	Like *wee* in English *week,* e.g., **ruido, bilingüismo.**

TRIPHTHONGS

Triphthong	Approximate sound
iai	Like *ya* in English *yard* combined with the *i* in *fight,* e.g., **estudiáis.**
iei	Like the English word *yea,* e.g., **estudiéis.**
uai, uay	Like *wi* in English *wide,* e.g., **averiguáis, guay.**
uei, uey	Like *wei* in English *weigh,* e.g., **amortigüéis, buey.**

CONSONANTS

Letter	Approximate sound
b	Generally like the English *b* in *boat, bring, obsolete,* when it is at the beginning of a word or preceded by *m,* e.g., **baile, bomba.** Between two vowels and when followed by *l* or *r,* it has a softer sound, almost like the English *v* but formed by pressing both lips together, e.g., **acaba, haber, cable.**
c	Before *a, o, u,* or a consonant, it sounds like the English *c* in *coal,* e.g., **casa, saco, cuba, acto.** Before *e* or *i,* it is pronounced like the English *s* in *six* in American Spanish and like the English *th* in *thin* in Castillian Spanish, e.g., **cerdo, cine.** If a word contains two *c*s, the first is pronounced like *c* in *coal,* and the second like *s* or *th* accordingly, e.g., **acción.**
ch	Like *ch* in English *cheese* or *such,* e.g., **chato, mucho.**
d	Generally like *d* in English *dog* or *th* in English *this,* e.g., **dedo, digo.** When ending a syllable, it is pronounced like the English *th,* e.g., **usted, libertad.**
f	Like *f* in English *fine, life,* e.g., **final.**
g	Before *a, o,* and *u;* the groups *ue* and *ui;* or a consonant, it sounds like *g* in English *gain,* e.g., **gato, gorra, aguja, guerra, guitar, digno.** Before *e* or *i,* like a strongly aspirated English *h,* e.g., **general, región.**
h	Always silent, e.g., **hoyo, historia.**
j	Like *h* in English *hat,* e.g., **joven, reja.**
k	Like *c* in English *coal,* e.g., **kilo.** It is found only in words of foreign origin.
l	Like *l* in English *lion,* e.g., **libro, límite.**
ll	In some parts of Spain and Spanish America, like the English *y* in *yet;* generally in Castillian Spanish, like the *lli* in English *million;* e.g., **castillo, silla.**
m	Like *m* in English *map,* e.g., **moneda, tomo.**
n	Like *n* in English *nine,* e.g., **nuevo, canto, determinación.**
ñ	Like *ni* in English *onion* or *ny* in English *canyon,* e.g., **cañón, paño.**
p	Like *p* in English *parent,* e.g., **pipa, pollo.**
q	Like *c* in English *coal.* This letter is only used in the combinations *que* and *qui* in which the *u* is silent, e.g., **queso, aquí.**
r	At the beginning of a word and when preceded by *l, n,* or *s,* it is strongly trilled, e.g., **roca, alrota, Enrique, desrabar.** In all other positions, it is pronounced with a single tap of the tongue, e.g., **era, padre.**
rr	Strongly trilled, e.g., **carro, arriba.**
s	Like *s* in English *so,* e.g., **cosa, das.**
t	Like *t* in English *tip* but generally softer, e.g., **toma, carta.**
v	Like *v* in English *mauve,* but in many parts of Spain and the Americas, like the Spanish **b,** e.g., **variar, mover.**
x	Generally like *x* in English *expand,* e.g., **examen.** Before a consonant, it is sometimes pronounced like *s* in English *so,* e.g., **excepción, extensión.** In the word **México,** and in other place names of that country, it is pronounced like the Spanish **j.**
y	When used as a consonant between vowels or at the beginning of a word, like the *y* in English *yet,* e.g., **yate, yeso, hoyo.**
z	Like Spanish **c** when it precedes **e** or **i,** e.g., **zapato, cazo, azul.**

AN OVERVIEW OF SPANISH GRAMMAR

ACCENTUATION/ACENTUACIÓN

Rules of accentuation

All words in Spanish (except adverbs ending in -mente) only have one stressed syllable. The stressed syllable is sometimes indicated by a written accent.

In words with no written accent, the ending of the word determines the placement of stress.

- Words that end in a consonant (except *n* or *s*) stress the last syllable: pared, añil, capaz.
  —The final y as part of a diphthong is treated as a consonant: carey, Paraguay.

- Words that end in a vowel or in *n* or *s* stress the next to the last (penultimate) syllable: casa, pasan, libros.

Note: Adverbs ending in -**mente** retain the original stress (and written accent) of the root word as well as stress the first syllable of the adverbial ending: claramente, difícilmente, últimamente.

The written accent is used in the following cases:

- Words that end in a vowel or the consonants *n* or *s* and that stress the last syllable: café, talón, anís.

- Words that end in a consonant (except *n* or *s*) and that stress the next to the last syllable: árbol, quídam.

- All words that stress the third from the last (antepenultimate) syllable: párvulo, máximo, ánimo.

Note: Verbs having unstressed pronouns attached to them preserve the written accent when they ordinarily carry one: llevóme, apuréla.

Other uses of the written accent

- The written accent is used to distinguish between two words with the same spelling but different meanings or functions:

él (pronoun)	el (article)
tú (pronoun)	tu (possessive adjective)
mí (pronoun)	{ mi (possessive adjective) mi (musical note)
sí (adverb) } sí (pronoun) }	si (conjunction)
sé (of the verb *ser*) } sé (of the verb *saber*) }	se (reflexive pronoun)
más (adverb)	mas (conjunction)
dé (of the verb *dar*)	de (preposition)
té (noun)	te (pronoun)
éste } ése } (pronouns) aquél }	este } ese } (adjectives) aquel }
sólo (adverb)	solo (adjective)

- The written accent is also used in the following cases:
  —**Quién, cuál, cúyo, cuánto, cuán, cuándo, cómo,** and **dónde** in interrogative and exclamatory sentences.
  —**Qué, cúyo, cuándo, cómo,** and **porqué** used as nouns: sin qué ni para qué, el cómo y el cuándo.
  —**Quién, cuál,** and **cuándo** having a distributive sense: quién más, quién menos.
  —**Aún** when it is interchangeable with **todavía**: no ha llegado aún.
  —The vowels *i* and *u* are accented when they are preceded or followed by another vowel and form a separate stressed syllable: llovía, baúl.
  —The conjunction o takes an accent when it comes between two arabic numerals to avoid mistaking it for zero (0): 3 ó 4.

ARTICLES / ARTÍCULOS

The article in Spanish is a variable part of speech, agreeing with the noun in gender and number.

Definite articles

	Masculine	Feminine
Singular	**el** libro (the book)	**la** cara (the face)
Plural	**los** libros (the books)	**las** caras (the faces)

The neuter article **lo** is used to give a substantive value to some adjectives: **lo** bello (the beautiful, what is beautiful, beautiful things); **lo** profundo de sus pensamientos (the profoundness of his thoughts).

Indefinite articles

	Masculine	Feminine
Singular	**un** hombre (a man)	**una** naranja (an orange)
Plural	**unos** hombres (some men)	**unas** naranjas (some oranges)

Special cases

- The masculine article is used with feminine nouns that begin with a stressed **a**: **el** alma (the soul); **un** ave (a bird).

- With reflexive verbs, the definite article is equivalent to an English possessive adjective in sentences like: me lavo **las** manos, I wash my hands; ponte **el** sombrero, put on your hat.

- When followed by **de** or an adjective, the Spanish definite article may be used as a pronoun equivalent to *the one* or *the ones:* el **del** sombrero blanco, the one in the white hat.

GENDER / GÉNERO

All nouns in Spanish have a gender: masculine, feminine, common, or epicene. Some adjectives having the value of a noun are in the neuter gender.

Note: For all practical purposes, common and epicene nouns are masculine or feminine and are treated as such in the entries of this dictionary.

Some observations

- Nouns denoting living beings usually have a different form for the masculine or feminine gender: **trabajador, trabajadora,** working man, working woman; **actor, actriz,** actor, actress; **oso, osa,** bear (male), bear (female); **buey, vaca,** ox, cow; **caballo, yegua,** horse, mare.

- Some nouns that denote persons have only one ending for both masculine and feminine genders. They are in the common gender, and the sex is indicated solely by the article: **un** pianista, **una** pianista, a pianist.

- Some masculine nouns and feminine nouns are used to denote animals of either sex. They are in the epicene gender, and the sex is indicated by the word **macho** or **hembra** following the noun: una serpiente **macho,** a male serpent; un rinoceronte **hembra,** a female rhinoceros.

- Nouns denoting material or spiritual things are never in the neuter gender but have either the masculine or feminine gender attributed to them. The reader is advised to look for the gender in the corresponding entries of this dictionary whenever a question arises.

FORMATION OF THE PLURAL / PLURAL

The plural of Spanish nouns and adjectives is formed by adding s or es to the singular word.

The plural is formed by adding s to:

- Words ending in an unstressed vowel: casa, **casas**; blanco, **blancos**.
- Words ending in an accented é: café, **cafés**.

The plural is formed by adding es to:

- Words ending in an accented á, í, ó, or ú: bajá, **bajaes**; rubí, **rubíes**.
  Exception: **Papá, mamá, chacó**, and **chapó** add s; maravedí has three forms for the plural: **maravedis, maravedíes**, and **maravedises**.
- The names of the vowels: a, **aes**; e, **ees**; i, **íes**, etc.
- Nouns and adjectives ending in a consonant: árbol, **árboles**; anís, **anises**; cañón, **cañones**.
  Exception: Nouns of more than one syllable ending in an s preceded by an unstressed vowel do not change in the plural: lunes, **lunes**; crisis, **crisis**. Observe that nouns and adjectives ending in z change the z to c in their written plurals: vez, **veces**; feliz, **felices**.

Proper names

When a proper name is used in the plural, all the preceding rules and exceptions are observed. Exception: Family names ending in z (Núñez, Pérez, etc.) do not change in the plural.

Nouns of foreign origin

Usually nouns of foreign origin form the plural according to the preceding rules. However, the plural of lord is **lores**, and the plural of cinc or zinc is **cincs** or **zincs**.
Latin words, such as ultimátum, déficit, fiat, and exequátur, have no plural form.

Compound nouns and adjectives

- When the elements of the compound noun or adjective are separate, only the first element takes the plural form: **ojos** de buey, **patas** de gallo.
- When the compound is imperfect, such as ricahembra, mediacaña, both the elements take the plural form: **ricashembras, mediascañas**.
- When the compound is perfect, the plural is formed at the end of the word: **ferrocarriles, patitiesos**.
- The plurals of cualquiera and quienquiera are **cualesquiera** and **quienesquiera**.

DIRECT AND INDIRECT OBJECTS / COMPLEMENTOS DIRECTO E INDIRECTO

Direct object

As a rule, the direct object is not preceded by a preposition. However, the positions of the subject and object in Spanish are often reversed, and the direct object is sometimes preceded by the preposition a to avoid confusion.

Examples and exceptions:

Construction with a	Construction without a
César venció a Pompeyo. (Proper noun—name of a person)	Plutarco os dará mil Alejandros. (Proper noun used as a common noun)
Ensilló a Rocinante. (Proper noun—name of an animal)	Ensilló el caballo. (Common noun of an animal)
Conquistó a Sevilla. Conozco Madrid. Uncertain use. (Proper nouns—names of places without the article)	Visitó La Coruña. Veremos El Escorial. (Proper nouns—names of places preceded by the article)

Busco al criado de mi casa.
(Common noun of a specified person)

Busco criados diligentes.
(Common noun of nonspecified persons)

Tienen por Dios al viento.
Temo al agua.
(Noun of a personified thing or of a thing to which an active quality is attributed)

Partiremos esta leña. Recojo el agua.
(Nouns of things in general)

No conozco a nadie.
Yo busco a otros, a alguien, a ti.
(Indefinite pronoun representing a person or personal pronoun)

No sabía nada. Di algo.
(Indefinite pronouns representing things)

Aquel a quien amo.

No sé quién vendrá.

Indirect object

The indirect object is always preceded by the prepositions **a** or **para**: Escribo una carta a mi madre. Compro un libro **para** mi hijo. (I write a letter to my mother. I buy a book for my son.)

ADJECTIVES/ADJETIVOS

The adjective in Spanish is a variable part of speech and must agree in gender and number with the noun it qualifies: libro **pequeño**, casa **pequeña**; libros **pequeños**, casas **pequeñas**.

Some adjectives, however, have the same ending for both masculine and feminine genders: hombre **fiel**, mujer **fiel**; hombres **fieles**, mujeres **fieles**.

Placement of the adjective

Predicate adjectives usually follow the verb: la nieve es **blanca**, the snow is white.

Nevertheless, the order of the sentence can be reversed for emphasis or in some fixed expressions: ¡**buena** es ésta!, that is a good one!; ¡**bueno** está lo bueno!, leave well enough alone.

Adjectives that directly modify a noun may either precede or follow it.

Special cases

- Adjectives that express a natural quality or a quality associated with a person or thing are placed before the noun: el **fiero** león, la **blanca** nieve.

- Indefinite, interrogative, and exclamative adjectives; the adjectives **medio, buen, mal, poco, mucho,** and **mero**; and adjectives expressing cardinal numbers are placed before the noun: **algún** día, some day; ¿**qué** libro prefiere usted?, which book do you prefer?; **dos** hombres, two men.

  Alguno, when placed after a noun, has a negative sense: no hay remedio **alguno**, there is no remedy.

- Some adjectives change meaning or connotation when they precede or follow a noun: un **simple** hombre, a mere man; un hombre **simple**, a simpleton.

- Some adjectives change in form when used before a noun. **Grande** may be shortened to **gran** when used in the sense of extraordinary or distinguished: un **gran** rey, a great king; una **gran** nación, a great nation.

- The masculine adjectives **alguno, ninguno, bueno, malo, primero,** and **tercero** drop the final o when placed before a noun: **algún** día, some day; **ningún** hombre, no man; **primer** lugar, first place; **tercer** piso, third floor.

- The masculine adjective **Santo** is shortened to **San** before all names of saints except Tomás, Toribio, and Domingo: **San** Juan, Saint John; **Santo** Tomás, Saint Thomas.

Comparative degree

The English comparatives—*more...than, less...than,* and adjective + *er than*—are expressed in Spanish as **más...que, menos...que**: Pedro es **más** (or **menos**) atlético **que** Juan, Peter is more (or less) athletic than John.

In a comparative expression, when **que** is followed by a conjugated verb or a number, it is replaced by **de lo que** and **de**, respectively: esto es más difícil **de lo que** parece, this is more difficult than it seems; hay más **de** diez personas, there are more than ten people.

The English comparatives, *as...as* and *so...as,* are expressed in Spanish as **tan...como**: mi casa es **tan** hermosa **como** la de usted, my house is as beautiful as yours.

Superlative degree

The English superlatives—*the most* (or *the least*)*...in* or *of* and adjective + *est...in* or *of*—are expressed in Spanish as **el más** (or **el menos**)**...de**: el barrio **más** populoso **de** la ciudad, the most populous quarter in the town.

- The absolute superlative is formed by placing **muy** before the adjective or by adding the ending **-ísimo** to the adjective: **muy** excelente, **excelentísimo**, most excellent.

- Adjectives ending in a vowel drop the vowel and add **-ísimo**: grande, **grandísimo**; alto, **altísimo**.

- Adjectives ending in **co** or **go**, change c to qu and g to gu and add **-ísimo**: poco, **poquísimo**; largo, **larguísimo**.

- Adjectives ending in **io** drop the ending and add **-ísimo**: limpio, **limpísimo**.

- Adjectives containing an accented diphthong—**ie** or **ue**—change ie to e and ue to o and add **-ísimo**: valiente, **valentísimo**; fuerte, **fortísimo**.

- Adjectives ending in **ble** change this ending to **bilísimo**: amable, **amabilísimo**.

- Some adjectives have special forms for the comparative and superlative degrees: bueno, mejor, óptimo; malo, peor, pésimo; grande, mayor, máximo; pequeño, menor, mínimo.

NUMERALS / NUMERALES

Observations

1) **Uno**, when it precedes a masculine noun, and **ciento**, when it precedes any noun and when used in a cardinal number, take the shortened forms **un** and **cien**: un libro; cien hombres; cien mil soldados.

2) The cardinal numbers between 20 and 30 are spelled **veintiuno, veintidós, veintitrés**, etc.

3) The cardinal numbers between 30 and 40, 40 and 50, etc. (under 100), use the conjunction **y**: treinta y uno, ochenta y tres.

4) The preceding rules apply to the spelling of any cardinal number over 100: **ciento veintiuno**, 121; **seiscientos cuarenta y dos**, 642; **cien mil cuarenta**, 100.040. Note that:
—**Millón, billón**, and the like take the indefinite article **un**; however, ciento, cien, and mil do not: un millón, a million; ciento, a hundred; mil, a thousand; cien mil, one hundred thousand.

5) Ordinal numbers between 10th and 20th are: **undécimo, duodécimo, decimotercero** or **decimotercio, decimocuarto, decimoquinto, decimosexto, decimoséptimo, decimoctavo**, and **decimonoveno** or **decimonono**.

6) The ordinal numbers between 20th and 30th, 30th and 40th, etc. are formed by adding the first nine ordinal numbers to **vigésimo, trigésimo, cuadragésimo**, etc.: **vigésimo primero**, twenty-first; **trigésimo segundo**, thirty-second; **cuadragésimo tercero**, forty-third.

7) Most ordinal numbers may also be formed by adding the endings **-eno, -ena**, and **-avo, -ava** to the cardinal numbers. The ordinal numbers ending in **-avo** (except octavo) are used only to express fractions: una **dozava** parte, one twelfth part; el **dozavo** de, a twelfth of.

8) The cardinal numbers (except **uno**) may be used as ordinals. However, from 2 to 10, preference is given to the ordinal numbers for the names of kings, chapters of books, etc.
—For the days of the month (except the first), only cardinal numbers are used: el **primero** de junio, el **dos** de octubre, el **catorce** de diciembre.

9) As a rule, cardinal numbers are placed before the noun; but when they are used as ordinal numbers, they are placed after the noun: **dos** libros, capítulo **quince**.

10) All the ordinal numbers and the cardinal numbers **uno, doscientos, trescientos,** through **novecientos** agree with the noun they qualify: la **primera** puerta, el **tercer** hombre, **una** casa, **doscientos** libros, **trescientas cuatro** personas.

PERSONAL PRONOUNS / PRONOMBRES PERSONALES
Subject pronouns

Person	Singular	Plural
1st	yo	nosotros, nosotras, nos
2nd	usted, tú	ustedes, vosotros, vosotras, vos
3rd	él, ella	ellos, ellas

- The subject pronoun in Spanish is used only for emphasis or to prevent ambiguity. When neither of these reasons for its use exists, its presence in the sentence makes the style heavy and should be avoided.

- Usted and ustedes are technically second person pronouns used out of courtesy. However, they take the verb in the third person.

- Nos is used by kings, bishops, etc. in their writings or proclamations in the same way as the English *royal we* and *us*. Nosotros is used by writers in the same way as the *editorial we* in English.

- Vos is used to address God, a saint, a king, etc. In some American countries tú is used.

Object pronouns

Direct Object Pronouns

Person	Singular	Plural
1st	me	nos
2nd	te, le, lo, la	os, los, las
3rd	le, lo, la	los, las

Indirect Object Pronouns (without a preposition)

Person	Singular	Plural
1st	me	nos
2nd	te, le	os, les
3rd	le	les

Object Pronouns (with a preposition)

Person	Singular	Plural
1st	mí	nosotros, nosotras
2nd	usted, ti	ustedes, vosotros, vosotras
3rd	él, ella, sí	ellos, ellas, sí

- Sí is equivalent to *himself, herself, itself,* and *themselves* relating to the subject of the sentence: esto es malo de sí, this is bad in itself; habla de sí mismo, he speaks of himself.

- When the indirect object pronouns le and les must precede another third person pronoun, they are replaced by se. Incorrect: le lo mandaron, les las quitaron. Correct: se lo mandaron, se las quitaron.

Reflexive Pronouns

Person	Singular	Plural
1st	me	nos
2nd	te	os
3rd	se	se

- Se may also be:
  —An indication of the passive voice.
  —An impersonal subject equivalent to the English *one, you, they, people:* **se** habló de todo, they talked about everything. However, when the verb is reflexive, **se** cannot be used this way. Instead, **uno, alguno,** or **alguien** may be substituted as the impersonal subject.

Observations:
- When the verb is a gerund or a form of the imperative or infinitive mood, the object pronoun or pronouns are placed after the verb: diciéndolo, dámelo, observarnos. In compound tenses, they are placed after the auxiliary verb: habiéndome dado, haberos comprendido.
  When the gerund or infinitive is subordinate to another verb, the pronouns may pass to the main verb: quieren molestarte or te quieren molestar; iban diciéndolo or lo iban diciendo.

- Direct and indirect object pronouns may be placed before or after the verb when the verb is in the indicative, subjunctive, or conditional mood. In everyday language, it is usual to place them before the verb.

- When there are two object pronouns, the indirect precedes the direct, and a reflexive pronoun precedes another pronoun: me lo dio, se las prometí.

- Object pronouns that follow the verb are incorporated into the verb: **diciéndolo, molestarte.**
  Sometimes in this union, the final letter of the verb must be dropped to avoid a metaplasm: correct: **unámonos,** incorrect: **unamosnos;** correct: **sentaos,** incorrect: **sentados.**

Order of placement
When two or more pronouns accompany the verb, either preceding or following it, the second person pronoun is placed before the first person pronoun, and this before the third person pronoun. The pronoun **se** always precedes the others. (**Te me** quieren arrebatar. **Nos lo** ofrecen. **Se te** conoce en la cara.)

POSSESSIVE PRONOUNS AND ADJECTIVES / POSESIVO (Adjetivo y pronombre)

- The Spanish possessive adjective and pronoun agree with the noun representing the possessed thing: **mi** sombrero, my hat; **mis** libros, my books; **tus** caballos, **vuestros** caballos, your horses.

- The third person possessive adjective or noun, especially in the form of **su,** is very ambiguous because it can mean *his, her, its,* and *their.* It is also equivalent to *your* when used in correlation with **usted** or **ustedes.** To prevent misunderstanding, the practice had been to add the possessor's name (or a pronoun representing it) preceded by **de:** su casa **de** Luis; su libro **de ellos;** su madre **de usted.** However, this use is now restricted to **su...de usted** or **su...de ustedes:** su libro **de usted,** su madre **de ustedes.** In most cases, it is preferable to reword the sentence to avoid ambiguity.

- **Nuestro** and **vuestro** denote only one possessor when the corresponding personal pronoun (**nosotros, nos,** or **vos**) denotes one person.

- In some sentences, the definite article replaces the possessive adjective: he dejado **los** guantes sobre la mesa, I have left my gloves on the table; te has olvidado **el** paraguas, you have forgotten your umbrella.

CONJUGATION OF VERBS / CONJUGACIÓN

Regular verbs in Spanish fall into three groups: **-ar** verbs (first conjugation), **-er** verbs (second conjugation), and **-ir** verbs (third conjugation).

Models of the three conjugations (simple tenses)

amar (to love)   temer (to fear)   recibir (to receive)

Indicative Mood

Present

am-o, -as, -a; -amos, -áis, -an
tem-o, -es, -e; -emos, -éis, -en
recib-o, -es, -e; -imos, -ís, -en

Preterite

am-é, -aste, -ó; -amos, -asteis, -aron
tem } -í, -iste, -ió; -imos, -isteis, -ieron
recib }

Imperfect

am-aba, -abas, -aba; -ábamos, -abais, -aban
tem } -ía, -ías, -ía; -íamos, -íais, -ían
recib }

Future

amar }
temer } -é, -ás, -á; -emos, -éis, -án
recibir }

Conditional

amar }
temer } -ía, -ías, -ía; -íamos, -íais, -ían
recibir }

Subjunctive Mood

Present

am-e, -es, -e; -emos, -éis, -en
tem } -a, -as, -a; -amos, -áis, -an
recib }

Imperfect
(s-form)

am-ase, -ases, -ase; -ásemos, -aseis, -asen
tem } -iese, -ieses, -iese; -iésemos, -ieseis,
recib } -iesen

Imperfect
(r-form)

am-ara, -aras, -ara; -áramos, -arais, -aran
tem } -iera, -ieras, -iera; -iéramos, -ierais,
recib } -ieran

Future

am-are, -ares, -are; -áremos, -areis, -aren
tem } -iere, -ieres, -iere; -iéremos, -iereis,
recib } -ieren

Past Participle

amado   temido   recibido

Gerund

amando   temiendo   recibiendo

Compound tenses are formed by the auxiliary verb **haber** and the past participle of the conjugated verb: **he comido**, I have eaten; **habrá llegado**, he will have arrived; **habías temido**, you had feared.

Irregular verbs

The conjugations of irregular verbs are given in the entries corresponding to their infinitives.

Orthographic-changing verbs

Some verbs undergo spelling changes to preserve their regularity to the ear: tocar, **toque**; llegar, **llegue**; vencer, **venzo**; lanzar, **lance**, etc. These orthographic-changing verbs are neither considered nor treated as irregular verbs in this dictionary.

PASSIVE VOICE / VOZ PASIVA

The Spanish language expresses the passive voice in two different ways:
1) By a form of the verb **ser** and a past participle: la serpiente **fue muerta** por Pedro, the snake was killed by Peter.
2) By the pronoun **se** preceding the verb: aquí **se habla** español, Spanish is spoken here.

The second form of the passive voice is often difficult to distinguish from the active voice in sentences where **se** is an impersonal subject.

EXPRESSING NEGATION / NEGACIÓN

Negation is expressed by the adverb **no**, which is equivalent to the English *no* and *not*.

- **No** is always placed before the verb: la casa **no es** mía, the house is not mine; el niño **no** come, the child does not eat.
  —Other words, even whole sentences, may be placed between **no** and the verb: no **se lo** daré, I will not give it to him; no **todos los presentes** estaban conformes, not all those present agreed.
  —Whenever the meaning may not be clearly understood, **no** must accompany the words it modifies. For example: tu madre **no puede** venir, your mother cannot come; tu madre **puede no** venir, your mother may not come.

- Words expressing negation: **jamás, nunca, nada, nadie, ninguno,** and the phrases **en mi vida, en todo el día,** etc. are substituted for **no** when they precede the verb: **jamás** volveré, **nunca** lo sabrás, **nada** me falta, a **nadie** veo, **ninguno** sobra.
  —However, when these words follow the verb, **no** must be used in the sentence and precede the verb: no volveré **jamás**, no lo sabrás **nunca**, no me falta **nada**, no veo a **nadie**, no sobra **ninguno**.
  —When the sentence contains many words that express negation, only one of them can be placed before the verb: **nadie** me ayudó nunca en nada, **nunca** me ayudó nadie en nada.
  —If the verb is preceded by **no**, all other negative words must follow the verb: No me ayudó **nunca nadie** en **nada**.

- **No** may be used without expressing negation:
  —In sentences subordinate to a verb expressing fear or possibility, **no** is substituted for a **que**: temía **no** viniese, I feared that he should come.
  —As an expletive in sentences like: Nadie dudará que la falta de precisión... **no** dimane de..., No one will doubt that the lack of precision comes from (or is due to)....

INTERROGATIVES / INTERROGACIÓN

Construction of the interrogative sentence

Sentences with no interrogative word:

- The subject is placed after the verb. If a compound tense is used, the subject follows the participle. Remember that in Spanish the subject is expressed only for emphasis or when its presence is necessary for meaning.

¿Ha llegado tu padre?
¿Viene alguien?
¿Trae cada uno su libro?
Llaman.— ¿Será él?
¿Vienes?
¿Viene usted?
¿Viene ella?

Sentences with an interrogative word:

- When the interrogative word is the subject, the sentence order is not reversed.
- When the interrogative word is an attribute, an object, or a complement, the sentence order is reversed.

¿Quién llama?
¿Qué dolor es comparable al mío?
¿Cuál es tu libro?
¿Qué quiere tu hermano?
¿Con quién habla usted?

Complement, object, or subject placed at the beginning of the sentence:

- For emphasis, a complement or object is placed at the beginning of a sentence. If a direct or indirect object is emphasized, it may be repeated by means of a pronoun: A este hombre, ¿lo conocían ustedes? A tu padre, ¿le has escrito? De este asunto, ¿han hablado ustedes?

- The subject can also be placed at the beginning of an interrogative sentence, but then the question is indicated only by the question marks and vocal intonation: ¿Los estudiantes estaban contentos? or Los estudiantes, ¿estaban contentos?

Interrogative sentences are punctuated with two question marks: the one (¿) at the beginning of the question and the other (?) at the end of the question.

THE INFINITIVE / INFINITIVO

The infinitive in Spanish has practically the same uses as the infinitive in English.

Exception: In some subordinate sentences that express what is ordered, expected, desired, etc., the subjunctive or indicative mood is used; whereas in English, the infinitive would be used: El capitán ordenó a los soldados **que trajesen** al prisionero. (The captain ordered the soldiers *to bring* the prisoner.) Me pidió **que pagase** la cuenta. (He asked me *to pay* the bill.) Esperan **que se irá** pronto. (They expect him *to go* away soon.)

The Spanish infinitive is used as a noun in the same way as the English infinitive and sometimes gerund are used as nouns. **Errar** es humano. (To err is human.) El **comer** es necesario para la vida. (Eating is necessary for life.)

PARTICIPLES / PARTICIPIOS

Past participle

- The past participle is always invariable when it is used to form a compound tense: he **recibido** una carta, los libros que he **recibido**.
  —When the past participle is used as an adjective or an attribute, it agrees with its noun in number and gender: un problema **resuelto**, la obra está **terminada**.
  —When the past participle is used with the verbs **tener, llevar, dejar,** etc., it is made to agree in number and gender with a related noun: tengo **resueltos** los problemas, I have the problems solved; llevo **escritas** cuatro cartas, I have four letters written; la dejó **hecha** una furia, when he left her, she was in a rage.

- Many past participles in Spanish have both a regular and an irregular form. As a rule, the irregular forms of the past participles are only used as adjectives and sometimes as nouns: Dios le ha **bendecido**, God has blessed him; una medalla **bendita**, a blessed medal.

Present participle

Very few Spanish verbs have a present participle (in the Latin sense). This participle has become an adjective. Only **concerniente, condescendiente, conducente, correspondiente,** and some others that can have the same complements and objects as the verb, retain something of their participial nature.

THE GERUND / GERUNDIO

Formation

The first conjugation adds **-ando** to the stem of the infinitive (amar, **amando**). The second and third conjugations add **-iendo** (temer, **temiendo**; recibir, **recibiendo**). The gerund does not change for number and gender.

Observations

- The gerund in Spanish never acts as a noun. It expresses an action occurring at the same time as or immediately preceding the action of the main verb: Lee **paseándose**, he reads while strolling; **viendo** a su padre, corrió hacia él, on seeing his father, he ran toward him; **habiendo estudiado** la proposición, me resuelvo a aceptarla, having studied the proposition, I resolve to accept it.

The gerund never expresses an action that occurs after the action of the main verb.

- When the gerund is related to the subject of the main sentence, it may be used only in an explanatory sense: el lobo, **huyendo de los perros,** se metió en el bosque. (The wolf, fleeing from the dogs, went into the woods.)

   The gerund is never used restrictively. *It is correct to say*: Los pasajeros, **llevando pasaporte,** pudieron desembarcar. (The passengers, having their passports, were able to disembark.) *It is incorrect to say*: Los pasajeros **llevando pasaporte** pudieron desembarcar. (Only the passengers having their passports could disembark.) This can be expressed as: Los pasajeros **que llevaban** pasaporte....

- When the gerund is related to the object of the main verb, the object then acts as the subject of the gerund. This use is only correct when the gerund expresses an action perceptible in its course, never a state, quality, or action not perceptible in its course. *It is correct to say*: Vi a un hombre **plantando** coles. (I saw a man planting cabbages.) *It is incorrect to say*: Envió una caja **conteniendo** libros. (He sent a box containing books.) In this case, it is necessary to say: Envió una caja **que contiene** libros.

- The gerund is often used in phrases that are independent of a main sentence, as in titles, captions, inscriptions on engravings, photographs, paintings, etc.: César **pasando** el Rubicón (Caesar passing the Rubicon); las ranas **pidiendo** rey (the frogs asking for a king).

- The gerund is frequently used as an adverb: Ella se fue **llorando** (she went away in tears); el tiempo pasa **volando** (time passes swiftly).

   As an adverb, the gerund may also express the way in which something is done or attained: hizo una cuerda **uniendo varias sábanas** (he made a rope by tying several sheets together).

ADVERBS / ADVERBIOS

Adverbs ending in -mente

Some adverbs are formed by adding -mente to the end of an adjective: fiel, **fielmente**. If the adjective can change gender, -mente is added to the feminine form: rico, rica, **ricamente**.

Placement of the adverb

Generally, when the adverb is qualifying an adjective or another adverb, it immediately precedes the word it qualifies: un libro **bien** escrito, a well-written book; tan **lindamente** ilustrado, so beautifully illustrated.

When the adverb modifies a verb, it may precede or follow the verb: **mañana** llegará mi padre or mi padre llegará **mañana**; my father will arrive tomorrow.

The negative adverb is always placed before the verb: **no** conozco a este hombre, I don't know this man; **no** lo conozco, I don't know him.

When a direct or indirect object pronoun precedes the verb, the adverb cannot separate the pronoun from the verb: **ayer** la vi or la vi **ayer,** I saw her yesterday. The adverb usually never separates an auxiliary verb from the principal verb: ha vencido **fácilmente** a su adversario, he has easily defeated his opponent.

Note: When a word is qualified by two or more adverbs that end in -mente, only the last adverb has the ending -mente, the others retain the adjective form: ella habló **clara, concisa** y **elegantemente**; she spoke clearly, concisely, and elegantly.

Comparative and superlative degrees

Adverbs can also be expressed in comparative and superlative degrees: **más claramente,** more clearly; **clarísimamente,** very clearly or most clearly.

SYNTAX / SINTAXIS

Sentence construction in Spanish is very free. As a general rule its elements, with the exception of object pronouns may be placed in any order.

Examples:

Pedro llegará a las tres.
Pedro a las tres llegará.
Llegará a las tres Pedro.
A las tres llegará Pedro.
A las tres Pedro llegará.

Traigo un regalo para ti.
Traigo para ti un regalo.
Un regalo traigo para ti.
Un regalo para ti traigo.
Para ti traigo un regalo.
Para ti un regalo traigo.

The use of any one of these constructions is a matter of style or of psychological or emotional intent. Nevertheless, the placement of the verb at the end of the sentence is considered affected, even though it is grammatically correct. It is rarely used in writing and not used at all in conversation.

Special cases

There are some cases in which the subject must be placed after the verb. The more important ones are:

- In some interrogative sentences.

- In exclamatory sentences beginning with **qué, cuál, cuán, cuánto**: ¡Qué alegría tendrá **Juan**! ¡Cuál sería **su sorpresa**!

- After **cualquiera que** and **quienquiera que**, used with the verb **ser**, and after **por...que** and **por muy...que**, when the intervening word is an attribute: Cualquiera que fuese **su estado**. Por muy hábil que sea **tu hermano**.

- In parenthetic sentences using the verbs **decir, preguntar, responder, exclamar**, etc.: Nadie — dijo **Juan** — lo creería.

- In sentences expressing a wish or desire, a condition, or a supposition: ¡Viva **la Reina**! Si se presenta **la ocasión**. Si lo quiere **usted** así.

- In sentences beginning with the adverbs or phrases **cuando, apenas, en cuanto**, etc.: Cuando llegue **tu padre**. Apenas lo oyó **Juan**. En cuanto estemos **todos** reunidos.

- In imperative sentences having **usted** as a subject or having a subject that is to be emphasized: Oiga **usted**. Ven **tú** si no viene **él**.

COMMON SPANISH SUFFIXES

-able, -ible	are equivalent to the English suffixes **-able, -ible.**
-ada	• is often equivalent to *-ful, -load:* **cucharada,** spoonful; **vagonada, carretada,** truckload. • indicates: —a blow with or of, a stroke of: **bofetada,** slap in the face; **puñalada,** stab. —an action peculiar to: **bufonada,** buffoonery. —a group or collection of: **manada,** herd, flock.
-ado, -ada	are often equivalent to *-ed* in words such as: **barbado,** bearded.
-ado, -ato	indicate office, state, term, or place, in nouns such as: **obispado,** bishopric; **decanato,** deanship; **reinado,** reign; **noviciado,** novitiate.
-ado, -ido	are the endings of the past participle. They take feminine and plural endings when the participle is used as an adjective.
-acho, -acha, -azo, -aza, -ón, -ona, -ote, -ota	are augmentative endings.
-aco, -aca, -acho, -acha, -ejo, -eja, -ucho, -ucha	are depreciative endings.
-azo	indicates a blow, shot, or explosion: **bastonazo,** blow with a cane; **pistoletazo,** pistol shot.
-dad, -idad, -ez, -eza	are usually equivalent to *-ity, -hood,* and *-ness:* **castidad,** chastity; **cortedad,** shortness; **niñez,** childhood; **pureza,** purity.
-al, -ar, -edo, -eda	denote field, orchard, grove, etc.: **arrozal,** rice field; **manzanar,** apple orchard; **rosaleda,** rose garden.
-dura	forms derivatives of verbs, often meaning action or the effect of action: **barredura,** sweeping; **barreduras,** sweepings.
-ería	• is equivalent to *-ness* in words such as: **tontería,** foolishness, a foolish act. • usually denotes: —profession, trade, occupation; place where something is made, sold, etc.: **herrería,** ironworks; **carpintería,** carpentry; **ingeniería,** engineering. —collection or ware: **ollería,** earthenware; **cristalería,** glassware.
-ero, -era	• often denote: —one having some trade, habit, or occupation: **zapatero,** shoemaker; **embustero,** liar; **tendero,** shopkeeper; **cajero,** cashier. —a tree or plant: **melocotonero,** peach tree. —a place: **achicharradero,** inferno, hot place. • form adjectives with various attributes: **dominguero,** Sunday (an attribute); **guerrero,** warlike.

-ía	• is equivalent to *-y* in words such as: **geometría,** geometry; **teología,** theology. • denotes office, employment, status, etc., in words such as: **soberanía,** sovereignty; **ciudadanía,** citizenry, citizenship.
-ico, -ica, -illo, -illa, -ito, -ita, -uelo, -uela,* -ete, -eta, -uco, -uca, -ucho, -ucha	are diminutive endings.
-ísimo	is the ending of the absolute superlative: **fortísimo,** very strong, strongest.
-izo, -ucho, -izco, -uzco	mean *tending to, somewhat:* **rojizo,** reddish; **malucho,** bad in health; **blanquizco,** whitish; **negruzco,** blackish.
-mente	is the adverbial ending equivalent to the English suffix *-ly:* **sabiamente,** wisely; **rápidamente,** swiftly.
-miento, -ción	have the meaning of *-ment, -tion,* or *-ing* in words denoting action or effect: **presentimiento,** presentiment; **coronamiento, coronación,** coronation, crowning.
-or, -ora, -dor, -dora	mean *that does* or *serves to do,* and are equivalent to *-ing* (in adjectives) and *-er* or *-or* (in nouns): **casa editora,** publisher, publishing house; **lector, lectora,** reader; **investigador,** investigator.
-ura	forms abstract nouns derived from adjectives: **altura,** height; **blancura,** whiteness.

*Includes the variants -cico, -ecico, -cillo, -ecillo, -zuelo, -ezuelo, etc.

Spanish verb conjugation tables

Models for the conjugation of regular verbs

Simple tenses

1st conjugation - AMAR

Pres Ind	amo, amas, ama, amamos, amáis. aman.
Past Ind	amé, amaste, amó, amamos, amasteis, amaron.
Imperf Ind	amaba, amabas, amaba, amábamos, amabais, amaban.
Fut Ind	amaré, amarás, amará, amaremos, amaréis, amarán.
Cond	amaría, amarías, amaría, amaríamos, amaríais, amarían.
Pres Subj	ame, ames, ame, amemos, améis, amen.
Imperf Subj	amara, amaras, amara, amáramos, amarais, amaran; amase, amases, amase, amásemos, amaseis, amasen.
Fut Subj	amare, amares, amare, amáremos, amareis, amaren.
Imperat	ama (tú), ame (él/Vd.), amemos (nos.) amad (vos.) amen (ellos/Vds.).
Gerund	amando.
Past Part	amado,-a.

2nd conjugation - TEMER

Pres Ind	temo, temes, teme, tememos, teméis, temen.
Past Ind	temí, temiste, temió, temimos, temisteis, temieron.
Imperf Ind	temía, temías, temía, temíamos, temíais, temían.
Fut Ind	temeré, temerás, temerá, temeremos, temeréis, temerán.
Cond	temería, temerías, temería, temeríamos, temeríais, temerían.
Pres Subj	tema, temas, tema, temamos, temáis, teman.
Imperf Subj	temiera, temieras, temiera, temiéramos, temierais, temieran; temiese, temieses, temiese, temiésemos, temieseis, temiesen.
Fut Subj	temiere, temieres, temiere, temiéremos, temiereis, temieren.
Imperat	teme (tú), tema (él/Vd.), temamos (nos.) temed (vos.) teman (ellos/Vds.).
Gerund	temiendo.
Past Part	temido,-a.

3rd conjugation - PARTIR

Pres Ind	parto, partes, parte, partimos, partís, parten.
Past Ind	partí, partiste, partió, partimos, partisteis, partieron.
Imperf Ind	partía, partías, partía, partíamos, partíais, partían.
Fut Ind	partiré, partirás, partirá, partiremos, partiréis, partirán.
Cond	partiría, partirías, partiría, partiríamos, partiríais, partirían.
Pres Subj	parta, partas, parta, partamos, partáis, partan.
Imperf Subj	partiera, partieras, partiera, partiéramos, partierais, partieran; partiese, partieses, partiese, partiésemos, partieseis, partiesen.
Fut Subj	partiere, partieres, partiere, partiéremos, partiereis, partieren.
Imperat	parte (tú), parta (él/Vd.), partamos (nos.) partid (vos.) partan (ellos/Vds.).
Gerund	partiendo.
Past Part	partido,-a.

Note that the imperative proper has forms for the second person (*tú* and *vosotros*) only; all other forms are taken from the present subjunctive.

Compound tenses

Pres Perf   he, has, ha, hemos, habeis, han amado/temido/partido
Pluperf   había, habías, había, habíamos, habíais, habían amado/temido/partido
Fut Perf   habré, habrás, habrá, habremos, habreis, habrán amado/temido/partido
Cond Perf   habría, habrías, habría, habríamos, habríais, habrían amado/temido/partido
Past Anterior hube, hubiste, hubo, hubimos, hubisteis, hubieron amado/temido/partido
Pres Perf Subj   haya, hayas, haya, hayamos, hayáis, hayan amado/temido/partido
Pluperf Subj hubiera, hubieras, hubiera, hubiéramos, hubierais, hubieran amado/temido/partido
  hubiese, hubieses, hubiese, hubiésemos, hubieseis, hubiesen amado/temido/partido.

Models for the conjugation of irregular verbs

Only the tenses which present irregularities are given here; other tenses follow the regular models above. Irregularities are shown in bold type.

1. SACAR (*c changes to* **qu** *before* **e**)
Past Ind   **saqué**, sacaste, sacó, sacamos, sacasteis, sacaron.
Pres Subj   **saque, saques, saque, saquemos, saquéis, saquen.**
Imperat   saca (tú), **saque** (él/Vd.), **saquemos** (nos.), sacad (vos.), **saquen** (ellos/Vds.).

2. MECER (*c changes to* **z** *before* **a** *and* **o**)
Pres Ind   **mezo**, meces, mece, mecemos, mecéis, mecen.
Pres Subj   **meza, mezas, meza, mezamos, mezáis, mezan.**
Imperat   mece (tú), **meza** (él/Vd.), **mezamos** (nos.), meced (vos.), **mezan** (ellos/Vds.).

3. ZURCIR (*c changes to* **z** *before* **a** *and* **o**)
Pres Ind   **zurzo**, zurces, zurce, zurcimos, zurcís, zurcen.
Pres Subj   **zurza, zurzas, zurza, zurzamos, zurzáis, zurzan.**
Imperat   zurce (tú), **zurza** (él/Vd.), **zurzamos** (nos.), zurcid (vos.), **zurzan** (ellos/Vds.).

4. REALIZAR (*z changes to* **c** *before* **e**)
Past Ind   **realicé**, realizaste, realizó, realizamos, realizasteis, realizaron.
Pres Subj   **realice, realices, realice, realicemos, realicéis, realicen.**
Imperat   realiza (tú), **realice** (él/Vd.), **realicemos** (nos.), realizad (vos.), **realicen** (ellos/Vds.).

5. PROTEGER (*g changes to* **j** *before* **a** *and* **o**)
Pres Ind   **protejo**, proteges, protege, protegemos, protegéis, protegen.
Pres Subj   **proteja, protejas, proteja, protejamos, protejáis, protejan.**
Imperat   protege (tú), **proteja** (él/Vd.), **protejamos** (nos.), proteged (vos.), **protejan** (ellos/Vds.).

6. DIRIGIR (*g changes to* **j** *before* **a** *and* **o**)
Pres Ind   **dirijo**, diriges, dirige, dirigimos, dirigís, dirigen.
Pres Subj   **dirija, dirijas, dirija, dirijamos, dirijáis, dirijan.**
Imperat   dirige (tú), **dirija** (él/Vd.), **dirijamos** (nos.), dirigid (vos.), **dirijan** (ellos/Vds.).

7. LLEGAR (*g changes to* **gu** *before* **e**)
Past Ind   **llegué**, llegaste, llegó, llegamos, llegasteis, llegaron.
Pres Subj   **llegue, llegues, llegue, lleguemos, lleguéis, lleguen.**
Imperat   llega (tú), **llegue** (él/Vd.), **lleguemos** (nos.), llegad (vos.), **lleguen** (ellos/
          Vds.).

8. DISTINGUIR (**gu** *changes to* **g** *before* **a** *and* **o**)
Pres Ind   **distingo**, distingues, distingue, distinguimos, distinguís, distinguen.
Pres Subj   **distinga, distingas, distinga, distingamos, distingáis, distingan.**
Imperat   distingue (tú), **distinga** (él/Vd.), **distingamos** (nos.), distinguid (vos.),
          distingan (ellos/Vds.).

9. DELINQUIR (**qu** *changes to* **c** *before* **a** *and* **o**)
Pres Ind   **delinco**, delinques, delinque, delinquimos, delinquís, delinquen.
Pres Subj   **delinca, delincas, delinca, delincamos, delincáis, delincan.**
Imperat   delinque (tú), **delinca** (él/Vd.), **delincamos** (nos.), delinquid (vos.),
          delincan (ellos/Vds.).

10. ADECUAR* (*unstressed* **u**)
Pres Ind   **adecuo, adecuas, adecua, adecuamos, adecuáis, adecuan.**
Pres Subj   **adecue, adecues, adecue, adecuemos, adecuéis, adecuen.**
Imperat   **adecua** (tú), **adecue** (él/Vd.), **adecuemos** (nos.), **adecuad** (vos.),
          adecuen (ellos/Vds.).

11. ACTUAR (*stressed* **ú** *in certain persons of certain tenses*)
Pres Ind   **actúo, actúas, actúa**, actuamos, actuáis, **actúan.**
Pres Subj   **actúe, actúes, actúe**, actuemos, actuéis, **actúen.**
Imperat   **actúa** (tú), **actúe** (él/Vd.), actuemos (nos.), actuad (vos.), **actúen** (ellos/
          Vds.).

12. CAMBIAR* (*unstressed* **i**)
Pres Ind   **cambio, cambias, cambia, cambiamos, cambiáis, cambian.**
Pres Subj   **cambie, cambies, cambie, cambiemos, cambiéis, cambien.**
Imperat   **cambia** (tú), **cambie** (él/Vd.), **cambiemos** (nos.), **cambiad** (vos.),
          cambien (ellos/Vds.).

13. DESVIAR (*stressed* **í** *in certain persons of certain tenses*)
Pres Ind   **desvío, desvías, desvía**, desviamos, desviáis, **desvían.**
Pres Subj   **desvíe, desvíes, desvíe**, desviemos, desviéis, **desvíen.**
Imperat   **desvía** (tú), **desvíe** (él/Vd.), desviemos (nos.), desviad (vos.), **desvíen**
          (ellos/Vds.).

14. AUXILIAR (**i** *can be stressed* **or** *unstressed*)
Pres Ind   **auxilío, auxilías, auxilía**, auxiliamos, auxiliáis, **auxilían.**
          auxilio, auxilias, auxilia, auxiliamos, auxiliáis, auxilian.
Pres Subj   **auxilíe, auxilíes, auxilíe**, auxiliemos, auxiliéis, **auxilíen.**
          auxilie, auxilies, auxilie, auxiliemos, auxiliéis, auxilien.
Imperat   **auxilía** (tú), **auxilíe** (él/Vd.), auxiliemos (nos.), auxiliad, (vos.), **auxilíen**
          (ellos/Vds.).
          auxilia (tú), auxilie (él/Vd.), auxiliemos (nos.), auxiliad (vos.), auxilien
          (ellos/Vds.).

15. AISLAR (*stressed* **í** *in certain persons of certain tenses*)
Pres Ind   **aíslo, aíslas, aísla**, aislamos, aisláis, **aíslan.**
Pres Subj   **aísle, aísles, aísle**, aislemos, aisléis, **aíslen.**
Imperat   **aísla** (tú), **aísle** (él/Vd.), aislemos (nos.), aislad (vos.), **aíslen** (ellos/Vds.).

16. AUNAR (*stressed* **ú** *in certain persons certain tenses*)
Pres Ind   **aúno, aúnas, aúna**, aunamos, aunáis, **aúnan.**
Pres Subj   **aúne, aúnes, aúne**, aunemos, aunéis, **aúnen.**

Imperat   **aúna** (tú), **aúne** (él/Vd.), aunemos (nos.), aunad (vos.), **aúnen** (ellos/ Vds.).

17. DESCAFEINAR (*stressed í in certain persons of certain tenses*)
Pres Ind   descafeíno, **descafeínas**, **descafeína**, descafeinamos, descafeináis, **descafeínan**.
Pres Subj   **descafeíne**, **descafeínes**, **descafeíne**, descafeinemos, descafeinéis, **descafeínen**.
Imperat   **descafeína** (tú), **descafeíne** (él/Vd.), descafeinemos (nos.), descafeinad (vos.), **descafeínen** (ellos/Vds.).

18. REHUSAR (*stressed ú in certain persons of certain tenses*)
Pres Ind   **rehúso**, **rehúsas**, **rehúsa**, rehusamos, rehusáis, **rehúsan**.
Pres Subj   **rehúse**, **rehúses**, **rehúse**, rehusemos, rehuséis, **rehúsen**.
Imperat   **rehúsa** (tú), **rehúse** (él/Vd.), rehusemos (nos.), rehusad (vos.), **rehúsen** (ellos/Vds.).

19. REUNIR (*stressed ú in certain persons of certain tenses*)
Pres Ind   **reúno**, **reúnes**, **reúne**, reunimos, reunís, **reúnen**.
Pres Subj   **reúna**, **reúnas**, **reúna**, reunamos, reunáis, **reúnan**.
Imperat   **reúne** (tú), **reúna** (él/Vd.), reunamos (nos.), reunid (vos.), **reúnan** (ellos/ Vds.).

20. AMOHINAR (*stressed í in certain persons of certain tenses*)
Pres Ind   **amohíno**, **amohínas**, **amohína**, amohinamos, amohináis, **amohínan**.
Pres Subj   **amohíne**, **amohínes**, **amohíne**, amohinemos, amohinéis, **amohínen**.
Imperat   **amohína** (tú), **amohíne** (él/Vd.), amohinemos (nos.), amohinad (vos.), **amohínen** (ellos/Vds.).

21. PROHIBIR (*stressed í in certain persons of certain tenses*)
Pres Ind   **prohíbo**, **prohíbes**, **prohíbe**, prohibimos, prohibís, **prohíben**.
Pres Subj   **prohíba**, **prohíbas**, **prohíba**, prohibamos, prohibáis, **prohíban**.
Imperat   **prohíbe** (tú), **prohíba** (él/Vd.), prohibamos (nos.), prohibid (vos.), **prohíban** (ellos/Vds.).

22. AVERIGUAR (*unstressed u; gu changes to gü before e*)
Past Ind   **averigüé**, averiguaste, averiguó, àveriguamos, averiguasteis, averiguaron.
Pres Subj   **averigüe**, **averigües**, **averigüe**, **averigüemos**, **averigüéis**, **averigüen**.
Imperat   averigua (tú), **averigüe** (él/Vd.), **averigüemos** (nos.), averiguad (vos.), **averigüen** (ellos/Vds.).

23. AHINCAR (*stressed í in certain persons of certain tenses; the c changes to qu before e*)
Pres Ind   **ahínco**, **ahíncas**, **ahínca**, ahincamos, ahincáis, **ahíncan**.
Past Ind   **ahinqué**, ahincaste, ahincó, ahincamos, ahincasteis, ahincaron.
Pres Subj   **ahínque**, **ahínques**, **ahínque**, ahinquemos, ahinquéis, **ahínquen**.
Imperat   **ahínca** (tú), **ahínque** (él/Vd.), **ahinquemos** (nos.), ahincad (vos.), **ahínquen** (ellos/Vds.).

24. ENRAIZAR (*stressed í in certain persons of certain tenses; the z changes to c before e*)
Pres Ind   **enraízo**, **enraízas**, **enraíza**, enraizamos, enraizáis, **enraízan**.
Past Ind   **enraicé**, enraizaste, enraizó, enraizamos, enraizasteis, enraizaron.
Pres Subj   **enraíce**, **enraíces**, **enraíce**, **enraicemos**, **enraicéis**, **enraícen**.
Imperat   **enraíza** (tú), **enraíce** (él/Vd.), **enraicemos** (nos.), enraizad (vos.), **enraícen** (ellos/Vds.).

25. CABRAHIGAR (*stressed í in certain persons of certain tenses; the g changes to gu before e*)
Pres Ind   **cabrahígo**, **cabrahígas**, **cabrahíga**, cabrahigamos, cabrahigáis, **cabrahígan**.
Past Ind   **cabrahigué**, cabrahigaste, cabrahigó, cabrahigamos, cabrahigasteis, cabrahigaron.

Pres Subj	**cabrahígue, cabrahígues, cabrahígue, cabrahiguemos, cabrahiguéis, cabrahíguen.**
Imperat	**cabrahíga** (tú), **cabrahígue** (él/Vd.), **cabrahiguemos** (nos.), cabrahigad (vos.), **cabrahíguen** (ellos/Vds.).

26. HOMOGENEIZAR (*stressed í in certain persons of certain tenses, the z changes to c before e*)

Pres Ind	**homogeneízo, homogeneízas, homogeneíza,** homogeneizamos, homogeneizáis, **homogeneízan.**
Past Ind	**homogeneicé,** homogeneizaste, homogeneizó, homogeneizamos, homogeneizasteis, homogeneizaron.
Pres Subj	**homogeneíce, homogeneíces, homogeneíce, homogeneicemos, homogeneicéis, homogeneícen.**
Imperat	**homogeneíza** (tú), **homogeneíce** (él/Vd.), **homogeneicemos** (nos.), homogeneizad (vos.), **homogeneícen** (ellos/Vds.).

27. ACERTAR (*e changes to ie in stressed syllables*)

Pres Ind	**acierto, aciertas, acierta,** acertamos, acertáis, **aciertan.**
Pres Subj	**acierte, aciertes, acierte,** acertemos, acertéis, **acierten.**
Imperat	**acierta** (tú), **acierte** (él/Vd.), acertemos (nos.), acertad (vos.), **acierten** (ellos/Vds.).

28. ENTENDER (*e changes to ie in stressed syllables*)

Pres Ind	**entiendo, entiendes, entiende,** entendemos, entendéis, **entienden.**
Pres Subj	**entienda, entiendas, entienda,** entendamos, entendáis, **entiendan.**
Imperat	**entiende** (tú), **entienda** (él/Vd.), entendamos (nos.), entended (vos.), **entiendan** (ellos/Vds.).

29. DISCERNIR (*e changes to ie in stressed syllables*)

Pres Ind	**discierno, disciernes, discierne,** discernimos, discernís, **disciernen.**
Pres Subj	**discierna, disciernas, discierna,** discernamos, discernáis, **disciernan.**
Imperat	**discierne** (tú), **discierna** (él/Vd.), discernamos (nos.), discernid (vos.), **disciernan** (ellos/Vds.).

30. ADQUIRIR (*i changes to ie in stressed syllables*)

Pres Ind	**adquiero, adquieres, adquiere,** adquirimos, adquirís, **adquieren.**
Pres Subj	**adquiera, adquieras, adquiera,** adquiramos, adquiráis, **adquieran.**
Imperat	**adquiere** (tú), **adquiera** (él/Vd.), adquiramos (nos.), adquirid (vos.), **adquieran** (ellos/Vds.).

31. CONTAR (*o changes to ue in stressed syllables*)

Pres Ind	**cuento, cuentas, cuenta,** contamos, contáis, **cuentan.**
Pres Subj	**cuente, cuentes, cuente,** contemos, contéis, **cuenten.**
Imperat	**cuenta** (tú), **cuente** (él/Vd.), contemos (nos.), contad (vos.), **cuenten** (ellos/Vds.).

32. MOVER (*o changes to ue in stressed syllables*)

Pres Ind	**muevo, mueves, mueve,** movemos, movéis, **mueven.**
Pres Subj	**mueva, muevas, mueva,** movamos, mováis, **muevan.**
Imperat	**mueve** (tú), **mueva** (él/Vd.), movamos (nos.), moved (vos.), **muevan** (ellos/Vds.).

33. DORMIR (*o changes to ue in stressed syllables or to u in certain persons of certain tenses*)

Pres Ind	**duermo, duermes, duerme,** dormimos, dormís, **duermen.**
Past Ind	dormí, dormiste, **durmió,** dormimos, dormisteis, **durmieron.**
Pres Subj	**duerma, duermas, duerma, durmamos, durmáis, duerman.**
Imperf Subj	**durmiera, durmieras, durmiera, durmiéramos, durmierais, durmieran;**
	durmiese, durmieses, durmiese, durmiésemos, durmieseis, durmiesen.

Fut Subj	**durmiere, durmieres, durmiere, durmiéremos, durmiereis, durmieren**.
Imperat	**duerme** (tú), **duerma** (él/Vd.), **durmamos** (nos.), dormid (vos.), **duerman** (ellos/Vds.).

34. SERVIR (*e weakens to* **i** *in certain persons of certain tenses*)

Pres Ind	**sirvo, sirves, sirve**, servimos, servís, **sirven**.
Past Ind	serví, serviste, **sirvió**, servimos, servisteis, **sirvieron**.
Pres Subj	**sirva, sirvas, sirva, sirvamos, sirváis, sirvan**.
Imperf Subj	**sirviera, sirvieras, sirviera, sirviéramos, sirvierais, sirvieran; sirviese, sirvieses, sirviese, sirviésemos, sirvieseis, sirviesen**.
Fut Subj	**sirviere, sirvieres, sirviere, sirviéremos, sirviereis, sirvieren**.
Imperat	**sirve** (tú), **sirva** (él/Vd.), **sirvamos** (nos.), servid (vos.), **sirvan** (ellos/Vds.).

35. HERVIR (*e changes to* **ie** *in stressed syllables or to* **i** *in certain persons of certain tenses*)

Pres Ind	**hiervo, hierves, hierve**, hervimos, hervís, **hierven**.
Past Ind	herví, herviste, **hirvió**, hervimos, hervisteis, **hirvieron**.
Pres Subj	**hierva, hiervas, hierva**, hirvamos, hirváis, **hiervan**.
Imperf Subj	**hirviera, hirvieras, hirviera, hirviéramos, hirvierais, hirvieran; hirviese, hirvieses, hirviese, hirviésemos, hirvieseis, hirviesen**.
Fut Subj	**hirviere, hirvieres, hirviere, hirviéremos, hirviereis, hirvieren**.
Imperat	**hierve** (tú), **hierva** (él/Vd.), **hirvamos** (nos.), hervid (vos.), **hiervan** (ellos/Vds.).

36. CEÑIR (*the* **i** *of certain endings is absorbed by* **ñ**; *the* **e** *changes to* **i** *in certain persons of certain tenses*)

Pres Ind	**ciño, ciñes, ciñe**, ceñimos, ceñís, **ciñen**.
Past Ind	ceñí, ceñiste, **ciñó**, ceñimos, ceñisteis, **ciñeron**.
Pres Subj	**ciña, ciñas, ciña, ciñamos, ciñáis, ciñan**.
Imperf Subj	**ciñera, ciñeras, ciñera, ciñéramos, ciñerais, ciñeran; ciñese, ciñeses, ciñese, ciñésemos, ciñeseis, ciñesen**.
Fut Subj	**ciñere, ciñeres, ciñere, ciñéremos, ciñereis, ciñeren**.
Imperat	**ciñe** (tú), **ciña** (él/Vd.), **ciñamos** (nos.), ceñid (vos.), **ciñan** (ellos/Vds.).

37. REÍR (*like* **ceñir**, *but the loss of* **i** *is not due to the influence of any consonant*)

Pres Ind	**río, ríes, ríe**, reímos, reís, **ríen**.
Past Ind	reí, reíste, **rió**, reímos, reísteis, **rieron**.
Pres Subj	**ría, rías, ría, riamos, riáis, rían**.
Imperf Subj	**riera, rieras, riera, riéramos, rierais, rieran; riese, rieses, riese, riésemos, rieseis, riesen**.
Fut Subj	**riere, rieres, riere, riéremos, riereis, rieren**.
Imperat	**ríe** (tú), **ría** (él/Vd.), **riamos** (nos.), reíd (vos.), **rían** (ellos/Vds.).

38. TAÑER (*the* **i** *ending is absorbed by* **ñ** *in certain persons of certain tenses*)

Past Ind	tañí, tañiste, **tañó**, tañimos, tañisteis, **tañeron**.
Imperf Subj	**tañera, tañeras, tañera, tañéramos, tañerais, tañeran; tañese, tañeses, tañese, tañésemos, tañeseis, tañesen**.
Fut Subj	**tañere, tañeres, tañere, tañéremos, tañereis, tañeren**.

39. EMPELLER (*the* **i** *ending is absorbed by* **ll** *in certain persons of certain tenses*)

Past Ind	empellí, empelliste, **empelló**, empellimos, empellisteis, **empelleron**.
Imperf Subj	**empellera, empelleras, empellera, empelléramos, empellerais, empelleran; empellese, empelleses, empellese, empellésemos, empelleseis, empellesen**.
Fut Subj	**empellere, empelleres, empellere, empelléremos, empellereis, empelleren**.

40. MUÑIR (*the i ending is absorbed by ñ in certain persons of certain tenses*)
Past Ind   muñí, muñiste, **muñó**, muñimos, muñisteis, **muñeron**.
Imperf Subj **muñera, muñeras, muñera, muñéramos, muñerais, muñeran;**
        muñese, muñeses, muñese, muñésemos, muñeseis, muñesen.
Fut Subj   **muñere, muñeres, muñere, muñéremos, muñereis, muñeren.**

41. MULLIR (*the i ending is absorbed by the ll in certain persons of certain tenses*)
Past Ind   mullí, mulliste, **mulló**, mullimos, mullisteis, **mulleron**.
Imperf Subj **mullera, mulleras, mullera, mulléramos, mullerais, mulleran;**
        mullese, mulleses, mullese, mullésemos, mulleseis, mullesen.
Fut Subj   **mullere, mulleres, mullere, mulléremos, mullereis, mulleren.**

42. NACER (*c changes to zc before a and o*)
Pres Ind   **nazco**, naces, nace, nacemos, nacéis, nacen.
Pres Subj   **nazca, nazcas, nazca, nazcamos, nazcáis, nazcan.**
Imperat   nace (tú), **nazca** (él/Vd.), **nazcamos** (nos.), naced (vos.), **nazcan** (ellos/
        Vds.).

43. AGRADECER (*c changes to zc before a and o*)
Pres Ind   **agradezco**, agradeces, agradece, agradecemos, agradecéis, agradecen.
Pres Subj   **agradezca, agradezcas, agradezca, agradezcamos, agradezcáis,**
        agradezcan.
Imperat   agradece (tú), **agradezca** (él/Vd.), **agradezcamos** (nos.), agradeced (vos.),
        agradezcan (ellos/Vds.).

44. CONOCER (*c changes to zc before a and o*)
Pres Ind   **conozco**, conoces, conoce, conemos, conocéis, conocen.
Pres Subj   **conozca, conozcas, conozca, conozcamos, conozcáis, conozcan.**
Imperat   conoce (tú), **conozca** (él/Vd.), **conozcamos** (nos.), conoced (vos.),
        conozcan (ellos/Vds.).

45. LUCIR (*c changes to zc before a and o*)
Pres Ind   **luzco**, luces, luce, lucimos, lucís, lucen.
Pres Subj   **luzca, luzcas, luzca, luzcamos, luzcáis, luzcan.**
Imperat   luce (tú), **luzca** (él/Vd.), **luzcamos** (nos.), lucid (vos.), **luzcan** (ellos/Vds.).

46. CONDUCIR (*c changes to zc before a and o; the Preterite is irregular*)
Pres Ind   **conduzco**, conduces, conduce, conducimos, conducís, conducen.
Past Ind   **conduje, condujiste, condujo, condujimos, condujisteis, condujeron.**
Pres Subj   **conduzca, conduzcas, conduzca, conduzcamos, conduzcáis,**
        conduzcan.
Imperf Subj **condujera, condujeras, condujera, condujéramos, condujerais,**
        condujeran;
        condujese, condujeses, condujese, condujésemos, condujeseis,
        condujesen.
Fut Subj   **condujere, condujeres, condujere, condujéremos, condujereis,**
        condujeren.
Imperat   conduce (tú), **conduzca** (él/Vd.), **conduzcamos** (nos.), conducid (vos.),
        conduzcan (ellos/Vds.).

47. EMPEZAR (*e changes to ie in stressed syllables and z changes to c before e*)
Pres Ind   **empiezo, empiezas, empieza**, empezamos, empezáis, **empiezan.**
Past ind   **empecé**, empezaste, empezó, empezamos, empezasteis, empezaron.
Pres Subj   **empiece, empieces, empiece, empecemos, empecéis, empiecen.**
Imperat   **empieza** (tú), **empiece** (él/Vd.), **empecemos** (nos.), empezad (vos.),
        empiecen (ellos/Vds.).

48. REGAR (*e changes to ie in stressed syllables; g changes to gu before e*)
Pres Ind   **riego, riegas, riega**, regamos, regáis, **riegan.**
Past Ind   **regué**, regaste, regó, regamos, regasteis, regaron.

Pres Subj   **riegue, riegues, riegue, reguemos, reguéis, rieguen**.
Imperat   **riega** (tú), **riegue** (él/Vd.), **reguemos** (nos.), regad (vos.), **rieguen** (ellos/Vds.).

49. TROCAR (*o changes to* **ue** *in stressed syllables;* **c** *changes to* **qu** *before* **e**)
Pres Ind   **trueco, truecas, trueca**, trocamos, trocáis, **truecan**.
Past Ind   **troqué**, trocaste, trocó, trocamos, trocasteis, trocaron.
Pres Subj   **trueque, trueques, trueque, troquemos, troquéis, truequen**.
Imperat   **trueca** (tú), **trueque** (él/Vd.), **troquemos** (nos.), trocad (vos.), **truequen** (ellos/Vds.).

50. FORZAR (*o changes to* **ue** *in stressed syllables;* **z** *changes to* **c** *before* **e**)
Pres Ind   **fuerzo, fuerzas, fuerza**, forzamos, forzáis, **fuerzan**.
Past Ind   **forcé**, forzaste, forzó, forzamos, forzasteis, forzaron.
Pres Subj   **fuerce, fuerces, fuerce, forcemos, forcéis, fuercen**.
Imperat   **fuerza** (tú), **fuerce** (él/Vd.), **forcemos** (nos.), forzad (vos.), **fuercen** (ellos/Vds.).

51. AVERGONZAR (*in stressed syllables* **o** *changes to* **ue** *and* **g** *to* **gü;** **z** *changes to* **c** *before* **e**)
Pres Ind   **avergüenzo, avergüenzas, avergüenza**, avergonzamos, avergonzáis, **avergüenzan**.
Past Ind   **avergoncé**, avergonzaste, avergonzó, avergonzamos, avergonzasteis, avergonzaron.
Pres Subj   **avergüence, avergüences, avergüence**, avergoncemos, avergoncéis, **avergüencen**.
Imperat   **avergüenza** (tú), **avergüence** (él/Vd.), **avergoncemos** (nos.), avergonzad (vos.), **avergüencen** (ellos/Vds.).

52. COLGAR (*o changes to* **ue** *in stressed syllables;* **g** *changes to* **gu** *before* **e**)
Pres Ind   **cuelgo, cuelgas, cuelga**, colgamos, colgáis, **cuelgan**.
Past Ind   **colgué**, colgaste, colgó, colgamos, colgasteis, colgaron.
Pres Subj   **cuelgue, cuelgues, cuelgue, colguemos, colguéis, cuelguen**.
Imperat   **cuelga** (tú), **cuelgue** (él/Vd.), **colguemos** (nos.), colgad (vos.), **cuelguen** (ellos/Vds.).

53. JUGAR (*u changes to* **ue** *in stressed syllables and* **g** *changes to* **gu** *before* **e**)
Pres Ind   **juego, juegas, juega**, jugamos, jugáis, **juegan**.
Past Ind   **jugué**, jugaste, jugó, jugamos, jugasteis, jugaron.
Pres Subj   **juegue, juegues, juegue, juguemos, juguéis, jueguen**.
Imperat   **juega** (tú), **juegue** (él/Vd.), **juguemos** (nos.), jugad (vos.), **jueguen** (ellos/Vds.).

54. COCER (*o changes to* **ue** *in stressed syllables and* **c** *changes to* **z** *before* **a** *and* **o**)
Pres Ind   **cuezo, cueces, cuece**, cocemos, cocéis, **cuecen**.
Pres Subj   **cueza, cuezas, cueza, cozamos, cozáis, cuezan**.
Imperat   **cuece** (tú), **cueza** (él/Vd.), **cozamos** (nos.), coced (vos.), **cuezan** (ellos/Vds.).

55. ELEGIR (*e changes to* **i** *in certain persons of certain tenses;* **g** *changes to* **j** *before* **a** *and* **o**)
Pres Ind   **elijo, eliges, elige**, elegimos, elegís, **eligen**.
Past Ind   elegí, elegiste, **eligió**, elegimos, elegisteis, **eligieron**.
Pres Subj   **elija, elijas, elija, elijamos, elijáis, elijan**.
Imperf Subj   **eligiera, eligieras, eligiera, eligiéramos, eligierais, eligiera**n; **eligiese, eligieses, eligiese, eligiésemos, eligieseis, eligiesen**.
Fut Subj   **eligiere, eligieres, eligiere, eligiéremos, eligiereis, eligieren**.
Imperat   **elige** (tú), **elija** (él/Vd.), **elijamos** (nos.), elegid (vos.), **elijan** (ellos/Vds.).

56. SEGUIR (*e changes to i in certain persons of certain tenses; gu changes to g before a and o*)

Pres Ind	**sigo, sigues, sigue,** seguimos, seguís, **siguen.**
Past Ind	seguí, seguiste, **siguió,** seguimos, seguisteis, **siguieron.**
Pres Subj	**siga, sigas, siga, sigamos, sigáis, sigan.**
Imperf Subj	**siguiera, siguieras, siguiera, siguiéramos, siguierais, siguieran; siguiese, siguieses, siguiese, siguiésemos, siguieseis, siguiesen.**
Fut Subj	**siguiere, siguieres, siguiere, siguiéremos, siguiereis, siguieren.**
Imperat	**sigue** (tú), **siga** (él/Vd.), **sigamos** (nos.), seguid (vos.), **sigan** (ellos/Vds.).

57. ERRAR (*e changes to ye in stressed syllables*)

Pres Ind	**yerro, yerras, yerra,** erramos, erráis, **yerran.**
Pres Subj	**yerre, yerres, yerre,** erremos, erréis, **yerren.**
Imperat	**yerra** (tú), **yerre** (él/Vd.), erremos (nos.), errad (vos.), **yerren** (ellos/Vds.).

58. AGORAR (*o changes to ue in stressed syllables and g changes to gü before e*)

Pres Ind	**agüero, agüeras, agüera,** agoramos, agoráis, **agüeran.**
Pres Subj	**agüere, agüeres, agüere,** agoramos, agoréis, **agüeren.**
Imperat	**agüera** (tú), **agüere** (él/Vd.), agoremos (nos.), agorad (vos.), **agüeren** (ellos/Vds.).

59. DESOSAR (*o changes to hue in stressed syllables*)

Pres Ind	**deshueso. deshuesas. deshuesa.** desosamos. desosáis. **deshuesan.**
Pres Subj	**deshuese. deshueses. deshuese.** desosemos. desoséis. **deshuesen.**
Imperat	**deshuesa** (tú). **deshuese** (él/Vd.). desosemos (nos.). desosad (vos.). **deshuesen** (ellos/Vds.).

60. OLER (*o changes to hue in stressed syllables*)

Pres Ind	**huelo, hueles, huele,** olemos, oléis, **huelen.**
Pres Subj	**huela, huelas, huela,** olamos, oláis, **huelan.**
Imperat	**huele** (tú), **huela** (él/Vd.), olamos (nos.), oled (vos.), **huelan** (ellos/Vds.).

61. LEER (*the i ending changes to y before o and e*)

Past Ind	leí, leíste, **leyó,** leímos, leísteis, **leyeron.**
Imperf Subj	**leyera, leyeras, leyera, leyéramos, leyerais, leyeran; leyese, leyeses, leyese, leyésemos, leyeseis, leyesen.**
Fut Subj	**leyere, leyeres, leyere, leyéremos, leyereis, leyeren.**

62. HUIR (*i changes to y before a, e, and o*)

Pres Ind	**huyo, huyes, huye,** huimos, huís, **huyen.**
Past Ind	hui, huiste, **huyó,** huimos, huisteis, **huyeron.**
Pres Subj	**huya, huyas, huya, huyamos, huyáis. huyan.**
Imperf Subj	**huyera, huyeras, huyera, huyéramos, huyerais, huyeran; huyese, huyeses, huyese, huyésemos, huyeseis, huyesen.**
Fut Subj	**huyere, huyeres, huyere, huyéremos, huyereis, huyeren.**
Imperat	**huye** (tú), **huya** (él/Vd.), **huyamos** (nos.), huid (vos.), **huyan** (ellos/Vds.).

63. ARGÜIR (*i changes to y before a, e, and o; gü becomes gu before y*)

Pres Ind	**arguyo, arguyes, arguye,** argüimos, argüís, **arguyen.**
Past Ind	argüí, argüiste, **arguyó,** argüimos, argüisteis, **arguyeron.**
Pres Subj	**arguya, arguyas, arguya, arguyamos, arguyáis. arguyan.**
Imperf Subj	**arguyera, arguyeras, arguyera, arguyéramos, arguyerais, arguyeran; arguyese, arguyeses, arguyese, arguyésemos, arguyeseis, arguyesen.**
Fut Subj	**arguyere, arguyeres, arguyere, arguyéremos, arguyereis, arguyeren.**
Imperat	**arguye** (tú), **arguya** (él/Vd.), **arguyamos** (nos.), argüid (vos.), **arguyan** (ellos/Vds.).

64. ANDAR

Past Ind   **anduve, anduviste, anduvo, anduvimos, anduvisteis, anduvieron**.
Imperf Subj   **anduviera, anduvieras, anduviera, anduviéramos, anduvierais, anduvieran;**
   anduviese, anduvieses, anduviese, anduviésemos, anduvieseis, anduviesen.
Fut Subj   **anduviere, anduvieres, anduviere, anduviéremos, anduviereis, anduvieren.**

65. ASIR

Pres Ind   **asgo,** ases, ase, asimos, asís, asen.
Pres Subj   **asga, asgas, asga, asgamos, asgáis, asgan**.
Imperat   ase (tú), **asga** (él/Vd.), **asgamos** (nos.), asid (vos.), **asgan** (ellos/Vds.).

66. CABER

Pres Ind   **quepo,** cabes, cabe, cabemos, cabéis, caben.
Past Ind   **cupe, cupiste, cupo, cupimos, cupisteis, cupieron**.
Fut Ind   **cabré, cabrás, cabrá, cabremos, cabréis, cabrán**.
Cond   **cabría, cabrías, cabría, cabríamos, cabríais, cabrían**.
Pres Subj   **quepa, quepas, quepa, quepamos, quepáis, quepan**.
Imperf Subj   **cupiera, cupieras, cupiera, cupiéramos, cupierais, cupieran;**
   cupiese, cupieses, cupiese, cupiésemos, cupieseis, cupiesen.
Fut Subj   **cupiere, cupieres, cupiere, cupiéremos, cupiereis, cupieren**.
Imperat   cabe (tú), **quepa** (él/Vd.), **quepamos** (nos.), cabed (vos.), **quepan** (ellos/Vds.).

67. CAER

Pres Ind   **caigo,** caes, cae, caemos, caéis, caen.
Past Ind   caí, caíste, **cayó,** caímos, caísteis, **cayeron**.
Pres Subj   **caiga, caigas, caiga, caigamos, caigáis, caigan**.
Imperf Subj   **cayera, cayeras, cayera, cayéramos, cayerais, cayeran;**
   cayese, cayeses, cayese, cayésemos, cayeseis, cayesen.
Fut Subj   **cayere, cayeres, cayere, cayéremos, cayereis, cayeren**.
Imperat   cae (tú), **caiga** (él/Vd.), **caigamos** (nos.), caed (vos.), **caigan** (ellos/Vds.).

68. DAR

Pres Ind   **doy,** das, da, damos, dais, dan.
Past Ind   **di, diste, dio, dimos, disteis, dieron**.
Pres Subj   **dé,** des, **dé,** demos, deis, den.
Imperf Subj   **diera, dieras, diera, diéramos, dierais, dieran;**
   diese, dieses, diese, diésemos, dieseis, diesen.
Fut Subj   **diere, dieres, diere, diéremos, diereis, dieren**.
Imperat   da (tú), **dé** (él/Vd.), demos (nos.), dad (vos.), den (ellos/Vds.).

69. DECIR

Pres Ind   **digo, dices, dice,** decimos, decís, **dicen**.
Past Ind   **dije, dijiste, dijo, dijimos, dijisteis, dijeron**.
Fut Ind   **diré, dirás, dirá, diremos, diréis, dirán**.
Cond   **diría, dirías, diría, diríamos, diríais, dirían**.
Pres Subj   **diga, digas, diga, digamos, digáis, digan**.
Imperf Subj   **dijera, dijeras, dijera, dijéramos, dijerais, dijeran;**
   dijese, dijeses, dijese, dijésemos, dijeseis, dijesen.
Fut Subj   **dijere, dijeres, dijere, dijéremos, dijereis, dijeren**.
Imperat   **di (tú), diga** (él/Vd.), **digamos** (nos.), decid (vos.), **digan** (ellos/Vds.).
Past Part   **dicho,-a**.

70. ERGUIR

Pres Ind   **irgo, irgues, irgue,** erguimos, erguís, **irgen;**
   yergo, yergues, yergue, erguimos, erguís, **yergen**.
Past Ind   erguí, erguiste, **irguió,** erguimos, erguisteis, **irguieron**.

Pres Subj	**irga, irgas, irga, irgamos, irgáis, irgan;**
	yerga, yergas, yerga, irgamos, irgáis, yergan.
Imperf Subj	**irguiera, irguieras, irguiera, irguiéramos, irguierais, irguieran;**
	irguiese, irguieses, irguiese, irguiésemos, irguieseis, irguiesen.
Fut Subj	**irguiere, irguieres, irguiere, irguiéremos, irguiereis, irguieren.**
Imperat	**irgue, yergue** (tú), **irga, yerga** (él/Vd.), **irgamos** (nos.), erguid (vos.),
	irgan, yergan (ellos/Vds.).

71. ESTAR

Pres Ind	**estoy,** estás, está, estamos, estáis, están.
Imperf	estaba, estabas, estaba, estábamos, estabais, estaban.
Past Ind	**estuve, estuviste, estuvo, estuvimos, estuvisteis, estuvieron.**
Fut Ind	estaré, estarás, estará, estaremos, estaréis, estarán.
Cond	estaría, estarías, estaría, estaríamos, estaríais, estarían.
Pres Subj	esté, estés, esté, estemos, estéis, estén.
Imperf Subj	**estuviera, estuvieras, estuviera, estuviéramos, estuvierais, estuvieran;**
	estuviese, estuvieses, estuviese, estuviésemos, estuvieseis,
	estuviesen.
Fut Subj	**estuviere, estuvieres, estuviere, estuviéremos, estuviereis, estuvieren.**
Imperat	está (tú), esté (él/Vd.), estemos (nos.), estad (vos.), estén (ellos/Vds.).

72. HABER

Pres Ind	**he, has, ha, hemos,** habéis, **han.**
Imperf Subj	había, habías, había, habíamos, habíais, habían.
Past Ind	hube, hubiste, hubo, hubimos, hubisteis, hubieron.
Fut Ind	habré, habrás, habrá, habremos, habréis, habrán.
Cond	habría, habrías, habría, habríamos, habríais, habrían.
Pres Subj	haya, hayas, haya, hayamos, hayáis, hayan.
Imperf Subj	hubiera, hubieras, hubiera, hubiéramos, hubierais, hubieran;
	hubiese, hubieses, hubiese, hubiésemos, hubieseis, hubiesen.
Fut Subj	hubiere, hubieres, hubiere, hubiéremos, hubiereis, hubieren.
Imperat	**he** (tú), **haya** (él/Vd.), **hayamos** (nos.), habed (vos.), **hayan** (ellos/Vds.).

73. HACER

Pres Ind	**hago,** haces, hace, hacemos, hacéis, hacen.
Past Ind	hice, hiciste, hizo, hicimos, hicisteis, hicieron.
Fut Ind	haré, harás, hará, haremos, haréis, harán.
Cond	haría, harías, haría, haríamos, haríais, harían.
Pres Subj	haga, hagas, haga, hagamos, hagáis, hagan.
Imperf Subj	hiciera, hicieras, hiciera, hiciéramos, hicierais, hicieran;
	hiciese, hicieses, hiciese, hiciésemos, hicieseis, hiciesen.
Fut Subj	hiciere, hicieres, hiciere, hiciéremos, hiciereis, hicieren.
Imperat	**haz** (tú), **haga** (él/Vd.), **hagamos** (nos.), haced (vos.), **hagan** (ellos/Vds.).
Past Part	**hecho,-a.**

74. IR

Pres Ind	**voy, vas, va, vamos, vais, van.**
Imperf Subj	iba, ibas, iba, íbamos, ibais, iban.
Past Ind	fui, fuiste, fue, fuimos, fuisteis, fueron.
Pres Subj	vaya, vayas, vaya, vayamos, vayáis, vayan.
Imperf Subj	fuera, fueras, fuera, fuéramos, fuerais, fueran;
	fuese, fueses, fuese, fuésemos, fueseis, fuesen.
Fut Subj	fuere, fueres, fuere, fuéremos, fuereis, fueren.
Imperat	**ve** (tú), **vaya** (él/Vd.), **vayamos** (nos.), id (vos.), **vayan** (ellos/Vds.).

75. OÍR

Pres Ind	**oigo, oyes, oye,** oímos, oís, **oyen.**
Past Ind	oí, oíste, **oyó,** oímos, oísteis, **oyeron.**
Pres Subj	**oiga, oigas, oiga, oigamos, oigáis, oigan.**

Imperf Subj	**oyera, oyeras, oyera, oyéramos, oyerais, oyeran**; **oyese, oyeses, oyese, oyésemos, oyeseis, oyesen**.
Fut Subj	**oyere, oyeres, oyere, oyéremos, oyereis, oyeren**.
Imperat	**oye** (tú), **oiga** (él/Vd.), **oigamos** (nos.), oíd (vos.), **oigan** (ellos/Vds.).

76. PLACER

Pres Ind	**plazco**, places, place, placemos, placéis, placen.
Past Ind	plací, placiste, plació *or* **plugo**, placimos, placisteis, placieron *or* **pluguieron**.
Pres Subj	**plazca, plazcas, plazca, plegue, plazcamos, plazcáis, plazcan**.
Imperf Subj	placiera, placieras, placiera *or* **pluguiera**, placiéramos, placierais, placieran placiese, placieses, placiese *or* **pluguiese**, placiésemos, placieseis, placiesen.
Fut Subj	placiere, placieres, placiere *or* **pluguiere**, placiéremos, placiereis, placieren.
Imperat	place (tú), **plazca** (él/Vd.), **plazcamos** (nos.), placed (vos.), **plazcan** (ellos/Vds.).

77. PODER

Pres Ind	**puedo, puedes, puede**, podemos, podéis, **pueden**.
Past Ind	**pude, pudiste, pudo, pudimos, pudisteis, pudieron**.
Fut Ind	**podré, podrás, podrá, podremos, podréis, podrán**.
Cond	**podría, podrías, podría, podríamos, podríais, podrían**.
Pres Subj	**pueda, puedas, pueda**, podamos, podáis, **puedan**.
Imperf Subj	**pudiera, pudieras, pudiera, pudiéramos, pudierais, pudieran**; **pudiese, pudieses, pudiese, pudiésemos, pudieseis, pudiesen**.
Fut Subj	**pudiere, pudieres, pudiere, pudiéremos, pudiereis, pudieren**.
Imperat	**puede** (tú), **pueda** (él/Vd.), podamos (nos.), poded (vos.), **puedan** (ellos/Vds.).

78. PONER

Pres Ind	**pongo**, pones, pone, ponemos, ponéis, ponen.
Past Ind	**puse, pusiste, puso, pusimos, pusisteis, pusieron**.
Fut Ind	**pondré, pondrás, pondrá, pondremos, pondréis, pondrán**.
Cond	**pondría, pondrías, pondría, pondríamos, pondríais, pondrían**.
Pres Subj	**ponga, pongas, ponga, pongamos, pongáis, pongan**.
Imperf Subj	**pusiera, pusieras, pusiera, pusiéramos, pusierais, pusieran**; **pusiese, pusieses, pusiese, pusiésemos, pusieseis, pusiesen**.
Fut Subj	**pusiere, pusieres, pusiere, pusiéremos, pusiereis, pusieren**.
Imperat	**pon** (tú), **ponga** (él/Vd.), **pongamos** (nos.), poned (vos.), **pongan** (ellos/Vds.).
Past Part	**puesto,-a**.

79. PREDECIR

Pres Ind	**predigo, predices, predice**, predecimos, predecís, **predicen**.
Past Ind	**predije, predijiste, predijo, predijimos, predijisteis, predijeron**.
Pres Subj	**prediga, predigas, prediga, predigamos, predigáis, predigan**.
Imperf Subj	**predijera, predijeras, predijera, predijéramos, predijerais, predijeran**; **predijese, predijeses, predijese, predijésemos, predijeseis, predijesen**.
Fut Subj	**predijere, predijeres, predijere, predijéremos, predijereis, predijeren**.
Imperat	**predice** (tú), **prediga** (él/Vd.), **predigamos** (nos.), predecid (vos.), **predigan** (ellos/Vds.).

80. QUERER

Pres Ind	**quiero, quieres, quiere**, queremos, queréis, **quieren**.
Past Ind	**quise, quisiste, quiso, quisimos, quisisteis, quisieron**.
Fut Ind	**querré, querrás, querrá, querremos, querréis, querrán**.
Cond	**querría, querrías, querría, querríamos, querríais, querrían**.
Pres Subj	**quiera, quieras, quiera**, queramos, queráis, **quieran**.

Imperf Subj	quisiera, **quisieras**, **quisiera**, **quisiéramos**, **quisierais**, **quisieran**;
	quisiese, **quisieses**, **quisiese**, **quisiésemos**, **quisieseis**, **quisiesen**.
Fut Subj	**quisiere**, **quisieres**, **quisiere**, **quisiéremos**, **quisiereis**, **quisieren**.
Imperat	**quiere** (tú), **quiera** (él/Vd.), queramos (nos.), quered (vos.), **quieran** (ellos/Vds.).

81. RAER

Pres Ind	rao, **raigo**, **rayo**, raes, rae, raemos. raéis, raen.
Past Ind	raí, raíste, **rayó**, raímos, raísteis, **rayeron**.
Pres Subj	**raiga**, **raigas**, **raiga**, **raigamos**, **raigáis**. **raigan**;
	raya, **rayas**, **raya**, **rayamos**, **rayáis**, **rayan**.
Imperf Subj	**rayera**, **rayeras**, **rayera**, **rayéramos**, **rayerais**, **rayeran**;
	rayese, **rayeses**, **rayese**, **rayésemos**, **rayeseis**, **rayesen**.
Fut Subj	**rayere**, **rayeres**, **rayere**, **rayéremos**, **rayereis**, **rayeren**.
Imperat	rae (tú), **raiga**, **raya** (él/Vd.), **raigamos**, **rayamos** (nos.), raed (vos.), **raigan**, **rayan** (ellos/Vds.).

82. ROER

Pres Ind	roo, **roigo**, **royo**, roes, roe, roemos, roéis, roen.
Past Ind	roí, roiste, **royó**, roímos, roísteis, **royeron**.
Pres Subj	roa, roas, roa, roamos, roáis, roan;
	roiga, **roigas**, **roiga**, **roigamos**, **roigáis**, **roigan**;
	roya, **royas**, **roya**, **royamos**, **royáis**, **royan**.
Imperf Subj	**royera**, **royeras**, **royera**, **royéramos**, **royerais**, **royeran**;
	royese, **royeses**, **royese**, **royésemos**, **royeseis**, **royesen**.
Fut Subj	**royere**, **royeres**, **royere**, **royéremos**, **royereis**, **royeren**.
Imperat	roe (tú), roa, **roiga**, **roya** (él/Vd.), roamos, **roigamos**, **royamos** (nos.), roed (vos.), roan, **roigan**, **royan** (ellos/Vds.).

83. SABER

Pres Ind	**sé**, sabes, sabe, sabemos, sabéis, saben.
Past Ind	**supe**, **supiste**, **supo**, **supimos**, **supisteis**, **supieron**.
Fut Ind	**sabré**, **sabrás**, **sabrá**, **sabremos**, **sabréis**, **sabrán**.
Cond	**sabría**, **sabrías**, **sabría**, **sabríamos**, **sabríais**, **sabrían**.
Pres Subj	**sepa**, **sepas**, **sepa**, **sepamos**, **sepáis**, **sepan**.
Imperf Subj	**supiera**, **supieras**, **supiera**, **supiéramos**, **supierais**, **supieran**;
	supiese, **supieses**, **supiese**, **supiésemos**, **supieseis**, **supiesen**.
Fut Subj	**supiere**, **supieres**, **supiere**, **supiéremos**, **supiereis**, **supieren**.
Imperat	sabe (tú), **sepa** (él/Vd.), **sepamos** (nos.), sabed (vos.), **sepan** (ellos/Vds.).

84. SALIR

Pres Ind	**salgo**, sales, sale, salimos, salís, salen.
Fut Ind	**saldré**, **saldrás**, **saldrá**, **saldremos**, **saldréis**, **saldrán**.
Cond	**saldría**, **saldrías**, **saldría**, **saldríamos**, **saldríais**, **saldrían**.
Pres Subj	**salga**, **salgas**, **salga**, **salgamos**, **salgáis**, **salgan**.
Imperat	**sal** (tú), **salga** (él/Vd.), **salgamos** (nos.), salid (vos.), **salgan** (ellos/Vds.).

85. SATISFACER

Pres Ind	**satisfago**, satisfaces, satisface, satisfacemos, satisfacéis, satisfacen.
Past Ind	**satisfice**, **satisficiste**, **satisfizo**, **satisficimos**, **satisficisteis**, **satisficieron**.
Fut Ind	**satisfaré**, **satisfarás**, **satisfará**, **satisfaremos**, **satisfaréis**, **satisfarán**.
Cond	**satisfaría**, **satisfarías**, **satisfaría**, **satisfaríamos**, **satisfaríais**, **satisfarían**.
Pres Subj	**satisfaga**, **satisfagas**, **satisfaga**, **satisfagamos**, **satisfagáis**, **satisfagan**.
Imperf Subj	**satisficiera**, **satisficieras**, **satisficiera**, **satisficiéramos**, **satisficierais**, **satisficieran**;
	satisficiese, **satisficieses**, **satisficiese**, **satisficiésemos**, **satisficieseis**, **satisficiesen**.
Fut Subj	**satisficiere**, **satisficieres**, **satisficiere**, **satisficiéremos**, **satisficiereis**, **satisficieren**.

Imperat **satisfaz,** satisface (tú), **satisfaga** (él/Vd.), **satisfagamos** (nos.), satisfaced (vos.), **satisfagan** (ellos/Vds.).
Past Part **satisfecho,-a.**

86. SER
Pres Ind **soy, eres, es, somos, sois, son.**
Imperf Subj **era, eras, era, éramos, erais, eran.**
Past Ind **fui, fuiste, fue, fuimos, fuisteis, fueron.**
Fut Ind **seré, serás, será, seremos, seréis, serán.**
Cond **sería, serías, sería, seríamos, seríais, serían.**
Pres Subj **sea, seas, sea, seamos, seáis, sean.**
Imperf Subj **fuera, fueras, fuera, fuéramos, fuerais, fueran; fuese, fueses, fuese, fuésemos, fueseis, fuesen.**
Fut Subj **fuere, fueres, fuere, fuéremos, fuereis, fueren.**
Imperat **sé** (tú), **sea** (él/Vd.), seamos (nos.), **sed** (vos.), sean (ellos/Vds.).
Past Part **sido.**

87. TENER
Pres Ind **tengo, tienes, tiene, tenemos, tenéis, tienen.**
Past Ind **tuve, tuviste, tuvo, tuvimos, tuvisteis, tuvieron.**
Fut Ind **tendré, tendrás, tendrá, tendremos, tendréis, tendrán.**
Cond **tendría, tendrías, tendría, tendríamos, tendríais, tendrían.**
Pres Subj **tenga, tengas, tenga, tengamos, tengáis, tengan.**
Imperf Subj **tuviera, tuvieras, tuviera, tuviéramos, tuvierais, tuvieran; tuviese, tuvieses, tuviese, tuviésemos, tuvieseis, tuviesen.**
Fut Subj **tuviere, tuvieres, tuviere, tuviéremos, tuviereis, tuvieren.**
Imperat **ten** (tú), **tenga** (él/Vd.), **tengamos** (nos.), tened (vos.), **tengan** (ellos/ Vds.).

88. TRAER
Pres Ind **traigo,** traes, trae, traemos, traéis, traen.
Past Ind **traje, trajiste, trajo, trajimos, trajisteis, trajeron.**
Pres Subj **traiga, traigas, traiga, traigamos, traigáis, traigan.**
Imperf Subj **trajera, trajeras, trajera, trajéramos, trajerais, trajeran; trajese, trajeses, trajese, trajésemos, trajeseis, trajesen.**
Fut Subj **trajere, trajeres, trajere, trajéremos, trajereis, trajeren.**
Imperat trae (tú), **traiga** (él/Vd.), traigamos (nos.), traed (vos.), **traigan** (ellos/ Vds.).

89. VALER
Pres Ind **valgo,** vales, vale, valemos, valéis, valen.
Fut Ind **valdré, valdrás, valdrá, valdremos, valdréis, valdrán.**
Cond **valdría, valdrías, valdría, valdríamos, valdríais, valdrían.**
Pres Subj **valga, valgas, valga, valgamos, valgáis, valgan.**
Imperat vale (tú), **valga** (él/Vd.), **valgamos** (nos.), valed (vos.), **valgan** (ellos/ Vds.).

90. VENIR
Pres Ind **vengo, vienes, viene,** venimos, venís, **vienen.**
Past Ind **vine, viniste, vino, vinimos, vinisteis, vinieron.**
Fut Ind **vendré, vendrás, vendrá, vendremos, vendréis, vendrán.**
Cond **vendría, vendrías, vendría, vendríamos, vendríais, vendrían.**
Pres Subj **venga, vengas, venga, vengamos, vengáis, vengan.**
Imperf Subj **viniera, vinieras, viniera, viniéramos, vinierais, vinieran; viniese, vinieses, viniese, viniésemos, vinieseis, viniesen.**
Fut Subj **viniere, vinieres, viniere, viniéremos, viniereis, vinieren.**
Imperat **ven** (tú), **venga** (él/Vd.), **vengamos** (nos.), venid (vos.), **vengan** (ellos/ Vds.).

91. VER

Pres Ind	veo, **ves**, **ve**, **vemos**, **veis**, **ven**.
Past Ind	**vi**, **viste**, **vio**, **vimos**, **visteis**, **vieron**.
Imperf Subj	**viera**, **vieras**, **viera**, **viéramos**, **vierais**, **vieran**;
	viese, **vieses**, **viese**, **viésemos**, **vieseis**, **viesen**.
Fut Subj	**viere**, **vieres**, **viere**, **viéremos**, **viereis**, **vieren**.
Imperat	**ve** (tú), vea (él/Vd.), veamos (nos.), **ved** (vos.), vean (ellos/Vds.).
Past Part	**visto,-a**.

92. YACER

Pres Ind	**yazco**, **yazgo**, **yago**, yaces, yace, yacemos, yacéis, yacen.
Pres Subj	**yazca**, **yazcas**, **yazca**,
	yazcamos, **yazcáis**, **yazcan**;
	yazga, **yazgas**, **yazga**, **yazgamos**, **yazgáis**, **yazgan**;
	yaga, **yagas**, **yaga**, **yagamos**, **yagáis**, **yagan**.
Imperat	yace, **yaz** (tú), **yazca**, **yazga**, **yaga** (él/Vd.), **yazcamos**, **yazgamos**,
	yagamos (nos.), yaced (vos.), **yazcan**, **yazgan**, **yagan** (ellos/Vds.).

A

a *prep (dirección)* to: **girar ~ la derecha,** to turn (to the) right. **2** *(destino)* to, towards. **3** *(distancia)* away: ~ *cien kilómetros de casa,* a hundred kilometres (away) from home. **4** *(lugar)* at, on: ~ *la entrada,* at the entrance. **5** *(tiempo)* at: ~ *las once,* at eleven; ~ *los tres días,* three days later; ~ *tiempo,* in time. **6** *(modo, manera)* ~ *ciegas,* blindly; ~ *pie,* on foot. **7** *(instrumento) escrito ~ mano/máquina,* handwritten/typewritten. **8** *(precio)* a: ~ *100 pesetas el kilo,* a hundred pesetas a kilo. **9** *(medida)* at: ~ *90 kilómetros por hora,* at 90 kilometres an hour. **10** *(finalidad)* to: *él vino* ~ *vernos,* he came to see us. **11** *(complemento directo) (no se traduce) vi ~ Juana,* I saw Juana. **12** *(complemento indirecto)* to: *te lo di ~ ti,* I gave it to you. **13** *(verbo + ~ + inf) aprender ~ nadar,* to learn (how) to swim. **14** *(como imperat) ¡~ dormir!,* bedtime! ▲ *a + el =* **al.**

abacería *f* grocer's (shop).

abad *m* abbot.

abadesa *f* abbess.

abadía *f (edificio)* abbey. **2** *(dignidad)* abbacy.

abajo *adv (lugar)* below, down: *ahí* ~, down there. **2** *(en una casa)* downstairs. **3** *(dirección)* down, downward: *calle* ~, down the street. − **4** *interj* down with!

abalanzarse [4] *p* to rush/spring forward: ~ *sobre/contra,* to rush at, pounce on.

abalorio *m (collar)* string of beads. **2** *(cuentecilla)* glass bead.

abandonado,-a *adj* abandoned. **2** *(descuidado)* neglected. **3** *(desaseado)* untidy.

abandonar(se) *t (desamparar)* to abandon, forsake. **2** *(lugar)* to leave, quit. **3** *(actividad)* to give up. − **4** *p (ceder)* to give in. **5** *(descuidarse)* to neglect o.s.

abanicar(se) [1] *t-p* to fan (o.s.).

abanico *m* fan. **2** *fig* range.

abaratar *t* to cut/reduce the price of.

abarcar [1] *t (englobar)* to cover, embrace. **2** *(abrazar)* to embrace. **3** AM *(acaparar)* to monopolize.

abarrotado,-a *adj* packed *(de,* with).

abarrotar *t* to pack *(de,* with).

abastecer(se) [43] *t* to supply. − **2** *p* to stock up *(de/con,* with).

abastecimiento *m* supplying, provision.

abasto *m* supply. **2** *(abundancia)* abundance. ●*fam dar* ~, to be sufficient for: *es que no doy* ~, I just can't cope. ▲ *1 often used in pl.*

abatido,-a *adj* dejected, depressed.

abatimiento *m* dejection.

abatir(se) *t (derribar)* to knock down; *(árbol)* to cut down. **2** *(bajar)* to lower. **3** *(desanimar)* to depress. **4** *(humillar)* to humiliate. − **5** *p (ave, avión)* to swoop *(sobre,* down on). **6** *(humillarse)* to humble o.s. **7** *(desanimarse)* to lose heart.

abdicación *f* abdication.

abdicar [1] *t* to abdicate, renounce.

abdomen *m* abdomen, belly.

abdominal *adj* abdominal. − **2** *mpl (ejercicios)* sit-ups.

abecé *m* ABC, alphabet. **2** *fig* rudiments *pl.*

abecedario *m* alphabet. **2** *(libro)* spelling book. **3** *fig* rudiments *pl.*

abedul *m* birch (tree).

abeja *f* bee. ■ ~ *reina,* queen bee.

abejorro *m* bumblebee. **2** *(coleóptero)* cockchafer.

aberración *f* aberration.

abertura *f* opening, gap.

abeto *m* fir (tree).

abierto,-a *pp* → **abrir.** − **2** *adj* open. **3** *(grifo)* (turned) on. **4** *(sincero)* frank. **5**

(tolerante) open-minded. ●*fig* **con los brazos abiertos,** with open arms.

abigarrado,-a *adj* gaudy.

abismar(se) *t* to confuse. − **2** *p* to become absorbed (**en,** in).

abismo *m* abyss.

abjurar *t* to abjure, forswear.

ablandar(se) *t* to soften. **2** *fig (calmar)* to soothe. − **3** *p* to soften (up), go soft/softer.

ablución *f* ablution.

abnegación *f* abnegation, self-denial.

abnegado,-a *adj* selfless, self-sacrificing.

abobado,-a *adj* stupid. **2** *(pasmado)* bewildered.

abochornado,-a *adj* ashamed.

abochornar(se) *t* to shame. **2** *(acalorar)* to make flushed. − **3** *p* to be ashamed.

abofetear *t* to slap.

abogacía *f* legal profession.

abogado,-a *m,f* lawyer, solicitor. ■ ~ **defensor,** counsel for the defense; ~ **laborista,** union lawyer.

abogar [7] *i* to plead. **2** *fig* to intercede.

abolengo *m* ancestry, lineage.

abolición *f* abolition.

abolir *t* to abolish. ▲ *Only used in forms which include the letter i in their endings:* **abolía, aboliré, aboliendo.**

abolladura *f* dent.

abollar *t* to dent.

abombado,-a *adj* convex.

abombar *t* to make convex.

abominable *adj* abominable, loathsome.

abominar *t* to abominate, loathe.

abonable *adj* payable.

abonado,-a *m,f (al teléfono, a revista)* subscriber; *(a teatro, tren, etc.)* season-ticket holder. − **2** *adj* FIN paid. **3** *(tierra)* fertilized.

abonar(se) *t* FIN to pay. **2** *(avalar)* to guarantee, answer for. **3** *(tierra)* to fertilize. **4** *(subscribir)* to subscribe. − **5** *p (a revista)* to subscribe (**a,** to); *(a teatro, tren, etc.)* to buy a season ticket (**a,** to).

abono *m* FIN payment. **2** *(aval)* guarantee. **3** *(para tierra)* fertilizer. **4** *(a revista)* subscription; *(a teatro, tren, etc.)* season-ticket.

abordaje *m* MAR collision.

abordar *t* MAR to run foul of. **2** *fig (persona, tema)* to approach.

aborigen *adj* aboriginal. − **2** *m* aborigine. ▲ *pl* **aborígenes.**

aborrecer [43] *t* to abhor, hate.

aborrecimiento *m* hate, loathing.

abortar *i (voluntariamente)* to abort; *(involuntariamente)* to miscarry. **2** *(fracasar)* to fail.

aborto *m (involuntario)* abortion; *(espontáneo)* miscarriage. **2** *fam (feo)* ugly person.

abotonar(se) *t-p* to button (up). − **2** *i (planta)* to bud.

abovedado,-a *adj* ARQ vaulted.

abovedar *t* ARQ to vault.

abrasador,-ra *adj* burning, scorching.

abrasar(se) *t (quemar)* to burn, scorch. **2** *(calentar)* overheat. − **3** *i-p* to burn (up): ~**se de calor,** to be weltering.

abrasivo,-a *adj-m* abrasive.

abrazadera *f* clamp, brace.

abrazar(se) [4] *t* to embrace. **2** *(ceñir)* to clasp. **3** *(incluir)* to include, comprise. **4** *(adoptar)* to adopt. − **5** *p* to embrace (each other).

abrazo *m* hug, embrace.

abrebotellas *m inv* bottle opener.

abrecartas *m inv* letter-opener, paper-knife.

abrelatas *m inv* tin-opener, US can-opener.

abrevadero *m* drinking trough.

abrevar *t (animales)* to water.

abreviación *f* abbreviation.

abreviar [12] *t* to shorten; *(texto)* to abridge; *(palabra)* to abbreviate.

abreviatura *f* abbreviation: **la** ~ **de etcétera es etc.,** etc. is the abbreviation of et caetera.

abridor *m* opener.

abrigar(se) [7] *t (contra el frío)* to wrap up, keep warm. **2** *(proteger)* to shelter, protect. **3** *(sospechas)* to harbour. − **4** *p (contra el frío)* to wrap o.s. up. **5** *(protegerse)* to take shelter.

abrigo *m (prenda)* coat, overcoat: **ropa de** ~, warm clothing. **2** *(refugio)* shelter. ●*fig* **ser de** ~, to be frightening.

abril *m* April.

abrillantador *m* polish.

abrillantar *t* to polish, burnish.

abrir(se) *t* to open. **2** *(cremallera)* to undo. **3** *(túnel)* to dig. **4** *(luz)* to switch/turn on. **5** *(grifo, gas)* to turn on. **6** *(encabezar)* to head, lead. − **7** *p* to open; *(flores)* to blossom. **8** *fig (sincerarse)* to open out. **9** *arg (largarse)* to clear off. ●~ **el apetito,** to whet one's appetite; ~ **paso,** to make way; *fam* **en un** ~ **y cerrar de ojos,** in the twinkling of an eye. ▲ *pp* **abierto,-a.**

abrochar(se) *t-p* to button (up): *abróchense los cinturones,* please fasten your seat-belts.

abrogar [7] *t* to abrogate.

abrojo *m* BOT thistle.

abroncar [1] *t (reprender)* to give a dressing-down (*a,* to). 2 *(abuchear)* to boo.

abrumador,-ra *adj* overwhelming, crushing.

abrumar *t* to overwhelm, crush: *la abrumó con sus atenciones,* his attentions made her feel uncomfortable.

abrupto,-a *adj (terreno)* rugged. 2 *(persona)* abrupt.

absceso *m* abscess.

absentismo *m* absenteeism.

ábside *m* apse.

absolución *f* absolution.

absoluto,-a *adj* absolute. − 2 *absolutamente adv* absolutely. ●*en* ~, not at all.

absolver [32] *t* to absolve; JUR to acquit. ▲ *pp absuelto,-a.*

absorbente *adj* absorbent. 2 *fig (trabajo)* absorbing, engrossing. − 3 *m* absorbent.

absorber *t* to absorb.

absorción *f* absorption.

absorto,-a *adj (pasmado)* amazed. 2 *(ensimismado)* absorbed/engrossed (*en,* in).

abstemio,-a *adj* abstemious, teetotal. − 2 *m,f* teetotaller.

abstención *f* abstention.

abstenerse [87] *p* to abstain/refrain (*de,* from).

abstinencia *f* abstinence. ■ *síndrome de* ~, withdrawal symptoms *pl.*

abstracción *f* abstraction.

abstracto,-a *adj* abstract: *en* ~, in the abstract.

abstraer(se) [88] *t* to abstract. − 2 *p* to become lost in thought.

absuelto,-a *pp →* **absolver.**

absurdo,-a *adj* absurd. − 2 *m* absurdity, nonsense.

abuchear *t* to boo.

abucheo *m* booing.

abuela *f* grandmother; *fam* grandma, granny. 2 *(vieja)* old woman.

abuelo *m* grandfather; *fam* granddad, grandpa. 2 *(viejo)* old man. 3 *pl* grandparents.

abulia *f* apathy.

abúlico,-a *adj* apathetic.

abultado,-a *adj* bulky, big.

abultamiento *m* swelling, protuberance.

abultar *t* to enlarge, increase. 2 *fig* to exaggerate. − 3 *i* to be bulky.

abundancia *f* abundance, plenty.

abundante *adj* abundant, plentiful.

abundar *i* to abound, be plentiful.

aburguesado,-a *adj* bourgeois.

aburguesarse *p* to become bourgeois.

aburrido,-a *adj (ser* ~*)* boring, tedious. 2 *(estar* ~*)* bored, weary.

aburrimiento *m* boredom.

aburrir(se) *t* to bore. − 2 *p* to get bored.

abusar *i (propasarse)* to go too far, abuse (*de,* -): ~ *de algn.,* to take unfair advantage of sb. 2 *(usar mal)* to misuse (*de,* -): ~ *de la bebida,* to drink too much.

abusivo,-a *adj* excessive, exorbitant.

abuso *m* abuse, misuse. 2 *(injusticia)* injustice. ■ ~ *de confianza,* betrayal of trust.

abusón,-ona *m,f fam (gorrón)* sponger. 2 *(injusto)* unfair person.

abyecto,-a *adj* abject.

acá *adv (lugar)* here, over here: *de* ~ *para allá,* to and fro, up and down. 2 *(tiempo)* until now: *de entonces* ~, since then.

acabado,-a *adj* finished; *(perfecto)* perfect: ~ *de hacer,* freshly made. 2 *(malparado)* worn-out: *una persona acabada,* a has-been. − 3 *m* finish, finishing touch.

acabar(se) *t* to finish (off); *(completar)* to complete: ~ *el trabajo,* to finish the work. 2 *(consumir)* to use up: ~ *las provisiones,* to run out of supplies. − 3 *i* to finish, end: ~ *en punta,* to have a pointed end. 4 *(*~ *+ por)/(*~ *+ gerundio)* to end up: ~ *por comprar/comprando el vestido,* to end up buying the dress. − 5 *p* to end, finish; *(no quedar)* to run out. ●~ *bien,* to have a happy ending; ~ *mal,* to end badly; ~ *con,* to destroy, put an end to; ~ *de,* to have just; *fam ¡acabáramos!,* at last!

acabose *m fam esto es el* ~, this is the end.

acacia *f* acacia.

academia *f (institución)* academy. 2 *(escuela)* school.

académico,-a *adj* academic: *estudios académicos,* academic qualifications. − 2 *m,f* academician.

acaecer [43] *i* to happen, come to pass.

acalambrarse *p* to get cramps.

acallar *t* to silence, hush. 2 *fig* to pacify.

acalorado,-a *adj* heated. **2** *fig (persona)* excited; *(debate)* heated, angry. **– 3** *acaloradamente adv* warmly; *fig* excitedly.

acaloramiento *m* heat. **2** *fig* passion.

acalorar(se) *t* to warm up, heat up. **2** *fig* to excite; *(pasiones)* to inflame. **– 3** *p* to get warm/hot. **4** *fig* to get excited; *(debate)* to get heated.

acampada *f* camping.

acampanado,-a *adj* bell-shaped; *(prendas)* flared.

acampar *i-t* to camp.

acanalado,-a *adj* grooved. **2** ARQ fluted.

acanalar *t* to groove. **2** ARQ to flute.

acantilado,-a *adj (costa)* rocky. **2** *(fondo del mar)* shelving. **– 3** *m* cliff.

acaparador,-ra *adj* hoarding. **– 2** *m,f* hoarder. **3** *(monopolizador)* monopolizer.

acaparamiento *m* hoarding. **2** *(monopolio)* monopolizing.

acaparar *t* to hoard; *(mercado)* to corner, buy up. **2** *(monopolizar)* to monopolize: *fig acaparó la atención de todos,* he/she commanded the attention.

acaramelado,-a *adj* spoony, oversweet. **2** *fig (pareja)* lovey-dovey.

acariciar(se) [12] *t* to caress, fondle. **2** *(esperanzas etc.)* to cherish. **– 3** *p* to caress each other.

acarrear *t (causar)* to cause, bring. **2** *(transportar)* to carry, transport.

acarreo *m* carriage, transport.

acartonarse *p* to go stiff/hard.

acaso *adv* perhaps, maybe. ●*por si ~,* just in case.

acatar *t (leyes etc.)* to obey. **2** *(personas)* to respect. **3** AM to notice.

acatarrarse *p* to catch a cold.

acaudalado,-a *adj* rich, wealthy.

acaudalar *t* to accumulate, amass.

acaudillar *t* to lead.

acceder *i (consentir)* to consent (*a,* to), agree (*a,* to). **2** *(tener entrada)* to enter: *por aquí se accede al jardín,* this leads to the garden. **3** *(alcanzar)* to accede (*a,* to): *~ al poder,* to come to power.

accesible *adj* accessible.

accésit *m* consolation prize. ▲ *pl accésits or accesis.*

acceso *m (entrada)* access, entry. **2** *(ataque)* fit, outburst. ■ *carretera de ~,* approach road; *vía de ~,* slip road.

accesorio,-a *adj-m* accessory: *accesorios del automóvil,* car accessories.

accidentado,-a *adj (turbado)* agitated: *vida accidentada,* stormy/troubled life.

2 *(terreno)* uneven, rough. **– 3** *m,f* casualty, accident victim.

accidental *adj* accidental.

accidentarse *p* to have an accident.

accidente *m* accident. **2** *(terreno)* unevenness. **3** MED fit. ●*por ~,* by chance.

acción *f* action; *(acto)* act, deed. **2** *(efecto)* effect: *la ~ del agua sobre la piel,* the effect of water on the skin. **3** COM share. **4** JUR action, lawsuit. **5** TEAT plot. **6** MIL action. ■ *~ de gracias,* thanksgiving; *película de ~,* adventure film.

accionar *t (máquina)* to drive, work. **–** *i* to gesticulate.

accionista *mf* shareholder, stockholder.

acebo *m* holly.

acechar *t* to watch, spy on: *un gran peligro nos acecha,* great danger looms ahead.

acecho *m* watching. ●*al ~,* in wait, on the watch.

aceite *m* oil.

aceitoso,-a *adj* oily. **2** *(grasiento)* greasy.

aceituna *f* olive. ■ *~ rellena,* stuffed olive.

aceitunado,-a *adj* olive-coloured.

acelerado,-a *adj* accelerated, fast, quick. **– 2** *f* acceleration.

acelerador *m* AUTO accelerator.

acelerar(se) *t* to accelerate. **2** *(aumentar)* to speed up. **– 3** *p (azorarse)* to get upset.

acelga *f* chard.

acento *m (tilde)* accent (mark). **2** *(tónico)* stress. **3** *(pronunciación)* accent: *~ andaluz,* Andalusian accent. **4** *(énfasis)* emphasis, stress.

acentuación *f* accentuation.

acentuado,-a *adj* accented. **2** *(resaltado)* strong, marked.

acentuar(se) [11] *t* to accent. **2** *(resaltar)* to emphasize, stress. **– 3** *p* to stand out.

acepción *f* meaning.

aceptable *adj* acceptable.

aceptación *f* acceptance. **2** *(aprobación)* approval: *tener poca ~,* not to be popular.

aceptar *t* to accept, receive. **2** *(aprobar)* to approve of.

acequia *f* irrigation ditch.

acera *f* pavement, US sidewalk. ●*fam ser de la ~ de enfrente,* to be gay/queer.

acerado,-a *adj* steel, steely. **2** *fig (mordaz)* sharp, incisive.

acerbo,-a *adj (al gusto)* bitter, sour. **2** *(cruel)* cruel, bitter.

acerca *~ de, adv* about, concerning.

acercamiento *m* coming together.

acercar(se) [1] *t* to bring near/nearer. – 2 *p* to approach, come near/nearer.

acero *m* steel. ■ ~ *inoxidable,* stainless, steel.

acérrimo,-a *adj* staunch.

acertado,-a *adj (opinión etc.)* right, correct. 2 *(conveniente)* suitable.

acertante *adj* winning. – 2 *mf* winner.

acertar [27] *t* to get right. 2 *(adivinar)* to guess: ~ *la quiniela,* to win the pools. – 3 *t-i (dar con)* to succeed *(con,* in), be right *(con,* about): *acertó (con) la casa,* he found the right house. – 4 *i (~ + a + inf)* to happen, chance: *yo acertaba a estar allí,* I happened to be there.

acertijo *m* riddle.

acervo *m (montón)* heap. 2 *(haber común)* common property.

acetato *m* acetate.

acetona *f* acetone.

achacar [1] *t* to impute; attribute.

achacoso,-a *adj* ailing, unwell.

achaque *m (indisposición)* ailment. 2 *(excusa)* excuse, pretext.

acharolado,-a *adj* varnished.

achatado,-a *adj* flattened.

achatar *t* to flatten.

achicar(se) [1] *t (amenguar)* to diminish, reduce. 2 *(amilanar)* to intimidate. 3 *(agua)* to drain; *(en barco)* to bale out. – 4 *p (amenguarse)* to get smaller. 5 *(amilanarse)* to lose heart.

achicharrar(se) *t-p* to scorch; *(comida)* to burn: *hace un sol que achicharra,* it's roasting.

achicoria *f* chicory.

achispado,-a *adj* tipsy.

achispar(se) *t* to make tipsy. – 2 *p* to get tipsy.

achuchado,-a *adj fam* difficult.

achuchar *t (estrujar)* to crush. 2 *(empujar)* to push violently.

achuchón *fam m* push, shove. 2 *(indisposición)* indisposition.

acicalarse *p* to dress up.

acicate *m* spur. 2 *fig* incentive.

acidez *f* sourness; QUÍM acidity. ■ ~ *de estómago,* heartburn.

ácido,-a *adj (sabor)* sharp, tart. 2 QUÍM acidic. – 3 *m* acid. 4 *arg* acid, LSD.

acierto *m (adivinación)* correct guess. 2 *(logro)* good shot. 3 *(casualidad)* chance. 4 *(éxito)* success. 5 *(habilidad)* skill.

aclamación *f* acclamation, acclaim.

aclamar *t* to acclaim.

aclaración *f* explanation.

aclarar(se) *t (cabello, color)* to lighten. 2 *(líquido)* to thin. 3 *(enjuagar)* to rinse. 4 *(explicar)* to explain. – 5 *p (entender)* to understand. 6 *(el tiempo)* to clear up. ●~*se la voz,* to clear one's throat.

aclimatación *f* acclimatization, US acclimation.

aclimatar(se) *t* to acclimatize *(a,* to). – 2 *p* to become acclimatized *(a,* to).

acné *f* acne.

acobardar(se) *t* to frighten. – 2 *p* to become frightened.

acodar(se) *t (plantas)* to layer. 2 *(doblar)* to bend. – 3 *p* to lean/rest one's elbow.

acogedor,-ra *adj (persona)* welcoming. 2 *(lugar)* cosy, warm.

acoger(se) [5] *t (recibir)* to receive; *(a invitado)* to welcome. 2 *(proteger)* to shelter, protect. 3 *(ideas etc.)* to accept, take to. – 4 *p (refugiarse)* to take refuge; *fig* to take refuge *(a,* in). 5 *(a una ley etc.)* to have recourse to.

acogida *f* reception, welcome. 2 *fig* shelter. 3 *(aceptación)* popularity.

acojonado,-a* *adj (asustado)* shit-scared*. 2 *(asombrado)* amazed.

acojonante* *adj* bloody great.

acojonar(se)* *t (atemorizar)* to scare (the shit out of)*. 2 *(asombrar)* to amaze. – 3 *p* to shit o.s., get the wind up.

acolchar *t* to quilt. 2 *(rellenar)* to pad.

acometer *t (embestir)* to attack. 2 *(tos etc.)* to be seized by. 3 *(emprender)* to undertake.

acometida *f* attack, assault.

acomodación *f* accommodation, adaptation.

acomodado,-a *adj (conveniente)* suitable. 2 *(rico)* well-to-do. 3 *(precio)* reasonable.

acomodador,-ra *m,f m* usher, *f* usherette.

acomodar(se) *t (colocar)* to arrange. 2 *(adaptar)* to apply, adapt. 3 *(alojar)* to lodge, accommodate. – 4 *p (instalarse)* to make o.s. comfortable. 5 *(avenirse)* to adapt o.s. *(a/con,* to).

acomodaticio,-a *adj* easy-going.

acomodo *m (empleo)* job, employment. 2 *(alojamiento)* lodging.

acompañamiento *m* accompaniment. 2 *(comitiva)* retinue.

acompañanta *f* (female) companion, chaperon(e).

acompañante *adj* accompanying. – 2 *mf* companion. 3 MÚS accompanist.

acompañar(se) *t* to accompany. 2 *(adjuntar)* to enclose. – 3 *p* MÚS to accom-

pany o.s. (*a,* on). •*fml* ~ *en el sentimiento,* to express one's condolences.
acompasado,-a *adj* rhythmic; *(paso)*
measured; *(habla)* slow.
acomplejado,-a *adj* with a complex. –
2 *m,f* person with a complex.
acomplejar(se) *i* to give a complex. – 2
p to develop a complex (*por,* about).
acondicionador *m* conditioner. ■ ~ *de
aire,* air conditioner; ~ *del cabello,* hair
conditioner.
acondicionar *t* to fit up, set up; *(mejorar)*
to improve.
acongojado,-a *adj* distressed.
acongojar(se) *t* to distress, grieve. – 2 *p*
to be distressed/grieved.
aconsejar(se) *t* to advise. – 2 *p* to seek
advice.
acontecer *i* to happen.
acontecimiento *m* event, happening.
acopio *m* storing. •*hacer* ~ *de,* to store
up.
acoplar(se) *t* *(juntar)* to fit (together) to
join. 2 TÉC to couple, connect. – 3 *p* to
pair, mate.
acoquinar(se) *t* to frighten. – 2 *p* to become frightened.
acorazado,-a *adj* armoured. – 2 *m* battleship.
acordado,-a *adj* agreed.
acordar(se) [31] *t* to agree. 2 *(decidir)* to
decide. 3 *(conciliar)* to reconcile. 4 MÚS
to attune. – 5 *p* to remember (*de,* -).
acorde *adj* in agreement. – 2 *m* MÚS
chord.
acordeón *m* accordion.
acordonar *t* *(atar)* to lace, tie. 2 *(rodear)*
to surround, draw a cordon around.
acorralar *t* to corner.
acortar *t* to shorten.
acosar *t* to pursue, chase.
acoso *m* pursuit, chase.
acostar(se) [31] *t* to put to bed. – 2 *p* to
go to bed. •*fam* ~*se con,* to sleep with.
acostumbrado,-a *adj* *(persona)* accustomed, used. 2 *(hecho)* usual, customary.
acostumbrar(se) *t* *(habituar)* to accustom to. 2 *(soler)* to be in the habit of:
no acostumbro a fumar por la mañana,
I don't usually smoke in the morning.
– 3 *p* to become accustomed.
acotación *f* *(en escrito)* marginal note. 2
(topográfica) elevation mark.
acotar *t* *(área)* to enclose. 2 *(topográfia)* to
mark with elevations. 3 *fig* to delimit,
restrict.

ácrata *adj-mf* anarchist.
acre *adj* acrid. 2 *fig (lenguaje)* bitter. – 3
m (medida) acre.
acrecentar(se) [27], **acrecer(se)** [43] *t-
p* to increase.
acreditado,-a *adj* reputable, well-
known.
acreditar(se) *t* to give credit to. 2 *(probar)* to prove to be. 3 FIN to credit. – 4
p to gain a reputation.
acreedor,-ra *adj* deserving. – 2 *m,f* FIN
creditor.
acribillar *t* to riddle. 2 *fig* to harass: ~ *a
algn. a preguntas,* to bombard sb. with
questions.
acrílico,-a *adj* acrylic.
acrimonia, acritud *f* acrimony.
acrobacia *f* acrobatics.
acróbata *mf* acrobat.
acrónimo *m* acronym.
acta *f* minutes *pl,* record (of proceedings). 2 *(certificado)* certificate. 3 *pl (me-
morias)* transactions. ■ ~ *notarial,* affidavit.
actitud *f* attitude.
activar(se) *t* to activate; *(acelerar)* to expedite. – 2 *p* to become activated.
actividad *f* activity.
activista *adj-mf* POL activist.
activo,-a *adj* active. – 2 *m* FIN assets *pl.*
■ ~ *disponible,* liquid assets *pl.*
acto *m* act. 2 *(ceremonia)* ceremony,
meeting, public function. 3 TEAT act.
•~ *seguido,* immediately afterwards;
en el ~, at once.
actor *m* actor.
actor,-ra *m,f* JUR plaintiff. – 2 *adj parte
actora,* prosecution.
actriz *f* actress.
actuación *f* performance. 2 JUR law proceedings *pl.*
actual *adj* present, current. 2 *(actualizado)* up-to-date. – 3 *m fml* this month: *el
doce del* ~, the 12th of this month. – 4
actualmente adv (hoy en día) nowadays;
(ahora) at present.
actualidad *f* present (time). 2 *(hechos)*
current affairs *pl.* •*en la* ~, at present.
■*temas de* ~, current affairs.
actualizar [11] *t* to bring up to date.
actuar *t* to actuate, work. – 2 *i* to act (*de,*
as). 3 CINEM TEAT to perform, act.
acuarela *f* watercolour.
acuario *m* aquarium.
acuartelar *t* MIL *(alojar)* to quarter. 2 *(retener)* to confine to barracks.
acuático,-a *adj* aquatic, water.

acuchillar *t (seres vivos)* to knife, stab. **2** *(prendas)* to slash. **3** *(madera)* to plane (down).

acuciante *adj* pressing, urging.

acuclillarse *p* to squat, crouch (down).

acudir *i (ir)* to go; *(venir)* to come. **2** *(ayudar)* to attend/help. **3** *(recurrir)* to resort.

acueducto *m* aqueduct.

acuerdo *m* agreement. ●*¡de* ~!, all right!, O.K.!; *de* ~ *con,* in accordance with; *de común* ~, by mutual agreement; *estar de* ~, to agree. ■ ~ *marco,* framework agreement.

acullá *adv fml* far away.

acumulación *f* accumulation.

acumulador,-ra *adj* accumulative. – **2** *m* FÍS accumulator.

acumular *t* to accumulate.

acunar *t* to rock.

acuñar *t (monedas)* to coin, mint. **2** *(poner cuñas)* to wedge.

acuoso,-a *adj* watery.

acupuntura *f* acupuncture.

acurrucarse [1] *p* to curl up.

acusación *f* accusation; JUR charge.

acusado,-a *adj-m,f* accused.

acusar(se) *t* to accuse; JUR charge *(de,* with). **2** *(manifestar)* to give away. – **3** *p (confesarse)* to confess. **4** *(acentuarse)* to become more pronounced. ●~ *recibo de,* to acknowledge receipt of.

acusativo *m* accusative.

acuse *m* ~ *de recibo,* acknowledgement of receipt.

acusica *adj-mf,* **acusón,-ona** *adj-m,f fam* telltale.

acústica *f* acoustics.

acústico,-a *adj* acoustic.

adagio *m* proverb. **2** MÚS adagio.

adalid *m* leader.

adamascado,-a *adj* damask.

adaptable *adj* adaptable.

adaptación *f* adaptation.

adaptar(se) *t* to adapt. **2** *(ajustar)* to adjust. – **3** *p* to adapt o.s. *(a,* to).

adecentar(se) *t-p* to tidy (o.s.) (up).

adecuado,-a *adj* adequate, suitable.

adecuar [10] *t* to adapt, make suitable.

adefesio *m fam (disparate)* nonsense, absurdity. **2** *(persona)* freak.

adelantado,-a *adj (precoz)* precocious. **2** *(aventajado)* advanced. **3** *(desarrollado)* developed. **4** *(reloj)* fast. ●*por* ~, in advance.

adelantamiento *m* AUTO overtaking. ●*hacer un* ~, to overtake.

adelantar(se) *t* to move forward. **2** *(reloj)* to put forward. **3** *(pasar delante)* to pass; AUTO to overtake. **4** *(dinero)* to pay in advance. – **5** *i (progresar)* to make progress. **6** *(reloj)* to be fast. – **7** *p (ir delante)* to go ahead. **8** *(llegar temprano)* to be early. **9** *(anticiparse)* to get ahead *(a,* of). **10** *(reloj)* to gain, be fast.

adelante *adv* forward, further. – **2** *interj* come in! ●*en* ~, henceforth; *más* ~, later on.

adelanto *m* advance: *los adelantos de la ciencia,* the progress of science. **2** COM advanced payment.

adelgazamiento *m* slimming.

adelgazar(se) [4] *t* to make slim. – **2** *p* to slim.

ademán *m* gesture. **2** *pl* manners. ●*hacer* ~ *de,* to look as if one is about to.

además *adv* besides. **2** *(también)* also. ●~ *de,* besides.

adentrarse *p* to penetrate. ●~ *en algo,* to go into sth.

adentro *adv* inside. – **2** *mpl* inward mind *sing: para sus adentros,* in his heart.

adepto *m* follower, supporter.

aderezar [4] *t* CULIN to season; *(ensalada)* to dress. **2** *(adornar) (personas)* to make beautiful; *(cosas)* to embellish. **3** *(preparar)* to prepare.

aderezo *m* CULIN seasoning; *(de ensalada)* dressing. **2** *(preparación)* preparation. **3** *(joyas)* set of jewellery.

adeudar(se) *t* to owe. **2** FIN to debit, charge. – **3** *p* to get into debt.

adherencia *f* adherence.

adherente *adj* adherent, adhesive.

adherir(se) [35] *i* to stick *(a,* to). – **2** *p* to follow. **3** *fig* to follow.

adhesión *f* adhesion, adherence. **2** *(apoyo)* support.

adhesivo,-a *adj-m* adhesive.

adición *f* addition.

adicionar *t* to add. **2** *(sumar)* to add up.

adicto,-a *adj (drogas)* addicted *(a,* to). **2** *(dedicado)* fond *(a,* of). **3** *(partidario)* supporting. – **4** *m,f (drogas)* addict. **5** *(partidario)* supporter.

adiestramento *m* training, instruction.

adiestrar(se) *t* to train, instruct. – **2** *p* to train o.s.

adinerado,-a *adj* rich, wealthy.

¡adiós! *interj* goodbye! **2** *(hasta luego)* see you later. ▲ *pl adioses.*

aditivo,-a *adj-m* additive.

adivinador,-ra *m,f* fortune-teller.

adivinanza *f* riddle, puzzle.

adivinar *t* to guess. **2** *(predecir)* to forecast. **3** *(enigma)* to solve.

adivino,-a *m,f* fortune-teller.

adjetivar *t* to use as an adjective. **2** *fig* to label.

adjetivo,-a *m* adjective. − **2** *adj* adjective, adjectival.

adjudicación *f* award, awarding.

adjudicar(se) [1] *t* to award: *¡adjudicado!,* sold! − **2** *p* to appropriate.

adjunto,-a *adj (en carta)* enclosed. **2** *(asistente)* assistant. − **3** *m,f* assistant teacher.

administración *f* administration. **2** *(cargo)* post of administrator. **3** *(oficina)* branch. ■ ~ *de Correos,* Post Office; ~ *de Hacienda,* tax office; ~ *de lotería,* lottery office; ~ *pública,* public administration.

administrador,-ra *m,f* administrator: *es muy buena administradora,* she knows how to stretch money.

administrar(se) *t* to administer. **2** *(aplicar)* to give: *le administró un antibiótico,* he gave him an antibiotic. − **3** *p* to manage one's own money.

administrativo,-a *adj* administrative. − **2** *m,f (funcionario)* official; *(de empresa, banco)* office worker.

admirable *adj* admirable.

admiración *f* admiration. **2** *(signo de)* exclamation mark.

admirar(se) *t* to admire. **2** *(sorprender)* to amaze, surprise. − **3** *p* to be astonished.

admisión *f* admission.

admitir *t (dar entrada, reconocer)* to admit. **2** *(aceptar)* to accept. **3** *(permitir)* to allow.

adobado,-a *adj* marinated.

adobar *t* to marinate.

adocenado,-a *adj* commonplace, ordinary.

adoctrinar *t* to indoctrinate.

adolecer [43] *i (sufrir)* to be ill. ●~ *de,* to suffer from.

adolescencia *f* adolescence.

adolescente *adj-mf* adolescent.

adonde *adv* where.

adónde *adv interr* where.

adondequiera ~ *(que),* *adv* wherever.

adopción *f* adoption.

adoptar *t* to adopt.

adoptivo,-a *adj* adoptive.

adoquín *m* cobble, paving stone.

adoración *f* adoration, worship.

adorar *t* to adore, worship.

adormecer(se) [43] *t* to put to sleep. **2** *(calmar)* to soothe. − **3** *p (dormirse)* to doze off. **4** *(entumecerse)* to go to sleep, go numb.

adormidera *f* opium poppy.

adormilarse *p* to doze, drowse.

adornar *t* to adorn, decorate; *fig* to embellish.

adorno *m* decoration.

adosado,-a *adj* semidetached: *casas adosadas,* semidetached houses.

adosar *t* to lean *(a,* against).

adquirir [30] *t* to acquire; *(comprar)* to buy.

adquisición *f* acquisition; *(compra)* buy, purchase.

adquisitivo,-a *adj* acquisitive.

adrede *adv* purposely, on purpose.

adrenalina *f* adrenalin.

adscribir *t (atribuir)* to attribute. **2** *(a un trabajo)* to appoint. ▲ *pp* **adscrito,-a.**

aduana *f* customs *pl.* ●*pasar por la* ~, to go through customs.

aduanero,-a *adj* customs. − **2** *m* customs officer.

aducir [46] *t* to adduce, allege.

adueñarse *p* ~ *de,* to seize.

adulación *f* adulation, flattery.

adular *t* to adulate, flatter.

adulteración *f* adulteration.

adulterado,-a *adj* adulterated.

adulterar *t* to adulterate.

adulterio *m* adultery.

adúltero,-a *adj* adulterous. − **2** *m,f m* adulterer, *f* adulteress.

adulto,-a *adj-m,f* adult: *los adultos,* the grown-ups.

adusto,-a *adj* scorched, burnt. **2** *fig (seco)* harsh, stern.

advenedizo,-a *adj-m,f* parvenu.

advenimiento *m* advent, coming. **2** *(al trono)* accession.

adventismo *m* Adventism.

adverbio *m* adverb.

adversario,-a *adj* opposing. − **2** *m,f* adversary, opponent.

adversidad *f* adversity.

adverso,-a *adj* adverse. **2** *(opuesto)* opposite.

advertencia *f* warning. **2** *(consejo)* advice. **3** *(nota)* notice.

advertido,-a *adj* capable, knowledgeable.

advertir [35] *t (darse cuenta)* to notice. **2** *(llamar la atención)* to warn. **3** *(aconsejar)* to advise.

adviento *m* advent.

adyacente *adj* adjacent.
aéreo,-a *adj* aerial. **2** AV air. ■*tráfico* ~, air traffic.
aereobús *m* airbus.
aerodinámico,-a *adj* aerodynamic. – **2** *f* aerodynamics.
aeródromo *m* aerodrome, US airfield.
aeromodelismo *m* aeroplane modelling.
aeronáutica *f* aeronautics.
aeronave *f* airship.
aeroplano *m* aeroplane, airplane.
aeropuerto *m* airport.
aerosol *m* aerosol, spray.
aerostático,-a *adj* aerostatic. – **2** *f* aerostatics.
afabilidad *f* affability.
afable *adj* affable, kind.
afamado,-a *adj* famous, renowned.
afán *m* (*anhelo*) eagerness: *con* ~, keenly. **2** (*esfuerzo*) hard work.
afanar(se) *t fam* to nick, pinch. – **2** *p* ~*se en*, to work hard at. **3** ~*se por*, to strive to.
afanoso,-a *adj* (*anheloso*) eager. **2** (*tarea*) hard, laborious.
afear *t* to make ugly. **2** *fig* (*vituperar*) to reproach.
afección *f* affection, fondness. **2** MED illness.
afectación *f* affectation.
afectado,-a *adj* affected. **2** (*fingido*) pretended.
afectar(se) *t* to affect. **2** (*impresionar*) to move. – **3** *p* (*impresionarse*) to be affected/moved.
afectividad *f* affectivity.
afecto,-a *adj* affectionate, fond (*a*, of). – **2** *m* affection: *con todo mi* ~, with all my love.
afectuoso,-a *adj* affectionate. – **2** *afectuosamente adv* affectionately; (*en cartas*) yours sincerely.
afeitado *m* shave, shaving.
afeitadora *f* electric shaver/razor.
afeitar(se) *t-p* to shave.
afelpado,-a *adj* velvety.
afeminado,-a *adj* effeminate.
aferrado,-a *adj fig* clutching, clinging.
aferrar(se) *i-p fig* to cling.
afianzar(se) [4] *t* (*clavar etc.*) to strengthen. **2** *fig* to consolidate: ~ *un régimen*, to consolidate a regime. – **3** *p* to steady o.s.
afición *f* (*inclinación*) liking: *tiene* ~ *por la música*, he's fond of music. ■*la* ~, the fans *pl*.

aficionado,-a *adj* keen, fond. **2** (*no profesional*) amateur. – **3** *m,f* fan, enthusiast. **4** (*no profesional*) amateur.
aficionar(se) *t* to make fond (*a*, of). – **2** *p* to become fond (*a*, of).
afilado,-a *adj* sharp. **2** (*con punta*) pointed.
afilalápices *m inv* pencil sharpener.
afilar *t* to sharpen.
afiliación *f* affiliation.
afiliado,-a *adj-m,f* affiliate, member.
afiliar [12] *t* to affiliate. – **2** *p* to join (*a*, to), become affiliated (*a*, to).
afín *adj* (*semejante*) similar. **2** (*relacionado*) related. **3** (*próximo*) adjacent, next.
afinar *t* to perfect, polish. **2** MÚS to tune. **3** (*puntería*) to sharpen.
afinidad *f* affinity.
afirmación *f* statement, assertion.
afirmar(se) *t* (*afianzar*) to strenghten. **2** (*aseverar*) to state, say. – **3** *p* (*ratificarse*) to steady o.s.
afirmativo,-a *adj* affirmative. – **2** *f* affirmative answer.
aflicción *f* affliction, grief.
afligido,-a *adj* afflicted, grieved.
afligir(se) [6] *t* to afflict, grieve. – **2** *p* to grieve, be distressed.
aflojar(se) *t* (*soltar*) to loosen. **2** *fam fig* (*dinero*) to pay up. – **3** *i* (*disminuir*) to weaken. – **4** *p* to come loose. ●*fam la mosca*, to fork out, cough up.
afluencia *f* inflow, influx: ~ *de público*, flow of people. **2** (*abundancia*) affluence.
afluente *m* (*río*) tributary.
afluir [62] *i* to flow (*a*, into).
afonía *f* loss of voice.
afónico,-a *adj* hoarse. ●*estar* ~, to have lost one's voice.
aforismo *m* aphorism.
afortunado,-a *adj* lucky, fortunate. **2** (*dichoso*) happy.
afrenta *f fml* affront, outrage.
afrentar *t* to affront, outrage.
afrodisiaco,-a, afrodisíaco,-a *adj-m* aphrodisiac.
afrontar *t* to face.
afuera *adv* outside: *vengo de* ~ , I've just been outside. – **2** *interj* out of the way! – **3** *fpl* outskirts.
agachar(se) *t* to lower. – **2** *p* (*encogerse*) to cower. **3** (*protegerse*) to duck (down).
agalla *f* (*de pez*) gill. **2** BOT gall. **3** *pl fam* courage *sing*, guts.
agarradero *m* (*asa*) handle. **2** *fig* protection.

agarrado,-a *adj* stingy. • *bailar* ~, to dance cheek to cheek.

agarrar(se) *t (con la mano)* to clutch, seize. **2** *(pillar)* to catch. − **3** *p* to hold on, cling *(a,* to). •*fig* ~*se a un clavo ardiendo,* to clutch at a straw.

agarrón *m* AM *(altercado)* quarrel, fight.

agarrotado,-a *adj (apretado)* tight. **2** *(músculo)* stiff.

agarrotar(se) *t (oprimir)* to squeeze. − **2** *p (los músculos)* to stiffen.

agasajar *t* to wine and dine.

agasajo *m (acogida)* warm welcome. **2** *(regalo)* gift.

ágata *f* agate. ▲ *Takes el and un in sing.*

agencia *f* agency. ■ ~ *de viajes,* travel agency.

agenciarse [12] *p* to manage: *me las agenciaré como pueda,* I'll manage.

agenda *f (libro)* diary. **2** *(orden del día)* agenda.

agente *mf* agent. ■ ~ *de cambio y bolsa,* stockbroker; ~ *de policía,* policeman.

ágil *adj* agile.

agilidad *f* agility.

agilizar [4] *t* to make agile. **2** *fig* to speed up.

agitación *f* agitation. **2** *fig* excitement.

agitador,-ra *m,f* agitator. − **2** *m* QUÍM agitator.

agitanado,-a *adj* gypsy-like.

agitar(se) *t* to agitate; *(botella)* to shake; *(pañuelo)* to wave. **2** *fig* agitate, excite. − **3** *p (inquietarse)* to become agitated/disturbed. **4** *(mar)* to become rough.

aglomeración *f* agglomeration. **2** *(de gente)* crowd.

aglomerado *m* agglomerate.

aglutinar(se) *t-p* to agglutinate.

agnóstico,-a *adj-m,f* agnostic.

agobiado,-a *adj (doblado)* bent over. **2** *fig (cansado)* exhausted: ~ *de trabajo,* up to one's eyes in work.

agobiar(se) [12] *t (doblar)* to weigh down. **2** *fig* to overwhelm. − **3** *p* to worry too much, get worked up.

agobio *m* burden, fatigue.

agolparse *p* to crowd, throng.

agonía *f* dying breath. **2** *(sufrimiento)* agony, grief. **3** AM *(desazón)* anxiety.

agonizante *adj-mf* dying (person).

agonizar [4] *i* to be dying.

agosto *m* August. •*fig hacer su* ~, to make a packet/pile.

agotado,-a *adj (cansado)* exhausted. **2** *(libros)* out of print; *(mercancías)* sold out.

agotador,-ra *adj* exhausting.

agotamiento *m* exhaustion.

agotar(se) *t* to exhaust. − **2** *p (cansarse)* to become exhausted. **3** *(acabarse)* to run out; COM to be sold out.

agraciado,-a *adj* attractive. **2** *(ganador)* winning.

agraciar [12] *t (embellecer)* to make more attractive. **2** *fml (conceder)* to bestow.

agradable *adj* nice, pleasant.

agradar *i* to please: *esto me agrada,* I like this.

agradecer [43] *t* to thank for, be grateful for: *siempre se agradece un descanso,* a rest is always welcome.

agradecido,-a *adj* grateful, thankful: *le quedaría muy* ~ *si ...,* I should be very much obliged if ... .

agradecimiento *m* gratitude, thankfulness.

agrado *m* pleasure: *no es de su* ~, it isn't to his liking.

agrandar(se) *t* to enlarge. **2** *(exagerar)* to exaggerate. − **3** *p* to enlarge, become larger.

agrario,-a *adj* agrarian.

agravante *m* added difficulty. **2** JUR aggravating circumstance.

agravar(se) *t* to aggravate. − **2** *p* to get worse.

agraviar [12] *t* to offend, insult.

agravio *m* offence, insult.

agredir *t* to attack. ▲ *Used only in forms which include the letter i in their endings: agredía, agrediré, agrediendo.*

agregado,-a *adj* aggregate. − **2** *m,f* EDUC assistant teacher. − **3** *m* attaché.

agregar(se) [7] *t (añadir)* to add. **2** *(unir)* to gather. − **3** *p* to join.

agresión *f* aggression.

agresividad *f* aggressiveness.

agresivo,-a *adj* aggressive.

agresor,-ra *m,f* aggressor.

agreste *adj* rural, country. **2** *(persona)* uncouth, coarse.

agriar(se) [12] *t* to sour. **2** *fig (persona)* to embitter. − **3** *p* to turn sour.

agrícola *adj* agricultural.

agricultor,-ra *m,f* farmer.

agricultura *f* agriculture, farming.

agridulce *adj* bittersweet. **2** CULIN sweet and sour.

agrietar(se) *t-p* to crack.

agrio,-a *adj* sour. − **2** *mpl* citrus fruits.

agronomía *f* agronomy.

agrónomo,-a *m,f* agronomist.

agropecuario,-a *adj* farming, agricultural.

agrumarse *p* to curdle, clot.

agrupación *f* grouping (together). **2** *(asociación)* association.

agrupar(se) *t (congregar)* to gather. − **2** *p* to group together. **3** *(asociarse)* to associate.

agua *f* water. ●*claro como el* ~, obvious; *estar con el* ~ *en el cuello,* to be up to one's neck in it; *hacérsele la boca* ~ *a uno,* to make one's mouth water; *nunca digas de esta* ~ *no beberé,* never say never; *(parturienta) romper aguas,* to break one's water bag. ■ ~ *corriente,* running water; ~ *de colonia,* (eau de) cologne; ~ *dulce,* fresh water; ~ *potable,* drinking water; ~ *salada,* salt water; *aguas jurisdiccionales,* territorial waters; *aguas residuales,* sewage *sing.* ▲ *Takes el and un in sing.*

aguacate *m* avocado (pear).

aguacero *m* heavy shower, downpour.

aguado,-a *adj* watered down.

aguador,-ra *m,f* water carrier.

aguafiestas *mf inv* killjoy.

aguafuerte *m* ART etching.

aguantar(se) *t (contener)* to hold (back). **2** *(sostener)* to hold. **3** *(soportar)* to tolerate. − **4** *p (contenerse)* to restrain o.s. **5** *(resignarse)* to resign o.s.

aguante *m (paciencia)* patience. **2** *(fuerza)* strength.

aguar [22] *t* to water down. ●~ *la fiesta a algn.,* to spoil sb.'s fun.

aguardar *t-i* to wait (for), await: *no sé lo que me aguarda el futuro,* I don't know what the future will bring me.

aguardiente *m* liquor, brandy.

aguarrás *m* turpentine.

agudeza *f* sharpness. **2** *(viveza)* wit. **3** *(ingenio)* witticism.

agudizar(se) [4] *t-p (afilar)* to sharpen. **2** *(enfermedad)* to worsen.

agudo,-a *adj (afilado)* sharp. **2** *(dolor)* acute. **3** *(ingenioso)* witty. **4** *(voz)* high-pitched. **5** *(palabra)* oxytone.

agüero *m* omen.

aguijón *m* ZOOL sting. **2** BOT thorn, prickle. **3** *fig (estímulo)* sting, spur.

aguijonear *t* to goad. **2** *fig* to spur on.

águila *f* eagle. ▲ *Takes el and un in sing.*

aguileño,-a *adj* aquiline: *nariz aguileña,* hook nose.

aguilucho *m* eaglet.

aguinaldo *m* Christmas bonus.

aguja *f* needle. **2** *(de reloj)* hand. **3** *(de tocadiscos)* stylus. **4** ARQ steeple. **5** *(de tren)* point, US switch. ●*buscar una* ~ *en un pajar,* to look for a needle in a haystack.

agujerear *t* to pierce, perforate.

agujero *m* hole.

agujetas *fpl* stiffness *sing.*

aguzar [4] *t (afilar)* to sharpen. **2** *(estimular)* to spur on. ●~ *el oído,* to prick up one's ears.

ahí *adv* there, in that place. ●*de* ~ *que,* hence, therefore; *por* ~, *(lugar)* round there; *(aproximadamente)* more or less.

ahijado,-a *m,f* godchild; *m* godson, *f* goddaughter.

ahijar(se) [15] *t-p* to adopt.

ahínco *m* eagerness: *con* ~, eagerly.

ahíto,-a *adj (de comida)* stuffed. **2** *(harto)* fed up. − **3** *m* indigestion.

ahogado,-a *adj* drowned. **2** *(sitio)* stuffy. − **3** *m,f* drowned person.

ahogar(se) [7] *t* to drown. **2** *(plantas)* to soak. **3** *fig (reprimir)* to stifle: ~ *las lágrimas,* to hold back one's tears. − **4** *p* to be drowned. **5** *(sofocarse)* to choke. **6** *(motor)* to be flooded. ●*fig* ~*se en un vaso de agua,* to make a mountain out of a molehill.

ahogo *m (al respirar)* breathing trouble. **2** *(congoja)* anguish. **3** *(penuria)* financial difficulty.

ahondar *t* to deepen. − **2** *t-i* to go deep: ~ *en un problema,* to examine a problem in depth.

ahora *adv* now. **2** *(hace un momento)* a while ago. **3** *(dentro de un momento)* shortly. ●~ *bien,* but, however; ~ *o nunca,* now or never; *hasta* ~, until now, so far; *por* ~, for the time being.

ahorcado,-a *m,f* hanged person.

ahorcar(se) [1] *t-p* to hang (o.s.).

ahorrador,-ra *adj* thrifty.

ahorrar *t* to save. **2** *(evitar)* to spare.

ahorros *mpl* savings. ■ *caja de* ~, savings bank.

ahuecar [1] *t* to hollow out. **2** *(descompactar)* to fluff out. **3** *(voz)* to deepen. ●*fam* ~ *el ala,* to clear off.

ahumado,-a *adj* smoked; *(bacon)* smoky. − **2** *m (proceso)* smoking.

ahumar [16] *t-i* to smoke.

ahuyentar *t* to drive/scare away.

airarse [15] *p* to get angry.

aire *m* air. **2** *(viento)* wind: *hace* ~, it's windy. **3** *(aspecto)* air, appearance. **4** *(estilo)* style. **5** MÚS air, melody. ● *al* ~ *libre,* in the open air, outdoors; *cam-*

biar de aires, to change one's surroundings; *darse aires,* to put on airs; *saltar por los aires,* to blow up. ■ ~ *acondicionado,* air conditioning.

airear(se) *t (ventilar)* to air. 2 *(un asunto)* to publicize. − 3 *p* to take some fresh air.

airoso,-a *adj (lugar)* windy. 2 *(persona)* graceful. •*salir* ~, to be successful *(de, in)*.

aislado,-a *adj* isolated. 2 TÉC insulated.

aislamiento *m* isolation. 2 TÉC insulation.

aislante *adj* insulating. − 2 *m* insulator.

aislar(se) [15] *t* to isolate. 2 TÉC to insulate. − 3 *p* to isolate o.s. *(de,* from).

¡ajá! *interj* good!

ajar(se) *t* to spoil. − 2 *p (piel)* to become wrinkled.

ajedrez *m* chess.

ajenjo *m* BOT wormwood. 2 *(licor)* absinthe.

ajeno,-a *adj* another's: *jugar en campo* ~, to play away from home. 2 *(distante)* detached: ~ *a la conversación,* not involved in the conversation. 3 *(impropio)* inappropriate.

ajetreado,-a *adj* busy, hectic.

ajetreo *m* activity, bustle.

ají *m* AM red pepper, chili.

ajillo *m al* ~, fried with garlic.

ajo *m* garlic. •*fig estar en el* ~, to be in on it. ■ *cabeza de* ~, head of garlic; *diente de* ~, clove of garlic.

ajuar *m (de novia)* trousseau. 2 *(de bebé)* layette. 3 *(muebles)* household furniture.

ajustado,-a *adj (justo)* right. 2 *(apretado)* tight, close-fitting.

ajustar(se) *t (adaptar)* to adjust; TÉC to fit. 2 *(ceñir)* to fit tight. 3 *(acordar)* to arrange. − 4 *p (ceñirse)* to fit. 5 *(ponerse de acuerdo)* to come to an agreement. •COM ~ *cuentas,* to settle up; *fig* to settle an old score.

ajuste *m* adjustment; TÉC assembly. 2 COM settlement. ■ TV *carta de* ~, test card; *fig de cuentas,* settling of scores.

ajusticiar [12] *t* to execute.

al *contraction of a + el.*

ala *f* wing. 2 *(de sombrero)* brim. 3 *(de hélice)* blade. 4 DEP winger. •*cortarle las alas a algn.,* to clip sb.'s wings; *dar alas a,* to encourage.

alabanza *f* praise.

alabar(se) *t* to praise. − 2 *p* to boast.

alabastro *m* alabaster.

alacena *f* cupboard.

alacrán *m* ZOOL scorpion.

alado,-a *adj* winged.

alambicar [1] *t* to distil. 2 *fig (estilo)* to make over-subtle.

alambique *m* still.

alambrado,-a *adj* wire fenced. − 2 *f* wire fence.

alambrar *t* to fence (off) with wire.

alambre *m* wire.

alameda *f* poplar grove. 2 *(paseo)* avenue.

álamo *m* poplar.

alarde *m* display. •*hacer* ~ *de,* to flaunt, show off.

alardear *i* to boast.

alargado,-a *adj* long.

alargar(se) [7] *t* to lengthen. 2 *(estirar)* to stretch. 3 *(prolongar)* to prolong. 4 *(dar)* to hand, pass. − 5 *p* to lengthen.

alarido *m* screech, yell.

alarma *f* alarm. ■ *falsa* ~, false alarm.

alarmante *adj* alarming.

alarmar(se) *t* to alarm. − 2 *p* to be alarmed.

alarmista *mf* alarmist.

alba *f* dawn, daybreak. 2 REL alb. ▲ *Takes el and un in sing.*

albacea *mf* JUR *m* executor, *f* executrix.

albahaca *f* basil.

albañil *m* mason, bricklayer.

albarán *m* COM delivery note.

albaricoque *m* apricot.

albedrío *m* will. ■ *libre* ~, free will.

alberca *f* reservoir.

albergar(se) [7] *t* to lodge, house. 2 *(sentimientos)* to cherish. − 3 *p* to stay.

albergue *m* hostel. 2 *(refugio)* shelter. ■ ~ *juvenil,* youth hostel.

albino,-a *adj-m,f* albino.

albóndiga, albondiguilla *f* meatball.

albor *m (luz)* dawn. 2 *pl (comienzo)* beginning *sing.*

alborada *f* dawn, break of day. 2 MIL reveille.

alborear *i* to dawn.

albornoz *m* bathrobe.

alborotado,-a *adj* agitated, excited. 2 *(desordenado)* untidy. 3 *(irreflexivo)* reckless.

alborotar(se) *t* to agitate, excite. 2 *(desordenar)* to make untidy. 3 *(sublevar)* to incite to rebel. − 4 *i* to make a racket. − 5 *p* to get excited.

alboroto *m (gritería)* din, racket. 2 *(desorden)* uproar, commotion.

alborozar [4] *t* to delight.

alborozo *m* joy, merriment.

¡albricias! *interj* great!

albufera *f* lagoon.

álbum *m* album.

albur *m* chance.

alcachofa *f* artichoke.

alcahuete,-a *m,f m* procurer, *f* procuress.

alcalde *m* mayor.

alcaldesa *f* lady mayor. **2** *(mujer del alcalde)* mayoress.

alcaldía *f* *(cargo)* mayorship. **2** *(oficina)* mayor's office.

alcalino,-a *adj* alkaline.

alcance *m* reach: *al ~ de uno,* within one's reach. **2** *(de arma)* range. **3** *(trascendencia)* scope, importance. **4** *(inteligencia)* intelligence: *persona de pocos alcances,* person of low intelligence.

alcancía *f* money-box.

alcanfor *m* camphor.

alcantarilla *f* sewer.

alcantarillado *m* sewer system.

alcanzar [4] *t* to reach; *(persona)* to catch up with: *~ a ver,* to see; *~ a oír,* to hear. **2** *(pasar)* to pass, hand over: *alcánzame el pan,* pass me the bread. **3** *(entender)* to understand. **4** *(conseguir)* to attain, achieve. **5** *(ser suficiente)* to be sufficient/enough *(para,* for).

alcaparra *f* caper.

alcatraz *m* *(ave)* gannet.

alcázar *m* *(fortaleza)* fortress. **2** *(palacio)* palace.

alce *m* ZOOL elk, moose.

alcista *adj* *(en bolsa)* bullish. **– 2** *mf* bull.

alcoba *f* bedroom.

alcohol *m* alcohol.

alcohólico,-a *adj-m,f* alcoholic.

alcoholímetro *m* breathalyzer®.

alcoholismo *m* alcoholism.

alcoholizar(se) *t-p* [4] to alcoholize. **– 2** *p* to become an alcoholic.

alcornoque *m* BOT cork oak. **2** *fig* blockhead.

alcurnia *f* lineage, ancestry.

aldaba *f* *(llamador)* door knocker. **2** *(pestillo)* bolt, crossbar.

aldea *f* hamlet, village.

aldeano,-a *m,f* villager.

aleación *f* alloy.

aleatorio,-a *adj* random, chance.

aleccionar *t* to teach, instruct.

alegación *f* allegation, plea.

alegar [7] *t* to allege, plead.

alegato *m* *(argumento)* claim, plea. **2** *(razonamiento)* reasoned allegation.

alegoría *f* allegory.

alegrar(se) *t* to make happy. **2** *(avivar)* to brighten (up). **– 3** *p* to be happy. **4** *fam* to get tipsy.

alegre *adj* happy. **2** *(color)* bright. **3** *(música)* lively. **4** *(espacio)* cheerful. **5** *(borracho)* tipsy. ■ *fam ~ de cascos,* scatterbrained.

alegría *f* happiness. **2** *(irresponsabilidad)* irresponsibility.

alejado,-a *adj* far away, remote.

alejamiento *m* *(separación)* distance, separation. **2** *(enajenación)* estrangement.

alejar(se) *t* to remove, move away. **2** *(separar)* to separate, estrange. **– 3** *p* to go/move away.

¡aleluya! *interj* hallelujah, alleluia.

alentador,-ra *adj* encouraging.

alentar [27] *t* to encourage.

alergia *f* allergy.

alérgico,-a *adj* allergic.

alero *m* ARQ eaves *pl.*

alerta *adv* on the alert. **– 2** *f* alert. **– 3** *m* alert, warning. **– 4** *interj* look out! ●*dar la (voz de) ~,* to give the alert.

alertar *t* to alert *(de,* to).

aleta *f* *(de pescado)* fin. **2** ANAT wing.

aletargar(se) [7] *t* to make drowsy. **– 2** *p* to get drowsy.

aletear *i* to flutter.

alevín *m* *(pescado)* fry, young fish. **2** *(principiante)* beginner.

alevosía *f* treachery, perfidy.

alfabético,-a *adj* alphabetic(al).

alfabeto *m* alphabet.

alfalfa *f* alfalfa, lucerne.

alfarería *f* pottery.

alfarero,-a *m,f* potter.

alféizar *m* windowsill.

alfeñique *m* CULIN sugar paste. **2** *fig* weakling.

alférez *m* second lieutenant, ensign.

alfil *m* *(ajedrez)* bishop.

alfiler *m* *(costura)* pin. **2** *(joya)* brooch. ● *no caber ni un ~,* to be crammed full. ■ *~ de corbata,* tiepin.

alfilerazo *m* pinprick.

alfiletero *m* pin box.

alfombra *f* carpet, rug. **2** *(de baño)* bathmat. **3** *(alfombrilla)* rug, mat.

alfombrar *t* to carpet.

alforjas *fpl* saddlebag *sing.* **2** *fig* provisions.

alga *f* BOT alga; *(marina)* seaweed. ▲ *Takes el and un in sing.*

algarabía *f* hubbub.

algarroba *f* *(fruto)* carob bean. **2** *(planta)* vetch.

álgebra *f* algebra. ▲ *Takes* **el** *and* **un** *in sing.*

álgido,-a *adj (frío)* icy. **2** *fig* culminating: **el punto** ~, the height.

algo *pron indef* something; *(negación, interrogación)* anything: **vamos a tomar** ~, let's have something to eat/drink. — **2** *adv (un poco)* quite, somewhat: **te queda** ~ **grande,** it's a bit too big for you.

algodón *m* cotton. ■ ~ **hidrófilo,** cotton wool.

algodonero,-a *adj* cotton.

algoritmo *m* algorithm.

alguacil *m* bailiff.

alguien *pron* somebody, someone; *(interrogativo, negativo)* anybody, anyone.

algún *adj* → **alguno,-a.** ▲ *Before sing masculine nouns.*

alguno,-a *adj* some; *(interrogativo, negativo)* any: **alguna vez,** sometimes; ~ **que otro,** some, a few; **no vino persona alguna,** nobody came. — **2** *pron indef* someone, somebody; *(interrogativo, negativo)* anybody.

alhaja *f* jewel. **2** *(cosa)* valuable thing. •*irón* **menuda** ~, he's a fine one!

alhelí *m* wallflower. ▲ *pl* **alhelíes.**

aliado,-a *adj* allied. — **2** *m,f* ally.

alianza *f (pacto)* alliance. **2** *(anillo)* wedding ring.

aliar(se) [13] *t-p* to ally.

alias *adv-m inv* alias.

alicaído,-a *adj fig* weak. **2** *(deprimido)* depressed.

alicates *mpl* pliers.

aliciente *m* incentive, inducement.

alienación *f* alienation.

alienar *t* to alienate.

aliento *m* breath(ing). **2** *(ánimo)* spirit, courage.

aligerar *t (descargar)* to lighten. **2** *(aliviar)* to alleviate. **3** *(acelerar)* to speed up.

alijo *m* contraband.

alimaña *f* vermin.

alimentación *f (acción)* feeding. **2** *(alimento)* food.

alimentar(se) *t* to feed: **el pescado alimenta mucho,** fish is very nutritious. **2** *fig (pasiones etc.)* to encourage. — **3** *p* ~**se de,** to live on.

alimenticio,-a *adj* nutritious.

alimento *m* food.

alinear(se) *t-p* to align, line up.

aliñar *t* to season; *(ensalada)* to dress.

aliño *m* seasoning; *(ensalada)* dressing.

alisar *t* to smooth.

alistamiento *m* MIL enlistment, enrolment.

alistar(se) *t-p* MIL to enlist.

aliviar(se) [12] *t (aligerar)* to lighten. **2** *fig (enfermedad, dolor)* to relieve. **3** *(consolar)* to comfort. **4** *(apresurar)* to hurry. — **5** *p* to get better.

alivio *m (aligeramiento)* lightening. **2** *(mejoría)* relief. **3** *(consuelo)* comfort.

aljibe *m* cistern.

allá *adv (lugar)* there: **más** ~, further (on). **2** *(tiempo)* back: ~ **por los años sesenta,** back in the sixties. ● ~ **tú/vosotros,** that's your problem. ■ **el más** ~, the beyond.

allanamiento *m* ~ **de morada,** unlawful entry; *(robo)* housebreaking.

allanar(se) *t* to level, flatten. **2** *(dificultad etc.)* to overcome. **3** *(pacificar)* to pacify, subdue. — **4** *p (acceder)* to agree.

allegado,-a *adj* close. — **2** *m,f* relative.

allegar(se) [7] *t* to gather, collect. — **2** *p (acceder)* to agree.

allende *adv fml* beyond.

allí *adv (lugar)* there: ~ **abajo/arriba,** down/up there. **2** *(tiempo)* then, at that moment.

alma *f* soul. ●**no había ni un** ~, there was not a soul; **ser el** ~ **de la fiesta,** to be the life and soul of the party. ▲ *Takes* **el** *and* **un** *in sing.*

almacén *m* warehouse. **2** *(habitación)* storeroom. **3** *pl* department store *sing.*

almacenaje *m* storage, warehousing.

almacenar *t* to store, warehouse. **2** *(acumular)* to store up.

almanaque *m* almanac.

almeja *f* clam.

almendra *f* almond. ■ ~ **garapiñada,** sugared almond.

almendro *m* almond tree.

almiar *m* haystack.

almíbar *m* syrup.

almibarar *t* to preserve in syrup. **2** *fig* to sweeten.

almidón *m* starch.

almidonar *t* to starch.

alminar *m* minaret.

almirante *m* admiral.

almizcle *m* musk.

almohada *f* pillow. •*fam* **consultar algo con la** ~, to sleep on sth.

almohadilla *f* small cushion. **2** COST sewing cushion. **3** *(tampón)* inkpad.

almohadón *m* cushion.

almorzar [50] *i* to (have) lunch. — **2** *t* to have for lunch.

almuecín, almuédano *m* muezzin.
almuerzo *m* lunch.
alocado,-a *adj* foolish, wild, reckless.
alocución *f* address.
alojamiento *m* lodging, accommodation.
alojar(se) *t* to lodge. — **2** *p* to be lodged, stay.
alondra *f* lark.
alpargata *f* rope-soled sandal, espadrille.
alpinismo *m* mountaineering.
alpinista *mf* mountaineer, mountain climber.
alpiste *m* birdseed.
alquilar *t* to hire; *(casa)* to rent.
alquiler *m* hiring; *(casa)* renting: *de ~,* for hire/rent. **2** *(cuota)* hire; *(casa)* rent.
alquimia *f* alchemy.
alquimista *mf* alchemist.
alquitrán *m* tar.
alrededor *adv (lugar)* (a)round: *mira ~,* look around. — **2** *mpl* surrounding area *sing.* •*~ de,* around, about.
alta *f (a un enfermo)* discharge: *dar de ~,* to discharge from hospital. **2** *(entrada, admisión)* admission: *darse de ~ en un club,* to join a club. ▲ *Takes el and un in sing.*
altanería *f* arrogance.
altanero,-a *adj* arrogant.
altar *m* altar.
altavoz *m* loudspeaker.
alteración *f (cambio)* alteration. **2** *(excitación)* agitation. **3** *(alboroto)* disturbance. •*~ del orden público,* breach of the peace.
alterar(se) *t (cambiar)* to alter, change. **2** *(enfadar)* to annoy. **3** *(preocupar)* to disturb, upset. — **4** *p (cambiar)* to change. **5** *(deteriorarse)* to go bad/off. **6** *(enfadarse)* to lose one's temper.
altercado *m* argument.
alternar *t-i (sucederse)* to alternate. — **2** *i* to socialize. **3** *(en salas de fiesta, bar)* to entertain.
alternativa *f* alternative, option.
alternativo,-a *adj* alternate.
alterne *m (copeo)* drinking. ■ *bar de ~,* hostess bar.
alteza *f* highness.
altibajos *mpl* ups and downs: *los ~ de la vida,* the ups and downs of life.
altillo *m* ARQ attic. **2** GEOG hillock.
altiplanicie *f,* **altiplano** *m* high plateau.
altísimo,-a *adj* very high. — **2** *m* REL *El Altísimo,* The Almighty.
altisonante *adj* grandiloquent.

altitud *f* height, altitude.
altivez *f* haughtiness, arrogance.
altivo,-a *adj* haughty, arrogant.
alto,-a *adj* high: *tacón ~,* high heel. **2** *(estatura)* tall: *un hombre ~,* a tall man. **3** *(voz, sonido)* loud: *en voz alta,* aloud. — **4** *m (elevación)* height, hillock. **5** *(parada)* halt, stop: *dar el ~,* to call to a halt, stop. — **6** *adv* high (up). **7** *(voz)* loud, loudly. — **8** *interj* halt!, stop! ■ *alta fidelidad,* high fidelity; *alta mar,* high seas; *altas horas,* late at night; *~ horno,* blast furnace; *clase alta,* upper class.
altramuz *m* lupin.
altruismo *m* altruism.
altruista *mf* altruist.
altura *f* height. **2** *(altitud)* altitude. **3** *(nivel)* level. **4** *fig* elevation, excellence. **5** *pl* REL heavens. •*fig a la ~ de las circunstancias,* worthy of the occasion.
alubia *f* bean.
alucinación *f* hallucination.
alucinado,-a *adj arg* amazed, spaced out.
alucinante *adj* hallucinatory. **2** *arg* mind-blowing.
alucinar *i arg* to be amazed/spaced out.
alucinógeno,-a *adj* hallucinogenic. — **2** *m* hallucinogen.
alud *m* avalanche.
aludir *i* to allude (*a,* to).
alumbrado *m* lighting, lights *pl.* ■ *~ público,* street lighting.
alumbramiento *m fig* childbirth.
alumbrar(se) *t* to give light to, illuminate. **2** *(enseñar)* to enlighten. — **3** *i* give light. **4** *(parir)* to give birth. — **5** *p fam (embriagarse)* to get tipsy.
aluminio *m* aluminium.
alumnado *m (de colegio)* pupils *pl;* *(de universidad)* student body.
alumno,-a *m,f (de colegio)* pupil; *(de universidad)* student.
alunizar [4] *i* to land on the moon.
alusión *f* allusion, reference.
alusivo,-a *adj* allusive, referring (*a,* to).
aluvión *m* flood.
alza *f (de precios)* rise, increase. **2** *(de rifle)* backsight. ▲ *Takes el and un in sing.*
alzacuello *m* clerical collar.
alzada *f (caballo)* height. **2** JUR appeal to a higher administrative body.
alzamiento *m* raising, lifting. **2** *(rebelión)* uprising, insurrection.
alzaprima *f (palanca)* lever. **2** *(cuña)* wedge.

alzar(se) [4] *t (levantar)* to raise, lift. **2** *(construir)* to build. **3** *(quitar)* to remove: ~ *la mesa,* to clear the table. **4** AM *(refugiar)* to shelter. – **5** *p (levantarse)* to rise, get up. **6** *(sublevarse)* to rise, rebel. **7** AM *(refugiarse)* to take shelter. ●*~se con,* to run away with.

ama *f (señora)* lady of the house. **2** *(propietaria)* landlady. ■ ~ *de casa,* housewife; ~ *de llaves,* housekeeper; ~ *de leche,* wet nurse. ▲ *Takes el and un in sing.*

amabilidad *f* kindness, affability.

amable *adj* kind, nice.

amado,-a *m,f* (be)loved.

amadrinar *t* to be the godmother of.

amaestrado,-a *adj* trained: *ratón ~,* performing mouse.

amaestrar *t* to train.

amagar(se) [7] *t (dejar ver)* to show signs of. **2** *(amenazar)* to threaten: *le amaga un gran riesgo,* great danger is in store for him. **3** *(fingir)* to simulate. – **4** *i (ser inminente)* to threaten, be imminent. **5** *(enfermedad)* to show the first signs.

amago *m* hint, symptom.

amainar *i (viento)* to die down. **2** *fig* to calm down.

amalgama *f* amalgam.

amalgamar *t* to amalgamate.

amamantar *t* to breast-feed, suckle.

amanecer [43] *i* to dawn. **2** *(estar, aparecer)* to be/appear at dawn. – **3** *m* dawn, daybreak: *al ~,* at daybreak. ▲ *1 only used in the 3rd pers. It does not take a subject.*

amanerado,-a *adj* affected, mannered.

amansar *t* to tame.

amante *adj* loving, fond *(de,* of). – **2** *mf* lover.

amañar(se) *t (falsear)* to fiddle, cook up. – **2** *p fam* to manage.

amaño *m* skill. **2** *pl* machinations.

amapola *f* poppy.

amar *t* to love.

amarar *t* to land at sea.

amargado,-a *adj* embittered, resentful. – **2** *m,f* bitter person.

amargar [7]*i* to taste bitter. – **2** *t* to make bitter. **3** *fig* to spoil: ~ *la existencia a algn.,* to make sb.'s life a misery.

amargo,-a *adj* bitter. **2** *fig (carácter)* sour.

amargura *f* bitterness. **2** *(dolor)* sorrow, grief.

amariconado,-a * *adj* queer*.

amarillento,-a *adj* yellowish.

amarillo,-a *adj-m* yellow.

amarra *f* mooring cable.

amarrar *t* to tie, fasten. **2** MAR to moor.

amasar *t* CULIN to knead; *(cemento)* to mix. **2** *(reunir)* to amass. **3** *fam fig* to cook up.

amateur *adj-mf* amateur.

amazona *f* Amazon. **2** *(jinete)* horsewoman.

ambages *mpl hablar sin ~,* to speak plainly.

ámbar *m* amber.

ambición *f* ambition, aspiration.

ambicionar *t* to want: *siempre ambicionó ser rico,* it was always his ambition to be rich.

ambicioso,-a *adj* ambitious.

ambidextro,-a *adj* ambidextrous.

ambientación *f* setting.

ambiental *adj* environmental.

ambiente *adj* environmental. – **2** *m* environment, atmosphere. ■ *temperatura ~,* room teperature.

ambigüedad *f* ambiguity.

ambiguo,-a *adj* ambiguous.

ámbito *m (espacio)* sphere: *en el ~ nacional,* nationwide. **2** *(marco)* field: *en el ~ de la informática,* in the computer science field.

ambivalencia *f* ambivalence.

ambos,-as *adj-pron pl* both.

ambulancia *f* ambulance.

ambulante *adj* itinerant, travelling.

ambulatorio *m* surgery, clinic.

amedrentar *t* to frighten, scare.

amén *m* amen. ●~ *de,* besides, in addition to.

amenaza *f* threat, menace.

amenazar [4] *t-i* to threaten: *fig el edificio amenaza ruina,* the building is on the verge of collapse.

amenguar [22] *t (disminuir)* to reduce. **2** *(deshonrar)* to dishonour, disgrace.

amenidad *f* amenity, pleasantness.

amenizar [4] *t* to make pleasant, liven up.

ameno,-a *adj* pleasant, entertaining.

americana *f* jacket.

americanismo *m* Spanish-American word/expression.

ametralladora *f* machine gun.

ametrallar *t* to machine-gun.

amianto *m* asbestos *inv.*

amigable *adj* amicable, friendly.

amígdala *f* tonsil.

amigdalitis *f inv* tonsillitis *inv.*

amigo,-a *adj* friendly. **2** *(aficionado)* fond *(de,* of). – **3** *m,f* friend. **4** *(novio)* *m* boyfriend, *f* girlfriend. ●*hacerse ~ de,* to make friends with.

amilanar(se) *t* to frighten. – **2** *p* to become depressed.

aminorar *t* to reduce. ●*~ el paso,* to slow down.

amistad *f* friendship. **2** *pl* friends.

amistoso,-a *adj* friendly. – **2** *amistosamente adv* amicably.

amnistía *f* amnesty.

amnistiar [13] *t* to amnesty.

amo *m (señor)* master. **2** *(dueño)* owner.

amodorrarse *p* to become drowsy.

amolar [31] *t* to sharpen. **2** *fam* to bother, annoy.

amoldar(se) *t* to adapt, adjust. – **2** *p* to adapt o.s.

amonestación *f (reprensión)* reproof. **2** *(advertencia)* warning.

amonestar *t (reprender)* to reprove. **2** *(advertir)* to warn.

amoniaco, amoníaco *m* ammonia.

amontonar(se) *t* to heap/pile (up). – **2** *p* to heap/pile (up). **3** *(gente)* to crowd together.

amor *m* love. **2** *(en tarea)* care. **3** *pl (asuntos)* love affair *sing.* ●*con/de mil amores,* willingly; *hacer el ~,* to make love. ■ *~ propio,* self-esteem.

amoratado,-a *adj (de frío)* blue with cold. **2** *(de un golpe)* black and blue.

amordazar [4] *t (persona)* to gag; *(perro)* to muzzle.

amorío *m* love affair.

amoroso,-a *adj* loving, affectionate.

amortajar *t* to shroud.

amortiguador *m* AUTO shock absorber. **2** TÉC damper.

amortiguar [22] *t* to alleviate. **2** *(golpe etc.)* to deaden. **3** *(sonido)* to muffle.

amortización *f (pago)* redemption. **2** *(recuperación)* amortization.

amortizar [4] *t (pagar)* to redeem. **2** *(recuperar)* to amortize.

amotinado,-a *m,f* mutineer, rioter.

amotinar(se) *t* to incite to rebellion. – **2** *p* to rebel, mutiny.

amparar(se) *t* to protect, shelter. – **2** *p* to take shelter, protect o.s. **3** *(acogerse)* to avail o.s. of the protection (*en,* of).

amparo *m* protection, shelter, support.

amperio *m* ampère.

ampliación *f* enlargement. **2** ARQ extension. ■ *~ de capital,* increase in capital; *~ de estudios,* furthering of studies.

ampliar [13] *t* to enlarge, extend. **2** *(estudios)* to further.

amplificación *f* amplification.

amplificar [1] *t* to amplify.

amplio,-a *adj (extenso)* ample. **2** *(espacioso)* roomy. **3** *(ancho)* wide.

amplitud *f (extensión)* extent. **2** *(espacio)* room, space. ■ *~ de miras,* broadmindedness.

ampolla *f* MED blister. **2** *(burbuja)* bubble. **3** *(para líquidos)* ampoule.

ampuloso,-a *adj* inflated, pompous.

amputación *f* amputation.

amueblar *t* to furnish.

amuermado,-a *adj fam (aburrido)* bored. **2** *(atontado)* dopey.

amuermar *t fam (aburrir)* to bore. **2** *(atontar)* to make feel dopey.

amuleto *m* amulet. ■ *~ de la suerte,* lucky charm.

amurallar *t* to wall.

anacoreta *mf* anchorite.

anacronismo *m* anachronism.

ánade *m* duck.

anagrama *m* anagram.

anal *adj* anal.

anales *mpl* annals.

analfabetismo *m* illiteracy.

analfabeto,-a *adj-m,f* illiterate.

analgésico,-a *adj-m* analgesic.

análisis *m inv* analysis. ■ *~ de orina,* urine analysis; *~ de sangre,* blood test.

analítico,-a *adj* analytic(al).

analizar [4] *t* to analyse.

analogía *f* analogy.

análogo,-a *adj* analogous, similar.

ananá, ananás *f* pineapple. ▲ *The pl of ananá is ananaes and the pl of ananás is ananases.*

anaquel *m* shelf.

anaranjado,-a *adj-m* orange.

anarquía *f* anarchy.

anárquico,-a *adj* anarchic(al).

anarquista *adj-mf* anarchist.

anatomía *f* anatomy.

anca *f* haunch. ■ *ancas de rana,* frogs' legs. ▲ *Takes el and un in sing.*

ancestral *adj* ancestral.

ancho,-a *adj* broad, wide. **2** *(prenda)* loose-fitting. – **3** *m* breadth, width. ●*fam a sus anchas,* comfortable, at one's ease; *fam quedarse tan ~,* to behave as if nothing had happened.

anchoa *f* anchovy.

anchura *f* breadth, width.

anciano,-a *adj* old, aged. – **2** *m,f* old people.

ancla *f* anchor. ▲ *Takes el and un in sing.*

anclar *i* to anchor.

áncora *f* anchor. ▲ *Takes el and un in sing.*

andadas *fpl fam volver a las* ~, to go back to one's old tricks.

andaderas *fpl* baby-walker *sing.*

andadura *f* walking.

andamio *m* scaffolding.

andanada *f* MAR broadside. 2 *(reprensión)* reprimand. 3 *(en plaza de toros)* grand stand.

andante *adj* walking. 2 MÚS andante. ■ *caballero* ~, knight errant.

andanza *f* event. 2 *pl* adventures.

andar [64] *i (moverse)* to walk: *andaba por la calle principal,* I was walking along the main street. 2 *(trasladarse algo)* to move: *este coche anda despacio,* this car goes very slowly. 3 *(funcionar)* to work, run, go: *este reloj no anda,* this watch doesn't work. 4 *(estar)* to be: *anda por los cincuenta,* he's around fifty years old. – 8 *m* walk, pace. ●~ *de puntillas,* to tiptoe; ~/~*se con cuidado,* to be careful; *fig* ~*se por las ramas,* to beat about the bush.

andariego,-a *adj* roving, walking. – 2 *m,f* rover, walker.

andarín,-ina *m,f* good walker.

andas *fpl* portable platform *sing.* ●*fig llevar a algn. en* ~, to pamper sb.

andén *m* platform.

andrajo *m* rag, tatter.

andrajoso,-a *adj* ragged, in tatters.

andrógino,-a *adj* androgynous, androgyne.

andurriales *mpl* out-of-the-way place *sing.*

anécdota *f* anecdote.

anegar(se) [7] *t (inundar)* to flood. 2 *(ahogar)* to drown. – 3 *p (inundarse)* to be flooded. 4 *(ahogarse)* to be drowned.

anejo,-a *adj* attached, joined (*a,* to)

anemia *f* an(a)emia.

anestesia *f* an(a)esthesia.

anestesiar *t* [12] to an(a)esthetize.

anestésico,-a *adj-m* an(a)esthetic.

anexar *t* to annex.

anexión *f* annexion, annexation.

anexo,-a *adj* attached, joined (*a,* to). – 2 *m* annex.

anfeta *m arg* → **anfetamina.**

anfetamina *f* amphetamine.

anfibio,-a *adj* amphibious. – 2 *m* amphibian.

anfiteatro *m* amphitheatre.

anfitrión,-ona *m,f m* host, *f* hostess.

ánfora *f* amphora.

ángel *m* angel. ●*tener* ~, to be charming. ■ ~ *custodio/de la guarda,* guardian angel; DEP *salto del* ~, swallow dive.

angelical, angélico,-a *adj* angelic(al).

angina *f* angina. ●*tener anginas,* to have a sore throat. ■ ~ *de pecho,* angina pectoris.

anglicano,-a *adj-m,f* Anglican.

anglófilo,-a *adj-m,f* Anglophile.

anglosajón,-ona *adj-m,f* Anglo-Saxon.

angosto,-a *adj* narrow.

angostura *f* narrowness.

anguila *f* eel.

angula *f* elver.

angular *adj* angular. ■ *piedra* ~, cornerstone.

ángulo *m* angle. 2 *(rincón)* corner.

angustia *f* anguish, affliction, distress.

angustiar(se) [12] *t* to distress. 2 *(preocupar)* to worry. – 3 *p (afligirse)* to become distressed. 4 *(preocuparse)* to worry.

angustioso,-a *adj* distressing.

anhelante *adj* longing, yearning.

anhelar *i* to long/yearn for.

anhelo *m* longing, yearning.

anheloso,-a *adj* longing.

anidar *i (pájaro)* to nest, nestle. – 2 *t fig* to shelter.

anilla *f (aro)* ring. 2 *pl* DEP rings.

anillar *t (dar forma)* to make into a ring. 2 *(sujetar)* to ring.

anillo *m* ring. ●*venir como* ~ *al dedo,* to be opportune. ■ ~ *de boda,* wedding ring.

ánima *f* soul. ▲ *Takes el and un in sing.*

animación *f (actividad)* activity. 2 *(viveza)* liveliness.

animado,-a *adj (movido)* animated, lively. 2 *(concurrido)* full of people.

animadversión *f* ill feeling.

animal *adj* animal. 2 *fig (persona)* stupid. – 3 *m* animal. 4 *fig (persona)* blockhead. ■ ~ *de carga,* beast of burden.

animalada *f* stupidity.

animar(se) *t (alegrar a algn.)* to cheer up. 2 *(alegrar algo)* to brighten up. 3 *(alentar)* to encourage. – 4 *p (persona)* to cheer up. 5 *(fiesta etc.)* to brighten up. 6 *(decidirse)* to make up one's mind.

anímico,-a *adj estado* ~, frame/state of mind.

ánimo *m (espíritu)* spirit; *(mente)* mind. 2 *(intención)* intention, purpose. 3 *(valor)* courage. – 4 *interj* cheer up!

animosidad *f* animosity, ill will.

animoso,-a *adj* brave, courageous.
aniquilación *f* annihilation, destruction.
aniquilar *t* to annihilate, destroy.
anís *m* BOT anise. **2** *(bebida)* anisette.
aniversario *m* anniversary.
ano *m* anus.
anoche *adv* last night.
anochecer [43] *i* to get dark. **2** to be/ reach at nightfall: *anochecimos en Burgos,* we were in Burgos at dusk. — **3** *m* nightfall, dusk, evening. ▲ *1 only used in the 3rd person. It does not take a subject.*
anodino,-a *adj* MED anodyne. **2** *(ineficaz)* ineffective. **3** *(soso)* insipid, dull. — **4** *m* MED anodyne.
anomalía *f* anomaly.
anómalo,-a *adj* anomalous.
anonadar(se) *t* to overwhelm. — **2** *p* to be overwhelmed.
anonimato *m* anonymity.
anónimo,-a *adj* anonymous. — **2** *m (carta)* anonymous letter. **3** *(anonimato)* anonymity. ■ *sociedad anónima,* limited company, US incorporated company.
anorak *m* anorak. ▲ *pl* **anoraks**.
anorexia *f* anorexia.
anormal *adj* abnormal.
anotación *f* *(acotación)* annotation. **2** *(nota)* note.
anotar *t* *(acotar)* to annotate. **2** *(apuntar)* to take down, write.
anquilosado,-a *adj* anchylosed, ankylosed.
anquilosar(se) *t-p* to anchylose, ankylose.
ansia *f* *(sufrimiento)* anguish. **2** *(deseo)* eagerness, longing. ▲ *Takes el and un in sing.*
ansiar [13] *t* to long/yearn for.
ansiedad *f* anxiety.
ansioso,-a *adj* *(desasosegado)* anguished. **2** *(deseoso)* eager, longing *(por/de,* to).
antagónico,-a *adj* antagonistic.
antagonista *adj* antagonistic. — **2** *mf* antagonist.
antaño *adv* formerly, in olden times, long ago.
ante *prep* before, in the presence of. **2** *(considerando)* in the face of: ~ *estas circunstancias,* under the circumstances. — **3** *m* ZOOL elk, moose. **4** *(piel)* suede. ● ~ *todo, (primero)* first of all; *(por encima de)* above all.
anteanoche *adv* the night before last.
anteayer *adv* the day before yesterday.
antebrazo *m* forearm.
antecámara *f* antechamber.

antecedente *adj-m* antecedent. — **2** *mpl* record *sing.* ■ *antecedentes penales,* criminal record *sing.*
anteceder *t* to antecede, precede.
antecesor,-ra *m,f (en un cargo)* predecessor. **2** *(antepasado)* ancestor.
antedicho,-a *adj* aforesaid, aforementioned.
antelación *f* previousness ● *con* ~, in advance.
antemano *de* ~, *adv* beforehand.
antena *f* RAD TV aerial. **2** ANAT antenna.
anteojo *m* telescope. **2** *pl (binóculos)* binoculars. **3** *(gafas)* glasses, spectacles.
antepasado,-a *adj* foregone. — **2** *m* ancestor.
antepecho *m (pretil)* parapet. **2** *(de ventana)* windowsill.
antepenúltimo,-a *adj* antepenultimate.
anteponer [78] *t* to place before. ▲ *pp* *antepuesto,-a.*
anterior *adj* anterior, foregoing, former, previous: *el día* ~, the day before. — **2** *anteriormente adv* previously, before.
anterioridad *f* priority. ● *con* ~, prior to, before.
antes *adv (tiempo)* before, earlier. **2** *(lugar)* in front, before. — **3** *conj* ~ **(bien),** on the contrary. — **4** *adj* before. ● *cuanto* ~, as soon as possible.
antesala *f* anteroom, antechamber.
antiadherente *adj* nonstick.
antiaéreo,-a *adj* anti-aircraft.
antibiótico,-a *adj-m* antibiotic.
anticiclón *m* anticyclone, high pressure area.
anticipación *f* anticipation, advance. ● *con* ~, in advance.
anticipar(se) *t* to anticipate, advance, hasten. **2** *(dinero)* to advance. — **3** *p (llegar antes)* to occur before the regular time. **4** *(adelantarse)* to beat to it: *él se me anticipó,* he beat me to it.
anticipo *m* foretaste. **2** *(adelanto)* advance payment.
anticlerical *adj-mf* anticlerical.
anticoncepción *f* contraception.
anticonceptivo,-a *adj-m* contraceptive.
anticongelante *adj-m* antifreeze.
anticuado,-a *adj* antiquated, old-fashioned, obsolete, out-of-date.
anticuario *m* antiquary, antique dealer.
anticuerpo *m* antibody.
antídoto *m* antidote.
antifaz *m* mask.
antigualla *f* antique. **2** *(pasado de moda)* out-of-date object.

antigüedad *f (período)* antiquity. **2** *(en empleo)* seniority. **3** *pl* antiquities, antiques.

antiguo,-a *adj* ancient, old. **2** *(en empleo)* senior. **3** *(pasado)* old-fashioned. — **4** *mpl* the ancients. — **5** *antiguamente adv* anciently, in old times.

antílope *m* antelope.

antiniebla *adj inv luces* ~, foglamps.

antiparras *fpl fam* specs, glasses.

antipatía *f* antipathy, dislike, aversion.

antipático,-a *adj* disagreeable, unpleasant.

antipirético,-a *adj-m* antipyretic.

antípoda *adj* antipodean, antipodal. — **2** *mf* antipodean. — **3** *f (punto)* antipodes. ▲ *Often used in plural.*

antirreglamentario,-a *adj* against the rules.

antirrobo *adj inv* antitheft. ■ *alarma* ~, *(para casa)* burglar alarm; *(para coche)* antitheft device.

antítesis *f inv* antithesis.

antojadizo,-a *adj* capricious, fanciful.

antojarse *p (encapricharse)* to take a fancy to. **2** *(suponer)* to think, imagine. ▲ *Only used with the personal pronouns me, te, le, nos and os.*

antojo *m (capricho)* whim; *(de embarazada)* craving. **2** *(en la piel)* birthmark. ●*a su* ~, arbitrarily.

antología *f* anthology.

antónimo,-a *adj* antonymous. — **2** *m* antonym.

antorcha *f* torch.

antro *m fig* dump, hole.

antropología *f* anthropology.

anual *adj* annual.

anuario *m* yearbook.

anudar *t* to knot, tie. **2** *fig* to join, bring together.

anulación *f* annulment, cancellation.

anular *adj* ring-shaped. — **2** *m (dedo)* ~, ring finger. — **3** *t* to annul, cancel.

anunciación *f* Annunciation.

anunciar(se) [12] *t (avisar)* to announce. **2** *(hacer publicidad)* to advertise, advert. — **3** *p* to advertise o.s.

anuncio *m (aviso)* announcement. **2** *(publicidad)* advertisement. **3** *(cartel)* poster.

anverso *m* obverse.

anzuelo *m* fish-hook. **2** *fig* lure. ●*tragar/morder/picar el* ~, to swallow the bait.

añadido,-a *adj* added. — **2** *m* addition.

añadidura *f* addition. ●*por* ~, besides, in addition.

añadir *t* to add (*a*, to).

añejo,-a *adj (vino)* mature.

añicos *mpl* bits, shatters. ●*hacerse* ~, to be smashed.

año *m* year. **2** *pl* years, age *sing*: **tengo 20 años,** I'm 20 years old. ■ ~ *bisiesto,* leap year; *años luz,* light years.

añoranza *f* longing.

añorar *t* to long for, miss. — **2** *i* to pine.

aojar *t* to bewitch.

aorta *f* aorta.

apabullar *t (aplastar)* to crush, flatten. **2** *fig* to squelch, silence.

apacentar(se) [27] *t-p* to graze.

apacible *adj* gentle, mild.

apaciguamiento *m* pacification, appeasement.

apaciguar(se) [22] *t* to pacify, appease, calm. — **2** *p* to calm down.

apadrinar *t (en bautizo)* to act as godfather to. **2** *(en duelo)* to act as second to. **3** *(artista)* to sponsor.

apagado,-a *adj (luz etc.)* out, off. **2** *(persona)* spiritless. **3** *(color)* dull.

apagar(se) [7] *t (fuego)* to extinguish, put out. **2** *(luz)* to turn out/off. **3** *(desconectar)* to switch off. **4** *(color)* to soften. — **5** *p (luz)* to go out.

apagón *m* power cut, blackout.

apalabrar *t* to agree to.

apalancado,-a *adj arg* ensconced.

apalancarse [1] *p arg* to ensconce o.s.: *se apalancaron delante de la tele,* they settled down in front of the telly.

apalear *t* to beat, cane, thrash.

apañado,-a *adj (hábil)* skilful. **2** *(apropiado)* suitable. ●*irón estar* ~, to be in for a surprise.

apañar(se) *t (recoger)* to take. **2** *(robar)* to steal. **3** *(ataviar)* to smarten up. **3** *(ropa)* to patch, mend. — **4** *p* to manage: *ya se apañará sola,* she'll manage on her own.

apaño *m (remiendo)* mend, repair. **2** *(habilidad)* skill.

aparador *m (escaparate)* shop window. **2** *(mueble)* sideboard, cupboard, buffet.

aparato *m* apparatus, set. **2** *(dispositivo)* device. **3** *(exageración)* exaggeration. **4** *(ostentación)* pomp, display, show. ■ ~ *de radio,* radio set; ~ *de televisión,* television set; ANAT ~ *digestivo,* digestive system.

aparatoso,-a *adj (pomposo)* pompous, showy. **2** *(espectacular)* spectacular.

aparcamiento *m (acción)* parking. **2** *(en la calle)* place to park. **3** *(en parking)* car park, US parking lot.

aplacar

aparcar [1] *t* to park.
aparcero,-a *m,f* sharecropper.
aparear *t (cosas)* to pair, match. **2** *(animales)* to mate.
aparecer(se) [43] *i-p* to appear. **2** *(dejarse ver)* to show/turn up.
aparecido *m* spectre.
aparejador,-ra *m,f (de obras)* clerk of works; *(perito)* quantity surveyor.
aparejar *t (preparar)* to prepare, get ready. **2** *(caballos)* to saddle. **3** MAR to rig out.
aparejo *m (equipo)* gear, equipment. **2** *(arreos)* harness. **3** MAR rigging. **4** *(polea)* block and tackle.
aparentar *t (simular)* to feign, pretend. **2** *(tener aspecto de)* to look like. — **3** *i* to show off.
aparente *adj* apparent. **2** *(conveniente)* suitable. — **3** *aparentemente adv* apparently.
aparición *f* appearance. **2** *(visión)* apparition.
apariencia *f* appearance, aspect. ●*fig* **guardar las apariencias,** to keep up appearances.
apartado,-a *adj (lejano)* distant. **2** *(aislado)* isolated, cut off. — **3** *m* post-office box. **4** *(párrafo)* section.
apartamento *m* small flat/apartment. **2** AM flat.
apartar(se) *t-p (alejar)* to move away: ~ **la mirada,** to look away. **2** *(separar)* separate, set apart.
aparte *adv* apart, aside, separately: *eso se paga ~,* you have to pay for that separately. — **2** *adj (distinto)* special: *eso es caso ~,* that's completely different. — **3** *m* TEAT aside. **4** LING paragraph: *punto y ~,* full stop, new paragraph.
apasionado,-a *adj* ardent, passionate.
apasionamiento *m* passion.
apasionante *adj* exciting, fascinating.
apasionar(se) *t* to excite, fascinate. — **2** *p* to get excited, become enthusiastic *(por/de,* about).
apatía *f* apathy.
apático,-a *adj* apathetic.
apeadero *m (de trenes)* halt.
apear(se) *t (desmontar)* to take down. **2** *(terreno)* to survey. **3** ARQ to prop up. **4** *fam* to dissuade. — **5** *p* to dismount, get off.
apechugar [7] *i ~ con,* to put up with.
apedrear *t* to throw stones at.
apegado,-a *adj* attached *(a,* to).

apegarse [7] *p* to become very fond *(a,* of), attach o.s. *(a,* to).
apego *m* attachment, affection, liking, fondness.
apelación *f* appeal.
apelar *i* to appeal.
apellidar(se) *t* to call. — **2** *p* to be called (by surname).
apellido *m* family name, surname.
apelmazado,-a *adj* heavy, stodgy.
apelmazar(se) [4] *t* to compress, squeeze together. — **2** *p* to go lumpy.
apelotonar(se) *t* to pile up; *(gente)* to cluster. — **2** *p* to crowd together.
apenado,-a *adj* troubled.
apenar(se) *t* to make sad. — **2** *p* to be grieved.
apenas *adv (casi no)* scarcely, hardly. **2** *(tan pronto como)* as soon as, no sooner. ●~ *si,* hardly.
apéndice *m* appendix.
apendicitis *f inv* appendicitis *inv.*
apercibir(se) *t* to prepare before hand. **2** *(avisar)* to warn, advise. **3** *(ver)* to perceive, see. — **4** *p* to get ready.
aperitivo *m (bebida)* apéritif. **2** *(comida)* appetizer.
apertura *f (comienzo)* opening. **2** POL liberalization.
apesadumbrar *t* to sadden, distress.
apestar *i* to stink. — **2** *t* to infect with the plague.
apetecer [43] *t* to feel like, fancy: *¿te apetece ir al cine?,* do you fancy going to the cinema?
apetecible *adj* desirable. **2** *(comida)* tasty.
apetencia *f* appetite, hunger.
apetito *m* appetite. ●*abrir el ~,* to whet one's appetite.
apetitoso,-a *adj* appetizing, savoury. **2** *(comida)* tasty.
apiadar(se) *t* to inspire pity. — **2** *p* to take pity *(de,* on).
ápice *m (punta)* apex. **2** *fig* tiny piece. ● *ni un ~,* not a bit.
apicultor,-ra *m,f* beekeeper.
apicultura *f* beekeeping.
apilar(se) *t-p* to pile/heap up.
apiñar(se) *t* to pack, press together, jam. — **2** *p* to crowd *(en,* into).
apio *m* celery.
apisonadora *f* steamroller.
apisonar *t* to roll.
aplacar(se) [1] *t* to placate, soothe. — **2** *p* to become appeased.

aplanar(se) *t (igualar)* to smooth, level, make even. **2** *(deprimir)* to depress. **– 3** *p* to be depressed.

aplastante *adj* crushing, overwhelming. ■*triunfo ~,* landslide victory.

aplastar(se) *t* to flatten. **2** fig *(vencer)* to crush. **– 3** *p* to be crushed.

aplaudir *t* to clap, applaud. **2** *(aprobar)* to approve, praise.

aplauso *m* applause.

aplazamiento *m* adjournment, postponement; *(de pago)* deferment.

aplazar [4] *t* to adjourn, postpone, put off; *(un pago)* to defer.

aplicación *f* application. **2** *(adorno)* appliqué.

aplicado,-a *adj (práctico)* applied. **2** *(estudioso)* studious, diligent. ■ *ciencias aplicadas,* applied sciences.

aplicar(se) [1] *t* to apply. **– 2** *p (usar)* to apply. **3** *(esforzarse)* to apply o.s.

aplomo *m* assurance, self-possession.

apocado,-a *adj* spiritless.

apocar [1] *t (intimidar)* to intimidate. **2** *(humillar)* to humiliate.

apócrifo,-a *adj* apocryphal.

apodar(se) *t* to nickname. **– 2** *p* to be nicknamed.

apoderado,-a *adj* authorized. **– 2** *m,f* agent, representative.

apoderar(se) *t* to authorize. **– 2** *p* to take possession *(de,* of).

apodo *m* nickname.

apogeo *m* ASTRON apogee. **2** fig *(punto culminante)* summit, height.

apolillado,-a *adj* moth-eaten.

apolillar(se) *t* to eat, make holes in. **– 2** *p* to become moth-eaten.

apolítico,-a *adj* apolitical.

apología *f* apology, defence.

apólogo *m* apologue.

apoltronarse *p* to grow lazy.

apoplejía *f* apoplexy, stroke.

aporrear *t* to beat.

aportación *f* contribution.

aportar *t* to contribute **– 2** *i* MAR to reach port. ●*~ su granito de arena,* to chip in one's small contribution.

aposentar(se) *t* to lodge. **– 2** *p* to take lodging.

aposento *m (cuarto)* room. **2** *(hospedaje)* lodgings *pl.*

aposición *f* apposition.

aposta *adv* on purpose.

apostar(se) [31] *t-i-p* to bet.

apostasía *f* apostasy.

apostilla *f* note.

apóstol *m* apostle.

apostrofar *t* to apostrophize. **2** *(reñir)* to scold.

apóstrofe *m & f* apostrophe. **2** *(reprimenda)* insult.

apoteosis *f inv* apotheosis.

apoyar(se) *t* to lean. **2** *(fundar)* to base, found. **3** fig *(defender)* to back, support. **– 4** *p* to lean *(en,* on). **5** *(basarse)* to be based *(en,* on).

apoyo *m* support.

apreciable *adj* appreciable, noticeable. **2** *(estimable)* valuable.

apreciación *f (valorización)* appraisal. **2** *(juicio)* appreciation.

apreciar(se) [12] *t (valorar)* to appraise. **2** *(sentir aprecio)* to regard highly. **3** *(reconocer valor)* to appreciate. **– 4** *p* to be noticeable.

aprecio *m* esteem, regard. ●*sentir ~ por algn.,* to be fond of sb.

aprehender *t (apresar)* to apprehend. **2** *(confiscar)* to seize.

aprehensión *f* apprehension, arrest. **2** *(de contrabando)* seizure.

apremiante *adj* urgent, pressing.

apremiar [12] *t* to urge, press. **2** JUR to compel, constrain.

apremio *m* pressure, urgency. **2** JUR constraint.

aprender *t* to learn.

aprendiz,-za *m,f* apprentice, trainee.

aprendizaje *m* learning.

aprensión *f* apprehension.

aprensivo,-a *adj* apprehensive.

apresar *t (tomar por fuerza)* to seize, capture. **2** *(asir)* to clutch.

aprestar(se) *t-p* to make ready. **– 2** *t (tejidos)* to finish.

apresto *m* preparation. **2** *(tejidos)* finish.

apresurado,-a *adj* hasty, hurried. **– 2** *apresuradamente adv* hurriedly, in great haste.

apresuramiento *m* hurry.

apresurar(se) *t-p* to hurry up.

apretado,-a *adj* tight. **2** *(ocupado)* busy: *un día muy ~,* a very busy day.

apretar(se) [27] *t (estrechar)* to squeeze, hug. **2** *(tornillo, nudo)* to tighten. **3** *(comprimir)* to compress, press together, pack tight. **4** *(acosar)* to spur, urge. **5** *(activar)* to press: *~ el gatillo,* to pull the trigger. **6** *(aumentar)* to increase. **– 7** *i (prendas)* to fit tight: *esta falda me aprieta,* this skirt is to tight on me. **– 8** *p (apiñar)* to narrow. **9** *(agolparse)* to crowd together. ●*~ a correr,* to start running; ~ *el paso,* to quicken one's pace; *~se el cinturón,* to tighten one's belt.

apretón *m* squeeze. ■ ~ *de manos,* handshake.

apretujar(se) *t* to squeeze. − 2 *p* squeeze together.

aprieto *m* straits *pl,* difficulty, scrape, fix. •*poner a algn. en un ~,* to put sb. in an awkward situation; *salir del ~,* to get out of trouble.

aprisa *adv* quickly.

aprisco *m* sheepfold.

aprisionar *t* to imprison. 2 *(sujetar)* to hold fast.

aprobación *f* approval.

aprobado,-a *adj* approved, passed. − 2 *m* EDUC pass mark.

aprobar [31] *t* to approve. 2 *(estar de acuerdo)* to approve of. 3 *(examen, ley)* to pass.

apropiación *f* appropriation.

apropiado,-a *adj* fit, proper, appropriate.

apropiar(se) [12] *t (acomodar)* to make suitable. − 2 *p* to appropriate, take possession of.

aprovechado,-a *adj* well used/spent. 2 *(diligente)* diligent, advanced. 3 *(sinvergüenza)* opportunistic. − 4 *m,f* opportunist.

aprovechar(se) *t* to make good use of. 2 *(sacar provecho)* to benefit from: ~ *la oportunidad,* to seize the opportunity. − 3 *i* to be useful. − 4 *p* to take advantage *(de,* of). •*¡que aproveche!,* enjoy your meal!

aprovisionar *t* to supply, provide.

aproximación *f* approximation.

aproximado,-a *adj* approximate. − 2 *aproximadamente adv* approximately, roughly.

aproximar(se) *t* to bring near. − 2 *p* to draw near.

aproximativo,-a *adj* approximate, rough.

aptitud *f* aptitude, ability.

apto,-a *adj (apropiado)* suitable. 2 *(capaz)* capable, able. •CINEM ~ *para todos los públicos,* U-certificate film, US rated G; CINEM *no ~,* for adults only.

apuesta *f* bet, wager.

apuesto,-a *adj* good-looking.

apuntador,-ra *m,f* TEAT prompter.

apuntalar *t* to prop (up).

apuntar(se) *t (señalar)* to point at. 2 *(arma)* to aim. 3 *(anotar)* to note down. 4 *(estar encaminado)* to be aimed at. 5

(insinuar) to suggest. 6 *(sujetar)* to stitch, pin/tack lightly. 7 TEAT to prompt. − 8 *i* to begin to appear: *cuando apunta el día,* when day breaks. − 9 *p (inscribirse)* to enrol.

apunte *m* note. 2 *(dibujo)* sketch. 3 *pl (de clase)* notes.

apuñalar *t* to stab.

apurado,-a *adj (necesitado)* in need: ~ *de dinero,* hard up for money. 2 *(dificultoso)* awkward. 3 *(exacto)* accurate, precise. ■ *afeitado ~,* close shave.

apurar(se) *t (terminar)* to finish up: ~ *una copa,* to drain a glass. 2 *(apremiar)* to urge. 3 *(purificar)* to purify. 4 *(averiguar)* to investigate minutely. 5 AM *(dar prisa)* to hurry. − 6 *p* to get/be worried. 7 AM *(darse prisa)* to hurry. •*fig si me apuras ...,* if you insist ... .

apuro *m* fix, tight spot; *(de dinero)* hardship. 2 *(vergüenza)* embarrassment. • *estar en un ~,* to be in a tight spot.

aquejar *t* to afflict, affect.

aquel,-lla *adj* that. 2 *pl* those. ▲ *pl aquellos,-as.*

aquél,-lla *m,f pron* that one; *(el anterior)* the former. 2 *pl* those; *(los anteriores)* the former. ▲ *pl aquéllos,-as.*

aquello *pron neut* that, that thing.

aquí *adv (lugar)* here: *por ~ por favor,* this way please. 2 *(tiempo)* now: *de ~ en adelante,* from now on. •*de ~ para allá,* up and down, to and fro; *de ~ (que),* hence; *fig hasta ~ podíamos llegar,* that's the end of it.

aquiescencia *f* acquiescence.

aquietar(se) *t-p* to calm down.

aquilatar *t* to assay. 2 *fig (evaluar)* to assess.

ara *f* altar. •*en aras de,* for the sake of.

arado *m* plough, US plow.

arancel *m* tariff, duty.

arancelario,-a *adj* tariff, duty.

arándano *m* bilberry, blueberry.

arandela *f* TÉC washer.

araña *f* ZOOL spider. 2 *(lámpara)* chandelier. ■ *tela de ~,* spider's web.

arañar *t (raspar)* to scratch.

arañazo *m* scratch.

arar *t* to plough, US plow.

arbitraje *m* arbitration. 2 DEP refereeing.

arbitrar *t* to arbitrate. 2 DEP to referee.

arbitrariedad *f (acción)* arbitrary act. 2 *(condición)* arbitrariness.

arbitrario,-a *adj* arbitrary.

arbitrio *m (voluntad)* will. 2 *(decisión)* power, choice. 3 *pl* taxes.

árbitro *m* arbiter, arbitrator. 2 DEP referee.

árbol *m* BOT tree. 2 TÉC axle. 3 MAR mast.

arbolado,-a *adj* wooded. – 2 *m* woodland.

arboleda *f* grove, woodland.

arbotante *m* flying buttress.

arbusto *m* shrub, bush.

arca *f* chest. 2 *(caja de caudales)* strongbox, safe. ■ ~ *de Noé,* Noah's ark; *arcas públicas,* Treasury *sing.* ▲ *Takes el and un in sing.*

arcada *f* ARQ arcade. 2 *(vómitos)* retching.

arcaico,-a *adj* archaic.

arcángel *m* archangel.

arcano,-a *adj* hidden. – 2 *m* secret, mystery.

arce *m* maple tree.

archipiélago *m* archipelago.

archivador,-ra *m,f* archivist. – 2 *m* filing cabinet.

archivar *t (ordenar)* to file. 2 INFORM to save. 3 *(arrinconar)* to shelve.

archivo *m* file. 2 *(documentos)* archives *pl.* 3 *(mueble)* filing cabinet.

arcilla *f* clay.

arcipreste *m* archpriest.

arco *m* ARQ arch. 2 MAT arc. 3 MÚS DEP bow. ■ ~ *iris,* rainbow; ~ *voltaico,* electric arc.

arder *i* to burn. 2 *(resplandecer)* to glow. 3 *fig* to burn: ~ *de pasión,* to burn with passion. ●*fam la cosa está que arde,* things are getting pretty hot.

ardid *m* scheme, trick.

ardiente *adj (encendido)* burning, hot. 2 *fig* passionate, fiery.

ardilla *f* squirrel.

ardor *m* burning, heat. 2 *(ansia)* ardour, fervour. ■ ~ *de estómago,* heartburn.

ardoroso,-a *adj* burning. 2 *fig* ardent, passionate.

arduo,-a *adj* arduous.

área *f (zona)* area. 2 *(medida)* are.

arena *f* sand. 2 *(lugar)* arena, circus.

arenal *m* sands *pl,* sandy area.

arenga *f* harangue.

arenisca *f* sandstone.

arenoso,-a *adj* sandy.

arenque *m* herring.

arete *m (anillo)* small ring. 2 *(pendiente)* earring.

argamasa *f* mortar.

argentado,-a *adj* silvery.

argolla *f (aro)* ring.

argot *m (popular)* slang. 2 *(técnico)* jargon.

argucia *f* sophism.

argüir [63] *t (deducir)* to deduce. 2 *(probar)* to prove. – 3 *i (discutir)* to argue.

argumentación *f* argumentation, argument.

argumentar *t (deducir)* to deduce. – 2 *i (discutir)* to argue.

argumento *m* argument. 2 *(de novela, obra, etc.)* plot.

arguyo *pres indic→* **arguir.**

aria *f* aria.

aridez *f* aridity.

árido,-a *adj* arid. 2 *fig* dry. – 3 *mpl* dry goods.

Aries *m* Aries.

arisco,-a *adj* unsociable, unfriendly.

arista *f* edge.

aristocracia *f* aristocracy.

aristócrata *mf* aristocrat.

aritmética *f* arithmetic.

arlequín *m* harlequin.

arma *f* weapon, arm. 2 *pl (profesión)* army. 3 *pl (heráldica)* arms, armorial bearings. ■ ~ *blanca,* knife, steel; ~ *de fuego,* firearm; *licencia de armas,* firearms licence. ▲ *Takes el and un in sing.*

armada *f* navy.

armado,-a *adj* armed: *ir* ~, to be armed.

armador,-ra *m,f* shipowner.

armadura *f (defensa)* armour. 2 *(armazón)* framework.

armamentista *adj* arms. ■ *la carrera* ~, the arms race.

armamento *m* armament.

armar(se) *t* to arm. 2 *(montar)* to assemble, put together. 3 MAR to fit out. 4 *(crear)* to create. – 5 *p* to arm o.s. ●*fig* ~*se de,* to provide o.s. with: ~*se de paciencia,* to summon up one's patience; ~*se de valor,* to pluck up courage; *fam va a* ~*se la gorda,* there's going to be real trouble.

armario *m* cupboard, wardrobe, US closet.

armatoste *m (cosa)* monstrosity. 2 *(persona)* useless great oaf.

armazón *f* frame, framework.

armería *f (tienda)* gunsmith's (shop). 2 *(arte)* gunsmith's craft. 3 *(museo)* armoury.

armiño *m* ermine.

armisticio *m* armistice.

armonía *f* harmony.

armónico,-a *adj* harmonic. – 2 *m* MÚS harmonic. – 3 *f* harmonica, mouth organ.

armonioso,-a *adj* harmonious.

armonizar [4] *t-i* to harmonize.

arnés *m (armadura)* armour. **2** *pl* harness *sing.*

aro *m* hoop, ring. **2** *(juego)* hoop. **3** *(servilletero)* serviette ring.

aroma *m* aroma; *(del vino)* bouquet.

aromático,-a *adj* aromatic.

arpa *f* MÚS harp. ▲ *Takes el and un in sing.*

arpía *f* harpy. **2** *fam fig* shrew, old witch.

arpillera *f* sackcloth, burlap.

arpón *m* harpoon.

arquear(se) *t-p* to arch, bend.

arqueología *f* archaeology.

arqueólogo,-a *m,f* archaeologist.

arquero *m* archer.

arqueta *f* small chest.

arquetípico,-a *adj* archetypal.

arquitecto,-a *m,f* architect.

arquitectura *f* architecture.

arrabal *m* suburb. **2** *pl* outskirts.

arracimarse *p* to cluster.

arraigado,-a *adj* (deeply) rooted.

arraigar(se) [7] *i-p* to take root. — **2** *t* to establish, strengthen.

arraigo *m* taking root.

arrancar [1] *t* to uproot, pull out. **2** *(plumas, cabello)* to pluck. **3** *(con violencia)* to tear out, snatch. — **4** *i (partir)* to begin. **5** *(coche)* to start; *(tren)* to pull out. **6** *fig (provenir)* to stem *(de,* from). ●*~ a correr,* to break into a run.

arranque *m* starting. **2** *fig* outburst.

arrasar *t (destruir)* to raze, demolish. **2** *(aplanar)* to level.

arrastrado,-a *adj* wretched, miserable.

arrastrar(se) *t* to drag (along), pull (along). **2** *fig* to sway. — **3** *p* to trail (on the ground). **4** *fig (humillarse)* to creep, crawl.

arrastre *m* dragging. ■ *pesca de ~,* trawling.

arrayán *m* myrtle.

arrear *t (animales)* to drive. **2** *(apresurar)* to hurry up. **3** *(pegar)* to hit: *~ una bofetada a algn.,* to slap sb. in the face. — **4** *i* to move fast.

arrebatado,-a *adj (precipitado)* rash. **2** *(iracundo)* furious. **3** *(ruborizado)* blushing.

arrebatador,-ra *adj fig* captivating, fascinating.

arrebatar(se) *t* to snatch. **2** *fig (atraer)* to captivate. — **3** *p (enfurecerse)* to become furious. **4** CULIN to burn.

arrebato *m* fit, outburst.

arrebol *m (de nubes)* red glow. **2** *(de mejillas)* redness.

arreciar(se) [12] *i-p* to get stronger/worse.

arrecife *m* reef.

arredrar(se) *t* to frighten, intimidate. — **2** *p* to be frightened.

arreglar(se) *t (gen)* to settle, fix up: *el tiempo lo arregla todo,* time heals all wounds. **2** *(ordenar)* to tidy (up). **3** *(reparar)* to mend, fix up. **4** *fam* to sort out: *¡ya te arreglaré!,* I'll teach you! — **5** *p (componerse)* to get ready, dress up; *(cabello)* to do. **6** *fam* to manage: *arréglatelas como puedas,* do as best you can.

arreglo *m (regla)* rule, order. **2** *(de una disputa)* arrangement. **3** *(reparación)* mending, repair. ●*con ~ a,* according to.

arrellanarse *p* to sit back.

arremangar(se) [7] *t-p* to roll up (one's sleeves).

arremeter *i* to attack.

arremetida *f* attack, assault.

arremolinarse *p* to whirl. **2** *(gente)* to crowd/press together.

arrendamiento *m* renting, leasing, letting. **2** *(precio)* rent.

arrendar [27] *t* to rent, lease.

arrendatario,-a *m,f* lessee. **2** *(inquilino)* tenant.

arreos *mpl* harness *sing.*

arrepentido,-a *adj* regretful.

arrepentimiento *m* regret, repentance.

arrepentirse [35] *p* to regret *(de,* -).

arrestado,-a *adj* arrested.

arrestar *t* to arrest. **2** *(poner en prisión)* to imprison, jail.

arresto *m* arrest. **2** *pl* daring *sing.*

arriar [13] *t (velas)* to lower. **2** *(bandera)* to strike.

arriba *adv* up; *(encima)* on (the) top. **2** *(piso)* upstairs: *vive ~,* he/she lives upstairs. **3** *(en escritos)* above: *véase más ~,* see above. — **4** *interj* up!: *¡~ la República!,* long live the Republic! ●*cuesta ~,* uphill; *de ~ abajo,* from top to bottom; *hacia ~,* upwards; *fam patas ~,* upside down.

arribar *i* to reach port.

arribista *adj* ambitious. — **2** *mf* arriviste, social climber.

arriendo *m* lease. **2** *(de un piso)* renting.

arriero *m* muleteer.

arriesgado,-a *adj (arriesgado)* risky, dangerous. **2** *(atrevido)* bold, rash.

arriesgar(se) [7] *t-p* to risk. ●*fam ~ el pellejo,* to risk one's neck.

arrimadero *m (de pared)* wainscot.

arrimar(se) *t* to move closer. — **2** *p* to move/get close. ●*fig ~ a algn.,* to seek sb.'s protection; *fig ~ al sol que más calienta,* to get on the winning side.

arrimo *m* support, protection.

arrinconar(se) *t* to put in a corner. **2** *(acorralar)* to corner. **3** *fig (desestimar)* to ignore. **4** *(abandonar)* to lay aside. — **5** *p* *(aislarse)* to isolate o.s.

arrobamiento *m* ecstasy, rapture.

arrobar *t* to rapture.

arrobo *m* → **arrobamiento**.

arrodillado,-a *adj* on one's knees. ●*estar ~,* to be kneeling down.

arrodillarse *p* to kneel down.

arrogancia *f* arrogance.

arrogante *adj* arrogant.

arrogarse [7] *p* to arrogate.

arrojadizo,-a *adj* for throwing.

arrojado,-a *adj* thrown (out). **2** *(osado)* bold, fearless.

arrojar(se) *t (tirar)* to throw, fling: *"prohibido ~ basuras",* "no dumping". **2** *(echar con violencia)* to throw out. **3** *(cuentas etc.)* to show. — **4** *i* to vomit. — **5** *p* to throw o.s.: *se arrojó sobre él,* he/she jumped on him.

arrojo *m* boldness, dash, bravery.

arrollador,-ra *adj* overwhelming: *un éxito ~,* a resounding success.

arrollar *t (envolver)* to roll (up). **2** *(el viento)* to sweep away. **3** *(al enemigo)* to rout. **4** *(atropellar)* to run over.

arropar(se) *t-p* to wrap (o.s.) up.

arrostrar *t* to face.

arroyo *m (río)* stream. **2** *(en la calle)* gutter.

arroz *m* rice. ■ *~ con leche,* rice pudding; *~ integral,* brown rice.

arrozal *m* rice field.

arruga *f* wrinkle.

arrugar(se) [7] *t-p* to wrinkle. ●*~ el ceño/entrecejo,* to frown.

arruinar(se) *t* to bankrupt, ruin. — **2** *p* to be bankrupt/ruined.

arrullar *t (pájaro)* to coo. **2** *(adormecer)* to lull.

arrullo *m (de pájaro)* cooing. **2** *(nana)* lullaby.

arrumaco *m* caress.

arsenal *m* MAR shipyard. **2** *(de armas)* arsenal.

arsénico *m* arsenic.

arte *m* art **2** *(habilidad)* craft, skill. **3** *(astucia)* cunning. **4** *(pesca)* fishing gear. ●*con malas artes,* by evil means. ■ *bellas artes,* fine arts.

artefacto *m* device. ■ *~ explosivo,* bomb.

arteria *f* artery.

arteriosclerosis *f inv* arteriosclerosis.

artero,-a *adj* artful, crafty.

artesa *f* trough.

artesanía *f* craftsmanship.

artesano,-a *m,f* artisan, craftsman.

artesonado,-a *adj* panelled. — **2** *m* panelled ceiling.

ártico,-a *adj-m* Arctic.

articulación *f* articulation. **2** ANAT TÉC joint.

articulado,-a *adj* articulate. — **2** *m* articles *pl.*

articular(se) *t-p* to articulate.

articulatorio,-a *adj* articulatory.

articulista *mf* columnist.

artículo *m* article. ■ *~ de fondo,* editorial.

artífice *mf (artista)* craftsman. **2** *(autor)* author: *fig Pepe ha sido el ~ de todo esto,* this is all Pepe's doing.

artificial *adj* artificial.

artificio *m (habilidad)* skill. **2** *(astucia)* artifice. **3** *(mecanismo)* device. ■ *fuegos de ~,* fireworks.

artificioso,-a *adj (hábil)* skilful. **2** *(astuto)* crafty.

artilugio *m* device, gadget. **2** *fig (trampa)* trick.

artillería *f* artillery.

artillero *m* artilleryman.

artimaña *f* trick.

artista *mf* artist. ■ *~ de cine,* film star.

artístico,-a *adj* artistic.

artritis *f inv* arthritis *inv.*

artrosis *f inv* arthrosis *inv.*

arveja *f,* **arvejo** *m* AM chickpea.

arzobispo *m* archbishop.

as *m* ace.

asa *f* handle. ▲ *Takes el and un in sing.*

asado,-a *adj* roast(ed). — **2** *m* roast.

asador *m* roaster.

asalariado,-a *adj* salaried. — **2** *m,f* wage earner.

asalariar [12] *t* to employ.

asalmonado,-a *adj* salmon-coloured.

asaltante *adj* assaulting. — **2** *mf* attacker.

asaltar *t* to assault, attack.

asalto *m* assault, attack. **2** *(boxeo)* round. ●*tomar por ~,* to take by storm.

asamblea *f* assembly, meeting.

asar(se) *t-p* to roast.

ascendencia *f* ancestry.

ascendente *adj* ascending, ascendant. –
2 *m* ascendant.

ascender [28] *t* to promote. – 2 *i (subir)*
to climb. 3 *(de categoría)* to be promoted. 4 *(sumar)* to amount (*a*, to).

ascendiente *adj* ascending, ascendant.
– 2 *mf* ancestor.

ascensión *f* ascension.

ascenso *m* rise, promotion.

ascensor *m* lift, US elevator.

asceta *mf* ascetic.

ascético,-a *adj* ascetic.

asco *m* disgust. ●*dar* ~, to be disgusting;
estar hecho un ~, to be filthy.

ascua *f* red hot coal. ●*estar en ascuas*, to
be on tenterhooks. ▲ *Takes el and un in
sing.*

aseado,-a *adj* clean, neat, tidy.

asear *t* to clean, tidy.

asediar [12] *t* to besiege. 2 *fig* to impor-
tunate.

asedio *m* siege.

asegurado,-a *adj* insured.

asegurador,-ra *m,f* insuring.

asegurar(se) *t (fijar)* to secure. 2 COM to
insure. 3 *(garantizar)* to assure, guarantee. – 4 *p (cerciorarse)* to make sure.
5 COM to insure o.s.

asemejar(se) *t* to make alike. – 2 *p* to
to look like.

asenso *m* assent, consent.

asentar(se) [27] *t* to place. 2 *(fijar)* to fix,
set. 3 *(afirmar)* to affirm, assume. 4
(anotar) to enter, note down. 5 *(golpes)*
to give. – 6 *p (establecerse)* to settle
(down). 7 *(aves)* to perch.

asentimiento *m* assent, consent, acquiescence.

asentir [35] *i* to assent, agree; *(con la cabeza)* to nod.

aseo *m* cleaning, tidying up. ■ *(cuarto
de)* ~, bathroom.

asepsia *f* asepsis.

aséptico,-a *adj* aseptic. 2 *fig* cool.

asequible *adj* accesible: *a un precio* ~,
at a reasonable price.

aserción *f* assertion, statement.

aserradero *m* sawmill.

aserrar [27] *t* to saw.

aserrín *m* sawdust.

aserto *m* → **aserción**.

asesinar *t* to kill, murder.

asesinato *m* killing, murder.

asesino,-a *adj* murderous. – 2 *m,f* killer.

asesor,-ra *m,f* adviser, consultant.

asesoramiento *m (acción)* advising. 2
(consejo) advice.

asesorar(se) *t* to advise, give advice. –
2 *p* to consult.

asestar *t (arma)* to aim. 2 *(golpe)* to deal.
3 *(tiro)* to fire.

aseveración *f* asseveration, assertion.

aseverar *t* to asseverate, affirm.

asfaltado *m (acción)* asphalting. 2 *(pavimento)* asphalt, Tarmac®.

asfaltar *t* to asphalt.

asfalto *m* asphalt.

asfixia *f* asphyxia, suffocation.

asfixiar(se) [12] *t-p* to asphyxiate, suffocate.

así *adv (de esta manera)* thus, (in) this
way. 2 *(de esa manera)* (in) that way:
por decirlo ~, so to speak; *y* ~ *sucesivamente*, and so on. 3 *(tanto)* as: ~ *usted como yo*, both you and I. 4 *(por tanto)* therefore: *llovía*, ~ *que cogimos el
paraguas*, it was raining, so we took
our umbrella. 5 *(tan pronto como)* as
soon as: ~ *que lo sepa*, as soon as I
know. – 6 *adj* such: *un hombre* ~, a
man like that. ●~ ~, so-so; ~ *sea*, so
be it; *aun* ~, even so.

asidero *m* handle. 2 *fig* excuse, pretext.

asiduidad *f* assiduity.

asiduo,-a *adj* assiduous, frequent.

asiento *m (silla etc.)* seat. 2 *(emplazamiento)* site. 3 *(sedimento)* sediment. 4
fig (orden) establishment. 5 COM entry.
6 *(de vasija)* bottom.

asignación *f* assignment. 2 *(remuneración)* allocation, allowance.

asignar *t* to assign, allot. 2 *(nombrar)* to
appoint.

asignatura *f* EDUC subject. ■ ~ *pendiente*, failed subject.

asilar *t (recoger)* to give shelter. 2 POL to
give political asylum.

asilo *m* asylum. ■ ~ *de ancianos*, old
people's home; POL ~ *político*, political
asylum.

asimetría *f* asymmetry.

asimétrico,-a *adj* asymmetric.

asimilación *f* assimilation.

asimilar(se) *t* to assimilate. – 2 *p* to be
assimilated.

asimismo *adv (también)* also. 2 *(de esta
manera)* likewise.

asir(se) [65] *t* to seize, grasp. – 2 *p* to
hold on (*a*, to).

asistencia *f (presencia)* attendance, presence. 2 *(público)* audience, public. 3
(ayuda) assistance.

asistenta *f* cleaning lady.

asistente *adj* attending. — **2** *mf* assistant. — **3** *m* MIL batman. ■ ~ *social,* social worker.

asistir *i* to attend, be present: ~ *a la escuela,* to attend school. — **2** *t* to assist, help.

asma *f* asthma. ▲ *Takes* **el** *and* **un** *in sing.*

asmático,-a *adj-m,f* asthmatic.

asno *m* ass, donkey.

asociación *f* association.

asociado,-a *adj* associated. — **2** *m,f* associate, partner.

asociar(se) [12] *t* to associate. — **2** *p* to be associated.

asolador,-ra *adj* razing, ravaging, devastating.

asolar [31] *t* *(destruir)* to devastate.

asomar(se) *i* to appear. — **2** *t* to show, put out. — **3** *p* to lean out; *(balcón)* to come out *(a,* on).

asombrado,-a *adj* amazed, astonished.

asombrar(se) *t* to amaze, astonish. — **2** *p* to be astonished/amazed.

asombro *m* amazement, astonishment.

asombroso,-a *adj* amazing, astonishing.

asomo *m* sign, indication. ●*ni por* ~, by no means.

asonancia *f* assonance.

aspa *f* X-shaped figure or cross. **2** *(de molino)* arm; *(de ventilador)* blade.

aspaviento *m* fuss. ●*hacer aspavientos,* to make a fuss.

aspecto *m* aspect. **2** *(apariencia)* look, appearance.

aspereza *f* roughness, coarseness.

asperjar *t* to sprinkle.

áspero,-a *adj* rough, coarse.

aspersión *f* sprinkling.

áspid(e) *m* asp.

aspillera *f* MIL loophole.

aspiración *f* *(al respirar)* inhalation. **2** *fig* *(ambición)* aspiration, ambition.

aspirador *m,* **aspiradora** *f* vacuum cleaner.

aspirante *adj* sucking. — **2** *mf* candidate.

aspirar *t* *(al respirar)* to inhale, breathe in. **2** *(absorber)* to suck/draw in. **3** LING to aspirate. — **4** *i* to aspire *(a,* to).

aspirina® *f* aspirin®.

asqueroso,-a *adj* *(sucio)* dirty, filthy. **2** *(desagradable)* disgusting.

asta *f* *(de bandera)* staff. **2** *(de lanza)* haft. **3** *(cuerno)* horn. ● *bandera a media* ~, flag at half-mast. ▲ *Takes* **el** *and* **un** *in sing.*

astenia *f* asthenia.

asterisco *m* asterisk.

asteroide *adj-m* asteroid.

astilla *f* splinter.

astillar *t* to splinter.

astillero *m* shipyard, dockyard.

astringente *adj-m* astringent.

astro *m* star.

astrología *f* astrology.

astrólogo,-a *m,f* astrologer.

astronauta *mf* astronaut.

astronomía *f* astronomy.

astrónomo,-a *m,f* astronomer.

astucia *f* astuteness, cunning.

astuto,-a *adj* astute, cunning.

asueto *m* short holiday.

asumir *t* to assume.

asunción *f* assumption.

asunto *m* matter, subject. **2** *(negocio)* affair, business. ■ POL *asuntos exteriores,* Foreign Affairs.

asustadizo,-a *adj* easily frightened.

asustar(se) *t* to frighten. — **2** *p* to be frightened.

atacar [1] *t* to attack. **2** *(criticar)* to criticize. **3** *(armas)* to tamp down.

atado,-a *adj* *(tímido)* shy. — **2** *m* bundle.

atadura *f* tying. **2** *fig* *(enlace)* tie. **3** *fig* *(impedimento)* hindrance.

atajar *i* to take a shortcut. — **2** *t* *(interrumpir)* to interrupt. **3** *(entorpecer el paso)* to halt.

atajo *m* shortcut.

atalaya *f* watchtower. — **2** *m* watcher, lookout.

atañer [38] *i* to concern *(a,* to).

ataque *m* attack. **2** MED fit. ■ ~ *aéreo,* air raid.

atar *t* to tie, fasten. ●*fig* ~ *cabos,* to put two and two together.

atardecer [43] *i* to get/grow dark. — **2** *m* evening, dusk. ▲ *1 only used in the 3rd pers. It does not take a subject.*

atareado,-a *adj* busy.

atarear(se) *t* to keep busy. — **2** *p* to be busy.

atascadero *m* obstacle.

atascar(se) [1] *t* *(bloquear)* to block, obstruct. **2** *fig* to hamper. — **3** *p* *(bloquearse)* to be obstructed. **4** *fig* *(estancarse)* to get tangled up.

atasco *m* obstruction. **2** *(de tráfico)* traffic jam.

ataúd *m* coffin.

ataviar(se) [13] *t* to dress (up). **2** *(adornar)* to adorn. — **3** *p* to get dressed up.

atavío *m* *(adorno)* decoration. **2** *(vestido)* dress.

atavismo *m* atavism.

ateísmo *m* atheism.
atemorizar(se) [4] *t* to frighten. — **2** *p* to become frightened.
atención *f* attention. **2** *(cortesía)* courtesy. ●*llamar la* ~, to attract attention.
atender [28] *t* to pay attention/attend to. **2** *(cuidar)* to take care of. **3** *(tener en cuenta)* to bear in mind. — **4** *i* to pay attention (*a,* to).
ateneo *m* athenaeum.
atenerse [87] *p* *(ajustarse)* to abide (*a,* by). **2** *(acogerse)* to rely (*a,* on).
atentado *m* attack, assault. ■ ~ *terrorista,* terrorist attack.
atentar [27] *i* ~ *a/contra,* to commit a crime against.
atento,-a *adj* attentive. **2** *(amable)* polite, courteous. — **3** *atentamente* *adv* attentively. **4** *(amablemente)* politely; *(en carta)* *le saluda atentamente,* your sincerely/faithfully.
atenuante *adj* attenuating.
atenuar [11] *t* to attenuate.
ateo,-a *adj-m,f* atheist.
aterciopelado,-a *adj* velvety.
aterido,-a *adj* stiff with cold.
aterrador,-ra *adj* terrifying.
aterrar(se) *t* *(asustar)* to terrify. **2** *(derribar)* to pull down, demolish. — **3** *p* to be terrified. ▲ **2** *follows conjugation model* [27].
aterrizaje *m* landing.
aterrizar [4] *t* to land.
aterrorizar(se) [4] *t* to terrify. — **2** *p* to be terrified.
atesorar *t* to hoard. **2** *fig* to possess.
atestación *f* attestation, testimony.
atestar *t* JUR to testify. **2** *(atiborrar)* to cram, pack (*de,* with). ▲ **2** *follows conjugation model* [27].
atestiguar [22] *t* to attest.
atiborrar(se) *t* to pack, cram, stuff (*de,* with). — **2** *p* to stuff o.s (*de,* with).
ático *m* penthouse.
atinado,-a *adj* right, accurate.
atinar *i-t* to guess right.
atisbar *t* to peep at, spy on, observe.
atisbo *m* *(indicio)* inkling.
atizador *m* poker.
atizar [4] *t* *(fuego)* to poke, stir. **2** *fig* *(pasiones)* to rouse.
atlas *m inv* atlas.
atleta *mf* athlete.
atlético,-a *adj* athletic.
atletismo *m* athletics.
atmósfera *f* atmosphere.
atmosférico,-a *adj* atmospheric.

atolladero *m* bog. **2** *fig* fix, jam.
atollar(se) *i-p* to get stuck in the mud.
atolondrado,-a *adj* stunned.
atolondrar(se) *t* to confuse. — **2** *p* to become confused.
atómico,-a *adj* atomic.
átomo *m* atom.
atónito,-a *adj* astonished, amazed.
átono,-a *adj* atonic, unstressed.
atontado,-a *adj* stunned, confused. **2** *(tonto)* stupid, silly.
atontar *t* to stun, stupefy. **2** *(confundir)* to confuse, bewilder.
atorar(se) *t* to obstruct, choke. — **2** *p* to be blocked/choked.
atormentar(se) *t-p* to torment (o.s.).
atornillar *t* to screw.
atosigar [4] *t* *(envenenar)* to poison. **2** *(apremiar)* to harass, pester.
atrabiliario,-a *adj* bad-tempered.
atracador,-ra *m,f* *(de banco)* (bank) robber; *(en la calle)* attacker, mugger.
atracar(se) [1] *t* *(robar)* to hold up, rob. **2** *(de comida)* to gorge. — **3** *i* MAR to come alongside. — **4** *p* *(de comida)* to gorge o.s. (*de,* on).
atracción *f* attraction. ■ *parque de atracciones,* funfair.
atraco *m* hold-up, robbery.
atracón *m fam* binge.
atractivo,-a *adj* attractive. — **2** *m* attraction, charm.
atraer [88] *t* to attract. **2** *(captivar)* to captivate, charm.
atragantarse *p* to choke (*con,* on).
atrancar(se) [1] *t* *(puerta)* to bar, bolt. **2** *(obstruir)* to obstruct.
atrapar *t* to seize, capture, catch.
atrás *adv* back. **2** *(tiempo)* ago: *días* ~, several days ago. — **3** *interj* stand/move back! ●*ir hacia* ~, to go backwards; *volverse* ~, to change one's mind, back out.
atrasado,-a *adj* late. **2** *(pago)* overdue. **3** *(reloj)* slow. **4** *(país)* backward, underdeveloped.
atrasar(se) *t* to delay. — **2** *i* *(reloj)* to be slow. — **3** *p* *(tren etc.)* to be late. **4** *(quedarse atrás)* to stay behind.
atraso *m* delay. **2** *(reloj)* slowness. **3** *pl* COM arrears.
atravesar(se) [27] *t* to cross (over). **2** *(poner oblicuamente)* to put/lay across. **3** *(bala etc.)* to pierce, run through. — **4** *p* to be in the way. ●*fam* ~*se algn. a uno,* not to be able to bear/stand sb.
atrayente *adj* attractive.

atreverse *p* to dare, venture.
atrevido,-a *adj* (*osado*) daring, bold. **2** (*indecoroso*) risqué.
atrevimiento *m* daring, boldness. **2** (*insolencia*) effrontery, insolence.
atribución *f* power, authority.
atribuir(se) [62] *t* to attribute, ascribe. – **2** *p* to assume.
atribular(se) *t* to grieve, afflict. – **2** *p* to be grieved/afflicted.
atributo *m* attribute, quality.
atril *m* lectern.
atrincherar(se) *t-p* to entrench (o.s.).
atrio *m* (*patio*) atrium. **2** (*vestíbulo*) vestibule.
atrocidad *f* atrocity. **2** (*disparate*) silly remark.
atrofia *f* atrophy.
atrofiarse [12] *p* to atrophy.
atropellado,-a *adj* hasty, precipitate.
atropellar(se) *t* to trample. **2** AUTO to knock down. **3** *fig* (*oprimir*) to hurry over; (*sentimientos*) to outrage; (*derechos*) to disregard. – **4** *p* to speak/act hastily.
atropello *m* (*accidente*) running over. **2** *fig* outrage, abuse.
atroz *adj* (*bárbaro*) atrocious. **2** *fam* enormous, huge, awful.
atuendo *m* attire.
atún *m* tunny, tuna.
aturdido,-a *adj* (*confundido*) stunned. **2** (*atolondrado*) reckless.
aturdimiento *m* (*confusión*) confusion. **2** (*atolondramiento*) recklessness.
aturdir(se) *t* to stun. **2** *fig* to confuse. – **3** *p* to be confused.
aturrullar *t* to confuse.
atusar *t* (*recortar*) to trim. **2** (*alisar*) to smooth (down).
audacia *f* audacity.
audaz *adj* audacious, bold.
audición *f* (*acción*) hearing. **2** TEAT audition. **3** MÚS concert.
audiencia *f* (*recepción*) audience. **2** JUR high court.
audífono *m* hearing aid.
audiovisual *adj* audio-visual.
auditor *m* auditor.
auditoría *f*. (*proceso*) auditing. **2** (*empleo*) auditorship.
auditorio *m* (*público*) audience. **2** (*lugar*) auditory.
auge *m* (*del mercado*) boom. **2** (*de precios*) boost. **3** (*de fama etc.*) peak. •*estar en* ~, to be on the increase.
augurar *t* to augur.
augurio *m* augury.

aula *f* classroom; (*en universidad*) lecture room. ▲ *Takes el and un in sing.*
aullar [16] *i* to howl.
aullido *m* howl.
aumentar *t* to augment, increase. **2** (*óptica*) to magnify. **3** (*fotos*) to enlarge. – **4** *i* to rise.
aumento *m* increase. **2** (*óptica*) magnification. **3** (*fotos*) enlargement. **4** (*salario*) rise. •*ir en* ~, to be on the increase.
aun *adv* even. •~ *cuando,* although, even though.
aún *adv* yet, still.
aunar(se) [16] *t-p* to unite, combine.
aunque *conj* (al)though.
¡aúpa! *interj* up!, get up!
aura *f* (*aire*) gentle breeze. **2** (*halo*) aura. ▲ *Takes el and un in sing.*
áureo,-a *adj* golden.
aureola, auréola *f* aureole, halo.
auricular *m* (*teléfono*) receiver, earpiece. **2** (*dedo*) little finger.
aurora *f* dawn.
auscultar *t* to sound (with a stethoscope).
ausencia *f* absence.
ausentarse *p* to leave.
ausente *adj* absent. – **2** *mf* absentee.
auspicio *m* auspice.
austeridad *f* austerity.
austero,-a *adj* austere.
austral *adj* austral, southern.
auténtico,-a *adj* authentic, genuine.
auto *m* JUR decree, writ. **2** *fam* (*coche*) car.
autobús *m* bus.
autocar *m* coach.
autocracia *f* autocracy.
autócrata *mf* autocrat.
autóctono,-a *adj* indigenous.
autodidáctico,-a *adj* self-taught. – **2** *m,f* self-taught person.
autoescuela *f* driving school.
autógrafo,-a *adj* autographic. – **2** *m* autograph.
autómata *m* automaton.
automático,-a *adj* automatic.
automatizar [4] *t* to automate.
automóvil *m* automobile, car.
automovilismo *m* motoring.
automovilista *mf* motorist.
autonomía *f* autonomy.
autónomo,-a *adj* autonomous.
autopista *f* motorway, US highway.
autopsia *f* autopsy.
autor,-ra *m,f* author. **2** (*de crimen*) perpetrator.

autoridad *f* authority.

autorización *f* authorization.

autorizar [4] *t* to authorize.

autostop *m* hitch-hiking. ●*hacer* ~, to hitch-hike.

auxiliar [14] *t* to help, assist. – **2** *adj* auxiliary. – **3** *m* assistant.

auxilio *m* help, aid, assistance. ■ *primeros auxilios,* first aid *sing.*

aval *m* guarantee.

avalancha *f* avalanche.

avalar *t* to guarantee.

avance *m* advance. **2** *(pago)* advance payment. ■ TV ~ *informativo,* news preview.

avanzar(se) [4] *i-p* to advance.

avaricia *f* avarice.

avaro,-a *adj* avaricious, miserly. – **2** *m,f* miser.

avasallador,-ra *adj* overwhelming.

avasallar *t* to subjugate, subdue.

ave *f* bird. ■ ~ *de rapiña,* bird of prey. ▲ *Takes* el *and* un *in sing.*

avecinarse *p* to approach *(a,* de*).*

avejentar *t* to age prematurely.

avellana *f* hazelnut.

avemaría *f* Hail Mary. ●*en un* ~, in a twinkle.

avena *f* oats *pl.*

avenencia *f* agreement, accord.

avengo *pres indic* → **avenir**.

avenida *f* avenue. **2** *(de río)* flood.

avenir(se) [90] *t* to reconcile. – **2** *p* to agree.

aventajado,-a *adj (sobresaliente)* outstanding. **2** *(provechoso)* advantageous.

aventajar *t (exceder)* to surpass. **2** *(ir en cabeza)* to lead.

aventar [27] *t* AGR to winnow. **2** *(viento)* to blow.

aventura *f* adventure. **2** *(riesgo)* hazard, risk. **3** *(relación amorosa)* love (affair).

aventurado,-a *adj* venturesome, risky.

aventurar(se) *t* to hazard, risk. – **2** *p* to venture, dare.

aventurero,-a *adj* adventurous. – **2** *m,f* *m* adventurer, *f* adventuress.

avergonzado,-a *adj* ashamed, embarrassed.

avergonzar(se) [51] *t* to shame. – **2** *p* to be ashamed/embarrassed.

avería *f (en productos)* damage. **2** TÉC failure. **3** AUTO breakdown.

averiado,-a *adj (en productos)* damaged. **2** TÉC faulty, not working. **3** AUTO broken down.

averiar(se) [13] *t (productos)* to damage. **2** TÉC to cause to malfunction. **3** AUTO to cause a breakdown to. – **4** *p (productos)* to be damaged. **5** TÉC to malfunction. **6** AUTO to break down.

averiguación *f* inquiry, investigation.

averiguar [22] *t* to inquire, investigate, find out about.

aversión *f* aversion. ●*sentir* ~ *por,* to loathe.

avestruz *m* ostrich.

avezar(se) [4] *t-p* to get used *(a,* to*).*

aviación *f* aviation. **2** MIL air force.

aviador,-ra *m,f* aviator, *m* airman, *f* airwoman.

aviar [13] *t (proveer)* to provide *(de,* with*):* *con esto me avío,* I'll manage with this. **2** *(arreglar)* to tidy. **3** *(apresurar)* to hurry up. **4** *(preparar)* to prepare.

avícola *adj* poultry.

avicultura *f* aviculture.

avidez *f* avidity.

ávido,-a *adj* avid, eager.

avieso,-a *adj* perverse.

avinagrado,-a *adj* vinegary.

avinagrar(se) *t-p* to turn sour.

avío *m* preparation. **2** *pl* gear *sing,* tackle *sing.*

avión *m* (air)plane. ●*por* ~, airmail.

avioneta *f* light plane.

avisar *t (informar)* to inform. **2** *(advertir)* to warn. **3** *(mandar llamar)* to call for: ~ *al médico,* to send for the doctor.

aviso *m (información)* notice. **2** *(advertencia)* warning. ●*estar sobre* ~, to be on the alert.

avispa *f* wasp.

avispado,-a *adj* clever, smart.

avispar(se) *t-p* to smarten up.

avispero *m* wasps' nest. **2** MED carbuncle.

avistar *t* to see, sight.

avituallamento *m* provisioning.

avituallar *t* to provision *(de,* with*).*

avivar(se) *t (anhelos)* to enliven. **2** *(pasiones)* to intensify. **3** (paso) to quicken. **4** (colores) to brighten. – **5** *i-p* to become brighter/livelier.

avizor *adj* alert, watchful. ● *estar ojo* ~, to be on the alert.

avizorar *t* to watch, spy on.

axioma *m* axiom.

axila *f.* armpit, axilla.

¡ay! *interj (dolor)* ouch!, ow! **2** *(pena)* alas!: *¡* ~ *de mí!,* woe is me!

ayer *adv* yesterday. **2** *(pasado)* past. **− 3** *m* past. •*antes de* ~, the day before yesterday.

ayuda *f* help, aid, assistance. ■ ~ *de cámara,* valet.

ayudante *mf* aid, assistant. **2** MIL adjutant.

ayudar(se) *t* to help, aid, assist. **− 2** *p* *(apoyarse)* to make use (*de/con,* of). **3** *(unos a otros)* to help (one another).

ayunar *i* to fast.

ayunas *fpl en* ~, without having eaten breakfast.

ayuno *m* fast(ing).

ayuntamiento *m* *(corporación)* town council. **2** *(edificio)* town hall.

azabache *m* jet.

azada *f* hoe.

azafata *f (de avión)* air hostess. **2** *(de congresos)* hostess.

azafrán *m* saffron.

azahar *m (de naranjo)* orange blossom; *(de limonero)* lemon blossom.

azar *m* chance. •*al* ~, at random. ■ *juegos de* ~, games of chance.

azararse *p* to be embarrassed.

azaroso,-a *adj* risky, hazardous.

azor *m* goshawk.

azoramiento *m* embarrassment.

azorar *t* to embarrass. **− 2** *p* to be embarrassed.

azotaina *f fam* spanking.

azotar *t (con látigo)* to whip. **2** *(golpear)* to beat.

azote *m (instrumento)* whip. **2** *(golpe)* lash. **3** *(manotada)* smack. **4** *fig* scourge.

azotea *f* flat roof. •*fam estar mal de la* ~, to have a screw loose.

azúcar *m & f* sugar. ■ *terrón de* ~, lump of sugar.

azucarar *t* to sugar, sweeten. **2** *(bañar)* to coat/ice with sugar.

azucarero,-a *adj* sugar. **− 2** *m & f* sugar bowl.

azucena *f* white lily.

azufre *m* sulphur.

azul *adj-m* blue. ■ ~ *celeste,* sky blue; ~ *marino,* navy blue; *príncipe* ~, Prince Charming.

azulado,-a *adj* blue, bluish.

azulejo *m* glazed tile.

azulgrana *adj* blue and scarlet. **2** DEP related to Barcelona Football Club.

azuzar [4] *t fam* to egg on. •~ *los perros a algn.,* to set the dogs on sb.

B

baba *f (saliva)* spittle. **2** *(de caracol)* slime. ●*fam* **caérsele a uno la** ~, to be delighted.

babear *i* to drool.

babel *m & f* bedlam.

babero *m* bib.

bable *m* Asturian dialect.

babor *m* port (side).

babosa *f* ZOOL slug.

babosear *t* to slobber, dribble.

baboso,-a *adj* drooling. **2** *fam fig* sloppy.

baca *f* roof rack.

bacalao *m* cod.

bache *m (en carretera)* pothole. **2** *(de aire)* air pocket. **3** *fig* bad patch.

bachiller *mf* one who has the Spanish certificate of secondary education.

bachillerato *m* ~ **unificado polivalente,** Spanish certificate of secondary education.

bacilo *m* bacillus.

bacon *m* bacon.

bacteria *f* bacterium.

báculo *m (palo)* staff. **2** *(de obispo)* crosier. **3** *fig* support, relief.

bádminton *m* badminton.

baf(f)le *m* loudspeaker.

bagaje *m* baggage. **2** *fig* experience, background.

bagatela *f* bagatelle, trifle.

bahía *f* bay.

bailador,-ra *adj* dancing. — **2** *m,f* dancer.

bailar [15] *t-i* to dance. **2** *(girar)* to spin. **3** *(ser grande)* to be too big.

bailarín,-ina *adj* dancing. — **2** *m,f* dancer.

baile *m* dance. **2** *(de etiqueta)* ball. ■ ~ *de disfraces,* masked ball.

baja *f* fall, drop. **2** MIL casualty. **3** *(por enfermedad)* sick leave. ●*darse de* ~, *(de un club)* to resign *(de,* from); *(en una suscripción)* to cancel *(de,* -); *(por enfermedad)* to take sick leave.

bajada *f* descent: *subidas y bajadas,* ups and downs. **2** *(en carretera etc.)* slope.

bajamar *f* low tide.

bajar(se) *t* to bring/get down. **2** *(recorrer de arriba abajo)* to come/go down. **3** *(inclinar)* to lower; *(cabeza)* to bow. **4** *(voz)* to lower. **5** *(precios)* to reduce. — **6** *i* to go/come down. **7** *(apearse)* to get off *(de,* -). — **8** *p* to come/go down. **9** *(apearse)* to get off *(de,* -). **10** *(agacharse)* to bend down.

bajeza *f (acción)* vile deed. **2** *fig* lowliness.

bajo *adv (abajo)* below. **2** *(voz)* softly, in a low voice. — **3** *prep* under: ~ **ningún concepto,** under no circumstances. **4** *(temperatura)* below.

bajo,-a *adj* low. **2** *(persona)* short. **3** *(inclinado)* bent down. **4** *(ojos)* downcast. **5** *(tosco)* vulgar. **6** *(territorio, río)* lower. **7** *(inferior)* poor, low: *la clase baja,* the lower classes. — **8** *m* lowland. **9** MAR sandbank. **10** MÚS bass. ■ *bajos/planta baja,* ground floor.

bajón *m fig* fall. **2** *(de salud)* relapse.

bala *f* bullet. ●*fam* **como una** ~, like a shot. ■ ~ *de cañón,* cannonball; ~ *perdida,* stray bullet; *fam fig* madcap.

balada *f* ballad.

baladí *adj* trivial. ▲ *pl* **baladíes**.

balance *m* oscillation, rocking. **2** COM balance (sheet). **3** *(cálculo)* total.

balancear(se) *i-p (mecerse)* to rock; *(en columpio)* to swing; *(barco)* to roll. — **2** *i fig* to hesitate, waver.

balanceo *m* swinging, rocking, rolling.

balancín *m* rocking chair.

balanza *f (aparato)* scales *pl.* **2** COM balance. ■ ~ *de pagos,* balance of payments.

balar *i* to bleat.

balaustrada *f* balustrade, banisters *pl.*

balazo *m* shot. **2** *(herida)* bullet wound.

balbucear *i* to stutter. **2** *(niño)* to babble.

balbuceo *m* stammering. **2** *(niño)* babbling.

balbucir *i* → **balbucear**.

balcón *m* balcony.

baldado,-a *adj (inválido)* crippled. **2** *fam (cansado)* shattered.

baldar *t (lisiar)* to cripple. **2** *fam (cansar)* to wear out.

balde *m* bucket, pail. ●*de* ~, free, for nothing; *en* ~, in vain.

baldío,-a *adj (tierra)* uncultivated. **2** *(vano)* vain. − **3** *m* wasteland.

baldón *m* insult, affront.

baldosa *f* floor tile.

balido *m* bleating.

baliza *f* MAR buoy. **2** AER beacon.

ballena *f* whale.

ballesta *f* HIST crossbow. **2** AUTO spring.

ballet *m* ballet.

balneario *m* spa, health resort.

balompié *m* football.

balón *m* DEP ball, football. **2** *(para gas)* bag. ■ ~ *de oxígeno,* oxygen cylinder.

baloncesto *m* basketball.

balsa *f* pool, pond. **2** MAR raft. ●*como una* ~ *de aceite, (mar)* like a millpond; *fig* very peaceful.

balsámico,-a *adj* balsamic, balmy.

bálsamo *m* balsam, balm.

baluarte *m* bastion.

bambolear(se) *i* to swing.

bambolla *f* pretence.

bambú *m* bamboo. ▲ *pl* **bambúes**.

banal *adj* trivial.

banalidad *f* triviality.

banana *f* banana.

banca *f* COM banking; *(bancos)* (the) banks *pl.* **2** *(asiento)* bench.

bancario,-a *adj* banking.

bancarrota *f* bankruptcy. ●*hacer* ~, to go bankrupt.

banco *m* bank. **2** *(asiento)* bench; *(de iglesia)* pew. **3** *(mesa)* bench. ■ ~ *de carpintero,* workbench; ~ *de datos,* data bank; ~ *de peces,* shoal of fish; ~ *de sangre,* blood bank.

banda *f (faja)* sash. **2** *(gente armada)* gang. **3** *(musical)* band. **4** *(de pájaros)* flock. **5** *(lado)* side. ●*cerrarse en* ~, to stand firm. ■ RAD ~ *de frecuencia,* radio band; CINEM ~ *sonora,* sound track; DEP *saque de* ~, throw-in; ~ *transportadora,* conveyor belt.

bandada *f* flock.

bandazo *m* lurch, heavy roll.

bandeja *f* tray. ●*fig poner/dar en* ~, to give on a silver platter.

bandera *f* flag. ●*arriar la* ~, to strike one's colours, surrender.

bandería *f* faction, party.

banderín *m* pennant, small flag.

banderita *f* little flag. ●*el día de la* ~, flag day.

bandido,-a *m,f* bandit.

bando *m (facción)* faction, party. **2** *(edicto)* edict, proclamation.

bandolera *f* bandolier.

bandolerismo *m* banditry.

bandolero *m* bandit.

banquero,-a *m,f* banker.

banqueta *f (taburete)* (foot)stool. **2** *(banco)* little bench.

banquete *m* banquet, feast.

banquillo *m* JUR dock. **2** DEP bench.

bañador *m (mujer)* bathing/swimming costume; *(hombre)* swimming trunks *pl.*

bañar(se) *t* to bathe. **2** *(cubrir)* to coat. − **3** *p* to bathe; *(nadar)* to swim.

bañera *f* bath(tub).

bañista *mf* bather, swimmer.

baño *m* bath. **2** *(bañera)* bath(tub). **3** *(capa)* coat(ing). **4** *(aseo)* bathroom. **5** *pl (balneario)* spa *sing.* ■ ~ *(de) María,* bain-marie.

baptisterio *m* baptistry.

baqueta *f (armas)* ramrod. **2** *pl* MÚS drumsticks.

bar *m (cafetería)* café, snack bar; *(de bebidas alcohólicas)* bar. ▲ *pl* **bares**.

barahúnda *f* uproar.

baraja *f* pack, deck.

barajar *t (naipes)* to shuffle. **2** *fig (nombres)* to juggle.

baranda, barandilla *f* handrail, banister.

baratija *f* trinket, knick-knack.

baratillo *m* piece of junk.

barato,-a *adj* cheap. − **2** *adv* cheap(ly).

baratura *f* cheapness.

baraúnda *f* → **barahúnda**.

barba *f* ANAT chin. **2** *(pelo)* beard. ●*hacer la* ~, *(molestar)* to annoy; *(adular)* to fawn on; *por* ~, a head. ■ ~ *cerrada,* thick beard.

barbaridad *f (crueldad)* cruelty. **2** *(disparate)* piece of nonsense: ¡qué ~!, how awful!

barbarie *f (rusticidad)* ignorance. **2** *(crueldad)* cruelty, brutality.

barbarismo *m* barbarism.

bárbaro,-a *adj* HIST barbarian. **2** *(cruel)* cruel. **3** *(temerario)* daring. **4** *fam (grande)* enormous. **5** *fam (esplendido)* tremendous, terrific.

barbecho *m* fallow land.

barbería *f* barber's (shop).

barbero *m* barber.

barbilla *f* chin.

barbudo,-a *adj* bearded.

barca *f* small boat.

barcaza *f* lighter.

barco *m* boat, vessel, ship. ∎ ~ *cisterna,* tanker; ~ *de vapor,* steamer.

baremo *m* ready reckoner. **2** *(tarifas)* scale, table.

barítono *m* baritone.

barlovento *m* windward.

barman *m* barman. ▲ *pl* **bármanes**.

barniz *m* varnish.

barnizado,-a *adj* varnished.

barnizar [4] *t* to varnish.

barómetro *m* barometer.

barón *m* baron.

baronesa *f* baroness.

barquero,-a *m,f m* boatman, *f* boatwoman.

barquillo *m* wafer.

barra *f* bar. **2** MEC lever, bar. **3** *(de pan)* loaf. **4** *(en tribunal)* bar, rail. **5** *(de arena)* sandbank. ∎ ~ *de labios,* lipstick; DEP ~ *fija,* horizontal bar.

barrabasada *f* mischief.

barraca *f* hut, shanty. **2** *(de feria)* stall.

barranco *m (precipicio)* precipice. **2** *(torrentera)* gully.

barrena *f* drill; *(para madera)* bit.

barrenar *t* to drill, bore. **2** *(desbaratar)* to foil, thwart.

barrendero,-a *m,f* street sweeper.

barreño *m* large bowl.

barrer *t* to sweep. ●*fig* ~ *para adentro,* to look after number one.

barrera *f* barrier. ∎ ~ *del sonido,* sound barrier.

barriada *f* suburb.

barrica *f* (medium-sized) barrel.

barricada *f* barricade.

barrido *m* sweeping.

barriga *f* belly.

barrigón,-ona, barrigudo,-a *adj* big-bellied.

barril *m* barrel, keg.

barrilete *m* keg. **2** *(carpintería)* clamp.

barrio *m* neighbourhood; *(zona)* district. ●*fam irse al otro* ~, to kick the bucket. ∎ ~ *histórico,* old town; *barrios bajos,* slums.

barrizal *m* mire.

barro *m (lodo)* mud. **2** *(arcilla)* clay: *objetos de* ~, earthenware *sing.*

barroco,-a *adj-m* baroque.

barrote *m* thick bar. **2** *(de escalera, silla)* rung.

barruntar *t* to conjecture.

bartola *a la* ~ *adv,* carelessly: *tumbarse a la* ~, to lie back lazily.

bártulos *mpl* things, stuff *sing.* ●*liar los* ~, to pack up.

barullo *m* noise, din.

basa *f* base, foundation. **2** ARQ base.

basalto *m* basalt.

basar(se) *t* to base (*en,* on). − **2** *p* to be based (*en,* on).

basca *f* nausea. **2** *fam (pandilla)* crowd.

báscula *f* scale; *(de baño)* scales *pl.*

basculante *adj* tilting. **2** *(camión)* tip-up.

bascular *t* to tilt.

base *f* base. **2** *fig* basis. ●*a* ~ *de,* on the basis of. ∎ ~ *aérea,* air base; ~ *de operaciones,* field headquarters *pl.*

básico,-a *adj* basic.

basílica *f* basilica.

básquet *m* basketball.

basta *f* basting stitch. − **2** *interj* enough!, stop it!

bastante *adj* enough, sufficient. **2** *(abundante)* quite a lot. − **3** *adv* enough. **4** *(un poco)* fairly, quite.

bastar(se) *i* to be sufficient/enough. − **2** *p* ~*se a sí mismo,* to be self-sufficient.

bastardilla *adj* italics *pl.*

bastardo,-a *adj* bastard. **2** *(despreciable)* base, mean.

bastidor *m* frame. **2** *(de coche)* chassis. **3** TEAT wing. ●*fig entre bastidores,* behind the scenes.

bastilla *f* hem.

bastimento *m* supply of provisions. **2** MAR vessel.

bastión *m* bastion.

basto,-a *adj (grosero)* coarse, rough. **2** *(sin pulimentar)* rough, unpolished. − **3** *mpl (baraja española)* clubs.

bastón *m* stick, walking stick. **2** *(insignia)* baton.

basura *f* rubbish, US garbage. ∎ *cubo de la* ~, dustbin.

basurero *m* dustman, US garbage man.

bata *f* dressing gown. **2** *(de trabajo)* overall; *(médicos etc.)* white coat.

batacazo *m* violent bump/crash.

batalla *f* battle. ●*fam de* ~, ordinary, everyday: *zapatos de* ~, everyday shoes. ∎ ~ *campal,* pitched battle.

batallar *i* to battle.
batallón *m* battalion.
batata *f* BOT sweet potato.
bate *m* bat.
batería *f* MIL battery. 2 TEAT footlights *pl*.
3 *(de orquesta)* percussion; *(de conjunto)*
drums *pl*. — 4 *mf* drummer. ■ ~ *de co-*
cina, pots and pans *pl*.
batiborrillo, batiburrillo *m* jumble.
batido,-a *adj (camino)* beaten. 2 *(seda)*
shot. 3 *(huevos)* beaten. — 4 *m* CULIN
milk shake.
batidor,-ra *adj* beating. — 2 *f* CULIN *(ma-*
nual) whisk; *(automática)* blender.
batiente *adj* beating. — 2 *m (marco)* jamb.
3 *(hoja)* leaf. ●*reírse a mandíbula* ~, to
laugh one's head off.
batín *m* short dressing gown.
batir(se) *t (huevos)* to beat; *(nata, claras)*
to whip. 2 *(palmas)* to clap. 3 *(metales)*
to hammer. 4 *(alas)* to flap. 5 *(derribar)*
to knock down. 6 *(atacar)* to beat, defeat. 7 DEP to break: ~ *la marca*, to
break the record. 8 MIL to range, reconnoitre. — 9 *p* to fight.
batista *f* cambric, batiste.
baturrillo *m* hodge-podge.
batuta *f* baton. ●*llevar la* ~, to lead.
baúl *m* trunk.
bautismo *m* baptism, christening.
bautizar [4] *t* to baptize, christen. 2 *(po-*
ner nombre a) to name 3 *(el vino)* to water down.
bautizo *m* baptism, christening.
baya *f* berry.
bayeta *f* baize. 2 *(paño)* cloth.
bayo,-a *adj* bay, whitish yellow. — 2 *m*
(caballo) bay.
bayoneta *f* bayonet.
baza *f (naipes)* trick. 2 *(ocasión)* chance.
●*fig meter* ~, to butt in.
bazar *m* bazaar.
bazo *m* spleen.
bazofia *f (de comida)* scraps *pl*, leftovers
pl. 2 *(basura)* rubbish.
beatería *f* sanctimoniousness.
beatificar [1] *t* to beatify.
beatitud *f* beatitude.
beato,-a *adj (feliz)* happy. 2 *(devoto)* devout. — 3 *m,f* lay brother.
bebé *m* baby. ■ ~ *probeta*, test-tube
baby.
bebedero,-a *adj* drinkable. — 2 *m (abre-*
vadero) water trough. 3 *(pico de vasija)*
spout. 3 *(vasija)* drinking dish.
bebedizo,-a *adj* drinkable. — 2 *m* potion.

bebedor,-ra *adj* drinking. — 2 *m,f* hard
drinker.
beber *t* to drink. ●~ *a la salud de algn.*,
to toast sb.; *fig* ~ *los vientos por*, to
long for.
bebida *f* drink, beverage. ●*darse a la* ~,
to take to drink.
bebido,-a *adj* half-drunk, tipsy.
beca *f* grant, scholarship, award.
becar [1] *t* to award a grant/scholarship
to.
becario,-a *m,f* grant/scholarship holder.
becerro *m* calf.
bedel *m* beadle, head porter.
befa *f* jeer, scoff.
begonia *f* begonia.
béisbol *m* baseball.
bejuco *m* liana, reed.
beldad *f* beauty.
belén *m* REL nativity scene, crib. 2 *fig*
mess, chaos.
bélico,-a *adj* warlike, bellicose.
beligerante *adj-mf* belligerent (person).
bellaco,-a *adj (malo)* wicked. 2 *(astuto)*
cunning, sly. — 3 *m,f* knave, scoundrel.
belleza *f* beauty.
bello,-a *adj* beautiful. 2 *(bueno)* fine, noble. ■ *bellas artes*, fine arts.
bellota *f* acorn.
bemol *adj-m* MÚS flat.
benceno *m* benzene.
bencina *f* benzine.
bendecir [79] *t* to bless.
bendición *f* blessing. 2 *pl* wedding ceremony *sing*.
bendito,-a *adj (bienaventurado)* blessed. 2
(feliz) happy. — 3 *m,f* simple person.
beneficencia *f* beneficence, charity.
beneficiar(se) [12] *t* to benefit, favour. 2
(mina) to work. 3 COM to sell at a discount. — 4 *p* to benefit. 5 COM to profit.
beneficio *m (ganancia)* profit. 2 *(bien)*
benefit. ■ ~ *neto*, clear profit.
beneficioso,-a *adj* beneficial, useful.
benéfico,-a *adj* charitable: *función be-*
néfica, charity performance.
benemérito,-a *adj* well-deserving, worthy.
beneplácito *m* approval, consent.
benevolencia *f* benevolence, kindness.
benévolo,-a *adj* benevolent, kind.
bengala *f* flare.
benigno,-a *adj* benign, gentle.
benjamín,-ina *m,f* youngest child.
berberecho *m* cockle.

berbiquí m brace: ~ **y barrena,** brace and bit. ▲ pl **berbiquíes.**
berenjena f aubergine, US eggplant.
bergante m scoundrel, rascal.
bergantín m brig.
berlina f (carruaje) berlin. 2 AUTO saloon.
bermejo,-a adj bright red.
bermellón m vermilion.
bermudas fpl Bermuda shorts.
berrear i (becerro) to bellow. 2 (gritar) to howl, bawl.
berrido m (becerro) bellowing. 2 (grito) howl, shriek.
berrinche m rage, tantrum, anger.
berro m (water)cress.
berza f cabbage.
besamel adj-f bechamel. ■ **salsa** ~, white sauce.
besar(se) t to kiss. – **2** p to kiss one another. 3 fam (chocar) to collide.
beso m kiss. 2 fam (choque) bump.
bestia f beast. – **2** mf brute. – **3** adj brutish.
bestial adj beastly, bestial. 2 fam enormous. 3 fam (extraordinario) great, fantastic.
bestialidad f bestiality, brutality. 2 (tontería) stupidity. 3 fam (gran cantidad) tons pl: **una** ~ **de comida,** tons of food.
bestiario m bestiary.
besugo m sea bream. ●fig **sostener un diálogo para besugos,** to talk at cross purposes.
besuquear t to kiss again and again.
betún m (para zapatos) shoe polish. 2 QUÍM bitumen.
biberón m baby bottle.
Biblia f Bible.
bíblico,-a adj biblical.
bibliografía f bibliography.
biblioteca f library. 2 (mueble) bookcase, bookshelf.
bibliotecario,-a m,f librarian.
bicarbonato m bicarbonate.
bíceps m inv biceps inv.
bicha f snake.
bicho m bug, insect. 2 fig odd character. ■ ~ **raro,** oddball.
bici f fam bike.
bicicleta f bicycle.
bicoca f fam bargain.
bidé m bidet.
bidón m can, drum.
biela f AUTO connecting rod.
bien adv well. 2 (acertadamente) right, correctly. 3 (con éxito) successfully. 4 (de acuerdo) O.K., all right. 5 (de buena gana) willingly. 6 (mucho) very; (bastante) quite. 7 (fácilmente) easily: ~ **se ve que** ..., it is easy to see that ... . – **8** m good: **hombre de** ~, honest man. 9 (da bienestar) benefit: **hacer** ~, to do good; **en** ~ **de,** for the sake of. 10 pl property sing, possessions. ●**ahora** ~, now then; ~ **que,** although; **más** ~, rather; **no** ~, as soon as; **si** ~, although. ■ **bienes inmuebles,** real estate sing; **bienes muebles,** movables, personal property sing; fam **gente** ~, the upper classes pl.
bienal adj biennial.
bienaventurado,-a adj REL blessed. 2 (afortunado) fortunate.
bienaventuranza f happiness, bliss.
bienestar m well-being, comfort.
bienhechor,-ra adj beneficent, beneficial. – **2** m,f m benefactor, f benefactress.
bienio m biennium.
bienvenida f welcome. ●**dar la** ~ **a,** to welcome.
bies m inv bias.
bifurcación f bifurcation. 2 (de la carretera) fork.
bifurcarse [1] p to fork, branch off.
bigamia f bigamy.
bígamo,-a adj bigamous. – **2** m,f bigamist.
bigote m moustache. 2 (gato) whiskers pl.
bilingüe adj bilingual.
bilingüismo m bilingualism.
bilioso,-a adj bilious.
bilis f bile. 2 fig spleen. ●fig **descargar la** ~ **contra,** to vent one's spleen on.
billar m billiards. 2 (mesa) billiard table. 3 pl billiard room.
billete m (moneda) note. 2 (de tren, autobús, sorteo, etc.) ticket. ■ ~ **de ida,** one-way ticket; ~ **de ida y vuelta,** return ticket, US round-trip ticket.
billón m billion, US trillion.
bimensual adj twice-monthly.
bimestral adj every two months.
bimotor adj twin-engine.
bingo m (juego) bingo. 2 (sala) bingo hall.
binoculares mpl field glasses, binoculars.
binóculo m pince-nez.
biodegradable adj biodegradable.
biografía f biography.
biología f biology.
biólogo,-a m,f biologist.
biombo m (folding) screen.
bioquímica f biochemistry.

biplano *m* biplane.

biquini *m* bikini.

birlar *t fam* to pinch, nick.

birlibirloque *m por arte de* ~, as if by magic.

birria *f fam* monstrosity: *este libro es una* ~, this book is rubbish.

biruji *m fam* chilly wind.

bis *adv* twice; *viven en el 23* ~, they live at 23A. − **2** *m inv* encore.

bisabuelo,-a *m,f* great-grandparent; *m* great-grandfather, *f* great-grandmother.

bisagra *f* hinge.

bisector,-triz *adj* bisecting. − **2** *f* bisector, bisectrix.

bisel *m* bevel (edge).

bisexual *adj-mf* bisexual.

bisiesto *adj año* ~, leap year.

bisnieto,-a *m,f* great-grandchild; *m* great-grandson, *f* great-granddaughter.

bisonte *m* bison.

bisoñé *m* toupee, hairpiece.

bisoño,-a *adj-m,f* inexperienced (person).

bisté, bistec *m* steak.

bisturí *m* scalpel. ▲ *pl* **bisturíes**.

bisutería *f* imitation jewellery.

bitácora *f* binnacle.

bíter *m* bitters *pl*.

bizantino,-a *adj* Byzantine. **2** *fig (discusión)* idle. **3** *fig (decadente)* decadent.

bizarro,-a *adj (valiente)* courageous. **2** *(generoso)* generous.

bizco,-a *adj-m,f* cross-eyed (person).

bizcocho *m* sponge cake.

bizquear *i* to squint. − **2** *t (guiñar)* to wink.

blanco,-a *adj* white. **2** *(complexión)* fair. **3** *(pálido)* pale. − **4** *m (color)* white. **5** *(objetivo)* target, mark; *fig* aim, goal. **6** *(hueco)* blank, gap; *(en escrito)* blank space. ●*dar en el* ~, to hit the mark; *fig* to hit the nail on the head; *quedarse en* ~, to fail to grasp the point.

blancura *f* whiteness.

blandir *t* to brandish, wave. ▲ *Only used in forms which include the letter i in their endings:* **blandía, blandiré, blandiendo**.

blando,-a *adj (tierno)* soft, bland. **2** *fig (benigno)* gentle, mild. **3** *(cobarde)* cowardly.

blandura *f* softness. **2** *fig (dulzura)* gentleness, sweetness.

blanqueador,-ra *adj* whitening. − **2** *m* whitewash.

blanquear *t* to whiten. **2** *(con cal)* to whitewash. − **3** *i* to whiten, turn white.

blanqueo *m* whitening. **2** *(con cal)* whitewashing.

blasfemar *i (decir palabrotas)* to swear, curse. **2** *(contra Dios)* to blaspheme *(contra,* against).

blasfemia *f (palabrota)* curse. **2** *(contra Dios)* blasphemy.

blasfemo,-a *adj* blasphemous. − **2** *m,f* blasphemer.

blasón *m* heraldry. **2** *(escudo)* coat of arms. **3** *fig* honour, glory.

blasonar *t* to emblazon. − **2** *i* to boast.

bledo *m* common amaranth. ●*fam me importa un* ~, I couldn't care less.

blindado,-a *adj* armoured, armour-plated. ■ *coche* ~, bullet-proof car; *(furgoneta)* security van; *puerta blindada,* reinforced door.

blindaje *m* armour.

blindar *t* to armour.

bloc *m* (note)pad.

blonda *f* blond lace.

bloque *m* block. **2** *(papel)* (note)pad. **3** POL bloc. ■ ~ *de pisos,* block of flats.

bloquear(se) *t* MIL to blockade. **2** *(cortar)* to block. **3** *(precios, cuentas)* to freeze. − **4** *p* to freeze.

bloqueo *m* MIL blockade. **2** *(precios, cuenta)* freezing.

blusa *f* blouse.

blusón *m* loose blouse, smock.

boa *f* boa.

boato *m* pomp, ostentation.

bobada *f* silliness, foolishness. ●*decir bobadas,* to talk nonsense.

bobear *i* to talk nonsense, play the fool.

bóbilis *de* ~ ~ *adv,* for nothing.

bobina *f* real, bobbin. **2** ELEC coil.

bobinar *t* to wind.

bobo,-a *adj* silly, foolish. − **2** *m,f* fool, dunce.

boca *f* mouth. **2** *(abertura)* entrance, opening. ●*andar en* ~ *de todos,* to be the talk of the town; *no decir esta* ~ *es mía/no abrir* ~, not to say a word; *se me hace la* ~ *agua,* it makes my mouth water. ■ ~ *a* ~, kiss of life, mouth-to-mouth resucitation; ~ *abajo/arriba,* face downwards/upwards; ~ *de un río,* mouth of a river; ~ *del estómago,* pit of the stomach.

bocacalle *f* entrance to a street. **2** *(calle secundaria)* side street.

bocadillo *m* sandwich. **2** *(en cómics)* (speech) balloon.

bocado *m* mouthful. **2** *(piscolabis)* snack, tidbit. ●~ *de rey,* tidbit, delicacy.

bocamanga *f* cuff.

bocanada *f (de humo)* puff. **2** *(de líquido)* mouthful.

bocata *m arg* sandwich.

bocazas *mf inv* bigmouth.

boceto *m* sketch; *(proyecto)* outline.

bochorno *m* sultry/close weather, stifling heat. **2** *(rubor)* blush. **3** *fig* embarrassment, shame.

bochornoso,-a *adj* hot, sultry. **2** *fig* disgraceful, shameful.

bocina *f* horn. • *tocar la ~,* to blow/ sound one's horn.

boda *f* marriage, wedding. ■ *bodas de plata/oro,* silver/golden wedding *sing.*

bodega *f* (wine) cellar. **2** *(tienda)* wine shop. **3** *(almacén)* pantry. **4** MAR hold.

bodegón *m* still-life painting.

bodrio *m fam* rubbish, trash: *¡vaya ~ de película!,* what a useless film!

bofetada *f,* **bofetón** *m* slap.

bofia *f arg la ~,* the fuzz *pl,* the cops *pl.*

boga *f* vogue. • *estar en ~,* to be in fashion.

bogar [7] *i* to row. **2** *(navegar)* to sail.

bogavante *m* lobster.

bohemio,-a *adj-m,f* bohemian.

bohío *m am* hut.

boicot *m* boycott. ▲ *pl* **boicots**.

boicotear *t* to boycott.

boina *f* beret.

boite *f* nightclub.

boj *m* box tree. ▲ *pl* **bojes**.

bol *m* bowl.

bola *f* ball. **2** *fam* fib, lie. ■ *~ de nieve,* snowball; *queso de ~,* Edam cheese.

bolero,-a *adj* lying. – **2** *m,f* liar. – **3** *m (baile)* bolero. – **4** *f* bowling alley.

boletín *m* bulletin.

boleto *m* ticket. **2** *(quiniela)* coupon.

boli *m fam* ballpen, Biro®.

boliche *m* bowling, skittles *pl.* **2** *(bolera)* bowling alley.

bólido *m* ASTRON fireball. **2** *fam* racing car.

bolígrafo *m* ball point (pen), Biro®.

bollo *m* CULIN bun, roll. **2** *(abolladura)* dent. **3** *(chichón)* bump. • *fig no está el horno para bollos,* this is not the right time.

bolo *m* skittle, ninepin. **2** *(necio)* dunce, idiot. **3** *pl* skittles.

bolsa *f* bag. **2** *(de dinero)* purse. **3** *(beca)* grant: *~ de estudios/viaje,* scholarship. **4** *(en prenda)* bag. **5** FIN stock exchange: *jugar a la ~,* to play the market. **6** AM jacket. • *¡la ~ o la vida!,* your money

or your life! ■ *~ de agua caliente,* hot water bottle; *(en periódico) ~ de trabajo,* job section.

bolsillo *m* pocket. • *fig sacar el dinero de tu/su propio ~,* to pay for it out of one's own pocket.

bolso *m* handbag, US purse.

bomba *f (explosivo)* bomb. **2** TÉC pump. • *a prueba de ~,* bombproof. ■ *~ aspirante,* suction pump; *fig atómica,* atomic bomb; *fig noticia ~,* bombshell.

bombacho *m (pantalón) ~,* knickerbockers *pl.*

bombardear *t* to bombard, bomb.

bombardeo *m* bombardment, bombing.

bombear *t* MIL to bombard. **2** *(agua)* to pump.

bombero *m* fireman.

bombilla *f* (light) bulb.

bombo *m* MÚS bass drum. **3** *(elogio)* buildup. **4** *(para sorteo)* lottery box. • *dar ~,* to praise excessively.

bombón *m* chocolate. **2** *fam* knock-out.

bonachón,-ona *adj* kind, good-natured. – **2** *m,f* kind soul.

bonanza *f* calm sea. **2** *fig* prosperity.

bondad *f* goodness. **2** *(afabilidad)* kindness. **3** *(amabilidad)* kindness: *tenga la ~ de contestar,* please write back.

bondadoso,-a *adj* kind, good, good-natured.

bonete *m* REL biretta, cap. **2** EDUC college cap.

boniato *m* sweet potato.

bonificación *f (descuento)* allowance, discount. **2** *(mejoría)* improvement.

bonificar [1] *t* COM to allow, discount. **2** *(mejorar)* to improve.

bonito,-a *adj* pretty, lovely. – **2** *m (pez)* (Atlantic) bonito.

bono *m* FIN bond. **2** *(vale)* voucher. ■ *~ del tesoro/Estado,* Exchequer bill.

boquear *i (inspirar)* to gasp. **2** *(expirar)* to breathe one's last. – **3** *t (pronunciar)* to utter.

boquerón *m (pescado)* anchovy.

boquete *m* narrow opening.

boquiabierto,-a *adj* open-mouthed.

boquilla *f (de pipa, instrumento)* mouthpiece. **2** *(sujeta cigarrillos)* cigarette holder. **3** *(filtro de cigarrillo)* tip.

borbollón *m* bubbling up. • *a borbollones,* hastily, tumltuously.

borbotar, borbotear *i* to boil over.

borbotón *m →* **borbollón**.

borda *f* MAR gunwale. • *arrojar por la ~,* to throw overboard.

bordado,-a *adj* embroidered. − **2** *m* embroidering, embroidery.

bordar *t* to embroider. **2** *fig* to perform exquisitely.

borde *adj (tonto)* silly. − **2** *m (extremo)* edge. **3** *(de prenda)* hem.

bordear *t* to skirt. **2** *(aproximarse)* to border, verge.

bordillo *m* kerb.

bordo *m* MAR board. ●*a* ~, on board.

boreal *adj* boreal, northern.

bórico,-a *adj* boric.

borla *f* tassel.

borrachera *f* drunkenness.

borracho,-a *adj* drunk. − **2** *m,f* drunkard. ●~ *como una cuba,* blind drunk.

borrador *m (apunte)* rough copy. **2** *(de pizarra)* duster. **3** *(goma)* eraser. **4** *(libro)* blotter.

borrar *t (con goma etc.)* to erase, rub out. **2** *(tachar)* to cross out/off.

borrasca *f* storm.

borrascoso,-a *adj* stormy.

borrego,-a *m,f* lamb. **2** *(ignorante)* simpleton.

borrico,-a *m* ass, donkey. − **2** *m,f fam* ass, dimwit.

borrón *m (mancha)* ink blot. **2** *fig* blemish.

borroso,-a *adj* blurred, hazy.

boscaje *m* thicket.

bosque *m* forest, wood.

bosquejar *t* to sketch, outline.

bosquejo *m (dibujo)* sketch; *(plan etc.)* outline.

bostezar [4] *i* to yawn.

bostezo *m* yawn.

bota *f* boot. **2** *(de vino)* wineskin. ●*fam fig* **ponerse las botas,** to stuff o.s.

botánica *f* botany.

botánico,-a *adj* botanical. − **2** *m,f* botanist.

botar *t* to throw. **2** AM *(despedir)* to fire. − **3** *i (pelota)* to bounce. **4** *(saltar)* to jump.

botarate *m* fool, harebrain. **2** AM spendthrift.

bote *m* MAR small boat. **2** *(salto)* bounce. **3** *(recipiente)* tin, can; *(para propinas)* jar/box for tips. ●*de* ~ *en* ~, jam-packed. ■ ~ *salvavidas,* lifeboat.

botella *f* bottle.

botellín *m* small bottle.

boticario *m* chemist, US druggist.

botija *f* earthenware jar.

botijo *m* earthen jar with spout and handle.

botín *m (zapato)* ankle boot. **2** *(cubierta)* gaiter. **3** *(de robo)* booty, loot.

botiquín *m* first-aid kit.

botón *m* button. **2** *(tirador)* knob: ~ *de puerta,* doorknob. **3** BOT bud. ■ BOT ~ *de oro,* buttercup.

botones *m inv* buttons.

boutique *f* boutique.

bóveda *f* vault. ■ ~ *celeste,* vault of heaven; ~ *de cañón,* barrel vault.

bovino,-a *adj* bovine.

boxeador *m* boxer.

boxear *i* to box.

boxeo *m* boxing.

boya *f* MAR buoy. **2** *(corcho)* float.

boyante *adj* MAR buoyant. **2** *fig* prosperous, successful.

bozal *m* muzzle.

bozo *m* fuzz.

bracear *i* to move/swing the arms. **2** *(nadar)* to swim. **3** *fig (forcejear)* to struggle.

bracero *m* labourer.

bracete *de* ~, *adv* arm-in-arm.

bragas *fpl* panties, knickers.

braguero *m* truss.

bragueta *f* fly, flies *pl*.

bramar *i* to bellow, roar.

bramido *m* bellow, roar.

brandi *m* brandy. ▲ *pl* **brandis**.

brasa *f* live coal. ■ *carne a la* ~, barbecued meat.

brasero *m* brazier.

bravata *f* bluster, bragging.

bravío,-a *adj (feroz)* ferocious, wild. **2** *(persona)* uncouth.

bravo,-a *adj (valiente)* brave, courageous. **2** *(bueno)* fine, excellent. **3** *(fiero)* fierce, ferocious. **4** *(mar)* rough. **5** *(enojado)* angry, violent. − **6** *interj* well done!, bravo! ■ *toro* ~, fighting bull.

bravura *f (valentía)* bravery, courage. **2** *(fiereza)* fierceness, ferocity.

braza *f (medida)* fathom. **2** *(natación)* breast stroke.

brazada *f (natación)* stroke.

brazal *m* armband.

brazalete *m* bracelet.

brazo *m* arm; *(de animal)* foreleg; *(río, candelabro, árbol)* branch. **2** *fig* power, might. **3** *pl* hands, workers. ●*a* ~ *partido,* *(sin armas)* hand to hand; *(con empeño)* tooth and nail; *asidos del* ~, arm in arm; *cruzarse de brazos,* to fold one's arms; *fig* to remain idle.

brea *f* tar, pitch.

brebaje *m* beverage.

brecha *f* break, opening. **2** *fig* breach.

bregar [7] *i* (*luchar*) to fight, struggle. **2** (*ajetrearse*) to work hard. − **3** *t* (*amasar*) to knead.

breña *f*, **breñal** *m* bushy/craggy ground.

breva *f* (*higo*) early fig. **2** (*cigarro*) flat cigar. **3** *fig* (*ganga*) cushy job/number.

breve *adj* short, brief. − **2** *f* MÚS breve. ●*en* ∼, soon, shortly.

brevedad *f* brevity, briefness. ●*con la mayor* ∼, as soon as possible.

breviario *m* REL breviary. **2** (*compendio*) compendium.

brezo *m* heath, heather.

bribón,-ona *adj* roguish. − **2** *m,f* rogue.

brida *f* bridle. **2** TÉC flange.

brigada *f* MIL brigade. **2** (*de policía*) squad.

brillante *adj* brilliant: *fig un alumno* ∼, a brilliant student. − **2** *m* (*diamante*) diamond.

brillantez *f* (*resplandor*) dazzle. **2** *fig* success, splendour.

brillantina *f* brilliantine, (hair) grease.

brillar *i* (*resplandecer*) to shine. **2** (*centellear*) to sparkle; (*estrella*) to twinkle. **3** *fig* to be outstanding.

brillo *m* (*resplandor*) shine. **2** (*estrella*) twinkling. ● *sacar* ∼, to shine.

brincar [1] *i* to jump, hop.

brinco *m* jump, hop.

brindar(se) *i* to toast (*por*, to). − **2** *t* (*ofrecer*) to offer: ∼ *a algn. una cosa*, to offer sth. to sb. − **3** *p* offer/volunteer (*a*, to).

brindis *m inv* toast.

brío *m* (*pujanza*) strength. **2** (*resolución*) determination. **3** (*valentía*) courage.

brisa *f* breeze.

brisca *f* Spanish card game.

brizna *f* bit, piece; (*de hierba*) blade.

broca *f* spindle. **2** (*barrena*) drill, bit.

brocado *m* brocade.

brocha *f* paintbrush: *pintor de* ∼ *gorda*, house painter. ■ ∼ *de afeitar*, shaving brush.

broche *m* COST fastener. **2** (*joya*) brooch.

brocheta *f* skewer.

broma *f* joke. ●*gastar una* ∼ *a algn.*, to play a joke on sb. ■ ∼ *pesada*, practical joke.

bromear *i* to joke.

bromista *adj* fond of joking. − **2** *mf* joker.

bronca *f* row, quarrel. ●*armar una* ∼, to cause a row/rumpus.

bronce *m* bronze.

bronceado,-a *adj* bronzed. **2** (*piel*) tanned. − **3** *m* (sun)tan.

broncear(se) *t* to bronze. − **2** *p* to get (sun)tan.

bronco,-a *adj* (*tosco*) coarse, rough. **2** (*metal*) brittle. **3** (*voz, sonido*) hoarse, harsh.

bronquio *m* bronchus.

bronquitis *f inv* bronchitis.

brotar *i* to sprout, bud. **2** (*agua*) to spring. **3** (*estallar*) to break out.

brote *m* bud, sprout. **2** (*estallido*) outbreak.

bruces *de* ∼, *adv* face downwards. ●*caer de* ∼, to fall headlong.

bruja *f* witch, sorceress. **2** *fam* old hag.

brujería *f* witchcraft, sorcery.

brujo *m* wizard, sorcerer.

brújula *f* compass.

bruma *f* mist, fog.

brumoso,-a *adj* hazy, misty.

bruno,-a *adj* dark brown.

bruñido,-a *adj* burnished. − **2** *m* burnishing.

bruñir [40] *t* to burnish, polish.

brusco,-a *adj* (*persona*) brusque, abrupt. **2** (*repentino*) sudden.

brusquedad *f* (*carácter*) brusqueness, abruptness. **2** (*rapidez*) suddenness.

brutal *adj* brutal, beastly, savage. **2** *fig* (*enorme*) colossal. **3** *fig* (*magnífico*) great, terrific.

brutalidad *f* (*crueldad*) brutality. **2** (*necedad*) stupidity.

bruto,-a *adj* (*cruel*) brutal. **2** (*necio*) stupid, ignorant. **3** (*tosco*) rough, coarse. **4** FIN gross. **5** (*peso*) gross. **6** (*piedra*) rough. **7** (*petroleo*) crude. − **8** *m* brute, beast.

bucal *adj* oral, mouth.

buceador,-ra *m,f* diver.

bucear *i* to dive.

buche *m* (*de aves*) crow, crop. **2** *fam* (*del hombre*) belly. **3** (*pecho*) bosom.

bucle *m* curl, ringlet.

bucólico,-a *adj* bucolic.

budín *m* pudding.

buen *adj* → **bueno,-a**. ▲ *Used in front of a sing masculine noun: buen chico/chico bueno.*

buenaventura *f* good luck/fortune. ●*decirle a algn. la* ∼, to tell sb's fortune.

bueno,-a *adj* good. **2** (*amable*) kind. **3** (*agradable*) nice, polite. **4** (*apropiado*) right, suitable. **5** (*de salud*) well. **6** (*grande*) big; (*considerable*) considerable: *un buen número de participantes*, quite a few participants. − **7** *interj* (*sorpresa*) well, very well; (*de acuerdo*) all right!

●*estar* ~, to be in good health; *fam* to be good-looking; *por la buenas,* willingly; *fam de buenas a primeras,* from the very start; *fam ¡ésta sí que es buena!,* that's a good one! ■ *buenos días,* good morning; *buenas noches,* good evening; *buenas tardes,* good afternoon. ▲ → **buen.**

buey *m* ox, bullock. ■ *carne de* ~, beef; ~ *marino,* sea cow.

búfalo *m* buffalo.

bufanda *f* (thick) scarf.

bufar *i* (*toro*) to snort. 2 (*persona*) to be fuming: ~ *de coraje,* to be fuming with rage.

bufé *m* buffet. ■ ~ *libre,* self-service buffet meal.

bufete *m* (*mesa*) writing desk. 2 (*de abogado*) lawyer's office: *abrir* ~, to set up as a lawyer.

bufido *m* angry snort/roar.

bufo,-a *adj* farcical, clownish. ■ *ópera* ~, opera bouffe.

bufón,-ona *adj* buffoon. – 2 *m,f* buffoon, jester.

buharda, buhardilla *f* (*ventana*) dormer window. 2 (*desván*) garret, attic.

búho *m* owl.

buhonero *m* pedlar, hawker.

buitre *m* vulture.

bujía *f* (*vela*) candle. 2 (*candelero*) candlestick. 3 AUTO spark plug.

bula *f* (*documento*) papal bull. 2 (*sello*) bulla.

bulbo *m* bulb.

buldog *m* bulldog.

bulevar *m* boulevard.

bulla *f* (*ruido*) noise, uproar, racket. 2 (*multitud*) crowd.

bullanga *f* tumult, racket.

bullicio *m* (*ruido*) noise, stir. 2 (*tumulto*) uproar.

bullicioso,-a *adj* (*ruidoso*) noisy. 2 (*animado*) busy.

bullir [41] *i* to boil, bubble up. 2 (*animales*) to swarm. 3 *fig* (*moverse*) to bustle about.

bulo *m* hoax, false report.

bulto *m* (*tamaño*) volume, size, bulk. 2 (*forma*) shape, form. 3 (*elevación*) swelling, lump. 4 (*fardo*) bundle, pack. ●*a* ~, broadly, roughly; *fig escurrir el* ~, to dodge the question.

búnker *m* bunker.

buñuelo *m* doughnut. 2 *fig* botch-up, bungle.

buque *m* MAR ship, vessel. ■ ~ *cisterna,* tanker; ~ *de guerra,* warship; ~ *de vapor,* steamer; ~ *de vela,* sailboat; ~ *mercante,* merchant ship.

burbuja *f* bubble.

burbujear *i* to bubble.

burdel *m* brothel.

burdo,-a *adj* coarse.

burgués,-esa *m,f* bourgeois, middle-class.

burguesía *f* bourgeoisie, middle class.

buril *m* burin.

burla *f* (*mofa*) mockery, gibe. 2 (*broma*) joke. 3 (*engaño*) deception, trick.

burlador,-ra *adj* mocking, deceiving. – 2 *m* ladies' man.

burlar(se) *t* to deceive, trick. 2 (*eludir*) to dodge, evade. – 3 *p* to mock. ●~*se de,* to make fun of, laugh at.

burlesco,-a *adj* burlesque, comical.

burlón,-ona *adj* mocking. – 2 *m,f* mocker, joker.

buró *m* writing desk, bureau.

burocracia *f* bureaucracy.

burócrata *mf* bureaucrat.

burrada *f* drove of asses. 2 *fig* foolishness, blunder.

burro,-a *m,f* donkey, ass. 2 *fig* (*trabajador*) drudge. 3 (*ignorante*) ignorant person.

bursátil *adj* stock market/exchange.

busca *f* search, hunt. ●*ir en* ~ *de,* to search for.

buscador,-ra *adj* searching. – 2 *m,f* searcher, seeker. – 3 *m* (*anteojo*) finder.

buscar [1] *t* to look/search for: ~ *una palabra en el diccionario,* to look up a word in the dictionary; *ir a* ~ *algo,* to go and get sth. ●*fam buscársela,* to be looking for trouble; *fam buscarse la vida,* to try and earn one's living.

buscavidas *mf inv* snooper, busybody.

buscón,-ona *m,f* (*ladrón*) petty thief. – 2 *f* prostitute.

búsqueda *f* search, quest.

busto *m* (*arte*) bust. 2 (*pecho*) (*de mujer*) bust; (*de hombre*) chest.

butaca *f* (*sillón*) armchair. 2 TEAT seat. ■ *patio de butacas,* stalls *pl,* US orchestra.

butano *m* butane. ■ *bombona de* ~, (butane) gas cylinder.

butifarra *f* kind of pork sausage.

buzo *m* diver.

buzón *m* letter-box, US mailbox. ●*echar una carta al* ~, to post a letter.

byte *m* INFORM byte.

C

cabal *adj* exact, precise. ●*estar en sus cabales,* to be in one's right mind.

cábala *f* cab(b)ala. **2** *(suposición)* guess, divination. **3** *(superstición)* plot. ▲ **2** *usually pl.*

cabalgadura *f* riding horse. **2** *(bestia de carga)* beast of burden.

cabalgar [7] *i* to ride.

cabalgata *f* cavalcade.

caballa *f* mackerel.

caballar *adj* equine, horse.

caballeresco,-a *adj* chivalrous.

caballería *f* mount, steed. **2** MIL cavalry. **3** HIST knighthood.

caballeriza *f* stable. **2** *(personal)* stable hands *pl.*

caballero,-a *adj* riding. — **2** *m* gentleman. **3** HIST knight. ■ ~ *andante,* knight errant.

caballerosidad *f* gentlemanly behaviour.

caballete *m (de pintor)* easel. **2** ARQ ridge. **3** TÉC trestle. **4** *(de nariz)* bridge.

caballito *m* small horse. **2** *pl (tiovivo)* merry-go-round *sing.,* US carousel *sing.* ■ ~ *de mar,* sea horse; ~ *del diablo,* dragonfly.

caballo *m* ZOOL horse. **2** TÉC horsepower. **3** *(ajedrez)* knight. **4** *(naipes)* queen. **5** arg *(heroína)* junk, horse. ●*a* ~, on horseback; *montar a* ~, to ride; *fig a* ~ *entre ...,* halfway between ... .

cabaña *f* cabin, hut, hovel. **2** *(ganado)* cattle.

cabaret *m* cabaret, nightclub. ▲ *pl* cabarets.

cabecear *i (negar)* to shake one's head. **2** *(dormirse)* to nod. **3** *(animal)* to move the head. **4** NÁUT to pitch. — **5** *t* DEP to head.

cabecera *f* top, head. **2** *(de cama)* bedhead.

cabecilla *mf* leader.

cabellera *f* (head of) hair. **2** *(de cometa)* tail.

cabello *m* hair. **2** *pl* corn silk *sing.* ■ ~ *de ángel,* sweet made of gourd and syrup.

cabelludo,-a *adj* hairy. ■ *cuero* ~, scalp.

caber [66] *i* to fit *(en,* into): *en esta lata caben diez litros,* this can holds ten litres; *no cabe más,* there is no room for more. **2** *(ser posible)* to be possible. ●*no cabe duda,* there is no doubt; *fig no me cabe en la cabeza,* I can't believe it.

cabestrillo *m* sling.

cabestro *m (dogal)* halter. **2** *(animal)* leading ox.

cabeza *f* head. **2** *(talento)* brightness. **3** *(persona)* chief, leader. **4** *(de región)* seat: ~ *de partido,* county seat. ●*a la* ~ *de,* at the front/top of; ~ *abajo,* upside down; ~ *arriba,* the right way up; *(diez mil) por* ~, (ten thousand) a head/per person; *volver la* ~, to look round; *fig estar mal de la* ~, to be mad; *fig irse la* ~, to feel dizzy; *fig no tener ni pies ni* ~, to be absurd. ■ ~ *de ajo,* bulb of garlic; ~ *de familia,* head of the family; *dolor de* ~, headache; *fam* ~ *de chorlito,* scatterbrain.

cabezada *f* blow on the head, butt. **2** *(saludo)* nod. ●*echar una* ~, to have a snooze.

cabezal *m* TÉC head. **2** *(almohada)* bolster.

cabezón,-ona *adj* bigheaded. **2** *(terco)* pigheaded.

cabezonada *f fam* pigheaded action.

cabezota *adj* pigheaded. — **2** *m,f* bighead. **3** *(terco)* pigheaded person.

cabezudo,-a *adj* bigheaded. **2** *(terco)* pigheaded. — **3** *m* bigheaded dwarf (in a procession).

cabida *f* capacity, room.

cabildo *m* town council.

cabina *f* cabin, booth. ■ ~ *telefónica,* telephone box, US telephone booth.

cabizbajo,-a *adj* crestfallen.

cable *m* cable. ●*fam echarle un ~ a algn.,* to give sb. a hand.

cablegrafiar *t* to cable.

cabo *m* end, extremity. **2** *fig* end: *al ~ de un mes,* in a month. **3** *(cuerda)* strand. **4** GEOG cape. **5** MIL corporal. ●*de ~ a rabo,* from head to tail; *llevar a ~,* to carry out.

cabotaje *m* cabotage, coasting trade.

cabra *f* goat. ●*fam loco,-a como una ~,* as mad as a hatter.

cabrahigar [25] *t* to hang skewered figs on.

cabré *indic fut* → **caber.**

cabrear(se)* *t* to make angry. − **2** *p* to get worked up.

cabreo* *m* anger: *agarrar/coger/pillar un ~,* to fly off the handle.

cabrero *m* goatherd.

cabrestante *m* capstan.

cabrío,-a *adj* goat(ish). ■ *macho ~,* he-goat.

cabriola *f (brinco)* caper, hop. **2** *(voltereta)* somersault.

cabrito *m* kid.

cabrón,-ona *m* ZOOL billy goat. − **2*** *m,f fig m* bastard*, *f* bitch*.

cabuya *f* AM string, rope.

caca *f fam (excremento)* shit. **2** *(en lenguaje infantil)* poopoo.

cacahuete *m* peanut.

cacao *m* BOT cacao. **2** *(polvo, bebida)* cocoa. **3** *fam (jaleo)* mess, cockup.

cacarear *i* to cackle. **2** *fam* to strut about.

cacareo *m* cackling. **2** *fam* boasting, bragging.

cacatúa *f* cockatoo.

cacería *f* hunt, hunting party.

cacerola *f* saucepan.

cacha *f fam* thigh. ●*estar cachas,* to be hunky.

cachalote *m* cachalot, sperm whale.

cacharro *m (de cocina)* crock, piece of crockery. **2** *fam (cosa)* thing, piece of junk. **3** *fam (coche)* banger.

cachaza *f* slowness, phlegm.

cachear *t* to search, frisk.

cachemir *m,* **cachemira** *f* cashmere.

cachete *m (bofetada)* slap.

cachiporra *f* cudgel.

cachirulos *mpl fam* thingumabobs.

cacho *m fam* bit, piece.

cachondearse *p* to poke fun (*de,* at).

cachondeo *m fam* laugh. ●*¡vaya ~!,* what a laugh!

cachondo,-a *adj (excitado)* hot, randy, horny. **2** *fam* funny.

cachorro,-a *m,f (de perro)* puppy; *(de otros animales)* cub.

cacique *m (indio)* cacique. **2** *(déspota)* tyrant. ▲ *f* **cacica.**

caciquismo *m* caciquism. **2** *(despotismo)* despotism.

caco *m fam* thief.

cacofonía *f* cacophony.

cacto, cactus *m inv* cactus.

cada *adj* each, every: *~ cual/uno,* each/every one; *ocho de ~ diez,* eight out of (every) ten. ●*¿ ~ cuánto?,* how often?; *~ vez más,* more and more.

cadalso *m (patíbulo)* scaffold. **2** *(plataforma)* platform.

cadáver *m* corpse, cadaver.

cadavérico,-a *adj* cadaverous. **2** *fig* deadly, pale.

cadena *f* chain. **2** *(industrial)* line. **3** *(montañosa)* range. **4** *(musical)* music centre. **5** TV channel; RAD chain of stations. **6** *pl* AUTO tyre chains. ●*tirar de la ~ del wáter,* to flush the toilet. ■ ~ *de fabricación,* production line; ~ *de montaje,* assembly line; ~ *perpetua,* life imprisonment.

cadencia *f* cadence, rhythm. **2** MÚS cadenza.

cadencioso,-a *adj* rhythmic(al).

cadera *f* hip.

cadete *m* cadet.

caducar [1] *i* to expire.

caducidad *f* expiry, loss of validity. ■ *fecha de ~,* expiry date.

caduco,-a *adj (pasado)* expired, out-of-date. **2** *(viejo)* decrepit. **3** BOT deciduous.

caer(se) [67] *i* to fall: *~ de cabeza/espalda,* to fall on one's head/back; *~ de rodillas,* to fall on one's knees; *dejar ~,* to drop. **2** *(derrumbar)* to fall down. **3** *(hallarse)* to be located: *el camino cae a la derecha,* the road is on the right. **4** *(coincidir fechas)* to be: *el día cuatro cae en jueves,* the fourth is a Thursday. **5** *(el sol)* to go down. − **6** *p* to fall (down). ●*~ bien/mal, (sentar)* to agree/not to agree with; *(prenda)* to suit/not to suit; *(persona)* to like/not to like; *~ en la cuenta de,* to realize; *fig ~ enfermo,-a,* to fall ill.

café *m* coffee. **2** *(cafetería)* café.

cafeína *f* caffeine.

cafetal *m* coffee plantation.

cafetera *f* coffeepot.

cafetería f cafeteria, café.

cafre adj-mf savage.

cagada* f (mierda) shit*. **2** fig (error) fuck-up*, cockup*.

cagar(se)* [7] i to shit*. – **2** p to shit* o.s. ●~ **de miedo,** to be shit-scared*.

caída f fall: **a la ~ del sol,** at sunset. **2** (pérdida) loss: **la ~ del cabello,** hair loss. **3** (de precios) fall, drop. **4** (de tejidos) hang. ■ ~ **de ojos,** demure look.

caído,-a adj fallen. **2** (desanimado) downhearted. ●~ **de hombros,** with drooping shoulders; fig ~ **del cielo,** out of the blue.

caigo indic pres → **caer.**

caimán m alligator.

caja f box. **2** (de madera) chest; (grande) crate. **3** (de bebidas) case. **4** (en comercio) cash desk; (en banco) cashier's desk. **5** AUTO body. **6** (tipografía) case. ●**hacer ~,** to take a lot. ■ ~ **de ahorros/pensiones,** savings bank; AUTO ~ **de cambios,** gearbox; ~ **de caudales,** strongbox; ~ **fuerte,** safe; AV ~ **negra,** black box; ~ **registradora,** cash register.

cajero,-a m,f cashier. ■ ~ **automático,** cash point.

cajetilla f packet (of cigarettes).

cajón m (en mueble) drawer. **2** (caja grande) crate. ■ fig ~ **de sastre,** jumble.

cal f lime.

cala f cove. **2** (trozo) slice.

calabacín m (pequeño) courgette, US zucchini. **2** (grande) marrow, US squash.

calabaza f gourd, pumpkin. ●fig **dar calabazas a algn.,** to fail sb.

calabozo m (prisión) jail. **2** (celda) cell.

calado,-a adj fam soaked. – **2** m (del agua) depth. **3** COST openwork, embroidery. ●~ **hasta los huesos,** soaked to the skin.

calafatear t NÁUT to caulk.

calamar m squid. ■ **calamares a la romana,** squid fried in batter.

calambre m cramp.

calamidad f calamity, disaster.

calamitoso,-a adj calamitous, miserable.

calandria f (ave) lark. **2** TÉC calender.

calaña f pey kind, sort.

calar(se) t (mojar) to soak, drench. **2** (agujerear) to go through, pierce. **3** COST to do openwork on. **4** TÉC to do fretwork on. **5** fam to rumble: ¡**te tengo calado,-a!,** I've got your number! – **6** i NÁUT to draw. – **7** p to get soaked. **8** (sombrero) to pull down. **9** AUTO to stop, stall.

calavera f skull. – **2** m fig madcap, reckless fellow.

calaverada f reckless escapade.

calcar [1] t fig to trace. **2** fig to copy.

calce m (llanta) rim. **2** (cuña) wedge.

calceta f (prenda) stocking. **2** (punto) knitting. ●**hacer ~,** to knit.

calcetín m sock.

calcificar(se) [1] to calcify.

calcinar t to calcine; fig to burn.

calcio m calcium.

calco m (de dibujo) tracing. **2** (imitación) copy.

calcomanía f transfer.

calculador,-ra adj calculating. – **2** m,f calculator.

calcular t to calculate.

cálculo m calculation, estimate. **2** (conjetura) conjecture, guess. **3** pl MED gallstones.

caldeamiento m heating, warming.

caldear t to warm, heat. **2** fig (excitar) to heat/warm up.

caldera f boiler.

calderilla f small change.

caldero m small cauldron.

caldo m CULIN stock, broth. **2** pl wines.

calé adj-m gypsy.

calefacción f heating. ■ ~ **central,** central heating.

calefactor m heater.

calendario m calendar.

calentador m heater.

calentamiento m heating: **ejercicios de ~,** warming-up exercises.

calentar(se) [27] t to warm up; (agua, horno) to heat. **2** DEP to warm up. **3** (excitar sexualmente) to arouse. **4** (pegar) to beat. – **5** p (escalfarse) to get hot/warm. **6** (enfadarse) to become angry. **7** (excitarse sexualmente) to get horny. ●~**se los sesos,** to get hot under the collar.

calentura f fever, temperature.

calenturiento,-a adj feverish.

calibrar t (graduar) to calibrate. **2** (medir) to gauge.

calibre m (de arma) calibre. **2** TÉC bore, gauge. **3** fig importance.

calicanto m stonework, masonry.

calidad f quality: **vino de ~,** good-quality wine. **2** (cualidad) kind, quality: **distintas calidades de papel,** different types of paper. **3** (condición) rank, capacity: **en ~ de ministro,** as a Minister.

cálido,-a adj warm.

calidoscopio *m* kaleidoscope.

caliente *adj* warm, hot. **2** *fam (excitado)* hot, randy.

calificable *adj* qualifiable.

calificación *f* qualification. **2** EDUC mark.

calificado,-a *adj (cualificado)* qualified. **2** *(de mérito)* eminent.

calificar [1] *t (etiquetar)* to describe *(de,* as). **2** EDUC to mark, grade.

calificativo,-a *adj* GRAM qualifying. — **2** *m* qualifier, epithet.

caligrafía *f* calligraphy.

cáliz *m* REL chalice. **2** BOT calyx.

caliza *f* limestone.

callado,-a *adj* silent, quiet.

callar(se) *i-p* to stop talking: *¡cállate!,* shut up! — **2** *t (esconder)* to keep to o.s.: *él calló su opinión,* he kept his opinion to himself.

calle *f* street, road. **2** DEP lane. ●*echar/ poner a algn. de patitas en la* ~, to throw/kick sb. out; *llevar/traer a algn. por la* ~ *de la amargura,* to give sb. a tough time. ■ ~ *mayor,* high/main street.

callejear *i* to wander the streets.

callejero,-a *adj* (in the) street. **2** *(persona)* fond of going out. — **3** *m* street directory.

callejón *m* back street/alley. ■ ~ *sin salida,* cul-de-sac.

callejuela *f* narrow street, lane.

callista *mf* chiropodist.

callo *m* MED callus, corn. **2** *pl* CULIN tripe *sing.*

calma *f* calm. **2** COM slack period. **3** *fam (cachaza)* slowness, phlegm. ●*perder la* ~, to lose one's patience.

calmante *adj* soothing. — **2** *m* painkiller.

calmar(se) *t* to calm (down). **2** *(dolor)* to relieve, soothe. — **3** *i* to fall calm. — **4** *p (persona)* to calm down. **5** *(dolor etc.)* to abate.

calmoso,-a *adj* calm, quiet. **2** *(lento)* slow, sluggish.

caló *m* gypsy language.

calor *m* heat, warmth: *hace* ~, it is hot; *tengo* ~, I feel warm/hot. **2** *fig* enthusiasm, ardour.

caloría *f* calorie.

calumnia *f* calumny, slander.

calumniador,-ra *adj* slanderous. — **2** *m,f* slanderer.

calumniar [12] *t* to calumniate, slander.

calumnioso,-a *adj* slanderous.

caluroso,-a *adj (tiempo)* warm, hot. **2** *fig* warm, enthusiastic.

calva *f* bald patch. **2** *(sitio)* clearing.

calvario *m* Calvary.

calvicie, calvez *f* baldness.

calvo,-a *adj* bald. **2** *(terreno)* bare, barren. — **3** *m,f* bald person.

calzada *f* road(way), US pavement.

calzado *m* footwear, shoes *pl.*

calzador *m* shoehorn.

calzar(se) [4] *t* to put shoes on. **2** *(llevar calzado)* to wear. — **3** *p* to put (one's shoes) on.

calzón *m* trousers *pl.*

calzoncillos *mpl* (under)pants, briefs.

cama *f* bed. ●*guardar* ~, to stay in bed. ■ ~ *doble/sencilla,* double/single bed; ~ *turca,* couch.

camada *f* brood, litter.

camafeo *m* cameo.

camaleón *m* chameleon.

camandulero,-a *adj-m,f* phoney.

cámara *f* chamber, room. **2** *(institución)* chamber. **3** AGR granary. **4** POL house. **5** *(de rueda)* inner tube. **6** ~ *(fotográfica),* camera. ●*a* ~ *lenta,* in slow motion. ■ POL ~ *alta/baja,* upper/lower house; ~ *de aire,* air chamber.

camarada *mf* colleague; *(de colegio)* schoolmate. **2** POL comrade.

camaradería *f* companionship.

camarero,-a *m,f m* waiter, *f* waitress. **2** *(en barco, avión) m* steward, *f* stewardess. — **3** *f* maid.

camarilla *f* clique; POL pressure group.

camarón *m* (common) prawn.

camarote *m* cabin.

camastro *m* old bed.

cambalache *m* swap, exchange.

cambiar(se) [12] *t* to change: ~ *en,* to change into; ~ *por,* to exchange for. **2** *(de sitio)* to shift; *(de casa)* to move. **3** *(moneda extranjera)* to (ex)change. — **4** *i* to change. **5** *(viento)* to veer. — **6** *p* to change: ~*se de ropa,* to get changed.

cambio *m* change: *no me has devuelto el* ~, you haven't given me back my change. **2** *(alteración)* alteration. **3** *(de valores, monedas)* price, quotation. **4** *(tren)* switch. **5** AUTO ~ *(de marchas)* gear change. ●*a* ~ *de,* in exchange for; *en* ~, *(por otro lado)* on the other hand; *(en lugar de)* instead. ■ AUTO *caja de* ~, gearbox; AUTO ~ *automático,* automatic transmission; COM *letra de* ~, bill of exchange; COM *libre* ~, free trade.

cambista *mf* moneychanger.

camelar(se) *t-p (cortejar)* to court, flirt with. **2** *(engañar)* to cajole.

camelia f camellia.
camello m ZOOL camel. 2 *(drogas)* (drug)pusher.
camelo m *(galanteo)* courting, flirting. 2 *fam (chasco)* hoax, sham.
camerino m TEAT dressing room.
camilla f *(litera)* stretcher. 2 *(cama)* small bed. ■ *(mesa)* ~, table with a heater underneath.
camillero m stretcher-bearer.
caminante mf traveller, walker.
caminar i-t to walk.
caminata f long walk, trek.
camino m path, track; *(ruta)* way. 2 *(viaje)* journey. 3 *fig (medio)* way. ●*abrirse* ~, to make a way for o.s.; *ponerse en* ~, to set off (on a journey); *fig ir por (el) buen/mal* ~, to be on the right/ wrong track.
camión m lorry, US truck.
camionero,-a m,f lorry driver, US truck driver.
camioneta f van.
camisa f shirt. ●*en mangas de* ~, in one's shirtsleeves; *fig cambiar de* ~, to change sides; *fig meterse en* ~ *de once varas,* to meddle in other people's business. ■ ~ *de dormir,* nightgown, nightdress; ~ *de fuerza,* straitjacket.
camisería f shirt shop.
camiseta f *(ropa interior)* vest. 2 *(sudadera)* T-shirt. 3 DEP shirt.
camisón m nightdress, nightgown, nightie.
camorra f row, quarrel.
camorrista adj quarrelsome. — 2 mf troublemaker.
campamento m camp.
campana f bell. 2 *fam (extractora)* hood. ■ ~ *de buzo,* diving bell.
campanada f stroke (of a bell). 2 *fig* scandal, sensational event.
campanario m belfry.
campanilla f small bell. 2 ANAT uvula. 3 BOT bell flower.
campanilleo m ringing.
campante adj carefree: *se quedó tan* ~, he/she didn't bat an eyelid.
campanudo,-a adj *(forma de campana)* bell-shaped. 2 *(escrito, orador)* pompous.
campaña f campaign. 2 *(campo)* countryside. ■ ~ *electoral,* election campaign; *tienda de* ~, tent.
campar i *(sobresalir)* to excel, stand out. 2 *(acampar)* to (en)camp.
campechano,-a adj frank, open, good-humoured.

campeón,-ona m,f champion.
campeonato m championship.
campero,-a adj country, rural.
campesino,-a adj country, rural. — 2 m,f peasant.
campestre adj country, rural.
camping m camp site. ●*ir de/hacer* ~, to go camping. ▲ *pl* **campings**.
campiña f countryside.
campo m country, countryside: *vivir en el* ~, to live in the country. 2 *(agricultura)* field: *los campos de maíz,* the cornfields. 3 DEP field. 4 MIL field. 5 *(espacio)* space; *fig* field, scope: *en el* ~ *de la medicina,* in the field of medicine. ●*dejarle a algn. el* ~ *libre,* to leave the field open for sb.; *ir a* ~ *traviesa/través,* to cut across the fields. ■ ~ *de batalla,* battlefield; ~ *de concentración,* concentration camp; ~ *de fútbol,* football pitch; ~ *de golf,* golf links; ~ *visual,* visual field; ~ *magnético,* magnetic field; *casa de* ~, country house.
camuflaje m camouflage.
camuflar t to camouflage.
can m lit dog.
cana f grey hair. ●*echar una* ~ *al aire,* to let one's hair down.
canal m *(artificial)* canal. 2 *(marítimo)* channel. — 3 m & f *(de tejado)* gutter. 4 TÉC channel. 5 *(animal)* open carcass. ●*abrir en* ~, to slit open.
canalizar [4] t *(agua, área)* to canalize. 2 *(riego)* to channel. 3 *fig* to direct; *(dinero)* to channel.
canalla f riffraff. — 2 m rascal, scoundrel, cad.
canallada f dirty trick.
canalón m downpipe, US downspout.
canapé m *(sofá)* couch, sofa. 2 CULIN canapé. ▲ *pl* **canapés**.
canario,-a adj-m,f GEOG Canarian. — 2 m *(pájaro)* canary.
canasta f basket.
canastilla f small basket. 2 *(de bebé)* layette.
canasto m large basket. — 2 *pl interj* good heavens!
cancel m storm door.
cancela f ironwork gate.
cancelación f cancellation.
cancelar t to cancel.
cáncer m cancer. 2 ASTROL ASTRON Cancer.
cancerígeno,-a adj carcinogenic. — 2 m carcinogen.
canceroso,-a adj cancerous.

cancha f sports ground; *(tenis)* court. **2** AM plot of land.

canciller m chancellor.

cancillería f chancellery.

canción f song. ■ ~ *de cuna,* lullaby.

cancionero m *(poemas)* collection of poems. **2** MÚS songbook.

candado m padlock.

candela f candle, taper. **2** AM *(lumbre)* lit firewood/coal.

candelabro m candelabrum.

candelero m candlestick. ●*estar en el* ~, to be high in office.

candente *adj* incandescent, red-hot. ■ *cuestión/tema* ~, pressing issue.

candidato,-a m,f candidate.

candidatura f candidacy. **2** *(conjunta)* list of candidates.

candidez f candour, innonce.

cándido,-a *adj* candid, ingenuous.

candil m oil lamp.

candilejas fpl footlights.

candor m candour, innocence.

candoroso,-a *adj* candid, ingenuous.

canela f cinnamon.

canelones mpl cannelloni.

cangrejo m *(de mar)* crab. **2** ~ *(de río),* freshwater crayfish.

caníbal *adj-mf* cannibal.

canibalismo m cannibalism.

canica f marble: *jugar a las canicas,* to play marbles.

canícula f dog days pl.

canijo,-a *adj* weak, sickly.

canilla f ANAT long bone. **2** *(de barril)* tap. **3** *(carrete)* reel.

canino,-a *adj-m* canine (tooth).

canje m exchange.

canjear t to exchange.

cano,-a *adj* grey, grey-haired.

canoa f canoe.

canódromo m greyhound track.

canon m canon.

canonizar [4] t to canonize.

canoso,-a *adj* grey-haired.

cansado,-a *adj* tired, weary. **2** *(pesado)* boring, tiring.

cansancio m tiredness, weariness.

cansar(se) t to tire. **2** *(molestar)* to annoy: *me cansan sus discursos,* I'm fed up with his speeches. — **3** p to get tired.

cantamañanas mf inv fam bullshitter.

cantante *adj* singing. — **2** mf singer.

cantar t-i to sing **2** fam to squeak, confess. — **3** i fam *(oler mal)* to stink. — **4** m song.

cántaro m pitcher. **2** *(contenido)* pitcherful. ●*llover a cántaros,* to rain cats and dogs.

cante m MÚS singing. **2** fam blunder: *¡vaya* ~ *!,* what a clanger! ■ ~ *hondo/jondo,* flamenco.

cantera f quarry. **2** DEP young players pl.

cántico m canticle.

cantidad f quantity, amount. — **2** adv fam a lot: *me gusta* ~, I love it. **3** *fam* ~ *de,* lots of: *había* ~ *de comida,* there was lots of food.

cantilena f *(canción)* song, ballad. **2** fam *(repetición)* annoying repetition: *la misma* ~, the same old story.

cantimplora f water bottle.

cantina f canteen, cafeteria.

cantinero,-a m,f canteen keeper.

canto m *(arte)* singing. **2** *(canción)* song. **3** *(extremo)* edge: *de* ~, sideways. **4** *(de cuchillo)* blunt edge. **5** *(esquina)* corner. **6** *(piedra)* stone. ■ ~ *del cisne,* swansong; ~ *rodado,* boulder.

cantón m canton.

cantor,-ra *adj* singing. — **2** m,f singer. ●*pájaro* ~, songbird.

canturrear, canturriar [12] i to hum, croon.

canutas fpl fam *pasarlas* ~, to have a hard time.

caña f *(planta)* reed. **2** (tallo) cane. **3** ANAT bone marrow. **4** *(de calzado)* leg. **5** *(de pescar)* fishing rod. **6** *(de cerveza)* glass of draught beer. ●*fam dar/meter* ~, *(coche)* to go at full speed; *(persona)* to do sb. over. ■ ~ *de azúcar,* sugar cane.

cañada f GEOG glen, dell, hollow. **2** *(sendero)* cattle track.

cañamazo m *(arpillera)* burlap.

cáñamo m BOT hemp. **2** *(tela)* hempen cloth.

cañaveral m cane plantation.

cañería f piping.

cañizal, cañizar m → **cañaveral**.

caño m tube. **2** *(chorro)* jet. **3** *(galería)* gallery. **4** NÁUT narrow channel.

cañón m *(de artillería)* cannon. **2** *(de arma)* barrel. **3** *(tubo)* tube, pipe. **4** *(de chimenea)* flue. **5** GEOG canyon. **6** *(de pluma)* quill. ●*fig al pie del* ~, without yielding; *fam estar* ~, to be/look terrific.

cañonero,-a *adj* armed.

caoba f mahogany.

caos m inv chaos.

caótico,-a *adj* chaotic.
capa *f (prenda)* cloak, cape. **2** *(pretexto)* pretence, disguise. **3** *(baño)* coat: *una ~ de pintura,* a coat of paint. **4** GEOG layer. **5** *(estrato social)* stratum. ●*andar de ~ caída,* to be on the decline; *fam so ~ de,* under pretence of.
capacho *m* basket, hamper.
capacidad *f (cabida)* capacity, content. **2** *(habilidad)* capability, ability.
capacitación *f* training.
capacitar *t* to train, qualify.
capar *t* to geld, castrate.
caparazón *m* shell. **2** *fig* shelter.
capataz *mf m* foreman, *f* forewoman.
capaz *adj (grande)* spacious, roomy. **2** *(hábil)* capable *(de,* of), able *(de,* to).
capazo *m* large flexible basket.
capcioso,-a *adj* captious, insidious.
capea *f* amateur bullfight.
capear *t (tauromaquia)* to play the bull with the cape. **2** *fig* to dodge. ●*~ la tormenta,* to weather the storm.
capellán *m* chaplain.
caperuza *f (prenda)* hood. **2** *(tapa)* cap.
capicúa *adj-m (número) ~,* palindromic number.
capilar *adj* capillary.
capilla *f* chapel. **2** MÚS choir. ■ *~ ardiente,* funeral chapel.
capirotazo *m* flip, flick.
capirote *m* hood.
capital *adj (principal)* capital. **— 2** *m* FIN capital. **— 3** *f* capital, chief town.
capitalismo *m* capitalism.
capitalista *adj-mf* capitalist.
capitalizar [4] *t* to capitalize.
capitán,-ana *m,f* captain.
capitanear *t* to captain. **2** *(dirigir)* to lead.
capitel *m* capital, chapiter.
capitoste *mf pey* bigwig.
capitulación *f* MIL capitulation. **2** *(acuerdo)* agreement. **3** *pl* marriage settlement *sing.*
capitular *i* MIL to capitulate. **— 2** *t-i (acordar)* to come to an agreement.
capítulo *m* chapter.
capó *m* bonnet, US hood.
capón *m (pollo)* capon. **2** *(golpe)* rap on the head.
caporal *m* head, leader.
capota *f* folding top.
capote *m (prenda)* cloak with sleeves. **2** *(de torero)* bullfighter's cape.
capricho *m* caprice, whim, fancy.
caprichoso,-a *adj* capricious, whimsical, fanciful.

cápsula *f* capsule. **2** *(de arma)* cartridge.
captación *f (de ondas)* reception. **2** *(comprensión)* understanding.
captar(se) *t* to attract. **2** *(ondas, agua)* to pick up. **3** *(comprender)* to understand. **— 4** *p* to draw, attract.
captura *f* capture, seizure.
capturar *t* to capture, seize.
capucha *f* hood.
capuchino,-a *adj-m,f* Capuchin. **— 2** *m (café)* cappuccino, white coffee.
capuchón *m (de estilográfica etc.)* cap.
capullo *m (de insectos)* cocoon. **2** BOT bud. **3*** *fam (estúpido)* silly bugger.
caqui *adj* khaki. **— 2** *m* BOT persimmon.
cara *f* face; *fig* look. **2** *(lado)* side; *(de moneda)* right side. ●*~ o cruz,* heads or tails; *dar la ~,* to face the consequences; *de ~ a,* opposite, facing; *echar en ~,* to reproach for; *tener buena/mala ~,* to look well/bad; *verse las caras,* to come face to face; *fam ~ de pocos amigos,* unfriendly face. ■ *~ a ~,* face to face; *~ dura,* cheeky person.
carabela *f* caravel.
carabina *f* carbine, rifle. **2** *fam* chaperon(e).
carabinero *m* customs guard.
¡caracho! *interj* goodness me!, damn it!
caracol *m* snail. **2** *(de mar)* winkle. **3** *(del oído)* cochlea. ■ *escalera de ~,* winding/spiral staircase.
caracola *f* conch.
carácter *m* character. **2** *(condición)* nature: *asistió en ~ de invitado,* he attended as a guest. **3** *(imprenta)* letter. ●*tener buen/mal ~,* to be good-natured/bad-tempered. ▲ *pl* **caracteres**.
característico,-a *adj-f* characteristic.
caracterizar(se) [4] *t* to characterize. **— 2** *p (distinguirse)* to be characterized. **3** TEAT to dress up *(de,* as).
caracterología *f* study of character.
carajillo *m fam* coffee with a dash of brandy.
¡carajo!* *interj* shit!*
¡caramba! *interj* good gracious!
carámbano *m* icicle.
carambola *f (billar)* cannon, US carom. ●*por ~,* by chance.
caramelo *m* sweet, US candy. **2** *(azúcar quemado)* caramel. ●*a punto de ~,* syrupy.
carantoñas *fpl* caresses. ●*hacer ~ a algn.,* to butter sb. up.
carátula *f (máscara)* mask. **2** *(cubierta)* cover.

caravana f caravan. 2 (atasco) traffic jam.

¡caray! interj good heavens!

carbón m coal. 2 (lápiz) charcoal. ■ ~ de leña/vegetal, charcoal; papel ~, carbon paper.

carbonato m carbonate.

carboncillo m charcoal.

carbonería f charcoal shop/store.

carbonero,-a adj coal. – 2 m,f coal dealer. – 3 f coal cellar.

carbónico,-a adj carbonic. ■ anhídrico ~, carbon dioxide; agua carbónica, mineral water.

carbonizar(se) [4] t-p to carbonize, burn.

carbono m carbon. ■ dióxido de ~, carbon dioxide.

carburador m carburet(t)or.

carburante m fuel.

carca adj-mf fam square, straight. 2 POL reactionary.

carcajada f burst of laughter, guffaw. ●reírse a carcajadas, to laugh one's head off.

carcamal mf pey old fogey.

cárcel f jail, gaol, prison: en la ~, in jail.

carcelero m jailer, gaoler, warder.

carcoma f woodworm.

carcomer(se) t to eat away at. 2 fig to undermine. – 3 p to be consumed (de, with).

carcomido,-a adj worm-eaten.

cardar t to card. 2 (peluquería) to backcomb.

cardenal m REL cardinal. 2 (equimosis) bruise.

cardíaco,-a adj cardiac, heart.

cardinal adj cardinal. ■ punto/número ~, cardinal point/number.

cardo m BOT thistle. 2 fam (arisco) cutting person. 3 fam (feo) ugly person. ■ ~ borriquero, cotton thistle; fam fig cutting person.

carear(se) t (comparar) to confront, compare. – 2 p (enfrentarse) to meet face to face.

carecer i [43] ~ de, to lack.

carenar t to careen.

carencia f lack (de, of).

carente ~ de, adv lacking (in).

careo m confrontation.

carestía f (falta) scarcity. 2 (precio alto) high cost.

careta f mask.

carey m (animal) sea turtle. 2 (concha) tortoiseshell.

carga f load. 2 (peso) burden. 3 (flete) cargo, freight. 4 (tributo) tax. 5 fig duty. ■ ~ eléctrica, electric charge.

cargado,-a adj loaded. 2 (tiempo) sultry, cloudy. 3 (bebida fuerte) strong. 4 fig burdened: ~ de responsabilidades, loaded with responsibility. ■ ~ de espaldas, round-shouldered.

cargador m loader. 2 AM porter. 3 (instrumento) charger.

cargamento m load, cargo.

cargante adj fam boring, annoying.

cargar(se) [7] t to load (de, with); (llenar) to fill (de, with). 2 COM ELEC MIL to charge. 3 (imputar) to ascribe. 4 fig (con responsabilidad etc.) to burden. 5 fam fig (molestar) to bother, annoy. – 6 i to load. 7 ARQ to rest. 8 (hacerse cargo de) to carry (con, -); fig to shoulder (con, with): yo cargo con toda la responsabilidad, I take full responsibility. – 9 p to load o.s. with. 10 (el cielo) to get cloudy/overcast. 11 EDUC fam to fail. 12 fam (destrozar) to smash, ruin. 13 fam (matar) to knock off. ●~ las tintas, to exaggerate; ~se de paciencia, to summon up all one's patience; fam ~se con el muerto, to be left holding the baby; (ser culpado) to get the blame.

cargo m (peso) loading. 2 fig (obligación) burden, weight. 3 (colocación) post, position. 4 (gobierno, custodia) charge, responsibility: tiene dos empleados a su ~, he has two employees. 5 FIN charge, debit. 6 JUR (falta) charge, accusation. ●hacerse ~ de, (responsabilizarse de) to take charge of; (entender) to take into consideration, realize.

cariar(se) [12] t to cause to decay. – 2 p to decay.

caricatura f caricature.

caricaturizar [4] t to caricature.

caricia f caress, stroke.

caridad f charity. ■ obra de ~, charitable deed.

caries f inv caries inv, cavity.

cariño m love, affection, fondness. 2 (querido) darling. ●coger ~ a algn./algo, to grow fond of sb./sth.

cariñoso,-a adj loving, affectionate. – 2 cariñosamente adv affectionately.

carisma m charisma.

caritativo,-a adj charitable.

cariz m aspect, look.

carmesí adj-m crimson.

carmín adj-m carmine.

carnada f bait.

carnal *adj* carnal. **2** *(pariente)* first. ■ *primo,-a* ~, first cousin.

carnaval *m* carnival. ■ *martes de* ~, Shrove Tuesday.

carne *f* ANAT flesh. **2** CULIN meat. **3** *(de fruta)* pulp. ●*en* ~ *viva,* raw; *ser de* ~ *y hueso,* to be only human; *ser uña y* ~, to be hand in glove. ■ ~ *asada,* roasted meat; ~ *picada,* mincemeat; *fig* ~ *de gallina,* goose flesh/bumps.

carné *m* card. ■ ~ *de conducir,* driving licence; ~ *de identidad,* identity card. ▲ *pl carnés.*

carnero *m* ram. **2** CULIN mutton.

carnet *m* → **carné.**

carnicería *f* butcher's (shop). **2** *fig* carnage, slaughter.

carnicero,-a *adj* carnivorous. **2** *fig* bloodthirsty, sanguinary. − **3** *m,f* butcher.

carnívoro,-a *adj* carnivorous.

carnoso,-a *adj* fleshy.

caro,-a *adj (costoso)* expensive, dear. − **2** *adv* at a high price.

carpa *f (pez)* carp. **2** *(toldo)* marquee. ■ *salto de* ~, jack-knife.

carpeta *f* folder, file.

carpintería *f* carpentry. **2** *(taller)* carpenter's shop.

carpintero *m* carpenter. ■ *pájaro* ~, woodpecker.

carraca *f (instrumento)* rattle. **2** *(ave)* roller. **3** *fam (coche)* banger.

carraspear *i* to clear one's throat.

carraspera *f* hoarseness.

carrasposo,-a *adj* rough, coarse.

carrera *f (paso)* run(ning). **2** *(trayecto)* route. **3** *(camino)* road. **4** DEP race. **5** *(estudios)* university education: *hacer la* ~ *de medicina,* to study medicine. **6** *(profesión)* career. **7** *(de media)* ladder. ●*euf (prostitución) hacer la* ~, to walk the streets. ■ ~ *de armamentos/armamentística,* arms race; ~ *de coches/automóviles,* car race.

carreta *f* cart.

carretada *f (carga)* cartload. **2** *fam (montón)* heaps *pl.*

carrete *m* bobbin, reel. **2** ELEC coil. **3** *(de película)* spool.

carretera *f* road. ■ ~ *comarcal,* B road; ~ *nacional,* A/main road; *red de carreteras,* road network.

carretero *m (conductor)* carter. **2** *(constructor)* cartwright.

carretilla *f* wheelbarrow. ●*fig saber algo de* ~, to know sth. parrot fashion.

carretón *m* small cart.

carril *m (ferrocarril)* rail. **2** AUTO lane. **3** *(surco)* furrow.

carrillo *m* cheek. ●*comer a dos carrillos,* to gulp one's food.

carro *m* cart. **2** AM car. **3** MIL tank. **4** *(de máquina de escribir)* carriage. ●*fam ¡para el* ~*!,* hold your horses!

carrocería *f* AUTO body.

carromato *m* long two-wheeled cart with a tilt.

carroña *f* carrion.

carroza *f* coach, carriage. **2** *(de carnaval)* float. − **3** *adj-mf fam* out-of-date (person).

carruaje *m* carriage, coach.

carta *f* letter. **2** *(naipe)* card. **3** *(minuta)* menu. **4** JUR chart. ●*echar una* ~, to post a letter; *echar las cartas a algn.,* to tell sb.'s fortune; *fig poner las cartas sobre la mesa,* to put one's cards on the table; *fig tomar cartas en un asunto,* to take part in an affair. ■ ~ *blanca,* carte blanche; ~ *certificada,* registered letter; TV ~ *de ajuste,* test card; ~ *de recomendación,* letter of introduction.

cartabón *m* set square.

cartapacio *m* notebook. **2** *(carpeta)* folder, file.

cartearse *p* to correspond/exchange letters.

cartel *m* poster. **2** *(póster)* placard. ●*tener* ~, to be popular.

cartelera *f (para carteles)* hoarding, US billboard. **2** *(en periódicos)* entertainment section.

cárter *m* TÉC housing. **2** AUTO crankcase.

cartera *f (monedero)* wallet. **2** *(de colegial)* satchel, schoolbag. **3** *(de ejecutivo)* briefcase. **4** *fig* portfolio: *ministro sin* ~, Minister without portfolio.

carterista *mf* pickpocket.

cartero,-a *m,f m* postman, *f* postwoman.

cartílago *m* cartilage.

cartilla *f (para aprender)* first reader. **2** *(cuaderno)* book. ■ ~ *de ahorros,* savings book; ~ *del seguro,* social security card.

cartografía *f* cartography.

cartón *m* cardboard. **2** *(de cigarrillos)* carton. **3** ART sketch. ■ ~ *piedra,* papier mâché.

cartuchera *f* cartridge holder/box.

cartucho *m* cartridge. **2** *(de monedas)* roll (of coins). **3** AM *(bolsa)* paper bag. **4** AM *(cono)* paper cone.

cartulina *f* (thin) cardboard.

casa *f (edificio)* house. **2** *(hogar)* home: *vete a* ~, go home. **3** *(linaje)* house: *la*

~ *de los Austria,* the House of Hapsburg. **4** *(empresa)* firm, company. ●*llevar la* ~, to run the house; *fig como Pedro por su* ~, as if he/she owned the place; *fig echar/tirar la* ~ *por la ventana,* to go all out. ■ ~ *consistorial,* town hall; ~ *de huéspedes,* boarding-house; ~ *de socorro,* first aid post; ~ *solariega,* manor; *euf* ~ *de citas,* brothel.

casaca *f* long coat.

casado,-a *adj-m,f* married (person): *los recién casados,* the newlyweds.

casamentero,-a *adj* matchmaking. – **2** *m,f* matchmaker.

casamiento *m* marriage. **2** *(ceremonia)* wedding.

casar(se) *t-i* to marry. **2** *(colores)* to go well (together). – **3** *p* to get married. ●*fam* ~*se de penalty,* to have a shotgun wedding.

cascabel *m* jingle/tinkle bell. ●*fam ser un* ~, to be a rattlebrain.

cascada *f* cascade, waterfall.

cascado,-a *adj fig* worn-out, aged. **2** *(voz)* harsh, hoarse.

cascajo *m* gravel. ●*estar hecho,-a un* ~, to be a wreck.

cascanueces *m inv* nutcracker.

cascar(se) [1] *t (quebrantar)* to crack. **2** *(la salud)* to harm. **3** *(pegar)* to beat, thrash. – **4** *i fam (morir)* to peg out. **5** *fam (charlar)* to chat away. – **6** *p* to crack.

cáscara *f (de huevo, nuez)* shell. **2** *(de fruta)* skin. **3** *(de grano)* husk.

cascarón *m* eggshell.

cascarrabias *mf inv fam* grumpy, US crank.

casco *m* helmet. **2** *(cráneo)* skull. **3** *(auricular)* headphone. **4** *(envase)* empty bottle. **5** MAR hull. **6** *(caballería)* hoof. ●*ser alegre de cascos,* to be scatter-brained. ■ ~ *urbano,* city centre.

cascote *m* piece of rubble/debris.

caserío *m (casa)* country house. **2** *(pueblo)* hamlet.

casero,-a *adj (persona)* home-loving. **2** *(productos)* home-made. – **3** *m,f (dueño)* *m* landlord, *f* landlady. **4** *(administrador)* keeper.

caseta *f (de feria)* stall. **2** *(de bañistas)* bathing hut, US bath house. **3** DEP changing room.

casete *m (magnetófono)* cassette player/recorder. – **2** *f (cinta)* cassette (tape).

casi *adv* almost, nearly: ~ *nunca,* hardly ever. ●*fam* ¡~ *nada!,* peanuts!

casilla *f (casa)* hut. **2** *(de casillero)* pigeonhole. **3** *(cuadrícula)* square. ●*fig sacar a algn. de sus casillas,* to drive sb. mad.

casillero *m* pigeonholes *pl.*

casino *m* casino.

caso *m (ocasión)* case, occasion. **2** *(suceso)* event, happening. ●*en* ~ *de que,* in case; *en todo* ~, anyhow, at any rate; *hacer* ~ *de/a,* to pay attention to; *hacer/venir al* ~, to be relevant.

caspa *f* dandruff.

¡cáspita! *interj* dear me!

casquete *m (prenda)* skullcap. ■ ~ *esférico,* fragment of a sphere; ~ *polar,* polar cap.

casquillo *m* TÉC ferrule, metal tip. **2** *(de cartucho)* cap.

casquivano,-a *adj* feather-brained.

cassette *m-f* → **casete**.

casta *f (grupo social)* caste. **2** *(linaje)* lineage, descent. **3** *fig (de cosa)* quality.

castaña *f* BOT chestnut. **2** *(de pelo)* knot, bun. **3** *fam (bofetada)* slap.

castañal, castañar *m* chestnut grove.

castañeta *f* snap of the fingers.

castañetear *t* to play the castanets to. – **2** *i (dientes)* to chatter. **3** *(los dedos)* to snap one's fingers.

castaño,-a *adj* chestnut-coloured; *(pelo)* brown. – **2** *m* BOT chestnut tree.

castañuela *f* castanet.

castellanizar [4] *t* to Hispanicize.

castellano,-a *adj-m,f* Castilian (person). – **2** *m* Spanish/Castilian (language).

castidad *f* chastity.

castigar [7] *t* to punish. **2** JUR DEP to penalize. **3** *(dañar)* to harm.

castigo *m* punishment. **2** JUR DEP penalty.

castillo *m* castle.

castizo,-a *adj* pure, authentic.

casto,-a *adj* chaste.

castor *m* beaver.

castrar *t* to castrate. **2** *(podar)* to prune.

castrense *adj* military.

casual *adj* accidental, chance. – **2** *m* chance. – **3** *casualmente adv* by chance. ●*por un* ~, just by chance.

casualidad *f* chance, coincidence. ●*de/por* ~, by chance.

casulla *f* chasuble.

cataclismo *m* cataclysm.

catacumbas *fpl* catacombs.

catador,-ra *m,f* taster. ■~ *de vinos,* wine taster.

catalán,-ana *adj-m,f* Catalan, Catalonian. – **2** *m* Catalan.

catalejo *m* spyglass.
catálisis *f inv* catalysis *inv.*
catalogación *f* cataloguing.
catalogar [7] *t* to catalog(ue).
catálogo *m* catalog(ue).
catamarán *m* catamaran.
cataplasma *f* poultice.
cataplines* *mpl* nuts.
catapulta *f* catapult.-
catar *t* to taste.
catarata *f* waterfall. **2** MED cataract.
catarro *m* catarrh, cold.
catastro *m* cadastre, cadaster.
catástrofe *f* catastrophe.
catastrófico,-a *adj* catastrophic.
cate *m fam* EDUC failed subject, fail.
catear *t* EDUC to fail, US flunk.
catecismo *m* catechism.
cátedra *f* *(de universidad)* professorship; *(de instituto)* post of head of department.
catedral *adj-f* cathedral.
catedrático,-a *m,f* *(de universidad)* professor; *(de instituto)* head of department.
categoría *f* category, rank. **2** *(tipo)* type. ●*de ~,* important, prominent; *de primera ~,* first-class.
categórico,-a *adj* categoric(al).
catequizar [4] *t* to catechize. **2** *(persuadir)* to persuade.
caterva *f pey* throng, crowd.
cateto,-a *m,f* *(palurdo)* dimwit. **2** *m* *(de triángulo)* cathetus.
catolicismo *m* Catholicism.
católico,-a *adj-m,f* Catholic.
catorce *adj* fourteen; *(catorceavo)* fourteenth. **– 2** *m* fourteen.
catre *m* cot.
cauce *m* river bed. **2** *(canal)* channel.
caucho *m* rubber.
caudal *adj* *(de la cola)* caudal. **– 2** *m* *(de río)* flow. **3** *fig* *(riqueza)* fortune, wealth.
caudaloso,-a *adj* *(río)* deep, plentiful. **2** *fig* *(persona)* wealthy.
caudillo *m* chief, leader.
causa *f* cause. **2** JUR lawsuit. ●*a/por ~ de,* because of, on account of; *hacer ~ común con,* to make common cause with.
causante *adj* causal, causing. **– 2** *mf* cause.
causar *t* to cause, bring about. **2** *(proporcionar)* to give: *me causa un gran placer ...,* it's a pleasure for me to ... .
cáustico,-a *adj* caustic.
cautela *f* caution, wariness.
cauteloso,-a *adj* cautious, wary.

cauterizar [4] *t* to cauterize, fire.
cautivador,-ra *adj* captivating. **2** *(encantador)* charming.
cautivar *t* to take prisoner, capture. **2** *(atraer)* to captivate, charm.
cautiverio *m,* **cautividad** *f* captivity.
cautivo,-a *adj-m,f* captive.
cauto,-a *adj* cautious.
cava *f* *(bebida)* cava, champagne. **2** *(bodega)* wine cellar.
cavar *t* to dig.
caverna *f* cavern, cave.
cavernícola *adj* cave dwelling. **– 2** *mf* cave dweller, caveman.
cavernoso,-a *adj* cavernous. **2** *(voz etc.)* hollow, deep.
caviar *m* caviar.
cavidad *f* cavity.
cavilación *f* pondering, musing.
cavilar *t* to ponder, brood over.
cayado *m* *(de pastor)* crook. **2** *(de obispo)* crozier.
cayo *m* cay, key.
caza *f* *(acción)* hunting. **2** *(animales)* game. **– 3** *m* AV fighter. ■ *~ mayor/menor,* big/small game.
cazador,-ra *adj* hunting. **– 2** *m,f* hunter. **– 3** *f* *(chaqueta)* (waist-length) jacket. ■ *~ furtivo,* poacher.
cazadotes *m inv* fortune hunter.
cazar *t* [4] to hunt. **2** *fam* *(coger)* to catch.
cazatorpedero *m* (torpedo-boat) destroyer.
cazo *m* *(cucharón)* ladle. **2** *(cacerola)* pot, pan.
cazuela *f* casserole.
cebada *f* barley.
cebar(se) *t* *(animal)* to fatten (up). **2** *(pistola)* to prime. **3** *fig* *(pasiones etc.)* to nourish. **– 4** *p* *(dedicarse)* to devote o.s. *(a,* to). **5** *(ensañarse)* to make prey *(en,* on).
cebo *m* *(para animales)* food. **2** *(para pescar)* bait.
cebolla *f* onion.
cebolleta *f,* **cebollino** *m* *(especia)* chives *pl.* **2** *(cebolla)* spring onion.
cebra *f* zebra. ■ *paso ~,* zebra crossing, US crosswalk.
cecear *i* to lisp.
ceceo *m* lisp.
cecina *f* salted/dried beef.
ceder *t* *(dar)* to cede. **– 2** *i* *(rendirse)* to yield *(a,* to). **3** *(caerse)* to fall, give way: *cedieron las paredes,* the walls caved in. ●AUTO *~ el paso,* to give way, US yield way.

cedro *m* cedar.

cédula *f* document. ■ AM ~ *personal,* identity card.

céfiro *m* zephyr.

cegador,-ra *adj* blinding.

cegar(se) [48] *t* to blind: *fig cegado,-a por la ira,* blind with rage. **2** *(puerta, ventana)* to wall up. − **3** *i* to go blind. − **4** *p fig* to become blinded.

cegato,-a *adj-m,f* short-sighted (person).

ceguedad, ceguera *f* blindness.

ceja *f* (eye)brow. ●*tener algo entre* ~ *y* ~, to have sth. in one's head.

cejar *i* to back up. **2** *fig* to give way.

celada *f (emboscada)* ambush. **2** *(casco)* helmet.

celador,-ra *adj* watching. − **2** *m,f* attendant; *(de cárcel)* warden.

celar *t (la ley)* to observe. **2** *(vigilar)* to watch over. **3** *(encubrir)* to hide, conceal.

celda *f* cell.

celebración *f (fiesta)* celebration. **2** *(de una reunión etc.)* holding. **3** *(aplauso)* praise, applause.

celebrar(se) *t (festejar)* to celebrate. **2** *(reunión)* to hold. **3** *(alabar)* to praise. **4** *(estar contento)* to be happy about: *celebro lo de tu ascenso,* I congratulate you on your promotion. **5** REL *(misa)* to say. − **6** *p* to take place, be held.

célebre *adj* well-known, famous.

celebridad *f* celebrity.

celeridad *f* celerity, speed.

celeste *adj* celestial. ■ *azul* ~, sky blue.

celestial *adj* celestial, heavenly. **2** *fig (delicioso)* heavenly.

celestina *f* procuress.

celibato *m* celibacy.

célibe *adj-mf* celibate.

celo *m (entusiasmo)* zeal. **2** *(cuidado)* care. **3** *pl* jealousy *sing.* ●*tener celos de algo/ algn.,* to be jealous of sth./sb.

celo® *m* sellotape®, US Scotch tape®.

celosía *f* lattice.

celoso,-a *adj (entusiasta, cuidadoso)* zealous. **2** *(envidioso)* jealous. **3** *(receloso)* suspicious.

celta *adj* Celtic. − **2** *mf* Celt.

célula *f* cell.

celular *adj* cell, cellular.

celulitis *f inv* cellulitis.

celuloide *m* celluloid.

celulosa *f* cellulose.

cementerio *m* cemetery, graveyard. ■ ~ *de coches,* scrapyard.

cemento *m* concrete, cement. ■ ~ *armado,* reinforced concrete.

cena *f* supper; *(formal)* dinner. ■ *la Santa Cena,* the Last Supper.

cenagal *m* marsh, swamp.

cenagoso,-a *adj* muddy.

cenar *i* to have supper/dinner. − **2** *t* to have for supper/dinner.

cencerro *m* cowbell. ●*estar como un* ~, to be nuts.

cenefa *f* border, fringe.

cenicero *m* ashtray.

ceniciento,-a *adj* ashen, ash-grey. − **2** *f* Cinderella.

cenit *m* zenith.

ceniza *f* ash, ashes *pl.* **2** *pl (restos)* ashes.

censo *m* census. ■ ~ *electoral,* electoral roll.

censor *m* censor.

censura *f* censorship: *pasar por la* ~, to be censured. **2** *(crítica)* censure.

censurar *t* to censor. **2** *(criticar)* to censure, criticize.

centavo,-a *adj-m* hundredth (part).

centella *f (rayo)* lightning. **2** *(chispa)* spark, flash.

centelleante *adj* sparkling, flashing.

centellear *i* to sparkle, flash.

centelleo *m* sparkling, flashing.

centena *f,* **centenar** *m* hundred.

centenario,-a *adj* centennial. − **2** *m,f (persona)* centenarian. − **3** *m (aniversario)* centenary.

centeno *m* rye.

centésimo,-a *adj-m,f* hundredth.

centígrado,-a *adj* centigrade.

centímetro *m* centimetre.

céntimo *m* centime, cent. ●*estar sin un* ~, to be penniless.

centinela *m & f* MIL sentry. **2** *(guardián)* watch.

centolla *f,* **centollo** *m* spider crab.

centrado,-a *adj* centred. **2** *fig (equilibrado)* balanced. **3** *fig (atento)* devoted *(en, to).*

central *adj* central. − **2** *f (oficina principal)* head office, headquarters *pl.* **3** ELEC power station. ■ ~ *telefónica,* telephone exchange.

centralismo *m* centralism.

centralita *f* switchboard.

centralización *f* centralization.

centralizar [4] *t* to centralize.

centrar(se) *t* to centre. − **2** *p* to be centred *(en,* on). **3** *(concentrarse)* to concentrate *(en,* on).

céntrico,-a *adj* in the centre, US downtown: *una calle céntrica,* a street in the centre.

centrifugar [7] to centrifuge. 2 *(ropa)* to spin-dry.

centrífugo,-a *adj* centrifugal.

centro *m* centre, middle. 2 *(asociación)* centre, association. ■ ~ *ciudad,* city centre, US downtown; ~ *comercial,* shopping centre; ~ *de mesa,* centrepiece; ~ *docente,* school; DEP *delantero* ~, centre forward; DEP *medio* ~, centre half.

centrocampista *mf* midfield player.

centuplicar [1] *t* multiply a hundredfold.

céntuplo,-a *adj-m* centuple, hundredfold.

centuria *f* century.

ceñido,-a *adj* close-fitting.

ceñir(se) [36] *t (estrechar)* to cling to, fit tight. 2 *(rodear)* to hug around the waist. — 3 *p (concentrarse)* to limit o.s. *(a,* to): ~*se al tema,* to keep to the subject. 4 *(moderarse)* to adjust o.s.

ceño *m* frown. ●*fruncir/arrugar el* ~, to frown.

ceñudo,-a *adj* frowning.

cepa *f (de vid)* vine. 2 *(tronco)* stump; *(de vid)* rootstalk. 3 *fig (origen)* origin. ●*de buena* ~, of good quality.

cepillar(se) *t* to brush. 2 *(madera)* to plane. — 3 *p* to brush. 4 *fam (matar)* to do in. 5 *fam (acabarse)* to finish: *se cepilló todo el pastel,* he/she gobbled up the whole cake. 6* *(tirarse a)* to lay.

cepillo *m* brush. 2 *(de madera)* plane. 3 *(para limosnas)* alms box. ■ ~ *de dientes,* toothbrush; ~ *del pelo,* hairbrush; ~ *de ropa,* clothes brush; ~ *de uñas,* nailbrush.

cepo *m (rama)* bough. 2 *(de yunque)* stock. 3 *(de reo)* pillory. 4 *(trampa)* trap. 5 AUTO clamp.

cera *f* wax; *(de abeja)* beeswax. 2 *(de la oreja)* earwax.

cerámica *f* ceramics, pottery: *una* ~, a piece of pottery.

cerca *adv* near, close: *aquí* ~, near here. — 2 *f (valla)* fence. ●~ *de, (cercano a)* near; *(casi)* nearly, about: ~ *de un año,* nearly a year; *de* ~, closely: *lo vi de* ~, I saw it close up.

cercado,-a *adj* fenced in. — 2 *m* enclosure.

cercanía *f* proximity, nearness.

cercano,-a *adj* near(by).

cercar [1] *t* to fence in. 2 *(rodear)* to surround. 3 MIL to besiege.

cercenar *t* to clip, cut off the edges of. 2 *(acortar)* to curtail.

cerciorar(se) *t* to assure, affirm. — 2 *p* to make sure *(de,* of).

cerco *m* circle. 2 *(marco)* frame. 3 MIL siege.

cerda *f (de caballo)* horsehair; *(de cerdo)* bristle. 2 *(animal)* sow.

cerdo *m (animal)* pig. 2 *(carne)* pork.

cereal *adj-m* cereal.

cerebral *adj* cerebral, brain. 2 *(frío)* calculating.

cerebro *m* ANAT brain. 2 *fig* brains *pl.*

ceremonia *f* ceremony.

ceremonial *adj-m* ceremonial.

ceremonioso,-a *adj* ceremonious, formal.

cereza *f* cherry.

cerezo *m* cherry tree.

cerilla *f* match.

cerner(se) [28], **cernir(se)** [29] *t (harina)* to sift. 2 *fig* to observe. — 3 *i (plantas)* to bud, blossom. 4 *(llover)* to drizzle. — 5 *p (pájaro)* to hover. 6 *(amenazar)* to threaten.

cero *m* zero: *ganar dos a* ~, to win two nil. 2 *(cifra)* naught, nought. ●*bajo* ~, below zero; *ser un* ~ *a la izquierda,* to be useless.

cerrado,-a *adj* shut, closed. 2 *(oculto)* obscure. 3 *(persona)* uncommunicative.

cerradura *f* lock. ■ ~ *de seguridad,* security lock.

cerrajería *f (oficio)* locksmith's trade. 2 *(negocio)* locksmith's (shop).

cerrajero *m* locksmith.

cerrar(se) [27] *t* to close, shut. 2 *(grifo, gas)* to turn off. 3 *(luz)* to switch off. 4 *(cremallera)* to zip (up). 5 *(un negocio definitivamente)* to close down. 6 *(carta)* to seal. — 7 *i* to shut. — 8 *p* to close, shut. 9 *(obstinarse)* to stand fast. ●~ *la boca,* to shut up.

cerrazón *f* obstinacy. 2 *(estupidez)* dimness. 3 METEOR stormy sky.

cerro *m* hill. ●*fig irse por los cerros de Úbeda,* to beat around the bush.

cerrojo *m* bolt. ●*echar/correr el* ~, to bolt.

certamen *m* competition, *(literario)* literary contest.

certero,-a *adj (disparo)* accurate, good. 2 *(seguro)* certain, sure.

certeza, certidumbre *f* certainty.

certificación *f* certificate. 2 *(de envío etc.)* registration.

certificado,-a *adj* certified. **2** *(envío)* registered. **— 3** *m (documento)* certificate. **4** *(carta)* registered letter; *(paquete)* registered package.

certificar [1] *t* to certify. **2** *(carta, paquete)* to register.

cerumen *m* earwax.

cervecería *f (bar)* pub, bar. **2** *(destilería)* brewery.

cerveza *f* beer, ale.

cervical *adj* cervical, neck.

cerviz *f* cervix. ●*doblar la* ~, to humble o.s.

cesante *adj* ceasing. **— 2** *mf* civil servant out of office.

cesar *i* to cease, stop. **2** *(en un empleo)* to leave. ●*sin* ~, incessantly.

cese *m* cessation. **2** *(despido)* dismissal.

cesión *f* cession.

césped *m* lawn, grass: *cortar el* ~, to mow the lawn.

cesta *f* basket. **2** DEP pelota/jai-alai basket. ■ ~ *de la compra*, shopping basket.

cesto *m* basket. ■ ~ *de los papeles*, wastepaper basket.

cetáceo *m* cetacean.

cetrino,-a *adj (color)* sallow, greenish yellow. **2** *fig* melancholic.

cetro *m* sceptre.

chabacanería *f* coarseness, vulgarity.

chabacano,-a *adj* coarse, vulgar.

chabola *f* shack.

chacal *m* jackal.

chacha *f fam pey* nurse(maid).

cháchara *f fam* prattle, idle talk. **2** *pl* trinkets.

chachi *adj arg* great, terrific.

chafar(se) *t (aplastar)* to flatten. **2** *(arrugar)* to crumple. **3** *fam (interrumpir)* to butt in on. **— 4** *p* to be flattened.

chaflán *m* chamfer.

chal *m* shawl.

chalado,-a *adj (loco)* mad. ●*estar* ~ *por*, to be mad about.

chalán,-ana *adj-m,f* horse-dealer.

chalé, chalet, *m* chalet. ▲ *pl chalés*.

chaleco *m* waistcoat, US vest. ■ ~ *salvavidas*, life jacket.

chalupa *f* boat.

chamarilero,-a *m,f* second-hand dealer.

chambelán *m* chamberlain.

chambón,-ona *adj (torpe)* clumsy. **2** *(con suerte)* lucky. **— 3** *m,f* clumsy person.

champán, champaña *m* champagne.

champú *m* shampoo. ▲ *pl champúes or champús*.

chamuscar(se) [1] *t* to singe, scorch. **— 2** *p* to be singed.

chamusquina *f* scorching. **2** *fig* quarrel.

chancear(se) *i-p* to joke, jest.

chanchi *adj arg* → **chachi**.

chancho *m* AM pig.

chanchullo *m fam* fiddle, wangle.

chancla *f (zapato viejo)* old shoe. **2** *(chancleta)* backless shoe/slipper.

chancleta *f* slipper.

chanclo *m (zueco)* clog. **2** *(elástico)* galosh.

chándal *m* track/jogging suit.

chanfaina *f (vegetal)* stewed vegetables *pl*. **2** *(de carne)* meat stew.

chanquete *m* transparent goby.

chantaje *m* blackmail. ●*hacer* ~, to blackmail.

chantajista *mf* blackmailer.

chanza *f* joke.

chapa *f (de metal, madera)* sheet. **2** *(tapón)* bottle top. **3** *(medalla)* badge, disc: MIL ~ *de identificación*, identity disc. **4** AM *(cerradura)* lock. **5** AUTO bodywork. **6** *pl* game of tossing up coins.

chapado,-a *adj* plated: ~ *en plata*, silver-plated. ●*fig* ~ *a la antigua*, old-fashioned.

chapar *t (metal)* to plate. **2** *(madera)* to veneer, finish. **3** *fig (encajar)* to come out with.

chaparrón *m* downpour, heavy shower.

chapotear *i* to splash. **— 2** *t (humedecer)* to moisten.

chapoteo *m* splashing. **2** *(humidificación)* moistening.

chapucería *f (tosquedad)* shoddiness. **2** *(chapuza)* botched job.

chapucero,-a *adj (trabajo)* botched; *(persona)* bungling. **— 2** *m,f (patoso)* bungler. **3** *(embustero)* liar.

chapurr(e)ar *t* to speak badly: ~ *el francés*, to have a smattering of French.

chapuza *f* botch, botch-up. ●*hacer una* ~, to botch up.

chapuzar(se) [4] *t-i* to duck. **— 2** *p* to dive in.

chapuzón *m* duck, dive. ●*darse un* ~, to have a dip.

chaqué *m* morning coat. ▲ *pl chaqués*.

chaqueta *f* jacket. ●*fam fig cambiar de* ~, to change sides.

chaquetón *m* winter jacket.

charada *f* charade.

charanga *f* brass band.

charca *f* pool, pond.

charco *m* puddle, pond. ●*pasar el* ~, to cross the pond.

charcutería *f* pork butcher's shop, delicatessen.

charla *f (conversación)* talk. **2** *(conferencia)* talk, lecture.

charlar *i* to chat, talk.

charlatán,-ana *adj (hablador)* talkative. **2** *(chismoso)* gossipy. — **3** *m,f (parlanchín)* chatterbox. **4** *(embaucador)* charlatan.

charlatanería *f* verbosity.

charol *m (barniz)* varnish. **2** *(cuero)* patent leather.

charola *f* AM tray.

charrán *m* rogue.

charretera *f* epaulette.

charro,-a *adj (tosco)* coarse. **2** *(hortera)* cheap, flashy.

chárter *adj-m inv* charter.

chascar [1] *t (lengua)* to click; *(dedos)* to snap. — **2** *i (madera)* to crack.

chascarrillo *m* crack, joke.

chasco *m (broma)* trick. **2** *(decepción)* disappointment.

chasis *m inv* chassis.

chasquear *t (bromear)* to play a trick on. **2** *(engañar)* to deceive. **3** *(decepcionar)* to disappoint. — **4** *i (madera, látigo)* to crack, snap. **5** *(decepcionarse)* to be disappointed.

chasquido *m (de látigo, madera)* crack; *(de la lengua)* click.

chatarra *f* scrap iron, iron slag. **2** *fam (monedas)* small change.

chatarrero,-a *m,f* scrap dealer.

chato,-a *adj (nariz)* snub; *(persona)* snub-nosed. **2** *(objeto)* flat. — **3** *m (vaso)* small glass. — **4** *m,f (persona)* snub-nosed person. **5** *fam (cariño)* love, dear.

chauvinismo *m* chauvinism.

chaval,-la *fam adj* young. — **2** *m,f* kid, youngster; *m* lad, *f* lass.

chaveta *f* cotter (pin). ●*perder la* ~, to go off one's rocker.

che *f* name of the digraph ch. ▲ *pl* **ches**.

chelín *m* shilling.

cheque *m* cheque, US check. ●*extender un* ~, to issue a cheque. ■ ~ *abierto/ cruzado/en blanco,* open/crossed/blank cheque; ~ *al portador,* cheque payable to bearer; ~ *de viaje/viajero,* traveler's cheque; *talonario de cheques,* cheque book.

chequeo *m* checkup.

chicha *f (lenguaje infantil)* meat. **2** AM liquor. ■MAR *calma* ~, dead calm.

chícharo *m* AM chickpea.

chicharra *f* cicada.

chicharrón *m* CULIN pork crackling. **2** *fig (moreno)* sunburnt person.

chichón *m* bump, lump.

chicle *m* chewing gum.

chico,-a *adj* small, little. — **2** *m,f* kid, youngster. — **3** *m (aprendiz)* office boy. — **4** *f (criada)* maid.

chicote *m* AM whip. ·

chiflado,-a *adj* mad, crazy.

chifladura *f* craziness, madness.

chiflar(se) *i (silbar)* to hiss, whistle. — **2** *p* to go mad/crazy.

chilaba *f* jellabah.

chillar *i* to scream. **2** *fig* to shout. **3** *(colores)* to be loud/gaudy.

chillido *m* shriek, screech, scream.

chillón,-ona *adj* screaming. **2** *(color)* loud, garish.

chimenea *f* chimney. **2** *(hogar)* fireplace. **3** *(de barco)* funnel.

chimpancé *m* chimpanzee. ▲ *pl* **chimpancés**.

china *f (piedra)* pebble. **2** *(seda)* China silk. **3** *(porcelana)* china. **4** *arg (droga)* deal.

chinchar(se) *fam t* to annoy, pester. — **2** *p* to grin and bear it. ●*¡chínchate!,* so there!

chinche *m & f* ZOOL bedbug. **2** *fig* bore, nuisance.

chincheta *f* drawing pin, US thumbtack.

chinchilla *f* ZOOL chinchilla.

chinela *f* slipper.

chingado,-a *adj* AM unsuccessful, vain.

chip *m* INFORM chip. **2** *pl fam* crisps.

chipirón *m* baby squid.

chiquero *m* pigsty.

chiquillada *f* childish prank.

chiquillo,-a *m,f* kid, youngster.

chiquito,-a *adj* tiny, very small. — **2** *m* small glass of wine. ●*no andarse con chiquitas,* not to beat about the bush.

chiringuito *m fam (en playa)* refreshment stall; *(en carretera)* roadside snack bar.

chirinola *f (fruslería)* trifle. ●*estar de* ~, to be in good spirits.

chiripa *f* fluke, stroke of luck.

chirlo *m (herida)* wound on the face. **2** *(cicatriz)* scar on the face.

chirriar [13] *i (al freír comida etc.)* to sizzle. **2** *(rueda, frenos)* to screech; *(puerta)* to creak. **3** *(aves)* to squawk. **4** *fig (persona)* to sing badly.

chirrido *m (de rueda, frenos)* screech. **2** *(de aves)* squawk.

chisme *m (comentario)* piece of gossip. **2** *(trasto)* knick-knack; *(de cocina etc.)*

gadget: *¿cómo funciona este* ~*?,* how does this thing work?

chismear *i* to gossip.

chismorreo *m* gossip(ing).

chismoso,-a *adj* gossipy. — **2** *m,f* gossip.

chispa *f* spark(le). **2** *(un poco)* bit. **3** METEOR droplet. **4** *fig (ingenio)* wit. ●*fig echar chispas,* to be raging; *fig tener* ~, to be witty/funny. ■ ~ *eléctrica,* spark.

chispazo *m* spark, flash.

chispeante *adj* sparkling.

chispear *i* to spark. **2** METEOR to drizzle lightly. **3** *fig (relucir)* to sparkle. ▲ **2** *only used in the 3rd pers. It does not take a subject.*

chisporrotear *i* to spark, splutter.

chisporroteo *m* sparkling, spluttering.

chistar *i* to speak. ●*no* ~, not to say a word.

chiste *m* joke. ●*explicar/contar un* ~, to tell a joke. ■ ~ *verde,* blue/dirty joke.

chistera *f (sombrero)* top hat. **2** *(de pescador)* fish basket.

chistoso,-a *adj* witty, funny.

chita *f* ANAT anklebone. **2** *(juego)* jacks *pl.* ●*a la* ~ *callando,* quietly; *(con disimulo)* on the quiet.

¡chitón! *interj* hush!, silence!

chivar(se) *t fam (molestar)* to annoy, pester. **2** *(delatar)* to denounce, give away. — **3** *p* to tell: ~*se a la policía,* to inform the police.

chivatazo *m fam* informing. ●*dar el* ~, to inform, squeal.

chivato,-a *m,f fam (delator)* informer. — **2** *m (dispositivo)* gadget. **3** ZOOL kid.

chivo,-a *m,f* male kid. ●*fam estar como una chiva,* to be crazy. ■ ~ *expiatorio,* scapegoat.

choc *m* shock.

chocante *adj (divertido)* funny. **2** *(sorprendente)* surprising. **3** *(raro)* strange.

chocar [1] *i (colisionar)* to collide *(contra/con,* with), crash *(contra/con,* into). **2** *(pelear)* to fight. **3** *fig (sorprender)* to surprise: *esto me choca,* I am surprised at this. — **4** *t (las manos)* to shake. **5** *(copas)* to clink. ●*¡chócala!/¡choca esos cinco!,* put it there!

chocarrería *f* coarse humour.

chocarrero,-a *adj* coarse, vulgar.

chochear *i* to dodder. **2** *(de cariño)* to be tender.

chochera, chochez *f* dotage. **2** *(cariño)* tenderness.

chocho,-a *adj* doting. **2** *(de cariño)* tender. — **3*** *m* cunt*.

choclo *m* AM tender maíz, corn on the cob. **2** *(guisado)* stew made with tender maize/corn.

chocolate *m* chocolate. **2** *arg (hachís)* dope, hash. ●*fam fig las cosas claras y el* ~ *espeso,* let's get things clear. ■ ~ *a la taza,* drinking chocolate; ~ *con leche,* milk chocolate; *tableta de* ~, bar of chocolate.

chocolatina *f* small bar of chocolate.

chófer, chofer *m (particular)* chauffeur; *(de autocar etc.)* driver. ▲ *pl* **chóferes.**

chollo *m fam* bargain, snip.

chopo *m* poplar.

choque *m* collision, crash. **2** *(enfrentamiento),* clash; MIL skirmish. **3** *(discusión)* dispute, quarrel. **4** MED shock.

chorizar *t fam* to pinch, nick.

chorizo *m* highly-seasoned pork sausage. **2** *fam (ratero)* thief, pickpocket.

chorlito *m (ave)* plover.

chorrada *f fam (necedad)* piece of nonsense: *decir chorradas,* to talk rubbish. **2** *(regalito)* little something.

chorrear *i (a chorros)* to spout, gush. **2** *(gotear)* to drip. **3** AM to steal.

chorro *m* jet, spout. ●*a chorros,* in abundance: *hablar a chorros,* to talk nineteen to the dozen. ■ *avión a* ~, jet plane; ~ *de voz,* loud voice.

chotear(se) *t-p fam* to make fun *(de,* of).

choteo *m fam* fun, joking.

choza *f* hut.

christmas *m inv* Christmas card.

chubasco *m* heavy shower.

chubasquero *m* raincoat.

chuchería *f (trasto)* trinket, knick-knack. **2** *(bocado)* tidbit, delicacy.

chucho *m fam* dog.

chueca *f (del tronco)* stump. **2** *(de hueso)* head.

chufa *f* chufa, groundnut. ■ *horchata de* ~, drink made from chufas.

chulear(se) *t-p (burlar)* to make fun of. — **2** *i (presumir)* to brag *(de,* about).

chulería *f (jactancia)* bragging. **2** *(gracia)* wit.

chuleta *f* chop, cutlet. **2** *fam* EDUC crib (note), US trot.

chulo,-a *adj (engreído)* cocky. **2** *fam (bonito)* nice: *¡qué vestido tan* ~*!,* what a nice dress! — **3** *m,f (presuntuoso)* show-off. — **4** *m (proxeneta)* pimp.

chumbera *f* prickly pear.

chunga *f* fun, joke. ●*estar de* ~, to be joking; *tomar a* ~, to make fun of.

chungo,-a *adj fam* naff: *lo tenemos ~,* we've got problems.

chunguearse *p* to joke, make fun of.

chupachup® *m inv* lollipop.

chupado,-a *adj* skinny, emaciated. **– 2** *f (a caramelo)* suck; *(a cigarro)* puff.

chupar(se) *t* to suck, draw. **2** *(absorber)* to absorb, soak up. **3** *(hacienda)* to drain, sponge on. **4** *fam (aprovecharse)* to milk. **– 5** *i* to suck. **– 6** *i-t* AM *(pitar)* to blow. **– 7** *p* to grow thin. ●*~se el dedo,* to suck one's thumb; *~se los dedos,* to lick one's fingers; *fam ~ del bote,* to scrounge; *fam ¡chúpate ésa!,* stick that in your pipe and smoke it!

chupatintas *m inv fam* office drudge.

chupete *m* dummy, soother, US pacifier.

chupón,-ona *adj* sucking. **2** *(gorrón)* sponging. **– 3** *m* BOT sucker. **– 4** *m,f (gorrón)* sponger.

churra *f fam* fluke, good luck.

churrasco *m* barbecued meat.

churrería *f* fritter shop.

churro *m* fritter, US cruller. **2** *fam (chapuza)* botch.

churumbel *m fam* kid.

chusco,-a *adj* funny, witty. **– 2** *m (de pan)* chunk of bread.

chusma *f* riffraff.

chut *m* DEP shot, kick.

chutar(se) *i* DEP to shoot. **– 2** *p arg* to fix, shoot up. ●*... y va que chuta,* ... and no problem.

chuzo *m* short pike. ●*fig llover chuzos,* to rain pitchforks.

cianuro *m* cyanide.

ciático,-a *adj* sciatic. **– 2** *f* sciatica.

cibernética *f* cybernetics.

cicatería *f* stinginess, niggardliness.

cicatero,-a *adj* stingy, niggardly.

cicatriz *f* scar.

cicatrizar(se) [4] *t-p* to heal.

cíclico,-a *adj* cyclic(al).

ciclismo *m* cycling.

ciclista *adj* cycle, cycling. **– 2** *mf* cyclist.

ciclo *m* cycle.

ciclocross *m inv* cyclo-cross.

ciclomotor *m* moped.

ciclón *m* cyclone.

ciclostil *m* cyclostyle.

ciego,-a *adj* blind. **2** *(conducto)* blocked up. **– 3** *m,f (persona)* blind person. **– 4** *m* ANAT caecum, blind gut. ●*a ciegas,* blindly.

cielo *m* sky. **2** *fig* heaven. **3** METEOR climate, weather. ●*a ~ raso,* in the open (air); *como caído del ~,* out of the blue;

despejarse el ~, to clear up; *poner a algo/algn. por los cielos,* to praise sth./ sb.; *poner el grito en el ~,* to hit the ceiling. ■ *~ raso,* ceiling.

ciempiés *m inv* centipede.

cien *adj* (one) hundred: *~ libras,* one hundred pounds. ●*~ por ~,* a hundred per cent; *fam fig ponerse a ~,* to be up to a hundred. ▲ *Only used in front of pl nouns.* → **ciento.**

ciénaga *f* marsh, bog.

ciencia *f* science. **2** *(saber)* knowledge, learning. ●*a ~ cierta,* with certainty. ■ *~ ficción,* science fiction; *ciencias empresariales,* business studies; *ciencias exactas,* mathematics *sing.*

cieno *m* mud, slime.

científico,-a *adj* scientific. **– 2** *m,f* scientist.

ciento *adj-m* (one) hundred. ●*por ~,* per cent; *fam ~ y la madre,* a crowd. ▲ → **cien.**

ciernes *en ~, adv* blossoming: *la política urbanística está en ~,* the town-planning policy is in its early stages.

cierre *m (acción)* closing, shutting. **2** *(de prenda)* fastener. **3** *(mecanismo)* catch. **4** *(de fábrica)* lockout; *(de tienda)* closedown.

cierto,-a *adj (seguro)* certain, sure. **2** *(verdadero)* true. **3** *(algún)* (a) certain, some: *~ día,* one day. **– 4** *adv* certainly. ●*estar en lo ~,* to be right; *por ~,* by the way.

ciervo *m* deer.

cierzo *m* north wind.

cifra *f (número)* figure, number. **2** *(cantidad)* amount. **3** *(código)* cipher, code.

cifrar *t (codificar)* to encode. **2** *(compendiar)* to summarize. **3** *fig (poner)* to place *(en, -).*

cigala *f* Dublin Bay prawn.

cigarra *f* cicada.

cigarrillo *m* cigarette.

cigarro *m* cigar.

cigüeña *f (ave)* stork. **2** TÉC crank.

cigüeñal *m* crankshaft.

cilindrada *f* cylinder capacity.

cilíndrico,-a *adj* cylindric(al).

cilindro *m* cylinder.

cima *f* summit. ●*dar ~ a,* to carry out, complete.

címbalo *m* cymbal.

cimbr(e)ar(se) *t (hacer vibrar)* to make quiver. **2** *(zarandearse)* to sway. **– 3** *p* to sway.

cimbreo *m* quiver. **2** *(de persona)* sway.

cimentar [27] *t* ARQ to lay the foundations of. **2** *fig* to found, establish.
cimiento *f* ARQ foundation. **2** *fig* basis.
cinc *m* zinc. ▲ *pl* **cines**.
cincel *m* chisel.
cincelado *m* chiselling.
cincelar *t* to chisel, engrave.
cinco *adj*·five; *(quinto)* fifth. **– 2** *m* five.
cincuenta *adj* fifty; *(cincuentavo)* fiftieth. **– 2** *m* fifty.
cincuentena *f* (group of) fifty.
cincuentenario *m* fiftieth anniversary.
cine *m (lugar)* cinema, US movie theatre: *ir al* ~, to go to the cinema, US go to the movies. **2** *(arte)* cinema.
cineclub *m* small film society. ▲ *pl* **cineclubs**.
cinema *m* → **cine**.
cinematografía *f* film making, cinematography.
cinética *f* kinetics.
cíngaro,-a *adj-m,f* gypsy.
cínico,-a *adj* cynical. **– 2** *m,f* cynic.
cinismo *m* cynicism.
cinta *f* band; *(decorativa)* ribbon. **2** TÉC tape. **3** CINEM film. **4** *(casete)* tape. **■** ~ *magnética*, magnetic tape; ~ *magnetofónica*, recording tape; ~ *métrica*, tape measure; ~ *transportadora*, conveyor belt.
cinto *m* belt, girdle.
cintura *f* waist.
cinturón *m* belt. **●** *fig apretarse el* ~, to tighten one's belt. **■** ~ *de seguridad*, safety belt.
ciprés *m* cypress.
circo *m* circus. **2** GEOG cirque.
circuito *m* circuit.
circulación *f* circulation. **2** *(de vehículos)* traffic. **●** *poner en/retirar de (la)* ~, to put into/withdraw from circulation. **■** *código de (la)* ~, highway code.
circular *adj* circular. **– 2** *f (carta)* circular letter. **– 3** *t-i* to circulate, go round; *(trenes etc.)* to run; *(coches)* to drive.
círculo *m* circle. **2** *(asociación)* club. **■** ~ *vicioso*, vicious circle.
circuncidar *t* to circumcise.
circuncisión *f* circumcision.
circundar *t* to surround.
circunferencia *f* circumference.
circunflejo,-a *adj* circumflex.
circunlocución *f*, **circunloquio** *m* circumlocution.
circunscribir(se) *t* to circumscribe. **– 2** *p* to confine o.s. *(a,* to). ▲ *pp* **circunscrito,-a**.

circunscripción *f* district, territory.
circunscrito,-a *pp* → **circunscribir**.
circunspección *f* circumspection.
circunspecto,-a *adj* circumspect, cautious.
circunstancia *f* circumstance. **●** *fam poner cara de circunstancias*, to look grave.
circunstancial *adj* circumstantial.
circunvalación *f* *carretera de* ~, ring road, US belt(way); *(autobús)* *línea de* ~, circular route.
circunvalar *t* to surround, encircle.
cirio *m* wax candle. **●** *fam armar un* ~, to kick up a rumpus.
cirro *m* cirrus.
cirrosis *f inv* cirrhosis.
ciruela *f* plum. **■** ~ *claudia*, greengage; ~ *pasa*, prune.
ciruelo *m* plum tree.
cirugía *f* surgery.
cirujano,-a *m,f* surgeon.
cisco *m (carbón)* coal dust, slack. **2** *(bullicio)* row. **●** *hacer* ~, to shatter; *meter* ~, to kick up a stink.
cisma *m & f* REL schism. **2** *(desacuerdo)* discord, split.
cismático,-a *adj-m,f* schismatic.
cisne *m* swan. **■** *canto del* ~, swan song.
cisterna *f* cistern, tank. **■** *camión* ~, tanker.
cistitis *f inv* cystitis.
cita *f (para negocios, médico, etc.)* appointment. **2** *(compromiso)* engagement, date. **3** *(mención)* quotation. **●** *darse* ~, to meet; *tener una* ~, to have an appointment/engagement.
citación *f (mención)* quotation. **2** JUR citation, summons.
citar(se) *t* to make an appointment/date with. **2** *(mencionar)* to quote. **3** JUR to summon. **– 4** *p* to arrange to meet *(con,* -).
cítara *f* zither, sitar.
cítrico,-a *adj* citric. **– 2** *mpl* citrus fruits.
ciudad *f* city, town.
ciudadanía *f* citizenship.
ciudadano,-a *adj* civic. **– 2** *m,f* citizen.
ciudadela *f* citadel, fortress.
cívico,-a *adj* civil, polite.
civil *adj* civil. **■** *(guardia)* ~, civil guard.
civilización *f* civilization.
civilizado,-a *adj* civilized.
civilizar(se) [4] *t* to civilize. **– 2** *p* to become civilized.
civismo *m* civility.

cizaña *f* BOT bearded darnel. ●*fig* **meter ~,** to sow discord.

clamar *i* to clamour. **– 2** *t* to cry out for: **~ venganza,** to cry out for revenge.

clamor *m* clamour.

clamoroso,-a *adj* clamorous.

clan *m* clan. ▲ *pl* **clanes.**

clandestino,-a *adj* clandestine, underground, secret.

clara *f* (egg) white. **2** *(bebida)* shandy.

claraboya *f* skylight.

clarear(se) *t* to make clear. **– 2** *i* to dawn. **3** METEOR to clear up. **– 4** *p* to become transparent. ▲ **2** *only used in the 3rd pers. It does not take a subject.*

clarete *m* claret (wine).

claridad *f* clarity; *(luz)* light. **2** *(inteligibilidad)* clearness.

clarificar [1] *t* to clarify.

clarín *m* bugle. **– 2** *mf* bugler.

clarinete *m* clarinet. **– 2** *mf* clarinettist.

clarividencia *f* *(percepción paranormal)* clairvoyance. **2** *(comprensión)* lucidity.

clarividente *mf* clairvoyant. **2** *(perspicaz)* lucid.

claro,-a *adj* clear. **2** *(color)* light. **3** *(salsa etc.)* thin. **4** *(evidente)* clear. **– 5** *adv* clearly. **– 6** *m* gap, space; *(de bosque)* clearing. **– 7** *interj* of course! ●**estar ~,** to be clear; **poner en ~,** to make plain, clear up; *fam* **más ~ que el agua,** as clear as daylight.

claroscuro *m* chiaroscuro.

clase *f* *(grupo)* class. **2** *(aula)* classroom. **3** *(tipo)* type, sort. ●**asistir a ~,** to attend class; **dar ~,** to teach; **toda ~ de,** all sorts of. ■ **~ alta/media/baja,** upper/middle/lower class; **~ de conducir,** driving lesson; **~ obrera,** working class.

clasicismo *m* classicism.

clásico,-a *adj* classic(al). **– 2** *m* classic.

clasificación *f* classification. **2** *(distribución)* sorting, filing. **3** DEP league, table.

clasificar(se) [1] *t* to class, classify. **2** *(distribuir)* to sort, file. **– 3** *p* DEP to qualify.

clasista *adj-mf* class-conscious (person).

claudicación *f* submission, yielding.

claudicar [1] *i* to yield, give in.

claustro *m* ARQ cloister. **2** EDUC *(profesores)* staff; *(junta)* staff meeting.

claustrofobia *f* claustrophobia.

cláusula *f* clause.

clausura *f* *(cierre)* closure. **2** REL enclosure.

clausurar *t* *(terminar)* to close. **2** *(cerrar)* to close (down): **~ un local,** to close down a bar.

clavado,-a *adj* *(con clavos)* nailed, nail-studded. **2** *fam (preciso)* exact, precise. **3** *(fijo)* firmly fixed. ●**dejar ~ (a algn.),** to leave (sb.) dumbfounded.

clavar(se) *t* *(con clavos)* to nail. **2** *fig* to fix: **~ los ojos en,** to rivet one's eyes on. **3** *fam (cobrar caro)* to sting. **– 4** *p* to get: **~se una astilla (en el dedo),** to get a splinter (in one's finger).

clave *f* *(de un enigma etc.)* key. **2** *(de signos)* code. **3** MÚS key: **en ~ de sol,** in the key of G. **– 4** *m* *(instrumento)* harpsichord. ■ **palabra ~,** key word; **hombre ~,** key man. ▲ *1 is inv.*

clavel *m* carnation.

clavetear *t* to stud with nails.

clavicordio *m* clavichord.

clavícula *f* clavicle, collarbone.

clavija *f* TÉC peg. **2** ELEC plug.

clavo *m* nail. **2** BOT clove. ●**dar en el ~,** to hit the nail on the head.

claxon *m* horn, hooter. ▲ *pl* **cláxones.**

clemencia *f* clemency, mercy.

clemente *adj* clement, merciful.

cleptomanía *f* kleptomania.

clerical *adj* clerical.

clérigo *m* clergyman, priest.

clero *m* clergy.

cliché *m* *(imprenta)* plate. **2** *(fotografía)* negative. **3** *fig* cliché.

cliente *mf* client, customer.

clientela *f* customers *pl*, clientele.

clima *m* climate. **2** *fig* atmosphere.

climatizado,-a *adj* air-conditioned.

climatizar [4] to air-condition.

clímax *m inv* climax.

clínica *f* clinic. **2** *(hospital)* private hospital.

clínico,-a *adj* clinical.

clip *m* *(para papel)* clip. **2** *(para pelo)* hairgrip, US bobby pin. ▲ *pl* **clips.**

clítoris *m inv* clitoris.

cloaca *f* sewer.

cloquear *i* to cluck.

clorhídrico,-a *adj* hydrochloric.

cloro *m* chlorine.

clorofila *f* chlorophyll.

cloroformizar *t* to chloroform.

cloroformo *m* chloroform.

club *m* club, society. ▲ *pl* **clubs** *or* **clubes.**

clueco,-a *adj-m,f* broody (hen).

coacción *f* coercion.

coaccionar *t* to coerce.

coactivo,-a *adj* coercive.

coagular(se) *t-p* to coagulate, clot.

coágulo *m* coagulum, clot.

coalición *f* coalition.

coartada *f* alibi.

coartar *t* to limit, restrict.

coba *f fam* soft soap. ●*dar ~ a algn.,* to soft-soap sb.

cobalto *m* cobalt. ■ *bomba de ~,* cobalt bomb.

cobarde *adj* cowardly. − 2 *mf* coward.

cobardía *f* cowardice.

cobertizo *m* shed.

cobertor *m (colcha)* bedspread. 2 *(manta)* blanket.

cobertura *f* cover(ing).

cobijar(se) *t* to cover. 2 *fig* to shelter. − 3 *p* to take shelter.

cobra *f* cobra.

cobrador,-ra *m,f* collector. 2 *(de autobús) m* conductor, *f* conductress.

cobrar *t (fijar precio por)* to charge; *(cheques)* to cash; *(salario)* to earn. 2 *(caza)* to retrieve. 3 *(adquirir)* to gain, get: *~ cariño,* to take a liking; *~ fuerzas,* to gather strength. ●*¡vas a ~!,* you're in for it!

cobre *m* copper.

cobrizo,-a *adj* copper.

cobro *m* cashing, collection.

coca *f arg* cocaine. 2 *fam (bebida)* Coke®.

cocaína *f* cocaine.

cocción *f* cooking; *(en agua)* boiling; *(en horno)* baking.

cocear *i* to kick.

cocer(se) [54] *t-p* to cook; *(hervir)* to boil; *(en horno)* to bake.

coche *m* car, automobile. 2 *(de tren, de caballos)* carriage, coach. ■ *~ cama,* sleeping car; *~ de alquiler,* hired car; *~ de carreras,* racing car; *~ de época,* vintage car; *~ fúnebre,* hearse; *~ restaurante,* dining car.

cochera *f* depot.

cochero *m* coachman.

cochinada *f (porquería)* dirty thing. 2 *fig* dirty trick.

cochinería *f (suciedad)* dirt, filth. 2 *fig* dirty trick.

cochinilla *f* cochineal.

cochinillo *m* sucking pig.

cochino,-a *adj (sucio)* filthy. 2 *(miserable)* bloody: *¡~ trabajo!,* damn work! − 3 *m,f* ZOOL *m* pig, *f* sow. 4 *fam (persona)* dirty person.

cocido,-a *adj* cooked; *(en agua)* boiled. − 2 *m* CULIN stew.

cociente *m* quotient.

cocina *f* kitchen. 2 *(gastronomía)* cooking: *~ española,* Spanish cooking/cuisine. 3 *(aparato)* cooker, US stove. ■ *~ casera,* home cooking; *~ de mercado,* food in season; *~ económica,* cooking range.

cocinar *t* to cook. 2 AM to bake.

cocinero,-a *m,f* cook.

coco *m* BOT *(árbol)* coconut palm. 2 *(fruta)* coconut. 3 *fam (fantasma)* bogeyman. 3 *arg (cabeza)* hard nut. ●*fam comer el ~ a algn.,* to brainwash sb; *fam comerse el ~,* to get worked up.

cocodrilo *m* crocodile.

cocotero *m* BOT coconut palm.

cóctel *m* cocktail. 2 *(fiesta)* cocktail party.

codazo *m* poke with the elbow.

codear(se) *i (empujar)* to elbow. − 2 *p ~se con,* to rub shoulders with.

codicia *f* greed.

codiciar [12] *t* to covet, long for.

codicioso,-a *adj* covetous, greedy.

código *m* code.

codo *m* ANAT elbow. 2 TÉC bend. ●*alzar/ empinar el ~,* to knock them back; *hablar por los codos,* to talk too much.

codorniz *f* quail.

coeficiente *m* coefficient. ■ *~ de inteligencia,* intelligence quotient.

coerción *f* coertion, restraint.

coercitivo,-a *adj* coercive.

coetáneo,-a *adj-m,f* contemporary.

coexistencia *f* coexistence.

coexistir *i* to coexist.

cofia *f* bonnet.

cofradía *f* brotherhood.

cofre *m* trunk, chest.

cogedor *m* dustpan.

coger [5] *t (asir)* to seize, take hold of. 2 *(apresar)* to capture. 3 *(tomar)* to take: *~ un empleo,* to take a job. 4 *(tren etc.)* to catch. 5 *(tomar prestado)* to borrow. 6 *(recolectar frutos etc.)* to pick. 7 *(enfermedad)* to catch. 8* AM to fuck*. ●*fig algo por los pelos,* to just make sth; *~ por sorpresa,* to catch by surprise; *(de media, etc.) ~ puntos,* to pick up stitches.

cognición *f* cognition.

cogollo *m (de lechuga etc.)* heart. 2 *(brote)* shoot. ●*fig el ~,* the cream, the best.

cogote *m* back of the neck, nape.

cohabitar *i* to cohabit.

cohechar *t* to bribe, suborn.

cohecho *m* bribery, subornation.

coherencia *f* coherence, coherency.

coherente *adj* coherent, connected.

cohesión *f* cohesion.

cohete *m* rocket.
cohibido,-a *adj* restrained.
cohibir(se) [21] *t* to restrain. − **2** *p* to feel embarrassed.
cohombro *m* cucumber.
coincidencia *f* coincidence.
coincidir *i* to coincide.
coito *m* coitus, intercourse.
cojear *i* to limp, hobble. **2** *(muebles)* to be rickety.
cojera *f* limp, lameness.
cojín *m* cushion.
cojinete *m* TÉC bearing. ■ ~ *de bolas,* ball bearing.
cojo,-a *adj* lame, crippled. **2** *(mueble)* wobbly. − **3** *m,f* lame person, cripple.
cojón* *m* ANAT ball*, bollock*. − **2** *interj* fuck it!* ●*por cojones,* like it or not; *tener cojones,* to have guts/balls*.
cojonudo,-a* *adj* fucking great*.
col *f* cabbage. ■ ~ *de Bruselas,* Brussels sprout.
cola *f* tail. **2** *(de vestido)* train. **3** *(fila)* queue, US line. **4** *(pegamento)* glue. ●*hacer* ~, to queue up; *fig tener/traer* ~, to have serious consequences. ■ ~ *de caballo,* BOT horsetail; *(peinado)* ponytail.
colaboración *f* collaboration. **2** *(prensa)* contribution.
colaboracionista *mf* collaborationist.
colaborador,-ra *m,f* collaborator. **2** *(prensa)* contributor.
colaborar *i* to collaborate. **2** *(prensa)* to contribute.
colación *f* *(comparación)* collation. **2** *(refrigerio)* light meal. ●*sacar a* ~, to mention, bring up.
colada *f* wash, laundry. **2** *(con lejía)* bleaching. **3** TÉC tapping. **4** *(volcánica)* outflow.
colador *m* *(de té, café)* strainer. **2** *(de caldo, alimentos)* colander.
colapso *m* MED collapse. **2** *fig* breakdown.
colar(se) [31] *t* to strain, filter. **2** *(con lejía)* to bleach. **3** *(lavar)* to wash. − **4** *fam* *p* to slip/sneak in. **5** *(equivocarse)* to slip up. **6** *(enamorarse)* to fall *(por,* for).
colcha *f* bedspread.
colchón *m* mattress.
colchoneta *f* small mattress.
colear *i* to wag the tail. **2** *fam* to drag on: *el asunto aún colea,* we haven't heard the last of it yet.
colección *f* collection.
coleccionar *t* to collect, make a collection of.

coleccionista *mf* collector.
colecta *f* collection.
colectividad *f* community.
colectivo,-a *adj* collective.
colector,-ra *adj* collecting. − **2** *m (caño)* water pipe. **3** *(cloaca)* main sewer.
colega *mf* colleague.
colegiado,-a *adj* collegiate. − **2** *m,f* collegiate. − **3** *m* DEP referee.
colegial,-la *adj* school. − **2** *m,f m* schoolboy, *f* schoolgirl.
colegiarse [12] *p* to join/form a professional association.
colegio *m* *(escuela)* school. **2** *(asociación)* college, body, association. ■ ~ *electoral,* polling station; ~ *mayor,* hall of residence; ~ *privado/de pago,* public school; ~ *público/estatal,* state school.
colegir [55] *t* to infer, conclude.
cólera *f* anger, rage. − **2** *m* MED cholera. ●*montar en* ~, to fly into a temper.
colérico,-a *adj* choleric, irascible.
coleta *f* pigtail.
colgador *m* (coat) hanger.
colgadura *f* hangings *pl,* drapery.
colgante *adj* hanging.
colgar(se) [52] *t* to hang (up). **2** *(abandonar)* to give up: ~ *los libros,* to give up studying. − **3** *i* to hang *(de,* from). **4** *(teléfono)* to put down, hang up: *¡no cuelgue!,* hold on!
colibrí *m* humming bird.
cólico *m* colic.
coliflor *f* cauliflower.
colilla *f* cigarette end/butt.
colina *f* hill(ock).
colindante *adj* adjacent, neighbouring.
colindar *i* to be adjacent *(con,* to).
colirio *m* eyewash, collyrium.
colisión *f* collision, clash.
colisionar *i* to collide, crash, clash.
collado *m* hill(ock). **2** *(paso entre montañas)* wide mountain pass.
collar *m* necklace. **2** *(cuello)* collar.
colmado,-a *adj* full, abundant. − **2** *m* grocer's (shop).
colmar *t* *(vaso, copa)* to fill to the brim. **2** *fig (ambiciones etc.)* to fulfil. ●~ *de,* to fill/to stuff with.
colmena *f* beehive.
colmenar *m* apiary.
colmillo *m* eye/canine tooth.
colmo *m* height, limit. ●*¡esto es el* ~*!,* this is too much!
colocación *f* *(acto)* location. **2** *(situación)* situation. **3** *(empleo)* employment.

colocado,-a *adj (empleado)* employed. **2** *arg (embriagado)* sozzled; *(drogado)* stoned, high.

colocar(se) [1] *t* to place, put. **2** *(emplear)* to give work to. **3** FIN to invest. **4** *(mercancías)* to sell well. — **5** *p (situarse)* to place o.s. **6** *(trabajar)* to get a job *(de, as)*. **7** *arg (embriagarse)* to get sozzled; *(drogarse)* to get stoned.

colofón *m (apéndice)* colophon. **2** *fig (remate)* crowning, climax.

colon *m* colon.

colonia *f (grupo)* colony. **2** *(vacaciones infantiles)* summer camp. **3** *(perfume)* cologne.

colonial *adj* colonial. — **2** *mpl* imported foodstuffs.

colonización *f* colonization.

colonizador,-ra *adj* colonizing. — **2** *m,f* colonizer, colonist.

colonizar [4] *t* to colonize.

colono *m (habitante)* colonist, settler. **2** AGR tenant farmer.

coloquial *adj* colloquial.

coloquio *m* talk, discussion.

color *m* colour. **2** *fig (carácter)* character. •*fig verlo todo de ~ de rosa,* to see life through rose-coloured spectacles.

colorado,-a *adj* coloured. **2** *(color)* red(dish). •*ponerse ~,* to blush.

colorante *adj* colouring. — **2** *m* colouring, dye.

color(e)ar *t* to colour.

colorete *m* rouge.

colorido *m* colour.

colorín *m* bright colour. •*... y ~ colorado este cuento se ha acabado,* ... and that's the end of the story.

colosal *adj* colossal, giant, huge.

columbrar *t (vislumbrar)* to glimpse. **2** *(conjeturar)* to guess, conjecture.

columna *f* column. ■ *~ vertebral,* vertebral/spinal column.

columnata *f* colonnade.

columpiar(se) *t-p* to swing.

columpio *m* swing.

coma *f* GRAM MÚS comma. **2** *(matemáticas)* point. — **3** *m* MED coma.

comadre *f (partera)* midwife. **2** *(madrina)* godmother. **3** *fam (vecina)* neighbour. **4** *(amiga)* (female) friend.

comadrear *i* to gossip, chat.

comadreja *f* weasel.

comadreo *m* gossiping, chatting.

comadrona *f* midwife.

comandancia *f (grado)* command. **2** *(edificio)* headquarters *inv.*

comandante *m (oficial)* commander. **2** *(graduación)* major.

comandar *t* to command.

comandita *f* COM silent partnership.

comando *m* commando.

comarca *f* area, region.

comba *f (curvatura)* bend. **2** *(cuerda)* skipping rope. •*saltar a la ~,* to skip (rope).

combar(se) *t-p* to bend.

combate *m* combat, battle. **2** *(boxeo)* fight.

combatiente *adj* fighting. — **2** *mf* fighter.

combatir *i* to fight, struggle *(contra, against)*. — **2** *t (luchar contra)* to fight.

combinación *f* combination. **2** *(prenda)* slip.

combinar(se) *t-p* to combine.

combustible *adj* combustible. — **2** *m* fuel.

combustión *f* combustion, burning.

comecocos *m inv arg (de tragaperras)* pacman. **2** *(asunto, libro, etc.)* soul-destroyer.

comedero *m* feeding trough.

comedia *f* TEAT comedy, play. **2** *fig* farce, pretence.

comediante,-a *m,f m* actor, *f* actress. **2** *fig* hypocrite.

comedido,-a *adj (educado)* courteous, polite. **2** *(moderado)* moderate.

comedirse [34] *p* to restrain o.s.

comedor,-ra *adj* heavy-eating: *ser (muy) ~,* to eat a lot. — **2** *m* dining room. **3** *(muebles)* dining-room suite.

comendador *m* commander.

comensal *mf* table companion.

comentar *t (por escrito)* to comment on; *(oralmente)* to talk about.

comentario *m (observación)* remark, comment. **2** *pl* gossip *sing.*

comentarista *mf* commentator.

comenzar [47] *t-i* to begin, start.

comer(se) *t* to eat. **2** *(color)* to fade. **3** *(corroer)* to corrode. **4** *fig (gastar)* to eat away. — **5** *i* to eat. **6** *(comida principal)* to have a meal. — **7** *p fig (saltarse)* to omit; *(párrafo)* to skip; *(palabra)* to swallow: *se come las palabras,* he/she slurs. •*~se las uñas,* to bite one's nails; *dar de ~,* to feed; *fam ~se algo con los ojos,* to devour sth. with one's eyes.

comercial *adj* commercial.

comercializar [4] *t* to commercialize, market.

comerciante *mf* merchant. **2** *(interesado)* moneymaker.

comerciar [12] *i (comprar y vender)* to trade, deal. **2** *(hacer negocios)* to do business *(con,* with).

comercio *m (ocupación)* commerce, trade. **2** AM *(tienda)* shop, store. ■ *libre* ~, free trade.

comestible *adj* edible. — **2** *mpl* groceries, food *sing.* ■ *tienda de comestibles,* grocer's (shop).

cometa *m* ASTRON comet. — **2** *f* kite.

cometer *t (crimen)* to commit; *(falta, error)* to make.

cometido *m (encargo)* task. **2** *(deber)* duty.

comezón *f* itch(ing).

cómic *m* comic.

comicios *mpl* POL elections.

cómico,-a *adj* comic. — **2** *mf* comedian, comic.

comida *f* food. **2** *(desayuno etc.)* meal. **3** *(almuerzo)* lunch.

comidilla *f* gossip, talk.

comience *pres subj/imperat* → **comenzar**.

comienzo *m* start, beginning.

comillas *fpl* inverted commas.

comilón,-ona *adj-m,f* big eater, glutton. — **2** *f* big meal.

comino *m* BOT cu(m)min. ●*no valer un* ~, not to be worth tuppence.

comisaría *f* ~ *(de policía),* police station.

comisario *m* ~ *(de policía),* police inspector.

comiscar [1] *t-i fam* to nibble (on).

comisión *f (retribución)* commission. **2** *(comité)* committee. **3** *(encargo)* assignment.

comisionado,-a *adj* commissioned. — **2** *m,f* commissioner, US constable.

comisionar *t* to commission.

comisura *f* corner, angle.

comité *m* committee.

comitiva *f* suite, retinue.

como *adv (lo mismo que)* as: *negro* ~ *la noche,* as dark as night. **2** *(de tal modo)* like: *hablas* ~ *un político,* you talk like a politician. **3** *(según)* as: ~ *dice tu amigo,* as your friend says. **4** *(en calidad de)* as: ~ *invitado,* as a guest. — **5** *conj (así que)* as soon as. **6** *(si)* if: ~ *lo vuelvas a hacer,* if you do it again. **7** *(porque)* as, since: ~ *llegamos tarde no pudimos entrar,* since we arrived late we couldn't get in. ●~ *quiera que,* since, as, inasmuch; ~ *no sea,* unless it is; ~ *si nada/ tal cosa,* as if nothing had happened; *fam tanto* ~, as much as.

cómo *adv interrog* how: *¿*~ *está usted?,* how do you do? **2** *(por qué)* why: *¿*~ *no viniste?,* why didn't you come? **3** *(admiración)* how: *¡*~ *corre el tiempo!,* time flies!

cómoda *f* chest of drawers.

comodidad *f* comfort. **2** *(facilidad)* convenience.

comodín *m (carta)* joker. **2** *fig* excuse.

cómodo,-a *adj* comfortable, cosy. **2** *(útil)* convenient, handy.

comodón,-ona *adj* comfort loving. — **2** *m,f* comfort lover.

compacto *adj* compact, dense.

compadecer(se) [43] *t* to pity, feel sorry for. — **2** *p* to have pity *(de,* on).

compadre *m (padrino)* godfather. **2** *(amigo)* mate, pal.

compaginar(se) *t* to arrange. — **2** *p* to go together, match.

compañerismo *m* companionship, fellowship.

compañero,-a *m,f* companion, fellow, mate.

compañía *f* company. ●*hacer* ~ *a algn.,* to keep sb. company. ■ ~ *de seguros/ teatro,* insurance/theatre company.

comparación *f* comparison.

comparar *t* to compare.

comparativo,-a *adj* comparative.

comparecer [43] *i* JUR to appear.

comparsa *f (teatro)* extras *pl.* **2** *(de carnaval)* masquerade. — **3** *mf* walk-on, extra.

compartim(i)ento *m* compartment.

compartir *t (dividir)* to divide up, split. **2** *(poseer en común)* to share.

compás *m* (pair of) compasses. **2** MÚS time. ●*llevar el* ~, to keep/beat time.

compasión *f* compassion, pity. ●*tener* ~ *(de algn.),* to feel sorry (for sb.).

compasivo,-a *adj* compassionate, sympathetic.

compatibilidad *f* compatibility.

compatible *adj* compatible.

compatriota *mf* compatriot; *m* fellow countryman, *f* fellow countrywoman.

compeler *t* to compel, force.

compendiar [12] *t* to summarize, abridge, sum up.

compendio *m* summary, digest.

compenetración *f fig* mutual understanding. **2** FÍS interpenetration.

compenetrarse *p* to understand each other. **2** FÍS to interpenetrate.

compensación *f* compensation.

compensar *t (indemnizar)* to compensate. **2** *(resarcir)* to make up for. **3** *fam* to be worthwhile: *este trabajo no me compensa,* this job's not worth my time.

competencia *f (rivalidad)* competition. **2** *(competidores)* competitors *pl.* **3** *(habilidad)* competence, ability. **4** *(incumbencia)* field, scope; *no es de mi* ~, it's not within my province.

competente *adj (capaz)* competent, capable. **2** *(adecuado)* adequate.

competer *i (corresponder)* to be up to. **2** *(incumbir)* to be the duty/business of.

competición *f* competition.

competidor,-ra *adj* competing. − **2** *m,f* competitor.

competir [34] *i* to compete *(con,* with/against; *en,* in; *por,* for).

competitivo,-a *adj* competitive.

compilar *t* to compile.

compinche *mf fam* chum, pal.

complacencia *f* pleasure, satisfaction.

complacer(se) [76] *t* to please. − **2** *p* to take pleasure *(en/de/por,* in). **3** *fml* to be pleased to: *me complace anunciar ...,* it gives me great pleasure to announce...

complaciente *adj* obliging.

complejidad *f* complexity.

complejo,-a *adj-m* complex.

complementar(se) *t* to complement. − **2** *p* to complement each other.

complementario,-a *adj* complementary.

complemento *m* complement. **2** GRAM object.

completar *t* to complete. **2** *(acabar)* to finish.

completo,-a *adj (terminado)* complete. **2** *(total)* full. − **3** *completamente adv* completely. ●*al* ~, full up, filled to capacity.

complexión *f* constitution, build.

complicación *f* complication. ●*buscarse complicaciones,* to make life difficult for o.s.

complicado,-a *adj* complicated.

complicar(se) [1] *t* to complicate. **2** *(implicar)* to involve *(en,* in). − **3** *p* to become complicated/involved. ●~*se la vida,* to make life difficult for o.s.

cómplice *mf* accomplice.

complicidad *f* complicity.

complot *m* plot, conspiracy.

componenda *f* shady deal.

componente *adj-m* component.

componer(se) [78] *t (formar)* to compose. **2** *(reparar)* to fix, repair. **3** *(ador-*

nar) to adorn, trim. **4** *(riña)* to settle. **5** *(ataviar)* to dress/make up. − **6** *p (consistir)* to consist *(de,* of). ●*fam componérselas,* to manage, make do. ▲ *pp compuesto,-a.*

comportamiento *m* behaviour, conduct.

comportar(se) *t* to bear, tolerate. − **2** *p* to behave, act. ●*saber* ~*se,* to know how to behave.

composición *f* composition. **2** *(acuerdo)* agreement. ●*hacer* ~ *de lugar,* to weigh the pros and cons.

compositor,-ra *m,f* composer.

compostura *f (reparación)* repair, mending. **2** *(dignidad)* composure, dignity. **3** *(ajuste)* settlement, adjustment. **4** *(convenio)* agreement.

compota *f* compote.

compra *f* purchase, buy. ●*ir de compras,* to go shopping. ■ ~ *a crédito,* credit purchase; ~ *a plazos,* hire purchase.

comprar *t* to buy. **2** *(sobornar)* to bribe, buy off.

compraventa *f* buying and selling, dealing.

comprender *t (entender)* to understand. **2** *(contener)* to comprehend, comprise, embrace.

comprensible *adj* understandable.

comprensión *f* understanding.

comprensivo,-a *adj (que entiende)* understanding. **2** *(que contiene)* comprehensive.

compresa *f (higiénica)* sanitary towel. **2** *(vendaje)* compress.

compresión *f* compression.

compresor,-ra *adj* compressing. − **2** *m* compressor.

comprimido,-a *adj* compressed. − **2** *m* tablet.

comprimir *t (apretar)* to compress. **2** *(reprimir)* to restrain.

comprobación *f* verification, check.

comprobante *m* receipt, voucher.

comprobar [31] *t* to verify, check.

comprometedor,-ra *adj* compromising. **2** *(persona)* troublemaking.

comprometer(se) *t (juzgar un tercero)* to submit to arbitration. **2** *(exponer a riesgo)* to compromise, risk. **3** *(obligar)* to engage. − **4** *p (prometer)* to commit o.s. ●~*se a hacer algo,* to undertake to do sth.

compromiso *m (obligación)* commitment. **2** *(acuerdo)* agreement. **3** *(dificultad)* difficult situation, bind. ●*poner (a* *algn.) en un* ~, to put (sb.) in a tight spot.

compuerta *f* sluice, floodgate.

compuesto,-a *pp* → **componer.** – **2** *adj* compound. **3** *(reparado)* repaired, mended. **4** *(elegante)* dressed up. – **5** *m* *(químico, farmacéutico, etc.)* compound.

compulsar *t (cotejar)* to collate. **2** JUR *(hacer copia)* to make a certified true copy.

compungido,-a *adj* remorseful.

compungirse [6] *p* to feel remorseful.

compuse *pt indef* → **componer.**

computador,-ra *m,f* computer.

computar *t* to compute, calculate.

cómputo *m* computation, calculation.

comulgar [7] *i* to receive Holy Communion. **2** *fig (compartir ideas etc.)* to share *(con, -)*.

común *adj* common. **2** *(compartido)* shared. – **3** *m* community. – **4** *comúnmente adv (normalmente)* commonly, usually, generally; *(frecuentemente)* often. ●*por lo* ~, generally.

comuna *f* commune.

comunal *adj* communal.

comunicación *f* communication. **2** *(comunicado)* communication; *(oficial)* communiqué. **3** *(telefónica)* connection. **4** *pl* communications. ■ *medios de* ~, (news) media.

comunicado *m* communiqué. ■~ *a la prensa,* press release.

comunicar(se) [1] *t-i-p* to communicate. – **2** *i (teléfono)* to be engaged, US be busy. ●~ *con algn.,* to get in touch with sb.

comunicativo,-a *adj* communicative. **2** *(de carácter)* open, unreserved.

comunidad *f* community. ■ ~ *de propietarios,* owners' association.

comunión *f* communion. ■ *la Sagrada* ~, the Holy Communion.

comunismo *m* communism.

comunista *adj-mf* communist.

con *prep* with. **2** *(a pesar de)* in spite of: ~ *ser tan fuerte ...,* in spite of his being so strong ... . **3** *(dirección)* to, towards. **4** *(relación)* to. ●~ *que,* as long as, if; ~ *tal (de) que,* provided that; ~ *todo,* nevertheless.

conato *m (intento)* attempt. **2** *(tendencia)* tendency.

concadenar *t* to concatenate, link together.

concavidad *f* concavity.

cóncavo,-a *adj* concave.

concebible *adj* conceivable.

concebir [34] *t-i (engendrar)* to conceive. – **2** *t fig (comprender)* to understand. **3** *(comenzar a sentir)* to experience.

conceder *t* to grant; *(premio)* to award. **2** *(admitir)* to concede, admit.

concejal,-la *m,f* town councillor.

concejalía *f* councillorship.

concenciar(se) [12] *t* to make aware. – **2** *p* to become aware.

concentración *f* concentration. **2** *(de gente)* gathering, rally.

concentrar(se) *t-p* to concentrate.

concéntrico,-a *adj* concentric.

concepción *f* conception.

concepto *m (idea)* concept. **2** *(opinión)* opinion, view. ●*bajo ningún* ~, under no circumstances; *en* ~ *de,* by way of.

conceptualizar [4] *t* to conceptualize.

conceptuar [11] *t* to deem, judge, think.

concerniente *adj* concerning, relating. ●*fml en lo* ~ *a,* with regard to.

concernir [29] *i* to concern. ●*por lo que a mí concierne,* as far as I am concerned. ▲ *Used only in indic pres, indic imperf and subj pres and in non-personal forms.*

concertar(se) [27] *t (acuerdo)* to conclude. **2** *(ordenar las partes)* to plan, arrange. **3** MÚS to harmonize. – **4** *i (concordar)* to agree. – **5** *p* to reach an agreement.

concertista *mf* soloist.

concesión *f* concession. **2** *(de premio)* awarding.

concesionario,-a *adj* concessionary. – **2** *m,f* concessionaire.

concha *f (caparazón)* shell. **2** *(ostra)* oyster.

conchabar(se) *t (unir)* to blend. – **2** *p* *(confabularse)* to plot, scheme.

conciencia *f (moral)* conscience. **2** MED consciousness; *(conocimiento)* awareness. ●*a* ~, conscientiously; *con la* ~ *tranquila,* with a clear conscience; *remorder la* ~ *a algn.,* to weigh on sb.'s conscience.

concienzudo,-a *adj* conscientious.

concierto *m* MÚS concert. **2** *(acuerdo)* agreement. ●*sin orden ni* ~, any old how.

conciliábulo *m* secret meeting.

conciliación *f* conciliation.

conciliador,-ra *adj* conciliatory.

conciliar(se) [12] *t* to conciliate. **2** *(enemigos)* to reconcile. – **3** *p* to win. ●~ *el sueño,* to get to sleep.

concilio *m* council.

concisión f conciseness.
conciso,-a adj concise, brief.
concitar t to excite, incite, stir up, raise.
conciudadano,-a m,f fellow citizen.
cónclave, conclave m REL conclave. 2 fig (reunión) private meeting.
concluir(se) [62] t-i-p to finish. − 2 t (deducir) to conclude, infer.
conclusión f conclusion, end. ●*llegar a una ~,* to come to a conclusion.
concluyente adj conclusive, decisive.
concomitancia f concomitance.
concomitante adj concomitant.
concordancia f concordance, agreement.
concordar [31] t to make agree, harmonize. − 2 i to agree, match, tally.
concordato m concordat.
concordia f concord, harmony.
concretar(se) t (precisar) to specify: ~ *una hora,* to fix/set a time. 2 (resumir) to summarize. − 3 p to limit o.s. (a, to).
concreto,-a adj concrete. 2 (definido) specific, definite. ●*en ~,* exactly.
concubina f concubine.
conculcar [1] t to infringe.
concupiscencia f concupiscence.
concurrencia f (confluencia) concurrence. 2 (público) audience. 3 (rivalidad) competition. 4 (auxilio) aid.
concurrido,-a adj (lugar público) busy.
concurrir i (gente a un lugar) to converge (en, on). 2 (coincidir) to coincide. 3 (contribuir) to contribute (en, to). 4 (convenir) to concur. 5 (competir) to take part in a competition.
concursante mf (a concurso) contestant, participant. 2 (a empleo) candidate.
concursar i (competir) to compete. 2 (a empleo) to be a candidate.
concurso m competition; (de belleza, deportivo) contest. 2 (concurrencia) concourse.
condado m county.
conde m count.
condecoración f decoration, medal.
condecorar t to decorate.
condena f (castigo) sentence. ●*cumplir una ~,* to serve a sentence.
condenación f condemnation. 2 REL damnation.
condenado,-a adj-mf convicted. − 2 mf convict. ●*trabajar como un ~,* to slog one's guts out.
condenar t JUR (castigar) to condemn; (sentenciar) to convict. 2 (desaprobar) to condemn. 3 (tabicar) to wall up.

condensación f (acción) condensing. 2 (efecto) condensation.
condensador,-ra adj condensing. − 2 m ELEC condenser.
condensar(se) t-p to condense.
condesa f countess.
condescendencia f acquiescence, condescension.
condescender [28] i to acquiesce, comply (a, with).
condescendiente adj condescending.
condición f (situación) condition. 2 (naturaleza) nature: *de ~ apacible,* of an easy-going nature. 3 (circunstancia) circumstance. 4 (estado social, calidad de) status, position: *de ~ humilde,* of humble origen. ●*a ~ de que,* provided (that); *condiciones de trabajo,* work conditions.
condicional adj conditional.
condicionar t to condition.
condimentar t to season, flavouring.
condimento m seasoning, flavouring.
condolerse [32] p to sympathize (with), feel sorry (for).
condón m condom, rubber.
cóndor m condor.
conducción f FÍS conduction. 2 (transporte) transportation. 3 (por tubería) piping; (eléctrica) wiring. 4 AUTO driving.
conducir(se) [46] t (guiar) to lead; (coche, animales) to drive. 2 (negocio) to manage. 3 (transportar) to transport; (líquidos) to convey. − 4 i to lead (a, -): *esto no conduce a nada,* this leads nowhere. − 5 p (comportarse) to behave, act.
conducta f conduct, behaviour.
conducto m conduit. 2 ANAT duct. 3 fig channel: *por conductos oficiales,* through official channels. ●*por ~ de,* through.
conductor,-ra adj conducting. 2 FÍS conductive. − 2 m,f AUTO driver. − 4 m FÍS conductor.
conectar t to connect. 2 (aparato eléctrico) to switch/plug on.
conejo m rabbit. ■ *~/conejillo de Indias,* guinea pig.
conexión f TÉC connection. 2 fig relationship.
confabulación f confabulation. 2 (conspiración) plot.
confabular(se) i to confabulate. − 2 p to plot.
confección f COST dressmaking. 2 (realización) making, creation.
confeccionar t to make (up). 2 (plato) to cook.

confederación f confederation, confederacy.

confederar(se) t-p to confederate.

conferencia f (charla) talk, lecture. **2** POL conference. **3** (teléfono) long-distance call. ■ ~ de prensa, press conference.

conferenciante mf lecturer.

conferenciar [12] i to confer (sobre/con, on/with).

conferir [35] t to confer.

confesar(se) [27] t-p to confess. ●~ de plano, to make a clean breast of it.

confesión f confession.

confesonario m confessional.

confesor m confessor.

confeti m confetti inv . ▲ pl confetis.

confiado,-a adj confiding, unsuspecting. **2** (seguro) self-confident.

confianza f (seguridad) confidence. **2** (fe) trust. **3** (familiaridad) familiarity. **4** (ánimo) encouragement. ●de ~, reliable; en ~, confidentially; tomarse (demasiadas/muchas) confianzas, to take liberties.

confiar(se) [13] i to trust (en, -). **2** (secreto) to confide. – **3** t (depositar) to entrust. – **4** p to be trustful. **5** (confesarse) to make confessions.

confidencia f confidence, secret.

confidencial adj confidential.

confidente,-a adj trustworthy, reliable. – **2** m,f m confidant, f confidante. **3** euf (de la policía) informer.

configuración f configuration, shape.

configurar t to form, shape.

confín m limit, boundary.

confinamiento m confinement. **2** (exilio) exile.

confinar(se) i (territorio) to border (on). – **2** t JUR to confine. – **3** p to shut o.s. away.

confirmación f confirmation.

confirmar t to confirm. ●la excepción confirma la regla, the exception proves the rule.

confiscar [1] t to confiscate.

confitar t to candy; (carne) to preserve.

confite m sweet, US candy.

confitería f sweet shop, US candy shop. **2** AM café.

confitero,-a m,f confectioner.

confitura f preserve.

conflagración f conflagration.

conflicto m conflict. ■ ~ laboral, labour dispute.

confluencia f confluence.

confluir [62] i to converge. **2** (ríos, caminos) to meet.

conformación f shape, structure.

conformar(se) t (dar forma) to shape. **2** (concordar) to conform. – **3** i (concordar) to agree (con, with). – **4** p to resign o.s. (con, to), be content (con, with).

conforme adj (concorde) according; estar ~, to agree. **2** (resignado) easy-going. – **3** adv in accordance with. **4** (según) as: ~ lo vi, as I saw it. – **5** m approval.

conformidad f (acuerdo) agreement. **2** (aprobación) approval. **3** (resignación) patience, resignation. ●en ~ con, in conformity with.

conformismo m conformity.

conformista adj-mf conformist.

confort m comfort. ●(en anuncio) "todo ~", "all mod. cons.".

confortable adj comfortable.

confortar t (dar vigor) to invigorate. **2** (consolar) to comfort.

confraternidad f confraternity.

confraternizar [4] i to fraternize.

confrontación f confrontation. **2** (comparación) comparison.

confrontar(se) t (carear) to bring face to face. **2** (cotejar) to compare (con, with). – **3** i (lindar) to border. – **4** p to face.

confundir(se) t (mezclar) to mix up. **2** (equivocar) to confuse (con, with). **3** (no reconocer) to mistake (con, for): le confundí con su hermana, I mistook her for her sister. **4** (turbar) to confound. – **5** p (mezclarse) to mingle. **6** (equivocarse) to be mistaken, make a mistake. **7** (turbarse) to be confounded.

confusión f (desorden) confusion. **2** (equivocación) mistake. **3** (turbación) confusion.

confuso,-a adj confused. **2** (recuerdos) vague. **3** (mezclado) mixed up.

congelación f freezing; MED frostbite.

congelado,-a adj frozen; MED frostbitten. – **2** pl frozen food sing.

congelador m freezer.

congelar(se) t-p to freeze. ●FIN ~ precios, to freeze prices.

congeniar [12] i to get along well.

congénito,-a adj congenital.

congestión f congestion. ■ ~ cerebral, stroke.

congestionar(se) t to congest. – **2** p to become congested.

conglomerado m conglomerate.

conglomerar(se) t-p to conglomerate.

congoja *f (angustia)* anguish. **2** *(pena)* grief.

congraciar(se) [12] *t* to win over. − **2** *p* to ingratiate o.s. (*con*, with).

congratulación *f fml* congratulation.

congratular(se) *t-p fml* to congratulate (o.s.) (*de/por*, on).

congregación *f* congregation.

congregar(se) [7] *t-p* to congregate.

congresista *mf* member of a congress; *m* congressman, *f* congresswoman.

congreso *m* congress. ■ ~ *de los Diputados*, GB Parliament, US Congress.

congrio *m* conger (eel).

congruencia *f (conveniencia)* congruity. **2** MAT congruence.

congruente *adj (conveniente)* coherent. **2** MAT congruent.

cónico,-a *adj* conical.

conífero,-a *adj* coniferous. − **2** *f* conifer.

conjetura *f* conjecture, guess.

conjeturar *t* to conjecture, guess.

conjugación *f* conjugation.

conjugar [7] *t* to conjugate.

conjunción *f* conjunction.

conjuntivitis *f inv* conjunctivitis.

conjunto,-a *adj* joint. − **2** *m (grupo)* group, collection. **3** *(todo)* whole. **4** *(prenda)* outfit. **5** MÚS *(clásico)* ensemble; *(pop)* band. **6** MAT set. − **7** *conjuntamente adv* jointly. ●*en* ~, as a whole, altogether.

conjura, conjuración *f* plot, conspiracy.

conjurar(se) *t* to exorcise. − **2** *i-p* to conspire (*contra*, against).

conjuro *m* exorcism.

conllevar *t (implicar)* to imply. **2** *(enfermedad)* to put up with.

conmemoración *f* commemoration.

conmemorar *t* to commemorate.

conmemorativo,-a *adj* commemorative.

conmigo *pron* with/to me: ~ *mismo,-a,* with/to myself; *hablaba* ~, he/she was talking to me.

conmiseración *f* commiseration, pity.

conmoción *f* commotion. **2** MED concussion. **3** *(levantamiento)* riot.

conmocionar *t* to shock. **2** MED to concuss.

conmovedor,-ra *adj* moving, touching.

conmover(se) [32] *t* to move, touch. **2** *(cosa)* to stir. − **3** *p* to be moved/touched.

conmutación *f* commutation.

conmutador *m* ELEC switch.

conmutar *t* to exchange. **2** JUR to commute. **3** ELEC to commutate.

connotación *f* connotation.

connotar *t* to connote.

cono *m* cone.

conocedor,-ra *adj-m,f* expert (*de*, in).

conocer(se) [44] *t* to know. **2** *(tener noticia de algn.)* to be acquainted with; *(por primera vez)* to meet. **3** *(reconocer)* to recognize. − **4** *p (a sí mismo)* to know o.s.; *(a otra persona)* to be acquainted with each other. ●~ *al dedillo/palmo a palmo,* to know sth. really well; ~ *de vista,* to know by sight.

conocido,-a *adj* known. **2** *(famoso)* well-known. − **3** *m,f* acquaintance.

conocimiento *m (saber)* knowledge. **2** *(madurez)* understanding. **3** *(conciencia)* consciousness. ●*perder/recobrar el* ~, to lose/regain consciousness; *tener* ~ *de,* to have an understanding of.

conque *conj* so.

conquista *f* conquest.

conquistador,-ra *adj* conquering. − **2** *m,f* conqueror. − **3** *m (ligón)* lady-killer.

conquistar *t (con las armas)* to conquer. **2** *(título)* to win. **3** *(ligar con)* to win over.

consabido,-a *adj fml* usual. **2** *(ya sabido)* well-known.

consagración *f* consecration.

consagrado,-a *adj* REL consecrate(d). **2** *(reconocido)* recognized.

consagrar(se) *t* REL to consecrate. **2** *(palabra)* to authorize. − **3** *p* to devote o.s. (*a*, to).

consanguíneo,-a *adj* related by blood. − **2** *m,f* blood relation.

consanguinidad *f* consanguinity.

consciencia *f* → **conciencia**.

consciente *adj* conscious.

consecución *f* attainment.

consecuencia *f* consequence, result. ●*a* ~ *de,* because of, owing/due to; *en/por* ~, consequently, therefore.

consecuente *adj (siguiente)* consequent. **2** *(resultante)* resulting. **3** *(coherente)* consistent.

consecutivo,-a *adj* consecutive.

conseguir [56] *t (cosa)* to obtain; *(objetivo)* to attain, get. **2** *(lograr)* succeed in, manage to: *¡lo conseguí!,* I did it! ▲ **2** *is always* ~ + *inf.*

consejero,-a *m,f* adviser. **2** POL counsellor.

consejo *m (recomendación)* advice: *te daré un* ~, I'll give you a piece of advice. **2** *(junta)* council, board. ■ ~ *de adminis-*

tración, board of directors; ~ *de gue-rra,* courtmartial; ~ *de ministros,* cabinet.

consenso *m (acuerdo)* consensus.

consentido,-a *adj-m,f* spoiled (child).

consentimiento *m* consent.

consentir(se) [35] *t (permitir)* to allow, permit, tolerate. **2** *(a un niño)* to spoil. **– 3** *i* to consent *(en,* to), give way. **– 4** *p* to crack.

conserje *m* porter.

conserva *f (en lata)* tinned/canned food. **2** *(dulces)* preserves *pl.*

conservación *f* conservation. **2** *(mantenimiento)* maintenance.

conservador,-ra *adj* POL conservative. **– 2** *m,f* POL conservative. **3** *(de museos)* curator.

conservadurismo *m* POL conservatism.

conservante *m* preservative.

conservar *t (alimentos)* to preserve. **2** *(mantener)* to keep, maintain.

conservatorio *m* conservatory, conservatoire.

considerable *adj* considerable.

consideración *f* consideration. **2** *(respeto)* regard. ●*de* ~, important: *herido,-a de* ~, seriously injured; *tomar en* ~, to take into consideration.

considerado,-a *adj (atento)* considerate. **2** *(apreciado)* respected. ●*estar bien/mal* ~, to be well/badly thought of.

considerar *t (reflexionar)* to consider, think over. **2** *(respetar)* to treat with consideration. **3** *(juzgar)* to judge.

consigna *f (en estación etc.)* left-luggage office, US check-room. **2** *(señal, lema)* watchword; MIL orders *pl.*

consignación *f (asignación)* allocation. **2** COM consignment.

consignar *t (poner)* to consign. **2** *(destinar dinero etc.)* to allocate; *(cantidad)* to assign. **3** *(por escrito)* to note down.

consignatario *m (depositario)* trustee. **2** COM consignee.

consigo *pron (singular)* with him/her/it: ~ *mismo,-a,* with himself/herself. **2** *(plural) (tercera pers)* with them; *(segunda pers)* with you: ~ *mismos,-as,* with themselves/yourselves. **3** *(usted)* with yourself: ~ *mismo,-a,* with yourself.

consiguiente *adj* consequent. ●*por* ~, therefore.

consistencia *f (dureza)* consistency. **2** *(coherencia)* coherence.

consistente *adj* consistent.

consistir *i* to consist *(en,* of).

consistorial *adj* consistorial.

consistorio *m* town council.

consola *f* console (table).

consolación *f* consolation, comfort.

consolador,-ra *adj* consoling, comforting.

consolar(se) [31] *t* to console, comfort. **– 2** *p* to take comfort *(con,* from).

consolidación *f* consolidation.

consolidar(se) *t-p* to consolidate.

consomé *m* clear soup, consommé.

consonancia *f* fig harmony.

consonante *adj-f* consonant.

consorcio *m* consortium, partnership.

consorte *mf (cónyuge)* spouse. **2** *pl* JUR accomplices.

conspicuo,-a *adj (destacable)* conspicuous. **2** *(ilustre)* outstanding.

conspiración *f* conspiracy, plot.

conspirador,-ra *m,f* conspirator.

conspirar *i* to conspire.

constancia *f (perseverancia)* constancy, perseverance. **2** *(evidencia)* evidence.

constante *adj (invariable)* constant, steady. **2** *(persona)* steadfast. ■ *constantes vitales,* vital signs.

constar *i (consistir en)* to consist *(de,* of). **2** *(ser cierto)* to be a fact; *(figurar)* to be, figure: *me consta que ha llegado,* I am absolutely certain that he/she has arrived.

constatación *f* verification.

constatar *t* to verify, confirm.

constelación *f* constellation.

consternación *f* consternation.

consternar(se) *t* to consternate, dismay. **– 2** *p* to be dismayed/aghast.

constipado,-a *adj* suffering from a cold. **– 2** *m* MED cold, chill.

constiparse *p* to catch a cold.

constitución *f* constitution.

constitucional *adj* constitutional.

constituir(se) [62] *t* to constitute. **2** *(ser)* to be. **– 3** *p* to set o.s. up.

constitutivo,-a *adj* constitutive; *(esencial)* essential. **– 2** *m* constituent.

constituyente *adj* constituent, component.

constreñimiento *m* constraint.

constreñir [36] *t* to constrain. **2** MED to constipate.

constricción *f* constriction.

construcción *f* construction. **2** *(edificio)* building.

constructor,-ra *adj* construction, building. **– 2** *m,f* constructor, builder.

construir [62] *t* to construct, build.

consuegro,-a *m,f m* son-daughter-in-law's father, *f* son-daughter-in-law's mother.

consuelo *m* consolation, comfort.

consuetudinario,-a *adj* habitual, customary.

cónsul *mf* consul.

consulado *m (oficina)* consulate. **2** *(cargo)* consulship.

consular *adj* consular.

consulta *f* consultation. **2** MED surgery; *(despacho)* consulting room: *horas de ~,* surgery hours.

consultar *t* to consult (with); *(un libro)* to look it up in.

consultorio *m* doctor's office. **2** *(en periódicos)* problem page, advice column.

consumación *f* consummation; *(de un crimen)* perpetration.

consumado,-a *adj* consummate(d).

consumar *t (matrimonio)* to consummate.

consumición *f* consumption. **2** *(bebida)* drink.

consumido,-a *adj* thin, emaciated.

consumidor,-ra *adj* consuming. — **2** *m,f* consumer.

consumir(se) *t (gastar, afligir)* to consume. **2** *(destruir)* to destroy. — **3** *p (gastarse, afligirse)* to be consumed. **4** *(destruirse)* to be destroyed.

consumismo *m* consumerism.

consumo *m* consumption. ■ *artículos de ~,* staple commodities.

consunción *f* consumption.

consuno *de ~, adv* together, with one accord.

contabilidad *f (profesión)* accounting. **2** *(en empresa etc.)* book-keeping. ●*llevar la ~,* to keep the books.

contabilizar [4] *t* to enter in the books.

contable *adj* countable. — **2** *mf* book-keeper, accountant.

contactar *t* to contact, get in touch (*con,* with).

contacto *m* contact. **2** AUTO ignition. ●*mantenerse en ~ con,* to keep in touch with.

contado,-a *adj (raro)* scarce. ●*al ~,* with cash, cash down.

contador,-ra *adj* counting. — **2** *m,f (contable)* accountant, book-keeper. — **3** *m* meter.

contagiar(se) [17] *t (enfermedad)* to transmit, pass on. — **2** *p* to get infected, catch.

contagio *m* contagion, infection.

contagioso,-a *adj* contagious, infectious.

contaminación *f* contamination; *(atmosférica)* pollution.

contaminar(se) *t* to contaminate; *(agua, aire)* to pollute. — **2** *p* to become contaminated/polluted.

contante *adj dinero ~,* (ready) cash.

contar [31] *t (calcular)* to count. **2** *(explicar)* to tell. — **3** *i* to count. ●*a ~ desde,* starting from; *~ con algn.,* to rely on sb.; *(incluirlo)* to count sb. in.

contemplación *f* contemplation. ●*no andarse con contemplaciones,* to make no bones about it.

contemplar *t-i* to contemplate.

contemplativo,-a *adj* contemplative.

contemporáneo,-a *adj-m* contemporary.

contemporizar [4] *i* to compromise.

contención *f* containment. ■ *muro de ~,* retaining wall.

contencioso,-a *adj* contentious. — **2** *m* legal action, case.

contender [28] *i* to contend.

contener [87] *t* to contain, hold. **2** *(reprimir)* to restrain, hold back.

contenido,-a *m* content, contents *pl.* — **2** *adj fig* moderate, temperate.

contentar(se) *t (satisfacer)* to please. — **2** *p* to be pleased.

contento,-a *adj* happy (*con,* with). — **2** *m* happiness.

contestación *f (respuesta)* answer, reply.

contestador *m ~ (automático),* answering machine.

contestar *t* to answer. — **2** *i (replicar)* to answer back.

contexto *m* context. **2** *fig* environment.

contienda *f* contest, dispute.

contigo *pron* with you.

contiguo,-a *adj* contiguous, adjoining.

continencia *f* continence.

continental *adj* continental.

continente *m* continent. **2** *(recipiente)* container.

contingencia *f* contingency. **2** *(riesgo)* risk, hazard.

contingente *adj* contingent. — **2** *m (parte proporcional)* contingent. **3** *(cuota)* quota, share.

continuación *f* continuation. ●*a ~,* next.

continuar [11] *t-i* to continue, carry on: *Pablo continúa en Francia,* Pablo is still in France.

continuidad *f* continuity.

continuo,-a *adj* continuous. – **2** *m* continuum. – **3** *continuamente adv* continuously. ■ AUTO *(línea) continua,* solid white line.

contonearse *p* to strut, swagger.

contoneo *m* strut(ting), swagger(ing).

contorno *m* outline; *(perímetro)* perimeter. **2** *(afueras)* surroundings *pl.* ▲ **2** *usually pl.*

contorsión *f* contortion.

contra *prep* against. – **2** *m* con. – **3** *f fam* drawback. ●*los pros y los contras,* the pros and cons; *llevar la* ~, to contradict *(a, -).*

contraalmirante *m* rear admiral.

contraatacar [1] *t* to counterattack.

contraataque *m* counterattack.

contrabajo *m* *(instrumento)* double bass. **2** *(voz)* low bass.

contrabandista *mf* smuggler.

contrabando *m* smuggling, contraband.

contracción *f* contraction.

contracepción *f* contraception.

contracorriente *f* crosscurrent. ●*ir a* ~, to go against the tide.

contracultura *f* counterculture.

contradecir(se) [69] *t* to contradict. – **2** *p* to contradict o.s. ▲ *pp contradicho,-a.*

contradicción *f* contradiction.

contradicho,-a *pp* → **contradecir.**

contradictorio,-a *adj* contradictory.

contraer [88] *t (encoger)* to contract. **2** *(enfermedad)* to catch. ●~ *matrimonio,* to get married.

contrafuerte *m (de zapato)* stiffener. **2** *(de montaña)* spur. **3** ARQ buttress.

contrahecho,-a *adj* deformed, hunchbacked.

contraindicación *f* contraindication. ●*(en medicamentos) "contraindicaciones, ninguna",* "may be used safely by anyone".

contralto *mf* contralto.

contraluz *m & f* view against the light.

contramaestre *m (capataz)* foreman. **2** MAR boatswain.

contraorden *f* countermand.

contrapartida *f* COM balancing entry. **2** *fig* compensation.

contrapelo *a* ~, *adv* against the grain, the wrong way.

contrapesar *t* to counterbalance, counterpoise. **2** *fig* to balance.

contrapeso *m* counterweight. **2** *fig* counterbalance.

contraponer [78] *(oponer)* to set in opposition *(a,* to). **2** *fig (contrastar)* to contrast. ▲ *pp contrapuesto,-a.*

contraportada *f* back page.

contraposición *f (contraste)* contrast. **2** *(oposición)* opposition.

contraproducente *adj* counterproductive.

contrapuesto,-a *pp* → **contraponer.**

contrapunto *m* counterpoint.

contrariar [13] *t* to oppose. **2** *(disgustar)* to annoy. **3** *(dificultar)* to obstruct.

contrariedad *f (oposición)* opposition. **2** *(disgusto)* annoyance. **3** *(dificultad)* setback.

contrario,-a *adj (opuesto)* contrary, opposite. **2** *(perjudicial)* harmful. – **3** *m,f* opponent, adversary. ●*al* ~, on the contrary; *llevar la contraria,* to oppose.

contrarreloj *adj-f* against the clock. ■ *(etapa)* ~, time trial.

contrarrestar *t (hacer frente)* to resist, oppose. **2** *(neutralizar)* counteract, neutralize.

contrarrevolución *f* counter-revolution.

contrasentido *m* contradiction.

contraseña *f* password.

contrastar *t* to contrast. **2** *(pesos y medidas)* to check. **3** *(oro y plata)* to hallmark. – **4** *i* to contrast *(con,* with).

contraste *m (oposición)* contrast. **2** *(pesos y medidas)* verification. **3** *(oro y plata)* hallmark.

contrata *f* contract.

contratación *f (contrato)* hiring. **2** *(pedido)* total orders *pl.*

contratar *t (servicio etc.)* to sign a contract for. **2** *(empleado)* to hire.

contratiempo *m* setback; *(accidente)* mishap.

contratista *mf* contractor.

contrato *m* contract. ■ ~ *de alquiler,* lease, leasing agreement.

contravención *f* contravention, infringement.

contravenir [90] *t* to contravene, infringe.

contraventana *f* (window) shutter.

contrayente *adj-mf* contracting (party).

contribución *f* contribution. **2** *(impuesto)* tax. ■ ~ *urbana,* community charge.

contribuir [62] *t-i* to contribute.

contribuyente *adj* taxpaying. – **2** *mf* taxpayer.

contrincante *m* competitor, rival.

contrito,-a *adj* contrite, repentant.

control *m* control. **2** *(sitio)* checkpoint. ■ ~ *a distancia,* remote control; ~ *de natalidad,* birth control; ~ *de pasaportes,* passport control.

controlador,-ra *m,f* air traffic controller.

controlar(se) *t-p* to control (o.s.).

controversia *f* controversy.

controvertido,-a *adj* controversial.

contumaz *adj* obstinate, stubborn.

contundencia *f (fuerza)* force. **2** *fig (convicción)* conviction.

contundente *adj fig (convincente)* forceful, decisive.

contusión *f* contusion, bruise.

contusionar *t* to contuse, bruise.

convalecencia *f* convalescence.

convalecer [43] *i* to convalesce, recover *(de,* from).

convaleciente *adj-mf* convalescent.

convalidación *f* EDUC validation. **2** *(documentos)* ratification.

convalidar *t* EDUC to validate. **2** *(documentos)* to ratify.

convecino,-a *adj* neighbouring. — **2** *m,f* neighbour.

convector *m* convector.

convencer(se) [2] *t* to convince. — **2** *p* to become convinced.

convencimiento *m* conviction.

convención *f* convention.

convencional *adj* conventional.

convencionalismo *m* conventionalism, conventionality.

convenido,-a *adj* agreed, set.

conveniencia *f (comodidad)* convenience. **2** *(ventaja)* advantage. **3** *pl* proprieties.

conveniente *adj (cómodo)* convenient. **2** *(ventajoso)* advantageous. **3** *(aconsejable)* advisable.

convenio *m* agreement.

convenir [90] *i (ser oportuno)* to suit. **2** *(ser aconsejable)* to be advisable: *conviene que te presentes,* you'd better be there. **3** *(opinar igual)* to agree. **4** *(venir juntos)* to come together. ●*a ~,* negotiable.

convento *m (de monjas)* convent; *(de monjes)* monastery.

convergencia *f* convergence.

convergente *adj* convergent, converging.

converger [5], **convergir** [6] *i* to converge, come together.

conversación *f* conversation, talk. ●*dar ~,* to keep sb. chatting.

conversador,-ra *adj* talkative. — **2** *m,f* AM gabber.

conversar *i* to converse, talk.

conversión *f* conversion.

convertir(se) [29] *t* to convert. — **2** *p ~se en,* to become.

convexidad *f* convexity.

convexo,-a *adj* convex.

convicción *f* conviction: *tengo la ~ de que ...,* I firmly believe that ... .

convicto,-a *adj* convicted.

convidado,-a *m,f* guest.

convidar *t* to invite. **2** *(incitar)* to prompt.

convincente *adj* convincing.

convite *m (invitación)* invitation. **2** *(comida)* banquet.

convivencia *f* living together. **2** *fig* coexistence.

convivir *i* to live together. **2** *fig* to coexist.

convocar [1] *t* to convoke, summon, call together. ■ ~ *oposiciones,* to hold competitive examinations.

convocatoria *f* convocation, summons. **2** EDUC examination, sitting.

convoy *m (escolta)* convoy. **2** *(tren)* train. ▲ *pl* **convoyes.**

convoyar *t* to convoy.

convulsión *f* convulsion. **2** *fig* upheaval.

conyugal *adj* conjugal. ■ *vida ~,* married life.

cónyuge *mf* spouse, consort. **2** *pl* husband and wife.

coñac *m* cognac, brandy. ▲ *pl* **coñacs.**

coño* *m* cunt*. — **2** *interj (sorpresa)* fuck me!*; *(disgusto)* for fuck's sake!*

cooperación *f* cooperation.

cooperar *i* to cooperate *(a/en,* in; *con,* with).

cooperativa *f* cooperative (society).

coordenado,-a *adj* coordinated. — **2** *f* coordinate.

coordinación *f* coordination.

coordinado,-a *adj* coordinated.

coordinador,-ra *adj* coordinating. — **2** *m,f* coordinator. — **3** *f (comité)* coordinating committee.

coordinar *t* to coordinate.

copa *f* glass. **2** *(de árbol)* top. **3** *(trofeo)* cup. ●*ir(se) de copas,* to go (out) drinking; *tomar una ~,* to have a drink.

copar *t* POL to take.

copartícipe *mf* joint partner, collaborator.

copete *m (cabello)* tuft. **2** *(de caballo)* forelock. **3** *(de mueble, montaña)* top. **4** *fig* arrogance. ●*de alto ~,* of high rank.

copia *f* copy. **2** *(abundancia)* abundance.

copiar [12] *t* to copy. **2** EDUC to cheat. **3** *(dictado etc.)* to take down.

copiloto *m* AV copilot; AUTO co-driver.

copión,-ona *fam m,f* cheat. **2** *(imitador)* copycat.

copioso,-a *adj fml* plentiful, abundant.

copista *mf* copyist.

copla *f (verso)* verse. **2** *pl* folk songs.

copo *m* flake; *(de nieve)* snowflake; *(de algodón)* ball (of cotton).

coproductor,-ra *m,f* co-producer.

copropietario,-a *m,f* joint owner, co-owner.

cópula *f (nexo)* link. **2** *(coito)* copulation.

copular *i* to copulate (*con,* with).

copulativo,-a *adj* copulative.

coque *m* coke.

coquetear *i* to flirt.

coquetería *f* coquetry, flirting.

coqueto,-a *adj* flirtatious. **– 2** *f* coquette, flirt.

coraje *m (valor)* courage. **2** *(ira)* anger.

coral *adj* choral. **– 2** *m* ZOOL coral. **3** MÚS choral(e).

coraza f *(armadura)* armour. **2** *(caparazón)* shell.

corazón *m* ANAT heart. **2** *(de fruta)* core. ●*de (todo)* ~, sincerely; *llevar el ~ en la mano,* to wear one's heart on one's sleeve; *me dice el ~ que ... ,* I have a feeling that ... .

corazonada *f* hunch, feeling. **2** *(impulso)* impulse.

corbata *f* tie.

corbatín *m* bow tie.

corbeta *f* corvette.

corcel *m* steed, charger.

corchea *f* quaver.

corchete *m* COST hook and eye. **2** *(signo impreso)* square bracket.

corcho *m* cork. **2** *(tabla)* cork mat.

¡córcholis! *interj* goodness me!

cordel *m* rope, cord.

cordero,-a *m,f* lamb. **– 2** *m* lambskin.

cordial *adj* cordial, friendly. **– 2** *m (bebida)* cordial. **– 3 cordialmente** *adv* heartily, cordially.

cordialidad *f* cordiality, friendliness.

cordillera *f* mountain range.

cordón *m* rope, string; *(de zapatos)* (shoe)lace. **2** *(cadena humana)* cordon. ■ ~ *umbilical,* umbilical cord.

cordoncillo *m (en tela)* rib(bing). **2** *(de moneda)* milling.

cordura *f* good sense.

corear *t* to say in chorus.

coreografía *f* choreography.

corista *f* chorus girl.

cornada *f* thrust with a horn. ●*sufrir una* ~, to be gored.

cornamenta *f* horns *pl*; *(del ciervo)* antlers *pl*. **2** *fam (de marido)* cuckold's horns *pl*.

córnea *f* cornea.

corneja *f* crow.

córner *m* DEP corner.

corneta *f* cornet; MIL bugle. **– 2** *mf* cornet player; MIL bugler.

cornisa *f* cornice.

cornucopia *f* cornucopia.

cornudo,-a *adj (animal)* horned, antlered. **2*** *(marido)* cuckolded. **– 3*** *m* cuckold.

coro *m* MÚS choir. **2** TEAT chorus. ●*a* ~, all together.

corola *f* corolla.

corolario *m* corollary.

corona *f* crown. **2** *(de flores etc.)* wreath.

coronación *f* coronation.

coronar *t* to crown.

coronel *m* colonel.

coronilla *f* crown (of the head). ●*fam estar hasta la* ~, to be fed up (*de,* with).

corpiño *m* bodice.

corporación *f* corporation.

corporal *adj* corporal, body.

corpóreo,-a *adj* corporeal, bodily.

corpulencia *f* corpulence.

corpulento,-a *adj* corpulent, stocky.

corpúsculo *m* corpuscle.

corral *m* yard; *(de granja)* farmyard, US corral.

correa *f (de piel)* strap. **2** *(de perro)* lead. **3** TÉC belt.

correaje *m* straps *pl*, belts *pl*.

corrección *f* correction. **2** *(educación)* courtesy. **3** *(represión)* rebuke.

correccional *m* reformatory.

correctivo,-a *adj-m* corrective.

correcto,-a *adj* correct. **2** *(educado)* polite, courteous.

corrector,-ra *adj* corrective. **– 2** *m,f (de pruebas impresas)* proofreader.

corredera *f* TÉC track. ■ *puerta/ventana* ~, sliding door/window.

corredizo,-a *adj* sliding. ■ *nudo* ~, slip knot.

corredor,-ra *adj* running. **– 2** *m,f* DEP runner. **– 3** *m* broker. ■ ~ *de bolsa,* stockbroker; ~ *de fincas,* estate agent.

corregible *adj* correctable, rectifiable.

corregir(se) [55] *t (amendar)* to correct. **2** *(reprender)* to reprimand. **– 3** *p* to mend one's ways.

correlación *f* correlation.

correo *m (servicio, correspondencia)* post, US mail. **2** *(persona)* courier. **3** *pl (oficina)* post office *sing.* •*a vuelta de* ~, by return (of post); *echar al* ~, to post, US mail. ■ *apartado de correos,* (post office) box; ~ *aéreo,* airmail; ~ *certificado,* registered post; *(tren)* ~, mail train.

correoso,-a *adj (flexible)* flexible, pliant. **2** *(comida)* tough, chewy.

correr(se) *i* to run. **2** *(viento)* to blow. **3** *(agua)* to flow. **4** *(tiempo)* to pass. **5** *(noticias)* to spread. **6** *(darse prisa)* to hurry. **7** *(estar en uso)* to be valid. **– 8** *t (recorrer)* to travel through. **9** *(carrera)* to run. **10** *(deslizar)* to close; *(cortina)* to draw. **11** *(estar expuesto)* to run. **12** *(avergonzar)* to ashame. **13** AM *(expulsar)* to let off, fire. **– 14** *p* to move over; *(objeto)* to shift. **15*** *(tener orgasmo)* to come. •~ *con los gastos,* to foot the bill; ~ *la voz,* to pass it on; ~ *prisa,* to be urgent; *dejar* ~ *algo,* to let sth. pass.

correría *f* raid, foray.

correspondencia *f* correspondence. **2** *(cartas)* post, US mail. **3** *(de trenes etc.)* connection.

corresponder(se) *i (equivaler)* to correspond *(a/con,* to/with). **2** *(pertenecer)* to belong, pertain. **3** *(devolver)* to return. **– 4** *p (ajustarse)* to correspond. **5** *(cartearse)* to correspond. **6** *(amarse)* to love each other.

correspondiente *adj* corresponding *(a,* to). **2** *(apropiado)* suitable, appropriate. **3** *(respectivo)* own.

corresponsal *mf* correspondent.

corretaje *m* brokerage.

corretear *i* to run about.

correve(i)dile *mf inv* tell-tale.

corrida *f (carrera)* race. ■ ~ *de toros,* bullfight.

corrido,-a *adj (peso)* heavy. **2** *(continuo)* full: *balcón* ~, full balcony. **3** *fig (avergonzado)* abashed. •*de* ~, without stopping.

corriente *adj (común)* ordinary. **2** *(agua)* running. **3** *(fecha)* current, present: *el cinco del* ~, the tenth of the present month. **– 4** *f (masa de agua)* current, stream. **5** *(de aire)* draught, US draft. **6** ELEC current. **7** *(de arte etc.)* current, trend. •*al* ~, up to date; *estar al* ~, to be in the know; *llevar/seguir la* ~ *a algn.,* to humour sb.; *salirse de lo* ~, to

be out of the ordinary. ■ *Corriente del Golfo,* Gulf Stream.

corrimiento *m* slipping. ■ ~ *de tierras,* landslide.

corro *m* circle, ring. **2** *(juego)* ring-a-ring-a-roses.

corroboración *f* corroboration.

corroborar *t* to corroborate.

corroer(se) [82] *t* to corrode. **2** *fig* to eat away/up. **– 3** *p* to become corroded. **4** *fig* to be eaten up *(de,* with).

corromper(se) *t (estropear)* to spoil; *(pudrir)* to turn bad. **2** *(pervertir)* to corrupt. **3** *(sobornar)* to bribe. **– 4** *p (pudrirse)* to go bad. **5** *(pervertirse)* to become corrupted.

corrosivo,-a *adj-m* corrosive. **2** *fig* caustic.

corrupción *f* corruption. **2** *(putefracción)* rot, decay. ■ ~ *de menores,* corruption of minors.

corruptor,-ra *adj* corrupting. **– 2** *m,f* corrupter.

corsario *m* corsair, pirate.

corsé *m* corset.

corsetería *f* ladies' underwear shop.

corta *f* felling (of trees).

cortacésped *m & f* lawnmower.

cortacircuito *m* circuit breaker.

cortado,-a *adj* cut; *(en lonchas)* sliced. **2** *(estilo)* concise, clipped. **3** *fam (aturdido)* dumbfounded. **– 4** *m* coffee with a dash of milk.

cortadura *f* cut.

cortafuego *m* firebreak.

cortante *adj* cutting, sharp. **2** *(aire)* biting.

cortapisa *f* condition, restriction.

cortaplumas *m inv* penknife.

cortar(se) *t* to cut; *(carne)* to carve; *(árbol)* to cut down. **2** *(dividir)* to divide. **3** COST to cut out. **4** *(interrumpir)* to cut off, interrupt: *nos han cortado el teléfono,* our telephone has been disconnected. **– 5** *p (herirse)* to cut. **6** *(el pelo) (por otro)* to have one's hair cut; *(uno mismo)* to cut one's hair. **7** *(leche)* to sour, curdle. **8** *(aturdirse)* to be dumbfounded. •*fam* ~ *por lo sano,* to take drastic measures.

cortaúñas *m inv* nail clipper.

corte *f (del rey etc.)* court. **2** *(séquito)* retenue. **3** AM JUR court. **– 4** *m* cut. **5** *(filo)* edge. **6** COST cross section. **7** *fam (respuesta brusca)* rebuff. •*hacer la* ~ *a,* to court, pay court to. ■ ~ *y confección,* dressmaking; *las Cortes,* (Spanish) Parliament *sing.*

cortedad *f* shortness.

cortejar *t* to court.

cortejo *m (acompañantes)* entourage. 2 *(galanteo)* courting.

cortés *adj* courteous, polite.

cortesía *f* courtesy, politeness.

corteza *f (de árbol)* bark. 2 *(de pan)* crust. 3 *(de fruta)* peel, skin. 4 *(de queso)* rind. ■ ~ *terrestre,* the earth's crust.

cortijo *m* farm(house).

cortina *f* curtain. ●*fig* ~ *de humo,* smoke screen.

cortinaje *m* drapery.

cortisona *f* cortisone.

corto,-a *adj* short. 2 *fig (tonto)* thick. ●*fam quedarse* ~, to underestimate. ■ ~ *de vista,* short-sighted.

cortocircuito *m* short circuit.

cortometraje *m* short (film).

corvo,-a *adj* arched, curved.

corzo,-a *m,f m* roe buck, *f* roe deer.

cosa *f* thing. 2 *(asunto)* matter. 3 *pl fam (manías)* hang-ups. ●*como si tal* ~, as if nothing had happened; ~ *de,* about; *fam (persona) ser poquita* ~, to be a weedy person.

coscorrón *m* blow on the head.

cosecha *f* harvest, crop. 2 *(tiempo)* harvest time. 3 *(año del vino)* vintage. ●*de su propia* ~, of his own invention.

cosechadora *f* combine harvester.

cosechar *t-i* to harvest, gather. 2 *fig (éxitos etc.)* to reap.

coser *t* to sew. 2 MED to stitch up. 3 *fig (atravesar)* to pierce: ~ *a balazos,* to riddle with bullets. ■ *máquina de* ~, sewing machine.

cosmético,-a *adj-m* cosmetic.

cosmonauta *mf* cosmonaut.

cosmopolita *adj-mf* cosmopolitan.

cosmos *m inv* cosmos.

cosquillas *fpl* tickles, tickling *sing.* ●*hacer* ~ *a,* to tickle.

cosquillear *t* to tickle.

cosquilleo *m* tickling.

costa *f* coast; *(playa)* seaside. 2 FIN cost, price. 3 *pl* JUR costs. ●*a* ~ *de,* at the expense of; *a toda* ~, at all costs.

costado *m* side. 2 MIL flank.

costal *m* sack. ●*ser harina de otro* ~, to be another kettle of fish.

costar [31] *i* to cost. 2 *(ser difícil)* to be difficult: *me cuesta el italiano,* I find Italian difficult. ●*cueste lo que cueste,* at any cost; *fam* ~ *un ojo de la cara,* to cost an arm and a leg.

coste *m* cost, price. ■ ~ *de (la) vida,* cost of living.

costear(se) *t* MAR to coast. 2 COM to pay for. – 3 *p* to pay one's way.

costero,-a *adj* coastal.

costilla *f* rib. 2 CULIN cutlet.

costo *m* cost, price. 2 *arg (hachís)* dope.

costoso,-a *adj* costly, expensive. 2 *(difícil)* hard.

costra *f* crust. 2 MED scab.

costumbre *f (hábito)* habit: *tengo la* ~ *de comer temprano,* it is my habit to have lunch early. 2 *(tradición)* custom: *es una* ~ *rusa,* it's a Russian custom. 3 *pl* ways.

costura *f (cosido)* sewing. 2 *(línea de puntadas)* seam. ■ *alta* ~, haute couture.

costurera *f* seamstress.

costurero *m* sewing basket.

cotejar *t* to collate, compare.

cotejo *m* collation, comparison.

cotidiano,-a *adj* daily, everyday.

cotilla *f (faja)* corset. – 2 *mf* busybody.

cotillear *i fam* to gossip.

cotilleo *m fam* gossip(ing).

cotización *f* COM quotation.

cotizar(se) [4] *t* COM to quote. – 2 *p* to sell at.

coto *m* reserve. 2 *(poste)* boundary mark. 3 *(límite)* restriction. ■ ~ *de caza,* game preserve.

cotorra *f* (small) parrot. 2 *fam fig* chatterbox.

cotorrear *i* to chatter, gossip.

covacha *f* small cave. 2 AM hovel.

coyote *m* coyote.

coyuntura *f* ANAT joint, articulation. 2 *(circunstancia)* juncture. ■ ~ *económica/ política/social,* economic/political/social situation.

coz *f* kick. ●*dar coces/una* ~, to kick.

crac *m (quiebra)* crash.

cráneo *m* cranium, skull.

crápula *f (borrachera)* drunkenness. 2 *(disipación)* dissipation.

cráter *m* crater.

creación *f* creation.

creador,-ra *adj* creative. – 2 *m,f* creator, maker.

crear *t* to create. 2 *(fundar)* to found, establish. 3 *(inventar)* to invent.

creatividad *f* creativity.

crecer(se) [43] *i (persona, planta)* to grow. 2 *(incrementar)* to increase. 3 *(corriente, marea)* to rise. – 4 *p* to become conceited.

creces *fpl* increase *sing.* ●*con* ~, fully, in full.

crecido,-a *adj* large; *(persona)* grown. **2** *(marea)* swollen. − **3** *f* spate.

crecimiento *m* growth, increase.

credencial *adj* credential. − **2** *fpl* credentials.

crédito *m* COM credit. **2** *(asenso)* credence. **3** *(fama)* reputation. ●*dar* ~ *a*, to believe.

credo *m* REL creed. **2** *(creencias)* credo.

credulidad *f* credulity.

crédulo,-a *adj* credulous, gullible.

creencia *f* belief.

creer [61] *t* to believe *(en,* in). **2** *(suponer, opinar)* to think, suppose.

creíble *adj* credible, believable.

creído,-a *adj* arrogant. ●*ser un* ~, to be full of o.s.

crema *f* cream. **2** *(natillas)* custard. − **3** *adj* cream, cream-coloured.

cremación *f* cremation.

cremallera *f (de vestido)* zipper, zip (fastener). **2** TÉC rack.

crematorio *m* crematorium.

cremoso,-a *adj* creamy.

crepitar *i* to crackle.

crepuscular *adj* twilight.

crepúsculo *m* twilight.

crespo,-a *adj (pelo)* frizzy. **2** *(estilo)* obscure.

crespón *m* crepe.

cresta *f* crest. **2** *(de gallo)* comb.

creta *f* chalk.

cretino,-a *m,f* cretin.

cretona *f* cretonne.

creyente *adj* believing. − **2** *mf* believer.

cría *f (acto de criar)* nursing; *(de animal)* breeding. **2** *(cachorro)* young. **3** *(camada)* brood.

criadero *m (de plantas)* nursery; *(de animales)* breeding ground/farm; *(minero)* seam.

criado,-a *adj (animal)* reared; *(persona)* bred. − **2** *m,f* servant. ●*bien* ~, well-bred; *mal* ~, ill-bred.

crianza *f (de animales)* breeding. **2** *(lactancia)* nursing.

criar [13] *t (educar niños)* to bring up. **2** *(nutrir)* to nurse. **3** *(animales)* to breed. **4** *(producir)* to have, grow; *(vinos)* to make.

criatura *f* creature. **2** *(niño)* baby, child.

criba *f* sieve. ●*fig pasar por la* ~, to screen.

cribar *t (colar)* to sift. **2** *fig* to screen.

cric *m* jack.

cricquet *m* cricket.

crimen *m (delito)* crime. **2** *(asesinato)* murder. ▲ *pl* **crímenes**.

criminal *adj-mf* criminal.

criminalista *mf (abogado)* criminal lawyer. **2** *(estudioso)* criminologist.

crin *f* mane.

crío,-a *m,f fam* kid.

cripta *f* crypt.

crisálida *f* chrysalis.

crisantemo *m* chrysanthemum.

crisis *f inv* crisis. **2** *(ataque)* fit, attack: ~ *de asma,* asthma attack.

crisma *m & f* chrism. **2** *fam* head.

crisol *m* crucible. **2** *fig* melting pot.

crispar(se) *t* ANAT to contract. **2** *(irritar)* to annoy. − **3** *p* to get annoyed.

cristal *m* crystal. **2** *(vidrio)* glass. **3** *(de ventana)* (window) pane. ■ ~ *de aumento,* magnifying glass.

cristalería *f (fábrica)* glassworks. **2** *(tienda)* glassware shop. **3** *(conjunto)* glassware.

cristalino,-a *adj* transparent, clear. − **2** *m* crystalline lens.

cristalizar(se) [4] *t-i-p* to crystallize.

cristiandad *f* Christendom.

cristianismo *m* Christianity.

cristianizar [4] *t* to convert to Christianity.

cristiano,-a *adj-m,f* Christian.

Cristo *m npr* Christ.

criterio *m* criterion. **2** *(juicio)* judgement. **3** *(opinión)* opinion.

crítica *f (juicio, censura)* criticism. **2** *(prensa)* review: *escribir una* ~, to write a review. **3** *(conjunto de críticos)* critics *pl*.

criticar [1] *t* to criticize. − **2** *i (murmurar)* to gossip.

crítico,-a *adj* critical. − **2** *m,f* critic.

criticón,-ona *fam adj* fault-finding. − **2** *m,f* fault-finder.

croar *i* to croak.

croissant *m* croissant. ▲ *pl* **croissants**.

crol *m* crawl.

cromar *t* to chrome.

cromático,-a *adj* chromatic.

cromo *m (metal)* chromium. **2** *(estampa)* picture card, transfer. ●*fam ir hecho,-a un* ~, to look a real sight.

cromosoma *m* chromosome.

crónica *f* chronicle. **2** *(en periódico)* article.

crónico,-a *adj* chronic.

cronista *mf* chronicler. **2** *(periodista)* reporter.

cronología *f* chronology.

cronológico,-a *adj* chronological.

cronometrar *t* to time.

cronómetro *m* chronometer.

croqueta *f* croquette.

croquis *m inv* sketch, outline.

cruce *m* cross(ing). **2** AUTO crossroads. **3** *(de razas)* crossbreeding. **4** *(interferencia telefónica etc.)* crossed line.

crucero *m (buque)* cruiser. **2** *(viaje)* cruise. **3** ARQ transept.

crucial *adj* crucial.

crucificar [1] *t* to crucify. **2** *fig* to torture.

crucifijo *m* crucifix.

crucigrama *m* crossword (puzzle).

crudeza *f (sin cocer)* rawness. **2** *(crueldad)* crudeness.

crudo,-a *adj (sin cocer)* raw; *(poco hecho)* underdone. **2** *(cruel)* crude. **3** *(color)* off-white. **4** *(clima)* harsh. − **5** *m (petróleo)* crude (oil).

cruel *adj* cruel. **2** *(duro)* harsh.

crueldad *f* cruelty. **2** *(dureza)* harshness.

cruento,-a *adj* bloody.

crujido *m (de puerta)* creak. **2** *(seda, papel)* rustle. **3** *(de dientes)* grinding.

crujiente *adj (alimentos)* crunchy. **2** *(seda)* rustling.

crujir *i (puerta)* to creak. **2** *(seda, hojas)* to rustle. **3** *(dientes)* to grind.

crustáceo *m* crustacean.

cruz *f* cross. **2** *(de moneda)* tails *pl*. ●*hacerse cruces de,* to be astonished at. ■ *Cruz Roja,* Red Cross.

cruzado,-a *adj* crossed. **2** *(animal)* crossbred. **3** *(prenda)* double-breasted. − **4** *f* HIST Crusade. − **5** *m* HIST crusader.

cruzamiento *m* crossing. **2** *(de animales)* cross-breeding.

cruzar(se) [4] *t* to cross. **2** GEOM to intersect. **3** *(animales)* to cross. **4** *(miradas, palabras)* to exchange. − **5** *p* to cross, pass each other. ●*~ los brazos/~se de brazos,* to fold one's arms.

cuadernillo *m* booklet.

cuaderno *m* notebook, exercise book.

cuadra *f (establo)* stable. **2** AM *(manzana)* block.

cuadrado,-a *adj-m* square. ●*elevar (un número) al ~,* to square (a number).

cuadragésimo,-a *adj-m,f* fortieth.

cuadrangular *adj* quadrangular.

cuadrante *m (reloj)* sundial. **2** *(instrumento)* quadrant.

cuadrar(se) *t* to square. − **2** *i (ajustarse)* to suit *(con, -).* **3** COM to balance. − **4** *p* MIL to stand at attention. **5** *fig* to stand fast.

cuadriculado,-a *adj* squared.

cuadricular *t* to divide into squares.

cuadrilla *f* party. **2** *(de bandidos etc.)* gang.

cuadro *m (cuadrado)* square. **2** *(pintura)* painting. **3** *(descripción)* description. **4** *(escena, paisaje)* sketch. **5** *(personal)* staff. **6** *(gráfico)* chart. **7** *(bancal)* bed, patch. ●*a cuadros,* checkered. ■ *~ de mandos,* control panel; *~ facultativo,* medical staff; *~ sinóptico,* diagram.

cuadrúpedo,-a *adj-m* quadruped.

cuádruple *adj* quadruple, fourfold.

cuajar(se) *t* to coagulate; *(leche)* to curdle; *(sangre)* to clot. **2** *(adornar)* to fill with. − **3** *i (lograrse)* to be a success: *la cosa no cuajó,* it didn't come off. − **4** *p* to coagulate; *(leche)* to curdle.

cuajo *m* rennet. ●*de ~,* by the roots.

cual *pron rel (persona)* who; *(cosa)* which. − **2** *adv fml* as, like. ▲ *pl* **cuales.**

cuál *pron-adj interrog* which (one). **2** *(valor distributivo)* some. ▲ *pl* **cuáles.**

cualidad *f* quality.

cualificar [1] *t* to qualify.

cualquier *adj indef* → **cualquiera.** ▲ *Used in front of a noun (but an adjective may be used between it and the noun).* ▲ *pl* **cualesquier.**

cualquiera *adj indef* any: *una dificultad ~,* any difficulty. − **2** *pron indef* anybody: *~ te lo puede decir,* anybody can tell you. − **3** *pron rel (persona)* whoever; *(cosa)* whatever; *(negativo)* nobody. − **4** *mf pey* nobody: *ser un ~,* to be a nobody. ●*~ que,* whatever, whichever. ▲ *pl* **cualesquiera.**

cuan *adv* as.

cúan *adv* how.

cuando *adv* when. − **2** *conj* when. **3** *(condicional)* provided if. ●*aun ~,* even though; *de (vez en) ~,* now and then.

cuándo *adv interrog* when.

cuantía *f* amount.

cuantioso,-a *adj* large.

cuanto *m* quantum.

cuanto,-a *adj-pron* as much as: *gasta ~ gana,* he/she spends every penny he earns. − **2** *adv ~ antes,* as soon as possible; *~ más,* the more; *en ~,* as soon as; *en ~ a,* as far as; *por ~,* insofar as. ●*unos,-as cuantos,-as,* some, a few. ▲ *pl* **cuantos,-as.**

cuánto,-a *adj-pron interrog* how much; *(para plural)* how many: *¿~ cuesta?,* how much does it cost?; *¿cuántos hay?,* how many are there? − **2** *adv* how: *¡~ me alegro!,* I'm so glad! ▲ *pl* **cuántos,-as.**

cuáquero,-ra *adj-m,f* Quaker.

cuarenta *adj* forty; *(cuadragésimo)* fortieth. — **2** *m* forty. •*cantarle las* ~ *a*
algn., to give sb. a piece of one's mind.

cuarentena *f (cuarenta)* forty. **2** MED
quarantine.

cuarentón,-ona *adj-m,f* forty-year-old
(person).

cuaresma *f* Lent.

cuartear *t (dividir en cuatro)* to quarter. **2**
(rajar) to crack.

cuartel *m* MIL barracks. •*no dar* ~, to
show no mercy. ■ ~ *general,* headquarters *inv.*

cuartelillo *m* post, station.

cuarteto *m* quartet.

cuartilla *f* sheet of paper.

cuarto,-a *adj-m,f* fourth. — **2** *m (parte)*
quarter: *un* ~ *de hora,* a quarter of an
hour. **3** *(habitación)* room. **4** *pl fam (di-*
nero) money. ■ *(de luna)* ~ *creciente/*
menguante, first/last quarter; ~ *de*
baño, bathroom; ~ *de estar,* living
room.

cuarzo *m* quartz.

cuatrero *m* cattle thief, rustler.

cuatro *adj inv* four; *(cuarto)* fourth. — **2** *m*
four. •*decir* ~ *cosas a algn.,* to say a
few things to sb.

cuatrocientos,-as *adj-m* four hundred.

cuba *f* cask, barrel. •*estar como una* ~,
to be (as) drunk as a lord.

cubalibre *m* rum/gin and coke.

cubata *m fam* → **cubalibre**.

cubertería *f* cutlery.

cubeta *f (recipiente)* tray. **2** *(cubo)* bucket.

cúbico,-a *adj* cubic.

cubierta *f* cover(ing). **2** *(de libro)* jacket.
3 ARQ roof. **4** *(de neumático)* outer tyre.
5 AV MAR deck.

cubierto,-a *pp* → **cubrir**. — **2** *m (techum-*
bre) cover. **3** *(en la mesa)* place setting.
4 *(menú)* meal at a fixed price. •*estar a*
~, to be under cover; *ponerse a* ~, to
take cover.

cubilete *m (molde)* mould. **2** *(de dados)*
dice cup.

cubismo *m* cubism.

cubito *m* ~ *(de hielo),* ice cube.

cubo *m* bucket. **2** *(figura)* cube. **3** *(de rue-*
da) hub. ■ ~ *de la basura,* rubbish bin,
US garbage can.

cubrecama *m* bedspread.

cubrir(se) *t* to cover. **2** *(esconder)* to hide.
3 ARQ to put a roof on. **4** *(llenar)* to fill.
5 *(montar)* to mount. — **6** *p (abrigarse)* to
cover o.s. **7** *(protegerse)* to protect o.s. **8**

(cielo) to become overcast. ▲ *pp* **cubier-**
to,-a.

cucaña *f* greasy pole. **2** *fam* easy-pick-
ings *pl.*

cucaracha *f* cockroach.

cuchara *f* spoon.

cucharada *f* spoonful. ■ ~ *(sopera),* ta-
blespoonful.

cucharilla *f* teaspoon. ■ ~ *de café,* coffee spoon.

cucharón *m* ladle.

cuchichear *i* to whisper.

cuchicheo *m* whispering.

cuchilla *f (hoja)* blade. ■ ~ *de afeitar,* razor blade.

cuchillada *f* stab, slash.

cuchillo *m* knife. ■ ~ *de pan,* breadknife.

cuchitril *m (establo)* pigsty. **2** *fam* hovel.

cuclillas *en* ~, *adv* crouching.

cuclillo *m* cuckoo.

cuco,-a *adj fam* cute. **2** *(taimado)* shrewd.

cucurucho *m* paper cone. **2** *(helado)* cornet, cone.

cuello *m* neck. **2** *(de prenda)* collar. **3** *(de*
botella) bottleneck. •*fam fig estar meti-*
do,-a hasta el ~, to be up to one's neck
in it.

cuenca *f (escudilla)* wooden bowl. **2** ANAT
(eye) socket. **3** GEOG basin.

cuenco *m* earthenware bowl.

cuenta *f (bancaria)* account. **2** *(factura)*
bill. **3** *(cálculo)* count(ing). **4** *(de collar*
etc.) bead. •*en resumidas cuentas,* in
short; *por* ~ *de,* for account of; *tener en*
~, to take into account. ■ ~ *atrás,*
countdown; ~ *corriente,* current account.

cuentagotas *m inv* dropper.

cuentakilómetros *m inv* speedometer.

cuentista *adj-mf fam* over-dramatic (person).

cuento *m* story, tale. •*el* ~ *de la lechera,*
counting one's chickens before they are
hatched; *venir a* ~, to be pertinent; *fam*
vivir del ~, to live by one's wits. ■ ~
chino, tall story; ~ *de hadas,* fairy tale.

cuerda *f* rope, string. **2** MÚS string. **3** *(de*
reloj) spring: *dar* ~ *a un reloj,* to wind
up a watch. ■ ~ *floja,* tightrope; *cuer-*
das vocales, vocal chords.

cuerdo,-a *adj-m,f* sane (person).

cuerno *m* horn; *(de antena)* antlers *pl.* **2**
MIL wing. •*fam poner cuernos a algn.,*
to be unfaithful to sb.; *fam romperse los*
cuernos, to break one's back.

cuero *m (de animal)* skin, hide. **2** *(curtido)*
leather. •*fam en cueros,* starkers. ■ ~
cabelludo, scalp.

cuerpo *m* body. 2 *(constitución)* build. 3 *(figura)* figure. 4 *(tronco)* trunk. 5 *(grupo)* body; MIL corps: *el ~ de bomberos,* the fire brigade. 6 *(cadáver)* corpse. 7 *(parte principal)* main part: *el ~ del libro,* the main body of the book. •*de ~ entero,* full-length; *estar de ~ presente,* to lie in state.

cuervo *m* raven. ■ *~ marino,* cormorant.

cuesta *f* slope. •*a cuestas,* on one's back/shoulders; *fig la ~ de enero,* the January squeeze. ■ *~ abajo/arriba,* downhill/uphill.

cuestación *f* charity collection.

cuestión *f (pregunta)* question. 2 *(asunto)* business. 3 *(discusión)* dispute, quarrel. •*fig ser ~ de vida o muerte,* to be a matter of life or death.

cuestionar *t* to question.

cuestionario *m* questionnaire.

cueva *f* cave.

cuévano *m* hamper.

cuidado *m (atención)* care, carefulness. 2 *(recelo)* worry. — 3 *interj* look out! •*al ~ de,* in care of; *tener ~,* to be careful. ■ *cuidados intensivos,* intensive care *sing.*

cuidadoso,-a *adj (atento)* careful. 2 *(celoso)* cautious.

cuidar(se) *t-i* to look after, care for, mind. — 2 *p* to take care of o.s.

cuita *f* trouble, sorrow.

culata *f (de arma)* butt. 2 AUTO head. 3 *(carne)* haunch, hindquarters *pl.*

culatazo *m* kick, recoil.

culebra *f* snake.

culebrear *i* to twist, wriggle.

culebrón *m* television serial, soap opera.

culinario,-a *adj* culinary, cooking.

culminación *f* culmination, climax.

culminante *adj* culminating, climatic; *(punto)* highest.

culminar *i* to climax. — 2 *t* to finish.

culo *m* bottom, arse*. 2 *(ano)* anus. 3 *(de recipiente)* bottom. •*fam caer de ~,* to fall flat on one's bottom; *fam fig ir de ~,* to be rushed off one's feet; *¡vete a tomar por el ~!*,* fuck off!*

culpa *f (culpabilidad)* guilt, blame. 2 *(falta)* fault: *esto es ~ mía,* it's my fault. •*echar la ~ a,* to blame; *tener la ~,* to be to blame for.

culpabilidad *f* guilt, culpabilility.

culpable *adj* guilty. — 2 *mf* offender, culprit.

culpar(se) *t-p* to blame (o.s.).

cultismo *m* cultism.

cultivado,-a *adj* cultivated. 2 *fig (con cultura)* cultured, refined.

cultivar *t* to cultivate, farm. 2 *(ejercitar facultades)* to work at: *~ la memoria,* to improve one's memory. •*fig ~ las amistades,* to cultivate friendships.

cultivo *m* cultivation, farming. 2 BIOL culture.

culto,-a *adj* cultured, learned. 2 *(estilo)* refined. — 3 *m* worship. •*rendir ~ a,* to pay homage to, worship.

cultura *f* culture.

cultural *adj* cultural.

cumbre *f (de montaña)* summit, top. 2 *(culminación)* pinnacle. 3 *(reunión)* summit.

cumpleaños *m inv* birthday.

cumplido,-a *adj* completed. 2 *(abundante)* large, ample. 3 *(educado)* polite. — 4 *m* compliment.

cumplidor,-ra *adj* dependable.

cumplimentar *t (felicitar)* to congratulate. 2 *(ejecutar)* to carry out.

cumplimiento *m* fulfilment. 2 *(cumplido)* compliment. ■*~ de la ley,* observance of the law.

cumplir(se) *t (llevar a cabo)* to carry out. 2 *(promesa)* to keep. 3 *(años)* to be: *mañana cumplo veinte años,* I'll be twenty tomorrow. — 4 *i* to do one's duty. — 5 *p (realizarse)* to be fulfilled.

cúmulo *m* heap, pile. 2 METEOR cumulus.

cuna *f* cradle. 2 *(linaje)* birth, lineage. 3 *fig (origen)* cradle, beginning.

cundir *i (extenderse)* to spread: *cundió el pánico,* panic spread. 2 *(dar de sí)* to increase in volume.

cuneta *f (de carretera)* verge. 2 *(zanja)* ditch.

cuña *f* wedge. •*hacer ~,* to be wedged in.

cuñado,-a *m,f m* brother-in-law, *f* sister-in-law.

cuño *m (troquel)* die. 2 *(sello)* stamp.

cuota *f (pago)* membership fee, dues *pl.* 2 *(porción)* quota, share.

cupe *pret indic →* **caber.**

cupé *m* coupé.

cuplé *m* popular lyric song.

cupo *m* quota.

cupón *m* coupon.

cúpula *f* cupola, dome.

cura *m* priest. — 2 *f* cure, healing. ■ *primeras curas,* first aid *sing.*

curación *f* cure, healing.

curado,-a *adj* cured. 2 *(curtido)* cured, salted; *(piel)* tanned.

curandero,-a *m,f* quack.
curar(se) *t (sanar)* to cure. **2** *(herida)* to dress; *(enfermedad)* to treat. **3** *(carne, pescado)* to cure; *(piel)* to tan; *(madera)* to season. — **4** *i (cuidar)* to take care (*de,* of). — **5** *p (recuperarse)* to recover (*de,* from), get well. **6** *(herida)* to heal up.
curativo,-a *adj* curative.
curia *f* curia.
curiosear *i-t* to pry (into).
curiosidad *f* curiosity. **2** *(aseo)* cleanliness.
curioso,-a *adj (indiscreto)* curious, inquisitive. **2** *(aseado)* clean, tidy. **3** *(extraño)* strange. — **4** *m,f* busybody.
currante *mf arg* worker.
currar *i arg* to grind, slave.
curre *m arg* job.
currículo, currículum *m* curriculum (vitae). ▲ *pl* **currículos** or **currícula**.
curry *m* curry.
cursar *t (estudiar)* to study. **2** *(enviar)* to send, dispatch. **3** *(tramitar)* to make an application.
cursi *adj-mf* affected (person).
cursilería *f* bad taste.
cursillo *m* short course.
curso *m (dirección)* course, direction. **2** EDUC course: ~ **académico,** academic/school year. **3** *(río)* flow, current. ●*estar en* ~, to be under way; *fig dejar que las cosas sigan su* ~, to let things take their course. ■*año/mes en* ~, current year/month.
cursor *m* INFORM cursor. **2** TÉC slide.
curtido,-a *adj* tanned. — **2** *m (operación)* tanning. **4** *mpl* tanned leather.
curtidor,-ra *m,f* tanner.
curtir(se) *t (piel)* to tan. **2** *(acostumbrar)* to harden. — **3** *p (por el sol)* to get tanned. **4** *(acostumbrarse)* to become hardened.
curva *f* curve. **2** *(de carretera)* bend. ■ ~ *cerrada,* sharp bend.
curvatura *f* curvature.
curvo,-a *adj* curved, bent.
cuscurro *m* crust of bread.
cúspide *f* summit. **2** *fig* peak.
custodia *f* custody, care. **2** REL monstrance.
custodiar [12] *t* to keep, take care of.
custodio *m* custodian, guard.
cutáneo,-a *adj* cutaneous, skin.
cutícula *f* cuticle.
cutis *m inv* skin, complexion.
cuyo,-a *pron* whose, of which. ●*en* ~ *caso,* in which case. ▲ *pl* **cuyos,-as.**

D

dabute(n) *adj arg* great, terrific.
dactilografía *f* typing, typewriting.
dádiva *f* gift, present.
dadivoso,-a *adj* generous, open-handed.
dado,-a *adj* given: *en un momento* ~, at a given moment, at a certain point. – **2** *m* die. ●~ *que*, given that; *ser* ~ *a*, to be keen on, be fond of.
daga *f* dagger.
dalia *f* dahlia.
daltonismo *m* colour blindness.
dama *f* lady. **2** *(en damas)* king; *(en ajedrez)* queen. **3** *pl* draughts, *us* checkers. ■ ~ *de honor*, bridesmaid; *primera* ~, first lady.
damasco *m* damask.
damisela *f* young lady, damsel.
damnificado,-a *adj* injured. – **2** *m,f* victim.
damnificar [1] *t* to injure, harm.
danza *f* dance.
danzar [4] *t-i* to dance *(con,* with).
danzarín,-ina *m,f* dancer.
dañado,-a *adj* damaged, spoiled.
dañar(se) *t (cosa)* to damage; *(persona)* to hurt, harm. – **2** *p (cosa)* to become damaged; *(persona)* to get hurt. **3** *(estropearse)* to spoil, go bad.
dañino,-a *adj* harmful, damaging.
daño *m* damage, harm, injury. ●*hacer* ~, *(doler)* to hurt; *(lastimar)* to hurt, injure: *hacerse* ~, to hurt o.s. ■ *daños y perjuicios,* damages.
dar(se) [68] *t* to give; *(entregar)* to deliver, hand over. **2** *(luz, gas)* to turn on. **3** *(producir)* to produce, bear. **4** *(reloj)* to strike. **5** *(película)* to show; *(teatro)* to perform. **6** *(pegar)* to hit. **7** *(considerar)* to assume *(por,* -), consider *(por,* -). **8** *(pintura, barniz)* to apply, put on. – **9** *i (caer)* to fall *(de,* on, *en,* -). **10** *(mirar a)* to overlook *(a,* -). – **11** *p (entregarse)* to

give in, surrender. **12** *(chocar)* to crash *(contra/con,* into). ●*da lo mismo,* it's all the same; ~ *a luz,* to give birth; ~ *algo por bueno,* to consider sth. valid; ~ *con algn./algo,* to find sb./sth.; ~ *de comer,* to feed; ~ *de sí,* to give, stretch; ~ *que hacer,* to give trouble; ~ *un paseo,* to take a walk; ~*se por vencido,-a,* to give in.
dardo *m* dart.
dársena *f* inner harbour, dock.
datar *t* to date, put a date on. – **2** *i* to date back *(de,* to/from).
dátil *m* date.
dato *m* fact, piece of information. **2** *pl* data; *(información)* information *sing.* ■ *datos personales,* personal details.
de *prep (posesión)* of, 's, s': *el libro de Juan,* Juan's book. **2** *(tema)* of, on, about. **3** *(materia)* of, out of. **4** *(origen, procedencia)* from. **5** *(modo)* on, in, as: ~ *pie,* standing up. **6** *(tiempo)* at, by: ~ *día,* by day: ~ *noche,* at night. **7** ~ + *inf.* if. ▲ → **del.**
deambular *i* to wander, stroll.
debacle *f* disaster.
debajo *adv* underneath, below. ●~ *de,* under, beneath.
debate *m* debate, discussion.
debatir(se) *t* to debate, discuss. – **2** *p* to struggle.
debe *m* debit.
deber(se) *m* duty, obligation. **2** *pl* homework *sing.* – **3** *t (dinero)* to owe. **4** *(obligación)* must, to have to; *(recomendación)* should: *deberías ir al médico,* you should see the doctor. – **5** *aux (conjetura)* ~ *de,* must: *deben de ser las seis,* it must be six o'clock; *no deben de haber llegado,* they can't have arrived. – **6** *p* to be due.
debido,-a *adj* owed. **2** *(apropiado)* due, just, proper. – **3** *debidamente adv* duly,

properly. •*como es* ~, right, properly;
~ *a*, due/owing to.
débil *adj* weak, feeble. **2** *(ruido)* faint. **3**
(luz) dim.
debilidad *f* weakness. •*tener* ~ *por*, to
have a weakness for.
debilitación *f*, **debilitamiento** *m* weakening.
debilitar(se) *t-p* to weaken.
débito *m* debt.
debut *m* debut.
debutar *i* to make one's debut.
década *f* decade.
decadencia *f* decadence, decline.
decadente *adj* decadent.
decaer [67] *i* to decline, decay, fall.
decaído,-a *adj* *(débil)* weak. **2** *(triste)* sad,
depressed.
decaimiento *m* *(debilidad)* weakness. **2**
(tristeza) sadness.
decálogo *m* decalogue.
decano,-a *m,f* dean.
decantar(se) *t* *(vasija)* to decant. — **2** *p*
(preferir) to prefer *(hacia/por,* -).
decapitar *t* to behead, decapitate.
decena *f* (group of) ten.
decencia *f* *(decoro)* decency, propriety. **2**
(honestidad) honesty.
decente *adj* *(decoroso)* decent, proper. **2**
(honesto) honest. **3** *(limpio)* tidy, proper.
decepción *f* disappointment.
decepcionante *adj* disappointing.
decepcionar *t* to disappoint, let down.
decidir(se) *t* *(asunto)* to decide, settle. **2**
(convencer) to persuade. — **3** *p* to make
up one's mind.
decimal *adj-m* decimal.
décimo,-a *adj-m,f* tenth. — **2** *m* (tenth
part of a) lottery ticket.
decimoctavo,-a *adj-m,f* eighteenth.
décimocuarto,-a *adj-m,f* fourteenth.
decimonono,-a *adj-m,f* nineteenth.
decimoquinto,-a *adj-m,f* fifteenth.
decimoséptimo,-a *adj-m,f* seventeenth.
decimosexto,-a *adj-m,f* sixteenth.
decimotercero,-a *adj-m,f* thirteenth.
decir(se) [69] *t* to say; *(contar)* to tell. —
2 *p* to say to o.s. — **3** *m* saying. •*como
quien dice/si dijéramos*, so to speak; ~
para sí, to say to o.s.; *es* ~, that is to
say; *querer* ~, to mean; *se dice ...*, they
say ..., it is said ... . ▲ *pp* **dicho,-a.**
decisión *f* *(resolución)* decision. **2** *(firmeza)* determination, resolution.
decisivo,-a *adj* decisive, final.
declamar *i-t* to declaim, recite.

declaración *f* declaration, statement. **2**
JUR evidence.
declarar(se) *t* to declare, state. **2** JUR to
find. — **3** *i* to declare. **4** JUR to testify. —
5 *p* to declare o.s. **6** *(a una mujer)* to propose. **7** *(fuego, guerra)* to start, break
out.
declinación *adj* GRAM declension. **2** AS-
TRON declination.
declinar *i* to decline. **2** *(decaer)* to decay,
fall off. — **3** *t* to decline.
declive *m* slope. **2** *fig* decline. •*en* ~, on
the decline.
decolorar *t* to discolour, bleach.
decomisar *t* to confiscate.
decoración *f*, **decorado** *m* decoration.
2 TEAT scenery, set.
decorador,-ra *m,f* decorator.
decorar *t* to decorate, adorn, embellish.
decorativo,-a *adj* decorative, ornamental.
decoro *m* decorum, decency. **2** *(respeto)*
respect, honour.
decoroso,-a *adj* decorous, decent. **2** *(respetable)* respectable, honourable.
decrecer [43] *i* to decrease, diminish.
decreciente *adj* decreasing, diminishing.
decrépito,-a *adj* decrepit.
decretar *t* to decree, order.
decreto *m* decree.
dedal *m* thimble.
decidido,-a *adj* decided. **2** *(audaz)* determined. — **3** *decididamente adv* decidedly.
dedicación *f* dedication.
dedicar(se) [1] *t* to dedicate. — **2** *p* to devote o.s. *(a,* to).
dedicatoria *f* dedication.
dedo *m* *(de la mano)* finger; *(del pie)* toe.
■ ~ *anular*, ring finger; ~ *del corazón*,
middle finger; ~ *gordo*, thumb; ~ *índice*, forefinger, index finger; ~ *meñique*, little finger.
deducción *f* deduction.
deducir [46] *t* to deduce. **2** *(dinero)* to deduct.
deductivo,-a *adj* deductive.
defecar [1] *t-i* to defecate.
defectivo,-a *adj* defective.
defecto *m* defect, fault.
defectuoso,-a *adj* defective, faulty.
defender(se) [28] *t* to defend. **2** *(afirmar)*
to assert, maintain. — **3** *p* *(espabilarse)* to
manage.
defendido,-a *adj* defended. — **2** *m,f* JUR
defendant.

delirar

defensa *f* defence. − **2** *mf* DEP back. ●*en ~ propia,* in self-defence.
defensivo,-a *adj* defensive. ●*estar a la ~,* to be on the defensive.
defensor,-ra *adj* defending. − **2** *m,f* defender.
deferencia *f* deference.
deficiencia *f* deficiency.
deficiente *adj* deficient, faulty. − **2** *mf ~ (mental),* mentally retarded person.
déficit *m inv* deficit. **2** *fig* shortage.
definición *f* definition.
definido,-a *adj* defined, definite.
definir *t* to define.
definitivo,-a *adj* definitive, final.
deformación *f* deformation, distortion.
deformar(se) *t* to deform, distort. − **2** *p* to become deformed.
deforme *adj* deformed, misshapen.
deformidad *f* deformity.
defraudación *f (estafa)* fraud, cheating. **2** *(decepción)* disappointment.
defraudar *t (estafar)* to defraud, cheat. **2** *(decepcionar)* to disappoint, deceive.
defunción *f* death, decease.
degeneración *f* degeneration.
degenerado,-a *adj-m,f* degenerate.
degenerar *i* to degenerate.
deglutir *t-i* to swallow.
degollar [31] *t* to slit the throat of.
degradación *f* degradation, debasement. **2** MIL demotion.
degradar(se) *t* to degrade, debase. **2** MIL to demote. − **3** *p* to demean o.s.
degüello *m* throat cutting.
degustación *f* tasting.
degustar *t* to taste, sample.
dehesa *f* pasture.
deidad *f* deity, divinity.
deificar [1] *t* to deify. **2** *fig* glorify.
dejadez *f* neglect, slovenliness; *(negligencia)* negligence. **2** *(pereza)* laziness.
dejado,-a *adj* untidy, slovenly; *(negligente)* negligent. **2** *(perezoso)* lazy.
dejar(se) *t* to leave; *(persona)* to abandon; *(lugar, trabajo)* to quit; *(hábito)* to give up. **2** *(permitir)* to allow, let. **3** *(prestar)* to lend. **4** *(legar)* to bequeath. **5** *(~ de + inf),* to stop: *~ de llover,* to stop raining. − **6** *aux (no ~ de + inf),* not to fail to: *no dejes de hacerlo,* don't forget to do it. − **7** *p (abandonarse)* to neglect o.s. **8** *(olvidar)* to forget: *me he dejado las llaves en casa,* I left my keys at home. **9** *(cesar)* to stop *(de, -).* ●*~ caer,* to drop; *~ en paz,* to leave alone; *~ mal,* to let down; *~ plantado,*

-a, to stand up; *~se llevar (por algo),* to get carried away (with sth.).
deje *m* accent. **2** *fig* aftertaste.
del *contraction of de + el →* **de.**
delantal *m* apron.
delante *adv (enfrente)* in front of, before, facing, opposite: *la casa de ~,* the house across the street; *~ de mis ojos,* before my eyes. ●*~ de,* in front of; *por ~,* ahead.
delantero,-a *adj* front, fore. − **2** *m* DEP forward. − **3** *f (frente)* front. **4** DEP forward line. **5** *(ventaja)* lead, advantage. ●*coger/tomar la delantera,* to get ahead, overtake.
delatar *t* to denounce, inform on. **2** *(revelar)* to reveal.
delator,-ra *adj* accusing, denouncing. − **2** *m,f* accuser, denouncer.
delco *m* AUTO distributor.
delegación *f* delegation. **2** COM branch.
delegado,-a *adj* delegated. − **2** *m,f* delegate, deputy.
delegar [7] *t* to delegate.
deleitar(se) *t* to delight, please. − **2** *p* to take delight *(con,* in).
deleite *m* pleasure, delight.
deletrear *t* to spell (out).
deletreo *m* spelling (out).
delfín *m* HIST dauphin. **2** ZOOL dolphin.
delgadez *f* thinness, slenderness.
delgado,-a *adj* thin, slender.
deliberación *f* deliberation.
deliberado,-a *adj* deliberate, intentional.
deliberar *t* to decide. − **2** *i* to deliberate, consider.
delicadeza *f* delicacy. **2** *(tacto)* thoughtfulness. ●*tener la ~ de,* to be thoughtful enough to.
delicado,-a *adj* delicate. **2** *(con tacto)* considerate, toughtful. **3** *(difícil)* difficult. **4** *(frágil)* fragile. **5** *(enfermizo)* frail.
delicia *f* delight, pleasure.
delicioso,-a *adj* delicious, delightful.
delictivo,-a *adj* criminal. ■ *hecho ~,* crime.
delimitar *t* to delimit, mark off/out.
delincuencia *f* delinquency.
delincuente *adj-mf* delinquent.
delineante *mf m* draughtsman, *f* draughtswoman.
delinear *t* to delineate, outline.
delinquir [9] *i* to break the law.
delirante *adj* delirious, raving.
delirar *i* to rave, be delirious. **2** *fig* to talk nonsense.

delirio *m* delirium. 2 *fig* nonsense. ■ *delirios de grandeza,* delusions of grandeur.

delito *m* offence, crime.

delta *m* delta.

demacrado,-a *adj* emaciated, thin, scrawny.

demacrarse *p* to waste away, become emaciated.

demagogia *f* demagogy.

demagógico,-a *adj* demagogic(al).

demagogo,-a *m,f* demagogue.

demanda *f* petition, request. 2 COM demand. 3 JUR lawsuit. ●*presentar una ∼ contra algn.,* to take legal action against sb.

demandado,-a *m,f* defendant.

demandante *mf* claimant.

demandar *t* JUR to sue. 2 *(pedir)* to demand, ask for.

demarcación *f* demarcation, boundary line.

demás *adj-pron* other, rest (of the): *los ∼ libros,* the other books. – 2 *adv* besides. ●*lo ∼,* the rest; *los ∼,* the others, the other people; *por lo ∼,* for the rest; *y ∼,* and so on.

demasía *f* excess. ●*en ∼,* too much, excessively.

demasiado,-a *adj* too much; *(plural)* too many. – 2 *adv* too (much).

demencia *f* insanity, madness.

demente *adj* mad, insane. – 2 *mf* lunatic, maniac.

democracia *f* democracy.

demócrata *adj* democratic. – 2 *mf* democrat.

democrático,-a *adj* democratic.

democratización *f* democratization.

democratizar [4] *t* to democratize.

demografía *f* demography.

demoledor,-ra *adj* demolishing, devastating.

demoler [32] *t* to demolish, pull/tear down.

demolición *f* demolition.

demonio *m* demon, devil. ●*fam de mil demonios,* horrific; *fam ¡qué ∼!,* what the devil!; *fam ser un ∼,* to be a devil.

demora *f* delay.

demorar(se) *t (retardar)* to delay, hold up. – 2 *i (detenerse)* to stay, remain. – 3 *i-p* AM to delay.

demostración *f* demonstration. 2 *(ostentación)* show. 3 *(prueba)* proof.

demostrar [31] *t* to demonstrate. 2 *(ostentar)* to show. 3 *(probar)* to prove.

demostrativo,-a *adj-m* demonstrative.

demudar(se) *t* to change, alter. – 2 *p (palidecer)* to turn pale. 3 *(alterarse)* to look upset.

denegación *f* denial, refusal.

denegar [48] *t* to deny, refuse.

denigrante *adj* insulting.

denigrar *t* to denigrate, disparage. 2 *(insultar)* to insult, revile.

denodado,-a *adj* bold, brave.

denominación *f* denomination.

denominador *m* denominator.

denominar *t* to denominate, name.

denostar [31] *t* to insult, abuse.

denotar *t* to denote, mean.

densidad *f* density.

denso,-a *adj* dense, compact, thick.

dentado,-a *adj* toothed; *(cuchillo)* serrated. ■ *rueda dentada,* cog wheel.

dentadura *f* (set of) teeth *pl.* ■ *∼ postiza,* false teeth.

dental *adj* dental.

dentellada *f* bite. 2 *(señal)* toothmark.

dentera *f fig* envy. ●*dar ∼ a algn.,* to set sb.'s teeth on edge.

dentición *f* teething.

dentífrico,-a *adj* tooth. – 2 *m* toothpaste. ■ *pasta dentífrica,* toothpaste.

dentista *mf* dentist.

dentro *adv* inside, within, in; *(de edificio)* indoors. ●*∼ de lo posible,* as far as possible; *∼ de poco,* shortly; *por ∼,* (on the) inside.

denuesto *m* insult, affront.

denuncia *f* denunciation, accusation. ●*presentar una ∼,* to lodge a complaint.

denunciar [12] *t* to denounce, condemn; *(delito)* to report.

deparar *t* to provide, offer.

departamento *m (sección)* department, section. 2 *(provincia)* district, province. 3 *(de tren)* compartment. 4 AM *(piso)* apartment.

departir *i fml* to chat, talk.

depauperar(se) *t* to impoverish. 2 *(organismo)* to weaken. – 3 *p* to become impoverished.

dependencia *f* dependence, dependency. 2 *(de servicios)* outbuildings *pl.*

depender *i* to depend/rely *(de,* on): *depende de ti,* it's up to you.

dependiente,-a *adj* depending, dependent. – 2 *m,f* shop assistant.

depilación *f* depilation, hair removal.

depilar(se) *t-p* to depilate.

depilatorio,-a *adj-m* depilatory. ■ *crema depilatoria,* hair-removing cream.

deplorable *adj* deplorable.

deplorar *t* to deplore, lament, regret.

deponer [78] *t* to lay down, set aside. 2 *(destituir)* to depose, remove from office. 3 JUR to declare, testify. ●~ *las armas,* to lay down arms. ▲ *pp depuesto,-a.*

deportación *f* deportation.

deportar *t* to deport.

deporte *m* sport. 2 *(pasatiempo)* recreation. ●*por* ~, as a hobby.

deportista *mf m* sportsman, *f* sportswoman.

deportividad *f* sportsmanship.

deportivo,-a *adj* sports, sporting. 2 *(imparcial)* sportsmanlike.

deposición *f* deposition. 2 JUR testimony. 3 *(defecación)* defecation.

depositar(se) *t* to deposit. – 2 *p (poso)* to settle.

depositario,-a *m,f* depositary, trustee. 2 *(tesorero)* treasurer.

depósito *m* deposit, trust. 2 *(poso)* sediment, deposit. 3 *(almacén)* depot, store, warehouse. 4 *(tanque)* tank. ■ ~ *de cadáveres,* mortuary; ~ *de gasolina,* petrol tank.

depravación *f* depravity.

depravado,-a *adj-m,f* depraved (person).

depre *f fam* depression.

deprecar [1] *t* to beg.

depreciar [12] *t* to depreciate.

depredador,-ra *adj* pillaging. – 2 *m,f* pillager.

depresión *f* depression. ■ ~ *nerviosa,* nervous breakdown.

depresivo,-a *adj* depressive.

deprimente *adj* depressing.

deprimido,-a *adj* depressed.

deprimir(se) *t* to depress. – 2 *p* to become depressed.

deprisa *adv* quickly.

depuesto,-a *pp* → **deponer.**

depurador *m* purifier.

depurar *t* to purify. 2 POL to purge.

derecho,-a *adj* right(-hand): *a la derecha,* to the right. 2 *(recto)* straight. 3 *(de pie)* standing, upright. – 4 *f* right (side). 5 *(mano)* right hand. 6 POL right wing. – 7 *m (poder, oportunidad)* right. 8 *(ley)* law. 9 EDUC law. 10 *pl* fees, taxes, duties. ■ ~ *civil,* civil law; *derechos humanos,* human rights.

deriva *f* drift. ●*ir a la* ~, to drift.

derivación *f* derivation. 2 ELEC shunt.

derivado,-a *adj* derived. – 2 *m* derivative. – 3 *f* MAT derivative.

derivar(se) *t* to lead, direct. – 2 *i-p* to derive. 3 MAR to drift.

dermatología *f* dermatology.

derogación *f* abolition, repeal.

derogar [7] *t* to abolish, repeal.

derramamiento *m* spilling. ■ ~ *de sangre,* bloodshed.

derramar(se) *t* to pour out, spill. 2 *(sangre, lágrimas)* to shed – 3 *p* to spill.

derrame *m* pouring out, spilling. 2 *(de sangre, lágrimas)* shedding. ■ MED ~ *cerebral,* cerebral hemorrhage.

derretir(se) *t-p* to melt. – 2 *p fig (de amor)* to burn (*de,* with).

derribar *t (edificio)* to pull down, demolish. 2 *(persona)* to fell, knock down. 3 MIL to shoot down. 4 *fig (gobierno)* to overthrow.

derribo *m (acción)* demolition. 2 *(material)* debris.

derrocar [1] *t (derribar)* to pull down, demolish. 2 *(gobierno)* to overthrow.

derrochador,-ra *adj* wasteful. – 2 *m,f* squanderer.

derrochar *t* to waste, squander. 2 *fig* to be full of.

derroche *m* waste, squandering.

derrota *f* defeat, rout. 2 *(camino)* path, road. 3 MAR ship's route/course.

derrotado,-a *adj* defeated. 2 *fam (cansado)* tired.

derrotar *t* to defeat.

derrotero *m* MAR course. 2 *fig* path, course of action.

derrotista *adj-mf* defeatist.

derruir [62] *t* to pull down, demolish.

derrumbamiento *m* falling down, collapse. 2 *(techo)* caving in. 3 *(de tierras)* landslide.

derrumbar(se) *t* to pull down, demolish. – 2 *p* to collapse. 3 *(techo)* to cave in.

desaborido,-a *adj* tasteless, insipid. 2 *fig (persona)* dull. – 3 *m,f* dull person.

desabrido,-a *adj* tasteless, insipid. 2 *(persona)* gruff, surly, rude. 3 *(tiempo)* unpleasant.

desabrigado,-a *adj* unsheltered.

desabrochar(se) *t-p* to undo, unfasten.

desacatar *t* to show disrespect towards. 2 *(desobedecer)* to disobey.

desacato *m* disrespect. 2 *(desobediencia)* disobedience.

desacertado,-a *adj* wrong, mistaken.

desacierto *m* mistake, blunder.

desaconsejar *t* to advise against.

desacostumbrar(se) *t* to break of the habit of. – **2** *p* to lose a habit.

desacreditar *t* to discredit, bring discredit on.

desactivar *t* to defuse.

desacuerdo *m* disagreement.

desafiante *adj* challenging, defiant.

desafiar [13] *t* to challenge.

desafinado,-a *adj* out of tune.

desafinar(se) *i* to be out of tune. – **2** *p* to get out of tune.

desafío *m* challenge. **2** *(duelo)* duel.

desaforado,-a *adj* violent, lawless. **2** *fig* huge, enormous.

desafortunado,-a *adj* unlucky, unfortunate.

desagradable *adj* disagreeable, unpleasant.

desagradar *t* to displease.

desagradecido,-a *adj* ungrateful.

desagradecimiento *m* ingratitude.

desagrado *m* displeasure, discontent. ●*con ~,* reluctantly.

desagravio *m* ammends *pl,* compensation.

desagüe *m* drain.

desaguisado *m* offence. **2** *fig (destrozo)* damage.

desahogado,-a *adj (espacioso)* roomy, spacious. ■ *posición desahogada,* comfortable circumstances.

desahogar(se) [7] *t* to vent. – **2** *p* relieve one's feelings, pour one's heart out, let off steam: *¡desahógate!,* don't bottle it up!

desahogo *m* relief. **2** *(comodidad)* comfort, ease.

desahuciar [12] *t* to take away all hope from. **2** JUR *(inquilino)* to evict.

desahucio *m* eviction.

desairar *t (desatender)* to slight, snub. **2** *(desestimar)* to reject.

desaire *m* slight, snub.

desajustar *t* to disarrange.

desajuste *m* disarrangement. **2** *(desacuerdo)* disagreement.

desalentador,-ra *adj* discouraging.

desalentar [27] *t* to discourage. – **2** *p* to lose heart.

desaliento *m* discouragement.

desaliñado,-a *adj* untidy, unkempt.

desaliño *m* untidiness.

desalmado,-a *adj (malvado)* wicked. **2** *(cruel)* cruel, heartless.

desalojar *t (persona)* to eject, remove. **2** *(inquilino)* to evict. **3** *(ciudad)* to evacuate. **4** *(edificio)* to clear. – **5** *i* to move out.

desalojo *m (de persona)* ejection, removal. **2** *(de inquilino)* eviction. **3** *(de lugar)* evacuation, clearing.

desamparado,-a *adj (niño)* helpless, defenceless. **2** *(lugar)* exposed. **3** *(casa etc.)* abandoned.

desamparar *t* to abandon, desert, leave helpless.

desamparo *m* abandonment, desertion. **2** *(estado)* defencelessness, helplessness.

desamueblado,-a *adj* unfurnished.

desandar [64] *t* to go back over. ●*~ lo andado,* to retrace one's steps.

desangrarse(se) *t* to bleed. – **2** *p* to bleed heavily, lose blood.

desanimado,-a *adj* despondent, downhearted. **2** *(aburrido)* dull.

desanimar(se) *t* to discourage, dishearten. – **2** *p* to become discouraged, disheartened.

desánimo *m* despondency, downheartedness.

desapacible *adj* unpleasant, disagreeable.

desaparecer(se) [43] *t* to make disappear. – **2** *i-p* to disappear, vanish.

desaparición *f* disappearance.

desapego *m* aloofness, indifference, detachment.

desapercibido,-a *adj* unprepared, unready. ●*pasar ~,* to go unnoticed.

desaplicado,-a *adj* lazy. – **2** *m,f* lazybones *inv.*

desaprensivo,-a *adj* unscrupulous.

desaprobación *f* disapproval.

desaprobar [31] *t* to disapprove of.

desaprovechar *t* to waste, not take advantage of. – **2** *i* to lose ground, fall back. ●*~ una ocasión,* to miss an opportunity.

desarmado,-a *adj* unarmed. **2** *(desmontado)* dismantled, taken to pieces.

desarmar *t* to disarm. **2** *(desmontar)* to dismantle, take apart.

desarme *m* disarmament. ■ *~ nuclear,* nuclear disarmament.

desarraigado,-a *adj* uprooted.

desarraigar(se) [7] *t* to uproot. **2** *(hábito)* to eradicate. – **3** *p* to become uprooted.

desarraigo *m* uprooting. **2** *(de hábito etc.)* eradication.

desarrapado,-a *adj-m,f* → **desharrapado,-a.**

desarreglar t make untidy, mess up, upset.

desarreglo m mess, untidiness, disorder.

desarrollado,-a adj developed.

desarrollar(se) t (gen) to develop. 2 (rollo) to unroll, unwind. 3 (realizar) to carry out. — 4 p (crecer) to develop, grow. 5 (ocurrir) to take place.

desarrollo m development.

desarticular t MED to disarticulate, put out of joint. 2 fig (organización) to break up.

desaseado,-a adj (desordenado) untidy. 2 (sucio) dirty. 3 (dejado) slovenly, unkempt.

desasir(se) [65] t to release, let go. — 2 p to rid o.s. (de, of).

desasnar t fam to teach good manners to.

desasosiego m disquiet, uneasiness, anxiety.

desastrado,-a adj (desordenado) untidy. 2 (sucio) dirty. 3 (dejado) slovenly, unkempt.

desastre m disaster.

desastroso,-a adj disastrous.

desatado,-a adj loose, untied. 2 fig wild, violent.

desatar(se) t to untie, undo. — 2 p to come untied/undone. 3 fig (desmadrarse) to lose all restraint. 4 (tormenta) to break.

desatascar t to unblock.

desatender [28] t to pay no attention to. 2 (no hacer caso) to neglect, disregard.

desatento,-a adj inattentive. 2 (descortés) discourteous, impolite.

desatinado,-a adj rash, reckless. 2 (tonto) foolish.

desatino m (error) mistake, blunder. 2 (locura) folly. 3 (tontería) nonsense.

desatornillar t to unscrew.

desatrancar t to unbar.

desautorización f withdrawal of authority, disavowal.

desautorizado,-a adj unauthorized, discredited.

desautorizar [4] t to deprive of authority.

desavenencia f disagreement, quarrel.

desavenirse p to disagree, quarrel.

desayunar(se) t-i-p to (have) breakfast.

desayuno m breakfast.

desazón f fig anxiety, uneasiness.

desazonado,-a adj fig anxious, uneasy.

desbancar [1] t to break, bust. 2 fig to supplant, replace.

desbandada f scattering. ●a la ~, helter-skelter, in disorder.

desbandarse p to scatter, disband.

desbarajuste m disorder, confusion.

desbaratar t to destroy, ruin. 2 (malgastar) to waste, squander.

desbarrar i fig (hablar) to talk nonsense. 2 (actuar) act foolishly.

desbloquear t to unblock. 2 FIN to unfreeze.

desbocado,-a adj (arma) widemouthed. 2 (jarra) with a chipped mouth. 3 (caballo) runaway.

desbocar(se) [1] t (jarra) to break the mouth of. — 2 p (caballo) to run away. 3 (persona) to let out a stream of abuse.

desbordamiento m overflow, flooding.

desbordante adj overflowing.

desbordar(se) t fig to surpass, go beyond. — 2 i-p to overflow. — 3 p to lose one's self-control.

desbravar t (caballo) to tame, break in. — 2 i-p to become less wild/fierce. 3 (licor) to go flat.

desbrozar [4] t to clear of rubbish/undergrowth.

descabalgar [7] i to dismount.

descabellado,-a adj wild, crazy.

descabezar [7] t to behead. 2 (planta) to top, cut the top off. ●~ un sueño, to take a nap.

descafeinado,-a adj decaffeinated. 2 fam watered-down. ■ café ~, decaffeinated coffee.

descalabrado,-a adj wounded/injured in the head.

descalabrar(se) t to wound in the head. 2 (herir) to hurt. — 3 p to hurt one's head.

descalabro m misfortune, damage, loss.

descalificar [1] t to disqualify.

descalzar(se) [4] t to take off sb.'s shoes. — 2 p to take off one's shoes.

descalzo,-a adj barefoot(ed).

descamisado,-a adj shirtless, ragged. — 2 m,f wretch.

descampado,-a adj open. — 2 m piece of open land.

descansado,-a adj rested, refreshed. 2 (tranquilo) easy.

descansar i to (have a) rest, take a break. 2 (dormir) to sleep. 3 (confiar) to rely (sobre, on), put trust (sobre, in). 4 (apoyarse) to rest (sobre, on), be supported (sobre, by). — 5 t to rest. ●~ en paz, to rest in peace; ¡descansen armas!, order arms!

descansillo *m* landing.

descanso *m* rest, break. **2** *(alivio)* relief. **3** TEAT interval.

descapotable *adj-m* convertible.

descarado,-a *adj-m,f* shameless (person), cheeky (person).

descarga *f* unloading. **2** ELEC discharge. **3** *(de fuego)* discharge, volley.

descargador *m* unloader. **2** *(estibador)* docker.

descargar(se) [7] *t* to unload. **2** *fig (conciencia)* to ease. **3** *(de obligaciones)* to free, discharge. **4** *(golpe)* to strike. **5** *(enfado)* to vent. **6** *(arma)* to fire, discharge. — **7** *p* to unburden o.s.

descargo *m* unloading. **2** COM acquittance. **3** JUR discharge. **4** *(excusa)* excuse. ●*en su* ~, in his defence.

descarnado,-a *adj* blunt.

descaro *m* impudence, effrontery, cheek.

descarriar(se) [13] *t* to send the wrong way. — **2** *p* to lose one's way. **3** *fig* to go astray.

descarrilamiento *m* derailment.

descarrilar *i* to be derailed, run off the rails.

descarrío *m fig* going astray.

descartar(se) *t* to discard, reject. — **2** *p* *(de cartas)* to discard.

descastado,-a *adj* unaffectionate. **2** *(desagradecido)* ungrateful.

descendencia *f* offspring.

descender [28] *i* to descend, go/come down. **2** *(temperatura)* to drop, fall. **3** *(derivar)* to derive. — **4** *t* to take down, bring down.

descendiente *adj* descendent. — **2** *mf (generación)* descendant; *(hijos)* offspring.

descenso *m* descent, coming down. **2** *(de temperatura)* drop, fall. **3** *(declive)* decline, fall.

descentrado,-a *adj* off-centre. **2** *fig* disoriented.

descentralizar [4] *t* to decentralize.

descentrar(se) *t* to put out of centre. **2** *fig* to disorientate. — **3** *p* to become uncentred. **4** *fig* to become disorientated.

descifrar *t* to decipher, decode.

desclavar *t* to remove the nails from.

descocado,-a *adj fam* bold, brazen.

descojonante* *adj* fucking hilarious*.

descojonarse* *p* to piss o.s. laughing*.

descolgar(se) [52] *t* to unhang, take down. **2** *(bajar)* to lower, let down. — **3** *p (aparecer)* to show up unexpectedly. **4** *(de una ventana)* to slip/let o.s. down.

descollar [31] *i* to stand out, excel.

descolonización *f* decolonization.

descolorido,-a *adj* discoloured, faded.

descomedido,-a *adj* excessive, immoderate. **2** *(descortés)* rude, impolite.

descomponer(se) [78] *t* to break down. **2** TÉC to break. **3** *(desordenar)* to mess up, upset. **4** FÍS *(fuerza)* to resolve. — **5** *p* to decompose, rot. **6** TÉC to break down, develop a fault. **7** *(enfermar)* to be indisposed. **8** *(enfadarse)* to lose one's temper. ▲ *pp* **descompuesto,-a.**

descomposición *f* decomposition, decay. **2** TÉC *(de fuerzas)* resolution. **3** MED looseness of bowels.

descompuesto,-a *pp* → **descomponer.** — **2** *adj* decomposed. **3** *(estropeado)* out of order. **4** *(alterado)* upset.

descomunal *adj* huge, enormous.

desconcertado,-a *adj* disconcerted, upset.

desconcertante *adj* disconcerting, upsetting.

desconcertar(se) [27] *t* to disconcert. — **2** *p* to be disconcerted/confused.

desconchado *m* chipping/peeling off.

desconchar(se) *t* to scrape off. — **2** *p* to peel/chip off.

desconchón *m* bare patch.

desconcierto *m* disorder, confusion.

desconectado,-a *adj* disconnected.

desconectar(se) *t* to disconnect. — **2** *p fam* to stop listening, turn off.

desconexión *f* disconnection.

desconfiado,-a *adj* distrustful, suspicious.

desconfianza *f* mistrust, suspicion.

desconfiar [13] *i* to distrust *(de, -)*.

descongelar *t* to thaw. **2** *(nevera)* to defrost.

descongestión *f* relief of congestion.

descongestionar *t* to relieve of congestion. **2** *fig* to clear.

desconocer [44] *t* not to know.

desconocido,-a *adj* unknown. **2** *(extraño)* strange, unfamiliar. — **3** *m,f* stranger. ●*estar* ~, to be unrecognizable; *lo* ~, the unknown.

desconocimiento *m* ignorance.

desconsideración *f* lack of consideration.

desconsiderado,-a *adj* inconsiderate, rude, discourteous.

desconsolado,-a *adj* disconsolate, grief-stricken, dejected.

desconsolar(se) [31] *t* to distress, grieve. − **2** *p* to become distressed.

desconsuelo *m* affliction, grief.

descontado,-a *adj* discounted. **2** *(excluido)* left out. ●*dar por* ~, to take for granted; *por* ~, needless to say, of course.

descontar [31] *t* to discount, deduct. **2** *(excluir)* to leave out.

descontento,-a *adj* displeased, unhappy. − **2** *m* discontent, displeasure.

descontrol *m fam* lack of control.

descontrolado,-a *adj* out of control.

descontrolarse *p* to lose control.

desconvocar [1] *t* to cancel, call off.

descorazonador,-ra *adj* disheartening.

descorazonar(se) *t* to dishearten, discourage. − **2** *p* to lose heart, become discouraged.

descorchar *t* to uncork.

descorrer *t* to draw back.

descortés *adj* impolite, rude.

descortesía *f* discourtesy, rudeness.

descoser(se) *t* to unstitch, rip. − **2** *p* to become unstitched, rip.

descosido,-a *adj* ripped, unstitched. − **2** *m* open seam. ●*fam como un* ~, like mad.

descoyuntar(se) *t* to dislocate, disjoint. − **2** *p* to get out of joint.

descrédito *m* discredit.

descreído,-a *adj* unbelieving, incredulous. − **2** *m,f* unbeliever.

descremado,-a *adj* skimmed. ■ *leche descremada,* skim(med) milk.

describir *t* to describe. ▲ *pp descrito,-a.*

descripción *f* description.

descrito,-a *pp* → **describir**.

descuartizar [4] *t* to quarter, cut into pieces.

descubierto,-a *pp* → **descubrir**. − **2** *adj* uncovered; *(sin sombrero)* bareheaded. − **3** *m* COM overdraft. ●*al* ~, in the open; COM *en* ~, overdrawn.

descubridor,-ra *m,f* discoverer.

descubrimiento *m* discovery.

descubrir(se) *t* to discover. **2** *(revelar)* to make known. **3** *(averiguar)* to find out. − **4** *p* to take off one's hat. ▲ *pp descubierto,-a.*

descuento *m* discount.

descuidado,-a *adj* careless, negligent. **2** *(desaseado)* slovenly.

descuidar(se) *t* to relieve. **2** *(distraer)* to distract. − **3** *i-p* to be careless.

descuido *m* neglect. **2** *(negligencia)* negligence, carelessness. **3** *(desaliño)* slovenliness. **4** *(despiste)* oversight. **5** *(desliz)* slip, error.

desde *prep* from, since. ●~ ... *hasta,* from ... to; ~ *ahora,* from now on; ~ *entonces,* since then, ever since; ~ *luego,* of course, certainly; ~ *que,* since.

desdecir(se) [79] *i* not to live up *(de,* to). − **2** *p* to go back on one's word. ▲ *pp desdicho,-a.*

desdén *m* disdain, scorn.

desdentado,-a *adj* toothless.

desdeñar *t* to disdain, scorn.

desdeñoso,-a *adj* disdainful, contemptuous, scornful.

desdicha *f* misfortune.

desdichado,-a *adj* unfortunate, wretched.

desdicho,-a *pp* → **desdecir(se)**.

desdoblar *t* to unfold, spread open.

deseable *adj* desirable.

desear *t* to desire, wish (for), want.

desecar [1] *t* to desiccate, dry (up).

desechable *adj* disposable.

desechar *t* to cast aside. **2** *(rechazar)* to refuse, decline.

desecho *m* refuse, reject, scrap. ●*de* ~, cast-off.

desembalar *t* to unpack.

desembarazar(se) [4] *t* to free. **2** *(habitación)* to evacuate. − **3** *p* to rid o.s. *(de,* of).

desembarcadero *m* landing-stage, wharf, pier.

desembarcar [1] *i* to disembark, land, go ashore.

desembarco *m* landing.

desembargar [7] *t* to raise an embargo from.

desembocadura *f (de río)* mouth. **2** *(salida)* outlet, exit.

desembocar [1] *i (río)* to flow *(en,* into). **2** *(calle)* to end *(en,* at), lead *(en,* into). **3** *fig* to lead *(en,* to).

desembolsar *t* to disburse, pay out.

desembolso *m* disbursement, payment. **2** *(gasto)* expenditure.

desembragar [7] *t* to disengage.

desembuchar *t fam* to let/blurt out.

desempaquetar *t* to unpack.

desempatar *t* to break a tie between; DEP to play off.

desempate *m* breaking the tie; DEP play-off.

desempeñar *t* to redeem, take out of pawn. **2** *(obligación)* to discharge, fulfil. **3** *(cargo)* to fill, hold. **4** *(papel)* to play.

desempleado,-a *adj-m,f* unemployed (person).

desempleo *m* unemployment. ●*cobrar el ~,* to be on the dole.

desempolvar *t* to dust. 2 *fig* to unearth.

desencadenar(se) *t* to unchain. 2 *(desatar)* to free, unleash. — 3 *p (desatarse)* to break loose. 4 *(tormenta, guerra)* to break out. 5 *(acontecimientos)* to start.

desencajar(se) *t* to take apart. — 2 *p (cara)* to become distorted/twisted.

desencaminar *t* to mislead.

desencantar *t* to disenchant. 2 *(desilusionar)* to disillusion.

desencanto *m* disenchantment. 2 *(desilusión)* disillusionment, disappointment.

desenchufar *t* to unplug, disconnect.

desenfadado,-a *adj* free and easy, carefree.

desenfado *m (soltura)* confidence. 2 *(facilidad)* ease.

desenfocado,-a *adj* out of focus.

desenfocar [1] *t* to take out of focus.

desenfrenado,-a *adj (caballo)* unbridled. 2 *(persona)* wild. 3 *(conducta)* licentious, wanton.

desenfreno *m* licentiousness.

desenfundar *t* to draw/pull out.

desenganchar *t* to unhook, unfasten. 2 *(caballerías)* to uncouple, unhitch.

desengañar(se) *t* to put wise. 2 *(desilusionar)* to disappoint. — 3 *p* to be disappointed. ●*¡desengáñate!,* (let's) face it!

desengaño *m* disillusion, disappointment.

desengrasar *t* to remove the grease from, clean.

desenlace *m* outcome, end. 2 *(de narración)* ending.

desenmascarar *t* to unmask.

desenredar(se) *t* to untangle, disentangle. — 2 *p* to disentangle o.s.

desenrollar *t* to unroll, unwind.

desenroscar [1] *t* to unscrew, uncoil.

desentenderse [28] *p* to pretend not to understand (*de, -*). 2 *(despreocuparse)* to take no part (*de,* in), cease to be interested (*de,* in).

desenterrar [27] *t* to unearth; *(cadáver)* to disinter, exhume. 2 *fig (recuerdos)* to recall.

desentonar *i* to be out of tune. 2 *fig* not to match.

desentrañar *t fig* to find out, solve, unravel.

desentrenado,-a *adj* out of training.

desentumecer(se) [43] *t* to free from numbness. — 2 *p* to shake off numbness.

desenvainar *t* to unsheathe, draw.

desenvoltura *f* confidence. 2 *(atrevimiento)* boldness.

desenvolver(se) [32] *t* to unwrap. — 2 *p (transcurrir)* to develop, go. 3 *(espabilarse)* to manage. ▲ *pp* **desenvuelto,-a.**

desenvuelto,-a *pp* → **desenvolver(se).** — 2 *adj* confident, natural.

deseo *m* wish, desire, longing.

deseoso,-a *adj* desirous, eager.

desequilibrado,-a *adj-m,f* unbalanced (person).

desequilibrar(se) *t* to unbalance. — 2 *p* to become unbalanced.

desequilibrio *m* lack of balance, imbalance. ■ *~ mental,* mental disorder.

deserción *f* desertion.

desertar *i* MIL to desert. 2 *(abandonar)* to abandon.

desértico,-a *adj* desert.

desertización *f* desertification.

desertor,-ra *m,f* deserter.

desesperación *f* despair, desperation. 2 *(irritación)* exasperation.

desesperado,-a *adj* hopeless, desperate. 2 *(irritado)* exasperated.

desesperante *adj* despairing. 2 *(irritante)* exasperating.

desesperar(se) *t* to make despair. 2 *(irritar)* to exasperate. — 3 *i-p* to despair. 4 *(irritarse)* to be exasperated.

desestabilizar [4] *t* to destabilize.

desestimar *t* to disregard, undervalue. 2 JUR to reject, refuse.

desfachatez *f* cheek, nerve.

desfalcar [1] *t* to embezzle.

desfalco *m* embezzlement.

desfallecer [43] *i* to faint. 2 *(decaer)* to lose heart.

desfallecido,-a *adj* faint, weak.

desfallecimiento *m* faintness. 2 *(desmayo)* fainting fit.

desfasado,-a *adj* out-dated; *(persona)* old-fashioned.

desfavorable *adj* unfavourable.

desfigurar *t (cara)* to disfigure. 2 *fig* to distort, misrepresent.

desfiladero *m* defile, gorge, narrow pass.

desfilar *t* to march past, parade. 2 *(irse)* to file out.

desfile *m* parade.

desfogar(se) [7] *t* to (give) vent (to). – **2** *p* to let off steam.

desgana *f* lack of appetite. **2** *(indiferencia)* indifference. ●*con* ~, reluctantly.

desganado,-a *adj* not hungry. **2** *(indiferente)* indifferent. ●*estar* ~, to have no appetite.

desgarbado,-a *adj* ungainly, ungraceful, clumsy.

desgarrador,-ra *adj* rending. **2** *fig* heart-breaking.

desgarrar *t* to tear, rend. **2** *fig (corazón)* to break.

desgarrón *m* tear, rip.

desgastar(se) *t* to wear out/away; *(tacones)* to wear down. **2** *(debilitar)* to weaken. – **3** *p (persona)* to wear o.s. out.

desgaste *m* wear (and tear); *(metal)* corrosion. **2** *(debilitamiento)* weakening.

desgracia *f* misfortune. **2** *(mala suerte)* bad luck, mischance. **3** *(pérdida de favor)* disfavour. **4** *(accidente)* mishap, accident. ●*caer en* ~, to lose favour, fall into disgrace; *por* ~, unfortunately; *¡qué* ~*!*, how awful!

desgraciado,-a *adj* unfortunate, unlucky. **2** *(infeliz)* unhappy. – **3** *m,f* wretch, unfortunate person.

desgraciar(se) [12] *t* to spoil. – **2** *p* to be ruined/spoiled. **3** *(fracasar)* to fail.

desgranar *t* to shell.

desgravar *t* to deduct.

desgreñado,-a *adj* dishevelled.

desguazar [4] *t (barco)* to break up; *(coche)* to scrap.

deshabitado,-a *adj* uninhabited.

deshacer(se) [73] *t* to undo, unmake. **2** *(nudo)* to loosen. **3** *(destruir)* to destroy. **4** *(planes)* to upset. **5** *(disolver)* to dissolve; *(fundir)* to melt. – **6** *p* to come undone. **7** *(disolverse)* to dissolve; *(fundirse)* to melt. **8** *(librarse)* to get rid of *(de,* of*)*. ●~ *en elogios,* to be full of praise; ~ *en llanto,* to cry one's eyes out. ▲ *pp deshecho,-a.*

desharrapado,-a *adj* ragged, in tatters, shabby.

deshecho,-a *pp* → **deshacer(se)**. – **2** *adj* undone, unmade. **3** *(destruido)* destroyed. **4** *(disuelto)* dissolved; *(fundido)* melted. **5** *fig (cansado)* shattered, exhausted.

desheredar *t* to disinherit.

deshidratar(se) *t* to dehydrate. – **2** *p* to become dehydrated.

deshielo *m* thaw; *(de congelador)* defrosting.

deshilachado,-a *adj* frayed.

deshilvanado,-a *adj fig* disconnected, incoherent.

deshinchar(se) *t* to deflate. **2** *(enfado)* to appease. – **3** *p* to become deflated. **4** *(persona)* to lose heart.

deshojar(se) *t* to strip the petals/leaves of. – **2** *p* to lose its petals/leaves.

deshollinador *m* chimney sweep.

deshollinar *t* to sweep.

deshonesto,-a *adj* dishonest. **2** *(inmoral)* immodest, indecent.

deshonor *m*, **deshonra** *f* dishonour, disgrace.

deshonrar *t* to dishonour, disgrace. **2** *(injuriar)* to insult, defame. **3** *(violar)* to rape.

deshonroso,-a *adj* dishonourable.

deshora *f* inconvenient time. ●*a* ~, inopportunely, at the wrong time.

deshuesar *t* to bone.

deshumanizar [4] *t* to dehumanize.

desidia *f* negligence, idleness.

desierto,-a *adj* uninhabited; *(vacío)* empty, deserted. – **2** *m* desert.

designación *f* designation, appointment.

designar *t (nombrar)* to assign, appoint. **2** *(fijar)* to set.

designio *m* design, plan.

desigual *adj* unequal. **2** *(irregular)* uneven, irregular. **3** *(variable)* changeable.

desigualdad *f* inequality, difference. **2** *(irregularidad)* unevenness. **3** *(inconstancia)* changeability

desilusión *f* disillusion(ment), disappointment.

desilusionado,-a *adj* disappointed, disillusioned.

desilusionar *t* to disillusion, disappoint.

desinfección *f* disinfection.

desinfectante *adj-m* disinfectant.

desinfectar *t* to disinfect.

desinflar(se) *t-p* to deflate. – **2** *p fam* to cool off.

desintegrar *t* to disintegrate.

desinterés *m* unselfishness. **2** *(indiferencia)* indifference.

desinteresado,-a *adj* unselfish.

desinteresarse *p* to lose interest *(de,* in*)*.

desintoxicar(se) [1] *t-p* to detoxicate (o.s.).

desistir *i* to desist, give up. **2** JUR to waive.

desleal *adj* disloyal.

deslealtad *f* disloyalty.

desleír [37] *t (sólido)* to dissolve; *(líquido)* to dilute.

deslenguado,-a *adj* insolent, foulmouthed.

desligar(se) [7] *t* to untie, unfasten. **2** *fig* to separate *(de,* from). **– 3** *p* to break away.

deslindar *t* to delimit, set out the boundaries of. **2** *fig* to clarify.

desliz *m* slide, slip. **2** *fig (error)* slip, blunder, false step.

deslizante *adj* sliding.

deslizar(se) [4] *t-i* to slide, slip (in). **– 2** *p* to slip; *(sobre agua)* to glide. **3** *(salir)* to slip out of; *(entrar)* to slip into. **4** *(río)* to flow.

deslucir [45] *t* to tarnish, dull. **2** *fig* to spoil.

deslumbramiento *m* dazzle, glare.

deslumbrante *adj* dazzling, glaring.

deslumbrar *t* to dazzle, daze.

desmadrarse *p fam* to go wild.

desmadre *m fam* havoc, hullabal(l)oo.

desmán *m* excess, outrage.

desmandarse *p* to go too far, get out of hand.

desmantelar *t* to dismantle. **2** MAR to unmast.

desmañado,-a *adj* clumsy, awkward.

desmaquillador,-ra *adj* cleansing. **– 2** *m* make-up remover.

desmaquillar(se) *t-p* to remove one's make-up.

desmayar(se) *i fig* to lose heart. **– 2** *p* MED to faint.

desmayo *m* discouragement. **2** MED fainting fit.

desmedido,-a *adj* excessive, disproportionate.

desmejorar(se) *t* to impair, make worse. **– 2** *i-p* to get worse. ●*estar desmejorado,-a,* to look unwell.

desmelenarse *p fam* to let one's hair down.

desmembrar [3] *t* to dismember. **2** *fig* to split, divide.

desmemoriado,-a *adj-m,f* forgetful/absent-minded (person).

desmentir [35] *t* to deny. **2** *(contradecir)* to contradict. **3** *(desmerecer)* not to live up to.

desmenuzar [4] *t* to crumble, break pieces. **2** *fig* to scrutinize, look into.

desmesurado,-a *adj* excessive, disproportionate.

desmontar *t* to dismantle, take down/apart. **2** *(edificio)* to knock down. **3** *(arma)* to uncock. **– 4** *i (del caballo)* to dismount *(de,* -).

desmoralizar(se) [4] *t* to demoralize. **– 2** *p* to become demoralized.

desmoronamiento *m* crumbling, disintegration.

desmoronar(se) *t* to crumble. **– 2** *p* to crumble, fall to pieces. **3** *fig* to lose heart.

desnaturalizado,-a *adj* adulterated. **2** QUÍM denatured. **3** *(persona)* unnatural. ■ *alcohol ~,* denatured alcohol.

desnaturalizar [4] *t* to adulterate. **2** QUÍM to denature.

desnivel *m* unevenness. **2** *(cuesta)* slope, drop.

desnivelado,-a *adj* uneven.

desnivelar(se) *t* to make uneven. **– 2** *p* to become uneven.

desnucar(se) [1] *t* to break the neck of. **– 2** *p* to break one's neck.

desnudar(se) *t* to undress. **– 2** *p* to get undressed.

desnudez *f* nudity, nakedness.

desnudo,-a *adj* naked, nude. **2** *fig* plain, bare. **– 3** *m* ART nude.

desnutrición *f* malnutrition, undernourishment.

desnutrido,-a *adj* undernourished.

desobedecer [43] *t* to disobey.

desobediencia *f* disobedience.

desobediente *adj* disobedient.

desocupación *f (ociosidad)* leisure. **2** *(desempleo)* unemployment.

desocupado,-a *adj (libre)* free, vacant. **2** *(ocioso)* unoccupied. **3** *(desempleado)* unemployed.

desocupar *t* to vacate, leave, empty.

desodorante *adj-m* deodorant.

desolación *f* desolation. **2** *(tristeza)* affliction, grief.

desolador,-ra *adj* desolating.

desolar(se) [31] *t* to devastate. **– 2** *p* to be grieved.

desollar [31] *t* to skin, flay. **2** *fig (persona)* to injure. ●*fig ~ vivo,-a,* to tear to pieces.

desorbitado,-a *adj* exorbitant.

desorden *m* disorder, disarray, mess: *en ~,* in disarray. **2** *(alteración)* disturbance, riot.

desordenado,-a *adj* untidy, messy. **2** *(desaseado)* slovenly. **3** *(vida)* licentious.

desordenar *t* to untidy, disarrange, mess up; *(alterar)* to disturb.

desorganización *f* disorganization.

desorganizar [4] *t* to disorganize, disrupt.

desorientado,-a *adj* disoriented. 2 *fig* confused.

desorientar(se) *t* to disorientate. — 2 *p* to lose one's bearings.

despabilado,-a *adj (despierto)* wide awake. 2 *(listo)* smart, sharp.

despabilar(se) *t* to smarten, enliven. — 2 *p (despertarse)* to wake up. 3 *(animarse)* to liven up.

despachar(se) *t (terminar)* to finish, *(completar)* to complete. 2 *(resolver)* to resolve, get through. 3 *(enviar)* to send, dispatch. 4 *(despedir)* to fire. 5 *(en tienda)* to serve; *(vender)* to sell. 6 *(asunto)* to deal with. 7 *fam fig (matar)* to kill. — 8 *p fam* to speak one's mind. ●~*se a gusto,* to get a load off one's mind.

despacho *m (envío)* sending, dispatch. 2 *(oficina)* office; *(estudio)* study. 3 *(venta)* sale. 4 *(tienda)* shop, office. 5 *(comunicación)* message, dispatch. ■ ~ *de localidades,* box office; *mesa de* ~, desk.

despachurrar(se) *t fam* to crush, squash. — 2 *p* to get crushed/squashed.

despacio *adv* slowly. — 2 *interj* easy there!

despampanante *adj* astounding.

desparejado,-a *adj* without a partner, odd.

desparpajo *m* ease. 2 *(descaro)* nerve, impudence.

desparramar(se) *t-p* to spread, scatter, spill.

despatarrar(se) *t* to astonish. — 2 *p* to open one's legs wide. 3 *(caer)* to fall with one's legs apart.

despavorido,-a *adj* terrified.

despecho *m* spite. ●*a* ~ *de,* in spite of, despite.

despechugarse [7] *p fam* to show one's chest.

despectivo,-a *adj* contemptuous. 2 GRAM pejorative.

despedazar [4] *t* to tear/cut into pieces.

despedida *f* farewell, goodbye. ■ ~ *de soltero/soltera,* stag night/hen party.

despedir(se) [34] *t (lanzar)* to throw. 2 *(emitir)* to emit, give off. 3 *(del trabajo)* to dismiss, fire. 4 *(decir adiós)* to say goodbye to. — 5 *p (decirse adiós)* to say goodbye *(de,* to). 6 *fig* to forget, give up *(de,* -). ●~*se a la francesa,* to take French leave; *salir despedido,-a,* to shoot off.

despegado,-a *adj* detached, unglued. 2 *fig* cool, indifferent.

despegar(se) [7] *t* to unstick, unglue. — 2 *i (avión)* to take off. — 3 *p* to come unstuck/unglued.

despego *m* coolness, indifference.

despegue *m* takeoff.

despeinado,-a *adj* dishevelled, unkempt.

despeinar(se) *t* to ruffle the hair of. — 2 *p* to ruffle one's hair.

despejado,-a *adj* assured, self-confident. 2 *(espacioso)* wide, spacious. 3 METEOR cloudless, clear.

despejar(se) *t* to clear, remove. 2 *(despertar)* to wake up. — 3 *p* METEOR to clear up. 4 *(persona)* to clear one's head.

despelotarse* *p* to strip off.

despelote* *m* strip. 2 *(de risa)* laugh, guffaw.

despensa *f* pantry, larder. 2 *(víveres)* store of provisions.

despeñadero *m* cliff, precipice.

despeñar(se) *t-p* to throw (o.s.) over a cliff.

desperdiciar [12] *t* to waste, squander.

desperdicio *m* waste. 2 *pl* leavings, refuse *sing.*

desperdigar(se) [7] *t-p* to scatter, disperse.

desperezarse [4] *p* to stretch (o.s).

desperfecto *m* slight damage. 2 *(defecto)* flaw, defect.

despertador *m* alarm clock.

despertar(se) [27] *t* to wake, awaken. 2 *(apetito)* to excite. — 3 *i-p* to wake up, awake.

despiadado,-a *adj* pitiless, ruthless, merciless.

despido *m* dismissal, sacking.

despierto,-a *adj* awake. 2 *(espabilado)* lively, smart.

despilfarrador,-ra *m,f* squanderer, spendrift.

despilfarrar *t* to waste, squander, spend lavishly.

despilfarro *m* waste, extravagance, lavishness.

despistado,-a *adj-m,f* absent-minded (person). ●*hacerse el* ~, to pretend not to understand.

despistar(se) *t* to throw off one's scent. — 2 *p (perderse)* to get lost. 3 *(distraerse)* to get distracted.

despiste *m* slip, mistake.

desplante *m* impudent remark/act.

desplazamiento *m (traslado)* moving. 2 *(viaje)* trip.

desplazar(se) [4] *t (trasladar)* to move. −
2 *p* to go travel (*a*, to).

desplegar [48] *t* to unfold, spread (out).
2 *(actividad)* to display. 3 MIL to deploy.
4 *(mostrar)* to show, display.

desplomarse *p* to fall down. 2 *(pared)* to
tumble down. 3 *(persona)* to collapse.

desplumar *t* to pluck. 2 *fig* to fleece,
swindle.

despoblación *f* depopulation.

despoblar(se) [31] *t* to depopulate. − 2
p to become depopulated, deserted.

despojar(se) *t* to despoil, deprive (*de*,
of). 2 JUR to dispossess. − 3 *p (de ropa)*
to take off (*de*, -). 4 *fig* to free o.s. (*de*,
of).

despojo *m (botín)* plunder. 2 *pl (de animal)* offal *sing*. 3 *pl (sobras)* leavings,
scraps. 4 *pl (de persona)* mortal remains.

desposado,-a *adj-m,f fml* newly-wed.

desposar(se) *fml t* to marry. − 2 *p* to get
married.

desposeer(se) [61] *t* to dispossess. − 2
p to give up (*de*, -).

desposorios *mpl fml (boda)* marriage
sing. 2 *(compromiso)* betrothal *sing*.

déspota *mf* despot, tyrant.

despotismo *m* despotism. ■ ~ *ilustrado,* enlightened despotism.

despotricar [1] *i* to rave (*contra*, about).

despreciable *adj* despicable, contemptible.

despreciar [12] *t* to despise, scorn. 2 *(desestimar)* to spurn, reject.

desprecio *m* contempt, scorn.

desprender(se) *t* to detach, unfasten. −
2 *p* to withdraw (*de*, from), renounce.
3 *(soltarse)* to come off. 4 *(deducirse)* to
follow, be inferred.

desprendido,-a *adj* generous, disinterested.

desprendimiento *m* generosity, unselfishness. 2 *(de tierra)* landslide.

despreocupación *f* nonchalance. 2 *(negligencia)* negligence, carelessness.

despreocuparse *p* not to care/worry
any more about.

desprestigiar(se) [12] *t* to discredit. − 2
p to lose one's prestige.

desprestigio *m* discredit, loss of prestige.

desprevenido,-a *adj* unprepared. ●*coger a algn.* ~, to take sb. by surprise.

desproporción *f* disproportion.

desproporcionado,-a *adj* disproportionate.

despropósito *m* absurdity, nonsense.

desprovisto,-a *adj* lacking (*de*, -), devoid (*de*, of).

después *adv* afterwards, later: *iremos* ~,
we'll go later. 2 *(entonces)* then: *y* ~ *dijo
que sí,* and then he said yes. 3 *(luego)*
next. ●~ *de (que),* after; ~ *de todo,* after all; *poco* ~, soon after.

despuntar *t* to blunt. − 2 *i (planta)* to
sprout, bud. 3 *fig* to be witty, clever. 4
(destacar) to excel. ●~ *el día,* to dawn.

desquiciar [12] *t* to unhinge. 2 *(descomponer)* to upset, unsettle.

desquitar(se) *t* to compensate. − 2 *p
(vengarse)* to take revenge (*de*, on), get
even (*de*, with).

desquite *m* compensation. 2 *(venganza)*
revenge, retaliation.

destacado,-a *adj* outstanding.

destacamento *m* detachment.

destacar(se) [1] *t* MIL to detach. 2 to
point out. − 3 *p* to stand out.

destajo *m* piecework. ●*a* ~, by the
piece.

destapar *t* to open, uncover. 2 *(botella)*
to uncork. 3 *(quitar la tapa)* to take off
the lid of.

destape *m fam* strip. ●*película de* ~,
blue movie.

destartalado,-a *adj* tumbledown, ramshackle.

destellar *i* to sparkle, gleam.

destello *m* sparkle, gleam, flash.

destemplado,-a *adj* MÚS out of tune. 2
(tiempo) unpleasant. ●*sentirse* ~, not to
feel well.

destemplar(se) *t* to disturb the harmony of. 2 MÚS to put out of tune. − 3
p MED to feel indisposed.

desteñir(se) [36] *t* to discolour. − 2 *i-p*
to lose colour, fade.

desternillarse *p fam* ~ *de risa,* to split
one's sides laughing.

desterrado,-a *adj* exiled, banished. − 2
m,f exile, outcast.

desterrar [27] *t* to exile, banish.

destetar *t* to wean.

destiempo *a* ~, *adv* inopportunely, at
the wrong time.

destierro *m* banishment, exile.

destilación *f* distillation.

destilar *t* to distil. 2 *(filtrar)* to filter. 3 *fig*
to exude, reveal.

destilería *f* distillery.

destinado,-a *adj* destined (*a*, to), bound
(*a*, for).

destinar *t* to assign, allot. 2 *(a un cargo)*
to appoint.

destinatario,-a *m,f (de carta)* addressee. **2** *(de mercancías)* consignee.

destino *m (sino)* destiny, fate. **2** *(lugar)* destination. **3** *(empleo)* employment, post. ●*con* ~ *a,* bound for, going to.

destitución *f* dismissal.

destituir [62] *t* to dismiss.

destornillador *m* screwdriver.

destornillar(se) *t* to unscrew. − **2** *p fig* to go crazy.

destreza *f* skill, dexterity.

destripar *t (animal)* to gut, disembowel. **2** *(cosa)* to tear/cut open. **3** *fig (despachurrar)* to crush.

destronar *t* to dethrone.

destrozado,-a *adj* smashed, broken, shattered.

destrozar [4] *t* to smash, break in pieces, shatter.

destrozo *m* destruction, damage.

destrucción *f* destruction.

destructivo,-a *adj* destructive.

destructor,-ra *adj* destructive. − **2** *m* MAR destroyer.

destruir [62] *t* to destroy, ruin.

desunir *t* to divide, separate. **2** *fig* to cause discord.

desuso *m* disuse. ●*caer en* ~, to become obsolete.

desvaído,-a *adj (color)* pale, dull. **2** *(borroso)* blurred.

desvalido,-a *adj-m,f* helpless/destitute (person).

desvalijar *t* to rob, hold up.

desvalorización *f* devaluation.

desvalorizar [4] *t* to devalue.

desván *m* loft, attic.

desvanecer(se) [43] *t* to make vanish/disappear. **2** *(nubes etc.)* to dispel. **3** *fig (recuerdo etc.)* to efface. − **4** *p* to vanish, disappear. **5** *(demayarse)* to faint, swoon.

desvanecimiento *m* dizziness, faintness.

desvariar [13] *i* to be delirious, rave, talk nonsense.

desvarío *m (delirio)* delirium. **2** *(locura)* nonsense, raving. **3** *(capricho)* fancy, whim.

desvelar(se) *t* to keep awake. **2** *(revelar)* to reveal. − **3** *p* to be unable to sleep. **4** *(dedicarse)* to devote o.s. (*por,* to).

desvelo *m* sleeplessness, wakefulness. **2** *(dedicación)* devotion, dedication.

desvencijado,-a *adj* rickety, loose.

desventaja *f* disadvantage, drawback.

desventura *f* misfortune, misery.

desventurado,-a *adj-m,f* unfortunate (person).

desvergonzado,-a *adj* shameless, impudent.

desvergüenza *f* shamelessness, impudence.

desvestir(se) [34] *t-p* to undress.

desviación *f* deviation. **2** *(de carretera)* diversion, detour.

desviar(se) [13] *t* to deviate. **2** *(golpe)* to deflect. **3** *(carretera)* to divert. **4** *(tema)* to change. − **5** *p* to go off course; *(coche)* to take a detour.

desvío *m* diversion, detour.

desvirgar [7] *t* to deflower.

desvirtuar [11] *t* to impair, diminish the value/quality of.

desvivirse *p* to do one's utmost (*por,* for). **2** *(desear)* to long (*por,* for).

detallado,-a *adj* detailed.

detallar *t* to detail, give the details of. **2** *(especificar)* to specify. **3** COM to retail, sell at retail prices.

detalle *m* detail, particular. **2** *(delicadeza)* gesture. ●*¡qué* ~*!,* how nice!; *tener un* ~, to be considerate/thoughtful; *vender al* ~, to sell on retail.

detectar *t* to detect.

detective *mf* detective.

detector *m* detector.

detención *f* stop. **2** JUR detention, arrest.

detener(se) [87] *t* to stop. **2** *(retener)* to keep, retain. **3** *(retrasar)* to delay. **4** JUR to detain, arrest. − **5** *p* to stop, halt.

detenido,-a *adj (minucioso)* careful. **2** JUR under arrest. − **3** *m,f* JUR prisoner.

detenimiento *m* care, thoroughness.

detergente *adj-m* detergent.

deteriorar(se) *t* to damage, spoil. − **2** *p* to get damaged.

deterioro *m* damage, deterioration.

determinación *f (valor)* determination. **2** *(decisión)* decision. **3** *(firmeza)* firmness.

determinado,-a *adj* determinate. **2** *(concreto)* fixed, set. **3** GRAM definite.

determinante *adj-m* determinant.

determinar *t (decidir)* to resolve, decide. **2** *(fijar)* to fix, set, appoint. **3** *(causar)* to bring about.

detestable *adj* detestable, hateful.

detestar *t* to detest, hate, abhor.

detonación *f* detonation.

detonador *m* detonator.

detonante *adj* detonating. − **2** *m* detonator. **3** *fig* trigger.

detractor,-ra *adj-m,f* detractor, slanderer.

detrás *adv* behind, at the back: ~ *de la puerta,* behind the door; *el jardín está* ~, the garden is at the back. **2** *(después)* then, afterwards: *llegaron* ~ *de él,* they arrived after him. •*ir* ~ *de,* to go after; *fig por* ~, behind one's back.

detrimento *m* detriment. •*en* ~ *de,* to the detriment of.

deuda *f* debt.

deudor,-ra *m,f* debtor.

devaluación *f* devaluation.

devaluar [11] *t* to devaluate.

devanar(se) *t* to wind, reel. – **2** *p fam* ~*se los sesos,* to rack one's brains.

devaneo *m (delirio)* delirium, nonsense. **2** *(amorío)* flirting.

devastación *f* devastation, destruction.

devastador,-ra *adj* devastating.

devastar *t* to devastate, lay waste, ruin.

devengar [7] *t (sueldo)* to earn. **2** *(interés)* to draw, accrue.

devoción *f* devotion. **2** REL piety, devoutness.

devolución *f* return, restitution. **2** JUR devolution.

devolver [32] *t* to give back, pay back, return. **2** *fam (vomitar)* to vomit. ▲ *pp* *devuelto,-a.*

devorador,-ra *adj* devouring. – **2** *m,f* devourer. ■ *devoradora de hombres,* man-eater.

devorar *t* to devour.

devoto,-a *adj* devout, pious. **2** *(dedicado)* devoted.

devuelto,-a *pp* → **devolver.**

di *indef indic* → **dar.** – **2** *imperat* → **decir.**

día *m* day. **2** *(con luz)* daylight, daytime. •*¡buenos días!,* good morning!; *cada* ~*/todos los días,* every day; *del* ~, fresh; ~ *a* ~, day by day; ~ *de año nuevo,* New Year's Day; ~ *de fiesta,* (bank) holiday; ~ *laborable,* workday; ~ *libre,* day off; *días alternos,* every other day; *hoy (en)* ~, today, now, nowadays; *poner al* ~, to bring up to date; *vivir al* ~, not to save a penny.

diabetes *f inv* diabetes.

diablesa *f* she-devil.

diablo *m* devil, demon. **2** *(malvado)* wicked person. •*¡al* ~ *con ...!,* to hell with ...!; *¡diablos!,* the devil!; *¿qué diablos ...?,* what the hell ...?

diablura *f* mischief.

diabólico,-a *adj* diabolic(al), devilish.

diácono *m* deacon.

diadema *f* diadem. **2** *(adorno)* hairband.

diáfano,-a *adj* diaphanous, see-through.

diafragma *m* diaphragm.

diagnosis *f inv* diagnosis.

diagnosticar [1] *t* to diagnose.

diagnóstico,-a *adj* diagnostic. – **2** *m* diagnosis.

diagonal *adj-f* diagonal.

diagrama *m* diagram.

dialecto *m* dialect.

dialogar [7] *i-t* to dialogue.

diálogo *m* dialogue.

diamante *m* diamond.

diámetro *m* diameter.

diana *f* MIL reveille. **2** *(blanco)* bull's eye.

diapasón *m* diapason, tuning fork.

diapositiva *f* slide.

diario,-a *adj* daily. – **2** *m (prensa)* (daily) newspaper. **3** *(íntimo)* diary, journal. – **4** *diariamente adv* daily, every day. •*a* ~, daily, every day.

diarrea *f* diarrhoea.

diatriba *f* diatribe.

dibujante *mf* sketcher, drawer. **2** TÉC *m* draughtsman, *f* draughtswoman.

dibujar(se) *t* to draw, sketch. **2** *(describir)* to describe. – **3** *p* to appear, be outlined.

dibujo *m* drawing, sketch. **2** *(modelo)* pattern. ■ *dibujos animados,* cartoons.

diccionario *m* dictionary.

dicha *f* happiness. **2** *(suerte)* fortune, good luck.

dicharachero,-a *adj* talkative.

dicho,-a *pp* → **decir.** – **2** *adj* said, mentioned. – **3** *m* saying, proverb. •~ *y hecho,* no sooner said than done; *mejor* ~, or rather; *propiamente* ~, strictly speaking.

dichoso,-a *adj* happy. **2** *(con suerte)* lucky. **3** *fam* damn(ed), cursed: *¡este* ~ *calor!,* this damn heat!

diciembre *m* December.

dictado *m* dictation. •*escribir al* ~, to take dictation.

dictador *m* dictator.

dictadura *f* dictatorship.

dictamen *m (opinión)* opinion. **2** *(informe)* report.

dictaminar *i* to give judgement/an opinion *(sobre,* on).

dictar *t* to dictate. **2** *(inspirar)* to inspire, suggest. **3** *(leyes)* to make.

didáctico,-a *adj* didactic, teaching. – **2** *f* didactics.

diecinueve *adj* nineteen; *(decimonono)* nineteenth. – **2** *m* nineteen.

dieciocho *adj* eighteen; *(decimoctavo)* eighteenth. – **2** *m* eighteen.

dieciséis *adj* sixteen; *(decimosexto)* sixteenth. – **2** *m* sixteen.

diecisiete *adj* seventeen; *(decimoséptimo)* seventeenth. – **2** *m* seventeen.

diente *m* tooth. **2** *(de ajo)* clove. •*apretar los dientes,* to set one's teeth; **hincar el** ~ **en,** to backbite, slander; *fig* to attack. ■ ~ *de leche,* milk tooth; ~ *picado,* decayed tooth.

diestro,-a *adj* right(-hand). **2** *(hábil)* dexterous, skilful. – **3** *f* right(-hand). – **4** *m* bullfighter. – **5** *diestramente adv* skillfully. •*a* ~ *y siniestro,* right, left and centre.

dieta *f* diet. **2** *(asamblea)* assembly. **3** *pl* expenses allowance *sing.* **4** *pl* doctor's fees.

dietario *m* family account book. **2** *(crónica)* chronicle.

dietético,-a *adj* dietetic. – **2** *f* dietetics.

diez *adj* ten; *(décimo)* tenth. – **2** *m* ten.

diezmar *t* to decimate.

diezmo *m* tithe.

difamación *f* defamation, slander.

difamar *t* to defame, slander.

diferencia *f* difference. •*a* ~ *de,* unlike.

diferenciar(se) [12] *t* to differentiate, distinguish (*entre,* between). **2** *(hacer diferente)* to make different. – **3** *p* to differ, be different. **4** *(destacarse)* to distinguish o.s.

diferente *adj* different.

diferido,-a *adj* recorded. ■ *retransmisión en* ~, recorded transmission.

diferir [35] *t* to defer, postpone, put off. – **2** *i* to differ, be different (*de/entre,* from).

difícil *adj* difficult, hard. **2** *(improbable)* unlikely. – **3** *difícilmente adv* with difficulty.

dificultad *f* difficulty. **2** *(obstáculo)* obstacle.

dificultar *t* to make difficult, hinder.

dificultoso,-a *adj* difficult, hard.

difundir(se) *t* *(luz)* to diffuse. **2** *fig (noticia)* to spread. **3** RAD to broadcast. – **4** *p (luz)* to be diffused. **5** *fig (noticia)* to spread.

difunto,-a *adj* deceased, late. – **2** *m,f* deceased. ■ *Día de los difuntos,* All Souls'/Saint's Day.

difusión *f (de luz)* diffusion. **2** *fig (de noticia)* spreading. **3** RAD broadcast(ing).

difuso,-a *adj* diffuse.

digerir [35] *t* to digest. **2** *fig (sufrir)* to suffer.

digestión *f* digestion.

digestivo,-a *adj* digestive. – **2** *m* digestive drink.

digital *adj* digital. ■ *reloj* ~, digital watch/clock.

dígito *m* digit.

dignarse *p* to deign/condescend (*a,* to).

dignatario,-a *m,f* dignitary.

dignidad *f* dignity. **2** *(cargo)* rank.

dignificar [1] *t* to dignify.

digno,-a *adj (merecedor)* worthy, deserving: ~ *de confianza,* trustworthy. **2** *(adecuado)* fitting, suitable. **3** *(respetable)* respectable.

digo *pres indic* → **decir.**

dije *m* trinket.

dilación *f* delay, postponement.

dilapidar *t* to squander.

dilatación *f* dilatation, expansion.

dilatado,-a *adj* dilated, expanded. **2** *(vasto)* vast, extensive, large.

dilatar(se) *t-p* to dilate, expand. – **2** *t (propagar)* to spread. **3** *(diferir)* to put off, delay.

dilema *m* dilemma.

diligencia *f (cualidad)* diligence, care. **2** *(trámite)* errand, steps *pl;* JUR proceeding. **3** *(carreta)* stagecoach.

diligente *adj* diligent. **2** *(rápido)* quick.

dilucidar *t* to clear up, elucidate.

diluir(se) [62] *t-p* to dilute.

diluviar [12] *i* to pour with rain. ▲ *Only used in the 3rd pers. It does not take a subject.*

diluvio *m* flood.

dimensión *f* dimension, size.

diminutivo,-a *adj-m* diminutive.

diminuto,-a *adj* little, tiny.

dimisión *f* resignation.

dimitir *t* to resign.

dinámica *f* dynamics.

dinámico,-a *adj* dynamic.

dinamismo *m* dynamism.

dinamita *f* dynamite.

dinamo, dínamo *f* dynamo.

dinastía *f* dynasty.

dineral *m* fortune.

dinero *m* money. **2** *(fortuna)* wealth. ■ ~ *al contado/contante (y sonante),* ready money, cash; ~ *suelto,* loose change.

dintel *m* lintel.

diocesano,-a *adj-m* diocesan.

diócesis *f inv* diocese.

dios *m* god. •*a la buena de Dios*, at random, haphazardly; *Dios mediante,* God willing; *¡Dios mío!,* my God!, good heavens!; *fam* **ni Dios,** not a soul; *fam* **todo Dios,** everybody.

diosa *f* goddess.

dióxido *m* dioxide.

diploma *m* diploma.

diplomacia *f* diplomacy.

diplomático,-a *adj* diplomatic, tactful. — 2 *m,f* diplomat.

diptongo *m* diphthong.

diputado,-a *m,f* deputy, representative.

dique *m* dam mole, dike. 2 *fig* barrier. ■ ~ **seco,** dry dock.

dirección *f* (*rumbo*) direction; (*sentido*) way. 2 (*cargo*) directorship, leadership. 3 (*junta*) board of directors, management. 4 (*domicilio*) address. 5 AUTO steering. ■ AUTO ~ **asistida,** power steering.

directivo,-a *adj* directive, managing. — 2 *m,f* director, manager. — 3 *f* board of directors, management.

directo,-a *adj* direct, straight. — 2 *m* DEP straight hit. — 3 *f* AUTO top gear. ●TV **en** ~, live.

director,-ra *adj* directing, managing. — 2 *m,f* director, manager. 3 (*de colegio*) *m* headmaster, *f* headmistress. 4 (*universidad*) principal. 5 (*de orquesta*) conductor.

directorio *m* directory.

dirigente *adj* leading, governing. — 2 *m,f* leader.

dirigir(se) [6] *t* to direct. 2 (*negocio*) to manage, run. 3 (*orquesta*) to conduct. 4 (*carta*) to address. — 5 *p* (*ir*) to go (*a,* to), make one's way (*a,* to), make (*a,* for). 6 (*hablar*) to address (*a,* -), speak (*a,* to).

dirimir *t* to annul, nullify. 2 (*resolver*) to settle.

discernimiento *m* discernment, judgement.

discernir [29] *t* to discern, distinguish.

disciplina *f* discipline. 2 (*doctrina*) doctrine. 3 (*asignatura*) subject.

disciplinado,-a *adj* disciplined.

disciplinar *t* to discipline, train.

discípulo,-a *m,f* disciple, follower. 2 (*alumno*) pupil.

disco *m* disc. 2 DEP discus. 3 (*de música*) record. 4 INFORM disk. ■ ~ **duro,** hard disk.

díscolo,-a *adj* ungovernable, unruly.

disconforme *adj* disagreeing.

discordancia *f* disagreement.

discorde *adj* discordant, in disagreement. 2 MÚS dissonant.

discordia *f* discord, disagreement.

discreción *f* discretion. ●*a* ~, at will.

discrecional *adj* optional. ■ *parada* ~, request stop.

discrepancia *f* discrepancy. 2 (*desacuerdo*) dissent, disagreement.

discreto,-a *adj* discreet, prudent. 2 (*sobrio*) sober. 3 (*moderado*) reasonable, moderate.

discriminación *f* discrimination.

discriminar *t* to discriminate.

disculpa *f* excuse, apology. ●*pedir disculpas a algn.,* to apologize to sb.

disculpar(se) *t* to excuse. — 2 *p* to apologize (*por,* for).

discurrir *i* to wander, roam. 2 (*río*) to flow. 3 (*tiempo*) to pass. 4 *fig* (*reflexionar*) to reason, meditate. — 5 *t* (*idear*) to invent, contrive.

discurso *m* speech, discourse. 2 (*razonamiento*) reasoning. 3 (*del tiempo*) course.

discusión *f* (*charla*) discussion. 2 (*disputa*) argument.

discutir *t-i* to discuss. 2 (*disputar*) to argue.

disecar [1] *t* to dissect. 2 (*animales*) to stuff.

disección *f* dissection, anatomy. 2 (*taxidermia*) taxidermy.

diseminar(se) *t-p* to disseminate, scatter, spread.

disentir [35] *i* to dissent, disagree.

diseñar *t* to design.

diseño *m* design.

disertación *f* dissertation, discourse.

disertar *t* to discourse (*sobre,* on/upon).

disfraz *m* disguise. 2 (*vestido*) fancy dress.

disfrazar(se) [4] *t-p* to disguise (o.s.).

disfrutar *t-p* to enjoy (o.s.).

disgregación *f* disintegration, break-up.

disgregar [7] *t* to disintegrate, break up.

disgustado,-a *adj* displeased, upset.

disgustar(se) *t* to displease, upset, annoy. — 2 *p* to be displeased/upset. 3 (*pelearse*) to quarrel (*con,* with).

disgusto *m* displeasure, annoyance. 2 (*pelea*) argument, quarrel. ●*a* ~, against one's will; **llevarse un** ~, to get upset.

disidente *adj-mf* dissenter.

disimular *t* to disguise, conceal.

disimulo *m* pretence, dissimulation.

disipación *f* dissoluteness, dissipation.

disipado,-a *adj* dissipated, wasted.

disipar(se) *t* to dissipate. 2 (*derrochar*) to squander. 3 (*desvanecer*) to dispel. — 4 *p* (*desaparecer*) to vanish.

dislocación *f* dislocation.

dislocar(se) [1] *t-p* to dislocate.

disminución *f* drop, decrease.

disminuir(se) [62] *t-i-p* to diminish, reduce, decrease.

disociar [12] *t* to dissociate.

disolución *f* dissolution, breaking up. **2** *(anulación)* invalidation. **3** *(disipación)* dissipation.

disoluto,-a *adj-m,f* dissolute (person).

disolver(se) [32] *t-p* to dissolve. ▲ *pp di-suelto,-a.*

disonancia *f* dissonance.

dispar *adj* unlike, different.

disparador *m* *(de arma)* trigger. **2** *(de cámara)* release.

disparar(se) *t* to discharge, fire, let off: ~ *un tiro,* to fire a shot. **2** *(lanzar)* to hurl, throw. — **3** *p* *(precio)* to shoot up. **4** *(correr)* to dash off. **5** *(arma)* to go off.

disparatado,-a *adj* absurd, foolish.

disparate *m* absurdity, nonsense, crazy idea. **2** *(error)* blunder, mistake. **3** *(enormidad)* enormity.

disparo *m* shot.

dispensa *f* dispensation, exemption.

dispensar *t* to dispense, give, grant. **2** *(eximir)* to exempt. **3** *(perdonar)* to forgive, pardon. ●*dispense,* pardon me.

dispensario *m* dispensary.

dispersar(se) *t-p* to disperse, scatter.

dispersión *f* dispersion, scattering.

displicencia *f* coolness, indifference.

disponer(se) [78] *t* to dispose, arrange. **2** *(preparar)* to prepare, get ready. **3** *(ordenar)* to order, decree. **4** *i* to have *(de, -).* — **5** *p* *(prepararse)* to get ready *(a,* for). ▲ *pp dispuesto,-a.*

disponibilidad *f* resources *pl,* money on hand.

disponible *adj* ready, available. **2** *(sobrante)* spare. **3** *(a mano)* on hand.

disposición *f* disposition, disposal. **2** *(talento)* gift, talent. **3** *(orden)* order. **4** *(colocación)* arrangement. **5** *(estado de ánimo)* frame of mind. ●*a su* ~, at your disposal/service; *estar en* ~ *de,* to be ready to.

dispositivo,-a *adj* preceptive. — **2** *m* TÉC device, contrivance.

dispuesto,-a *pp* → **disponer**. — **2** *adj* disposed. **3** *(preparado)* prepared, ready. **4** *(despabilado)* bright, clever.

disputa *f* dispute, argument.

disputar *t* to dispute. **2** *(discutir)* to argue. **3** *(competir)* to contest. **4** DEP *(partido)* to play.

distancia *f* distance. **2** *fig (diferencia)* difference. ●*guardar las distancias,* to keep one's distance.

distanciar(se) [12] *t* to distance, separate. — **2** *p* to become distant.

distante *adj* distant, far, remote.

distar *i* to be distant *(de,* from). ●~ *mucho de,* to be far from.

distinción *f* distinction. **2** *(elegancia)* refinement.

distinguido,-a *adj* distinguished. **2** *(elegante)* elegant.

distinguir(se) [8] *t* to distinguish. **2** *(ver)* to see. **3** *(preferir)* to single out. — **4** *p* *(destacar)* to excel, stand out. **5** *(ser visible)* to be visible.

distintivo,-a *adj* distinctive. — **2** *m* *(insignia)* badge; *(marca)* mark.

distinto,-a *adj* distinct. **2** *(diferente)* different.

distracción *f* *(divertimiento)* amusement, pastime. **2** *(despiste)* distraction, absent-mindedness. **3** *(error)* oversight.

distraer(se) [88] *t* to amuse, entertain. **2** *(atención)* to distract. **3** *(fondos)* to embezzle. — **4** *p* *(divertirse)* to amuse o.s. **5** *(despistarse)* to be inattentive/absent-minded.

distraído,-a *adj* absent-minded, inattentive.

distribución *f* distribution. **2** *(colocación)* arrangement.

distribuir [62] *t* to distribute. **2** *(colocar)* to arrange.

distrito *m* district.

disturbio *m* disturbance, riot.

disuadir *t* to dissuade, deter.

disuelto,-a *pp* → **disolver**.

diurno,-a *adj* daily, diurnal.

divagación *f* digression.

divagar [7] *i* to digress, ramble.

diván *m* divan, couch.

divergencia *f* divergence.

diversidad *f* diversity, variety.

diversión *f* fun, amusement, entertainment.

diverso,-a *adj* different. **2** *pl* several, various.

divertido,-a *adj* entertaining, fun.

divertir(se) [35] *t* to amuse, entertain. — **2** *p* to enjoy/amuse o.s., have a good time.

dividir *t* to divide, split (up) *(en,* in).

divinidad *f* divinity, god, deity.

divinizar [4] *t* to deify.

divino,-a *adj* divine, heavenly. **2** *fam (bonito)* beautiful, gorgeous.

divisa f badge, emblem. **2** (de escudo) device. **3** (moneda) foreign currency.

divisar t to perceive, make out.

división f division.

divo,-a m,f opera star. – **2** f prima donna.

divorciar(se) [12] t to divorce. – **2** p to get divorced.

divorcio m divorce.

divulgación f spreading. **2** (de conocimientos) popularization.

divulgar [7] t to divulge, spread. **2** (conocimiento) to popularize.

dobladillo m hem.

doblar(se) t to double. **2** (plegar) to fold. **3** (esquina) to turn, go round. **4** (película) to dub. – **5** i (girar) to turn: ~ *a la derecha,* to turn right. **6** (campana) to toll. – **7** p (plegarse) to fold. **8** (torcerse) to bend. **9** (rendirse) to give in.

doble adj double – **2** m double: *gana el* ~ *que yo,* he/she earns twice as much as I do. – **3** mf CINEM double; m stunt man, f stunt woman. – **4** adv double. •ver ~, to see double.

doblegar(se) [7] t (doblar) to bend, fold. **2** (vencer) to force to yield, subdue. – **3** p (inclinarse) to bend over, stoop. **4** (rendirse) to yield, submit.

doblez m (pliegue) fold. – **2** m & f fig (duplicidad) duplicity, deceitfulness.

doce adj twelve; (duodécimo) twelfth. – **2** m twelve.

docena f dozen.

docente adj teaching.

dócil adj docile, obedient.

docto,-a adj-m,f learned (person).

doctor,-ra m,f doctor.

doctorado m doctorate.

doctrina f doctrine.

documentación f documentation, papers pl.

documento m document.

dogma m dogma.

dogmático,-a adj dogmatic.

dólar m dollar.

dolencia f ailment, illness.

doler(se) [32] i to ache, hurt: *me duele la cabeza,* my head aches. **2** fig to feel hurt. – **3** p (arrepentirse) to repent, feel sorry (de, for). **4** (lamentarse) to complain (de, of).

dolido,-a adj fig hurt, grieved.

dolor m pain, ache. **2** fig pain, sorrow, grief. ■ ~ *de cabeza,* headache.

dolorido,-a adj sore, aching. **2** fig sorrowful, grief-stricken.

doloroso,-a adj painful.

doma f taming, breaking.

domador,-ra m,f tamer, horse-breaker.

domar t to tame, break in.

domesticar [1] t to domesticate; (animal) to tame.

doméstico,-a adj domestic. – **2** m,f domestic, house servant.

domiciliar [12] t to house, lodge. **2** FIN to pay by standing order.

domicilio m address. ■ *servicio a* ~, house deliveries pl.

dominante adj dominant. **2** (que avasalla) domineering.

dominar t to dominate. **2** (avasallar) to domineer. **3** (controlar) to control. **4** (tema) to master. **5** (paisaje) to overlook, command. – **6** i (destacar) to stand out.

domingo m Sunday. ■ ~ *de Ramos,* Palm Sunday; ~ *de Resurrección,* Easter Sunday.

dominio m dominion. **2** (poder) domination, control. **3** (de tema) mastery. **4** (terreno) domain.

don m gift, present. **2** (talento) talent. **3** (título) don. ▲ **3** *is a courtesy title placed before the first names of men.*

donación f donation.

donaire m grace, elegance.

donar t to donate.

donativo m gift, donation.

doncella f maiden, maid. **2** (criada) maidservant.

donde adv-pron where, in which. •*de* ~, from where, whence; *hasta* ~, up to where; fam ¡*vaya por* ~!, fancy that!

dónde pron interrog where: ¿~ *está?,* where is it?

dondequiera adv everywhere, wherever.

doña f doña. ▲ *Courtesy title placed before first names of women.*

dorado,-a adj gilt, golden. – **2** m gilding.

dorar t to gild. **2** CULIN to brown.

dormilón,-ona fam adj sleepyheaded. – **2** m,f sleepyhead.

dormir(se) [33] i to sleep. – **2** p to fall asleep. •fam ~ *a pierna suelta,* to sleep like a log.

dormitar i to doze, nap.

dormitorio m bedroom. **2** (colectivo) dormitory.

dorso m back, reverse.

dos adj two; (segundo) second: *las* ~, two o'clock. – **2** m two. •*cada* ~ *por tres,* every five minutes; *de* ~ *en* ~, two abreast, in twos.

doscientos,-as adj-m two hundred.

dosel *m* canopy.
dosis *f inv* dose.
dotación *f* endowment, funds *pl*. **2** *(tripulación)* complement, crew. **3** *(personal)* staff, personnel.
dotar *t (dar dote)* to give a dowry. **2** *(donar)* to endow, provide.
dote *m &.f* dowry. − **2** *f* gift, talent.
doy *pres indic* → **dar**.
dragado *m* dredging.
dragar [7] *t* to dredge.
dragón *m* dragon.
drama *m* drama.
dramático,-a *adj* dramatic.
dramaturgo,-a *m,f* playwright, dramatist.
drástico,-a *adj* drastic.
drenaje *m* drainage.
drenar *t* to drain.
driblar *i* to dribble.
droga *f* drug. **2** AM *(embuste)* lie. ■ ~ *blanda/dura,* soft/hard drug.
drogadicción *f* drug addiction.
drogadicto,-a *m,f* drug addict.
drogar(se) [7] *t* to drug. − **2** *p* to take drugs.
drogata *mf arg* junkie.
droguería *f* hardware and household goods shop.
dromedario *m* dromedary.
ducado *m* dukedom.
ducha *f* shower. ●*darse/tomar una* ~, to take/have a shower.
duchar(se) *t* to shower. − **2** *p* to take a shower.
dúctil *adj* ductile.
dudar *i* to be doubtful. **2** *(titubear)* to hesitate. − **3** *t* to doubt: *lo dudo,* I doubt it. ●~ *de algn.,* to suspect sb.
dudoso,-a *adj* doubtful, uncertain. **2** *(vacilante)* hesitant, undecided. **3** *(sospechoso)* suspicious, dubious.

duelo *m* duel. ●*batirse en* ~, to fight a duel.
duende *m* goblin, elf, gnome. **2** *(encanto)* charm: *es una chica con* ~, she's got charm.
dueño,-a *m,f* owner. **2** *(de casa, piso)* *m* landlord, *f* landlady.
dulce *adj* sweet. **2** *fig* soft, gentle. − **3** *m* CULIN sweet. **4** *(pastel)* cake. ■ *agua* ~, fresh water; ~ *de membrillo,* quince jelly.
dulcificar [1] *t* to sweeten. **2** *fig* to soften.
dulzura *f* sweetness. **2** *fig* softness, gentleness.
duna *f* dune.
dúo *m* duet.
duodécimo,-a *adj-m,f* twelfth.
dúplex *adj-m inv* duplex.
duplicado,-a *adj-m* duplicate.
duplicar(se) [1] *t gen* to duplicate; *(cantidad)* to double. − **2** *p* to double.
duplicidad *f* duplicity.
duque *m* duke.
duquesa *f* duchess.
duración *f* duration, length.
duradero,-a *adj* durable, lasting.
durante *adv* during, in, for: *viví allí* ~ *una año,* I lived there for a year.
durar *i* to last, go on: *la película duró tres horas,* the film went on for three hours.
durazno *m* AM peach.
dureza *f* hardness, toughness. **2** *fig (de carácter)* toughness, harshness. **3** MED corn.
durmiente *adj* sleeping. ■ *bella* ~, sleeping beauty.
duro,-a *adj* hard, tough. **2** *(difícil)* hard, difficult. **3** *(cruel)* tough, hardhearted. **4** *(resistente)* strong. − **5** *m* five-peseta coin. **6** *fam* tough guy. − **7** *adv* hard: *dale* ~, hit him/her hard. ●*fam lo que faltaba para el* ~, just what I/we needed!

E

e *conj* and. ▲ *Used instead y before words beginning with* **i** *or* **hi**.

ebanista *mf* cabinet-maker.

ébano *m* ebony.

ebrio,-a *adj* intoxicated, drunk.

ebullición *f* boiling. ■ *punto de* ~, boiling point.

eccema *m* eczema.

echar(se) *t (lanzar)* to throw. **2** *(del trabajo)* to sack, dismiss. **3** *(despedir de sí)* to throw out. **4** *(correo)* to post. **5** *(brotar)* to grow, sprout. **6** *(poner)* to put. **7** *(emanar)* to give out/off. **8** *fam (en el cine, teatro)* to show. − **9** *i-p* ~*(se) a* + *inf*, to begin to: ~*se a correr*, to run off. − **10** *p (lanzarse)* to throw o.s. **11** *(tenderse)* to lie down. ●~ *cuentas*, to reckon; ~ *de menos*, to miss; ~ *el pestillo/la llave*, to bolt/lock; ~ *en cara*, to blame; ~ *una mano*, to lend a hand; ~ *una mirada*, to have a quick look/glance; ~*(se) a perder*, to spoil.

echarpe *m* shawl.

ecléctico,-a *adj-m,f* eclectic.

eclesiástico,-a *adj* ecclesiastic(al). − **2** *m* clergyman.

eclipsar(se) *t* to eclipse. − **2** *p* to be eclipsed. **3** *fig (desaparecer)* to disappear.

eclipse *m* eclipse.

eco *m* echo. ●*fig tener* ~, to spread, be widely accepted. ■ *ecos de sociedad*, gossip column *sing*.

ecografía *f* scan.

ecología *f* ecology.

ecológico,-a *adj* ecological.

ecologista *adj* ecological. − **2** *mf* ecologist.

economato *m* company store.

economía *f (administración)* economy. **2** *(ciencia)* economics. **3** *pl* savings: *hacer economías*, to save up.

económico,-a *adj* economic. **2** *(barato)* cheap, economical.

economista *mf* economist.

economizar [4] *t* to economize, save.

ecosistema *m* ecosystem.

ecuación *f* equation.

ecuador *m* equator.

ecuánime *adj (temperamento)* calm, placid. **2** *(juicio, opinión)* fair, impartial.

ecuatorial *adj* equatorial.

ecuestre *adj* equestrian.

edad *f* age: *¿qué* ~ *tiene usted?*, how old are you? ■ ~ *media*, Middle Ages *pl*; *mayor/menor de* ~, of/under age.

edición *f* edition. **2** *(publicación)* publication.

edicto *m* edict.

edificación *f* building, construction.

edificar [1] *t* to build. **2** *fig* to edify, uplift.

edificio *m* building.

editar *t* to publish; *(discos)* to release.

editor,-ra *adj* publishing. − **2** *m,f* publisher.

editorial *adj* publishing. − **2** *m (artículo)* editorial, leading article. − **3** *f* publishing house.

edredón *m* eiderdown, continental quilt.

educación *f* education. **2** *(crianza)* upbringing. **3** *(cortesía)* manners *pl*, politeness.

educado,-a *adj* polite.

educar [1] *t* to educate, teach. **2** *(criar)* to bring up. **3** *(en la cortesía etc.)* to teach manners.

educativo,-a *adj* educational.

edulcorante *m* sweetener.

efectividad *f* effectiveness.

efectivo,-a *adj* real. − **2** *m (dinero)* cash. **3** *(de plantilla)* personnel. − **4** *efectivamente adv* quite!, yes indeed! ●*hacer algo* ~, to carry sth. out. ■ *dinero en* ~, cash.

efecto *m* effect. **2** *(impresión)* impression. **3** *(fin)* aim, object. **4** DEP spin: *dar ~ a la pelota,* to put some spin on the ball. **5** COM bill, draft. **6** *pl* personal belongings. ●*en ~,* in fact, indeed; *hacer ~,* to be impressive. ▪ *efectos especiales,* special effects.

efectuar(se) [1] *t* to carry out, make. – **2** *p (realizarse)* to be carried out; *(acto etc.)* to take place.

efeméride *m* anniversary. **2** *pl (en periódico etc.)* list of the day's anniversaries.

efervescencia *f* effervescence. **2** *fig* high spirits *pl.*

efervescente *adj* effervescent. **2** *fig* high-spirited.

eficacia *f* effectiveness, efficacy.

eficaz *adj* efficient.

eficiencia *f* efficiency.

eficiente *adj* efficient.

efigie *f* effigy.

efímero,-a *adj* ephemeral, brief.

efusión *f* effusion. **2** *fig* warmth.

efusivo,-a *adj* effusive, warm.

égloga *f* eclogue.

egocéntrico,-a *adj* egocentric, self-centred.

egoísmo *m* selfishness.

egoísta *adj-mf* selfish (person).

egolatría *f* self-worship.

eje *m* axis. **2** TÉC shaft, spindle. **3** AUTO axle.

ejecución *f (de una orden etc.)* carrying out, execution. **2** MÚS performance. **3** *(ajusticiamiento)* execution.

ejecutar *t (una orden etc.)* to carry out. **2** MÚS to perform. **3** *(ajusticiar)* to execute.

ejecutivo,-a *adj* executive. – **2** *m,f* board member, executive. – **3** *f* the executive.

ejemplar *adj* exemplary. – **2** *m (copia)* copy: *~ gratuito,* free copy. **3** *(prototipo)* specimen.

ejemplificar [1] *t* to illustrate, exemplify.

ejemplo *m* example. ●*dar ~,* to set an example; *por ~,* for instance.

ejercer [2] *t (profesión etc.)* to practise. **2** *(usar)* to exercise.

ejercicio *m* exercise. **2** FIN year.

ejercitar(se) *t* to practice. **2** *(enseñar)* to train. – **3** *p (aprender)* to train; MIL to exercise.

ejército *m* army.

el *art m sing* the. **2** *~ + de,* the one: *(posesivo) ~ de tu amigo,-a,* your friend's; *(lugar de origen) ~ de Valencia,* the one from Valencia. **3** *~ + que,* the one: *~ que vino ayer,* the one who came yesterday.

él *pron pers m sing (sujeto) (persona)* he: *~ vive,* he lives; *(cosa, animal)* it. **2** *(objeto) (persona)* him; *(cosa, animal)* it. **3** *(posesivo) de ~,* his: *es de ~,* it's his. ▲ *f ella; pl ellos.*

elaboración *f* manufacture, production.

elaborar *t* to make, manufacture.

elasticidad *f* elasticity.

elástico,-a *adj-m* elastic. **2** *pl* braces.

elección *f (nombramiento)* election. **2** *(opción)* choice. **3** *pl* elections. ▪ *elecciones generales,* general election *sing.*

electo,-a *adj* elect.

electorado *m* electorate, voters *pl.*

electoral *adj* electoral. ▪ *campaña ~,* election campaign; *colegio ~,* polling station.

electricidad *f* electricity.

electricista *mf* electrician.

eléctrico,-a *adj* electric(al).

electrizar [4] *t* to electrify. **2** *fig* to thrill, excite.

electrocardiograma *m* electrocardiogram.

electrocutar(se) *t* to electrocute. – **2** *p* to be electrocuted.

electrodoméstico *m* (home) electrical appliance.

electrónico,-a *adj* electronic. – **2** *f* electronics.

elefante *m* elephant.

elegancia *f* elegance, smartness.

elegante *adj* elegant, stylish.

elegía *f* elegy.

elegido,-a *adj* chosen. **2** POL elected.

elegir [55] *t* to chose. **2** POL to elect.

elemental *adj (del elemento)* elemental. **2** *(obvio)* elementary, obvious. **3** *(primordial)* essential.

elemento *m* element. **2** *(parte)* component, part. **3** *(individuo)* type, sort. **4** *pl (atmosféricos)* elements. **5** *pl (fundamentos)* rudiments. ●*fig estar uno en su ~,* to be in one's element.

elenco *m (catálogo)* index, catalogue. **2** TEAT cast.

elepé *m* LP (record).

elevación *f* elevation, rise.

elevado,-a *adj* elevated, raised. **2** *(alto)* tall, high; *(número)* high. **3** *fig* lofty, noble.

elevador,-ra *adj* elevating. – **2** *m* AM lift, US elevator.

elevar *t* to elevate, raise, lift. **2** *(matemáticas)* to raise.

elidir *t* to elide.
eliminación *f* elimination.
eliminar *t* to eliminate.
eliminatorio,-a *adj* eliminatory. – **2** *f* heat, qualifying round.
elite *f* elite.
elixir *m* elixir.
ella *pron pers f sing (sujeto)* she: ~ *vive,* she lives; *(cosa, animal)* it. **2** *(objeto)* her; *el coche de* ~, her car; *(cosa, animal)* it. **3** *(posesivo) de* ~, hers. ▲ *m* **él**; *pl* **ellas**.
ello *pron pers neut sing* it; *¡no se hable más de* ~!, (and) that's final!
ellos,-as *pron pers m,fpl (sujeto)* they. **2** *(complemento)* them. **3** *(posesivo) de* ~, theirs.
elocución *f* elocution.
elocuencia *f* eloquence.
elocuente *adj* eloquent.
elogiar [12] *t* to praise, eulogize.
elogio *m* praise, eulogy.
elucidar *t* to elucidate, explain.
eludir *t* to elude, avoid.
emanar *i* to emanate.
emancipación *f* emancipation.
emancipar(se) *t* to emancipate, free. – **2** *p* to become emancipated/free.
embadurnar *t* to daub, besmear.
embajada *f* embassy. **2** *(mensaje)* message.
embajador,-ra *m,f* ambassador.
embalaje *m* packing.
embalar(se) *t* to pack. – **2** *i-p* to speed up.
embaldosar *t* to tile.
embalsamar *t* to embalm.
embalsar *t* to dam up.
embalse *m* dam, reservoir.
embarazada *adj-f* pregnant (woman).
embarazar [4] *t (dejar preñada)* to make pregnant. **2** *(estorbar)* to hinder. **3** *(turbar)* to embarrass.
embarazo *m (preñez)* pregnancy. **2** *(obstáculo)* obstruction. **3** *(turbación)* embarrassment, constraint.
embarazoso,-a *adj* embarrassing.
embarcación *f* boat, craft.
embarcadero *m* pier, jetty, quay.
embarcar(se) [1] *t-p* to embark. ●*fig ~se en un asunto,* to get involved in an affair.
embargar [7] *t* JUR to seize. **2** *(emociones)* to overcome.
embargo *m* JUR seizure of property. **2** COM embargo. ●*sin* ~, nevertheless, however.
embarnizar [4] *t* to varnish.

embarque *m (de personas)* boarding; *(de mercancías)* loading. ■ *tarjeta de* ~, boarding card.
embarrado,-a *adj* muddy.
embarrancar(se) [1] *i-p* MAR to run aground. **2** *fig* to get bogged down.
embarullar(se) *t-p* to muddle, make a mess of.
embastar *t* to baste, tack.
embaucador,-ra *m,f* impostor.
embaucar [1] *t* to deceive.
embebecer(se) [43] *t* to delight. – **2** *p* to be delighted.
embeber(se) *t* to soak up. – **2** *p* to become absorbed.
embelesar *t* to charm, captivate.
embellecer [43] *t* to embellish.
embestida *f* onslaught.
embestir [34] *t* to assault. **2** *(atacar)* to attack *(contra, -)*.
emblema *m* emblem.
embocadura *f (de río)* mouth. **2** MÚS mouthpiece. **3** *(de vino)* taste, flavour.
émbolo *m* piston.
embolsar(se) *t-p* to pocket.
emborrachar(se) *t-p* to get drunk.
emboscada *f* ambush.
embotar(se) *t-p* to blunt. **2** *fig* to dull.
embotellado,-a *adj* bottled. – **2** *m* bottling.
embotellar *t* to bottle. **2** *fig* to stop, obstruct.
embozo *m* muffler, mask. **2** *fig* reserve.
embragar [7] *i* to engage the clutch.
embrague *m* clutch.
embravecer(se) [43] *t* to enrage. – **2** *p* to get enraged. **3** *(el mar)* to become rough.
embriagado,-a *adj* intoxicated, drunk.
embriagar(se) [7] *t-p* to get drunk.
embriaguez *f* drunkenness.
embrión *m* embryo.
embrollar(se) *t* to confuse, muddle. – **2** *p* to get confused/muddled.
embrollo *m (confusión)* muddle, mess. **2** *(mentira)* lie. **3** *fig* embarrassing situation.
embromar *t* to play jokes on. **2** AM to annoy.
embrujar *t* to haunt; *(a persona)* to bewitch.
embrujo *m* spell, charm. **2** *(fascinación)* attraction.
embrutecer(se) [43] *t* to make dull. – **2** *p* to become dull.
embudo *m* funnel. **2** *fig* trick.
embuste *m* lie, trick.

embustero,-a *adj* lying. — 2 *m,f* liar.

embutido *m* processed cold meat, cold cut.

emergencia *f (imprevisto)* emergency. 2 *(salida)* emergence.

emerger [5] *i* to emerge.

emigración *f* emigration.

emigrante *adj-mf* emigrant.

emigrar *i* to emigrate; *(aves)* to migrate.

eminencia *f* eminence. 2 *(elevación)* height.

eminente *adj* eminent. 2 *(elevado)* high.

emir *m* emir.

emirato *m* emirate.

emisario,-a *m,f* emissary.

emisión *f* emission. 2 FIN issue: ~ *de bonos,* bond issue. 3 RAD TV transmission, broadcast(ing).

emisor,-ra *adj* emitting. — 2 *m* radio transmitter. — 3 *f* broadcasting station. — 4 *m,f* emitter.

emitir *t* to emit. 2 FIN to issue. 3 RAD TV to broadcast.

emoción *f* emotion, feeling.

emocionante *adj* moving, touching.

emocionar(se) *t* to move, touch. — 2 *p* to be moved/touched.

emotivo,-a *adj* emotional.

empacar [1] *t* to pack. 2 AM to annoy.

empachar(se) *t (comer demasiado)* to give indigestion. 2 *(impedir)* to obstruct. — 3 *p* to have indigestion.

empacho *m (indigestión)* indigestion. 2 *(turbación)* embarrassment.

empadronar(se) *t-p* to register.

empalagar [7] *i (dulces)* to cloy. 2 *fig* to bother.

empalagoso,-a *adj (dulces)* cloying, oversweet. 2 *(persona)* smarmy.

empalizada *f* fence.

empalmar *t* to join. 2 *fig (planes etc.)* to combine. — 3 *i (enlazar)* to connect.

empalme *m* connection.

empanada *f* pie.

empanadilla *f* pasty.

empanado,-a *adj* breaded.

empañado,-a *adj (cristal)* steamed up. 2 *(voz)* faint.

empañar(se) *t (cristal)* to steam up. 2 *(bebés)* to put a nappy on. 3 *fig* to taint. — 4 *p (cristal)* to steam up. 5 *fig* to become tainted.

empapar(se) *t* to soak. — 2 *p* to get soaked.

empapelar *t (envolver)* to wrap up in paper. 2 *(una pared)* to paper.

empaque *m (de paquete)* packing. 2 *(de una persona)* presence.

empaquetar *t (paquetes, personas)* to pack. 2 *(castigar)* to punish.

emparedado,-a *adj* confined. — 2 *m* sandwich.

emparejar *t (cosas)* to match; *(personas)* to pair off. 2 *(nivelar)* to make level. — 3 *i (ser parejo)* to be even. 4 *(alcanzar)* to catch up.

emparentado,-a *adj* related by marriage *(con,* to).

emparentar [3] *i* to become related by marriage *(con,* to).

emparrado *m* vine arbour.

empastar *t* to fill.

empaste *m* filling.

empatar *t* to tie, draw; DEP to equalize: *estar empatados,-as,* to be equal.

empate *m* tie, draw.

empecinado,-a *adj* stubborn.

empedernido,-a *adj* confirmed, inveterate.

empedrado,-a *adj* cobbled. — 2 *m* cobblestones *pl.*

empedrar [27] *t* to cobble.

empeine *m (pubis)* groin. 2 *(pie, calzado)* instep.

empeñar(se) *t* to pawn. 2 *(palabra)* to pledge. — 3 *p (endeudarse)* to get into debt. 4 *(insistir)* to insist *(en,* on).

empeño *m (insistencia)* determination. 2 *(deuda)* pledge. ●*con* ~, eagerly; *tener* ~ *en,* to be eager to. ■ *casa de empeños,* pawn-shop.

empeorar(se) *i* to worsen. — 2 *t* to make worse. — 3 *p* to get worse.

empequeñecer [43] *t* to diminish, make smaller.

emperador *m* emperor.

emperatriz *f* empress.

emperejilarse, emperifollarse *p* to get dolled up.

empero *conj lit* yet, however.

empezar [47] *t-i* to begin, start.

empinado,-a *adj (alto)* very high. 2 *(inclinado)* steep. 3 *(orgulloso)* stiff.

empinar(se) *t* to raise, lift. — 2 *p (persona)* to stand on tiptoe; *(animal)* to rear. 3 *(alcanzar altura)* to tower. ●~ *el codo,* to drink heavily.

empírico,-a *adj* empiric(al). — 2 *m,f* empiricist.

emplazamiento *m* JUR summons. 2 *(localización)* location.

emplazar [4] *t (citar)* to call together; JUR to summons. 2 *(situar)* to locate, place.

empleado,-a *m,f* employee, clerk. ■ ~ **de hogar,** servant.

emplear *t* to employ. 2 *(dinero)* to spend. 3 *(tiempo)* to invest. *irón* ●*le está bien empleado,* it serves him/her right.

empleo *m* occupation, job. 2 *(uso)* use.

empobrecer(se) [43] *i* to impoverish. — 2 *p* to become poor.

empobrecimiento *m* impoverishment.

empollar *t (las gallinas)* to brood, hatch. 2 *fam* to swot (up).

empollón,-ona *fam pey adj* swotty. — 2 *m,f* swot.

empolvar(se) *t* to cover with dust. — 2 *p* to powder one's face.

emponzoñar *t* to poison. 2 *fig* to corrupt.

empotrar *t* to embed.

emprendedor,-ra *adj* enterprising.

emprender *t* to begin. ●~ *la marcha,* to start out; *fam* **emprenderla con algn.,** to pick on sb.

empresa *f (compañía)* firm, company. 2 *(acción)* enterprise, venture.

empresarial *adj* managerial.

empresario,-a *m,f* employer, manager. ■ ~ **de pompas fúnebres,** undertaker; ~ **de teatro,** impresario.

empréstito *m* loan.

empujar *t* to push. 2 *fig* to force.

empuje *m* push. 2 *(presión)* pressure. 3 *(energía)* energy, drive.

empujón *m* push, shove. ●*a empujones,* by fits and starts.

empuñar *t* to clutch, grasp.

emular *t* to emulate.

émulo,-a *adj-m,f* emulator.

en *prep (lugar, tiempo)* in, on, at: ~ *casa,* at home; ~ *Valencia,* in Valencia. 2 *(transporte)* by, in: *ir ~ coche/~ avión,* to go by car/to fly. 3 *(tema, materia)* at, in: *experto,-a ~ política,* expert in politics. ●~ *seguida,* at once, straight away. ↔ *enseguida.*

enaguas *fpl* petticoat *sing.*

enajenación *f,* **enajenamiento** *m* distraction. ■ ~ *mental,* insanity.

enajenar(se) *t (propiedad)* to alienate. 2 *(turbar)* to drive mad. — 3 *p (desposeerse)* to deprive o.s. (*de,* of). 4 *(de una amistad)* to alienate. 5 *(enloquecer)* to go mad.

enaltecer [43] *t* to praise.

enamorado,-a *adj* in love. — 2 *m,f* lover.

enamorar(se) *t* to win the heart of. — 2 *p* to fall in love (*de,* with).

enano,-a *adj-m,f* dwarf.

enarbolar(se) *t (izar)* to hoist. — 2 *p (caballo)* to rear up. 3 *(enojarse)* to get angry.

enardecer(se) [43] *t (excitar)* to excite. — 2 *p* to become excited.

enardecimiento *m* excitement, passion.

encabezamiento *m* heading. 2 *(en escritos)* headline.

encabezar [4] *t (en escrito)* to head. 2 *(ser líder)* to lead.

encabritarse *p* to rear up. 2 *(barco)* to rise; *(coche, avión)* to stall. 3 *fig (enojarse)* to get cross.

encadenamiento *m* TÉC chaining. 2 *(unión)* connection.

encadenar *t* to chain. 2 *(enlazar)* to connect, link up. 3 *fig (atar)* to tie down.

encajar(se) *t (ajustar)* to encase. 2 *(comentario etc.)* to get in. — 3 *p (vestido)* to slip into.

encaje *m* COST lace. 2 *(acto)* fit(ting).

encajonar(se) *t* to put in a box, encase. 2 *(en espacio)* to squeeze. — 3 *p (río)* to narrow.

encalar *t* to whitewash.

encallar *i* MAR to run aground. 2 *fig* to flounder, fail.

encalmarse *p (viento)* to drop. 2 *(animal)* to be overheated.

encaminar(se) *t (guiar, orientar)* to direct. — 2 *p (dirigirse)* to head (*a/hacia,* for/towards).

encandilar *t (deslumbrar)* to dazzle. 2 *(el fuego)* to stir. 3 *fig (fascinar)* to fascinate. 4 *fig (amor etc.)* to kindle.

encanecer(se) [43] *i-p (pelo)* to go grey. 2 *fig* to grow old.

encantado,-a *adj (contento)* pleased, delighted. 2 *(embrujado)* haunted. 3 *(distraído)* absent-minded. ●*fml* ~ *(de conocerlo/a),* pleased to meet you.

encantador,-ra *adj* enchanting, charming, delightful. — 2 *m,f m* enchanter, *f* enchantress.

encantamiento *m* spell, charm, enchantment.

encantar *t (hechizar)* to cast a spell on. 2 *fam (gustar)* to delight: *me encanta la natación,* I love swimming.

encanto *m (hechizo)* enchantment. 2 *pl (gracias)* charm *sing,* delight *sing.* 3 *fam* dear: *lo que tú digas,* ~, whatever you say, darling.

encapotado,-a *adj* overcast, cloudy.

encapotarse *p (persona)* to frown, look grim. 2 METEOR to become overcast/cloudy. ▲ 2 only used in the 3rd pers. It does not take a subject.

encapricharse *p* to take a fancy (*con*, to).

encapuchado,-a *adj* hooded.

encaramar(se) *t* to raise. **2** *fig (elogiar)* to praise. **3** *fig (elevar)* to promote. — **4** *p (subirse)* to climb up.

encarar(se) *t (afrontar)* to face, confront. **2** *(arma)* to point, aim. — **3** *i-p (cara a cara)* to face, confront. ●~*se con,* to face up to.

encarcelar *t* to imprison, jail.

encarecer [43] *t (precios)* to put up the price of. **2** *fig (elogiar)* to praise. **3** *fig (recomendar)* to urge, strongly recommend.

encargado,-a *adj* in charge. — **2** *m,f m* manager, *f* manageress.

encargar(se) [7] *t (encomendar)* to entrust. **2** *(recomendar)* to recommend. **3** COM *(solicitar)* to order. — **4** *p* to take charge *(de,* of).

encargo *m (recado)* errand; *(tarea)* job. **2** COM order, commission.

encariñado,-a *adj* attached *(con,* to).

encariñarse *p* to become fond *(con,* of).

encarnado,-a *adj* red. ●*ponerse ~,* to blush.

encarnar *i* REL to become incarnate. — **2** *t (personificar)* to embody. **3** TEAT to play.

encarnizado,-a *adj* bloody, fierce.

encarnizar(se) [4] *t* to make cruel, infuriate. — **2** *p* to be cruel *(con/en,* to). ●~*se con,* to attack savagely.

encarrilar *t* to direct, guide. **2** *(vehículo)* to put back on the rails.

encasillar *t (poner en casillas)* to pigeonhole. **2** *(clasificar)* to classify.

encausar *t* to prosecute.

encauzar [4] *t* to channel. **2** *fig* to direct, guide.

encenagado,-a *adj* muddy. **2** *fig (vicioso)* depraved.

encenagarse [7] *p* to get covered in mud. **2** *fig (en el vicio)* to wallow.

encendedor *m* lighter.

encender(se) [28] *t* to light, set fire to; *(cerilla)* to strike; *(vela)* to light. **2** *(luz, radio, tv)* to turn/switch on. **3** *fig (excitar)* to inflame. — **4** *p (incendiarse)* to catch fire. **5** *(luz)* to go/come on. **6** *fig (excitarse)* to flare up. **7** *(ruborizarse)* to blush.

encendido,-a *adj* glowing. **2** *(rostro)* red, flushed. — **3** *m* AUTO ignition.

encerado,-a *adj* waxed. — **2** *m* blackboard.

encerar *t* to wax.

encerrar(se) [27] *t* to shut in/up. **2** *fig (contener)* to contain. — **3** *p* to shut o.s. in/up; *(con llave)* to lock o.s. in. **4** *(recogerse)* to go into seclusion.

encestar *t* to put in a basket.

encharcado,-a *adj* flooded, swamped.

encharcar(se) [1] *t* to flood, swamp. — **2** *p* to swamp, get flooded.

enchufado,-a *m,f fam* wirepuller. ●*ser un/una ~,* to have good contacts; *(en la escuela)* teacher's pet.

enchufar(se) *t* ELEC to connect, plug in. **2** *fam fig* to pull strings for: *enchufó a su hija en su empresa,* he/she got his daughter a job in his/her company. — **3** *p fam fig* to get a sinecure.

enchufe *m* ELEC *(hembra)* socket; *(macho)* plug. **2** *fam fig (cargo)* sinecure, easy job; *(influencias)* contacts *pl.*

encía *f* gum.

enciclopedia *f* encyclop(a)edia.

encierro *m (toros)* bullpen. **2** *(prisión)* locking up. **3** *(protesta)* sit-in.

encima *adv* on top, above: *¿llevas cambio ~?,* do you have any change on you? **2** *(además)* in addition, besides. ●~ *de,* on, upon; *estar algn. ~ de otro,* to be on sb.'s back; *por ~, (a más altura)* above; *(de pasada)* superficially; *por ~ de,* over, above; *por ~ de todo,* above all; *fig quitarse algo/algn. de ~,* to get rid of sth./sb.

encina *f* evergreen oak.

encinta *adj* pregnant.

enclaustrar *t* to cloister.

enclavar *t (clavar)* to nail. **2** *(atravesar)* to pierce, transfix. **3** *(ubicar)* to locate.

enclave *m* enclave.

enclenque *adj (flaco)* skinny. — **2** *mf (débil)* weak person; *(enfermizo)* sickly person.

encoger(se) [5] *t (contraer)* to shrink, contract. — **2** *i-p (contraerse)* to contract; *(prenda)* to shrink. ●~*se de hombros,* to shrug one's shoulders.

encogido,-a *adj* awkward, shy.

encolar *t* to glue, stick.

encolerizar(se) [4] *t* to anger, irritate. — **2** *p* to get angry.

encomendar(se) [3] *t-p* to entrust (o.s.) *(a,* to).

encomienda *f* assignment.

enconado,-a *adj* MED inflamed. **2** *fig* angry.

enconarse *p* MED to become inflamed. **2** *fig* to get angry.

encontrar(se) [31] *t (hallar)* to find. **2** *(persona)* to come *(a,* across); *(chocar)* to bump (*a*, into). **3** *(creer)* to think: *no lo encuentro justo,* I don't think it's fair. — **4** *p (hallarse)* to be. **5** *(persona)* to meet. **6** *(sentirse)* to feel. ●~*se con,* to come across, meet up with.

encontrón, encontronazo *m* collision. **2** *(riña)* quarrel.

encopetado,-a *adj (presumido)* presumptuous, stuck-up. **2** *fig (de clase alta)* upper-class.

encordonar *t* to tie up with cord.

encorvado,-a *adj* bent.

encorvar(se) *t* to bend, curve. — **2** *p* to bend over.

encrespar(se) *t (pelo)* to curl, frizz. **2** *(enfurecer)* to infuriate. — **3** *p (pelo)* to stand on end. **4** *(enfurecerse)* to get cross.

encrucijada *f* crossroads *pl.* ●*fig estar en la ~,* to be at crisis point.

encrudecer(se) *i-p* [43] to get colder.

encuadernación *f* bookbinding. **2** *(cubierta)* binding.

encuadernador,-ra *m,f* bookbinder.

encuadernar *t* to bind.

encuadrar *t (cuadro)* to frame. **2** *fig* to fit into.

encubierto,-a *pp* → **encubrir**.

encubridor,-ra *m,f* accessory, abettor.

encubrir *t (ocultar)* to conceal, hide; *(a un criminal)* to shelter. ▲ *pp* **encubierto,-a**.

encuentro *m* meeting, encounter. **2** DEP match. **3** *(choque)* collision. ●*salir al ~ de algn.,* to go to meet sb.

encuesta *f* poll, survey. **2** *(pesquisa)* inquiry.

encumbrar(se) *t fig* to exalt, elevate. — **2** *p* to rise to a high position.

endeble *adj fml* feeble.

endémico,-a *adj* endemic; *fig* chronic.

endemoniado,-a *adj (diabólico)* diabolical. **2** *(poseso)* possessed.

enderezar(se) [4] *t (poner derecho)* to straighten out. **2** *(poner vertical)* to set upright. **3** *(guiar)* to direct, guide. — **4** *p* to straighten up.

endeudarse *p* to get into debt.

endiablado,-a *adj (maldito)* wretched. **2** *(perverso)* devilish. **3** *(feo)* ugly.

endibia *f* endive.

endilgar [7] *t fam (trabajo etc.)* to palm off onto. **2** *(golpe)* to land.

endiosar(se) *t* to deify. — **2** *p fig* to become haughty/proud.

endocrinología *f* endocrinology.

endomingado,-a *adj* in one's Sunday best.

endosar *t* to endorse.

endulzar [4] *t* to sweeten. **2** *fig (suavizar)* to alleviate, sof.en.

endurecer(se) [43] *t-p* to harden.

endurecimiento *m* hardening.

enemigo,-a *adj* enemy. — **2** *m,f* enemy.

enemistar(se) *t* to make enemies of. — **2** *p* to become enemies. ● ~*se con algn.,* to fall out with sb.

energía *f* energy. **2** *fig* vigour. ■ ~ *eléctrica,* electric power.

enérgico,-a *adj* energetic. **2** *fig* vigorous.

energúmeno,-a *m,f fam m* madman, *f* mad woman.

enero *m* January.

enervar(se) *t* to enervate. — **2** *p fam* to exasperate.

enésimo,-a *adj* nth. **2** *fam* umpteenth: *te lo digo por ~ vez,* this is the umpteenth time I've told you.

enfadado,-a *adj* angry, US mad.

enfadar(se) *t* to make angry. — **2** *p* to get angry *(con,* with).

enfado *m* anger, irritation.

enfadoso,-a *adj* annoying.

enfangar(se) [7] *t* to cover with mud. — **2** *p* to get muddy. **3** *fig* to get involved in dirty business.

énfasis *m & f inv* emphasis.

enfático,-a *adj* emphatic.

enfatizar [4] *t* to emphasize.

enfermar *i* to fall ill, be taken ill.

enfermedad *f* illness, disease.

enfermería *f* infirmary, sick bay.

enfermero,-a *m,f m* male nurse, *f* nurse.

enfermizo,-a *adj* sickly, unhealthy.

enfermo,-a *adj-m,f* sick (person).

enfervorizar [4] *t* to arouse fervour/passions.

enfilar *t (poner en fila)* to line up. **2** *(tomar dirección)* to make for: ~ *la calle,* to go down/along the street. **3** *(dirigir)* to direct.

enflaquecer(se) [43] *t (poner flaco)* to make thin. **2** *fig* to weaken. — **3** *i-p* to become thin.

enfocar [1] *t* to focus (on). **2** *(luz)* to shine a light on. **3** *fig (problema etc.)* to approach.

enfoque *m* focus(ing). **2** *fig* approach, point of view.

enfrascar(se) [1] *t* to bottle. — **2** *p (aplicarse)* to become absorbed *(en,* in).

enfrentamiento *m* confrontation.

enfrentar(se) *t (afrontar)* to face, confront. **2** *(encarar)* to bring face to face. — **3** *p (encararse)* to face (up) *(a,* to).

enfrente *adv* opposite, facing: *la casa de* ~, the house opposite.

enfriamiento *m* cooling. **2** MED cold, chill.

enfriar(se) [13] *t* to cool (down). **– 2** *p (lo caliente)* to cool down. **3** *(tener frío)* to get cold. **4** MED to get/catch a cold. **5** *fig* to cool off.

enfundar *t* to put in its case; *(espada)* to sheathe.

enfurecer(se) [43] *t* to infuriate, enrage. **– 2** *p* to get furious (*con/contra/por,* at). **3** *(el mar)* to become rough.

enfurruñarse *p fam* to get angry.

engalanar(se) *t* to adorn, deck out. **– 2** *p* to dress up.

enganchar(se) [43] *t* to hook. **2** *(animales)* to hitch. **3** *(vagones)* to couple. **4** *(a persona)* to attract. **– 5** *p* to get caught. **6** MIL to enlist. **7** *arg (a drogas)* to get hooked.

enganche *m* hook. **2** *(vagones)* coupling. **3** MIL enlistment.

engañabobos *mf inv fam* con man, trickster. **– 2** *m (trampa)* con trick.

engañar(se) *t* to deceive; *(al marido, a la esposa)* to be unfaithful to. **2** *(estafar)* to cheat. **3** *(mentir)* to lie to. **– 4** *p* to deceive o.s. **5** *(equivocarse)* to be wrong. ●*fig* ~ *el hambre,* to stave off hunger.

engaño *m* deceit. **2** *(estafa)* fraud. **3** *(mentira)* lie. **4** *(error)* mistake.

engarzar [4] *t (trabar)* to string. **2** *(joyas)* to link. **3** *fig (palabras, frases)* to string together.

engaste *m* setting, mounting.

engatusar *t fam* to cajole, coax.

engendrar *t* to engender, beget. **2** *fig* to generate, give rise to.

engendro *m* foetus. **2** *(ser informe)* malformed child. **3** *fig pey* monstrosity.

englobar *t* to include, comprise.

engolfarse *p* to get deeply absorbed (*en,* in).

engomar *t* to gum, glue.

engordar *t* to fatten. **– 2** *i (persona)* to put on weight. **3** *(alimento)* to be fattening.

engorro *m* bother, nuisance.

engorroso,-a *adj* bothersome, annoying.

engranaje *m* TÉC gears *pl,* gearing. **2** *fig* machinery.

engranar *i* TÉC to engage. **2** *fig (enlazar)* to connect, link.

engrandecer [43] *t* to increase, enlarge. **2** *fig (exaltar)* to elevate. **3** *fig (alabar)* to laud.

engrasar *t* to grease, oil, lubricate. **2** *fig (sobornar)* to bribe.

engreído,-a *adj* vain, conceited.

engreír(se) [37] *t* to make vain/conceited. **– 2** *p* to become vain/conceited.

engrosar [31] *t (hacer grueso)* to thicken. **2** *fig (aumentar)* to increase, enlarge. **– 3** *i (engordar)* to get fat.

engullir [41] *t* to gobble up.

enhebrar *t* to thread.

enhiesto,-a *adj* erect, upright.

enhorabuena *f* congratulations *pl.* **– 2** *adv* happily. ●*dar la* ~ *a,* to congratulate.

enigma *m* enigma, puzzle.

enigmático,-a *adj* enigmatic(al).

enjabonar *t* to soap. **2** *fig* to soft-soap.

enjambre *m* swarm.

enjaular *t* to cage. **2** *fam* to put inside/in jail.

enjoyar *t* to adorn with jewels.

enjuagar(se) [7] *t-p* to rinse.

enjuague *m* rinse. **2** *(líquido)* mouthwash. **3** *fig* scheme, plot.

enjuiciar [12] *t* to judge. **2** JUR *(causa)* to sue; *(criminal)* to indict, prosecute.

enjuto,-a *adj* thin, skinny.

enlace *m (conexión)* link, connection. **2** *(boda)* marriage. **3** *(intermediario)* liaison. ■ ~ *sindical,* shop steward, US union delegate.

enladrillar *t* to pave with bricks.

enlatar *t* to can, tin.

enlazar [4] *t (unir)* to link, connect. **– 2** *i (trenes etc.)* to connect.

enloquecedor,-ra *adj* maddening.

enloquecer(se) [43] *i (volverse loco)* to go mad. **2** *fam (gustar)* to be mad/wild about. **– 3** *t (volver loco)* to drive mad. **– 4** *p* to go mad.

enlosar *t* to pave (with tiles).

enlutado,-a *adj* (in) mourning.

enmarañar(se) *t (enredar)* to tangle. **2** *fig* to embroil, muddle up. **– 3** *p* to get tangled. **4** *fig* to get embroiled. **5** METEOR to become overcast.

enmascarar(se) *t* to mask, disguise. **– 2** *p* to put on a mask.

enmendar(se) [27] *t* to correct; *(daño)* to repair. **2** JUR to amend. **– 3** *p* to reform, mend one's ways.

enmienda *f* correction; *(de daño)* repair. **2** JUR amendment.

enmohecerse [43] *p* to go mouldy.

enmoquetar *t* to carpet.

enmudecer [43] *i* to become dumb.

ennegrecer(se) [43] *t* to blacken, darken. – **2** *p* to blacken.

ennoblecer(se) [43] *t* to ennoble. **2** *fig* (*dignificar*) to dignify. – **3** *p* to become noble.

enojado,-a *adj* angry, cross.

enojar(se) *t* to anger, annoy. – **2** *p* to get angry/cross.

enojo *m* anger, annoyance, irritation.

enojoso,-a *adj* annoying, irritating.

enorgullecer(se) [43] *t* to fill with pride. – **2** *p* to be/feel proud. ●~*se de algo,* to pride o.s. on sth.

enorme *adj* enormous, huge.

enormidad *f* enormity. **2** (*desatino*) nonsense.

enrabiar(se) [12] *t* to enrage, infuriate. – **2** *p* to get enraged/infuriated.

enraizar(se) [24] *i-p* BOT to take root. **2** *fig* (*persona*) to put down roots.

enrarecer(se) [43] *t* to rarefy. – **2** *i-p* to become scarce.

enredadera *f* creeper.

enredar(se) *t* (*prender*) to catch in a net. **2** (*para cazar*) to set. **3** (*enmarañar*) to tangle up, entangle. **4** *fig* (*engatusar*) to involve (*en,* in). – **5** *i* (*travesear*) to be mischievous. – **6** *p* (*hacerse un lío*) to get tangled up. **7** (*complicarse*) to get complicated/confused; (*en discusión*) to get caught up. **8** (*amancebarse*) to have an affair.

enredo *m* (*maraña*) tangle. **2** (*engaño*) deceit. **3** (*confusión*) mix-up, mess. **4** (*amoroso*) love affair. **5** *pl* (*trastos*) bits and pieces.

enrejado *m* railings *pl.* **2** (*celosía*) trellis.

enrejar *t* (*puerta, ventana*) to put a grating on. **2** (*vallar*) to fence.

enrevesado,-a *adj* complicated, difficult.

enriquecer(se) [43] *t* (*hacer rico*) to make rich. **2** *fig* to enrich. – **3** *p* to become rich.

enrojecer(se) [43] *t* (*volver rojo*) to redden; (*metal*) to make red-hot. – **2** *p* (*ruborizarse*) to go red, blush. **3** (*volverse rojo*) to turn red; (*metal*) to get red-hot.

enrollado,-a *adj* rolled up. **2** *fam* great: *una tía muy enrollada,* a great woman. ●*fam estar* ~ *con algn.,* to be deep in conversation with sb.; (*salir juntos*) to go out with sb.

enrollar(se) *t* to roll up. – **2** *p fam* (*hablar*) to go on and on.

enroscar(se) [1] *t* to coil; (*cable*) to twist. **2** (*tornillo*) to screw. – **3** *p* to coil; (*cable*) to roll up; (*serpiente*) to coil itself.

ensaimada *f type of* pastry.

ensalada *f* salad.

ensaladera *f* salad bowl.

ensaladilla *f* ~ *rusa,* Russian salad.

ensalmo *m* spell.

ensalzar [4] *t* (*enaltecer*) to exalt. **2** (*elogiar*) to praise, extol.

ensambladura *f* joint.

ensamblaje *m* assembly.

ensamblar *t* to join, assemble.

ensanchamiento *m* widening, broadening.

ensanchar *t* to widen, enlarge; COST to let out. – **2** *p fig* (*envanecerse*) to become conceited.

ensanche *m* widening, enlargement. **2** (*de ciudad*) urban development.

ensangrentado,-a *adj* bloodstained, bloody.

ensangrentar(se) [27] *t* to stain with blood. – **2** *p* to be covered with blood.

ensañar(se) *t* to enrage. – **2** *p* to be cruel (*con,* to).

ensartar *t* to string together. **2** *fig* to reel off.

ensayar *t* TEAT to rehearse; MÚS to practise. **2** (*probar*) to try out, test.

ensayo *m* TEAT rehearsal; MÚS practise. **2** (*prueba*) test, experiment. **3** (*literario*) essay. ■ ~ *general,* dress rehearsal.

enseguida *adv* at once, straight away. ▲ Also **en seguida**.

ensenada *f* cove, inlet.

enseñanza *f* education, teaching. ■ ~ *primaria/secundaria/superior,* primary/secondary/higher education.

enseñar *t* (*en escuela etc.*) to teach. **2** (*educar*) to educate. **3** (*mostrar*) to show. ●*fig* ~ *los dientes,* to bare one's teeth.

enseres *mpl* belongings, goods.

ensillar *t* to saddle (up).

ensimismarse *p* (*absorberse*) to become engrossed. **2** (*abstraerse*) to become lost in thought.

ensoberbecer(se) [43] *t* to make arrogant. – **2** *p* to become arrogant. **3** MAR to get rough.

ensombrecer(se) [43] *t* to cast a shadow over. – **2** *p* to darken.

ensordecedor,-ra *adj* deafening.

ensordecer [43] *t* to deafen. – **2** *i* to go deaf.

ensortijarse *p* to curl.

ensuciar(se) [12] *t* to dirty. **2** *fig* (*reputación etc.*) to damage. – **3** *p* to get dirty.

ensueño *m* daydream, fantasy.

entablar *t (poner tablas)* to plank, board. **2** *(conversación)* to begin, start; *(amistad)* to strike up. ■ ~ *acción/demanda,* to take legal action.

entallar *t (esculpir)* to carve. **2** COST to take in at the waist: *una camisa entallada,* a fitted shirt.

entarimado *m* parquet floor.

ente *m* being. **2** *(institución)* entity, body.

enteco,-a *adj* weak, puny.

entendederas *fpl fam* brains.

entender(se) [28] *m* understanding, opinion. — **2** *t (comprender)* to understand. **3** *(discurrir)* to think. **4** *(oír)* to hear. — **5** *i* to be an expert *(en/de,* in). — **6** *p (conocerse)* to know what one is doing. **7** *fam (llevarse bien)* to get along well together. **8** *fam (relación amorosa)* to have an affair. ●*dar a ~ que ...,* to imply that ...; *fam no entiendo ni jota,* I don't understand a word of it.

entendido,-a *m,f* expert.

entendimiento *m* understanding, comprehension.

enterado,-a *adj* knowledgeable, well-informed. — **2** *m,f fam* expert.

enterar(se) *t* to inform *(de,* about/of); *(poner al corriente)* to acquaint *(de,* with). — **2** *p* to find out *(de,* about).

entereza *f* entirety. **2** *fig (de carácter etc.)* integrity.

enternecedor,-ra *adj* moving, touching.

enternecer(se) [43] *t (ablandar)* to soften. **2** *(conmover)* to move, touch. — **3** *p* to be moved/touched.

entero,-a *adj (completo)* entire, whole. **2** *fig (de carácter etc.)* firm. **3** *(robusto)* robust. — **4** *m* FIN point.

enterrador *m* gravedigger.

enterrar(se) [27] *t* to bury. **2** *fig (olvidar)* to forget. — **3** *p fig* to bury o.s.

entibiar [12] *t* to cool, make lukewarm.

entidad *f* entity. ●*de ~,* important.

entierro *m* burial. **2** *(ceremonia)* funeral.

entoldado *m* awning. **2** *(para fiestas etc.)* marquee.

entonación *f* intonation.

entonar *t (nota)* to pitch; *(canción)* to sing. **2** *(el organismo)* to tone up. **3** *(colores)* to be in harmony.

entonces *adv* then. ●*por (aquel) ~,* at that time.

entontecer(se) [43] *i* to befuddle. — **2** *p* to become confused.

entornar *t (ojos)* to half-close. **2** *(puerta)* to leave ajar.

entorpecer [43] *t* to make numb/dull. **2** *fig* to obstruct.

entorpecimiento *m* dullness. **2** *fig* obstruction.

entrada *f* entrance, entry. **2** *(ingreso)* ticket, admission. **3** *(pago inicial)* down payment. **4** *(en libro cuentas)* entry. **5** INFORM input. **6** *pl (cabellos)* receding hairline *sing.* ●*"prohibida la ~",* "no admittance".

entrante *adj* entering, coming: *el mes ~,* next month. — **2** *m* CULIN starter.

entrañable *adj* beloved.

entrañas *fpl* ANAT entrails. **2** *fig* heart *sing.* ●*no tener ~,* to be heartless.

entrar(se) *i* to come/go in. **2** *(en una sociedad etc.)* to join *(en, -)*. **3** *(encajar)* to fit. **4** *(empezar) (año, estación)* to begin; *(período)* to enter. **5** *(venir)* to come over: *me entró dolor de cabeza,* I got a headache. — **6** *p* to get in. ●*fam fig entrado,-a en edad/en años,* well on in years; *fam fig no me entra en la cabeza,* I can't believe it.

entre *prep (dos términos)* between; *(más de dos términos)* among(st). **2** *(sumando)* counting: ~ *niños y adultos somos doce,* there are twelve of us all together. ●*de ~,* among; ~ *tanto,* meanwhile.

entreabrir *t (ojos)* to half open. **2** *(puerta etc.)* to leave ajar. ▲ *pp* **entreabierto,-a**.

entreacto *m* interval.

entrecejo *m* space between the eyebrows; *(ceño)* frown.

entrecot, entrecó *m* fillet steak.

entredicho *m* prohibition, ban.

entredós *m* COST insertion. **2** *(mueble)* cabinet. ▲ *pl* **entredoses**.

entrega *f* handing over; COM delivery. **2** *(de posesiones)* surrender. **3** *(libros etc.)* instalment. **4** *fig (devoción)* selflessness. ■ ~ *contra reembolso,* cash on delivery.

entregar(se) [7] *t* to hand over; *(deberes etc.)* to hand in; COM to deliver. **2** *(posesiones)* to surrender. — **3** *p (rendirse)* to give in, surrender. **4** *(dedicarse)* to devote o.s. *(a,* to).

entrelazar [4] *t* to entwine, interweave.

entremés *m* CULIN hors d'oeuvres. **2** TEAT interlude.

entremeter(se) *t* to insert, place between. — **2** *p* → **entrometerse**.

entrenador,-ra *m,f* trainer, coach.

entrenamiento *m* training.

entrenar(se) *t-p* to train.

entreoír [75] *t* to hear vaguely.

entrepierna *f* crotch.

entresacar [1] *t* to select.

entresuelo *m* mezzanine; GB first floor, US second floor.

entretanto *adv* meanwhile.

entretejer *t* to interweave, intertwine.

entretela *f* interfacing, interlining. **2** *pl fam* heart *sing*, entrails.

entretener(se) [87] *t (retrasar)* to delay, detain. **2** *(divertir)* to entertain, amuse. — **3** *p (retrasarse)* to be delayed. **4** *(divertirse)* to amuse o.s., keep o.s. occupied.

entretenido,-a *adj (divertido)* entertaining, amusing. **2** *(complicado)* time-consuming.

entretenimiento *m* entertainment, amusement.

entretiempo *m* period between seasons.

entrever [91] *t* to glimpse. **2** *(conjeturar)* to guess. ▲ *pp* **entrevisto,-a.**

entrevista *f (prensa)* interview. **2** *(reunión)* meeting.

entrevistar(se) *t* to interview. — **2** *p* to have an interview/meeting *(con,* with).

entrevisto,-a *pp* → **entrever.**

entristecer(se) [43] *t* to sadden. — **2** *p* to be sad *(por,* about).

entrometerse *p* to meddle, interfere *(en,* in).

entrometido,-a *adj* interfering, nosy. — **2** *m,f* meddler, busybody.

entromparse *p fam* to get sloshed.

entronizar [4] *t* to enthrone. **2** *fig* to worship.

entuerto *m* wrong, injustice.

entumecer(se) [43] *t* to numb. — **2** *p* to go numb/dead. **3** *(mar, río)* to swell.

entumecimiento *m* numbness. **2** *(mar, río)* swelling.

enturbiar(se) [12] *t* to make muddy. **2** *fig* to cloud, muddle. — **3** *p* to get muddy. **4** *fig* to get confused/muddled.

entusiasmar(se) *t* to captivate, excite. — **2** *p* to get enthusiastic *(con,* about).

entusiasmo *m* enthusiasm. ●*con* ~, keenly, enthusiastically.

entusiasta *mf* lover, fan *(de,* of).

enumerar *t* to enumerate, count.

enunciado *m* enunciation. **2** LING statement.

enunciar [12] *t* to enounce, state.

envainar *t* to sheathe.

envalentonar(se) *t* to make bold/daring. — **2** *p* to become bold/daring.

envanecer(se) [43] *t* to make vain. — **2** *p* to get conceited/vain.

envasar *t (paquetes)* to pack; *(botellas)* to bottle; *(latas)* to can, tin. ●~ *al vacío,* to vacuum-pack.

envase *m (acto)* packing; *(botellas)* bottling; *(latas)* canning. **2** *(recipiente)* container. ■ ~ *sin retorno,* nonreturnable container.

envejecer [43] *t* to age. — **2** *i* to grow old.

envejecido,-a *adj* aged, old-looking.

envenenamiento *m* poisoning.

envenenar *t* to poison.

envergadura *f (de pájaro)* spread. **2** *(de avión)* span. **3** *fig* importance.

envés *m (de página)* back. **2** *(de tela)* wrong side. **3** BOT reverse.

enviado,-a *m,f* messenger, envoy. ■ *(prensa)* ~ *especial,* special correspondent.

enviar [13] *t* to send; COM to dispatch; *(por barco)* to ship.

enviciar(se) [12] *t* to corrupt, vitiate. — **2** *p* to become addicted.

envidia *f* envy. ●*tener* ~ *de,* to envy.

envidiable *adj* enviable.

envidiar [12] *t* to envy.

envidioso,-a *adj* envious.

envilecer(se) [43] *t* to debase, degrade. — **2** *i* to lose value. — **3** *p* to degrade o.s.

envío *m* sending; COM dispatch, shipment. **2** *(remesa)* consignment; *(paquete)* parcel. ■ ~ *contra reembolso,* cash on delivery; *gastos de* ~, postage and packing.

enviudar *i (hombre)* to become a widower; *(mujer)* to become a widow.

envoltorio *m (de caramelo etc.)* wrapper. **2** *(lío)* bundle.

envoltura *f* wrapping.

envolver(se) [32] *t (cubrir)* to cover; *(con papel)* to wrap (up). **2** *fig (implicar)* to involve. — **3** *p* to wrap o.s. up *(en,* in). **4** *fig (implicarse)* to become involved *(en,* in). ▲ *pp* **envuelto,-a.**

enyesar *t* to plaster. **2** MED to put in plaster.

enzarzar(se) [4] *t fig* to sow discord. — **2** *p fig* to squabble: ~ *en una discusión,* to get into an argument.

épico,-a *adj* epic, heroic. — **2** *f* epic poetry.

epidemia *f* epidemic.

epidémico,-a *adj* epidemic.

epidermis *f inv* epidermis, skin.

epifanía *f* Epiphany, Twelfth Night.

epígrafe *m (cita)* epigraph. **2** *(título)* title, heading.

epilepsia *f* epilepsy.

epílogo *m* epilogue. **2** *(resumen)* summary.

episcopado *m* *(obispos)* episcopacy. **2** *(lugar)* bishopric.

episodio *m* *(literario)* episode. **2** *(suceso)* incident.

epístola *f* epistle, letter.

epitafio *m* epitaph.

epíteto *m* epithet.

epítome *m* abstract, summary.

época *f* time, age. **2** HIST period, epoch. **3** AGR season. •*por aquella* ~, about that time.

epopeya *f* epic poem.

equidad *f* equity, justice, fairness.

equidistar *i* to be equidistant *(de,* from).

equilibrado,-a *adj* balanced. **2** *(persona)* sensible.

equilibrar(se) *t-p* to balance.

equilibrio *m* balance. •*perder el* ~, to lose one's balance.

equilibrista *mf* tightrope walker, trapeze artist. **2** AM POL opportunist.

equino,-a *adj* equine, horse.

equinoccio *m* equinox.

equipaje *m* luggage, baggage. **2** *(instrumental)* equipment, outfit. **3** MAR crew. •*hacer el* ~, to pack, do the packing.

equipar(se) *t* to equip. — **2** *p* to kit o.s. out.

equiparar *t* to compare, liken *(con,* to).

equipo *m* *(prestaciones)* equipment. **2** *(ropas, utensilios)* outfit, kit. **3** *(de personas)* team. ■ ~ *de alta fidelidad,* hi-fi stereo system; ~ *de salvamento,* rescue team.

equitación *f* horsemanship, horse riding.

equitativo,-a *adj* equitable, fair.

equivalente *adj-m* equivalent.

equivaler [89] *i* *(ser igual)* to be equivalent/equal *(a,* to). **2** *(significar)* to be tantamount *(a,* to).

equivocación *f* mistake, error.

equivocado,-a *adj* mistaken, wrong. — **2** *equivocadamente adv* by mistake.

equivocar(se) [1] *t* to mistake. — **2** *p* to be mistaken/wrong; *(de dirección, camino etc.)* to go wrong.

equívoco,-a *adj* equivocal, ambiguous. — **2** *m* equivocation, ambiguity.

era *f* era, age. **2** AGR threshing floor. **3** *(cuadro de jardín)* bed, plot. — **4** *imperf indic* → **ser**.

erección *f* erection. **2** *(institución)* foundation, establishment.

erecto,-a *adj* erect.

eremita *m* hermit.

eres *pres indic* → **ser**.

erguir(se) [70] *t* to raise (up straight), erect. — **2** *p* *(ponerse derecho)* to straighten up. **3** *(engreírse)* to swell with pride.

erigir(se) [6] *t* to erect, build. **2** *(instituir)* to establish. — **3** *p* to establish o.s.

erizado,-a *adj* bristly, prickly.

erizar(se) [4] *t* to make stand on end. — **2** *p* to stand on end.

erizo *m* hedgehog. ■ ~ *marino/de mar,* sea urchin.

ermita *f* hermitage.

ermitaño,-a *m,f* hermit. — **2** *m* ZOOL hermit crab.

erógeno,-a *adj* erogenous.

erosión *f* erosion, wearing away. **2** *fig* wear and tear.

erosionar *t* to erode. **2** *(gastar)* to wear away.

erótico,-a *adj* erotic.

erotismo *m* eroticism.

erradicar [1] *t* to eradicate; *(enfermedad)* to stamp out.

errado,-a *adj* mistaken.

errante *adj* errant, wandering.

errar [57] *t* *(objetivo)* to miss, get wrong. — **2** *i* *(vagar)* to wander, rove. **3** *(divagar)* to be mistaken.

errata *f* erratum, misprint. ■ *fe de erratas,* errata *pl.*

erróneo,-a *adj* erroneous, wrong.

error *m* error, mistake.

eructar *i* to belch, burp.

eructo *m* belch, burp.

erudición *f* erudition, learning.

erudito,-a *adj* erudite, learned. — **2** *m,f* scholar.

erupción *f* *(volcánica)* eruption. **2** *(cutánea)* rash.

es *pres indic* → **ser**.

esbeltez *f* slenderness. **2** *(elegancia)* gracefulness.

esbelto,-a *adj* slim, slender. **2** *(elegante)* graceful.

esbozar [4] *t* to sketch, outline.

esbozo *m* sketch, outline.

escabechar *t* to pickle. **2** *fig (el cabello)* to dye. **3** *fam (matar)* to do in. **4** *fam (suspender)* to fail.

escabeche *m* pickle: *sardinas en* ~, pickled sardines.

escabechina *f* massacre, slaughter.

escabroso,-a *adj* *(desigual)* uneven. **2** *fig (áspero)* harsh, rude. **3** *(indecente)* indecent.

escabullirse [13] *p* *(deslizarse)* to slip through. **2** *(persona)* to slip away.

escacharrar(se) *fam t-p* to break. – **2** *p* to be ruined.

escala *f (escalera)* ladder, stepladder. **2** *(graduación)* scale. **3** MAR port of call; AV stopover. ●*a gran* ~, on a large scale; *hacer* ~, to stop over *(en,* in). ■ ~ *móvil,* sliding scale; ~ *musical,* scale.

escalada *f* climb(ing). ●*fig la* ~ *del terrorismo,* the rise of terrorism.

escalador,-ra *m,f* climber.

escalafón *m (según graduación)* ladder; *(según salarios)* salary/wage scale.

escalar *t* to climb, scale.

escaldado,-a *adj* scalded. **2** *fig* wary, cautious. ●*salir* ~, to get one's fingers burnt.

escaldar(se) *t* to scald. – **2** *p* to get scalded.

escalera *f* stair, staircase. **2** *(escala)* ladder. **3** *(naipes)* run, sequence. ■ ~ *de caracol,* spiral staircase; ~ *mecánica/ automática,* escalator.

escalerilla *f* MAR gangway; AV boarding ramp.

escalfar *t* to poach: *huevos escalfados,* poached eggs.

escalinata *f* stoop.

escalofriante *adj* chilling, blood-curdling.

escalofrío *m (de frío)* shiver; *(de miedo)* shudder; *(de fiebre)* chill.

escalón *m (peldaño)* step. **2** *fig* degree. **3** MIL echelon.

escalope *m* escalope.

escama *f* scale. **2** *(de jabón)* flake.

escamar(se) *t* to scale. **2** *fig* to make suspicious. – **3** *p* to become suspicious.

escamotear *t* to whisk away. **2** *fam (robar)* to lift, pinch.

escamoteo *m* sleight of hand. **2** *fam (robo)* pilfering.

escampar *t* to clear out. – **2** *i* METEOR to stop raining, clear up.

escandalizar(se) [4] *t* to scandalize, shock. – **2** *i* to make a racket. – **3** *p* to be shocked *(de/por,* at).

escándalo *m* scandal. **2** *(alboroto)* racket. ●*armar un* ~, to kick up a fuss.

escandaloso,-a *adj* scandalous. **2** *(alborotado)* noisy.

escaño *m* bench. **2** POL seat.

escapada *f fam* quick trip. **2** DEP breakaway.

escapar(se) *i-p* to escape, flee, run away. – **2** *p (gas etc.)* to leak (out). **3** *(autobús etc.)* to miss. ●*fig escapársele a uno algo,* to go unnoticed; *fam ~se por un pelo,* to have a narrow escape.

escaparate *m* shop window. **2** AM *(armario)* wardrobe.

escapatoria *f* escape. **2** *(excusa)* excuse. ●*no hay* ~, there is no way out.

escape *m* escape, flight. **2** *(de gas etc.)* leak(age). **3** *(tubo de)* ~, exhaust pipe.

escaquearse *p fam* to shirk, skive off.

escarabajo *m* beetle.

escaramuza *f* skirmish. **2** *(riña)* dispute.

escarbar *t (suelo)* to scratch. **2** *(dientes, orejas)* to clean out. **3** *(fuego)* to poke. **4** *fig (inquirir)* to inquire into.

escarceo *m* small wave. **2** *(prueba)* attempt. **3** *pl (del caballo)* prancing *sing.*

escarcha *f* rime, frost.

escarchar *i* METEOR to be frosty/freezing. – **2** *t* CULIN to ice; *(frutas)* to crystallize. ▲ *1 used in the 3rd person only. It does not take a subject.*

escarlata *adj-m* scarlet.

escarlatina *f* scarlatina, scarlet fever.

escarmentar(se) [27] *t* to punish. – **2** *i-p* to learn one's lesson: *para que escarmientes,* that'll teach you a lesson.

escarmiento *m* punishment, lesson.

escarnecer [43] *t* to scoff at, mock.

escarnio *m* derision, mockery.

escarola *f* curly endive, US escarole.

escarpado,-a *adj (inclinado)* steep. **2** *(abrupto)* rugged.

escasear *i* to be/get scarce. – **2** *t* to be sparing with.

escasez *f* scarcity, lack, shortage.

escaso,-a *adj* scarce, scant: *andar ~ de dinero,* to be short of money. **2** *(mezquino)* miserly.

escatimar *t* to stint, skime on.

escatología *f* REL eschatology. **2** *(de excrementos)* scatology.

escena *f fig* scene. **2** TEAT stage. ●*poner en* ~, to stage.

escenario *m* stage. **2** *fig* scene.

escenografía *m* set.

escepticismo *m* scepticism.

escéptico,-a *adj* sceptical. – **2** *m,f* sceptic.

escindir(se) *t* to split, divide. – **2** *p* to split (off).

escisión *f* split, division.

esclarecer [43] *t* to light up. **2** *fig* to clear up, make clear. – **3** *i (amanecer)* to dawn.

esclavitud *f* slavery, servitude.

esclavizar [4] *t* to enslave.

esclavo,-a *m,f* slave. ●*ser ~ de algo,* to be a slave to sth.

esclusa *f* lock, sluicegate.

escoba *f* brush, broom.
escobilla *f* small brush. **2** AUTO windscreen wiper blade.
escocedura *f* chafe, soreness.
escocer(se) [54] *i* to smart, sting. **2** *fig* to hurt. − **3** *p (dolerse)* to hurt, be sore.
escoger [5] *t* to choose, select. ●~ *del montón,* to choose from the pile.
escogido,-a *adj* chosen, selected.
escolar *adj* school, scholastic. − **2** *mf m* schoolboy, *f* schoolgirl.
escolástico,-a *adj* scholastic.
escollera *f* breakwater.
escollo *m* MAR reef, rock. **2** *fig* difficulty.
escolta *f* escort. **2** MAR convoy.
escoltar *t* to escort. **2** MAR to convoy.
escombros *mpl (de derribo etc.)* rubble *sing.*
esconder(se) *t* to hide, conceal. − **2** *p* to hide *(de,* from).
escondite *m* hiding place. ●*jugar al ~,* to play hide-and-seek.
escondrijo *m* hiding place.
escopeta *f* shotgun. ■ ~ *de aire comprimido,* airgun.
escoplo *m* chisel.
escora *f (puntal)* loadline. **2** *(inclinación)* list.
escorbuto *m* scurvy.
escoria *f* slag, dross. **2** *fig* dregs *pl.*
escorpión *m* scorpion. **2** *Escorpión,* ASTROL ASTRON Scorpio.
escotado,-a *adj* low-necked.
escotar *t* COST to cut a low neckline in. **2** *(gastos)* to share.
escote *m* low neckline. **2** *(parte a pagar)* share.
escotilla *f* hatchway.
escotillón *m* TEAT trapdoor. **2** MAR small hatch.
escozor *m* irritation, smarting. **2** *fig* pain, grief.
escribano *m* notary. **2** *(pájaro)* bunting.
escribiente *m* (office) clerk.
escribir(se) *t-i* to write. **2** *(deletrear)* to spell. − **3** *p* to hold correspondence, write to each other. ▲ *pp escrito,-a.*
escrito,-a *pp* → **escribir.** − **2** *adj* written, stated. − **3** *m* writing, document. ●*por ~,* in writing.
escritor,-ra *m,f* writer.
escritorio *m* writing desk. **2** *(oficina)* office. ■ *objetos de ~,* stationery.
escritura *f* writing. ■ ~ *de propiedad,* title deed; *Sagradas Escrituras,* Holy Scriptures.
escrúpulo *m (recelo)* scruple, doubt. **2** *(aprensión)* fussiness.

escrupuloso,-a *adj* scrupulous. **2** *(aprensivo)* finicky.
escrutar *t* to scrutinize. **2** *(votos)* to count.
escrutinio *m (examen)* scrutiny, examination. **2** *(de votos)* count.
escuadra *f (instrumento)* square. **2** MIL squad.
escuadrilla *f* squadron.
escuadrón *m* squadron.
escucha *f* listening. ●*estar a la ~ de,* to listen out for. ■ *escuchas telefónicas,* phone tapping *sing.*
escuchar(se) *t (oír)* to hear. **2** *(atender)* to listen to. − **3** *p* to speak in an affected way.
escudería *f* racing team.
escudero *m* squire, page.
escudilla *f* bowl.
escudo *m* shield. ■ ~ *de armas,* coat of arms.
escuela *f* school. ■ ~ *privada,* private school; ~ *pública,* state school.
escueto,-a *adj* bare, plain, strict. − **2** *escuetamente adv* simply.
esculpir *t* to sculpt; *(madera)* to carve.
escultor,-ra *m,f m* sculptor, *f* sculptress.
escultura *f* sculpture.
escupidera *f* spittoon.
escupir *i* to spit. − **2** *t* to spit out. **3** *fam fig (confesar)* to come clean. ●~ *a algn.,* to scoff at sb.
escurreplatos *m inv* plate rack.
escurridizo,-a *adj* slippery. ■ *lazo ~,* slipknot.
escurridor *m* strainer, colander. **2** *(de platos)* dish rack.
escurrir(se) *t (platos)* to drain; *(ropa)* to wring out; *(comida)* to strain. − **2** *i* to drip. **3** *(deslizar)* to slip. − **4** *p (escapar) fam* to run/slip away. **5** *(decir demasiado)* to let sth. slip.
ese,-a *adj m,f* that: ~ *coche,* that car. ▲ *pl esos,-as.*
ése,-a *pron m,f* that one: *toma ~,* take that one. ▲ *pl ésos,-as.*
esencia *f* essence. ■ *quinta ~,* quintessence.
esencial *adj* essential.
esfera *f* sphere. **2** *(de reloj)* dial.
esférico,-a *adj* spherical.
esfinge *f* sphinx.
esforzado,-a *adj* energetic.
esforzar(se) [50] *t (fortalecer)* to strengthen. − **2** *p* to try hard, strive.
esfuerzo *m* effort. **2** *(valor)* courage.

esfumarse *p* to fade away. **2** *fam (largarse)* to disappear.

esgrima *f* fencing.

esgrimir *t (arma)* to wield, brandish. **2** *fig (un argumento)* to put forward.

esguince *m* MED sprain. **2** *(gesto)* swerve. **3** *(gesto de disgusto)* frown.

eslabón *m* link. ■ *el ~ perdido,* the missing link.

eslip *m (ropa interior)* men's briefs *pl,* underpants *pl.* **2** *(bañador)* trunks *pl.* ▲ *pl eslips.*

eslogan *m* slogan. ▲ *pl eslóganes.*

eslora *f* length.

esmaltado,-a *adj* enamelled. − **2** *m* enamelling.

esmaltar *t* to enamel.

esmalte *m* enamel. ■ *~ de uñas,* nail polish/varnish.

esmerado,-a *adj* careful.

esmeralda *f* emerald.

esmerar(se) *t* to polish. − **2** *p* to take great care *(en,* over).

esmeril *m* emery.

esmero *m* great care.

esmoquin *f* dinner jacket. ▲ *pl esmóquines.*

esnifar *t arg* to sniff.

esnob *mf* snob. ▲ *pl esnobs.*

esnobismo *m* snobbery, snobbishness.

eso *pron neut* that. ●*(hora) a ~ de las ...,* around ...; *¡~ es!,* that's it!

esófago *m* oesophagus.

esos,-as *adj m,f pl* those.

ésos,-as *pron m,f pl* those ones.

esotérico,-a *adj* esoteric.

espabilarse *p* to wake up.

espaciar(se) [12] *t* to space. − **2** *p* to spread o.s.

espacio *m* space: *necesitamos más ~,* we need more room. **2** *(de tiempo)* length. ■ *~ televisivo/radiofónico,* TV/radio programme.

espacioso,-a *adj* spacious, roomy.

espada *f* sword. **2** *(naipe)* spade. ●*fig entre la ~ y la pared,* between the devil and the deep blue sea.

espadachín *m* swordsman. **2** *pey (presuntuoso)* bully.

espadaña *f* bell gable.

espaguetis *mpl* spaghetti *sing.*

espalda *f* ANAT back, shoulders *pl.* **2** *(natación)* backstroke. ●*de espaldas,* backwards; *fig a espaldas de,* behind one's back; *fig dar la ~a,* to turn one's back on.

espaldar *m (de silla)* back. **2** *(para plantas)* trellis.

espantada *f* stampede.

espantajo, espantapájaros *m* scarecrow. ▲ *espantapájaros* is inv.

espantar(se) *t (asustar)* to frighten, scare. **2** *(ahuyentar)* to frighten away. − **3** *p* to get/feel frightened.

espanto *m (miedo)* fright, dread. **2** *(asombro)* astonishment.

espantoso,-a *adj (terrible)* frightful, dreadful. **2** *(asombroso)* astonishing.

españolada *f pey* something pseudo-Spanish.

esparadrapo *m* sticking plaster.

esparcimiento *m* scattering. **2** *(recreo)* amusement.

esparcir(se) [3] *t (separar)* to scatter. **2** *(divulgar)* to spread. **3** *(divertir)* to recreate. − **4** *p* to amuse o.s.

espárrago *m* asparagus. ■ *~ triguero,* wild asparagus.

esparto *m* esparto grass.

espasmo *m* spasm.

espasmódico,-a *adj* spasmodic.

espátula *f* spatula.

especia *f* spice.

especial *adj* special. ●*en ~,* especially.

especialidad *f* speciality.

especialista *adj-mf* specialist.

especialización *f* specialization.

especializar(se) [4] *i-p* to specialize *(en,* in).

especie *f (de animales, plantas)* species. **2** *(tipo)* kind, sort. **3** *(tema)* matter, notion.

especificar [1] *t* to specify.

específico,-a *adj* specific. − **2** *m* patent medicine.

espécimen *m* specimen. ▲ *pl especímenes.*

espectacular *adj* spectacular.

espectáculo *m* spectacle. **2** *(de TV, radio etc.)* performance. **3** *(escándalo)* scandal. ●*irón dar/montar un ~,* to make a scene.

espectador,-ra *m,f* DEP spectator; TEAT CINEM member of the audience; TV viewer.

espectro *m* FÍS spectre. **2** *(fantasma)* spectrum.

especulación *f* speculation.

especulador,-ra *m,f* speculator.

especular *t (reflexionar)* to speculate about. − **2** *i (comerciar)* to speculate *(en,* on). **3** *(conjeturar)* to guess *(sobre,* about).

espejismo *m* mirage.

espejo *m* mirror.

espeleología *f* potholing, speleology.

espeluznante *adj* hair-raising, terrifying.

espera *f* wait(ing). **2** *(paciencia)* patience. ●*en ~ de ...,* waiting for ... . ■ *sala de ~,* waiting-room.

esperanza *f* hope. ■ *~ de vida,* life expectancy.

esperanzador,-ra *adj* encouraging.

esperar *t (confiar)* to hope for, expect: *espero que sí,* I hope so; *espero ganar la carrera,* I hope to win the race. **2** *(aguardar)* to wait for, await: *espera un momento,* wait a moment.

esperma *m* sperm.

espermatozoide *m* spermatozoid.

esperpento *m (cosa fea)* fright, sight. **2** *(absurdo)* absurdity.

espesar(se) *t-p* to thicken.

espeso,-a *adj* thick, dense.

espesor *m* thickness, density.

espesura *f* thickness. **2** *(bosque)* thicket, dense wood.

espía *mf* spy.

espiar [13] *t* to spy.

espiga *f* spike; *(de trigo)* ear. **2** *(clavija)* peg.

espigar(se) [7] *t* to glean. – **2** *p* to shoot up.

espigón *m* breakwater, jetty. **2** *(punta)* sharp point.

espina *f (de planta)* thorn. **2** *(de pez)* fishbone. **3** *fig* scruple, suspicion. ●*dar mala ~,* to arouse one's suspicion. ■ *~ (dorsal),* spinal column, spine, backbone.

espinacas *fpl* spinachs.

espinazo *m* spine, backbone.

espinilla *f* shinbone. **2** *(grano)* blackhead.

espinoso,-a *adj (planta)* thorny. **2** *(pez)* spiny. **3** *fig* arduous, difficult.

espionaje *m* spying, espionage.

espiral *adj-f* spiral.

espirar *t-i* to exhale, breathe out.

espiritismo *m* spiritualism.

espiritista *mf* spiritualist.

espíritu *m* spirit; *(alma)* soul. **2** *(fantasma)* ghost. **3** *(licores)* spirits *pl*. ■ *el Espíritu Santo,* the Holy Ghost.

espiritual *adj* spiritual.

espléndido,-a *adj* splendid, magnificent. **2** *(liberal)* lavish.

esplendor *m fig* splendour. **2** *(resplandor)* radiance.

esplendoroso,-a *adj* splendid, radiant.

espliego *m* lavender.

espolvorear *t* to powder.

esponja *f* sponge.

esponjar(se) *t* to make spongy. – **2** *p (envanecerse)* to swell with pride. **3** *(físicamente)* to glow with health.

esponjoso,-a *adj* spongy.

esponsales *mpl fml* betrothal *sing*.

espontaneidad *f* spontaneity.

espontáneo,-a *adj (cosa)* spontaneous. **2** *(persona)* natural, unaffected. – **3** *m,f* spectator who spontaneously joins in.

esporádico,-a *adj* sporadic.

esposar *t* to handcuff.

esposas *fpl* handcuffs.

esposo,-a *m,f* spouse; *m* husband, *f* wife. **2** *pl* husband and wife.

espuela *f* spur.

espulgar [7] *t* to delouse. **2** *fig (examinar)* to examine closely.

espuma *f* foam; *(de jabón)* lather; *(de cerveza)* froth, head; *(olas)* surf. **2** *(impurezas)* scum. ■ *~ de afeitar,* shaving foam.

espumadera *f* spoon for skimming.

espumoso,-a *adj* foamy, frothy; *(jabón)* lathery; *(vino)* sparkling.

esputo *m* sputum, spit.

esqueje *m* cutting.

esquela *f (carta)* short letter. ■ *~ mortuoria,* announcement of a death.

esquelético,-a *adj* skeletal. **2** *fam (delgado)* skinny.

esqueleto *m* skeleton. **2** ARQ framework. ●*fam mover el ~,* to shake it about.

esquema *m (plan)* outline; *(gráfica)* diagram.

esquematizar [4] *t* to outline.

esquí *m (tabla)* ski. **2** *(deporte)* skiing. ■ *~ acuático,* water-skiing. ▲ *pl esquís*.

esquiador,-ra *m,f* skier.

esquiar [13] *i* to ski.

esquila *f* small bell.

esquilar *t* to clip; *(ovejas)* to shear.

esquimal *adj-mf* Eskimo.

esquina *f* corner. ●*doblar la ~,* to turn the corner.

esquinazo *m dar ~ a algn.,* to give sb. the slip.

esquirol *m* blackleg, scab.

esquivar *t (persona)* to avoid, shun. **2** *(golpe)* to dodge.

esquivez *f* coldness, aloofness.

esquivo,-a *adj* cold, aloof.

esquizofrenia *f* schizophrenia.

esquizofrénico,-a *adj* schizophrenic.

esta *adj* → **este,-a**.

está *pres indic* → **estar**.

ésta *pron* → **éste,-a**.
estabilidad *f* stability.
estabilizar(se) [4] *t* to stabilize, make stable/steady. – 2 *p* to become stable.
estable *adj* stable, steady.
establecer(se) [43] *t* to establish. 2 *(ordenar)* to state, decree. – 3 *p* to settle; *(un negocio)* to set up in business.
establecimiento *m (acto)* establishment, founding. 2 *(edificio)* establishment, shop, store. 3 JUR statute.
establo *m* stable.
estaca *f (palo con punta)* stake, picket. 2 *(garrote)* stick, cudgel.
estacada *f* fence. 2 MIL stockade. ●*dejar a algn. en la* ~, to leave sb. in the lurch.
estación *f (del año)* season. 2 *(de tren)* station. ■ ~ *balnearia*, spa, ~ *de esquí*, ski resort; ~ *de servicio*, service station.
estacionar(se) *t* to station. – 2 *p (estancarse)* to be stationary. 3 AUTO to park.
estadio *m* stadium. 2 *(fase)* stage, phase.
estadista *mf m* statesman, *f* stateswoman. 2 MAT statistician.
estadística *f (ciencia)* statistics: *una* ~, a figure/statistic.
estado *m (situación)* state, condition: *su* ~ *es grave*, his condition is serious. 2 *(en orden social)* status. 3 POL state. 4 *(resumen)* return, summary. ●*estar en* ~, to be pregnant. ■ ~ *civil*, marital status; MIL ~ *mayor*, staff.
estafa *f* fraud.
estafador,-ra *m,f* racketeer, swindler.
estafar *t* to swindle.
estafeta *f* post-office branch.
estalactita *f* stalactite.
estallar *i* to explode. 2 *(rebelión, epidemia)* to break out.
estallido *m* explosion. 2 *fig* outbreak.
estambre *m* COST worsted, woolen yarn. 2 BOT stamen.
estamento *m* class, stratum.
estampa *f (imagen)* picture. 2 *fig* appearance. 3 *(impresión)* print.
estampado,-a *adj* stamped; *(vestido)* printed. – 2 *m (tela)* print.
estampar *t (imprimir)* to print. 2 *(metales)* to stamp. 3 *(dejar huella)* to engrave. 4 *fam (arrojar)* to hurl.
estampida *f* stampede.
estampido *m* bang.
estampilla *f* (rubber) stamp. 2 AM postage stamp.
estancar(se) [1] *t* to hold up. – 2 *p* to stagnate.

estancia *f (permanencia)* stay. 2 *(aposento)* room. 3 AM farm.
estanco *m* tobacconist's (shop).
estándar *adj* standard(ized). – 2 *m* standard. ▲ *pl* **estándares**.
estandarizar [4] *t* to standardize.
estandarte *m* standard, banner.
estanque *m* pool, pond. 2 *(para proveer agua)* reservoir.
estanquero,-a *m,f* tobacconist.
estante *m* shelf; *(para libros)* bookcase.
estantería *f* shelving, shelves *pl*.
estaño *m* tin.
estar(se) [71] *i* to be: *está de profesor pero es ingeniero*, he works as a teacher but he's an engineer; *estamos a dos de noviembre*, it's the second of November. – 2 *aux* ~ + *gerundio*, to be: ~ *comiendo*, to be eating. – 3 *p (permanecer)* to spend. ●*está bien*, it's all right; ~ *al caer*, to be just round the corner; ~ *de más*, not to be needed; ~ *por hacer*, to remain to be done; *estarle bien a uno*, to be becoming to sb.; *no* ~ *para bromas*, not to be in the mood for jokes; *fam* ~ *a matar*, to be at daggers drawn; *fam estoy que no puedo más*, I can't take anymore. ▲ *When followed by an adjective it expresses a quality neither permanent nor inherent: Pilar está resfriada. If it is followed by a noun it always takes a preposition: está sin trabajo*.
estás *pres indic* → **estar**.
estatal *adj* state.
estático,-a *adj* static.
estatua *f* statue.
estatura *f* stature, height.
estatuto *m* statute.
este,-a *adj m,f* this: ~ *libro*, this book. – 2 *m* east. ▲ *pl 1 estos,-as*.
éste,-a *pron m,f* this one. ●*éste ... aquél ...*, the former ... the latter ... . ▲ *pl éstos,-as*.
esté *pres subj* → **estar**.
estela *f* MAR wake; AV vapour trail. 2 *fig* trail.
estelar *adj (sideral)* stellar. 2 *fig* star: *la figura* ~, the star.
estepa *f* steppe.
estercolar *t* to dung, manure.
estercolero *m* dunghill, manure.
estéreo *m* stereo.
estereofónico,-a *adj* stereo(phonic).
estereotipado,-a *adj* stereotyped, standard.
estéril *adj* sterile.
esterilidad *f* sterility.

esterilizar [4] *t* to sterilize.

esterilla *f* small mat.

esterlina *adj* **libra** ~, sterling pound.

esternón *m* sternum, breastbone.

esteticista *mf* beautician.

estético,-a *adj* aesthetic. **– 2** *f* aesthetics.

estetoscopio *m* stethoscope.

estevado,-a *adj* bow-legged.

estibar *t* to stow.

estiércol *m* dung, manure.

estigma *m* stigma.

estilarse *p* to be fashionable.

estilete *m* (*punzón*) stylus. **2** (*cuchillo*) stiletto.

estilista *mf* stylist.

estilizar [4] *t* to stylize.

estilo *m* style. ●*algo por el* ~, something like that. **2** GRAM speech. **3** (*natación*) stroke.

estilográfica *f* fountain pen.

estima *f* esteem.

estimación *f* esteem.

estimado,-a *adj* (*apreciado*) esteemed. **2** (*valorado*) valued. ●(*en carta*) ~ **señor/ señora,** Dear Sir/Madam.

estimar *t* (*apreciar*) to esteem; (*objeto*) to value. **2** (*juzgar*) to consider.

estimulante *adj* stimulating. **– 2** *m* stimulant.

estimular *t* to stimulate. **2** *fig* to encourage.

estímulo *m* stimulus. **2** *fig* encouragement.

estío *m* *fml* summer.

estipendio *m* stipend, fee.

estipulación *f* stipulation.

estipular *t* to stipulate.

estirado,-a *adj* stretched; (*brazo etc.*) stretched out; (*pelo*) straight. **2** *fig* stiff, conceited.

estirar(se) *t* to stretch, pull out. **– 2** *i* (*crecer*) to shoot up. **– 3** *p* (*desperezarse*) to stretch. ●*fam* ~ **las piernas,** to stretch one's legs; *fam* ~ **la pata,** to kick the bucket.

estirpe *f* stock, lineage.

estival *adj* summer.

esto *pron neut* this. ●~ *de ...*, the business about ... .

estocada *f* stab, thrust.

estofa *f* class: **gente de baja** ~, low-class people.

estofado,-a *adj* stewed. **– 2** *m* stew.

estofar *t* to stew.

estoico,-a *adj-m,f* stoic.

estomacal *adj* (of the) stomach. **– 2** *m* digestive liqueur.

estómago *m* stomach.

estopa *f* (*fibra*) tow. **2** (*tela*) burlap.

estoque *m* sword.

estorbar *t* (*dificultar*) to hinder, obstruct. **2** (*molestar*) to annoy.

estorbo *m* (*obstáculo*) obstruction. **2** (*molestia*) hindrance; (*persona*) nuisance.

estornudar *i* to sneeze.

estornudo *m* sneeze.

estos,-as *adj m,f pl* these.

éstos,-as *pron m,f pl* these (ones). ●*fam* **en éstas,** just then.

estoy *pres indic* → **estar.**

estrado *m* dais, platform. **2** *pl* law courts.

estrafalario,-a *adj fam* eccentric.

estrago *m* havoc, ruin, ravage. ●*hacer estragos en,* to play havoc with/on.

estragón *m* tarragon.

estrambótico,-a *adj fam* outlandish.

estrangular *t* to strangle.

estraperlista *mf* black marketeer.

estraperlo *m* black market.

estratagema *f* MIL stratagem. **2** *fig* trick.

estrategia *f* strategy.

estratégico,-a *adj* strategic.

estrato *m* stratum.

estraza *f* rag. ■ **papel de** ~, brown paper.

estrechar(se) *t* to narrow; (*vestido*) to take in. **2** (*abrazar*) to embrace. **3** *fig* (*obligar*) to compel. **– 4** *p* (*apretarse*) to squeeze. **5** *fig* (*gastos etc.*) to economize. ●~ *la mano,* to shake hands (*de,* with); *fig* ~ *los lazos de amistad,* to tighten the bond of friendship.

estrechez *f* narrowness; (*vestido, zapatos*) tightness. **2** *fig* (*económica*) want, need. **3** *fig* (*rigidez*) strictness. **4** *fig* (*apuro*) tight spot. ■ ~ *de miras,* narrow-mindedness.

estrecho,-a *adj* narrow; (*vestido, zapatos*) tight. **2** *fig* (*amistad etc.*) close. **3** *fig* (*mezquino*) mean. **4** *fig* (*estricto*) narrow. **– 5** *m* GEOG straits *pl*: ~ *de Gibraltar,* Straits of Gibraltar.

estregar [48] *t* (*con paño*) to rub; (*con cepillo*) to scrub.

estrella *f* star. ●*fig* **tener buena/mala** ~, to be lucky/unlucky; *fig* **ver las estrellas,** to see stars. ■ ~ *de cine,* film star; ~ *de mar,* starfish; ~ *fugaz,* shooting star.

estrellado,-a *adj* (*cielo*) starry, star-spangled. **2** (*forma*) star-shaped. **3** (*hecho pedazos*) smashed.

estrellar(se) *t* to cover with stars. **2** *fam (hacer pedazos)* to smash (to pieces), shatter. − **3** *p* to smash, shatter. **4** *(chocar)* to crash (*contra/en,* into).

estremecer(se) [43] *t* to shake. **2** *fig (asustar)* to startle, frighten. − **3** *p (de miedo, frío)* to tremble.

estremecimiento *m* shake, shudder; *(de miedo, frío)* shiver, trembling.

estrenar(se) *t* to use/wear for the first time. **2** TEAT to perform for the first time; CINEM to release. − **3** *p* to make one's debut.

estreno *m (de algo)* first use. **2** *(persona)* debut. **3** TEAT first performance; CINEM new release, première.

estreñimiento *m* constipation.

estreñir(se) [36] *t* to constipate. − **2** *p* to become constipated.

estrépito *m* din, noise.

estrepitoso,-a *adj* noisy. **2** *(éxito)* resounding.

estrés *m* stress. ▲ *pl* **estreses**.

estría *f (ranura)* groove. **2** ARQ flute. **3** *(en la piel)* stretch mark.

estriar(se) *t (hacer ranuras)* to groove. **2** ARQ to flute. − **3** *p* to be grooved/fluted.

estribación *f* spur, counterfort.

estribar *i (apoyarse)* to rest (*en,* on). **2** *fig (basarse)* to lie (*en,* in).

estribillo *m* refrain. **2** *(muletilla)* pet phrase.

estribo *m* stirrup. **2** *(de carruaje)* step. **3** AUTO running board, footboard. **4** ARQ buttress. ●*perder los estribos,* to lose one's head.

estribor *m* starboard.

estricto,-a *adj* strict, severe.

estridente *adj* strident, shrill.

estrofa *f* strophe, stanza.

estropajo *m* scourer.

estropear(se) *t (máquina)* to damage. **2** *(plan etc.)* to spoil, ruin. − **3** *p (máquina)* to break down. **4** *(plan, etc.)* to fail.

estropicio *m (rotura)* breakage. **2** *(jaleo)* fuss.

estructura *f* structure.

estructurar *t* to structure, organize.

estruendo *m (ruido)* great noise, din. **2** *(confusión)* uproar.

estrujar *t* to squeeze. **2** *fig (sacar partido)* to drain.

estuario *m* estuary.

estuche *m* case, box

estudiante *mf* student.

estudiar [12] *t-i* to study.

estudio *m* study: *estar en ~,* to be under consideration. **2** *(apartamento)* studio (flat). **3** *pl (conocimientos)* studies, education *sing:* **hacer/realizar sus estudios,** to study. **4** *pl* CINEM studio *sing.*

estudioso,-a *adj* studious.

estufa *f* heater.

estupefacto,-a *adj* astounded, dumbfounded.

estupendo,-a *adj* marvellous, wonderful. − **2** *interj* great!, super!

estupidez *f* stupidity.

estúpido,-a *adj* stupid, silly. − **2** *m,f* berk, idiot.

estupor *m* stupor, amazement, astonishment.

esvástica *f* swastika.

etapa *f* period, stage. **2** DEP leg, stage.

etarra *adj* (of) ETA. − **2** *mf* member of ETA.

etcétera *f* etcetera, and so on.

éter *m* ether. **2** *(celestial)* ether, heavens *pl.* ▲ *pl* **éteres**.

etéreo,-a *adj* ethereal.

eternidad *f* eternity. **2** *fam* ages *pl:* **tardaste una ~,** you took ages.

eternizar(se) [4] *t* to etern(al)ize. **2** *fam* to prolong endlessly. − **3** *p* to be interminable.

eterno,-a *adj* eternal, everlasting.

ético,-a *adj* ethical. − **2** *f* ethics.

etimología *f* etymology.

etiqueta *f (rótulo)* label. **2** *(formalidad)* etiquette, formality. ■ *traje de ~,* evening/formal dress.

etiquetar *t* to label, put a label on.

étnico,-a *adj* ethnic.

eucalipto *m* eucalyptus.

eucaristía *f* Eucharist.

eufemismo *m* euphemism.

euforia *f* euphoria, elation.

eufórico,-a *adj* euphoric, elated.

eunuco *m* eunuch.

evacuación *f* evacuation.

evacuar [10] *t (lugar)* to evacuate. **2** ANAT to empty.

evadir(se) *t (peligro etc.)* to avoid. **2** *(capital)* to evade. − **3** *p (escaparse)* to escape.

evaluar [11] *t* to evaluate, assess.

evangélico,-a *adj* evangelic(al).

evangelio *m* gospel.

evaporación *f* evaporation.

evaporar(se) *t-p* to evaporate.

evasión *f (fuga)* escape. **2** *fig* evasion. ■ *~ fiscal/de impuestos,* tax evasion.

evasivo,-a *adj* evasive. − **2** *f* evasive answer: *contestar con una* ~, not to give a straight answer.

eventual *adj (casual)* chance. **2** *(trabajo)* casual, temporary. − **3** *mf* casual/temporary worker. − **4** *eventualmente adv* by chance.

eventualidad *f* eventuality, contingency.

evidencia *f* obviousness. ●*poner a algn. en* ~, to make a fool of sb.

evidenciar [12] *t* to show, make evident, prove.

evidente *adj* evident, obvious.

evitar *t* to avoid.

evocación *f* evocation, recollection.

evocar [1] *t* to evoke, call up. **2** *(a espíritu)* to invoke.

evolución *f* evolution.

evolucionar *i* to evolve.

exabrupto *m* sharp comment, sudden outburst.

exacerbar(se) *t (agravar)* to exacerbate. **2** *(enfadar)* to exasperate, irritate. − **3** *p (agravarse)* to become exacerbated. **4** *(enfadarse)* to feel exasperated.

exactitud *f* exactness, accuracy.

exacto,-a *adj* exact, accurate. − **2** *interj* precisely! − **3** *exactamente adv* exactly, precisely.

exageración *f* exaggeration.

exagerado,-a *adj* exaggerated. **2** *pey (excesivo)* excessive.

exagerar *t* to exaggerate. **2** *pey (exceder)* to overdo.

exaltación *f* exaltation.

exaltado,-a *adj* exalted. **2** *(excitado)* hotheaded.

exaltar(se) *t (ascender)* to raise. **2** *(alabar)* to exalt, praise. − **3** *p (excitarse)* to get overexcited.

examen *m* examination. **2** *(estudio)* inquiry, investigation. ●*presentarse a un* ~, to take/sit an exam. ■ ~ *de conciencia,* soul searching; ~ *de conducir,* driving test; ~ *médico,* checkup. ▲ *pl* *exámenes.*

examinador,-ra *adj* examining. − **2** *m,f* examiner.

examinar(se) *t* to examine. **2** *(considerar)* to look into, consider. − **3** *p* to take/sit an examination.

exánime *adj fml* lifeless.

exasperación *f* exasperation.

exasperar(se) *t* to exasperate. − **2** *p* to get exasperated.

excavación *f* excavation, digging. **2** *(arqueológica)* dig.

excavador,-ra *adj* excavator, digger. − **2** *f* digger.

excavar *t* to excavate, dig.

excedencia *f* leave (of absence).

exceder(se) *t* to exceed, surpass. − **2** *i-p* to go too far: ~ *en sus funciones,* to exceed one's authority.

excelencia *f* excellence. ●*por* ~, par excellence; *Su Excelencia,* Your Excellency.

excelente *adj* excellent.

excelso,-a *adj* lofty, sublime.

excentricidad *f* eccentricity.

excéntrico,-a *adj* eccentric.

excepción *f* exception. ●*a/con* ~ *de,* with the exception of, except for; *de* ~, exceptional. ■ POL *estado de* ~, state of emergency.

excepcional *adj* exceptional.

excepto *adv* except (for), apart from.

exceptuar [11] *t* to except, leave out.

excesivo,-a *adj* excessive.

exceso *m* excess; COM surplus. ●*con* ~, too much; *en* ~, in excess, excessively.

excitación *f (acción)* excitation. **2** *(sentimiento)* excitement.

excitante *adj* exciting. **2** MED stimulating. − **3** *m* stimulant.

excitar(se) *t* to excite. **2** *(emociones)* to stir up. − **3** *p* to get excited.

exclamación *f* exclamation; *(grito)* cry. ■ *(signo de)* ~, exclamation mark.

exclamar *t-i* to exclaim, cry out.

exclamativo,-a, exclamatorio,-a *adj* exclamatory.

excluir [62] *t* to exclude, shut out.

exclusión *f* exclusion.

exclusive *adv* exclusive(ly).

exclusivo,-a *adj* exclusive. − **2** *f* COM sole right. **3** *(prensa)* exclusive. − **4** *exclusivamente adv* exclusively.

excombatiente *adj-m* ex-serviceman, US veteran.

excomulgar [7] *t* to excommunicate.

excomunión *f* excommunication.

excremento *m* excrement.

exculpar *t* to exonerate; JUR to acquit.

excursión *f* excursion, trip. ●*ir de* ~, to go on an excursion/a trip.

excursionismo *m* hiking.

excursionista *mf* tripper; *(a pie)* hiker.

excusa *f* excuse.

excusado,-a *adj (de pagar)* exempt. **2** *(reservado)* private. − **3** *m* toilet.

excusar(se) *t* to excuse. **2** *(evitar)* to avoid. **3** *(eximir)* to exempt (*de*, from). — **4** *p* to apologize, excuse o.s.

exento,-a *pp* → **eximir**. — **2** *adj* free (*de*, from). **3** JUR exempt.

exequias *fpl* obsequies, funeral rites.

exfoliar [12] *t* to exfoliate.

exhalación *f* exhalation. **2** *(estrella)* shooting star.

exhalar(se) *t* *(gases, vapores, etc.)* to exhale. **2** *fig* *(suspiros)* to heave. — **3** *p fig* *(persona)* to rush.

exhaustivo,-a *adj* exhaustive, thorough.

exhausto,-a *adj* exhausted.

exhibición *f* *(exposición)* exhibition. **2** CINEM showing.

exhibicionista *mf* exhibitionist.

exhibir(se) *t* to exhibit, show. **2** JUR to produce. — **3** *p* to show off.

exhortar *t* to exhort.

exigencia *f* demand. **2** *(requisito)* requirement.

exigente *adj* demanding, exacting.

exigir [6] *t* *(a algn.)* to demand; *(cosa)* to require.

exil(i)ado,-a *adj* exiled, in exile. — **2** *m,f* exile.

exil(i)ar(se) [12] *t* to exile, send into exile. — **2** *p* to go into exile.

exilio *m* exile.

eximir(se) *t-p* to exempt/free (o.s.) (*de*, from). ▲ *pp* **exento,-a** or **eximido,-a**.

existencia *f* existence, life. **2** *pl* stock *sing*, stocks. ●*en* ~, in stock.

existencial *adj* existential.

existir *i* to exist, be.

éxito *m* success. ●*tener* ~, to be successful.

éxodo *m* exodus.

exonerar *t* to exonerate. **2** *(despedir)* to dismiss.

exorbitante *adj* exorbitant.

exorcista *mf* exorcist.

exorcizar [4] *t* to exorcise.

exótico,-a *adj* exotic.

expandir(se) *t-p* *(dilatar)* to expand. **2** *(divulgar)* to spread.

expansión *f* *(dilatación)* expansion. **2** *(difusión)* spreading. **3** *(recreo)* relaxation, recreation.

expansionarse *p* *(dilatarse)* to expand. **2** *(divertirse)* to amuse o.s.

expansivo,-a *adj* *(gas etc.)* expansive. **2** *(franco)* open, frank.

expatriar(se) [14] *t* to expatriate. — **2** *p* to emigrate.

expectación *f* expectation.

expectativa *f* expectation, hope. **2** *(posibilidad)* prospect: *estar a la* ~, to be on the lookout. ■ ~ *de vida,* life expectancy.

expectorar *t-i* to expectorate.

expedición *f* expedition; *(personas)* party. **2** *(envío)* dispatch.

expediente *m* JUR proceedings *pl*, action. **2** *(informe)* dossier, record. **3** *(recurso)* expedient. ●*fam* *cubrir el* ~, to go through the motions.

expedir [34] *t* *(certificado etc.)* to issue. **2** *(despachar)* to dispatch. **3** *(enviar)* to send off, remit.

expeditivo,-a *adj* expeditious.

expedito,-a *adj* free, clear.

expeler *t* to expel, eject. ▲ *pp* **expulso,-a** or **expelido,-a**.

expendeduría *f* tobacconist's (shop).

expensas *fpl* expenses. ●*a* ~ *de,* at the expense of.

experiencia *f* experience. **2** *(experimento)* experiment. ●*por* ~, from experience.

experimentación *f* experimentation.

experimentado,-a *adj* experienced. **2** *(método)* tested.

experimentar *t* *(probar)* to experiment, try. **2** *(sentir)* to experience; *(cambio)* undergo: ~ *una mejoría,* to improve.

experimento *m* experiment, test.

experto,-a *adj-m,f* expert.

expiación *f* expiation.

expiar [13] *t* to expiate.

expirar *i* to expire.

explanada *f* esplanade.

explanar *t* *(allanar)* to level, grade. **2** *(explicar)* to explain.

explayar(se) *t-p* to extend. — **2** *p* *(confiarse)* to confide (*con*, in). **3** *(divertirse)* to amuse o.s.

explicación *f* explanation.

explicar(se) [1] *t* to explain, expound. — **2** *p* *(comprender)* to understand: *no me lo explico,* I can't understand it.

explícito,-a *adj* explicit, express.

exploración *f* exploration. **2** MED probe.

explorador,-ra *adj* exploring. — **2** *m,f* explorer.

explorar *t* to explore. **2** MED to probe. **3** MIL to reconnoitre.

explosión *f* explosion, blast. **2** *fig* outburst.

explosionar *t-i* to explode.

explosivo,-a *adj-m* explosive.

explotación *f* exploitation. ■ ~ *agrícola,* farm; ~ *forestal,* forestry.

explotador,-ra *m,f* exploiter.

explotar *t (sacar provecho)* to exploit; *(mina)* to work; *(tierra)* to cultivate. − 2 *i (explosionar)* to explode, go off.

expoliación *f* plundering.

exponente *m* index, exponent.

exponer(se) [78] *t (explicar)* to expound, explain. 2 *(mostrar)* to expose, show, exhibit. 3 *(arriesgar)* to expose, risk. − 4 *p (arriesgarse)* to expose o.s. *(a,* to). ▲ *pp* **expuesto,-a**.

exportación *f* export(ation).

exportador,-ra *adj* exporting. − 2 *m,f* exporter.

exportar *t* to export.

exposición *f (de arte)* exhibition. 2 *(explicación)* account, explanation. 3 *(fotografía)* exposure. 4 *(riesgo)* risk. ■ *sala de exposiciones,* (art) gallery.

expósito,-a *adj-m,f* foundling.

exprés *adj* express. ■ *(café)* ~, expresso (coffee); *olla* ~, pressure cooker; *tren* ~, express (train).

expresar(se) *t-p* to express (o.s.).

expresión *f* expression. ■ ~ *corporal,* free expression.

expresivo,-a *adj (elocuente)* expressive. 2 *(afectuoso)* affectionate, warm.

expreso,-a *adj* express. − 2 *m (tren)* express (train). − 3 *expresamente adv (específicamente)* specifically. 4 *(adrede)* on purpose.

exprimidera *f,* **exprimidor** *m* squeezer.

exprimir *t* to squeeze.

expropiar [12] *t* to expropriate.

expuesto,-a *pp* → **exponer**. − 2 *adj (peligroso)* dangerous.

expulsar *t* to expel. 2 DEP to send off.

expulsión *f* expulsion. 2 *(dep)* sending off.

expulso,-a *pp* → **expeler**.

expurgar [7] *t* to expurgate. 2 *fig* to purge.

exquisito,-a *adj* exquisite.

extasiarse [13] *p* to be in ecstasy, be delighted.

éxtasis *m inv* ecstasy, rapture.

extender(se) [28] *t* to extend. 2 *(agrandar)* to enlarge. 3 *(mapa, papel)* to spread (out). 4 *(brazo etc.)* to stretch (out). 5 *(documento)* to draw up; *(cheque)* to make out; *(pasaporte, certificado)* to issue. − 6 *p (durar)* to extend, last. 7 *(terreno)* to spread out. 8 *fig* to enlarge.

extensión *f gen* extension. 2 *(dimensión)* extent, size.

extensivo,-a *adj* extendable, extensive.

extenso,-a *adj (amplio)* extensive, vast. − 2 *extensamente adv* extensively. 3 *fig* widely.

extenuado,-a *adj* exhausted.

extenuar(se) [11] *t* to exhaust; *(debilitar)* to weaken. − 2 *p* to exhaust o.s.

exterior *adj* exterior, outer. 2 *(extranjero)* foreign: *política* ~, foreign policy. − 3 *m* exterior, outside. 4 *(de una persona)* appearance. 5 *pl* CINEM location *sing.* − 6 *exteriormente adv* outwardly.

exteriorizar [4] *t* to show, reveal, manifest.

exterminar *t* to exterminate.

exterminio *m* extermination.

externo,-a *adj* external, outward: *parte externa,* outside. ●*"de uso* ~*",* "external use only".

extinción *f* extinction.

extinguir(se) [8] *t (fuego)* to extinguish, put out. 2 *(especie)* to wipe out. − 3 *p (fuego)* to go out. 4 *(especie)* to become extinct. ▲ *pp* **extinto,-a**.

extinto,-a *pp* → **extinguir**. − 2 *adj* extinguished. − 3 *m,f (muerto)* dead.

extintor *m* fire extinguisher.

extirpación *f* MED removal, extraction. 2 *fig* eradication.

extirpar *t* MED to remove, extract. 2 *fig* to eradicate.

extra *adj* extra. − 2 *mf* CINEM extra. − 3 *m (gasto)* extra expense. 4 *(plus)* bonus. ■ *paga* ~, bonus.

extracción *f* extraction.

extracto *m (substancia)* extract. 2 *(resumen)* summary. ■ ~ *de cuenta,* statement of account.

extractor,-ra *m,f* extractor.

extraer [88] *t* to extract.

extranjero,-a *adj* foreign, alien. − 2 *m,f* foreigner, alien. − 3 *m* foreign countries *pl,* abroad: *viajar al* ~, to travel/go abroad.

extrañar(se) *t (desterrar)* to banish, exile. 2 *(sorprender)* to surprise. 3 AM *(echar de menos)* to miss. − 4 *p (desterrarse)* to go into exile. 5 *(sorprenderse)* to be surprised *(de/por,* at).

extraño,-a *adj (no conocido)* alien, foreign. 2 *(particular)* strange, peculiar. − 3 *m,f* stranger.

extraordinario,-a *adj* extraordinary.

extrarradio *m* outskirts *pl.*

extraterrestre *adj* extraterrestrial, alien. − 2 *mf* alien.

extravagancia *f* extravagance, eccentricity.

extravagante *adj* extravagant, eccentric.

extraviado,-a *adj* missing, lost: *perro* ~, stray dog. **2** *(lugar)* out-of-the-way.

extraviar(se) [13] *t (persona)* to lead astray. **2** *(objeto)* to mislay. − **3** *p (persona)* to get lost. **4** *(objeto)* to get mislaid.

extravío *m (pérdida)* loss, mislaying. **2** *fig* deviation.

extremado,-a *adj* extreme.

extremar(se) *t* to carry to extremes. − **2** *p* to do one's best.

extremaunción *f* extreme unction.

extremidad *f (parte extrema)* extremity; *(punta)* end, tip. **2** *pl* ANAT limbs, extremities.

extremista *adj-mf* extremist.

extremo,-a *adj (superior)* extreme, utmost. **2** *(distante)* far. **3** *fig (intenso)* utmost. − **4** *m* extreme, end. **5** DEP wing. ●*en último* ~, as a last resort; *hasta tal* ~, to such a point.

extrínseco,-a *adj* extrinsic.

extrovertido,-a *adj* extraverted, extroverted. − **2** *m,f* extravert, extrovert.

exuberancia *f* exuberance.

exultar *i* to exult.

exvoto *m* votive offering.

eyaculación *f* ejaculation. ■ ~ *precoz,* premature ejaculation.

eyacular *i* to ejaculate.

F

fábrica *f (industria)* factory, plant. **2** *(fabricación)* manufacture. ■ ~ *de cerveza,* brewery; ~ *de conservas,* canning plant; *marca de* ~, trademark; *precio de* ~, factory/ex-works price.

fabricación *f* manufacture, production. ●*de* ~ *casera,* home-made; *de* ~ *propia,* our own make.

fabricante *mf* manufacturer.

fabricar [1] *t* to make, manufacture, produce. **2** *(inventar)* to fabricate, invent. ●~ *en serie,* to mass-produce.

fabuloso,-a *adj* fabulous, fantastic.

facción *f* POL faction. **2** *pl (rasgos)* (facial) features.

facha *f fam (aspecto)* appearance, look. **2** *(mamarracho)* mess, sight: *estar hecho una* ~, to look a mess/sight. — **3** *adj-mf pey* fascist.

fachada *f* façade, front. **2** *fam (apariencia)* outward show, window dressing.

fácil *adj* easy. **2** *(probable)* probable, likely. **3** *pey (mujer)* easy, loose.

facilidad *f* easiness, facility. **2** *(talento)* talent, gift. ■ *facilidades de pago,* easy terms.

facilitar *t (simplificar)* to make easy, facilitate. **2** *(proporcionar)* to provide/supply (-, with).

factible *adj* feasible, practicable.

factor *m* factor.

factoría *f* COM trading post. **2** *(fábrica)* factory, mill.

factura *f* invoice, bill. ●*pasar/presentar* ~ *a,* to invoice, send a bill to.

facturar *t* COM to invoice, charge. **2** *(equipaje)* to register, check in.

facultad *f (capacidad)* faculty, ability. **2** *(poder)* faculty, power. **3** *(universitaria)* faculty, school.

facultar *t* to empower, authorize.

facultativo,-a *adj (opcional)* optional. **2** *(profesional)* professional. — **3** *m,f* doctor, physician.

faena *f (tarea)* task, job. **2** *fam (mala pasada)* dirty trick. ●*fam estar metido,-a en* ~, to be hard at work. ■ *faenas de la casa,* housework *sing.*

faenar *i (pesca)* to fish.

faja *f (cinturón)* band, belt. **2** *(de mujer)* girdle. **3** *(banda)* sash. **4** *(correo)* wrapper. **5** *(franja)* strip.

fajo *m* bundle; *(de billetes)* wad.

falaz *adj (erróneo)* fallacious. **2** *(engañoso)* deceitful, false.

falda *f (prenda)* skirt. **2** *(regazo)* lap. **3** *(ladera)* slope. ■ ~ *escocesa,* kilt; ~ *pantalón,* culottes *pl.*

fallar *i-t* JUR to pass, pronounce. **2** *(premio)* to award. — **3** *i (fracasar, no funcionar)* to fail. **4** *(ceder)* to give way, collapse. ●~ *la puntería,* to miss one's aim; ~ *los cálculos,* to be wrong, miscalculate.

fallecer [43] *i fml* to pass away, die.

fallecimiento *m* decease, demise.

fallido,-a *adj* unsuccessful, frustrated.

fallo *m (error)* mistake, blunder; *(fracaso)* failure. **2** *(defecto)* fault, defect. **3** JUR judgement, sentence. **4** *(premio)* awarding.

falsear *t (informe etc.)* to falsify; *(hechos)* to distort. **2** *(falsificar)* to counterfeit, forge.

falsedad *f (hipocresía)* falseness, hypocrisy. **2** *(mentira)* falsehood, lie.

falsificación *f* falsification, forgery.

falsificador,-ra *adj* forging; *(de dinero)* counterfeiting. — **2** *m,f* forger; *(de dinero)* counterfeiter.

falsificar [1] *t* to falsify. **2** *(cuadro, firma)* to forge; *(dinero)* to counterfeit, forge.

falso,-a *adj* false, untrue. 2 *(persona)* insincere, treacherous.

falta *f (carencia)* lack, shortage, absence. 2 *(error)* mistake: ~ *de ortografía,* spelling mistake. 3 *(defecto)* fault, defect. 4 *(mala acción)* misdeed. 5 MED missed period. 6 JUR misdemeanour. 7 DEP *(fútbol) (tenis)* fault. ●*a/por ~ de algo,* for want/lack of sth.; *hacer ~,* to be necessary; *sin ~,* without fail. ■ ~ *de educación,* bad manners *pl.*

faltar *i (no estar) (cosa)* to be missing; *(persona)* to be absent. 2 *(haber poco)* to be lacking/needed. 3 *(no tener)* to lack, not have (enough): *me falta azúcar,* I haven't got enough sugar. 4 *(no acudir)* not to go, miss *(a, -).* 5 *(incumplir)* to break, not keep: ~ *a su palabra/promesa,* to break one's word/promise. 6 *(quedar)* to be left. ●*¡lo que me faltaba!,* that's all I needed!; *¡no faltaba más!, (por supuesto)* (but) of course!; *(por supuesto que no)* absolutely not!

falto,-a *adj* lacking, without, short. ●~ *de dinero,* short of money; ~ *de recursos,* without resources.

fama *f (renombre)* fame, renown. 2 *(reputación)* reputation. ●*de ~ mundial,* world-famous; *tener buena/mala ~,* to have a good/bad name.

famélico,-a *adj* starving, famished.

familia *f* family. 2 *(prole)* children *pl.* ●*estar en ~,* to be among friends.

familiar *adj (de la familia)* (of the) family. 2 *(conocido)* familiar, well-known. 3 GRAM colloquial. − 4 *mf* relation, relative.

familiaridad *f* familiarity, informality.

familiarizar(se) [4] *t-p* to familiarize *(con,* with).

famoso,-a *adj* famous, well-known.

fan *mf* fan, admirer. ●*ser un/una ~ de algo,* to be mad on sth.

fanático,-a *adj* fanatic(al). − 2 *m,f* fanatic.

fanatismo *m* fanaticism.

fanfarrón,-ona *adj fam* swanky, boastful. − 2 *m,f* show-off, swank, braggart.

fanfarronear *i fam (chulear)* to show off. 2 *(bravear)* to brag, boast.

fango *m (barro)* mud, mire. 2 *fig* degradation.

fantasear *t* to (day)dream.

fantasía *f* fantasy, fancy. ●*tener mucha ~,* to be too full of imagination.

fantasioso,-a *adj* imaginative.

fantasma *m (espectro)* phantom, ghost. 2 *fam (fanfarrón)* braggart, show-off.

fantástico,-a *adj* fantastic.

fantoche *m (títere)* puppet, marionette. 2 *pey (fanfarrón)* braggart, show-off. 3 *pey (mamarracho)* nincompoop, ninny.

fardar *i arg (presumir)* to show off, swank.

fardo *m (paquete)* bundle, pack. ●*fam estar hecho,-a un ~,* to look like a barrel.

farfullar *t* to gabble, jabber.

farmacéutico,-a *adj* pharmaceutical. − 2 *m,f (licenciado)* pharmacist. 3 *(en una farmacia)* chemist, US druggist, pharmacist.

farmacia *f (estudios)* pharmacology. 2 *(tienda)* chemist's (shop), US drugstore, pharmacy.

fármaco *m* medicine, medication.

faro *m (torre)* lighthouse, beacon. 2 *(coche)* headlight. 3 *fig (guía)* guiding light, guide.

farol *m (luz)* lantern; *(farola)* streetlamp, streetlight. 2 *arg (fardada)* bragging, swank; *(engaño)* bluff. ●*arg marcarse/tirarse un ~,* to brag, boast.

farola *f* streetlight, streetlamp; *(de gas)* gas lamp.

farsa *f* TEAT farce. 2 *(enredo)* sham, farce.

farsante *adj* lying, deceitful. − 2 *mf* fake, impostor.

fascículo *m* fascicle, instalment.

fascinación *f* fascination.

fascinador,-ra *adj* fascinating.

fascinar *t* to fascinate, captivate.

fascista *adj-mf* fascist.

fase *f* phase, stage.

fastidiado,-a *adj (hastiado)* sickened, disgusted. 2 *(molesto)* annoyed. 3 *(dañado)* damaged, in bad condition. 4 *fam (estropeado)* ruined, spoilt.

fastidiar(se) [12] *t (hastiar)* to sicken, disgust. 2 *(molestar)* to annoy, bother. 3 *(partes del cuerpo)* to hurt. 4 *fam (estropear)* to damage, ruin; *(planes)* to spoil, upset, mess up. − 5 *p (aguantarse)* to put up with. 6 *fam (estropearse)* to get damaged, break down: *se ha fastidiado el tocadiscos,* the record-player is bust. 7 *(lastimarse)* to hurt/injure o.s.: *me he fastidiado la mano,* I've hurt my hand. ●*fam ¡que se fastidie!,* that's his/her tough luck!; *fam ¡no fastidies!,* you're kidding!

fastidio *m (molestia)* bother, nuisance. 2 *(aburrimiento)* boredom.

fastidioso,-a *adj (molesto)* annoying, irksome. 2 *(aburrido)* boring, tedious.

fastuoso,-a *adj* splendid, lavish, ostentatious.

fatal *adj (inexorable)* fateful. **2** *(mortal)* deadly, fatal. **3** *fam (muy malo)* awful, horrible, terrible. **– 4** *adv fam* awfully, terribly.

fatalidad *f (destino)* fate. **2** *(desgracia)* misfortune.

fatídico,-a *adj (desastroso)* disastrous. **2** *fml (profético)* fateful, ominous.

fatiga *f (cansancio)* fatigue. **2** *pl (molestia)* troubles, difficulties.

fatigar(se) [7] *t* to wear out, tire. **2** *(molestar)* to annoy. **– 3** *p* to tire, get/become tired.

fatuo,-a *adj (necio)* fatuous. **2** *(vano)* vain, conceited.

favor *m* favour. ●*a ~ de,* in favour of; *por ~,* please; *tener algo a su ~,* to have sth. in one's favour.

favorable *adj* favourable; *(condiciones)* suitable.

favorecer [43] *t (ayudar)* to favour, help. **2** *(agraciar)* to flatter, suit.

favoritismo *m* favouritism.

favorito,-a *adj-m,f* favourite.

fe *f* faith. **2** JUR *(certificado)* certificate. ●*de buena/mala ~,* with good/dishonest intentions. ■ *~ de erratas,* errata.

fealdad *f* ugliness.

febrero *m* February.

febril *adj* MED feverish. **2** *(desasosegado)* hectic, restless.

fecha *f* date. **2** *(día)* day. **3** *pl (época)* time *sing: por esas fechas,* at that time. ●*con/de ~ ...,* dated ...; *hasta la ~,* so far. ■ *~ límite/tope,* deadline.

fechar *t* to date, put the date on.

fechoría *f* misdeed, misdemeanour; *(de niño)* mischief.

fecundación *f* fertilization. ■ *~ in vitro,* in vitro fertilization.

fecundar *t* to fertilize.

fecundo,-a *adj* fertile, fecund.

federación *f* federation.

federar(se) *t-p* to federate.

fehaciente *adj fml* authentic, reliable.

felicidad *f* happiness. ●*¡felicidades!,* congratulations!

felicitación *f (tarjeta)* greetings card. **2** *pl* congratulations.

felicitar *t* to congratulate *(por,* on). ●*~ a algn. las Navidades/por su santo,* to wish sb. merry Christmas/a happy Saint's Day; *¡te/os felicito!,* congratulations!

feligrés,-esa *m,f* parishioner.

felino,-a *adj-m* feline.

feliz *adj* happy. **2** *(acertado)* fortunate. ●*¡~ Navidad!,* Happy/Merry Christmas!

felpudo,-a *adj (textil)* plush, plushy. **– 2** *m* (door)mat.

femenino,-a *adj* feminine; *(sexo)* female.

feminismo *m* feminism.

feminista *adj-mf* feminist.

fenomenal *adj* phenomenal. **2** *fam (fantástico)* great, terrific. **3** *fam (enorme)* colossal, huge. **– 4** *adv* wonderfully, marvellously.

fenómeno *m* phenomenon. **2** *(prodigio)* genius. **3** *(monstruo)* freak. **– 4** *adj fam* fantastic, terrific.

feo,-a *adj (desagradable)* ugly. **2** *(malo)* nasty. **3** *(indigno)* improper, rude, not nice. **– 4** *m,f* ugly person. **– 5** *m (ofensa)* slight, snub: *hacerle un ~ a algn.,* to slight/snub sb.

féretro *m* coffin.

feria *f* COM fair. **2** *(fiesta)* fair, festival. ■ *~ de muestras,* trade exhibition/fair.

fermentar *i* to ferment.

ferocidad *f* ferocity, fierceness.

feroz *adj* fierce, ferocious.

férreo,-a *adj* ferreous. **2** *fig (tenaz)* iron: *voluntad férrea,* iron will.

ferretería *f (tienda)* ironmonger's (shop), hardware store. **2** *(género)* ironmongery, hardware. **3** *(ferrería)* forge.

ferrocarril *m* railway, US railroad.

ferroviario,-a *adj* rail(way). **– 2** *m,f (trabajador)* railway employee/worker.

fértil *adj* fertile, rich.

fertilidad *f* fertility.

fertilizante *adj* fertilizing. **– 2** *m (abono)* fertilizer.

fertilizar [4] *t* to fertilize.

ferviente *adj* fervent, passionate.

fervor *m* fervour.

fervoroso,-a *adj →* **ferviente**.

festejar *t (celebrar)* to celebrate. **2** *(agasajar)* to wine and dine, entertain. **3** *(cortejar)* to court, woo.

festejo *m* feast, entertainment. **2** *(galanteo)* courting, courtship. **3** *pl* festivities.

festín *m* feast, banquet.

festival *m* festival.

festividad *f (fiesta)* festivity, celebration. **2** *(día)* feast day, holiday.

festivo,-a *adj (alegre)* festive, merry. **2** *(agudo)* witty. ■ *día ~,* holiday.

fétido,-a *adj* stinking, fetid.

feto *m* foetus. **2** *fam (feo)* monster, ugly sod.

fiable *adj* reliable; *(persona)* trustworthy.

fiado,-a *adj* COM on credit. **2** *(confiado)* trusting.

fiador,-ra *m,f* guarantor. ●*salir/ser ~ de algn., (pagar fianza)* to stand bail for sb.; *(avalar)* to vouch for sb.

fiambre *adj* (served) cold. **2** *irón* stale, old. – **3** *m* cold cut. **4** *fam (cadáver)* stiff, corpse. ●*dejar ~ a algn.,* to do sb. in.

fiambrera *f* lunch box.

fianza *f (depósito)* deposit, security. **2** JUR bail. ●*bajo ~,* on bail.

fiar(se) [13] *t (asegurar)* to guarantee. **2** *(vender)* to sell on credit. **3** *(confiar)* to confide, entrust. – **4** *p (confiarse)* to trust *(de, -)*. ●*de ~,* trustworthy; *"no se fía", "no credit given".*

fibra *f (filamento)* fibre. **2** *(de madera)* grain. **3** *fig (carácter)* push, go.

ficción *f* fiction.

ficha *f (tarjeta)* index/file card. **2** *(teléfono)* token. **3** *(juegos)* counter; *(naipes)* chip; *(ajedrez)* piece, man; *(dominó)* domino. ■ *~ policíaca,* police record; *~ técnica,* specifications *pl*; CINEM credits *pl*.

fichaje *m* signing (up).

fichar *t (anotar)* to put on an index card, file. **2** *fam (conocer)* to size up: *lo tengo bien fichado,* I've got him sized up. **3** DEP to sign up. – **4** *i (al entrar)* to clock in; *(al salir)* to clock out. ●*estar fichado,-a por la policía,* to have a police record.

fichero *m (archivo)* card index. **2** *(mueble)* filing cabinet, file.

ficticio,-a *adj* fictitious.

fidedigno,-a *adj* trustworthy, reliable.

fidelidad *f (lealtad)* fidelity, faithfulness. **2** *(exactitud)* accuracy. ■ *alta ~,* high fidelity, hi-fi.

fideo *m* noodle. ●*fam estar como un ~,* to be as thin as a rake.

fiebre *f* MED fever. **2** *(agitación)* fever, excitement. ●*tener ~,* to have a temperature.

fiel *adj (leal)* faithful, loyal. **2** *(exacto)* accurate. – **3** *m (de balanza)* needle, pointer. ●*ser ~ a,* to be faithful to.

fieltro *m* felt.

fiero,-a *adj (animal) (salvaje)* wild; *(feroz)* fierce, ferocious. **2** *(persona)* cruel. **3** AM *(feo)* ugly. – **4** *f (animal)* wild animal/beast. **5** *fig (persona)* beast, brute. **6** *fig (genio)* wizard. **7** *(toro)* bull. ●*fam estar hecho,-a una fiera,* to be in a rage; *ser una fiera para algo,* to be brilliant at sth.

fiesta *f (vacaciones)* holiday. **2** *(reunión)* party. **3** *(festividad)* celebration, festivi-

ty. **4** REL feast. ●*hacer ~ un día,* to take a day off; *¡tengamos la ~ en paz!,* cut it out!; *fig estar de ~,* to be in a festive mood. ■ *~ de guardar/precepto,* day of obligation; *fig la ~ nacional,* bullfighting.

figura *f* figure. **2** *(forma)* shape. **3** CINEM TEAT character. ■ *~ decorativa,* figurehead.

figuración *f* imagination. ●*son figuraciones mías/tuyas/suyas ...,* it's just my/your/his ... imagination.

figurar(se) *t (representar)* to represent. **2** *(simular)* to simulate, pretend. – **3** *i (aparecer)* to appear, figure. **4** *(destacar)* to stand out, be important. – **5** *p (imaginarse)* to imagine, suppose. ●*¡figúrate!,* just imagine!, *ya me lo figuraba,* I thought as much.

figurativo,-a *adj* figurative.

figurín *m (dibujo)* sketch. **2** *(revista)* fashion magazine. **3** *pey* dandy, fop.

fijador,-ra *adj* fixing. – **2** *m (pelo)* hairspray, hair gel; *(dibujo etc.)* fixative.

fijar(se) *t (sujetar)* to fix, fasten. **2** *(pegar)* to stick, post. **3** *(establecer)* to set, determine. – **4** *p (darse cuenta)* to notice. **5** *(poner atención)* to pay attention, watch. ●*~ residencia,* to take up residence; *¡fíjate/fíjese!,* (just) fancy that! ●*~ la vista/los ojos,* to stare *(en,* at).

fijo,-a *adj (sujeto)* fixed, fastened. **2** *(establecido)* set, determined. **3** *(firme)* steady, stable, firm. **4** *(permanente)* permanent. **5** *(fotografía)* fast. – **6** *fijamente adv* fixedly.

fila *f* file, line. **2** *(de local)* row. **3** *pl* MIL ranks. ●*en ~ de uno/~ india,* in single file; *en primera ~,* in the front row; MIL *llamar a algn. a filas,* to call sb. up; *poner en ~,* to line up; MIL *¡rompan filas!,* fall out!, dismiss!

filatelia *f* philately, stamp collecting.

filete *m (de carne, pescado)* fillet; *(solomillo)* sirloin. **2** *(encuadernación)* fillet. **3** *(moldura)* fillet. **4** *(tornillo)* thread.

filiación *f (datos personales)* particulars *pl.* **2** POL affiliation.

filial *adj* filial. – **2** *adj-f* COM subsidiary, branch.

filigrana *f (orfebrería)* filigree. **2** *(papel)* watermark. **3** *pl fig* intricacy *sing,* intricate work *sing.*

film(e) *m* film, picture, US movie.

filmar *t* to film, shoot.

filo *m* (cutting) edge. ●*sacar ~ a algo,* to sharpen sth.; *fig al ~ de la medianoche,* on the stroke of midnight; *fig arma de doble* ~, double-edged argument.

filólogo,-a *m,f* philologist.

filón *m (mineral)* seam, vein. 2 *(buen negocio)* gold mine.

filosofía *f* philosophy.

filósofo,-a *m,f* philosopher.

filtración *f* filtration. 2 *(de información)* leak.

filtrar(se) *t-i* to filter. – 2 *p (información)* to leak (out).

filtro *m* filter. 2 *(poción)* philtre, love potion.

fin *m (final)* end. 2 *(objetivo)* purpose, aim. ●*a* ~ *de*, in order to, so as to; *a* ~ *de que*, so that; *al* ~ *y al cabo*, when all's said and done; *en* ~, anyway; *no tener* ~, to be endless; *¡por/al* ~*!*, at last! ■ ~ *de fiesta*, grand finale; ~ *de semana*, weekend.

final *adj* final, last. – 2 *m* end. – 3 *finalmente adv* finally. ●*al* ~, in the end; *al* ~ *del día*, at the end of the day.

finalidad *f* purpose, aim.

finalista *adj* in the final: *equipo* ~, team in the final. – 2 *mf* finalist.

finalizar [4] *t-i* to end, finish.

financiación *f* financing.

financiar [12] *t* to finance.

financiero,-a *adj* financial. – 2 *m,f* financier.

finanzas *fpl* finances.

finca *f* property, estate. ■ ~ *urbana*, building.

fingido,-a *adj* feigned, false.

fingir(se) [6] *t* to feign, pretend. – 2 *p* to pretend to be.

finiquito *m (acción)* settlement. 2 *(documento)* final discharge.

finito,-a *adj* finite.

fino,-a *adj* fine. 2 *(alimento)* choice, select. 3 *(sentidos)* sharp, acute. 4 *(delgado)* thin. 5 *(educado)* refined, polite. 6 *(sutil)* subtle. – 7 *m (vino)* dry sherry. ●*fam estar* ~, to be witty/shrewd; *fam irón ir* ~, to be plastered/stoned.

finura *f (calidad)* fineness. 2 *(agudeza)* sharpness, acuteness. 3 *(refinamiento)* refinement. 4 *(sutileza)* finesse.

firma *f (autógrafo)* signature. 2 *(acto)* signing. 3 *(empresa)* firm.

firmamento *m* firmament.

firmante *adj-mf* signatory. ●*el/la abajo* ~, the undersigned.

firmar *t* to sign.

firme *adj* firm, steady. – 2 *m (terreno)* road surface. – 3 *adv* hard. ●MIL *¡firmes!*, attention!; *fig mantenerse* ~, to hold one's ground. ■ *sentencia* ~, final judgement; *tierra* ~, terra firma.

firmeza *f* firmness, steadiness.

fiscal *adj* fiscal. – 2 *mf* JUR public prosecutor, US district attorney. 3 *fig* snooper.

fiscalizar [4] *t* to supervise, inspect.

fisco *m* exchequer, treasury.

fisgar [7] *t fam* to pry, snoop.

fisgón,-ona *adj (espía)* snooper; *(curioso)* busybody.

fisgonear *t* to pry, snoop.

físico,-a *adj* physical. – 2 *m,f (profesión)* physicist. – 3 *m (aspecto)* physique. – 4 *f (ciencia)* physics.

fisiología *f* physiology.

fisión *f* fission.

fisioterapia *f* physiotherapy.

fisonomía *f* physiognomy, appearance.

fisonomista *mf ser buen/mal* ~, to be good/no good at remembering faces.

fisura *f* fissure.

flaccidez, flacidez *f* flaccidity, flabbiness.

fláccido,-a, flácido,-a *adj* flaccid, flabby.

flaco,-a *adj* thin, skinny. 2 *fig* weak, frail. – 3 *m (defecto)* weak point/spot.

flagrante *adj* flagrant. ●*en* ~ *delito*, redhanded.

flamante *adj (vistoso)* splendid, brilliant. 2 *(nuevo)* brand-new.

flamear *i* to flame, blaze. 2 *(ondear)* to flutter, flap. – 3 *t* CULIN to flambé.

flan *m* caramel custard. ●*fam estar como un* ~, *(físico)* to feel tired and washed out; *(ánimo)* to be easily upset.

flanco *m* flank, side.

flaquear *i (ceder)* to weaken, give in. 2 *(fallar)* to fail. 3 *(desalentarse)* to lose heart. 4 *(disminuir)* to decrease.

flaqueza *f* weakness, frailty.

flash *m (fotografía)* flash. 2 *(noticia breve)* newsflash.

flato *m* wind, flatulence.

flauta *f* flute. – 2 *mf* flautist. ■ ~ *de Pan*, pipes *pl* of Pan; ~ *dulce*, recorder; ~ *travesera*, transverse/cross flute.

flautista *mf* flautist.

flecha *f* arrow. ●*salir como una* ~, to go off like a shot.

flechazo *m (disparo)* arrow shot. 2 *(herida)* arrow wound. 3 *fig (enamoramiento)* love at first sight.

fleco *m (adorno)* fringe. 2 *(deshilachado)* frayed edge.

flemón *m* gumboil, abcess.

flequillo *m* fringe, US bangs *pl*.

fletar *t* to charter, freight.

flexible *adj* flexible.

flexión *f* flexion. 2 LING inflection. 3 DEP press-up, US push-up. ▲ 3 *often pl*.

flexionar *t (músculo)* to flex; *(cuerpo)* to bend.

flipar(se) *arg t* to fascinate, drive wild. — 2 *p (drogas)* to get stoned.

flojear *i (disminuir)* to fall off, go down. 2 *(debilitarse)* to weaken, grow weak.

flojera *f fam* weakness, faintness.

flojo,-a *adj (suelto)* loose, slack. 2 *(débil)* weak: *un viento muy ~,* a light wind. 3 *(perezoso)* lazy, idle. — 4 *m,f* lazy person, idler. ●*arg me la trae floja,* I couldn't give a toss.

flor *f* flower. 2 *(piropo)* compliment: ●*a ~ de piel,* skin-deep; *en ~,* in blossom; *fig en la ~ de la vida,* in the prime of life; *fig la ~ y nata,* the cream (of society).

floreado,-a *adj* flowered, flowery.

florecer(se) [43] *i (plantas)* to flower, bloom; *(árboles)* to blossom. 2 *(prosperar)* to flourish, thrive. — 3 *p (pan etc.)* to go mouldy.

floreciente *adj* flourishing, prosperous.

florecimiento *m (plantas)* flowering, blooming; *(árboles)* blossoming. 2 *(auge)* flourishing.

florero *m* vase.

florido,-a *adj (con flores)* flowery. 2 *(selecto)* choice, select.

florista *mf* florist.

floristería *f* florist's (shop).

flota *f* fleet.

flotador *m* float. 2 *(de niño)* rubber ring.

flotar *i* to float. 2 *(ondear)* to wave, flutter.

flote *m* floating. ●*a ~,* afloat; *fig salir a ~,* to get back on one's feet, get out of difficulty.

fluctuar [11] *i* to fluctuate. 2 *(vacilar)* to hesitate.

fluidez *f* fluidity. 2 *fig* fluency.

fluido,-a *adj* fluid. 2 *fig* fluent. — 3 *m* FÍS fluid. ■ *~ eléctrico,* current.

fluir [62] *i* to flow.

fluorescente *adj* fluorescent. — 2 *m* fluorescent light.

foca *f* seal. 2 *fam (persona)* fat lump.

foco *m* centre, focal point. 2 FÍS MAT focus. 3 *(lámpara)* spotlight, floodlight. 4 AM (electric light) bulb. ■ *~ de atención,* focus of attention.

fofo,-a *adj* soft, spongy. 2 *(persona)* flabby.

fogón *m (cocina)* kitchen range, stove. 2 *(de máquina de vapor)* firebox.

fogosidad *f* ardour, fire.

fogoso,-a *adj* fiery, spirited.

follaje *m* foliage, leaves *pl*.

follar(se)* *arg i-p (copular)* to fuck*, screw*.

folletín *m (relato)* newspaper serial. 2 *fig (melodrama)* saga. ●*¡menudo ~!,* what a saga!

folleto *m (prospecto)* pamphlet, leaflet, brochure; *(explicativo)* instruction leaflet; *(turístico)* brochure.

follón *fam m (alboroto)* rumpus, shindy. 2 *(enredo, confusión)* mess, trouble. ●*armar (un) ~,* to kick up a rumpus.

follonero,-a *adj* troublemaking. — 2 *m,f* troublemaker.

fomentar *t* to promote, encourage, foster.

fonda *f* inn, small restaurant.

fondear *t (sondear)* to sound. 2 *(registrar)* to search. 3 *fig (examinar)* to get to the bottom of, delve into. — 4 *i* to anchor.

fondista *mf* innkeeper. 2 DEP long-distance runner.

fondo *m (parte más baja)* bottom. 2 *(parte más lejana)* end, back. 3 *(segundo término)* background. 4 FIN fund. 5 *(de libros etc.)* stock. 6 *pl (dinero)* funds, money *sing*. ●*a ~,* thoroughly; *fig en el ~,* deep down, at heart; *fig tocar ~,* to reach rock bottom. ■ *bajos fondos,* dregs of society; *doble ~,* false bottom; *~ común,* kitty; *~ del mar,* sea bed.

fontanería *f* plumbing.

fontanero,-a *m,f* plumber.

footing *m* jogging.

forajido,-a *m,f* outlaw, desperado.

forastero,-a *adj* foreign, alien. — 2 *m,f* stranger, outsider.

forcejear *i* to wrestle, struggle.

forense *adj* forensic, legal. — 2 *mf (médico) ~,* forensic surgeon.

forestal *adj* forest. ■ *repoblación ~,* reafforestation.

forja *f (fragua)* forge. 2 *(forjado)* forging. 3 *(ferrería)* ironworks, foundry.

forjar *t (metales)* to forge. 2 *fig (crear)* to create, make.

forma *f* form, shape. 2 *(manera)* way. 3 DEP form. 4 *pl (modales)* manners, social conventions. 5 *pl fam (de mujer)* curves. ●*de ~ que,* so that; *de todas formas,* anyway, in any case; *estar en baja ~,* to be off form; *estar en ~,* to be in shape, be fit; *ponerse en* ~, to get fit. ■ ~ *de pago,* method of payment; ~ *física,* physical fitness.

formación *f* formation. **2** *(educación)* upbringing. **3** *(enseñanza)* education, training.

formal *adj (serio)* serious, serious-minded. **2** *(cumplidor)* reliable, dependable. **3** *(cortés)* polite.

formalidad *f* formality. **2** *(seriedad)* seriousness. **3** *(fiabilidad)* reliability. **4** *(trámite)* formality, requisite.

formalizar(se) [4] *t (hacer formal)* to formalize. **2** *(contrato)* to legalize. **–** **3** *p* to become/grow serious.

formar(se) *t* to form. **2** *(integrar, constituir)* to form, constitute: ~ *parte de algo,* to be a part of sth. **3** *(educar)* to bring up. **4** *(enseñar)* to educate. **–** **5** *i* MIL *(colocarse)* to form up. **– 6** *p (desarrollarse)* to grow, develop. ●MIL *¡a* ~*!,* fall in!

formativo,-a *adj* formative. **2** *(educativo)* educational.

formato *m* format. **2** *(del papel)* size.

formidable *adj (tremendo)* tremendous, formidable. **2** *(maravilloso)* wonderful, terrific. **–** **3** *interj* great!

fórmula *f* formula. **2** *(receta)* recipe.

formular *t (una teoría)* to formulate. **2** *(quejas, peticiones)* to make. ●~ *un deseo,* to express a desire; ~ *una pregunta,* to ask a question.

formulario,-a *adj* routine: *una visita formularia,* a formal visit. **– 2** *m (documento)* form: ~ *de solicitud,* application form.

fornicar [1] *i* to fornicate.

fornido,-a *adj* strapping, hefty.

forrar(se) *t (por dentro)* to line. **2** *(por fuera)* to cover. **–** **3** *p fam (de dinero)* to make a packet.

forro *m (interior)* lining. **2** *(funda)* cover, case. ●*fam ni por el* ~, not in the slightest.

fortalecer(se) [43] *t* to fortify, strengthen. **–** **2** *p* to strengthen, become stronger.

fortalecimiento *m* fortification, strengthening.

fortaleza *f (vigor)* strength, vigour. **2** *(de espíritu)* fortitude. **3** MIL fortress, stronghold.

fortuito,-a *adj* chance, fortuitous.

fortuna *f (destino)* fortune, fate. **2** *(suerte)* luck. **3** *(capital)* fortune. ●*por* ~, fortunately.

forzar [50] *t (persona)* to force, compel. **2** *(cosa)* to force/break open. **3** *(violar)* to rape.

forzoso,-a *adj (inevitable)* inevitable, unavoidable. **2** *(obligatorio)* obligatory, compulsory. **–** **3** *forzosamente adv* inevitably.

forzudo,-a *adj* strong, brawny.

fosa *f (sepultura)* grave. **2** *(hoyo)* pit, hollow. **3** ANAT fossa. ■ *fosas nasales,* nostrils.

fosforecer [10] *i* to phosphoresce, glow.

fosforescente *adj* phosphorescent.

fósforo *m* phosphorus. **2** *(cerilla)* match.

foto *f fam* photo, picture.

fotocomposición *f* typesetting, US photosetting.

fotocopia *f* photoprint.

fotocopiar [12] *t* to photocopy.

fotogénico,-a *adj* photogenic.

fotografía *f (proceso)* photography. **2** *(retrato)* photograph.

fotografiar [13] *t* to photograph, take a photograph of.

fotográfico,-a *adj* photographic.

fotógrafo,-a *m,f* photographer.

fotomatón *m* automatic coin-operated photo machine.

fotomontaje *m* photomontage.

frac *m* dress coat, tails *pl.* ▲ *pl* **fracs** or **fraques**.

fracasado,-a *adj* unsuccessful. **–** **2** *m,f (persona)* failure.

fracasar *i* to fail, be unsuccessful, fall through.

fracaso *m* failure.

fracción *f* fraction. **2** POL faction.

fraccionar *t* to break/split up.

fractura *f* fracture.

fracturar(se) *t-p* to fracture, break.

fragancia *f* fragrance.

fragante *adj* fragrant, scented.

frágil *adj (quebradizo)* fragile, breakable. **2** *(débil)* frail, weak.

fragilidad *f* fragility. **2** *(debilidad)* frailty, weakness.

fragmentar(se) *t* to fragment, divide up. **– 2** *p* to break up.

fragmento *m (pedazo)* fragment, piece. **2** *(literario)* passage.

fraguar [10] *t (metal)* to forge. **2** *fig (plan)* to dream up, fabricate; *(conspiración)* to hatch. **–** **3** *i (endurecerse)* to set, harden.

fraile *m* friar, monk.

frambuesa *f* raspberry.

franco,-a *adj (persona)* frank, open. **2** *(cosa)* clear, obvious. **3** COM free. **– 4** *m* *(moneda)* franc. ●~ *de aduana,* duty-free; ~ *fábrica,* ex-works.

franela *f* flannel.

franja *f (banda)* band, strip. **2** *(de tierra)* strip. **3** COST fringe, border.

franqueable *adj* crossable, which can be crossed. **2** *(obstáculo)* surmountable.

franquear(se) *t (dejar libre)* to free, clear. **2** *(atravesar)* to cross; *fig* to overcome. **3** *(carta)* to frank. **– 4** *p* to unbosom o.s., open up one's heart. ●*a* ~ *en destino,* postage paid.

franqueo *m* postage.

franqueza *f (sinceridad)* frankness, openness. **2** *(confianza)* familiarity, intimacy.

franquicia *f* exemption. **2** COM franchise. ■ ~ *arancelaria,* exemption from customs duty.

frasco *m* flask.

frase *f* GRAM *(oración)* sentence. **2** *(expresión)* phrase. ■ ~ *hecha,* set phrase/expression, idiom.

fraternal *adj* fraternal, brotherly.

fraternidad *f* fraternity, brotherhood.

fraternizar [4] *i* to fraternize.

fraterno,-a *adj* fraternal, brotherly.

fratricida *adj* fratricidal. **– 2** *mf* fratricide.

fraude *m* fraud. ■ ~ *fiscal,* tax evasion.

fraudulento,-a *adj* fraudulent.

frecuencia *f* frequency.

frecuentar *t* to frequent, visit.

frecuente *adj (repetido)* frequent. **2** *(usual)* common. **– 3 frecuentemente** *adv* frequently, often.

fregadero *m* kitchen sink.

fregar [48] *t (lavar)* to wash. **2** *(frotar)* to scrub. **3** *(el suelo)* to mop. **4** AM *(molestar)* to annoy, irritate. ●~ *los platos,* to do the washing up.

fregona *f pey (sirvienta)* skivvy. **2** *(utensilio)* mop.

fregotear *t fam* to give a quick wipe to.

freidora *f* (deep) fryer.

freír [37] *t* to fry. **2** *fig* to annoy. ▲ *pp* *frito,-a.*

frenar *t* to brake. **2** *fig* to restrain, check.

frenazo *m* sudden braking. ●*dar un* ~, to jam on the brakes.

frenesí *m* frenzy. ▲ *pl* **frenesíes.**

frenético,-a *adj (exaltado)* frenzied, frenetic. **2** *(colérico)* wild, mad.

freno *m* brake. **2** *(de caballería)* bit. ●*morder el* ~, to champ at the bit; *poner* ~ *a algo,* to curb sth.

frente *m & f (parte delantera)* front. **– 2** *m* MIL front. **– 3** *f* ANAT forehead. **– 4** *adv* ~ *a,* in front of, opposite. ●*al* ~ *de,* at

the head of; ~ *a* ~, face to face; *hacer* ~ *a algo,* to face sth., stand up to sth.; *no tener dos dedos de* ~, to be as thick as two short planks.

fresa *f (planta)* strawberry plant. **2** *(fruto)* (wild) strawberry. **3** TÉC milling. **4** *(dentista)* drill. **– 5** *adj inv* red.

frescales *mf inv fam* cheeky devil.

fresco,-a *adj* cool, cold: *viento* ~, cool wind; *agua fresca,* cold water. **2** *(tela, vestido)* light, cool. **3** *(aspecto)* healthy, fresh. **4** *(comida)* fresh. **5** *(reciente)* fresh, new: *noticias frescas,* latest news *sing.* **6** *fig (impasible)* cool, calm, unworried. **7** *(desvergonzado)* cheeky, shameless. **– 8** *m (frescor)* fresh/cool air. **9** ART fresco. **– 10** *f (aire fresco)* fresh/cool air. **11** *fam (impertinencia)* cheeky remark. ●*al* ~, in the cool; *decirle cuatro frescas a algn.,* to tell sb. a few home truths; *hacer* ~, to be chilly; *¡qué* ~*!,* what a nerve!; *quedarse tan* ~, not to bat an eyelid; *¡sí que estamos frescos!,* now we're in a fine mess!; *tomar el fresco/la fresca,* to get some fresh air.

frescor *m* coolness, freshness.

frescura *f (frescor)* freshness, coolness. **2** *(desvergüenza)* cheek, nerve. **3** *(calma)* coolness, calmness. ●*¡qué* ~*!,* what a nerve!

fresno *m* ash tree.

fresón *m (planta)* strawberry plant. **2** *(fruto)* (large) strawberry.

frialdad *f* coldness.

fricción *f* friction. **2** *(friega)* rub(bing).

friccionar *t* to rub, massage.

friega *f* rub(bing).

frigidez *f* frigidity.

frigorífico,-a *adj* refrigerating. **– 2** *m (doméstico)* refrigerator, fridge. **3** *(cámara)* coldstorage room.

frijol, fríjol *m* (kidney) bean.

frío,-a *adj-m* cold. **– 2 fríamente** *adv* coldly, coolly. ●*hacer* ~, to be cold; *tener/pasar* ~, to be cold; *fam hace un* ~ *que pela,* it's freezing cold.

friolero,-a *adj* sensitive to the cold: *es muy* ~, he really feels the cold. **– 2** *f* trifle, trinket. **3** *fam (gran cantidad)* fortune: *gastarse la* ~ *de 30.000 pesetas en unos zapatos,* to spend a mere 30.000 pesetas on a pair of shoes.

frisar *t (refregar)* to rub. **– 2** *i (acercarse)* to approach, border *(con/en,* on). ●~ *con/en (una edad),* to be getting on for (an age).

frito,-a *pp →* **freír.** **– 2** *adj* CULIN fried. *fam* exasperated, fed up. **– 4** *m* fry, piece of fried food. ●*fam* **quedarse** ~, *(dormido)* to fall asleep; *(muerto)* to snuff it; **tener a uno** ~ **con algo,** to be sick to death of sth.

frivolidad *f* frivolity.

frívolo,-a *adj* frivolous.

frondoso,-a *adj* leafy, luxuriant.

frontera *f* frontier, border. **2** *fig* limit, bounds *pl*, borderline.

fronterizo,-a *adj* border(line).

frontón *m* DEP *(juego)* pelota. **2** DEP *(edificio)* pelota court. **3** ARQ pediment.

frotar *t* to rub.

fructífero,-a *adj* BOT fruit-bearing. **2** *fig* fruitful.

fructificar [1] *i* BOT to bear fruit, produce a crop. **2** *fig* to be fruitful.

frugal *adj* frugal.

frunce *m* shir, gather. ●*con frunces,* shirred, gathered.

fruncir [3] *t* COST to gather. **2** *(el ceño)* to frown, knit. **3** *(los labios)* to purse, pucker.

frustración *f* frustration.

frustrar(se) *t (cosa)* to frustrate, thwart. **2** *(persona)* to disappoint. — **3** *p (proyectos, planes)* to fail, go awry.

fruta *f* fruit. ■ ~ **del tiempo,** fresh fruit; ~ **escarchada,** candied fruit; ~ **seca,** dried fruit.

frutal *adj* fruit. — **2** *m* fruit tree.

frutería *f* fruit shop.

frutero,-a *adj* fruit. — **2** *m,f* fruiterer. — **3** *m* fruit dish/bowl.

fruto *m* fruit. ●*dar* ~, to bear fruit, *fig* to be fruitful; **sacar** ~ **de algo,** to profit from sth. ■ **frutos secos,** *(almendras etc.)* nuts; *(pasas etc.)* dried fruit *sing*.

fuego *m* fire. **2** *(lumbre)* light. **3** *(cocina)* burner, ring. **4** *(ardor)* ardour, zeal. ●*a* ~ **lento,** on a low flame; *(al horno)* in a slow oven; *¿me da* ~?, have you got a light?; *fig* **estar entre dos fuegos,** to be caught between two fires. ■ ~ **fatuo,** will-o'-the-wisp, Jack-o'-lantern; **fuegos artificiales,** fireworks.

fuente *f (manantial)* spring. **2** *(artificial)* fountain. **3** *(recipiente)* (serving) dish. **4** *fig* source: *de* ~ **desconocida,** from an unknown source.

fuera *adv* out, outside: *por* ~, on the outside. **2** *(alejado)* away: **estar** ~, to be away; *(en el extranjero)* to be abroad. **3** *(excepto)* except for, apart from. — **4** *m* DEP *(falta)* out. — **5** *pt subj* → **ser.** — **6** *pt subj* → **ir.** — **7** *interj* get out! ●*estar* ~ *de sí,* to be beside o.s.; ~ *de combate,* knocked out; ~ *de duda,* beyond

doubt; ~ *de lo normal,* extraordinary, very unusual. ■ ~ *de juego,* offside.

fuero *m* code of laws. **2** *(privilegio)* privilege. **3** *(jurisdicción)* jurisdiction. ●*en el* ~ *interno,* deep down, in one's heart of hearts.

fuerte *adj* strong. **2** *(intenso)* severe. **3** *(sonido)* loud. **4** *(importante)* main. **5** *(pesado)* heavy. **6** *(sujeto)* stiff. — **7** *m (fortificación)* fort. **8** *(punto fuerte)* forte, strong point. — **9** *adv* a lot, hard: *comer* ~, to eat a lot. ●*¡abrázame* ~!, hold me tight!; **estar** ~ *en algo,* to be good at something; *¡habla más* ~!, speak up! ■ *comida* ~, heavy meal; *plato* ~, main course; *fam fig* most important event.

fuerza *f* strength, force. — **2** *pl (el poder)* authorities: *las fuerzas vivas de la localidad,* the local authorities. ●*a* ~ *de,* by dint/force of; *a la* ~, by force; *por la* ~, against one's will. ■ ~ *de voluntad,* willpower; ~ *mayor,* force majeure; *fuerzas del orden público,* police force *sing*.

fuese *pt subj* → **ser.** — **2** *pt subj* → **ir.**

fuete *m* AM whip.

fuga *f (escapada)* flight, escape. **2** *(pérdida)* leak. **3** MÚS fugue. ●*darse a la* ~, to take flight; *poner en* ~, to put to flight. ■ ~ *de cerebros,* brain drain; ~ *de divisas,* flight of capital.

fugarse [7] *p* to flee, escape.

fugaz *adj* fleeting, brief.

fugitivo,-a *adj (en fuga)* fleeing. **2** *fig (efímero)* ephemeral, fleeting. — **3** *m,f* fugitive, runaway.

fui *pt indef* → **ser.** — **2** *pt indef* → **ir.**

fulano,-a *m,f* so-and-so; *m* what's his name, *f* what's her name. — **2** *m fam pey* fellow, guy. — **3** *f pey* whore, tart. ●*Don/Doña Fulano,-a de tal,* Mr/Mrs So-and-so; ~, *mengano y zutano,* Tom, Dick and Harry.

fulgor *m (resplandor)* brilliance, glow.

fullero,-a *adj* cheating. — **2** *m,f (naipes)* cheat, cardsharp(er).

fulminante *adj* fulminating. **2** *fig* staggering: *mirada* ~, withering look.

fulminar *t* to strike with lightning. **2** *fig* to strike dead. ●~ *a algn. con la mirada,* to look daggers at sb.

fumador,-ra *adj* smoking. — **2** *m,f* smoker. ●*los no fumadores,* nonsmokers.

fumar(se) *t-i-p* to smoke. ●*fam* ~*se las clases,* to play truant, US play hooky; *"no* ~", "no smoking".

fumigar [7] *t* to fumigate.

función *f* function. **2** *(cargo)* duties *pl.* **3** *(espectáculo)* performance. ●*en ~ de,* according to; *entrar en ~, (persona)* to take up one's duties; *estar en funciones,* to be in office; *presidente en funciones,* acting president. ■ *~ de noche,* late performance; *~ de tarde,* matinée.

funcionamiento *m* operation, working. ●*poner en ~,* to put into operation.

funcionar *i* to function, work. ●*hacer ~ algo,* to operate sth.; *"no funciona",* "out of order".

funcionario,-a *m,f* civil servant.

funda *f (flexible)* cover. **2** *(rígida)* case. **3** *(de arma blanca)* sheath. ■ *~ de almohada,* pillowcase.

fundación *f* foundation.

fundador,-ra *m,f* founder.

fundamental *adj* fundamental.

fundamentar *t fig* to base *(en,* on). **2** *(construcción)* to lay the foundations of.

fundamento *m (base)* basis, grounds *pl.* **2** *(seriedad)* seriousness; *(confianza)* reliability. **3** *pl (construcción)* foundations. ●*sin ~,* unfounded.

fundar(se) *t (crear)* to found; *(erigir)* to raise. **2** *(basar)* to base, found. **3** *p* to be founded. **4** *(teoría, afirmación)* to be based *(en,* on); *(persona)* to base o.s. *(en,* on).

fundición *f* melting. **2** *(de metales)* smelting, casting. **3** *(lugar)* foundry, smelting works *pl.* ■ *~ de acero,* steelworks *pl*; *hierro de ~,* cast iron.

fundidor *m* smelter.

fundir *t (un sólido)* to melt. **2** *(metal)* to found, cast; *(hierro)* to smelt. **3** *(bombilla, plomos)* to blow. **4** *(unir)* to unite, join.

fúnebre *adj (mortuorio)* funeral. **2** *(lúgubre)* mournful, lugubrious.

funeral *adj* funeral. **— 2** *m(pl) (entierro)* funeral *(sing).* **3** *(conmemoración)* memorial service.

funerala MIL *a la ~,* with reversed arms. ●*ojo a la ~,* black eye.

funerario,-a *adj* funerary, funeral. **— 2** *f (establecimiento)* undertaker's shop.

funesto,-a *adj* ill-fated, fatal.

funicular *m* funicular (railway).

furcia *f pey* whore, tart.

furgón *m* AUTO van, wag(g)on. **2** *(tren)* (goods) wag(g)on, US boxcar.

furgoneta *f* van.

furia *f* fury, rage. ●*ponerse hecho,-a una ~,* to become furious, fly into a rage.

furibundo,-a *adj* furious, enraged.

furioso,-a *adj* furious. ●*ponerse ~,* to get angry.

furor *m* fury, rage. ●*fig hacer ~,* to be all the rage.

furtivo,-a *adj* furtive. ■ *cazador ~,* poacher.

fusible *adj* fusible. **— 2** *m* fuse.

fusil *m* rifle, gun.

fusilamiento *m* shooting, execution.

fusilar *t (ejecutar)* to shoot, execute. **2** *(plagiar)* to plagiarize.

fusión *f (metales)* fusion, melting; *(hielo)* thawing, melting. **2** *(de intereses)* fusion. **3** COM merger, amalgamation.

fusionar(se) *t-p* to fuse. **2** COM to merge.

fustigar [7] *t (caballo)* to whip, lash. **2** *fig* to give a dressing-down to.

fútbol, futbol *m* football, US soccer. ■ *~ americano,* American football.

futbolín *m* table football.

futbolista *mf* footballer, football/soccer player.

futilidad *f* futility, triviality.

futuro,-a *adj* future. **— 2** *m* future.

G

gabacho,-a *adj-m, f pey* French.
gabán *m* overcoat.
gabardina *f (tela)* gabardine. **2** *(impermeable)* raincoat.
gabarra *f* barge, lighter.
gabinete *m (estudio)* study. **2** POL cabinet.
gacela *f* gazelle.
gaceta *f* gazette.
gacha *f (masa)* paste. **2** *pl* porridge *sing.*
gacho,-a *adj* dropping, bent.
gaélico,-a *adj-m* Gaelic.
gafas *fpl* spectacles, glasses. ■ ~ *de sol,* sunglasses.
gafe *adj-mf fam* jinx.
gaita *f* bagpipe. **2** *fam* bother.
gaitero,-a *m, f* piper, bagpipe player.
gaje *m* pay, wages *pl.* ■ *irón* **gajes del oficio,** occupational hazards.
gajo *m (de naranja)* section. **2** *(de árbol)* branch.
gala *f* best dress. **2** *(espectáculo)* gala. ●*hacer ~ de,* to make a show of.
galáctico,-a *adj* galactic.
galán *m* handsome man. **2** TEAT leading man. ■ ~ *de noche,* valet.
galante *adj* courteous, gallant.
galantear *t* to court, woo.
galantería *f* gallantry. **2** *(piropo)* compliment.
galápago *m* turtle.
galardón *m* prize.
galardonar *t* to reward.
galaxia *f* galaxy.
galeón *m* galleon.
galera *f* galley.
galerada *f* galley proof.
galería *f* gallery. **2** *(subterránea)* underground passage. **3** TEAT gallery. ■ *galerías comerciales,* shopping centre *sing.*
galgo *m* greyhound.

galimatías *m inv fam* gibberish.
galón *m* MIL stripe. **2** *(medida)* gallon.
galopar *i* to gallop.
galope *m* gallop.
galvanizar [4] *t* to galvanize.
gallardía *f* elegance, gracefulness. **2** *(valentía)* valour.
gallardo,-a *adj* elegant, graceful. **2** *(valiente)* brave, gallant.
galleta *f* biscuit, US cooky. **2** *fam (bofetada)* slap.
gallina *f* hen. — **2** *mf fam* chicken, coward. ■ *carne de ~,* gooseflesh.
gallinero *m* henhouse. **2** TEAT top gallery. **3** *fam* bedlam, madhouse.
gallo *m* cock, rooster. **2** *fig (canto)* false note. ■ ~ *de pelea,* fighting cock.
gama *f* range. **2** MÚS scale.
gamba *f* prawn.
gamberrada *f* act of hooliganism.
gamberro,-a *adj* loutish. — **2** *m, f* hooligan.
gamo *m* fallow deer.
gamuza *f* chamois.
gana *f* wish, desire. ● *de buena ~,* willingly; *de mala ~,* reluctantly; *tener ganas de,* to wish, feel like.
ganadería *f (cría)* cattle-raising. **2** *(ganado)* livestock. **3** *(marca)* cattle brand.
ganadero,-a *adj* cattle-raising. — **2** *m, f* cattle raiser/dealer.
ganado *m* cattle, livestock.
ganador,-ra *adj* winning. — **2** *m, f* winner.
ganancia *f* gain, profit.
ganar(se) *t (triunfar)* to win. **2** *(dinero)* earn. — **3** *t-p* to gain. — **4** *i (mejorar)* to improve. ●*~se la vida,* to earn one's living.
ganchillo *m* crochet needle. **2** *(labor)* crochet.

gancho *m* hook. **2** *(de pastor)* crook. ●*tener* ~, to be attractive.

gandul,-la *adj* idle, loafing. – **2** *m,f* idler, loafer.

gandulear *i* to idle, loaf around.

gandulería *f* idleness, laziness.

ganga *f* bargain.

ganglio *m* ganglion.

gangrena *f* gangrene.

gangrenarse *p* to become gangrenous.

ganso,-a *m* ZOOL goose, gander. – **2** *m,f* *fig* slow/lazy person.

garabatear *t-i* to scribble, scrawl.

garabato *m* *(gancho)* hook. **2** *(dibujo)* scrawl, scribble.

garaje *m* garage.

garante *adj* responsible. – **2** *mf* guarantor.

garantía *f* guarantee. **2** COM warranty, security.

garantizar [4] *t* to guarantee. **2** COM to warrant. **3** *(responder por)* to vouch for.

garbanzo *m* chickpea.

garbeo *m* *fam* walk. ●*dar(se) un* ~, to go for a walk.

garbo *m* gracefulness, jauntiness.

gardenia *f* gardenia.

garfio *m* hook.

garganta *f* ANAT throat. **2** GEOG gorge. **3** *(voz)* voice. ■ *dolor de* ~, sore throat.

gargantilla *f* necklace.

gárgaras *fpl* gargle *sing.*

gargarizar [4] *i* to gargle.

gárgola *f* gargoyle.

garita *f* sentry box.

garito *m* gambling den.

garra *f* *(de león etc.)* paw, claw; *(de halcón etc.)* talon. **2** *pey (de persona)* clutch. **3** *fig* force: *este libro no tiene* ~, this book has no bit to it.

garrafa *f* carafe.

garrafal *adj* monumental, enormous: *un error* ~, a terrible mistake.

garrapata *f* tick.

garrotazo *m* blow with a stick.

garrote *m* thick stick, cudgel. **2** *(pena capital)* garrotte. ●*dar* ~, to garrotte.

garza *f* heron.

gas *m* gas. **2** *pl* MED flatulence *sing.* ●*tener gases,* to have wind. ■ *agua con* ~, carbonated water.

gasa *f* gauze, chiffon.

gaseoso,-a *adj* gaseous. **2** *(bebida)* carbonated, fizzy. – **3** *f* pop, fizzy lemonade.

gasoil, gasóleo *m* diesel oil.

gasolina *f* petrol, US gas(oline).

gasolinera *f* petrol station.

gastado,-a *adj* spent. **2** *(usado)* used up.

gastar(se) *t* to spend. **2** *(usar)* to use, wear. – **3** *p* to run out, become used up.

gasto *m* expenditure, expense.

gatear *i* to creep, crawl.

gatillo *m* trigger.

gato,-a *m* (tom)cat. **2** *(de coche)* jack. – **3** *f* (she-)cat. ●*a gatas,* on all fours; *fam buscar tres pies al* ~, to complicate things; *fam dar* ~ *por liebre,* to take sb. in.

gastritis *f inv* gastritis.

gastronomía *f* gastronomy.

gatuno,-a *adj* catlike, feline.

gaveta *f* drawer.

gavilán *m* sparrow hawk.

gavilla *f* sheaf.

gaviota *f* (sea)gull.

gay *mf* gay.

gazapo *m* ZOOL young rabbit. **2** *fig (mentira)* lie. **3** *fig (error)* blunder, slip.

gazmoñería *f* prudishness, prudery.

gazpacho *m* cold soup *made of tomatoes and other vegetables.*

gel *m* gel. ■ ~ *de baño,* shower gel.

gelatina *f* gelatin(e). **2** CULIN jelly.

gema *f* gem, precious stone.

gemelo,-a *adj-m,f* twin. – **2** *mpl (botones)* cuff links. **3** *(anteojos)* binoculars.

gemido *m* groan, wail, moan.

Géminis *m* Gemini.

gemir [34] *i* to moan, groan, wail.

gendarme *m* gendarme.

gene *m* gene.

genealogía *f* genealogy.

genealógico,-a *adj* genealogical.

generación *f* generation.

generador *m* generator.

general *adj* general. **2** *(común)* common, usual. – **3** *m* MIL general.

generalizar(se) [4] *t* to generalize. – **2** *p* to become widespread.

generar *t* to generate.

genérico,-a *adj* generic.

género *m* *(clase)* kind, sort. **2** GRAM gender. **3** BIOL genus. **4** ART genre. **5** *(tela)* cloth. **6** COM article. ■ *géneros de punto,* knitwear *sing.*

generosidad *f* generosity.

generoso,-a *adj* generous.

génesis *f inv* genesis.

genial *adj* brilliant, inspired. **2** *fam* great.

genio *m* *(carácter)* temper, disposition. **2** *(persona)* genius. ●*tener mal* ~, to have a bad temper.

genitales *mpl* genitals.
genocidio *m* genocide.
gente *f* people. **2** *(familia)* family: *mi ~,* my family. ■ *pey* ~ *bien,* posh people.
gentil *adj-mf* heathen, pagan; *(no judío)* gentile. – **2** *adj* courteous, graceful. – **3 gentilmente** *adv* gracefully.
gentileza *f* grace. **2** *(cortesía)* politeness.
gentío *m* crowd.
gentuza *f pey* mob, rabble.
genuflexión *f* genuflexion.
genuino,-a *adj* genuine, true.
geografía *f* geography.
geográfico,-a *adj* geographic(al).
geología *f* geology.
geológico,-a *adj* geological.
geometría *f* geometry.
geométrico,-a *adj* geometric(al).
geranio *f* geranium.
gerencia *f* management, administration. **2** *(oficina)* manager's office.
gerente *mf m* manager, *f* manageress.
geriatría *f* geriatrics.
germen *m* germ. ▲ *pl* **gérmenes**.
germinar *i* to germinate.
gerundio *m* gerund.
gestación *f* gestation.
gestar(se) *t* to gestate. – **2** *p fig (sentimiento)* to grow; *(idea)* to develop; *(plan)* to be under way.
gesticulación *f* gesticulation, gestures *pl.*
gesticular *i* to gesticulate.
gestión *f (negociación)* negotiation. **2** *(de negocio)* administration, management. **3** *(diligencia)* step.
gestionar *t (negociar)* to negotiate. **2** *(negocio)* to run. **3** *(hacer diligencias)* to take steps to.
gesto *m* grimace, gesture.
gestor,-ra *m,f* manager, director. ■ *~ administrativo,* (business) agent.
gestoría *f* management. **2** *(administrativa)* (business) agency.
giba *f* hump, hunch.
gigante,-a *adj* giant, gigantic. – **2** *m,f* giant.
gigantesco,-a *adj* gigantic.
gilipollas* *adj-mf* arsehole*.
gimnasia *f* gymnastics.
gimnasio *m* gymnasium.
gimnasta *mf* gymnast.
gimotear *i* to whine, whimper.
gimoteo *m* whining, whimpering.
ginebra *f* gin.
ginecología *f* gynaecology.

gira *f (artística)* tour. **2** *(excursión)* trip, excursion.
girar *i* to rotate, whirl, spin. **2** *(torcer)* to turn. **3** *fig (conversación)* to deal with. – **4** *t-i* COM to draw.
girasol *m* sunflower.
giratorio,-a *adj* revolving.
giro *m* turn(ing). **2** *(dirección)* course, direction. **3** COM draft. **4** *(frase)* turn (of phrase). ■ *~ postal,* money order.
gitano,-a *adj-m,f* gypsy.
glacial *adj* glacial. **2** *(helado)* ice-cold.
glaciar *m* glacier.
glándula *f* gland.
glicerina *f* glycerin.
global *adj* total.
globo *m (esfera)* globe, sphere. **2** *(tierra)* world, earth. **3** *(de aire)* balloon. ■ *~ aerostático,* hot air/gas balloon; *~ ocular,* eyeball; *~ terráqueo,* globe.
glóbulo *m* globule. ■ *~ blanco/rojo,* white/red corpuscle.
gloria *f* glory. **2** *(fama)* fame, honour. **3** *(cielo)* heaven. **4** *(placer)* bliss, delight. **5** *(esplendor)* boast. ●*irón* **cubrirse de ~,** to make a fool of o.s.
glorieta *f* arbour, bower. **2** *(de calles)* roundabout.
glorificar [1] *t* to glorify.
glorioso,-a *adj* glorious.
glosa *f* gloss, comment.
glosar *t* to gloss, comment on.
glosario *m* glossary.
glotón,-ona *adj* gluttonous. – **2** *m,f* glutton.
glotonería *f* gluttony.
glucosa *f* glucose.
gobernador,-ra *adj* governing. – **2** *m,f* governor.
gobernante *adj* governing, ruling. – **2** *mf* ruler, leader.
gobernar(se) [27] *t gen* to govern. **2** *(país)* to rule. **3** *(dirigir)* to lead, direct. **4** *(barco)* to steer. **5** *(negocio)* to run, handle. – **6** *p* to manage one's affairs.
gobierno *m* POL government. **2** *(dirección)* direction, control. **3** *(timón)* rudder. ■ *para su ~,* for your own information.
goce *m* enjoyment.
gol *m* goal. ●*marcar un ~,* to score a goal.
golear *t* DEP to hammer.
golf *m* golf.
golfo,-a *adj-m,f (pilluelo)* street urchin. – **2*** *f* whore*. – **3** *m* GEOG gulf, large bay.
golondrina *f* swallow.

golosina *f* sweet.

goloso,-a *adj* sweet-toothed.

golpe *m* blow, knock. **2** *(coches)* bump. **3** *fig (desgracia)* blow. **4** *fam (robo)* hold-up. ●*al primer* ~ *de vista,* at first glance; *de* ~ *(y porrazo),* suddenly; *de un* ~, all at once. ■ ~ *de Estado,* coup d'état.

golpear *t* to hit, blow.

goma *f* gum, rubber. **2** *(de borrar)* rubber, eraser. **3** *arg (condón)* French letter.

gomaespuma *f* foam rubber.

gomina *f* hair cream.

góndola *f* gondola.

gordo,-a *adj* fat. **2** *(voluminoso)* bulky. **3** *(grueso)* thick. **4** *(grave)* serious. − **5** *m,f* fatty. ■ *el* ~, the first prize.

gordura *f* fatness, obesity.

gorgorito *m* trill.

gorila *m* gorilla.

gorjear *i* to trill.

gorjeo *m* trill.

gorra *f* cap, bonnet. ●*fam vivir de* ~, to live at another's expense.

gorrino,-a *adj* dirty. − **2** *m,f* (little) pig.

gorrión *m* sparrow

gorro *m* cap. **2** *(de bebé)* bonnet.

gorrón,-ona *adj fam* sponging. − **2** *m,f* sponger, parasite.

gota *f* drop. **2** MED gout.

gotear *i* to dribble, drip, leak. ▲ *Only used in the 3rd pers. It does not take a subject.*

gotera *f* leak.

gótico,-a *adj* Gothic.

gozada *f fam* delight.

gozar(se) [4] *t-i* to enjoy (o.s.). − **2** *p* to take pleasure (*en,* in).

gozne *m* hinge.

gozo *m* joy, delight, pleasure.

grabación *f* recording.

grabado,-a *adj* engraved, stamped. − **2** *m* engraving, print. **3** *(ilustración)* picture.

grabador,-ra *adj* recording. − **2** *f* tape recorder. − **3** *m,f* engraver.

grabar *t* to engrave. **2** *(sonido)* to record.

gracia *f* grace(fulness). **2** *(encanto)* charm. **3** *(elegancia)* elegance. **4** *(chiste)* joke, wittiness. ●*gracias a,* thanks to, owing to; *hacer/tener* ~, to be funny; *¡(muchas) gracias!,* thank you (very much); *¡qué* ~*!,* how funny!

gracioso,-a *adj* graceful, charming. **2** *(bromista)* witty, facetious. **3** *(divertido)* funny, amusing. − **4** *m,f* TEAT jester, clown, fool.

grada *f* step. **2** *(asiento)* row of seats.

gradación *f* gradation.

gradería *f* rows *pl* of seats.

grado *m* gen degree. **2** *(estado)* stage. **3** EDUC *(clase)* class, grade. **4** EDUC *(título)* degree. **5** *(peldaño)* step. ●*de buen/mal* ~, willingly/unwillingly.

graduable *adj* adjustable.

graduación *f* graduation, grading. **2** *(de licor etc.)* strength. **3** MIL rank, degree of rank. **4** EDUC admission to a degree.

graduado,-a *adj* graduated, graded. − **2** *m,f* EDUC graduate.

gradual *adj* gradual.

graduar(se) [11] *t* gen to graduate. **2** EDUC to give a diploma/degree to. **3** *(medir)* to gauge, measure. − **4** *p* to take a degree.

grafía *f* graphic symbol. **2** *(escritura)* writing.

gráfico,-a *adj* graphic. **2** *fig (vívido)* vivid, lifelike. − **3** *f* graph, diagram. − **4** *m (dibujo)* sketch.

grafología *f* graphology.

gragea *f* pill, tablet.

grajo *m* rook, crow.

grama *f* AM grass.

gramática *f* grammar.

gramo *m* gram(me).

gramófono *m* gramophone.

gran *adj* → **grande**. ▲ *Used in front of a sing masculine noun:* ~ *chico/chico grande*.

grana *f* (small) seed. **2** *(insecto)* cochineal. **3** *(color)* scarlet colour. **4** *(paño)* scarlet cloth.

granada *f* BOT pomegranate. **2** MIL grenade, shell.

granado,-a *adj (ilustre)* illustrious. **2** *(maduro)* mature, expert. **3** *(espigado)* tall, grown.

granar *i* to seed.

granate *adj-m* maroon.

grande *adj* large, big. − **2** *m* grandee, nobleman. ▲ → **gran**.

grandeza *f* bigness, largeness. **2** *(tamaño)* size. **3** *(majestad)* greatness, grandeur.

grandilocuencia *f* grandiloquence.

grandiosidad *f* grandeur, magnificence, grandness.

grandioso,-a *adj* grandiose, grand, magnificent.

granel *(a)* ~, *adv* loose, in bulk.

granero *m* granary, barn.

granito *m* granite.

granizado *m* iced drink.

granizada *f* hailstorm.

granizar [4] *i* to hail, sleet. ▲ *Only used in the 3rd pers. It does not take a subject.*
granizo *m* hail.
granja *f* farm.
granjear(se) *t-p* to win, obtain, earn.
granjero,-a *m,f* farmer.
grano *m* grain; *(de café)* bean. **2** MED pimple, spot. **3** *pl* cereals. ●*fam ir al* ~, to come to the point.
granuja *m* urchin, rascal.
granulado,-a *adj* granulated.
grapa *f* staple, cramp.
grapadora *f* stapler.
graso,-a *adj* greasy. **2** *(alimentos)* fatty. — **3** *f* grease, fat.
grasiento,-a *adj* greasy, oily.
gratificación *f* gratification. **2** *(recompensa)* recompense, reward.
gratificar [1] *t* to gratify. **2** *(recompensar)* to reward, tip.
gratinar *t* to grill.
gratis *adv* free.
gratitud *f* gratitude, gratefulness.
grato,-a *adj* agreeable, pleasant. — **2** *gratamente adv* pleasantly.
gratuito,-a *adj* free (of charge). **2** *(arbitrario)* arbitrary, gratuitous.
grava *f (guijas)* gravel. **2** *(piedra machacada)* broken stone.
gravamen *m (carga)* burden, obligation. **2** *(impuesto)* tax, duty. ▲ *pl* **gravámenes**.
gravar *t* to tax.
grave *adj (que pesa)* heavy. **2** *(serio)* grave, serious. **3** *(difícil)* difficult. **4** *(solemne)* solemn. **5** GRAM *(acento)* grave. **6** *(voz)* deep, low.
gravedad *f* gravity. **2** *(importancia)* importance, seriousness. **3** *(de sonido)* depth.
grávido,-a *adj fml (lleno)* full. **2** *(embarazada)* pregnant.
gravitar *i* FÍS to gravitate. **2** *fig (amenazar)* to loom (*sobre*, over).
graznar *i (cuervo)* to caw, croak. **2** *(oca)* to cackle, gaggle.
graznido *m (de cuervo)* caw, croak. **2** *(de oca)* cackle, gaggle.
gremio *m* guild, corporation.
greña *f* tangled mop of hair.
gresca *f* noise, racket.
grey *f (rebaño)* flock, herd. **2** *(de personas)* group.
grieta *f* crack, crevice. **2** *(en la piel)* chap.
grifo *m* tap.
grillarse *p* to sprout.
grillete *m* fetter, shackle.

grillo *m* ZOOL cricket. **2** *(de patata)* sprout. **3** *(grilletes)* fetters *pl*.
grima *f* displeasure, disgust.
gringo,-a *adj-m,f* AM *pey* North American (person).
gripe *f* flu, influenza.
gris *adj-m* grey, US gray.
grisáceo,-a *adj* greyish.
gritar *i* to shout, cry out, scream.
griterío *m* shouting, uproar.
grito *m* shout, cry, scream. ●*fam a* ~ *pelado*, at the top of one's voice.
grosella *f* red currant. ■ ~ *silvestre*, gooseberry.
grosería *f* coarseness, rudeness.
grosero,-a *adj* coarse, rough. **2** *(maleducado)* rude. — **3** *m,f* boor, churl.
grosor *m* thickness.
grotesco,-a *adj* grotesque, ridiculous.
grúa *f* crane, derrick. **2** AUTO breakdown van, US towtruck.
grueso,-a *adj* thick. **2** *(gordo)* bulky, fat, stout. — **3** *m* bulk, mass. **4** *(parte principal)* main body.
grulla *f* crane.
grumete *m* cabin boy.
grumo *m (de sangre)* clot. **2** *(de líquido)* lump. **3** *(de leche)* curd.
gruñido *m* grunt, growl, grumble.
gruñir [40] *i* to grunt. **2** *(chirriar)* to creak.
gruñón,-ona *adj* grumbling, cranky. — **2** *m,f* grumbler.
grupo *m* group.
gruta *f* cavern, grotto, cave.
guadaña *f* scythe.
guante *m* glove.
guantón *m* AM slap.
guapo,-a *adj* handsome, good-looking. **2** *arg (bonito)* nice, smart.
guarda *mf* guard, keeper. — **2** *f* custody, care. **3** *(de la ley etc.)* observance. **4** *(de libro)* flyleaf. **5** AUTO guard plate.
guardabarrera *mf* gatekeeper.
guardabarros *m inv* mudguard.
guardabosque *m* gamekeeper.
guardacostas *m inv* coastguard ship.
guardaespaldas *m inv* bodyguard.
guardagujas *m inv* pointsman.
guardameta *mf* goalkeeper.
guardamuebles *m inv* furniture warehouse.
guardapolvo *m* dust cover. **2** *(mono)* overalls *pl*.
guardar(se) *t (cuidar)* to keep, watch over, guard. **2** *(conservar)* to lay up, store. **3** *(leyes etc.)* to observe, obey. —

4 *p (precaverse)* to keep (*de,* from), guard (*de,* against). **5** *(evitar)* to avoid.

guardarropa *m (armario)* wardrobe. **2** *(local)* cloakroom. **– 3** *mf* cloakroom attendant.

guardavía *m* linekeeper.

guardería *f* crèche, nursery.

guardia *mf* guard. **– 2** *f (defensa)* defense, protection. **3** *(servicio)* duty. **4** *(tropa)* guard. ●*estar de* ~, to be on duty. ■ ~ *civil,* Civil Guard; ~ *urbano,* policeman; *médico de* ~, doctor on duty.

guardián,-ana *m,f* guardian, keeper.

guarecer(se) [43] *t* to shelter, protect. **– 2** *p* to take shelter, refuge.

guarida *f* ZOOL haunt, den, lair. **2** *pey (refugio)* den.

guarismo *m* cipher, figure.

guarnecer [43] *t (decorar)* to adorn, decorate, garnish. **2** *(proveer)* to furnish, provide. **3** MIL to garrison. **4** *(joya)* to set. **5** *(caballo)* to harness.

guarnición *f (de joya)* setting. **2** CULIN garnish. **3** MIL garrison.

guarrada *f,* **guarrería** *f* dirty thing. **2** *(mala pasada)* dirty trick.

guarro,-a *adj* dirty, filthy. **– 2** *m (cerdo)* hog. **– 3** *f (cerda)* saw.

guasa *f* jest, fun. ●*estar de* ~, to be in a jesting mood.

guasearse *p* to make fun (*de,* of).

guasón,-ona *adj* funny. **– 2** *m,f* jester, mocker.

guateque *m* party.

guay *adj fam* super.

gubernamental, gubernativo,-a *adj* government(al).

guedeja *f* long hair. **2** *(de león)* mane.

guerra *f* war.

guerrear *i* to war.

guerrero,-a *adj* warlike. **– 2** *m,f* warrior, soldier.

guerrilla *f (guerra)* guerrilla warfare. **2** *(banda)* guerrilla band.

guerrillero,-a *m,f* guerrilla.

gueto *m* ghetto.

guía *mf* guide, leader. **– 2** *f (libro)* guidebook. **3** *(de bicicleta)* handle bar. ■ ~ *de teléfonos,* (telephone) directory.

guiar(se) [13] *t* to guide, lead. **2** *(vehículo)* to drive, steer. **3** *(avión)* to pilot. **-- 4** *p* to be guided (*por,* by).

guijarro *m* pebble, cobble.

guillotina *f* guillotine.

guinda *f* sour cherry.

guindilla *f* red pepper.

guiñapo *m* rag, tatter.

guiñar *t* to wink.

guiño *m* wink.

guión *m* GRAM hyphen, dash. **2** *(de discurso)* notes *pl.* **3** CINEM script.

guionista *mf* scriptwriter.

guiri *mf arg* foreigner.

guirigay *m (lenguaje)* gibberish. **2** *(griterío)* hubbub, confusion.

guirnalda *f* garland, wreath.

guisa *f fml* manner, way. ●*a* ~ *de,* as, like.

guisado,-a *adj* CULIN cooked, prepared. **– 2** *m* stew.

guisante *m* pea.

guisar *t* to cook, stew.

guiso *m* stew.

guita *f arg* bread, brass.

guitarra *f* guitar.

guitarrista *mf* guitarist.

gula *f* gluttony.

gusanillo *f* little worm. ●*fam matar el* ~, to have a snack.

gusano *m* worm; *(oruga)* caterpillar. **2** *fig (persona)* miserable, wretch. ■ ~ *de (la) seda,* silkworm.

gustar *t (agradar)* to like: *me gusta,* I like it. **2** *(probar)* to taste. ●*fml cuando guste,* whenever you want.

gusto *m gen* taste. **2** *(sabor)* flavour. **3** *(placer)* pleasure. **4** *(capricho)* whim, fancy. ●*con mucho* ~, with pleasure; *dar* ~, to please, delight; *de buen/mal* ~, in good/bad taste; *tanto* ~, delighted, pleased to meet you.

gustoso,-a *adj (sabroso)* tasty, savoury, palatable. **2** *(agradable)* agreeable, pleasant. **3** *(con gusto)* glad, willing, ready. **– 4** *gustosamente adv* with pleasure, gladly, willingly.

gutural *adj* guttural.

H

haba *f* broad bean.

habano *m* Havana cigar.

haber [72] *verbo aux* to have: ~ *hecho,* to have done. **2** *(obligación)* to have *(de, to),* must: *has de venir hoy,* you must come today. **– 3** *t (poseer)* to have. **– 4** *i* to be: *hay un puente,* there is a bridge. **– 5** *m (cuenta corriente)* credit. **6** *(posesiones)* property. **7** *(sueldo)* salary. ●*habérselas con algn.,* to be up against sb. ▲ **4** *only used in the 3rd person. It does not take a subject.*

habichuela *f* French bean.

hábil *adj (aptitud)* skilful. **2** *(despabilado)* clever. **– 3 hábilmente** *adv* skilfully. ■ *día* ~, working day.

habilidad *f (aptitud)* skill. **2** *(astucia)* cleverness. **3** *(objeto)* craft.

habilidoso,-a *adj* skilful.

habilitar *t (espacio)* to fit out. **2** *(capacitar)* to entitle. **3** FIN to finance.

habitación *f* room. **2** *(dormitorio)* bedroom.

habitante *mf* inhabitant.

habitar *t* to live in. **– 2** *i* to live.

hábito *m (costumbre)* habit, custom. **2** *(vestido)* habit.

habitual *adj* usual, habitual, customary. **2** *(asiduo)* regular.

habituar(se) [11] *t* to accustom *(a,* to). **– 2** *p* to become accustomed *(a,* to).

habla *f (facultad)* speech. **2** *(idioma)* language: *países de* ~ *hispana,* Spanish-speaking countries. ●*al* ~!, speaking! ▲ *Takes* **el** *and* **un** *in sing.*

hablado,-a *adj* spoken.

hablador,-ra *adj-m,f (parlanchín)* talkative (person). **2** *(chismoso)* gossip(y).

habladuría *f* piece of gossip.

hablante *mf* speaker.

hablar *i* to speak, talk *(con,* to). **– 2** *t (idioma)* to speak. ●~ *alto/bajo/claro,* to speak loud/softly/plainly; ~ *en broma,* to be joking; *¡ni* ~!, certainly not!; *fam* ~ *por los codos,* to be a chatterbox.

hacendado,-a *m,f* landowner.

hacer(se) [73] *t (producir)* to make; *(comida)* to prepare. **2** *(construir)* to build. **3** *(efectuar, recorrer)* to do. **4** *(causar)* to cause. **5** *(obligar)* to make: *hazle callar,* make him/her shut up. **6** *(creer, suponer)* to think: *le hacía en Roma,* I thought he/she was in Rome. **7** *(aparentar)* to act: ~ *el imbécil,* to act stupid. **– 8** *i (representar)* to play *(de,* -). **9** *(clima)* to be: *hace buen día,* it's a fine day. **10** *(tiempo pasado)* ago: *hace tres años,* three years ago. **11** *(fingirse)* to pretend to be, act as. **– 12** *p (volverse)* to become: ~*se viejo,-a,* to grow old. **13** *(crecer)* to grow. ●~ *bien/mal,* to do the right/wrong thing; ~ *cola,* to queue up; ~ *conocer/saber,* to make known; ~ *gracia,* to tickle; ~ *la cama,* to make the bed; ~ *la(s) maleta(s),* to pack; ~ *lugar,* to make room; ~ *pedazos,* to ruin; ~ *recados,* to run errands; ~ *sombra,* to cast a shadow; ~ *tiempo,* to kill time; ~*se con,* to get hold of; ~*se a un lado,* to step aside; *fam* ~ *se el/la sordo,-a,* to turn a deaf ear; *euf* ~ *de vientre/del cuerpo,* to evacuate one's bowels. ▲ pp **hecho,-a.** **9** *and* **10** *only used in the 3rd person. They do not take a subject.*

hacha *f* axe. ▲ *Takes* **el** *and* **un** *in sing.*

hachís *m* hashish.

hacia *prep (dirección)* towards, to. **2** *(tiempo)* at about/around. ●~ *abajo,* downward(s); ~ *adelante,* forward(s); ~ *arriba,* upward(s); ~ *atrás,* backward(s).

hacienda *f (bienes)* property. **2** *(finca)* estate, property. ■ ~ *pública,* public funds/finances *pl.*

hacinar *t* to pile up.

hada f fairy. ▲ *Takes* **el** *and* **un** *in sing.*

¡hala! *interj (dar prisa)* go on! **2** *(infundir ánimo)* come on! **3** *(sorpresa)* oh dear!

halagar [7] *t* to flatter.

halago *m* compliment.

halagüeño,-a *adj (adulador)* flattering. **2** *(promesa, futuro)* promising.

halcón *m* falcon.

¡hale! *interj* get going!

hallar(se) *t (encontrar)* to find. **2** *(averiguar)* to find out. **3** *(ver, notar)* to see, observe. — **4** *p (estar)* to be.

hallazgo *m (descubrimiento)* finding, discovery. **2** *(cosa descubierta)* find.

halo *m* halo, aura.

halterofilia *f* weight-lifting.

hamaca *f* hammock.

hambre *f* hunger, starvation. ●*tener* ~, to be hungry; *pey* *ser un muerto de* ~, to be a good-for-nothing. ▲ *Takes* **el** *and* **un** *in sing.*

hambriento,-a *adj-m,f* hungry (person): *fig* ~ *de justicia,* longing for justice.

hampa *f* underworld.

hámster *m* hamster.

hándicap *m* handicap.

hangar *m* hangar.

harapiento,-a *adj* ragged, tattered.

harapo *m* rag, tatter.

harem, **harén** *m* harem.

harina *f* flour. ●*fig eso es* ~ *de otro costal,* that's another kettle of fish.

hartar(se) *t (atiborrar)* to satiate, fill up. **2** *(fastidiar)* to annoy. **3** *(causar)* to overwhelm *(de,* with). — **4** *p (atiborrarse)* to eat one's fill. **5** *(cansarse)* to get fed up *(de,* with).

harto,-a *adj (repleto)* full. **2** *fam (cansado)* tired of, fed up with.

hasta *prep (tiempo)* until, till, up to. **2** *(lugar)* as far as. **3** *(cantidad)* up to, as many as. — **4** *conj* ~ *(que),* until. ●*¡*~ *luego!,* see you later!

hastiar(se) [13] *t* to make sick/tired *(de,* of). — **2** *p* to get sick/tired *(de,* of).

hastío *m (repugnancia)* disgust. **2** *fig* boredom.

hay *pres indic* → **haber.**

haya *f* BOT beech. — **2** *pres subj* → **haber.**

haz *m* bundle; *(de hierba, leña)* sheaf. **2** *(de luz)* beam. — **3** *f (cara)* face. — **4** *imperat* → **hacer.**

hazaña *f* deed, exploit.

hazmerreír *m* laughing stock.

he *adv* ~ *ahí/aquí,* there/here you have. — **2** *pres indic* → **haber.**

hebilla *f* buckle.

hebra *f (de hilo)* (piece of) thread. **2** *(de carne)* sinew. **3** *fig* thread.

hebreo,-a *adj-m,f* Hebrew.

hecatombe *f* hecatomb. **2** *(desgracia)* disaster, catastrophe.

hechicería *f (arte)* sorcery, witchcraft. **2** *(hechizo)* spell, charm.

hechicero,-a *adj* bewitching. — **2** *m,f m* sorcerer, wizard, *f* sorceress, witch.

hechizar [4] *t (embrujar)* to bewitch. **2** *fig (cautivar)* to charm.

hechizo *m (embrujo)* charm, spell. **2** *fig (embelesamiento)* fascination.

hecho,-a *pp* → **hacer.** — **2** *adj* made: *un bistec* ~, a well-cooked steak. **3** *(persona)* mature. — **4** *m (realidad)* fact. **5** *(suceso)* event, incident. — **6** *interj* ¡done! ●*¡bien* ~!, well done!; *dicho y* ~, no sooner said than done; ~ *a mano/máquina,* hand-/machine-made. ■ ~ *consumado,* fait accompli.

hechura *f (forma)* shape. **2** COST cut.

hectárea *f* hectare.

hectolitro *m* hectolitre.

hectómetro *m* hectometre.

heder [28] *i* to stink.

hedor *m* stink, stench.

hegemonía *f* hegemony.

helado,-a *adj* frozen; MED frostbitten. **2** *(pasmado)* dumbfounded. — **3** *m* ice cream. — **4** *f* METEOR frost, freeze. ●*fam fig quedarse* ~, to be flabbergasted.

helar(se) [27] *t-p* to freeze; MED to frostbite. — **2** *i* METEOR to freeze: *anoche heló,* there was a frost last night. ▲ **2** only used in the 3rd person. It does not take a subject.

helecho *m* fern.

helénico,-a *adj* Hellenic, Greek.

hélice *f* helix. **2** AV MAR propeller.

helicóptero *m* helicopter.

hematoma *m* haematoma, bruise.

hembra *f* female. **2** *(mujer)* woman. **3** *(de tornillo)* nut. **4** *(de enchufe)* socket. **5** *(corchete)* eye.

hemisferio *m* hemisphere.

hemorragia *f* haemorrhage.

henchir(se) [34] *t (llenar)* to fill. — **2** *p (atiborrarse)* to stuff o.s.

hender(se) [28] *t-p* to cleave, split, crack.

hendidura *f* cleft, crack.

hendir(se) [29] *t-p* → **hender.**

heno *m* hay.

hepático,-a *adj* hepatic.

hepatitis *f inv* hepatitis.

heptágono *m* heptagon.

heráldico,-a *adj* heraldic. − **2** *f* heraldry.
herbaje *m* grass, pasture.
herbario,-a *adj* herbal. − **2** *m* herbarium.
herbicida *m* weedkiller, herbicide.
herbívoro,-a *adj* herbivorous. − **2** *m,f* herbivore.
herbolario,-a *m,f (persona)* herbalist. − **2** *m (tienda)* herbalist's (shop).
herboristería *f* herbalist's (shop).
heredad *f* property, estate.
heredar *t* to inherit.
heredero,-a *m,f m* heir, *f* heiress.
hereditario,-a *adj* hereditary.
hereje *mf* heretic.
herejía *f* heresy.
herencia *f* inheritance. **2** *(genética)* heredity.
herida *f* wound.
herido,-a *adj-m,f* wounded (person), injured (person).
herir [35] *t* to wound, injure, hurt.
hermafrodita *adj-mf* hermaphrodite.
hermanar *t* to unite.
hermanastro,-a *m,f m* stepbrother, *f* stepsister.
hermandad *f (congregación)* fraternity, brotherhood, sisterhood. **2** *(parentesco)* brotherhood.
hermano,-a *m,f m* brother, *f* sister. ■ ~ *político,-a*, brother-/sister-in-law.
hermético,-a *adj* hermetic(al), airtight. **2** *fig* impenetrable.
hermetismo *m* hermetism. **2** *fig* secrecy.
hermoso,-a *adj* beautiful, lovely.
hermosura *adj* beauty.
hernia *f* hernia, rupture.
herniarse [12] *p* to rupture o.s.
héroe *m* hero.
heroico,-a *adj* heroic.
heroína *f (mujer)* heroine. **2** *(droga)* heroin.
heroinómano,-a *m,f* heroin addict.
heroísmo *m* heroism.
herradura *f* horseshoe.
herramienta *f* tool.
herrar [27] *t (caballo)* to shoe. **2** *(ganado)* to brand.
herrería *f (taller)* forge, ironworks. **2** *(tienda)* blacksmith's shop.
herrero *m* blacksmith.
hervidero *m* boiling. **2** *(manantial)* spring of water. **3** *fig (multitud)* swarm.
hervir [35] *t-i* to boil.
hervor *m* boiling, bubbling.
heterodoxo,-a *adj-m,f* heterodox (person).

heterogéneo,-a *adj* heterogeneous.
hexágono *m* hexagon.
hez *f* scum, dregs *pl*. **2** *pl* excrements. ▲ *pl heces*.
hibernación *f* hibernation.
hibernar *i* to hibernate.
híbrido,-a *adj* hybrid.
hidalgo,-a *adj* noble. − **2** *m* nobleman, gentleman.
hidratación *f* hydration. **2** *(de la piel)* moisturizing.
hidratante *adj-m* moisturizing.
hidratar *t* to hydrate. **2** *(piel)* to moisturize.
hidrato *m* hydrate. ■ ~ *de carbono*, carbohydrate.
hidráulico,-a *adj* hydraulic.
hidroavión *m* hydroplane, seaplane.
hidrógeno *m* hydrogen.
hiedra *f* ivy.
hiel *f* bile.
hielo *m* ice. ●*romper el* ~, to break the ice.
hiena *f* hy(a)ena.
hierático,-a *adj* REL hieratic(al). **2** *(rígido)* rigid.
hierba *f* grass. **2** *arg (marihuana)* grass. ■ *mala* ~, weed; ~ *mate*, maté.
hierbabuena *f* mint.
hierro *m* iron. ●*fig ser de* ~, to be strong as an ox. ■ ~ *colado/fundido*, cast iron; ~ *forjado*, wrought iron.
hígado *m* liver.
higiene *f* hygiene.
higiénico,-a *adj* hygienic. ■ *papel* ~, toilet paper.
higo *m* fig. ■ ~ *chumbo*, prickly pear.
higuera *f* fig tree.
hijastro,-a *m,f* stepchild; *m* stepson, *f* stepdaughter.
hijo,-a *m,f* child; *m* son, *f* daughter: *hijos,* children. ■ ~ *político,-a*, son-in-law/daughter-in-law; ~ *único,-a*, only child.
hilacha *f*, **hilacho** *m* unravelled thread.
hilado,-a *adj* spun. − **2** *m (operación)* spinning. **3** *(hilo)* thread.
hilador,-ra, **hilandero,-a** *m,f* spinner.
hilar *t* to spin.
hilaridad *f fml* hilarity.
hilera *f* line, row.
hilo *m* thread. **2** *(lino)* linen. **3** *(telefónico)* wire. ●*con un* ~ *de voz*, in a thin voice; *fig seguir el* ~ *de la conversación*, to follow a conversation.
hilván *m* tacking, basting.
hilvanar *t* to tack, baste. **2** *fig* to throw.

himno *m* hymn. ■ ~ *nacional,* national anthem.

hincapié *m* hacer ~ *en,* to insist on.

hincar [1] *t* to drive (in). ●~ *el diente,* to bite; *fig* to get one's teeth (*a,* into).

hincha *f (antipatía)* dislike. — 2 *mf* fan, supporter.

hinchado,-a *adj* inflated. 2 MED swollen. 3 *fig (persona)* vain.

hinchar(se) *t* to inflate, blow up. — 2 *p* MED to swell. 3 *(engreírse)* to get conceited. 4 *fam (comer)* to stuff o.s.

hinchazón *f* swelling, inflation.

hinojo *m* fennel.

hipar *i* to hiccup, have the hiccups.

hipermercado *m* hypermarket.

hípico,-a *adj* horse, equine.

hipnosis *f inv* hypnosis.

hipnotizar [4] *t* to hypnotize.

hipo *m* hiccup, hiccough.

hipocondría *f* hypochondria.

hipocondríaco,-a *adj-m,f* hypochondriac.

hipocresía *f* hypocrisy.

hipócrita *adj* hypocritical. — 2 *mf* hypocrite.

hipódromo *m* racetrack, racecourse.

hipoteca *f* mortgage.

hipotecar [1] *t* to mortgage. 2 *fig* to jeopardize.

hipótesis *f inv* hypothesis.

hipotético,-a *adj* hypothetic(al).

hippie *adj-mf* hippy.

hirviente *adj* boiling, seething.

hispánico,-a *adj* Hispanic, Spanish.

hispanidad *f* Spanishness. 2 *(mundo hispánico)* Spanish/Hispanic world.

hispano,-a *adj* Spanish, Hispanic. 2 *(de América)* Spanish-American. — 3 *m,f* Spaniard. 4 *(de América)* Spanish American, US Hispanic.

hispanoamericano,-a *adj* Spanish American.

hispanohablante *adj-mf* Spanish-speaking (person).

histeria *f* hysteria. ■ ~ *colectiva,* mass hysteria.

histérico,-a *adj* hysteric(al).

historia *f (estudio)* history. 2 *(narración)* story, tale.

historiador,-ra *m,f* historian.

historial *m* MED record. 2 *(currículo)* curriculum (vitae).

historiar [13] *t* to chronicle.

histórico,-a *adj* historical. 2 *(importante)* historic.

historieta *f (cuento)* short story, tale. 2 *(viñetas)* comic strip.

hito *m (mojón)* milestone. 2 *(blanco)* target. ●*mirar de ~ en ~,* to stare at.

hobby *m* hobby.

hocico *m* snout.

hockey *m* hockey.

hogar *m (de chimenea)* hearth. 2 *fig* home.

hogareño,-a *adj (vida)* home, family. 2 *(persona)* home-loving.

hogaza *f* large loaf (of bread).

hoguera *f* bonfire.

hoja *f* gen leaf. 2 *(pétalo)* petal. 3 *(de papel)* sheet, leaf; *(impreso)* handout. 4 *(de libro)* leaf, page. 5 *(de metal)* sheet. 6 *(de cuchillo)* blade. ■ ~ *de afeitar,* razor blade; ~ *de ruta,* waybill; ~ *de servicios,* record of service.

hojalata *f* tin(plate).

hojaldre *m & f* puff pastry.

hojarasca *f* fallen/dead leaves *pl.* 2 *(frondosidad)* foliage. 3 *fig* trash; *(palabras)* verbiage.

hojear *t* to leaf/flick through.

hojuela *f* pancake. ●*fig miel sobre hojuelas,* so much the better.

¡hola! *interj* hello!, hullo!, US hi! 2 AM *(al teléfono)* hello.

holgado,-a *adj (desocupado)* idle. 2 *(ropa)* loose, baggy. 3 *(espacio)* roomy. 4 *(de dinero)* comfortable, well-off.

holgar(se) [52] *i (descansar)* to rest. 2 *(estar ocioso)* to be idle. — 3 *p (alegrarse)* to be pleased *(con/de,* by). 4 *(divertirse)* to enjoy o.s. ●*huelga decir que ...,* needless to say (that) ... .

holgazán,-ana *adj* idle, lazy. — 2 *m,f* lazybones *inv,* layabout.

holgazanear *i* to idle, lounge about.

holgazanería *f* idleness, laziness.

holgorio *m* revelry, meriment.

holgura *f (ropa)* looseness. 2 *(espacio)* roominess. 3 *(bienestar)* affluence, comfort.

hollar [31] *t (comprimir)* to tread (on), trample down. 2 *(pisar)* to trample on. 3 *fig* to humiliate.

hollín *m* soot.

holocausto *m* holocaust.

hombre *m* man. 2 *(especie)* man(kind). 3 *fam (marido)* husband. — 4 *interj* what a surprise!: ¡~, claro!, well, of course!, you bet! ■ ~ *anuncio,* sandwich man; ~ *de estado,* statesman; ~ *de negocios,* businessman; *fig* ~ *de paja,* front man; *fam* ~ *del saco,* bogey man.

hombrear *i* to act the man. **2** *(con hombros)* to push with one's shoulders.

hombrera *f* shoulder pad. **2** MIL epaulette.

hombro *m* shoulder. ●*arrimar el ~,* to help out; *encogerse de hombros,* to shrug (one's shoulders).

hombruno,-a *adj* mannish, manly.

homenaje *m* homage, tribute.

homenajear *t* to pay tribute to.

homeopatía *f* homeopathy.

homicida *adj* homicidal: *el arma ~,* the murder weapon. **– 2** *mf* killer.

homicidio *m* homicide, murder.

homogeneidad *f* homogeneity, uniformity.

homogeneizar [26] *t* to homogenize.

homogéneo,-a *adj* homogeneous, uniform.

homologar [7] *t* to give official approval to. **2** DEP to ratify.

homólogo,-a *adj* comparable. **– 2** *m,f* opposite number.

homónimo *m* homonym.

homosexual *adj-mf* homosexual.

homosexualidad *f* homosexuality.

hondo,-a *adj* deep. **– 2** *m* bottom, the depths *pl.* **– 3** *f* sling. ■ *cante ~,* flamenco (music).

hondonada *f* hollow, ravine.

hondura *f* depth.

honestidad *f (honradez)* honesty. **2** *(recato)* modesty.

honesto,-a *adj (honrado)* honest, upright. **2** *(recatado)* modest.

hongo *m* fungus. **2** *(sombrero)* bowler (hat).

honor *m* honour. **2** *pl* title *sing.* **3** *(agasajo)* honours. ●*en ~ a la verdad,* to be fair.

honorable *adj* honourable.

honorario,-a *adj* honorary. **– 2** *mpl* fee *sing.*

honra *f* honour, dignity. **2** *(respeto)* respect. ●*¡y a mucha ~!,* and (I'm) proud of it!

honradez *f* honesty.

honrado,-a *adj* honest. **2** *(decente)* upright.

honrar(se) *t (respetar)* to honour. **2** *(enaltecer)* to do credit to. **– 3** *p* to be honoured.

honroso,-a *adj (que honra)* honourable. **2** *(decoroso)* respectable.

hora *f* hour. **2** *(tiempo)* time. **3** *(cita)* appointment. ●*a altas horas,* in the small hours. ■ *~ oficial,* standard time; *~*

punta, rush hour; *horas extras,* overtime (hours); *hora punta,* rush hour.

horadar *t* to perforate.

horario *m* timetable, schedule: *tengo ~ de mañana,* I work mornings.

horca *f (patíbulo)* gallows *pl.* **2** AGR hayfork.

horcajadas *a ~, adv* astride.

horchata *f* sweet milky drink *made from chufa nuts or almonds.*

horizontal *adj* horizontal.

horizonte *m* horizon.

horma *f* mould. **2** *(de zapato)* last. ●*encontrar uno la ~ de su zapato,* to meet one's match.

hormiga *f* ant.

hormigón *m* concrete. ■ *~ armado,* reinforced concrete.

hormigonera *f* concrete mixer.

hormigueo *m* itch.

hormiguero *m* anthill.

hormona *f* hormone.

hornada *f* batch.

horno *m* oven. **2** TÉC furnace. **3** *(cerámica, ladrillos)* kiln. ■ *alto ~,* blast furnace; *~ (de) microondas,* microwave oven. ●*fam no estar el ~ para bollos,* not to be the right time.

horóscopo *m* horoscope.

horquilla *f (alfiler)* hairgrip, hairpin. **2** AGR pitchfork. **3** *(de bicicleta)* fork.

horrendo,-a *adj* awful, frightful.

hórreo *m* granary.

horrible *adj* horrible, dreadful.

horripilante *adj* hair-raising, horrifying.

horror *m (repulsión)* horror. **2** *(temor)* hate. **3** *fig (atrocidad)* atrocity. **4** *fam fig* awful lot.

horrorizar(se) [4] *t* to horrify, terrify. **– 2** *p* to be horrified.

horroroso,-a *adj* horrible. **2** *(feo)* ugly. **3** *fam (malísimo)* dreadful, awful.

hortalizas *fpl* vegetables, greens.

hortelano,-a *m,f* market gardener, US truck farmer. ●*el perro del ~,* the dog in the manger.

hortensia *f* hydrangea.

hortera *arg adj* common, vulgar, tacky.

horterada *f arg* tacky thing/act.

horticultura *f* horticulture.

hosco,-a *adj* sullen, surly. **2** *(lugar)* gloomy.

hospedaje *m* lodging; *(precio)* cost of lodging.

hospedar(se) *t* to lodge. **– 2** *p* to stay *(en,* at).

hospicio *m* (*de huérfanos*) orphanage. 2 (*de pobres, peregrinos*) hospice.

hospital *m* hospital.

hospitalario,-a *adj* (*acogedor*) hospitable. 2 MED hospital.

hospitalidad *f* hospitality.

hospitalizar [4] *t* to go/send into hospital, hospitalize.

hostal *m* hostel.

hostelería *f* catering business.

hostia *f* REL host, Eucharistic wafer. 2* (*choque*) bash. − 3* *interj* damn it! •*ser la ~**, (*fantástico*) to be bloody amazing*; (*penoso*) to be bloody useless*.

hostiar* *t* to bash.

hostigar [7] *t* (*azotar*) to whip. 2 (*perseguir*) to plague, persecute. 3 (*molestar*) to pester.

hostil *adj* hostile.

hostilidad *f* hostility.

hotel *m* hotel.

hotelero,-a *adj* hotel. − 2 *m,f* hotel keeper.

hoy *adv* today. 2 (*presente*) now. •*de ~ en adelante,* from now on; *~ (en) día,* nowadays; *~ por ~,* at the present time.

hoya *f* hole, pit. 2 GEOG valley, dale.

hoyo *m* hole.

hoyuelo *m* dimple.

hoz *f* AGR sickle. 2 GEOG ravine.

hucha *f* moneybox. 2 *fig* savings *pl.*

hueco,-a *adj* (*vacío*) empty. 2 (*mullido*) spongy, soft. 3 (*presumido*) vain. 4 (*estilo etc.*) affected. − 5 *m* (*cavidad*) hollow. 6 (*de tiempo*) free time; (*de espacio*) gap. 7 (*vacante*) vacancy.

huelga *f* strike. ■ *~ de celo,* work-to-rule; *~ general,* general strike; *~ de hambre,* hunger strike. ▲ *also→ holgar.*

huelguista *mf* striker.

huella *f* (*de pie*) footprint; (*roderas*) track. 2 *fig* trace, sign. •*dejar ~,* to leave one's mark. ■ *~ dactilar,* fingerprint.

huérfano,-a *adj-mf* orphan.

huerta *f* market garden, US truck garden.

huerto *m* vegetable/kitchen garden; (*de frutales*) orchard.

hueso *m* ANAT bone. 2 *fig* (*cosa difícil*) drudgery; (*persona*) pain in the neck. 3 AM job. •*fig un ~ duro de moler/roer,* a hard nut to crack.

huésped,-da *m,f* (*invitado*) guest. 2 (*en hotel*) lodger, boarder. ■ *casa de huéspedes,* guesthouse.

hueste *f* army, host.

huesudo,-a *adj* bony.

huevo *m* egg. 2* *pl* balls* *pl.* ■ *~ duro,* hard-boiled egg; *~ escalfado,* poached egg; *~ estrellado/frito,* fried egg; *~ pasado por agua,* soft-boiled egg; *huevos revueltos,* scrambled eggs.

huida *f* flight, escape.

huir [62] *i* to flee, run away (*de,* from). 2 (*evitar*) to avoid (*de,* -). from.

hule *m* oilcloth, oilskin.

hulla *f* coal. ■ *~ blanca,* water power.

humanidad *f* humanity. 2 (*especie*) mankind. 3 (*benignidad*) benevolence, kindness. 4 *pl* EDUC humanities.

humanista *mf* humanist.

humanitario,-a *adj* humanitarian.

humanizar(se) [4] *t* to humanize. − 2 *p* to become more human.

humano,-a *adj* human. 2 (*benigno*) humane. − 3 *m* human (being).

humareda *f* cloud of smoke.

humeante *adj* (*de humo*) smoky, smoking. 2 (*de vaho*) steaming.

humear *i* (*humo*) to smoke. 2 (*vaho*) to steam. − 3 *t* AM (*fumigar*) to fumigate.

humedad *f* humidity. 2 (*de vapor*) moisture. 3 (*sensación*) dampness.

humedecer(se) [43] *t* to moisten, dampen. − 2 *p* to become damp/wet.

húmedo,-a *adj* humid. 2 (*impregnado*) damp, moist.

humildad *f* humility, humbleness.

humilde *adj* humble.

humillación *f* humiliation.

humillante *adj* humiliating.

humillar(se) *t* to humiliate, humble. − 2 *p* to humble o.s.

humo *m* smoke. 2 (*vapor*) steam, vapour. 3 *pl fig* conceit *sing.*

humor *m* (*ánimo*) mood. 2 (*gracia*) humour. 3 (*líquido*) humour. •*tener para algo,* to feel like (doing) sth. ■ *buen/mal ~,* good/bad humour; *~ negro,* black comedy; *sentido del ~,* sense of humour.

humorismo *m* humour.

humorístico,-a *adj* humorous, funny, amusing.

hundimiento *m* (*barco*) sinking. 2 (*tierra*) subsidence. 3 (*edificio*) collapse.

hundir(se) *t* (*sumir*) to submerge. 2 (*barco*) to sink. 3 (*derrumbar*) to cause to collapse. 4 *fig* (*abatir*) to demoralize. 5 (*arruinar*) to ruin. − 6 *p* (*sucumbir*) to be destroyed. 7 (*barco*) to sink. 8 (*derrumbarse*) to collapse. 9 (*arruinarse*) to be ruined.

huracán *m* hurricane.

huraño,-a *adj* sullen, unsociable.

hurgar [7] *t* *(remover)* to poke. **2** *(fisgar)* to stir up. **3** *(incitar)* to poke at. ●~*se las narices,* to pick one's nose.

hurón *m* ferret.

¡hurra! *interj* hurray!, hurrah!

hurtadillas *a* ~, *adv* stealthily, on the sly.

hurtar *t* *(robar)* to steal, pilfer. **2** *(desviar)* to dodge. **3** *(plagiar)* to plagiarize.

hurto *m* petty theft.

husmear *t* to sniff out, scent. **2** *fig* to pry into.

huso *m* spindle.

¡huy! *interj* ouch!, ow!

I

iceberg *m* iceberg.

ida *f* going, departure.

idea *f* idea. **2** *(noción)* notion. **3** *(ingenio)* imagination. ●*fam ni ~,* no idea, not a clue.

ideal *adj-m* ideal.

idealista *adj* idealistic. − **2** *mf* idealist.

idealizar [4] *t* to idealize.

idear *t* *(concebir)* to imagine, conceive, think. **2** *(inventar)* to design.

idéntico,-a *adj* identical.

identidad *f* identity.

identificación *f* identification.

identificar(se) [1] *t-p* to identify.

ideología *f* ideology.

idílico,-a *adj* idyllic.

idilio *m* *fig* love affair.

idioma *m* language.

idiota *adj* idiotic, stupid. − **2** *mf* idiot.

idiotez *f* idiocy, stupidity.

idiotizar(se) [4] *t* to daze. − **2** *p* to get dazed.

ido,-a *adj* *(loco)* mad. **2** *(despistado)* absent-minded.

idólatra *adj* idolatrous. − **2** *mf m* idolater, *f* idolatress.

idolatrar *t* to worship. **2** *fig* to idolize.

ídolo *m* idol.

idóneo,-a *adj* suitable, fit. **2** *(apto)* qualified.

iglesia *f* church.

iglú *m* igloo. ▲ *pl* **iglúes.**

ignición *f* ignition.

ignorancia *f* ignorance.

ignorante *adj* ignorant. − **2** *mf* ignoramus.

ignorar *t* not to know, be ignorant of.

igual *adj* equal: *a partes iguales,* into equal parts. **2** *(lo mismo)* the same: *es ~ de alto que tú,* he is as tall as you. **3** *(empatados)* even. − **4** *m* equal. **5** MAT equal(s) sign. **6** *pl* DEP even. − **7** *adv* probably: *~ no vienen,* they may not come. **8** *igualmente,* equally. **9** *(también)* also. ●*es ~,* it doesn't matter; *¡igualmente!,* the same to you!

igualar(se) *t* to equalize. **2** *(allanar)* to level; *(pulir)* to smooth. **3** *(comparar)* to match. − **4** *i-p* to be equal.

igualdad *f* equality.

ilegal *adj* illegal.

ilegítimo,-a *adj* illegitimate.

ileso,-a *adj* unharmed, unhurt.

ilícito,-a *adj* illicit, unlawful.

ilimitado,-a *adj* unlimited.

ilógico,-a *adj* illogical.

iluminación *f* illumination.

iluminar *t* to illuminate, light (up). **2** *fig* to enlighten.

ilusión *f* *(delusión)* illusion. **2** *(esperanza)* hope. **3** *(sueño)* dream. ●*forjarse/hacerse ilusiones,* to build up one's hopes.

ilusionado,-a *adj* excited. ●*estar ~,* to be looking forward to.

ilusionarse *p* *(esperanzarse)* to build up one's hopes. **2** *(entusiasmarse)* to be excited *(con,* about).

iluso,-a *adj* deluded, deceived. − **2** *m,f* dupe.

ilustración *f* *(estampa)* illustration. **2** *(instrucción)* learning, erudition.

ilustrado,-a *adj* *(libro etc.)* illustrated. **2** *(culto)* learned, erudite.

ilustrador,-ra *adj* illustrative. − **2** *m,f* illustrator.

ilustrar(se) *t* to illustrate. **2** *(aclarar)* to explain. **3** *(instruir)* to enlighten. − **4** *p* to learn.

ilustrativo,-a *adj* illustrative.

ilustre *adj* illustrious, distinguished.

imagen *f* image. **2** TV picture.

imaginación *f* imagination, fantasy.

imaginar(se) *t-p* to imagine. **2** *(suponer)* to suppose.
imaginario,-a *adj* imaginary.
imaginativo,-a *adj* imaginative.
imán *m* magnet.
iman(t)ar *t* to magnetize.
imbécil *adj-mf* stupid (person).
imbecilidad *f* stupidity, imbecility.
imitación *f* imitation.
imitador,-ra *adj* imitative. — **2** *m,f* imitator.
imitar *t* to imitate; *(gestos)* to mimic.
impaciencia *f* impatience.
impacientar(se) *t* to make lose patience, exasperate. — **2** *p* to get impatient.
impaciente *adj* impatient.
impacto *m* impact. ■ ~ *de bala,* bullet hole.
impagado,-a *adj* unpaid.
impar *adj-m* odd (number).
imparcial *adj* impartial, fair.
impartir *t* to impart.
impasible *adj* impassive.
impávido,-a *adj* dauntless, fearless.
impecable *adj* impeccable, faultless.
impedido,-a *adj* disabled, handicapped, crippled. — **2** *m,f* cripple, disabled/handicapped person.
impedimento *m* impediment; *(obstáculo)* hindrance, obstacle.
impedir [34] *t (estorbar)* to impede, hinder. **2** *(obstaculizar)* to prevent. ●~ *el paso,* to block the way.
impeler *t* to drive forward, propel. **2** *(incitar)* to impel, incite.
impenetrable *adj* impenetrable. **2** *fig (cosa)* incomprehensible. **3** *(persona)* reserved.
impensable *adj* unthinkable.
imperar *i* to rule, prevail.
imperativo,-a *adj* imperative.
imperceptible *adj* imperceptible.
imperdible *m* safety pin.
imperdonable *adj* unforgivable, inexcusable.
imperecedero,-a *adj fml* everlasting.
imperfección *f* imperfection. **2** *(defecto)* defect, fault.
imperfecto,-a *adj* imperfect.
imperial *adj* imperial.
imperialista *adj-mf* imperialist.
imperio *m* empire. **2** *(altivez)* haughtiness. ●*fam* **valer un** ~, to be worth a fortune.
imperioso,-a *adj (dominante)* imperious. **2** *(necesario)* urgent, pressing.

impermeabilidad *f* impermeability.
impermeabilizar [4] *t* to waterproof.
impermeable *adj* impervious. **2** *(ropa)* waterproof. — **3** *m* raincoat.
impersonal *adj* impersonal.
impertinencia *f* impertinence. **2** *(palabras)* impertinent remark.
impertinente *adj-mf* impertinent (person).
imperturbable *adj* impassive.
ímpetu *m (impulso)* impetus. **2** *(violencia)* violence.
impetuoso,-a *adj* impetuous.
implacable *adj* implacable, relentless.
implantar *t* to implant; *(reforma)* to introduce.
implicación *f* implication.
implicar [1] *t (involucrar)* to implicate, involve (**en,** in). **2** *(conllevar)* to imply. **3** *(obstar)* to contradict.
implícito,-a *adj* implicit.
implorar *t* to implore, entreat, beg.
imponente *adj* impressive. — **2** *adv fam (muy bien)* terrific.
imponer(se) [78] *t* to impose. **2** *(infundir)* to inspire. **3** *(instruir)* to instruct (**en,** in). **4** FIN to deposit. — **5** *p* to impose one's authority (**a,** on). ▲ *pp* **impuesto,-a**.
imponible *adj* taxable, subject to taxation.
importación *f* import(ation).
importador,-ra *adj* importing. — **2** *m,f* importer.
importancia *f* importance.
importante *adj* important.
importar *i (convenir)* to matter: *no me importa,* I don't care. — **2** *t* COM *(traer de fuera)* to import.
importe *m* price, cost.
importunar *t* to importune, pester, tease.
importuno,-a *adj (inoportuno)* inopportune. **2** *(molesto)* bothersome, troublesome.
imposibilidad *f* impossibility.
imposibilitado,-a *adj (incapaz)* unable. **2** *(inválido)* disabled, crippled.
imposibilitar(se) *t (impedir)* to make impossible, prevent. — **2** *p* to become disabled.
imposible *adj* impossible. ●*hacer lo* ~, to do the impossible, do one's utmost.
imposición *f (carga)* imposition. **2** *(cantidad)* deposit; *(impuesto)* tax.
impostor,-ra *m,f (tramposo) m* impostor, *f* impostress. **2** *(calumniador)* slanderer.

impostura f (trampa) imposture. 2 (calumnia) slander.

impotencia f impotence.

impotente adj impotent.

impracticable adj unfeasible. 2 (camino etc.) impassable.

imprecación f imprecation, curse.

imprecisión f inaccuracy.

impreciso,-a adj vague, indefinite.

impredecible adj unpredictable.

impregnar(se) t to impregnate. – 2 p to be pervaded.

imprenta f (arte) printing. 2 (taller) printer's, printing house. 3 fig press.

imprescindible adj essential, indispensable.

impresión f (huella) impression, imprint. 2 (imprenta) printing. 3 fig (efecto) impression. 4 (opinión) impression.

impresionable adj emotional.

impresionante adj impressive, striking.

impresionar(se) t (afectar) to impress, affect. 2 (conmover) to touch, move. 3 (discos) to cut. 4 (fotografías) to expose. – 5 p (estar afectado) to be impressed. 6 (conmoverse) to be touched/moved.

impreso,-a pp → **imprimir**. – 2 adj printed. – 3 m (forumulario) form. 4 pl (en carta etc.) printed matter sing.

impresor,-ra m,f printer. – 2 f (máquina) printer.

imprevisible adj unforeseeable.

imprevisto,-a adj unforeseen. – 2 m (incidente) unforeseen event. 3 pl COM incidental expenses.

imprimir t to print. 2 (dejar huella) to stamp. 3 fig (en el ánimo) to fix. ▲ pp **imprimido,-a** or **impreso,-a**.

improbable adj improbable, unlikely.

ímprobo,-a adj (deshonesto) dishonest. 2 (trabajo) arduous, laborious.

improcedente adj unsuitable. 2 JUR inadmissible.

improductivo,-a adj unproductive.

impropio,-a adj (incorrecto) improper. 2 (inadecuado) unsuitable.

improvisación f improvisation.

improvisado,-a adj improvised.

improvisar t-i to improvise.

improviso,-a adj unforeseen, unexpected. ●de ~, suddenly, all of a sudden.

imprudencia f imprudence, rashness.

imprudente adj-mf imprudent/rash (person).

impúdico,-a adj (indecente) immodest. 2 (desvergonzado) shameless.

impuesto,-a pp → **imponer**. – 2 adj imposed. 3 (informado) informed. – 4 m tax, duty. ■ ~ sobre el valor añadido (IVA), value added tax (VAT); ~ sobre la renta, income tax; (tienda) libre de impuestos, duty-free (shop).

impugnación f refutation.

impugnar t to impugn, refute.

impulsar t to impel; TÉC to drive forward.

impulsivo,-a adj impulsive.

impulso m impulse. 2 (fuerza, velocidad) momentum. ●coger ~, to gather momentum.

impune adj unpunished. – 2 **impunemente** adv with impunity.

impunidad f impunity.

impureza f impurity.

impuro,-a adj impure.

imputar t to impute, ascribe.

inaccesible adj unreachable.

inactividad f inactivity.

inactivo,-a adj inactive.

inadaptado,-a adj maladjusted. – 2 m,f misfit.

inadecuado,-a adj unsuitable. 2 (inapropiado) inappropriate.

inadmisible adj unacceptable.

inadvertido,-a adj (no visto) unseen, unnoticed. 2 (distraído) inattentive.

inagotable adj inexhaustible.

inaguantable adj intolerable, unbearable.

inalterable adj unalterable. 2 (impasible) impassive, imperturbable.

inanimado,-a adj inanimate, lifeless.

inapetencia f lack/loss of appetite.

inapreciable adj (sin poder apreciar) invaluable, priceless. 2 (insignificante) insignificant.

inasequible adj unattainable. 2 (precio) prohibitive. 3 (persona) unapproachable.

inaudito,-a adj (nunca oído) unheard-of. 2 (monstruoso) outrageous.

inauguración f inauguration, opening.

inaugural adj inaugural, opening.

inaugurar t to inaugurate.

incalculable adj incalculable.

incandescente adj incandescent.

incansable adj indefatigable, untiring, tireless.

incapacidad f incapacity. 2 (incompetencia) incompetence. ■ ~ laboral, (industrial) disability.

incapacitar t to incapacitate. 2 (sin aptitud legal) to make unfit (para, for).

incapaz *adj* incapable (*de,* of). **2** *(incompetente)* incompetent.

incautarse *p* JUR to seize, confiscate. **2** *(apoderarse)* to appropriate.

incauto,-a *adj (imprudente)* unwary, reckless, heedless. **2** *(fácil de engañar)* gullible.

incendiar(se) [12] *t* to set on fire, set fire to. **– 2** *p* to catch fire.

incendiario,-a *adj* incendiary. **– 2** *m,f* arsonist.

incendio *m* fire. **■** ~ *intencionado/provocado,* arson.

incentivo *m* incentive.

incertidumbre *f* uncertainty.

incesante *adj* incessant, unceasing.

incesto *m* incest.

incidencia *f* incidence. **2** *(repercusión)* repercussion, consequence.

incidente *adj* incidental. **– 2** *m* incident, event.

incidir *i (incurrir en falta etc.)* to fall (*en,* into). **2** *(proyectil, luz)* to hit (*en,* -). **3** *(causar efecto)* to affect.

incierto,-a *adj (falso)* uncertain, doubtful. **2** *(inconstante)* inconstant, unpredictable. **3** *(desconocido)* unknown.

incineración *f (basuras)* incineration; *(cadáveres)* cremation.

incinerar *t (basura)* to incinerate; *(cadáveres)* to cremate.

incipiente *adj* incipient, nascent.

incisión *f* incision, cut.

incisivo,-a *adj* incisive, cutting. **2** *fig* sarcastic. **■** *(diente)* ~, incisor.

inciso,-a *adj (estilo)* jerky. **– 2** *m* interpolated remark.

incitación *f* incitement, encouragement.

incitante *adj (estimulante)* inciting. **2** *(provocativo)* provocative.

incitar *t* to incite, excite, rouse.

incivilizado,-a *adj* uncivilized.

inclemencia *f* inclemency, harshness. **2** METEOR hard weather.

inclinación *f (pendiente)* slant, slope. **2** *(tendencia)* liking, propension. **3** *(saludo)* bow; *(asentimiento)* nod.

inclinado,-a *adj* inclined, slanted.

inclinar(se) *t* to incline, slant; *(el cuerpo)* to bow; *(la cabeza)* to nod. **2** *fig (persuadir)* to dispose, move. **– 3** *p* to lean, slope. **4** *fig (propender a)* to be/feel inclined (*a,* to).

incluido,-a *adj* included.

incluir [62] *t* to include. **2** *(contener)* to contain, comprise: *este precio incluye*

todos los gastos, this is an all-in price. **3** *(en carta etc.)* to enclose.

inclusión *f* inclusion.

inclusive *adv* inclusive.

incluso *adv* inclusive(ly). **– 2** *prep* even.

incógnito,-a *adj* unknown. **– 2** *m* incognito. **– 3** *f* MAT unknown (quantity). **4** *fig (misterio)* mystery. **●** *de* ~, incognito.

incoherencia *f* incoherence.

incoherente *adj* incoherent, disconnected.

incoloro,-a *adj* colourless

incombustible *adj* incombustible, fireproof.

incomestible, incomible *adj* uneatable, inedible.

incomodar(se) *t (causar molestia)* to inconvenience. **2** *(fastidiar)* to annoy, bother. **3** *(enojar)* to anger. **– 4** *p (enfadarse)* to get annoyed/angry.

incomodidad *f,* **incomodo** *m* discomfort. **2** *(molestia)* inconvenience. **3** *(malestar)* unrest, uneasiness.

incómodo,-a *adj* uncomfortable. **●** *sentirse* ~, to feel uncomfortable/awkward.

incomparable *adj* incomparable.

incomparecencia *f* non-appearance.

incompatibilidad *f* incompatibility.

incompatible *adj* incompatible.

incompetencia *f* incompetence.

incompleto,-a *adj* incomplete. **2** *(inacabado)* unfinished.

incomprensible *adj* incomprehensible.

incomprensión *f* lack of understanding.

incomunicar [1] *t (un lugar)* to isolate, cut off. **2** *(una habitación)* to shut off. **3** *(un preso)* to put in solitary confinement.

inconcebible *adj* inconceivable, unthinkable.

incondicional *adj* unconditional. **– 2** *mf* staunch supporter.

inconexo,-a *adj* disconnected.

inconformista *adj-mf* nonconformist.

inconfundible *adj* unmistakable.

incongruente *adj* incongruous.

inconsciencia *f* MED unconsciousness. **2** *(irreflexión)* thoughtlessness.

inconsciente *adj* MED unconscious. **2** *(irreflexivo)* thoughtless.

inconsistencia *f* inconsistency.

inconstancia *f* inconstancy, fickleness.

inconstante *adj* inconstant, fickle.

incontable *adj* countless, uncountable.

incontinencia *f* incontinence.

incontrolado,-a *adj* uncontrolled.

inconveniencia *f* inconvenience. 2 *(grosería)* rude remark. ●*decir/cometer una ~*, to be tactless.

inconveniente *adj* inconvenient. − 2 *m (desventaja)* drawback; *(dificultad)* problem.

incordiar [12] *t* to pester, bother.

incorporación *f (unión)* incorporation. 2 *(el cuerpo)* sitting up.

incorporar(se) *t (unir)* to incorporate. 2 *(levantar cuerpo)* to help to sit up. − 3 *p (levantarse)* to sit up. 4 *(funcionarios etc.)* to join. ●*~se a filas,* to join up.

incorrección *f* incorrectness.

incorrecto,-a *adj* incorrect.

incorregible *adj* incorrigible.

incorruptible *adj* incorruptible.

incrédulo,-a *adj* incredulous. 2 REL unbelieving. − 3 *m,f* disbeliever. 4 REL unbeliever.

increíble *adj* incredible, unbelievable.

incrementar *t* to increase.

incremento *m* increase, rise.

increpar *t* to rebuke, scold.

incruento,-a *adj* bloodless.

incrustación *f* incrustation, encrustation. 2 *(artística)* inlaying, inlay.

incrustar(se) *t* to incrust, encrust. 2 *(arte)* to inlay. − 3 *p* to become embedded *(en,* in).

incubadora *f* incubator.

incubar *t* to incubate.

inculcar [1] *t* to instil.

inculpar *t* to accuse, blame for.

inculto,-a *adj (persona)* uneducated. 2 *(terreno)* uncultivated, untilled.

incultura *f* lack of culture.

incumbencia *f* incumbency, duty, concern. ●*no es de mi ~,* it does not concern me.

incumbir *i* to be incumbent *(a,* upon), be the duty *(a,* of).

incumplir *t* not to fulfil.

incurable *adj* incurable.

incurrir *i (merecer)* to incur *(en,* -), become liable to. 2 *(causar)* to bring *(en,* about).

incursión *f* raid, incursion.

indagación *f* investigation, inquiry.

indagar [7] *t* to investigate, inquire into.

indecencia *f* indecency, obscenity.

indecente *adj* indecent, obscene.

indecisión *f* indecision, irresolution.

indeciso,-a *adj (sin decidir)* undecided. 2 *(dudoso)* hesitant, indecisive.

indecoroso,-a *adj* indecorous.

indefenso,-a *adj* defenceless.

indefinido,-a *adj* undefined, vague.

indelicadeza *f* tactless act.

indemne *adj (persona)* unharmed, unhurt; *(cosa)* undamaged.

indemnización *f (acción)* indemnification. 2 *(compensación)* indemnity, compensation.

indemnizar [4] *t* to indemnify, compensate *(de/por,* for).

independencia *f* independence.

independiente *adj* independent. 2 *(individualista)* self-sufficient. − 3 *independientemente* *adv* independently. 4 *(aparte de)* regardless *(de,* of).

independizar(se) [4] *t* to make independent. − 2 *p* to become independent.

indescifrable *adj* indecipherable.

indescriptible *adj* indescribable.

indeterminación *f* indecision, irresolution.

indeterminado,-a *adj (por determinar)* indeterminate. 2 *(persona)* irresolute.

indicación *f* indication. 2 *(observación)* hint. 3 *(prescripción)* instruction.

indicador,-ra *adj* indicating. − 2 *m* indicator; TÉC gauge.

indicar [1] *t* to indicate, point out, show. 2 *(aconsejar)* to advise. 3 *(esbozar)* to outline.

indicativo,-a *adj-m* indicative.

índice *m* index. 2 *(dedo)* index finger, forefinger. 3 *(indicio)* sign, indication. ■ *~ de natalidad/mortalidad,* birth/death rate.

indicio *m* sign, indication.

indiferencia *f* indifference.

indiferente *adj* indifferent.

indígena *adj* indigenous, native. − 2 *mf* native.

indigente *adj fml* indigent. − 2 *mf* poor person: *los indigentes,* the needy.

indigestarse *p* to have/get indigestion. 2 *fam fig (no agradar)* to be disagreeable.

indigestión *f* indigestion.

indigesto,-a *adj* indigestible.

indignación *f* indignation.

indignado,-a *adj* indignant *(por,* at/about).

indignante *adj* outrageous, infuriating.

indignar(se) *t* to infuriate, make angry. − 2 *p* to become indignant *(por,* at/about).

indigno,-a *adj* unworthy *(de,* of). 2 *(vil)* low, undignified.

indirecta *f* hint, insinuation. ●*lanzar/tirar una ~,* to drop a hint.

indirecto,-a *adj* indirect.

indiscreción f indiscretion.
indiscreto,-a adj-m,f indiscreet (person).
indiscriminado,-a adj indiscriminate.
indiscutible adj unquestionable, indisputable.
indispensable adj indispensable, essential.
indisponer(se) [78] t (plan, proyecto) to upset, spoil. **2** (malquitar) to set (contra, against). **3** (físicamente) to make unwell. − **4** p to become ill. ●~se con algn., to fall out with sb. ▲ pp indispuesto,-a.
indisposición f MED indisposition, illness. **2** (reticencia) reluctance.
indispuesto,-a pp → indisponer. − **2** adj MED indisposed, ill. **3** (enemistado) on bad terms (con, with).
indistinto,-a adj inconsequential.
individual adj individual. ■ habitación/dormitorio ~, single room.
individualizar [4] t to individualize.
individuo,-a adj individual. − **2** m person. **3** pey bloke, guy.
indocumentado,-a adj without identification papers. − **2** m,f arg (persona) dead loss.
índole f (carácter) disposition, nature. **2** (tipo) type, kind.
indolente adj (perezoso) indolent, lazy. **2** (indiferente) indifferent.
indomable adj indomitable, untamable.
inducir [46] t (incitar) to induce, lead. **2** (inferir) to infer, deduce. **3** ELEC to induce.
indudable adj doubtless, unquestionable. − **2** indudablemente adv certainly.
indulgencia f indulgence, leniency.
indulgente adj indulgent, lenient.
indultar t JUR to pardon. **2** (eximir) to exempt.
indulto m pardon, amnesty.
indumentaria f clothing, clothes pl.
industria f industry.
industrial adj industrial. − **2** mf industrialist.
industrializar(se) [4] t to industrialize. − **2** p to become industrialized.
inédito,-a adj (libro) unpublished. **2** (desconocido) unknown. **3** (nuevo) new.
inefable adj ineffable.
ineficacia f inefficiency.
ineficaz adj inefficient.
ineludible adj unavoidable, inevitable.
ineptitud f incompetence.
inepto,-a adj-m,f incompetent (person).
inequívoco,-a adj unmistakable.

inercia f inertia. ●hacer algo por ~, to do sth. out of habit.
inerte adj inert.
inesperado,-a adj unexpected, unforeseen.
inestabilidad f instability, unsteadiness. ■ ~ atmosférica, changeable weather.
inestable adj unstable, unsteady.
inestimable adj inestimable, invaluable.
inevitable adj inevitable, unavoidable.
inexactitud f incorrectness, inaccuracy.
inexacto,-a adj inexact, inaccurate.
inexistente adj non-existent, inexistent.
inexperiencia f inexperience.
inexperto,-a adj inexperienced.
inexplicable adj inexplicable.
infalible adj infallible.
infame adj infamous, vile.
infamia f infamy.
infancia f childhood.
infante,-a m,f m prince, f princess.
infantería f infantry.
infantil adj child, children's. **2** (aniñado) childlike; pey childish.
infarto m infarction, infarct. ■ ~ de miocardio, heart attack.
infatigable adj indefatigable, tireless.
infección f infection.
infeccioso,-a adj infectious.
infectar(se) t to infect. − **2** p to become infected.
infeliz adj unhappy. − **2** mf (bondadoso) simpleton.
inferior adj (situado debajo) lower. **2** (cantidad) less, lower: número ~ a diez, a number less than ten. **3** (en calidad) inferior (a, to). − **4** mf subordinate.
inferioridad f inferiority. ●en ~ de condiciones, at a disadvantage.
inferir t [35] (deducir) to infer, conclude. **2** (conducir a) to cause.
infernal adj infernal, hellish.
infestar t (invadir animales, plantas) to infest. **2** (infectar) to infect. **3** fig (llenar) to overrun, invade.
infidelidad f infidelity.
infiel adj (desleal) unfaithful (a/con/para, to). **2** (inexacto) inexact. − **3** mf REL infidel.
infierno m hell.
infiltrar(se) t-p to infiltrate.
ínfimo,-a adj (bajo) lowest, smallest. **2** (malo) worst.
infinidad f infinity. **2** (gran cantidad) great number: una ~ de posibilidades, an endless number of possibilities.

infinito,-a *adj* infinite. – **2** *m* infinity. – **3** *adv (muchísimo)* infintely.

inflación *f* inflation.

inflamable *adj* inflammable.

inflamación *f* inflammation.

inflamar(se) *t (encender)* to set on fire. **2** *fig (pasiones etc.)* to excite, arouse. – **3** *p* MED to become inflamed.

inflar(se) *t* to inflate, blow up. **2** *fig (hechos, noticias)* to exaggerate. – **3** *p (engreírse)* to get conceited. **4** *fam (hartarse)* to stuff o.s. (*de,* with).

inflexible *adj* inflexible, stiff.

inflexión *f* inflection, inflexion.

infligir [6] *t* to inflict.

influencia *f* influence. ●*tener influencias,* to be influential.

influenciar [12] *i* to influence.

influente *adj* → **influyente**.

influir [62] *i* to influence.

influjo *m* influence.

influyente *adj* influential.

información *f* information. **2** *(noticia)* piece of news.

informal *adj (desenfadado)* informal. **2** *(persona)* unreliable.

informalidad *f (desenfado)* informality. **2** *(en persona)* unreliability.

informar(se) *t (dar noticia)* to report, inform. – **2** *i (dictaminar)* to report (*de,* on). – **3** *p (procurarse noticias)* to find out.

informático,-a *adj* computer, computing. – **2** *f* computer science, computing. – **3** *m,f* (computer) technician.

informativo,-a *adj* informative. – **2** *m* news bulletin.

informatizar [4] *t* to computerize.

informe *adj* shapeless, formless. – **2** *m* report. **3** *pl* references.

infortunio *f (desgracia)* misfortune. **2** *(contratiempo)* mishap, mischance.

infracción *f* offence; *(de ley)* infraction, infringement, breach.

infractor,-ra *m,f* offender.

infraestructura *f* infraestructure.

in fraganti *adv* in the act.

infranqueable *adj* insurmountable.

infrarrojo,-a *adj* infrared.

infravalorar *t* underestimate.

infringir [6] *t* to infringe; *(ley)* to break.

infructuoso,-a *adj* fruitless, unsuccessful.

ínfulas *fpl* conceit *sing.* ●*darse ~,* to put on airs.

infundado,-a *adj* groundless.

infundir *t* to instil, arouse. ▲ *pp* **infundido,-a** *o* **infuso,a**.

infusión *f* infusion: *~ de manzanilla/ menta,* camomile/mint tea.

infuso,-a *pp* → **infundir**. – **2** *adj* inspired.

ingeniar(se) [12] *t* to think up. – **2** *p* to manage.

ingeniería *f* engineering.

ingeniero,-a *m,f* engineer.

ingenio *m (talento)* talent; *(chispa)* wit. **2** *(individuo)* genius. **3** *(habilidad)* ingenuity. **4** *(aparato)* device. ●*aguzar el ~,* to sharpen one's wits.

ingenioso,-a *adj* ingenious, clever; *(con chispa)* witty.

ingenuidad *f* ingenuousness, naïveté.

ingenuo,-a *adj-m,f* naïve (person).

ingerir [35] *t (comida)* to eat; *(bebida)* to drink.

ingle *f* groin.

ingratitud *f* ingratitude.

ingrato,-a *adj (desagradecido)* ungrateful, thankless. **2** *(desagradable)* unpleasant.

ingrávido,-a *adj* weightless.

ingrediente *m* ingredient.

ingresar *t (dinero)* to deposit, pay in. – **2** *i (entrar)* to enter; *(club etc.)* to become a member (*en,* of); *(ejército)* to join up. **3** *(en hospital)* to admit.

ingreso *m (entrada)* entry. **2** *(admisión)* admission (*en,* to). **3** *(a cuenta bancaria)* deposit. **4** *pl (sueldo, renta)* income *sing.*

íngrimo,-a *adj* AM alone.

inhabilitar *t (incapacitar)* to disable. **2** JUR to disqualify.

inhalar *t* to inhale, breathe in.

inherente *adj* inherent (*a,* in).

inhibir(se) *t* to inhibit. – **2** *p (abstenerse)* to keep out (*de,* of).

inhóspito,-a *adj* inhospitable.

inhumación *f* burial.

inhumano,-a *adj* inhuman, cruel.

iniciación *f* initiation, introduction (*a,* to).

iniciador,-ra *adj* initiatory. – **2** *m,f* initiator. **3** *(pionero)* pioneer.

inicial *adj-f* initial.

iniciar(se) [12] *t (introducir)* to initiate (*en,* in). **2** *(empezar)* to begin. – **3** *p* to learn.

iniciativa *f* initiative.

inicio *m* beginning, start.

inimaginable *adj* unimaginable.

ininteligible *adj* unintelligible.

ininterrumpido,-a *adj* uninterrupted.

injerir(se) *t* to insert. – **2** *p* to interfere (*en,* in).

injertar *t* to graft.

injuria *f* insult, affront. **2** *(daño)* damage.

injuriar [12] *t (insultar)* to insult. **2** *(dañar)* to damage.

injusticia *f* injustice, unfairness.

injustificado,-a *adj* unjustified.

injusto,-a *adj* unjust, unfair.

inmediaciones *fpl* neighbourhood *sing*, environs.

inmediato,-a *adj (poco después)* immediate. **2** *(contiguo)* next to, adjoining.

inmejorable *adj* unsurpassable.

inmensidad *f* immensity. **2** *(gran cantidad)* great number.

inmenso,-a *adj* immense, vast.

inmerecido,-a *adj* undeserved.

inmigración *f* immigration.

inmigrante *adj-mf* immigrant.

inmigrar *i* to immigrate.

inminente *adj* imminent, near.

inmiscuirse [62] *p* to interfere, meddle.

inmobiliario,-a *adj* property, real estate. **− 2** *f* estate agency.

inmoral *adj* immoral.

inmoralidad *f* immorality.

inmortal *adj-mf* immortal.

inmortalizar(se) [4] *t* to immortalize. **− 2** *p* to be immortal.

inmóvil *adj* still, motionless. **2** *fig (constante)* determined, steadfast.

inmovilizar [4] *t* to immobilize.

inmueble *m* building.

inmundo,-a *adj (sucio)* dirty, filthy. **2** *fig* nasty.

inmune *adj* MED immune (*a,* to). **2** *(exento)* exempt (*de,* from).

inmunidad *f* immunity.

inmunizar [4] *t* to immunize.

inmutable *adj* unchangeable, immutable.

inmutarse *p* to change one's expression.

innato,-a *adj* innate, inborn.

innecesario,-a *adj* unnecessary.

innegable *adj* undeniable.

innocuo *adj* innocuous, harmless.

innovación *f* innovation.

innovador,-ra *adj* innovatory.

innovar *t* to innovate.

innumerable *adj* innumerable, countless.

inocencia *f* innocence. **2** *(ingenuidad)* naïveté.

inocente *adj-mf* innocent (person). **2** *(ingenuo)* naïve (person).

inodoro,-a *adj* odourless. **− 2** *m* toilet.

inofensivo,-a *adj* inoffensive, harmless.

inolvidable *adj* unforgettable.

inoportuno,-a *adj* inopportune, untimely.

inorgánico,-a *adj* inorganic.

inoxidable *adj* rustproof.

inquebrantable *adj* unbreakable. **2** *fig* firm, irrevocable.

inquietante *adj* worrying, disturbing.

inquietar(se) *t-p* to worry.

inquieto,-a *adj (agitado)* restless. **2** *(preocupado)* worried, anxious.

inquietud *f (agitación)* restlessness. **2** *(preocupación)* worry, anxiety.

inquilino,-a *m,f* tenant.

inquirir [30] *t* to inquire, investigate.

insaciable *adj* insatiable.

insalubre *adj* unhealthy, unwholesome.

insano,-a *adj* insane, mad.

insatisfacción *f* dissatisfaction.

insatisfecho,-a *adj* unsatisfied.

inscribir(se) *t (grabar)* to inscribe. **2** *(apuntar)* to register, record. **− 3** *p (matricularse)* to enrol. ▲ *pp* **inscrito,-a**.

inscripción *f (grabado)* inscription. **2** *(registro)* enrolment, registration.

inscrito,-a *pp →* **inscribir(se)**.

insecticida *adj-m* insecticide.

insecto *m* insect.

inseguridad *f* insecurity. **2** *(duda)* uncertainty. **3** *(peligro)* unsafety.

inseguro,-a *adj* insecure. **2** *(que duda)* uncertain. **3** *(peligroso)* unsafe.

insensatez *f* stupidity.

insensato,-a *adj* stupid, foolish.

insensible *adj* insensitive. **2** MED insensible, numb.

inseparable *adj-mf* inseparable.

inserción *f* insertion.

insertar *t* to insert, introduce.

insigne *adj* famous, eminent.

insignia *f* badge. **2** MAR pennant.

insignificante *adj* insignificant.

insinuación *f* insinuation, hint.

insinuar(se) [11] *t* to insinuate. **− 2** *p* to worm one's way (*en,* into).

insípido,-a *adj* tasteless. **2** *fig* dull, flat.

insistencia *f* insistence, persistence.

insistir *i* to insist (*en,* on), persist (*en,* in).

insociable *adj* unsociable.

insolación *f* sunstroke.

insolencia *f* insolence, cheekiness.

insolente *adj-mf (irrespetuoso)* insolent (person). **2** *(arrogante)* haughty (person).

insólito,-a *adj* unusual.

insoluble *adj* insoluble.

insolvente *adj-mf* insolvent, bankrupt.
insomnio *m* insomnia.
insonorizar [4] *t* to soundproof.
insoportable *adj* unbearable, intolerable.
insostenible *adj* untenable, indefensible.
inspección *f* inspection.
inspeccionar *t* to inspect, oversee.
inspector,-ra *m,f* inspector.
inspiración *f* inspiration. 2 *(inhalación)* inhalation.
inspirar(se) *t (aspirar)* to inhale, breathe in. 2 *(infundir)* to inspire. – 3 *p* to be inspired (*en,* by).
instalación *f* installation. 2 *(equipo)* equipment.
instalador,-ra *m,f* installer, fitter.
instalar(se) *t* to install. 2 *(equipar)* to fit up. – 3 *p (establecerse)* to settle.
instancia *f (solicitud)* request; *(escrito)* application form. ●*a ~/instancias de,* at the request of.
instantáneo,-a *adj* instantaneous. – 2 *f (foto)* snapshot. ■ *café ~,* instant coffee.
instante *m* instant, moment. ●*al ~,* immediately.
instar *t (insistir)* to press, urge. – 2 *i (urgir)* to be pressing, urgent.
instaurar *t (restaurar)* to restore, renew. 2 *(establecer)* to establish.
instigar [7] *t* to incite.
instintivo,-a *adj* instinctive.
instinto *m* instinct.
institución *f* institution, establishment. ■ *~ benéfica,* charitable foundation.
instituir [62] *t* to institute.
instituto *m* institute. 2 EDUC state secondary school, US high school. ■ *~ de belleza,* beauty salon.
instrucción *f (educación)* instruction, education. 2 MIL drill. 3 *pl* directions, orders.
instructivo,-a *adj* instructive.
instruir [62] *t* to instruct. 2 *(educar)* to teach.
instrumental *adj* instrumental. – 2 *m* equipment.
instrumento *m* instrument.
insubordinarse *p* to rebel.
insuficiencia *f (falta)* insufficiency. 2 *(no adecuado)* incompetence.
insuficiente *adj* insufficient. 2 EDUC fail.
insulso,-a *adj* insipid.
insultar *t* to insult.
insulto *m* insult.

insuperable *adj* insuperable, unsurpassable.
insurrección *f* insurrection, uprising.
intacto,-a *adj* intact.
intachable *adj* blameless, faultless.
integración *f* integration.
integral *adj-f* integral.
integrar(se) *t* to compose, make up. – 2 *p* to integrate.
integridad *f* integrity. 2 *(honradez)* honesty.
íntegro,-a *adj* whole, entire. 2 *(honrado)* honest, upright.
intelectual *adj-mf* intellectual.
inteligencia *f* intelligence. 2 *(comprensión)* understanding.
inteligente *adj* intelligent, clever.
intemperie *f* bad weather. ●*a la ~,* in the open (air), outdoors.
intempestivo,-a *adj* untimely, inopportune.
intención *f* intention. ●*tener ~ de,* to intend. ■ *buena/mala ~,* good/ill will.
intencionado,-a *adj* intentional, deliberate.
intendente *m* supervisor. 2 MIL quartermaster general.
intensidad *f* intensity; *(de viento)* force.
intensificar [1] *t* to intensify.
intensivo,-a *adj* intensive. ■ *curso ~,* crash course.
intenso,-a *adj* intense; *(dolor)* acute.
intentar *t* to try, attempt.
intento *m* attempt, try.
intercalar *t* to intercalate, insert.
intercambiar [12] *t* to exchange, swap.
intercambio *m* exchange, interchange.
interceder *i* to intercede.
interceptar *t* to intercept; *(tráfico)* to hold up.
intercesión *f* intercession, mediation.
interés *m* interest. ■ *intereses creados,* vested interests.
interesado,-a *adj* interested, concerned. 2 *(egoísta)* selfish, self-interested. – 3 *m,f* interested person.
interesante *adj* interesting.
interesar(se) *t* to interest. – 2 *p ~se en/ por algo,* to be interested in sth. 3 *~se por algn.,* to ask about sb.
interferencia *f* interference. 2 *(radio)* jamming.
interferir [35] *t* to interfere with. 2 *(radio)* to jam.
interino,-a *adj* provisional, temporary. 2 *(cargo)* acting. – 3 *m,f* stand-in.

interior *adj* interior, inner, inside. **2** *(de la nación)* domestic, internal. **3** GEOG inland. **– 4** *m* inside, inner part. **5** *(alma)* soul. ■ *habitación ~,* inner room; *Ministerio del Interior,* Home Office, US Department of the Interior.
interiorizar [4] *t* to internalize.
interlocutor,-ra *m,f* speaker, interlocutor.
intermediario,-a *adj* intermediate. **– 2** *m,f* COM middleman.
intermedio,-a *adj* intermediate. **– 2** *m* intermission, interval.
interminable *adj* interminable, endless.
intermitente *adj* intermittent. **– 2** *m* AUTO indicator, blinker.
internacional *adj* international.
internado,-a *adj* interned. **– 2** *m* boarding school.
internar(se) *t* to intern. **– 2** *p (penetrar)* to penetrate.
interno,-a *adj* internal. **2** *(política)* domestic. **– 3** *m,f* boarder.
interponer(se) [78] *t* to interpose. **– 2** *p* to intervene. ▲ *pp* **interpuesto,-a**.
interpretación *f* interpretation. **2** MÚS TEAT performance.
interpretar *t* to interpret. **2** *(obra, pieza)* to perform; *(papel)* to play; *(canción)* to sing.
intérprete *mf (traductor)* interpreter. **2** *(actor, músico)* performer.
interpuesto,-a *pp* → **interponer**.
interrogación *f* interrogation, questioning. ■ *(signo de) ~,* question mark.
interrogante *adj* interrogating, questioning. **– 2** *m* question mark.
interrogar [7] *t* to question. **2** *(a testigo etc.)* to interrogate.
interrumpir *t* to interrupt.
interrupción *f* interruption.
interruptor *m* switch.
interurbano,-a *adj* inter-city. ■ *conferencia/llamada interurbana,* trunk/ long-distance call.
intervalo *m (de tiempo)* interval. **2** *(de espacio)* gap.
intervención *f* intervention. **2** MED operation.
intervenir [90] *i (tomar parte)* to take part *(en,* in). **2** *(interponer)* to intervene. **3** *(mediar)* to mediate. **– 3** *t* MED to operate on. **4** *(cuentas)* to audit.
interventor,-ra *m,f* supervisor, inspector. ■ *~ (de cuentas),* auditor.
intestino,-a *adj (interior)* internal. **– 2** *m* intestine.

intimar(se) *t (notificar)* to notify. **– 2** *i-p* to become close *(con,* to).
intimidad *f* intimacy. **2** *(vida privada)* private life. ●*en la ~,* in private.
intimidar *t* to intimidate, daunt.
íntimo,-a *adj* intimate. **2** *(vida)* private. **3** *(amistad)* close.
intolerable *adj* intolerable, unbearable.
intolerancia *f* intolerance.
intoxicación *f* poisoning; *(alimenticia)* food poisoning.
intoxicar [1] *t* to poison.
intranquilidad *f* restlessness, uneasiness.
intranquilizar(se) [4] *t* to worry, upset. **– 2** *p* to get worried.
intranquilo,-a *adj* restless, worried, uneasy.
intransigencia *f* intransigence.
intratable *adj (asunto)* intractable. **2** *(persona)* unsociable.
intrepidez *f* fearlessness, courage.
intrépido,-a *adj* intrepid, bold.
intriga *f* intrigue. **2** *(de película etc.)* plot.
intrigar [7] *t (interesar)* to intrigue. **– 2** *i (maquinar)* to plot, scheme.
intrincado,-a *adj* intricate, complicate.
intrínseco,-a *adj* intrinsic.
introducción *f* introduction.
introducir(se) [46] *t* to introduce. **2** *(insertar)* to insert. **– 3** *p (entrometerse)* to work one's way *(en,* into).
intromisión *f* interference, meddling.
introspección *f* introspection.
introvertido,-a *adj* introverted. **– 2** *m,f* introvert.
intruso,-a *adj* intrusive. **– 2** *m,f* intruder.
intuición *f* intuition.
intuir [62] *t* to know by intuition.
intuitivo,-a *adj* intuitive.
inundación *f* flood(ing).
inundar *t* to flood.
inútil *adj* useless. **– 2** *mf fam (persona)* good-for-nothing.
inutilizar [4] *t* to make/render useless. **2** *(máquina)* to put out of action.
invadir *t* to invade, overrun.
invalidar *t* to invalidate.
invalidez *f (nulidad)* invalidity. **2** MED disablement, disability.
inválido,-a *adj (nulo)* invalid. **2** *(persona)* disabled, handicapped. **– 3** *m,f* disabled/handicapped (person).
invariable *adj* invariable.
invasión *f* invasion.
invasor,-ra *adj* invading. **– 2** *m,f* invader.

invencible *adj* insurmountable; *(ejército etc.)* invincible.
invención *f (invento)* invention. **2** *(mentira)* fabrication.
inventar *t (crear)* to invent. **2** *(imaginar)* to imagine. **3** *(mentir)* to make up, fabricate.
inventario *m* inventory. •*hacer el* ~, to do the stocktaking.
inventiva *f* inventiveness.
invento *m* invention.
inventor,-ra *m,f* inventor.
invernáculo, invernadero *m* greenhouse, hothouse.
invernal *adj* wintry, winter.
invernar [27] *i* to winter. **2** *(animales)* to hibernate.
inverosímil *adj* unlikely.
inversión *f* inversion. **2** FIN investment.
inverso,-a *adj* inverse, opposite. •*a la inversa, (al contrario)* on the contrary; *(en dirección opuesta)* in the opposite direction.
inversor,-ra *m,f* investor.
invertebrado,-a *adj-m* invertebrate.
invertido,-a *adj* inverted. − **2** *m* homosexual.
invertir [35] *t (orden)* to invert. **2** *(dirección)* to reverse. **3** *(tiempo)* to spend. **4** FIN to invest (*en,* in).
investigación *f* investigation, enquiry. **2** *(científica)* research.
investigador,-ra *adj* investigating. − **2** *m,f (científico)* researcher. **3** *(detective)* investigator.
investigar [7] *t (indagar)* to investigate. **2** *(ciencia)* to do research on.
investir [34] *t* to invest.
inviable *adj* not viable, unfeasible.
invidente *adj-mf* blind (person).
invierno *m* winter.
invisible *adj* invisible.
invitación *f* invitation.
invitado,-a *m,f* guest.
invitar *t* to invite.
invocar [1] *t* to invoke, implore.
involucrar *t* to involve (*en,* in).
involuntario,-a *adj* involuntary.
invulnerable *adj* invulnerable.
inyección *f* injection. •*poner una* ~ *a algn.,* to give sb. an injection.
inyectar *t* to inject (*en,* into).
ir(se) [74] *i* to go: ~ *de compras,* to go shopping. **2** *(camino etc.)* to lead: *este camino va a la aldea,* this road leads you to the village. **3** *(funcionar)* to work: *el*

ascensor no va, the lift is out of order. **4** *(sentar bien)* to suit: *el rojo te va,* red suits you. − **5** *verbo aux* (~ + *a* + *infin*) going to: *voy a salir,* I'm going out. **6** (~ + *gerundio*) ~ *andando,* to go on foot. **7** (~ + *pp*) ~ *cansado,-a,* to be tired. − **8** *p (marcharse)* to go away, leave. **9** *(deslizarse)* to slip. **10** *(gastarse)* to go, disappear. •~ *a pie/en tren/en coche,* to go on foot/by train/by car; ~*se de la lengua,* to tell it all; ~*se a pique,* to sink; *fig* to fall through; ~*se por las ramas,* to get sidetracked; *fam vas que chutas,* you're set.
ira *f* anger, wrath, rage.
iracundo,-a *adj* irritable, angry.
irascible *adj* irascible, irritable.
iris *m inv* iris.
ironía *f* irony.
irónico,-a *adj* ironic(al).
ironizar [4] *t* to ridicule, be ironical about.
irracional *adj* irrational.
irradiar [12] *t* to irradiate, radiate.
irreal *adj* unreal.
irrebatible *adj* irrefutable.
irreflexivo,-a *adj (acto)* rash; *(persona)* impetuous.
irregular *adj* irregular.
irrelevante *adj* irrelevant.
irremediable *adj* irremediable, hopeless.
irremisible *adj* unpardonable, unforgivable.
irreprochable *adj* irreproachable.
irresistible *adj* irresistible. **2** *(insoportable)* unbearable.
irresponsable *adj-mf* irresponsible (person).
irreverente *adj* irreverent.
irreversible *adj* irreversible.
irrisorio,-a *adj* derisory, ridiculous. **2** *(insignificante)* insignificant.
irritable *adj* irritable.
irritación *f* irritation.
irritar(se) *t* to irritate. − **2** *p* to lose one's temper.
irrompible *adj* unbreakable.
irrumpir *i* to burst (*en,* into).
irrupción *f* irruption.
isla *f* island.
isleño,-a *m,f* islander.
itinerante *adj* itinerant.
itinerario *m* itinerary.
izar [4] *t* to hoist.
izquierdo,-a *adj* left. **2** *(zurdo)* left-handed. − **3** *f* left: *mano izquierda,* left hand. •*a la* ~, to the left.

J

jabalí *m* wild boar. ▲ *pl* **jabalíes**.

jabón *m* soap. ■ ~ *de afeitar/tocador*, shaving/toilet soap.

jabonar *t* → **enjabonar**.

jabonera *f* soapdish.

jabonoso,-a *adj* soapy.

jaca *f* pony, cob.

jacinto *m* hyacinth.

jactancia *f* boastfulness, boasting, bragging.

jactancioso,-a *adj* boastful. — 2 *m,f* braggart.

jactarse *p* to boast, brag (*de,* about).

jadeante *adj* panting, breathless.

jadear *i* to pant, gasp.

jadeo *m* panting, gasping.

jalar *t* (*tirar de un cabo*) to pull, heave. 2 *fam* (*comer*) to wolf down.

jalea *f* jelly.

jalear *t* (*animar*) to cheer (on), clap and shout at. 2 (*caza*) to urge on.

jaleo *m* (*alboroto*) din, racket. 2 (*escándalo*) fuss, commotion. 3 (*riña*) row. 4 (*confusión*) muddle.

jalón *m* (*estaca*) marker pole. 2 *fig* (*hito*) milestone.

jalonar *t* (*señalar con estacas*) to stake out. 2 *fig* (*marcar*) to mark.

jamás *adv* never, ever: ~ *he escrito un libro,* I have never written a book; *el mejor libro que* ~ *se haya escrito,* the best book ever written. ●~ *de los jamases,* never ever, never on your life; *nunca* ~, never ever; *por siempre* ~, for ever (and ever).

jamón *m* ham. ■ ~ *de York/en dulce,* boiled ham; ~ *serrano,* cured ham.

jaque *m* check. ●*dar* ~ *a,* to check. ■ ~ *mate,* checkmate.

jaqueca *f* migraine, headache. ●*fig dar* ~ *a algn.,* to bore sb., be a pain in the neck to sb.

jarabe *m* syrup. ■ ~ *para la tos,* cough syrup/mixture.

jarana *f fam* (*juerga*) wild party, spree. 2 (*jaleo*) racket, din. ●*armar* ~, to make a racket; *ir de* ~, to go on a spree.

jarcia *f* (*naútica*) rigging, ropes *pl.* 2 (*pesca*) fishing tackle.

jardín *m* garden. ■ ~ *de infancia,* nursery school.

jardinero,-a *m,f* gardener. — 2 *f* (*mueble*) (*para tiestos*) planter, flower stand; (*en ventana*) window box.

jardinería *f* gardening.

jarra *f* jug, US pitcher. ●*fig de/en jarras,* arms akimbo, hands on hips. ■ ~ *de cerveza,* beer mug; ~ *de leche,* milk-churn.

jarro *m* (*recipiente*) jug. 2 (*contenido*) jugful.

jarrón *m* vase. 2 ART urn.

jaspeado,-a *adj* mottled, speckled.

jaula *f* (*para animales*) cage. 2 (*embalaje*) crate. 3 (*niños*) playpen.

jauría *f* pack of hounds. 2 *fig* gang.

jazmín *m* jasmine.

jefatura *f* (*cargo, dirección*) leadership. 2 (*sede*) central office; MIL headquarters *inv.*

jefe,-a *m,f* head, chief, boss. 2 COM *m* manager, *f* manageress. 3 POL leader. 4 MIL officer in command. ■ ~ *de estación,* station master; ~ *de Estado,* Head of State; ~ *de Estado Mayor,* Chief of Staff; ~ *de redacción,* editor-in-chief; ~ *de taller,* foreman.

jerarca *m* hierarch.

jerarquía *f* hierarchy. 2 (*grado*) scale. 3 (*categoría*) rank.

jerga *f* (*técnica*) jargon. 2 (*vulgar*) slang.

jergón *m* straw mattress. 2 *fig* (*torpe*) country bumpkin.

jerigonza *f* → **jerga**. 2 (*extravagancia*) oddness.

jeringuilla *f* (hypodermic) syringe.

jeroglífico,-a *adj* hieroglyphic. — **2** *m* hieroglyph(ic). **3** *(juego)* rebus.

jersey *m* sweater, pullover, jumper. ▲ *pl* **jerseyes** or **jerséis**.

jesuítico,-a *adj* Jesuitic. **2** *fig* cautious.

jeta *f fam (cara)* mug, face. **2** *(hocico)* snout. **3** *(descaro)* cheek. — **4** *mf pl* rogue *sing*. ●**poner** ~, to pull a face; **tener** ~, to be cheeky, have a nerve.

jícara *f* small cup.

jilguero *m* goldfinch.

jilipollas* *mf inv* → **gilipollas***.

jinete *m* rider, horseman.

jira *f (pedazo de tela)* strip of cloth. **2** *(merienda)* picnic.

jirafa *f* giraffe. **2** *fig (alto)* tall person.

jirón *m (trozo desgarrado)* shred, strip. **2** *(pedazo suelto)* bit, scrap. ●**hecho,-a jirones,** in shreds/tatters.

jocosidad *f* humour.

jocoso,-a *adj* funny, humorous, comic.

joder(se)* *arg t (copular)* to fuck*, screw*. **2** *(fastidiar)* to piss off*. **3** *(echar a perder, estropear)* to fuck up*. **4** *(lastimar)* to hurt. — **5** *p (aguantarse)* to put up with it. **6** *(echarse a perder)* to fuck up*, ruin. **7** *(lastimarse)* to hurt, fuck up*. **8** *(estropearse)* to go bust. — **9** *interj* bloody hell!, fuck*! ●**¡hay que ~se!,** you'll just have to grin and bear it!; **¡la jodiste!,** you screwed it up!; **¡no me jodas!,** come on, don't give me that!; **¡que se joda(n)!,** to hell with him/her/them!

jodido,-a* *arg adj (maldito)* bloody, fucking*. **2** *(molesto)* annoying. **3** *(enfermo)* in a bad way; *(cansado)* knackered, exhausted. **4** *(estropeado, roto)* fucked up*, done for, kaput, buggered*. **5** *(difícil)* complicated.

jolgorio *m fam (juerga)* binge. **2** *(algazara)* fun. ●**¡qué ~!,** what fun!

¡jolín!, ¡jolines! *interj fam (sorpresa)* gosh!, good grief! **2** *(enfado)* blast!, damn!

jornada *f (duración de un trabajo, una diversión)* day. **2** *(camino recorrido en un día)* day's journey. **3** MIL expedition. **4** *pl* conference *sing*, congress *sing*. ■~ **completa,** full-time; **media** ~, part-time.

jornal *m* day's wage. ●**trabajar a** ~, to be paid by the day.

jornalero,-a *m,f* day labourer.

joroba *f (deformidad)* curvature, hump. **2** *fam (fastidio)* nuisance, drag. — **3** *interj* drat!

jorobado,-a *adj* hunchbacked, humpbacked. — **2** *m,f* hunchback, humpback.

jorobar(se) *fam t (fastidiar)* to annoy, bother. **2** *(romper)* to smash up, break. **3** *(estropear)* to ruin, wreck. — **4** *p (aguantarse)* to put up with it. ●**me joroba,** it really gets up my nose; **¡no jorobes!,** *(fastidio)* stop pestering me!; *(incredulidad)* pull the other one!

jota *f* the letter ~ **2** *(cantidad mínima)* jot, scrap. ●**ni** ~, not an iota.

joven *adj* young. — **2** *mf m* youth, young man, *f* girl, young woman.

jovial *adj* jovial, good-humoured.

jovialidad *f* joviality, cheerfulness.

joya *f* jewel, piece of jewellery. ●*fig* **ser una** ~, to be a real treasure/godsend.

joyería *f (tienda)* jewellery shop, jeweller's (shop). **2** *(comercio)* jewellery trade.

joyero,-a *m,f* jeweller. — **2** *m* jewel case/box.

juanete *m* bunion.

jubilación *f (acción)* retirement. **2** *(dinero)* pension.

jubilado,-a *adj-m,f* retired (person).

jubilar(se) *t-p (retirarse)* to retire. — **2** *t* to pension off; *fam fig* to get rid of, ditch. — **3** *i fml (alegrarse)* to rejoice.

júbilo *m* jubilation, joy.

jubiloso,-a *adj* jubilant, joyful.

judicial *adj* judicial, juridical.

judío,-a *adj* Jewish. **2** *fam* mean, stingy. — **3** *m,f* Jew. — **4** *f (planta)* bean. ■ ~ **blanca/pinta,** haricot/kidney bean; ~ **verde,** French/green bean.

juego *m* game. **2** DEP sport; *(tenis)* game. **3** *(apuestas)* gambling. **4** *(conjunto de piezas)* set. **5** *(movimiento)* play. ●*fig* **a** ~, matching; *fig* **descubrirle el** ~ **a algn.,** to see through sb.; *fig* **hacer/seguir el** ~ **a algn.,** to play along with sb.; *fig* **hacer** ~, to match; *fig* **poner algo en** ~, to put sth at stake. ■ ~ **de café/té,** coffee/tea service; ~ **de ingenio,** guessing game; ~ **de manos,** sleight of hand; ~ **de palabras,** play on words, pun; **juegos malabares,** juggling *sing*.

juerga *f fam* binge, rave-up. ●**de** ~, living it up, having a good time; **ir(se) de juerga,** to go on a binge.

juerguista *adj-mf* fun-loving (person).

jueves *m inv* Thursday.

juez *mf* JUR judge. ■ ~ **de banda/línea,** linesman; ~ **de paz,** justice of the peace.

jugada *f* play; *(ajedrez)* move; *(billar)* shot; *(dardos)* throw. **2** FIN speculation. **3** *fam* dirty trick. ●**hacerle una mala** ~ **a algn.,** to play a dirty trick on sb.

jugador,-ra *m,f* player. **2** *(apostador)* gambler. **3** FIN speculator.

jugar(se) [53] *i* to play. **2** *(burlarse)* to make fun *(con,* of). – **3** *t (hacer uso) (una pieza)* to move; *(una carta)* to play. – **4** *t-p (apostar)* to bet, stake. – **5** *p (arriesgar)* to risk. ●*jugársela a algn.,* take sb. for a ride; *jugársela al marido/a la mujer,* to two-time one's husband/wife; *¿quién juega?,* whose go/turn is it?; *fig ~(se) el todo por el todo,* to stake everything one has.

jugarreta *f fam* dirty trick.

jugo *m* juice. ●*fig sacar el ~ a algo,* to make the most of sth.; *fig sacarle el ~ a algn.,* to exploit sb., bleed sb. dry.

jugoso,-a *adj* juicy. **2** *fig (rentable)* profitable.

juguete *m* toy. ●*fig ser el ~ de algn.,* to be sb.'s plaything.

juguetear *i* to play, frolic.

jugueteo *m* playing, frolicking.

juguetería *f (tienda)* toy shop. **2** *(comercio)* toy business.

juguetón,-ona *adj* playful, frolicsome.

juicio *m* judgement. **2** *(sensatez)* reason, common sense. **3** JUR trial, lawsuit. **4** REL judgement. ●*dejar algo a ~ de algn.,* to leave sth. to sb.'s discretion; *emitir un ~ sobre algo,* to express an opinion about sth.; *en su sano ~,* in one's right mind; *llevar a algn. a ~,* to take legal action against sb., sue sb.; *quitar/trastornar el ~ a algn.,* to drive sb. insane.

juicioso,-a *adj* judicious, sensible, wise.

julio *m* July.

jumento *m* ass, donkey.

junco *m* BOT rush. **2** *(bastón)* walking stick, cane.

jungla *f* jungle.

junio *m* June.

junta *f (reunión)* meeting, assembly, conference. **2** *(conjunto de personas)* board, council, committee. **3** *(sesión)* session, sitting. **4** MIL junta. **5** TÉC joint. ■ *~ administrativa,* administrative board; *~ de empresa,* works council; *~ directiva,* board of directors.

juntar(se) *t (unir)* to join/put together; *(piezas)* to assemble. **2** *(coleccionar)* to collect. **3** *(reunir) (dinero)* to raise; *(gente)* to gather together. – **4** *p (unirse a)* to join, get together; *(ríos, caminos)* to meet. **5** *(amancebarse)* to move in with. ●*fig ~se con algo,* to find o.s. with sth.

junto,-a *adj* together. – **2** *adv* near, close. **3** *(al mismo tiempo)* at the same time. ●*~ a,* near, close to; *~ con,* together with; *todo ~,* all at once.

jura *f (acción)* oath; *(ceremonia)* swearing-in, pledge.

jurado,-a *adj* sworn. – **2** *m* JUR *(tribunal)* jury; *(miembro del tribunal)* juror, member of the jury. **3** *(en un concurso)* panel of judges, jury.

juramentar *t* to swear (in).

juramento *m* JUR oath. **2** *(blasfemia)* swearword, curse(word). ●*tomar ~ a algn.,* to swear sb. in. ■ *~ de fidelidad,* oath of allegiance; *~ falso,* perjury.

jurar(se) *t* to swear, take an oath. – **2** *i (blasfemar)* to curse, swear. ●*~ en falso,* to commit perjury; *~ en vano,* to take the name of the Lord in vain; *~ fidelidad,* to pledge allegiance; *jurársela(s) a algn.,* to have it in for sb.

jurídico,-a *adj* juridical, legal.

jurisconsulto *m* jurist, legal expert.

jurisdicción *f* jurisdiction.

jurisdiccional *adj* jurisdictional. ■ *aguas jurisdiccionales,* territorial waters.

jurisprudencia *f* jurisprudence.

jurista *mf* jurist, lawyer.

justicia *f* justice, fairness.

justiciero,-a *adj* severe.

justificable *adj* justifiable.

justificación *f* justification.

justificante *adj* justifying. – **2** *m* voucher, written proof.

justificar(se) [1] *t-p* to justify (o.s.). ●*~se con algn.,* to apologize to sb. (for sth.).

justo,-a *adj (con justicia)* just, fair, right. **2** *(apretado, escaso)* tight. **3** *(exacto)* right, accurate. – **4** *m,f* just/fair person. – **5** *adv (exactamente)* exactly, precisely. **6** *(suficiente)* just enough. – **7** *justamente adv (con exactitud)* precisely, exactly. **8** *(con justicia)* fairly, justly. ●*ir ~ , (de dinero/tiempo)* to be tight (for money/time); *ser ~, (de inteligencia)* to be dim.

juvenil *adj* youthful, young. – **2** *adj-mf* DEP under 18.

juventud *f (edad)* youth. **2** *(aspecto joven)* youthfulness. **3** *(conjunto de jóvenes)* young people, youth. ●*conservar la ~,* to keep one's youthful look.

juzgado *m* court, tribunal. ●*fam fig ser de ~ de guardia,* to be absolutely scandalous. ■ *~ de guardia,* (police) court.

juzgar [7] *i* to judge. **2** *(considerar)* to consider, think.

K

kárate *m* karate.
kilo *m* kilogram. **2** *arg* million pesetas.
kilogramo *m* kilogram(me).
kilolitro *m* kilolitre.
kilométrico,-a *adj* kilometric. — **2** *m* runabout ticket.

kilómetro *m* kilometre.
kilovatio *m* kilowatt.
kiosko *m* → **quiosco**.
kiwi *m* kiwi.
kleenex® *m* Kleenex®, tissue.
koala *m* koala.

L

la *art def f sing* the: ~ *casa,* the house. — **2** *pron pers f sing (objeto)* her: ~ *miré,* I looked at her; *(cosa, animal)* it: ~ *cogí,* I took it. — **3** *m* MÚS la(h), A.

laberinto *m* labyrinth, maze.

labia *f fam* glibness.

labio *m* lip.

labor *f (trabajo)* work, task. **2** COST embroidery, needlework; *(punto)* knitting. **3** AGR farmwork.

laboral *adj* labour. ■ *jornada* ~, working day.

laborable *adj* AGR arable. **2** *(de trabajo)* working. ■ *día* ~, workday.

laboratorio *m* laboratory.

laboriosidad *f* diligence, industry.

laborioso,-a *adj* industrious, diligent. **2** *(trabajoso)* arduous.

laborista *adj* Labour. — **2** *mf* Labour (Party) member.

labrador,-ra *m,f* farmer, peasant.

labranza *f* farming.

labrar *t (metal)* to work; *(madera)* to carve; *(piedra)* to cut. **2** AGR to plough.

laca *f (resina)* lacquer. **2** *(barniz)* shellac. **3** *(para pelo)* hair lacquer/spray.

lacayo *m* lackey, footman.

lacerar *t* to lacerate, tear. **2** *fig* to harm, damage.

lacio,-a *adj (marchito)* withered. **2** *(flojo)* languid. **3** *(cabello)* straight; *(sin vingor)* lank.

lacónico,-a *adj* laconic.

lacra *f* trace, mark, scar. **2** *(defecto)* fault, defect.

lacrar *t* to seal.

lacre *m* sealing wax.

lacrimógeno,-a *adj* tearful: *una historia lacrimógena,* a tear jerker. ■ *gas* ~, tear-gas.

lacrimoso,-a *adj* lachrymose, tearful.

lactancia *f* lactation.

lactante *adj* lactational. — **2** *mf* breast-fed baby.

lácteo,-a *adj* milk(y). ■ *Vía Láctea,* Milky way.

ladear(se) *t-p* to tilt.

ladera *f* slope, hillside.

ladino,-a *adj* shrewd, sly.

lado *m* side. **2** *(aspecto)* aspect. ● *al* ~, close by, near by; *al* ~ *de,* beside; *dar de* ~ *a algn.,* to avoid sb.; *dejar a un* ~, to set aside; *hacerse a un* ~, to get out of the way; *por un* ~ *... por otro...,* on the one hand ... on the other hand...

ladrar *i* to bark.

ladrido *m* bark, barking.

ladrillo *m* brick.

ladrón,-ona *m,f* thief.

lagartija *f* small lizard.

lagarto *m* lizard.

lago *m* lake.

lágrima *f* tear.

lagrimal *m* corner of the eye.

laguna *f* small lake, lagoon. **2** *fig (blanco)* blank, gap.

laico,-a *adj* lay, secular. — **2** *m,f* lay person.

lamentable *adj* lamentable, deplorable, regrettable.

lamentación *f* wail, lamentation.

lamentar(se) *t* to deplore, regret, be sorry for. — **2** *p* to complain, grieve.

lamento *m* wail, moan, cry.

lamer *t* to lick.

lámina *f* sheet. **2** *(ilustración)* (full-page) illustration.

lámpara *f* lamp. **2** RAD valve.

lamparón *m* stain.

lana *f* wool.

lanar *adj* wool-bearing. ■ *ganado* ~, sheep.

lancero *m* lancer.

lancha *f* launch, (motor)boat.

langosta *f* (insecto) locust. **2** (crustáceo) lobster.

langostino *m* prawn, shrimp.

languidecer [43] *i* to languish.

languidez *f* weakness, languor.

lánguido,-a *adj* weak, languid.

lanza *f* lance, spear. **2** (de carro) shaft.

lanzadera *f* shuttle.

lanzagranadas *m inv* grenade launcher.

lanzamiento *m* cast, throwing. **2** AER launching.

lanzar(se) [4] *t* to throw, fling, hurl. **2** (nave) to launch. **3** *fig* (grito) to let out. **4** *fig* (mirada) to fire. — **5** *p* to throw o.s.

lapa *f* ZOOL limpet. **2** *pey* (persona) bore.

lápida *f* tombstone, slab.

lapidar *t* to throw stones at, stone to death.

lápiz *m* pencil. ■ *lápices de colores,* coloured pencils/crayons; ~ *de labios,* lipstick.

lapso *m* lapse. **2** (error) slip.

largar(se) [7] *t* to let go. **2** *fig* (dar) to give. **3** (decir) to let out. — **4** *p fam* to get out, leave. ●*¡lárgate!,* get out!

largo,-a *adj* long. **2** (extenso) large. **3** (astuto) shrewd. — **4** *m* length: *tiene dos metros de ~,* it's two metres long. — **5** *interj* get out! — **6** *largamente adv* at length; long, for a long time. **7** largely. ●*a la larga,* in the long run; *a lo ~ de,* along, throughout; ~ *y tendido,* at length; *pasar de ~,* to pass by; *tener para ~,* to have a long wait ahead.

largometraje *m* feature film, full-length film.

largura *f* length.

laringe *f* larynx.

laringitis *f inv* laryngitis.

larva *f* larva.

las *art def fpl* the: ~ *casas,* the houses. — **2** *pron pers fpl* (objeto directo) them: ~ *vi,* I saw them.

lascivia *f* lasciviousness, lewdness.

lascivo,-a *adj* lascivious, lewd.

lasitud *f* lassitude, weariness.

lástima *f* pity, compassion, grief. ●*por ~,* out of pity; *¡qué ~!,* what a pity!; *tener ~ a algn.,* to feel sorry for sb.

lastimar(se) *t* to hurt, injure. **2** (ofender) to offend. — **3** *p* to get hurt.

lastre *m* ballast. **2** *fig* dead weight, burden.

lata *f* (hojalata) tinplate. **2** (envase) tin, can. **2** (fastidio) bore, nuisance. ●*dar la ~,* to annoy; *en ~,* canned, tinned.

latente *adj* latent.

lateral *adj* lateral, side. — **2** *m* AUTO side lane.

latido *m* beat.

latifundio *m* large estate.

latigazo *m* lash. **2** (sonido) crack. **3** MED whiplash injury. **4** *fam* (trago) swig.

látigo *m* whip.

latín *m* Latin.

latir *i* to beat, throb.

latitud *f* latitude.

latón *m* brass.

latoso,-a *adj fam* tiresome.

latrocinio *m fml* theft, robbery.

laúd *m* lute.

laudable *adj* laudable, praiseworthy.

laureado,-a *adj* laureate.

laurel *m* bay.

lava *f* lava.

lavabo *m* washbasin. **2** (cuarto de baño) washroom. **3** (público) toilet.

lavadero *m* wash room, laundry.

lavado *m* wash(ing).

lavadora *f* washing machine.

lavandera *f* washerwoman, laundress.

lavandería *f* laundry.

lavar(se) *t* (manos etc.) to wash. **2** (platos) to wash up. **3** (limpiar) to clean. — **4** *p* to wash o.s. ●~ *en seco,* to dry-clean.

lavaplatos *m inv* → **lavavajillas.**

lavativa *f* enema.

lavavajillas *m inv* dishwasher.

laxante *adj-m* laxative.

laxar *t* to laxate, loosen.

laxitud *f* laxity, laxness.

lazada *f* (nudo) knot. **2** (lazo) bow.

lazarillo *m* guide. ■ *perro ~,* guide dog.

lazo *m* bow. **2** (nudo) knot. **3** *fig* (vínculo) tie, bond. **4** (trampa) snare, trap. ■ ~ *corredizo,* slip-knot.

le *pron pers m* (objeto directo) him; (usted) you. — **2** *pron pers mf* (objeto indirecto) him; (a ella) her; (a cosa, animal) it; (a usted) you.

leal *adj* loyal, faithful. **2** (justo) fair.

lealtad *f* loyalty, faithfulness.

lección *f* lesson. ●*fig dar una ~ a algn.,* to teach sb. a lesson.

lechal *adj* sucking. ■ *cordero ~,* sucking lamb.

lechar *t* AM to milk.

leche *f* milk. **2** *fam* (golpe) knock. **3** *fam* (suerte) luck. ●*fam tener mala ~,* to have a nasty temper. ■ ~ *condensada,* condensed milk; ~ *descremada,* skim(med) milk.

lechería *f* dairy.
lechero,-a *adj* milk. — **2** *m,f m* milkman, dairyman, *f* milkmaid, dairymaid.
lecho *m* bed.
lechón *m* sucking pig.
lechuga *f* lettuce.
lechuza *f* barn owl.
lector,-ra *m,f* reader. **2** *(universitario)* lecturer. — **3** *m* TÉC reader.
lectura *f* reading. **2** *(interpretación)* interpretation.
leer [61] *t* to read.
legado *m* *(herencia)* legacy, bequest. **2** *(persona)* legate, representative.
legajo *m* dossier.
legal *adj* legal. **2** *fam (persona)* honest.
legalidad *f* legality, lawfulness.
legalizar [4] *t* to legalize.
legaña *f* sleep.
legañoso,-a *adj* bleary-eyed.
legar [7] *t* to will, bequeath. **2** *fig* to pass on.
legendario,-a *adj* legendary.
legión *f* legion.
legionario *m* legionary, legionnaire.
legislación *f* legislation.
legislar *t* to legislate.
legislativo,-a *adj* legislative.
legislatura *f* legislature.
legitimar *t* to legitimate.
legítimo,-a *adj* JUR legitimate. **2** *(genuino)* genuine, real.
lego,-a *adj* lay, secular. **2** *(ignorante)* ignorant.
legua *f* league.
legumbre *f* legume.
lejanía *f* distance.
lejano,-a *adj* distant, remote, far.
lejía *f* bleach.
lejos *adv* far, far away/off. ● *a lo ~,* in the distance, far away; *de ~,* from afar.
lelo,-a *adj fam* stupid, dull.
lema *m* motto, slogan.
lencería *f* *(ropa blanca)* linen (goods). **2** *(tienda)* linen-draper's shop. **3** *(de mujer)* underwear, lingerie.
lengua *f* ANAT tongue. **2** *(idioma)* language. **3** *(de tierra)* strip. ● *fig morderse la ~,* to hold one's tongue; *fig no tener pelos en la ~,* not to mince one's words; *fig tener algo en la punta de la ~,* to have sth. on the tip of one's tongue. ■ *~ materna,* mother tongue.
lenguado *m* sole.
lenguaje *m* *gen* language. **2** *(habla)* speech.

lente *m & f* lens. — **2** *mpl* glasses, spectacles. ■ *~ de aumento,* magnifying glass; *lentes de contacto,* contact lenses.
lenteja *f* lentil.
lentejuela *f* sequin.
lentitud *f* slowness.
lento,-a *adj* slow.
leña *f* firewood. **2** *fam fig (paliza)* thrashing. ● *fig echar ~ al fuego,* to add fuel to the fire.
leñador,-ra *m,f* woodcutter, lumberjack.
leño *m* log. — **2** *fig (lerdo)* blockhead. ● *dormir como un ~,* to sleep like a log.
Leo *m inv* Leo.
león,-ona *m,f m* lion, *f* lioness.
leonera *f* lion 's den. — **2** *(cuarto)* untidy room.
leopardo *m* leopard.
lepra *f* leprosy.
leproso,-a *adj* leprous. — **2** *m,f* leper.
lerdo,-a *adj* clumsy.
les *pron pers mf pl (objeto indirecto)* them; *(a ustedes)* you. — **2** *pron pers mpl (objeto directo)* them; *(ustedes)* you.
lesbiana *f* lesbian.
lesión *f* wound, injury.
lesionar *t* to wound, injure.
letal *adj* lethal, deadly.
letargo *m* lethargy.
letra *f* *(del alfabeto)* letter. **2** *(de imprenta)* printing type, character. **3** *(escritura)* handwriting. **4** *(de canción)* words *pl.* **5** *pl* EDUC arts; *(literatura)* letters. ● *al pie de la ~,* literally; ■ COM *~ de cambio,* bill of exchange, draft; *~ mayúscula,* capital letter; *~ minúscula,* small letter.
letrado,-a *adj* learned, erudite. — **2** *m,f* lawyer.
letrero *m* sign, notice.
letrina *f* letrine.
leucemia *f* leukaemia.
leva *f* MIL levy. **2** MAR weighing anchor.
levadizo,-a *adj* liftable.
levadura *f* yeast.
levantamiento *m* *(supresión)* lifting, raising. **2** *(insurrección)* insurrection, uprising, revolt.
levantar(se) *t* to raise, lift, hoist. **2** *(construir)* to erect, build. **3** *(mesa)* to clear. — **4** *p (ponerse de pie)* to rise, stand up. **5** *(de la cama)* to get up, rise. **6** *(sublevarse)* to rebel. ● *~ acta,* to draw up a statement; *~ la sesión,* to adjourn; *fig ~se con el pie izquierdo,* to get out of bed on the wrong side.
levante *m* East. **2** *(viento)* east wing. **3** GEOG east coast of Spain.

levantisco,-a *adj* turbulent, rebellious.
levar *t* to set sail.
leve *adj* light. **2** *fig (poco importante)* slight, trifling.
levita *m* levite.
léxico,-a *adj* lexical. — **2** *m (diccionario)* lexicon. **2** *(vocabulario)* vocabulary.
lexicografía *f* lexicography.
ley *f gen* law; *(del parlamento)* act, bill. **2** *(de metal)* purity. ●*aprobar una ~,* to pass a bill; *fig con todas las de la ~,* properly. ■ *plata de ~,* sterling silver.
leyenda *f* legend. **2** *(inscripción)* inscription.
liar(se) [13] *t (atar)* to tie up; *(envolver)* to wrap up, bind. **2** *(cigarrillo)* to roll. **3** *(engañar)* to muddle up. **4** *(complicar)* to involve. — **5** *p (complicarse)* to get mixed up. **6** *fam (con algn.)* to have an affair *(con,* with).
libelo *m* libel.
libélula *f* dragon-fly.
liberación *f* liberation, freeing, release.
liberal *adj-mf* liberal.
liberar *t* to liberate, free.
libertad *f* liberty, freedom.
libertador,-ra *m,f* liberator.
libertinaje *m* licentiousness.
libertino,-a *adj-m,f* libertine.
libra *f* pound. **2** ASTROL ASTRON *Libra,* Libra. ■ *~ esterlina,* pound sterling.
libramiento *m* order for payment.
librar(se) *t* to free, deliver, save. **2** *(batalla)* to give. — **3** *p* to get rid *(de,* of), escape *(de,* from).
libre *adj* free. **2** *(asiento)* vacant. **3** *(sin ocupación)* disengaged, at leisure. ■ *~ albedrío,* free will.
librecambio *m* free trade.
librería *f (tienda)* bookshop. **2** *(estantería)* bookshelf.
librero,-a *m,f* bookseller.
libreta *f* notebook.
libro *m* book. ●COM *llevar los libros,* to keep the accounts. ■ POL *~ blanco,* white paper; *~ de bolsillo,* paperback; COM *~ de caja,* cash-book; *~ de reclamaciones,* complaints book.
licencia *f (permiso)* licence, permission. **2** *(documento)* licence, permit. **3** MIL discharge. ■ *~ fiscal,* business permit.
licenciado,-a *m,f* graduate. — **2** *m* MIL discharged soldier.
licenciar(se) *t* EDUC to grant a degree to. **2** MIL to discharge. — **3** *p* to graduate.
licenciatura *f* bachelor's degree.
licencioso,-a *adj* licentious, dissolute.

liceo *m* secondary school. **2** *(sociedad)* literary/recreational society.
licitar *t* to bid for.
lícito,-a *adj* licit, lawful.
licor *m (líquido)* liquid. **2** *(alcohólico)* liquor, spirits *pl.*
licuar [10] *t* to liquefy.
lid *f* contest, fight. **2** *fig (controversia)* dispute. ●*experto,-a en estas lides,* experienced in these matters.
líder *mf* leader.
lidia *f* fight. **2** *(de toros)* bullfight.
lidiar [12] *i (pelear)* to fight *(con/contra,* against), struggle *(con/contra,* with/against). **2** *fig* to deal *(con,* with). — **3** *t (toros)* to fight.
liebre *f* hare.
lienzo *m (tela)* linen. **2** ART canvas, painting.
liga *f (para media)* garter. **2** *(mezcla)* mixture. **3** *(alianza)* league, alliance. **4** DEP league.
ligadura *f* tie, bond.
ligamento *m* ligament.
ligar *t (atar)* to tie, bind. **2** *(metales)* to alloy. **3** *(unir)* to join, unite. **4** CULIN to thicken. — **5** *i fam (conquistar)* pick up *(con, -).*
ligereza *f (livianidad)* lightness. **2** *(prontitud)* swiftness. **3** *(agilidad)* agility. **4** *fig (frivolidad)* flippancy, frivolity.
ligero,-a *adj (liviano)* light. **2** *(rápido)* swift. **3** *(ágil)* agile. **4** *fig (frívolo)* flippant, thoughtless. ●*a la ligera,* lightly.
lija *f (papel)* sandpaper.
lila *adj-m-f* lilac.
lima *f (utensilio)* file. **2** *(fruta)* sweet lime.
limadura *f* filing.
limar *t* to file. **2** *fig* to polish up. ● *fig ~ asperezas,* to smooth things off.
limeta *f* AM (round) vase.
limitación *f* limitation, limit.
limitar(se) *t* to limit, cut down, restrict. — **2** *i* to border *(con,* on). — **3** *p* to limit o.s. *(a,* to).
límite *m* limit, bound. **2** *(frontera)* border.
limítrofe *adj* bordering.
limón *m* lemon.
limonada *f* lemonade.
limonero *m* lemon tree.
limosna *f* alms *pl,* charity. ●*pedir ~,* to beg.
limpiacristales *mf inv* window cleaner.
limpiabotas *m inv* bootblack.
limpiar [12] *t* to clean, cleanse. **2** *(con paño)* to wipe. **3** *fig (purificar)* to purify. **4** *fam (robar)* to pinch, nick.

límpido,-a *adj* limpid.
limpieza *f* cleanness, cleanliness. **2** *(acción)* cleaning. **3** *(pureza)* purity. **4** *(honradez)* honesty, fairness. **5** *(precisión)* precision, accuracy.
limpio,-a *adj* clean. **2** *(claro)* neat, tidy. **3** *(puro)* pure. **4** *(honesto)* honest, fair. **5** *(juego)* fair. **6** COM net: *ganó 40.000 limpias,* he/she made 40,000 clear profit. ●*dejar ~,* to leave broke; *poner en ~,* to make a clean copy; *sacar en ~,* to conclude, infer.
linaje *m* lineage. **2** *fig (clase)* kind, sort.
linaza *f* linseed.
lince *m* ZOOL lynx. **2** *fig (persona)* sharp-eyed person.
linchamiento *m* lynching.
linchar *t* to lynch.
lindante *adj* bordering *(con,* on).
lindar *i* to border *(con,* on).
linde *m & f* limit, boundary.
lindero,-a *adj* bordering. **− 2** *m →* **linde**.
lindeza *f (belleza)* prettiness. **2** *pl irón* insults.
lindo,-a *adj* pretty, nice, lovely. ●*de lo ~,* a great deal.
línea *f* line. **2** *(tipo)* figure. ●*guardar la ~,* to keep one's figure.
lineal *adj* linear.
lingote *m* ingot.
lingüista *mf* linguist.
lino *m (tela)* linen. **2** BOT flax.
linterna *f* lantern, lamp. ■ *~ (eléctrica),* flashlight.
lío *m (atado)* bundle, parcel. **2** *fig (embrollo)* tangle, muddle, mess. ●*armar un ~,* to make a fuss; *hacerse un ~,* to get tangled up; *meterse en un ~,* to get o.s. into a mess; *¡qué ~!,* what a mess!; *tener un ~ con algn.,* to be having an affair with sb.
liquidación *f* clearance sale.
liquidar *t* COM *(deuda)* to liquidate. **2** COM *(mercancías)* to sell off. **3** *fam (matar)* to kill.
líquido,-a *adj-m* liquid.
lírico,-a *adj* lyric(al). **− 2** *m,f* lyric poet. **− 3** *f* lyric poetry.
lirio *m* lily.
lirismo *m* lyricism.
lirón *m* dormouse.
lisiado,-a *adj* crippled. **− 2** *m,f* cripple.
liso,-a *adj* smooth, even. **2** *(pelo)* straight. **3** *(color)* plain. **− 4** *adj-m,f* AM *(sinvergüenza)* cheeky/shameless (person).
lisonja *f* (piece of) flattery.
lisonjear *t* to flatter.

lisonjero,-a *adj* flattering.
lista *f (raya)* strip. **2** *(tira)* slip. **3** *(relación)* list, register. ●*pasar ~,* to call the roll. ■ *~ de correos,* poste restante; *~ negra,* blacklist.
listado,-a *adj* striped. **− 2** *m (lista)* list.
listo,-a *adj (preparado)* ready, prepared. **2** *(inteligente)* clever, smart. **3** *(diligente)* quick, prompt.
listón *m (de madera)* lath. **2** DEP bar.
litera *f* bunk bed; *(en barco)* bunk; *(tren)* couchette.
literal *adj* literal.
literario,-a *adj* literary.
literato,-a *m,f* writer, man/woman of letters.
literatura *f* literature.
litigar [7] *t* JUR to litigate. **− 2** *i (disputar)* to argue, dispute.
litigio *m* JUR litigation, lawsuit. **2** *(disputa)* dispute.
litoral *adj* coastal. **− 2** *m* coast.
litro *m* litre.
liturgia *f* liturgy.
liviano,-a *adj (ligero)* light. **2** *fig (inconstante)* frivolous. **3** *fig (lascivo)* lewd.
lívido,-a *adj* livid.
llaga *f* ulcer, sore. ●*poner el dedo en la ~,* to touch a sore spot/point.
llama *f (de fuego)* flame, blaze. **2** ZOOL llama.
llamada *f* call. **2** *(a la puerta)* knock, ring.
llamamiento *m* call, summons, appeal.
llamarada *f* flash, sudden blaze/flame. **2** *fig (sonrojo)* sudden flush, blush.
llamar(se) *t* to call. **2** *(convocar)* to summon. **3** *(dar nombre)* to name. **− 4** *i (a la puerta)* to knock. **− 5** *p (tener nombre)* to be called/named: *me llamo Juan,* my name is Juan. ●*~ la atención,* to catch the attention; *~ la atención a,* to warn; *~ (por teléfono),* to telephone, ring up.
llamativo,-a *adj* showy, flashy.
llaneza *f (sencillez)* plainness, simplicity. **2** *(franqueza)* frankness.
llano,-a *adj (plano)* flat, even, level. **2** *(franco)* open, frank. **3** *(sencillo)* simple. **− 4** *m (llanura)* plain.
llanta *f* (wheel) rim.
llanto *m* crying, weeping.
llanura *f* plain.
llave *f (de puerta etc.)* key. **2** TÉC wrench. ●*bajo ~,* under lock and key; *cerrar con ~,* to lock. ■ *~ de contacto,* ignition key; *~ de paso,* stopcock; *~ inglesa,* monkey wrench; *~ maestra,* master key.

llavero *m* key ring.

llavín *m* latchkey.

llegada *f* arrival. **2** DEP finishing line.

llegar(se) [7] *i* to arrive (*a,* at/in), get (*a,* at), reach (*a,* -): ~ *a casa,* to arrive home. **2** (*alcanzar*) to reach. **3** (*ser suficiente*) to be enough, suffice. **4** (*cifra*) to amount (*a,* to), cost: *este modelo llega a los cuarenta millones,* this model costs forty million. **5** (*suceder*) to come, arrive: *llegó el momento,* the moment arrived/came. **6** (~ *a* + *infin.*) *llegó a decir que no lo quería,* he even said he didn't want it; ~ *a ver,* to manage to see. − **7** *p* (*acercarse*) to approach, come near. **8** (*ir*) to go (*a,* to): *llégate al estanco,* nip to the tobacconist's.

llenar(se) *t* to fill (up); (*formulario*) to fill in; (*tiempo*) to fill, occupy. **2** (*satisfacer*) to fulfil, please. **3** *fig* (*de insultos*) to heap (*de,* on); (*de favores etc.*) to shower (*de,* with). − **4** *p* to fill (up). **5** (*de gente*) to get crowded. **6** (*de comida*) to overeat.

lleno,-a *adj* full (*de,* of), filled (*de,* with). **2** (*de gente*) crowded (*de,* with). − **3** *m* TEAT full house. ●*de* ~, fully; ~ *hasta el borde,* brimful.

llevadero,-a *adj* bearable, tolerable.

llevar(se) *t* (*transportar*) to carry. **2** (*prenda*) to wear, have on. **3** (*conducir*) to take, lead, guide. **4** (*aguantar*) to bear, endure. **5** (*libros, cuentas*) to keep. **6** (*dirigir*) to be in charge of, manage. **7** (*pasar tiempo*) to be: *llevo un mes aquí,* I have been here for a month. **8** (~ + *participio*) to have: *llevo hechas cuatro cartas,* I've done four letters. **9** (*exceder*) to be ahead: *te llevo tres años,* I'm three years older than you. **10** (*paso*) to keep. **11** (*vida*) to lead. − **12** *p* to take off, carry away. **13** (*premio*) to win, carry off. **14** (*recibir*) to get: *~se un susto,* to get a shock. **15** (*estar de moda*) to be fashionable: *este color ya no se lleva,* this colour is not fashionable anymore. **16** (*entenderse*) to get on (*con,* with). **17** MAT to carry over. ●*~ adelante,* to carry on; ~ *las de perder,* to be at a disadvantage; *~se un chasco,* to be disappointed.

llorar *i* to cry, weep. **2** *fam* (*quejarse*) to moan. − **3** *t* to mourn. ●*~ a lágrima viva/moco tendido,* to cry one's heart out.

lloro *m* tears *pl,* weeping.

llorón,-ona *adj* weeping. − **2** *m,f* crybaby.

lloroso,-a *adj* tearful, weeping.

llover [32] *i* to rain. ●*~ a cántaros,* to rain cats and dogs. ▲ *Only used in the 3rd pers. It does not take a subject.*

llovizna *f* drizzle, sprinkle.

lloviznar *i* to drizzle, sprinkle. ▲ *Only used in the 3rd pers. It does not take a subject.*

lluvia *f* rain. **2** *fig* shower.

lluvioso,-a *adj* rainy, wet.

lo *art neut* the: ~ *bueno,* the good thing. − **2** *pron pers m & neut* (*objeto directo*) him; (*cosa, animal*) it; (*usted*) you. ●*~ cual,* which; ~ *que,* what.

loa *f* praise.

loable *adj* laudable, praiseworthy.

loar *t* to praise, extol.

lobo,-a *m,f m* wolf, *f* she-wolf. ●*oscuro como la boca del* ~, pitch-dark. ■ *fig* ~ *de mar,* old salt.

lóbrego,-a *adj* dark, gloomy, sad.

lóbulo *m* lobe, lobule.

local *adj* local. − **2** *m* premises *pl.*

localidad *f* (*ciudad*) village, town. **2** TEAT (*asiento*) seat.

localizar *t* (*encontrar*) to locate, find. **2** (*fuego, dolor*) to localize.

loco,-a *adj* mad, crazy, insane. − **2** *m,f* lunatic, insane person. ●*¡ni* ~*!,* no way!; *volverse* ~, to go crazy. ■ ~ *de remate,* stark mad.

locomotora *f* engine, locomotive.

locuaz *adj* loquacious, talkative.

locución *f* locution, phrase, idiom.

locura *f* madness, insanity, folly.

locutor,-ra *m,f* announcer.

lodo *m* mud, mire.

lógico,-a *adj* logical. − **2** *f* logic. − **3** *m,f* logician.

lograr *t* to get, obtain. **2** (*objetivo*) to attain, achieve. **3** (*tener éxito*) to succeed: *logré hacerlo,* I managed to do it.

logro *m* (*éxito*) success, achievement. **2** (*beneficio*) gain, profit.

loma *f* (hill)ock.

lombriz *f* earthworm.

lomo *m* ANAT back. **2** CULIN loin. ●*ir a ~ de,* to ride.

lona *f* canvas, sailcloth.

loncha *f* slice.

longaniza *f* pork sausage.

longevidad *f* longevity, long life.

longitud *f* length. **2** GEOG longitude.

longitudinal *adj* longitudinal.

lonja *f* (*mercado*) exchange, market. **2** ARQ raised porch. **3** (*loncha*) slice, rasher.

lontananza *f* (*fondo*) background. ●*en* ~, in the distance.

loro *m* parrot.

los *art def mpl* the: ~ *niños,* the boys. — **2** *pron pers mpl* them: ~ *vi,* I saw them.

losa *f* flagstone, slab. **2** *(de sepulcro)* gravestone.

lote *m (parte)* share, portion. **2** COM lot.

lotería *f* lottery. ●*tocarle la* ~ *a algn.,* to win a prize in the lottery; *fig* to be very lucky.

loza *f (cerámica)* pottery. **2** *(cocina)* crockery.

lozanía *f (frondosidad)* luxuriance. **2** *(vigor)* bloom, freshness, vigour.

lozano,-a *adj (frondoso)* luxuriant. **2** *(vigoroso)* blooming, fresh, vigorous.

lubricante *m* lubricant.

lubricar [1] *t* to lubricate.

lucero *m* (bright) star.

lucha *f* fight, struggle. **2** DEP wrestling. ■ ~ *de clases,* class struggle.

luchador,-ra *m,f* fighter. **2** DEP wrestler.

luchar *i* to fight. **2** DEP to wrestle.

lucidez *f* lucidity.

lúcido,-a *adj* clear, lucid.

luciérnaga *f* glow-worm.

lucimiento *m* brilliance.

lucir(se) [45] *i* to shine, glow. **2** *(sobresalir)* to excel. — **3** *t (mostrar) (cualidades)* to show, display; *(ropa)* to sport. — **4** *p (aventajarse)* to be brilliant/successful. **5** *(presumir)* to show off. **6** *irón (meter la pata)* to excel as.

lucrarse *p* to (make a) profit.

lucrativo,-a *adj* lucrative, profitable.

lucro *m* gain, profit. ■ *afán de* ~, greed for profit.

luego *adv (después)* afterwards, next. **2** *(más tarde)* later. **3** *(prontamente)* presently, immediately. — **4** *conj* therefore, then. ●*desde* ~, of course; *hasta* ~, so long, see you later.

lugar *m* place. **2** *(ciudad)* spot, town. **3** *(ocasión)* opportunity. **4** *(posición)* position. **5** *(espacio)* space. ●*dar* ~ *a,* to give rise to; *en* ~ *de,* instead of; *en primer* ~, firstly; *fuera de* ~, out of place; *fig* irrelevant; *hacer* ~, to make a room; *tener* ~, to take place, happen.

lugareño,-a *m,f* local.

lugarteniente *m* deputy.

lúgubre *adj* lugubrious, gloomy, dismal.

lujo *m* luxury. ●*de* ~, de luxe.

lujoso,-a *adj* luxurious, costly.

lujuria *f* lewdness, lust.

lujurioso,-a *adj* licentious, lustful.

lumbre *f* fire. **2** *(para cigarrillo)* light.

lumbrera *f* luminary. **2** *fig (persona)* eminence.

luminoso,-a *adj* bright, shining.

luna *f* ASTRON moon. **2** *(cristal)* window pane. **3** *(espejo)* mirror plate. ●*fig estar en la* ~, to be absent-minded. ■ ~ *llena,* full moon; *fig* ~ *de miel,* honey moon.

lunar *adj* lunar. — **2** *m (en la piel)* mole, beauty spot. ●*de lunares,* spotted.

lunes *m inv* Monday.

lupa *f* magnifying glass.

lustrar *t* to polish, shine.

lustre *m (brillo)* polish, shine, lustre. **2** *fig (esplendor)* glory.

luto *m* mourning. **2** *fig* grief. ●*estar de* ~, to mourn; *ir de* ~, to be in mourning.

luxación *f* dislocation.

luz *f* light. **2** *pl* knowledge *sing,* enlightenment *sing.* **3** *fam (electricidad)* electricity. ●*a todas luces,* evidently; *dar a* ~, to give birth to; *sacar a la* ~, to bring to light. ■ AUTO *luces de cruce,* dipped headlights; AUTO *luces de posición,* sidelights; ~ *del día,* daylight.

maca *f (en fruta)* bruise. **2** *(señal)* flaw, blemish.

macabro,-a *adj* macabre.

macanudo,-a *adj fam* great, terrific.

macarrón *m* macaroon. ■ *macarrones al gratén,* macaroni cheese.

macedonia *f* fruit salad.

macerar *t* to macerate.

maceta *f* plant pot, flowerpot.

macetero *m* flowerpot stand.

machaca *mf arg* dogsbody.

machacar [1] *t* to crush. — **2** *i fam (insistir en)* to harp on. **3** *fam (estudiar)* to swot.

machete *m* machete.

machismo *m* male chauvinism.

machista *mf* male chauvinist.

macho *adj* male. **2** *(robusto)* strong, robust. **3** *(viril)* manly, viril. — **4** *m* ZOOL male. **5** TÉC male piece/part; *(del corchete)* hook. **6** *fam* mate: *¿qué hay, ~?,* how's it going, mate? ■ *~ cabrío,* he-goat.

macizo,-a *adj* solid. — **2** *m (de flores)* bed. **3** *(de edificios)* group. **4** *(montañoso)* massif, mountain mass.

macramé *m* macramé.

macrobiótica *f* macrobiotics.

mácula *f (mancha)* spot, stain. **2** *(defecto)* blemish.

macuto *m* knapsack. ■ *fam radio ~,* bush telegraph, grapevine.

madeja *f* skein, hank. **2** *(persona)* limp, listless person.

madera *f* wood; ARQ timber. **2** *(de caballerías)* horn, rind. **3** *fig (talento)* talent. ●*¡toca ~!,* touch wood!

madero *m* piece of timber. **2** *arg (policía)* cop.

madrastra *f* stepmother.

madre *f gen* mother. **2** *(del río)* bed. **3** *(acequia)* main channel. **4** *(de vino, café)* dregs *pl.* **5** *(alcantarilla)* main sewer. ●*fam ¡~ mía!,* good heavens!; *la ~ que te parió/matriculó*,* you bastard!*; *¡tu ~!*,* up yours!* ■ *futura ~,* mother-to-be; *~ alquilada,* surrogate mother; *~ política,* mother-in-law.

madriguera *f (de conejo etc.)* hole, burrow. **2** *(de gente)* den, hideout.

madrina *f (de bautizo)* godmother. **2** *(de boda)* bridesmaid.

madroño *m* strawberry tree.

madrugada *f (alba)* dawn. **2** *(después de medianoche)* early morning. ●*de ~,* at daybreak/dawn.

madrugador,-ra *adj* early rising. — **2** *m,f* early riser.

madrugar [7] *i* to get up early.

madurar *t* to mature. **2** *(fruta)* to ripen. **3** *fig (plan etc.)* to think out. — **4** *i* to mature.

madurez *f* maturity. **2** *(de la fruta)* ripeness.

maduro,-a *adj* mature. **2** *(fruta)* ripe.

maestro,-a *adj (principal)* main. — **2** *m,f* teacher. — **3** *m (perito)* master. **4** MÚS *(compositor)* composer; *(director)* conductor. ■ *llave maestra,* master-key; *~ de obras,* foreman; *obra maestra,* masterpiece; *pared maestra,* structural wall.

mafia *f* mafia.

magdalena *f* bun, cake.

magia *f* magic. ■ *~ negra,* black magic.

mágico,-a *adj* magic(al). **2** *(maravilloso)* wonderful. — **3** *m,f* magician.

magisterio *m* teaching.

magistrado,-a *m,f* judge.

magistral *adj* EDUC of teaching. **2** *(superior)* masterly; *(tono)* magisterial.

magistratura *f* magistracy.

magnate *m* magnate.

magnético,-a *adj* magnetic.

magnetismo *m* magnetism.

magnetófono *m* tape recorder.

magnificencia *f* magnificence, splendour.

magnífico,-a *adj* magnificent, splendid.

magnitud *f* magnitude, greatness.

mago,-a *m,f* magician, wizard. ■ *los Reyes Magos,* the Three Kings/Wise Men.

magrear *t fam* to grope.

magro,-a *adj (flaco)* thin. **2** *(sin grasa)* lean. **– 3** *m (de cerdo)* lean meat. **– 4** *f (de jamón)* slice of ham.

magulladura *f* bruise, contusion.

magullar(se) *t* to bruise. **– 2** *p* to get bruised.

mahometano,-a *adj-m,f* Mohammedan.

mahonesa *f* → **mayonesa**.

maíz *m* maize, US corn.

majara, majareta *adj-mf fam* loony. ●*volverse* ∼, to go crazy.

majestad *f* majesty.

majestuosidad *f* majesty.

majestuoso,-a *adj* majestic, stately.

majo,-a *adj* pretty, lovely. **2** *(simpático)* nice. **3** *(tratamiento)* darling. **– 4** *f* belle.

mal *m* evil, wrong: *el bien y el* ∼, good and evil. **2** *(daño)* harm. **3** *(enfermedad)* illness, disease. **– 4** *adv* badly, wrong: *lo hizo* ∼, he did it wrong. **– 5** *adj* bad. ●*encontrarse* ∼, to feel ill; *menos* ∼ *que ...,* it's a good job that ...; *tomar a* ∼, to take badly. ▲ **5** *(adj)* used in front of a sing masculine noun: *mal día/día malo*.

malabarismo *m* juggling.

malabarista *mf* juggler.

malaleche* *adj-mf* bad-tempered (person). **– 2** *f* bad temper.

malapata *fam mf* jinx. **– 2** *f fam* bad luck.

malasombra *mf* clumsy person. **– 2** *f* clumsiness.

malbaratar *t (productos)* to undersell. **2** *(malversar)* to squander.

malcarado,-a *adj* grim-faced.

malcriar [13] *t* to spoil.

maldad *f* badness, evil. **2** *(acto)* evil/wicked thing.

maldecir [79] *t-i* to curse, damn. ●∼ *de,* to speak ill of.

maldición *f* curse.

maldito,-a *adj* cursed, damned. **2** *fam (que causa molestia)* damned, bloody.

maleante *mf* delinquent, criminal.

malear(se) *t (dañar)* to spoil, damage. **2** *(pervertir)* to corrupt. **– 3** *p* to become corrupted.

maleducado,-a *adj-m,f* bad mannered (person).

maleficio *m* spell, charm.

malentendido *m* misunderstanding.

malestar *m (incomodidad)* discomfort. **2** *fig (inquietud)* uneasiness.

maleta *f* suitcase, case. ●*hacer la* ∼, to pack.

maletero *m* AUTO boot, US trunk. **2** *(mozo)* porter.

maletín *m* briefcase.

malévolo,-a *adj* malevolent.

maleza *f (malas hierbas)* weeds *pl*. **2** *(arbustos)* thicket.

malformación *f* malformation.

malgastador,-ra *m,f* spendthrift, squanderer.

malgastar *t* to waste, squander.

malhablado,-a *adj-m,f* foul-mouthed (person).

malhechor,-ra *adj* criminal. **– 2** *m,f* wrongdoer, criminal.

malherir [35] *t* to wound seriously.

malhumor *m* bad temper/mood.

malhumorado,-a *adj* bad-tempered.

malicia *f (mala intención)* malice. **2** *(maldad)* evil, maliciousness. **3** *(astucia)* slyness, sagacity. **4** *(sospecha)* suspicion.

malicioso,-a *adj-m,f* malicious (person).

maligno,-a *adj* malignant.

malintencionado,-a *adj-m,f* ill-intentioned (person).

malla *f (red)* mesh, network. **2** *(prenda)* leotard. **3** AM swimming costume.

malo,-a *adj* bad. **2** *(malvado)* wicked. **3** *(travieso)* naughty. **4** *(nocivo)* harmful. **5** *(enfermo)* ill, sick. **6** *(difícil)* difficult. ●*estar de malas,* to be out of luck; *estar* ∼, to be ill; *lo malo es que ...,* the trouble is that ...; *por las malas,* by force. ■ *mala voluntad,* ill will. ▲ → **mal**.

malogrado,-a *adj (desaprovechado)* wasted. **2** *(difunto)* ill-fated.

malograr(se) *t* to waste. **– 2** *p* to fail, fall through.

malparado,-a *adj* hurt, injured. ●*salir* ∼, to end up in a sorry state.

malpensado,-a *adj-m,f* nasty-minded (person).

malsano,-a *adj* unhealthy, sickly.

malsonante *adj* ill-sounding. **2** *(grosero)* offensive.

malta *f* malt.

maltratar *t* to ill-treat, mistreat.

maltrecho,-a *adj* damaged, battered; *(persona)* injured.

malva *adj (color)* mauve. **– 2** *f* BOT mallow. ●*criar malvas,* to be pushing up the daisies.

malvado,-a *adj-m,f* wicked/evil (person).

malversación f misappropriation, embezzlement.

malvivir i to live very badly.

mama f (teta) breast; (de animal) udder. 2 fam (madre) mum(my).

mamá f fam mum(my).

mamar(se) t (leche) to suck. 2 fig (aprender de pequeño) to grow up with. — 3 p fam to get drunk.

mamarracho m fam (ridículo) sight. 2 (tonto) stupid.

mamífero,-a adj mammalian, mammal. — 2 m mammal.

mamón,-ona* adj pillock*, prick*.

mamotreto m (libro de apuntes) memorandum book. 2 (armatoste) monstrosity.

mampara f screen.

maná m manna.

manada f (vacas, elefantes) herd; (ovejas) flock; (lobos, perros) pack. 2 (que cabe en la mano) handful.

manager mf m manager, f manageress.

manantial m spring.

manar i (salir) to flow, run. 2 fig (abundar) to abound. — 3 t (salir) to run with.

manazas mf inv fam clumsy person.

mancha f stain, spot. 2 fig blemish. ■ ~ solar, sunspot.

manchar(se) t to stain. — 2 p to get dirty.

manco,-a adj one-handed. 2 (defectuoso) faulty. — 3 m,f one-handed person.

mancomunidad f community, association.

mandado,-a m (recado) order, errand. — 2 m,f person who carries out an order.

mandamás mf fam bigwig, boss.

mandamiento m order, command. 2 JUR warrant. ■ los Diez Mandamientos, the Ten Commandments.

mandar t (ordenar) to order; (encargarse de) to be in charge of. 2 (enviar) to send. ●~ recuerdos, to send regards; fam ~ a algn. a paseo, to send sb. packing; fam ¿mande?, pardon?

mandarina adj mandarin (orange), tangerine.

mandato m (orden) order, command. 2 JUR writ, warrant. 3 POL mandate, term of office.

mandíbula f jaw. ●reír a ~ batiente, to laugh one's head off.

mando m (autoridad) command; POL authorities pl. 2 (para mecanismos) control. ●estar al ~ de, to be in charge of. ■ ~ a distancia, remote control.

mandón,-ona adj-m,f bossy (person).

mandril m ZOOL mandril. 2 TÉC mandrel.

manecilla f (de reloj) hand.

manejable adj manageable, easy-to-handle.

manejar t (manipular) to handle, operate. 2 (dirigir) to run. 3 AM to drive.

manejo m (uso) handling. 2 (funcionamiento) running. 3 (de negocio) management. 4 (ardid) trick. 5 AM (de coche) driving.

manera f way, manner. 2 pl (educación) manners. ●a mi/tu ~, in my/your way; de ~ que, so that; de ninguna ~, by no means; de todas maneras, at any rate, anyhow; fam de mala ~, rudely.

manga f sleeve: en mangas de camisa, in shirtsleeves. 2 (manguera) hose (pipe). 3 (de pescar) casting net. 4 CULIN icing/forcing bag. ●sacarse algo de la ~, to pull sth. out of one's hat; ser de/tener ~ ancha, to be too indulgent.

mangar [7] t arg to knock off, pinch.

mango m handle. 2 BOT mango.

mangonear i fam pey (manipular) to be bossy. 2 (interferir) to meddle.

manguera f watering/gardening hose. 2 (de bombero) fire hose.

manguito m (de manos) muff. 2 (de manga) oversleeve. 3 TÉC sleeve.

manía f MED mania. 2 (ojeriza) dislike. 3 (pasión) craze. ●fam cogerle/tomarle ~ a algn., to take a dislike to sb.

maniaco,-a, maníaco,-a adj-m,f MED manic. 2 fam maniac.

maniático,-a adj-m,f fussy/cranky (person).

manicomio m mental hospital.

manicura f manicure.

manifestación f (de protesta etc.) demonstration. 2 (expresión) manifestation. 3 (declaración) statement, declaration.

manifestante mf demonstrator.

manifestar(se) [27] t-p (en la calle etc.) to demonstrate. 2 (declarar) to declare (o.s.). — 3 t (expresar) to manifest.

manifiesto,-a adj obvious, evident. — 2 m manifesto. ●poner de ~, to make evident.

manilla f (grillete) handcuff. 2 (de reloj) hand.

manillar m handlebar.

maniobra f manoeuvre.

maniobrar i to manoeuvre.

manipulación f manipulation.

manipular t to manipulate. 2 (mercancías) to handle. 3 fig to interfere with.

maniquí *m* (*muñeco*) dummy. – 2 *mf* (*modelo*) mannequin, model. ▲ *pl* **maniquíes**.

manitas *adj-mf inv fam* clever hands *inv*.

manivela *f* crank.

manjar *m* dish, food.

mano *f* hand. 2 ZOOL forefoot, forepaw. 3 (*de reloj*) hand. 4 (*de pintura etc.*) coat. 5 (*serie*) series. 6 *fig* (*habilidad*) skill. ●*cogidos,-as de la(s) mano(s),* hand in hand; *dar/tender la ~ a,* (*saludar*) to shake hands with; (*ayudar*) to offer one's hand to; *de segunda ~,* secondhand; *echar una ~,* to lend a hand; *hecho,-a a ~,* handmade; *tener ~ izquierda,* to be tactful; *fam coger/pillar a algn. con las manos en la masa,* to catch sb. red-handed. ▪ *apretón de manos,* handshake; *~ de obra,* labour(er).

manojo *m* bunch.

manopla *f* (*guante*) nitten.

manosear *t* to finger.

manotazo *m* cuff, slap.

mansalva *a ~, adv* safely.

mansarda *f* attic.

mansedumbre *f* meekness, gentleness. 2 (*animales*) tameness.

mansión *f* mansion.

manso,-a *adj* (*animal*) tame. 2 (*persona*) meek, mild, gentle.

manta *f* blanket. – 2 *mf fam* (*perezoso*) lazybones *inv*. ●*a ~,* abundantly. ▪ *~ de viaje,* travelling rug.

manteca *f* fat. ▪ *~ de cerdo,* lard; *~ de vaca,* butter.

mantecado *m* (*pastelito*) shortcake. 2 (*helado*) dairy ice cream.

mantecoso,-a *adj* greasy, buttery.

mantel *m* tablecloth.

mantelería *f* table linen.

mantener(se) [87] *t* (*conservar*) to keep. 2 (*sostener*) to support, hold up. 3 (*tener lugar, celebrar*) to hold. 4 (*ideas etc.*) to defend, maintain. 5 (*sustentar*) to support. – 6 *p* (*alimentarse*) to support o.s. 7 (*continuar*) to continue. ●*~se en sus trece,* to stick to one's guns.

mantenimiento *m* maintenance. 2 (*alimento*) sustenance.

mantequilla *f* butter.

manto *m* mantle, cloak.

mantón *m* large shawl. ▪ *~ de Manila,* embroidered silk shawl.

manual *adj-m* manual. ▪ *trabajos manuales,* handicrafts.

manufactura *f* (*obra*) manufacture. 2 (*fábrica*) factory.

manufacturar *t* to manufacture.

manuscrito,-a *adj* handwritten, manuscript. – 2 *m* manuscript.

manutención *f* maintenance. 2 (*alimenticia*) feeding.

manzana *f* BOT apple. 2 (*de casas*) block.

manzanilla *f* çamomile. 2 (*infusión*) camomile tea.

manzano *m* apple tree.

maña *f* skill. 2 (*astucia*) trick.

mañana *f* morning. – 2 *m* tomorrow, future. – 3 *adv* tomorrow. ●*pasado ~,* the day after tomorrow; *por la ~,* in the morning.

mañoso,-a *adj* dexterous, skilful. 2 (*astuto*) crafty.

mapa *m* map. ●*fam borrar del ~,* to get rid of.

mapamundi *m* map of the world.

maqueta *f* scale model. 2 (*de libro, disco*) dummy.

maquillaje *m* make-up.

maquillar(se) *t-p* to make (o.s.) up.

máquina *f* machine. ▪ *~ de afeitar (eléctrica),* (electric) razor/shaver; *~ de escribir,* typewriter; *~ fotográfica/de fotos,* camera; *~ tragaperras,* slot machine.

maquinación *f* machination.

maquinar *t* to scheme, plot.

maquinaria *f* machinery.

maquinista *mf* machinist. 2 (*de tren*) engine driver.

mar *m & f* sea. 2 (*marejada*) swell. 3 *fam* very, a lot: *la ~ de dificultades,* a lot of difficulties. ●*en alta ~,* on the high seas; *hacerse a la ~,* to put (out) to sea; *la ~ de,* very; *fam ¡pelillos a la ~!,* let bygones be bygones! ▪ *~ adentro,* out to sea; *~ de fondo,* groundswell; *~ gruesa,* heavy sea.

marabunta *f* swarm of ants. 2 *fam fig* mob.

maratón *m* marathon.

maravilla *f* wonder, marvel. ●*a las mil maravillas,* wonderfully well.

maravillar(se) *t* to astonish, dazzle. – 2 *p* to wonder, marvel.

maravilloso,-a *adj* wonderful, marvellous.

marca *f* (*señal*) mark, sign. 2 (*comestibles, productos del hogar*) brand; (*otros productos*) make. 3 DEP record. ●*de ~,* topquality. ▪ *~ registrada,* registered trademark.

marcado,-a *adj* (*señalado*) marked. 2 (*evidente*) distinct, evident.

marcador *m* DEP scoreboard.
marcapasos *m inv* pacemaker.
marcar [1] *t* to mark; *(ganado)* to brand.
2 DEP *(hacer tanto)* to score. **3** DEP *(al contrario)* to mark. **4** *(pelo)* to set. **5** *(aparato)* to indicate. **6** *(teléfono)* to dial. ●~ *el paso,* to mark time.
marcha *f* march. **2** *(progreso)* course, progress. **3** *(partida)* departure. **4** *(velocidad)* speed. **5** AUTO gear. **6** MÚS march. **7** *fam (energía)* go: **tener mucha** ~, to be wild. ●**a marchas forzadas,** against the clock; **a toda** ~, at full speed. ■ AUTO **cambio de marchas,** gearshift; DEP ~ **atlética,** walking race; AUTO ~ **atrás,** reverse (gear).
marchar(se) *i (ir)* to go, walk. **2** *(funcionar)* to work, run. − **3** *p* to leave. ●**¡marchando!,** on your way!
marchitar(se) *t-p* to shrivel, wither.
marchito,-a *adj* shrivelled, withered.
marchoso,-a *arg adj* fun-loving, wild. − **2** *m,f* raver, fun-lover.
marcial *adj* martial.
marciano,-a *adj-m,f* Martian.
marco *m (de cuadro, ventana, etc.)* frame. **2** *fig* framework, setting. **3** *(moneda)* mark.
marea *f* tide. ■ ~ **alta/baja,** high/low tide; ~ **negra,** oil slick.
mareado,-a *adj* sick. **2** *(aturdido)* dizzy, giddy.
marear(se) *t* MAR to sail. − **2** *t-i (molestar)* to annoy, bother. − **3** *p* to get sick.
maremagno, maremágnum *m* mess, confusion.
maremoto *m* seaquake.
mareo *m* sickness. **2** *(aturdimiento)* dizziness.
marfil *m* ivory.
margarina *f* margarine.
margarita *f* BOT daisy. **2** *(de máquina)* daisywheel.
margen *m & f (extremidad)* border, edge. **2** *(de río)* bank. **3** *(papel)* margin. **4** COM margin. ●**dar** ~ **para,** to give scope for.
marginación *f* exclusion.
marginado,-a *adj* excluded. − **2** *m,f* drop-out.
marginar *t* to leave out, exclude.
maría *f fam* EDUC easy subject. **2** *fam* housewife. **3** *arg (marihuana)* marijuana, pot.
marica*, maricón* *m* queer*.
mariconada* *f* dirty trick.
mariconera *f fam* man's clutch bag.
marido *m* husband.

marihuana *f* marijuana.
marimandona *f fam* domineering woman.
marimorena *f fam* row. ●**armarse la** ~, to kick up a racket.
marinero,-a *adj* sea. − **2** *m* sailor. ●*fam* ~ **de agua dulce,** landlubber.
marino,-a *adj* marine. − **2** *m* seaman. − **3** *f (zona)* seacoast. **4** *(pintura)* seascape. **5** *(barcos)* seamanship. ■ **azul** ~, navy blue; **marina de guerra,** navy.
marioneta *f* puppet, marionette.
mariposa *f* butterfly. **2** *(lámpara)* oil lamp. **3*** *(marica)* queer*. ●**nadar** ~, to do (the) butterfly.
mariposear *i (ser inconstante)* to be fickle. **2** *(vagar)* to flutter around.
mariquita *f* ZOOL ladybird. − **2*** *m (marica)* queer*.
mariscal *m* marshal. ■ ~ **de campo,** field marshal.
marisco *m* shellfish.
marisma *f* salt marsh.
marisquería *f* seafood restaurant.
marítimo,-a *adj* maritime, sea.
marketing *m* marketing.
marmita *f* cooking pot.
mármol *m* marble.
marmota *f* ZOOL marmot. ●*fam* **dormir como una** ~, to sleep like a log.
marqués,-esa *m,f m* marquis, *f* marchioness.
marquesina *f* canopy.
marquetería *f* marquetry, inlaid work.
marranada *f* filthy thing/act.
marrano,-a *adj (sucio)* dirty. − **2** *m* ZOOL pig. **3** *fam (sucio)* dirty pig.
marrón *adj-m* brown. ■ ~ **glacé,** marron glacé.
marroquinería *f* leather goods.
marta *f* marten; *(piel)* sable.
Marte *m* Mars.
martes *m inv* Tuesday. ●~ **y trece,** Friday the thirteenth.
martillear *t* to hammer.
martillo *m* hammer.
mártir *mf* martyr.
martirio *m* martyrdom. **2** *fig* torture, torment.
martirizar [4] *t* to martyr. **2** *fig* to torment, torture.
marxismo *m* Marxism.
marzo *m* March.
mas *conj* but.
más *adv (comparativo)* more. **2** *(con números o cantidades)* more than: ~ **de tres,** more than three. **3** *(superlativo)* most: **el**

~ *caro,* the most expensive. **4** *(después de pron interrog/indef)* else: ¿*algo* ~?, anything else? — **5** *m (signo)* plus. ●*a lo* ~, at the most; *como el que* ~, as well as anyone; *de* ~, spare, extra; *estar de* ~, to be unwanted; *es* ~, what's more; ~ *bien,* rather; *ni* ~ *ni menos,* exactly; *por* ~ *(que),* however much; *sin* ~ *ni* ~, without reason. ■ *el* ~ *allá,* the beyond.

masa *f* mass. **2** CULIN dough. **3** *(mortero)* mortar. **4** ELEC ground. **5** *(de cosas)* volume. **6** *(multitud)* crowd of people. **7** AM *(pastel)* cake.

masacre *f* massacre.

masaje *m* massage.

masajista *mf m* masseur, *f* masseuse.

mascar [1] *t-i* to chew, masticate.

máscara *f* mask. **2** *pl* masquerade *sing.*

mascarilla *f* mask. **2** *(cosmética)* face pack. **3** MED face mask.

mascota *f* mascot.

masculino,-a *adj* male. **2** *(para hombres)* men's. **3** GRAM masculine. — **4** *m* masculine.

mascullar *t* to mumble, mutter.

masivo,-a *adj* massive.

masón,-ona *m,f* Mason, Freemason.

masonería *f* Masonry, Freemasonry.

masoquismo *m* masochism.

masoquista *adj* masochistic. — **2** *mf* masochist.

masticar [1] *t* to masticate, chew.

mástil *m (asta)* mast. **2** MAR mast.

masturbación *f* masturbation.

masturbar(se) *t-p* to masturbate.

mata *f (arbusto)* shrub, bush. **2** *(ramita)* sprig. **3** AM *(bosque)* forest. ●*a salto de* ~, any old how. ■ ~ *de pelo,* head of hair.

matadero *m* slaughterhouse, abattoir.

matador,-ra *adj* killing. — **2** *m* matador, bullfighter.

matanza *f* slaughter.

matarife *m* slaughterer.

matarratas *m inv (raticida)* rat poison. **2** *(aguardiente)* rotgut.

matar(se) *t* to kill; *(asesinar)* to murder. — **2** *p* to kill o.s. ●*estar a* ~ *con,* to be at daggers drawn with; *matarlas callando,* to be a wolf in a sheep's clothing.

matasellos *m inv* postmark.

mate *adj (sin brillo)* matt, dull. — **2** *m (ajedrez)* checkmate. **3** *(hierba)* maté.

matemáticas *fpl* mathematics *sing.*

matemático,-a *adj* mathematical. — **2** *m,f* mathematician.

materia *f* matter. **2** FÍS material, substance. **3** EDUC subject.

material *adj* material. — **2** *m* material, equipment. — **3** *materialmente adv* materially, physically. ■ ~ *escolar,* teaching material(s); ~ *de oficina,* office equipment.

materialista *adj* materialistic. — **2** *mf* materialist.

materializar(se) [4] *t-p* to materialize.

maternal *adj* maternal, motherly.

maternidad *f* maternity, motherhood.

materno,-a *adj* maternal.

matinal *adj* morning. — **2** *f* matinée.

matiz *m (color)* shade, tint. **2** *fig* nuance.

matización *f fig* nuances *pl.*

matizar [1] *t (colores)* to blend. **2** *fig (palabras etc.)* to tinge. **3** *fig (precisar)* to be more explicit about.

matojo *m* bush, small shrub.

matón,-ona *m,f fam* bully, thug.

matorral *m* bush, thicket.

matraca *f* wooden rattle. **2** *(molestia)* pest, nuisance.

matriarcal *adj* matriarchal.

matrícula *f (lista)* list, roll. **2** *(registro)* registration. **3** AUTO registration number; *(placa)* number plate, US licence plate.

matricular(se) *t-p* to register, enrol.

matrimonio *m (acto)* marriage. **2** *(pareja)* married couple.

matriz *adj* principal. — **2** *f* ANAT womb. **3** TÉC mould. **4** *(original)* original, master copy. **5** *(de talonario)* stub.

matrona *f* matron. **2** *(comadrona)* midwife.

matutino,-a *adj* morning.

maullar [16] *i* to mew, miaow.

maullido *m* mewing, miaow.

mausoleo *m* mausoleum.

máxima *f* maxim.

máxime *adv fml* especially.

máximo,-a *adj-m* maximum. — **2** *f* METEOR maximum temperature.

mayo *m* May. **2** *(palo)* maypole.

mayonesa *f* mayonnaise.

mayor *adj (comparativo)* bigger, greater, larger; *(persona)* older; *(hermanos, hijos)* elder. **2** *(superlativo)* biggest, greatest, largest; *(persona)* oldest; *(hermanos, hijos)* eldest. **3** *(de edad)* mature, elderly. **4** *(adulto)* grown-up. — **5** *mayormente adv* chiefly, principally. ●*al por* ~, wholesale; *ser* ~ *de edad,* to be of age.

■ *calle* ~, high street; *colegio* ~, hall of residence.

mayoral *m (pastor)* head shepherd. **2** *(cochero)* coachman. **3** *(capataz)* foreman.

mayordomo *m* butler.

mayoría *f* majority. ■ ~ *de edad,* (age of) majority.

mayorista *mf* wholesaler.

mayúsculo,-a *adj (enorme)* huge. **2** *(letra)* capital. – **3** *f* capital letter.

maza *f* mace.

mazapán *m* marzipan.

mazmorra *f* dungeon.

mazo *m* mallet.

mazorca *f* spike, cob.

me *pron pers sing* me: *no* ~ *lo digas,* don't tell me. **2** *(reflexivo)* myself: ~ *veo en el espejo,* I can see myself in the mirror.

meada* *f* piss*, slash*.

mear(se)* *i* to (have a) piss. – **2** *p* to wet o.s.

¡mecachis! *interj fam* darn it!

mecánica *f (ciencia)* mechanics. **2** *(mecanismo)* mechanism.

mecánico,-a *adj* mechanical. – **2** *m,f* mechanic.

mecanismo *m* mechanism.

mecanizar [4] *t* to mechanize.

mecanografía *t* typing.

mecanografiar [13] *t* to type.

mecanógrafo,-a *m,f* typist.

mecedora *f* rocking chair.

mecer(se) [2] *t-p* to rock.

mecha *f (de vela)* wick. **2** MIL fuse. **3** *(de pelo)* lock.

mechero *m* (cigarette) lighter.

mechón *m (de pelo)* lock. **2** *(de hilos)* tuft.

medalla *f* medal.

medallón *m* medallion.

media *f* stocking. **2** *(promedio)* average. **3** MAT mean. ●*hacer* ~, to knit.

mediación *f* mediation.

mediado,-a *adj* half-full. ●*a mediados de,* about the middle of.

mediador,-ra *m,f* mediator.

medianero,-a *adj* dividing. ■ *pared medianera,* party wall.

mediano,-a *adj* average. **2** *(mediocre)* mediocre. **3** *(de tamaño)* middle-sized.

medianoche *f* midnight.

mediante *adj* by means of. ●*fml Dios* ~, God willing.

mediar [12] *i (interponerse)* to mediate, intervene. **2** *(tiempo)* to elapse.

medicación *f* medication, medical treatment.

medicar(se) *t* to medicate. – **2** *p* to take medicine.

medicina *f* medicine.

medición *f* measuring, measurement.

médico,-a *adj* medical. – **2** *m,f* doctor, physician. ■ ~ *de cabecera,* general practitioner.

medida *f* measure. **2** *(acción)* measurement. **3** *(prudencia)* moderation. ●*a (la)* ~ *de,* according to; *a* ~ *que,* as; *tomar/ adoptar medidas,* to take steps.

medidor *m* AM *(contador)* meter.

medieval *adj* medi(a)eval.

medievo *m* Middle Ages *pl.*

medio,-a *adj (mitad)* half: *las dos y media,* half past two. **2** *(intermedio)* middle: *a media tarde,* in the middle of the afternoon. **3** *(promedio)* average. – **4** *m (mitad)* half. **5** *(centro)* middle. **6** *(contexto)* environment. **7** *pl (recursos)* means. – **8** *adv* half: ~ *terminado,-a,* half-finished. ●*por todos los medios,* by all means; *quitar algo/algn. de en* ~, to get sth./sb. out of the way. ■ ~ *ambiente,* environment; *medios de comunicación,* (mass) media; *término* ~, average.

mediocre *adj* mediocre.

mediodía *m* noon, midday. **2** *(hora del almuerzo)* lunchtime.

medioevo *m* Middle Ages *pl.*

medir(se) [34] *t* to measure. **2** *(comparar)* to gauge. **3** *(moderar)* to weight. **4** *(versos)* to scan. – **5** *p* to measure o.s.

meditabundo,-a *adj* pensive, thoughtful.

meditación *f* meditation.

meditar *t-i* to meditate, think.

médium *mf inv* medium.

medrar *i* to grow. **2** *fig* to flourish.

médula, medula *f* marrow.

medusa *f* jellyfish.

megáfono *m* megaphone.

megalítico,-a *adj* megalithic.

mejilla *f* cheek.

mejillón *m* mussel.

mejor *adj-adv (comparativo)* better: *es* ~ *no hablar de esto,* it's better not to talk about this. **2** *(superlativo)* best: *mi* ~ *amigo,-a,* my best friend. ●*a lo* ~, perhaps, maybe; ~ *dicho,* rather; *tanto* ~, so much the better.

mejora *f,* **mejoramiento** *m* improvement.

mejorar(se) *t* to better, improve. – **2** *i-p* to recover, get better. **3** METEOR to clear up.

mejoría *f* improvement.

mejunje *m* unpleasant brew.

melancolía *f* melancholy.

melancólico,-a *adj-m,f* melancholic (person).

melaza *f* molasses.

melena *f (de cabello)* long hair. **2** *(de león, caballo)* mane.

melenudo,-a *adj-m,f* long-haired (person).

melindre *m* CULIN honey fritter. **2** *fig* affectation.

melindroso,-a *adj* finicky, affected.

mella *f (hendedura)* nick, notch. **2** *(hueco)* hollow, gap. •*hacer* ~, to make an impression.

mellizo,-a *adj-m,f* twin.

melocotón *m* peach.

melodía *f* melody.

melódico,-a *adj* melodic.

melón *m* melon.

meloso,-a *adj* sweet, honeyed.

membrana *f* membrane.

membrete *m* letterhead.

membrillo *m (árbol)* quince tree. **2** *(fruta)* quince. **3** *(dulce)* quince preserve/jelly.

memo,-a *adj fam* silly, foolish. – **2** *m,f* fool, simpleton.

memorable *adj* memorable.

memorándum *m* notebook. ▲ *pl* **memorándums**.

memoria *f* memory. **2** *(informe)* report. **3** *(inventario)* inventory. **4** *pl (biografía)* memoirs. •*de* ~, by heart; *hacer* ~ *de*, to try to remember.

memorial *m* notebook.

menaje *m* household equipment.

mención *f* mention.

mencionar *t* to mention, cite.

mendigar *i* to beg.

mendigo,-a *m,f* beggar.

mendrugo *m* hard crust (of bread).

menear(se) *t* to shake; *(cola)* to wag. **2** *fam (el cuerpo)* to wiggle. – **3** *p* to move.

menester *m (necesidad)* need. • *euf hacer sus menesteres*, to do one's business.

menestra *f* vegetable stew.

mengano,-a *m,f* so-and-so.

menguar [22] *i* to diminish, decrease. **2** *(luna)* to wane. **3** *(puntos)* to decrease.

menopausia *f* menopause.

menor *adj (comparativo)* smaller, lesser; *(persona)* younger. **2** *(superlativo)* smallest, least; *(persona)* youngest. – **3** *mf* minor. •*al por* ~, retail. ■ ~ *de edad*, under age.

menos *adv (comparativo)* less, fewer. **2** *(superlativo)* least, fewest. **3** *(para hora)* to: *las tres* ~ *cuarto*, a quarter to three. – **4** *m* minus. •*a* ~ *que*, unless; *al/a lo/ por lo* ~, at least; *de* ~, missing, wanting; *¡* ~ *mal!*, thank God!

menoscabar *t (mermar)* to reduce. **2** *(deteriorar)* to impair. **3** *fig* to discredit.

menospreciar [12] *t (no valorar)* to undervalue, underrate. **2** *(despreciar)* to despise.

mensaje *m* message.

mensajero,-a *m,f* messenger. ■ *paloma mensajera*, carrier pigeon.

menstruación *f* menstruation.

menstruar [11] *i* to menstruate.

mensual *adj* monthly.

mensualidad *f* monthly salary.

menta *f* mint.

mentado,-a *fml adj (mencionado)* aforementioned. **2** *(famoso)* famous.

mental *adj* mental.

mentalidad *f* mentality.

mentalizar(se) [4] *t* to make aware. – **2** *p (concienciarse)* to become aware.

mentar [27] *t* to name, mention.

mente *f* mind. •*tener una cosa en* ~, to have intention of doing sth.

mentecato,-a *adj* idiot. – **2** *m,f* fool.

mentir [35] *i* to lie, tell lies.

mentira *f* lie. •*parece* ~, it's unbelievable. ■ ~ *piadosa*, white lie.

mentiroso,-a *adj* lying. – **2** *m,f* liar.

mentís *m inv* denial.

mentón *m* chin.

menú *m* menu. ▲ *pl* **menús**.

menudear *t* to repeat frequently. – **2** *i* to happen frequently.

menudencia *f (bagatela)* trifle. **2** *(exactitud)* exactness. **3** *pl* pork products.

menudillos *mpl* giblets.

menudo,-a *adj (pequeño)* small, tiny. **2** *irón* fine: *¡* ~ *lío!*, what a fine mess! – **3** *mpl (moneda)* change *sing*. **4** *(de res)* offal *sing*; *(de ave)* giblets. •*a* ~, often, frequently.

meñique *adj* little. ■ *(dedo)* ~, little finger.

meollo *m (encéfalo)* brains *pl*. **2** *(médula)* marrow. **3** *fig (quid)* substance.

mercado *m* market. ■ *Mercado Común*, Common Market; ~ *de valores*, stockmarket; ~ *negro*, black market.

mercadotecnia *f* marketing.

mercancía *f* goods *pl*.

mercante *adj* merchant.

mercantil *adj* mercantile, commercial.

merced f favour. ●a ~ de, at the mercy of. ■ fml **Vuestra Merced,** you, sir/madam.

mercenario,-a adj-m,f mercenary.

mercería f (artículos) haberdashery, US notions pl. **2** (tienda) haberdasher's shop, US notions store.

mercurio m quicksilver, mercury.

merecer(se) [41] t-i to deserve.

merecido,-a adj deserved. − **2** m (just) deserts pl.

merendar [27] i to have an afternoon snack, have tea.

merendero m tearoom, snack bar. **2** (en el campo) picnic spot.

merengue m meringue. **2** (alfeñique) weak person.

meridiano,-a adj (de mediodía) meridian. **2** fig (claro) obvious. − **3** m meridian.

merienda f afternoon snack, tea.

mérito m merit, worth.

meritorio,-a adj meritorious, worthy. − **2** m,f unpaid trainee.

merluza f hake. ●fam coger/agarrar una ~, to get pissed.

merma f decrease, reduction.

mermar(se) t-i-p to decrease, diminish.

mermelada f jam; (de agrios) marmalade.

mero,-a adj mere, pure. − **2** m (pez) grouper.

merodear i MIL to maraud. **2** (vagar) to harass.

mes m month.

mesa f table. ●levantar/quitar/recoger la ~, to clear the table; poner la ~, to set the table. ■ ~ de trabajo, desk; ~ electoral, electoral college; ~ redonda, round table.

meseta f GEOG tableland, plateau. **2** (descansillo) staircase landing.

mesón m (venta) inn, tavern.

mestizo,-a adj half-breed.

mesurar(se) t to moderate. − **2** p to restrain o.s.

meta f (portería) goal; (de carreras) finish(ing) line. **2** fig aim, purpose.

metabolismo m metabolism.

metafísica f metaphysics.

metáfora f metaphor.

metal m metal. **2** MÚS brass.

metálico,-a adj metallic. − **2** m cash. ●pagar en ~, to pay (in) cash.

metalurgia f metallurgy.

metamorfosis f inv metamorphosis.

meteorito m meteorite.

meteorología f meteorology.

meter(se) t to put (in). **2** (hacer) to make: ~ miedo a, to frighten. **3** fam (dar) to give: me metieron una multa, I got a ticket. **4** COST to take in. − **5** p (entrar) to get/come in. **6** (entrometerse) to meddle with. **7** (dedicarse) to go into: ~se en política, to go into politics.

meticuloso,-a adj meticulous.

metódico,-a adj methodical.

metodista adj-mf Methodist.

método m method.

metraje m length, footage.

metralla f shrapnel.

metralleta f submachine gun.

métrico,-a adj metric(al). − **2** f metrics.

metro m metre. **2** (transporte) underground, tube, US subway.

metrópoli f metropolis.

metropolitano,-a adj metropolitan. − **2** m fml underground, tube, US subway.

mezcla f (acción) mixing, blending. **2** (producto) mixture, blend. **3** (argamasa) mortar.

mezclar(se) t to mix, blend. **2** (desordenar) to mix up. − **3** p (cosas) to get mixed up; (personas) to get involved.

mezcolanza f mixture, hotchpoch.

mezquindad f meanness, stinginess. **2** (acción) mean thing.

mezquino,-a adj (avaro) stingy, niggardly. **2** (bajo) low, base. **3** (infeliz) miserable.

mezquita f mosque.

mi adj pos my. − **2** m MÚS E.

mí pron pers me. **2** (~ mismo) myself.

miaja f crumb. **2** fam fig bit.

miau m miaow, mew.

michelín m fam spare tyre.

mico m (long-tailed) monkey.

microbio m microbe.

micrófono m microphone.

microscopio m microscope.

miedo m fear. ●dar ~, to be scary; dar ~ a algn., to frighten sb.; tener ~, to be afraid; fam de ~, great, terrific.

miedoso,-a adj fearful, afraid.

miel f honey.

miembro m (extremidad) limb. **2** (pene) penis. **3** (socio) member.

mientras adv while. **2** (por el contrario) whereas. ●~ que, while, ~ tanto, meanwhile.

miércoles m inv Wednesday.

mierda f shit. **2** (porquería) dirt, filth.

mies f corn, grain. **2** (cosecha) harvest time. **3** pl cornfields.

miga f crumb. **2** (trocito) bit. **3** fig (substamcia) substance. ●*hacer buenas/malas migas con*, to get along well/badly with.

migaja f crumb. **2** fam fig bit.

migración f migration.

migraña f migraine.

mijo m millet.

mil adj thousand. **2** (milésimo) thousandth. − **3** m a/one thousand.

milagro m miracle, wonder.

milagroso,-a adj miraculous. **2** (asombroso) marvellous.

milenario,-a adj millenial. − **2** m millenium.

milenio m millenium.

milésimo,-a adj-m,f thousandth.

mili f fam military service.

milicia f (disciplina) art of warfare. **2** (profesión) militia.

miligramo m milligram.

milímetro m millimetre.

militante adj-mf militant.

militar adj military. − **2** m military man, soldier. − **3** i MIL to serve. **4** POL to be a militant.

milla f mile.

millar m thousand.

millón m million.

millonario,-a adj-m,f millionaire.

mimar t to spoil.

mimbre m wicker.

mímica f (arte) mimicry. **2** (representación) pantomime.

mimo m TEAT mime. **2** (cariño) pampering.

mina f mine. **2** (paso subterráneo) underground passage. **3** (de lápiz) lead; (de bolígrafo) refill.

minar t to mine.

mineral adj-m mineral.

minería f mining.

minero,-a adj mining. − **2** m,f miner.

miniatura f miniature.

minifalda f miniskirt.

mínimo,-a adj minimal, lowest. − **2** m minimum. − **3** f minimum temperature. ●*como* ~, at least. ■ ~ *común múltiplo*, lowest common multiple.

ministerio m ministry, US department.

ministro,-a m,f minister. ■ *primer,-ra* ~, prime minister.

minoría f minority.

minuciosidad f (detallismo) minuteness.

minucioso,-a adj (detallado) minute, detailed. **2** (persona) meticulous. − **3** *minuciosamente* adv in detail.

minúsculo,-a adj small.

minusválido,-a adj-m,f handicapped/disabled (person).

minuta f (borrador) draft. **2** (factura) lawyer's bill. **3** (lista) roll, list. **4** CULIN menu.

minutero m minute hand.

minuto m minute. ●*al* ~, at once.

mío,-a adj pos my, of mine: *un pariente* ~, a relative of mine. − **2** pron pos mine: *este libro es* ~, that book is mine. ●*fam los míos*, my people/folks.

miope adj-mf shortsighted (person).

miopía f myopia, shortsightedness.

mira f (visual) sight. − **2** interj look. ●*con miras a*, with a view to.

mirado,-a adj (cauto) cautious. **2** (cuidadoso) careful. **3** (considerado) highly regarded. − **4** f look. ●*bien* ~, after all; *echar una mirada a*, to have a look at.

mirador m (balcón) bay window. **2** (con vistas) viewpoint.

miramiento m consideration.

mirar(se) i to look at. **2** (considerar) to consider, have in mind. **3** (dar a) to look, face. − **4** p (reflexionar) to think twice. **5** (a uno mismo) to look o.s. ●~ *con buenos/malos ojos*, to like/dislike; ~ *por*, to look after; fam *¡mira quién habla!*, look who's talking!

mirilla f peephole.

mirlo m blackbird.

mirón,-ona adj pey peeping. **2** (espectador) onlooking. − **3** m,f pey voyeur. **4** (espectador) onlooker.

mirra f myrrh.

misa f mass.

misal m missal.

miscelánea f miscellany.

miserable adj miserable. **2** (canalla) wretched.

miseria f misery. **2** (pobreza) extreme poverty.

misericordia f mercy, pity, compassion.

misil, mísil m missile.

misión f mission.

misionero,-a adj mission. − **2** m,f missionary.

mismo,-a adj same. **2** (enfático) (propio) own; (uno ~) oneself: *sus mismos amigos no lo entienden*, not even his/her own friends understand; *yo* ~, I myself. − **3** pron same: *es el* ~ *que vimos ayer*, it's the same one that we saw yesterday.

misterio m mystery.

misterioso,-a adj mysterious.

misticismo *m* mysticism.

místico,-a *adj-m,f* mystic.

mitad *f* half. **2** *(en medio)* middle. •*a la/ a ~ de,* halfway through.

mitigar [7] *t* to mitigate, relieve.

mitin *m* meeting, rally. ▲ *pl* **mítines**.

mito *m* myth.

mitología *f* mythology.

mitológico,-a *adj* mythological.

mixto,-a *adj* mixed.

mobiliario *m* furniture.

mocedad *f fml* youth.

mochila *f* rucksack, backpack.

mochuelo *m* ZOOL little owl. **2** *fam fig (fastidio)* bore.

moción *f* motion. ■ *~ de censura,* vote of censure.

moco *m* mucus. **2** *(de vela)* drippings *pl.* •*fam no es ~ de pavo,* it's not to be taken lightly.

mocoso,-a *adj* with a running nose. – **2** *m,f fam* brat.

moda *f* fashion. •*estar de ~,* to be in fashion; *pasado de ~,* old-fashioned.

modales *mpl* manners.

modalidad *f* form, category.

modelar *t* to model, shape.

modelo *adj-m* model. – **2** *mf* (fashion) model.

moderación *f* moderation.

moderador,-ra *adj* moderating. – **2** *m,f* chairperson; *m* chairman, *f* chairwoman.

moderar(se) *t* to moderate. – **2** *p* to restrain/control o.s.

modernizar(se) [4] *t-p* to modernize.

moderno,-a *adj* modern.

modestia *f* modesty.

modesto,-a *adj-m,f* modest (person).

módico,-a *adj* moderate. **2** *(precio)* reasonable.

modificación *f* modification.

modificar(se) [1] *t-p* to modify.

modismo *m* idiom.

modista *mf* dressmaker.

modo *m* manner, way. **2** GRAM mood. **3** *pl* manners. •*de cualquier ~,* anyway; *de ningún ~,* by no means; *de todos modos,* anyhow, at any rate.

modoso,-a *adj* quiet, well-behaved.

modulación *f* modulation.

modular *t-i* to modulate.

mofa *f* mockery.

mofar(se) *i-p* to scoff *(de,* at).

mofeta *f* skunk.

moflete *m* chubby cheek.

mogollón *m fam* load, heap.

moho *m* mould. **2** *(de metales)* rust.

moisés *m* wicker cradle.

mojado,-a *adj* wet.

mojar(se) *t* to wet. – **2** *p* to get wet. **3** *fam (comprometerse)* to commit o.s.

mojón *m* landmark, milestone.

molar *i arg (gustar)* **me mola cantidad,** it's magic, I'm really into it. **2** *(presumir)* to show off.

molde *m* mould.

moldeado,-a *adj* moulded. – **2** *(de pelo)* soft perm.

moldear *t* to mould.

mole *f* mass, bulk.

molécula *f* molecule.

moler [32] *t* to grind, mill. **2** *(cansar)* to wear out. •*~ a palos,* to beat up.

molestar(se) *t* to disturb, bother. – **2** *p* to bother. **3** *(ofenderse)* to take offence.

molestia *f* nuisance, bother. **2** MED slight pain. •*tomarse la ~ (de hacer algo),* to take the trouble (to do sth.).

molesto,-a *adj* annoying, troublesome. **2** *(enfadado)* annoyed. **3** *(incómodo)* uncomfortable.

molido,-a *adj* ground, milled. **2** *fam (cansado)* worn-out.

molinero,-a *m,f* miller.

molinillo *m* grinder, mill. ■ *~ de café,* coffee grinder.

molino *m* mill. ■ *~ de viento,* windmill.

mollera *f fam* brains *pl,* sense. •*duro de ~, (tonto)* thick; *(testarudo)* pigheaded.

molusco *m* mollusc.

momentáneo,-a *adj* momentary.

momento *m* moment, instant. •*al ~,* at once; *de/por el ~,* for the present.

momia *f* mummy.

mona *f* ZOOL monkey. **2** *fam (imitador)* copycat. •*fam coger una ~,* to get pissed.

monada *f (gesto)* silly way of acting. **2** *(cosa bonita)* charming thing. **3** *(zalamería)* caress.

monaguillo *m* altar boy.

monarca *m* monarch.

monarquía *f* monarchy.

monárquico,-a *adj* monarchic(al). – **2** *m,f* monarchist.

monasterio *m* monastery.

monda *f (piel)* peel, skin. •*fam ser la ~,* to be amazing.

mondadientes *m inv* toothpick.

mondar *t (limpiar)* to clean. **2** *(pelar)* to peel.

moneda *f gen* currency, money. **2** *(pieza)* coin. ■ ~ *falsa,* counterfeit money; ~ *suelta,* small change.

monedero *m* purse.

monetario,-a *adj* monetary. — **2** *m* collection of coins and medals.

mongolismo *m* mongolism, Down's syndrome.

monigote *m* rag/paper doll.

monitor,-ra *m* monitor. — **2** *m,f (profesor)* instructor.

monja *f* nun.

monje *m* monk.

mono,-a *adj (bonito)* pretty, cute. — **2** *m* ZOOL monkey. **3** *fig* ugly person. **4** *(prenda)* overalls *pl.* **5** *arg (síndrome abstinencia)* cold turkey.

monóculo *m* monocle.

monogamia *f* monogamy.

monografía *f* monograph.

monolingüe *adj* monolingual.

monólogo *m* monologue.

monopatín *m* skateboard.

monopolio *m* monopoly.

monopolizar [4] *t* to monopolize.

monosílabo,-a *adj* monosyllabic. — **2** *m* monosyllable.

monotonía *f* monotony.

monótono,-a *adj* monotonous.

monserga *fam f (lenguaje)* boring talk. **2** *(pesadez)* gibberish, gabble.

monstruo *m* monster. **2** *fam (genio)* genius.

monstruoso,-a *adj* monstrous. **2** *(grande)* massive, huge.

monta *f* value. ●*de poca* ~, of little value.

montacargas *m inv* goods lift, US freight elevator.

montaje *m* assembling. **2** CINEM mounting. **3** TEAT staging. ■ ~ *fotográfico,* montage.

montaña *f* mountain. ■ ~ *rusa,* big dipper.

montañismo *m* mountaineering, mountain climbing.

montañoso,-a *adj* mountainous.

montar(se) *i (subir)* to mount, get on. **2** *(caballo, bicicleta)* to ride *(en, -).* — **3** *t (cabalgar)* to ride. **4** *(poner encima)* to put on, mount. **5** *(sobreponer)* to overlap. **6** *(nata, claras)* to whip. **7** *(máquinas)* to assemble. **8** *(joyas)* to set. **9** *(negocio)* to set up. **10** CINEM to edit, mount. **11** TEAT to stage. **12** COM to amount to: *el total monta diez mil pesetas,* the total amounts to ten thousand pesetas. — **13**

p (subirse) to get on. **14** *fam (armarse)* to break out: *se montó un buen jaleo,* there was a right to-do. ●~ *en cólera,* to fly into a rage; *fam* **montárselo,** to have things nicely worked out.

monte *m* mountain, mount. **2** *(bosque)* woodland. ■ ~ *de piedad,* assistance fund.

montepío *m* assistance fund.

montículo *m* mound, hillock.

montón *m* heap, pile. **2** *fam (gran cantidad)* piles *pl,* great quantity. ●*ser del* ~, to be nothing special.

montura *f (cabalgadura)* mount. **2** *(silla)* saddle. **3** *(armadura)* mounting.

monumento *m* monument.

moño *m* bun. ●*fam* **estar hasta el** ~, to be fed up to the back teeth.

moquear *i* to have a runny nose.

moqueta *f* fitted carpet.

moquillo *m (de perro)* distemper; *(de gallina)* pip.

mora *f* BOT *(de moral)* mulberry. **2** *(zarzamora)* blackberry.

morada *f fml* abode, dwelling.

morado,-a *adj-m* dark purple. ●*fam* **pasarlas moradas,** to have a tough time.

moral *adj* moral. — **2** *f (reglas)* morals *pl.* **3** *(ánimo)* morale, spirits *pl.* — **4** *m* BOT mulberry tree.

moraleja *f* moral.

moralidad *f* morality.

moralizar [4] *t-i* to moralize.

morbidez *f* softness, tenderness.

mórbido,-a *adj* soft, delicate. **2** *(malsano)* morbid.

morbo *m*, **morbosidad** *f* sickness. **2** *fam (interés malsano)* morbidity.

morboso,-a *adj (enfermo)* sick, ill. **2** *(malsano)* morbid, diseased.

morcilla *f* black pudding. ●*que le den* ~*,* he/she can drop dead for all I care.

mordacidad *f* mordacity, sharpness.

mordaz *adj* mordant, sarcastic.

mordaza *f* gag.

mordedura *f* bite.

morder [32] *t* to bite.

mordisco *m* bite.

moreno,-a *adj (pelo)* dark-haired. **2** *(piel)* dark-skinned. **3** *(bronceado)* (sun)tanned. — **4** *m* suntan.

morera *f* white mulberry.

morfema *m* morpheme.

morfina *f* morphine.

morfología *f* morphology.

moribundo,-a *adj-m,f* moribund.

morir(se) [32] *i-p* to die. ●~*se de ham-bre,* to starve; *fig* to be starving. ▲ *pp muerto,-a.*

mormón,-ona *m,f* Mormon.

moro,-a *adj* Moorish. **2** *(musulmán)* Moslim. **– 3** *m* Moor. **4** *(musulmán)* Moslim.

moroso,-a *adj* FIN in arrears. **2** *(lento)* slow.

morral *m* *(para bestias)* nosebag. **2** *(de cazador)* gamebag. **3** MIL haversack.

morrear(se) *t-i-p* *fam* to snog, smooch.

morriña *f* homesickness.

morro *m* *(cosa redonda)* knob, round end. **2** *fam* *(de persona)* mouth, (thick) lips. **3** *(de animal)* snout, nose. ●*fam* ¡*vaya* ~!, what a cheek!

morsa *f* walrus.

Morse *m* Morse code.

mortaja *f* shroud.

mortal *adj* mortal. **2** *(mortífero)* fatal, lethal. **– 3** *mf* mortal.

mortalidad *f* mortality. ■ *índice de* ~, death rate.

mortandad *f* massacre, slaughter.

mortero *m* mortar.

mortífero,-a *adj* deadly, fatal, lethal.

mortificación *f* mortification.

mortificar(se) [1] *t-p* to mortify (o.s.).

mortuorio,-a *adj* mortuary.

mosaico *m* mosaic.

mosca *f* fly. ●*fam aflojar/soltar la* ~, to fork out; *fam estar* ~, to be cross. ■ *fig* ~ *muerta,* hypocrite.

moscardón *m* blowfly.

moscatel *adj-m* muscat(el).

mosquearse *p* *fam* *(resentirse)* to get cross. **2** *(sospechar)* to smell a rat.

mosquetón *m* short carbine.

mosquitero *m* mosquito net. **2** *(pájaro)* chiffchaff, warbler.

mosquito *m* mosquito.

mostacho *m* moustache.

mostaza *f* mustard.

mosto *m* *(del vino)* must. **2** *(bebida)* grape juice.

mostrador *m* counter.

mostrar *t* to show. **2** *(exponer)* to exhibit, display. **3** *(señalar)* to point out.

mota *f* *(granillo)* mote, speck. **2** *(defecto)* slight defect/fault.

mote *m* nickname.

motín *m* riot, uprising.

motivar *t* *(causar)* to cause, give rise to. **2** *(estimular)* to motivate.

motivo *m* *(causa)* motive, reason. **2** *(de dibujo, música)* (leit)motif. ●*con* ~ *de,*

(debido a) owing to; *(en ocasión de)* on the occassion of.

moto *f fam* motorbike.

motocicleta *f* motorbike.

motociclismo *m* motorcycling.

motor,-ra *adj* motor, motive. **– 2** *m* BIOL motor. **3** TÉC engine. **– 4** *f* small motorboat. ■ ~ *de explosión,* internal combustion engine; ~ *de reacción,* jet engine.

motorista *mf* motorcyclist.

motorizar(se) [4] *t* to motorize. **– 2** *p* to get o.s a car/motorbike.

motricidad *f* motivity.

motriz *adj* motive. ■ *fuerza* ~, motive power. ▲ *Only with feminine nouns.*

mover(se) [32] *t* to move. **2** *(hacer obrar)* to drive, work. **3** *(suscitar)* to incite. **– 4** *p* to move. **5** *fam* *(solucionar gestiones etc.)* to take every step.

movida *f arg* action.

móvil *adj* movable, mobile. **– 2** *m* moving body. **3** *(motivo)* motive, inducement.

movilidad *f* mobility.

movilización *f* mobilization.

movilizar [4] *t* to mobilize.

movimiento *m gen* movement; TÉC motion. **2** FIN operations *pl.* ●*en* ~, in motion. ■ ~ *de caja,* turnover; ~ *sísmico,* earth tremor.

moviola *f* editing projector

mozárabe *adj* Mozarabic. **– 2** *mf* Mozarab.

mozo,-a *adj* young. **2** *(soltero)* unmarried. **– 3** *m* young man. **4** *(camarero)* waiter. **5** *(de hotel)* buttons. **6** *(de estación)* porter. **– 7** *f* girl, lass.

muchacho,-a *m,f* boy, lad, *f* girl, lass.

muchedumbre *f* multitude, crowd.

mucho,-a *adj* *(abundante)* a lot of, much: *hace* ~ *calor,* it's very hot. **2** *pl* a lot of, many: ¿*tienes muchos libros?,* have you got many books? **– 3** *pron* a lot. **4** *pl* many: *muchos de ellos,* many of them. **– 5** *adv* a lot, much. **6** *(frecuentemente)* often. ●*por* ~ *que,* however much.

muda *f* *(de ropa)* change of clothes. **2** *(animal)* moult(ing).

mudanza *f* *(de residencia)* removal. **2** *(cambio)* change.

mudar(se) *t* to change. **2** *(trasladar)* to change, move. **3** *(plumas)* to moult. **4** *(voz)* to break. **5** *(piel)* to shed. **– 6** *p* to change: ~*se de ropa,* to change one's clothes. **7** *(de residencia)* to move.

mudo,-a *adj-m,f* dumb (person).

mueble *adj m* piece of furniture. **2** *pl* furniture.

mueca *f* grimace.

muela *f (para moler)* millstone. **2** *(para afilar)* grindstone. **3** *(diente)* tooth. ■ *dolor de muelas,* toothache; ~ *del juicio,* wisdom tooth.

muelle *adj* soft. **– 2** *m* MAR dock. **3** *(elástico)* spring.

muérdago *m* mistletoe.

muerte *f* death. ●*dar* ~, to kill; *de mala* ~, miserable, wretched.

muerto,-a *pp* → **morir**. **– 2** *adj* dead. **3** *fam (cansado)* tired. **4** *(marchito)* faded, withered. **– 5** *m,f* dead person; *(cadáver)* corpse. **6** *(víctima)* victim. ●*hacer el* ~, to float on one's back. ■ AUTO *punto* ~, neutral.

muesca *f (concavidad)* mortise. **2** *(corte)* nick, notch.

muestra *f (ejemplar)* sample. **2** *(modelo)* model, pattern. **3** *(señal)* proof, sign. **4** *(rótulo)* sign. ●*dar muestras de,* to show signs of.

muestrario *m* collection of samples.

mugido *m (vaca)* moo. **2** *(toro)* bellow.

mugir [6] *i* to moo. **2** *(toro)* to bellow.

mugre *f* grease, filth.

mujer *f* woman. **2** *(esposa)* wife.

mujeriego,-a *adj* woman-chasing.

mulato,-a *adj-m,f* mulatto.

muleta *f* crutch. **2** *fig* support.

muletilla *f (bastón)* cross-handled cane. **2** *(frase repetida)* pet phrase, cliché.

mullir [41] *t (esponjar)* to soften. **2** *(la tierra)* to break up.

mulo,-a *m,f m* mule, *f* she-mule.

multa *f* fine; AUTO ticket.

multar *t* to fine.

multicolor *adj* multicoloured.

multimillonario,-a *adj-m,f* multimillionaire.

múltiple *adj* multiple. **2** *pl* many.

multiplicación *f* multiplication.

multiplicar(se) [1] *t-p* to multiply.

múltiplo,-a *adj-m,f* multiple.

multitud *f* multitude, crowd.

multitudinario,-a *adj* multitudinous.

mundanal, mundano,-a *adj* of the world, mundane.

mundial *adj* worldwide, world. **– 2** *m* world championship.

mundo *m* world. **2** *(baúl)* trunk. ●*correr/ver* ~, to knock around; *todo el* ~, everybody. ■ *el otro* ~, the hereafter.

munición *f* ammunition.

municipal *adj* municipal. **– 2** *mf m* policeman, *f* policewoman.

municipio *m* municipality. **2** *(ayuntamiento)* town council.

muñeca *f* ANAT wrist. **2** *(juguete)* doll.

muñeco *m (marioneta)* puppet. **2** *(monigote)* dummy.

muñequera *f* wristband.

muñón *m* ANAT stump. **2** TÉC gudgeon.

mural *adj-m* mural.

muralla *f* wall.

murciélago *m* bat.

murmullo *m* murmur(ing), whisper(ing). **2** *(de hojas etc.)* rustle.

murmuración *f* gossip, backbiting.

murmurar *i (susurrar)* to murmur, whisper. **2** *(hojas etc.)* to rustle. **– 3** *t-i (comentar)* to gossip.

muro *m* wall.

musa *f* Muse.

musaraña *f* ZOOL shrew. **2** *(animalito)* small animal. ●*estar pensando en las musarañas,* to be daydreaming.

muscular *adj* muscular.

músculo *m* muscle.

museo *m* museum.

musgo *m* moss.

música *f* music. ■ ~ *de fondo,* background music; *fig* ~ *celestial,* double Dutch.

musical *adj-m* musical.

músico,-a *adj* musical. **– 2** *m,f* musician.

musitar *i* to whisper.

muslo *m* thigh.

mustio,-a *adj (plantas)* withered, faded. **2** *(persona)* sad, melancholy.

musulmán,-ana *adj-m,f* Muslim, Moslem.

mutación *f* change. **2** *(biología)* mutation.

mutilado,-a *adj-m,f* mutilated/crippled (person).

mutilar *t* to mutilate.

mutis *m* TEAT exit. ●*hacer* ~, *(salir)* to make o.s. scarce; *(callar)* to say nothing.

mutualidad *f (reciprocidad)* mutuality. **2** *(asociación)* mutual benefit society.

mutuo,-a *adj* mutual, reciprocal.

muy *adv.* very. ●*(en carta)* ~ *señor mío,* dear sir; *fam ser* ~ *hombre/mujer,* to be a real man/woman.

N

nacer [42] *i* to be born. **2** *(río)* to rise. **3** *(tener su origen)* to originate, start.

nacido,-a *adj-m,f* born.

naciente *adj (nuevo)* new. **2** *(creciente)* growing. ■ *sol* ~, rising sun.

nacimiento *m* birth. **2** *(de río)* source. **3** *fig* origin, beginning.

nación *f* nation.

nacional *adj* national. **2** *(productos, mercados)* domestic.

nacionalizar(se) [4] *t* to naturalize. **2** ECON to nationalize. — **3** *p* to become naturalized, take up citizenship.

nada *pron* nothing: *no quiero* ~, I want nothing, I don't want anything. — **2** *adv* (not) at all: *no me gusta* ~, I don't like it at all. — **3** *f* nothingness. ●*como si* ~, just like that; *gracias, –de* ~, thanks, –don't mention it.

nadador,-ra *m,f* swimmer.

nadar *i* to swim.

nadie *pron* nobody, not ... anybody.

nalga *f* buttock.

naranja *f* BOT orange. — **2** *adj-m (color)* orange.

naranjada *f* orangeade.

naranjo *m* orange tree.

narcotraficante *mf* drug trafficker.

nariz *f* ANAT nose. **2** *fig (sentido)* sense of smell. — **3** *pl interj fam* not on your life! ●*fam estar hasta las narices de,* to be fed up to the back teeth with.

narración *f* narration, account.

narrar *t* to narrate.

nata *f* cream. **2** *(de leche hervida)* skin.

natación *f* swimming.

natal *adj* natal. ■ *país* ~, native country; *pueblo/ciudad* ~, home town.

natalidad *f* birth-rate.

nativo,-a *adj-m,f* native.

natural *adj* natural. **2** *(fruta, flor)* fresh. **3** *(sin elaboración)* plain. — **4** *m (tempera-mento)* nature, disposition. ●*al* ~, *(en la realidad)* in real life; CULIN in its own juice.

naturaleza *f* nature. **2** *(forma de ser)* nature, character. **3** *(complexión)* physical constitution. ●*en plena* ~, in the wild. ■ ART ~ *muerta,* still life.

naturalidad *f (sencillez)* naturalness. **2** *(espontaneidad)* ease, spontaneity.

naufragar [7] *i (barco)* to be wrecked. **2** *(persona)* to be shipwrecked. **3** *fig* to fail.

naufragio *m* shipwreck. **2** *fig* failure.

náufrago,-a *adj* (ship)wrecked. — **2** *m,f* shipwrecked person, castaway.

náusea *f* nausea, sickness. ●*me da* ~, it makes me sick. ▲ *Often pl.*

nauseabundo,-a *adj* nauseating, sickening.

náutico,-a *adj* nautical. — **2** *f* navigation, seamanship.

navaja *f (cuchillo)* penknife, pocketknife. **2** *(molusco)* razor-shell. ■ ~ *de afeitar,* razor.

navajazo *m* stab.

nave *f (náutica)* ship, vessel. **2** *(espacial)* spaceship, spacecraft. **3** ARQ nave. ■ ~ *lateral,* aisle; ~ *industrial,* industrial premises *pl.*

navegación *f* navigation.

navegante *adj* sailing. — **2** *mf* navigator.

navegar [7] *i* to navigate, sail.

Navidad *f* Christmas.

naviero,-a *adj* shipping. — **2** *m,f (propietario)* shipowner.

navío *m* vessel, ship.

neblina *f* mist.

nebuloso,-a *adj* cloudy, hazy. **2** *fig* nebulous, vague. — **3** *f* ASTRON nebula.

necedad *f* stupidity, foolishness.

necesario,-a *adj* necessary. ●*es* ~ *hacerlo,* it has to be done; *hacerse* ~, *(algo)* to be required; *(persona)* to become vital/essential; *si fuera/es* ~, if need be.

neceser *m (de aseo)* toilet bag. **2** *(de maquillaje)* make-up bag/kit. **3** *(de costura)* sewing kit.

necesidad *f* necessity, need. **2** *(hambre)* hunger. **3** *(pobreza)* poverty, want. ●*de* ~, essential; *euf* **hacer sus necesidades,** to relieve o.s.

necesitado,-a *adj* needy, poor.

necesitar *t* to need. ●*"se necesita chico,-a",* "boy/girl wanted".

necio,-a *adj* silly, stupid. – **2** *m,f* fool, idiot.

necrología *f* obituary.

nefasto,-a *adj (desgraciado)* unlucky, ill-fated. **2** *(perjudicial)* harmful, fatal.

negación *f* negation. **2** *(negativa)* refusal.

negado,-a *adj* dull. – **2** *m,f* nohoper. ●*ser* ~ *para algo,* to be hopeless/useless at sth.

negar(se) [48] *t* to deny. **2** *(no conceder)* to refuse. – **3** *p* to refuse *(a,* to). ●~ *con la cabeza,* to shake one's head.

negativo,-a *adj-m* negative. – **2** *f* refusal.

negligencia *f* negligence, carelessness.

negligente *adj* negligent, neglectful, careless.

negociación *f* negotiation. ■ ~ *colectiva,* collective bargaining.

negociante *mf* dealer.

negociar [12] *i (comerciar)* to do business, deal. – **2** *t* FIN POL to negotiate.

negocio *m gen* business. **2** *(transacción)* deal, transaction. **3** *(asunto)* affair. ●*buen* ~, COM profitable deal; *irón* bargain; *hacer* ~, to make a profit.

negro,-a *adj gen* black. **2** *(oscuro)* dark. **3** *(bronceado)* suntanned. – **4** *m,f m* black (man), *f* black (woman). – **5** *m (color)* black. **6** *(escritor)* ghostwriter. – **7** *f* MÚS crotchet; US quarter note. ●*fig* **verlo todo** ~, to be very pessimistic.

negrura *f* blackness.

nene,-a *m,f* baby.

nervio *m* nerve. **2** *(de la carne)* tendon, sinew.

nervioso,-a *adj* nervous. ●*poner* ~ *a algn.,* to get on sb.'s nerves; *ponerse* ~, to get all excited.

neto,-a *adj (peso, cantidad)* net. **2** *(claro)* neat, clear.

neumático,-a *adj* pneumatic, tyre. – **2** *m* tyre.

neura *f fam* depression. – **2** *adj-mf fam* neurotic.

neurólogo,-a *m,f* neurologist.

neurótico,-a *adj-m,f* neurotic.

neutralidad *f* neutrality.

neutro,-a *adj* neutral. **2** GRAM neuter.

nevado,-a *adj gen* covered with snow; *(montaña)* snow-capped. – **2** *f* snowfall.

nevar [27] *i* to snow. ▲ *Only used in the 3rd person. It does not take a subject.*

nevera *f* fridge, refrigerator.

nexo *m* connexion, link.

ni *conj* neither, nor: *no tengo tiempo* ~ *dinero,* I have got neither time nor money. **2** *(ni siquiera)* not even: ~ *por dinero,* not even for money. ●*¡*~ *hablar!,* no way!

nido *m* nest.

niebla *f* fog. ●*fig* **envuelto,-a en** ~, confused, cloudy.

nieto,-a *m,f* grandchild; *m* grandson, *f* granddaughter.

nieve *f* snow.

nimiedad *f (cualidad)* smallness, triviality. **2** *(cosa nimia)* trifle.

ningún *adj* → **ninguno,-a.** ●*de* ~ *modo,* in no way. ▲ *Used before a sing masculine noun.*

ninguno,-a *adj* no, not any. – **2** *pron (persona)* nobody, no one: ~ *lo vio,* no one saw it. **3** *(objeto)* not any, none: ~ *me gusta,* I don't like any of them. ●*en ninguna parte,* nowhere; *ninguna cosa,* nothing; ~ *de nosotros/ellos,* none of us/them. ▲ → **ningún.**

niñera *f* nursemaid, nanny.

niñería *f (chiquillada)* childishness, childish behaviour. **2** *(cosa nimia)* trifle.

niñez *f* childhood, infancy.

niño,-a *m,f gen* child. **2** *(muchacho) m* (small) boy, *f* (little) girl. **3** *(bebé)* baby. ●*de* ~, as a child; *desde* ~, from childhood.

niqui *m* T-shirt.

níspero *m (fruto)* medlar. **2** *(árbol)* medlar tree.

nitidez *f (transparencia)* limpidness, transparency. **2** *(claridad)* accuracy, precision. **3** *(de imagen)* sharpness.

nítido,-a *adj (transparente)* limpid, transparent. **2** *(claro)* accurate, precise. **3** *(imagen)* sharp.

nivel *m (altura)* level, height. **2** *(categoría)* standard, degree. **3** *(instrumento)* level. ●*a* ~ *del mar,* at sea level. ■ ~ *de vida,* standard of living.

nivelar *t* to level out/off.

no *adv* no, not: ~, ~ *quiero,* no, I don't want. **2** *(prefijo)* non: *la* ~ *violencia,* nonviolence. – **3** *m* no: *un* ~ *rotundo,* a definite no. ●*¡a que* ~!, I bet you don't; *es rubia, ¿~?,* she's blonde, isn't she?; *~ obstante,* notwithstanding.

noble *adj* noble. – **2** *mf m* nobleman, *f* noblewoman.

nobleza *f (cualidad)* nobility, honesty, uprightness. **2** *(los nobles)* nobility.

noche *f* night. ●*buenas noches, (saludo)* good evening; *(despedida)* good night; *esta ~,* tonight; *hacerse de ~,* to grow dark; *por la ~,* at night, in the evening; *son las nueve de la ~,* it's nine p.m.; *fig de la ~ a la mañana,* overnight.

nochebuena *f* Christmas Eve.

nochevieja *f* New Year's Eve.

noción *f* notion, idea. **2** *pl* smattering *sing,* basic knowledge *sing.*

nocivo,-a *adj* noxious, harmful.

noctámbulo,-a *m,f* sleepwalker. **2** *fam (trasnochador)* nightbird.

nocturno,-a *adj* night, evening. **2** ZOOL nocturnal.

nogal *m* walnut tree.

nombramiento *m* appointment.

nombrar *t* to name, appoint.

nombre *m* name. **2** LING noun. **3** *(reputación)* reputation. ●*a ~ de,* addressed to; *en ~ de,* on behalf of; *fig llamar a las cosas por su ~,* to call a spade a spade; *fig no tiene ~,* it's unspeakable. ■ *~ artístico,* stage name; *~ de pila,* Christian name; *~ propio,* proper noun.

nómina *f (plantilla)* payroll. **2** *(sueldo)* salary, pay cheque. ●*estar en ~,* to be on the staff.

nominación *f* nomination.

nominar *t* to nominate.

nominativo,-a *adj* nominal.

non *adj (número)* odd. ●*pares y nones,* odds and evens.

nonagenario,-a *adj-m,f* nonagenarian.

nonagésimo,-a *adj-m,f* ninetieth.

nor(d)este *m* northeast.

nórdico,-a *adj (del norte)* northern. **2** *(escandinavo)* Nordic.

noria *f (para agua)* water-wheel. **2** *(de feria)* big wheel.

norma *f* norm, rule.

normal *adj* normal, usual, average.

normalidad *f* normality.

normalizar(se) [4] *t* to normalize, restore to normal. – **2** *p* to return to normal.

normativo,-a *adj* normative. – **2** *f* rules *pl.*

noroeste *m* northwest.

norte *m* north. **2** *fig (guia)* aim, goal. ●*fig sin ~,* aimless(ly).

nos *pron pers pl (complemento)* us: *~ ha visto,* he/she has seen us. **2** *(reflexivo)* ourselves: *~ lavamos,* we wash ourselves. **3** *(recíproco)* each other: *~ queremos mucho,* we love each other very much.

nosotros,-as *pron pers m,f pl (sujeto)* we: *~ lo vimos,* we saw it. **2** *(complemento)* us: *con ~,* with us.

nostalgia *f* nostalgia. **2** *(morriña)* homesickness.

nostálgico,-a *adj* nostalgic.

nota *f (anotación)* note. **2** *(calificación)* mark, grade. **3** *(cuenta)* bill. **4** *fig (detalle)* element, quality. **5** MÚS note. ●*tener/ sacar buenas notas,* to get good marks; *tomar ~ de algo, (apuntar)* to note sth. down; *fig (fijarse)* to take note of sth.

notable *adj (apreciable)* noticeable; *(digno de notar)* outstanding, remarkable.

notar(se) *t (percibir)* to notice, note. **2** *(sentir)* to feel. – **3** *p (percibirse)* to be noticeable/evident, show. **4** *(sentirse)* to feel. ●*hacerse ~,* to draw attention to o.s.; *se nota que ...,* one can see that ...

notaría *f (profesión)* profession of notary (public). **2** *(despacho)* notary's office.

notario,-a *m,f* notary (public), public solicitor.

noticia *f* news *pl: una ~,* a piece of news. ●*dar la ~,* to break the news.

noticiario *m* news (bulletin).

notificación *f* notification. ■ *~ judicial,* summons *sing.*

notificar [1] *t* to notify, inform.

notorio,-a *adj* well-known.

novato,-a *adj (persona)* inexperienced, green. – **2** *m,f (principiante)* novice, beginner. **3** *(universidad)* fresher.

novecientos,-as *adj* nine hundred; *(ordinal)* nine hundredth. – **2** *m* nine hundred.

novedad *f (cualidad)* newness. **2** *(cosa nueva)* novelty. **3** *(cambio)* change, innovation. **4** *(noticia)* news *pl.*

novela *f* novel. ■ *~ corta,* short story; *~ negra/policíaca,* detective story; *~ rosa,* romance.

novelar *t* to novelize, convert into a novel. – **2** *i* to write novels.

novelista *mf* novelist.

noveno,-a *adj-m,f* ninth.

noventa *adj* ninety; *(nonagésimo)* ninetieth. – **2** *m* ninety.

noviazgo *m* engagement.

noviembre *m* November.

novio,-a *m,f (amigo) m* boyfriend, *f* girlfriend. **2** *(prometido) m* fiancé, *f* fiancée. **3** *(en boda) m* bridegroom, *f* bride.

nubarrón *m* storm cloud.

nube *f* cloud. **2** *fig (multitud)* swarm, crowd. ●*fig poner a algn. por las nubes,* to praise sb. to the skies.

nublado,-a *adj* cloudy, overcast.

nublar(se) *t* to cloud. − **2** *p* to cloud over.

nubosidad *f* cloudiness.

nuboso,-a *adj* cloudy.

nuca *f* nape of the neck.

núcleo *m* nucleus. **2** *(parte central)* core. **3** *(grupo de gente)* circle, group.

nudillo *m* knuckle. ▲ *Often in pl.*

nudo *m* knot. **2** *fig (vínculo)* link, tie. **3** *(punto principal)* crux, core. **4** *(de comunicaciones)* centre; *(de ferrocaril)* junction. ●*hacer un ~,* to tie a knot; *fig hacérsele a uno un ~ en la garganta,* to get a lump in one's throat.

nuera *f* daughter-in-law.

nuestro,-a *adj pos* our, of ours: ~ *amigo,-a,* our friend; *un amigo,-a ~,* a friend of ours. − **2** *pron pos* ours: *este libro es ~,* this book is ours. ●*fam los nuestros,* our side, our people.

nueve *adj* nine; *(noveno)* ninth. − **2** *m* nine.

nuevo,-a *adj* new. **2** *(adicional)* further. − **3** *m,f* newcomer; *(principiante)* beginner; *(universidad)* fresher. − **4** *nuevamente adv* again. ●*de ~,* again, *estar (como)*

~, *(objeto)* to be as good as new; *(persona)* to feel like a new man/woman; *fam ¿qué hay de ~?,* what's new?

nuez *f* BOT walnut. ■ ~ *(de Adán),* Adam's apple; ~ *moscada,* nutmeg.

nulidad *f (ineptitud)* incompetence. **2** *(persona)* nonentity. **3** JUR nullity.

nulo,-a *adj (inepto)* useless, totally inept. **2** *(sin valor)* null and void, invalid.

numeración *f* numeration. ■ ~ *arábiga,* Arabic numerals *pl;* ~ *romana,* Roman numerals *pl.*

numerar(se) *t* to number. − **2** *p* MIL to number off.

numérico,-a *adj* numerical.

número *m* number. **2** *(prensa)* number, issue. **3** *(de zapatos)* size. **4** *(en espectáculo)* sketch, act. ●*en números redondos,* in round figures; *fam montar un ~,* to make a scene. ■ ~ *atrasado,* back number; *(prensa)* ~ *extraordinario,* special edition/issue; ~ *fraccionario/ quebrado,* fraction; ~ *impar/ordinal/ par/primo,* odd/ordinal/even/prime number.

numeroso,-a *adj* numerous, large.

nunca *adv* never. **2** *(en interrogativa)* ever: *¿has visto ~ cosa igual?,* have you ever seen anything like it? ●*casi ~,* hardly ever; *más que ~,* more than ever; ~ *jamás,* never ever; ~ *más,* never again.

nupcias *fpl fml* wedding *sing,* nuptials.

nutrición *f* nutrition.

nutrir(se) *t-p* to feed.

nutritivo,-a *adj* nutritious, nourishing.

Ñ

ñame *m* AM yam.
ñandú *m* AM nandu, American ostrich.
ñoñería, ñoñez *f (cosa)* insipidness. 2 *(persona)* fussiness.

ñoño,-a *adj (cosa)* insipid. 2 *(persona)* fussy. 3 AM old.
ñoqui *m* gnocchi *pl.*

o *conj* or. ●~ ... ~ ..., either ... or ...; ~
sea que, that is (to say).

oasis *m inv* oasis.

obcecación *f* blindness.

obedecer [43] *t (acatar)* to obey. **2** *(responder)* to respond to. — **3** *i (provenir)* to
be due (*a,* to).

obediencia *f* obedience.

obediente *adj* obedient.

obesidad *f* obesity.

obeso,-a *adj* obese:

obispo *m* bishop.

objeción *f* objection. ●*poner una* ~, to
raise an objection.

objetar *t* to object.

objetividad *f* objectivity.

objetivo,-a *adj* objective. — **2** *m (fin)* objective, aim, goal. **3** MIL target. **4** *(fotografía)* lens.

objeto *m* object. **2** *(fin)* aim, purpose, object. **3** *(tema)* theme, subject, matter.
●*con* ~ *de,* in order to; *tener por* ~, to
be designed to. ■ *objetos perdidos,* lost
property *sing.*

objetor,-ra *adj* objecting, dissenting. — **2**
m,f MIL objector.

oblicuo,-a *adj* oblique.

obligación *f (deber)* obligation. **2** FIN
bond. ●*tener* ~ *de,* to have to.

obligar [7] *t* to oblige, force.

obligatorio,-a *adj* compulsory, obligatory.

obra *f (trabajo)* (piece of) work. **2** ART
work; *(literatura)* book; TEAT play. **3**
(acto) deed. **4** *(institución)* institution,
foundation. **5** *(construcción)* building
site. **6** *pl (arreglos)* repairs. ●*"en obras",*
"building works". ■ *mano de* ~, labour; ~ *benéfica,* charity; ~ *maestra,*
masterpiece.

obrar *i (proceder)* to act, behave. — **2** *t (trabajar)* to work.

obrero,-a *adj* working. — **2** *m,f* worker,
labourer.

obscenidad *f* obscenity.

obsceno,-a *adj* obscene.

obscurecer(se) [43] *t (ensombrecer)* to
darken. **2** *fig (ofuscar)* to cloud. — **3** *i* to
get dark. — **4** *p (nublarse)* to become
cloudy. ▲ **3** *used only in the 3rd person.
It does not take a subject.*

obscuridad *f* darkness. **2** *fig* obscurity.

obscuro,-a *adj* dark. **2** *fig (origen, idea)*
obscure; *(futuro)* uncertain, gloomy;
(asunto) shady. ●*a obscuras,* in the
dark.

obsequiar [12] *t (dar regalos)* to give. **2**
(agasajar) to entertain.

obsequio *m* gift, present.

observación *f* observation.

observador,-ra *adj* observant. — **2** *m,f*
observer.

observar *t (mirar)* to observe. **2** *(notar)* to
notice. **3** *(cumplir)* to obey.

observatorio *m* observatory. ■ ~ *meteorológico,* weather station.

obsesión *f* obsession.

obsesionar(se) *t* to obsess. — **2** *p* to get
obsessed.

obsesivo,-a *adj* obsessive.

obseso,-a *adj-m,f* obsessed (person).
■ ~ *sexual,* sex maniac.

obstaculizar [4] *t* to obstruct, hinder.

obstáculo *m* obstacle, hindrance.

obstante *no* ~, *adv* nevertheless, all the
same.

obstetricia *f* obstetrics.

obstinación *f* obstinacy, stubbornness.

obstinado,-a *adj* obstinate, stubborn.

obstinarse *p* to persist (*en,* in).

obstruir(se) [62] *t (obstaculizar)* to block,
obstruct. — **2** *p* to get blocked up.

obtención *f* obtaining.

obtener(se) [87] *t (alcanzar)* to obtain, get. – **2** *p (provenir)* to come (*de,* from).

obturador *m (de cámara)* shutter.

obturar *t* to plug, stop.

obtuso,-a *adj* obtuse.

obvio,-a *adj* obvious.

oca *f* goose.

ocasión *f (momento)* occasion. **2** *(oportunidad)* opportunity, chance. **3** COM bargain. ●*dar ~ a algo,* to give rise to sth.; *de ~, (segunda mano)* secondhand; *(barato)* bargain; *en cierta ~,* once.

ocasional *adj (de vez en cuando)* occasional. **2** *(fortuito)* accidental, by chance.

ocasionar *t (causar)* to cause, occasion.

ocaso *m (anochecer)* sunset. **2** *(occidente)* west. **3** *fig (declive)* fall, decline.

occidental *adj* western. – **2** *mf (persona)* westerner.

occidente *m* the West.

océano *m* ocean.

ochenta *adj* eighty; *(octagésimo)* eightieth. – **2** *m* eighty.

ocho *adj* eight; *(octavo)* eighth. – **2** *m* eight. ●*a los ~ días,* in a week('s time).

ochocientos,-as *adj* eight hundred; *(ordinal)* eight hundredth. – **2** *m* eight hundred.

ocio *m* leisure, idleness.

ocioso,-a *adj (inactivo)* idle. **2** *(inútil)* pointless, useless. – **3** *m,f* idler.

octagésimo,-a *adj-m,f* eightieth.

octavilla *f* leaflet.

octavo,-a *adj-m,f* eighth.

octubre *m* October.

oculista *mf* oculist.

ocultar [62] *t* to conceal/hide (*a,* from).

oculto,-a *adj* concealed, hidden.

ocupación *f* occupation.

ocupado,-a *adj (persona)* busy. **2** *(asiento)* taken; *(aseos, teléfono)* engaged; *(puesto de trabajo)* filled. **3** MIL occupied.

ocupante *mf* occupant.

ocupar(se) *t gen* to occupy, take. **2** *(llenar)* to take up. **3** *(desempeñar)* to hold, fill. **4** *(trabajadores)* to employ. **5** *(habitar)* to live in. – **6** *p (emplearse)* to occupy o.s. (*de/en/con,* with). **7** *(vigilar)* to look after (*de,* -). **8** *(reflexionar)* to look into (*de,* -). ●*~se de un asunto,* to deal with a matter.

ocurrencia *f (agudeza)* witty remark. **2** *(idea)* idea.

ocurrente *adj* bright, witty.

ocurrir(se) *i* to happen, occur. – **2** *p* to think, occur to.

odiar [12] *t* to hate, loathe.

odio *m* hatred, loathing.

odioso,-a *adj* hateful, detestable.

odontólogo,-a *m,f* dental surgeon, odontologist.

oeste *m* west.

ofender(se) *t* to offend. – **2** *p* to be offended (*con/por,* by), take offence (*con/por,* at).

ofensa *f* insult.

ofensivo,-a *adj* offensive, rude. – **2** *f* MIL offensive.

oferta *f* offer. **2** FIN IND bid, tender. **3** *(suministro)* supply. ●*de ~,* on (special) offer. ■ *~ y demanda,* supply and demand.

oficial *adj* official. – **2** *m* MIL officer. **3** *(empleado)* clerk. **4** *(obrero)* skilled worker.

oficina *f* office. ■ *horas de ~,* business hours; *~ de empleo,* job centre, US job office; *~ pública,* government office.

oficinista *mf* office worker.

oficio *m (ocupación)* job, occupation; *(especializado)* trade. **2** *(función)* role, function. **3** *(comunicación oficial)* official letter/note. **4** REL service. ●*de ~,* by trade.

oficioso,-a *adj (noticia, fuente)* unofficial. **2** *(persona)* officious.

ofrecer(se) [43] *t (dar) (premio, amistad)* to offer; *(banquete, fiesta)* to hold; *(regalo)* to give. **2** *(presentar)* to present. – **3** *p (prestarse)* to offer, volunteer.

ofuscación *f* blinding, dazzling.

ofuscar [1] *t (deslumbrar)* to dazzle. **2** *fig (confundir)* to blind.

oídas *de oídas, adv* by hearsay.

oído *m (sentido)* hearing. **2** *(órgano)* ear. ●*de ~,* by ear.

oír [75] *t* to hear. ●*¡oye!,* hey!; *fam como lo oyes,* believe it or not.

ojal *m* buttonhole.

¡ojalá! *interj* if only, I wish: *~ fuera rico,-a,* I wish I were rich.

ojeada *f* glance, quick look. ●*echar una ~, (mirar)* to take a quick look (*a,* at); *(vigilar)* to keep an eye (*a,* on).

ojear *t (mirar)* to have a quick look at.

ojeras *fpl* bags under the eyes.

ojeroso,-a *adj* with rings under the eyes, haggard.

ojo *m* eye. **2** *(agujero)* hole. – **3** *interj* careful, look out. ●*fig a ~,* at a rough guess; *fig mirar con buenos ojos,* to look favourably on; *fig saltar a los ojos,* to be evident. ■ *~ de la cerradura,* keyhole; *~ morado,* black eye.

ola *f* wave.

¡olé!, ¡ole! *interj* bravo!
oleada *f* wave. 2 *fig* influx.
oleaje *m* swell.
oler [60] *t-i* to smell (*a*, of).
olfatear *t* (*oler*) to sniff, smell. 2 *fig* (*indagar*) to nose/pry into. 3 (*sospechar*) to suspect.
olfato *m* sense of smell. 2 *fig* (*intuición*) a good nose, instinct, flair.
olimpiada *f* Olympiad. ▪ *las Olimpiadas,* the Olympic Games.
oliva *adj-f* olive.
olivo *m* olive (tree).
olla *f* saucepan, pot. ▪ ~ *exprés/a presión,* pressure cooker.
olor *m* smell. ▪ ~ *corporal,* body odour.
oloroso,-a *adj* fragrant, sweet-smelling.
olvidar(se) *t-p* to forget.
olvido *m* (*desmemoria*) oblivion. 2 (*descuido*) forgetfulness, absent-mindedness. 3 (*lapsus*) oversight, lapse.
ombligo *m* navel.
omiso,-a *adj* negligent. ●*hacer caso ~ de,* to take no notice of.
omitir *t* (*no decir*) to omit, leave out. 2 (*dejar de hacer*) to neglect, overlook.
omnipotente *adj* omnipotent, almighty.
once *adj* eleven; (*undécimo*) eleventh. – 2 *m* eleven.
onda *f* wave. 2 (*en el agua*) ripple. ▪ ~ *expansiva,* shock wave.
ondear *i* (*bandera*) to flutter. 2 (*agua*) to ripple. ●~ *a media asta,* to be flying at half mast.
ondulación *f* undulation, wave. 2 (*agua*) ripple.
ondular *t* (*el pelo*) to wave. – 2 *i* (*moverse*) to undulate.
opaco,-a *adj* opaque.
opción *f* (*elección*) option, choice. 2 (*derecho*) right; (*posibilidad*) opportunity, chance.
ópera *f* opera.
operación *f* operation. 2 FIN transaction, deal.
operador,-ra *m,f* operator. 2 CINEM (*de la cámara*) *m* cameraman, *f* camerawoman; (*del proyector*) projectionist.
operario,-a *m,f* operator, worker.
operar(se) *t* MED to operate (*a*, on). 2 (*producir*) to bring about. – 3 *i* (*hacer efecto*) to operate, work. 4 FIN to deal, to do business (with). – 5 *p* MED to have an operation (*de*, for).
opinar *i* to think, be of the opinion.
opinión *f* (*juicio*) opinion, (point of) view. ●*cambiar de ~,* to change one's mind.

opíparo,-a *adj fml* lavish.
oponente *adj* opposing. – 2 *mf* opponent.
oponer(se) [78] *t* to oppose. 2 (*resistencia*) to offer. – 3 *p* (*estar en contra*) to oppose (*a*, -). 4 (*ser contrario*) to be in opposition (*a*, to), contradict. ▲ *pp* **opuesto,-a.**
oportunidad *f* opportunity, chance. 2 (*ganga*) bargain.
oportunista *adj-mf* opportunist.
oportuno,-a *adj* (*a tiempo*) opportune, timely. 2 (*conveniente*) appropriate.
oposición *f* opposition. 2 (*examen*) competitive examination.
opresión *f* oppression. ▪ ~ *en el pecho,* tightness of the chest.
opresor,-ra *adj* oppressive, oppressing. – 2 *m,f* oppressor.
oprimir *t* to squeeze, press. 2 *fig* to oppress.
optar *i* (*elegir*) to choose. 2 (*aspirar*) to apply (*a*, for).
optativo,-a *adj* optional.
óptico,-a *adj* optic(al). – 2 *m,f* optician. – 3 *f* (*tienda*) optician's (shop). 4 FÍS optics.
optimismo *m* optimism.
optimista *adj* optimistic. – 2 *mf* optimist.
óptimo,-a *adj* very best, optimum.
opuesto,-a *pp* → **oponer.** – 2 *adj* (*contrario*) opposed, contrary. 3 (*de enfrente*) opposite.
opulencia *f* opulence, luxury.
opulento,-a *adj* opulent.
oración *f* REL prayer. 2 GRAM clause, sentence. ▪ *partes de la ~,* parts of speech.
orador,-ra *m,f* speaker, orator.
oral *adj* oral. ●MED *por vía ~,* to be taken orally.
orar *i* to pray.
órbita *f* orbit. 2 (*ojo*) socket.
orden *m* (*arreglo*) order. 2 *fig* (*campo*) sphere. – 3 *f* (*mandato, cuerpo*) order. 4 JUR warrant. ●*de primer ~,* first-rate; *por ~ de,* by order of. ▪ ~ *de arresto/detención,* warrant for arrest; ~ *de pago,* money order; ~ *judicial,* court order; ~ *público,* law and order.
ordenación *f* (*disposición*) arrangement, organizing. 2 REL ordination.
ordenador,-ra *adj* ordering. – 2 *m* INFORM computer. ▪ ~ *personal,* personal computer.
ordenar *t* (*arreglar*) to put in order; (*habitación*) to tidy up. 2 (*mandar*) to order

to. **3** REL to ordain. ●*fig* ~ *las ideas,* to collect one's thoughts.

ordeñar *t* to milk.

ordinario,-a *adj (corriente)* ordinary, common. **2** *(grosero)* vulgar, common. ●*de* ~, usually.

orégano *m* oregano.

oreja *f* ear.

orejudo,-a *adj* big-eared.

orfanato *m* orphanage.

organismo *m (ser viviente)* organism. **2** *(entidad pública)* organization, body.

organización *f* organization.

organizador,-ra *adj* organizing. — **2** *m,f* organizer.

organizar(se) [4] *t* to organize. — **2** *p fig* to set up.

órgano *m* organ.

orgasmo *m* orgasm.

orgía *f* orgy.

orgullo *m (propia estima)* pride. **2** *(arrogancia)* arrogance, haughtiness.

orgulloso,-a *adj (satisfecho)* proud. **2** *(arrogante)* arrogant, haughty.

orientación *f (dirección)* orientation. **2** *(enfoque)* approach. **3** *(guía)* guidance. ■ ~ *profesional,* career/vocational guidance.

orientador,-ra *adj* advisory, guiding. — **2** *m,f* guide, adviser, counsellor.

oriental *adj* eastern, oriental.

orientar(se) *t (dirigir)* to orientate, direct. **2** *(guiar)* to guide, give directions. — **3** *p (encontrar el camino)* to get one's bearings, find one's way about. **4** *(dirigirse)* to tend towards.

oriente *m* east, orient.

orificio *m* hole, opening.

origen *m* origin: *de* ~ *español,* of Spanish extraction.

original *adj-mf* original.

originario,-a *adj* original. ●*ser* ~ *de, (persona)* to come from; *(costumbre)* to originate in.

originar(se) *t* to cause, give rise to. — **2** *p* to originate, have its origin.

orilla *f (borde)* edge. **2** *(del río)* bank; *(del mar)* shore. ●*a la* ~ *del mar,* by the sea.

orina *f* urine.

orinar(se) *i* to urinate. — **2** *p* to wet o.s.

oriundo,-a *adj* native of. ●*ser* ~ *de,* to come from, originate from/in.

ornamentar *t* to adorn, embellish.

oro *m* gold. ●*de* ~, gold(en).

orquesta *f* orchestra. **2** *(banda)* dance band.

ortografía *f* spelling, orthography.

oruga *f* caterpillar.

os *pron pers pl (complemento directo)* you: ~ *veo mañana,* I'll see you tomorrow. **2** *(complemento indirecto)* to you: ~ *lo mandaré,* I'll send it to you. **3** *(reflexivo)* yourselves: ~ *hacéis daño,* you're hurting yourselves. **4** *(recíproco)* each other: ~ *queréis mucho,* you love each other very much.

osadía *f (audacia)* daring, boldness. **2** *(desvergüenza)* impudence.

osado,-a *adj (audaz)* daring, bold. **2** *(desvergonzado)* shameless.

osar *i* to dare.

oscilación *f (de precios)* fluctuation. **2** FÍS oscillation.

oscilar *i (variar)* to vary, fluctuate. **2** FÍS to oscillate.

oscurecer(se) *t-p* → **obscurecer(se)**.

oscuridad *f* → **obscuridad**.

oscuro,-a *adj* → **obscuro**.

oso *m* bear.

ostensible *adj* ostensible, obvious.

ostentación *f* ostentation.

ostentar *t (jactarse)* to show off, flaunt. **2** *(poseer)* to hold. ●~ *el cargo de,* to hold the position of.

ostentoso,-a *adj* ostentatious.

ostra *f* oyster. — **2** *pl interj* crikey!, US gee!

otoño *m* autumn, US fall.

otorgar [7] *t (conceder)* to grant, give *(a,* to); *(premio)* to award *(a,* to). **2** JUR to execute, draw up.

otro,-a *adj-pron indef* another, other. ●*entre otras cosas,* amongst other things; *otra cosa,* something else; ~ *día,* another day; ~ *tanto,* as much.

ovación *f* ovation, cheering, applause.

ovacionar *i* to give an ovation *(a,* to), applaud *(a,* –).

oval, ovalado,-a *adj* oval.

oveja *f* sheep, ewe.

ovillo *m* ball (of wool). ●*fig hacerse un* ~, to curl up into a ball.

OVNI *m* UFO.

oxidado,-a *adj* rusty.

oxidarse *p* to rust, go rusty.

oye *pres indic* → **oír**.

oyente *mf* RAD listener. **2** *pl* audience *sing*.

P

pabellón *m (tienda)* tent. **2** ARQ pavilion. **3** *(dosel)* canopy. **4** *(bandera)* flag. **5** ANAT (external) ear.

pabilo, pábilo *m* wick.

pábulo *m* food, support. ●*dar ~ a,* to encourage.

pacer [42] *i-t* to graze.

pachorra *f fam* phlegm, slowness.

pachucho,-a *adj* overripe. **2** *fig* weak, feeble.

paciencia *f* patience. ●*tener ~,* to be patient.

paciente *adj-mf* patient.

pacificar [1] *t* to pacify. **2** *(calmar)* to appease.

pacífico,-a *adj* peaceful.

pacotilla *f fam de ~ ,* shoddy.

pactar *t* to agree (to).

pacto *m* pact, agreement.

padecer [43] *t-i* to suffer *(de,* from).

padecimiento *m* suffering.

padrastro *m* stepfather.

padre *m* father. **2** *pl* parents. — **3** *adj fam* terrific. ■ *~ político,* father-in-law.

padrenuestro *m* Lord's Prayer.

padrino *m* godfather. **2** *(de boda)* best man. **3** *(patrocinador)* sponsor.

padrón *m* census.

paella *f* paella.

paga *f (sueldo)* pay.

pagadero,-a *adj* payable.

pagado,-a *adj* pleased, proud. ●*~ de sí mismo,* self-satisfied.

paganismo *m* paganism.

pagano,-a *adj-m,f* pagan. — **2** *m,f fam* one who pays.

pagar [7] *t* to pay (for). ●*~ al contado,* to pay cash; *fam ¡me las pagarás!,* you'll pay for this!

pagaré *m* promissory note.

página *f* page. ■ *páginas amarillas,* yellow pages.

pago *m* payment. **2** *(recompensa)* reward. ●*en ~ por,* in payment/return for.

país *m* country.

paisaje *m* landscape.

paisano,-a *m,f m* countryman, *f* countrywoman. **2** *(compatriota) m* fellow countryman, *f* fellow countrywoman. — **3** *m* civilian. ●*de ~,* in plain clothes.

paja *f* straw. **2** *fig (relleno)* padding, waffle. **3*** *(masturbación)* wank*.

pajarita *f (prenda)* bow tie. **2** *(de papel)* paper bird.

pájaro *m* ZOOL bird. **2** *fig* slyboots. ●*fam matar dos pájaros de un tiro,* to kill two birds with one stone. ■ *~ bobo,* penguin; *~ carpintero,* woodpecker; *fig ~ de cuenta,* big shot.

paje *m* page.

pala *f* shovel. **2** *(de cocina)* slice. **3** DEP bat. **4** *(de hélice etc.)* blade.

palabra *f* word. ●*dar/empeñar uno su ~,* to give/pledge one's word; *en una ~,* in a word, to sum up; *tener la ~,* to have the floor; *fig ser de pocas palabras,* not to be very talkative.

palabrota *f* swearword. ●*decir palabrotas,* to swear.

palacio *m* palace.

paladar *m* palate. **2** *fig (gusto)* taste, relish.

paladear *t* to savour, relish.

paladín *m* HIST paladin. **2** *fig* champion.

palanca *f* lever. **2** *(manecilla)* handle. ■ *~ de cambio,* gear lever, gearstick.

palangana *f* washbasin.

palco *m* box.

paleta *f (de pintor)* palette. **2** *(de albañil)* trowel. **3** *(de hélice etc.)* blade. **4** DEP bat.

paletilla *f* ANAT shoulder blade. **2** CULIN shoulder.

paleto,-a *m,f pey* country bumpkin.
paliar [12] *t* to palliate, alleviate.
palidecer [43] *i* to turn pale.
palidez *f* paleness, pallor.
pálido,-a *adj* pale,
palillo *m (mondadientes)* toothpick. **2** MÚS drumstick. ■ *palillos (chinos),* chopsticks.
palio *m* canopy.
palique *m fam* chat, small talk.
paliza *f* beating, thrashing. **2** *(derrota)* defeat. **3** *fam (pesadez)* bore. ●*dar/pegar una ~ a algn.,* to beat sb. up; *fam dar la ~ a algn.,* to bore sb.
palizada *f* palisade, stockade.
palma *f* BOT palm (tree). **2** *(de la mano)* palm. **3** *pl (aplausos)* clapping *sing,* applause *sing.* ●*batir palmas,* to clap; *fig llevarse la ~,* to win, triumph.
palmada *f (golpe)* slap, pat. **2** *(aplauso)* clapping. ●*dar palmadas,* to clap.
palmario,-a *adj* obvious, evident.
palmatoria *f* candlestick.
palmera *f* palm (tree).
palmo *m* span. ●*~ a ~,* inch by inch; *fam dejar (a algn.) con un ~ de narices,* to let (sb.) down.
palmotear *t* to clap.
palo *m* stick, pole. **2** MAR mast. **3** *(golpe)* blow. **4** *(de naipes)* suit. **5** AM *(árbol)* tree. ●*dar palos,* to hit, strike; *fig a ~ seco,* on its own; *fig dar palos de ciego,* to grope about in the dark.
paloma *f* dove, pigeon. ■ *~ mensajera,* carrier pigeon.
palomar *m* pigeon loft; *(rústico)* dovecote.
palomitas *fpl* popcorn *sing.*
palpable *adj* palpable. **2** *fig (evidente)* obvious, evident.
palpar *t* to touch, feel.
palpitación *f* palpitation.
palpitante *adj* palpitating, throbbing. **2** *fig* burning.
palpitar *i* to palpitate, throb.
pálpito *m* AM presentiment.
paludismo *m* malaria.
palurdo,-a *adj pey* uncouth, rude. – **2** *m,f* boor, churl.
pampa *f* pampas *pl.*
pamplina *f* nonsense.
pan *m* bread. **2** *(de metal)* leaf, foil. ●*ganarse el ~,* to earn one's living; *fig llamar al ~, ~ y al vino, vino,* to call a spade a spade. ■ *~ de molde,* packet sliced bread; *~ integral,* wholemeal/

wholewheat bread; *~ rallado,* breadcrumbs *pl; fig ~ comido,* a piece of cake.
pana *f* corduroy.
panadería *f* bakery, baker's (shop).
panadero,-a *m,f* baker.
panal *m* honeycomb.
pancarta *f* placard.
pandereta *f* small tambourine.
pandero *m* tambourine.
pandilla *f* gang, band.
panecillo *m* roll.
panegírico,-a *adj* panegyric(al). – **2** *m* panegyric.
pánfilo,-a *adj (lento)* slow. **2** *(tonto)* stupid. – **3** *m,f* fool.
panel *m* panel.
panfleto *m* pamphlet, lampoon.
pánico *m* panic.
panocha *f* corncob; *(de trigo)* ear.
panoplia *f* panoply.
panorama *m* panorama, view.
panqueque *m* AM pancake.
pantalón *m* trousers *pl.* ■ *~ corto,* short (trousers). ▲ *Often pl.*
pantalla *f* screen. **2** *(de lámpara)* shade.
pantano *m* marsh.
pantanoso,-a *adj* marshy.
panteón *m* pantheon. ■ *~ familiar,* family vault.
panteonero *m* AM gravedigger.
pantera *f* panther.
pantomima *f* pantomime.
pantorrilla *f* calf.
pantufla *f* slipper.
panza *f* paunch, belly.
pañal *m* nappy, napkin, US diaper.
paño *m* cloth (material). **2** *(para polvo)* duster. **3** *pl (prendas)* clothes. **4** *(de pared)* panel, stretch. ●*en paños menores,* in one's underwear.
pañuelo *m* handkerchief. **2** *(chal)* shawl.
papa *m* pope.
papá *m fam* dad(dy).
papada *f* double chin.
papagayo *m* parrot. **2** *fig* chatterbox.
papamoscas *m inv* fly-catcher.
papanatas *mf inv* simpleton.
paparrucha *f fam (mentira)* fib. **2** *(tontería)* nonsense.
papel *m* (piece/sheet of) paper. **2** CINEM TEAT role, part. ●*desempeñar el ~ de,* to play the part of; *hacer mal/buen ~,* to do badly/well. ■ *~ de calcar,* tracing-paper; *~ de estado,* government securities *pl; ~ de estaño/plata,* aluminium/tin foil; *~ de lija,* sandpaper; *~ higié-*

nico, toilet paper; ~ *moneda,* paper money; ~ *pintado,* wallpaper; ~ *secante,* blotting-paper.

papeleo *m fam* red tape.

papelera *f* wastepaper basket. **2** *(en la calle)* litter bin.

papelería *f* stationer's.

papeleta *f (de empeño)* ticket. **2** *(para votar)* ballot paper. **3** *(de exámen)* report. **4** *fam (problema)* tricky problem: *¡vaya ~!,* what an awful situation!

paperas *fpl* mumps.

papilla *f* pap. •*fam echar la primera ~,* to be as sick as a dog; *fam hacer ~ a algn.,* to make mincemeat of sb.

papiro *m* papyrus.

paquebote *m* packet boat.

paquete *m* package; *(caja)* packet. **2** *(conjunto)* set, packet. **3** *fam (torpón)* wally, useless tool. •*ir de ~,* to ride pillion. ■ ~ *postal,* parcel.

par *adj* equal. **2** MAT even. − **3** *m* pair. **4** *(título)* peer. •*a la ~,* *(al mismo tiempo)* at the same time; *(juntos)* together; *de ~ en ~,* wide open; *sin ~,* matchless.

para *prep (finalidad)* for, (in order) to: *es ~ Pepe,* it's for Pepe; ~ *ahorrar dinero,* (in order) to save money. **2** *(dirección)* toward: *¿~ dónde vas?,* where are you going? **3** *(tiempo, fechas límites)* by: ~ *Navidad,* by Christmas. •*dar ~,* to be sufficient for; *hay ~ rato,* it will be some time before it's over; ~ *entonces,* by then; ~ *que,* in order that, so that; *¿~ qué?,* what for?

parabién *m* congratulations *pl.*

parábola *f* REL parable. **2** MAT parabola.

parabrisas *m inv* windscreen.

paracaídas *m inv* parachute. •*tirarse en ~,* to parachute.

paracaidista *mf* DEP parachutist. **2** MIL paratrooper.

parachoques *m inv* AUTO bumper, US fender. **2** *(de tren)* buffer.

parada *f* stop, halt. **2** *(de autobús etc.)* stop. **3** *(pausa)* pause. **4** DEP catch. ■ ~ *de taxis,* taxi/cab stand; ~ *discrecional,* request stop.

paradero *m* whereabouts *pl.*

parado,-a *adj* stopped. **2** *(quieto)* still, motionless. **3** *fig (lento)* slow, awkward. **4** *fam (desempleado)* unemployed. − **5** *m,f* unemployed person.

paradoja *f* paradox.

paradójico,-a *adj* paradoxical.

parador *m* state-run hotel.

paráfrasis *f inv* paraphrase.

paraguas *m inv* umbrella.

paraíso *m* paradise.

paraje *m* spot, place.

paralelo,-a *adj-m* parallel. − **2** *fpl* DEP parallel bars.

paralelogramo *m* parallelogram.

parálisis *f inv* paralysis.

paralítico,-a *adj-m,f* paralytic.

paralización *f* paralysation. **2** COM stagnation.

paralizar(se) [1] *t* to paralyse. **2** *(tráfico)* to bring to a standstill. − **3** *p* to be paralysed. **2** *fig* to come to a standstill.

paramento *m (adorno)* ornament, decoration. **2** ARQ face.

parámetro *m* parameter.

páramo *m* moor.

parangón *m fml* comparison.

parangonar *t fml* to compare.

paraninfo *m* assembly hall of a university.

parapetarse *p* to take shelter/cover. **2** *fig* to take refuge.

parapeto *m* ARQ parapet. **2** *(terraplén)* barricade.

parapsicología *f* parapsychogy.

parar(se) *t* to stop. **2** DEP to catch. − **3** *i* to stop. **4** *(llegar)* to lead: *¿adónde iremos a ~?,* what is the world coming to? **5** *(estar)* to be: *nunca paro en casa,* I'm never at home. **6** *(alojarse)* to lodge. − **7** *p* to stop. **8** AM *(levantarse)* to stand up. •*ir a ~ a,* to end up at/in; *no ~,* to be always on the go; *~se en seco,* to stop dead; *sin ~,* nonstop, without stopping; *fig ~ los pies a algn.,* to put sb. in his/her place.

pararrayos *m inv* lightning conductor.

parasitario,-a *adj* parasitic.

parásito,-a *adj* parasitic. − **2** *m* BIOL parasite. **3** *fam (persona)* hanger-on. **4** *pl* RAD interference *sing.*

parasol *m* parasol, sunshade.

parcela *f (de tierra)* plot. **2** *fig* portion.

parche *m* patch. **2** *(emplasto)* plaster. **3** *fig (chapuza)* botch.

parcial *adj* partial.

parcialidad *f* partiality.

parco,-a *adj (escaso)* frugal, sparing. **2** *(moderado)* moderate, sober.

pardo,-a *adj-m* drab, dark grey.

parecer(se) [43] *i* to seem, look (like): *parece fácil,* it seems/looks easy; *parece un mono,* it looks like a monkey. **2** *(opinar)* to think: *me parece que sí,* I think so; *¿qué te parece?,* what do you think? **3** *(aparentar)* to look as if: *parece que va a llover,* it looks as if it's going to rain. − **4** *p* to be alike, look like: *se parece a su padre,* he/she looks like his/her father. − **5** *m (opinión)* opinion, mind. ●*al* ~, apparently; *según parece,* as it seems. ▲ **3** *used only in the 3rd pers. It does not take a subject.*

parecido,-a *adj* similar. − **2** *m* resemblance, likeness. ■ *bien/mal* ~, good-looking/ugly.

pared *f* wall. ■ ~ *maestra/medianera,* main/partition wall.

pareja *f gen* pair. **2** *(de personas)* couple. **3** *(de baile)* partner. ●*hacer buena* ~, to be two of a kind.

parejo,-a *adj (igual)* equal, like. **2** *(liso)* even, smooth.

parentela *f* relatives *pl,* relations *pl.*

parentesco *m* kinship, relationship.

paréntesis *m inv* parenthesis, brackets *pl.* **2** *fig (interrupción)* break, interruption. ●*entre* ~, in parenthesis/brackets.

paria *mf* pariah.

paridad *f* parity, equality.

pariente,-a *m,f* relative, kinsman.

parir *t-i* to give birth to.

parlamentar *i* to talk.

parlamentario,-a *adj* parliamentary. − **2** *m,f* member of parliament.

parlamento *m* parliament. **2** *(discurso)* speech.

parlanchín,-ina *adj* talkative. − **2** *m,f* chatterbox.

parlotear *i fam* to prattle (on).

paro *m* stop(page). **2** *(desempleo)* unemployment. ●*estar en el* ~, to be out of work.

parodia *f* parody.

parodiar [12] *t* to parody.

parpadear *i (ojos)* to blink, wink. **2** *(luz)* to twinkle.

párpado *m* eyelid.

parque *m* park.

parra *f* grapevine.

parrafada *f fam (conversación)* chat. **2** *(discurso)* speech.

párrafo *m* paragraph.

parranda *f fam* spree. ●*ir(se) de* ~, to go out on a spree.

parricida *mf* parricide.

parricidio *m* parricide.

parrilla *f* grill. **2** TÉC grate. ●CULIN *a la* ~, grilled.

parrillada *f* (dish of) grilled fish/seafood/meat.

párroco *m* parish priest.

parroquia *f* parish. **2** *(iglesia)* parish church. **3** *fam (clientela)* customers *pl,* clientele.

parroquiano,-a *m,f (fiel)* parishioner. **2** *fam (cliente)* customer, client.

parsimonia *f (moderación)* parsimony. **2** *(calma)* calmness. **3** *(lentitud)* slowness.

parsimonioso,-a *adj (moderado)* parsimonious. **2** *(calmado)* calm. **3** *(lento)* slow, unhurried.

parte *f gen* part; *(en una partición)* portion, lot. **2** *(en negocio)* share, interest. **3** JUR party. **4** *(lugar)* place, region. − **5** *m (comunicado)* official communication. ●*dar* ~, to report; *de* ~ *a* ~, through; *de* ~ *de,* on behalf of, from; *¿de* ~ *de quien?,* who's calling?; *en ninguna* ~, nowhere; *en* ~, partly; *estar de* ~ *de,* to support; *llevar la mejor/peor* ~, to have the best/worst of it; *por todas partes,* everywhere; *por una* ~, *... por otra,* on the one hand..., on the other hand... .

partera *f* midwife.

parterre *m* flowerbed.

partición *f* partition, division.

participación *f* participation, share. **2** *(comunicado)* announcement.

participante *adj* participating. − **2** *mf* participant.

participar *t (notificar)* to notify, inform. − **2** *i (tomar parte)* to participate, share.

partícipe *adj* participant. − **2** *mf* participant. ●*hacer* ~ *de algo,* *(notificar)* to inform about sth.; *(hacer paticipar)* to share with.

participio *m* participle.

partícula *f* particle.

particular *adj* particular. **2** *(extraordinario)* noteworthy, extraordinary. − **3** *m (individuo)* private, citizen. **4** *(detalle)* particular.

particularidad *f* particularity.

partida *f (salida)* departure, leave. **2** *(documento)* certificate. **3** FIN entry, item. **4** *(remesa)* lot, shipment. **5** *(juego)* game. **6** *(de soldados)* squad, gang. ●*jugar una mala* ~, to play a mean trick.

partidario,-a *adj* supporting. − **2** *m,f* supporter.

partido *m (grupo)* party, group. **2** *(provecho)* profit, advantage. **3** DEP *(equipo)* team; *(partida)* game, match. ●*sacar de,* to profit from; *ser un buen* ~, to be a good catch; *tomar* ~, to take sides.

partir(se) *t* to divide, split. **2** *(romper)* to break, crack. **3** *(repartir)* to share, distribute. − **4** *i (irse)* to leave, set out/off.

– 5 *p* to split (up), break (up). ●*a ~ de hoy,* from today onwards; *fig ~ la cara a algn.,* to smash sb.'s face in; *fam ~se de risa,* to split one's sides laughing.

partitura *f* score.

parto *m* childbirth, delivery. ●*estar/ir de ~,* to be in labour.

párvulo,-a *m,f* little child.

pasa *f* raisin. ■ *~ de Corinto,* currant.

pasacalle *m* lively march.

pasada *f* passage. **2** COST long stitch. **3** *(punto)* pick. ●*de ~, (de paso)* in passing; *(rápidamente)* hastily. ■ *mala ~,* mean trick.

pasado,-a *adj* past, gone by. **2** *(año, semana, etc.)* last. **3** *(después)* after: *pasadas las once,* after eleven. **4** *(estropeado)* (gone) bad. **– 5** *m* past. ■ *~ de moda,* out of date/fashion; *~ mañana,* the day after tomorrow.

pasador *m (de puerta etc.)* bolt, fastener. **2** *(de pelo)* hair-pin. **3** *(colador)* strainer, colander.

pasaje *m* passage. **2** *(pasajeros)* passengers *pl.* **3** *(calle)* lane, alley.

pasajero,-a *adj* passing. **– 2** *m,f* passenger.

pasamano *m* handrail.

pasaporte *m* passport.

pasar(se) *i (ir)* to go/walk past. **2** *(tiempo)* to pass, go by. **3** *(entrar)* to come/go in. **4** *(cesar)* to come to an end. **5** *(límite)* to exceed *(de, -).* **6** *(ocurrir)* to happen. **– 7** *t* to pass. **8** *(trasladar)* to carry across. **9** *(mensaje)* to give. **10** *(página)* to turn. **11** *(calle etc.)* to cross. **12** *(límite)* to go beyond. **13** *(aventajar)* to surpass, beat. **14** AUTO to overtake. **15** *(tolerar)* to tolerate, overlook. **16** *(examen)* to pass. **17** *(película)* to show. **– 18** *p (desertar)* to pass over *(a,* to). **19** *(excederse)* to go too far *(de, -).* **20** *(pudrirse)* to go off. **21** *(olvidarse)* to forget. **22** *(ir)* to go by, walk past *(por, -).* ●*ir pasando,* to get along; *~ a,* to go on to; *~ por,* to be considered; *pasarlo bien,* to have a good time; *¿qué pasa?,* what is the matter?, what happens?; *~ sin,* to do without. ▲ **6** *used only in the 3rd pers. It does not take a subject.*

pasarela *f* walkway.

pasatiempo *m* pastime, hobby.

pascua *f (cristiana)* Easter; *(judía)* Passover. **2** *pl* Christmas. ●*felices Pascuas,* merry Christmas; *fam estar alegre como unas pascuas,* to be as happy as a sandboy; *... y santas pascuas,* ... and that's that. ■ *~ de Resurrección,* Easter.

pase *m* pass, permit. **2** CINEM showing.

pasear(se) *i-p* to take a walk. **– 2** *t* to (take for a) walk.

paseo *m* walk, stroll. **2** *(en coche)* drive. **3** *(calle)* avenue, promenade. ●*dar un ~,* to go for a walk.

pasillo *m* corridor.

pasión *f* passion.

pasional *adj* passionate.

pasionaria *f* passion flower.

pasivo,-a *adj* passive. **– 2** *m* COM liabilities *pl.*

pasmar(se) *t* to astonish, amaze. **– 2** *p* to be astonished/amazed.

pasmo *m* amazement, astonishment.

pasmoso,-a *adj* astonishing, amazing.

paso *m* (foot)step, pace. **2** *(distancia)* pace. **3** *(camino)* passage, way. **4** *(avance)* progress, advance. **5** *(trámite)* step, move. ●*abrirse ~,* to force one's way through; *de ~,* by the way; *marcar el ~,* to mark time; *~ a ~,* step by step; *"prohibido el ~",* "no entry"; *fig a dos pasos,* just round the corner; *fig dar un ~ en falso,* to make a wrong move. ■ *~ a nivel,* level crossing.

pasta *f (masa)* paste. **2** CULIN pasta. **3** *(pastelito)* cake. **4** *fam (dinero)* dough, money. ●*fam ser de buena ~,* to be good-natured.

pastar *t-i* to pasture, graze.

pastel *m* pie, cake: *~ de manzana,* apple pie. **2** ART pastel. **3** *fam (conspiración)* plot.

pastelería *f* confectioner's (shop).

pastelero,-a *m,f* pastrycook.

pastilla *f (medicina)* tablet, pill. **2** *(de chocolate)* bar. **3** *(de jabón)* cake, bar. ●*fam a toda ~,* at full tilt.

pasto *m* pasture. **2** AM *(hierba)* grass. ●*ser ~ de las llamas,* to go up in flames.

pastor,-ra *m,f m* shepherd, *f* shepherdess.

pastoso,-a *adj* pasty, doughy. **2** *(voz)* mellow.

pata *f gen* leg. **2** *(garra)* paw. **3** *(pezuña)* hoof. **4** ZOOL female duck. ●*a cuatro patas,* on all fours; *patas arriba,* upside down; *fam a ~,* on foot; *fam estirar la ~,* to die; *fam meter la ~,* to put one's foot in it; *fam tener mala ~,* to have bad luck. ■ *~ de gallo,* crow's feet.

patada *f* kick. ●*a patadas,* in abundance; *fam sentar como una ~ en el estómago,* to be like a kick in the teeth.

patalear *i* to stamp one's feet.

pataleo *m* stamping.

pataleta *f fam* tantrum.

patán *m* boor.

patata *f* potato. ■ *patatas fritas,* chips.

patatús *m fam* fainting fit, swoon.

patear *t* to kick. – **2** *i* to stamp one's feet.

patentar *t* to patent.

patente *adj* patent, evident. – **2** *f* patent.

patentizar *t* to show, reveal, make evident.

paternal *adj* paternal.

paternidad *f* paternity. **2** *(autoría)* authorship.

paterno,-a *adj* paternal.

patético,-a *adj* pathetic.

patíbulo *m* scaffold, gallows.

patidifuso,-a *adj irón* astonished, amazed.

patillas *fpl* sideboards, US sideburns.

patín *m* skate. ■ ~ *de ruedas,* roller-skate.

patinar *t-i* to skate. – **2** *i (vehículo)* to skid.

patinazo *m* skid. **2** *fam (error)* blunder.

patinete *m* scooter.

patio *m* court(yard). **2** TEAT pit.

patitieso,-a *adj fam* astonished, amazed.

patituerto,-a *adj fam* crook-legged.

patizambo,-a *adj-m,f* knock-kneed (person).

pato *m* duck. ●*fam pagar el* ~, to carry the can.

patología *f* pathology.

patraña *f* hoax.

patria *f* homeland. ■ ~ *chica,* home town.

patriarca *m* patriarch.

patrimonio *m* heritage, patrimony.

patriota *mf* patriot.

patriotismo *m* patriotism.

patrocinar *t* to-sponsor.

patrocinio *m* patronage.

patrón,-ona *m,f* patron. **2** REL patron saint. **3** *(jefe)* employer, boss, *m* master, *f* mistress. – **4** COST pattern. **5** *(modelo)* standard. ■ ~ *oro,* gold standard.

patronato *m* REL patronage. **2** *(consejo)* board, council.

patrulla *f* patrol. **2** *(banda)* gang, band.

patrullar *i* to patrol.

paulatino,-a *adj* slow, gradual.

pausa *f* pause. **2** MÚS rest.

pausado,-a *adj* slow, calm, deliberate.

pauta *f (norma)* rule, standard. **2** MÚS staff. **3** *(modelo)* model, example.

pava *f* turkey hen. ●*fam pelar la* ~, to court (at a window). ■ ~ *real,* peahen.

pavimentar *t (calle)* to pave. **2** *(suelo)* to tile.

pavimento *m (calle)* roadway. **2** *(suelo)* flooring.

pavo *m* turkey. ■ ~ *real,* peacock.

pavonear(se) *i-p* to show off, swagger.

pavor *m* fear.

pavoroso,-a *adj* frightening.

payasada *f* buffoonery, clowning.

payaso *m* clown.

paz *f* peace. ●*dejar en* ~, to leave alone; *estar en* ~, to be even/quits.

peaje *m* toll.

peana *f* pedestal, stand.

peatón *m* pedestrian.

peca *f* freckle.

pecado *m* sin. ■ ~ *capital,* deadly/capital sin.

pecador,-ra *adj* sinful, sinning. – **2** *m,f* sinner.

pecaminoso,-a *adj* sinful, wicked.

pecar [1] *i* to sin.

pecera *f (redonda)* fishbowl; *(rectangular)* aquarium, fish tank.

pechera *f* shirt front. **2** *(de delantal)* bib.

pecho *m* chest. **2** *(busto)* breast. **3** *(seno)* bosom. ●*dar el* ~, to nurse, suckle; *fig tomar a* ~, to take to heart.

pechuga *f* breast.

pecoso,-a *adj* freckled.

peculiar *adj* peculiar.

peculiaridad *f* peculiarity.

peculio *m* savings *pl.*

pecuniario,-a *adj* pecuniary.

pedagogía *f* pedagogy.

pedagógico,-a *adj* pedagogic(al).

pedal *m* pedal.

pedalear *i* to pedal.

pedante *adj* pedantic. – **2** *mf* pedant.

pedantería *f* pedantry.

pedazo *m* piece, bit. ●*hacer pedazos,* to break to pieces.

pedernal *m* flint.

pedestal *m* pedestal.

pedestre *adj* pedestrian.

pediatra *mf* pediatrician.

pedicuro,-a *m,f* chiropodist.

pedido *m* COM order. **2** *(petición)* request, petition.

pedigüeño,-a *adj* pestering. – **2** *m,f* pest.

pedir [34] *t* to ask (for). **2** *(mendigar)* to beg. **3** COM to order. **4** *(cuenta etc.)* to call to. ●*a* ~ *de boca,* just as desired; ~ *prestado,-a,* to borrow.

pedo *m* fart. **2** *fam (borrachera)* drunkenness. ●*fam estar/ir* ~, to be drunk.

pedrada f blow with a stone.

pedregal m stony ground.

pedregoso,-a adj stony, rocky.

pedrera f quarry.

pedrería f gems pl.

pedrisco m hail(storm).

pedrusco m rough stone.

pega f fam (dificultad) snag. ●de ~, sham, worthless; **poner pegas a todo,** to find fault with everything.

pegadizo,-a adj sticky, adhesive. 2 (canción) catchy.

pegajoso,-a adj sticky, clammy.

pegar(se) [7] t-i (con goma) to glue, stick. 2 (atar) to tie, fasten. 3 (golpear) to hit. — 4 t (fuego) to set. — 5 p to stick (together). 6 (golpearse) to come to blows.

peinado m hair style.

peinar(se) t to comb (one's hair). ●fig ~ canas, to be old.

peine m comb.

peineta f ornamental comb.

peladilla f sugared almond.

pelado,-a adj bald, bare. 2 (cabeza) hairless. 3 (terreno) barren, treeless. 4 fam (sin dinero) penniless. — 5 m fam haircut.

pelagatos m inv fam poor devil.

pelaje m (de animal) coat, fur.

pelar(se) t to cut/shave the hair of. 2 (ave) to pluck. 3 (fruta etc.) to peel. — 4 p (perder pelo) to lose the hair. 5 (cortarse el pelo) to get one's hair cut.

peldaño m step.

pelea f fight, quarrel.

pelear(se) i-p to fight, quarrel; (a golpes) to come to blows.

pelele m straw puppet. 2 fig puppet.

peletería f fur shop, furrier's.

peletero,-a m,f furrier.

peliagudo,-a adj difficult, tricky.

pelícano m pelican.

película f film. ■ ~ del oeste, western; ~ muda, silent movie.

peligrar i to be in danger.

peligro m danger.

peligroso,-a adj dangerous.

pelirrojo,-a adj red-haired. — 2 m,f redhead.

pellejo m (piel) skin. 2 (odre) wineskin. ●salvar el ~, to save one's skin.

pellizcar [1] t to pinch, nip.

pellizco m pinch, nip.

pelo m hair. 2 (de barba) whisker. 3 (de animal) coat, fur. ●fig no tener pelos en la lengua, to be speak one's mind; fig tomar el ~ a algn., to pull sb.'s leg.

pelota f ball. ●fam en pelotas, naked. ■ ~ vasca, pelota.

pelotera f fam dispute, quarrel.

pelotilla f small ball. ●fam hacer la ~, to fawn on.

pelotón m squad.

peltre m pewter.

peluca f wig.

peluche m plush.

peludo,-a adj hairy.

peluquería f (de mujeres) hairdresser's (shop); (de hombres) barber's (shop).

peluquero,-a m,f (de mujeres) hairdresser; (de hombres) barber.

pelusa f fluff.

pelvis f pelvis.

pena f (castigo) penalty, punishment. 2 (tristeza) grief, sorrow. 3 (lástima) pity. 4 (dificultad) hardship, trouble. 5 AM (vergüenza) shame. ●a duras penas, with a great difficulty; dar ~, to arouse pity; valer la ~, to be worth while. ■ ~ capital, capital punishment.

penacho m tuft (of feathers), crest.

penal adj penal. — 2 m penitentiary.

penalidad f trouble, hardship.

penalizar [4] t to penalize.

penar t (castigar) to punish, penalize. — 2 i (padecer) to suffer, grieve.

pendenciero,-a adj quarrelsome.

pender i to hang, dangle. 2 fig to depend (on).

pendiente adj hanging. 2 (por resolver) pending. — 3 f slope, incline. — 4 m earring. ●estar ~ de, to be waiting for.

pendón m banner, standard.

péndulo m pendulum.

pene m penis.

penetración f penetration. 2 (perspicacia) insight.

penetrante adj penetrating. 2 (perspicaz) acute.

penetrar t gen to penetrate. 2 (líquido) to permeate. 3 fig to grasp, understand. — 4 i to penetrate (en, in). 5 (entrar) to get (en, in). 6 fig to break, pierce.

penicilina f penicillin.

península f peninsula.

peninsular adj peninsular.

penique m penny.

penitencia f REL penance. 2 (virtud) penitence. 3 fam (pesadez) pain, bore.

penitenciaría f penitentiary.

penitente adj-mf penitent.

penoso,-a adj (doloroso) painful. 2 (trabajoso) laborious, hard.

pensado,-a *adj* thought-out. ●*mal* ~, evil-minded; *tener algo* ~, to have sth. planned/in mind.

pensador,-ra *adj* thinking. — 2 *m,f* thinker.

pensamiento *m* thought. 2 *(mente)* mind. 3 BOT pansy.

pensar [27] *t-i* gen to think (*en,* of/about; *sobre,* over/about). — 2 *t (considerar)* to consider. 3 *(imaginar)* to imagine. 4 *(tener la intención)* to intend.

pensativo,-a *adj* pensive, thoughtful.

pensión *f (dinero)* pension, allowance. 2 *(residencia)* boarding house. ■ *media* ~, half board; ~ *completa,* full board.

pensionado,-a *m,f* pensioner. — 2 *m* boarding school.

pensionista *mf (jubilado etc.)* pensioner. 2 *(residente)* boarder.

pentagrama *m* MÚS stave, staff.

Pentecostés *m* Pentecost.

penúltimo,-a *adj-m,f* penultimate.

penumbra *f* shadow.

penuria *f* shortage. 2 *(pobreza)* penury.

peña *f* rock, boulder. 2 *fam (de amigos)* group (of friends).

peñasco *m* large rock, crag.

peñón *m* craggy rock.

peón *m (trabajador)* unskilled labourer. 2 *(juguete)* spinning-top. 3 *(damas)* man. 4 *(ajedrez)* pawn. ■ ~ *caminero,* roadmender; ~ *de albañil,* hodman.

peonza *f* whipping-top.

peor *adj-adv (comparativo)* worse: *tu coche es* ~ *que el mío,* your car is worse than mine. 2 *(superlativo)* worst. ●*en el* ~ *de los casos,* at worst; ~ *es nada,* it's better than nothing.

pepino *m* cucumber. ●*fam me importa un* ~, I don't give a damn.

pepita *f (de fruta)* seed, pip. 2 *(de metal)* nugget.

pequeñez *f (de tamaño)* smallness. 2 *(insignificancia)* trifle.

pequeño,-a *adj* little, small. 2 *(joven)* young. — 3 *m,f* child. ●*de* ~, as a child; *ser el* ~, to be the youngest.

pera *f* pear.

peral *m* pear tree.

percal *m* percale.

percance *m* mishap.

percatarse *p* to notice (*de,* -).

percepción *f* perception.

perceptible *adj* perceptible, noticeable.

percha *f* perch. 2 *(de ropa)* hanger; *(fijo)* rack.

perchero *m* clothes rack.

percibir *t (notar)* to perceive, notice. 2 *(impuestos)* to collect.

percusión *f* percussion.

percusor, percutor *m* hammer, striker.

perder(se) [28] *t* gen to lose. 2 *(malgastar)* to waste. 3 *(tren etc.)* to miss. 4 *(arruinar)* to be the ruin of. 5 *(empeorar)* to get worse. 6 *fig (color)* to fade. — 7 *p* to go astray, get lost. 8 *(fruta etc.)* to be spoiled. 9 *(arruinarse)* to become ruined. ●*echar a* ~, to spoil; ~ *de vista,* to lose sight of; *salir perdiendo,* to come off worst.

perdición *f (moral)* perdition. 2 *(ruina)* loss, ruin.

pérdida *f* loss. 2 *(de tiempo)* waste. ●COM *pérdidas y ganancias,* profit and loss.

perdido,-a *adj* gen lost. 2 *(desorientado)* mislaid. 3 *(desperdiciado)* wasted. 4 *(bala)* stray. 5 *(vicioso)* vicious. — 6 *m,f* vicious person. — 7 *perdidamente adv* madly, desperately, hopelessly. ●*estar loco,-a* ~ *por,* to be madly in love with.

perdigón *m* pellet. 2 ZOOL young partridge.

perdiz *f* partridge.

perdón *m* pardon, forgiveness. ●*con* ~, by your leave; *pedir* ~, to apologize; ¡~!, sorry!

perdonar *t* to pardon, forgive. 2 *(deuda)* to remit. 3 *(excusar)* to excuse.

perdurar *t* to last, endure.

perecedero,-a *adj* perishable.

perecer [43] *i* to perish, die.

peregrinación *f*, **peregrinaje** *m* pilgrimage.

peregrinar *i* to go on a pilgrimage.

peregrino,-a *adj* travelling. 2 *(ave)* migratory. 3 *fig (raro)* strange, rare. — 4 *m,f* REL pilgrim.

perejil *m* parsley.

perenne *adj* perennial, perpetual.

perentorio,-a *adj* peremptory, urgent.

pereza *f* laziness, idleness. ●*tener* ~, to be/feel lazy.

perezoso,-a *adj* lazy, idle. — 2 *m,f* lazy person, idler. — 3 *m* ZOOL sloth.

perfección *f* perfection. ●*a la* ~, perfectly.

perfeccionar *t* to perfect. 2 *(mejorar)* to improve.

perfecto,-a *adj* perfect.

perfidia *f* perfidy.

pérfido,-a *adj* perfidious. — 2 *m,f* traitor.

perfil *m* gen profile. 2 *(silueta)* outline. ●*de* ~, in profile.

perfilar(se) *t* to profile. **2** *(dar forma)* to outline. — **3** *p fig (destacarse)* to stand out.

perforación *f* perforation. **2** TÉC drilling, boring. **3** *(agujero)* hole.

perforadora *f* drill.

perforar *t* to perforate. **2** TÉC to drill, bore.

perfumar *t* to perfume, scent.

perfume *m* perfume, scent.

perfumería *f* perfumery.

pergamino *m* parchment.

pericia *f* expertise, skill.

periferia *f gen* periphery. **2** *(afueras)* outskirts *pl*.

perifollo *m* BOT common chervil. **2** *pl fam (adornos)* frills, trimmings.

perilla *f* goatee. ●*fam de ~,* just right.

perímetro *m* perimeter.

periódico,-a *adj* periodic(al). — **2** *m* newspaper.

periodismo *m* journalism.

periodista *mf* journalist.

periodístico,-a *adj* journalistic.

periodo, período *m* period.

peripecia *f* vicissitude, incident.

periquito *m* parakeet.

perito,-a *adj-m* expert.

perjudicar [1] *t (a persona)* to damage; *(a cosa)* to harm.

perjudicial *adj* harmful.

perjuicio *m (moral)* injury; *(material)* damage. ●*en ~ de,* to the detriment to; *sin ~ de,* without prejudice to.

perjurar *i* to commit perjury.

perjurio *m* perjury.

perjuro,-a *adj* perjured. — **2** *m,f* perjurer.

perla *f* pearl. **2** *fig* gem. ●*fam de perlas,* just right.

permanecer [43] *i* to remain, stay.

permanencia *f (estancia)* stay. **2** *(continuidad)* permanence.

permanente *adj* permanent, lasting. — **2** *f (del pelo)* permanent wave.

permeable *adj* permeable, porous.

permiso *m* permission. **2** *(documento)* permit. **3** MIL leave. ●*con su ~,* by your leave. ■ *~ de conducir,* driving licence.

permitir(se) *t* to permit, allow, let. — **2** *p* to take the liberty of. ●*poder ~se,* to be able to afford.

permuta *f* exchange.

permutable *adj* exchangeable.

permutar *t* to exchange. **2** MAT to permute.

pernicioso,-a *adj* pernicious, harmful.

pernil *m* ham.

perno *m* bolt.

pernoctar *i* to spend the night.

pero *conj* but. — **2** *m* objection, fault. ●*poner peros,* to find fault.

perogrullada *f* platitude.

perorar *i* to deliver a speech.

perorata *f* long-winded speech.

perpendicular *adj-f* perpendicular.

perpetrar *t* to perpetrate, commit.

perpetuar(se) [11] *t* to perpetuate. — **2** *p* to be perpetuated.

perpetuidad *f* perpetuity.

perpetuo,-a *adj* perpetual, everlasting.

perplejidad *f* perplexity.

perplejo,-a *adj* perplexed.

perra *f* ZOOL bitch. **2** *fam (pataleta)* tantrum. **3** *pl fam* money *sing*.

perrera *f* kennel.

perrería *f fam* dirty trick.

perro,-a *m,f* ZOOL dog. **2** *fam (persona)* rotter. ●*"cuidado con el ~",* "beware of the dog".

persecución *f* pursuit. **2** *(represión)* persecution.

perseguir [56] *t* to pursue, chase. **2** *fig (seguir)* to follow. **3** *fig (pretender)* to be after.

perseverancia *f* perseverance.

perseverante *adj* persevering.

perseverar *i* to persevere, persist.

persiana *f* Venetian blind.

persignarse *p* to cross o.s.

persistencia *f* persistence.

persistente *adj* persistent.

persistir *i* to persist, persevere.

persona *f* person. ●*en ~,* in person.

personaje *m (estrella)* celebrity. **2** CINEM TEAT character.

personal *adj* personal. — **2** *m* personnel, staff.

personalidad *f* personality.

personarse *p* to go/appear in person.

personificar [1] *t* to personify.

perspectiva *f* perspective. **2** *(apariencia)* appearance. **3** *(vista)* view.

perspicacia *f* perspicacity.

perspicaz *adj* perspicacious.

persuadir(se) *i* to persuade, convince. — **2** *p* to be persuaded/convinced.

persuasión *f* persuasion.

persuasivo,-a *adj* persuasive.

pertenecer [43] *i* to belong (*a,* to). **2** *(concernir)* to concern.

pertenencia *f (bienes)* property. **2** *(afiliación)* membership.

perteneciente *adj* belonging, pertaining.

pértiga *f* pole. ■ *salto de ~,* pole vault.

pertinaz *adj* obstinate, stubborn.

pertinente *adj* pertinent, relevant.

pertrechar *t* to supply (*de,* with).

pertrechos *mpl* equipment *sing.* 2 MIL supplies.

perturbación *f* disturbance. ■ *~ mental,* mental disorder.

perturbado,-a *adj* disturbed. 2 *(loco)* insane.

perturbar *t* to disturb, perturb, upset.

perversidad *f* perversity.

perversión *f* perversion.

perverso,-a *adj* perverse.

pervertir(se) [35] *t* to pervert. – 2 *p* to become perverted.

pesa *f* weight.

pesadez *f* heaviness. 2 *(aburrimiento)* tiresomeness. 3 *(torpeza)* clumsiness.

pesadilla *f* nightmare.

pesado,-a *adj* heavy, weighty. 2 *(aburrido)* dull, tiresome, boring. 3 *(torpe)* clumsy. 4 *(sueño)* deep. ●*ponerse ~,* to be a nuissance.

pesadumbre *f* sorrow, grief.

pésame *m* condolence, expression of sympathy.

pesar *t* to weigh. – 2 *i* to be heavy. 3 *(sentir)* to be sorry, regret. – 4 *m (pena)* sorrow, grief. 5 *(arrepentimiento)* regret. ●*a ~ de,* in spite of.

pesaroso,-a *adj* sorry, regretful.

pesca *f* fishing.

pescadería *f* fishmonger's (shop), fish shop.

pescadero,-a *m,f* fishmonger.

pescado *m* CULIN fish.

pescador,-ra *adj* fishing. – 2 *m* fisherman.

pescar [1] *t* to catch. ●*ir a ~,* to go fishing.

pescuezo *m* neck.

pesebre *m (para animales)* manger, stall. 2 *(de Navidad)* crib.

peseta *f* peseta.

pesimismo *m* pessimism.

pesimista *adj* pessimistic. – 2 *mf* pessimist.

pésimo,-a *adj* abominable, very bad.

peso *m* weight. 2 *(balanza)* scales *pl,* balance. 3 *fig* load, burden.

pespunte *m* backstitch.

pespuntear *t* to backstitch.

pesquero,-a *adj* fishing. – 2 *m* fishing boat.

pesquisa *f* inquiry, investigation.

pestaña *f* eyelash. 2 TÉC flange.

pestañear *i* to wink, blink.

pestañeo *m* winking, blinking.

peste *f (epidemia)* plague. 2 *(mal olor)* stink, stench. 3 *(cosa mala)* pest. ●*echar pestes,* to curse.

pestilencia *f* pestilence. 2 *(mal olor)* stink, stench.

pestillo *m* bolt.

petaca *f (de cigarrillos)* cigarette case. 2 *(de tabaco)* tobacco pouch.

pétalo *m* petal.

petardo *m* MIL petard. 2 *(de verbena)* firecracker, banger. 3 *fam (persona fea)* ugly person.

petición *f* petition, request. ●*a ~ de,* on/ at request of.

petirrojo *m* robin.

peto *m* HIST breastplate. 2 *(prenda)* bib.

pétreo,-a *adj* stony, rocky.

petrificar(se) [1] *t* to petrify. – 2 *p* to become petrified.

petróleo *m* petroleum, oil.

petrolero *m* oil tanker.

petulancia *f* vanity.

petulante *adj* vain

pez *m* fish. ■ *fig ~ gordo,* big shot.

pezón *m* nipple.

pezuña *f* hoof.

piadoso,-a *adj* pious, devout. 2 *(clemente)* merciful, clement.

piano *m* piano. ■ *~ de cola,* grand piano; *~ vertical,* upright piano.

piar [13] *i* to chirp.

piara *f* herd of pigs.

pica *f* pike. 2 *(de toros)* goad. 3 *(naipes)* spade.

picadero *m* riding school.

picadillo *m* mince.

picado,-a *adj* perforated, pricked. 2 CULIN chopped; *(carne)* minced. 3 *(tabaco)* cut. 4 *(mar)* choppy. 5 *(diente)* decayed. 6 *fam (ofendido)* offended. – 7 *m* AER dive. ●*caer en ~,* to plummet.

picador *m* mounted bullfighter.

picadura *f (de insecto, serpiente)* bite; *(de abeja, avispa)* sting. 2 *(tabaco)* cut tobacco.

picaflor *m* hummingbird.

picante *adj (sabor)* hot, spicy. 2 *fig (pícaro)* spicy.

picapedrero *m* stonecutter.

picaporte *m (llamador)* door knocker. 2 *(pomo)* door handle.

picardía *f* naughtiness. 2 *(astucia)* slyness.

pícaro,-a *adj* knavish, roguish. **2** *(malicioso)* mischievous. **3** *(astuto)* sly. **– 4** *m,f* slyboots.

picar(se) [1] *t* to prick, pierce. **2** *(toro)* to goad. **3** *(insecto)* to bite; *(abeja, avispa)* to sting. **4** *(algo de comer)* to nibble. **5** CULIN to chop; *(carne)* to mince. **– 6** *t-i* *(sentir escozor)* to itch. **– 7** *p (fruta)* to begin to rot. **8** *(diente)* to begin to decay. **9** *(mar)* to get choppy. **10** *fig (enfadarse)* to take offense. ●*fig* **~ alto,** to aim high.

picazón *f* itch(ing).

pichón *m* pigeon.

pico *m (aves)* beak. **2** *fam (boca)* mouth. **3** *(punta)* corner. **4** *(de montaña)* peak. **5** *(herramienta)* pick(axe). **6** *(cantidad)* small surplus: *tres mil y* **~,** three thousand odd. ●*fam* **callar el ~,** to keep one's mouth shut.

picotazo *m (de pájaro)* peck. **2** *(de insecto)* bite; *(de abeja, avispa)* sting.

picotear *t-i* to peck (at).

pictórico,-a *adj* pictorial.

pie *m* ANAT foot. **2** *(fondo)* bottom. **3** *(base)* base, stand. ●*a* **~,** on foot; *al* **~** *de la letra,* word for word; *dar* **~,** to give occasion for; *en* **~,** standing; *fig no tener ni pies ni cabeza,* to be absurd.

piedad *f* piety. **2** *(caridad)* pity, mercy. ●*¡por* **~!,** for pity's sake!

piedra *f* stone. **2** METEOR hail(stone). ■ **~ angular,** cornerstone; **~ clave,** keystone; **~ de toque,** touchstone.

piel *f* skin. **2** *(de animal)* hide, pelt. **3** *(cuero)* leather. **4** *(pelaje)* fur. ■ **~ roja,** redskin.

pienso *m* fodder.

pierna *f* leg. ●*fam* **dormir a ~ suelta,** to sleep like a log.

pieza *f* piece, fragment. **2** TEAT play. **3** *(de ajedrez, damas)* piece, man. **4** AM *(habitación)* room. ■ *fam* **buena ~,** rogue.

pifia *f* blunder.

pigmentación *f* pigmentation.

pigmento *m* pigment.

pigmeo,-a *adj-m,f* pygmy.

pijama *m* pyjamas.

pila *f (recipiente)* stone trough/basin. **2** *(de bautismo)* font. **3** *fam (montón)* pile, heap. **4** ELEC battery. **5** AM *(fuente)* fountain. ■ *nombre de* **~,** first name.

pilar *m* pillar, column.

pilastra *f* pilaster.

píldora *f* pill. ●*fig* **dorar la ~,** to sugar the pill.

pileta *f* AM swimming pool.

pillaje *m* plunder, sack.

pillar *t (coger)* to catch. **2** *(robar)* to plunder.

pillo,-a *m,f* rogue, rascal.

pilón *m* basin.

piloto *m* pilot.

piltrafa *f* skinny meat. **2** *pl (restos)* scraps.

pimentón *m* red pepper.

pimienta *f (especia)* pepper.

pimiento *m* (green/red) pepper. ■ **~ morrón,** sweet pepper.

pimpollo *m* BOT shoot, sprout. **2** *fig* attractive youth.

pináculo *m* pinnacle.

pinar *m* pine grove.

pincel *m* (artist's) brush.

pincelada *f* brush stroke.

pinchar *t* to puncture.

pinchazo *m* puncture. **2** *(inyección)* jab.

pinche,-a *m,f* kitchen boy/girl.

pincho *m* thorn, prickle.

pineda *f* pine wood.

pingajo *m* *pey* rag, tatter.

pingüino *m* penguin.

pino *m* pine (tree).

pintalabios *m inv* lipstick.

pintar(se) *t* to paint. **2** *fig (describir)* to describe. **– 3** *p* to make up one's face.

pintor,-ra *m,f* painter. ■ **~ de brocha gorda,** house painter.

pintoresco,-a *adj* picturesque.

pintura *f (arte)* painting. **2** *(color, bote)* paint. **3** *(cuadro)* picture.

pinzas *fpl* tweezers, tongs. **2** *(de cangrejo)* claws.

piña *f (fruta)* pineapple. **2** *fig* cluster.

piñón *m* pine nut. **2** TÉC pinion.

pío,-a *adj* pious. **2** *(compasivo)* merciful.

piojo *m* louse.

piojoso,-a *adj* lousy.

pipa *f (de tabaco)* pipe. **2** *(de fruta)* pip, seed.

pipí *m fam* wee-wee.

pique *m* pique, resentment. ●*irse a* **~,** to sink; *fig* to fail.

piquete *m* picket.

piragua *f* pirogue, canoe.

pirámide *f* pyramid.

pirarse *p fam* to beat it.

pirata *m* pirate.

piratería *f* piracy.

pirómano,-a *adj* pyromaniacal. **– 2** *m,f* pyromaniac.

piropear *t* to compliment.

piropo *m* compliment, piece of flattery. ●*echar un* **~ a,** to pay a compliment to.

pirotecnia f pyrotechnics.

pirrarse p arg to long (*por,* for).

pirueta f pirouette, caper.

pis m fam wee-wee.

pisada f footstep. 2 *(huella)* footprint.

pisapapeles m inv paperweight.

pisar t to tread on, step on.

piscina f swimming-pool.

Piscis m inv Pisces.

piscolabis m inv snack.

piso m floor. 2 *(apartamento)* flat, apartment.

pisotear t to trample on.

pisotón m stamp on the foot.

pista f *(rastro)* trail, track. 2 *(indicio)* clue. 3 DEP track; *(de tenis)* court; *(de esquí)* slope, ski run. 4 *(de circo)* ring. 5 AER runway, landing field. ●*seguir la ~,* to be on the trail of. ■ ~ *de baile,* dance floor.

pistacho m pistachio (nut).

pistola f pistol.

pistolera f holster.

pistolero m gunman, bandit.

pistón m piston.

pitar i to blow a whistle, whistle at. — 2 t *(abuchear)* to boo at. — 3 t-i AM *(fumar)* to smoke.

pitillera f cigarette case.

pitillo m cigarette.

pito m whistle. 2 *(abucheo)* booing. ●*fam me importa un ~,* I don't give a damn.

pitonisa f fortune teller.

pitorrearse p fam to mock.

pivote m pivot.

pizarra f slate. 2 *(de escuela)* blackboard.

pizca f bit, jot, whit: *no sabe ni ~,* he/she hasn't an inkling.

pizpireta adj brisk, lively.

placa f plaque.

placentero,-a adj pleasant.

placer [76] t to please, content. — 2 m pleasure. 2 *(voluntad)* will.

placidez f placidity.

plácido,-a adj placid, calm.

plaga f plague, pest.

plagar [7] t to plague, infest.

plagiar [12] t to plagiarize.

plagio m plagiarism.

plan m plan, project. 2 *(dibujo)* drawing.

plana f *(de periódico)* page. 2 *(llanura)* plain.

plancha f *(de metal)* plate, sheet. 2 *(para planchar)* iron. ●*fam hacer una ~,* to put one's foot in it.

planchado m ironing.

planchar t to iron, press.

planeador m glider.

planear t to plan. — 2 i AER to glide.

planeta m planet.

planetario,-a adj planetary. — 2 m planetarium.

planicie f plain.

plano,-a adj plane. 2 *(llano)* flat, even. — 3 m *(superficie)* plane. 4 *(mapa)* plan, map. ●*levantar un ~,* to make a survey; *fig de ~,* openly. ■ *primer ~,* *(foto)* close-up; *(terreno)* foreground.

planta f BOT plant. 2 *(del pie)* sole. ■ *buena ~,* good looks; ~ *baja,* ground floor.

plantación f planting. 2 *(terreno)* plantation.

plantar(se) t to plant. 2 *(colocar)* to set up, place. 3 *(persona)* to stand up. — 4 p to stand firm. ●*dejar a uno plantado,* to keep someone waiting indefinitely.

planteamiento m *(exposición)* exposition. 2 *(de problema)* statement. 3 *(enfoque)* approach.

plantear t *(planear)* to plan, outline. 2 *(establecer)* to establish. 3 *(problema)* to state. 4 *(pregunta)* to pose, raise.

plantilla f *(de zapato)* insole. 2 *(patrón)* model, pattern. 3 *(personal)* staff.

plantón m dar un ~ a algn., to keep sb. waiting.

plañir [40] i to mourn.

plasma m plasma.

plasmar t to make, mould, shape.

plástico,-a adj-m plastic.

plata f silver. 2 AM money. ●*fam hablar en ~,* to speak frankly.

plataforma f platform.

plátano m banana. 2 *(árbol)* plane tree.

platea f orchestra stalls pl.

plateado,-a adj silver-plated. 2 *(color)* silvery.

platear t to silver, silver-plate.

platero,-a m,f silversmith.

plática f chat, talk.

platicar [1] i to chat, talk.

platillo m *(plato)* saucer. 2 *(de balanza)* pan. 3 MÚS cymbal. ■ ~ *volante,* flying saucer.

platino m platinum.

plato m plate, dish. 2 CULIN dish. 3 *(en comida)* course.

platónico,-a adj platonic.

plausible adj plausible.

playa f beach.

plaza f square. 2 *(mercado)* market-place. 3 *(fortaleza)* fortress. 4 *(empleo)* position.

5 *(ciudad)* town, city. ■ ~ *de toros,* bullring.

plazo *m* term, due date. ●*a plazos,* by instalments.

pleamar *f* high tide/water.

plebe *f* common people.

plebeyo,-a *adj-m,f* plebeian.

plebiscito *m* plebiscite.

plegable *adj* folding.

plegaria *f* prayer.

plegar(se) [48] *t* to fold. – **2** *p* to bend. **3** *fig (rendirse)* to yield, submit.

pleitear *t* to litigate.

pleito *m* litigation, lawsuit. **2** AM *(agarrón)* fight, quarrel.

plenilunio *m* full moon.

plenitud *f* fullness.

pleno,-a *adj* full, complete: *en* ~ *día,* in broad day. – **2** *m* full assembly.

pleuresía *f* pleurisy.

pliego *m* sheet of paper. **2** *(documento)* document. ■ ~ *de condiciones,* specifications (for a contract).

pliegue *m* fold. **2** COST pleat.

plomada *f* plumb line.

plomero *m* plumber.

plomo *m* lead. **2** ELEC fuse. **3** *fig* boring person. ●*a* ~, vertically; *caer a* ~, to fall flat.

pluma *f* feather. **2** *(de escribir)* quill pen; *(estilográfica)* fountain pen.

plumaje *m* plumage.

plumero *m* feather duster. **2** *(cresta)* crest, plume.

plumilla *f* nib.

plural *adj-m* plural.

pluralidad *f* plurality.

plus *m* extra (pay), bonus.

plusvalía *f* appreciation.

población *f* population. **2** *(ciudad)* city, town; *(pueblo)* village.

poblado,-a *adj* populated. **2** *(barba)* thick. – **3** *m* *(pueblo)* village.

poblar(se) *t* to people. **2** *(de árboles)* to plant with. – **3** *p* to become peopled.

pobre *adj-mf* poor (person).

pobreza *f* poverty.

pocilga *f* pigsty.

poco,-a *adj* little. **2** *pl* few: *unos pocos,* a few. – **3** *adv* little, not much. ●*a* ~ *de,* shortly after; *dentro de* ~, soon, presently; ~ *a* ~, little by little; ~ *más o menos,* more or less; *por* ~, nearly; *tener en* ~, to hold cheap.

podar *t* to prune.

poder [77] *t-i* to be able (to), can. – **2** *i* to be possible, may, might: *puede que*

llueva, it may rain. – **3** *m* power. **4** *(fuerza)* force, strength. ●*estar en el* ~, to be in the office; *no* ~ *con,* not to be able to cope with, *no* ~ *más,* to be unable to do more. ▲ **2** *used only in the 3rd pers. It does not take a subject.*

poderío *m* power.

poderoso,-a *adj* powerful.

podredumbre *f* rottenness.

podrido,-a *adj* rotten. **2** *fig* corrupt.

poema *m* poem.

poesía *f* poetry. **2** *(poema)* poem.

poeta *mf* poet.

poético,-a *adj* poetic.

poetisa *f* poetess.

polar *adj* polar. **2** ELEC pole. ■ *estrella* ~, pole star.

polea *f* pulley.

polémico,-a *adj* polemic(al). – **2** *f* polemics, dispute.

polen *m* pollen.

polichinela *m* Punch.

policía *f* police (force). – **2** *mf m* policeman, *f* policewoman. ■ ~ *secreta,* secret police.

policíaco,-a *adj* police. ■ *novela policíaca,* detective story.

poligamia *f* polygamy.

polígamo,-a *adj* polygamous. – **2** *m* polygamist.

polígloto,-a *adj-m,f* polyglot.

polilla *f* (clothes) moth.

pólipo *m* polyp.

polisílabo,-a *adj* polysyllabic.

politécnico,-a *adj* polytechnic.

política *f* politics. **2** *(manera)* policy.

político,-a *adj* politic(al). **2** *(cortés)* tactful. **3** *(parentesco)* -in-law: *padre* ~, father-in-law. – **4** *m,f* politician.

póliza *f* COM certificate, policy. ■ ~ *de seguros,* insurance policy.

polla *f* ZOOL young hen. **2*** *(órgano)* prick*.

pollera *f* AM skirt.

pollería *f* poultry shop.

pollo *m* chicken. **2** *fam (joven)* young man.

polo *m* pole. **2** DEP polo.

poltrona *f* easy chair.

polvareda *f* cloud of dust.

polvera *f* powder bowl.

polvo *m* dust. **2** *(para maquillar)* powder. **3*** screw*, fuck*.

pólvora *f* gunpowder.

polvoriento,-a *adj* dusty.

polvorín *m* powder magazine.

pomada *f* ointment.

pomo *m (de puerta)* knob. **2** *(de arma)* pommel.

pompa *f (de jabón)* bubble. **2** *(ostentación)* pomp. ■ *pompas fúnebres,* funeral.

pomposidad *f* pomposity.

pomposo,-a *adj* pompous.

pómulo *m* cheekbone.

ponche *m* punch.

ponderación *f* careful consideration.

ponderado,-a *adj* balanced, steady.

ponderar *t* to ponder, consider, think over. **2** *(alabar)* to praise highly.

poner(se) [78] *t gen* to place, put, set. **2** *(instalar)* to install. **3** *(huevos)* to lay. **4** *(suponer)* to suppose: *pongamos que es así,* let's suppose that it is so. **5** *(dinero)* to place, pay. **6** *(dar nombre)* to name, call. **7** *(~ + adj)* to make: *me pone enfermo,* it makes me sick. **8** CINEM TV to show. **9** *(carta etc.)* to send. **10** *(deber, trabajo)* to give, assign. − **11** *p* to place/put o.s. **12** *(sombrero, prenda)* to put on. **13** *(sol)* to set. **14** *(volverse)* to become, get, turn. **15** *(al teléfono)* to answer. ●*~ a,* to start/begin to; ~ *al corriente,* to get informed; ~ *al día,* to bring up to date; ~ *de manifiesto,* to make evident; ~ *de relieve,* to emphasize; ~ *en libertad,* to set free; ~ *en práctica,* to carry out; ~ *por las nubes,* to praise to the skies; ~ *reparos,* to make objections; ~*se a malas con algn.,* to fall out with sb.; ~*se de acuerdo,* to agree; ~*se perdido,-a,* to get dirty; ~*se en pie,* to stand up; *fam* ~ *como un trapo,* to pull to pieces. ▲ *pp puesto,-a.*

pongo *pres ind* → **poner.**

poniente *m* west. **2** *(viento)* west wind.

pontífice *m* pontiff, pope.

ponzoña *f* poison.

popa *f* poop, stern. ●*en/a ~,* aft.

populacho *m* mob.

popular *adj* popular.

popularidad *f* popularity.

popularizar [4] *t* to popularize.

populoso,-a *adj* populous.

por *prep gen* for. **2** *(causa)* because of. **3** *(tiempo)* at, for. **4** *(lugar)* along, in, on, by. **5** *(medio)* by: *enviar ~ avión,* to send by air. **6** *(autoría)* by: *escrito por él,* written by him. **7** *(distribución)* per: *cinco ~ ciento,* five per cent. **8** *(con pasiva)* by: *comprado por ella,* bought by her. ●*estar ~, (a punto de)* to be on the point of; *estar ~ hacer,* to remain to be done, not to have been done; ~ *aquí,* around here; *¡~ Dios!,* for heaven's sake!; ~ *lo*

visto, apparently; ~ *más/mucho que,* however much; ~ *mí,* as I am concerned; *¿~ qué?,* why?; ~ *supuesto,* of course; ~ *(lo) tanto,* therefore.

porcelana *f* porcelain. **2** *(vajilla)* china.

porcentaje *m* percentage.

porche *m* porch.

porción *f* portion, part. **2** *(cuota)* share.

pordiosero,-a *m,f* beggar.

porfía *f* insistence, obstinacy.

porfiar [13] *i* to insist, persist.

pormenor *m* detail.

pornografía *f* pornography.

pornográfico,-a *adj* pornographic.

poroso,-a *adj* porous.

porque *conj (de causa)* because: *no voy ~ no quiero,* I'm not going because I don't want to. **2** *(de finalidad)* in order that.

porqué *m* cause, reason.

porquería *f* dirt, filth.

porra *f* cudgel, club. ●*fam mandar a la ~,* to send packing.

porrazo *m* blow, knock.

porro *m* leek. **2** *arg* joint.

porrón *m* glass flask.

portaaviones *m inv* aircraft carrier.

portada *f* ARQ façade. **2** *(de libro)* cover.

portador,-ra *m,f* carrier, bearer, holder.

portaequipajes *m inv* luggage rack.

portal *m* doorway. **2** ARQ *(porche)* porch; *(zaguán),* entrance hall.

portalámparas *m inv* lamp-holder.

portamonedas *m inv* purse.

portarse *p* to behave, act.

portátil *adj* portable.

portavoz *mf* spokesman.

portazo *m* bang/slam (of a door).

porte *m* portage, carriage. **2** COM freight. **3** *(donaire)* bearing. **4** *(aspecto)* appearance. ■ ~ *pagado,* portage prepaid.

portento *m* wonder.

portentoso,-a *adj* prodigious, portentous.

portería *f* porter's lodge. **2** DEP goal.

portero,-a *mf* doorkeeper, porter. **2** DEP goalkeeper.

pórtico *m* portico.

porvenir *m* future.

pos *en ~ de, adv* after, in pursuit of.

posada *f* lodging-house, inn.

posadero,-a *m,f* innkeeper. − **2** *fpl fam* buttocks.

posar(se) *i* ART to pose. − **2** *p (pájaro)* to alight, perch, sit. **3** *(sedimento)* to settle.

posdata *f* postscript.

poseedor,-ra *m,f* owner, possessor.

poseer [61] *t* to own, possess.
posesión *f* possession.
posesionar(se) *t* to give possession. – 2 *p* to take possession (*de,* of).
posesivo,-a *adj-m* possessive.
posguerra *f* postwar period.
posibilidad *f* possibility. 2 *pl* (*dinero*) means.
posible *adj* possible. 2 *mpl* (*dinero*) means. ●*hacer todo lo* ~, to do one's best.
posición *f* position.
positivo,-a *adj* positive.
poso *m* sediment, dregs *pl*.
posponer [78] *t* to postpone, delay, put off. ▲ *pp* *pospuesto,-a*.
posta *f* (*de caballos*) relay. ●*a* ~, on purpose.
postal *adj* postal. – 2 *f* postcard. ■ *servicio* ~, postal service.
poste *m* post, pillar. ■ ~ *indicador,* signpost.
postergar [7] *t* to delay, postpone. 2 (*perjudicar*) to disregard someone's rights.
posteridad *f* posterity.
posterior *adj* back, rear. 2 (*tiempo*) later. – 3 *posteriormente adv* afterwards, later on.
postigo *m* small door. 2 (*de ventana*) (window) shutter.
postín *m fam* airs *pl*, importance. ●*darse* ~, to put on airs.
postizo,-a *adj* false. – 2 *m* switch (of hair).
postor *m* bidder.
postración *f* prostration.
postrar(se) *t-p* to prostrate (o.s.).
postre *m* dessert. ●*a la* ~, at last, finally.
postrero,-a *adj* last.
postrimerías *fpl* last (few) years *pl*.
postulante *m,f* petitioner, applicant.
postular *t* to postulate. 2 (*suplicar*) to beg, demand.
póstumo,-a *adj* posthumous.
postura *f* posture, position. 2 (*actitud*) bid.
potable *adj* drinkable.
potaje *m* stew.
pote *m* pot, jar.
potencia *f* potency. 2 (*poder*) power. 3 (*fuerza*) strength. 4 (*país*) power.
potencial *adj-m* potential.
potentado *m* potentate.
potente *adj* potent, powerful, mighty. 2 (*fuerte*) strong, vigorous.

potestad *f* power.
potestativo,-a *adj* optional.
potro,-a *m,f* colt, foal. – 2 *m* (*de tortura*) rack. – 3 *f fam* (*suerte*) luck. ●*tener potra,* to be lucky.
pozo *m* well. 2 (*mina*) shaft.
practicable *adj* practicable, feasible.
practicante *adj* practising. – 2 *m,f* doctor's assistant.
practicar [1] *t* to practice 2 (*hacer*) to make. – 3 *i* to practice.
práctico,-a *adj* practical. 2 (*hábil*) skilful, practised. – 3 *m* MAR pilot. – 4 *f* practice. 5 (*habilidad*) skill. 6 *pl* training. ●*poner en práctica,* to put into practice.
pradera *f* prairie, meadow.
prado *f* field, meadow, lawn.
preámbulo *m* preamble, preface.
prebenda *f* REL prebend. 2 (*sinecura*) sinecure.
precario,-a *adj* shaky, precarious.
precaución *f* precaution.
precaver(se) *t* to guard/provide against. – 2 *p* to be on one's guard.
precavido,-a *adj* cautious, wary.
precedente *adj* preceding, prior, foregoing. – 2 *m* precedent.
preceder *t-i* to precede, go ahead (*a,* of).
preceptivo,-a *adj* compulsory.
precepto *m* precept, rule; order. ■ *día de* ~, holiday.
preceptor,-ra *m,f* teacher, tutor.
preciado,-a *adj* valuable, precious.
preciar(se) [12] *t* to value, prize. – 2 *p* to be proud (*de,* of).
precintar *t* to seal with a strap.
precinto *m* strap, band.
precio *m* price. 2 *fig* (*valor*) value, worth. ●*fig no tener* ~, to be priceless.
precioso,-a *adj* precious. 2 (*bello*) beautiful.
precipicio *m* precipice.
precipitación *f* (*prisa*) rush, haste, hurry. 2 METEOR precipitation.
precipitado,-a *adj* hasty.
precipitar(se) *t* to precipitate, hasten, hurry. – 2 QUÍM to precipitate. – 3 *p* to be hasty/rash.
precisar *t* to fix, define. 2 (*necesitar*) to need. – 3 *i* to be necessary
precisión *f* precision, accuracy.
preciso,-a *adj* precise, exact, accurate. 2 (*necesario*) necessary: *es* ~, it is necessary. – 3 *precisamente adv* precisely, exactly. 4 (*justamente*) justo.
precocinado,-a *adj* precooked.

precoz *adj* precocious.
precursor,-ra *m,f* precursor.
predecesor,-ra *m,f* predecessor.
predecir [79] *t* to predict, foretell. ▲ *pp predicho,-a.*
predestinado,-a *adj* predestined.
prédica *f* sermon.
predicado *m* predicate.
predicador,-ra *m,f* preacher.
predicar [1] *t* to preach.
predicho,-a *pp* → **predecir**.
predilección *f* predilection.
predilecto,-a *adj* favourite.
predisponer [78] *t* to predispose. ▲ *pp predispuesto,-a.*
predisposición *f* predisposition.
predispuesto,-a *pp* → **predisponer**.
predominante *adj* predominant.
predominar *t* to predominate, prevail.
predominio *m* predominance.
preescolar *adj* pre-school.
prefabricado,-a *adj* prefabricated.
prefacio *m* preface.
preferencia *f* preference. ●AUTO ~ *(de paso),* right of way.
preferente *adj* preferential.
preferible *adj* preferable.
preferir [35] *t* to prefer: *yo preferiría no ir,* I'd rather not go.
prefijo *m* prefix. 2 *(telefónico)* code.
pregón *m* public announcement.
pregonar *t* to announce.
pregonero *m* town crier.
pregunta *f* question. ●*hacer una ~ a algn.,* to ask sb. a question.
preguntar(se) *t* to ask. − 2 *p* to wonder. ●*~ por algn.,* to ask after/about sb.
preguntón,-ona *m,f* nosey parker.
prehistórico,-a *adj* prehistoric.
prejuicio *m* prejudice.
prelado *m* prelate.
preliminar *adj-m* preliminary.
preludio *m* prelude.
prematrimonial *adj* premarital.
prematuro,-a *adj-m* premature (baby).
premeditación *f* premeditation. ●*con ~,* deliberately.
premeditado,-a *adj* deliberate.
premiar [12] *t (otorgar premio)* to award a prize *(a,* to). 2 *(recompersar)* to reward.
premio *m* prize. 2 *(recompensa)* reward.
premisa *f* premise.
premonición *f* premonition.
prenda *f (de vestir)* garment. 2 *(prueba)* token.

prendarse *p* to take a fancy *(de,* to).
prender(se) *t (agarrar)* to seize. 2 *(sujetar)* to attach; *(con agujas)* pin. 3 *(arrestar)* to arrest. 4 *(fuego)* to set. 5 AM to turn on the ligth. − 6 *i (planta)* to take root. 7 *(fuego etc.)* to catch. − 8 *p* to catch fire.
prensa *f* press.
prensar *t* to press.
preñado,-a *adj* pregnant.
preñar *t (mujer)* to make pregnant; *(animal)* to impregnate.
preocupación *f* worry.
preocupado,-a *adj* worried.
preocupar(se) *t-p* to worry.
preparación *f* preparation.
preparado,-a *adj* ready, prepared. − 2 *m (medicamento)* preparation.
preparar(se) *t* to prepare, get ready. − 2 *p* to get ready. 3 *(educarse)* to train.
preparativos *mpl* preparations, arrangements.
preponderante *adj* preponderant.
preposición *f* preposition.
prepotencia *f* power, dominance.
prepucio *m* foreskin.
prerrogativa *f* prerogative.
presa *f (acción)* capture. 2 *(cosa prendida)* prey. 3 *(embalse)* dam. ●*ser ~ de,* to be a victim of.
presagiar [12] *t* to predict, foretell.
presagio *m (señal)* omen. 2 *(adivinación)* premonition.
presbiterio *m* presbytery.
presbítero *m* priest.
prescindir *i* ~ *de,* to do without.
prescribir *t* to prescribe. ▲ *pp prescrito,-a.*
prescripción *f* prescription.
prescrito,-a *pp* → **prescribir**.
presencia *f* presence.
presencial *adj testigo* ~, eyewitness.
presenciar [12] *t* to be present at, witness.
presentación *f* presentation. 2 *(de personas)* introduction.
presentador,-ra *m,f* presenter, host.
presentar(se) *t* to present. 2 *(mostrar)* to display, show. 3 *(personas)* to introduce. − 4 *p (comparecer)* to present o.s.; *(candidato)* to stand. 5 *(ofrecerse)* to volunteer.
presente *adj-m* present. ●*hacer ~,* to remind of; *tener ~,* to bear in mind.
presentimiento *m* presentiment.

presentir [35] *t* to have a premonition of.

preservar *t* to preserve.

presidencia *f* presidency. **2** *(en reunión)* chairmanship.

presidente,-a *m,f* president. **2** *(en reunión)* *m* chairman, *f* chairwoman.

presidiario,-a *m,f* convict, prisoner.

presidio *m* prison, penitentiary.

presidir *t (reunión)* to chair. **2** *(país)* to be president of.

presilla *f* fastener.

presión *f* pressure. ■ ~ *arterial/sanguínea,* blood pressure.

presionar *t* to press. **2** *fig* to put pressure on.

preso,-a *adj* imprisoned. − **2** *m,f* prisoner.

prestación *f* service.

prestamista *mf* moneylender.

préstamo *m* loan.

prestar(se) *t (dejar prestado)* to lend, loan. **2** *(pedir prestado)* to borrow. **3** *(servicio)* to do, render. **4** *(ayuda)* to give. **5** *(atención)* to pay. **6** *(juramento)* to swear. − **7** *p (ofrecerse)* to lend o.s. **8** *(dar motivo)* to cause.

presteza *f* promptness.

prestidigitador,-ra *m,f* conjuror, magician.

prestigio *m* prestige.

prestigioso,-a *adj* prestigious.

presto,-a *adj (dispuesto)* ready. **2** *(rápido)* quick.

presumible *adj* probable.

presumido,-a *adj-m,f* vain (person).

presumir *t (suponer)* to presume, suppose. − **2** *i (vanagloriarse)* to be vain/conceited: *Pepe presume de guapo,* Pepe fancies himself.

presunción *f (suposición)* presumption. **2** *(vanidad)* conceit.

presunto,-a *adj* presumed, supposed.

presuntuoso,-a *adj* conceited, vain.

presuponer [78] *t* to presuppose. ▲ *pp* **presupuesto,-a.**

presupuestar *t* to budget for.

presupuesto,-a *pp* → **presuponer.** − **2** *m* FIN *(cómputo anticipado)* estimate; *(coste)* budget. **3** *(supuesto)* presupposition.

pretencioso,-a *adj-m,f* pretentious (person).

pretender *t* to *(querer)* to want to. **2** *(intentar)* to try to. **3** *(cortejar)* to court.

pretendiente,-a *m,f (enamorado)* suitor. **2** *(a cargo)* applicant.

pretensión *f* aim, aspiration. ●*tener muchas pretensiones,* to be pretentious.

pretérito,-a *adj* past. − **2** *m* preterite, past simple.

pretextar *t* to plead, allege.

pretexto *m* pretext, excuse.

prevalecer [43] *i* to prevail.

prevaler(se) [89] *i* to prevail. − **2** *p* to take advantage *(de,* of).

prevención *f* prevention. **2** *(medida)* precaution. **3** *(antipatía)* prejudice.

prevenir [90] *t (disponer)* to prepare. **2** *(prever)* to prevent. **3** *(advertir)* to warn.

preventivo,-a *adj* preventive.

prever [91] *t* to foresee, forecast. ▲ *pp* **previsto,-a.**

previo,-a *adj* previous, prior.

previsión *f (anticipación)* forecast. **2** *(precaución)* precaution.

previsor,-ra *adj* far-sighted.

previsto,-a *pp* → **prever.**

prieto,-a *adj* tight.

prima *f* bonus. **2** → **primo,-a 3.**

primacía *f* primacy.

primar *t (pagar)* to give a bonus to. − **2** *i* to be most important.

primario,-a *adj* primary.

primavera *f* spring. **2** BOT primrose.

primer *adj* → **primero,-a.** ▲ *Used in front of a sing masculine noun: primer día/día primero.*

primero,-a *adj-m,f* first. − **2** *adv* first. − **3** *f (clase)* first class. **4** AUTO first gear. ●*de primera,* great, first-class. ▲ → **primer.**

primicia *f* BOT first fruit. **2** *(noticia)* novelty.

primitivo,-a *adj* HIST primitive. **2** *(tosco)* coarse.

primo,-a *adj (materia)* raw. **2** MAT prime. − **3** *m,f* cousin. − **4** *m* simpleton. ●*hacer el ~,* to be taken for a ride.

primogénito,-a *adj-m,f* first-born, eldest.

primor *m (hermosura)* beauty. **2** *(habilidad)* care, skill.

primordial *adj* essential, fundamental.

princesa *f* princess.

principado *m* principality.

principal *adj* main, chief. − **2** *m (jefe)* chief. **3** *(piso)* first floor.

príncipe *m* prince.

principiante,-a *m,f* beginner.

principio *m (inicio)* beginning, start. **2** *(base)* principle. **3** *pl* rudiments. ●*al ~,* at first.

pringar [7] *i arg (morir)* to kick the bucket. **2** *(trabajar)* to work hard.

pringoso,-a *adj* greasy.

pringue *m* grease. **2** *(suciedad)* dirt.

prior,-ra *m,f m* prior, *f* prioress.

prioridad *f* priority.

prisa *f* hurry. ●*correr ~,* to be urgent; *tener ~,* to be in a hurry.

prisión *f* prison, jail. ● *en ~ preventiva,* remanded in custody.

prisionero,-a *m,f* prisoner.

prisma *m* prism.

prismático,-a *adj* prismatic. − **2** *mpl* binoculars, field glasses.

privación *f* deprivation, privation.

privado,-a *adj* private.

privar *t (despojar)* to deprive *(de,* of). **2** *(prohibir)* to forbid. **3** *fam (gustar)* to like. − **4** *i (estar de moda)* to be in fashion. **5** *fam (beber)* to booze.

privilegiado,-a *adj-m,f* privileged (person).

privilegio *m* privilege.

pro *m & f* advantage. − **2** *prep* in favour of. ●*pro(s) y contra(s),* the pros and cons.

proa *f* prow, bow.

probabilidad *f* probability.

probable *adj* probable, likely.

probador *m* fitting room.

probar [31] *t (demostrar)* to prove. **2** *(comprobar)* to test. **3** *(vino, comida)* to taste, try. **4** *(prendas)* to try on. − **5** *i* to attempt/try *(a,* to).

probeta *f* test-tube.

probidad *f* honesty, integrity.

problema *m* problem.

problemático,-a *adj* problematic.

procacidad *f* impudence, insolence.

procedencia *f* origin, source. **2** *(adecuación)* appropriateness, properness.

procedente *adj* coming *(de,* from). **2** *(adecuado)* appropriate, proper.

proceder *i (ejecutar)* to proceed. **2** *(venir de)* to come *(de,* from). **3** *(actuar)* to behave. **4** JUR to take proceedings. **5** *(ser adecuado)* to be proper/suitable/fitting. − **5** *m* behaviour.

procedimiento *m* procedure, method. **2** JUR proceedings *pl.*

procesado,-a *adj-m,f* JUR accused.

procesamiento *m* processing. ■ INFORM

· *~ de datos/textos,* data/word processing.

procesar *t* to process. **2** JUR to prosecute.

procesión *f* procession.

proceso *m* process. **2** *(en el tiempo)* time. **3** JUR trial.

proclama, proclamación *f* proclamation.

proclamar *t* to proclaim.

procrear *t* to procreate.

procurador,-ra *m,f* JUR attorney, GB solicitor.

procurar *t* to try to, attempt. **2** *(proporcionar)* (to manage) to get.

prodigar(se) [7] *t (gastar)* to lavish. − **2** *p* to bend over backwards to be helpful. **3** *(exhibirse)* to show off.

prodigio *m* prodigy, miracle.

prodigioso,-a *adj* prodigious. **2** *(maravilloso)* marvellous.

pródigo,-a *adj (derrochador)* wasteful. **2** *(generoso)* lavish. − **3** *m,f* spendthrift.

producción *f* production. ■ *~ en cadena,* mass production.

producir(se) [46] *t* to produce. **2** *(causar)* to cause. − **3** *p* to happen.

productividad *f* productivity.

productivo,-a *adj* productive.

producto *m* product.

productor,-ra *adj* productive. − **2** *m,f* producer. − **3** *f* CINEM production company.

proeza *f* heroic deed.

profanar *t* to profane.

profano,-a *adj* profane, secular. **2** *(no experto)* lay. − **3** *m,f* layman.

profecía *f* prophecy.

proferir [35] *t* to utter.

profesar *t-i* to profess.

profesión *f* profession.

profesional *adj-mf* professional.

profesor,-ra *m,f* teacher; *(de universidad)* lecturer.

profesorado *m* teaching staff.

profeta *m* prophet.

profetizar [4] *t* to prophesy, foretell.

profiláctico *m* condom.

prófugo,-a *adj-m,f* fugitive. − **2** *m* MIL deserter.

profundidad *f* depth.

profundizar [4] *t* to deepen. − **2** *t-i (discurrir)* to go deeply into.

profundo,-a *adj (hondo)* deep. **2** *fig* profound.

profusión *f* profusion.

progenie *f* *fml* lineage.

progenitor,-ra *m,f* progenitor, ancestor. — **2** *mpl* parents.

programa *m* programme, US program. **2** INFORM program.

programador,-ra *m,f* INFORM programmer.

programar *t* to programme, US to program. **2** INFORM to program.

progre *adj-mf fam* trendy, lefty.

progresar *i* to progress.

progresión *f* progression.

progresivo,-a *adj* progressive. — **2** *progresivamente, adv* progressively.

progreso *m* progress.

prohibición *f* prohibition, ban.

prohibir [21] *t* to forbid.

prohibitivo,-a *adj* prohibitive.

prohijar [20] *t* to adopt.

prohombre *m* outstanding man.

prójimo *m* fellow man. ■ *el ~,* mankind.

prole *f* offspring.

proletariado *m* proletariat.

proletario,-a *adj-m,f* proletarian.

proliferar *i* to proliferate.

prolífico,-a *adj* prolific.

prólogo *m* prologue.

prolongación *f* prolongation.

prolongar(se) [7] *t* to prolong. — **2** *p* to go on.

promediar [12] *t* to average out. — **2** *i* to mediate.

promedio *m* average.

promesa *f* promise.

prometedor,-ra *adj* promising.

prometer(se) *t* to promise. — **2** *i* to be promising. — **3** *p (pareja)* to get engaged. ●*~ el oro y el moro,* to promise the moon.

prometido,-a *m,f m* fiancé, *f* fiancée.

prominencia *f* prominence, knoll.

prominente *adj* prominent, projecting.

promiscuo,-a *adj* promiscuous.

promoción *f* promotion. **2** *(venta)* offer.

promocionar *t* to promote.

promontorio *m* promontory, headland.

promotor,-ra *m,f* promoter.

promover [32] *t* to promote.

promulgar [7] *t* to enact.

pronombre *m* pronoun.

pronosticar [1] *t* to predict, foretell.

pronóstico *m* forecast. **2** MED prognosis.

prontitud *f* quickness, promptness.

pronto,-a *adj* quick, fast. — **2** *m* sudden impulse. — **3** *adv* soon. ●*de ~,* suddenly; *lo más ~ posible,* as soon as possible; *por lo ~,* for the present.

pronunciación *f* pronunciation.

pronunciamiento *m* uprising, insurrection.

pronunciar(se) [12] *t* to pronounce. **2** *(discurso)* to make. — **3** *p* to declare o.s.

propagación *f* propagation, spreading.

propaganda *f* POL propaganda. **2** COM advertising.

propagar(se) *t-p* to spread.

propasarse *p* to go too far.

propensión *f* tendency.

propenso,-a *adj* inclined. **2** MED susceptible.

propiciar [12] *t* to favour.

propicio,-a *adj* apt, suitable.

propiedad *f (derecho)* ownership. **2** *(objeto)* property. **3** *(cualidad)* propriety. ●*con ~,* properly, appropriately.

propietario,-a *m,f* owner.

propina *f* tip.

propinar *t* to give.

propio,-a *adj (perteneciente)* own. **2** *(indicado)* proper, appropriate. **3** *(particular)* typical, peculiar: *es muy ~ de él,* it's very typical of him. **4** *(mismo) (él)* himself; *(ella)* herself, *(cosa, animal)* itself: *el ~ autor,* the author himself.

proponer(se) [78] *t* to propose, put forward. — **2** *p* to intend. ▲ *pp* **propuesto,-a.**

proporción *f* proportion. **2** *pl* size *sing*.

proporcionado,-a *adj* proportionate. **2** *(facilitado por)* supplied.

proporcionar *t* to proportion. **2** *(facilitar)* to supply, give.

proposición *f* proposition, proposal. **2** GRAM clause.

propósito *m (intención)* intention. **2** *(objetivo)* purpose, aim. ●*a ~, (por cierto)* by the way; *(adrede)* on purpose.

propuesto,-a *pp →* **proponer.** — **2** *f* proposal.

propulsar *t* to propel. **2** *fig* to promote.

prórroga *f* extension. **2** MIL deferment.

prorrogar [7] *t* to postpone; MIL to defer.

prorrumpir *i* to burst.

prosa *f* prose.

prosaico,-a *adj* prosaic.

prosapia *f* ancestry, lineage.

proscribir *t (exiliar)* to exile. **2** *(prohibir)* to ban. ▲ *pp* **proscri(p)to,-a.**

proseguir [56] *t-i* to continue, carry on.

prosista *mf* prose writer.

prospección *f* prospect. **2** COM survey.

prospecto *m* leaflet, prospectus.

prosperar *i* to prosper, thrive.
prosperidad *f* prosperity.
próspero,-a *adj* prosperous. ●~ *año nuevo,* happy New Year.
próstata *f* prostate (gland).
prostíbulo *m* brothel.
prostitución *f* prostitution.
prostituir [62] *t* to prostitute.
prostituta *f* prostitute.
protagonista *mf (de película etc.)* main character, leading role. **2** *fig* centre of attraction.
protagonizar [4] *t* to play the lead in.
protección *f* protection.
protector,-ra *adj* protecting. – **2** *m,f* protector.
proteger [5] *t* to protect, defend.
proteína *f* protein.
protesta *f* protest.
protestante *adj-mf* Protestant.
protestantismo *m* Protestantism.
protestar *t-i* to protest.
protocolo *m* protocol. **2** *(etiqueta)* etiquette.
prototipo *m* prototype.
protuberancia *f* protuberance.
provecho *m* profit, benefit. ●¡*buen* ~*!,* enjoy your meal!; *sacar* ~ *de,* to benefit from.
provechoso,-a *adj* profitable.
proveedor,-ra *m,f* supplier, purveyor.
proveer [61] *t* to supply with, provide. ▲ *pp provisto,-a.*
provenir [90] *i* to come.
proverbio *m* proverb, saying.
providencia *f* providence.
providencial *adj* providential.
provincia *f* province. ■ *capital de* ~, provincial capital.
provinciano,-a *adj-m,f pey* provincial.
provisión *f* provision.
provisional *adj* provisional, temporary.
provisto,-a *pp* → **proveer**. – **2** *adj* provided.
provocación *f* provocation.
provocador,-ra *adj* provoking. – **2** *m,f* instigator.
provocar [1] *t* to provoke. ●~ *un incendio (intencionado),* to commit arson.
provocativo,-a *adj* provocative.
proximidad *f* nearness, proximity.
próximo,-a *adj (cerca)* near, close to. **2** *(siguiente)* next: *el mes* ~, next month. – **3** *próximamente adv (pronto)* soon.
proyección *f* projection. **2** CINEM screening.

proyectar *t (luz)* to project. **2** CINEM to show. **3** *(planear)* to plan.
proyectil *m* projectile, missile.
proyecto *m* project. ■ ~ *de ley,* bill.
proyector *m (reflector)* searchlight. **2** CINEM projector.
prudencia *f* prudence, discretion.
prudente *adj* sensible, wise, prudent.
prueba *f* proof. **2** *(examen)* test. **3** COST fitting. **4** TÉC trial. **5** DEP event. **6** JUR evidence. **7** *pl* AM trick *sing.* ●*poner a* ~, to put to the test.
prurito *m* MED itching. **2** *fig* desire.
psicoanálisis *m inv* psychoanalysis.
psicología *f* psychology.
psicológico,-a *adj* psychological.
psicólogo,-a *m,f* psychologist.
psicópata *mf* psychopath.
psiquiatra *mf* psychiatrist.
psiquiatría *f* psychiatry.
psíquico,-a *adj* psychic(al).
púa *f* sharp point. **2** BOT thorn. **3** ZOOL quill. **4** *(de peine)* tooth. **5** MÚS plectrum.
pubertad *f* puberty.
pubis *m inv* pubes *pl.* **2** *(hueso)* pubis.
publicación *f* publication.
publicar [1] *t* to publish.
publicidad *f (hacer público)* publicity. **2** COM advertising.
publicitario,-a *adj* advertising.
público,-a *adj-m* public.
puchero *m* cooking pot. **2** CULIN meat and vegetable stew. ●*hacer pucheros,* to pout.
púdico,-a *adj* chaste, decent.
pudiente *adj-mf* rich (person).
pudor *m* chastity, decency.
pudrir(se) *t-p* to rot, decay.
pueblo *m (población)* village, (small) town. **2** *(gente)* people. **3** *(nación)* nation.
puente *m* bridge. **2** *(fiesta)* long weekend. ■ ~ *aéreo, (pasajeros)* shuttle service; *(emergencia)* airlift; ~ *colgante,* suspension bridge; ~ *levadizo,* drawbridge.
puerco,-a *adj fam* dirty, filthy. – **2** *m,f* pig, *f* sow. ■ ~ *de mar,* sea cow; ~ *espín,* porcupine.
puericultura *f* paeditriatics.
pueril *adj* puerile, childish.
puerro *m* leek.
puerta *f* door. **2** *(verja)* gate. ●*de* ~ *a* ~, (from) door to door; *fig por la* ~ *grande,* in a grand manner. ■ ~ *corredera/giratoria,* sliding/revolving door.
puerto *m* port, harbour. **2** *(de montaña)* (mountain) pass. ■ ~ *deportivo,* marina; ~ *franco,* free port.

pues *conj (ya que)* since, as. **2** *(por lo tanto)* therefore. **3** *(repetitivo)* then: *digo, ~ ...,* I say then ... . **4** *(enfático)* ~ *bien,* well then; *¡~ claro!,* of course!; ~ *no,* well no.

puesta *f* setting. ■ ~ *a punto,* tuning; ~ *de sol,* sunset.

puesto,-a *pp* → **poner**. — **2** *adj* set, put. **3** *(ropa)* on. — **4** *m* place. **5** *(de mercado)* stall; *(de feria etc.)* stand. **6** *(empleo)* position, post. **7** MIL post. ●~ *que,* since, as. ■ ~ *de socorro,* first-aid station.

púgil *m* boxer.

pugna *f* fight, battle.

pugnar *i* to fight, struggle.

puja *f (acción)* bidding. **2** *(cantidad)* bid.

pujante *adj* thriving.

pujanza *f* power, strength.

pujar *t (pugnar)* to struggle. **2** *(en subasta)* to bid higher.

pulcritud *f* neatness.

pulcro,-a *adj* neat, tidy, clean.

pulga *f* flea. ●*tener malas pulgas,* to have a nasty streak.

pulgada *f* inch.

pulgar *m* thumb.

pulido,-a *adj* neat, clean. **2** TÉC polished.

pulimentar *t* to polish.

pulir *t* to polish. **2** *(perfeccionar)* to refine.

pullover *m* pullover.

pulmón *m* lung.

pulmonía *f* pneumonia.

pulpa *f* pulp, flesh.

púlpito *m* pulpit.

pulpo *m* octopus.

pulsación *f* pulsation. **2** *(de corazón)* beat, throb. **3** *(mecanografía)* stroke.

pulsar *t* to press. **2** *(teclas)* to tap; MÚS to play. **3** MED to feel the pulse of. **4** *fig* to sound out. — **5** *i (corazón etc.)* to beat, throb.

pulsera *f* bracelet. **2** *(de reloj)* watch strap.

pulso *m* pulse. **2** *(seguridad de mano)* steady hand. **3** *fig* care, tact. ●*ganarse algo a ~,* to work hard for sth.

pulular *i* to swarm.

pulverizador *m* spray, atomizer.

pulverizar [4] *t (sólidos)* to pulverize. **2** *(líquidos)* to atomize, spray.

puma *m* puma.

pundonor *m* self-respect.

punta *f* tip; *(extremo afilado)* point. **2** *(pizca)* bit. **3** *pl* needlepoint *sing.* ●*de ~ en*

blanco, dressed up to the nines; *estar de ~ con algn.,* to be at odds with sb.; *sacar ~ a,* to sharpen.

puntada *f* stitch.

puntal *m* prop. **2** *fig* support.

puntapié *m* kick. ●*echar a puntapiés,* to kick out.

puntear *t* to dot. **2** *(guitarra)* to pluck.

puntera *f* toecap.

puntería *f* aim. ●*tener buena/mala ~,* to be a good/bad shot.

puntero *m* pointer.

puntiagudo,-a *adj* pointed.

puntilla *f* COST lace. ●*de puntillas,* on tiptoe.

puntilloso,-a *adj* punctilious.

punto *m* point. **2** *(marca)* dot. **3** *(de puntuación)* full stop, US period. **4** *(lugar)* spot. **5** COST stitch. ●*en ~,* sharp, on the dot; *a ~ de,* to be on the point of; *estar en su ~,* to be just right; *hasta cierto ~,* up to a certain point; ~ *por ~,* in detail. ■ *dos puntos,* colon; ~ *de vista,* point of view; ~ *y coma,* semicolon.

puntuación *f* punctuation. **2** *(en competición)* scoring. **3** EDUC marking.

puntual *adj* punctual. **2** *(exacto)* exact. **3** *(aislado)* specific. — **4** *puntualmente adv* punctually.

puntualidad *f* punctuality.

puntualizar [4] *t* to give full details of. **2** *(especificar)* to point out.

puntuar [11] *t* to punctuate. **2** EDUC to mark.

punzada *f (dolor)* sharp pain.

punzar [4] *t* to prick. **2** *fig* to torment.

punzón *m* punch.

puñado *m* handful. ●*a puñados,* by the score.

puñal *m* dagger.

puñalada *f* stab.

puñeta *f* nuisance. ●*¡puñetas!,* damn!

puñetazo *m* punch.

puño *m (mano)* fist. **2** *(mango)* handle. **3** *(de prenda)* cuff.

pupa *f* cold sore. **2** *fam (daño)* pain.

pupila *f* pupil.

pupilaje *m* AUTO garaging.

pupilo *m fml* pupil.

pupitre *m* desk.

purasangre *adj-mf* thoroughbred.

puré *m* purée. ■ ~ *de patatas,* mashed potatoes.

pureza *f* purity. **2** *(castidad)* chastity.

purga f purge.
purgar [7] t to purge.
purgatorio m purgatory.
purificar t to purify.
puritano,-a adj-m,f puritan.
puro,-a adj pure. **2** (mero) sheer, mere. **– 3** m cigar.
púrpura f purple.
purpurina f purpurin.
pus m pus.
pusilánime adj faint-hearted.

puta* f whore*, prostitute. ●de ~ **madre***, great, terrific.
putada* f dirty trick.
putativo,-a adj putative, supposed.
putear* i to go whoring*. **– 2** t to fuck/piss about*.
puto,-a* adj fucking*: *no tengo ni un ~ duro,* I haven't got a fucking penny.
putrefacción f putrefaction, rotting.
putrefacto,-a, **pútrido,-a** adj putrefied, rotten.

Q

que *pron rel (sujeto) (persona)* who, that: *la chica ~ vino,* the girl who came; *(cosa)* that, which. **2** *(complemento) (persona)* whom, who; *(cosa)* that, which: *el libro ~ me prestaste,* the book (that) you lent me. **3** *(complemento tiempo)* when; *(lugar)* where. — **4** *conj* that: *dice ~ está cansado,* he says (that) he's tired. — **5** *comp* than, that: *es más alto ~ su padre,* he is taller than his father. ●*¿a ~ no?,* I bet you can't; *¡~ te diviertas!,* enjoy yourself!; *~ yo sepa,* as far as I know; *yo ~ tú,* if I were you.

qué *pron interrog* what. **2** *(cuál)* which. **3** *(en exclamativas)* how, what: *¡~ bonito!,* how nice!; *¡~ flor!,* what a flower! ●*no hay de ~,* don't mention it; *¿para ~?,* what for?; *¿por ~?,* why?; *¡~ de coches!,* what a lot of cars!; *¡~ lástima!,* what a pity!; *¿~ hay/tal?,* how are things?; *¡y ~ !,* so what!

quebrada *f* gorge, ravine.

quebradero *m* *~ de cabeza,* worry, headache.

quebradizo,-a *adj* brittle.

quebrado,-a *adj (roto)* broken. **2** FIN bankrupt. **3** *(terreno)* rough. — **4** *m* MAT fraction.

quebrantar(se) *t* to break. **2** *(machacar)* to grind. **3** *(debilitar)* to weaken. — **4** *p* to break. **5** *(salud)* to be shattered.

quebranto *m (pérdida)* loss. **2** *(aflicción)* grief, pain. **3** *(lástima)* pity.

quebrar(se) [27] *t* to break. **2** *fig* to soften. — **3** *i* FIN to go bankrupt. — **4** *p* to break.

quedar(se) *i* to remain, be left: *queda poco,* there's not much left. **2** *(favorecer)* to look: *queda muy bien,* it looks very nice. **3** *(estar situado)* to be: *¿por dónde queda tu casa?,* whereabouts is your house? **4** *(acordar)* to agree *(en,* to). — **5** *p* to remain, stay, be. **6** *(retener)* to keep

(con, -). ●*~ atónito,-a,* to be astonished; *~ bien/mal,* to make a good/bad impression; *~se sin algo,* to run out of sth.; *todo quedó en nada,* it all came to nothing; *fam ~se con algn.,* to make a fool of sb.; *fam ~se sin blanca,* to be broke.

quedo,-a *adj* quiet, still. **2** *(voz)* low.

quehacer *m* task, chore. ■ *quehaceres domésticos,* housework *sing.*

queja *f (descontento)* complaint. **2** *(dolor)* moan, groan. **3** JUR *presentar una ~,* to lodge a complaint.

quejarse *p (de descontento)* to complain *(de,* about). **2** *(de dolor)* to moan, groan.

quejica *adj-mf fam* grumpy (person).

quejido *m (gemido)* groan, moan. **2** *(grito)* cry.

quejoso,-a *adj* complaining, plaintive.

quema *f (acción, efecto)* burning. **2** *(fuego)* fire. ●*huir de la ~,* to beat it, flee.

quemado,-a *adj* burnt, burned. **2** *fig (resentido)* embittered. **3** *fam (acabado)* spent, burnt-out. **4** *arg (sexualmente)* hot. ●*arg ir ~,* to be dying for it.

quemadura *f* burn.

quemar(se) *t* to burn. **2** *(incendiar)* to set on fire. **3** *fam (acabar)* to burn out. — **4** *i (muy caliente)* to burn. — **5** *p* to be/get burnt.

quemarropa *a ~, adv* point-blank.

quemazón *f (calor)* intense heat. **2** *(comezón)* itch(ing). **3** *(dicho picante)* smarting/cutting word.

quepo *pres indic →* **caber.**

querella *f* JUR charge. **2** *(queja)* complaint. **3** *(pelea)* dispute, quarrel.

querellarse *p* JUR to bring an action, lodge a complaint.

querer [80] *t (amar)* to love. **2** *(desear)* to want: *quiero que vengas,* I want you to come. **3** *(auxiliar)* would: *¿quieres ve-*

nir?, would you like to come? **4** *(ser conveniente)* to need. **5** *(posibilidad)* may: *parece que quiere llover,* it looks like it might rain. ●*lo hice sin* ~, I didn't mean to do it; *quieras o no,* like it or not; ~ *decir,* to mean; *fam está como quiere,* he/she is gorgeous.

querido,-a *adj* dear, beloved. — **2** *m,f (amante)* lover; *(mujer)* mistress. **3** *(apelativo) fam* darling.

queso *m* cheese. ■ ~ *de bola,* Edam; ~ *en lonchas,* cheese slices *pl;* ~ *rallado,* grated cheese.

quevedos *mpl* pince-nez.

quicio *m* hinge. ●*fam estar fuera de* ~, to be beside o.s.; *fam sacar a algn. de* ~, to get on sb.'s nerves.

quid *m* crux. ●*el* ~ *de la cuestión,* the crux of the matter.

quiebra *f* COM failure, bankruptcy. **2** *(rotura)* break, crack. **3** *(pérdida)* loss. **4** GEOG ravine.

quien *pron rel (sujeto)* who: *fue el jefe* ~ *me lo dijo,* it was the boss who told me. **2** *(complemento)* who(m): *las personas con quienes trabajo,* the people (who) I work with. **3** *(indefinido)* whoever, anyone who: ~ *quiera venir que venga,* whoever wants to can come. ●~ *más* ~ *menos,* everybody.

quién *pron interrog (sujeto)* who: *¿*~ *sabe?,* who knows? **2** *(complemento)* who(m): *¿con* ~ *hablas?,* who(m) are you talking to? **3** *de* ~, whose: *¿de* ~ *es esto?,* whose is this?

quienquiera *pron indef* whoever. ●~ *que sea,* whoever it may be. ▲ *pl quienesquiera.*

quieto,-a *adj (sin moverse)* still: *estarse* ~, to keep still. **2** *(sosegado)* quiet, calm.

quietud *f (sin movimiento)* stillness. **2** *(sosiego)* calm(ness).

quijada *f* jawbone.

quijotada *f* quixotic act.

quijotesco,-a *adj* quixotic.

quilate *m* carat. ●*fig de muchos quilates,* of great value.

quilo *m* → **kilo.**

quilla *f* keel.

quimera *f (ilusión)* wild fancy, fantasy, pipe dream. **2** *(riña)* quarrel.

quimérico,-a *adj* unrealistic, fantastic.

química *f* chemistry.

químico,-a *adj* chemical. — **2** *m,f* chemist.

quimono *m* kimono.

quina *f* → **quinina.**

quincalla *f* tinware.

quince *adj* fifteen; *(ordinal)* fifteenth. — **2** *m* fifteen.

quincena *f* fortnight.

quincuagésimo,-a *adj-m,f* fiftieth.

quiniela *f* football pools *pl.* ●*hacer la* ~, to do the pools.

quinientos,-as *adj (cardinal)* five hundred; *(ordinal)* five hundredth. — **2** *m* five hundred. ●*fam a las quinientas,* very late.

quinina *f* quinine.

quinqué *m* oil lamp.

quinqui *mf fam* delinquent, petty criminal.

quinta *f* country house, villa. **2** MIL conscription, US draft.

quintillizo,-a *m,f* quin(tuplet).

quinto,-a *adj-m,f* fifth. — **2** *m* MIL conscript, recruit. **3** *(cerveza)* small beer.

quiosco *m* kiosk. ■ ~ *(de periódicos),* newspaper stand.

quiquiriquí *m* cock-a-doodle-doo. ▲ *pl quiquiriquíes.*

quirófano *m* operating theatre.

quirúrgico,-a *adj* surgical.

quisquilloso,-a *adj* finicky, fussy, touchy.

quiste *m* cyst.

quitaesmaltes *m inv* nail varnish/polish remover.

quitamanchas *m inv* stain remover.

quitanieves *m inv* snowplough, US snowplow.

quitar(se) *t* to remove, take out/off. **2** *(restar)* to subtract. **3** *(robar)* to steal, rob of. **4** *(coger)* to take. **5** *(apartar)* to take away. **6** *(prendas)* to take off. **7** *(dolor)* to relieve. **8** *(mesa)* to clear. **9** *(impedir)* to stop, prevent. — **10** *p (apartarse)* to move away, come/get out. **11** *(desaparecer)* to go away, come out: *se me han quitado las ganas,* I don't feel like it any more. **12** *(prendas)* to take off. **13** *(renunciar)* to give up. ●*de quita y pon,* detachable; ~*se algo/a algn. de encima,* to get rid of sth./sb.; *(saludar)* ~*se el sombrero,* to tip one's hat.

quitasol *m* parasol, sunshade.

quite *m estar al* ~ , to be on the alert.

quizá, quizás *adv* perhaps, maybe.

R

rabadilla *f* ANAT coccyx. **2** *(de ave)* parson's nose.

rábano *m* radish.

rabia *f* MED rabies. **2** *(enfado)* rage, fury. ●*dar* ~, to make furious; *tener* ~ *a algn.,* to hate sb.

rabiar [12] *i* MED to have rabies. **2** *(enfadarse)* to rage, be furious. **3** *(sufrir)* to be in great pain. ●~ *por,* to be dying for.

rabieta *f fam* tantrum.

rabioso,-a *adj* rabid. **2** *(airado)* furious, angry. **3** *(excesivo)* terrible. — **4** *rabiosamente adv* furiously.

rabo *m* tail. ●*con el* ~ *entre piernas,* crestfallen.

racial *adj* racial.

racimo *m* bunch.

raciocinio *m (razón)* reason. **2** *(argumento)* reasoning.

ración *f* ration. **2** *(de comida)* portion.

racional *adj* rational.

racionamiento *m* rationing.

racionar *t* to ration.

racha *f (de viento)* gust. **2** *(período)* spell, patch.

radar *m* radar. ▲ *pl* **radares**.

radiación *f* radiation.

radiactividad *f* radioactivity.

radiactivo,-a *adj* radioactive.

radiador *m* radiator.

radiante *adj* radiant *(de,* with).

radiar [12] *t-i* to radiate. — **2** *t (retransmitir)* to broadcast.

radical *adj* radical. — **2** *m* GRAM root.

radicalizar(se) [4] *t-p (conflicto)* to intensify. **2** *(postura)* to harden.

radicar(se) [1] *i (encontrarse)* to be located *(en,* in); *fig* to lie *(en,* in): *el problema radica en la economía,* the problem lies in the economy. **2** *(arraigar)* to take root. — **3** *p* to settle (down).

radio *m* ANAT radius. **2** QUÍM radium. **3** *(de rueda)* spoke. **4** *(campo)* scope. — **5** *f fam (radiodifusión)* radio, broadcasting. **6** *fam (aparato)* radio.

radiocasete *m* radio-cassette.

radiodifusión *f* broadcasting.

radiofónico,-a *adj* radio.

radiografía *f (técnica)* radiography. **2** *(imagen)* X-ray.

radioyente *mf* listener.

raer [81] *t* to scrape (off).

ráfaga *f (de viento)* gust. **2** *(de disparos)* burst. **3** *(de luz)* flash.

raído,-a *adj* threadbare, worn.

rail, raíl *m* rail.

raíz *f* root. ●*a* ~ *de,* on the occasion of; *de* ~, entirely. ■ ~ *cuadrada,* square root.

raja *f* split, crack. **2** *(tajada)* slice.

rajar(se) *t* to split. **2** *(melón etc.)* to slice. **3** *fam* to cut up. — **4** *i (jactarse)* to show off. **5** *(hablar)* to chatter. — **6** *p (partirse)* to split, crack. **7** *fam (desistir)* to back out, quit.

rajatabla *a* ~, *adv* to the letter, strictly.

rallador *m* grater.

ralladura *f* grating.

rallar *t* to grate.

rama *f* branch. ●*andarse/irse por las ramas,* to beat about the bush.

ramaje *m* foliage, branches *pl*.

ramal *m (de cuerda)* strand. **2** *(de camino etc.)* branch.

rambla *f (lecho de agua)* watercourse. **2** *(paseo)* boulevard, avenue.

ramera *f* whore, prostitute.

ramificación *f* ramification.

ramificarse [1] *p* to ramify, branch (out).

ramillete *m* bouquet.

ramo *m (de flores)* bunch. **2** *(de árbol)* branch.

rampa f (calambre) cramp. **2** (declive) ramp.

rana f frog. ●fam **salir** ~, to be a disappointment.

rancio,-a adj (comestibles) stale; (mantequilla) rancid. **2** (linaje) old, ancient. ■ **vino** ~, old/mellow wine.

ranchero,-a m,f (granjero) rancher, farmer. − **2** f AM type of popular song.

rancho m MIL mess. **2** AM (granja) ranch.

rango m rank, class.

ranura f (canal) groove. **2** (para monedas, fichas) slot.

rapapolvo m fam ticking off.

rapar t (afeitar) to shave. **2** (pelo) to crop.

rapaz adj ZOOL predatory, of prey. **2** (persona) rapacious. − **3** f bird of prey.

rapaz,-za m,f lad, f lass.

rape m (pez) angler fish. **2** (rasura) quick shave. ●**al** ~, close-cropped.

rapidez f speed.

rápido,-a adj quick, fast. − **2** mpl (del río) rapids.

raptar t to kidnap.·

rapto m (secuestro) kidnapping. **2** (impulso) outburst.

raptor,-ra m,f kidnapper.

raqueta f racket. **2** (para nieve) snowshoe. **3** (en casinos) rake.

raquítico,-a adj med rachitic. **2** (exiguo) meagre. **3** (débil) weak.

rareza f (poco común) rarity, rareness. **2** (peculiaridad) oddity. **3** (extravagancia) eccentricity.

raro,-a adj (poco común) scarce: **raras veces,** seldom. **2** (peculiar) odd, strange. − **3 raramente** adv rarely, seldom.

ras a ~ **de,** adv (on a) level with.

rasante adj (tiro) grazing; (vuelo) low. − **2** f slope.

rascacielos m inv skyscraper.

rascar(se) [1] t-p to scratch (o.s.).

rasera f spatula.

rasgado,-a adj (luminoso) wide-open. **2** (ojos) almond-shaped.

rasgadura f tear.

rasgar(se) [7] t-p to tear, rip. ●fig ~**se las vestiduras,** to pull one's hair out.

rasgo m (línea) stroke. **2** (facción) feature. **3** (peculiaridad) characteristic. **4** (acto) act, feat. ●**a grandes rasgos,** in outline.

rasguear t (guitarra) to strum. − **2** i (al escribir) to scribble.

rasguño m scratch.

raso,-a adj (plano) flat, level; (liso) smooth. **2** (atmósfera) clear. − **3** m (tejido) satin. ●**al** ~, in the open air.

raspa f (de pescado) bone. **2** (de cereal) beard.

raspadura f scraping.

raspar t (rascar) to scrape (off). **2** (vino etc.) to be sharp. **3** (hurtar) to nick.

rasposo,-a adj (áspero) rough.

rastra f (rastro) trail, track. **2** (sarta) string. **3** (para pescar) trawl (net). ●**a rastras,** dragging; fig (sin querer) unwillingly.

rastrear t to trail, track, trace. **2** (río) to drag. **3** (zona) to comb, search. − **4** i AGR to rake. **5** AV to fly very low.

rastrero,-a adj creeping, dragging. **2** (de vuelo bajo) flying low. **3** (bajo) vile.

rastrillo m rake.

rastro m (instrumento) rake. **2** (señal) trace, track. **3** (vestigio) vestige. **4** (mercado) flea market.

rata f ZOOL rat. − **2** m fam (ratero) pickpocket. − **3** mf (tacaño) mean/stingy person.

ratero,-a m,f pickpocket.

raticida m rat poison.

ratificación f ratification.

ratificar(se) [1] t to ratify. − **2** p to be ratified.

rato m (momento) time, while, moment. ●**a ratos perdidos,** in spare time; **pasar el** ~, to kill time; **un buen** ~, a long time; (distancia) a long way; (diversión) a pleasant time.

ratón m mouse.

ratonera f (trampa) mousetrap. **2** (agujero) mousehole.

raudal m torrent, flood.

raya f (línea) line. **2** (de color) stripe: **a rayas,** striped. **3** (del pantalón) crease. **4** (del pelo) parting. **5** (pez) skate. **6** arg (de droga) fix, dose. ●**pasarse de la** ~, to overstep the mark; **tener a** ~, to keep within bounds.

rayado,-a adj striped. **2** (papel) ruled.

rayar t (líneas) to draw lines on, line, rule. **2** (superficie) to scratch. **3** (tachar) to cross out. **4** (subrayar) to underline. − **5** i to border (con/en, on) to border. ●**al** ~ **el día/alba,** at daybreak/dawn.

rayo m ray, beam. **2** (chispa) (stroke of) lightening. ●~ **de sol,** sunbeam.

rayuela f hopscotch.

raza f race. **2** (animal) breed.

razón f reason. **2** MAT ratio. ●**dar la** ~, to agree with; **perder la** ~, lo lose one's reason; "~ **aquí**", "enquire within"; **tener/no tener** ~, to be right/wrong. ■ ~ **social,** trade name.

razonable adj reasonable.

razonamiento *m* reasoning.

razonar *i (discurrir)* to reason. **2** *(explicar)* to reason out.

re *m* MÚS re, D.

reacción *f* reaction. ■ *avión a ~*, jet.

reaccionario,-a *adj-m,f* reactionary.

reacio,-a *adj* reluctant, unwilling.

reactivar *t* to reactivate.

reactivo *m* reagent.

reactor *m* reactor. **2** AV jet (plane).

readmitir *t* to readmit.

reafirmar *t* to reassert.

reajuste *m* readjustment; POL reshuffle.

real *adj* real. **2** *(regio)* royal. — **3** *m (de feria)* fairground. — **4** *realmente adv* really. **5** *(en realidad)* in fact, actually.

realce *m (adorno)* relief. **2** *(lustre)* prestige. ●*dar ~ a*, to enhance.

realeza *f* royalty.

realidad *f* reality. ●*en ~*, really, in fact.

realismo *m* realism.

realista *adj* realistic. — **2** *mf* realist.

realizable *adj* feasible.

realización *f* achievement, fulfilment.

realizar(se) [4] *t* to realize. **2** *(llevar a cabo)* to accomplish, carry out, do, fulfil. — **3** *p (persona)* to fulfil o.s.

realzar [4] *t fig* to heighten, enhance. **2** *(pintura)* to highlight.

reanimar(se) *t-p* to revive.

reanudar(se) *t* to renew, resume. — **2** *p* to be renewed/resumed.

reaparecer [43] *i* to reappear.

rearme *m* rearmament, rearming.

reavivar *t* to revive.

rebaba *f* rough edge.

rebaja *f* reduction. **2** *pl* sales.

rebajar(se) *t (disminuir)* to reduce; *(color)* to tone down. **2** *(bajar nivel)* to lower. **3** *(humillar)* to humiliate. — **4** *p* to humble o.s. ●*~se a*, to stoop to.

rebanada *f* slice.

rebaño *m* herd; *(de ovejas)* flock.

rebasar *t* to exceed, go beyond.

rebeca *f* cardigan.

rebelarse *p* to rebel, revolt.

rebelde *adj* rebellious. — **2** *mf* rebel.

rebeldía *f* rebelliousness. **2** JUR default.

rebelión *f* rebellion, revolt.

reblandecer [43] *t* to soften.

rebobinar *t* to rewind.

reborde *m* flange, rim.

rebosar *i* to overflow *(de,* with). — **2** *t-i (abundar)* to abound.

rebotar *i* to bounce, rebound; *(bala)* to ricochet. — **2** *t (clavo)* to clinch. **3** *(conturbar)* to put out. — **4** *p (conturbarse)* to get angry.

rebote *m* (re)bound. ●*fig de ~*, on the rebound.

rebozar [4] *t* to coat (in breadcrumbs/batter).

rebuscado,-a *adj* recherché.

rebuznar *i* to bray.

rebuzno *m* bray(ing).

recabar *t (solicitar)* to ask for. **2** *(obtener)* to attain, obtain.

recadero,-a *m,f* messenger.

recado *m (mensaje)* message. **2** *(encargo)* errand.

recaer [67] *i* to relapse. **2** *(corresponder)* to fall *(sobre,* on).

recaída *f* relapse.

recalcar *f* [1] to emphasize, stress.

recalentar [27] *t (volver a calentar)* to reheat, warm up. **2** *(calentar demasiado)* to overheat.

recambiar [12] *t* to change (over).

recambio *m* spare (part); *(de pluma/bolígrafo)* refill.

recapacitar *t* to think over.

recapitulación *f* recapitulation.

recapitular *t* to recapitulate.

recargable *adj* refillable.

recargado,-a *adj (sobrecargado)* overloaded. **2** *(exagerado)* overelaborate, exaggerated.

recargar [7] *t (volver a cargar)* to reload. **2** *(sobrecargar)* to overload. **3** *(exagerar)* to overelaborate. **4** FIN to increase.

recargo *m* extra charge.

recatado,-a *adj (prudente)* cautious. **2** *(púdico)* modest, shy.

recatar(se) *t* to hide. — **2** *p* to be cautious.

recato *m (cautela)* caution. **2** *(pudor)* modesty.

recauchutado,-a *adj neumático ~*, retread.

recaudación *f* collection. **2** *(cantidad recaudada)* takings *pl*. **3** *(oficina)* tax collector's office.

recaudador,-ra *m,f* tax collector.

recaudar *t* to collect.

recelar *t* to suspect.

recelo *m* suspicion.

receloso,-a *adj* suspicious.

recensión *f* review.

recepción *f gen* reception. **2** *(de documento, carta etc.)* receipt.

recepcionista *mf* receptionist.

receptáculo *m* receptacle.

receptor,-ra *adj* receiving. − 2 *m,f* receiver.

receso *m* recess.

receta *f* MED prescription. 2 CULIN recipe.

recetar *t* to prescribe.

rechazar [4] *t* to reject, turn down.

rechazo *m* rejection.

rechinar *i* to grate; *(dientes)* to grind.

rechistar *i* to clear one's throat. ●*fam* **hacer algo sin** ∼, to do sth. without complaining.

rechoncho,-a *adj* chubby.

recibidor *m* entrance hall.

recibimiento *m* reception, welcome.

recibir(se) *t gen* receive. 2 *(salir al encuentro)* to meet. − 3 *p* AM *(licenciarse)* to graduate. ●*(en carta)* **recibe un abrazo de,** with best wishes from.

recibo *m (resguardo)* receipt. 2 *(factura)* invoice, bill. ●*acusar* ∼ *de,* to acknowledge receipt of.

reciclar *t (materiales)* to recycle. 2 *(profesionales)* to retrain.

recién *adv* recently, newly; *(café, pan)* freshly. 2 AM just: ∼ **llegó,** he/she has just arrived. ∎∼ **nacido,** newborn baby; ∼ **casados,** newlyweds.

reciente *adj* recent. − 2 *recientemente adv* recently, lately.

recinto *m* enclosure, precinct. ∎ ∼ **ferial,** fairground.

recio,-a *adj (fuerte)* strong, robust. 2 *(grueso)* thick. 3 *(duro)* hard; *(clima)* harsh.

recipiente *m* vessel, container.

recíproco,-a *adj* reciprocal, mutual.

recital *m* recital, concert.

recitar *t* to recite.

reclamación *f (demanda)* claim, demand. 2 *(queja)* complaint, protest.

reclamar *t (pedir)* to demand. − 2 *i* to protest *(contra,* against).

reclamo *m (para cazar)* decoy. 2 *(silbato)* bird call. 3 *(anuncio)* advertisement. 4 *fig* inducement.

reclinar(se) *t* to lean *(en/sobre,* on). − 2 *p* to lean back.

recluir [62] *t* to shut away. 2 *(encarcelar)* to imprison.

reclusión *f* seclusion. 2 *(encarcelamiento)* imprisonment.

recluso,-a *m,f* prisoner.

recluta *m (voluntario)* recruit. 2 *(obligado)* conscript.

reclutamiento *m (voluntario)* recruitment. 2 *(obligatorio)* conscription.

reclutar *t (voluntarios)* to recruit. 2 *(obligatorio)* conscript.

recobrar(se) *t-p* to recover.

recochinearse *p fam* to make fun *(de,* of).

recodo *m* turn, bend, corner.

recogedor *m* dustpan.

recoger(se) [5] *t (coger)* to pick up. 2 *(juntar)* to gather. 3 *(ordenar)* to clear up. 4 *(ir a buscar)* to fetch, pick up. 5 *(dar asilo)* to take in *(a, -).* − 6 *p (irse a casa)* to go home. 7 *(irse a dormir)* to go to bed. 8 *(para meditar)* to retire. ●∼ **la mesa,** to clear the table; ∼**se el pelo,** to gather one's hair up.

recogido,-a *adj (apartado)* secluded. 2 *(pelo)* gathered up.

recolección *f (recopilación)* summary. 2 AGR harvest. 3 *(recaudación)* collection.

recolectar *t* to gather. 2 AGR to harvest.

recomendación *f* recommendation.

recomendar [27] *t* to recommend.

recompensa *f* reward, recompense.

recompensar *t (compensar)* to compensate. 2 *(remunerar)* to reward, recompense.

recomponer [78] *t* to repair, mend. ▲ *pp* **recompuesto,-a.**

reconcentrar(se) *t (concentrar)* to concentrate *(en,* to). 2 *(reunir)* to bring together. − 3 *p (ensimismarse)* to become absorbed in thought.

reconciliación *f* reconciliation.

reconciliar(se) *t* to reconcile. − 2 *p* to be reconciled.

recóndito,-a *adj* recondite.

reconfortar *t* to comfort. 2 *(animar)* to encourage.

reconocer(se) [44] *t gen* to recognize. 2 MIL to reconnoitre. 3 MED to examine. − 4 *p* to recognize each other. 5 *(admitir)* to admit.

reconocimiento *m gen* recognition. 2 MIL reconnaissance. 3 MED examination, check up.

reconquistar *t* to reconquer.

reconstituyente *m* tonic.

reconstruir [62] *t* to reconstruct.

reconvención *f* reproach.

reconvenir [90] *t* to reproach.

reconvertir [35] *t* to reconvert. 2 *(en industria)* to modernize.

recopilación *f (resumen)* summary. 2 *(colección)* compilation, collection.

recopilar *t* to compile, collect.

récord *adj-m* record.

recordar(se) [31] *t* to remember. **2** *(a otra persona)* to remind: ~ *algo a algn.,* to remind sb. of sth. — **3** *i-p* AM *(despertar)* to wake up.

recorrer *t (atravesar)* to cover, travel. **2** *(reconocer)* to go over. **3** *(reparar)* to mend, repair.

recorrido *m (trayecto)* journey. **2** *(distancia)* distance travelled.

recortar *t (muñecos, telas, etc.)* to cut out. **2** *(lo que sobra)* to cut off.

recorte *m* cutting. **2** *(de periódico)* press clipping. **3** *fig (reducción)* cut.

recostar(se) [31] *t* to lean. — **2** *p* to lie down.

recreación *f* recreation.

recrear(se) *t* to amuse, entertain. — **2** *p* to amuse o.s.

recreativo,-a *adj* recreational.

recreo *m* recreation, amusement. **2** *(en la escuela)* playtime.

recriminación *f* recrimination.

recriminar *t* to recriminate.

recrudecer(se) [43] *t-p* to worsen, aggravate.

rectangular *adj* rectangular.

rectángulo *m* rectangle.

rectificar [1] *t* to rectify. **2** AUTO to straighten up.

rectilíneo,-a *adj* straight.

rectitud *f* straightness. **2** *fig* uprightness.

recto,-a *adj* straight. **2** *(honesto)* just, honest. — **3** *m* ANAT rectum. — **4** *f* MAT straight line.

rector,-ra *adj* ruling, governing. — **2** *m,f* EDUC head; *(universidad)* vice-chancellor. — **3** *m* REL vicar.

rectoría *f (casa)* rectory. **2** *(cargo)* rectorship.

recubrir *t* to cover. ▲ *pp* **recubierto,-a**.

recuento *m* (re)count.

recuerdo *m* memory. **2** *(regalo)* souvenir. **3** *pl (saludos)* regards; *(en carta)* best wishes.

recular *i* to go back. **2** *fam (ceder)* to back down.

recuperación *f* recovery. **2** EDUC remedial lessons *pl*.

recuperar(se) *t-p* to recover. ●~ *el conocimiento,* to regain consciousness.

recurrir *i* JUR to appeal. **2** *(acogerse) (a algo)* to resort *(a,* to); *(a algn.)* to turn *(a,* to).

recurso *m* resort. **2** JUR appeal. **3** *pl* resources, means.

red *f* net. **2** *(sistema)* network. **3** *fig (trampa)* trap.

redacción *f (escritura)* writing. **2** *(estilo)* wording. **3** *(prensa)* editing. **4** *(oficina)* editorial office. **5** *(redactores)* editorial staff.

redactar *t* to write; *(definitivamente)* to word.

redactor,-ra *m,f* editor.

redada *f* raid.

redención *f* redemption.

redentor,-ra *adj* redeeming. — **2** *m,f* redeemer.

redicho,-a *adj* affected.

redil *m* fold, sheepfold.

redimir *t* to redeem.

rédito *m* interest.

redoblar *t (aumentar)* to redouble. **2** *(clavo etc.)* to clinch. — **3** *i (tambores)* to roll.

redoble *m* roll.

redonda *f (comarca)* region. **2** MÚS semibreve. ●*a la* ~, around.

redondear(se) *t* to (make) round. **2** *(cantidad)* to round off. — **3** *p (ponerse redondo)* to become round. **4** *(enriquecerse)* to acquire a fortune.

redondel *m* circle.

redondo,-a *adj* round. **2** *(rotundo)* categorical: *un no* ~, a flat refusal. **3** *(perfecto)* perfect, excellent: *un negocio* ~, an excellent business deal. — **4** *m (de carne)* topside.

reducción *f* reduction.

reducido,-a *adj* limited, small.

reducir(se) [46] *t* to reduce. **2** *(vencer)* to subdue. **3** MED to set. — **4** *i* AUTO to change down. — **5** *p* to economize.

reducto *m* redoubt.

redundancia *f* redundancy.

redundar *i (rebosar)* to overflow. **2** *(resultar)* to result *(en,* in), lead *(en,* to).

reedición *f* reprint, reissue.

reembolsar *t (pagar)* to reimburse; *(devolver)* to refund.

reembolso *m (pago)* reimbursement; *(devolución)* refund. ■ *contra* ~, cash on delivery.

reemplazar [4] *t* to replace.

reemplazo *m* replacement. **2** MIL call-up.

reemprender *t* to start again.

reencarnación *f* reincarnation.

reestructurar *t* to restructure, reorganize.

referencia *f* reference. **2** *pl* references. ●*con* ~ *a,* with reference to; *hacer* ~ *a,* to refer to.

referente *adj* concerning *(a,* -).

referir(se) [35] *t (expresar)* to relate, tell. — **2** *p (aludir)* to refer *(a,* to).

refilón *de* ~, *adv* obliquely. **2** *(de pasada)* briefly.

refinado,-a *adj* refined.

refinamiento *m* refinement. **2** *(pulcritud)* neatness.

refinar(se) *t (azúcar etc.)* to refine. **2** *(escrito etc.)* to polish. – **3** *p (pulirse)* to polish o.s.

refinería *f* refinery.

reflectar *t* to reflect.

reflector *m (cuerpo)* reflector. **2** ELEC searchlight.

reflejar(se) *t* to reflect. – **2** *p* to be reflected *(en,* in).

reflejo,-a *adj* reflected. **2** GRAM reflexive. **3** *(movimiento)* reflex. – **4** *m (imagen)* reflection. **5** *(destello)* gleam. ●*tener (buenos) reflejos,* to have good reflexes.

reflexión *f* reflection.

reflexionar *t* to reflect *(en/sobre,* on).

reflexivo,-a *adj* reflective. **2** GRAM reflexive.

reflujo *m* ebb tide.

reforma *f* reform. **2** *(mejora)* improvement. **3** *pl* alterations, repairs: *"cerrado por reformas"*, "closed for alterations".

reformar(se) *t* to reform. **2** ARQ to renovate. – **3** *p* to reform o.s.

reformatorio *m* reformatory.

reforzar [50] *t* to reinforce, strengthen.

refractar(se) *t-p* to refract.

refractario,-a *adj (cuerpo)* heat-resistant. **2** *(persona)* reluctant.

refrán *m* proverb, saying.

refregar [48] *t* to rub hard.

refrenar(se) *t-p* to restrain (o.s.).

refrescante *adj* refreshing.

refrescar(se) [1] *t* to cool, refresh. **2** *(en la memoria)* to brush up. – **3** *i (el tiempo)* to get cool. – **4** *p (tomar el fresco)* to take a breath of fresh air. **5** *(beber)* to have a drink.

refresco *m (bebida)* refreshment. **2** *(comida)* snack.

refriega *f* scuffle.

refrigeración *f* refrigeration. **2** *(aire acondicionado)* air conditioning.

refrigerador *m* fridge.

refrigerar *t (enfriar)* to refrigerate. **2** *(con aire acondicionado)* to air-condition.

refrigerio *m* refreshments *pl*, snack.

refrito *m fam (cosa rehecha)* rehash.

refuerzo *m* reinforcement, strengthening. **2** *pl* MIL reinforcements.

refugiado,-a *adj-m,f* refugee.

refugiar(se) [12] *t* to shelter. – **2** *p* to take refuge.

refugio *m* shelter, refuge. ■ ~ *atómico,* (nuclear) fallout shelter.

refundir *t* to recast. **2** *(comedia etc.)* to adapt.

refunfuñar *i* to grumble.

refutar *t* to refute, disprove.

regadera *f* watering can. ●*fam estar como una* ~, to be as mad as a hatter.

regadío *m* irrigated land.

regalado,-a *adj (de regalo)* given as a present. **2** *(suave)* delicate. **3** *(agradable)* comfortable.

regalar(se) *t* to give as a present. **2** *(halagar)* to flatter. **3** *(deleitar)* to delight. – **4** *p* to spoil o.s. *(con,* with).

regaliz *m* liquorice.

regalo *m* gift, present. **2** *(comodidad)* comfort. **3** *(exquisitez)* delicacy.

regañadientes *a* ~, *adv* reluctantly, grudgingly.

regañar *t fam* to scold, tell off. – **2** *i* to argue, quarrel.

regañina *f* scolding, telling-off.

regar [48] *t* to water. **2** *(esparcir)* to sprinkle.

regata *f (competición)* regatta. **2** AGR irrigation channel.

regatear *t* to bargain. – **2** *i* DEP to dribble.

regazo *m* lap.

regencia *f* regency.

regenerar *t* to regenerate.

regentar *t* POL to govern. **2** *(cargo)* to hold. **3** *(dirigir)* to manage.

regente *mf* POL regent. **2** JUR magistrate. **3** *(director)* manager.

regidor,-ra *m,f* town councillor. **2** TEAT stage manager.

régimen *m* POL regime. **2** MED diet. **3** *(condiciones)* rules *pl*. ▲ *pl regímenes*.

regimiento *m* regiment.

regio,-a *adj* royal. **2** *(magnífico)* magnificent.

región *f* region.

regional *adj* regional.

regir [55] *t (gobernar)* to govern, rule. **2** *(dirigir)* to manage, direct. – **3** *i (ley etc.)* to be in force; *(costumbre)* to prevail. ●*fam no* ~, to have a screw loose.

registrado,-a *adj* registered.

registrador,-ra *adj* registering.

registrar(se) *t (inspeccionar)* to search, inspect. **2** *(inscribir)* to register, record. **3** *(anotar)* to note. – **4** *p (matricularse)* to register, enrol. **5** *(detectarse)* to be recorded.

registro *m (inspección)* search, inspection. **2** *(inscripción)* registration. **3** JUR *(oficina)* registry; *(libro)* register. **4** MÚS register.

regla *f* rule. **2** *(instrumento)* ruler. **3** *(menstruación)* period. ●*en* ~, in order; *por* ~ *general,* as a rule.

reglamentación *f* regulations *pl.* **2** *(acción)* regulation.

reglamentar *t* to regulate.

reglamentario,-a *adj* statutory, prescribed.

reglamento *m* regulations *pl.*

regocijar(se) *t* to delight. − **2** *p* to be delighted.

regocijo *m (placer)* delight. **2** *(júbilo)* merriment.

regodearse *p fam* to delight *(con,* in).

regordete,-a *adj* plump, chubby.

regresar *i* to return, come/go back.

regresión *f* regression.

regreso *m* return. ●*estar de* ~, to be back.

reguero *m* trickle. ■ *como un* ~ *de pólvora,* like wildfire.

regulador,-ra *adj* regulating. − **2** *m* regulator.

regular *adj* regular. **2** *(pasable)* so-so, average. − **3** *t* to regulate.

regularidad *f* regularity.

regularizar [4] *t* to regularize.

regusto *m* aftertaste.

rehabilitar(se) *t* to rehabilitate.

rehacer(se) [73] *t* to do again. **2** *(reconstruir)* to remake, rebuild. **3** *(reparar)* to repair, mend. − **4** *p (reforzarse)* to regain strength. **5** *(serenarse)* to pull o.s. together. ▲ *pp* **rehecho,-a**.

rehén *mf* hostage.

rehogar [7] *t* to fry *slowly and partially.*

rehuir [62] *t* to avoid, shun.

rehusar [18] *t* to refuse, decline.

reimprimir *t* to reprint. ▲ *pp* **reimpreso,-a** or **reimprimido,-a**.

reina *f* queen.

reinado *m* reign.

reinar *i* to reign. **2** *(prevalecer)* to rule, prevail.

reincidir *i* to relapse *(en,* into).

reincorporar(se) *t* to reincorporate; *(a un trabajo)* to reinstate. − **2** *p* to rejoin.

reino *m* kingdom, reign.

reinserción *f* reintegration.

reintegrar(se) *t (restituir)* to reintegrate. **2** *(pago)* to refund. − **3** *p (volver a ejercer)* to return *(a,* to). **4** *(recobrarse)* to recover.

reintegro *m* FIN reimbursement.

reír(se) [37] *i-p* to laugh *(de,* at).

reiterar *t* to reiterate, repeat.

reivindicación *f* claim.

reivindicar [1] *t* to claim.

reja *f* grill, grating, grille. **2** AGR ploughshare.

rejilla *f (celosía)* grill(e). **2** *(de chimenea)* grate. **3** *(de silla)* wickerwork.

rejuvenecer(se) [43] *t* to rejuvenate. − **2** *p* to become rejuvenated.

relación *f* relation. **2** *(conexión)* link. **3** *(lista)* list. **4** *(relato)* account. ●*tener buenas relaciones,* to be well connected. ■ *relaciones públicas,* public relations.

relacionar(se) *t* to relate/connect *(con,* with). **2** *(relatar)* to tell. − **3** *p (tener amistad)* to get acquainted *(con,* with).

relajación *f* relaxation.

relajado,-a *adj* relaxed. **2** *(inmoral)* loose, dissolute.

relajar(se) *t* to relax. **2** *(aflojar)* to loosen, slacken. − **3** *p (descansarse)* to relax. **4** *(en las costumbres)* to let o.s. go. **5** *(dilatarse)* to slacken.

relamer(se) *t* to lick. − **2** *p* to lick one's lips.

relamido,-a *adj pej* affected.

relámpago *m* flash of lightning.

relampaguear *i* to flash. ▲ *Only used in the 3rd pers. It does not take a subject.*

relatar *t* to relate, tell.

relativo,-a *adj-m* relative.

relato *m* story, tale.

relax *m inv* relaxation. **2** *(prostitución)* call-girl service.

releer [61] *t* to reread.

relegar [7] *t* to relegate.

relevante *adj (significativo)* relevant. **2** *(importante)* excellent, outstanding.

relevar *t (sustituir)* to relieve. **2** *(eximir)* to exempt from. **3** *(destituir)* to dismiss. **4** *(engrandecer)* to exaggerate.

relevo *m* MIL relief. **2** DEP relay.

relicario *m* reliquary. **2** *(caja)* locket.

relieve *m* relief. ●*fig poner de* ~, to emphasize.

religión *f* religion.

religioso,-a *adj* religious. − **2** *m,f m* monk, *f* nun.

relinchar *i* to neigh, whinny.

reliquia *f* relic.

rellano *m* landing.

rellenar *t (volver a llenar)* to refill. **2** *(enteramente)* to cram. **3** *(cuestionario)* to fill in. **4** CULIN *(ave)* to stuff; *(pastel)* to fill.

relleno,-a *adj* stuffed. – **2** *m* CULIN *(aves)* stuffing; *(pasteles)* filling. **3** COST padding.

reló, reloj *m* clock; *(de pulsera)* watch. ●*contra* ~, against the clock. ■ ~ *de arena*, hourglass; ~ *de pared*, clock; ~ *de sol*, sundial; ~ *despertador*, alarm clock.

relojería *f (arte)* watchmaking. **2** *(tienda)* watchmaker's shop.

relojero,-a *m,f* watchmaker.

reluciente *adj* bright, shining, gleaming.

relucir [45] *i (brillar)* to shine. **2** *fig (destacar)* to excel. ●*sacar a* ~, to bring up.

relumbrante *adj* shining, dazzling.

remachar *t (clavo etc.)* to clinch. **2** *fig (confirmar)* to drive home.

remanente *m* remainder, residue.

remanso *m* backwater. ●*fig* ~ *de paz*, oasis of peace.

remar *i* to row.

remarcable *adj* remarkable.

remarcar [1] *t* to stress, underline.

rematado,-a *adj* absolute.

rematar *t* to finish off.

remate *m (final)* end. ●*de* ~, totally.

remedar *t* to imitate.

remediar [12] *t* to remedy. **2** *(reparar)* to repair. **3** *(socorrer)* to help, relieve. **4** *(evitar)* to avoid: *no lo puedo* ~, I can't help it.

remedio *m* remedy, cure. **2** *fig (solución)* solution. ●*no tener más* ~ *que ...* , to have no choice but to ... .

rememorar *t* to remember.

remendar [27] *t* to mend, repair. **2** COST to patch.

remendón,-ona *adj* mended. ■ *zapatero* ~, cobbler.

remero,-a *m,f* rower.

remesa *f (de dinero)* remittance. **2** *(de mercancías)* consignment, shipment.

remiendo *m* mend. **2** COST patch.

remilgado,-a *adj* affected.

remilgo *m* affectation.

reminiscencia *f* reminiscence.

remirado,-a *adj* over-cautious.

remisión *f (remite)* reference. **2** *(envío)* sending.

remite *m* sender's name and address.

remitente *mf* sender.

remitir(se) *t (enviar)* to remit, send. **2** *(referir)* to refer. **3** REL to forgive. **4** *(aplazar)* to postpone. – **5** *p* to refer *(a,* to).

remo *m* oar, paddle. **2** *(deporte)* rowing.

remodelación *f (modificación)* reshaping. **2** *(reorganización)* reorganization.

remojar *t* to soak *(en,* in).

remojo *m* soaking. ●*dejar/poner en* ~, to soak.

remolacha *f* beetroot. ■ ~ *azucarera*, sugar beet.

remolcador *m* MAR tug(boat). **2** AUTO tow truck.

remolcar [1] *t* to tow.

remolino *m* whirl; *(de agua)* whirlpool; *(de aire)* whirlwind. **2** *(de pelo)* cowlick.

remolón,-ona *adj* lazy, slack.

remolque *m (acción)* towing. **2** *(vehículo)* trailer. ●*a* ~, in tow.

remontar(se) *t (elevar)* to raise. **2** *(río)* to go up. **3** *(superar)* to overcome. – **4** *p (al volar)* to soar. **5** *(datar)* to go back *(a,* to).

remorder [32] *t* to cause remorse to.

remordimiento *m* remorse.

remoto,-a *adj* remote.

remover [32] *t (trasladar)* to move. **2** *(mezlar)* to stir. **3** *(conmover)* to disturb. **4** *(destituir)* to remove *(from office)*.

remuneración *f* remuneration.

remunerar *t* to remunerate, reward.

renacer [42] *i* to be reborn. **2** *fig* to revive.

renacimiento *m* rebirth. ■ *el Renacimiento*, the Renaissance.

renacuajo *m* tadpole.

rencilla *f* quarrel.

rencor *m* rancour.

rencoroso,-a *adj* rancorous.

rendición *f* surrender.

rendido,-a *adj (sumiso)* humble. **2** *(cansado)* worn out.

rendija *f* crack, split.

rendimiento *m (trabajo útil)* yield, output. **2** *(sumisión)* submissiveness. **3** *(cansancio)* exhaustion.

rendir(se) [34] *t (vencer)* to defeat. **2** *(cansar)* to exhaust. **3** *(restituir)* to render. **4** *(producir)* to yield, produce. **5** *(dar fruto)* to pay: *este negocio rinde poco*, this business doesn't pay. – **6** *i* AM to go a long way. – **7** *p* to surrender. ●~ *cuentas*, to account for one's actions; *fam* ¡*me rindo!*, I give up!

renegado,-a *adj-m,f* renegade.

renegar [48] *i (blasfemar)* to swear, curse. – **2** *t (negar)* to deny, disown. **3** *(abominar)* to detest.

renglón *m* line. ●*a* ~ *seguido*, right after.

reno *m* reindeer.

renombre *m* renown, fame.

renovación *f (de contrato etc.)* renewal. **2** *(de casa)* renovation.

renovar(se) [31] *t* to renew. **2** *(casa)* to renovate. **– 3** *p* to be renewed.

renquear *i* to limp; *(del pie)* to hobble. **2** *fig* to hardly manage.

renta *f (ingresos)* income. **2** *(beneficio)* interest. **3** *(alquiler)* rent. ■ ~ *per cápita,* per capita income.

rentabilidad *f* profitability.

rentabilizar [4] *t* to make profitable.

rentable *adj* profitable.

rentista *mf (experto)* financial expert. **2** *(que vive de rentas)* person of independent means.

renuncia *f* renouncement. **2** *(dimisión)* resignation.

renunciar [12] *t* to renounce, give up. **2** *(dimitir)* to resign. **3** *(trono)* to relinquish.

reñido,-a *adj (enemistado)* on bad terms. **2** *(de rivalidad)* bitter.

reñir [36] *i (discutir)* to quarrel, argue. **– 2** *t (reprender)* to scold.

reo *mf* offender, culprit.

reojo *mirar de* ~, to look out of the corner of one's eye (at).

repanchigarse, repantigarse [7] *p* to lounge, stretch out.

reparación *f* repair. **2** *(desagravio)* reparation.

reparar *t (arreglar)* to repair, mend. **2** *(desagraviar)* to make amends for. **3** *(reflexionar)* to consider. **4** *(corregir)* to correct. **– 5** *t-i (advertir)* ~ *en,* to notice, see. **6** *(remediar)* to make good.

reparo *m* objection. ●*no tener reparos en,* not to hesitate to; *poner reparos a,* to object to.

repartición *f* distribution.

repartidor,-ra *m,f* distributor.

repartir *t (distribuir)* to distribute. **2** *(entregar)* to give out; *(correo)* to deliver.

reparto *m* distribution. **2** *(distribución)* handing out; COM delivery. **3** TEAT cast.

repasar *t* to revise, go over. **2** *(máquina etc.)* to check. **3** COST to mend. **4** *fam (mirar)* to look over.

repaso *m* revision, check; *(lección)* review. **2** COST mending. **3** *(máquina etc.)* check, overhaul.

repatriar [14] *t* to repatriate.

repecho *m* hill. ●*a* ~, uphill.

repelente *adj* repellent, repulsive. ■ *irón niño,-a* ~, little know-all.

repeler *t (rechazar)* to repel, reject. **2** *(repugnar)* to disgust.

repente *m* sudden impulse. ●*de* ~, suddenly.

repentino,-a *adj* sudden. **– 2** *repentinamente adv* suddenly.

repercusión *f* repercussion.

repercutir *i (trascender)* to have repercussions (*en,* on). **2** *(rebotar)* to rebound. **3** *(sonido)* to echo.

repertorio *m (resumen)* repertory, index. **2** TEAT repertoire.

repesca *f fam* second chance; *(examen)* resit.

repetición *f* repetition.

repetidor *m* TÉC relay, booster station.

repetir [34] *t-i* to repeat.

repicar [1] *t (campanas)* to peal, ring out. **2** *(picar)* to chop, mince.

repique *m* peal, ringing.

repisa *f* ledge, shelf. ■ ~ *de la chimenea,* mantelpiece.

replegarse [48] *p* to fall back.

repleto,-a *adj* full up.

réplica *f* answer; *(objeción)* retort. **2** ART replica.

replicar [1] *t-i* to answer back, reply.

repoblación *f* repopulation. ■ ~ *forestal,* reafforestation.

repoblar [31] *t* to repopulate; *(bosque)* to reafforest.

repollo *m* cabbage.

reponer(se) [78] *t (devolver)* to put back, replace. **2** TEAT to put on again; CINEM to rerun. **3** *(replicar)* to reply. **– 4** *p* to recover. ▲ *pp repuesto,-a.*

reportaje *m* report.

reportar *t (ventajas etc.)* to bring. **2** *(refrenar)* to restrain.

reportero,-a *m,f* reporter.

reposado,-a *adj* calm, quiet.

reposapiés *m inv* footrest.

reposar *t-i* to rest.

reposición *f (restitución)* restoration. **2** TEAT revival; CINEM rerun.

reposo *m* rest.

repostar *t (provisiones)* to stock up with; *(combustible)* to fill up.

repostería *f (tienda)* confectioner's shop. **2** *(pastas)* cakes *pl.* **3** *(despensa)* pantry, larder.

reprender *t* to reprimand, scold.

represalia *f* reprisal, retaliation.

representación *f* representation. **2** TEAT performance.

representante *mf* representative.

representar *t* to represent. **2** TEAT to perform. **3** *(edad)* to appear to be. ●~ *mucho para algn.,* to mean a lot to sb.

representativo,-a *adj* representative.

represión *f* repression.

represivo,-a *adj* repressive.
reprimenda *f* reprimand.
reprimido,-a *adj-m,f* repressed (person).
reprimir(se) *t* to repress. **– 2** *p* to refrain o.s.
reprobar [31] *t (cosa)* to condemn; *(persona)* to reprove, censure.
reprochar *t* to reproach, censure.
reproche *m* reproach, criticism.
reproducción *f* reproduction.
reproducir(se) [46] *t-p* to reproduce.
reproductor,-ra *adj* reproducing. **2** ANAT reproductive.
reptar *i* to crawl. **2** *(adular)* to flatter.
reptil, réptil *m* reptile.
república *f* republic.
republicano,-a *adj-m,f* republican.
repudiar [12] *t* to repudiate.
repuesto,-a *pp →* **reponer. – 2** *adj (recuperado)* recovered. **– 3** *m (prevención)* store, supply. **4** *(recambio)* spare (part). ●*de ~,* spare, reserve.
repugnancia *f* repugnance.
repugnante *adj* repugnant.
repugnar *i* to disgust, revolt. **– 2** *t (negar)* to conflict.
repulsa *f* rebuff.
repulsión *f* repulsion, repugnance.
repulsivo,-a *adj* repulsive, revolting.
reputación *f* reputation.
reputar *t* to consider, deem.
requemar(se) *t-p* to scorch.
requerimiento *m* request. **2** JUR summons.
requerir [35] *t (necesitar)* to require. **2** *(solicitar)* to request. **3** *(persuadir)* to persuade.
requesón *m* cottage cheese.
requiebro *m* compliment.
requisa *f* inspection. **2** *(embargo)* requisition.
requisar *t* MIL to requisition. **2** *fam (apropiarse)* to grab.
requisito *m* requisite, requirement.
res *f* beast, animal.
resaca *f* hangover.
resaltar *i (sobresalir)* to project, jut out. **2** *fig* to stand out. ●*hacer ~,* to emphasize.
resbaladizo,-a *adj* slippery.
resbalar(se) *i-p (deslizarse)* to slide. **2** *(sin querer)* to slip; AUTO to skid. **3** *fig* to slip up.
resbalón *m* slip.
rescatar *t* to rescue. **2** *(recuperar)* to recover.
rescate *m* rescue. **2** *(dinero)* ransom.

rescindir *t* to rescind, cancel.
rescoldo *m* embers *pl*. **2** *fig* lingering doubt.
resecar(se) [1] *t-p* to dry up.
reseco,-a *adj* very dry. **2** *(flaco)* lean, thin.
resentido,-a *adj-m,f* resentful (person).
resentimiento *m* resentment.
resentirse [35] *p* to suffer (*de,* from). **2** *(enojarse)* to become resentful, feel resentment.
reseña *f (crítica)* review. **2** *(narración)* brief account.
reseñar *t (crítica)* to review. **2** *(narrar)* to give an account of.
reserva *f (de plazas)* booking, reservation. **2** *(provisión)* reserve. **3** *(cautela)* reservation. **4** *(discreción)* discretion. **5** *(vino)* vintage. **6** *(parque)* reserve. **7** MIL reserve. **8** *pl* COM stock(s). **– 9** *mf* DEP reserve, substitute. ●*sin ~,* openly.
reservado,-a *adj (plazas)* booked, reserved. **2** *(persona)* reserved, discreet. **– 3** *m* private room.
reservar(se) *t (plazas)* to book, reserve. **2** *(provisiones)* to keep, save. **3** *(ocultar)* to keep secret. **– 4** *p (conservarse)* to save o.s. (*para,* for). **5** *(cautelarse)* to withold.
resfriado *m* cold; *(poco importante)* chill.
resfriar(se) [13] *t* to cool. **– 2** *p* MED to catch a cold.
resguardar(se) *t-p* to protect (o.s.).
resguardo *m (protección)* protection. **2** *(recibo)* receipt.
residencia *f* residence. ■ *~ de estudiantes,* hall of residence, US dormitory.
residente *adj-mf* resident.
residir *i* to reside/live (*en,* in). **2** *fig* to lie (*en,* in).
residuo *m* residue. ■ *residuos radiactivos,* radioactive waste.
resignación *f* resignation.
resignar(se) *t-p* to resign (o.s.).
resina *f* resin.
resistencia *f* resistance. **2** *(capacidad)* endurance. **3** *(oposición)* reluctance, opposition.
resistente *adj* resistant (*a,* to). **2** *(fuerte)* tough.
resistir(se) *i* to resist. **– 2** *t (aguantar)* to bear, withstand. **3** *(tentación etc.)* to resist. **– 4** *p (forcejear)* to resist. **5** *(oponerse)* to offer resistance. **6** *fam (costar)* to struggle: *la física se le resiste,* he/she's struggling with physics.
resolución *f (ánimo)* resolution, decision. **2** *(solución)* solving.

resolver(se) [32] *t (decidir)* to resolve. **2** *(problema)* to solve. **3** QUÍM to dissolve. − **4** *p* to resolve, make up one's mind. ▲ *pp* **resuelto,-a.**

resollar [31] *i* to breathe heavily. **2** *(de cansancio)* to puff.

resonancia *f* resonance. **2** *fig* importance. ●*tener* ~, to cause a sensation.

resonar [31] *i* to resound. **2** *fig* to have repercussions.

resoplar *i* to breathe heavily. **2** *(de cansancio)* to puff and pant.

resoplido, resoplo *m* puff, pant.

resorte *m* spring. **2** *fig* means

respaldar(se) *t* to support, back (up). − **2** *p* to lean back *(en, on).*

respaldo *m* back. **2** *fig* support, backing.

respectar *i* to concern. ●*por lo que a mí respecta,* as far as I'm concerned. ▲ *Used only in the 3rd pers. sing.*

respectivo,-a *adj* respective.

respecto *m* relation. ●*con* ~ *a,* with regard to.

respetable *adj* respectable.

respetar *t* to respect.

respeto *m* respect. **2** *fam (miedo)* fear. ●*fml presentar sus respetos a algn.,* to pay one's respects to sb.

respetuoso,-a *adj* respectful.

respingo *m (sacudida)* start. **2** *fig* gesture of unwillingness.

respingón,-ona *adj nariz respingona,* snub nose.

respiración *f* breathing. **2** *(aliento)* breath. **3** *(aire)* ventilation.

respiradero *m* air vent. **2** *fig* rest.

respirar *i* to breathe. − **2** *i* to breathe (in). **3** *fig (relajar)* to breathe a sigh of relief.

respiratorio,-a *adj* respiratory.

respiro *m* breathing. **2** *(descanso)* breather. **3** *(prórroga)* respite.

resplandecer [43] *i* to shine.

resplandeciente *adj* resplendent.

resplandor *m (luz)* brightness. **2** *(esplendor)* splendour.

responder *t* to answer, reply. − **2** *i (corresponder)* to answer: ~ *a una descripción,* to fit a description. **3** *(replicar)* to answer back. ●~ *de/por,* to be responsible for.

respondón,-ona *adj* argumentative.

responsabilidad *f* responsibility.

responsabilizar(se) [4] *t* to make/hold responsible *(de,* for). − **2** *p* to assume responsibility *(de,* for).

responsable *adj* responsible. − **2** *mf (jefe)* head.

respuesta *f* answer, reply; *(reacción)* response.

resquebrajar(se) *t-p* to crack.

resquicio *m* crack, gap. **2** *fig* glimmer; *(oportunidad)* chance.

resta *f* substraction.

restablecer(se) [43] *t* to reestablish, restore. − **2** *p* MED to recover, get better.

restallar *i (látigo)* to crack. **2** *(hacer ruido)* to crackle.

restante *adj* remaining.

restañar *t* to staunch.

restar *t* MAT to subtract. **2** *(disminuir)* to reduce. − **3** *i* to be left, remain. ●~ *importancia a algo,* to play sth. down.

restauración *f* restoration.

restaurador,-ra *m,f* restorer.

restaurante *m* restaurant.

restaurar *t* to restore.

restituir [62] *t* to restore. **2** *(devolver)* to return, give back.

resto *m* remainder, rest. **2** *pl* remains; CULIN leftovers. ■ *restos mortales,* mortal remains.

restregar [48] *t* to rub hard.

restricción *f* restriction.

restrictivo,-a *adj* restrictive.

restringir(se) [6] *t-p* to restrict (o.s.).

resucitar *t-i* to resuscitate. **2** *fig* to revive.

resuelto,-a *pp* → **resolver.** − **2** *adj (decidido)* resolute, bold.

resuello *m* breathing.

resulta *f* consequence. ●*de resultas de,* as a result of.

resultado *m* result. ●*dar buen* ~, to work well.

resultar *i* to result. **2** *(ocurrir, ser)* to turn out to be: *resultó ser muy simpático,-a,* he/she turned out to be very nice. **3** *(salir)* to come out: ~ *bien/mal,* to come out well/badly. ●*resulta que,* it turns out that.

resumen *m* summary. ●*en* ~, in short, to sum up.

resumir *t* to summarize.

resurgimiento *m* resurgence.

resurgir [6] *i* to reappear, revive.

resurrección *f* resurrection.

retablo *m* altarpiece.

retaguarda, retaguardia *f* rearguard.

retahíla *f* string, series.

retal *m (trozo de tela)* oddment. **2** *(desperdicio)* remnant.

retama *f* broom.

retar *t* to challenge.

retardar *t (detener)* to slow down. **2** *(retrasar)* to delay.

retardo *m* delay.

retazo *m (retal)* remnant. **2** *(fragmento)* portion.

retén *m* MIL reserves *pl.* **2** *(previsión)* stock.

retener [87] *t (conservar)* to retain, keep back. **2** *(en la memoria)* to remember. **3** *(arrestar)* to detain, arrest. **4** FIN to deduct, withold.

retentiva *f* memory.

reticencia *f* reticence, reserve.

retina *f* retina.

retintín *m (sonido)* tinkling, ring. **2** *fig* innuendo, sarcastic tone.

retirada *f* MIL retreat, withdrawal.

retirado,-a *adj (apartado)* remote. − **2** *adj-m,f* MIL retired (officer).

retirar(se) *t (apartar)* to take away. − **2** *p* MIL to retreat. **3** *(apartarse)* to withdraw. **4** *(jubilarse)* to retire. ●*fml puede ~se,* you may leave.

retiro *m (jubilación)* retirement. **2** *(pensión)* pension. **3** *(lugar, recogimiento)* retreat.

reto *m* challenge. **2** AM insult.

retocar [1] *t* to touch up.

retoño *m* BOT sprout, shoot. **2** *fig* kid.

retoque *m* finishing touch.

retorcer(se) [54] *t* to twist. **2** *(tergiversar)* to distort. − **3** *p (de dolor)* to writhe; *(de risa)* to double up with laughter.

retorcido,-a *adj fig* twisted.

retórica *f* rhetoric.

retórico,-a *adj* rhetorical.

retornar(se) *t (restituir)* to return, give back. − **2** *i-p (volver)* to come/go back.

retorno *m* return. **2** *(recompensa)* reward.

retortijón *m* twisting. **2** *pl* MED cramps.

retozar [4] *i* to frolic, romp.

retractar(se) *t-p* to retract.

retraer(se) [88] *t (volver a traer)* to bring back. **2** *(reprochar)* to reproach. **3** *(disuadir)* to dissuade. − **4** *p (refugiarse)* to take refuge.

retraído,-a *adj* unsociable, withdrawn.

retransmisión *f* broadcast.

retransmisor *m* transmitter.

retransmitir *t* to broadcast.

retrasado,-a *adj (persona)* behind. **2** *(reloj)* slow. **3** *(tren)* late. **4** *(país)* backward. − **5** *m,f* mentally retarded person.

retrasar(se) *t (diferir)* to delay, put off. **2** *(reloj)* to put back. − **3** *i-p (ir atrás)* to fall behind: *va retrasado,-a en física,* he's behind in physics. **4** *(llegar tarde)* to be late. **5** *(reloj)* to be slow.

retraso *m* delay. **2** *(subdesarrollo)* backwardness.

retratar *t* ART to portray. **2** *(foto)* to photograph. **3** *fig* to describe.

retrato *m* ART portrait. **2** *(foto)* photograph. **3** *fig* description. ■ ~ *robot,* identikit/photofit picture.

retreta *f* retreat.

retrete *m* toilet, lavatory.

retribución *f (pago)* pay. **2** *(recompensa)* recompense, reward.

retribuir [41] *t (pagar)* to pay. **2** *(recompensar)* to remunerate, reward.

retroactivo,-a *adj* retroactive.

retroceder *i* to go back.

retroceso *m* backward movement.

retrógrado,-a *adj-m,f* reactionary.

retrospectivo,-a *adj-f* retrospective.

retrovisor *m* rear-view mirror.

retumbar *i* to resound.

reuma, reúma *m* rheumatism.

reumatismo *m* rheumatism.

reunión *f* meeting.

reunir(se) [19] *t-p* to meet.

revalidación *f* confirmation, ratification.

revalidar *t* to confirm, ratify.

revalorizar [4] *t* to revalue.

revancha *f* revenge.

revelación *f* revelation.

revelado *m* developing.

revelar *t* to reveal. **2** *(fotos)* to develop.

revender *t* to resell. **2** *(entradas)* to tout.

reventa *f* resale. **2** *(de entradas)* touting.

reventar(se) [27] *t-i-p* to burst. − **2** *t (molestar)* to annoy: *su amiga me revienta,* I hate his friend. − **3** *p (cansarse)* to tire o.s. out.

reventón *m* burst. **2** AUTO blowout.

reverberación *f* reverberation.

reverberar *i* to reverberate.

reverdecer [43] *i* to grow green again. **2** *fig* to revive.

reverencia *f* reverence. **2** *(gesto)* bow, curtsy.

reverenciar [12] *t* to revere, venerate.

reverendo,-a *adj-m,f* reverend.

reversible *adj* reversible.

reverso *m* reverse.

revertir [35] *i* to revert. **2** *(resultar)* to result *(en,* in).

revés *m* back, reverse. **2** *(bofetada)* slap. **3** *(contrariedad)* misfortune. ●*al/del ~, (al contrario)* the other way round; *(interior en exterior)* inside out; *(boca abajo)* upside down, the wrong way up; *(la parte de detrás delante)* back to front.

revestimiento *m* covering, coating.

revestir(se) [34] *t* to cover/coat (*de,* with). **2** *(disimular)* to conceal. **3** *(presentar)* to possess, have. **– 4** *p* to arm o.s.: ~*se de paciencia,* to arm o.s. with patience.

revisar *t* to revise, review, check.

revisión *f* revision. ■ ~ *de cuentas,* audit; ~ *médica,* checkup.

revisor,-ra *m,f* ticket inspector.

revista *f (publicación)* magazine, review. **2** *(inspección)* inspection. **3** TEAT revue.

revistero *m* magazine rack.

revitalizar [4] *t* to revitalize.

revivir *i* to revive.

revocar [1] *t (dejar sin efecto)* to revoke. **2** *(disuadir)* to dissuade. **3** *(enlucir)* to plaster. **4** *(repintar)* to whitewash.

revolcar(se) [49] *t (derribar)* to knock down/over. **2** *(vencer)* to floor. **– 3** *p* to roll about.

revolotear *i* to fly/flutter about.

revoloteo *m* fluttering.

revoltijo, revoltillo *m* mess, medley, jumble. **2** CULIN scrambled egg.

revoltoso,-a *adj (rebelde)* rebellious. **2** *(travieso)* mischievous, naughty. **– 3** *m,f (sedicioso)* troublemaker.

revolución *f* revolution.

revolucionar *t* to revolutionize.

revolucionario,-a *adj-m,f* revolutionary.

revolver(se) [32] *t (agitar)* to stir, shake. **2** *(desordenar)* to mess up. **3** *(producir náuseas)* to upset. **– 4** *p (moverse)* to move. **5** *(tiempo)* to turn stormy. ▲ *pp* *revuelto,-a.*

revólver *m* revolver. ▲ *pl* revólveres.

revuelo *m* fig commotion.

revuelta *f (revolución)* revolt, riot. **2** *(curva)* bend, turn.

revuelto,-a *pp →* revolver. **– 2** *adj (desordenado)* confused, mixed up. **3** *(intricado)* intricate. **4** *(revoltoso)* agitated.

rey *m* king. ■ *(día de) Reyes,* the Epiphany; *los Reyes Magos,* the Three Kings, the Three Wise Men.

reyerta *f* quarrel, row, fight.

rezagar(se) [7] *t* to leave behind. **2** *(atrasar)* to delay, put off. **– 3** *p* to fall/lag behind.

rezar [4] *t* to pray. **2** *fam* to say, read: *la carta reza así,* the letter says this.

rezo *m* prayer.

rezumar(se) *i* to ooze, leak. **2** *fig* to exude. **– 3** *p* to leak out.

ría *f* estuary; *(técnicamente)* ria.

riada *f* flood.

ribera *f (de río)* bank. **2** *(de mar)* (sea)-shore.

ribete *m* border, trimming.

ribetear *t* to edge, border.

ricacho,-a, ricachón,-ona *m,f fam* moneybags.

rico,-a *adj (acaudalado)* rich, wealthy. **2** *(abundante)* rich; *(tierra)* fertile. **3** *(sabroso)* tasty, delicious. **4** *fam* lovely. **5** *(tratamiento)* sunshine: *mira ~, haz lo que te dé la gana,* look sunshine, just do what you want.

rictus *m inv* rictus. **2** *(de dolor)* wince. **3** *(de mofa)* grin.

ridiculez *f* ridiculous thing/action. **2** *(nimiedad)* triviality.

ridiculizar [4] *t* to ridicule.

ridículo,-a *adj* ridiculous, absurd. **– 2** *m* ridicule. ●*hacer el ~,* to make a fool of o.s.; *poner a algn. en ~,* to make a fool of sb.

riego *m* irrigation, watering. ■ ~ *sanguíneo,* blood circulation.

riel *m* rail.

rienda *f* rein. **2** *(control)* restraint. ●*fig dar ~ suelta a,* to give free rein to.

riesgo *m* risk, danger.

rifa *f* raffle.

rifar *t* to raffle (off).

rigidez *f* stiffness. **2** *(severidad)* strictness.

rígido,-a *adj* rigid, stiff. **2** *(severo)* strict.

rigor *m* rigour. **2** *(severidad)* strictness. **3** *(dureza)* harshness. ●*de ~,* indispensable; *en ~,* strictly speaking.

riguroso,-a *adj* rigorous. **2** *(severo)* severe, strict.

rima *f* rhyme. **2** *pl* poems.

rimar *t-i* to rhyme.

rimbombante *adj* ostentatious.

rímel *m* mascara.

rincón *m* corner.

rinoceronte *m* rhinoceros.

riña *f (pelea)* fight. **2** *(discusión)* quarrel.

riñón *m* kidney. ●*fam costar un ~,* to cost a bomb.

río *m* river. ●*en ~ revuelto,* in troubled waters.

riqueza *f (cualidad)* richness. **2** *(abundancia)* wealth, riches *pl.*

risa *f* laugh. **2** *pl* laughter *sing.* ●*tomar a ~,* to treat as a joke.

risco *m* crag, cliff.

risotada *f* guffaw.

ristra *f* string: ~ *de ajos,* string of garlic.

risueño,-a *adj* smiling. **2** *(animado)* cheerful. **3** *(próspero)* bright.

ritmo *m* rhythm. **2** *fig* pace, speed: *trabajar a buen ~*, to work at a good pace.

rito *m* rite.

ritual *adj-m* ritual.

rival *mf* rival.

rivalidad *f* rivalry.

rivalizar [4] *i* to rival.

rizado,-a *adj (pelo)* curly. **2** MAR choppy. **— 3** *m* curling.

rizar(se) [4] *t-p (pelo)* to curl. **— 2** *t (papel)* to crease. ●*fig ~ el rizo,* to split hairs.

rizo *m* curl. **2** *(de agua)* ripple. **3** *(tejido)* terry towelling. **4** AV loop.

robar *t (banco, persona)* to rob; *(objeto)* to steal; *(casa)* to break into.

roble *m* oak (tree).

robo *m* theft, robbery; *(en casa)* burglary.

robot *m* robot.

robustecer [43] *t* to strengthen, fortify.

robusto,-a *adj* robust, strong.

roca *f* rock.

rocambolesco,-a *adj fam* incredible, fantastic.

roce *m (señal) (en superficie)* scuff mark; *(en piel)* chafing mark. **2** *(contacto físico)* light touch. **3** *(trato)* contact. **4** *(disensión)* friction.

rociador *m* sprayer.

rociar [13] *t* to spray. **2** *(arrojar)* to scatter. **— 3** *i* to fall (dew): *hoy ha rociado,* there's a dew this morning. ▲ **3** *used only in the 3rd pers. It does not take a subject.*

rocío *m* dew.

rockero,-a *adj* rock. **— 2** *m,f (cantante)* rock singer, *(fan)* rock fan.

rocoso,-a *adj* rocky.

rodado,-a *adj (vehículo)* wheeled. **2** *(caballo)* dappled **3** *(piedra)* rounded. **4** *(persona)* experienced. ■ *tráfico ~,* wheeled traffic.

rodaja *f* slice.

rodaje *m* CINEM filming, shooting. **2** AUTO running-in.

rodar [31] *i (dar vueltas)* to roll, turn. **2** *(caer)* to roll down. **3** *(rondar)* to wander about, roam. **4** *(vehículos)* to run (on wheels). **— 5** *t* CINEM to shoot. **6** AUTO to run in.

rodear(se) *t (cercar)* to surround, encircle. **2** *(hacer dar vuelta)* to make a detour. **— 3** *p* to sorrounds o.s. *(de,* with).

rodeo *m (desviación)* detour. **2** *(elusión)* evasiveness. **3** *(de ganado)* roundup; *(espectáculo)* rodeo.

rodera *f* tyre mark.

rodilla *f* knee. ●*ponerse de rodillas,* to kneel down.

rodillera *f* DEP knee pad. **2** COST knee patch.

rodillo *m* roller. **2** CULIN rolling pin.

rodríguez *m estar de ~,* to be a grass widower.

roedor,-ra *adj-m* rodent.

roer [82] *t* to gnaw.

rogar [52] *t* to request, ask, beg.

rojo,-a *adj-m-m,f* red.

rol *m* list, catalogue. **2** *(papel)* role.

rollizo,-a *adj* plump, chubby.

rollo *m* roll. **2** *fam (aburrimiento)* drag, bore. **3** *fam (amorío)* affair.

romance *adj-m* LING Romance (language). **— 2** *m (amorío)* romance.

románico,-a *adj-m* ARQ Romanesque. **2** LING Romance.

romántico,-a *adj-m,f* romantic.

rombo *m* rhombus. **2** *(naipes)* diamond.

romería *f* pilgrimage. **2** *(excursión)* picnic.

romero,-a *m* BOT rosemary. **— 2** *m,f (peregrino)* pilgrim.

rompecabezas *m inv (jigsaw)* puzzle. **2** *(problema)* riddle.

rompecorazones *mf inv fam* heartthrob.

rompeolas *m inv* breakwater.

romper(se) *t gen* to break; *(papel, tela)* to tear; *(cristal)* to smash. **2** *(gastar)* to wear out. **3** *(relaciones)* to break off. **— 4** *i* to begin/start *(a,* with): *~ a llorar,* to start to cry. ●*de rompe y rasga,* resolute, determined; *~ con algn.,* to quarrel with sb.; *~se la cabeza,* to rack one's brains. ▲ *pp roto,-a.*

rompiente *m* reef.

ron *m* rum.

roncar [1] *i* to snore.

ronco,-a *adj* hoarse. ●*quedarse ~,* to lose one's voice.

ronda *f (patrulla)* patrol, night watch. **2** *(de policía)* beat. **3** *(visita)* round. **3** *(de bebidas, cartas)* round. **4** *(músicos)* group of strolling minstrels. **5** AUTO ring road.

rondar *t-i (vigilar)* to patrol. **2** *(merodear)* to prowl around.

ronquear *i* to be hoarse.

ronquera *f* hoarseness.

ronquido *m* snore, snoring.

ronronear *i* to purr.

roña *f (suciedad)* filth, dirt. **— 2** *mf (tacaño)* scrooge.

roñoso,-a *adj (sucio)* filthy, dirty. **2** *(tacaño)* scrooge.

ropa *f* clothing, clothes *pl.* ■ *~ blanca,* linen; *~ interior,* underwear.

ropaje *m* clothing.

ropero *m* wardrobe.

roquero,-a *adj-m,f* → **rockero,-a**.

rosa *adj-m (color)* pink. — **2** *f* BOT rose. •*fresco,-a como una ~,* as fresh as a daisy. ■ *~ náutica/de los vientos,* compass rose.

rosado,-a *adj* rosy, pink. — **2** *adj-m (vino)* rosé.

rosal *m* rosebush.

rosaleda *f* rose garden.

rosario *m* rosary. **2** *fig* string. •*acabar como el ~ de la aurora,* to come to a bad end.

rosbif *m* roast beef.

rosca *f (en espiral)* thread. **2** *(anilla)* ring. •*fam pasarse de ~,* to go too far.

rosco *m* ring-shaped roll/pastry. •*arg no comerse un ~,* not to get one's oats.

rosquilla *f* doughnut.

rostro *m* *fml* face.

rotación *f* rotation.

rotativo,-a *adj* rotary. — **2** *m* newspaper.

rotatorio,-a *adj* rotary.

roto,-a *pp* → **romper**. — **2** *adj* broken. — **3** *m* hole, tear.

rotonda *f* rotunda.

rótula *f* knee-cap.

rotulador *m* felt-tip pen.

rotular *t* to label, letter.

rótulo *m (etiqueta)* label. **2** *(letrero)* sign. **3** *(anuncio)* poster, placard. ■ *~ luminoso,* illuminated sign.

rotundo,-a *adj* categorical. — **2** *rotundamente adv* flatly, roundly.

rotura *f* break(ing). **2** MED fracture.

roturar *t* to plough, US to plow.

rozadura *f* scratch.

rozar(se) [4] *t-i (tocar ligeramente)* to touch lightly. — **2** *t (raer)* to rub against. — **3** *p (tropezarse)* to trip over one's feet. **4** *(ser familiar)* to be familiar.

rubéola *f* German measles, rubella.

rubí *m* ruby. ▲ *pl* **rubíes**.

rubio,-a *adj* blond(e). ■ *tabaco ~,* Virginia tobacco.

rubor *m* blush, flush.

ruborizarse [4] *p* to blush, go red.

rúbrica *f* flourish (in signature). **2** *(título)* title.

rubricar [1] *t* to sign with a flourish. **2** *(respaldar)* to endorse.

rudeza *f* roughness, coarseness.

rudimentario,-a *adj* rudimentary.

rudimento *m* rudiment.

rudo,-a *adj* rough, coarse.

rueda *f* wheel. **2** *(círculo)* circle, ring. **3** *(rodaja)* round slice. **4** *(turno)* round. •*fam ir sobre ruedas,* to go like clockwork. ■ *~ de recambio,* spare wheel.

ruego *m* request.

rufián *m (proxeneta)* pimp. **2** *(canalla)* scoundrel.

rugido *m* roar, bellow; *(del viento)* howl.

rugir [6] *i* to roar, bellow; *(viento)* to howl.

rugoso,-a *adj* rough, wrinkled.

ruido *m* noise. **2** *(jaleo)* din, row. •*hacer/meter ~,* to make a noise; *mucho ~ y pocas nueces,* much ado about nothing.

ruidoso,-a *adj* noisy, loud.

ruin *adj pey* mean, base, despicable, vile. **2** *(pequeño)* petty, insignificant. **3** *(tacaño)* stingy.

ruina *f* ruin. •*amenazar ~,* to be about to collapse.

ruinoso,-a *adj* ruinous, disastrous.

ruiseñor *m* nightingale.

rulo *m (para pelo)* curler.

rumba *f* r(h)umba.

rumbo *m* course, direction. •*(con) ~ a,* bound for.

rumiante *adj-m* ruminant.

rumiar [12] *i* to ruminate. **2** *fig* to meditate.

rumor *m (murmullo)* murmur. **2** *(noticia, voz)* rumour.

rumorearse *i* to be rumoured. ▲ *Used only in the 3rd pers. It does not take a subject.*

runrún, runruneo *m* buzz, noise.

rupestre *adj* rock. ■ *pintura ~,* cave painting.

ruptura *f* breaking, breakage. **2** *fig* breaking-off.

rural *adj* rural, country.

rústico,-a *adj* rustic. — **2** *m* peasant. •*(libro) en rústica,* paper-backed (book).

ruta *f* route.

rutina *f* routine.

rutinario,-a *adj* routine.

S

sábado *m* Saturday.

sabana *f* savanna(h).

sábana *f* sheet.

sabandija *f* ZOOL bug. **2** *fig (persona)* swine, louse.

sabañón *m* chilblain.

sabático,-a *adj* sabbatical.

sabelotodo *mf inv pey* know-all.

saber [83] *m* knowledge. – **2** *t-i* to know. – **3** *i (sabor a)* to taste (*a*, of). **4** AM *(soler)* to be in the habit of. ●*hacer ~*, to inform; *que yo sepa*, as far as I know; *~ (hablar) un idioma*, to be able to speak a language: *¿sabes francés?*, do/can you speak French?; *fml a ~*, namely; *fam ¡y yo que sé!*, how should I know!

sabiduría *f* knowledge. **2** *(prudencia)* wisdom.

sabiendas *a ~*, *adv* knowingly.

sabihondo,-a *m,f pey* know-(it-)all.

sabio,-a *adj-m,f* learned (person).

sablazo *m (golpe)* blow with a sabre. **2** *fam (de dinero)* sponging.

sable *m* sabre.

sablear *t fam* to touch for money, scrounge money from.

sabor *m* taste, flavour. **2** *fig* feeling. ●*fig dejar (a algn.) mal ~ de boca*, to leave a bad taste in one's mouth.

saborear *t* to taste. **2** *fig* to savour.

sabotaje *m* sabotage.

sabotear *t* to sabotage.

sabroso,-a *adj* tasty. **2** *(agradable)* pleasant, delightful.

sabueso *m* bloodhound. **2** *(persona)* sleuth.

sacacorchos *m inv* corkscrew.

sacapuntas *m inv* pencil sharpener.

sacar [1] *t gen* to take out. **2** *(obtener)* to get. **3** *(resolver)* to make out, solve. **4** *(quitar)* to remove. **5** *(extraer)* to extract, pull out. **6** *(restar)* to subtract. **7** *(premio)* to win. **8** *(foto)* to take. **9** *(moda)* to introduce. **10** *(billete)* to buy. **11** DEP to serve. **12** AM *(quitar)* to remove. ●*~ a bailar*, to ask to dance; *~ a luz*, to bring to light; *(libro)* to publish; *~ a relucir*, to mention; *~ adelante*, to carry out; *(hijos)* to bring up; *~ de quicio/sí*, to infuriate; *~ de un apuro*, to bail out; *~ algo en limpio*, to make sense of sth.; *~ la lengua*, to stick one's tongue out.

sacarina *f* saccharin(e).

sacerdote *m* priest.

sacerdotisa *f* priestess.

saciar(se) [12] *t* to satiate; *(sed)* to quench. **2** *fig* to satisfy. – **3** *p* to satiate o.s., be satiated.

saciedad *f* satiety, satiation. ●*hasta la ~*, over and over (again).

saco *m* sack, bag. **2** *(contenido)* sackful, bagful. **3** AM coat. ■ *~ de dormir*, sleeping bag.

sacramento *m* sacrament.

sacrificar(se) [1] *t* to sacrifice. **2** *(reses)* to slaughter. – **3** *p* to sacrifice o.s. (*por*, for).

sacrificio *m* sacrifice.

sacrilegio *m* sacrilege.

sacristán,-ana *m,f* verger, sexton.

sacristía *f* vestry, sacristy.

sacudida *f* shake.

sacudidor *m* carpet beater.

sacudir(se) *t* to shake. **2** *(para quitar el polvo)* to shake off. **3** *(golpear)* to beat. – **4** *p* to shake off.

sádico,-a *adj* sadistic. – **2** *m,f* sadist.

sagacidad *f* sagacity.

sagaz *adj* clever, sagacious.

Sagitario *m inv* Sagittarius.

sagrado,-a *adj* sacred, holy.

sagrario *m* tabernacle.

sainete *m* TEAT comic sketch.

sal f salt. 2 fig wit. ■ *sales de baño,* bath salts.

sala f room. 2 *(de hospital)* ward. 3 JUR *(lugar)* courtroom; *(tribunal)* court. ■ ~ *de espera,* waiting room; ~ *de fiestas,* nightclub, discotheque.

salado,-a adj salted. 2 fam fig witty. 3 AM unlucky.

salamandra f salamander.

salar t to salt.

salario m salary, wages pl.

salazón f salted meat/fish.

salchicha f sausage.

salchichón m salami-type sausage.

saldar t *(cuenta)* to settle, balance. 2 *(rebajar)* to sell off.

saldo m *(de una cuenta)* balance. 2 *(pago)* liquidation, settlement. 3 *(mercancía)* remnant: *precios de* ~, bargain prices.

salero m saltcellar. 2 fig *(gracia)* charm, wit.

saleroso,-a adj charming, witty.

salida f *(acto)* departure. 2 DEP start. 3 *(excursión)* trip, outing. 4 *(puerta etc.)* exit, way out. 5 *(astro)* rising. 6 *(despacho)* dispatch. 7 FIN *(inversión)* outlay. 8 INFORM output. 9 fig *(ocurrencia)* witty remark. ■ ~ *de tono,* improper remark.

saliente adj projecting. – 2 m projection.

salir(se) [84] i gen to go out. 2 *(ir de dentro para fuera)* to come out: *ven, sal al jardín,* come out here into the garden. 3 *(partir)* to leave: *el autobús sale a las tres,* the bus leaves at three. 4 *(aparecer)* to appear: ~ *en los periódicos,* to be/appear in the newspapers. 5 *(proceder)* to come *(de,* from). 6 *(resultar)* to (turn out) to be: ~ *vencedor,-ra* to be the winner. 7 *(venir a costar)* to come to. 8 *(sobresalir)* to project, stand out. – 9 p *(líquido)* to leak (out). ●~ *adelante,* to be successful; ~ *bien/mal,* to turn out well/badly; ~ *con algn.,* to go out with sb.; ~ *con algo,* to come out with: *¡ahora me sales con esa!,* now you come out with this!; ~ *de dudas,* to make sure; fam ~ *pitando/disparado,-a,* to rush out; fam ~*se con la suya,* to get one's own way.

saliva f saliva.

salmo m psalm.

salmón m salmon.

salmonete m red mullet.

salmuera f brine.

salón m *(en casa)* drawing room, lounge. 2 *(público)* hall. ■ ~ *de actos,* assembly hall; ~ *de baile,* ballroom; ~ *de belleza,* beauty salon/parlour.

salpicadero m dashboard.

salpicadura f splash(ing).

salpicar [1] t to splash, spatter. 2 fig to sprinkle.

salpicón m CULIN cocktail.

salpimentar [1] t to season.

salsa f sauce.

salsera f gravy boat.

saltador,-ra adj jumping. – 2 m,f jumper.

saltamontes m inv grasshopper.

saltar(se) i to jump. 2 *(romperse)* to break. 3 *(desprenderse)* to come off. 4 fig *(enfadarse)* to blow up. – 5 t to jump (over). 6 *(omitir)* to skip, miss out. – 7 p *(ley etc.)* to ignore. ●~ *a la cuerda/comba,* to skip; ~ *en pedazos,* to break into pieces; fig ~ *a la vista,* to be obvious.

saltimbanqui mf *(titiritero)* puppeteer. 2 *(malabarista)* juggler.

salto m jump, leap. 2 DEP jump; *(natación)* dive. 3 fig gap. ●fig *a* ~ *de mata,* flying and hiding; fig *en un* ~, in a flash. ■ ~ *de agua,* waterfall, falls pl; ~ *de cama,* negligée; ~ *mortal,* somersault.

salubre adj salubrious, healthy.

salud f health. – 2 interj cheers!

saludable adj healthy, wholesome. 2 *(beneficioso)* good.

saludar t to say hello to; *(mostrando respeto)* to greet. 2 MIL to salute. ●*salúdale de mi parte,* give him/her my regards.

saludo m, **salutación** f greeting. ●*(en carta)* "*un (atento)* ~ *de ...*", "best wishes from ... ".

salvación f salvation.

salvado m bran.

salvador,-ra adj saving. – 2 m,f saviour.

salvaguardar t to safeguard *(de,* from).

salvaguardia f safeguard, protection. – 2 m guardian.

salvajada f atrocity.

salvaje adj gen wild; *(pueblo)* savage, uncivilized. – 2 mf savage.

salvam(i)ento m rescue.

salvar(se) t to save, rescue *(de,* from). 2 *(obstáculo)* to clear. 3 *(dificultad)* to overcome. 4 *(distancia)* to cover. 5 *(exceptuar)* to exclude. – 6 p *(sobrevivir)* to survive. 7 REL to be saved. ●*¡sálvese quien pueda!,* every man for himself!

salvavidas m inv lifebelt.

salvedad f exception.

salvia f sage.

salvo,-a adj unharmed, safe. – 2 adv except (for). ●*estar a* ~, to be safe.

salvoconducto m safe-conduct.

sambenito *m fig* stigma. ●*colgarle un ~ a algn.*, to give sb. a bad name.

san *adj* → **santo,-a**. ▲ *Used before all masculine names except those beginning To- and Do-.*

sanar *t-i* to heal, cure. − **2** *i (enfermo)* to recover, get better.

sanatorio *m* sanatorium.

sanción *f* sanction.

sancionar *t* to sanction.

sandalia *f* sandal.

sándalo *m* sandalwood.

sandía *f* watermelon.

sanear *t (tierra)* to drain. **2** *(edificio)* to clean. **3** *fig* to remedy, put right.

sangrar *t-i* to bleed. − **2** *t (texto)* to indent.

sangre *f* blood. ●*de ~ caliente/fría,* warm-/cold-blooded. ■ *~ fría,* sangfroid.

sangría *f (bebida)* sangria. **2** MED bleeding. **3** *(texto)* indentation.

sangriento,-a *adj* bloody. **2** *(cruel)* cruel.

sanguijuela *f* leech.

sanguinario,-a *adj* bloodthirsty.

sanidad *f* health. **2** *(servicios)* public health.

sanitario,-a *adj* sanitary. − **2** *m,f* health officer. − **3** *m* toilet. **4** *pl* bathroom fittings.

sano,-a *adj* healthy. **2** *(entero)* sound. ●*~ y salvo,* safe and sound.

santiamén *en un ~, adv* in the twinkling of an eye.

santidad *f* saintliness, holiness.

santificar [1] *t* to sanctify.

santiguar(se) [22] *t* to bless. − **2** *p* to cross o.s.

santo,-a *adj* holy, sacred. **2** *(para enfatizar)* blessed: *todo el ~ día,* the whole day long. − **3** *m,f* saint. − **4** *m (onomástica)* saint's day. ●*fam írsele a algn. el ~ al cielo,* to clean forget sth. ■ *~ y seña,* countersign. ▲ → **san**.

santuario *m* sanctuary.

saña *f (enojo)* rage, fury. **2** *(crueldad)* cruelty.

sapo *m* toad.

saque *m (tenis)* service. **2** *(fútbol)* kick-off.

saquear *t* to sack, plunder; *(en casas y comercios)* to loot.

saqueo *m* sacking, plundering; *(casa, comercio)* looting.

sarampión *m* measles *pl*.

sarcasmo *m* sarcasm.

sarcástico,-a *adj* sarcastic.

sardina *f* sardine.

sargento *m* sergeant.

sarna *f* MED scabies. **2** ZOOL mange.

sarro *m* MED tartar. **2** *(sedimiento)* deposit.

sarta *f* string.

sartén *f* frying pan, US skillet. ●*fig tener la ~ por el mango,* to have the upper hand.

sastre,-a *m,f m* tailor, *f* tailoress.

sastrería *f (tienda)* tailor's shop. **2** *(oficio)* tailoring.

satánico,-a *adj* satanic.

satélite *m* satellite.

satén *m* satin.

sátira *f* satire.

satírico,-a *adj* satiric(al).

satirizar [4] *t* to satirize.

sátiro *m* satyr.

satisfacción *f* satisfaction.

satisfacer(se) [85] *t* to satisfy. **2** *(deuda)* to pay. − **3** *p* to be satisfied. ▲ *pp* **satisfecho,-a**.

satisfactorio,-a *adj* satisfactory.

satisfecho,-a *pp* → **satisfacer**. − **2** *adj (contento)* satisfied, pleased. **3** *(presumido)* self-satisfied.

saturar *t* to saturate.

sauce *m* willow. ■ *~ llorón,* weeping willow.

sauna *f* sauna.

savia *f* sap.

saxofón, saxófono *m* saxophone.

sayo *m* cassock.

sazón *f (madurez)* ripeness. **2** *(sabor)* taste. **3** *(tiempo, ocasión)* season, time. ●*a la ~,* at that time.

sazonar(se) *t-p (madurar)* to ripen, mature. − **2** *t (comida)* to season, flavour.

se *pron (reflexivo) (a él mismo)* himself; *(a ella misma)* herself; *(de por sí)* itself; *(a usted mismo)* yourself; *(a ellos mismos)* themselves; *(a ustedes mismos)* yourselves. **2** *(recíproco)* one another, each other: *~ quieren,* they love each other. **3** *(en pasivas e impersonales) ~ dice que ...,* it is said that ..., *~ han abierto las puertas,* the doors have been opened. **4** *(objeto indirecto) (a él)* him; *(a ella)* her; *(cosa)* it; *(a usted/ustedes)* you; *(a ellos/ ellas)* them: *~ lo diré mañana,* (a usted) I'll tell you tomorrow; *(a él/ella)* I'll tell him/her tomorrow; *(a ellos/ellas)* I'll tell them tomorrow. ▲ **4** *is used before* **la, las, lo,** *instead of* **le** *or* **les**.

sé *pres indic* → **saber**. − **2** *imperat* → **ser**.

sebo *m* fat. **2** *(para velas)* tallow.

secador,-ra *m* dryer. − **2** *f* clothes-/tumble-dryer. ■ *~ de pelo,* hairdryer.

secano *m* dry land.

secante *adj* drying. — **2** *adj-f (geometría)* secant. — **3** *m (papel)* ~, blotting paper.

secar(se) *t* to dry; *(lágrimas, vajilla)* to wipe. — **2** *p* to dry. **3** *(planta)* to wither. **4** *(enflaquecer)* to become thin.

sección *f* section.

seccionar *t* to section.

seco,-a *adj gen* dry. **2** *(delgado)* skinny. **3** *(planta)* withered. **4** *(golpe, ruido)* sharp. ●*a secas,* simply, just.

secreción *f* secretion.

secretaría *f* (secretary's) office.

secretario,-a *m,f* secretary.

secreto,-a *adj-m* secret.

secta *f* sect.

sector *m* sector. **2** *(zona)* area.

secuaz *mf* follower, supporter.

secuela *f* consequence.

secuencia *f* sequence.

secuestrador,-ra *m,f* kidnapper. **2** *(de avión)* hijacker.

secuestrar *t* to kidnap. **2** *(avión)* to hijack.

secuestro *m* kidnapping. **2** *(de avión)* hijacking.

secular *adj-m* secular.

secundar *t* to support.

secundario,-a *adj* secondary.

sed *f* thirst. ●*tener* ~, to be thirsty.

seda *f* silk. ●*fig como una* ~, smoothly.

sedal *m* fishing line.

sedante *adj-m* sedative.

sede *f (oficina central)* headquarters central office. **2** *(del gobierno)* seat. ■ *la Santa Sede,* the Holy See.

sedentario,-a *adj* sedentary.

sedición *f* sedition.

sediento,-a *adj* thirsty.

sedimentar(se) *t-p* to settle.

sedimento *m* sediment.

sedoso,-a *adj* silky, silken.

seducción *f* seduction.

seducir [46] *t* to seduce.

seductor,-ra *adj* seductive. **2** *(atractivo)* captivating. — **3** *m,f* seducer.

segador,-ra *m,f* harvester, reaper. — **2** *f* harvester, reaper; *(de césped)* lawn mower.

segar [48] *t* to reap; *(césped)* to mow.

seglar *adj* secular, lay. — **2** *mf* lay person.

segmento *m* segment.

segregación *f* segregation.

segregar [7] *t* to segregate.

seguido,-a *adj* continuous. **2** *(consecutivo)* consecutive: *dos días seguidos,* two

days running. **3** *(recto)* straight. ●*en seguida,* at once, immediately.

seguidor,-ra *m,f* follower.

seguimiento *m* pursuit.

seguir(se) [56] *t-p gen* to follow. — **2** *t (perseguir)* to pursue, chase. **3** *(continuar)* to continue. — **4** *i (proseguir)* to go on.

según *prep* according to: ~ *lo que dicen,* according to what they say. **2** *(depende)* depending on: ~ *lo que digan,* depending on what they say. **3** *(como)* just as. **4** *(a medida que)* as.

segundero *m* second hand.

segundo,-a *adj-m,f* second. — **2** *m* second. ●*decir algo con segundas,* to say sth. with a double meaning.

seguridad *f* security. **2** *(física)* safety. **3** *(certeza)* certainty, sureness. **4** *(confianza)* confidence. ■ ~ *social,* National Health Service.

seguro,-a *adj* secure. **2** *(físicamente)* safe. **3** *(firme)* firm, steady. **4** *(cierto)* certain. **5** *(confiado)* confident. — **6** *m (contrato, póliza)* insurance. **7** *(mecanismo)* safety catch/device. — **8** *adv* for sure, definitely. **9** *seguramente (de cierto)* surely. **10** *(probablemente)* most likely, probably: *seguramente vendrá hoy,* he/she will probably come today. ●*sobre* ~, without risk. ■ ~ *de vida,* life insurance.

seis *adj* six; *(sexto)* sixth. — **2** *m* six.

seiscientos,-as *adj* six hundred; *(ordinal)* six hundredth. — **2** *m* six hundred.

seísmo *m* earthquake.

selección *f* selection. ■ DEP ~ *nacional,* national team.

seleccionar *t* to select.

selectividad *f* selectivity. **2** EDUC university entrance examination.

selecto,-a *adj* select. **2** *(escogido)* exclusive.

selector *m* selector button.

selva *f (bosque)* forest. **2** *(jungla)* jungle.

sellar *t* to stamp; *(lacrar)* to seal. **2** *(cerrar)* to close. **3** *fig* to conclude.

sello *m* stamp. **2** *(de estampar, precinto)* seal. **3** *(distintivo)* hallmark.

semáforo *m* traffic lights *pl.*

semana *f* week. ■ ~ *Santa,* Easter; *(estrictamente)* Holy Week.

semanal *adj* weekly.

semanario *m* weekly magazine.

semántica *f* semantics.

semblante *m (cara)* face. **2** *(expresión)* countenance. **3** *(apariencia)* look.

sembrar [27] *t* AGR to sow. **2** *(esparcir)* to scatter, spread.

semejante *adj* similar. **2** *(tal)* such: ~ *insolencia,* such insolence. — **3** *m* fellow being.

semejanza *f* similarity, likeness.

semejar(se) *i-p* to resemble, be alike.

semen *m* semen.

semental *m* stud.

semestre *m* six-month period, semester.

semicírculo *m* semicircle.

semilla *f* seed.

semillero *m* seedbed. **2** *fig* hotbed.

seminario *m* EDUC seminar. **2** REL seminary.

seminarista *m* seminarist.

sémola *f* semolina.

sempiterno,-a *adj* everlasting, eternal.

senado *m* Senate.

senador,-ra *m,f* senator.

sencillez *f* simplicity.

sencillo,-a *adj* simple. **2** *(persona)* natural, unaffected. **3** *(ingenuo)* naïve.

senda *f,* **sendero** *m* path.

sendos,-as *adj* each.

senectud *f* old age.

senil *adj* senile.

seno *m* breast. **2** *fig* bosom. **3** *(matriz)* womb. **4** *(cavidad)* cavity, hollow. **5** MAT sine.

sensación *f* sensation, feeling.

sensacional *adj* sensational.

sensacionalismo *m* sensationalism.

sensatez *f* (good) sense.

sensato,-a *adj* sensible.

sensibilidad *f* sensitivity.

sensibilizar [4] *t* to sensitize.

sensible *adj* sensitive. **2** *(manifiesto)* perceptible, noticeable.

sensiblería *f* mawkishness.

sensitivo,-a *adj* sensitive.

sensual *adj* sensual.

sensualidad *f* sensuality.

sentado,-a *adj* seated, sitting. ●*dar algo por* ~, to take sth. for granted.

sentar(se) [27] *t* to sit, seat. **2** *(establecer)* to establish. — **3** *i* *(quedar bien/mal)* to suit; *(comida)* to agree with: *esta corbata te sienta bien,* this tie suits you. **4** *(agradar)* to please. — **5** *p* to sit down.

sentencia *f* *(decisión)* judgement. **2** *(condena)* sentence. **3** *(aforismo)* proverb, maxim.

sentenciar [12] *t* to sentence *(a,* to).

sentido,-a *adj* felt. **2** *(sensible)* touchy. — **3** *m gen* sense. **4** *(dirección)* direction. ●*perder el* ~, to faint; *tener* ~, to make sense. ■ ~ *común,* common sense; ~ *del humor,* sense of humour.

sentimental *adj* sentimental.

sentimiento *m* feeling. **2** *(pena)* sorrow, grief.

sentir(se) [35] *m (sentimiento)* feeling. **2** *(opinión)* opinion. — **3** *t-p* to feel. — **4** *t (lamentar)* to regret. **5** *(oír)* to hear. ●*¡lo siento!,* I'm sorry!; ~ *frío/miedo,* to be cold/afraid; ~*se mal,* to feel ill.

seña *f (indicio, gesto)* sign. **2** *(señal)* mark. **3** *pl* address *sing.* ●*hacer señas,* to signal. ■ *señas personales,* particulars.

señal *f* sign, signal. **2** *(marca)* mark; *(vestigio)* trace. **3** *(cicatriz)* scar. **4** *(de pago)* deposit. ●*en* ~ *de,* as a sign/token of. ■ ~ *de comunicar,* engaged tone, US busy signal; ~ *de la cruz,* sign of the cross; ~ *de tráfico,* road sign.

señalado,-a *adj* distinguished, famous. **2** *(fijado)* appointed.

señalar(se) *t (marcar)* to mark. **2** *(hacer notar)* to point to. **3** *(con el dedo)* to point at. **4** *(designar)* to appoint; *(fecha, lugar)* to set, determine. — **5** *p* to distinguish o.s.

señalización *f* road signs *pl.*

señor,-ra *adj (noble)* distinguished. **2** *fam* fine: *es un* ~ *coche,* it's quite a car. — **3** *m* man; *(caballero)* gentleman. **4** *(amo)* master. **5** *(en tratamientos)* sir; *(delante apellido)* Mr. — **6** *f* woman; *fml* lady. **7** *(ama)* mistress. **8** *(esposa)* wife. **9** *(en tratamientos)* madam; *(delante apellido)* Mrs. ■ *Nuestro,-a Señor/Señora,* Our Lord/Lady.

señoría *f fml (para hombre)* lordship; *(para mujer)* ladyship.

señorío *m (mando)* dominion. **2** *(territorio)* estate. **3** *(en el porte)* elegance. **4** *(nobleza)* nobility.

señorito,-a *m (tratamiento)* master. **2** *pey* daddy's boy. — **3** *f* young lady. **4** *(delante apellido)* miss.

señuelo *m* decoy.

sepa *pres subj* → **saber.**

separación *f* separation.

separado,-a *adj* separate. **2** *(divorciado)* separated.

separar(se) *t-p* to separate. — **2** *t (guardar)* to set aside.

separatismo *m* separatism.

sepelio *m* burial, interment.

sepia *f* cuttlefish. — **2** *adj-m (color)* sepia.

septentrional *adj* northern.

séptico,-a *adj* septic.

septiembre *m* September.

séptimo,-a *adj-m,f* seventh.

sepulcral *adj* sepulchral. ■ *silencio* ~, deathly silence.

sepulcro *m* tomb.

sepultar *t* to bury.

sepultura *f* grave. ●*dar ~ a,* to bury.

sepulturero *m* gravedigger.

sequedad *f* dryness. **2** *fig* curtness.

sequía *f* drought. **2** AM thirst.

séquito *m* entourage, retinue.

ser [86] *i gen* to be. **2** *(pertenecer)* to belong *(de,* to). **3** *(proceder)* to come from. **— 4** *verbo aux* to be: *fue encontrado,-a por Juan,* it was found by Juan; *es de esperar que ...,* it is to be expected that ... . **— 5** *m (ente)* being. **6** *(valor)* core. ●*a no ~ que,* unless; *a poder ~,* if possible; *de no ~ por ...,* had it not been for ...; *érase una vez,* once upon a time; *es más,* furthermore; *sea como sea,* in any case; *~ de,* to be made of: *es de madera,* it's made of wood; *fam ~ muy suyo,-a,* to be an eccentric.

serenarse *p* to become calm. **2** METEOR to clear up.

serenidad *f* serenity, calm.

sereno,-a *adj (sosegado)* calm. **2** METEOR clear. **— 3** *m* night watchman.

serial *m* serial.

serie *f* series *inv.* ■ *fabricación en ~,* mass production.

seriedad *f (gravedad)* seriousness, gravity. **2** *(formalidad)* reliability.

serio,-a *adj* serious. **2** *(formal)* reliable. ●*en ~,* seriously.

sermón *m* sermon.

serpentina *f* streamer.

serpiente *f* snake. ■ *~ de cascabel,* rattlesnake.

serrar [27] *t* to saw.

serrería *f* sawmill.

serrín *m* sawdust.

serrucho *m* handsaw.

servicial *adj* obliging.

servicio *m* service. **2** *(criados)* servants *pl.* **3** *(juego)* set: *~ de té,* tea set. **4** *pl* toilet *sing.* ●*estar de ~,* to be on duty. ■ *~ a domicilio,* delivery service.

servidor,-ra *m,f* servant. **2** *(eufemismo)* me: *¿Francisco Reyes?,* —*~,* Francisco Reyes?, —yes? ●*fml ~ de usted,* at your service; *fml su seguro ~,* yours faithfully.

servidumbre *f* servitude. **2** *(criados)* servants *pl.*

servil *adj* servile.

servilismo *m* servility.

servilleta *f* napkin, serviette.

servir(se) [34] *t-i* to serve. **— 2** *i (ser útil)* to be useful. **— 3** *p (comida etc.)* to help

o.s. ●*~ de,* to be used as; *~ para,* to be used for; *~se de,* to make use of; *fml sírvase,* please.

sesenta *adj* sixty; *(ordinal)* sixtieth. **— 2** *m* sixty.

sesión *f* session, meeting. **2** CINEM showing. ■ *~ de tarde,* matinée.

seso *m* brain. **2** *fig* brains *pl.* ●*fig calentarse/devanarse los sesos,* to rack one's brains.

seta *f* mushroom; *(no comestible)* toadstool.

setecientos,-as *adj* seven hundred; *(ordinal)* seven hundredth. **— 2** *m* seven hundred.

setenta *adj* seventy; *(ordinal)* seventieth. **— 2** *m* seventy.

setiembre *m →* **septiembre**.

seto *m* hedge.

seudónimo *m* pseudonym; *(de escritores)* pen name.

severidad *f* severity.

severo,-a *adj* severe.

sexagésimo,-a *adj-m,f* sixtieth.

sexista *adj* sexist. **2** *(machista)* male chauvinist.

sexo *m* sex. **2** *(órganos)* genitals *pl.*

sexto,-a *adj-m,f* sixth.

sexual *adj* sexual.

sexualidad *f* sexuality.

short *m* shorts *pl.*

si *conj* if, whether. **2** *(para enfatizar)* but: *¡~ yo no quería!,* but I didn't want it! **— 3** *m* MÚS ti, si, B. ●*~ bien,* although; *por ~ acaso,* just in case. ▲ *pl of 3 is sis.*

sí *adv* yes. **2** *(enfático) (no se traduce) ~ que me gusta,* of course I like it. **— 3** *pron pers (él)* himself; *(ella)* herself; *(cosa)* itself; *(uno mismo)* oneself; *(plural)* themselves. **— 4** *m* yes. ●*estar fuera de ~,* to be beside o.s.; *volver en ~,* to regain consciousness; *un día ~ y otro no,* every other day. ▲ *pl of 4 is síes.*

sibarita *adj-mf* sybarite.

sidecar *m* sidecar.

siderurgia *f* iron and steel industry.

sidra *f* cider.

siega *f* harvest. **2** *(acción)* reaping.

siembra *f* sowing.

siempre *adv* always. ●*para ~,* forever, for good; *~ que/y cuando,* provided, as long as.

sien *f* temple.

sierra *f* saw. **2** GEOG mountain range.

siervo,-a *m,f* slave.

siesta *f* siesta, afternoon nap.

siete *adj* seven; *(séptimo)* seventh. **– 2** *m* seven. **3** *(rasgón)* tear.

sífilis *f inv* syphilis.

sifón *m (tubo encorvado)* siphon. **2** *(tubo acodado)* U-bend. **3** *(bebida)* soda (water).

sigiloso,-a *adj* secretive.

sigla *f* acronym.

siglo *m* century. ■ *el Siglo de Oro,* the Golden Age.

signatario,-a *adj-m,f* signatory.

significación *f* meaning. **2** *(trascendencia)* significance.

significado,-a *adj* well-known. **– 2** *m* meaning.

significar(se) [1] *t* to mean. **2** *(hacer saber)* to make known. **– 3** *p* to stand out.

significativo,-a *adj* significant.

signo *m* sign. **2** GRAM mark. ■ *~ de admiración/interrogación,* exclamation/question mark.

siguiente *adj* following, next.

sílaba *f* syllable.

silbar *i* to whistle. **2** *(abuchear)* to hiss.

silbato *m* whistle.

silbido *m* whistle.

silenciador *m* silencer.

silenciar [12] *t (sonido)* to muffle. **2** *(callar)* to hush.

silencio *m* silence. ●*guardar ~,* to keep quiet.

silencioso,-a *adj* quiet, silent.

silicona *f* silicone.

silla *f* chair. ■ *~ de montar,* saddle; *~ de ruedas,* wheelchair; *~ giratoria,* swivel chair; *~ plegable,* folding chair.

sillín *m* saddle.

sillón *m* armchair.

silo *m* silo.

silogismo *m* syllogism.

silueta *f* silhouette. **2** *(figura)* figure, shape.

silvestre *adj* wild.

sima *f* abyss, chasm.

simbólico,-a *adj* symbolic(al).

simbolizar [4] *t* to symbolize.

símbolo *m* symbol.

simetría *f* symmetry.

simétrico,-a *adj* symmetric(al).

simiente *f* seed.

símil *adj* similar. **– 2** *m (comparación)* comparison. **3** *(literario)* simile.

similar *adj* similar.

similitud *f* similarity.

simio *m* simian, monkey.

simpatía *f (cordialidad)* affection. **2** *(amabilidad)* pleasant manner. **3** *(afinidad)* affinity. ●*cogerle ~ a algn.,* to take a liking to sb.

simpático,-a *adj* pleasant, nice. ●*hacerse el ~,* to ingratiate o.s.

simpatizante *adj* supporting. **– 2** *mf* supporter.

simpatizar [4] *i* to get on *(con,* with).

simple *adj* simple. **2** *(mero)* mere. **– 3** *mf* simpleton. **– 4** *simplemente* *adv* simply.

simpleza *f (idiotez)* simple-mindedness. **2** *(tontería)* nonsense.

simplicidad *f* simplicity.

simplificar [1] *t* to simplify.

simposio *m* symposium.

simulacro *m* sham, pretence: *un ~ de ataque,* a mock attack.

simular *t* to simulate, feign.

simultáneo,-a *adj* simultaneous. **– 2** *simultáneamente* *adv* simultaneously.

sin *prep* without. ●*~ embargo,* nevertheless.

sinagoga *f* synagogue.

sincerarse *p* to open one's heart *(con,* to).

sinceridad *f* sincerity.

sincero,-a *adj* sincere.

síncope *m* syncope.

sincronizar [4] *t* synchronize.

sindicato *m* (trade) union.

síndrome *m* syndrome.

sinfín *m* endless number.

sinfonía *f* symphony.

singular *adj (único)* singular, single. **2** *(excepcional)* extraordinary. **3** *(raro)* peculiar. **– 4** *m* GRAM singular.

singularidad *f* singularity. **2** *(excepcionalidad)* strangeness. **3** *(rareza)* peculiarity.

singularizar(se) [4] *t* to distinguish, single out. **– 2** *p* to distinguish o.s.

siniestro,-a *adj* left, left-hand. **2** *(malo)* sinister. **– 3** *m* disaster; *(incendio)* fire. **– 4** *f* left hand.

sinnúmero *m* endless number.

sino *conj* but, except.

sinónimo,-a *adj* synonymous. **– 2** *m* synonym.

sinóptico,-a *adj* synoptic(al). ■ *cuadro ~,* diagram.

sinsabor *m* worry, trouble.

sintáctico,-a *adj* syntactic(al).

sintaxis *f inv* syntax.

síntesis *f inv* synthesis.

sintético,-a *adj* synthetic.

síntoma *m* symptom.

sintonizar [4] *t* to tune in to. − **2** *i fig* to get on well.

sinusitis *f inv* sinusitis.

sinvergüenza *mf* cheeky devil.

siquiera *conj* although. − **2** *adv* at least. ●*ni ~,* not even.

sirena *f* siren.

sirimiri *m* fine drizzle.

sirviente,-a *m,f* servant.

sisa *f* COST dart. **2** *(hurto)* petty theft.

sisar *t* COST to dart. **2** *(hurtar)* to pilfer, filch.

sisear *i* to hiss.

sistema *m* system.

sistemático,-a *adj* systematic.

sitiar [12] *t* to besiege.

sitio *m* place. **2** *(espacio)* space, room. **3** MIL siege. ●*hacer ~,* to make room *(a, for)*.

sito,-a *adj fml* located.

situación *f* situation. **2** *(posición)* position.

situar(se) [11] *t* to place, locate. − **2** *p* to be placed.

so *prep fml* under. ●*~ pena de,* under penalty of, on pain of.

sobaco *m* armpit.

sobar *t (ablandar)* to knead. **2** *(manosear)* to fondle.

soberanía *f* sovereignty.

soberano,-a *adj-m,f* sovereign.

soberbia *f* arrogance. **2** *(magnificiencia)* sumptuousness.

soberbio,-a *adj* arrogant. **2** *(magnífico)* superb.

sobón,-ona *adj-m,f fam* randy/fresh (person).

sobornar *t* to bribe.

soborno *m* bribery. **2** *(regalo)* bribe.

sobra *f* excess, surplus. **2** *pl* leftovers. ●*de ~, (no necesario)* superfluous; *(excesivo)* more than enough.

sobrado,-a *adj* abundant.

sobrar *i (quedar)* to be left over. **2** *(sin aprovechar)* to be more than enough. **3** *(estar de más)* to be superfluous.

sobre *prep (encima)* on, upon. **2** *(por encima)* over, above. − **3** *m* envelope. ●*~ todo,* above all.

sobrecarga *f* overload.

sobrecargar [7] *t* to overload.

sobrecogedor,-ra *adj* dramatic. **2** *(que da miedo)* frightening.

sobredosis *f inv* overdose.

sobrehilar *t* to whipstitch.

sobrellevar *t* to bear, endure.

sobremesa *f* after-dinner chat.

sobrenatural *adj* supernatural.

sobrentender(se) [28] *t* to deduce, infer. − **2** *p* to go without saying.

sobrepasar *t* to exceed.

sobreponer(se) [78] *t* to put on top. − **2** *p* to overcome *(a, -)*. ▲ *pp* **sobrepuesto,-a.**

sobrepujar *t* to surpass.

sobresaliente *adj* outstanding. − **2** *m (calificación)* A, first.

sobresalir [84] *i (exceder)* to stand out, excel. **2** *(abultar)* to protrude.

sobresaltar(se) *t* to startle. − **2** *p* to be startled.

sobresalto *m* start; *(de temor)* fright.

sobretodo *m* overcoat.

sobrevenir [90] *i* to happen, occur.

sobrevivir *i* to survive.

sobrevolar [31] *t* to fly over.

sobriedad *f* sobriety, moderation.

sobrino,-a *m,f m* nephew, *f* niece.

sobrio,-a *adj* sober, temperate.

socarrón,-ona *adj* sarcastic, sly.

socarronería *f* slyness.

socavar *t fig* to undermine.

sociable *adj* sociable, friendly.

social *adj* social.

socialdemocracia *f* social democracy.

socialismo *m* socialism.

socialista *adj-mf* socialist.

sociedad *f* society. **2** COM company. ■ *~ anónima,* limited company, US incorporated company; *~ limitada,* private limited company.

socio,-a *m,f* member. **2** COM partner.

sociología *f* sociology.

socorrer *t* to help, assist.

socorrismo *m* life-saving.

socorrista *mf* life-saver, lifeguard.

socorro *m* help, aid, assistance. − **2** *interj* help!

soda *f* soda (water).

sodomita *adj-mf* sodomite.

soez *adj* vulgar, crude.

sofá *m* sofa, settee. ▲ *pl* **sofás.**

sofisticado,-a *adj* sophisticated.

sofocante *adj* suffocating, stifling.

sofocar(se) [1] *t* to suffocate, smother. **2** *(incendio)* to put out, extinguish. − **3** *p* *(ruborizarse)* to blush.

sofoco *m* suffocation. **2** *(vergüenza)* embarrassment.

sofreír [37] *t* to fry lightly, brown. ▲ *pp* **sofrito,-a.**

sofrito,-a *pp* → **sofreír.** − **2** *m* fried tomato and onion sauce.

soga f rope, cord.

soja f soya bean.

sol m sun. **2** (luz) sunlight, sunshine. **3** MÚS sol, G. ●*tomar el* ~, to sunbathe.

solamente adv only.

solapa f (de prenda) lapel. **2** (de sobre, libro) flap.

solar adj solar. − **2** m (terreno) plot. **3** (casa) ancestral house.

solariego,-a adj noble. ■ *casa solariega,* manor-house.

soldado m soldier. ■ ~ *raso,* private.

soldadura f soldering, welding.

soldar [31] t to solder, weld.

soleado,-a adj sunny.

soledad f solitude. **2** (sentimiento) loneliness.

solemne adj solemn. **2** pey downright: *es una* ~ *estupidez,* it's downright stupidity.

solemnidad f solemnity. **2** pl formalities.

soler [32] i (presente) to be in the habit of. **2** (pasado) to use to. ▲ Only used in pres and past indic.

solera f fig tradition.

solfeo m solfa.

solicitante mf applicant.

solicitar t to request.

solícito,-a adj obliging.

solicitud f (petición) request; (de trabajo) application. **2** (diligencia) solicitude.

solidaridad f solidarity.

solidarizarse [4] p to support (con, -).

solidez f solidity.

solidificar(se) [1] t-p to solidify. **2** (pasta) to harden, set.

sólido,-a adj-m solid.

solista mf soloist.

solitario,-a adj (sin compañía) solitary. **2** (sentimiento) lonely. **3** (lugar) deserted. − **4** m solitaire. − **5** f MED tapeworm.

sollozar [4] i to sob.

sollozo m sob.

solo,-a adj alone. **2** (solitario) lonely. **3** (único) sole, single. − **4** m fam black coffee. **5** MÚS solo. ●*a solas,* alone, in private.

sólo adv → **solamente.**

solomillo m sirloin.

solsticio m solstice.

soltar(se) [31] t (desasir) to release. **2** (desatar) to untie, unfasten. **3** fam (decir) to come out with. − **4** p (desatarse) to come loose. **5** (desprenderse) to come off.

soltero,-a adj single, unmarried. − **2** m,f m bachelor, single man, f single woman.

solterón,-ona m,f pey m old bachelor, f old maid.

soltura f agility. **2** (al hablar) fluency.

soluble adj soluble.

solución f solution.

solucionar t to solve.

solvencia f FIN solvency. **2** (fiabilidad) reliability.

solventar t (solucionar) to solve. **2** FIN to settle.

sombra f shade. **2** (silueta) shadow. ■ ~ *de ojos,* eye shadow.

sombrero m hat. ■ ~ *de copa,* top hat; ~ *hongo,* bowler hat.

sombrilla f parasol, sunshade.

sombrío,-a adj (lugar) dark. **2** fig gloomy.

somero,-a adj superficial.

someter(se) t (subyugar) to subdue. **2** (probar) to subject (a, to): ~ *a prueba,* to put to test. − **3** p (rendirse) to surrender (a, to). **4** (tratamiento etc.) to undergo (a, -).

somier m spring mattress.

somnífero,-a adj sleep-inducing. − **2** m sleeping pill.

somnolencia f sleepiness, drowsiness.

son m sound. **2** (modo) manner. ●*sin ton ni* ~, without rhyme or reason.

sonado,-a adj (conocido) famous. **2** fam (loco) mad, crazy.

sonajero m baby's rattle.

sonámbulo,-a adj sleepwalker.

sonar(se) [31] i to sound. **2** (timbre etc.) to ring. **3** (reloj) to strike. **4** (conocer vagamente) to sound familiar. − **5** p to blow one's nose.

sonda f probe.

sondear t to sound, probe. **2** (encuestar) to sound out.

sondeo m sounding, probing. **2** (encuesta) poll.

soneto m sonnet.

sonido m sound.

sonoridad f sonority.

sonoro,-a adj (resonante) loud, resounding. **2** CINEM sound.

sonreír(se) [37] i-p to smile.

sonriente adj smiling.

sonrisa f smile.

sonrojar(se) t to make blush. − **2** p to blush.

sonrojo m blush(ing).

sonrosado,-a adj rosy, pink.

sonsacar [1] *t* to wheedle. **2** *(secreto)* to worm out.

soñador,-ra *adj* dreamy. — **2** *m,f* dreamer.

soñar [31] *t-i* to dream.

soñoliento,-a *adj* drowsy, sleepy.

sopa *f* soup. ■ ~ *boba,* gruel.

sopero,-a *adj* soup. — **2** *f* soup tureen.

sopesar *t* to try the weight of. **2** *fig* to weigh up.

sopetón *m* slap. ●*de* ~, all of a sudden.

soplar *i* to blow. — **2** *t* to blow (away). **3** *(delatar)* to split on. **4** *(apuntar)* to prompt. **5** *fam (robar)* to steal. **6** *fam (beber)* to down.

soplete *m* blowtorch.

soplo *m* blow, puff. **2** *(de viento)* puff. **3** MED souffle. **4** *fam (de secreto etc.)* tip-off.

soplón,-ona *m,f fam* informer, squealer.

soponcio *m* swoon, fainting fit.

sopor *m* drowsiness.

soportable *adj* bearable.

soportar *t* to support, bear. **2** *fig* to tolerate.

soporte *m* support.

soprano *mf* soprano.

sorber *t* to sip. **2** *(absorber)* to absorb.

sorbete *m* sorbet, iced fruit drink.

sorbo *m* sip, gulp.

sordera *f* deafness.

sórdido,-a *adj (sucio)* squalid. **2** *(vil)* sordid.

sordo,-a *adj* deaf. **2** *(sonido, dolor)* dull. — **3** *m,f* deaf person.

sordomudo,-a *adj-m,f* deaf and dumb (person).

sorna *f* sarcasm.

sorprendente *adj* surprising.

sorprender(se) *t* to surprise. — **2** *p* to be surprised *(de,* at).

sorpresa *f* surprise.

sortear *t* to draw/cast lots for; *(rifar)* to raffle. **2** *(obstáculos)* to get round.

sorteo *m* draw; *(rifa)* raffle.

sortija *f* ring.

sortilegio *m* sorcery.

sosegado,-a *adj* calm, quiet.

sosegar(se) [48] *t-p* to calm (down).

sosería *f* insipidity, dullness.

sosiego *m* calmness, peace.

soslayar *t* to slant. **2** *fig (evitar)* to avoid, dodge.

soslayo *al/de* ~, *adv* sideways.

soso,-a *adj* tasteless. **2** *fig* dull.

sospecha *f* suspicion.

sospechar *t* to suspect.

sospechoso,-a *adj* suspicious. — **2** *m,f* suspect.

sostén *m* support. **2** *(prenda)* bra(ssière).

sostener(se) [87] *t* to support, hold up. **2** *fig (soportar)* to endure. **3** *(opinión)* to maintain, affirm. — **4** *p (mantenerse)* to support o.s. **5** *(permanecer)* to stay.

sostenido,-a *adj* sustained. — **2** *adj-m* MÚS sharp.

sota *f (cartas)* jack, knave.

sotana *f* cassock.

sótano *m* cellar, basement.

soto *m* grove.

sprintar *t* to sprint.

stárter *m* choke.

stop *m* stop sign.

su *adj pos (de él)* his; *(de ella)* her; *(de usted/ ustedes)* your; *(de ellos)* their; *(de animales, cosas)* its.

suave *adj* soft. **2** *(liso)* smooth. **3** *(apacible)* gentle, mild. — **4** *suavemente adv* softly, smoothly.

suavidad *f* softness. **2** *(lisura)* smoothness. **3** *(docilidad)* gentleness, mildness.

suavizar [4] *t* to soften. **2** *(alisar)* to smooth.

subalterno,-a *adj-m,f* subordinate, subaltern.

subarrendar [27] *t* to sublet, sublease.

subasta *f* auction.

subastar *t* to auction.

subconsciente *adj-m* subconscious.

subdesarrollo *m* underdevelopment.

súbdito,-a *adj-m,f* subject.

subdividir *t* to subdivide.

subestimar *t* to undervalue.

subida *f (ascenso)* ascent; *(a montaña)* climb. **2** *(pendiente)* slope. **3** *(aumento)* rise. **4** *arg (drogas)* high.

subir(se) *i-p (ascender)* to go up. **2** *(montar) (vehículo)* get on; *(coche)* get into; *(caballo)* to mount. — **3** *i (elevarse, aumentar)* to rise. **4** *(categoría, puesto)* to be promoted. — **5** *t (escalar)* to climb. **6** *(mover arriba)* to carry/take up. ●*fig* ~*se por las paredes,* to hit the roof.

súbito,-a *adj* sudden. ●*de* ~, suddenly.

subjetivo,-a *adj* subjective.

subjuntivo *m* subjunctive.

sublevación *f* rising, revolt.

sublevar(se) *t* to incite to rebellion. **2** *(indignar)* to infuriate. — **3** *p* to rebel.

sublime *adj* sublime.

submarinismo *m* skin-diving.

submarinista *mf* skin-diver.

submarino,-a *adj-m* underwater. — **2** *m* submarine.

subnormal *adj-mf* mentally handicapped (person).

suboficial *m* noncommissioned officer.

subordinado,-a *adj-m,f* subordinate.

subordinar *t* to subordinate.

subrayar *t* to underline. **2** *(recalcar)* to emphasize.

subsanar *t* to rectify, correct.

subscribir(se) *t* to sign, subscribe. — **2** *p* to subscribe to. ▲ *pp* **subscrito,-a.**

subscripción *f* subscription.

subscrito,-a *pp* → **subscribir.**

subsidiario,-a *adj* subsidiary.

subsidio *m* allowance. ■ ~ *de paro,* unemployment benefit.

subsiguiente *adj* subsequent.

subsistencia *f* subsistence. **2** *pl* provisions.

subsistir *i* to subsist.

substancia *f* substance. **2** *fig* essence.

substancial *adj* substantial. **2** *(fundamental)* essential.

substantivo,-a *adj* substantive. — **2** *m* GRAM noun.

substitución *f* substitution, replacement.

substituir [62] *t* to substitute, replace.

substituto,-a *m,f* substitute.

substracción *f* substraction. **2** *(robo)* theft.

substraer [88] *t* *(restar)* to substract. **2** *(robar)* to steal.

subsuelo *m* subsoil.

subterfugio *m* subterfuge.

subterráneo,-a *adj* subterranean, underground. — **2** *m* underground passage.

suburbano,-a *adj* suburban.

suburbio *m* suburb; *(barrio pobre)* slums *pl.*

subvención *f* subsidy, grant.

subvencionar *t* to subsidize.

subversivo,-a *adj* subversive.

subyugar [7] *t* to subjugate.

succionar *t* to suck (in).

sucedáneo,-a *adj-m* substitute.

suceder *i* *(acontecer)* to happen, occur. **2** *(seguir)* to follow. **3** *(heredar)* to succeed. ▲ **1** used only in the 3rd person. It does not take a subject.

sucesión *f* succession. **2** *(descendientes)* heirs *pl.*

sucesivo,-a *adj* following, successive. — **2** *sucesivamente adv* successively: *y así* ~, and so on. ●*en lo* ~, from now on.

suceso *m* *(hecho)* event, happening. **2** *(incidente)* incident. **3** *(delito)* crime.

sucesor,-ra *m,f* successor.

suciedad *f* *(inmundicia)* dirt. **2** *(calidad)* dirtiness.

sucinto,-a *adj* concise, brief.

sucio,-a *adj* dirty.

suculento,-a *adj* juicy, succulent.

sucumbir *i* to succumb/yield *(a,* to). **2** *(morir)* to perish.

sucursal *f* branch (office).

sudar *i* to sweat. ●*fam* ~ *la gota gorda,* to sweat blood.

sudario *m* shroud.

sudeste *m* southeast.

sudoeste *m* southwest.

sudor *m* sweat.

sudoroso,-a *adj* sweating.

suegro,-a *m,f* *m* father-in-law, *f* mother-in-law.

suela *f* sole.

sueldo *m* salary, pay.

suelo *m* ground; *(de interior)* floor. **2** *(tierra)* soil. **3** *(terreno)* land.

suelto,-a *adj* *(no sujeto)* loose; *(desatado)* undone. **2** *(estilo etc.)* easy. **3** *(libre)* free. **4** *(desparejado)* odd. — **5** *m* *(noticia)* news item. **6** *(cambio)* small change.

sueño *m* *(acto)* sleep. **2** *(ganas de dormir)* sleepiness. **3** *(mientras se duerme)* dream. ■ *fig* ~ *dorado,* cherished dream.

suero *m* MED serum.

suerte *f* *(fortuna)* luck. **2** *(azar)* chance. **3** *fml* *(tipo)* sort, kind. ●*echar (a) suertes,* to cast lots; *tener* ~, to be lucky.

suéter *m* sweater.

suficiencia *f* capacity. **2** *(engreimiento)* arrogance.

suficiente *adj* *(bastante)* sufficient. **2** *(apto)* suitable. **3** *(engreído)* smug.

sufragar [7] *t* to defray, pay. **2** *(ayudar)* to aid, assist.

sufragio *m* suffrage. ●*en* ~ *de ...,* for the soul of ... .

sufrido,-a *adj* patient, long-suffering.

sufrimiento *m* suffering.

sufrir *t* *(padecer)* to suffer. **2** *(ser sujeto de)* to have; *(operación)* to undergo: ~ *un accidente,* to have an accident. **3** *(sostener)* to bear.

sugerencia *f* suggestion.

sugerir [35] *t* to suggest, hint.

sugestión *f* suggestion.

sugestionar *t* to influence.

sugestivo,-a *adj* suggestive.

suicida *adj* suicidal. — **2** *mf* suicide.

suicidarse *p* to commit suicide.

suicidio *m* suicide.

sujetador,-ra *adj* fastening. — **2** *m* bra, brassière.

sujetapapeles *m inv* paper clip.
sujetar(se) *t (someter)* to subject. **2** *(agarrar)* to hold. **3** *(para que no caiga)* to fix, secure. — **4** *p* to subject o.s. (*a,* to).
sujeto,-a *adj (sometido)* subject/liable (*a,* to). **2** *(agarrado)* fastened. — **3** *m* LING subject. **4** *(persona)* fellow.
sulfato *m* sulphate.
sulfurar(se) *t* to exasperate. — **2** *p* to get angry.
sulfuro *m* sulphide.
sultán *m* sultan.
suma *f (cantidad)* sum, amount. **2** MAT sum, addition. ●*en* ~, in short. ■ ~ *y sigue,* carried forward.
sumamente *adv* extremely.
sumar(se) *t* MAT to add (up). **2** *(total)* to total. — **3** *p* to join (*a,* in).
sumario,-a *adj* summary. — **2** *m (resumen)* proceedings *pl.* **3** JUR legal proceedings *pl.*
sumergible *adj* submergible, submersible.
sumergir(se) [6] *t* to submerge, submerse. — **2** *p fig* to become immersed (*en,* in).
sumidero *m* drain, sewer.
suministrar *t* to provide/supply with.
suministro *m* provision, supply.
sumir(se) *t (hundir)* to sink, plunge. — **2** *p* to immerse o.s. (*en,* in).
sumisión *f* submission.
sumiso,-a *adj* submissive, obedient.
súmmum *m* summit.
sumo,-a *adj* highest. ●*a lo* ~, at most.
suntuosidad *f* sumptuousness.
suntuoso,-a *adj* sumptuous.
supeditar *t* to subordinate (*a,* to).
súper *fam adj* super, great. — **2** *m (tienda)* supermarket.
superación *f* overcoming.
superar(se) *t* to surpass, exceed. **2** *(obstáculo etc.)* to overcome, surmount. — **3** *p* to excel o.s.
superávit *m inv* surplus.
superdotado,-a *adj* exceptionally gifted. — **2** *m,f* genius.
superficial *adj* superficial.
superficie *f* surface. **2** *(geometría)* area.
superfluo,-a *adj* superfluous.
superintendente *mf* superintendent.
superior *adj (encima de)* upper. **2** *(mayor)* greater. **3** *(mejor)* superior. — **4** *mf* superior.
superioridad *f* superiority.
superlativo,-a *adj-m* superlative.
supermercado *m* supermarket.

superponer [78] *t* to superpose. ▲ *pp* **superpuesto,-a.**
supersónico,-a *adj* supersonic.
superstición *f* superstition.
supersticioso,-a *adj* superstitious.
supervisar *t* to supervise.
supervivencia *f* survival.
superviviente *adj* surviving. — **2** *mf* survivor.
supino,-a *adj-m* supine.
suplantar *t* to supplant, replace.
suplementario,-a *adj* supplementary.
suplemento *m* supplement.
suplencia *f* substitution.
suplente *adj-mf* substitute.
supletorio,-a *adj* supplementary. — **2** *m (teléfono)* extension.
súplica *f* request.
suplicante *adj* beseeching. — **2** *mf* suppli(c)ant.
suplicar [1] *t* to beseech, beg.
suplicio *m (castigo)* torture. **2** *(dolor)* pain; *fig* torment.
suplir *t* to replace, substitute.
suponer [78] *t* to suppose. **2** *(dar por sentado)* to assume. **3** *(acarrear)* to entail. — **4** *m fam* supposition. ▲ *pp* **supuesto,-a.**
suposición *f* supposition, assumption.
supositorio *m* suppository.
supremacía *f* supremacy.
supremo,-a *adj* supreme.
supresión *f* suppression; *(de ley, impuesto)* abolition. **2** *(omisión)* omission; *(de palabra)* deletion.
suprimir *t* to suppress; *(ley, impuestos)* to abolish. **2** *(omitir)* to omit; *(palabras, texto)* to delete.
supuesto,-a *pp* → **suponer.** — **2** *adj* supposed, assumed. — **3** *m* supposition. ●*dar por* ~, to take for granted; *por* ~, of course.
supurar *i* to suppurate.
sur *m* south.
surcar [1] *t* AGR to furrow. ●~ *los mares,* to ply the seas.
surco *m (en tierra)* trench. **2** *(arruga)* wrinkle.
surgir [6] *i* to arise, appear. **2** *(agua)* to spring forth.
surtido,-a *adj* assorted. — **2** *m* assortment.
surtidor *m (fuente)* fountain. **2** *(chorro)* jet, spout. ■ ~ *de gasolina,* petrol pump.
surtir *t* to supply, provide. ●~ *efecto,* to work.
susceptibilidad *f* susceptibility.

susceptible *adj* susceptible. **2** *(sentido)* touchy.

suscitar *t* to cause.

suscribir *t* → **subscribir**.

suscripción *f* → **subscripción**.

suscrito,-a *pp* → **subscrito,-a**.

susodicho,-a *adj fml* above-mentioned.

suspender *t* *(levantar)* to hang (up). **2** *(aplazar)* to postpone. **3** EDUC to fail. **4** *(pagos)* to suspend.

suspense *m* suspense. ■ *película de* ~, thriller.

suspensión *f* *(acto)* hanging (up). **2** AUTO suspension. **3** *(aplazamiento)* postponement. **4** *(supresión)* suspension. ■ ~ *de pagos,* suspension of payments.

suspensivo,-a *adj* *puntos suspensivos,* (row of) dots, US suspension points.

suspenso,-a *adj* hanging, suspended. — **2** *m* EDUC fail.

suspicacia *f* suspiciousness, mistrust.

suspicaz *adj* suspicious, distrustful.

suspirar *i* to sigh. ●~ *por,* to long for.

suspiro *m* sigh.

sustancia *f* → **substancia**.

sustancial *adj* → **substancial**.

sustantivo,-a *adj* → **substantivo,-a**.

sustentar(se) *t* *(mantener)* to maintain. **2** *(sostener)* to hold up. **3** *(teoría, opinión)* to support, defend. — **4** *p* to sustain o.s.

sustento *m* sustenance.

sustitución *f* → **substitución**.

sustituir [62] *t* → **substituir**.

sustituto,-a *m,f* → **substituto,-a**.

susto *m* fright, scare.

sustracción *f* → **substracción**.

sustraer [88] *t* → **substraer**.

susurrar *i* to whisper. **2** *(agua)* to murmur. **3** *(hojas)* to rustle.

susurro *m* whisper. **2** *(agua)* murmur. **3** *(hojas)* rustle.

sutil *adj* thin, fine. **2** *fig* subtle.

sutileza *f* thinness. **2** *fig* subtlety.

suyo,-a *adj pos* *(de él/ella)* of his/hers: *¿es amigo* ~?, is he a friend of his/hers?; *(de usted/ustedes)* of yours; *(de animales/cosas)* of its; *(de ellos,-as)* of theirs. — **2** *pron pos* *(de él/ella)* his/hers; *(de usted/ustedes)* yours; *(de ellos,-as)* theirs: *éste es suyo,* this one is theirs. ●*salirse con la suya,* to get one's way; *fam* *hacer de las suyas,* to be up to one's tricks.

T

tabaco *m* *(planta, hoja)* tobacco. **2** *(cigarrillos)* cigarettes *pl*.

tábano *m* horsefly.

taberna *f* pub, bar.

tabernero,-a *m,f* bartender.

tabique *m* partition (wall). ■ ~ *nasal*, nasal bone.

tabla *f* board. **2** *(de madera)* plank, board. **3** ART panel. **4** COST pleat. **5** *(índice)* table. **6** MAT table. **7** *pl (ajedrez)* stalemate *sing*, draw *sing*. **8** *pl* TEAT stage *sing*. ●*fig a raja* ~, strictly, to the letter. ■ ~ *de materias*, (table of) contents *pl*.

tablado *m* *(suelo)* wooden floor. **2** *(plataforma)* wooden platform.

tablero *m* *(tablón)* panel, board. **2** *(en juegos)* board. **3** *(encerado)* blackboard.

tableta *f* *(pastilla)* tablet. **2** *(de chocolate)* bar.

tablilla *f* small board.

tablón *m* plank. **2** *(en construcción)* beam. ■ ~ *de anuncios*, notice board.

tabú *adj-m* taboo. ▲ *pl* **tabúes**.

taburete *m* stool.

tacañería *f* meanness, stinginess.

tacaño,-a *adj* mean, stingy. — **2** *m,f* miser.

tacha *f* *(defecto)* flaw, blemish, defect. **2** *(clavo grande)* large tack; *(decorativo)* large stud.

tachar *t* to cross out. ●*fig* ~ *de*, to accuse of.

tachón *m* crossing out.

tachuela *f* tack, stud.

tácito,-a *adj* tacit.

taciturno,-a *adj* *(callado)* taciturn, silent. **2** *(triste)* sullen. **3** *(lunático)* sulky, moody.

taco *m* *(tarugo)* plug, stopper. **2** *(para pared)* plug. **3** *(bloc de notas)* notepad, writing pad; *(calendario)* tear-off calendar; *(de entradas)* book; *(de billetes)* wad. **4** *(de billar)* cue. **5** CULIN cube, piece. **6** *fam (palabrota)* swearword. **7** *fam (años)* year. ●*armarse un* ~, to get all mixed up.

tacón *m* heel.

taconear *i* *(pisar)* to tap one's heels. **2** *(golpear)* to stamp one's heels.

taconeo *m* *(pisada)* heel tapping. **2** *(golpe)* stamping with the heels.

táctica *f* tactic(s) *pl*.

táctil *adj* tactile.

tacto *m* touch. **2** *fig (delicadeza)* tact. ●*tener* ~, to be tactful.

tafetán *m* taffeta.

tahúr,-ura *adj-m,f* cardsharp(er).

taimado,-a *adj* sly, crafty. — **2** *m,f* sly/crafty person.

tajada *f* *(rodaja)* slice. **2** *(corte)* cut; *(cuchillada)* stab. **3** *fam (borrachera)* drunkenness. ●*fig pillar una* ~, to get smashed; *fig sacar/llevarse* ~, to take one's share.

tajante *adj* sharp. **2** *fig* strong, sharp.

tajar *t* to cut, chop (off).

tajo *m* *(corte)* cut, slash. **2** *(escarpe)* steep cliff.

tal *adj* *(semejante)* such (a): *en tales condiciones*, in such conditions. **2** *(tan grande)* such, so: *es* ~ *su valor que ...,* he is so courageous that ... . **3** *(cosa sin especificar)* such and such: ~ *día*, such and such a day. **4** *(persona)* someone called: *te llamó un* ~ *García,* someone called García phoned you. — **5** *pron (alguno) (cosa)* something; *(persona)* someone, somebody. — **6** *conj* as. ●*como si* ~ *cosa,* as if nothing had happened; *con* ~ *(de) que,* so long as, provided; *de* ~ *manera que,* in such a way that; *¿qué* ~?, how are things?; ~ *cual,* just as it is; ~ *para cual,* two of a kind; ~ *vez,* perhaps, maybe; *y* ~ *y cual,* and so on.

tala *f* tree felling.

taladrar *t* to drill, drill a hole in. **2** *(billete)* to punch.

taladro *m (herramienta)* drill, bore; *(barrena)* gimlet. **2** *(agujero)* hole.

talante *m (semblante)* disposition. **2** *(voluntad)* willingness.

talar *t (árboles)* to fell, cut down. **2** *(lugar)* to devastate.

talco *m* talc. ■ *polvos de* ~, talcum powder *sing*.

talego *m (bolsa)* long bag/sack. **2** *(contenido)* bagful, sackful. **3** *arg (cárcel)* clink, hole. **4** *arg (mil pesetas)* one thousand peseta note.

talento *m* talent.

talismán *m* talisman, lucky charm.

talla *f (estatura)* height; *fig* stature. **2** *(de prenda)* size. **3** *(escultura)* carving, sculpture. **4** *(tallado)* cutting, carving; *(metal)* engraving.

tallar *t (madera, piedra)* to carve, shape; *(piedras preciosas)* to cut; *(metales)* to engrave. **2** *(medir)* to measure the (height of). **3** *(valorar)* to value, appraise.

tallarines *mpl* tagliatelle *sing*, noodles.

talle *m (cintura)* waist. **2** *(figura) (de hombre)* build, physique; *(de mujer)* figure.

taller *m (obrador)* (work)shop. **2** ART studio. **3** IND factory, mill.

tallo *m* stem, stalk.

talón *m* heel. **2** *(cheque)* cheque, US check.

talonario *m* cheque book, US check book.

tamaño,-a *adj* such a big, so big a. – **2** *m (medida)* size. ● *del* ~ *de,* as big as.

tambalear(se) *i-p (persona)* to stagger, totter; *(mueble)* to wobble.

también *adv (también)* also, too, as well, so: *Pedro* ~ *estaba,* Peter was also there/there too/there as well; *¿lo harás?* —*yo* ~, are you going to do it? —so am I. **2** *(además)* besides, in addition.

tambor *m* MÚS *(instrumento)* drum. **2** *(persona)* drummer. **3** *(de arma)* cylinder, barrel. **4** *(de lavadora)* drum. **5** *(de jabón)* drum.

tamiz *m* sieve. ● *pasar por el* ~, to sift.

tamizar [1] *t (harina, tierra)* to sieve. **2** *(luz)* to filter. **3** *fig (seleccionar)* to screen.

tampoco *adv* neither, nor, not ... either: *Juan no vendrá y María* ~, Juan won't come and María won't either/neither will María; *yo* ~, me neither.

tampón *m (de entintar)* inkpad. **2** MED tampon.

tan *adv (tanto)* such (as), so: *no me gusta* ~ *dulce,* I don't like it so sweet. **2** *(comparativo)* as ... as, so ... (that): *es* ~ *alto como tú,* he's as tall as you (are); *iba* ~ *deprisa que no lo ví,* he went by so fast that I didn't see him. ● *de* ~, so; ~ *siquiera,* even, just.

tanda *f (conjunto)* batch, lot; *(serie)* series, course. **2** *(turno)* shift. ● *por tandas,* in batches. ■ ~ *de palos,* thrashing.

tangente *f* tangent.

tangible *adj* tangible.

tanque *m (depósito)* tank, reservoir. **2** MIL tank. **3** *(vehículo cisterna)* tanker.

tantear *t (calcular)* to estimate, guess. **2** *(probar) (medidas)* to size up; *(pesos)* to feel. **3** *fig (examinar)* to try out, put to the test. – **4** *i* DEP to (keep) score. ● ~ *a algn.,* to sound sb. out.

tanteo *m (cálculo aproximado)* estimate, guess. **2** *(prueba)* reckoning, rough estimate; *(de medidas)* sizing up. **3** *(sondeo)* trial, test; *(de la actitud de una persona)* sounding. **4** DEP score.

tanto,-a *adj-pron (incontables)* so much; *(contables)* so many: *¡ha pasado* ~ *tiempo!,* it's been so long! **2** *(aproximadamente)* odd: *cincuenta y tantas personas,* fifty odd people. – **3** *adv (cantidad)* so much: *¡te quiero* ~!, I love you so much! **4** *(tiempo)* so long. **5** *(frecuencia)* so often. – **6** *m (punto)* point. **7** *(cantidad imprecisa)* so much, a certain amount. **8** *(poco)* bit. ● *a las tantas,* very late; *en/entre/mientras* ~, meanwhile; *estar al* ~, *(informado)* to be informed; *(alerta)* to be on the alert; *no es/hay para* ~, it's not that bad; *otro* ~, as much again, the same again; *por lo* ~, therefore; ~ *más/menos,* all the more/less; ~ *mejor/peor,* so much the better/worse; *uno,-a de tantos,-as,* run-of-the-mill; *¡y* ~!, oh, yes!, certainly!

tañer [38] *t (instrumento)* to play. **2** *(campanas)* to ring, toll.

tañido *m (de instrumento)* sound. **2** *(de campanas)* ringing, toll.

tapa *f (cubierta)* lid, top; *(de libro)* cover. **2** *(de zapato)* heelplate. **3** AUTO head. **4** CULIN *(comida)* appetizer, savoury. **5** *(de res)* round of beef.

tapadera *f* cover, lid. **2** *fig* cover, front.

tapar(se) *t* to cover; *(con tapa)* to put the lid/top on; *(con ropas/mantas)* to wrap up. **2** *(obstruir)* to obstruct; *(tubería)* to block. **3** *(ocultar)* to hide; *(vista)* to block. – **4** *p (cubrirse)* to cover o.s.; *(abrigarse)* to wrap up. ● ~*se los oídos,* to put one's fingers in one's ears.

tapete *m* table runner. ●*fig estar sobre el* ~, *(discutir)* to be under discussion; *poner sobre el* ~, *(plantear)* to bring up.

tapia *f (cerca)* garden wall; *(de adobe)* mud/adobe wall.

tapiar [12] *t (área)* to wall in/off; *(puerta, ventana)* to wall, close up.

tapicería *f* ART tapestry making; *(tapices)* tapestry. **2** *(de muebles)* upholstery. **3** *(tienda)* upholsterer's (work)shop.

tapicero,-a *m,f (de muebles, coche)* upholsterer. **2** ART tapestry maker.

tapiz *m (paño)* tapestry. **2** *(alfombra)* rug, carpet.

tapizar [4] *t (muebles)* to upholster. **2** *(una pared)* to cover. **3** *(cubrir con tapices)* to cover with tapestries.

tapón *m* stopper, plug; *(de botella)* cap, cork. **2** *(del oído)* (ear)wax. **3** *fam (persona)* shorty, stubby person. **4** *(baloncesto)* block. **5** AUTO traffic jam.

taponar *t (tubería, hueco)* to plug, stop. **2** *(el paso)* to block. **3** *(poner el tapón)* to put the plug in. **4** MED to tampon.

taquigrafía *f* shorthand, stenography.

taquígrafo,-a *m,f* shorthand writer, stenographer.

taquilla *f* ticket/booking office; CINEM TEAT box-office. **2** *(recaudación)* takings *pl.* **3** *(armario)* locker.

taquillero,-a *m,f* booking/ticket clerk. — **2** *adj fig* popular.

tara *f (peso)* tare. **2** *(defecto)* defect, blemish, fault.

tarado,-a *adj (defectuoso)* defective, damaged. **2** *(persona)* handicapped. — **3** *m,f fam* idiot, nitwit.

tarambana *adj fam* madcap.

tararear *t* to hum.

tardanza *f* delay.

tardar *t (emplear tiempo)* to take: *tardé tres años,* it took me three years. — **2** *i (demorar)* to take long: *se tarda más en tren,* it takes longer by train. ●*a más* ~, at the latest; *¿cuánto se tarda?,* how long does it take?; *no tardes,* don't be long.

tarde *f (hasta las seis)* afternoon: *son las 4 de la* ~, it is 4 o'clock in the afternoon. **2** *(después de las seis)* evening. — **3** *adv (hora avanzada)* late: *se está haciendo* ~, it's getting late. ●*de* ~ *en* ~, very rarely, not very often; *(más)* ~ *o (más) temprano,* sooner or later.

tardío,-a *adj* late, belated.

tardo,-a *adj* slow.

tarea *f* task, job. ■ *las tareas de la casa,* the chores, the housework *sing*; *tareas escolares,* homework *sing.*

tarifa *f (precio)* tariff, rate; *(en transporte)* fare. **2** *(lista de precios)* price list. ■ ~ *reducida,* reduced rate, special deal; ~ *turística,* tourist class rate.

tarima *f* platform, dais.

tarjeta *f* card. ■ *(~) postal,* postcard.

tarro *m (vasija)* jar, pot. **2** *fam (cabeza)* bonce.

tarta *f* cake, tart, pie.

tartaja *mf fam* stammerer, stutterer.

tartamudear *i* to stutter, stammer.

tartamudo,-a *adj* stuttering, stammering. — **2** *m,f* stutterer, stammerer.

tartera *f (fiambrera)* lunch box. **2** *(cazuela)* baking tin.

tarugo *m (de madera)* lump of wood. **2** *(de pan)* chunk of stale bread. **3** *fam (persona)* blockhead.

tasa *f (valoración)* valuation, appraisal. **2** *(precio)* fee, charge. **3** *(impuesto)* tax. **4** *(límite)* limit; *(medida)* measure. **5** *(índice)* rate.

tasar *t (valorar)* to value, appraise. **2** *(poner precio)* to set/fix the price of. **3** *(gravar)* to tax. **4** *(regular)* to regulate. **5** *(limitar)* to limit. **6** *(racionar)* to ration.

tasca *f* bar, pub. ●*ir de tascas,* to go on a pub crawl.

tatarabuelo,-a *m, f m* great-great-grandfather, *f* great-great-grandmother.

tatuaje *m (dibujo)* tattoo. **2** *(técnica)* tattooing.

tatuar [10] *t* to tattoo.

taurino,-a *adj* of/related to bullfighting.

Tauro *m* Taurus.

tauromaquia *f* tauromachy, (art of) bullfighting.

taxi *m* taxi.

taxímetro *m* taximeter, clock.

taxista *mf* taxi driver.

taza *f (recipiente)* cup. **2** *(contenido)* cupful. **3** *(de retrete)* bowl.

tazón *m* bowl.

te *pron pers* (to/for) you: *no quiero verte,* I don't want to see you; ~ *compraré uno,* I'll buy one for you, I'll buy you one. **2** *(reflexivo)* yourself: *lávate,* wash yourself. **3** *(sin traducción)*: *no* ~ *vayas,* don't go.

té *m* tea. ■ ~ *con limón,* lemon tea.

tea *f* torch.

teatral *adj* theatrical, dramatic. **2** *fig (exagerado)* stagy, theatrical.

teatro *m* theatre. **2** ART theatre, acting, stage. **3** *(literatura)* drama. **4** *fig (lugar)* scene, theatre. **5** *fig (exageración)* theatrics. ●*fig hacer* ~, to play-act.

tebeo *m* comic (book).

techar *t* to roof.

techo *m (construcción)* ceiling; *(de coche, tejado)* roof. **2** *fig* limit, end.

techumbre *f* roof, covering.

tecla *f* key. ●*tocar muchas teclas,* to try to do too many things at once.

teclado *m* keyboard.

teclear *i (piano)* to press the keys; *(máquina de escribir, ordenador)* to type, tap the keyboard. **2** *(tamborilear)* to drum, tap one's fingers.

técnico,-a *adj* technical. − **2** *m,f* technician, technical expert. − **3** *f (tecnología)* technics *pl,* technology. **4** *(habilidad)* technique, method.

tedio *m* tedium, boredom.

tedioso,-a *adj* tedious.

teja *f* tile. ●*fam a toca* ~, on the nail.

tejado *m* roof.

tejanos *mpl* jeans.

tejedor,-ra *adj* weaving. − **2** *m,f* weaver.

tejer *t (en telar)* to weave. **2** *(hacer punto)* to knit. **3** *(araña)* to spin. **4** *fig (plan)* to weave, plot.

tejido *m (tela)* fabric, textile. **2** ANAT tissue. **3** *fig* web. ■ ~ *adiposo/óseo,* fatty/bone tissue; ~ *de punto,* knitted fabric.

tela *f (textil)* material, fabric, cloth. **2** *(de la leche)* skin. **3** *fam (dinero)* dough. **4** ART painting. ●*fig poner en* ~ *de juicio,* to question. ■ ~ *metálica,* gauze.

telar *m* loom.

telaraña *f* cobweb, spider's web.

telediario *m* television news bulletin.

teledirigir [6] *t* to operate/guide by remote control.

telefonazo *m fam* buzz, ring. ●*dar un* ~ *(a algn.),* to give (sb.) a ring.

telefonear *i-t* to (tele)phone.

telefonista *mf* (telephone) operator.

teléfono *m* (tele)phone.

telegrafiar [13] *t* to telegraph, wire.

telégrafo *m* telegraph. **2** *pl* post office *sing.*

telegrama *m* telegram, cable.

telescopio *m* telescope.

televisar *t* to televise.

televisión *f (sistema)* television. **2** *fam (aparato)* television set.

televisor *m* television set.

telón *m* curtain. ■ ~ *de fondo,* TEAT backdrop; *fig* background.

tema *m* topic. **2** MÚS theme. **3** GRAM root, stem. ●*atenerse al* ~, to keep to the point; *salir(se) del* ~, to go off at a tangent. ■ ~ *de actualidad,* current affair.

temario *m (de examen)* programme; *(de conferencia)* agenda.

temblar [27] *i (de frío)* to shiver; *(de miedo)* to tremble *(de,* with); *(con sacudidas)* to shake. **2** *(voz)* to quiver.

temblor *m* tremor, shudder.

tembloroso,-a *adj (de frío)* shivering; *(de miedo)* trembling; *(con sacudidas)* shaking. **2** *(voz)* quivering.

temer *t* to fear, be afraid of. − **2** *i* to be afraid. **3** *(preocuparse)* to worry.

temerario,-a *adj* reckless, rash.

temeridad *f (actitud)* temerity, rashness. **2** *(acto temerario)* reckless act.

temeroso,-a *adj* fearful, timid. **2** *(medroso)* frightful. ●~ *de Dios,* God-fearing.

temible *adj* dreadful, fearful, frightening.

temor *m (de Dios)* fear. **2** *(recelo)* worry, apprehension. ●*tener* ~, to feel apprehensive.

témpano *m* ice floe.

temperamento *m* temperament, nature. ●*tener* ~, to have a strong character.

temperatura *f* temperature.

tempestad *f* storm. **2** *fig* turmoil, uproar. ●*fig una* ~ *en un vaso de agua,* a storm in a teacup.

tempestuoso,-a *adj* stormy.

templado,-a *adj (agua)* (luke)warm; *(clima, temperatura)* mild, temperate. **2** *(moderado)* moderate; *(sereno)* composed, unruffled. **3** MÚS tuned. **4** *(metal)* tempered. ●*nervios bien templados,* steady nerves.

templanza *f (moderación)* moderation, restraint. **2** *(del clima)* mildness.

templar *t* to moderate, temper. **2** *(algo frío)* to warm up; *(algo caliente)* to cool down. **3** *(cólera)* to appease; *(apaciguar)* to calm down. **4** *(cuerda, tornillo)* to tighten up. **5** *(bebida)* to dilute. **6** MÚS to tune. **7** *(metal)* to temper. **8** *(colores)* to match.

temple *m (fortaleza)* boldness, courage. **2** *(estado de ánimo)* frame of mind, mood. **3** *(de metal)* temper.

templo *m* temple.

temporada *f (en artes, deportes, moda)* season. **2** *(período)* period, time. ●*en plena* ~, at the height of the season; *por temporadas,* on and off. ■ ~ *alta,* high/peak season; ~ *baja,* low/off season.

temporal *adj (transitorio)* temporary, provisional. **− 2** *m* METEOR storm.

temprano,-a *adj-adv* early.

tenacidad *f* tenacity, perseverance. **2** *(de metal)* tensile strength.

tenaz *adj* tenacious; *(perseverante)* persevering, unflagging; *(persistente)* persistent, unremitting.

tenaza *f (herramienta)* pliers *pl*, pincers *pl*; *(para el fuego)* tongs *pl*. ▲ *gen pl*.

tendedero *m* clothesline, drying place.

tendencia *f* tendency, inclination. •*tener ~ a hacer algo,* to tend to do sth., have a tendency to do sth.

tendencioso,-a *adj* tendentious, biased.

tender(se) [28] *t (mantel)* to spread; *(red)* to cast; *(puente)* to throw; *(vía, cable)* to lay; *(velas)* to spread. **2** *(ropa, colada)* to hang out. **3** *(mano)* to stretch/hold out. **4** *(emboscada, trampa)* to lay, set. **5** *(tener tendencia)* to tend *(a,* to). **− 6** *p (tumbarse)* to lie down, stretch out.

tenderete *m (puesto)* stall. **2** *(montón)* heap, mess.

tendero,-a *m,f* shopkeeper.

tendón *m* tendon, sinew.

tenebroso,-a *adj (sombrío)* dark, gloomy. **2** *(siniestro)* sinister, shady.

tenedor *m* fork.

tenencia *f* JUR tenancy, possession.

tener(se) [87] *t* to have (got): *tenemos un examen,* we've got an exam. **2** *(poseer)* to own, possess. **3** *(sostener)* to hold: *lo tienes en la mano,* you're holding it. **4** *(coger)* to take. **5** *(sensación, sentimiento)* to be, feel. **6** *(mantener)* to keep. **7** *(medir)* to measure. **8** *(contener)* to hold, contain. **9** *(edad)* to be: *tiene diez años,* he is ten. **10** *(celebrar)* to hold: *~ una reunión,* to hold a meeting. **11** *(considerar)* to consider, think: *me tienen por estúpido,* they think I'm a fool. **− 12** *aux (obligación)* ~ *que,* to have (got) to, must: *tengo que irme,* I must leave. **− 13** *p (sostenerse)* to stand up. **14** *(dominarse)* to control o.s. •*no ~se,* to be tired out; *¿qué tienes?,* what's wrong with you?; *~ calor/frío,* to be hot/cold; *~ cariño a,* to be fond of; *~ compasión,* to take pity *(de,* on); *~ ganas de,* to feel like; *~ ilusión,* to be enthusiastic; *~ miedo,* to be frightened; *tenerla tomada con algn.,* to have it in for sb.

tenga *pres subj* → **tener.**

tengo *pres indic* → **tener.**

teniente *m* lieutenant. ■ *~ de alcalde,* deputy mayor.

tenis *m* tennis.

tenista *mf* tennis player.

tenor *m* MÚS tenor. **2** *(conforme)* tenor, purport. •*a ~ de,* according to.

tensar *t (cable, cuerda)* to tauten; *(arco)* to draw.

tensión *f* ELEC tension, voltage. **2** MED pressure. **3** *(de una situación)* tension; *(de una relación)* stress, strain.

tenso,-a *adj* tense. **2** *(relaciones)* strained.

tentación *f* temptation.

tentáculo *m* tentacle.

tentador,-ra *adj* tempting.

tentar [27] *t (palpar)* to feel, touch. **2** *(incitar)* to tempt. **3** *(atraer)* to attract, appeal.

tentativa *f* attempt.

tenue *adj (delgado)* thin, light. **2** *(luz, sonido)* subdued, faint.

teñir [36] *t* to dye. **2** *fig* to tinge.

teología *f* theology.

teorema *m* theorem.

teoría *f* theory. •*en ~,* theoretically.

teórico,-a *adj* theoretic(al). **− 2** *m,f* theoretician, theorist.

teorizar [4] *t* to theorize on.

terapia *f* therapy.

tercer *adj* → **tercero,-a.** ▲ *Used in front of a sing masculine noun.*

tercero,-a *adj-m,f* third. **− 2** *m (mediador)* mediator; *(persona ajena)* outsider, JUR third party.

terceto *m (poesía)* tercet. **2** MÚS trio.

terciar(se) [12] *i (mediar)* to mediate, arbitrate. **− 2** *p (ocasión)* to arise. •*si se tercia,* should the occasion arise.

tercio,-a *adj-m* (one) third.

terciopelo *m* velvet.

terco,-a *adj* obstinate, stubborn.

tergiversación *f* distortion.

tergiversar *t* to twist, distort.

terminal *adj* terminal. **− 2** *f (estación)* terminus.

terminante *adj (categórico)* categorical. **2** *(dato, resultado)* conclusive, definitive.

terminar(se) *t-i (acabar)* to finish. **− 2** *i (ir a parar)* to end up *(como,* as), end *(en,* in/with). **3** *(eliminar)* to put an end *(con,* to). **4** *(reñir)* to break up *(con,* with). **− 5** *p (acabarse)* to finish, end, be over. **6** *(agotarse)* to run out.

término *m* end, finish. **2** *(estación)* terminus. **3** *(límite)* limit, boundary. **4** *(plazo)* term, time. **5** *(palabra, argumento)* term. **6** *(lugar, posición)* place. •*dar ~ a,* to conclude; *en otros términos,* in other words; *en términos generales,* generally speaking; *llevar (algo) a buen/feliz ~,* to carry (sth.) through (successfully); *poner ~ a algo,* to put an end to sth.; *(por) ~ medio,* on average. ■ *~ municipal,* district.

termómetro *m* thermometer.

termo *m* (thermos) flask.

ternero,-a *m,f* calf. — **2** *f* CULIN veal.

ternura *f* tenderness.

terquedad *f* obstinacy, stubbornness.

terraplén *m* embankment.

terrateniente *mf* landowner.

terraza *f* (*balcón*) terrace. **2** (*azotea*) roof terrace. **3** (*de un café*) veranda.

terremoto *m* earthquake.

terreno,-a *adj* worldly, earthly. — **2** *m* (*tierra*) piece of) land, ground; (*solar*) plot, site; GEOG terrain; AGR (*de cultivo*) soil; (*campo*) field. **3** *fig* field, sphere. ●*fig estar en su propio ~,* to be on home ground; *fig saber uno el ~ que pisa,* to know what one's doing; *fig ser ~ abonado (para algo),* to be receptive (to sth.).

terrestre *adj* terrestrial, earthly. **2** (*por tierra*) by land.

terrible *adj* terrible, awful.

territorial *adj* territorial.

territorio *m* territory.

terrón *m* lump.

terror *m* terror. **2** CINEM horror.

terrorífico,-a *adj* terrifying, frightening.

terrorismo *m* terrorism.

terso,-a *adj* (*liso*) smooth. **2** (*estilo*) polished, fluent.

tertulia *f* get-together. ●*hacer ~,* to have a get-together.

tesis *f inv* thesis.

tesitura *f fig* attitude.

tesón *m* tenacity, firmness.

tesorería *f* (*oficina*) treasurer's office; (*cargo*) treasurer.

tesorero,-a *m,f* treasurer.

tesoro *m* treasure. **2** (*erario*) exchequer. **3** (*diccionario*) thesaurus.

testamentario,-a *adj* testamentary. — **2** *m,f m* executor, *f* executrix.

testamento *m* will, testament.

testar *i* to make/draw up one's will.

testarudo,-a *adj* obstinate, stubborn, pigheaded.

testículo *m* testicle.

testificar [1] *t* to testify.

testigo *mf* witness. — **2** *m* DEP baton. ●*poner (a algn.) por ~,* to call (sb.) to witness. ■ *~ de cargo/descargo,* wit-

ness for the prosecution/defence; *~ ocular/presencial,* eyewitness.

testimonio *m* testimony. **2** (*prueba*) evidence, proof. ●*dar ~,* to give evidence.

teta *f fam* tit(y), boob. **2** (*de vaca*) udder.

tetera *f* teapot.

tetina *f* (rubber) teat.

tétrico,-a *adj* gloomy, dull, dismal.

textil *adj-m* textile.

texto *m* text. ■ *libro de ~,* textbook.

textual *adj* textual. **2** (*exacto*) literal.

textura *f* (*textil*) texture. **2** (*minerales*) structure.

tez *f* complexion.

ti *pron pers* you. ▲ *Used only after prep.*

tía *f* aunt. **2** *fam* (*mujer*) girl, woman, bird.

tibia *f* tibia, shinbone.

tibieza *f* tepidity.

tibio,-a *adj* tepid, lukewarm.

tiburón *m* shark.

tic *m* tic, twitch. ▲ *pl tiques.*

tictac *m* tick-tock, ticking.

tiempo *m* time. **2** METEOR weather. **3** (*edad*) age: *¿cuánto/qué ~ tiene su niño?,* how old is your baby? **4** (*temporada*) season. **5** MÚS tempo, movement. **6** DEP (*parte*) half. **7** GRAM tense. ●*a su (debido) ~,* in due course; *al poco ~,* soon afterwards; *con ~,* in advance; *¿cuánto ~?,* how long?; *¿qué ~ hace?,* what's the weather like?

tienda *f* shop, US store. **2** (*de campaña*) tent.

tienta *f a tientas,* gropingly.

tiento *m* (*tacto*) tact, feel. **2** (*prudencia*) caution. ●*con ~,* tactfully.

tierno,-a *adj* (*blando*) tender, soft. **2** (*reciente*) fresh. **3** (*cariñoso*) affectionate, darling.

tierra *f* (*planeta*) earth. **2** (*superficie sólida*) land. **3** (*terreno cultivado*) soil, land. **4** (*país*) country. **5** (*suelo*) ground. **6** AM dust. ●*tocar ~,* MAR to reach harbour; AV to touch down; *fig echar ~ encima de,* to hush up. ■ *~ natal,* homeland.

tieso,-a *adj* (*rígido*) stiff, rigid. **2** (*erguido*) upright, erect. **3** *fam* (*engreído*) stiff, starchy.

tiesto *m* flowerpot.

tifón *m* typhoon.

tigre *m* tiger.

tijera *f* (pair of) scissors *pl.* ▲ *gen pl.*

tila *f* lime/linden blossom tea.

tildar *t* to call, brand.

tilín *m* ting-a-ling. ●*hacer ~,* to please: *Juana le hace ~,* he fancies Juana.

tilo *m* lime tree.

timador,-ra *m,f* swindler.

timar *t* to swindle, cheat.

timbrar *t* *(carta)* to stamp, mark; *(documento)* to seal.

timbre *m* *(de la puerta)* bell. **2** *(sello)* stamp.

timidez *f* shyness.

tímido,-a *adj* shy, timid.

timo *m* swindle, fiddle.

timón *m* rudder. **2** *(del arado)* beam. ●*fig* **empuñar/llevar el ~**, to be at the helm.

timonel *m* steersman.

timorato,-a *adj* shy, timid.

tímpano *m* eardrum.

tina *f* *(recipiente)* vat, tub. **2** *(bañera)* bath(tub).

tinaja *f* large earthenware jar.

tinglado *m* *(cobertizo)* shed. **2** *(tablado)* platform. **3** *fig (embrollo)* mess. **4** *fig (intriga)* intrigue. **5** *fig (mundillo)* setup, racket.

tiniebla *f* darkness. **2** *fig (ignorancia)* ignorance. ▲ *gen pl*.

tinta *f* ink. **2** *pl* colours. ●*fig* **medias tintas**, ambiguities; *fig* **(re)cargar las tintas**, to exaggerate; *fig* **saber algo de buena ~**, to have got sth. straight from the horse's mouth; *fig* **sudar ~**, to sweat blood.

tinte *m* *(colorante)* dye. **2** *(proceso)* dyeing. **3** *(tintorería)* dry-cleaner's. **4** *fig (matiz)* shade, colouring.

tintero *m* inkpot.

tintin(e)ar *i* *(vidrio)* to clink, chink. **2** *(campanillas)* to jingle, tinkle.

tintineo *m* *(de vidrio)* clink(ing), chink. **2** *(de campanillas)* jingling, ting-a-ling.

tinto *adj* *(vino)* red. **2** *(teñido)* dyed. — **3** *m* red wine.

tintorería *f* dry-cleaner's.

tiñoso,-a *adj* scabby, mang(e)y. **2** *fam (mezquino)* mean, stingy.

tío *m* uncle. **2** *fam* fellow, bloke, US guy.

tiovivo *m* merry-go-round, roundabout.

típico,-a *adj* typical, characteristic.

tipo *m* *(clase)* type, kind. **2** FIN rate. **3** ANAT *(de hombre)* build, physique; *(de mujer)* figure. **4** *fam (persona)* guy, fellow, bloke. ●**tener buen ~**, to have a good figure; *fig* **aguantar el ~**, to keep cool/calm.

tipografía *f* typography.

tiquete *f* AM ticket.

tira *f* strip. ●*fam* **la tira**, a lot, loads *pl*.

tirabuzón *m* *(rizo)* ringlet. **2** *(sacacorchos)* corkscrew.

tirada *f* *(impresión)* printing; *(edición)* edition. **2** *(distancia)* stretch. **3** *(serie)* (long) series. ●**de/en una ~**, in one go.

tirado,-a *fam adj (precio)* dirt cheap. **2** *(problema, asunto)* dead easy. **3** *(abandonado)* let down.

tirador,-ra *m,f (persona)* shooter. — **2** *m (de puerta, cajón)* knob, handle; *(cordón)* bell-pull.

tiranía *f* tyranny.

tiranizar [4] *t* to tyrannize.

tirano,-a *m,f* tyrant.

tirante *adj* taut, tight. **2** *fig (relación, situación)* tense. — **3** *mpl* braces, US suspenders.

tirantez *f* tautness, tightness. **2** *fig (de una relación/situación)* tension, strain.

tirar(se) *t (echar)* to throw; *(un tiro)* to fire; *(una bomba)* to drop; *(un beso)* to blow. **2** *(dejar caer)* to drop. **3** *(desechar)* to throw away. **4** *(derribar)* to knock down; *(casa, árbol)* to pull down; *(vaso, botella)* to knock over. **5** *(derramar)* to spill. **6** *(imprimir)* to print. **7** *(hacer) (foto)* to take; *(línea, plano)* to draw. — **8** *i (cuerda, puerta)* to pull **(de, -)**. **9** *(estufa, chimenea)* to draw. **10** *(en juegos)* to be a player's move/turn. **11** *(funcionar)* to work, run. **12** *(durar)* to last. **13** *(tender)* to tend **(a**, towards). **14** *(parecerse)* to take after **(a**, -). **15** *(ir)* to go, turn. — **16** *p (lanzarse)* to throw o.s. **17** *(tumbarse)* to lie down. **18** *(tiempo)* to spend. **19** *arg (fornicar)* to lay **(a**, -). ●**ir tirando**, *(espabilarse)* to manage; *(tener buena salud)* to be okay; **~ una moneda al aire**, to toss a coin; *fig* **tira y afloja**, give and take; *fig* **~ el dinero**, to squander money; *fig* **~ para**, to be attracted to.

tirita® *f* (sticking) plaster.

tiritar *i* to shiver, shake; *(dientes)* to chatter.

tiro *m (lanzamiento)* throw. **2** *(disparo, ruido)* shot. **3** *(caballerías)* team: **animal de ~**, draught animal. **4** *(de chimenea)* draught. **5** *(de escaleras)* flight. ●**a ~**, *(de arma)* within range; *(a mano)* within reach; **dar/pegar un ~**, to shoot, fire a shot; *fig* **de tiros largos**, all dressed up; *fam fig* **ni a tiros**, not for love or money. ■ **animal de ~**, draught animal; **~ al blanco**, target shooting.

tirón *m* pull, tug. ●*fam* **de un ~**, in one go.

tirotear *t* to shoot, snipe.

tiroteo *m* shooting, firing to and fro.

tirria *f fam* dislike.

tisana *f* infusion, tisane.

tisis *f inv* phthisis, consumption.

títere *m* puppet, marionette.

titilar *i (temblar)* to quiver. **2** *(luz)* to flicker; *(de estrella)* to twinkle.

titiritar *i* to tremble, shiver.

titubear *i (tambalearse)* to stagger, totter. **2** *(tartamudear)* to stammer. **3** *(vacilar)* to hesitate.

titubeo *m (tartamudeo)* stammering. **2** *(duda)* hesitation.

titulación *f* qualifications *pl.*

titular(se) *t* to call. — **2** *p* to be called. **3** EDUC to graduate *(en,* in). — **4** *adj* appointed, official. — **5** *mf (persona)* (office) holder. — **6** *m (prensa)* headline.

título *m* title. **2** *(de texto legal)* heading. **3** EDUC degree; *(diploma)* certificate, diploma. **4** *(titular de prensa)* headline. **5** *(banca)* bond, security. **6** *pl (méritos)* qualifications, qualities. ■ ~ *de propiedad,* deeds.

tiza *f* chalk: *una* ~, a piece of chalk.

tiznado,-a *adj* sooky, blackened.

tiznar *t* to blacken, soil with soot.

tizne *m* soot.

tizón *m* half-burnt stick, brand.

toalla *f* towel.

toallero *m* towel rail/rack.

tobillo *m* ankle.

toca *f (sombrero)* headdress; *(de monja)* wimple.

tocadiscos *m inv* record player.

tocado,-a *adj (fruta)* bad, rotten. **2** *fam (perturbado)* crazy, touched. **3** DEP injured. — **4** *m (peinado)* coiffure, hairdo. **5** *(prenda)* headdress.

tocador *m (mueble)* dressing table. **2** *(habitación)* dressing room, boudoir. ■ *artículos de* ~, toiletries; ~ *de señoras,* powder room.

tocante *tocante a, adv* concerning, about. ●*en lo* ~ *a,* with reference to.

tocar [1] *t* to touch. **2** *(sentir por el tacto)* to feel. **3** *(hacer sonar) (instrumento, canción)* to play; *(timbre)* to ring; *(bocina)* to blow, honk; *(campanas)* to strike. **4** DEP *(diana)* to hit. **5** *(mencionar)* to touch on. — **6** *i (corresponder)* to be one's turn. **7** *(caer en suerte)* to win. **8** *(tener que)* to have to. **9** *(afectar)* to concern, affect. **10** *(ser parientes)* to be a relative of. **11** AV MAR to call *(en,* at), stop over *(en,* at). ●~ *a su fin,* to be coming to an end.

tocinería *f* pork butcher's.

tocino *m* lard. ■ ~ *ahumado,* smoked bacon; ~ *de cielo,* sweet *made with egg yolk.*

tocón,-ona *adj fam* groper.

todavía *adv (a pesar de ello)* nevertheless. **2** *(tiempo)* still, yet: ~ *la quiere,* he still loves her; ~ *no lo quiere,* he doesn't want it yet. **3** *(para reforzar)* even: *esto* ~ *te gustará más,* you'll enjoy this even more.

todo,-a *adj (sin excluir nada)* all. **2** *(entero)* complete. **3** *pl (cada)* every. — **4** *m (totalidad)* whole. — **5** *pron (sin excluir nada)* all, everything. **6** *(cualquiera)* anybody. **7** *pl (cada uno)* everybody. — **8** *adv* completely, totally. ●*ante* ~, first of all; *con* ~, in spite of everything; *del* ~, completely; *estar en* ~, to be really with it; ~ *lo más,* at the most.

todopoderoso,-a *adj* almighty, all-powerful. ■ *el Todopoderoso,* the Almighty.

toga *f* robe, gown.

toldo *m* awning.

tolerable *adj* tolerable.

tolerancia *f* tolerance. **2** *(resistencia)* resistance.

tolerar *t* to tolerate. **2** *(inconvenientes)* to stand. **3** *(gente)* to put up with. **4** *(comida, bebida)* to take. **5** *(peso)* to bear.

toma *f (acción)* taking. **2** MED dose. **3** MIL capture. **4** *(grabación)* recording. **5** CINEM take, shot. ■ ~ *de posesión,* takeover.

tomado,-a *adj (voz)* hoarse. **2** AM *(bebido)* drunk.

tomar(se) *t-p* to take. **2** *(comer, beber)* to have. — **3** *t (el autobús, el tren)* to catch. **4** *(adquirir)* to acquire. — **5** *i (encaminarse)* to go, turn. ●~ *la costumbre,* to get into the habit; ~ *la palabra,* to speak; ~ *tierra,* to land; *fam tomarla con alguien,* to have it in for sb.

tomate *m* tomato. **2** *fam (jaleo)* fuss, commotion. **3** *fam (dificultad)* snag, catch. ●*fig ponerse como un* ~, to go as red as a beetroot.

tómbola *f* tombola.

tomillo *m* thyme.

tomo *m* volume.

ton *sin* ~ *ni son, adv* without rhyme or reason.

tonada *f* tune, song. **2** *(acento)* accent.

tonel *m* barrel, cask. ●*fam como un* ~, as fat as a pig.

tonelada *f* ton. ■ ~ *métrica,* metric ton.

tonelaje *m* tonnage.

tónico,-a *adj-m* tonic. — **2** *f (bebida)* tonic. **3** *(tendencia)* tendency, trend.

tono *m* tone. **2** MÚS key, pitch. ●*a* ~ *con,* in tune/harmony with; *bajar de* ~/~, to lower one's voice; *subir de* ~/*el*

~, to speak louder; *fig darse* ~, to put on airs; *fig fuera de* ~, inappropiate, out of place; *fig sin venir a* ~, for no good reason.

tontada *f* silly thing, nonsense. **2** *(insignificancia)* triffle.

tontaina *fam adj* foolish, silly. — **2** *mf* fool, nitwit.

tontear *i (decir tonterías)* to act the clown, fool about. **2** *(galantear)* to flirt.

tontería *f (calidad de tonto)* stupidity, silliness. **2** *(dicho, hecho)* silly/stupid thing. **3** *(insignificancia)* triffle. ●*decir tonterías*, to talk nonsense; *dejarse de tonterías*, to be serious.

tonto,-a *adj* silly, dumb. — **2** *m,f* fool, idiot. ●*hacer el* ~, to act the fool; *hacerse el* ~, to play dumb; *ponerse* ~, to get stroppy.

topar *t-i (chocar)* to bump (into). **2** *(hallar casualmente)* to run into.

tope *adj* top, maximum. — **2** *m (límite)* limit, end. — **3** *adv fam* incredibly.

tópico,-a *adj* MED external. — **2** *m* commonplace, cliché.

topo *m* mole.

topografía *f* topography.

topónimo *m* place name.

toque *m (acto)* touch. **2** *(tañido)* ringing. **3** *(advertencia)* warning (note). ■ ~ *de queda,* curfew.

tórax *m inv* thorax.

torbellino *m* whirlwind.

torcedura *f* twist(ing). **2** MED sprain.

torcer(se) [54] *t (cuerda etc.)* to twist. **2** *(doblar)* to bend. **3** *(inclinar)* to slant. — **4** *p* MED to sprain. **5** *(plan)* to fall through. ●~ *la esquina,* to turn the córner.

torcido,-a *adj* twisted. **2** *(ladeado)* slanted.

tordo *m (pájaro)* thrush.

torear *i-t* to fight (bulls). — **2** *t (a persona)* to tease, confuse.

toreo *m* bullfighting.

torero,-a *adj* relating to bullfighting. — **2** *m,f* bullfighter. — **3** *f* bolero (jacket).

tormenta *f* storm.

tormento *m (tortura)* torture. **2** *(dolor)* torment, pain.

tormentoso,-a *adj* stormy.

tornado *m* tornado.

tornasol *m* BOT sunflower. **2** *(luz)* iridescense. **3** *(colorante)* litmus.

tornear *t* to turn.

torneo *m* tournament.

tornillo *m* screw.

torniquete *m* turnstile. **2** MED tourniquet.

torno *m* lathe. ●*en* ~ *a, (alrededor de)* around; *(acerca de)* about, concerning.

toro *m* bull.

torpe *adj* clumsy. **2** *(de movimiento)* slow.

torpedo *m* torpedo.

torpeza *f* clumsiness. **2** *(de movimiento)* slowness.

torre *f* tower. **2** *(chalé)* country house. **3** *(ajedrez)* rook, castle.

torrente *m* mountain stream, torrent.

tórrido,-a *adj* torrid.

torrija *f type of* French toast.

torsión *f* twist(ing).

torso *m* torso.

torta *f* cake. **2** *fam (golpe)* blow, crack.

tortícolis *f inv* stiff neck.

tortilla *f* omelet(te). **2** AM tortilla, pancake.

tortillera* *f arg* dyke*, lesbian.

tórtola *f* dove.

tortuga *f (de tierra)* tortoise, US turtle. **2** *(marina)* turtle.

tortuoso,-a *adj* tortuous.

tortura *f* torture.

torturar(se) *t-p* to torture (o.s.).

tos *f* cough(ing). ■ ~ *ferina,* whooping cough.

tosco,-a *adj* rough. **2** *(persona)* uncouth.

toser *i* to cough.

tosquedad *f* roughness.

tostado,-a *adj* toasted; *(café)* roasted. **2** *(moreno)* tanned. **3** *(color)* brown. — **4** *f* (slice) of toast.

tostar(se) [31] *t* to toast; *(café)* to roast; *(carnes)* to brown. **2** *(piel)* to tan. **3** AM *(zurrar)* to tan. — **4** *p* to get brown/tanned.

tostón *m fam fig* bore, drag.

total *adj-m* total. — **2** *adv* in short.

totalidad *f* whole, totality.

totalitario,-a *adj* totalitarian.

tóxico,-a *adj* toxic. — **2** *m* toxicant, poison.

tozudez *f* stubbornness.

tozudo,-a *adj* stubborn.

traba *f fig* hindrance, obstacle.

trabajador,-ra *adj* working. **2** *(laborioso)* hard-working. — **3** *m,f* worker.

trabajar *i* to work. — **2** *t (materiales)* to work (on). **3** *(a algn.)* to (try to) persuade.

trabajo *m* work. **2** *(tarea)* task, job. **3** *(empleo)* job. **4** *(esfuerzo)* effort. **5** EDUC report, paper. ■ ~ *a destajo,* piecework;

trabajos forzados, hard labour *sing;* **trabajos manuales,** arts and crafts.

trabajoso,-a *adj* hard, laborious.

trabalenguas *m inv* tongue twister.

trabar(se) *t (unir)* to join. **2** *(amistad, conversación)* to strike up. **3** *(líquido, salsa)* to thicken. − **4** *p (mecanismo)* to jam. ●*trabársele la lengua a algn.,* to get tongue-tied.

trabazón *f (unión)* joining. **2** *(conexión)* connection, relation.

trabuco *m* blunderbuss.

traca *f* string of firecrackers.

tracción *f* traction. ■ ~ *delantera/trasera,* front-/rear-wheel drive.

tractor *m* tractor.

tradición *f* tradition.

tradicional *adj* traditional.

traducción *f* translation. ■ ~ *automática,* machine translation.

traducir [46] *t* to translate *(a/de,* into/from).

traductor,-ra *adj* translating. − **2** *m,f* translator.

traer [88] *t* to bring. **2** *(llevar consigo)* to carry. **3** *(causar)* to bring about. **4** *(vestir)* to wear. ●~ *entre manos,* to be busy with; *fam* **traérselas,** to be really difficult.

traficante *mf* trader, dealer. **2** *(ilegal)* trafficker.

traficar [1] *i* to deal. **2** *(de forma ilegal)* to traffic *(con,* in).

tráfico *m* traffic.

tragaluz *m* skylight.

tragaperras *f inv (máquina)* ~, slot machine.

tragar(se) [7] *t-p* to swallow (up).

tragedia *f* tragedy.

trágico,-a *adj* tragic. − **2** *m,f* tragedian.

trago *m (sorbo)* swig. **2** *(bebida)* drink. ●*echar un* ~, to have a drink; *fig pasar un mal* ~, to have a bad time of it.

tragón,-ona *adj* greedy. − **2** *m,f* glutton.

traición *f* treason, betrayal.

traicionar *t* to betray. **2** *(delatar)* to give away.

traicionero,-a *adj* treacherous.

traidor,-ra *adj* treacherous. − **2** *m,f* traitor.

tráiler *m* CINEM trailer. **2** AUTO articulated lorry, US trailer truck.

traje *m (de hombre)* suit. **2** *(de mujer)* dress. ■ ~ *de baño,* bathing suit/costume; ~ *de etiqueta,* full dress; ~ *de luces,* bullfighter's costume; ~ *sastre,* skirt and jacket.

trajín *m* comings and goings *pl.*

trajinar *t (acarrear)* to carry. − **2** *i (moverse)* bustle about.

trama *f (textil)* weft, woof. **2** *(argumento)* plot.

tramar *t (tejidos)* to weave. **2** *(preparar)* to plot.

tramitar *t* to negotiate, carry out.

trámite *m (paso)* step. **2** *(negociación)* procedures *pl.*

tramo *m* stretch, section. **2** *(de escalera)* flight.

tramontana *f* north wind.

tramoya *f* stage machinery.

tramoyista *mf* scene shifter.

trampa *f* trap. **2** *(abertura)* trapdoor. **3** *fig (engaño)* fiddle. ●*hacer trampa(s),* to cheat.

trampilla *f* trapdoor.

trampolín *m (de piscina)* springboard, diving board. **2** *(de esquí)* ski jump.

tramposo,-a *adj* deceitful, tricky. − **2** *m,f* trickster.

tranca *f (palo)* club, truncheon. **2** *(para puertas etc.)* bar. ●*a trancas y barrancas,* with great difficulty.

trance *m* critical moment. **2** *(éxtasis)* trance. ●*a todo* ~, at any risk.

tranquilidad *f* calmness, tranquillity.

tranquilizante *m* tranquillizer.

tranquilizar(se) [4] *t-p* to calm down.

tranquilo,-a *adj* calm. **2** *(sin ruidos)* quiet.

transacción *f* transaction.

transatlántico,-a *adj* transatlantic. − **2** *m* (ocean) liner.

transbordador *m* ferry.

transbordo *m (de vehículo)* change, US transfer; *(de barco)* tran(s)shipment.

transcribir *t* to transcribe. ▲ *pp* **transcrito,-a.**

transcurrir *i* to pass, elapse.

transcurso *m* course/passing (of time).

transeúnte *mf* pedestrian. **2** *(residente transitorio)* temporary resident.

transferencia *f* transference. **2** FIN transfer.

transferir [35] *t* to transfer.

transfigurar(se) *t* to transfigure. − **2** *p* to become transfigured.

transformación *f* transformation.

transformador *m* transformer.

transformar(se) *t* to transform. − **2** *p* to change. ●~ *en,* to become.

tránsfuga *mf* fugitive; MIL deserter. **2** POL turncoat.

transgredir *t* to transgress, break. ▲ *Only used in forms which include the letter* *i in their endings:* **transgredía, transgrediré, transgrediendo**.

transgresión *f* transgression.

transgresor,-ra *m,f* transgressor.

transición *f* transition.

transigencia *f* tolerance.

transigir *i* to compromise, be tolerant.

transistor *m* transistor.

transitable *adj* passable.

transitar *i* to travel (about).

transitivo,-a *adj* transitive.

tránsito *m (acción)* passage, transit. **2** AUTO traffic.

transitorio,-a *adj* transitory.

translúcido,-a *adj* translucent.

transmisión *f* transmission. **2** RAD TV broadcast. **3** TÉC drive.

transmisor,-ra *adj* transmitting. **– 2** *m,f* transmitter.

transmitir *t gen* to transmit. **2** RAD TV to broadcast.

transmutar(se) *t* to transmute. **– 2** *p* to change.

transparencia *f* transparency. **2** *(diapositiva)* slide.

transparentarse *p* to be transparent, show through.

transparente *adj* transparent.

transpiración *f* perspiration.

transpirar *i* to perspire.

transplante *m* → **trasplante**.

transponer(se) [78] *t (de sitio)* to move. **2** *(trasplantar)* to transplant. **3** *(desaparecer)* to disappear. **– 4** *p (astro)* to set. ▲ *transpuesto,-a*.

transportar *t* to transport; *(mercancías)* to ship.

transporte *m* transport.

transportista *mf* carrier.

transpuesto,-a *pp* → **transponer**.

transvasar *t* to decant.

transversal *adj* transverse, cross.

tranvía *m* tram(car).

trapacero,-a *adj* tricky. **– 2** *m,f* trickster.

trapecio *m* SP trapeze. **2** *(geometría)* trapezium.

trapero,-a *m,f* rag-and-bone man.

trapo *m (tela vieja)* rag. **2** *(paño)* cloth. **3** MAR sails *pl*. **– 4** *pl* clothes. ●*a todo ~*, at full sail; *fig* flat out; *poner (a algn.) como un ~ (sucio)*, to tear sb. apart.

tráquea *f* trachea.

tras *prep (después de)* after. **2** *(detrás)* behind.

trascendencia *f (importancia)* significance. **2** *(filosofía)* transcendence.

trascendental *adj (importante)* significant. **2** *(filosofía)* transcendent(al).

trascender [28] *i (olor)* to smell. **2** *(darse a conocer)* to become known. **3** *(tener consecuencias)* to have an effect. **– 4** *t (averiguar)* to discover.

trascribir *t* → **transcribir**.

trascrito,-a *pp* → **transcribir**.

trasero,-a *adj* back, rear. **– 2** *m fam* bottom, bun.

trasfondo *m* background.

trashumante *adj* transhumant.

trasiego *m* comings and goings *pl*.

trasladar(se) *t* to move. **2** *(de cargo etc.)* to transfer. **3** *(aplazar)* to postpone, adjourn. **– 4** *p (cosa)* to move *(de/a,* from/ to); *(persona)* to go.

traslado *m* move. **2** *(de cargo etc.)* transfer.

traslucir(se) *t-p fig* to show. **– 2** *p (material)* to be translucent.

trasluz *m* diffused light. ●*mirar algo al* ~, to hold sth. against the light.

trasnochador,-ra *m,f* night bird.

trasnochar *i* to stay up late.

traspapelarse *p* to get mislaid.

traspasar(se) *t* to go through, cross. **2** *(perforar)* to pierce. **3** *(negocio etc.)* to transfer. **– 4** *p* to exceed o.s. ●*"se traspasa"*, "for sale".

traspaso *m* transfer. **2** *(precio)* take-over fee.

traspié *m* stumble, trip.

trasplantar *t* to transplant.

trasplante *m* transplantation.

trasquilar *t (animales)* to shear.

trastada *f* dirty trick.

traste *m dar al* ~ *con,* to spoil, ruin.

trastienda *f* back room. **2** *fig* cunning.

trasto *m* piece of junk. **2** *(persona)* useless person. **3** *pl (utensilios)* tackle *sing*.

trastocarse [49] *p* to go mad.

trastornado,-a *adj (preocupado)* upset. **2** *(loco)* mad.

trastornar(se) *t (revolver)* to upset, turn upside down. **2** *(alterar)* to disturb. **3** *(enloquecer)* to drive crazy. **– 4** *p* to go mad.

trastorno *m (desorden)* confusion. **2** *(molestia)* trouble. **3** MED upset.

trata *f* slave trade/traffic.

tratable *adj* friendly, congenial.

tratado *m (pacto)* treaty. **2** *(estudio)* treatise.

tratamiento *m* treatment. **2** *(título)* title, form of address. ●MED *un* ~ *a base de...,* a course of... .

tratante *mf* dealer.

tratar(se) *t* to treat. 2 *(asunto)* to discuss. 3 *(manejar)* to handle. 4 INFORM to process. – 5 *i (relacionarse)* to be acquainted *(con,* with): **he tratado más con la hermana,** I'm more acquainted with her sister. 6 *(tener tratos)* to deal/negotiate *(con,* with). 7 *(intentar)* ~ *de,* to try to. 8 *(llamar)* ~ *de,* to address as. 9 *(versar)* ~ *de/sobre/acerca,* to be about. 10 COM to deal *(en,* in). – 11 *p (ser cuestión)* ~ *de,* to be a question/matter of.

trato *m (de personas)* manner, treatment: **tener un** ~ **agradable,** to have a pleasant manner. 2 *(contacto)* contact; *pey* dealings *pl.* 3 *(acuerdo)* agreement. 4 COM deal. 5 *(tratamiento)* title. ■ *malos tratos,* ill-treatment *sing;* ~ *diario,* daily contact.

trauma *m* trauma.

través *m (de madera)* crosspiece, crossbeam. 2 *fig (desgracia)* misfortune. – 3 *adv a* ~ *de,* through. 4 *de* ~, *(transversalmente)* crosswise; *(de lado)* sideways. – 5 *prep al/a* ~, across, over.

travesaño *m* crosspiece. 2 DEP crossbar.

travesía *f (viaje)* voyage, crossing. 2 *(calle)* (cross) street. 3 *(distancia)* distance.

travesti, travestí *mf* transvestite.

travesura *f* mischief. ●*hacer travesuras,* to get into mischief.

travieso,-a *adj* mischievous, naughty. – 2 *f (ferrocarril)* sleeper. 3 *(construcción)* trimmer.

trayecto *m (distancia)* distance, way. 2 *(recorrido)* route, itinerary.

trayectoria *f* trajectory. 2 *fig* line, course.

traza *f (apariencia)* looks *pl,* appearance. 2 *(mañas)* skill, knack. 3 ARQ plan, design. ●*no llevar/tener trazas de,* not to look as if.

trazado *m (plano)* layout, plan. 2 *(dibujo)* drawing, sketch. 3 *(de carretera, ferrocarril)* route, course.

trazar [4] *i* to draw. 2 *(parque)* to lay out; *(edificio)* to design. 3 *(describir)* to sketch.

trazo *m (línea)* line. 2 *(de una letra)* stroke. 3 *(rasgo facial)* feature.

trébol *m* clover, trefoil. 2 *(naipes)* club.

trece *adj* thirteen; *(ordinal)* thirteenth. – 2 *m* thirteen.

trecho *m (distancia)* distance, way. 2 AGR plot, patch.

tregua *f* truce. 2 *fig* respite, rest.

treinta *adj* thirty; *(ordinal)* thirtieth. – 2 *m* thirty.

tremendo,-a *adj (terrible)* terrible, dreadful. 2 *(muy grande)* huge, tremendous.

trémulo,-a *adj* shaky, quivering; *(llama, luz)* flickering.

tren *m* train. 2 MIL convoy. 3 TÉC set (of gears/wheels). 4 *fig (ritmo)* speed, pace. ●*vivir a todo* ~, to lead a grand life. ■ ~ *de cercanías,* suburban train; ~ *de lavado,* car wash; ~ *directo,* through train.

trencilla *f* braided ribbon.

trenza *f (peluquería)* plait, US braid. 2 COST braid.

trenzar [4] *t* to intertwine. 2 *(peluquería)* to plait, US braid.

trepador,-ra *adj* climbing, creeper. – 2 *m,f fam* go-getter, social climber.

trepar *t-i* to climb.

trepidar *i* to vibrate, shake.

tres *adj* three; *(tercero)* third. – 2 *m* three.

trescientos,-as *adj* three hundred; *(ordinal)* three hundredth. – 2 *m* three hundred.

tresillo *m* (three-piece) suite.

treta *f* trick, ruse.

triangular *adj* triangular.

triángulo *m* triangle.

tribu *f* tribe.

tribulación *f* tribulation.

tribuna *f (plataforma)* rostrum, dais. 2 DEP grandstand. ■ ~ *de (la) prensa,* press box.

tribunal *m* court. 2 *(de examen)* board of examiners.

tributación *f* taxation. 2 *(pago)* payment.

tributar *t* to pay.

tributario,-a *adj* tributary, tax. – 2 *m,f* taxpayer.

tributo *m* tax. ■ ~ *de amistad,* token of friendship.

tricotar *t* to knit.

trienio *m* triennium.

trifulca *f* rumpus, row.

trigal *m* wheat field.

trigésimo,-a *adj-m,f* thirtieth.

trigo *m* wheat.

trigonometría *f* trigonometry.

trigueño,-a *adj (pelo)* corn-coloured, dark blonde. 2 *(piel)* dark, swarthy. 3 *(persona)* olive-skinned.

trilla *f* threshing.

trillado,-a *adj fig (expresión)* overworked, well-worn. 2 *(camino)* beaten.

trillar *t* to thresh.

trillizo,-a *m,f* triplet.

trimestral *adj* quarterly, three-monthly.

trimestre *m* quarter, trimester. **2** EDUC term.

trinar *i* to warble. **2** *fam (enfadarse)* to rage, fume.

trinchar *t* to carve, slice (up).

trinchera *f* trench.

trineo *m* sleigh, sled(ge).

trino *m* trill.

trío *m* trio.

tripa *f* gut, intestine; *fam* tummy.

triple *adj-m* triple.

triplicado *m* triplicate. ●*por* ~, in triplicate.

triplicar [1] *t* to triple, treble.

tripudo,-a *adj fam* paunchy, potbellied.

tripulación *f* crew.

tripular *t* to man.

triquiñuela *f fam* trick, dodge.

triste *adj (infeliz)* sad, unhappy; *(futuro)* bleak. **2** *(oscuro, sombrío)* gloomy, dismal. **3** *(único)* single. **4** *(insignificante)* poor, humble. ●*hacer un* ~ *papel,* to cut a sorry figure.

tristeza *f* sadness. **2** *pl* problems, sufferings.

triturar *t* to grind (up); *(papel)* to shred. **2** *fig (físicamente)* to beat (up); *(moralmente)* to tear apart.

triunfal *adj* triumphant.

triunfalista *adj* boastful. **2** POL jingoistic, chauvinist(ic).

triunfar *i* to triumph, win. ●~ *en la vida,* to succeed in life.

triunfo *m (victoria)* triumph, victory; DEP win. **2** *(éxito)* success. **3** *(naipes)* trump.

trivial *adj* trivial, petty.

triza *f* bit, fragment. ●*hacer trizas,* to tear to shreds; *(gastar)* to wear out; *fam fig estar hecho,-a trizas,* to feel washed out.

trocar(se) [49] *t (permutar)* to exchange, barter. **2** *(transformar)* to turn *(en,* into), convert. − **3** *p (mudarse)* to change *(en,* into), switch round.

trocear *t* to cut up (into bit/pieces).

trofeo *m* trophy.

trola *f fam* lie, fib.

tromba *f* waterspout. ■ ~ *de agua,* violent downpour.

trombón *m* MÚS trombone. − **2** *mf* trombonist.

trompa *f* MÚS horn. **2** *(de elefante)* trunk. **3** *(de insecto)* proboscis. **4** *fam (borrachera)* drunkenness.

trompazo *m* bump.

trompeta *f* MÚS trumpet. − **2** *mf* trumpet player.

trompetista *mf* trumpet player.

trompicón *m (tropezón)* trip, stumble. **2** *(golpe)* blow, hit. ●*a trompicones,* in fits and starts.

tronada *f* thunderstorm.

tronar [31] *i* to thunder. ▲ *Only used in the 3rd pers. It does not take a subject.*

tronchar *t (árboles)* to cut down, fell. **2** *fig* to destroy. ●~*se de risa,* to split one's sides with laughter.

tronco *m* ANAT trunk, torso. **2** BOT *(tallo de árbol)* trunk; *(leño)* log. **3** *(linaje)* family stock. **4** *arg (compañero)* mate, pal, chum.

trono *m* throne.

tropa *f* MIL troops *pl,* soldiers *pl.* **2** *(muchedumbre)* crowd.

tropel *m* throng, mob. ●*en* ~, in a mad rush.

tropelía *f (atropello)* outrage. **2** *(delito)* crime.

tropezar [47] *i (trompicar)* to trip, stumble *(con,* on). **2** *(encontrar)* to come *(con,* across). **3** *fig (con dificultades)* to come up against; *(con una persona)* to disagree with.

tropezón *m (traspié)* trip, stumble. **2** *fig (error)* slip-up. **3** *fam (de comida)* chunk of meat.

tropical *adj* tropical.

trópico *m* tropic.

tropiezo *m (obstáculo)* trip. **2** *fig (error)* blunder, faux pas; *(revés)* setback, mishap. **3** *(riña)* quarrel.

trotamundos *mf inv* globe-trotter.

trotar *i* to trot.

trote *m (de caballo)* trot. **2** *fam (actividad)* chasing about, (hustle and) bustle. ●*de/ para todo* ~, for everyday use/wear; *no estar para (esos) trotes,* not to be up to that.

trozo *m* piece, chunk.

trucar [1] *t* to doctor, alter.

trucha *f* trout.

truco *m (ardid)* trick. **2** CINEM TV gimmick. **3** *(tranquillo)* knack.

truculento,-a *adj (cruel)* cruel. **2** *(excesivo)* sensationalistic.

trueno *m* thunder(clap). **2** *fam (joven)* madcap.

trueque *m* barter, exchange.

trufa *f* truffle.

truhán,-ana *m,f* rogue, crook.

truncar(se) [1] *t* to truncate. − **2** *t-p fig (escrito)* to leave unfinished, cut off; *(sentido)* to upset.

tu *adj pos* your: ~ *libro,* your book; *tus libros,* your books.

tú *pron pers* you. ●*de* ~ *a* ~, on equal terms.

tubérculo *m* BOT tuber. **2** MED tubercle.

tuberculosis *f inv* tuberculosis.

tubería *f (de agua)* piping, pipes *pl,* plumbing. **2** *(de gas, petróleo)* pipeline.

tubo *m* tube. **2** *(tubería)* pipe. ■ ~ *de escape,* exhaust pipe.

tuerca *f* nut.

tuerto,-a *adj* one-eyed, blind in one eye. − **2** *m,f* one-eyed person.

tuétano *m* marrow. ●*hasta los tuétanos,* through and through.

tufo *m (mal olor)* foul odour/smell, fug. **2** *(emanación)* fume, vapour.

tugurio *m* shepherd's hut. **2** *fig* hole.

tul *m* tulle.

tulipán *m* tulip.

tullir(se) [41] *t (maltratar)* to cripple. **2** *(de cansancio)* to wear/tire out. − **3** *p* to become crippled.

tumba *f* tomb, grave.

tumbar(se) *t (derribar)* to knock down/over. **2** *fam* EDUC to fail. − **3** *i (caer a tierra)* to fall down. − **4** *p (acostarse)* to lie/stretch down.

tumbo *m* jolt, bump. ●*dar tumbos,* to jolt, bump along.

tumor *m* tumour.

tumulto *m* tumult, commotion.

tunante,-a *adj-m,f* rascal, rogue.

tunda *f* thrashing, beating. **2** *fig (trabajo agotador)* exhausting job, drag.

túnel *m* tunnel.

tupido,-a *adj* dense, thick. **2** AM *(torpe)* clumsy.

turbación *f (alteración)* disturbance. **2** *(preocupación)* anxiety, worry. **3** *(desconcierto)* confusion, uneasiness.

turbar(se) *t (alterar)* to unsettle, disturb. **2** *(preocupar)* to upset, worry. **3** *(desconcertar)* to baffle, put off. − **4** *p (preocuparse)* to be(come) upset. **5** *(desconcertarse)* to be(come) confused/baffled.

turbina *f* turbine.

turbio,-a *adj (oscurecido)* cloudy, muddy. **2** *pey* shady, dubious. **3** *(turbulento)* turbulent.

turbulento,-a *adj* turbulent, troubled.

turgente *adj* turgid.

turismo *m* tourism. **2** *(industria)* tourist trade/industry. **3** AUTO private car. ●*hacer* ~, to go touring/sightseeing.

turista *mf* tourist.

turnar(se) *i* to alternate. − **2** *p* to take turns.

turno *m (tanda)* turn, go. **2** *(período de trabajo)* shift. ●*estar de* ~, to be on duty.

turquesa *adj-f* turquoise.

tutear *t* to *address as* **tú**. **2** *fig* to be on familiar terms with.

tutela *f* tutelage, guardianship. **2** *fig* protection, guidance.

tutor,-ra *m,f* guardian. **2** *fig* protector, guide. **3** EDUC tutor.

tuve *pret indic* → **tener**.

tuyo,-a *adj pos* of yours: *¿es amigo* ~?, is he a friend of yours? − **2** *pron pos* yours: *éste es* ~, this one is yours. **3** *pl los tuyos, (familiares)* your family *sing; (amigos)* your friends.

U

u *conj* or. ▲ *Used only before words starting (h)o*.

ubicación *f* location, position.

ubicar [1] *i-p* to be (situated).

ubre *f* udder.

ufanarse *p* to boast (*de,* of).

ufano,-a *adj (orgulloso)* conceited, arrogant. **2** *(satisfecho)* satisfied, happy.

ujier *m* usher.

úlcera *f* ulcer.

ulterior *adj* further. **2** *(siguiente)* subsequent. — **3** *ulteriormente adv* subsequently, afterwards.

ultimar *t* to finish, complete.

ultimátum *m* ultimatum. ▲ *pl* *ultimátums*.

último,-a *adj* last. **2** *(más reciente)* latest; *(de dos)* latter. **3** *(más alejado)* furthest; *(más abajo)* bottom, lowest; *(más arriba)* top; *(más atrás)* back. **4** *(definitivo)* final. — **5** *últimamente adv* lately, recently. ●*a la última,* up to date; *a últimos de,* towards the end of; *por* ~, finally; *fig estar en las últimas, (moribundo)* to be at death's door; *(arruinado)* to be down and out.

ultrajante *adj* outrageous, insulting.

ultrajar *t* to outrage, insult.

ultraje *m* outrage, insult.

ultramar *m* overseas (countries *pl*).

ultramarino,-a *adj* overseas. — **2** *m (tienda)* grocer's (shop). **3** *pl (comestibles)* groceries.

ultranza *a* ~, *adv (a muerte)* to the death. **2** *(a todo trance)* at all costs, at any price. **3** *(acérrimo)* out-and-out, extreme.

ultratumba *adv* beyond the grave. — **2** *f* afterlife.

ulular *i* to howl.

umbral *m* threshold.

umbrío,-a *adj* shady.

un,-a *art indef* a, an: ~ *coche,* a car; ~ *huevo,* an egg. **2** *pl* some: *unas flores,* some flowers. — **3** *adj* one.

unánime *adj* unanimous.

unanimidad *f* unanimity. ●*por* ~, unanimously.

uncir [3] *t* to yoke.

undécimo,-a *adj-m,f* eleventh.

ungir [6] *t* to anoint.

ungüento *m* ointment.

unicelular *adj* unicellular.

único,-a *adj (solo)* only: *la única vez,* the only time. **2** *(extraordinario)* unique.

unidad *f* unit. **2** *(cohesión)* unity.

unificar [1] *t* to unify.

uniformar *t (igualar)* to make uniform, standardize. **2** *(poner en uniforme)* to put into uniform.

uniforme *adj-m* uniform. — **2** *adj (superficie)* even.

uniformidad *f* uniformity. **2** *(de superficie)* evenness.

unión *f* union. **2** TÉC *(acoplamiento)* joining; *(junta)* joint.

unir *t (juntar)* to unite, join (together). **2** *(combinar)* to combine (*a,* with). **3** *(enlazar)* to link. ●*estar muy unidos,* to be very attached to one another.

unísono *m* harmony, unison. ●*al* ~, in unison.

universal *adj* universal.

universidad *f* university. ■ ~ *a distancia,* Open University.

universitario,-a *adj* university. — **2** *m,f* university student/graduate.

universo *m* universe.

uno,-a *adj (cardinal)* one; *(ordinal)* first. **2** *pl* some; *(aproximado)* about, around: *habrá unos veinte,* there must be around twenty. — **3** *pron* one: ~ *(de ellos),* one of them. **4** *(impersonal)* one, you. **5**

fam (persona) someone, somebody. **– 6** *m* one. **– 7** *f* one o'clock. ●*hacerle una a algn.,* to play a daily trick on sb.

untar(se) *t* to grease, smear: ~ *pan con mantequilla,* to spread butter on bread. **2** *fam (sobornar)* to bribe. **– 3** *p (mancharse)* to get stained/smeared. **4** *fam (forrarse)* to line one's pockets.

untuoso,-a *adj* unctuous, greasy, oily.

uña *f* nail. **2** *(garra)* claw; *(pezuña)* hoof. ●*ser ~ y carne,* to be inseparable.

uranio *m* uranium.

urbanidad *f* urbanity, politeness.

urbanismo *m* town planning.

urbanización *f (proceso)* urbanization. **2** *(conjunto residencial)* housing development/estate.

urbanizar [4] *t* to urbanize, develop. ■ *zona urbanizada,* built-up area.

urbano,-a *adj* urban, city. **– 2** *m,f fam m* (traffic) policeman, *f* (traffic) policewoman.

urbe *f* large city, metropolis.

urdimbre *f (textil)* warp. **2** *fig (trama)* intrigue.

urdir *t (textil)* to warp. **2** *fig (tramar)* to plot.

urgencia *f* urgency. **2** *(necesidad)* urgent need. **2** *(emergencia)* emergency.

urgente *adj* urgent. ■ *correo ~,* express mail.

urgir [6] *i* to be urgent/pressing.

urinario,-a *adj* urinary. **– 2** *m (retrete)* urinal.

urna *f* POL ballot box. **2** *(vasija)* urn. **3** *(caja)* glass case. ●*fig acudir a las urnas,* to vote.

urraca *f* magpie.

usado,-a *adj (gastado)* worn out, old. **2** *(de segunda mano)* secondhand, used.

usar(se) *t* to use. **2** *(prenda)* to wear. **– 3** *i* to make use *(de,* of). **– 4** *p* to be used/ in fashion.

uso *m* use. **2** *(ejercicio)* exercise: *el ~ de un privilegio,* the exercise of a privilege. **3** *(de prenda)* wearing. **4** *(costumbre)* usage, custom. **5** *(farmacia)* application: ~ *externo,* external application. ●*al ~,* in the style/fashion of; *hacer ~ de la palabra,* to take the floor. ■ *usos y costumbres,* ways and customs.

usted *pron pers fml* you. ▲ *pl* **ustedes**.

usual *adj* usual, common.

usuario,-a *m,f* user.

usufructo *m* usufruct.

usura *f* usury.

usurero,-a *m,f* usurer.

usurpación *f* usurpation.

usurpador,-ra *adj* usurping. **– 2** *m,f* usurper.

usurpar *t* to usurp.

utensilio *m (herramienta)* tool, utensil. **2** *(aparato)* device, implement.

útil *adj* useful. **– 2** *m (herramienta)* tool, instrument. ■ *día ~,* working day.

utilidad *f* utility, usefulness. **2** *(beneficio)* profit.

utilizable *adj* usable, fit/ready for use.

utilizar [4] *t* to use, utilize, make use of.

uva *f* grape. **2** *fig (humor)* mood. ● *fam de mala ~,* in a bad mood.

V

vaca f cow. **2** (carne) beef. ■ fig *las vacas gordas,* the years of plenty.

vacaciones fpl holiday(s) (pl). ●de ~, on holiday.

vacante adj vacant, unoccupied. – **2** f vacancy.

vaciado m casting, moulding.

vaciar [13] t (recipiente) to empty. **2** (contenido) to pour away/out. **3** (dejar hueco) to hollow out. **4** (moldear) to cast, mould.

vacilación f (duda) hesitation. **2** (oscilación) swaying, unsteadiness.

vacilante adj (dubitativo) hesitating. **2** (oscilante) swaying.

vacilar i (dudar) to hesitate. **2** (oscilar) to sway, stagger.

vacío,-a adj empty. **2** (no ocupado) unoccupied. **3** fig (vano) vain. **4** (hueco) hollow. – **5** m void, emptiness. **6** FÍS vacuum. **7** fig (hueco) gap, blank. ●envasado al ~, vacuum-packed; fig hacer el ~ a algn., to cold-shoulder sb.

vacuna f vaccine.

vacunación f vaccination.

vacunar t to vaccinate (contra, against).

vacuno,-a adj bovine. ■ ganado ~, cattle.

vadear t (río) to ford, wade. **2** fig (dificultad) to overcome.

vado m (de río) ford. ■ "~ permanente", "keep clear".

vagabundear i to wander, roam.

vagabundo,-a adj wandering, roving. – **2** m,f wanderer, tramp.

vagancia f idleness, vagrancy.

vagar [7] i to wander (about), roam (about).

vago,-a adj (holgazán) idle, lazy. **2** (impreciso) vague. – **3** m,f idler, loafer. ●hacer el ~, to laze around.

vagón m (para pasajeros) carriage, coach, US car. **2** (para mercancías) wagon, goods van, US boxcar, freight car. ■ ~ cama, sleeping-car.

vaguedad f vagueness.

vahído m dizziness, faintness.

vaho m vapour, steam. **2** (aliento) breath. **3** pl MED inhalation sing.

vaina f (funda) sheath, scabbard. **2** BOT pod, husk.

vainilla f vanilla.

vaivén m swaying, swinging. **2** (de la gente) coming and going, bustle. **3** fig (cambio) fluctuation.

vajilla f tableware, dishes pl, crockery. ■ una ~, a set of dishes.

vale m (comprobante) voucher. **2** (pagaré) IOU, promissory note.

valedero,-a adj valid.

valentía f bravery, courage.

valentón,-ona pey adj arrogant, boastful. – **2** m,f braggart, bully.

valer(se) [89] i to be worth: *no vale nada,* it is worthless. **2** (costar) to cost, amount to: *¿cuánto vale?,* how much is it? **3** (ser válido) to be valid, count. **4** (ganar) to win, earn. **5** (servir) to be useful, be of use: *no vale para director,* he's no use as a manager. – **6** p. to use, make use (of, de). **7** (espabilarse) to manage. ●hacer ~, to assert; *no vale,* it's no good; *¿vale?,* all right?, O.K.?; *vale más,* it is better; ~ la pena, to be worthwhile; *¡válgame Dios!,* good heavens!

valeroso,-a adj courageous, brave.

valía f value, worth.

validez f validity.

válido,-a adj valid.

valiente adj brave, courageous. **2** (fuerte) strong, vigorous. **3** fig (excelente) fine, excellent. – **4** mf brave person.

valija *f (maleta)* suitcase. **2** *(de correos)* mailbag. ■ ~ *diplomática,* diplomatic bag.

valioso,-a *adj* valuable.

valla *f* fence, barrier. **2** DEP hurdle. **3** *fig* obstacle. ■ ~ *publicitaria,* hoarding, US billboard.

vallado *m* fence, enclosure.

vallar *t* to fence (in), enclose.

valle *m* valley.

valor *m* value, worth. **2** *(precio)* price. **3** *(coraje)* courage, valour. **4** *(desvergüenza)* daring, nerve. **5** *pl* securities, bonds. ●*armarse de* ~, to pluck up courage; *dar* ~ *a,* to attach importance to; *¡qué* ~*!,* what a nerve!; *sin (ningún)* ~, worthless.

valoración *f* valuation, valuing.

valorar, valorizar [4] *t (tasar)* to value, appraise. **2** *(aumentar el valor)* to raise the value of.

vals *m* waltz.

válvula *f* valve.

vampiro *m* vampire. **2** *fig* bloodsucker.

vanagloria *f* vainglory.

vanagloriarse [12] *p* to boast *(de,* of).

vandalismo *m* vandalism.

vanidad *f* vanity, conceit.

vanidoso,-a *adj* vain, conceited.

vano,-a *adj (inútil)* vain, useless. **2** *(ilusorio)* illusory, futile. **3** *(frívolo)* frivolous. **4** *(arrogante)* vain, conceited. − **5** *m* opening. ●*en* ~, in vain.

vapor *m* vapour, steam. **2** *(barco)* steamship, steamer. ●CULIN *al* ~, steamed.

vaporizador *m* vaporizer, spray.

vaporizar(se) [4] *t-p* to vaporize.

vaporoso,-a *adj* vaporous. **2** *fig (ligero)* airy, light.

vapulear *t* to whip, thrash.

vapuleo *m* whipping, thrashing.

vaquería *f* dairy.

vaquero,-a *adj* cow, cattle. − **2** *m* cowherd, US cowboy. ■ *(pantalones) vaqueros,* (pair of) jeans.

vara *f* stick, rod. **2** *(mando)* staff, mace.

varadero *m* shipyard.

varar *i* to beach, dock.

variable *adj* variable, changeable.

variación *f* variation, change.

variado,-a *adj* varied, mixed.

variante *adj* variable. − **2** *f* variant.

variar [13] *t-i* to vary, change. ●*irón para* ~, as usual.

varicela *f* chickenpox.

variedad *f* variety, diversity. **2** *pl* TEAT variety show *sing.*

varilla *f* stick, rod. **2** *(de paraguas)* rib.

vario,-a *adj* varied, different. **2** *pl* some, several.

variz *f* varicose vein.

varón *m* male, man.

varonil *adj* manly, virile, male.

vas *pres indic* → **ir.**

vasija *f* vessel, pot, jar.

vaso *m* glass. **2** *(para flores)* vase. **3** ANAT vessel.

vástago *m* BOT shoot, bud. **2** *(descendencia)* offspring. **3** TÉC rod.

vasto,-a *adj* vast, immense, huge.

vaticinar *t* to predict, foretell.

vaticinio *m* prophecy, prediction.

vatio *m* watt.

vaya *pres subj & imperat* → **ir.**

¡vaya! *interj* well!: ~ *casa!,* what a house!

ve *pres indic* → **ver.** − **2** *imperat* → **ir.**

vecinal *adj* local. ■ *camino* ~, country road.

vecindad *f,* **vecindario** *m* neighbourhood. **2** *(vecinos)* neighbours *pl.*

vecino,-a *adj* nearby, next, neighbouring. − **2** *m,f* neighbour. **3** *(residente)* resident. **4** *(habitante)* inhabitant.

veda *f* prohibition. **2** *(de caza)* close season.

vedar *t* to prohibit, forbid. **2** *(impedir)* to prevent.

vega *f* fertile lowland.

vegetación *f* vegetation.

vegetal *adj-m* vegetable.

vegetar *i* to vegetate, live.

vegetariano,-a *adj-m,f* vegetarian.

vehemencia *f* vehemence.

vehemente *adj* vehement.

vehículo *m* vehicle. **2** *(coche)* car.

veinte *adj* twenty; *(vigésimo)* twentieth. − **2** *m* twentieth.

vejación *f* vexation.

vejar *t* to vex, annoy.

vejez *f* old age.

vela *f (vigilia)* watch, vigil. **2** *(desvelo)* wakefulness. **3** *(candela)* candle. **4** *(de barco)* sail. ●*pasar la noche en* ~, to have a sleepless night.

velada *f* evening (party).

velar(se) *i* to stay awake. **2** *(cuidar)* to watch *(por,* over), look *(por,* after). − **3** *t* to veil, hide. − **4** *p (fotografía)* to fog.

velatorio *m* wake, vigil.

veleidad *f (capricho)* caprice, whim. **2** *(inconstancia)* inconstancy.

veleidoso,-a *adj* inconstant, fickle.

veleta *f* weathercock. − **2** *mf fig (persona)* fickle person.

vello *m* hair.

velloso,-a *adj* downy, hairy.

velo *m* veil. •*fig correr/echar un ~ sobre,* to draw a veil over.

velocidad *f* speed, velocity. 2 AUTO *(marcha)* gear.

velódromo *m* cycle track.

veloz *adj* fast, quick, swift.

vena *f* ANAT vein. 2 *(de metal)* vein, seam. 3 *fig (inspiración)* poetical inspiration. •*estar en ~,* to be in the mood.

venablo *m* javelin, dart.

venado *m* ZOOL stag, deer. 2 CULIN venison.

vencedor,-ra *adj* DEP winning. 2 MIL conquering, victorious. — 3 *m,f* DEP winner. 4 MIL conqueror.

vencer [2] *t* DEP to beat. 2 MIL to defeat, conquer. 3 *(problema etc.)* to overcome. — 4 *i* DEP to win. 5 *(deuda)* to fall due. 6 *(plazo)* to expire.

vencido,-a *adj* defeated. 2 *(deuda)* due, payable.

venda *f* bandage.

vendaje *m* bandaging.

vendar *t* to bandage. •*fig ~ los ojos,* to blindfold.

vendaval *m* strong wind, gale.

vendedor,-ra *adj* selling. — 2 *m,f* seller, *m* salesman, *f* saleswoman.

vender(se) *t* to sell. 2 *fig (traicionar)* to betray. — 3 *p* to be sold: *se venden a peso,* they are sold by weight. 4 *(dejarse sobornar)* to sell o.s., accept a bribe. • *"se vende",* "for sale".

vendimia *f* grape harvest.

vendimiar [12] *t* to harvest.

vendré *fut indic* → **venir.**

veneno *m (química, vegetal)* poison; *(animal)* venom.

venenoso *adj* poisonous, venomous.

venerable *adj* venerable.

veneración *f* veneration, worship.

venerar *t* to venerate, worship.

venga *pres subj & imperat* → **venir.**

venganza *f* revenge, vengeance.

vengar(se) [7] *t* to avenge. — 2 *p* to take revenge *(de,* on).

vengo *pres indic* → **venir.**

venial *adj* venial.

venida *f* coming, arrival.

venidero,-a *adj* future, forthcoming. •*en lo ~,* in the future.

venir(se) [90] *i gen* to come. 2 *(llegar)* to arrive. — 3 *p* to come back. •*el mes que viene,* next month; *~ a menos,* to decline; *~ abajo,* to collapse; *~ al caso,* to be relevant; *~ al pelo,* to be opportune; *~ bien/mal,* to be/not to be suitable; *~ de,* to come from; *~ motivado,-a por,* to be caused by; *~se abajo,* to collapse, fall down.

venta *f* sale, selling. 2 *(hostal)* roadside inn. • *"en ~",* "for sale"; *poner a la ~,* to put up for sale. ■ *~ al por mayor/menor,* wholesale/retail sale.

ventaja *f* advantage.

ventajoso,-a *adj* advantageous. 2 *(beneficioso)* profitable.

ventana *f* window.

ventilación *f* ventilation.

ventilador *m* ventilator, fan.

ventilar *t* to air, ventilate. 2 *fig (tema)* to discuss; *(opinión)* to air.

ventisca *f* snowstorm, blizzard.

ventolera *f* gust of wind. 2 *fig* caprice, whim.

ventosidad *f* wind, flatulence.

ventoso,-a *adj* windy.

ventrículo *m* ventricle.

ventrílocuo,-a *m,f* ventriloquist.

ventura *f (felicidad)* happiness. 2 *(suerte)* luck, fortune. 3 *(hazar)* hazard, risk. •*por ~,* by chance.

venturoso,-a *adj* lucky, fortunate.

ver(se) [91] *t gen* to see. 2 *(mirar)* to look (at). 3 *(televisión)* to watch. 4 *(entender)* to understand. 5 *(visitar)* to visit. — 6 *p* to be seen. 7 *(con algn.)* to meet, see each other. 8 *(encontrarse)* to find o.s. •*a ~,* let's see; *es de ~,* it is worth seeing; *hacer ~,* to pretend; *hasta más ~,* see you; *no poder ~,* to detest; *no tener nada que ~ con,* to have nothing to do with; *se ve que,* apparently; *véase,* see; *~ venir,* to expect to happen; *~se obligado,-a a,* to be obliged to; *ya se ve,* of course. ▲ *pp* **visto,-a.**

vera *f* edge, verge. •*a la ~ de,* near, close to.

veracidad *f* veracity, truthfulness.

veraneante *mf* summer resident.

veranear *i* to spend the summer (holiday) *(en,* in/at).

veraneo *m* summer holiday.

veraniego,-a *adj* summer.

verano *m* summer (season).

veras *de ~, adv* really, truly.

veraz *adj* truthful, veracious.

verbal *adj* verbal, oral.

verbena *f* BOT verbena. 2 *(fiesta)* night party.

verbigracia *adv fml* for example.

verbo *m* verb.

verdad f truth. 2 (confirmación) es bonita, ¿~?, she's pretty, isn't she? •a decir ~, to tell the truth; en ~, really; ¿(no es) ~?, isn't that so?

verdadero,-a adj true, real.

verde adj gen green. 2 (fruta) unripe. 3 fam (chiste) blue, dirty. — 4 m (color) green. 5 (hierba) grass. •fam poner ~, to abuse. ■ fam viejo ~, dirty old man.

verdor m verdure, greenness.

verdoso,-a adj greenish.

verdugo m executioner.

verdulería f greengrocer's (shop).

verdulero,-a m,f greengrocer. — 2 f fig coarse woman.

verdura f vegetables pl, greens pl.

vereda f (foot)path.

veredicto m verdict.

vergel m flower and fruit garden.

vergonzoso,-a adj (acto) shameful, shocking. 2 (persona) bashful, shy.

vergüenza f shame. 2 (timidez) bashfulness. 3 (turbación) embarrassment. •tener/sentir ~, to be ashamed.

verídico,-a adj truthful, true: es ~, it is a fact.

verificar(se) [1] t to verify, confirm. 2 (probar) to prove. 3 (efectuar) to carry out. — 4 p (comprobarse) to come true. 5 (efectuarse) to take place.

verja f (reja) grating. 2 (cerca) railing.

verosímil adj likely, probable.

verosimilitud f probability, likeliness.

verruga f wart.

versado,-a adj versed, proficient.

versar i to deal (sobre, with), be (sobre, about).

versátil adj versatile.

versificar [1] t to versify. — 2 i to write in verse.

versión f version.

verso m verse.

vértebra f vertebra.

vertebrado,-a adj-m,f vertebrate.

vertedero m (rubbish) dump/tip.

verter [28] t to pour (out); (basura) to dump. 2 (derramar) to spill; (lágrimas) to shed. 3 (vaciar) to empty (out). — 4 i (corriente; río) to run, flow.

vertical adj-f vertical.

vértice m vertex.

vertiente f slope. 2 fig (aspecto) angle. 3 AM (fuente) fountain.

vertiginoso,-a adj dizzy, giddy.

vértigo m vertigo. 2 (turbación) dizziness, giddiness.

vesícula f vesicle.

vespa ® f (motor) scooter.

vespertino,-a adj evening.

vestíbulo m (de casa) hall, entrance. 2 (de hotel etc.) hall, lobby.

vestido m (de mujer) dress; (de hombre) costume, suit. ■ ~ de etiqueta, evening dress.

vestigio m vestige, trace, remains pl.

vestir(se) [34] t (llevar) to wear. 2 (a algn.) to dress (de, in). 3 (cubrir) to cover (de, with). — 4 i to dress: ~ de negro, to dress in black. 5 (ser elegante, lucir) to be elegant, look smart. — 6 p to dress, get dressed. •el mismo que viste y calza, the very same, none other; ~se de, to wear, dress in; (disfrazarse) to disguise o.s. as; ~se de punta en blanco, to dress up to the nines.

vestuario m wardrobe, clothes pl. 2 MIL uniform. 3 TEAT (camerino) dressing room. 4 DEP changing room.

veta f seam, vein. 2 fig streak.

veterano,-a adj-m,f veteran.

veterinario,-a m,f veterinary surgeon, vet, US veterinarian. — 2 adj veterinary. — 3 f veterinary medicine/science.

veto m veto.

vez f time. 2 (turno) turn; (ocasión) occasion. •a la ~, at the same time; a su ~, in turn; a veces, sometimes; alguna ~, sometimes; (en pregunta) ever; cada ~, every time; de una ~ para siempre, once for all; de ~ en cuando, from time to time; dos veces, twice; en ~ de, instead of; muchas veces, often; otra ~, again; pocas veces, seldom; tal ~, perhaps, maybe.

vía f (camino) road, way; (calle) street. 2 (de tren) track, line. 3 fig (modo) way, manner. •en ~ de, in process of. ■ ~ férrea, railway, track; ~ pública, thoroughfare.

viable adj viable.

viaducto m viaduct.

viajante m commercial traveller.

viajar i to travel.

viaje m journey, trip. 2 (por mar/aire, largo) voyage. 3 (concepto de viajar) travel. 4 (carga) load. •irse de ~, to go on a journey/trip. ■ cheque de ~, traveller's cheque; ~ de ida y vuelta, return trip, US round trip.

viajero,-a adj travelling. — 2 m,f traveller. 3 (pasajero) passenger.

viandante mf pedestrian, passer-by.

víbora f viper.

vibración f vibration.

vibrar t-i to vibrate.

vicario,-a *m,f* vicar.

viceversa *adv* vice versa.

viciar(se) [12] *t* to vitiate, corrupt, spoil. – **2** *p* to take to vice, become corrupted.

vicio *m* vice, corruption. **2** *(mala costumbre)* bad habit. ●*de/por* ~, for no reason at all, for the sake of it.

vicioso,-a *adj* vicious, corrupt, depraved. – **2** *m,f* depraved person.

vicisitud *f* vicissitude.

víctima *f* victim.

victoria *f* victory, triumph.

victorioso,-a *adj* victorious, triumphant.

vid *f* (grape)vine.

vida *f* life. **2** *(viveza)* liveliness. **3** *(tiempo)* lifetime. **4** *(modo de vivir)* (way of) life. **5** *(medios)* living, livelihood. ●*de por* ~, for life; *en mi/tu/su* ~, never; *en* ~ *de*, during the life of; *ganarse la* ~, to earn one's living; *¡* ~ *mía!*, my love!

vidente *mf* seer, soothsayer.

vídeo *m* video. **2** *(aparato)* video recorder, video. ■ *cinta de* ~, videotape.

videoaficionado,-a *m,f* video fan.

videocámara *f* video camera.

videocasete *m* video cassette.

videocinta *f* videotape.

videoclub *m* video club.

videojuego *m* video game.

videoteca *f* video library.

vidriera *f* glass window/door. **2** ART stained glass window.

vidrio *m* glass.

vidrioso,-a *adj* *(quebradizo)* brittle, glasslike. **2** *(resbaladizo)* slippery. **3** *(ojo)* glassy. **4** *fig (delicado)* touchy.

viejo,-a *adj* *(persona)* old, aged; *(cosa)* ancient, antique. – **2** *m,f* *m* old man, *f* old woman.

viento *m* wind.

vientre *m* belly, abdomen. **2** *(vísceras)* bowels *pl*. **3** *(de embarazada)* womb.

viernes *m* *inv* Friday. ■ *Viernes Santo*, Good Friday.

viga *f* *(de madera)* beam, rafter. **2** *(de acero etc.)* girder.

vigente *adj* in use, in force.

vigésimo,-a *adj-m,f* twentieth.

vigía *f* *(atalaya)* watchtower. – **2** *mf* lookout, *m* watchman, *f* watchwoman.

vigilancia *f* vigilance, watchfulness.

vigilante *adj* vigilant, watchful. – **2** *mf* *m* watchman, *f* watchwoman.

vigilar *t-i* *(ir con cuidado)* to watch. **2** *(con armas etc.)* to guard. **3** *(supervisar)* to oversee. **4** *(cuidar)* to look after.

vigor *m* vigour, strength. **2** *(validez)* force, effect. ●*en* ~, in force.

vigorizar [4] *t* to invigorate, strengthen, encourage.

vigoroso,-a *adj* vigorous, strong.

vil *adj* vile, base, despicable.

vileza *f* *(cualidad)* vileness, baseness. **2** *(acto)* vile act.

vilipendiar [12] *t* to revile, defame. **2** *(despreciar)* to despise.

villa *f* *(casa)* villa. **2** *(pueblo)* small town.

villancico *m* (Christmas) carol.

villano,-a *m,f* villain.

vilo *en* ~, *adv* *(supendido)* in the air. **2** *(inquieto)* in suspense.

vinagre *m* vinegar.

vinagreras *fpl* cruet (stand) *sing*.

vinculación *f* bond, link.

vincular *t* to link, bind. **2** *(relacionar)* to relate. **3** JUR to entail.

vínculo *m* tie, bond. **2** JUR entail. ■ *vínculos familiares*, family ties.

vindicación *f* vindication. **2** *(venganza)* revenge.

vindicar [1] *t* to vindicate. **2** *(vengar)* to avenge.

vine *pt indef indic* → **venir**.

vinícola *adj* wine-producing.

vino *m* wine. ■ ~ *de Jerez*, sherry; ~ *tinto*, red wine.

viña *f*, **viñedo** *m* vineyard.

violación *f* *(transgresión)* violation, infringement. **2** *(de persona)* rape.

violar *t* *(transgredir)* to violate, infringe. **2** *(persona)* to rape.

violencia *f* violence. **2** *(sentimiento)* embarrassment; *(situación)* embarrassing.

violentar(se) *t* *(obligar)* to force. **2** *(entrar)* to break into. – **3** *p* *(molestarse)* to get annoyed. **4** *(avergonzarse)* to be embarrassed, feel ashamed.

violento,-a *adj* violent. **2** *(vergonzoso)* embarrassing, awkward.

violeta *adj-m* *(color)* violet. – **2** *f* BOT violet.

violín *m* violin. – **2** *mf* violinist.

violinista *mf* violinist.

viraje *m* turn, bend.

virar *i* MAR to tack. **2** AUTO to turn round.

virgen *adj* *(persona)* virgin. **2** *fig* virgin, pure. **3** *(en estado natural)* unspoiled. **4** *(reputación)* unsullied. – **5** *f* virgin.

virginidad *f* virginity.

Virgo *m* *inv* Virgo.

viril *adj* virile, manly.

virilidad *f* virility.

virtual *adj* virtual.

virtud f virtue. 2 *(propiedad, eficacia)* property, quality.

virtuoso,-a adj virtuous. − 2 m,f virtuous person. 3 ART virtuoso.

viruela f smallpox. 2 *(marca)* pockmark.

virulencia f virulence.

virulento,-a adj virulent.

virus m inv virus.

viruta f shaving.

visado m visa.

víscera f internal organ. 2 pl viscera, entrails.

viscosidad f viscosity.

viscoso,-a adj viscous.

visera f *(de gorra)* peak; *(de casco)* visor.

visibilidad f visibility.

visible adj visible. 2 *(evidente)* evident.

visión f vision. 2 *(vista)* sight. •*ver visiones,* to dream, see things.

visionario,-a adj-m,f visionary.

visita f visit. 2 *(invitado)* visitor, guest. •*hacer una* ~, to pay a visit to.

visitante adj visiting. − 2 mf visitor.

visitar t to visit, pay a visit, call upon. 2 *(inspeccionar)* to inspect, examine.

vislumbrar t to glimpse, make out. 2 fig *(conjeturar)* to guess, conjecture.

viso m *(reflejo)* sheen, gloss. 2 *(ropa interior)* underskirt. 3 fig appearance.

visón m mink.

víspera f eve. 2 REL vespers. •*en vísperas de,* on the eve of.

vista f sight, vision. 2 *(ojo)* eye(s). 3 *(panorama)* view, scene. 4 *(aspecto)* aspect, looks pl. 5 *(intención)* intention. 6 *(propósito)* outlook, prospect. 7 JUR trial, hearing. •*a la* ~, at sight; *a primera/ simple* ~, at first sight; *bajar la* ~, to look down; *con vistas a,* overlooking; *conocer de* ~, to know by sight; *en* ~ *de,* in view of; *estar a la* ~, to be evident; *hacer la* ~ *gorda,* to overlook; *hasta la* ~, good-bye, so long; *perder de* ~, to lose sight of.

vistazo m glance, look. •*echar un* ~ *a,* to have a look at.

visto,-a pp → ver. − 2 adj seen. •*estar bien* ~, to be well looked upon; *estar mal* ~, to be frowned upon; *nunca* ~, extraordinary; *por lo* ~, as it seems.

vistoso,-a adj bright, showy, colourful.

visual adj visual. − 2 f line of sight.

vital adj vital. 2 *(esencial)* essential. 3 *(persona)* lively.

vitalicio,-a adj (for) life.

vitamina f vitamin.

vitorear t to cheer, acclaim.

vitrina f *(armario)* glass/display cabinet. 2 *(de exposición)* glass case, showcase. 3 *(escaparate)* shop window.

vituperar t to censure, condemn.

vituperio m insult, censure.

viudez f widowhood.

viudo,-a adj widowed. − 2 m,f m widower, f widow.

viva m cheer, shout. − 2 interj hurrah!

vivaracho,-a adj vivacious, lively.

vivaz adj *(vivo)* vivacious, lively. 2 *(perspicaz)* keen, quick-witted.

víveres mpl food sing, provisions, victuals.

vivero m *(de plantas)* nursery. 2 *(de peces)* fish farm.

viveza f *(persona)* liveliness, vivacity. 2 *(color, relato)* vividness. 3 *(al hablar)* vehemence. 4 *(agudeza)* sharpness. 5 *(en ojos)* sparkle.

vivienda f housing, accommodation. 2 *(morada)* dwelling. 3 *(casa)* house. 4 *(piso)* flat.

viviente adj living, alive.

vivificar [1] t to vivify, enliven.

vivir i to live, to be alive. − 2 t *(pasar)* to live (through). − 3 m living, life. •~ *de,* to live on; fam ~ *a lo grande,* to live it up, live in style.

vivo,-a adj alive, living. 2 *(color etc.)* bright, vivid. 3 *(animado)* lively. 4 *(dolor etc.)* acute, sharp. 5 *(listo)* quick-witted. − 6 m,f living person: *los vivos,* the living. •TV *en* ~, live.

vizconde m viscount.

vizcondesa f viscountess.

vocablo m word, term.

vocabulario m vocabulary.

vocación f vocation, calling.

vocal adj vocal. − 2 f vowel. − 3 mf *(de junta etc.)* member.

vocear i *(dar voces)* to shout, cry out. − 2 t *(divulgar)* to publish. 3 *(gritar)* to shout, call. 4 *(aclamar)* to cheer, acclaim.

vocerío m shouting, uproar.

vociferar i-t to vociferate, shout.

volador,-ra adj flying.

voladura f blowing up, demolition.

volante adj flying. − 2 m COST flounce. 3 AUTO steering wheel. 4 *(aviso, orden)* note, order.

volar [31] i to fly. 2 *(desaparecer)* to disappear. 3 *(noticia)* to spread rapidly. − 4 t *(hacer explotar)* to blow up.

volátil adj volatile.

volcán m volcano.

volcar(se) [49] *t-i* to turn over, upset. **2** MAR to capsize. **3** *(vaciar)* to empty out. **− 4** *p* to turn over, overturn. **5** *fig (entregarse)* to devote o.s.

voltaje *m* voltage.

voltereta *f* somersault.

voltio *m* volt.

volubilidad *f* changeability, fickleness.

voluble *adj* changeable, fickle.

volumen *m* volume. **2** *(tamaño)* size. ●*bajar/subir el* ~, to turn the volume down/up.

voluminoso,-a *adj* voluminous, bulky.

voluntad *f* will. **2** *(propósito)* intention, purpose. **3** *(deseo)* wish. ●*a* ~, at will; *buena* ~, goodwill.

voluntario,-a *adj* voluntary. **− 2** *m,f* volunteer. ●*ofrecerse* ~, to volunteer.

voluntarioso,-a *adj* willing.

voluptuoso,-a *adj* voluptuous.

voluta *f* volute. **2** *(de humo)* ring.

volver(se) [32] *t (dar vuelta a)* to turn (over); *(hacia abajo)* to turn upside down; *(de fuera a dentro)* to turn inside out. **2** *(convertir)* to turn, make: ~ *loco,-a,* to drive crazy. **3** *(devolver)* to give back; *(a su lugar)* to put back. **− 4** *i (regresar)* to go/come back, return. **− 5** *p (regresar)* to come/go back. **6** *(darse la vuelta)* to turn (round). **7** *(convertirse)* to turn, become. ●~ *a,* to do again; ~ *en sí,* to recover consciousness, come round; ~*se atrás,* to back out. ▲ *pp* *vuelto,-a.*

vomitar *t-i* to vomit.

vómito *m (resultado)* vomit. **2** *(acción)* vomiting.

vorágine *f* vortex, whirlpool.

voraz *adj* voracious. **2** *fig* fierce.

vosotros,-as *pron pers m,f pl* you.

votación *f* vote, ballot. **2** *(acto)* vote, voting. ●*someter algo a* ~, to put sth. to the vote, take a ballot on sth.

votante *mf* voter.

votar *i* to vote *(por/contra,* for/against).

voto *m* vote. **2** REL vow. **3** *(deseo)* wish, prayer.

voy *pres indic* → **ir**.

voz *f* voice. **2** *(grito)* shout. **3** *(en diccionario)* word. **4** GRAM voice. **5** *(rumor)* rumour, report. ●*dar voces,* to shout; *en* ~ *alta,* aloud; *en* ~ *baja,* in a low voice.

vuelco *m* overturning, upset.

vuelo *m* flight. **2** *(acción)* flying. **3** *(de vestido)* fullness, flare. **4** ARQ projection. ●*alzar el* ~, to take flight, *fig cazarlas/cogerlas al* ~, to be quick on the uptake.

vuelta *f* turn. **2** *(en un circuito)* lap, circuit. **3** *(paseo)* walk, stroll. **4** *(regreso)* return. **5** *(dinero de cambio)* change. **6** *(curva)* bend, curve. **7** *(reverso)* back, reverse. ●*a la* ~, on the way back; *dar la* ~, *(alrededor)* to go round; *(girar)* to turn (round); *(de arriba abajo)* to turn upside down; *(de dentro a fuera)* to turn inside out; *(cambiar de lado)* to turn over; *dar vueltas,* to turn; *estar de* ~, to be back; *fig dar vueltas a algo,* to worry about sth.; *fig no tener* ~ *de hoja,* to be beyond doubt; *fig poner de* ~ *y media,* to insult.

vuelto,-a *pp* → **volver**.

vuestro,-a *adj pos* your, of yours: *vuestra casa,* your house; *un amigo* ~, a friend of yours. **− 2** *pron pos* yours: *éstas son las vuestras,* these are yours.

vulgar *adj (grosero)* vulgar. **2** *(general)* common, general. **3** *(banal)* banal, ordinary.

vulgaridad *f (grosería)* vulgarity. **2** *(banalidad)* commonplace, platitude, triviality.

vulgarizar [4] *t* to popularize.

vulgo *m pey* mob.

vulnerable *adj* vulnerable.

vulnerar *t* to harm, damage. **2** *(ley etc.)* to violate.

vulva *f* vulva.

W

walkman® *m* walkman®.
wáter *m* *fam* toilet. ▲ *pl* *wáteres*.
waterpolo *m* water polo.
wélter *m* welterweight.

whisky *m* whisky; *(Irlandés)* whiskey.
windsurf *m* windsurfing.
windsurfista *mf* windsurfer.
wolfram, wolframio *m* wolfram.

xenofobia *f* xenophobia.
xerografía *f* xerography.

xilófono *m* xylophone.
xilografía *f (arte)* xylography. **2** *(impresión)* xylograph.

Y

y *conj* and. **2** *(hora)* past: *son las tres* ~ *cuarto,* it's a quarter past three. **3** *(en pregunta)* what about: *¿~ López?,* what about López? ●~ *eso que,* although, even though; *¿~ qué?,* so what?; *¿~ si ... ?,* what if ... ?; *¡~ tanto!,* you bet!, and how!

ya *adv* *(con pasado)* already: ~ *lo sabía,* I already knew. **2** *(con presente)* now: *es preciso actuar* ~, it is vital that we act now. **3** *(ahora mismo)* immediately, at once. — **4** *interj irón* oh yes! ●~ *entiendo,* I see; ~ *era. hora,* about time too; *¡~ está!,* there we are!, done!; ~ *no,* any more, no longer; ~ *que,* since.

yacer [92] *i* to lie, be lying.

yacimiento *m* bed, deposit.

yago *pres indic* → **yacer**.

yanqui *adj-mf pey* Yankee.

yarda *f* yard.

yate *m* yacht.

yedra *f* → **hiedra**.

yegua *f* mare.

yeguada *f* herd of horses.

yelmo *m* helmet.

yema *f* *(de huevo)* yolk. **2** BOT bud. **3** *(del dedo)* fingertip.

yerba *f* → **hierba**.

yermo,-a *adj* *(sin vegetación)* barren, uncultivated. **2** *(despoblado)* deserted, uninhabited. — **3** *m* *(terreno inculto)* barren land, wasteland. **4** *(terreno inhabitado)* wilderness.

yerno *m* son-in-law.

yerro *m* error, mistake.

yerto,-a *adj* stiff, rigid.

yeso *m* gypsum. **2** *(construcción)* plaster. **3** *(tiza)* chalk.

yo *pron pers* I, me: *soy* ~, it's me. — **2** *m el* ~, the ego/self.

yodo *m* iodine.

yoduro *m* iodide.

yogur *m* yog(h)urt.

yonqui *mf arg* junkie.

yóquey, yoqui *m* jockey.

yudo *m* judo.

yugo *m* yoke.

yunque *m* anvil.

yunta *f* yoke/team of oxen.

yute *m* jute.

yuxtaponer [78] *t* to juxtapose. ▲ *pp yuxtapuesto,-a.*

yuxtaposición *f* juxtaposition.

yuxtapuesto,-a *pp irreg* → **yuxtaponer**.

Z

zafar(se) *t (soltar)* to loosen, untie. **2** *(desembarazar)* to free, clear. **– 3** *p (librarse)* to get away *(de,* from), escape *(de,* from).

zafio,-a *adj* uncouth, rough, coarse.

zafiro *m* sapphire.

zaga *f* rear. ●*a/en la* ~, behind, at the rear.

zagal,-la *m,f (muchacho) m* lad, *f* lass. **2** *(pastor) m* shepherd, *f* shepherdess.

zaguán *m* hall(way).

zaherir [35] *t (sentimientos)* to hurt. **2** *(reprender)* to reprimand. **3** *(censurar)* to reproach. **4** *(burlarse)* to mock.

zahorí *m (adivino)* seer, clairvoyant; *(de agua)* water diviner. **2** *fig* mindreader. **▲** *pl zahoríes.*

zahúrda *f* pigsty.

zaino,-a *adj (traidor)* treacherous. **2** *(caballo)* chestnut; *(res vacuna)* black.

zalamería *f* cajolery, flattery.

zalamero,-a *adj* flattering, fawning. **– 2** *m,f* flatterer, fawner.

zamarra *f* sheepskin jacket.

zambo,-a *adj* knock-kneed.

zambomba *f* kind of *primitive* drum. **– 2** *interj fam* phew!

zambombazo *m fam (explosión)* bang, explosion. **2** *(golpe)* blow.

zambullida *f* dive, plunge.

zambullir(se) [41] *t (en el agua) (persona)* to duck; *(cosa)* to dip, plunge. **– 2** *p* to dive, plunge. **3** *(en una actividad)* to become absorbed *(en,* in).

zampar(se) *t-p* to wolf down.

zanahoria *f* carrot.

zanca *f* leg.

zancada *f* stride.

zancadilla *f* trip. **2** *fam (engaño)* ruse, trick. ●*ponerle/hacerle la* ~ *a algn.,* to trip sb. up.

zanco *m* stilt.

zancudo,-a *adj* longlegged. **2** *(ave)* wading. **– 3** *fpl (aves)* waders.

zanganear *i* to idle, laze around.

zángano,-a *m,f fam (persona)* idler, lazybones *inv.* **– 2** *m (insecto)* drone.

zanja *f* ditch, trench.

zanjar *t (abrir zanjas)* to dig a ditch/trench in. **2** *fig (asunto)* to settle.

zapatazo *m* blow with a shoe.

zapatear *t* to tap with the feet.

zapatería *f (tienda)* shoe shop. **2** *(oficio)* shoemaking.

zapatero,-a *m,f* shoemaker. **■** ~ *remendón,* cobbler.

zapatilla *f* slipper. **■** ~ *de ballet,* ballet shoe; ~ *de deporte,* running shoe.

zapato *m* shoe. **■** *zapatos de tacón,* high-heeled shoes.

zarabanda *f* saraband. **2** *fam (jaleo)* bustle, confusion, turmoil.

zaragata *f* row, rumpus.

zaranda *f* sieve.

zarandajas *fpl* odds and ends, trifles.

zarandear(se) *t (cribar)* to sieve. **2** *(sacudir)* to shake; *(empujar)* to jostle, knock about. **– 3** *p (ajetrearse)* to bustle/rush about. **4** *(contonearse)* to swagger, strut.

zarandeo *m (criba)* sieving. **2** *(sacudida)* shaking; *(empujones)* bustling/rushing about. **3** *(contoneo)* swaggering, strutting.

zarcillo *m (pendiente)* earring. **2** BOT tendril.

zarpa *f* claw, paw. ●*echar la* ~ *a,* to grab.

zarpar *i* to weigh anchor, set sail.

zarpazo *m* clawing. ●*dar/pegar un* ~, to claw.

zarrapastroso,-a *adj* scruffy. **– 2** *m,f* scruff.

zarza *f* bramble, blackberry bush.

zarzal *m* bramble patch.

zarzamora *f (zarza)* blackberry bush; *(fruto)* blackberry.

¡zas! *interj* crash!, bang!

zascandil *m* fusspot. **2** *(casquivano)* featherbrain. **3** *(entrometido)* busybody, meddler.

zascandilear *i* to fuss about. **2** to meddle.

zenit *m* zenith.

zigzag *m* zigzag. ▲ *pl* **zigzags, zigzagues.**

zigzagueante *adj* zigzag.

zigzaguear *i* to zigzag.

zinc *m* zinc.

zipizape *m* rumpus, scuffle.

zócalo *m (de pared)* skirting board. **2** *(pedestal)* plinth.

zodiacal *adj* zodiacal.

zodiaco, zodíaco *m* zodiac.

zombi, zombie *mf* zombie. ●*fam* **estar ~,** to be groggy; *(loco)* to be crazy.

zona *f* zone, area. ■ **~ verde,** park.

zonzo,-a *adj* AM silly.

zoo *m* zoo.

zoología *f* zoology.

zoológico,-a *adj* zoological. **– 2** *m* zoo. ■ *parque ~,* zoo.

zoólogo,-a *m,f* zoologist.

zopenco,-a *adj* daft, stupid. **– 2** *m,f* dope, half-wit.

zoquete *adj fam (lerdo)* stupid. **– 2** *mf fam (lerdo)* blockhead. **– 3** *m (tarugo)* block of wood.

zorrería *f fam* dirty trick.

zorro,-a *m,f (animal)* fox; *(piel)* fox-fur, fox-skin. **2** *(persona)* sly person, fox. **– 3** *f fam (prostituta)* whore. **– 4** *mpl (para el polvo)* duster *sing.* **– 5** *adj (astuto)* cunning, sly. ●*fam* **estar hecho unos zorros,** to be knackered; *fam* **no tener ni zorra (idea),** not to have the slightest idea.

zote *adj* dim-witted. **– 2** *mf* dimwit.

zozobra *f (náutica)* sinking, capsizing. **2** *fig (congoja)* worry, anxiety.

zozobrar *i (náutica)* to sink, capsize. **2** *(persona)* to worry, be anxious. **3** *(proyecto)* to fail, be ruined.

zueco *m* clog.

zumbado,-a *adj fam* crazy, mad.

zumbar(se) *i* to hum, buzz. **– 2** *t fam (pegar)* to thrash. **– 3** *t-p (burlarse)* to tease, make fun of.

zumbido *m* buzzing, humming.

zumbón,-ona *adj* teasing, joking. **– 2** *m,f* teaser, joker.

zumo *m* juice.

zurcido *m* darn, mend.

zurcir [3] *t* to darn, mend.

zurdo,-a *adj (persona)* left-handed; *(mano)* left. **– 2** *m,f* left-handed person. **– 3** *f (mano)* left hand.

zurra *f* beating, thrashing.

zurrar *t* to beat, thrash.

zurriagazo *m (latigazo)* lash, stroke. **2** *fig (desgracia)* mishap, stroke of bad luck.

zurriago *m* whip.

zurrón *m* shepherd's pouch/bag.

zutano,-a *m,f fam* so-and-so; *m* what's-his-name, *f* what's-her-name.

Geographical names and languages

[1] habitante sólo - inhabitant only
[2] adjetivo referente al país (y nombre del idioma si existe) pero no habitante - adjective refering to the country (language if it exists) but not inhabitant
[3] adjetivo, habitante e idioma (si existe) - adjective, inhabitant and language (if it exists)
[4] adjetivo y habitante pero no idioma - adjective and inhabitant but not language
[5] idioma sólo - language only

Adriático, mar	Adriatic Sea	argentino	Argentinian
Afganistán	Afghanistan	Armenia	Armenia
afgano	Afghan	armenio	Armenian
África	Africa	Ártico, océano	Arctic Ocean
africano	African	Asia	Asia
Albania	Albania	asiático	Asian
albano	Albanian	asturiano	Asturian
alemán	German	Asturias	Asturias
Alemania	Germany	Atlántico, océano	Atlantic Ocean
Alpes	Alps	Australia	Australia
Amazonas	Amazon	australiano	Australian
América	America	Austria	Austria
América del Norte	North America	austríaco	Austrian
América del Sur	South America	Azerbaiján	Azerbaijan
América Latina	Latin America	azerbaijano	Azerbaijani
Andalucía	Andalusia	Azores	Azores
andaluz	Andalusian		
Andes	Andes		
Andorra	Andorra	Bangladesh	Bangladesh
andorrano	Andorran	Balcanes	Balkans
Anglonormandas, Islas	Channel Islands	balear, baleárico	Balearic
		Baleares, Islas	Balearic Islands
anglosajón	Anglosaxon	Báltico, mar	Baltic Sea
Antártida	Antarctica	belga	Belgian
antillano	West Indian	Bélgica	Belgium
Antillas	West Indes	Belice	Belize
Apeninos	Apennines	Bielorrusia	Byelorussia
árabe	Arabian[4], Arabic[5]	bielorruso	Byelorussian
Arabia	Arabia	Bolivia	Bolivia
Arabia Saudí	Saudi Arabia	boliviano	Bolivian
Aragón	Aragon	Bosnia-Herzegovina	Bosnia-Herzegovina
aragonés	Aragonese	bosnio	Bosnian
Argel	Algiers	Brasil	Brazil
Argelia	Algeria	brasileño	Brazilian
argelino	Algerian	británico	British[2], Briton[1]
Argentina	Argentine		

Bulgaria	Bulgaria	Ecuador	Ecuador
búlgaro	Bulgarian	ecuatoriano	Ecuadorian
		Egeo, mar	Aegean Sea
		egipcio	Egyptian
Camboya	Cambodia	Egipto	Egypt
camboyano	Cambodian	Eire	Eire
Camerún	Cameroon	El Salvador	El Salvador
camerunés	Cameroonian	Emiratos Árabes Unidos	United Arab Emirates
Canadá	Canada		
canadiense	Canadian	Escandinavia	Scandinavia
Canal de La Mancha	English Channel	escandinavo	Scandinavian
		escocés	Scot[1], Scots[2], Scottish[2]
Canarias, Islas	Canary Islands		
Cantabria	Cantabria	Escocia	Scotland
cántabro	Cantabrian	eslavo	Slav
Caribe, mar	Caribbean (Sea)	Eslovenia	Slovenia
caribeño	Caribbean	esloveno	Slovenian, Slovene
castellano	Castilian	España	Spain
Castilla	Castile	español	Spaniard[1], Spanish[2]
catalán	Catalan[3], Catalonian[4]	Estados Unidos (de América)	United States (of America)
Cataluña	Catalonia	estadounidense	American
Ceilán	Ceylon	Estonia	Estonia
ceilanés	Ceylonese	estonio	Estonian
celta	Celt[1], Celtic[4]	etíope	Ethiopian
Cerdeña	Sardinia	Etiopía	Ethiopia
Ceuta	Ceuta	Europa	Europe
checo	Czech	europeo	European
checoslovaco	Chechoslovak(ian)	Extremadura	Estremadura
Checoslovaquia	Czechoslovakia	extremeño	Estremaduran
Chile	Chile		
chileno	Chilean		
China	China	Filipinas	Philippines
chino	Chinese	filipino	Philippine[5], Filipino[3]
Chipre	Cyprus		
chipriota	Cypriot(e)	finlandés	Finn[1], Finnish[2]
Colombia	Colombia	Finlandia	Finland
colombiano	Colombian	francés	French
Córcega	Corsica	Francia	France
Corea	Korea	Fuerteventura	Fuerteventura
coreano	Korean		
corso	Corsican		
Costa Rica	Costa Rica	Gales	Wales
costarricense	Costa Rican	galés	Welsh[2], Welshman[1]
Croacia	Croatia		
croata	Croat, Croatian	Galicia	Galicia
Cuba	Cuba	gallego	Galician
cubano	Cuban	Georgia	Georgia
		georgiano	Georgian
		Gibraltar	Gibraltar
danés	Dane[1], Danish[2]	gibraltareño	Gibraltarian
Danubio	Danube	Golfo de León	Gulf of Lions
Dinamarca	Denmark	Golfo de Vizcaya	Bay of Biscay
dominicano	Dominican	Gran Canaria	Gran Canaria, Grand Canary
dublinés	Dubliner[1]		

Gran Bretaña	(Great) Britain	Jordania	Jordan
Grecia	Greece	jordano	Jordanian
griego	Greek	Júpiter	Jupiter
Groenlandia	Greenland		
Guatemala	Guatemala		
guatemalteco	Guatemalan	Kenia, Kenya	Kenya
		keniano	Kenyan
		Kuwait	Kuwait
Haití	Haiti	kuwaití	Kuwaiti
haitiano	Haitian		
hebreo	hebrew		
Himalaya	Himalayas	Lanzarote	Lanzarote
hindú	Indian	Laos	Laos
Hispanoamérica	Spanish America	laosiano	Laotian
hispanoamericano	Spanish American	Latinoamérica	Latin America
Holanda	Holland	latinoamericano	Latin American
holandés	Dutch	Lejano Oriente	Far East
Honduras	Honduras	letón	Latvian
hondureño	Honduran	Letonia	Latvia
húngaro	Hungarian	libanés	Lebanese
Hungría	Hungary	Líbano	Lebanon
		Libia	Libya
		libio	Libyan
Ibiza	Ibiza	Liechtenstein	Liechtenstein
ibizenco	Ibizan	liechtenstiense	Liechtensteiner[1],
India	India		Liechtenstein[5]
Índico, océano	Indian Ocean	Lituania	Lithuania
indio	Indian	lituano	Lithuanian
Indochina	Indochina	londinense	Londoner
Indonesia	Indonesia	luso	Portuguese
indonesio	Indonesian	Luxemburgo	Luxembourg
Inglaterra	England	luxemburgués	Luxembourger
inglés	English		
Iraq	Irak, Iraq		
Irán	Iran	Macedonia	Macedonia
iraní	Iranian	macedonio	Macedonian
iraquí	Iraqi	Malasia	Malaysia
Irlanda	Ireland	malayo	Malaysian
Irlanda del Norte	Northern Ireland	Mallorca	Majorca
irlandés	Irish	Malvinas, Islas	Falkland Islands
islandés	Icelander[1],	marroquí	Moroccan
	Icelandic[2]	Marruecos	Morocco
Islandia	Iceland	Marte	Mars
Israel	Israel	Mediterráneo, mar	Mediterranean Sea
israelí	Israeli	mejicano	Mexican
israelita	Israelite	Méjico, México	Mexico
Italia	Italy	Melilla	Melilla
italiano	Italian	Menorca	Minorca
		menorquín	Minorcan
		Mercurio	Mercury
Jamaica	Jamaica	Misisipí	Mississippi
jamaicano,	Jamaican	Moldavia	Moldavia
jamaiquino		moldavo	Moldavian
Japón	Japan	Mónaco	Monaco
japonés	Japanese	monegasco	Monegasque

Montañas Rocosas	Rocky Mountains
Montenegro	Montenegro
montenegrino	Montenegrin
Muerto, mar	Dead Sea
Navarra	Navarre
navarro	Navarrese
Negro, mar	Black Sea
neoyorquino	New Yorker
neocelandés	New Zealander[1]
Nepal	Nepal
nepalí	Nepalese
Neptuno	Neptune
Nicaragua	Nicaragua
nicaragüense	Nicaraguan
Nigeria	Nigeria
nigeriano	Nigerian
Nilo	Nile
Norte, mar del	North Sea
norteamericano	North American
Noruega	Norway
noruego	Norwegian
Nueva Zelanda	New Zealand
Oceanía	Oceania
Oriente Medio	Middle East
Pacífico, océano	Pacific Ocean
País Vasco	Basque Country
Países Bajos	Netherlands
Pakistán, Paquistán	Pakistan
Pakistaní, Paquistaní	Pakistani
Palestina	Palestine
palestino	Palestinian
Panamá	Panama
panameño	Panamanian
Paraguay	Paraguay
paraguayo	Paraguayan
Península Ibérica	Iberian Peninsula
persa, pérsico	Persian
Perú	Peru
peruano	Peruvian
Pirineos	Pyrenees
Plutón	Pluto
Polinesia	Polynesia
polinesio	Polynesian
Polo Norte	North Pole
Polo Sur	South Pole
polaco	Pole[1], Polish[2]
Polonia	Poland
Portugal	Portugal

portugués	Portuguese
portorriqueño, puertorriqueño	Puerto Rican
Puerto Rico	Puerto Rico
Reino Unido	United Kingdom
República de Irlanda	Eire
República Dominicana	Dominican Republic
Rin	Rhine
Ródano	Rhone
Rojo, mar	Red Sea
Rumanía	Romania, Rumania
rumano	Romanian, Rumanian
Rusia	Russia
ruso	Russian
salvadoreño	Salvador(i)an
sardo	Sardinian
Saturno	Saturn
saudí, saudita	Saudi (Arabian)
Sena	Seine
serbio	Serb, Serbian
serbocroata	Serbo-Croat, Serbo-Croatian
Sicilia	Sicily
siciliano	Sicilian
Singapur	Singapore
Siria	Syria
sirio	Syrian
Sudamérica	South America
sudamericano	South American
Suecia	Sweden
sueco	Swede[1], Swedish[2]
Suiza	Switzerland
suizo	Swiss
Suráfrica	South Africa
surafricano	South African
Suriname	Surinam
surinamés	Surinamese
tailandés	Thai
Tailandia	Thailand
Taiwan	Taiwan
Támesis	Thames
Tenerife	Tenerife
Tierra	Earth
tunecino	Tunisian
Túnez	Tunisia
turco	Turk[1], Turkish[2]
Turquía	Turkey

Ucrania	Ukraine	Venezuela	Venezuela
ucraniano	Ukrainian	Venus	Venus
Urano	Uranus	Vietnam	Vietnam
Uruguay	Uruguay	vietnamita	Vietnamese
uruguayo	Uruguayan		
		Yugoslavia	Yugoslavia
Valencia	Valencia	yugoslavo	Yugoslav(ian)
valenciano	Valencian		
vasco	Basque		
Vaticano	Vatican	Zaire	Zaire
venezolano	Venezuelan	zairense	Zairian

APPENDICES
APÉNDICES

FALSE COGNATES AND "PART-TIME" COGNATES

Some of the following Spanish words appear to be cognates of English words, but they are not: e.g., **"sopa"** in Spanish does *not* mean "soap" in English, and **"parientes"** does *not* mean "parents" in English. Other words sometimes suggest an English equivalent, but can also have a very different meaning: e.g., **"real"** in Spanish can be interpreted at times to mean "real" in English but more often should be translated as "royal," and **"equipo"** in Spanish can mean "equipment" in English but is more often translated as "team."

In the Spanish-to-English column, certain English words are in brackets to indicate that *only sometimes* the Spanish word has the meaning of the bracketed English word. In the English-to-Spanish column the abbreviations—(a.) = adjective, (n.) = noun, and (v.) = verb—are used in a few cases for clarity.

Spanish-English

acre: sharp, sour, rude, harsh, [acre]

actual: current, present (re time)

admirar: to astonish, surprise, [admire]

apuntar: to point, aim; write down, make a note of

asignación: allowance, assignment, [assignation]

asistir: to attend, be present, to help, [to assist]

atender: to pay attention, take care of, [attend to]

carpeta: portfolio; file folder

carta: letter (re mail), charter, [playing card]

cigarro: cigarette

colegio: school (private or high school)

conferencia: lecture, interview, meeting, [conference]

constipado: suffering from a cold

contar: to tell, relate, [count]

contento: happy, glad, satisfied, [contented]

costumbre: custom

decepción: disillusionment, disappointment, [deception]

desgracia: misfortune, mishap, disfavor

desgraciado: unfortunate, wretched, unlucky

deshonesto: immodest, indecent

dirección: address (re mail), [direction]

disgusto: quarrel, annoyance, sorrow, [disgust]

distinto: different; clear; several; [distinct]

embarazada: pregnant

equipo: team; fittings; squad; [equipment]

equivocación: error, mistake

éxito: success

expedir: to issue (a decree); send, ship; dispatch, [expedite]

explanar: to level, grade (ground); [explain]

fábrica: factory, mill, structure, [fabric]

falta: shortage, lack; blemish; defect, [fault]

English-Spanish

acre: acre, unidad de medida

actual: verdadero, real

admire: considerar con placer, admirar

appoint: nombrar, señalar

assignation: asignación, destinación

assist: ayudar, asistir

attend: asistir a, cuidar, atender

carpet: alfombra

cart: carro, carreta
card: tarjeta, naipe, carta

cigar: puro

college: universidad

conference: junta, sesión, entrevista, conferencia

constipated: estreñido

count: (v.) contar

contented: satisfecho, tranquilo, contento

costume: vestuario, traje

deception: engaño, fraude, decepción

disgrace: (n.) deshonra, vergüenza, ignominia

disgraced: deshonrado, avergonzado

dishonest: engañoso, falso, poco honrado

direction: dirección

disgust: hastío, asco, repugnancia, disgusto

distinct: claro, visible; inequívoco; diferente, distinto

embarrassed: turbado, desconcertado

equipment: aparatos, equipo

equivocation: equívoco; subterfugio, engaño

exit: salida

expedite: acelerar, facilitar; apresurar, despachar

explain: explicar, aclarar

fabric: tela, textura; fábrica; construcción

fault: (n.) culpa; defecto, falta

formal: reliable, trustworthy; grave; definite; [formal]

frase: sentence, [phrase]

fray: priest, friar

golpe: blow

gracioso: amusing, witty; graceful, charming

grande: large, big, great, [grand]

honesto: decent, pure, virtuous; reasonable; [honest]

idioma: language, [idiom]

ignorar: to be unaware or ignorant of

largo: long

lectura: reading

leer: to read

liar: to tie, bind, roll up

media: stocking

ordinario: coarse, vulgar; usual, [ordinary]

parientes: relatives

probar: to test, taste, try out

quitar: to take away, deprive of, subtract

real: royal, [real]

realizar: to fulfill, achieve, carry out; [realize]

recordar: to remember, recall, remind, awaken

regular: ordinary; so-so, fairly well; systematic, [regular]

renta: interest, revenue, [rent]

repente: start, sudden movement

replicar: to reply, answer, retort, [replicate]

ropa: clothes, clothing

ruin: vile, mean; petty, stingy; little

salvo: safe; easily; omitted

sano: healthy; sound; whole; [sane]

sauce: willow

sensible: sentient; sensitive; perceptible; [sensible]

simpático: agreeable, pleasant, cogenial

sopa: soup

suceder: to happen, come about, [succeed]

suceso: event, incident

taller: workshop; laboratory; studio

tuna: prickly pear; idle and vagrant life

tutor: guardian, [tutor]

vagón: railway car or coach

vale: note, sales slip, coupon

formal: convencional, ceremonioso, formal

phrase: expresión, frase

fray: (v.) raerse, deshilacharse; (n.) alboroto, riña

gulp: (n.) trago

gracious: afable, cortés; atractivo; bondadoso

grand: magnífico; grandioso, majestuoso; grande

honest: honrado, íntegro, recto; sincero

idiom: modismo; lenguaje

ignore: no hacer caso de; desconocer

large: grande

lecture: (n.) conferencia; lección; plática

leer: (v.) mirar de soslayo, mirar con injuria; (n.) mirada de soslayo

liar: (n.) mentiroso, embustero

media: (pl. of medium) medios; medios de comunicación (radio, televisión, etc.)

ordinary: corriente, común, ordinario; mediocre

parents: padres

probe: (v.) tentar; examinar a fondo; sondear; penetrar

quit: abandonar, cesar, parar, dejar (de hacer algo)

real: (a.) verdadero, real

realize: darse cuenta de; comprender; efectuar, llevar a cabo; realizar

record: (v.) registrar, apuntar, asentar, inscribir; grabar en disco

regular: metódico, ordenado, regular

rent: (v.) alquilar; (n.) arrendamiento, renta; rasgadura

repent: arrepentirse

replicate: (v.) duplicar, repetir, replicar

rope: (n.) soga, cuerda

ruin: (v.) arruinar, estropear; (n.) ruina, destrucción

salvo: salva; pretexto

sane: cuerdo; razonable; sano

sauce: salsa, condimento

sensible: sensato, razonable, juicioso

sympathetic: compasivo; simpatizante

soap: jabón

succeed: lograr(se); medrar, salir bien; suceder

success: éxito

taller: más alto

tuna: atún

tutor: (n.) maestro particular, tutor

wagon: carro, carreta, carretón

vale: valle, cañada

MONETARY UNITS / UNIDADES MONETARIAS

Country / País	Name / Nombre	Subdivision / Subdivisión	Symbol / Símbolo
THE AMERICAS / LAS AMÉRICAS			
Argentina	austral	100 centavos	A
Bahamas	dollar / dólar bahameño	100 cents / centavos	B$
Barbados	dollar / dólar de Barbados	100 cents / centavos	$
Belize / Belice	dollar / dólar	100 cents / centavos	$
Bolivia	peso	100 centavos	$B
Brazil / Brasil	cruzado	100 centavos	$; Cr$
Canada / Canadá	dollar / dólar canadiense	100 cents / centavos	$
Chile	peso* / peso chileno*	1000 escudos	$
Colombia	peso	100 centavos	$; P
Costa Rica	colon / colón	100 centimos / céntimos	₡; ¢
Cuba	peso	100 centavos	$
Dominican Republic / República Dominicana	peso	100 centavos	RD$
Ecuador	sucre	100 centavos	S/
El Salvador	colon / colón	100 centavos	₡; ¢
Guatemala	quetzal	100 centavos	Q; Q
Guyana	dollar / dólar guayanés	100 cents / centavos	G$
Haiti / Haití	gourde	100 centimes / céntimos	Ø; G; Gde
Honduras	lempira	100 centavos	L
Jamaica	dollar / dólar jamaicano	100 cents / centavos	$
Mexico / México	peso	100 centavos	$
Nicaragua	cordoba / córdoba	100 centavos	C$
Panama / Panamá	balboa	100 centesimos / centésimos	B/
Paraguay	guarani / guaraní	100 centimos / céntimos	Ø; G
Peru / Perú	sol	100 centavos	S/; $
Puerto Rico	dollar / dólar	100 cents / centavos	$
Suriname / Surinam	guilder / gulder de Surinam	100 cents / centavos	g
Trinidad and Tobago / Trinidad y Tabago	dollar / dólar trinitario	100 cents / centavos	TT$
United States / Estados Unidos	dollar / dólar	100 cents / centavos	$
Uruguay	peso	100 centesimos / centésimos	$
Venezuela	bolivar / bolívar	100 centimos / céntimos	B

* The Chilean monetary unit, the escudo, was replaced by the peso in 1975.

* El escudo, la unidad monetaria chilena, fue reemplazado por el peso en 1975.

OTHER COUNTRIES / OTROS PAÍSES

Australia	dollar / dólar australiano	100 cents / centavos	$A
Austria	shilling / chelín	100 groschen	S; Sch
Belgium / Bélgica	franc / franco belga	100 centimes / céntimos	Fr; F
China	yuan / yüan	100 fen	$
East Germany / Alemania, R.D.	mark or ostmark / marco DDR	100 pfennigs	M; OM
Egypt / Egipto	pound / libra egipcia	100 piasters / piastras	£E
France / Francia	franc / franco	100 centimes / céntimos	Fr; F
Greece / Grecia	drachma / dracma	100 lepta	Dr
India	rupee / rupia	100 paise / paisas	Re; Rs
Ireland / Irlanda	pound / libra irlandesa	100 pence / peniques	£
Israel	pound / libra israelí	100 argorot	I£
Italy / Italia	lira	100 centesimi / centésimos	L; Lit
Japan / Japón	yen	100 sen	¥ ; Y
Portugal	escudo	100 centavos	$; Esc
Soviet Union / Unión Soviética	ruble / rublo	100 kopecks / kopeks	R; Rub
Spain / España	peseta	100 centimos / céntimos	Pta; P
United Kingdom / Reino Unido	pound / libra esterlina	100 pence / peniques	£
West Germany / Alemania, R.F.	deutsche mark	100 pfennigs	DM

WEIGHTS AND MEASURES

Metric System

Unit	Abbreviation	Approximate U.S. Equivalent	
LENGTH			
1 millimeter	mm	0.04	inch
1 centimeter	cm	0.39	inch
1 meter	m	39.37	inches
		1.094	yards
1 kilometer	km	3,281.5	feet
		0.62	mile
AREA			
1 square centimeter	sq cm (cm²)	0.155	square inch
1 square meter	m²	10.764	square feet
		1.196	square yards
1 hectare	ha	2.471	acres
1 square kilometer	sq km (km²)	247.105	acres
		0.386	square mile
VOLUME			
1 cubic centimeter	cu cm (cm³)	0.061	cubic inch
1 stere	s	1.308	cubic yards
1 cubic meter	m³	1.308	cubic yards
CAPACITY (Liquid Measure)			
1 deciliter	dl	0.21	pint
1 liter	l	1.057	quarts
1 dekaliter	dal	2.64	gallons
CAPACITY (Dry Measure)			
1 deciliter	dl	0.18	pint
1 liter	l	0.908	quart
1 dekaliter	dal	1.14	pecks
1 hectoliter	hl	2.84	bushels
CAPACITY (Cubic Measure)			
1 deciliter	dl	6.1	cubic inches
1 liter	l	61.02	cubic inches
1 dekaliter	dal	0.35	cubic foot
1 hectoliter	hl	3.53	cubic feet
1 kiloliter	kl	1.31	cubic yards
MASS AND WEIGHT			
1 gram	g, gm	0.035	ounce
1 dekagram	dag	0.353	ounce
1 hectogram	hg	3.527	ounces
1 kilogram	kg	2.2046	pounds
1 quintal	q	220.46	pounds
1 metric ton	MT, t	1.1	tons

PESAS Y MEDIDAS

Sistema métrico

Unidad	Abreviatura	Equivalente aproximado del sistema estadounidense	
LONGITUD			
1 milímetro	mm	0,04	pulgada
1 centímetro	cm	0,39	pulgada
1 metro	m	39,37	pulgadas
		1,094	yardas
1 kilómetro	Km	3.281,5	pies
		0,62	milla
ÁREA			
1 centímetro cuadrado	cm²	0,155	pulgada cuadrada
1 metro cuadrado	m²	10,764	pies cuadrados
		1,196	yardas cuadradas
1 hectárea	ha	2,471	acres
1 kilómetro cuadrado	Km²	247,105	acres
		0,386	milla cuadrada
VOLUMEN			
1 centímetro cúbico	cm³	0,061	pulgadas cúbicas
1 metro cúbico	m³	1,308	yardas cúbicas
CAPACIDAD (Medida líquida)			
1 decilitro	dl	0,21	pinta
1 litro	l	1,057	quarts
1 decalitro	Dl	2,64	galones
CAPACIDAD (Medida árida)			
1 decilitro	dl	0,18	pinta
1 litro	l	0,908	quart
1 decalitro	Dl	1,14	pecks
1 hectolitro	Hl	2,84	bushels
CAPACIDAD (Medida cúbica)			
1 decilitro	dl	6,1	pulgadas cúbicas
1 litro	l	61,02	pulgadas cúbicas
1 decalitro	Dl	0,35	pie cúbico
1 hectolitro	Hl	3,53	pies cúbicos
1 kilolitro	Kl	1,31	yardas cúbicas
MASA Y PESO			
1 gramo	g	0,035	onza
1 decagramo	Dg	0,353	onza
1 hectogramo	Hg	3,527	onzas
1 kilogramo	Kg	2,2046	libras
1 quintal métrico	q	220,46	libras
1 tonelada métrica	t	1,1	toneladas

U.S. Customary Weights and Measures /
Unidades de pesas y medidas estadounidenses

Linear measure / Medida de longitud

1 foot / pie	=	12 inches / pulgadas
1 yard / yarda	=	36 inches / pulgadas
	=	3 feet / pies
1 rod	=	5½ yards / yardas
1 mile / milla	=	5,280 feet / 5.280 pies
	=	1,760 yards / 1.760 yardas

Liquid measure / Medida líquida

1 pint / pinta	=	4 gills
1 quart / quart líquido	=	2 pints / pintas
1 gallon / galón	=	4 quarts / quarts líquidos

Area measure / Medida de superficie

1 square foot / pie cuadrado	=	144 square inches / pulgadas cuadradas
1 square yard / yarda cuadrada	=	9 square feet / pies cuadrados
1 square rod / rod cuadrado	=	30¼ square yards / yardas cuadradas
1 acre	=	160 square rods / rods cuadrados
1 square mile / milla cuadrada	=	640 acres

Dry measure / Medida árida

1 quart	=	2 pints / pintas áridas
1 peck	=	8 quarts
1 bushel	=	4 pecks

Some useful measures / Unas medidas útiles

Quantity / Cantidad

1 dozen / docena	=	12 units / unidades
1 gross / gruesa	=	12 dozen / docenas

Quantity of paper / Cantidad de papel

1 quire / mano	=	24 or 25 sheets / hojas
1 ream / resma	=	500 sheets / hojas
	=	20 quires / manos

Electricity / Electricidad

charge / carga	coulomb / culombio
power / potencia	watt / vatio
	kilowatt / kilovatio
resistance / resistencia	ohm / ohmio
strength / fuerza	ampere / amperio
voltage / voltaje	volt / voltio

NUMBERS / NUMERALES

Cardinal Numbers		Números cardinales	Cardinal Numbers		Números cardinales
zero	0	cero	twenty	20	veinte
one	1	uno	twenty-one	21	veintiuno
two	2	dos	twenty-two	22	veintidós
three	3	tres	twenty-three	23	veintitrés
four	4	cuatro	twenty-four	24	veinticuatro
five	5	cinco	twenty-five	25	veinticinco
six	6	seis	twenty-six	26	veintiséis
seven	7	siete	twenty-seven	27	veintisiete
eight	8	ocho	twenty-eight	28	veintiocho
nine	9	nueve	twenty-nine	29	veintinueve
ten	10	diez	thirty	30	treinta
eleven	11	once	forty	40	cuarenta
twelve	12	doce	fifty	50	cincuenta
thirteen	13	trece	sixty	60	sesenta
fourteen	14	catorce	seventy	70	setenta
fifteen	15	quince	eighty	80	ochenta
sixteen	16	dieciséis	ninety	90	noventa
seventeen	17	diecisiete	one hundred	100	cien, ciento
eighteen	18	dieciocho	five hundred	500	quinientos
nineteen	19	diecinueve	one thousand	1000	mil

Ordinal Numbers / Números ordinales

Ordinal Numbers		Números ordinales	
1st	first	1.º, 1.ª	primero, -a
2nd	second	2.º, 2.ª	segundo, -a
3rd	third	3.º, 3.ª	tercero, -a
4th	fourth	4.º, 4.ª	cuarto, -a
5th	fifth	5.º, 5.ª	quinto, -a
6th	sixth	6.º, 6.ª	sexto, -a
7th	seventh	7.º, 7.ª	séptimo, -a
8th	eighth	8.º, 8.ª	octavo, -a
9th	ninth	9.º, 9.ª	noveno, -a
10th	tenth	10.º, 10.ª	décimo, -a
11th	eleventh	11.º, 11.ª	undécimo, -a
12th	twelfth	12.º, 12.ª	duodécimo, -a
13th	thirteenth	13.º, 13.ª	decimotercero, -a decimotercio, -a
14th	fourteenth	14.º, 14.ª	decimocuarto, -a
15th	fifteenth	15.º, 15.ª	decimoquinto, -a
16th	sixteenth	16.º, 16.ª	decimosexto, -a
17th	seventeenth	17.º, 17.ª	decimoséptimo, -a
18th	eighteenth	18.º, 18.ª	decimoctavo, -a
19th	nineteenth	19.º, 19.ª	decimonoveno, -a decimonono, -a
20th	twentieth	20.º, 20.ª	vigésimo, -a
21st	twenty-first	21.º, 21.ª	vigésimo (-a) primero (-a)
22nd	twenty-second	22.º, 22.ª	vigésimo (-a) segundo (-a)
30th	thirtieth	30.º, 30.ª	trigésimo, -a
40th	fortieth	40.º, 40.ª	cuadragésimo, -a
50th	fiftieth	50.º, 50.ª	quincuagésimo, -a
60th	sixtieth	60.º, 60.ª	sexagésimo, -a
70th	seventieth	70.º, 70.ª	septuagésimo, -a
80th	eightieth	80.º, 80.ª	octogésimo, -a
90th	ninetieth	90.º, 90.ª	nonagésimo, -a
100th	hundredth	100.º, 100.ª	centésimo, -a

TEMPERATURE / LA TEMPERATURA

Fahrenheit and Celsius / Grados Fahrenheit y grados Celsius

To convert Fahrenheit to Celsius, subtract 32 degrees, multiply by 5, and divide by 9.

Para convertir grados Fahrenheit a grados Celsius (centígrados), réstese 32 grados, multiplíquese por 5 y divídase por 9.

$$104°F - 32 = 72 \times 5 = 360 \div 9 = 40°C$$

To convert Celsius to Fahrenheit, multiply by 9, divide by 5, and add 32 degrees.

Para convertir grados Celsius (centígrados) a grados Fahrenheit, multiplíquese por 9, divídase por 5 y agréguese 32 grados.

$$40°C \times 9 = 360 \div 5 = 72 + 32 = 104°F$$

At sea level, water boils at Al nivel del mar, se hierve el agua a	212°F / 100°C
Water freezes at Se congela el agua en	32°F / 0°C
Average human temperature Temperatura promedia del ser humano	98.6°F / 37°C

Some normal temperatures in the Americas / Algunas temperaturas normales en las Américas

	Winter / Invierno	Summer / Verano
North of the equator / Al norte del ecuador		
Churchill, Manitoba	-11°F / -23.9°C	63°F / 17.2°C
Montreal, Quebec	22°F / -5.6°C	79°F / 26.1°C
Anchorage, Alaska	12°F / -11.1°C	58°F / 14.4°C
Chicago, Illinois	24°F / -4.4°C	75°F / 23.9°C
New York, New York	32°F / 0°C	77°F / 25°C
Dallas, Texas	45°F / 7.2°C	86°F / 30°C
Los Angeles, California	57°F / 13.9°C	73°F / 22.8°C
Phoenix, Arizona	51°F / 10.6°C	94°F / 34.4°C
Tegucigalpa, Honduras	50°F / 10°C	90°F / 32°C
South of the equator / Al sur del ecuador		
Tierra del Fuego, Argentina	32°F / 0°C	50°F / 10°C
Sao Paulo, Brazil	57.2°F / 14°C	69.8°F / 21°C
Montevideo, Uruguay	55.4°F / 13°C	71.6°F / 22°C
Buenos Aires, Argentina	52.3°F / 11.3°C	73.8°F / 23.2°C
Lima, Peru	59°F / 15°C	77°F / 25°C

NORTH AMERICA / AMÉRICA DEL NORTE

CENTRAL AMERICA / AMÉRICA CENTRAL

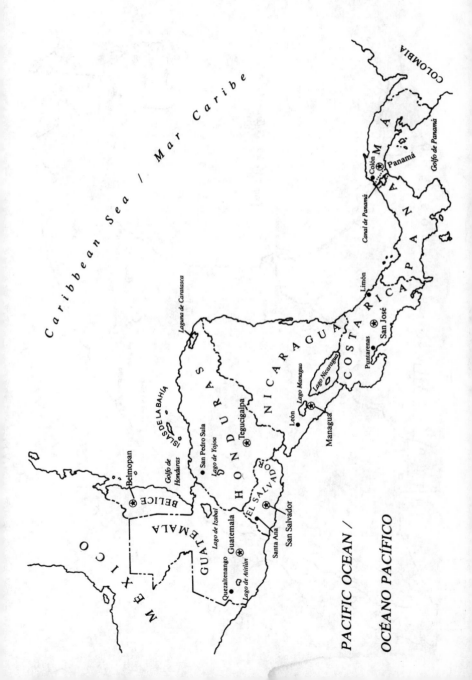

MEXICO / MÉXICO

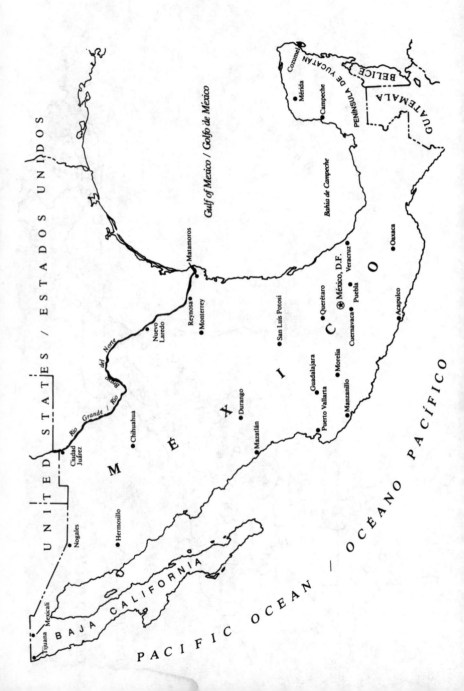

WEST INDIES / LAS ANTILLAS

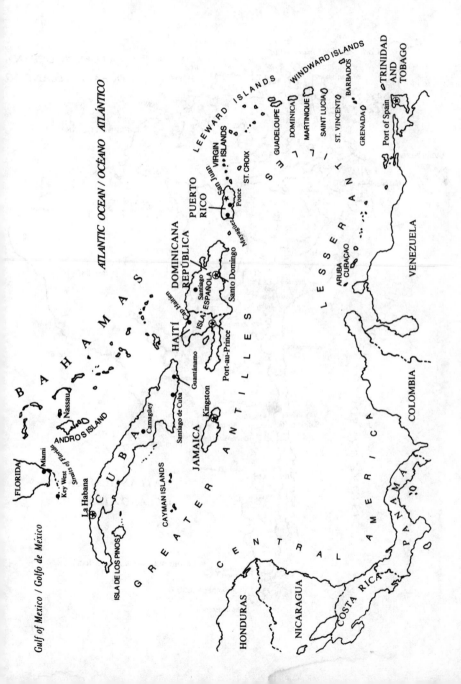

SOUTH AMERICA /AMÉRICA DEL SUR

Caribbean Sea/ Mar Caribe

CENTROAMÉRICA

Barranquilla

Maracaibo
Valencia
Caracas

Barquisimeto Orinoco

TRINIDAD AND
TOBAGO
Port of Spain

ATLANTIC OCEAN /
OCÉANO ATLÁNTICO

Río

VENEZUELA

Cuca

Medellín

Cali

Bogotá

Río Magdalena

GUYANA

Georgetown
Paramaribo

SURINAM

Cayenne
FRENCH GUIANA

COLOMBIA

ARCHIPIÉLAGO
DE COLÓN

ECUADOR

Quito

Río Negro

Guayaquil

Cuenca

Iquitos

Río Amazonas

B R A S I L

Fortaleza

Recife

P E R Ú

Lima
Callao

Cuzco

Lago Titicaca

La Paz

Cochabamba

B O L I V I A

Santa Cruz

Brasilia

Lago
de
Poopó

Sucre

Potosí

Antofagasta

Concepción

Paraná

Belo Horizonte

PACIFIC OCEAN / OCÉANO PACÍFICO

A

San Miguel
de Tucumán

PARAGUAY

Asunción

São Paulo

Río de Janeiro

R

Córdoba

G

Santa Fe

Paraná

Porto Alegre

Valparaíso

Mendoza

Santiago

Rosario

URUGUAY

C

Buenos Aires

Montevideo

H

La Plata

ATLANTIC OCEAN /

I

OCÉANO ATLÁNTICO

L

E

N

T

I

N

A

*Estrecho de
Magallanes*

FALKLAND ISLANDS / ISLAS MALVINAS

TIERRA DEL FUEGO

Cabo de Hornos

SPAIN AND PORTUGAL / ESPAÑA Y PORTUGAL

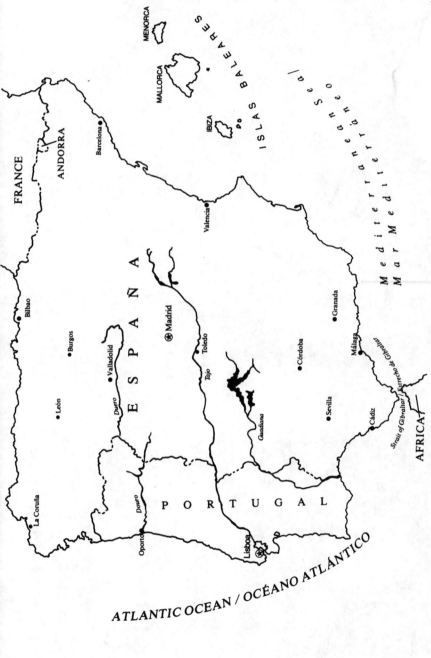

NTC'S LANGUAGE DICTIONARIES

The Best, By Definition

Spanish/English
Vox New College (Thumb-index & Plain-edge)
Vox Modern
Vox Compact
Vox Everyday
Vox Traveler's
Vox Super-Mini
Cervantes-Walls

Spanish/Spanish
Diccionario Básico Norteamericano
Vox Diccionario Escolar de la lengua española
El Diccionario del español chicano

French/English
NTC's New College French and English
NTC's Dictionary of *Faux Amis*
NTC's Dictionary of Canadian French

German/English
Schöffler-Weis
Klett's Modern (New Edition)
Klett's Super-Mini
NTC's Dictionary of German False Cognates

Italian/English
Zanichelli New College Italian and English
Zanichelli Super-Mini

Greek/English
NTC's New College Greek and English

Chinese/English
Easy Chinese Phrasebook and Dictionary

For Juveniles
Let's Learn English Picture Dictionary
Let's Learn French Picture Dictionary
Let's Learn German Picture Dictionary
Let's Learn Italian Picture Dictionary
Let's Learn Spanish Picture Dictionary
English Picture Dictionary
French Picture Dictionary
German Picture Dictionary
Spanish Picture Dictionary

English for Nonnative Speakers
Everyday American English Dictionary
Beginner's Dictionary of American English Usage

Electronic Dictionaries
Languages of the World on CD-ROM
NTC's Dictionary of American Idioms, Slang, a
 Colloquial Expressions (Electronic Book)

Other Reference Books
Robin Hyman's Dictionary of Quotations
British/American Language Dictionary
NTC's American Idioms Dictionary
NTC's Dictionary of American Slang and
 Colloquial Expressions
Forbidden American English
Essential American Idioms
Contemporary American Slang
NTC's Dictionary of Grammar Terminology
Complete Multilingual Dictionary of Computer
 Terminology
Complete Multilingual Dictionary of Aviation &
 Aeronautical Terminology
Complete Multilingual Dictionary of Advertisin
 Marketing & Communications
NTC's Dictionary of American Spelling
NTC's Classical Dictionary
NTC's Dictionary of Debate
NTC's Mass Media Dictionary
NTC's Dictionary of Word Origins
NTC's Dictionary of Literary Terms
Dictionary of Trade Name Origins
Dictionary of Advertising
Dictionary of Broadcast Communications
Dictionary of Changes in Meaning
Dictionary of Confusing Words and Meanings
NTC's Dictionary of English Idioms
NTC's Dictionary of Proverbs and Clichés
Dictionary of Acronyms and Abbreviations
NTC's Dictionary of American English
 Pronunciation
NTC's Dictionary of Phrasal Verbs and Other
 Idiomatic Verbal Phrases
Common American Phrases

Polish/English
The Wiedza Powszechna Compact Polish and
 English Dictionary

For further information or a current catalog, write:
National Textbook Company
a division of *NTC Publishing Group*
4255 West Touhy Avenue
Lincolnwood, Illinois 60646-1975 U.S.A.